Dragonball

STORY AND ART BY

AKIRA TORIYAMA

DRAGON BALL 3-IN-1 EDITION ④

SHONEN JUMP Manga Omnibus Edition
A compilation of the graphic novel volumes 10–12

STORY AND ART **AKIRA TORIYAMA**

TRANSLATION **Mari Morimoto**
ENGLISH ADAPTATION **Gerard Jones**
TOUCH-UP ART & LETTERING **Wayne Truman**
DESIGN **Sean Lee** (Manga Edition)
Shawn Carrico (Omnibus Edition)
EDITOR **Jason Thompson** (Manga Edition)
Mike Montesa (Omnibus Edition)

Printed in the U.S.A.

Published by VIZ Media, LLC
P.O. Box 77010
San Francisco, CA 94107

10 9 8 7 6 5
Omnibus edition first printing, March 2014
Fifth printing, May 2018

Dragonball

VOLUME 10

THE 22ND TENKA'ICHI BUDŌKAI

VOLUME 11

THE EYES OF TENSHINHAN

VOLUME 12

THE DEMON KING PICCOLO

STORY AND ART BY

AKIRA TORIYAMA

SHONEN JUMP Manga Omnibus Edition

CONTENTS

CAST OF CHARACTERS

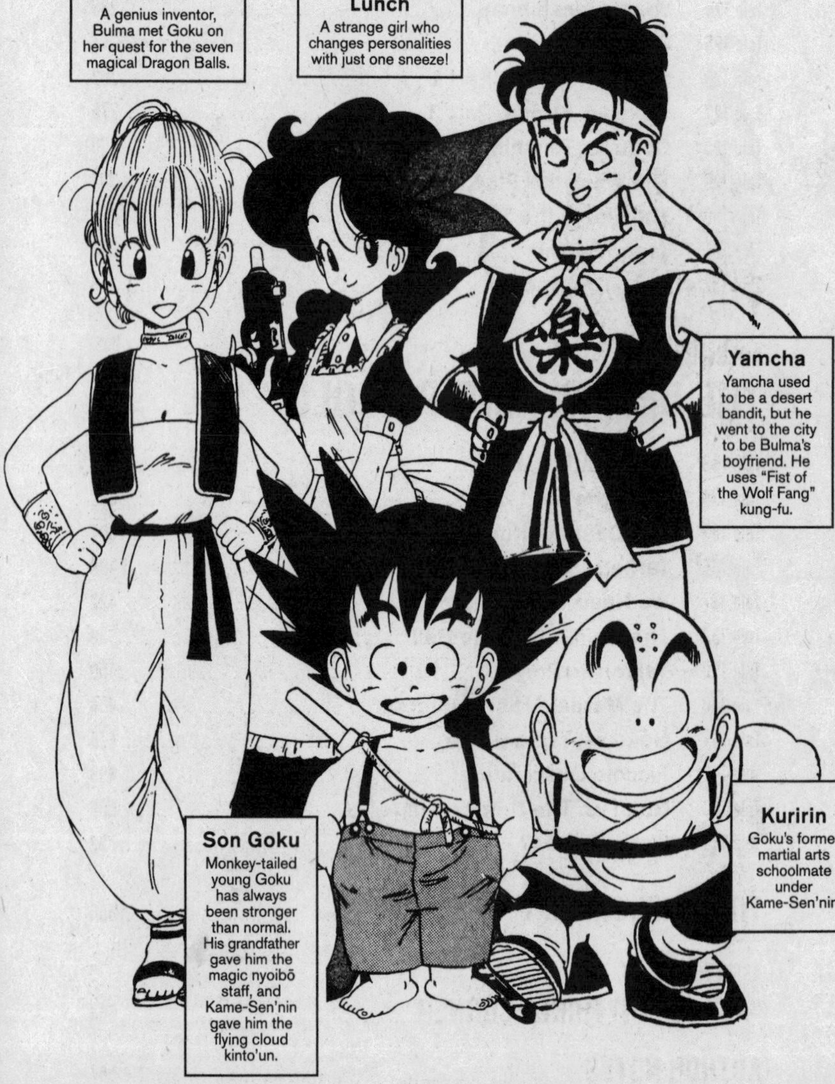

Bulma

A genius inventor, Bulma met Goku on her quest for the seven magical Dragon Balls.

Lunch

A strange girl who changes personalities with just one sneeze!

Yamcha

Yamcha used to be a desert bandit, but he went to the city to be Bulma's boyfriend. He uses "Fist of the Wolf Fang" kung-fu.

Son Goku

Monkey-tailed young Goku has always been stronger than normal. His grandfather gave him the magic nyoibō staff, and Kame-Sen'nin gave him the flying cloud kinto'un.

Kuririn

Goku's former martial arts schoolmate under Kame-Sen'nin.

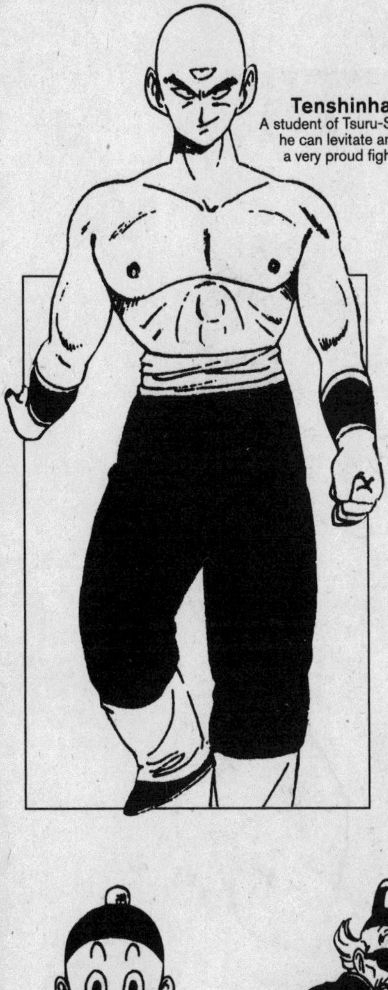

Tenshinhan
A student of Tsuru-Sen'nin, he can levitate and is a very proud fighter.

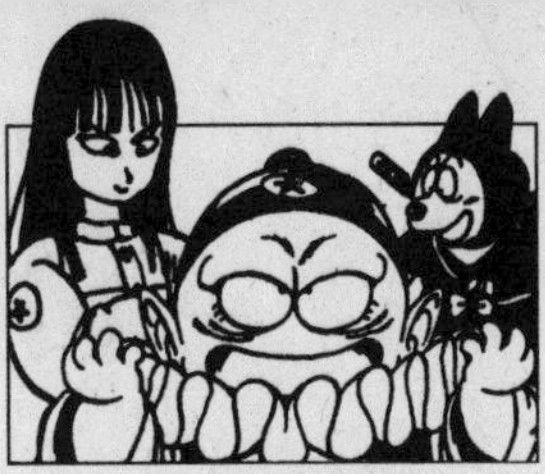

Pilaf and Co.
A power-hungry lord who wants the Dragon Balls so he can have his wish to rule the world granted. He is assisted by Mai and Soba.

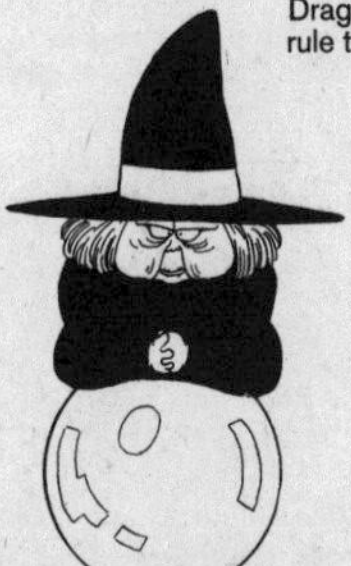

The All-Seeing Crone
Sometimes called "Baba Uranai," this old witch can see the future and locate anything, but her services don't come cheap. She is also Kame-Sen'nin's sister.

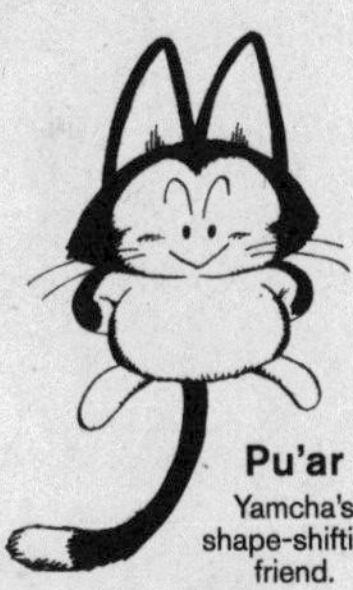

Pu'ar
Yamcha's shape-shifting friend.

Bora & Upa
A father and son who live in the Karin Sanctuary. When Bora was killed by assassin Taopaipai, Goku vowed to gather the Dragon Balls and wish him back to life.

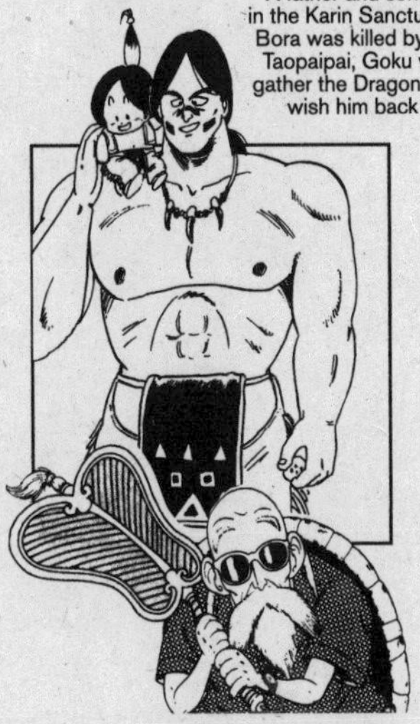

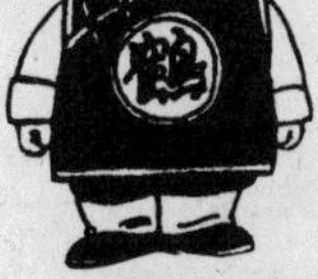

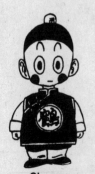

Chaozu
A student of Tsuru-Sen'nin, he can levitate and uses psychic powers.

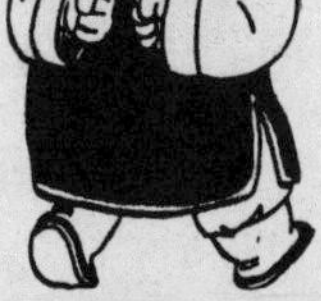

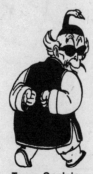

Tsuru-Sen'nin ("The Crane Hermit")
Rival of Kame-Sen'nin, he teaches a different style of martial arts that has a signature move known as *dodon-pa*. His brother Taopaipai was an evil assassin that was hired to kill Goku.

Kame-Sen'nin (The "Turtle Hermit")
A lecherous but powerful martial artist who trained Goku and taught him the *kamehameha* attack. He is also known as *Muten-Rōshi*, or "Invincible Old Master." In disguise as Jackie Chun, he narrowly defeated Goku at the last "Strongest Under the Heavens" martial arts tournament.

Dragonball

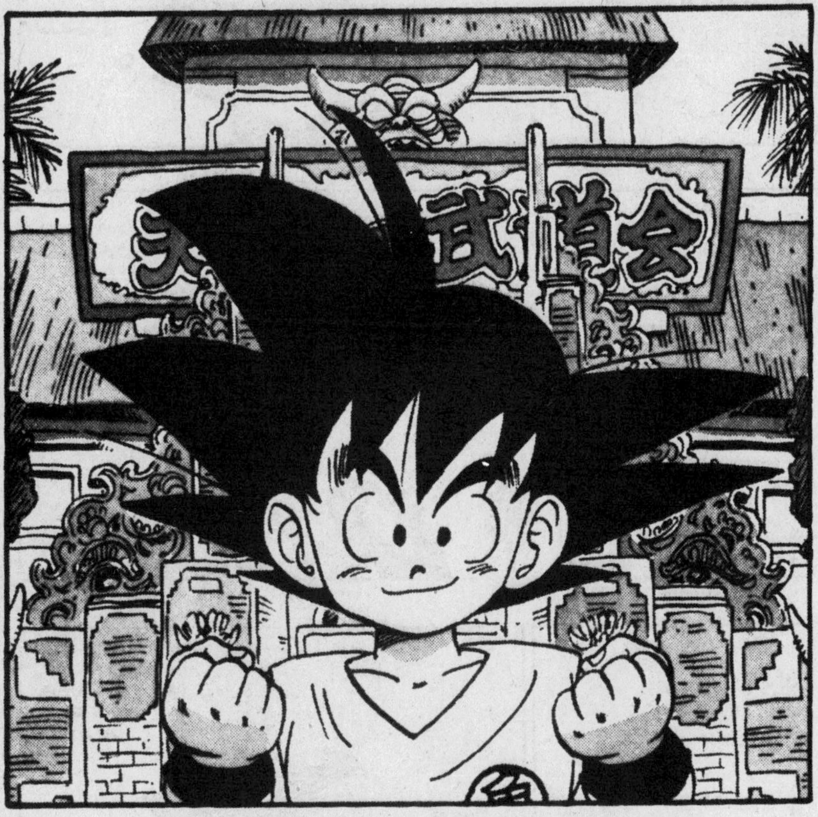

VOLUME 10

THE 22ND TENKA'ICHI BUDŌKAI

Tale 109 • A Second Helping of Pilaf

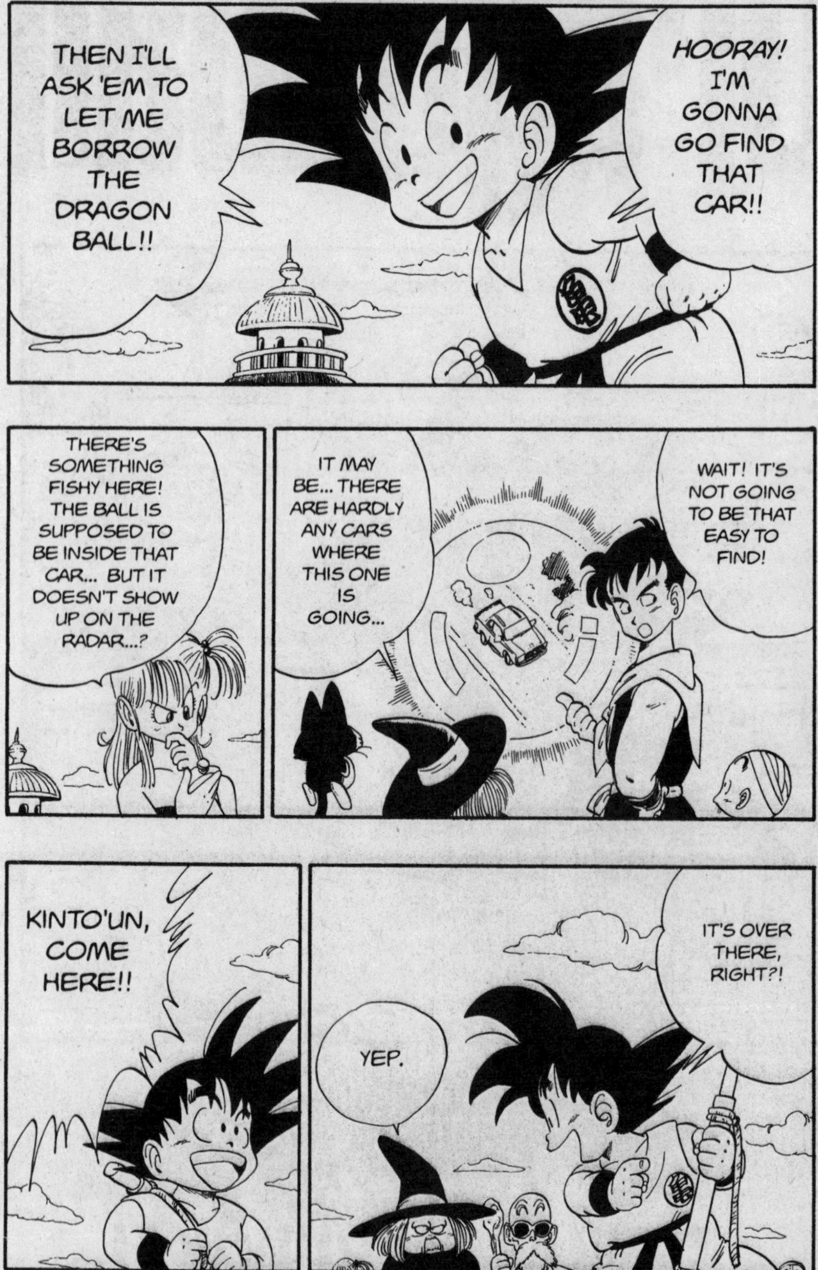
HOORAY! I'M GONNA GO FIND THAT CAR!!
THEN I'LL ASK 'EM TO LET ME BORROW THE DRAGON BALL!!
WAIT! IT'S NOT GOING TO BE THAT EASY TO FIND!
IT MAY BE... THERE ARE HARDLY ANY CARS WHERE THIS ONE IS GOING...
THERE'S SOMETHING FISHY HERE! THE BALL IS SUPPOSED TO BE INSIDE THAT CAR... BUT IT DOESN'T SHOW UP ON THE RADAR...?
IT'S OVER THERE, RIGHT?!
YEP.
KINTO'UN, COME HERE!!

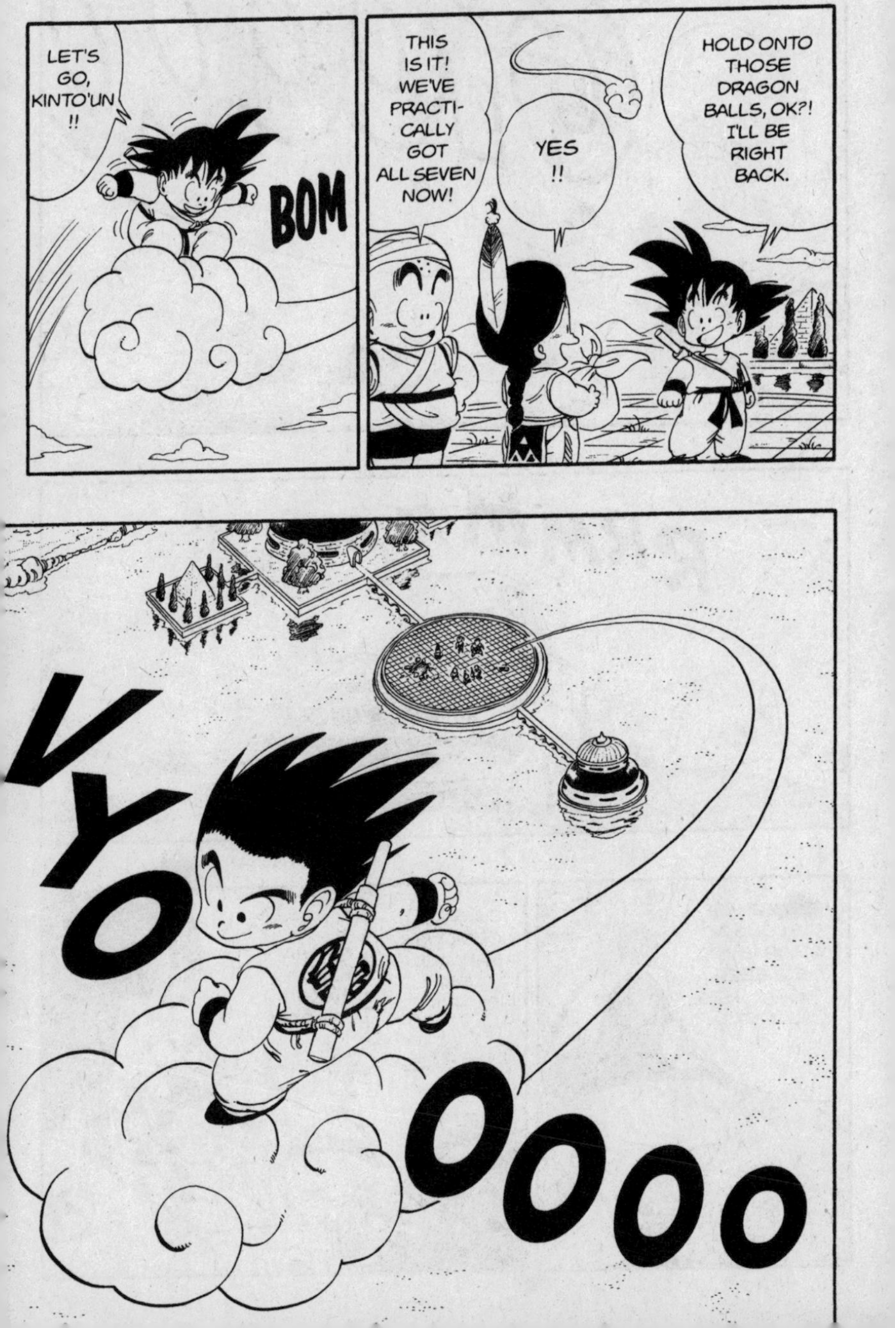
HOLD ONTO THOSE DRAGON BALLS, OK?! I'LL BE RIGHT BACK.
YES !!
THIS IS IT! WE'VE PRACTI-CALLY GOT ALL SEVEN NOW!
LET'S GO, KINTO'UN !!
BOM
VYOOOOO

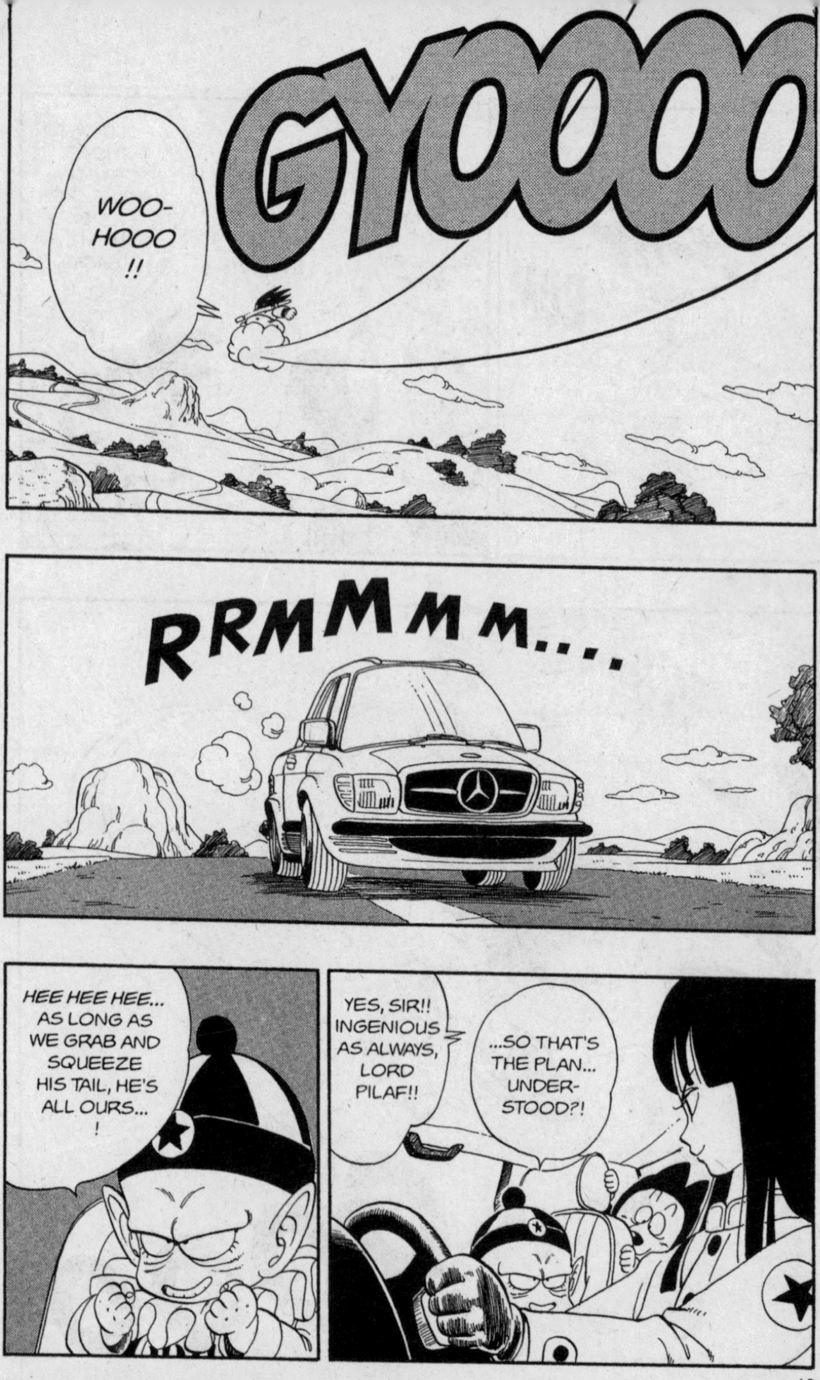
GYOOOO
WOO-HOOO !!
RRMMMM....
...SO THAT'S THE PLAN... UNDERSTOOD?!
YES, SIR!! INGENIOUS AS ALWAYS, LORD PILAF!!
HEE HEE HEE... AS LONG AS WE GRAB AND SQUEEZE HIS TAIL, HE'S ALL OURS... !

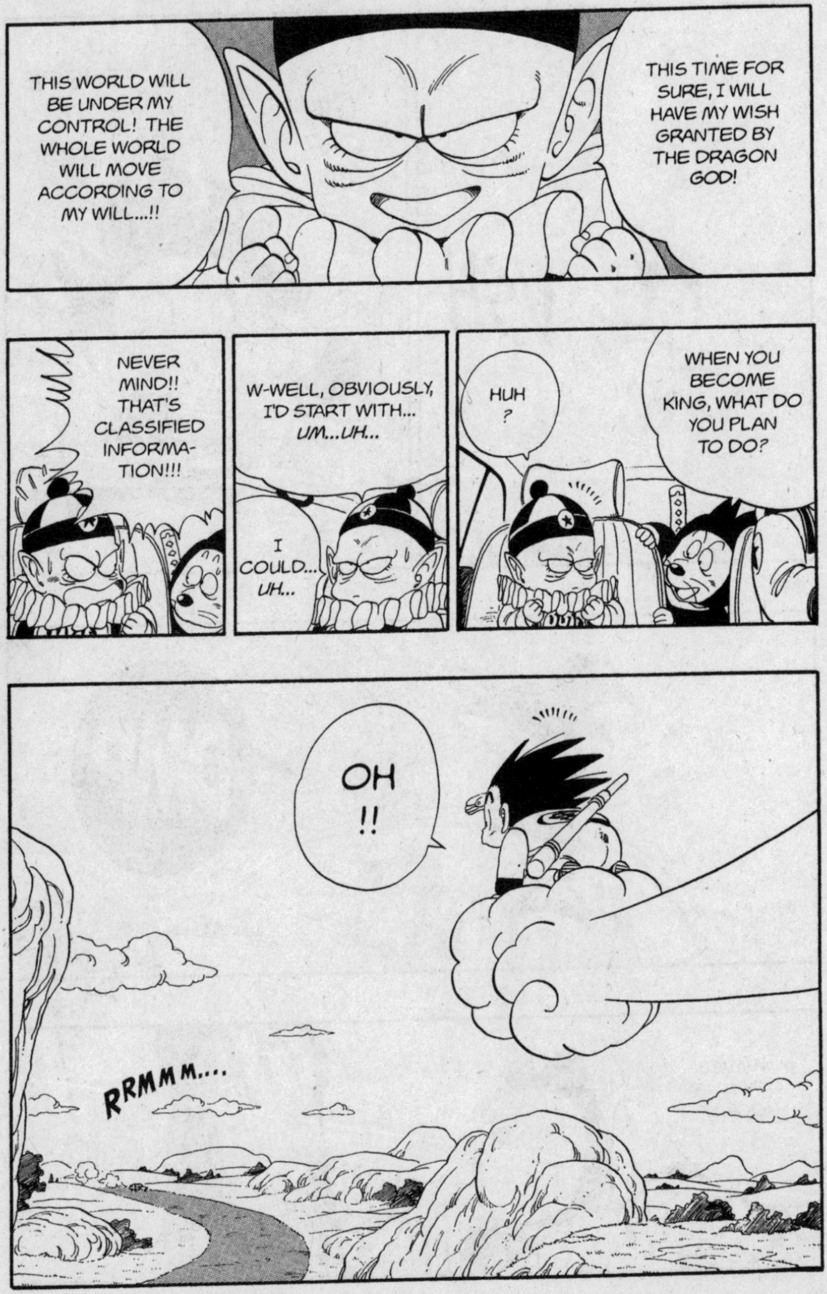
THIS TIME FOR SURE, I WILL HAVE MY WISH GRANTED BY THE DRAGON GOD!
THIS WORLD WILL BE UNDER MY CONTROL! THE WHOLE WORLD WILL MOVE ACCORDING TO MY WILL...!!
WHEN YOU BECOME KING, WHAT DO YOU PLAN TO DO?
HUH ?
W-WELL, OBVIOUSLY, I'D START WITH... UM...UH...
I COULD... UH...
NEVER MIND!! THAT'S CLASSIFIED INFORMATION!!!
OH !!
RRMMM....

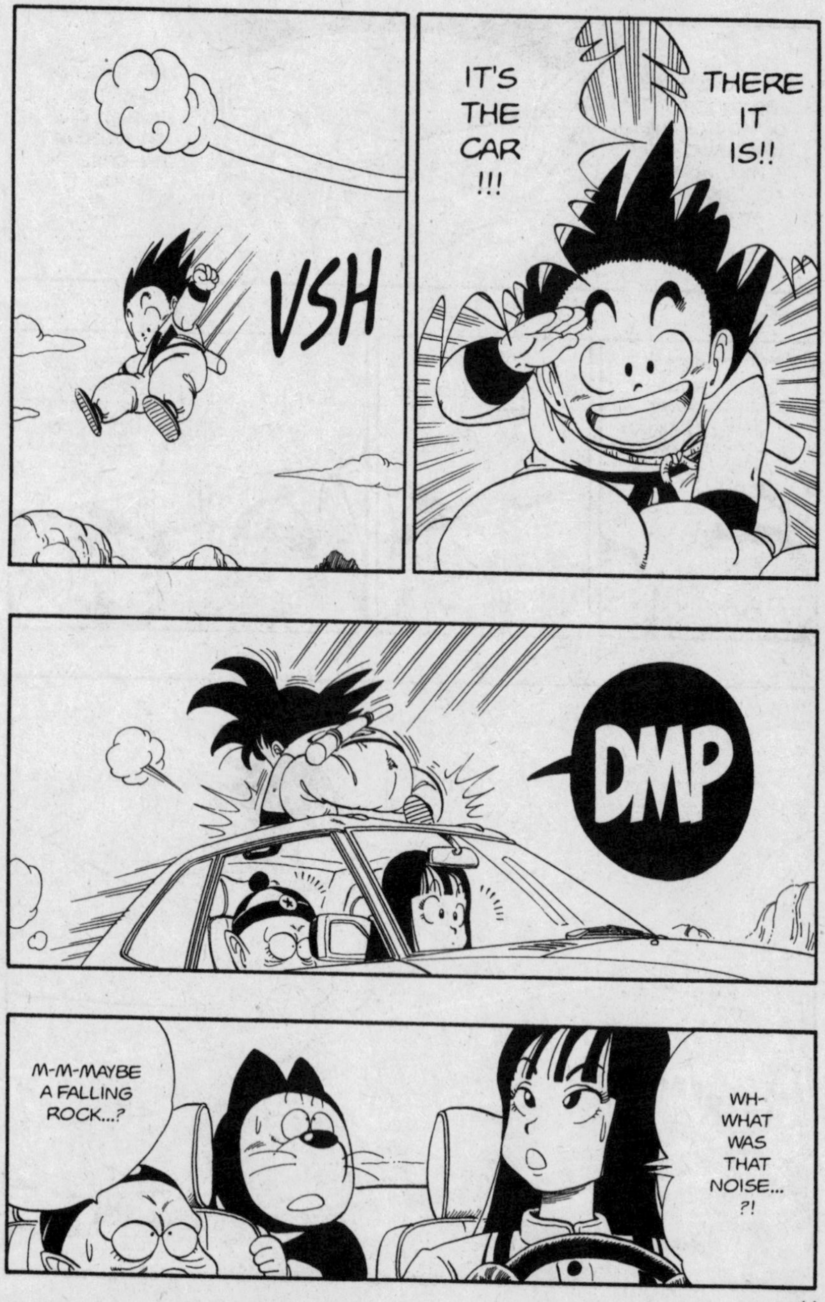
THERE IT IS!!
IT'S THE CAR !!!
VSH
DMP
WH- WHAT WAS THAT NOISE... ?!
M-M-MAYBE A FALLING ROCK...?

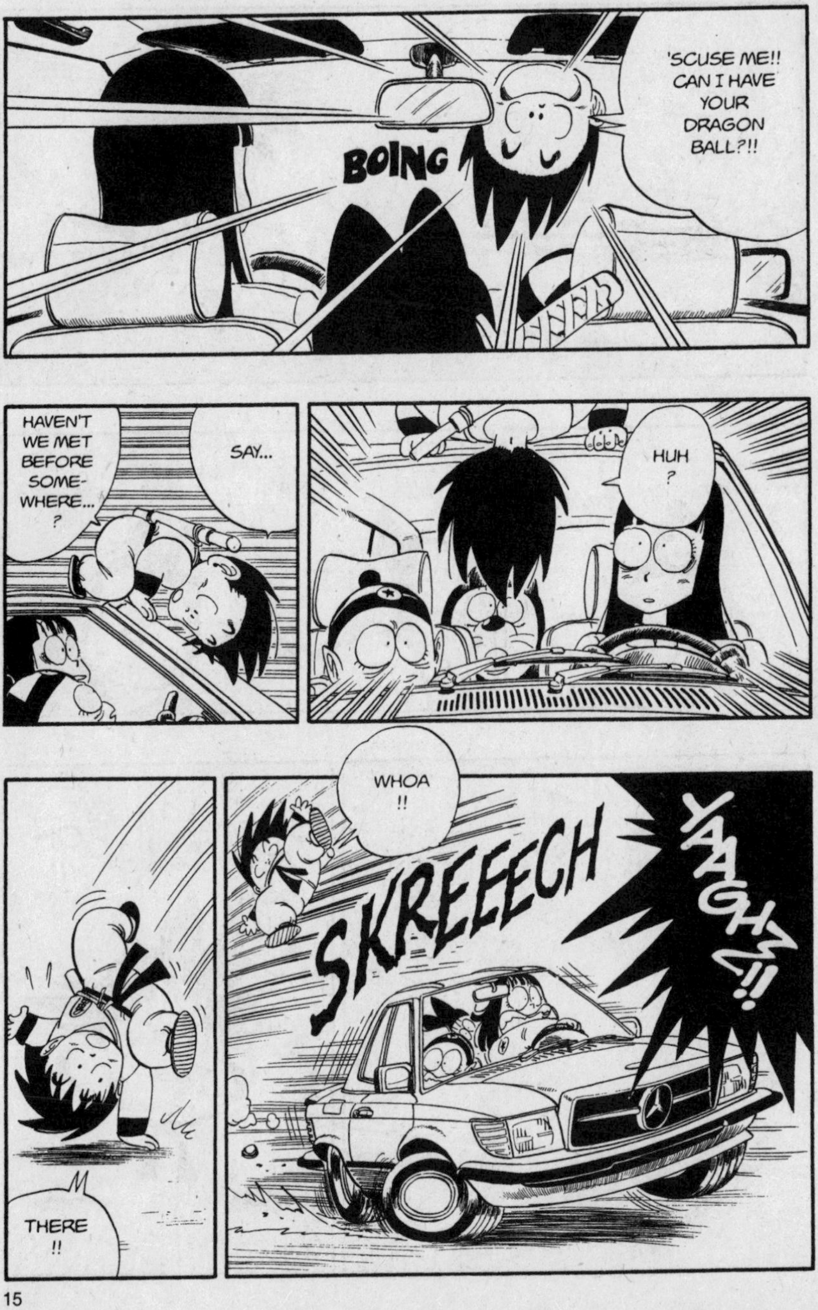
'SCUSE ME!! CAN I HAVE YOUR DRAGON BALL?!!
BOING
HUH ?
SAY...
HAVEN'T WE MET BEFORE SOME-WHERE... ?
YAAGHZZ!!
WHOA !!
SKREEECH
THERE !!

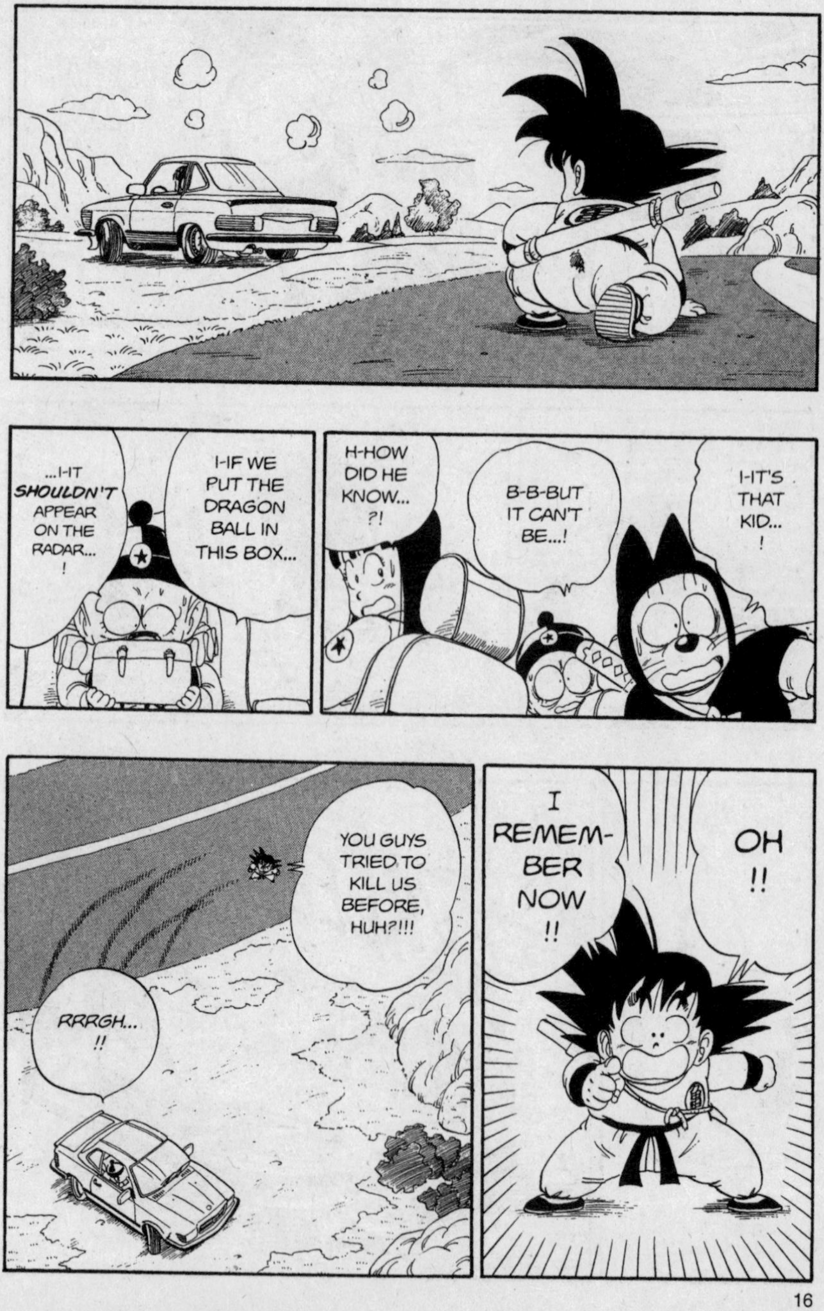

I-IT'S THAT KID...!
B-B-BUT IT CAN'T BE...!
H-HOW DID HE KNOW...?!
I-IF WE PUT THE DRAGON BALL IN THIS BOX...
...I-IT *SHOULDN'T* APPEAR ON THE RADAR...!
OH!!
I REMEM-BER NOW!!
YOU GUYS TRIED TO KILL US BEFORE, HUH?!!!
RRRGH...!!

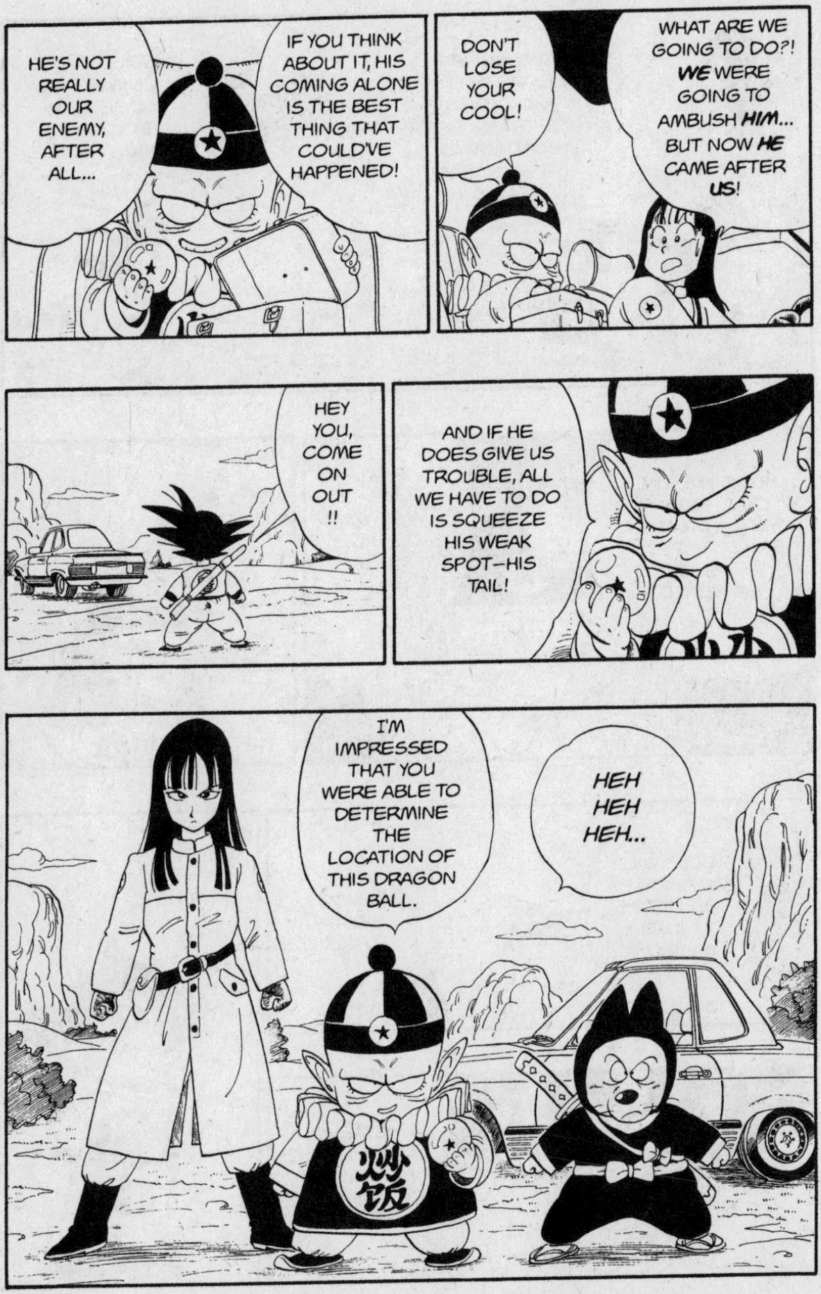
WHAT ARE WE GOING TO DO?! **WE** WERE GOING TO AMBUSH **HIM**... BUT NOW **HE** CAME AFTER **US**!
DON'T LOSE YOUR COOL!
IF YOU THINK ABOUT IT, HIS COMING ALONE IS THE BEST THING THAT COULD'VE HAPPENED!
HE'S NOT REALLY OUR ENEMY, AFTER ALL...
AND IF HE DOES GIVE US TROUBLE, ALL WE HAVE TO DO IS SQUEEZE HIS WEAK SPOT—HIS TAIL!
HEY YOU, COME ON OUT !!
HEH HEH HEH...
I'M IMPRESSED THAT YOU WERE ABLE TO DETERMINE THE LOCATION OF THIS DRAGON BALL.

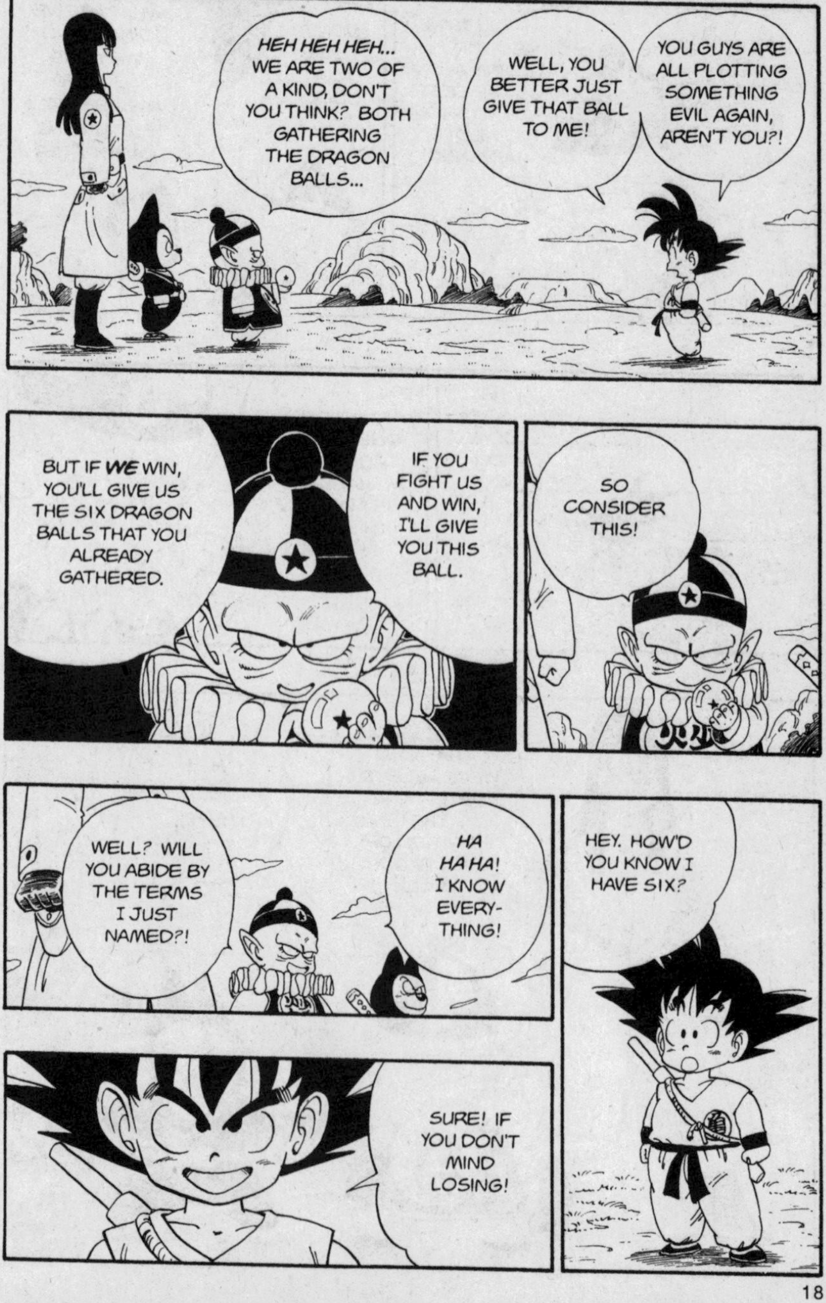
YOU GUYS ARE ALL PLOTTING SOMETHING EVIL AGAIN, AREN'T YOU?!
WELL, YOU BETTER JUST GIVE THAT BALL TO ME!
HEH HEH HEH... WE ARE TWO OF A KIND, DON'T YOU THINK? BOTH GATHERING THE DRAGON BALLS...
SO CONSIDER THIS!
IF YOU FIGHT US AND WIN, I'LL GIVE YOU THIS BALL.
BUT IF ***WE*** WIN, YOU'LL GIVE US THE SIX DRAGON BALLS THAT YOU ALREADY GATHERED.
HEY. HOW'D YOU KNOW I HAVE SIX?
HA HA HA! I KNOW EVERYTHING!
WELL? WILL YOU ABIDE BY THE TERMS I JUST NAMED?!
SURE! IF YOU DON'T MIND LOSING!

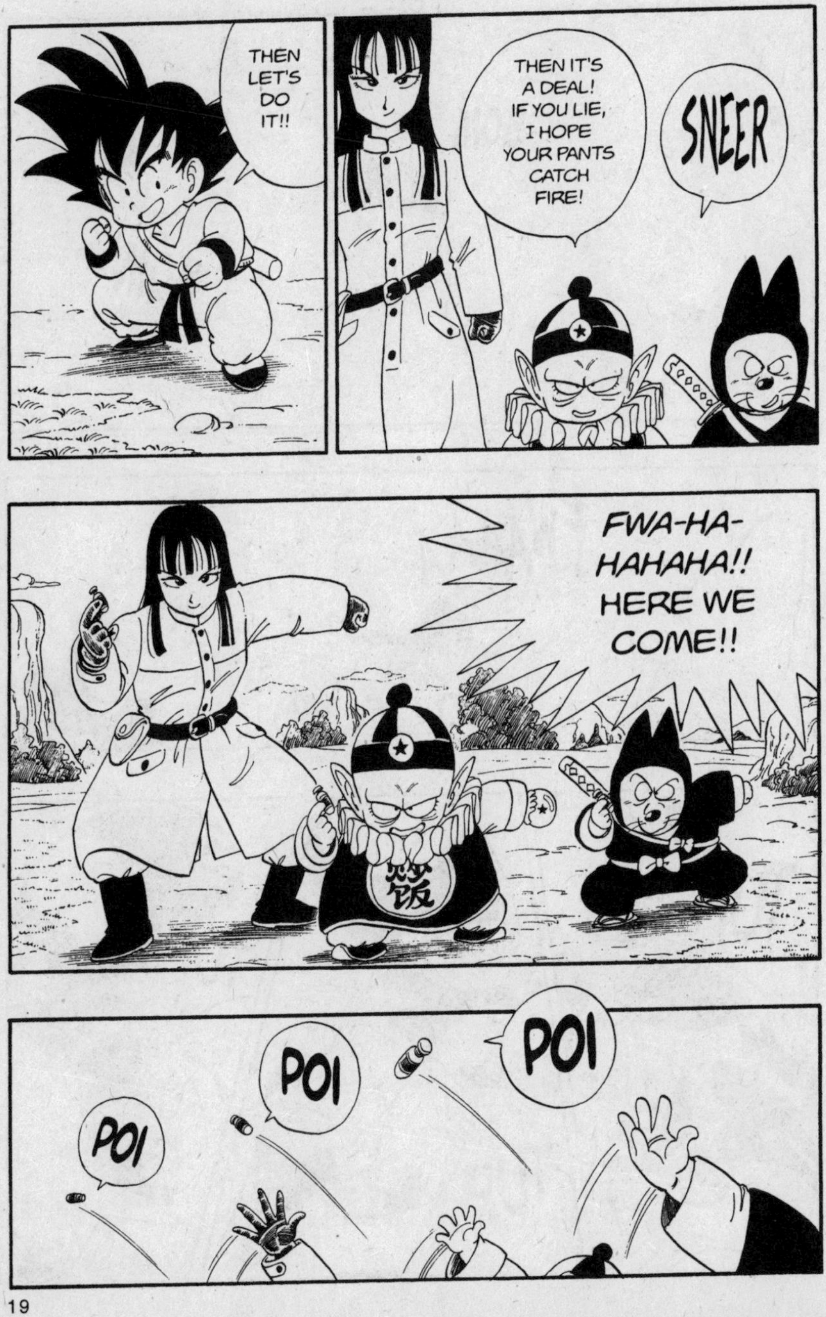
SNEER
THEN IT'S A DEAL! IF YOU LIE, I HOPE YOUR PANTS CATCH FIRE!
THEN LET'S DO IT!!
FWA-HA-HAHAHA!! HERE WE COME!!
POI
POI
POI

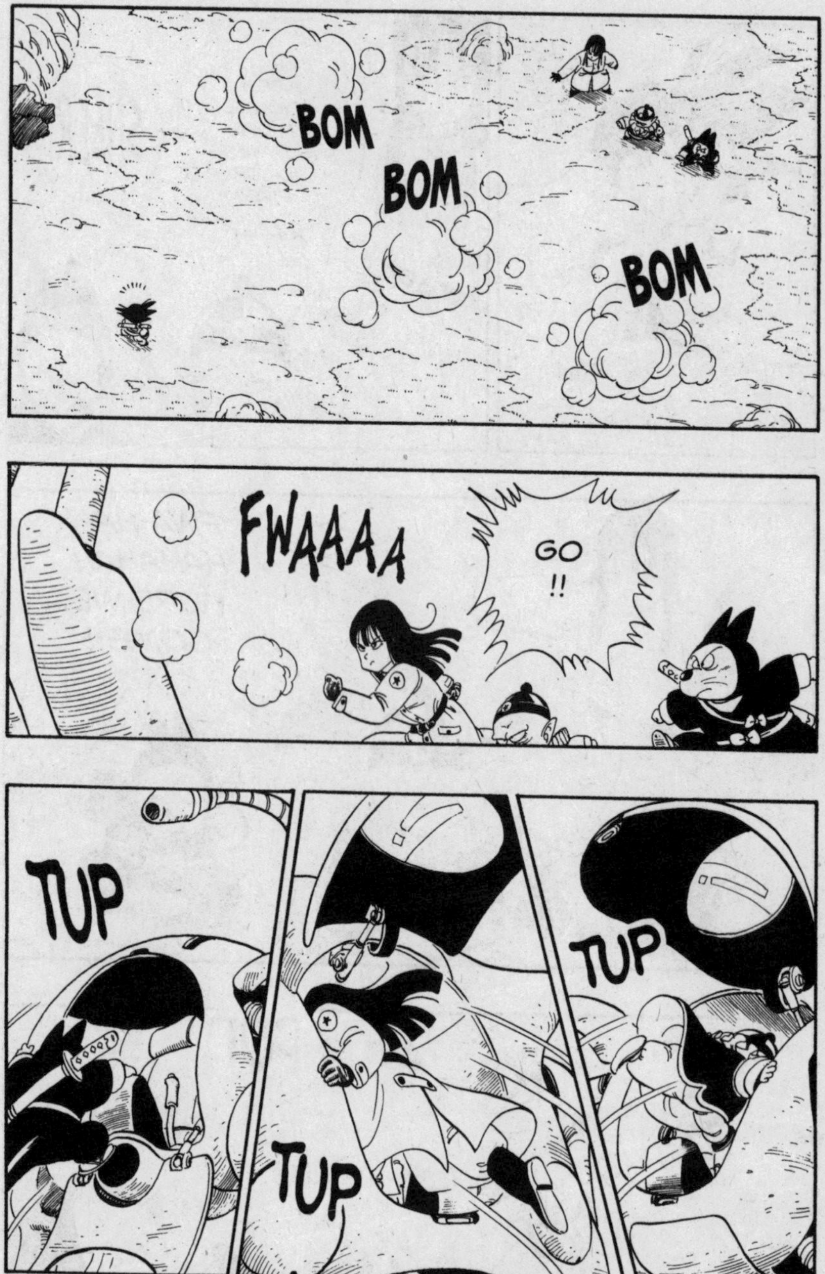
BOM
BOM
BOM
GO !!
FWAAAA
TUP
TUP
TUP

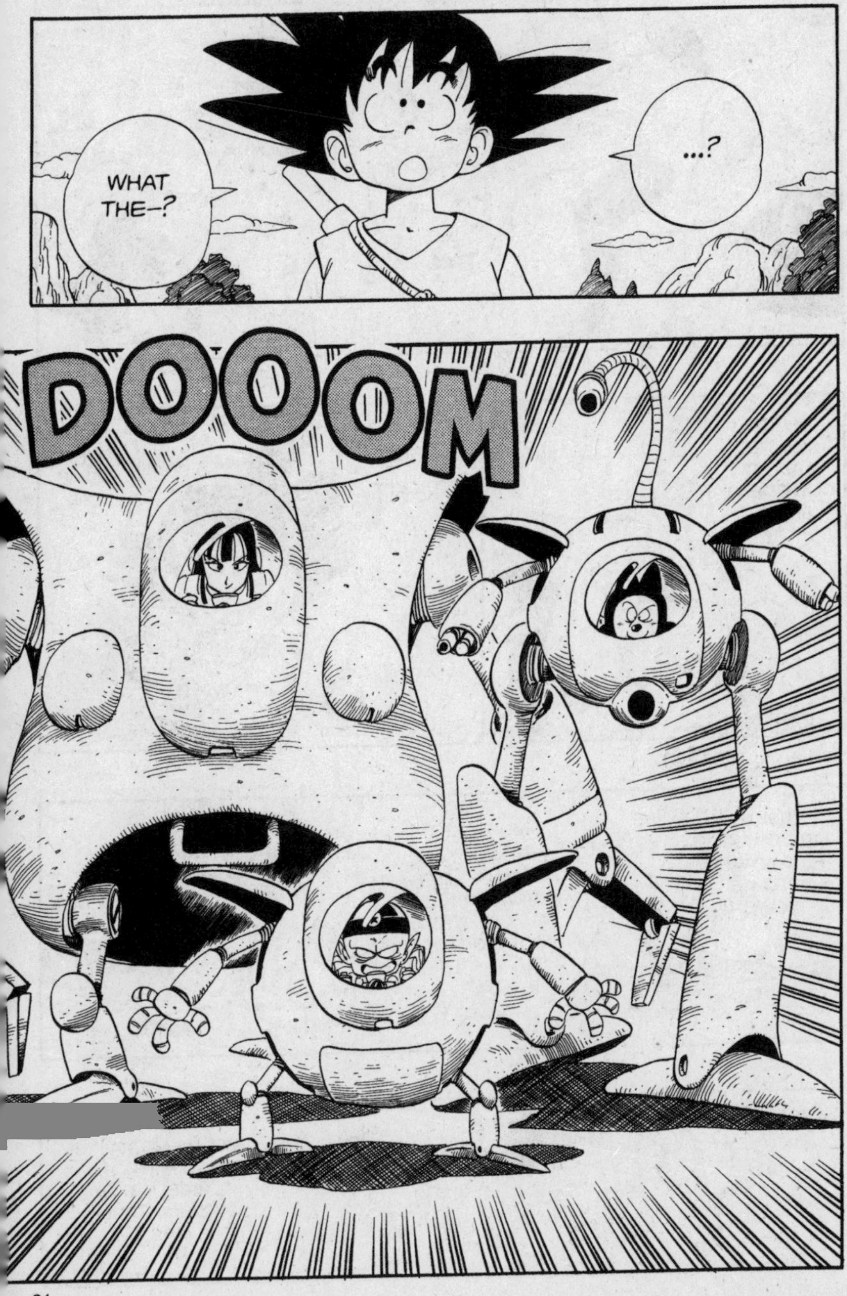
...?
WHAT THE–?
DOOOM

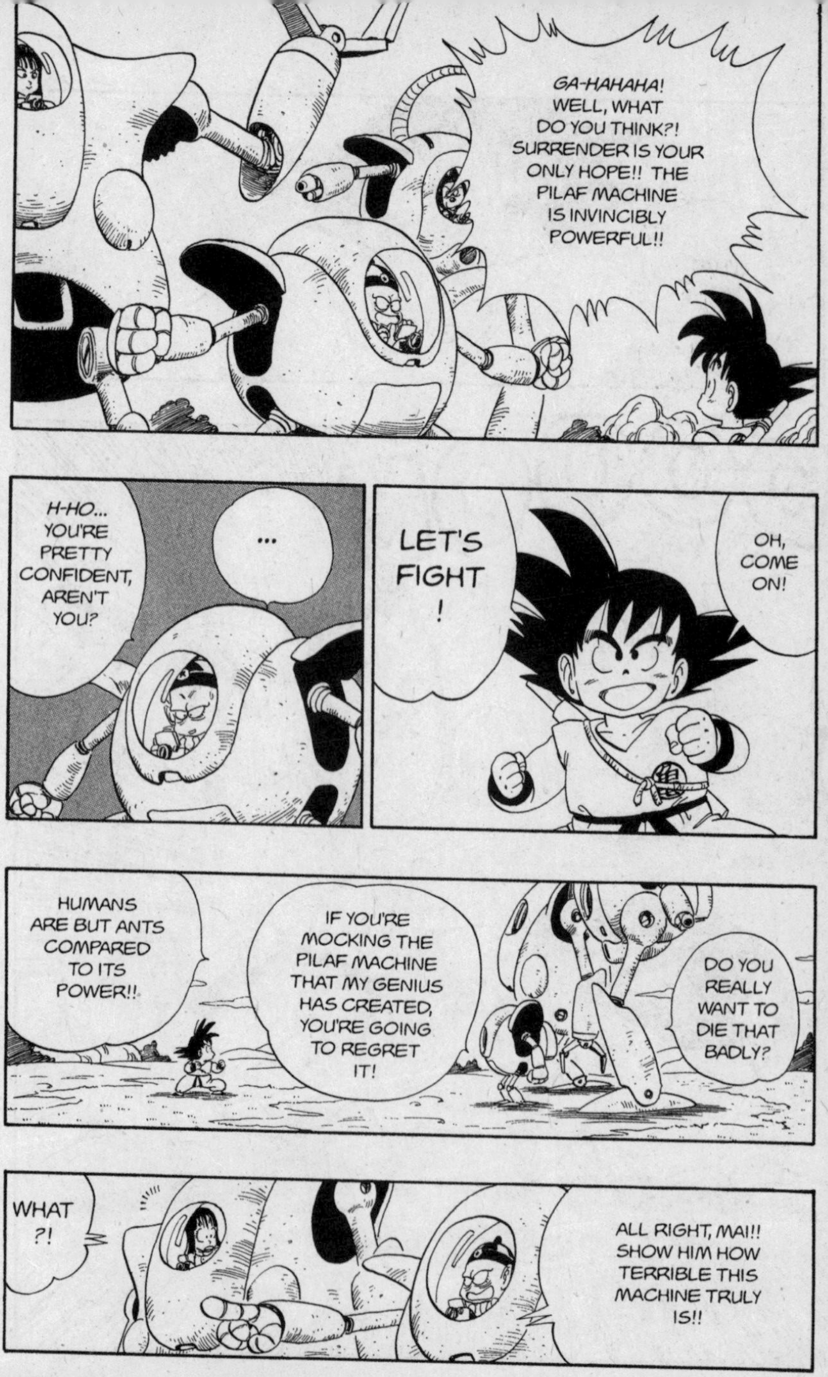
GA-HAHAHA! WELL, WHAT DO YOU THINK?! SURRENDER IS YOUR ONLY HOPE!! THE PILAF MACHINE IS INVINCIBLY POWERFUL!!
OH, COME ON!
LET'S FIGHT!
...
H-HO... YOU'RE PRETTY CONFIDENT, AREN'T YOU?
DO YOU REALLY WANT TO DIE THAT BADLY?
IF YOU'RE MOCKING THE PILAF MACHINE THAT MY GENIUS HAS CREATED, YOU'RE GOING TO REGRET IT!
HUMANS ARE BUT ANTS COMPARED TO ITS POWER!!
ALL RIGHT, MAI!! SHOW HIM HOW TERRIBLE THIS MACHINE TRULY IS!!
WHAT?!

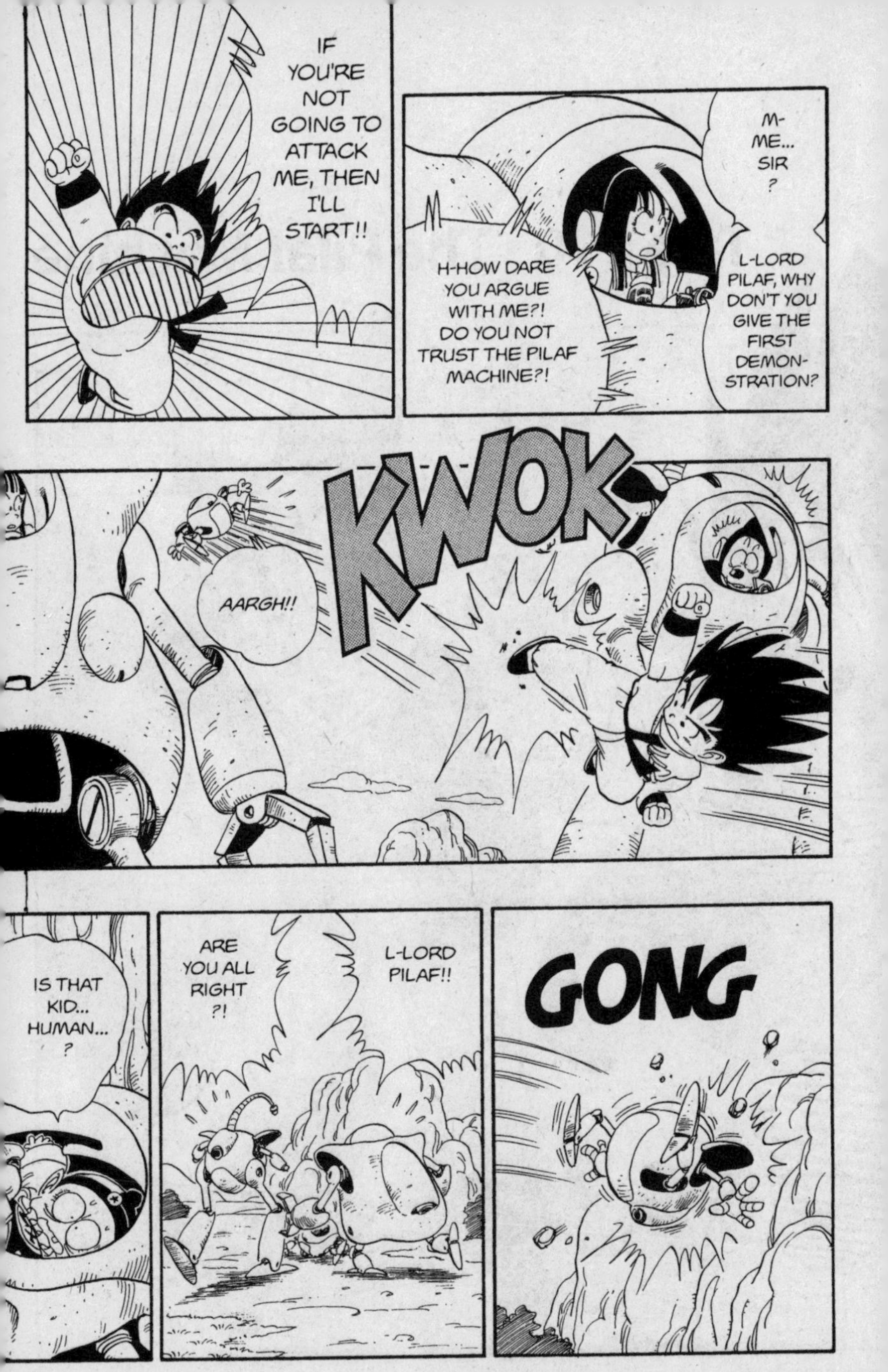
M-ME... SIR?
L-LORD PILAF, WHY DON'T YOU GIVE THE FIRST DEMONSTRATION?
H-HOW DARE YOU ARGUE WITH ME?! DO YOU NOT TRUST THE PILAF MACHINE?!
IF YOU'RE NOT GOING TO ATTACK ME, THEN I'LL START!!
KWOK
AARGH!!
GONG
L-LORD PILAF!!
ARE YOU ALL RIGHT?!
IS THAT KID... HUMAN...?

Tale 110 • The Pilaf Machine

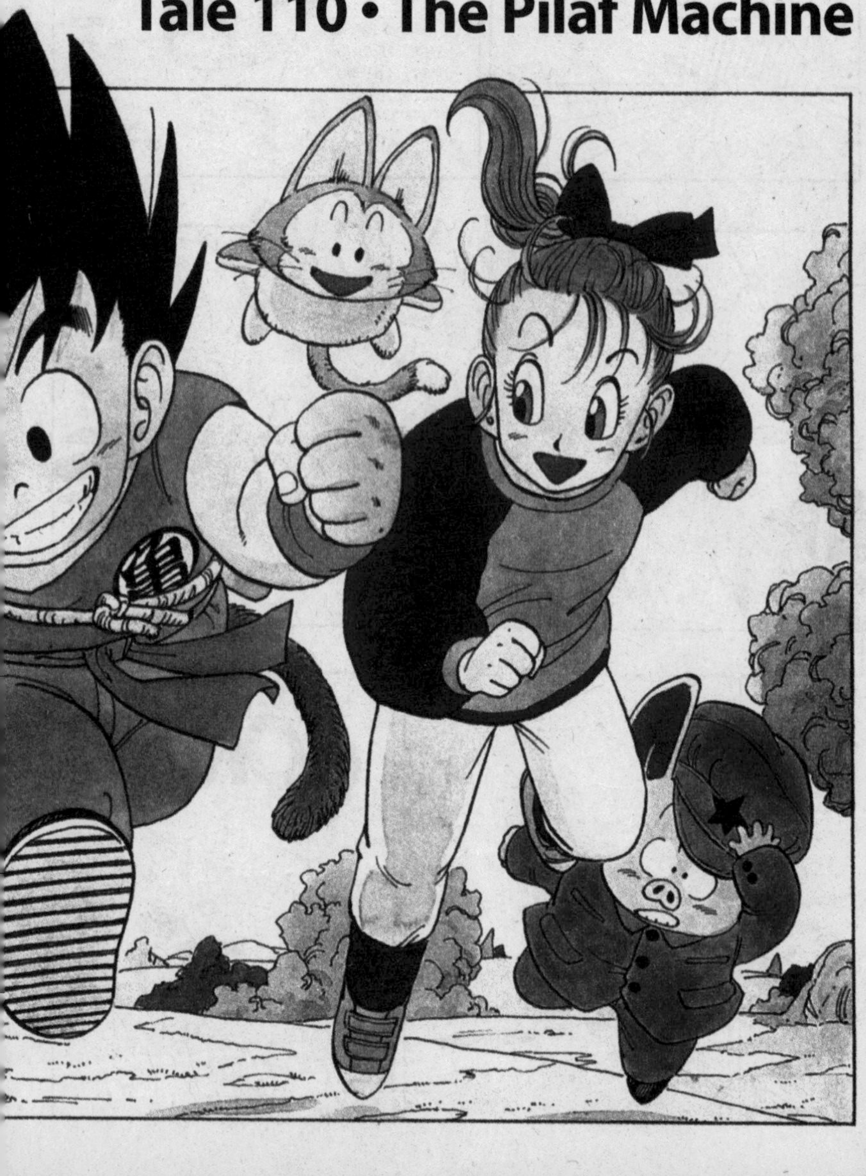

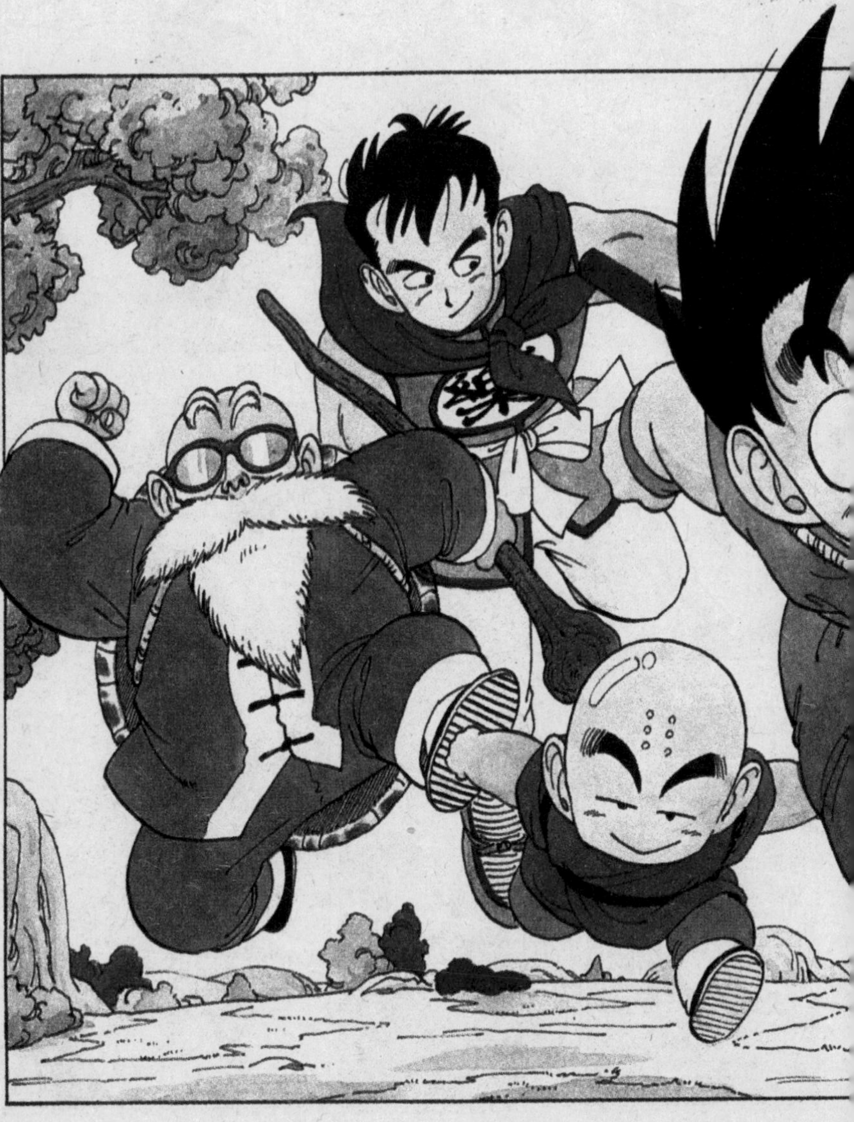

Tale 110 • The Pilaf Machine

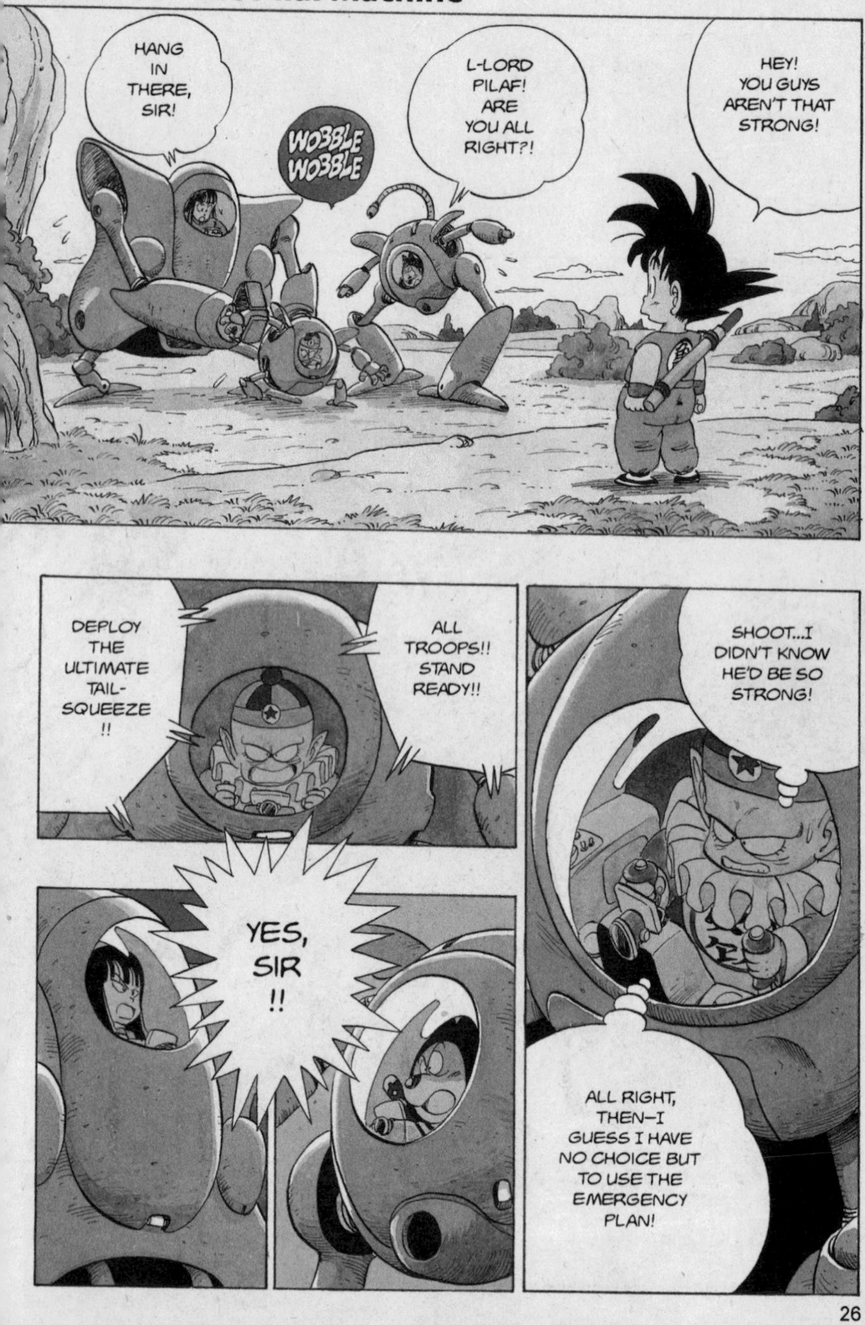
HEY! YOU GUYS AREN'T THAT STRONG!
L-LORD PILAF! ARE YOU ALL RIGHT?!
WOBBLE WOBBLE
HANG IN THERE, SIR!
SHOOT...I DIDN'T KNOW HE'D BE SO STRONG!
ALL RIGHT, THEN—I GUESS I HAVE NO CHOICE BUT TO USE THE EMERGENCY PLAN!
ALL TROOPS!! STAND READY!!
DEPLOY THE ULTIMATE TAIL-SQUEEZE !!
YES, SIR !!

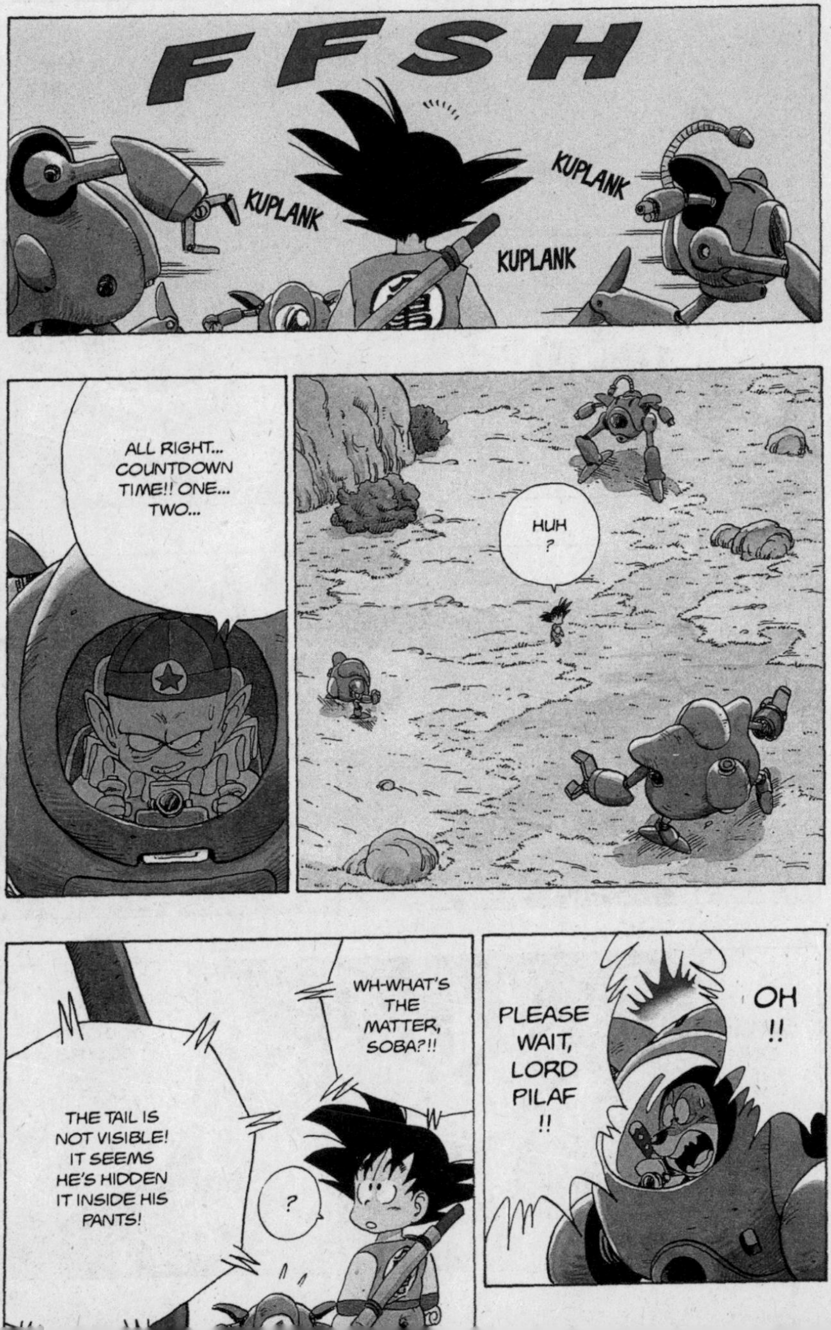
FFSH
KUPLANK
KUPLANK
KUPLANK
HUH ?
ALL RIGHT... COUNTDOWN TIME!! ONE... TWO...
OH !!
PLEASE WAIT, LORD PILAF !!
WH-WHAT'S THE MATTER, SOBA?!!
THE TAIL IS NOT VISIBLE! IT SEEMS HE'S HIDDEN IT INSIDE HIS PANTS!
?

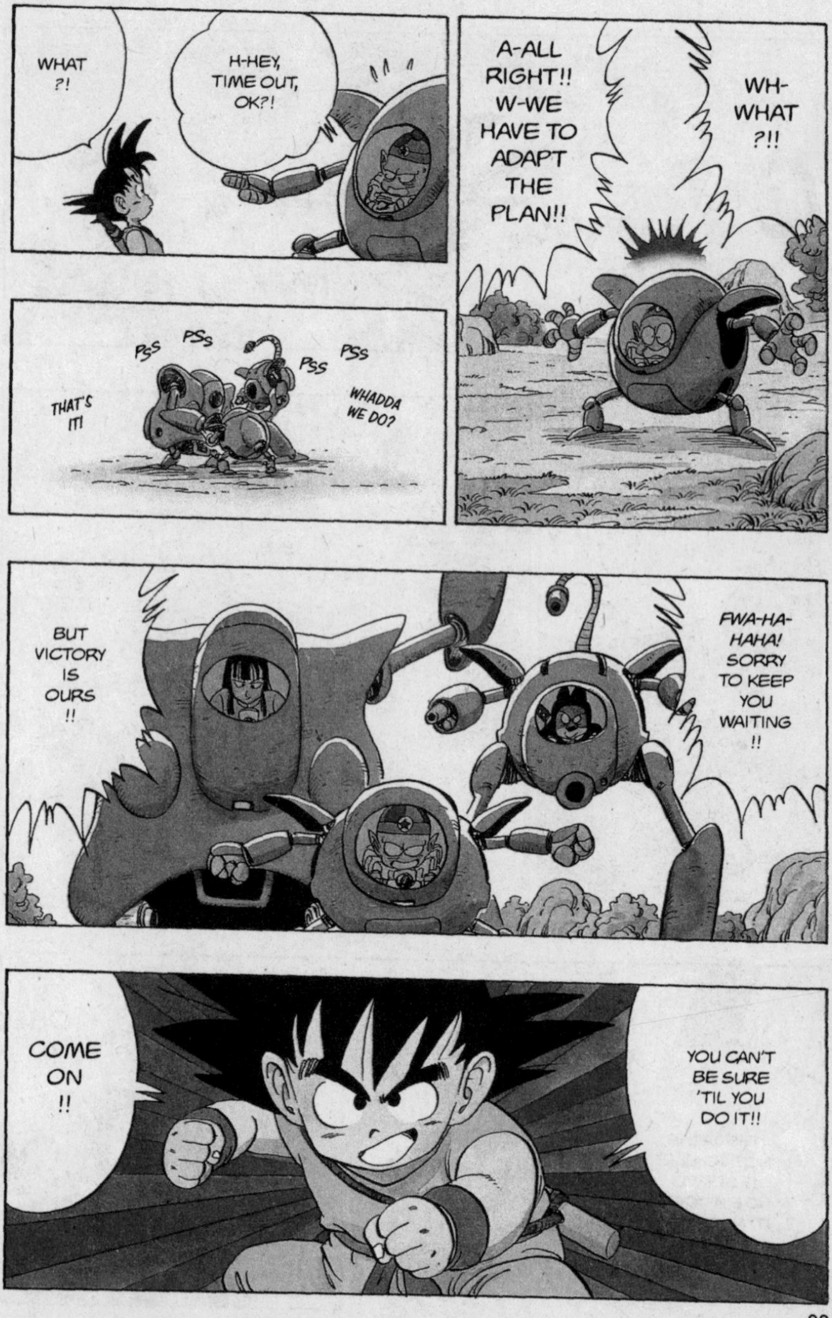

WH-WHAT?!!
A-ALL RIGHT!! W-WE HAVE TO ADAPT THE PLAN!!
H-HEY, TIME OUT, OK?!
WHAT?!
PSS
PSS
WHADDA WE DO?
PSS
PSS
THAT'S IT!
FWA-HA-HAHA! SORRY TO KEEP YOU WAITING!!
BUT VICTORY IS OURS!!
YOU CAN'T BE SURE 'TIL YOU DO IT!!
COME ON!!

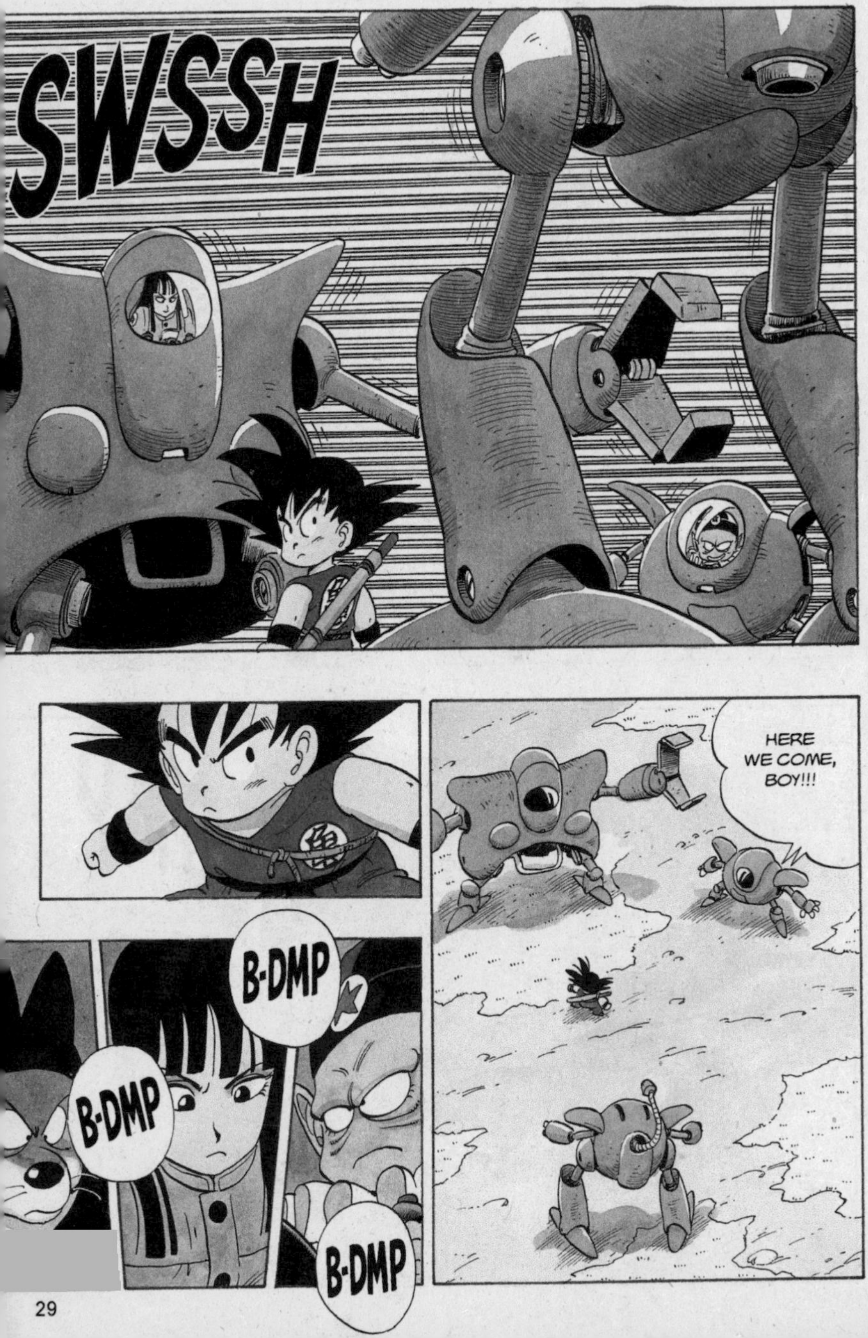
SWSSH
HERE WE COME, BOY!!!
B-DMP
B-DMP
B-DMP

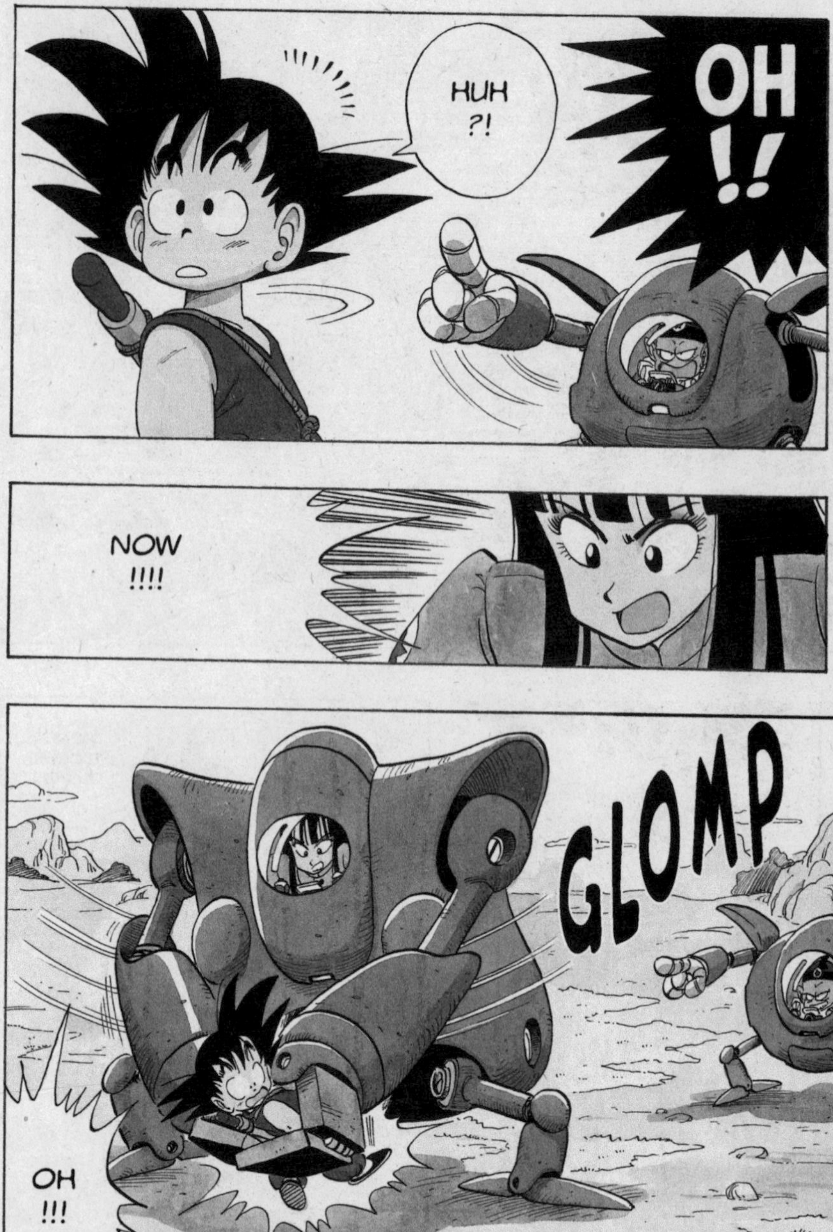
OH !!
HUH ?!
NOW !!!!
GLOMP
OH !!!

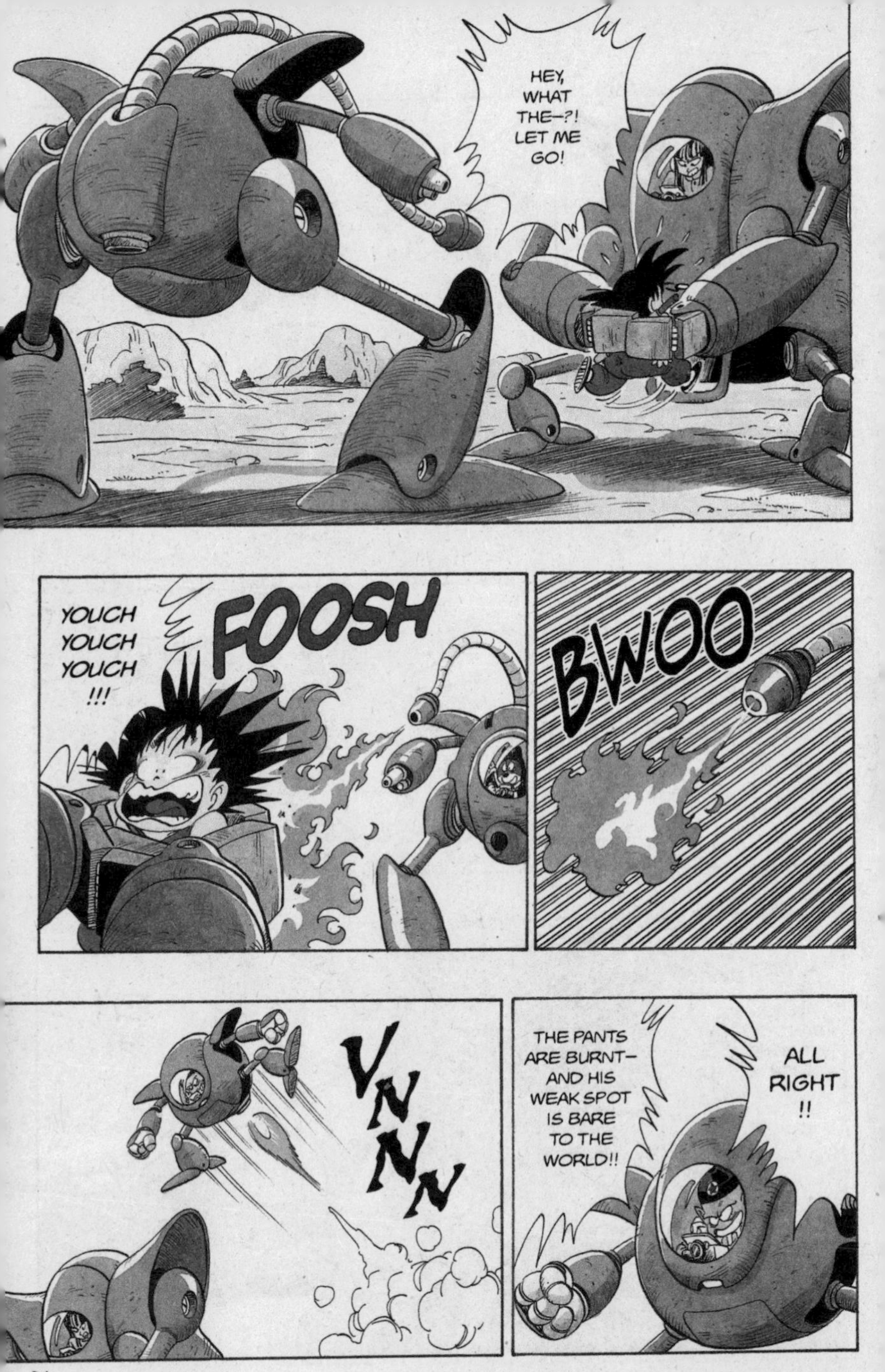
HEY, WHAT THE—?! LET ME GO!
BWOO
YOUCH YOUCH YOUCH !!!
FOOSH
ALL RIGHT !!
THE PANTS ARE BURNT— AND HIS WEAK SPOT IS BARE TO THE WORLD!!
VNNN

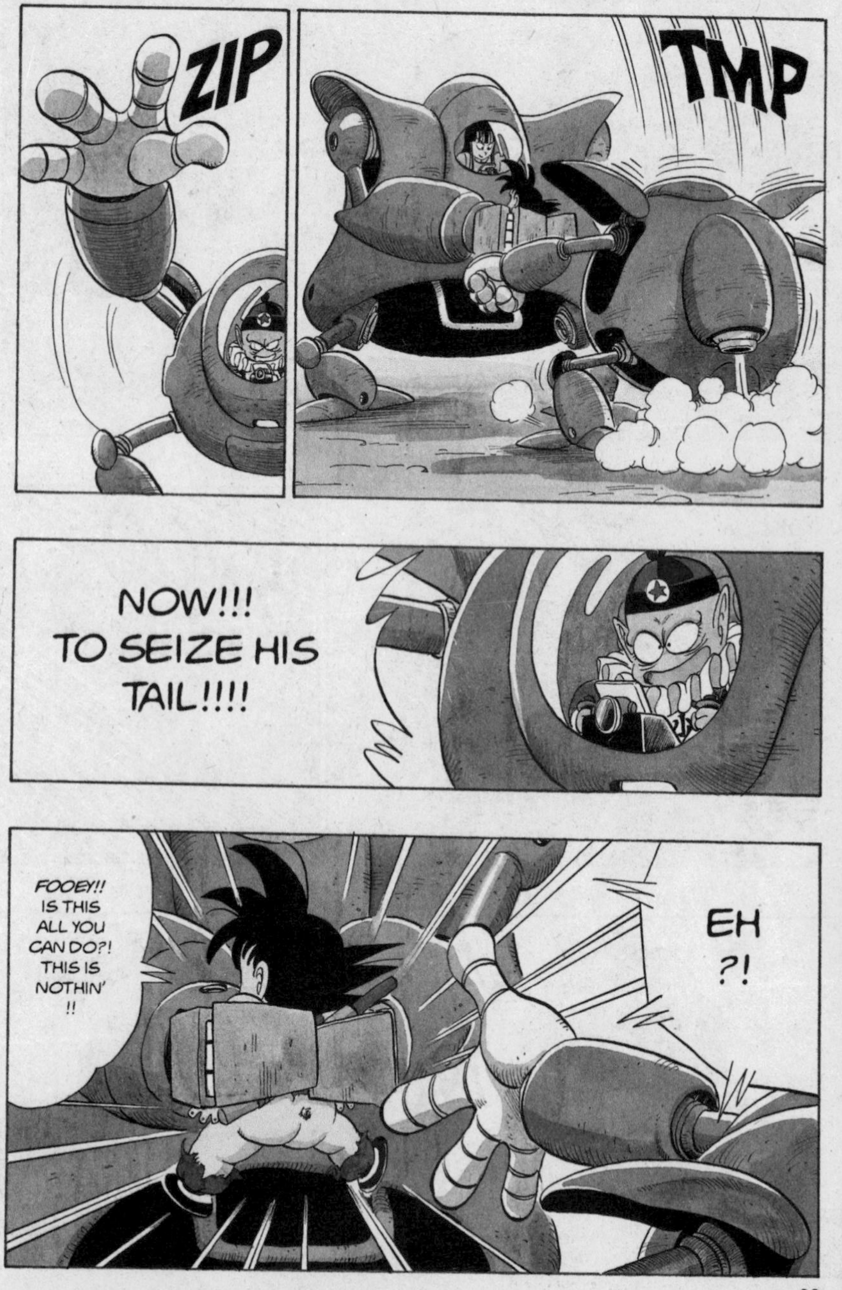
TMP
ZIP
NOW!!! TO SEIZE HIS TAIL!!!!
EH ?!
FOOEY!! IS THIS ALL YOU CAN DO?! THIS IS NOTHIN' !!

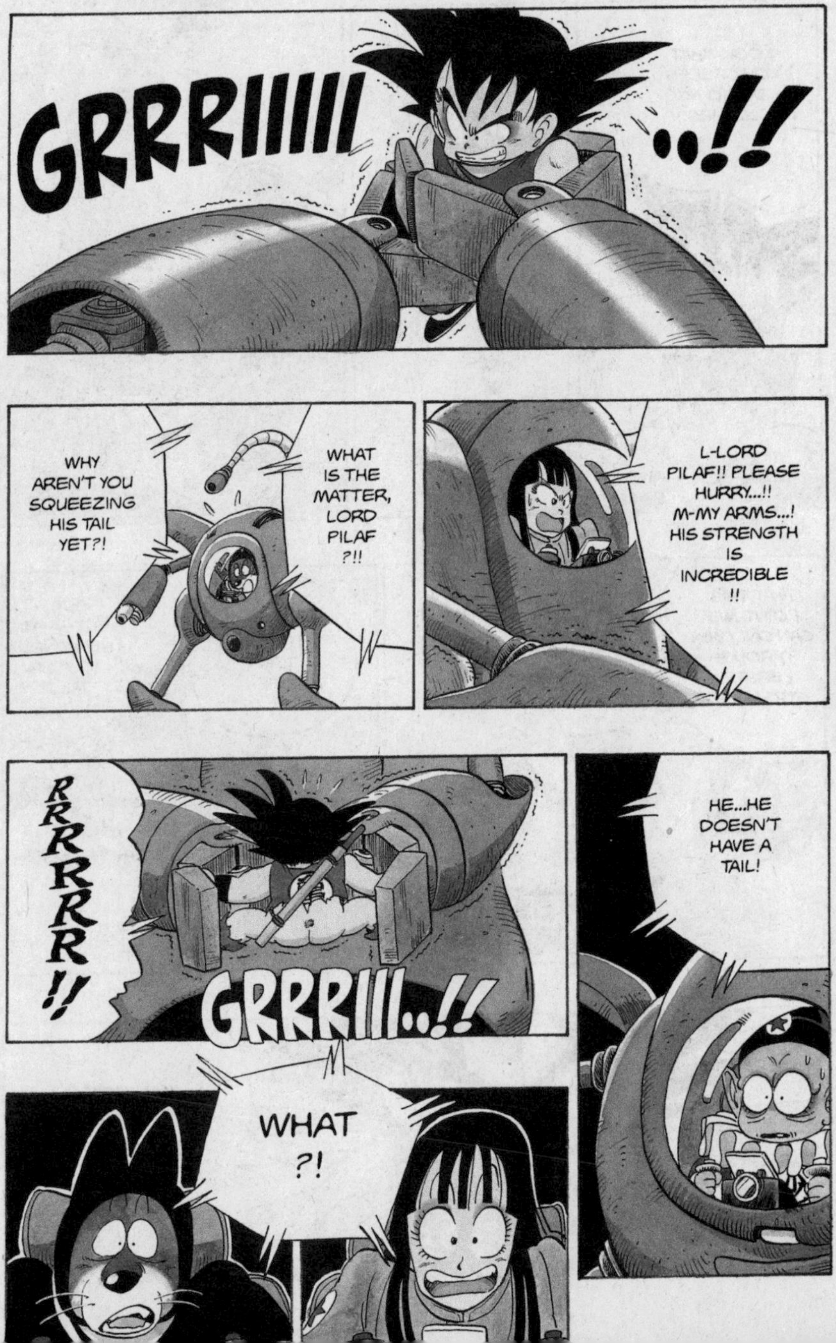
GRRRIIIII..!!
L-LORD PILAF!! PLEASE HURRY...!! M-MY ARMS...! HIS STRENGTH IS INCREDIBLE!!
WHAT IS THE MATTER, LORD PILAF?!!
WHY AREN'T YOU SQUEEZING HIS TAIL YET?!
HE...HE DOESN'T HAVE A TAIL!
RRRRRR!!
GRRRIII..!!
WHAT?!

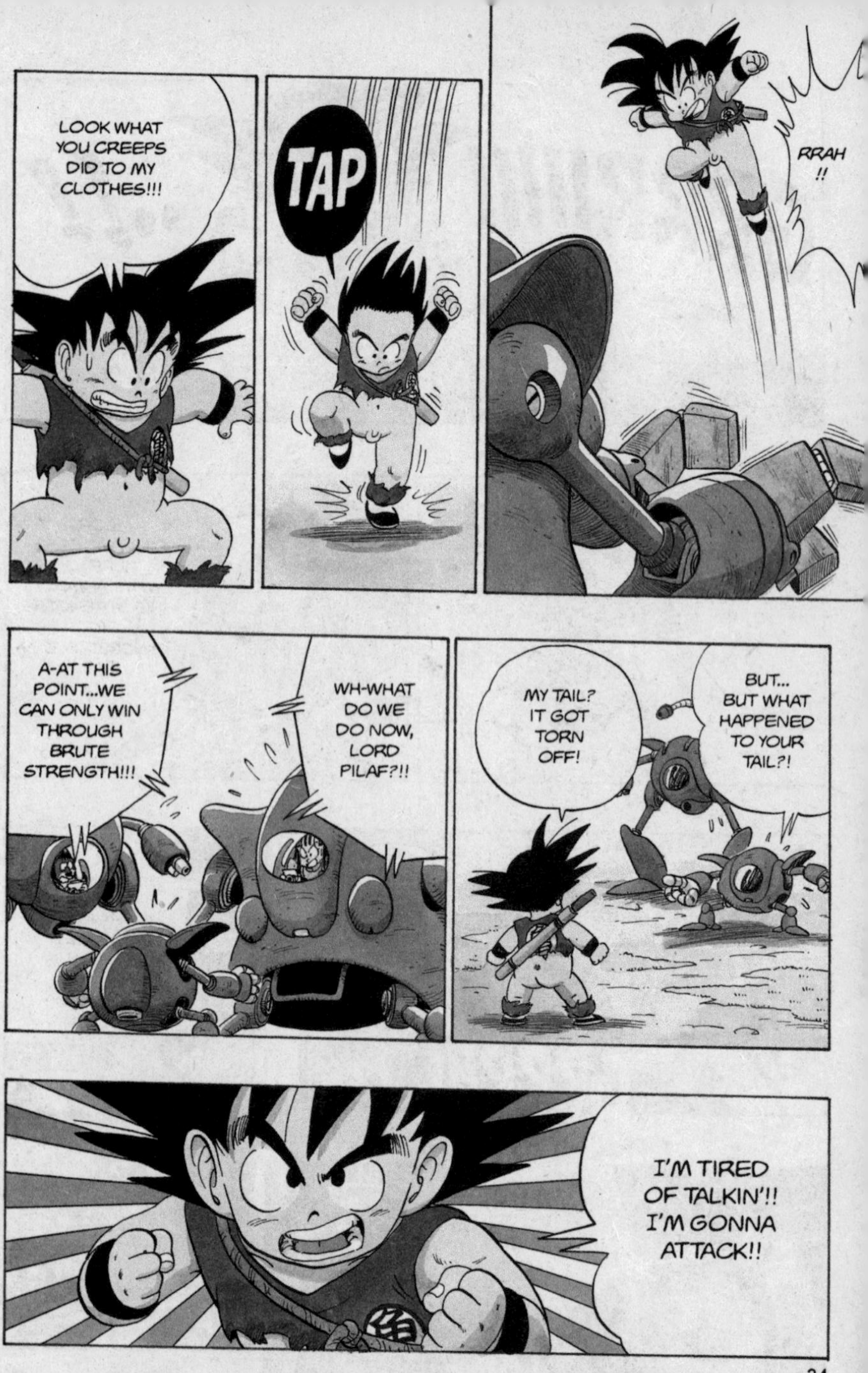

RRAH!!
TAP
LOOK WHAT YOU CREEPS DID TO MY CLOTHES!!!
BUT... BUT WHAT HAPPENED TO YOUR TAIL?!
MY TAIL? IT GOT TORN OFF!
WH-WHAT DO WE DO NOW, LORD PILAF?!!
A-AT THIS POINT...WE CAN ONLY WIN THROUGH BRUTE STRENGTH!!!
I'M TIRED OF TALKIN'!! I'M GONNA ATTACK!!

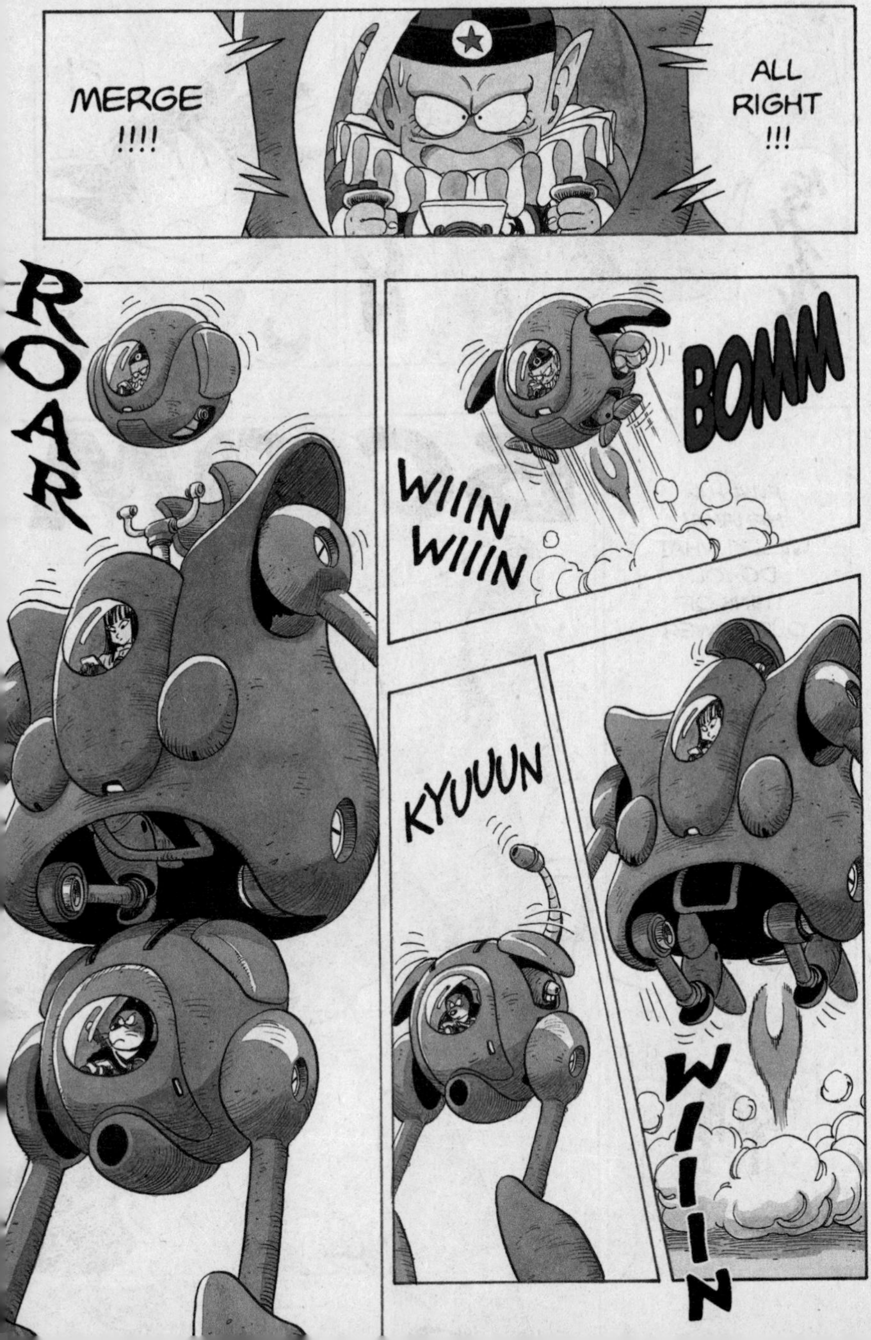
ALL RIGHT !!!
MERGE !!!!
BOMM
WIIIN WIIIN
WIIIN
KYUUUN
ROAR

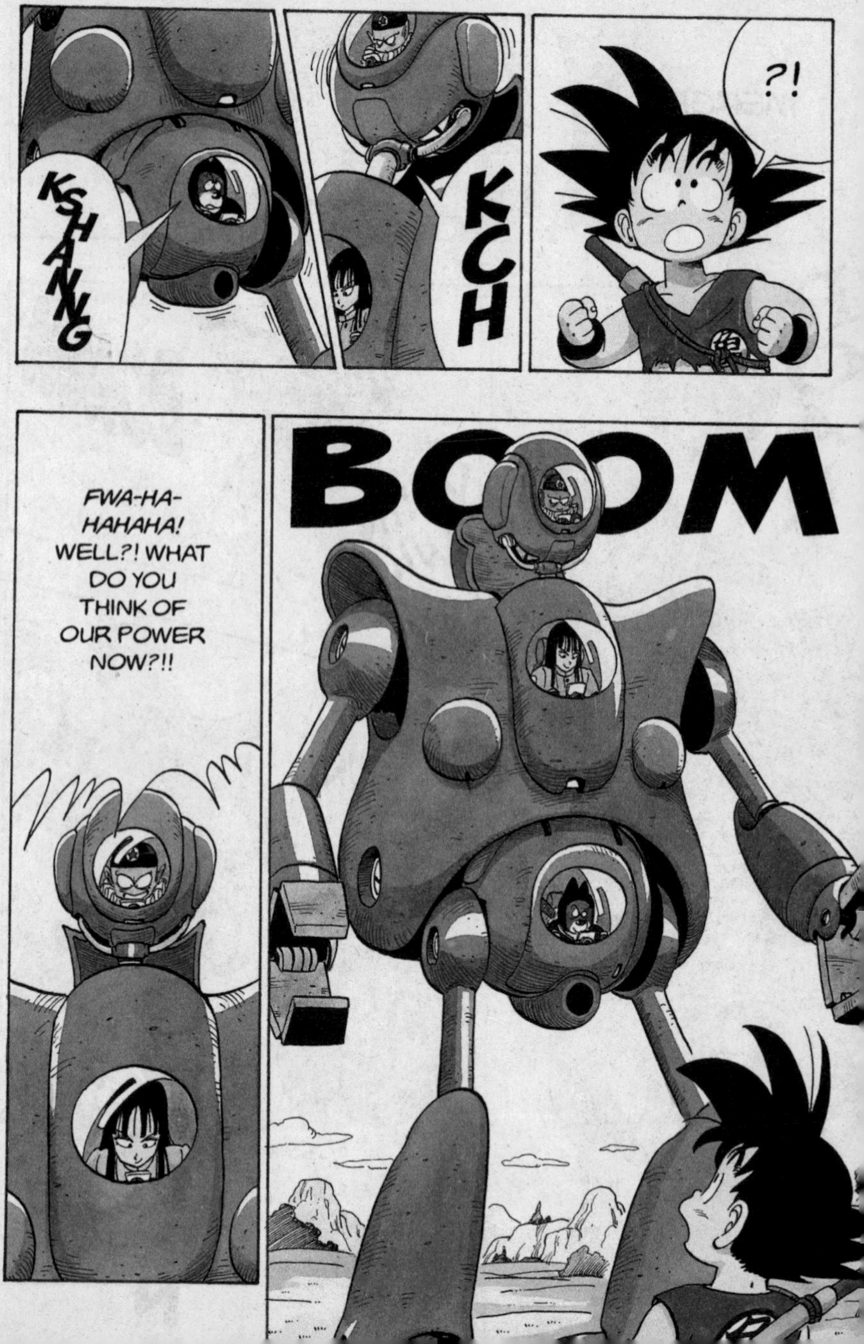
?!
KCH
KSHANNG
BOOM
FWA-HA-HAHAHA! WELL?! WHAT DO YOU THINK OF OUR POWER NOW?!!

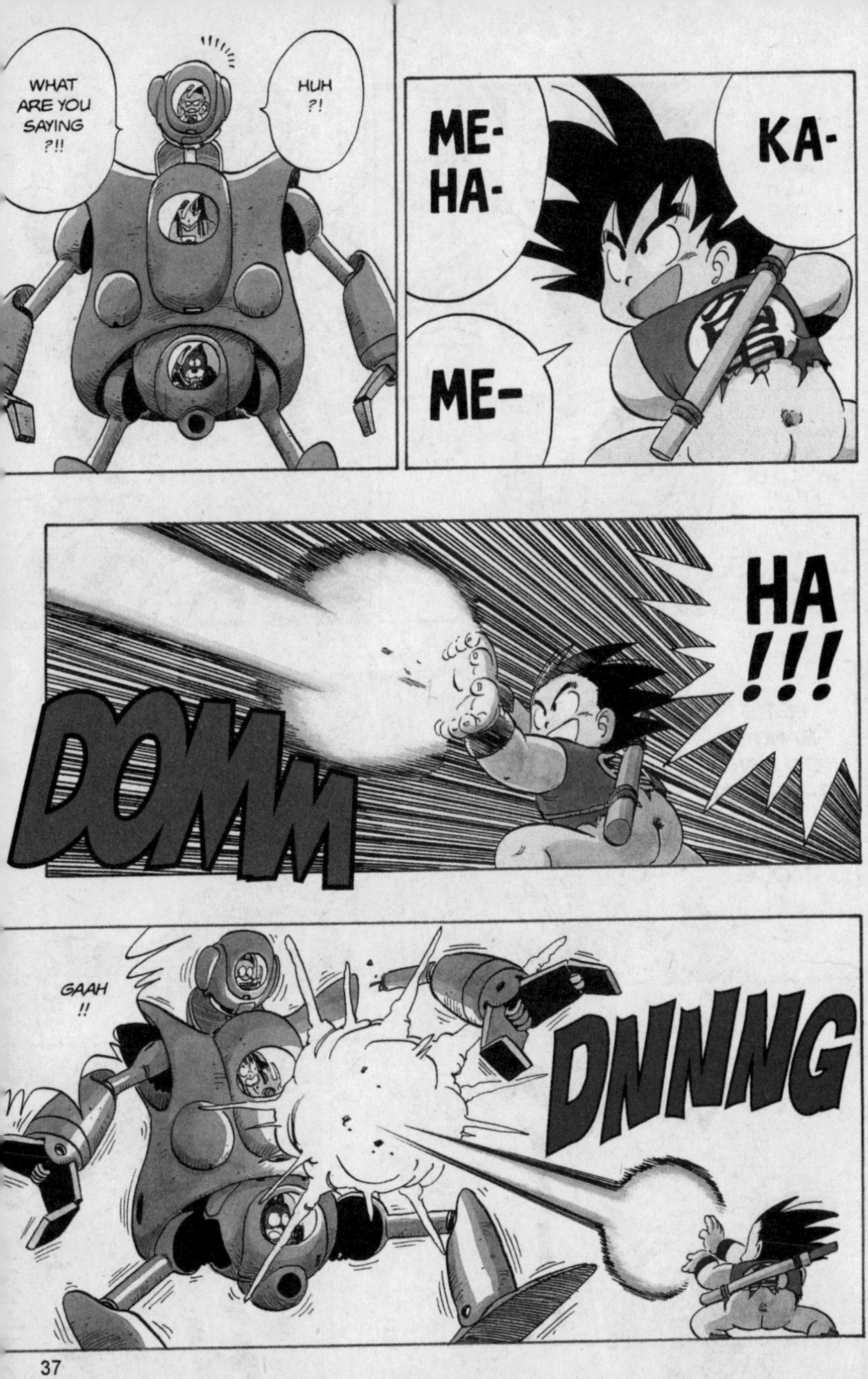
KA-
ME-
HA-
ME-
HUH ?!
WHAT ARE YOU SAYING ?!!
HA !!!
DOMM
DNNNG
GAAH !!

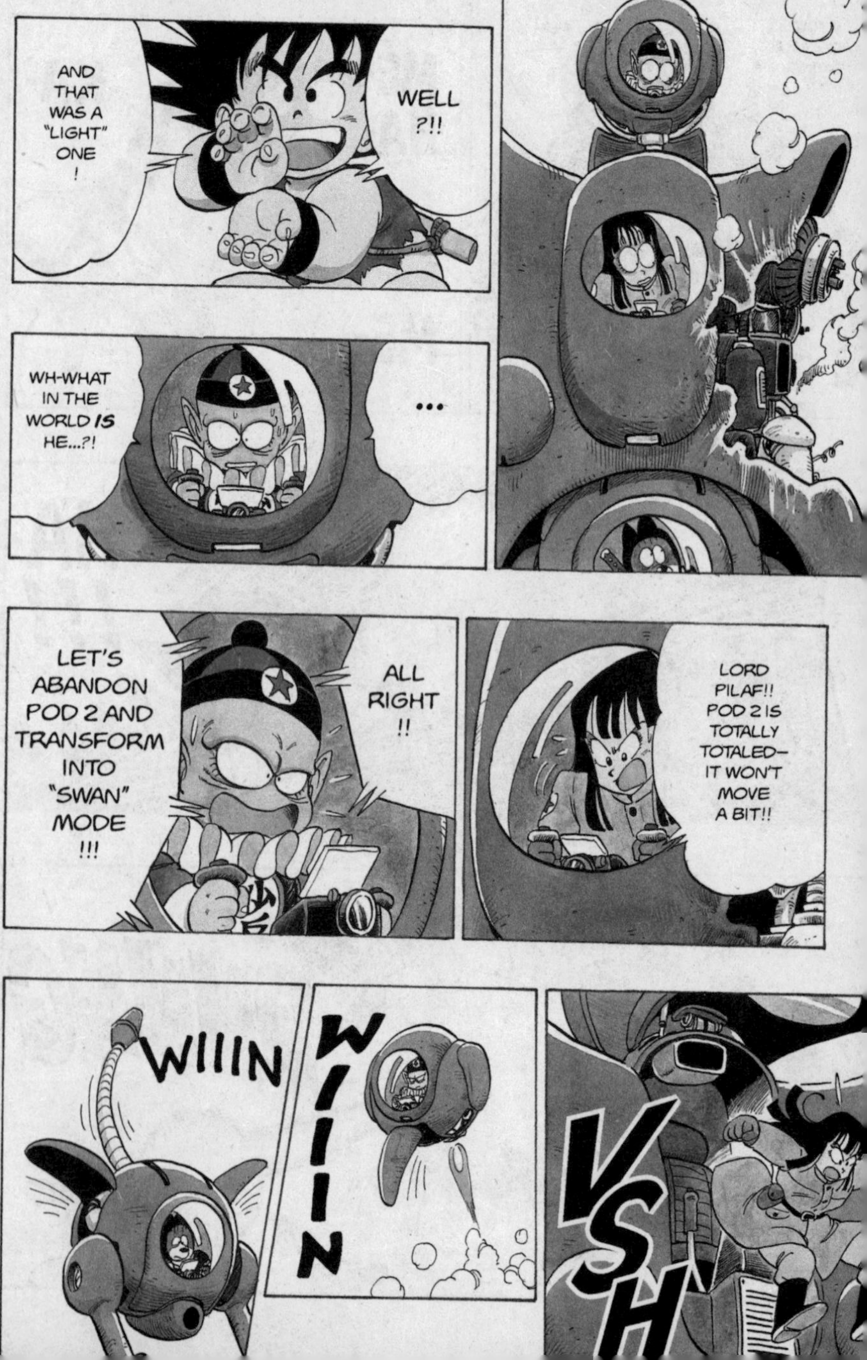
WELL ?!!
AND THAT WAS A "LIGHT" ONE !
...
WH-WHAT IN THE WORLD IS HE...?!
LORD PILAF!! POD 2 IS TOTALLY TOTALED— IT WON'T MOVE A BIT!!
ALL RIGHT !!
LET'S ABANDON POD 2 AND TRANSFORM INTO "SWAN" MODE !!!
VSH
WIIIN
WIIIN

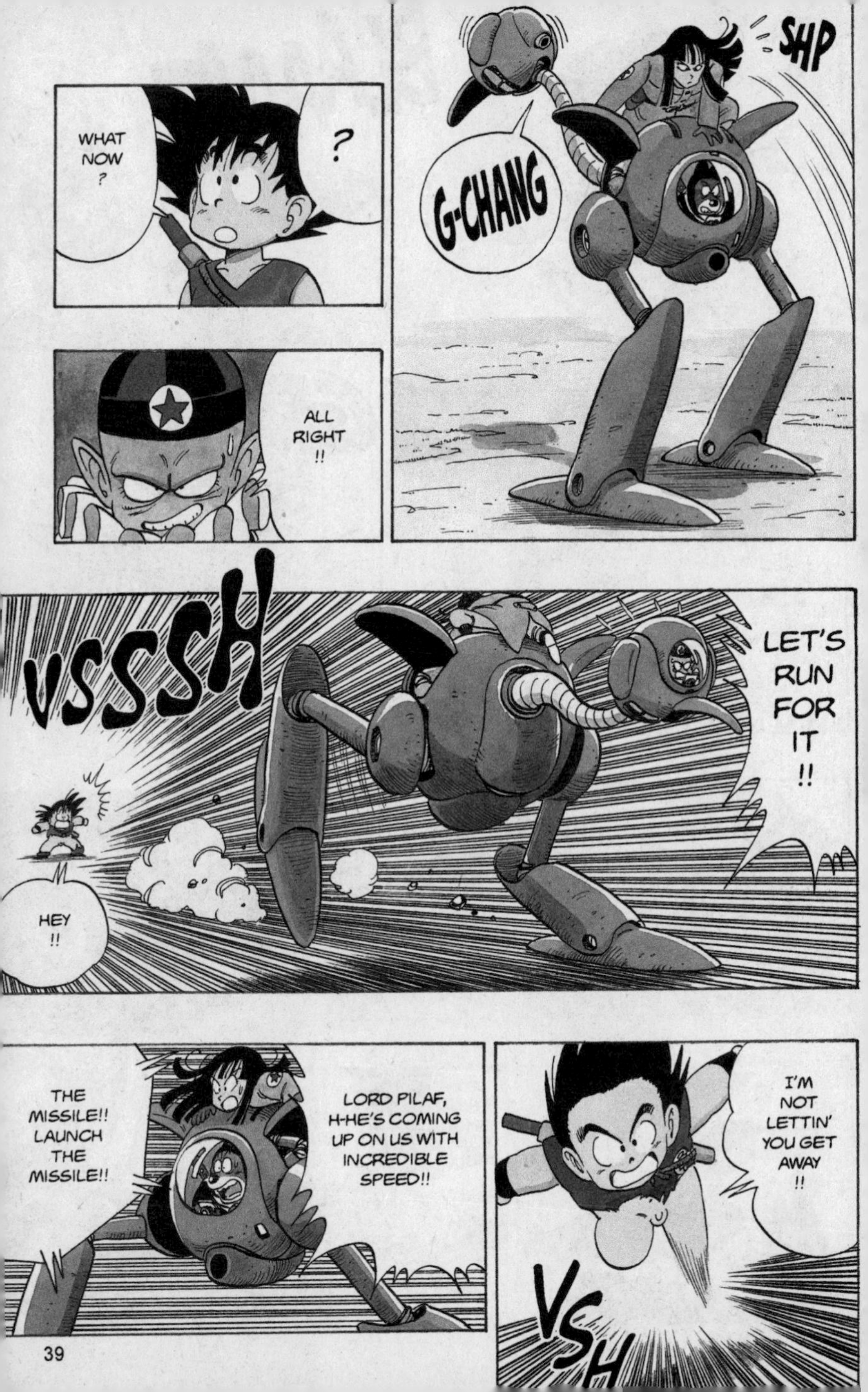
SHP
G-CHANG
?
WHAT NOW ?
ALL RIGHT !!
LET'S RUN FOR IT !!
VSSSH
HEY !!
I'M NOT LETTIN' YOU GET AWAY !!
VSH
LORD PILAF, H-HE'S COMING UP ON US WITH INCREDIBLE SPEED!!
THE MISSILE!! LAUNCH THE MISSILE!!

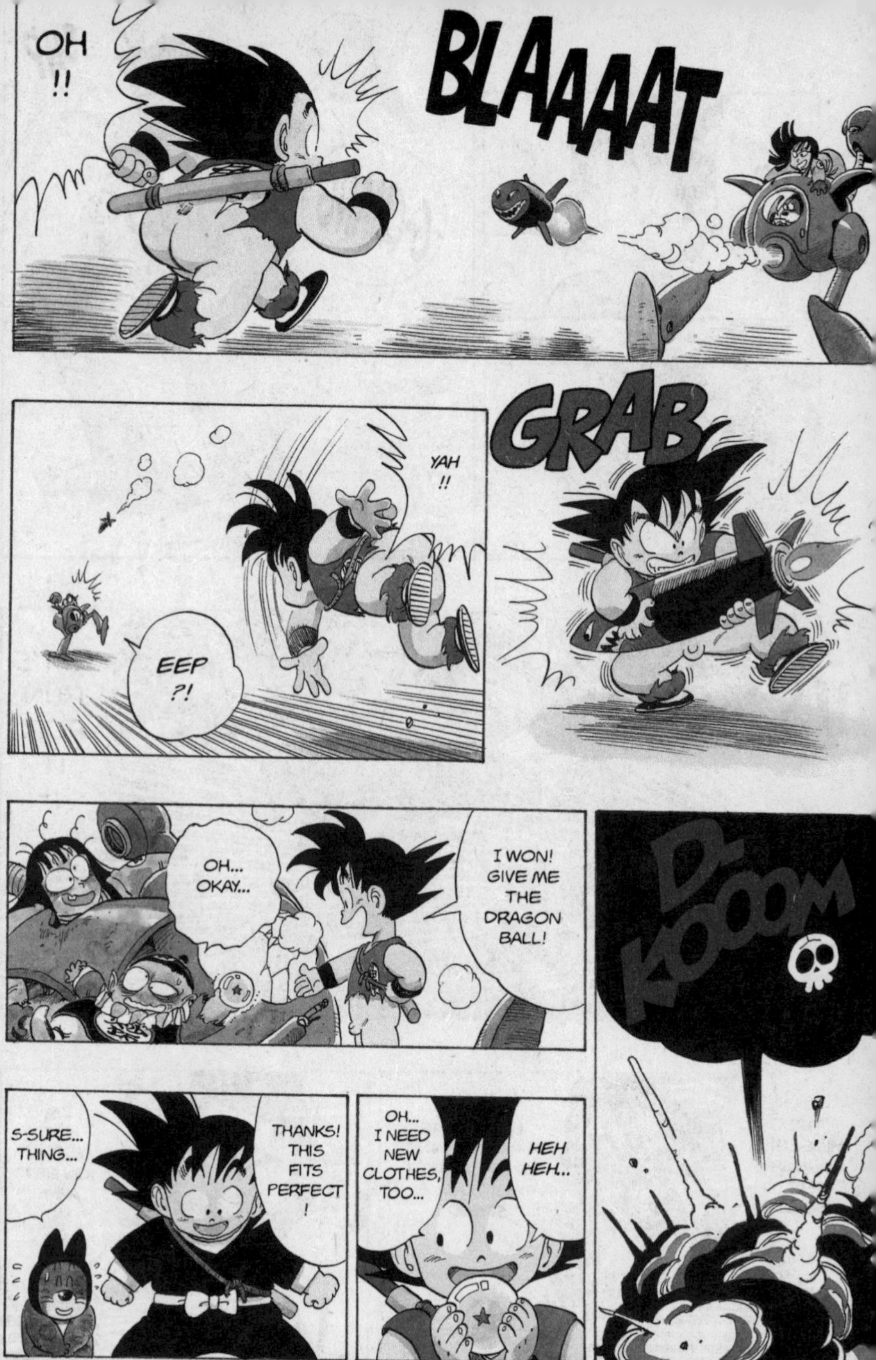
BLAAAAT
OH !!
GRAB
YAH !!
EEP ?!
D-KOOOM
I WON! GIVE ME THE DRAGON BALL!
OH... OKAY...
HEH HEH...
OH... I NEED NEW CLOTHES, TOO...
THANKS! THIS FITS PERFECT!
S-SURE... THING...

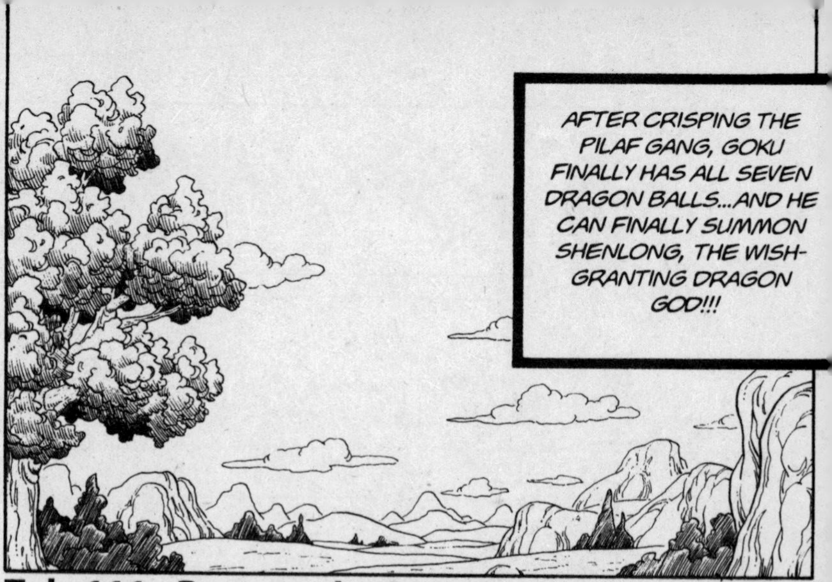
AFTER CRISPING THE PILAF GANG, GOKU FINALLY HAS ALL SEVEN DRAGON BALLS...AND HE CAN FINALLY SUMMON SHENLONG, THE WISH-GRANTING DRAGON GOD!!!

Tale 111 • Reenter the Dragon

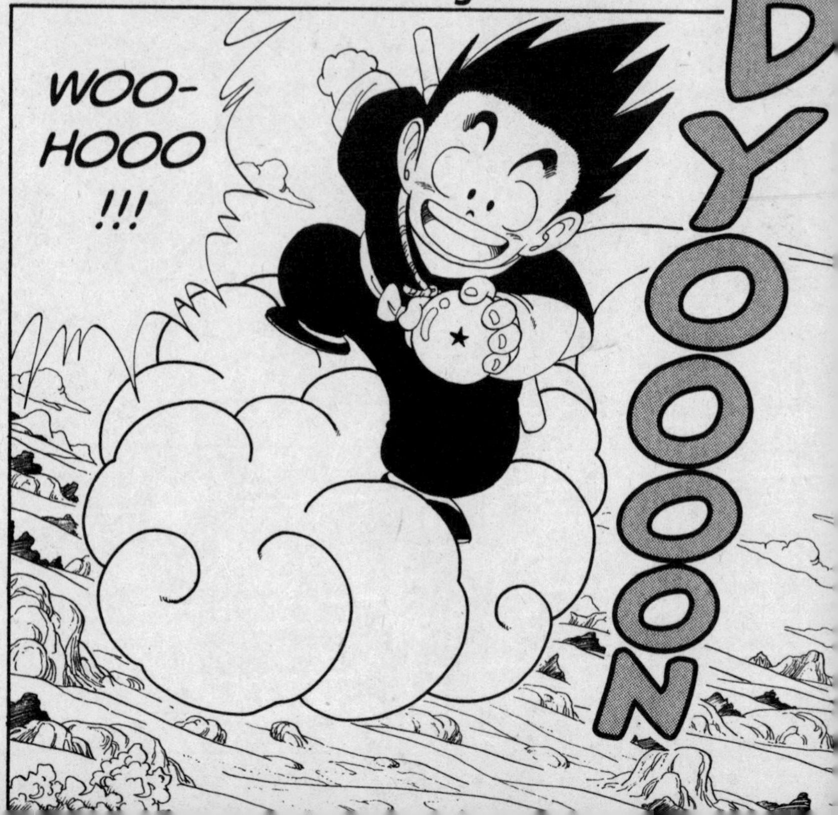
DYOOOOON
WOO-HOOO !!!

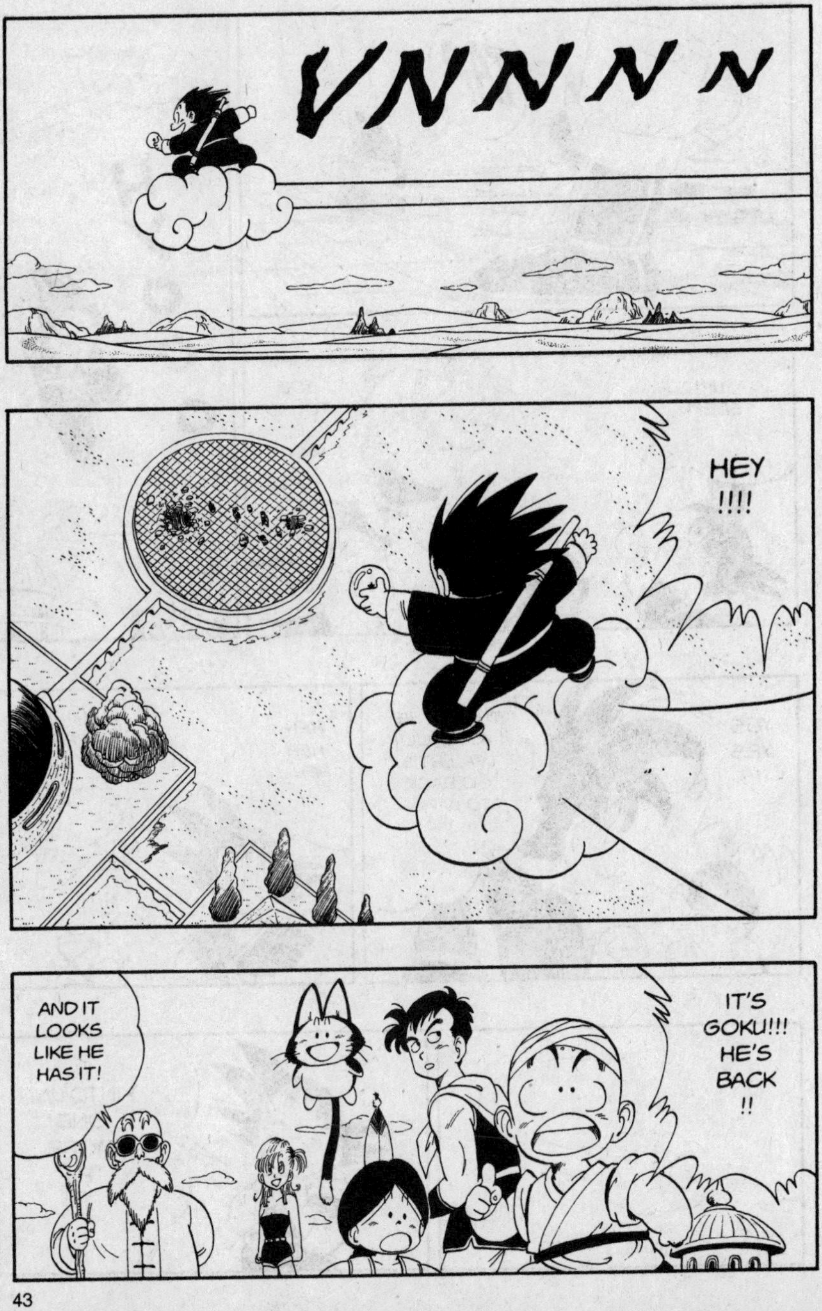
VNNNN
HEY !!!!
IT'S GOKU!!! HE'S BACK !!
AND IT LOOKS LIKE HE HAS IT!

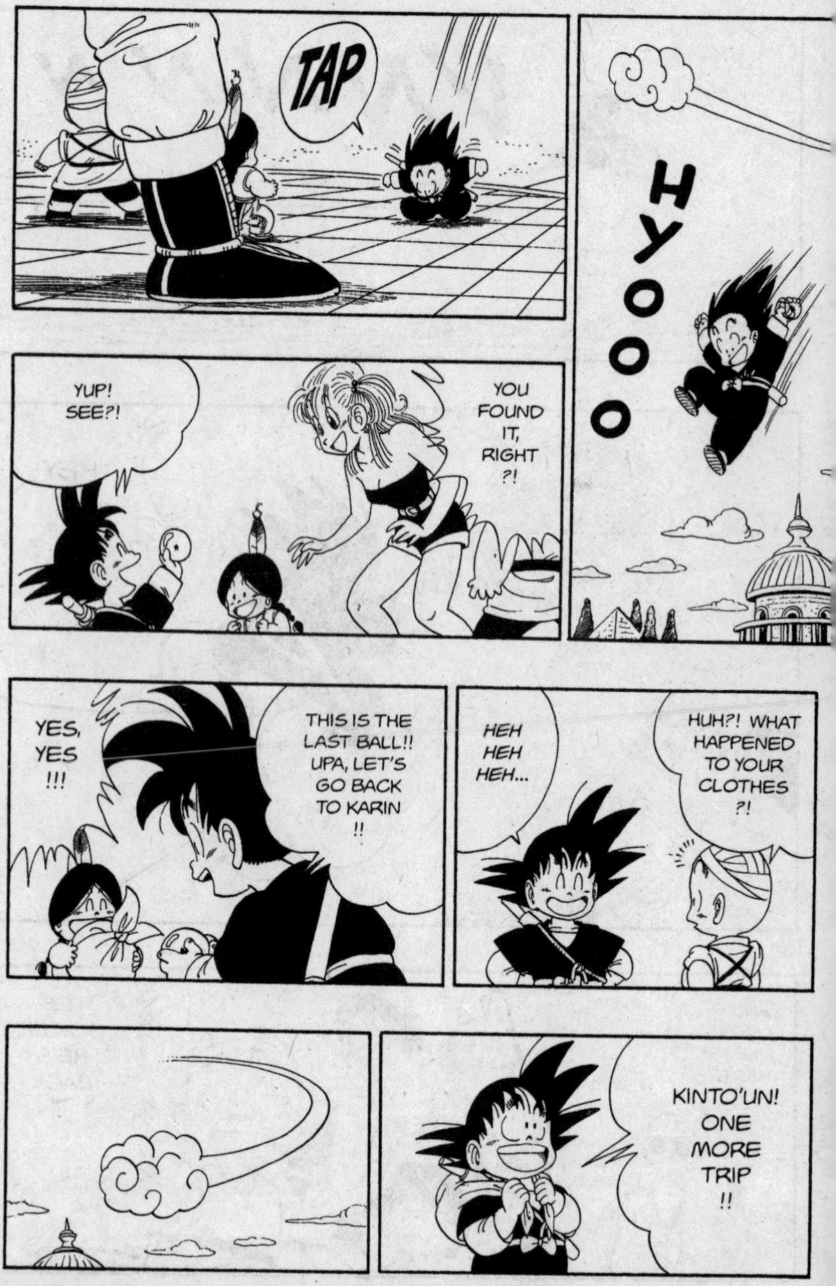
HYOOOO
TAP
YOU FOUND IT, RIGHT?!
YUP! SEE?!
HUH?! WHAT HAPPENED TO YOUR CLOTHES?!
HEH HEH HEH...
THIS IS THE LAST BALL!! UPA, LET'S GO BACK TO KARIN!!
YES, YES!!!
KINTO'UN! ONE MORE TRIP!!

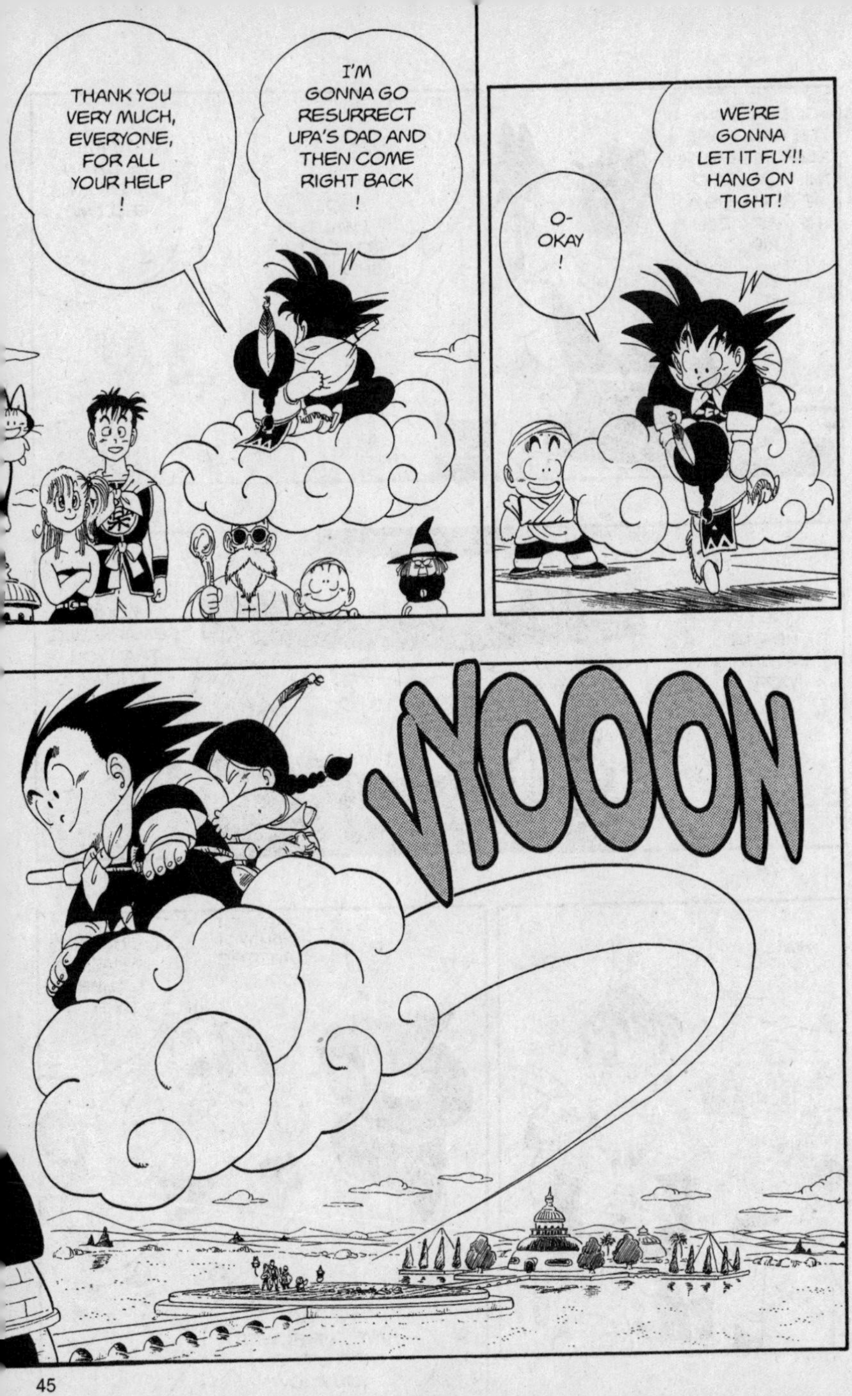
WE'RE GONNA LET IT FLY!! HANG ON TIGHT!
O-OKAY!
I'M GONNA GO RESURRECT UPA'S DAD AND THEN COME RIGHT BACK!
THANK YOU VERY MUCH, EVERYONE, FOR ALL YOUR HELP!
VYOOON

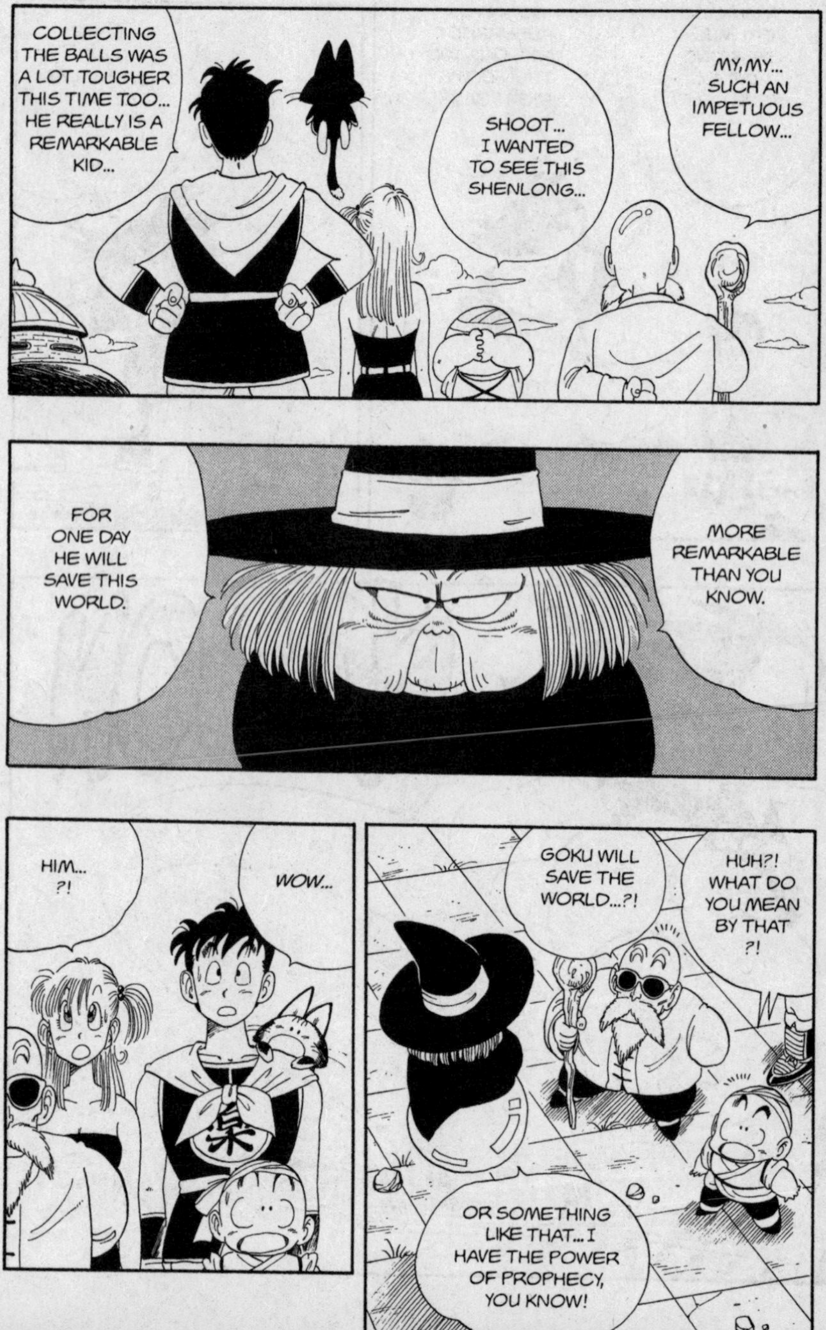
MY, MY... SUCH AN IMPETUOUS FELLOW...
SHOOT... I WANTED TO SEE THIS SHENLONG...
COLLECTING THE BALLS WAS A LOT TOUGHER THIS TIME TOO... HE REALLY IS A REMARKABLE KID...
MORE REMARKABLE THAN YOU KNOW.
FOR ONE DAY HE WILL SAVE THIS WORLD.
HUH?! WHAT DO YOU MEAN BY THAT ?!
GOKU WILL SAVE THE WORLD...?!
OR SOMETHING LIKE THAT... I HAVE THE POWER OF PROPHECY, YOU KNOW!
WOW...
HIM... ?!

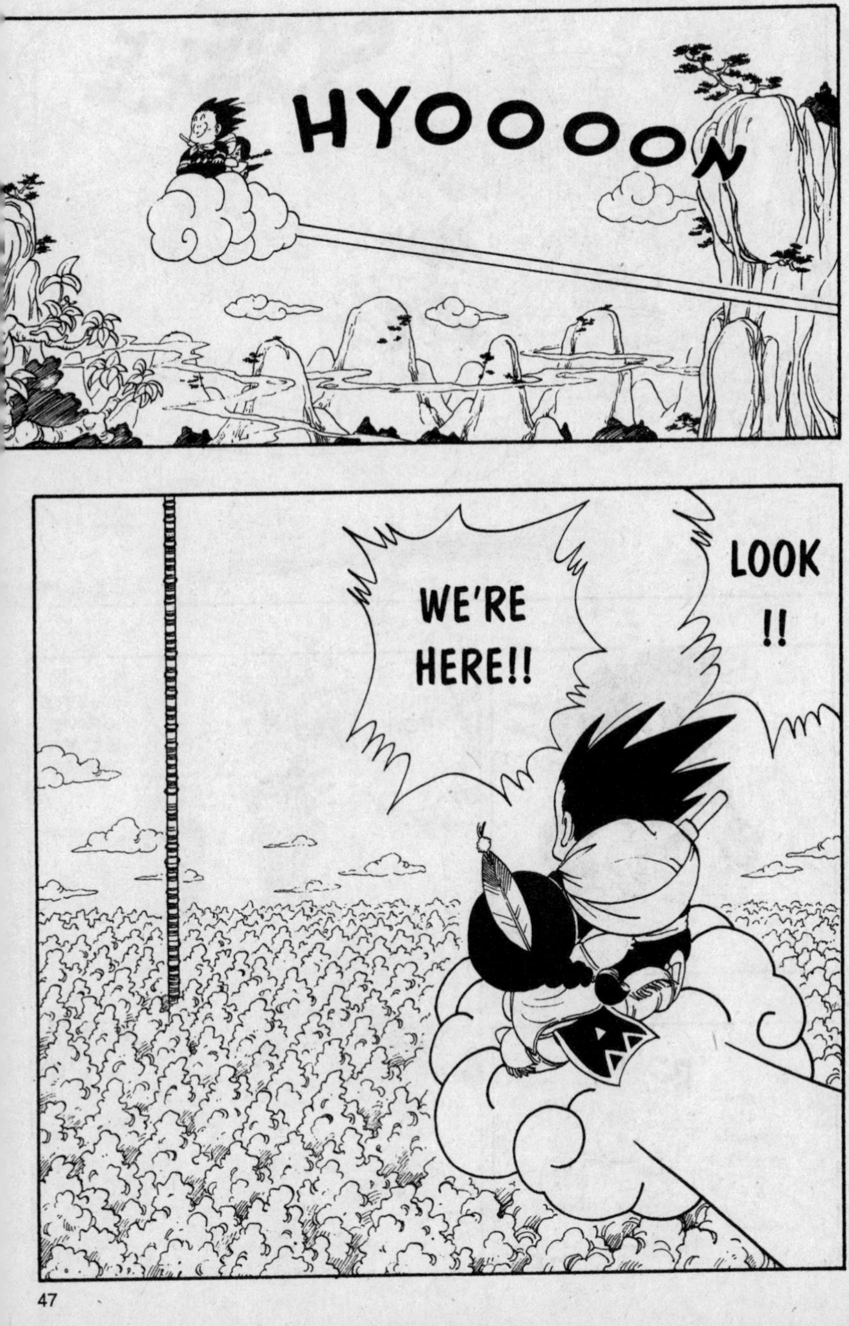
HYOOOOON
LOOK !!
WE'RE HERE!!

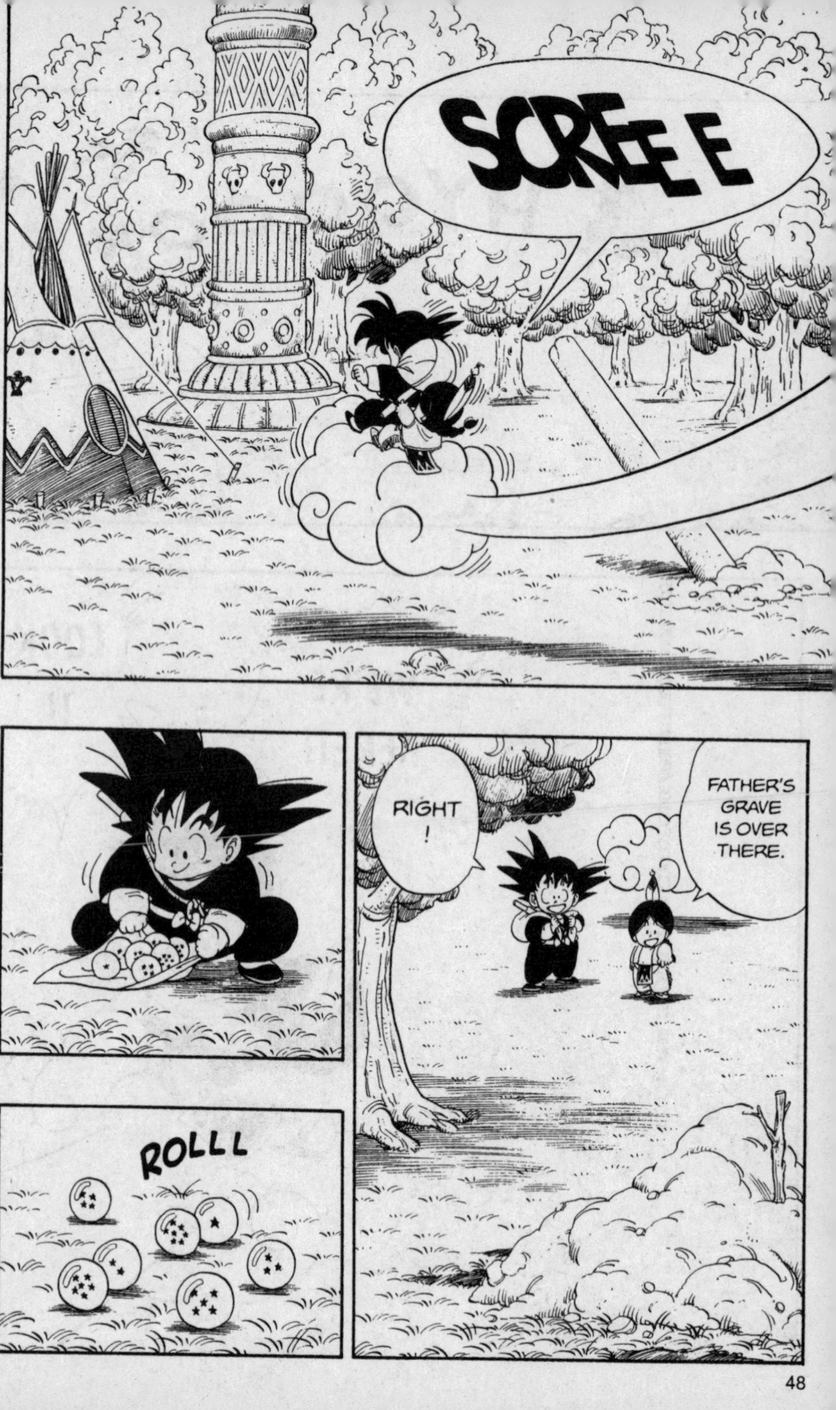
SCREEE E
FATHER'S GRAVE IS OVER THERE.
RIGHT !
ROLLL

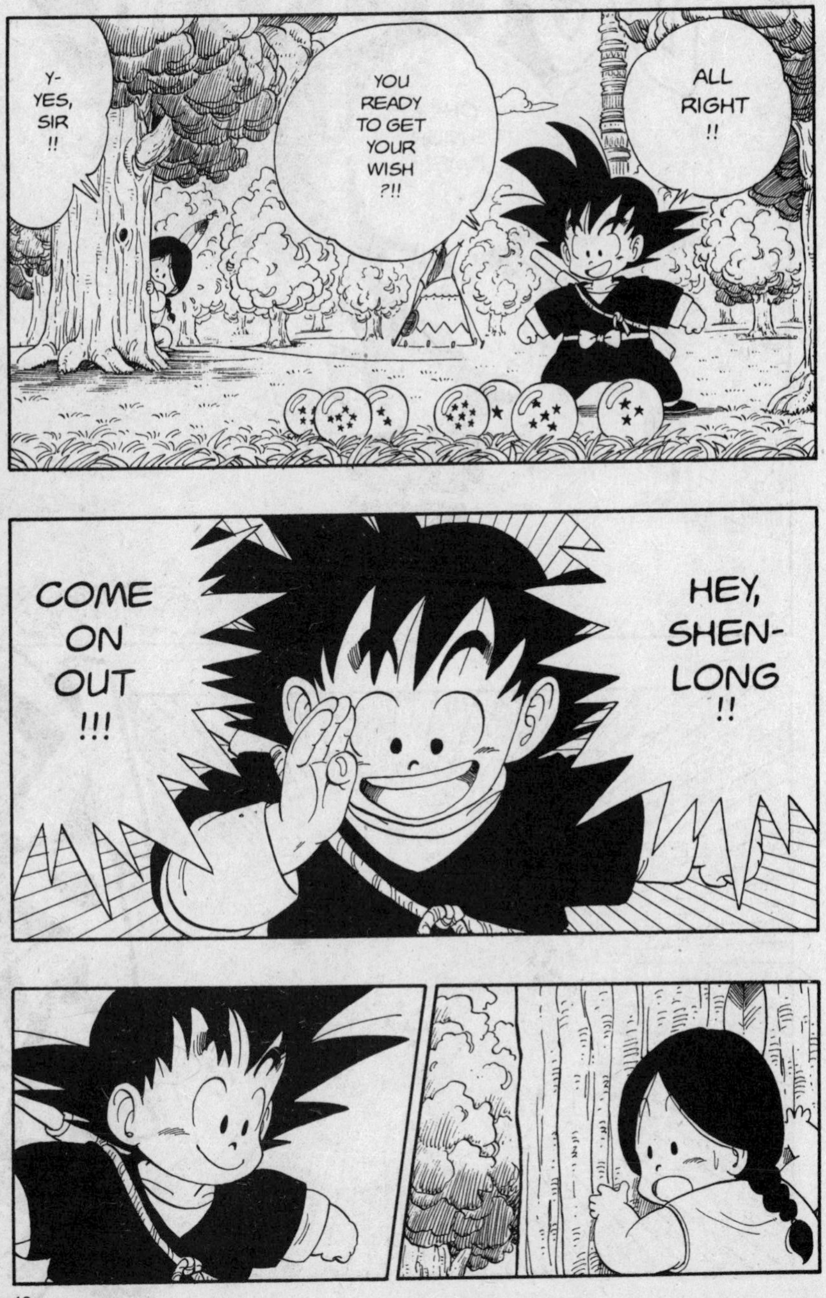
ALL RIGHT !!
YOU READY TO GET YOUR WISH ?!!
Y- YES, SIR !!
HEY, SHEN-LONG !!
COME ON OUT !!!

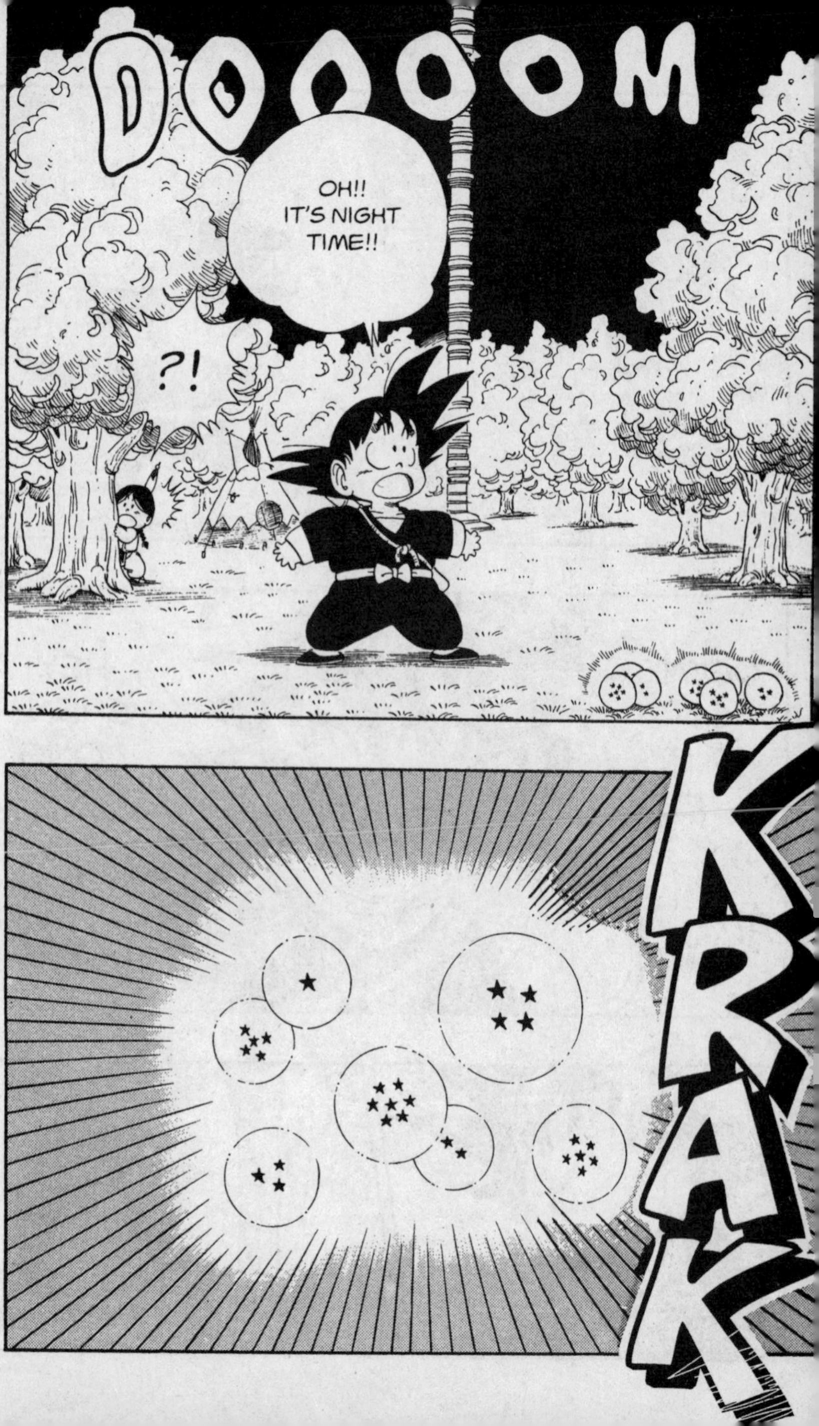
DOOOOM
OH!! IT'S NIGHT TIME!!
?!
KRAK

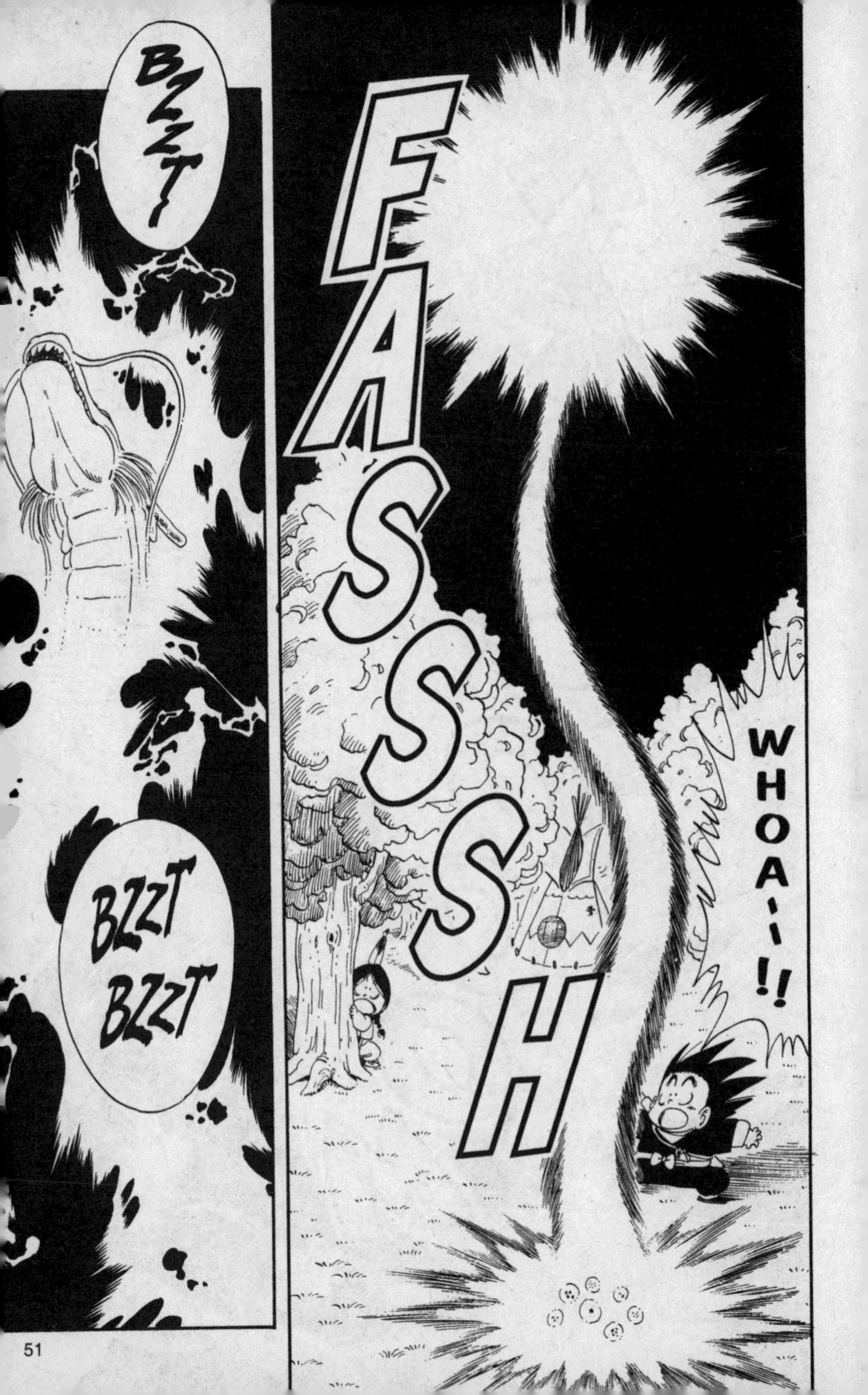
FASSSH
WHOA...!!
BZZZT
BZZT BZZT

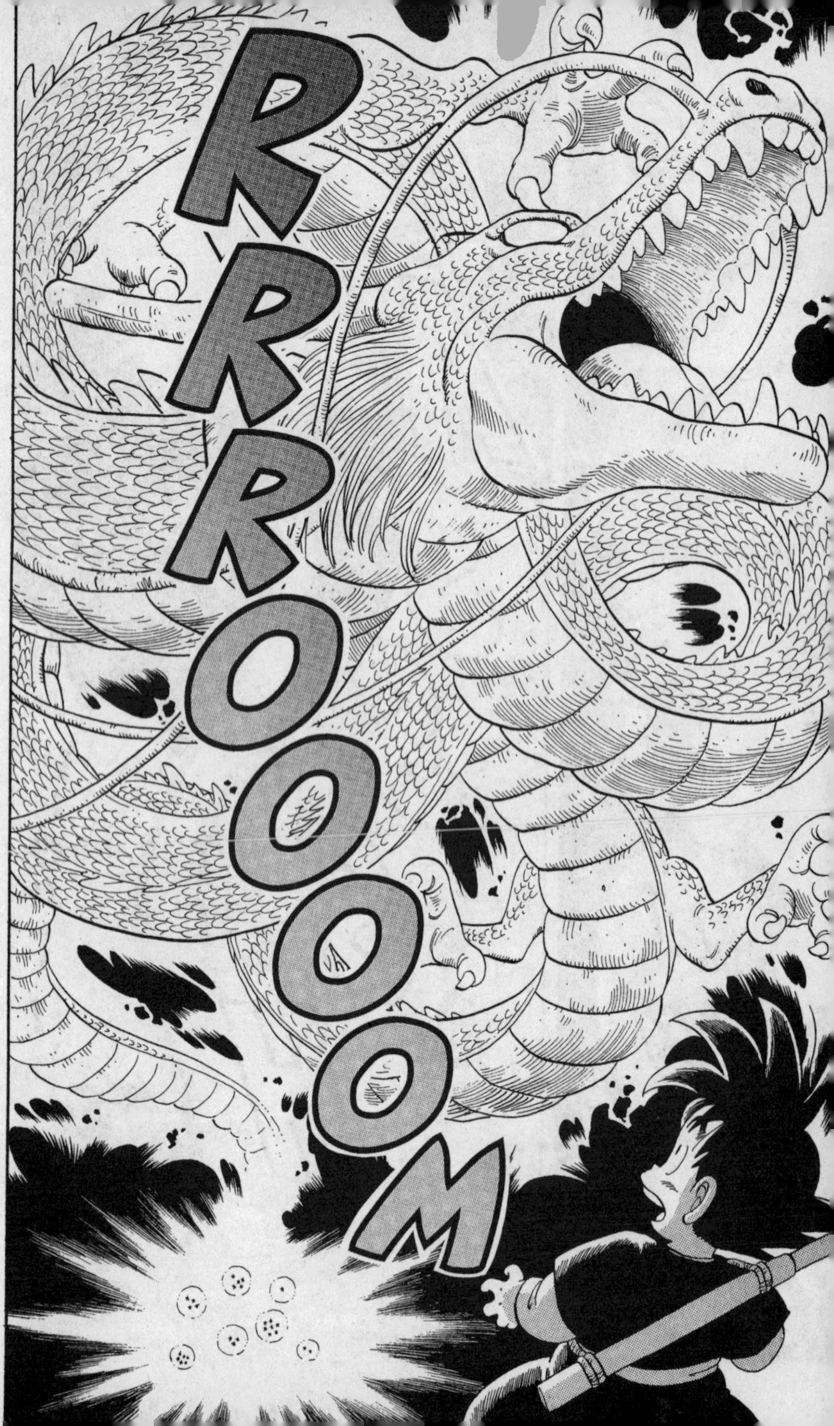
RRROOOOM

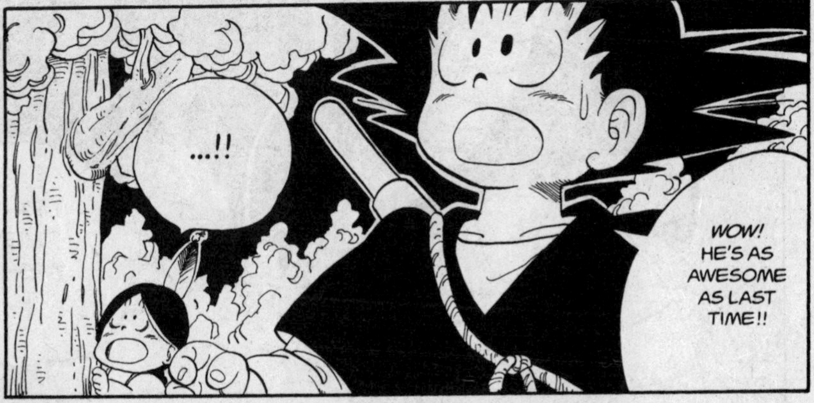
WOW! HE'S AS AWESOME AS LAST TIME!!
...!!

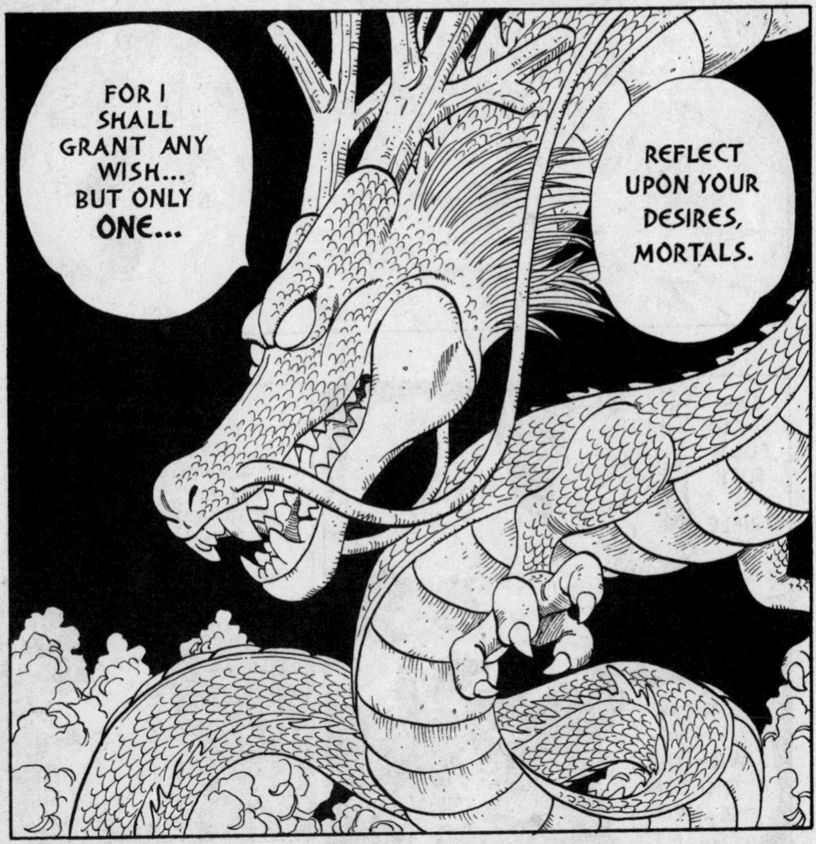
REFLECT UPON YOUR DESIRES, MORTALS.
FOR I SHALL GRANT ANY WISH... BUT ONLY ONE...

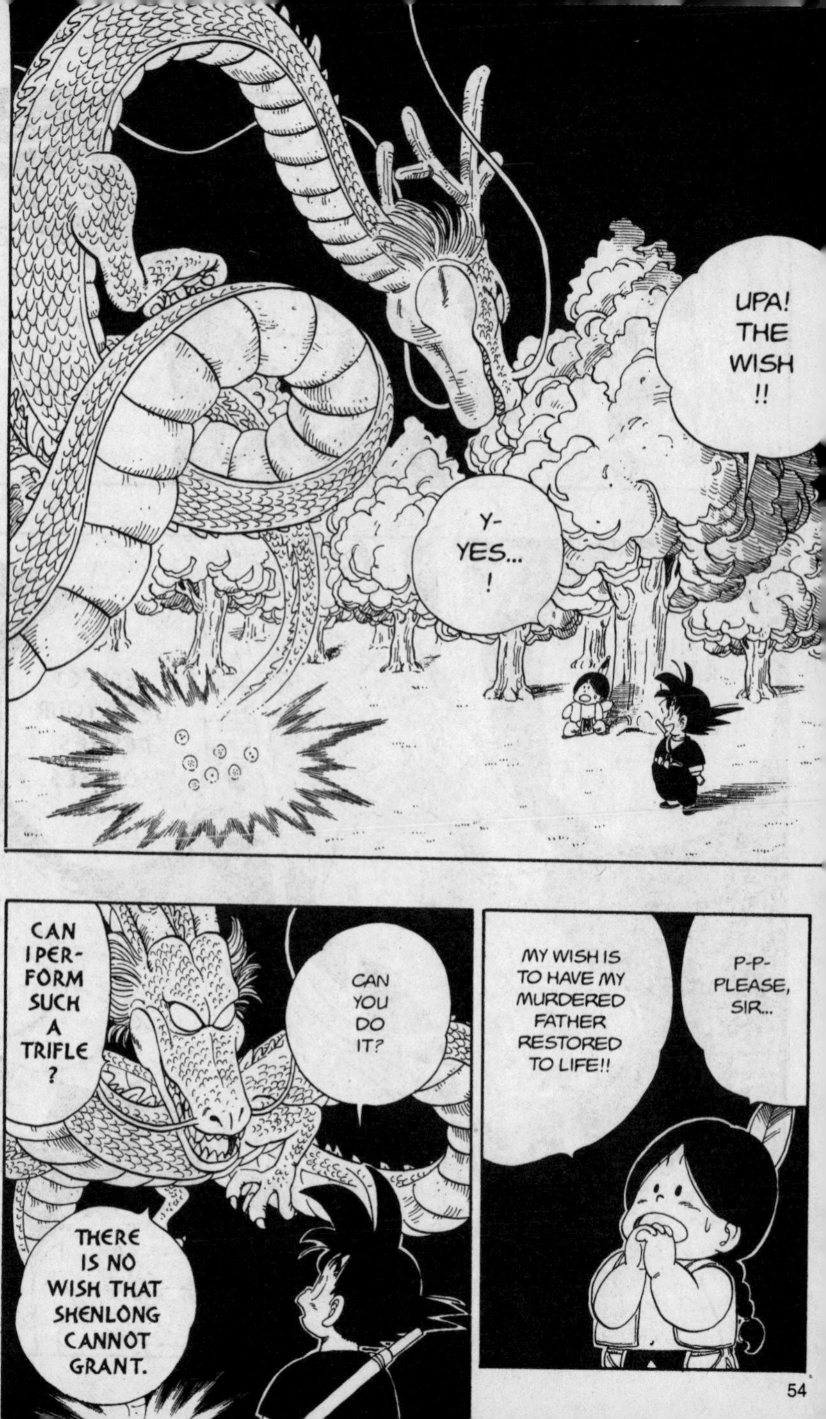
UPA! THE WISH!!
Y-YES...!
P-P-PLEASE, SIR...
MY WISH IS TO HAVE MY MURDERED FATHER RESTORED TO LIFE!!
CAN YOU DO IT?
CAN I PERFORM SUCH A TRIFLE?
THERE IS NO WISH THAT SHENLONG CANNOT GRANT.

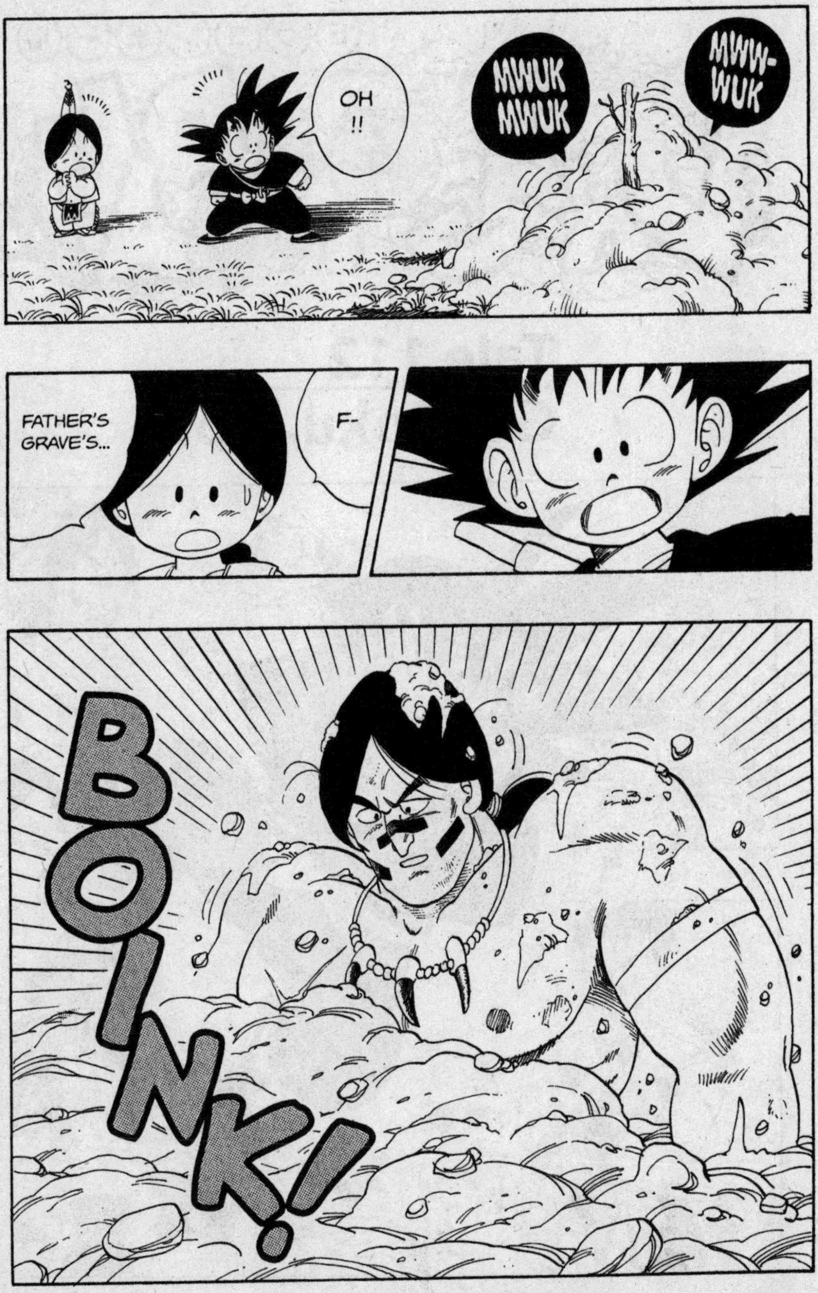
MWW-WUK
MWUK MWUK
OH !!
F-
FATHER'S GRAVE'S...
BOINK!

ドラゴンボール

DRAGON BALL

Tale 112

Go, Goku, Go!

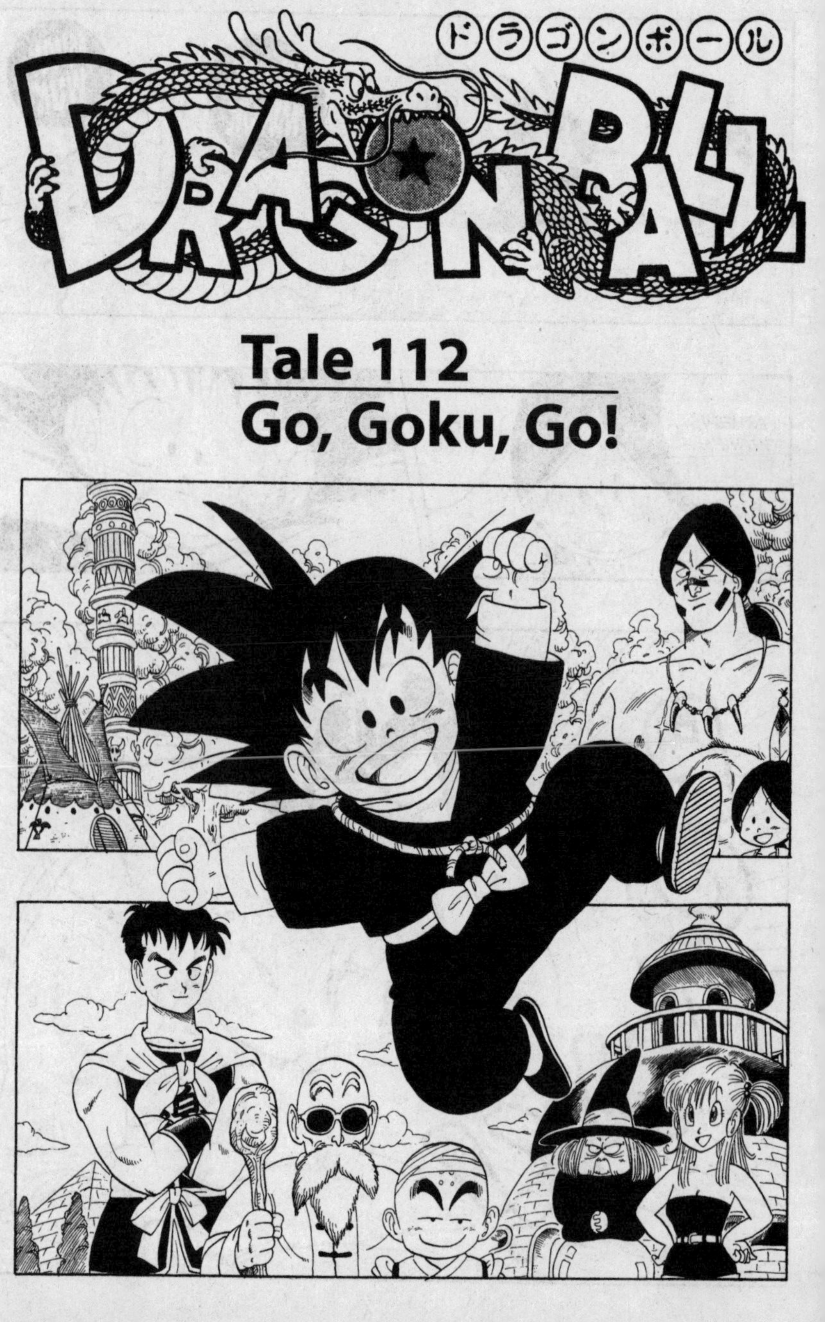

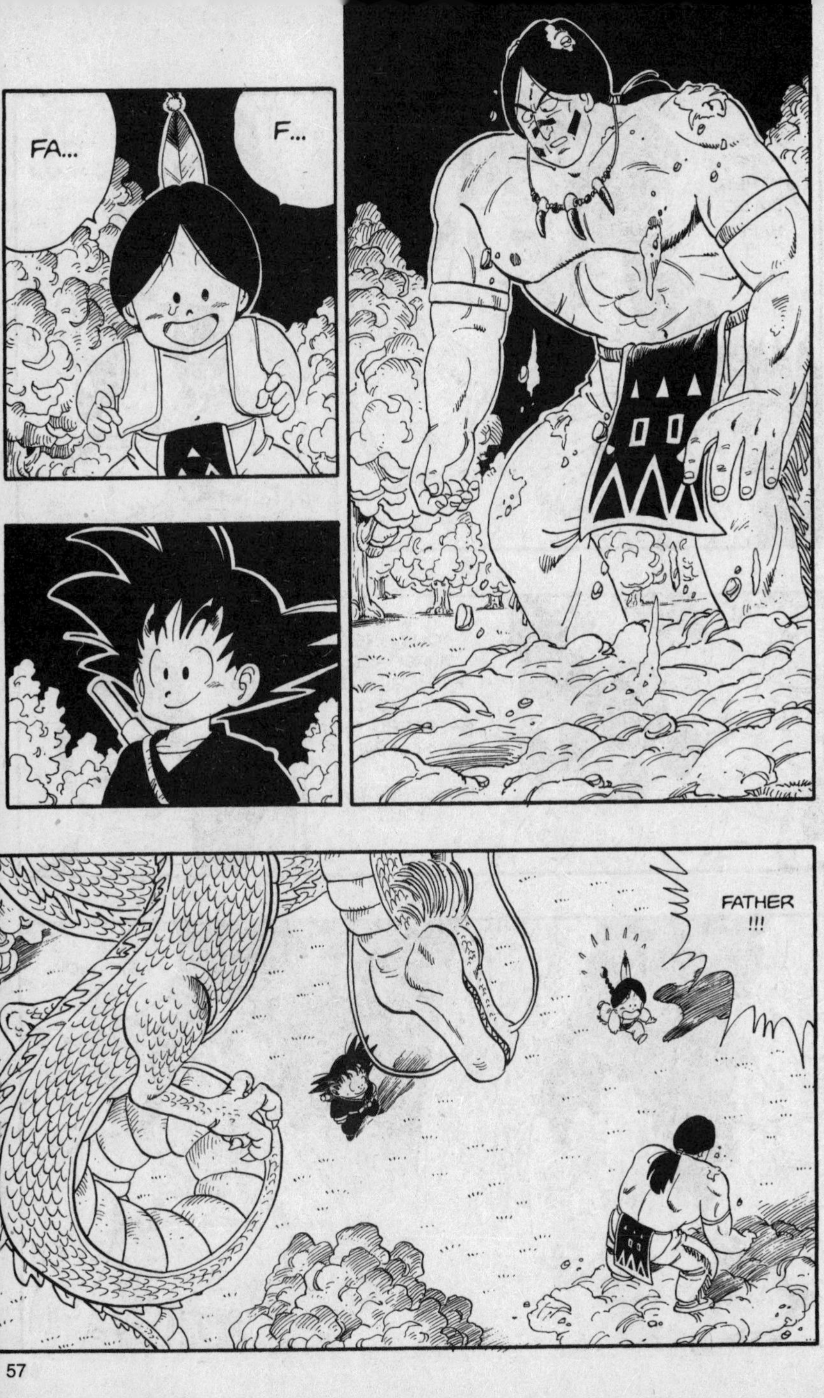
F...
FA...
FATHER !!!

I'M SO HAPPY, FATHER, I'M SO HAPPY !!!

...?!

UPA...!

OH, FATHER!!

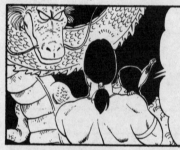

YOU WERE MURDERED, FATHER! BUT SON GOKU GATHERED THE DRAGON BALLS AND RESURRECTED YOU!!

I-I WAS...

THAT'S RIGHT...

HE...?! ASTOUNDING !!

YOUR WISH IS GRANTED.

FARE YOU WELL.

THAT ONE!

THE FOUR-STAR-BALL IS...

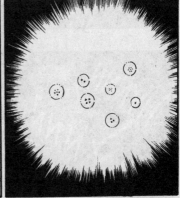

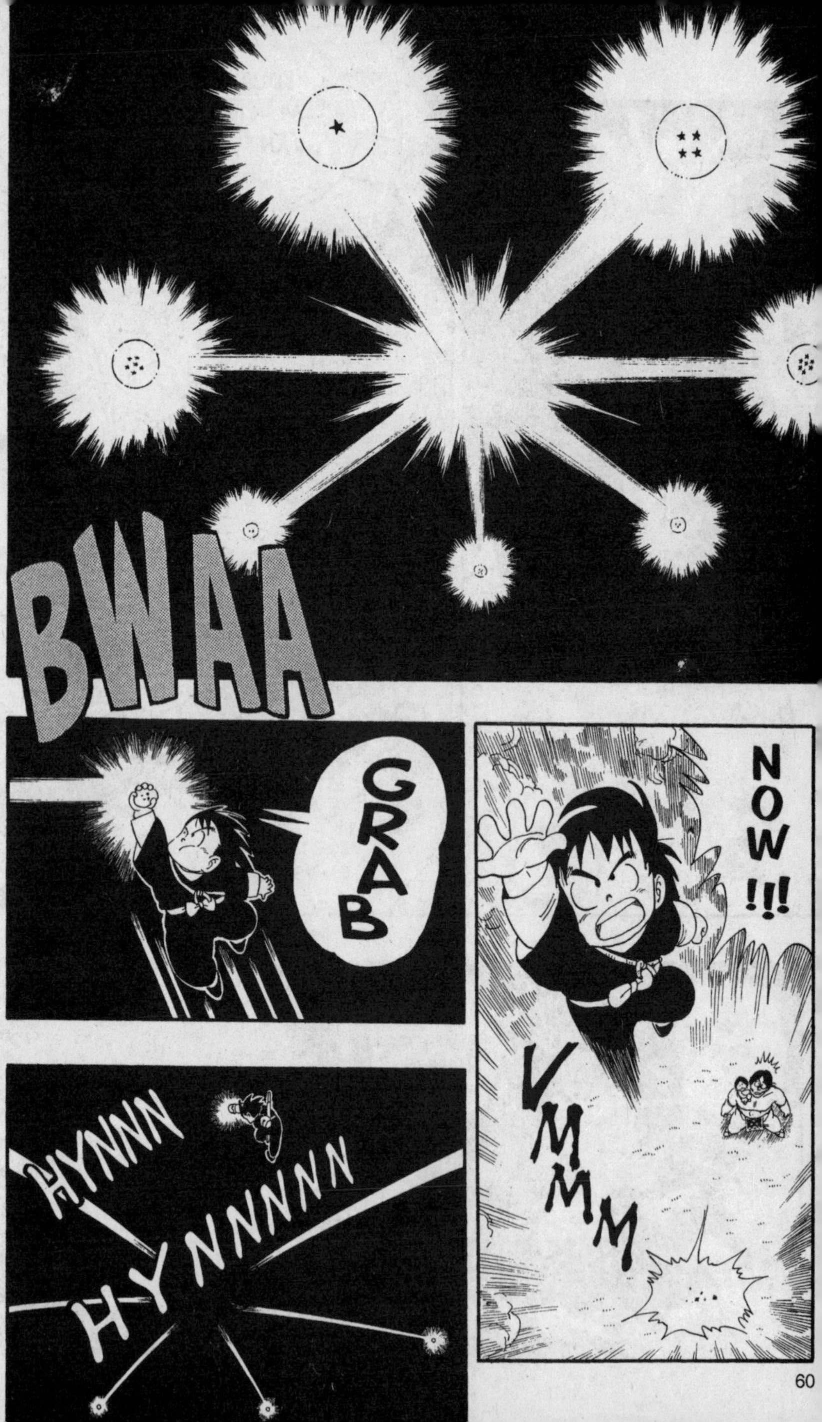
BWAA
NOW!!!
VMMM
GRAB
HYNNN
HYNNNNN

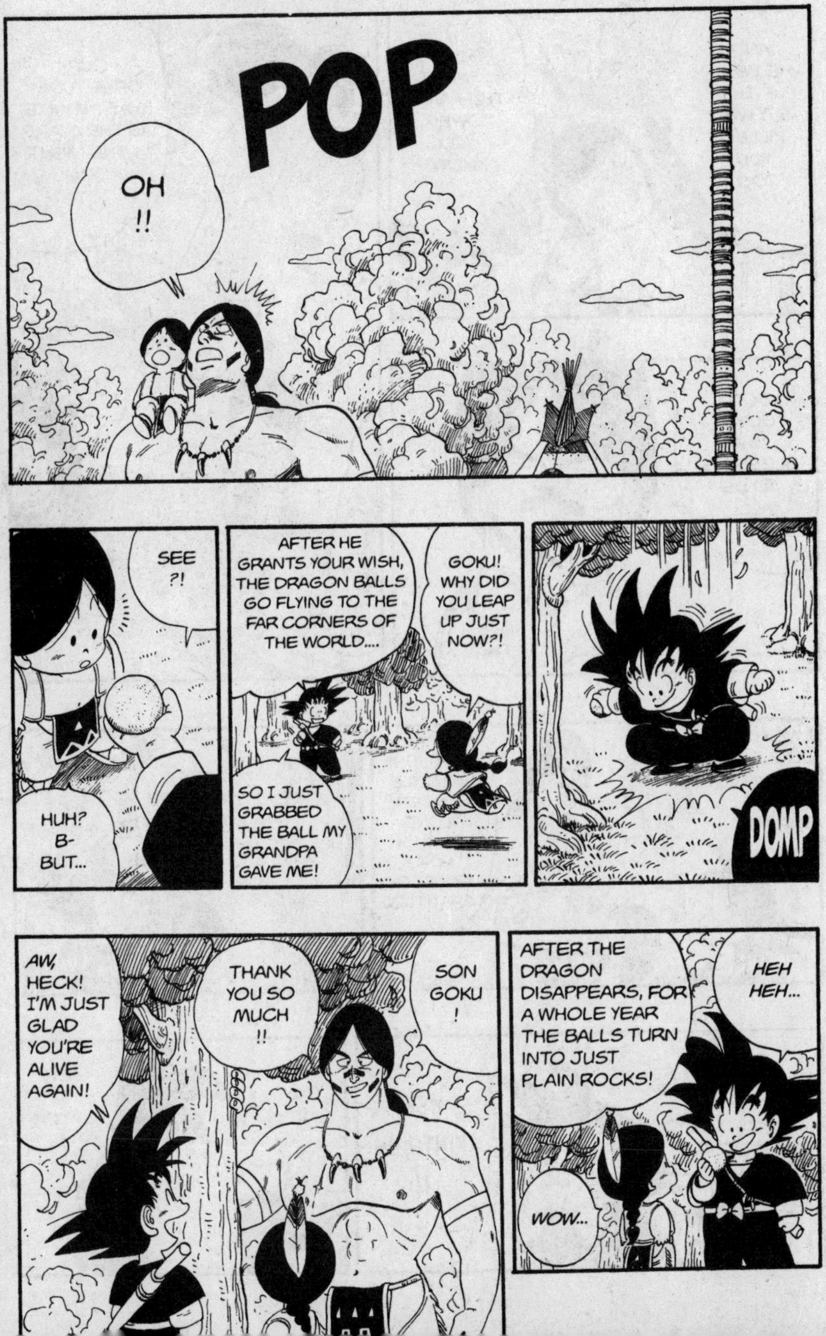
POP
OH !!
DOMP
GOKU! WHY DID YOU LEAP UP JUST NOW?!
AFTER HE GRANTS YOUR WISH, THE DRAGON BALLS GO FLYING TO THE FAR CORNERS OF THE WORLD....
SO I JUST GRABBED THE BALL MY GRANDPA GAVE ME!
SEE ?!
HUH? B- BUT...
HEH HEH...
AFTER THE DRAGON DISAPPEARS, FOR A WHOLE YEAR THE BALLS TURN INTO JUST PLAIN ROCKS!
WOW...
SON GOKU !
THANK YOU SO MUCH !!
AW, HECK! I'M JUST GLAD YOU'RE ALIVE AGAIN!

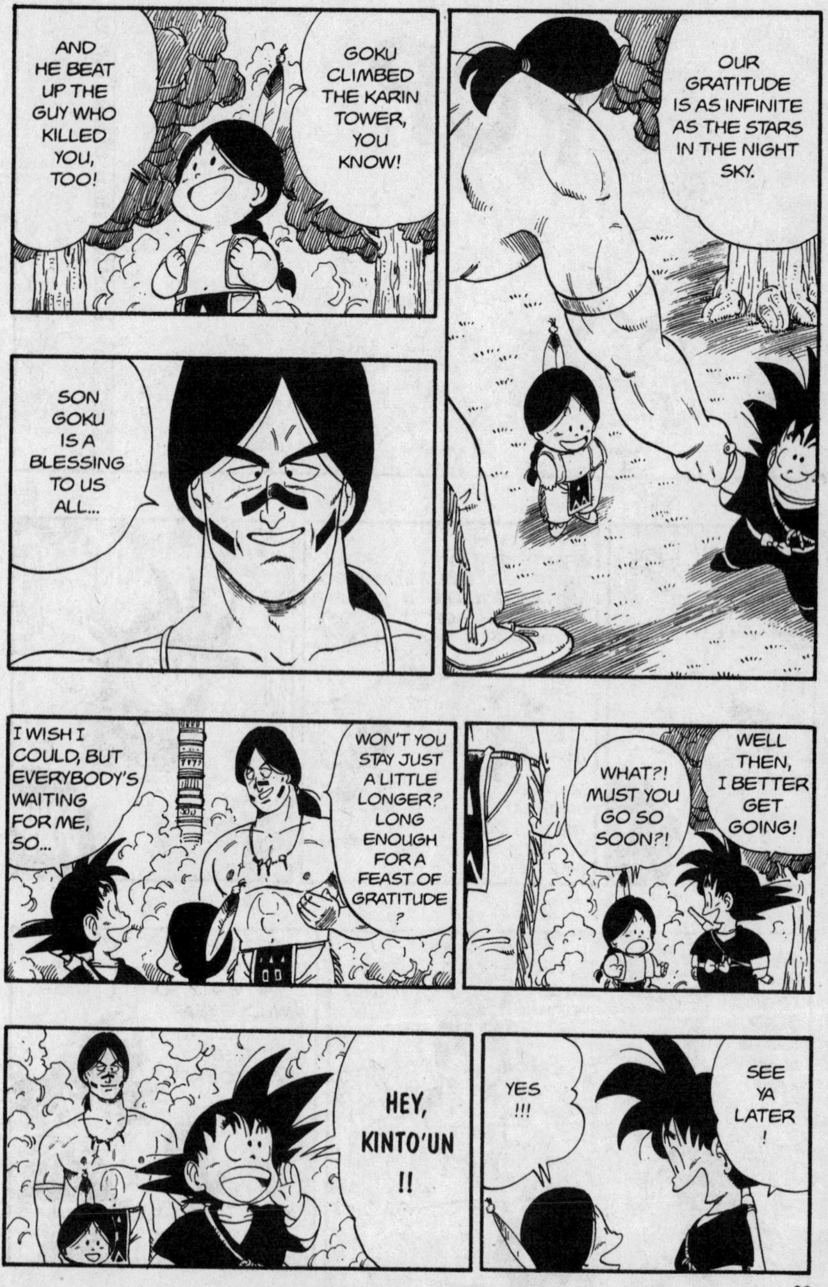
OUR GRATITUDE IS AS INFINITE AS THE STARS IN THE NIGHT SKY.
GOKU CLIMBED THE KARIN TOWER, YOU KNOW!
AND HE BEAT UP THE GUY WHO KILLED YOU, TOO!
SON GOKU IS A BLESSING TO US ALL...
WELL THEN, I BETTER GET GOING!
WHAT?! MUST YOU GO SO SOON?!
WON'T YOU STAY JUST A LITTLE LONGER? LONG ENOUGH FOR A FEAST OF GRATITUDE?
I WISH I COULD, BUT EVERYBODY'S WAITING FOR ME, SO...
SEE YA LATER!
YES!!!
HEY, KINTO'UN!!

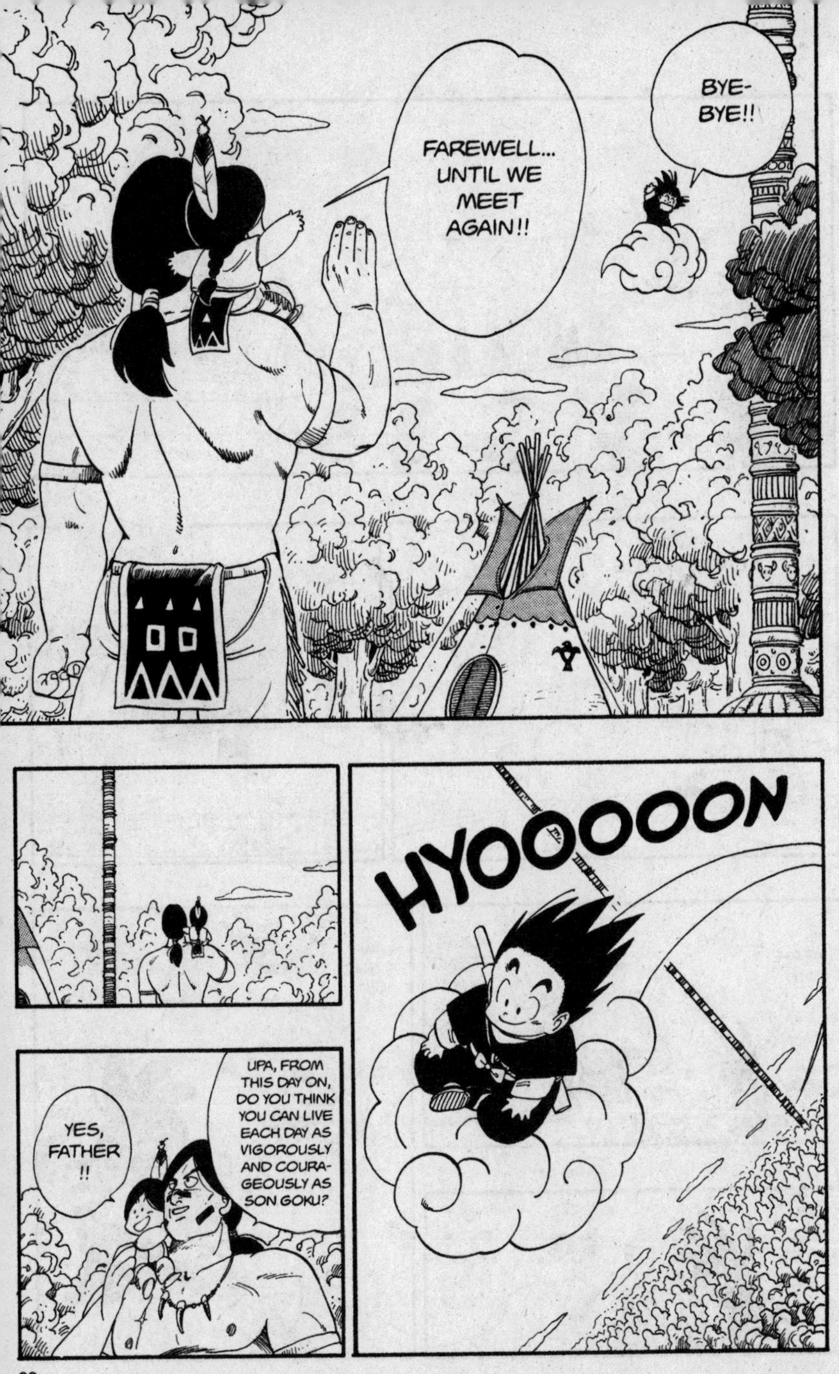
BYE-BYE!!
FAREWELL... UNTIL WE MEET AGAIN!!
HYOOOOOON
UPA, FROM THIS DAY ON, DO YOU THINK YOU CAN LIVE EACH DAY AS VIGOROUSLY AND COURAGEOUSLY AS SON GOKU?
YES, FATHER!!

WELL?! HOW'D IT GO?! WERE YOU ABLE TO REVIVE HIS DAD ALL RIGHT?!

HEY!

HE'S BACK!!

IT'S GOKU!!

YEAH!!!

YOUR FRIEND MUST BE OVERJOYED!!

AW-RIGHT!!

YUP! HE'S ALIVE!!

TEE HEE HEE...

YOU DID A GOOD THING INDEED.

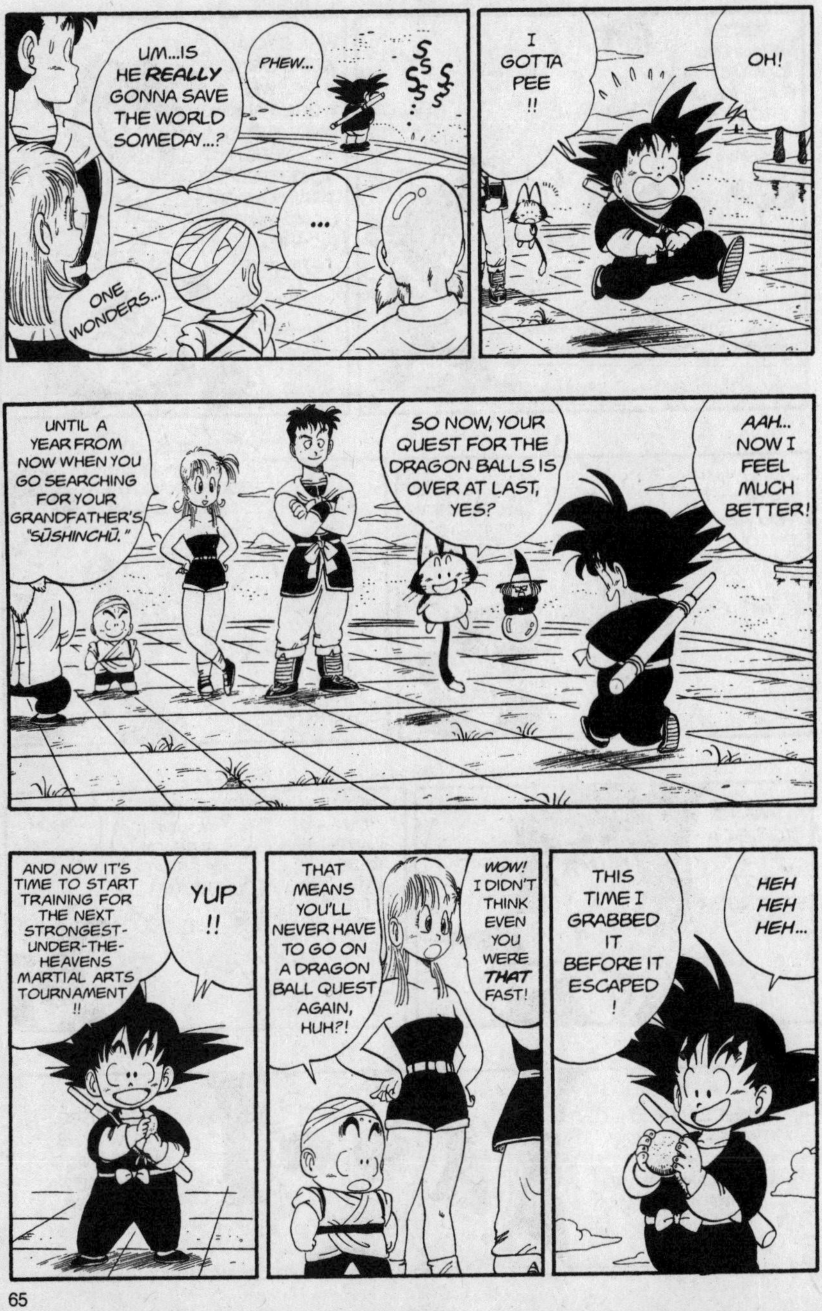
OH!
I GOTTA PEE!!
PHEW...
UM...IS HE REALLY GONNA SAVE THE WORLD SOMEDAY...?
...
ONE WONDERS...
AAH... NOW I FEEL MUCH BETTER!
SO NOW, YOUR QUEST FOR THE DRAGON BALLS IS OVER AT LAST, YES?
UNTIL A YEAR FROM NOW WHEN YOU GO SEARCHING FOR YOUR GRANDFATHER'S "SŪSHINCHŪ."
HEH HEH HEH...
THIS TIME I GRABBED IT BEFORE IT ESCAPED!
WOW! I DIDN'T THINK EVEN YOU WERE THAT FAST!
THAT MEANS YOU'LL NEVER HAVE TO GO ON A DRAGON BALL QUEST AGAIN, HUH?!
YUP!!
AND NOW IT'S TIME TO START TRAINING FOR THE NEXT STRONGEST-UNDER-THE-HEAVENS MARTIAL ARTS TOURNAMENT!!

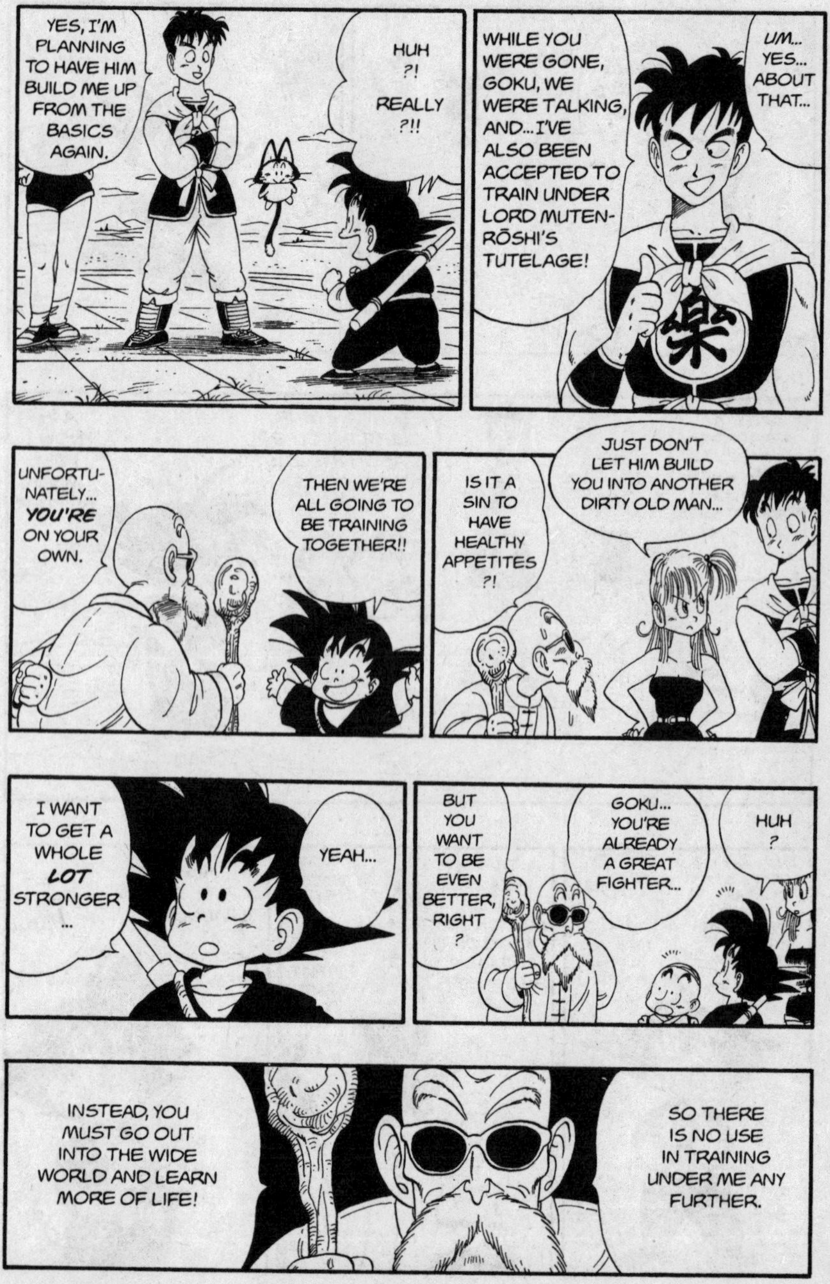
UM... YES... ABOUT THAT...
WHILE YOU WERE GONE, GOKU, WE WERE TALKING, AND...I'VE ALSO BEEN ACCEPTED TO TRAIN UNDER LORD MUTEN-RŌSHI'S TUTELAGE!
HUH ?! REALLY ?!!
YES, I'M PLANNING TO HAVE HIM BUILD ME UP FROM THE BASICS AGAIN.
JUST DON'T LET HIM BUILD YOU INTO ANOTHER DIRTY OLD MAN...
IS IT A SIN TO HAVE HEALTHY APPETITES ?!
THEN WE'RE ALL GOING TO BE TRAINING TOGETHER!!
UNFORTU-NATELY... *YOU'RE* ON YOUR OWN.
HUH ?
GOKU... YOU'RE ALREADY A GREAT FIGHTER...
BUT YOU WANT TO BE EVEN BETTER, RIGHT ?
YEAH...
I WANT TO GET A WHOLE *LOT* STRONGER ...
SO THERE IS NO USE IN TRAINING UNDER ME ANY FURTHER.
INSTEAD, YOU MUST GO OUT INTO THE WIDE WORLD AND LEARN MORE OF LIFE!

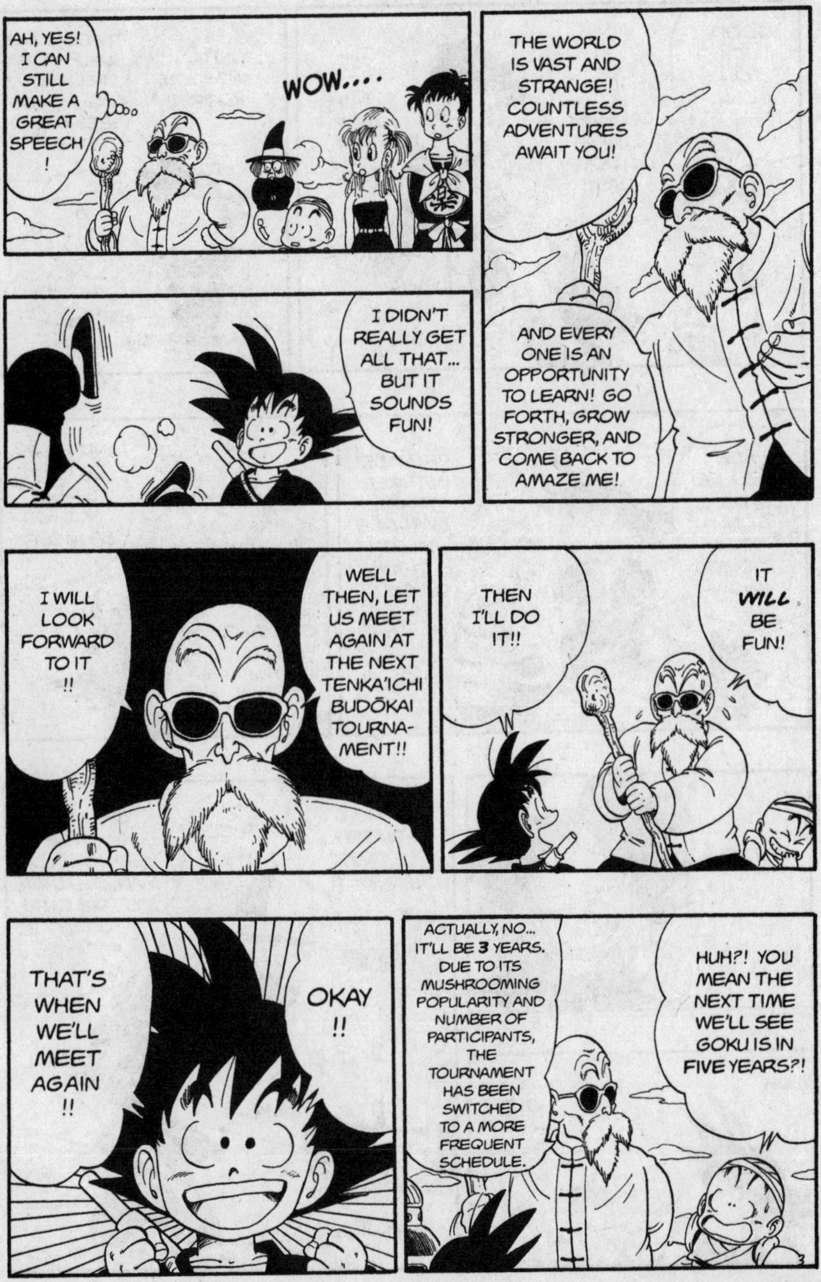
THE WORLD IS VAST AND STRANGE! COUNTLESS ADVENTURES AWAIT YOU!
AND EVERY ONE IS AN OPPORTUNITY TO LEARN! GO FORTH, GROW STRONGER, AND COME BACK TO AMAZE ME!
WOW....
AH, YES! I CAN STILL MAKE A GREAT SPEECH!
I DIDN'T REALLY GET ALL THAT... BUT IT SOUNDS FUN!
IT WILL BE FUN!
THEN I'LL DO IT!!
WELL THEN, LET US MEET AGAIN AT THE NEXT TENKA'ICHI BUDŌKAI TOURNAMENT!!
I WILL LOOK FORWARD TO IT!!
HUH?! YOU MEAN THE NEXT TIME WE'LL SEE GOKU IS IN FIVE YEARS?!
ACTUALLY, NO... IT'LL BE 3 YEARS. DUE TO ITS MUSHROOMING POPULARITY AND NUMBER OF PARTICIPANTS, THE TOURNAMENT HAS BEEN SWITCHED TO A MORE FREQUENT SCHEDULE.
OKAY!!
THAT'S WHEN WE'LL MEET AGAIN!!

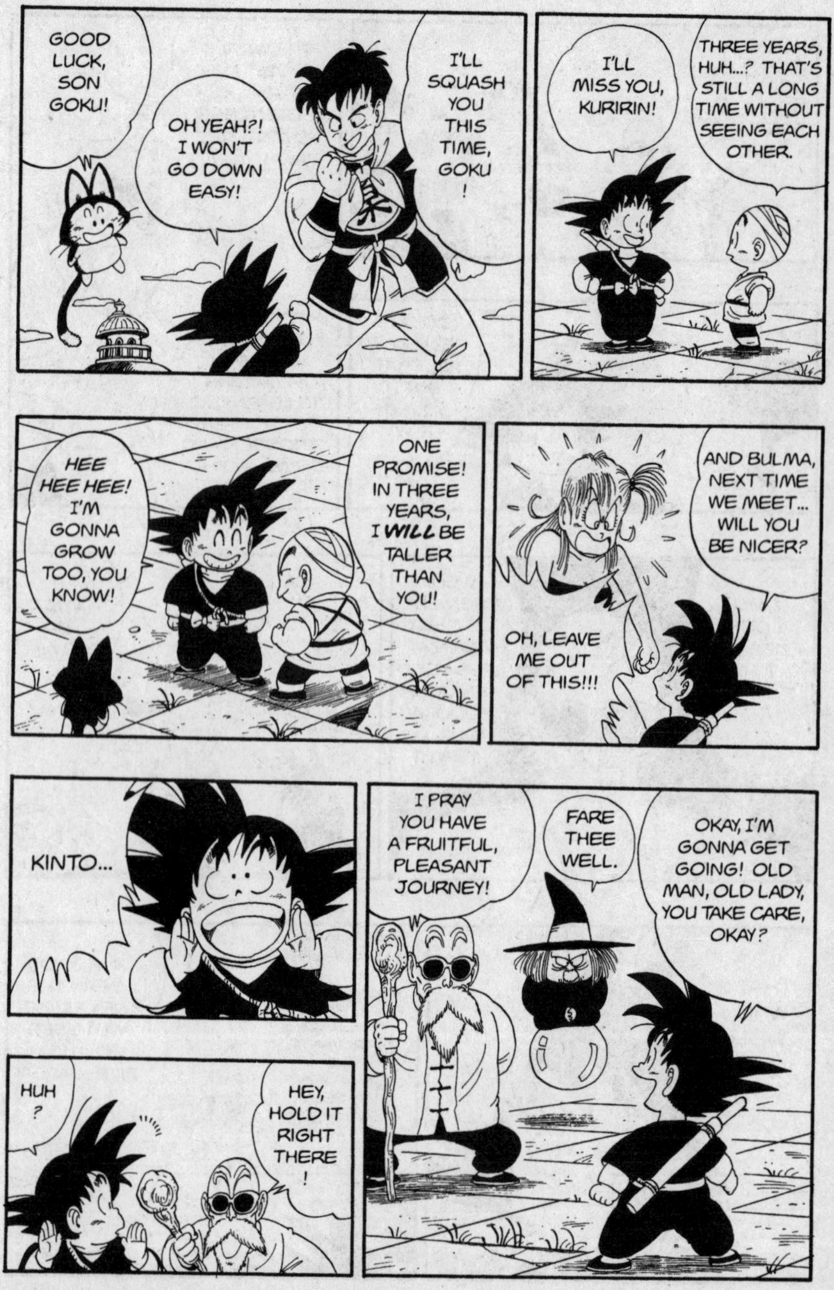
THREE YEARS, HUH...? THAT'S STILL A LONG TIME WITHOUT SEEING EACH OTHER.
I'LL MISS YOU, KURIRIN!
I'LL SQUASH YOU THIS TIME, GOKU!
OH YEAH?! I WON'T GO DOWN EASY!
GOOD LUCK, SON GOKU!
AND BULMA, NEXT TIME WE MEET... WILL YOU BE NICER?
OH, LEAVE ME OUT OF THIS!!!
ONE PROMISE! IN THREE YEARS, I **WILL** BE TALLER THAN YOU!
HEE HEE HEE! I'M GONNA GROW TOO, YOU KNOW!
OKAY, I'M GONNA GET GOING! OLD MAN, OLD LADY, YOU TAKE CARE, OKAY?
FARE THEE WELL.
I PRAY YOU HAVE A FRUITFUL, PLEASANT JOURNEY!
KINTO...
HEY, HOLD IT RIGHT THERE!
HUH?

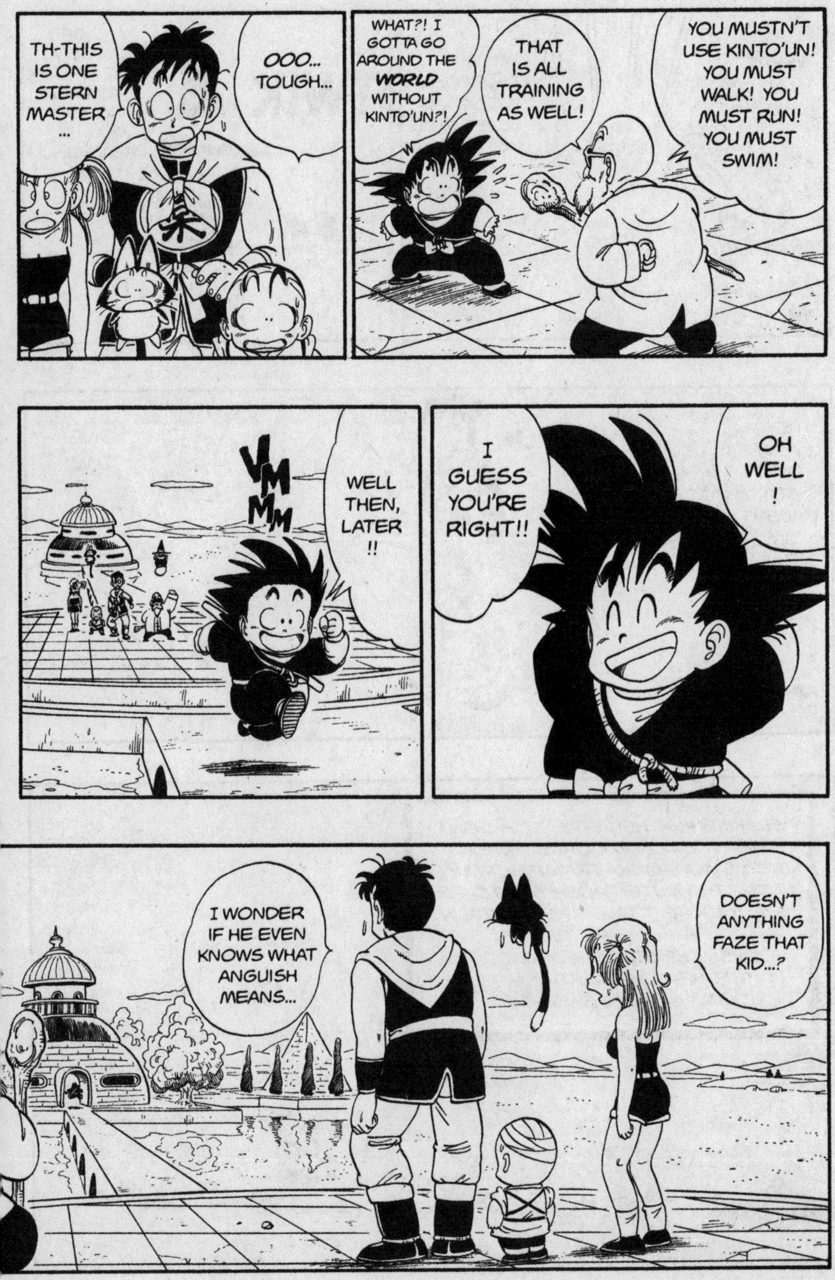
YOU MUSTN'T USE KINTO'UN! YOU MUST WALK! YOU MUST RUN! YOU MUST SWIM!
THAT IS ALL TRAINING AS WELL!
WHAT?! I GOTTA GO AROUND THE WORLD WITHOUT KINTO'UN?!
OOO... TOUGH...
TH-THIS IS ONE STERN MASTER ...
OH WELL !
I GUESS YOU'RE RIGHT!!
WELL THEN, LATER !!
VMMM
DOESN'T ANYTHING FAZE THAT KID...?
I WONDER IF HE EVEN KNOWS WHAT ANGUISH MEANS...

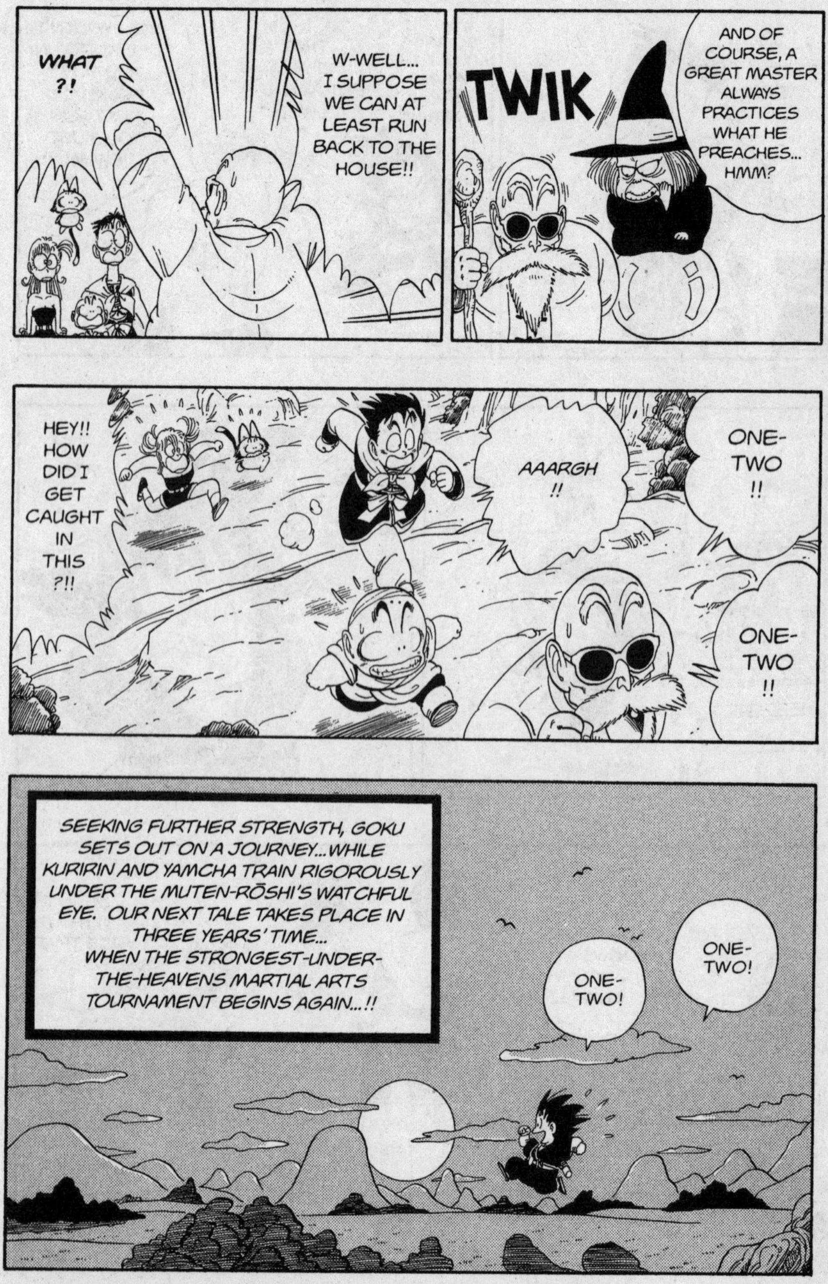
TWIK
AND OF COURSE, A GREAT MASTER ALWAYS PRACTICES WHAT HE PREACHES... HMM?
W-WELL... I SUPPOSE WE CAN AT LEAST RUN BACK TO THE HOUSE!!
WHAT ?!
ONE-TWO !!
ONE-TWO !!
AAARGH !!
HEY!! HOW DID I GET CAUGHT IN THIS ?!!
ONE-TWO!
ONE-TWO!
SEEKING FURTHER STRENGTH, GOKU SETS OUT ON A JOURNEY...WHILE KURIRIN AND YAMCHA TRAIN RIGOROUSLY UNDER THE MUTEN-RŌSHI'S WATCHFUL EYE. OUR NEXT TALE TAKES PLACE IN THREE YEARS' TIME... WHEN THE STRONGEST-UNDER-THE-HEAVENS MARTIAL ARTS TOURNAMENT BEGINS AGAIN...!!

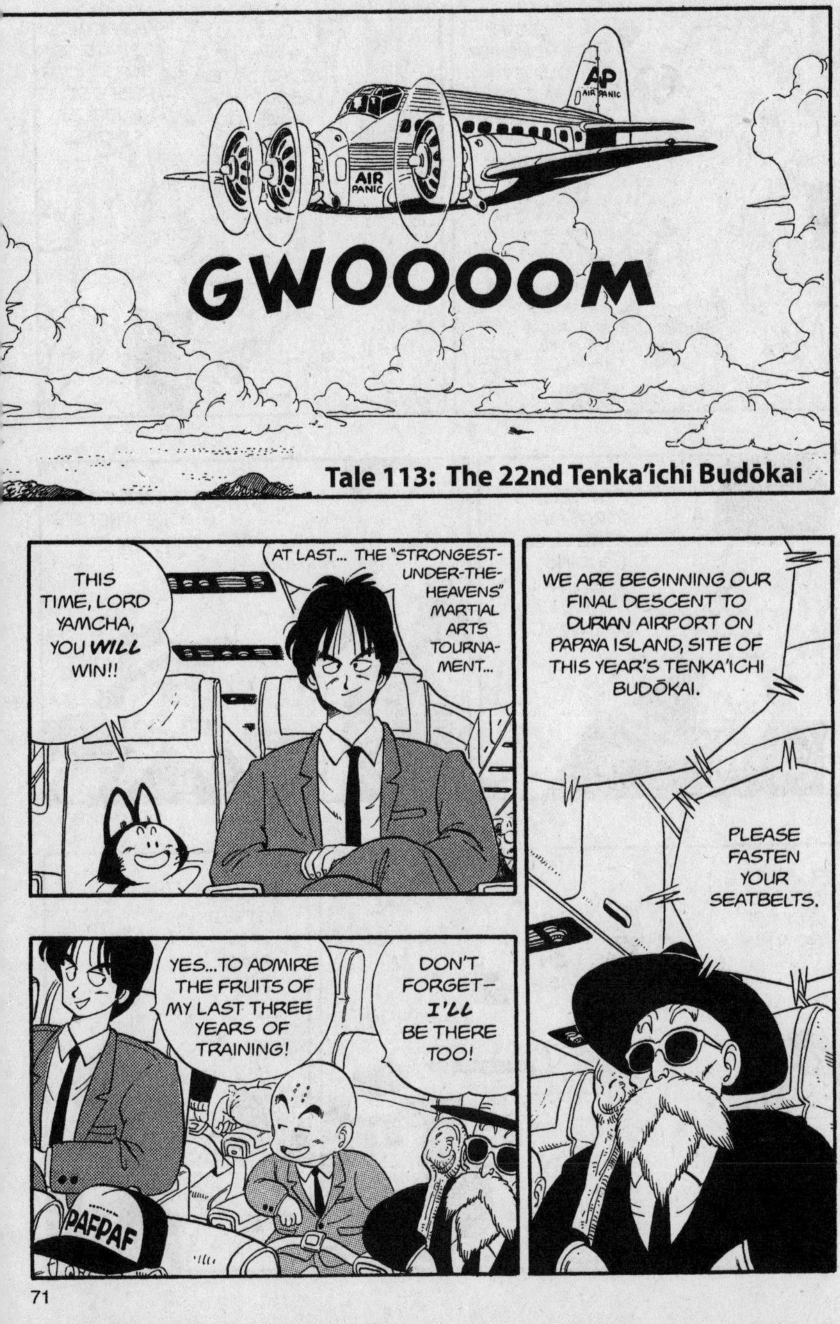
GWOOOOM
AIR PANIC
Tale 113: The 22nd Tenka'ichi Budōkai
WE ARE BEGINNING OUR FINAL DESCENT TO DURIAN AIRPORT ON PAPAYA ISLAND, SITE OF THIS YEAR'S TENKA'ICHI BUDŌKAI.
PLEASE FASTEN YOUR SEATBELTS.
AT LAST... THE "STRONGEST-UNDER-THE-HEAVENS" MARTIAL ARTS TOURNAMENT...
THIS TIME, LORD YAMCHA, YOU **WILL** WIN!!
YES...TO ADMIRE THE FRUITS OF MY LAST THREE YEARS OF TRAINING!
DON'T FORGET—**I'LL** BE THERE TOO!
PAFPAF

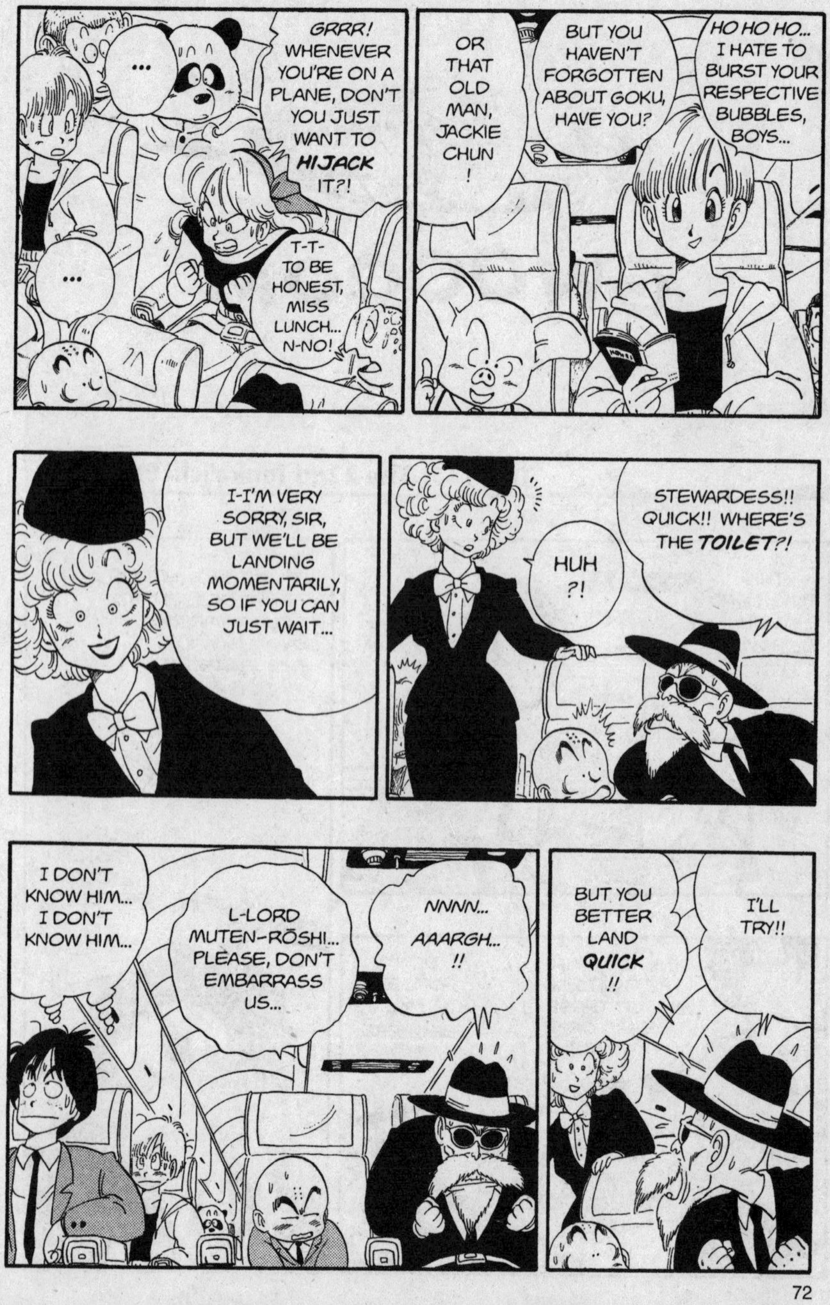
HO HO HO... I HATE TO BURST YOUR RESPECTIVE BUBBLES, BOYS...
BUT YOU HAVEN'T FORGOTTEN ABOUT GOKU, HAVE YOU?
OR THAT OLD MAN, JACKIE CHUN!
GRRR! WHENEVER YOU'RE ON A PLANE, DON'T YOU JUST WANT TO HIJACK IT?!
...
T-T-TO BE HONEST, MISS LUNCH... N-NO!
...
STEWARDESS!! QUICK!! WHERE'S THE TOILET?!
HUH?!
I-I'M VERY SORRY, SIR, BUT WE'LL BE LANDING MOMENTARILY, SO IF YOU CAN JUST WAIT...
I'LL TRY!!
BUT YOU BETTER LAND QUICK!!
NNNN... AAARGH...!!
L-LORD MUTEN-RŌSHI... PLEASE, DON'T EMBARRASS US...
I DON'T KNOW HIM... I DON'T KNOW HIM...

ドラゴンボール
DRAGON BALL

Tale 113
The 22nd Tenka'ichi Budōkai

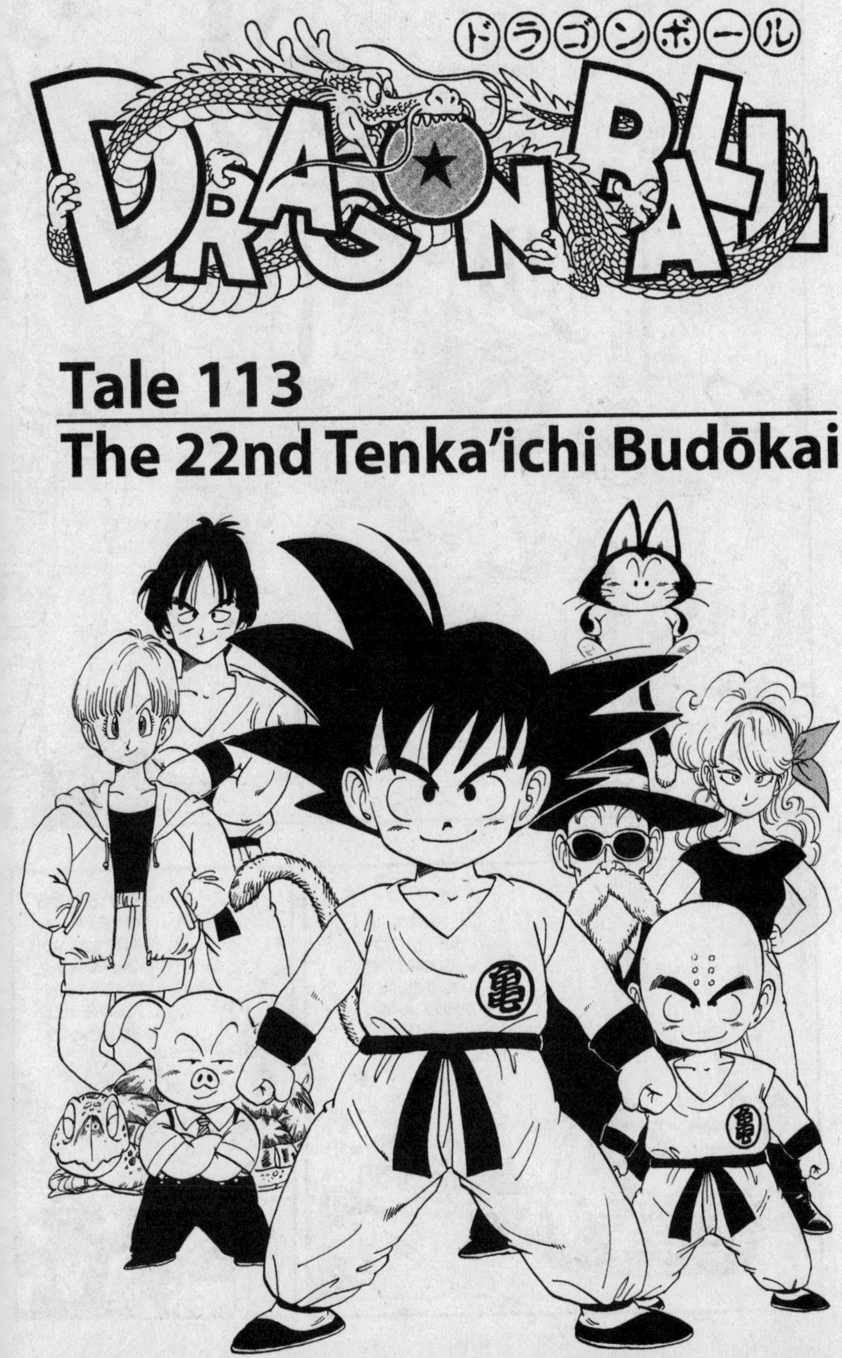

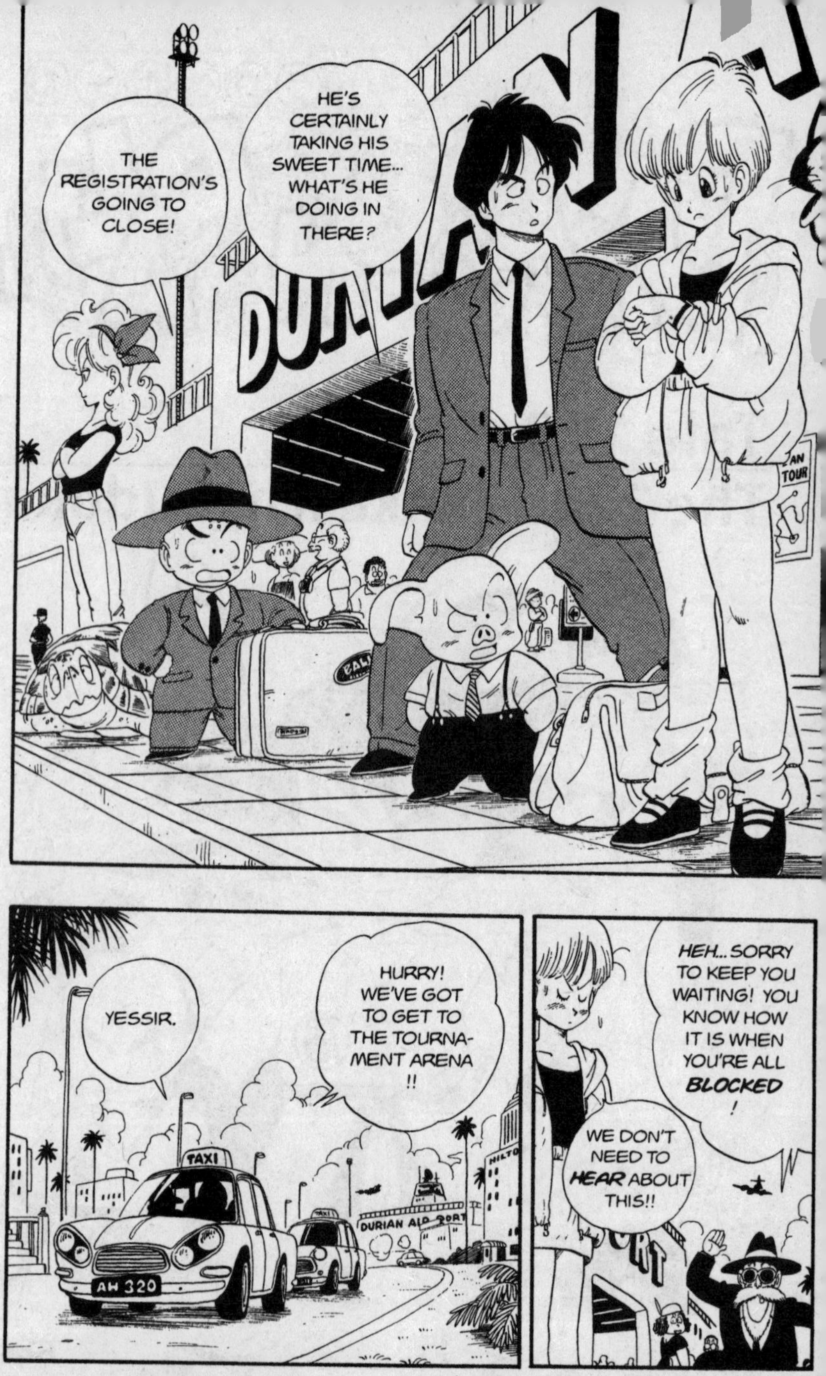
HE'S CERTAINLY TAKING HIS SWEET TIME... WHAT'S HE DOING IN THERE?
THE REGISTRATION'S GOING TO CLOSE!
HEH... SORRY TO KEEP YOU WAITING! YOU KNOW HOW IT IS WHEN YOU'RE ALL *BLOCKED*!
WE DON'T NEED TO *HEAR* ABOUT THIS!!
HURRY! WE'VE GOT TO GET TO THE TOURNAMENT ARENA!!
YESSIR.
TAXI
AW 320

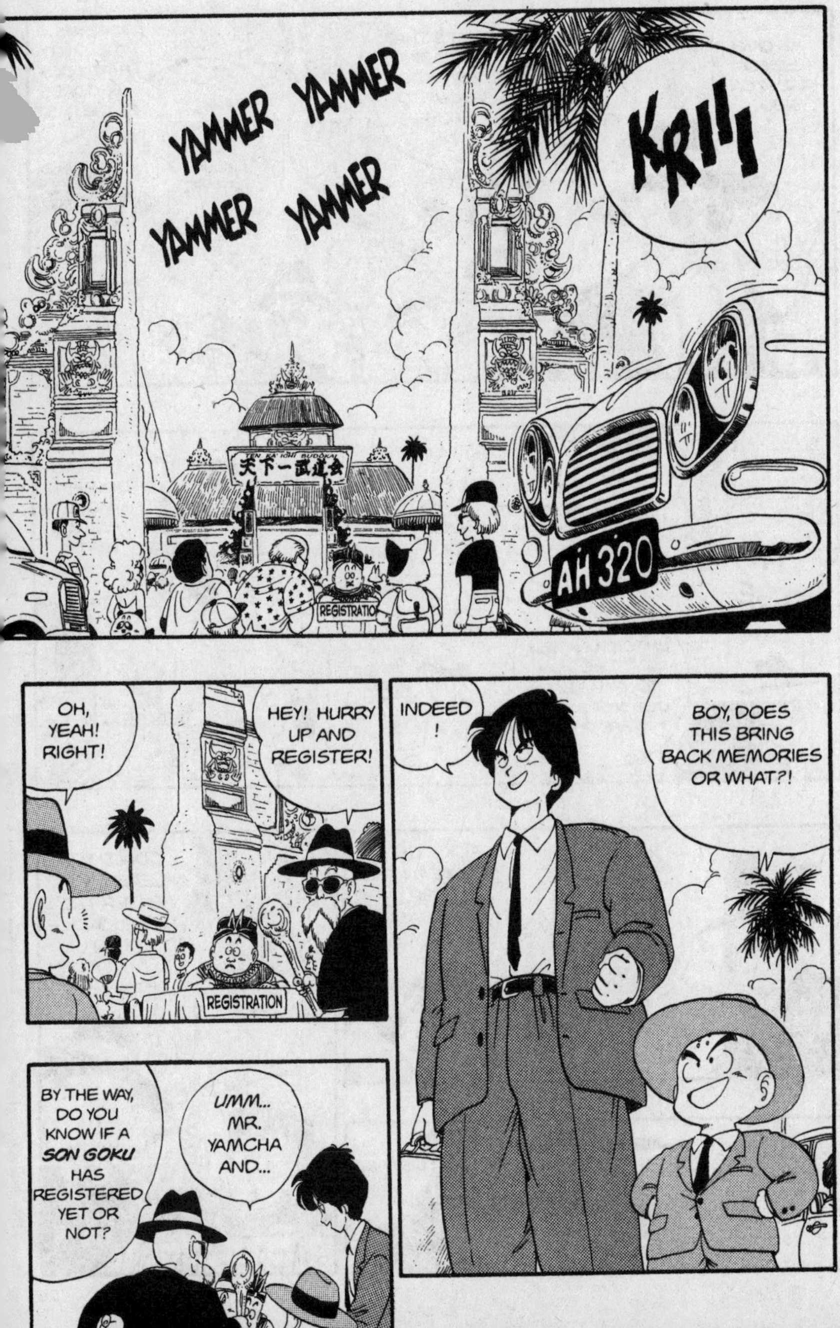
KRII
YAMMER YAMMER
YAMMER YAMMER
AH 320
TEN KA'ICHI BUDOKAI
天下一武道会
REGISTRATIO
BOY, DOES THIS BRING BACK MEMORIES OR WHAT?!
INDEED!
HEY! HURRY UP AND REGISTER!
OH, YEAH! RIGHT!
REGISTRATION
UMM... MR. YAMCHA AND...
BY THE WAY, DO YOU KNOW IF A *SON GOKU* HAS REGISTERED YET OR NOT?

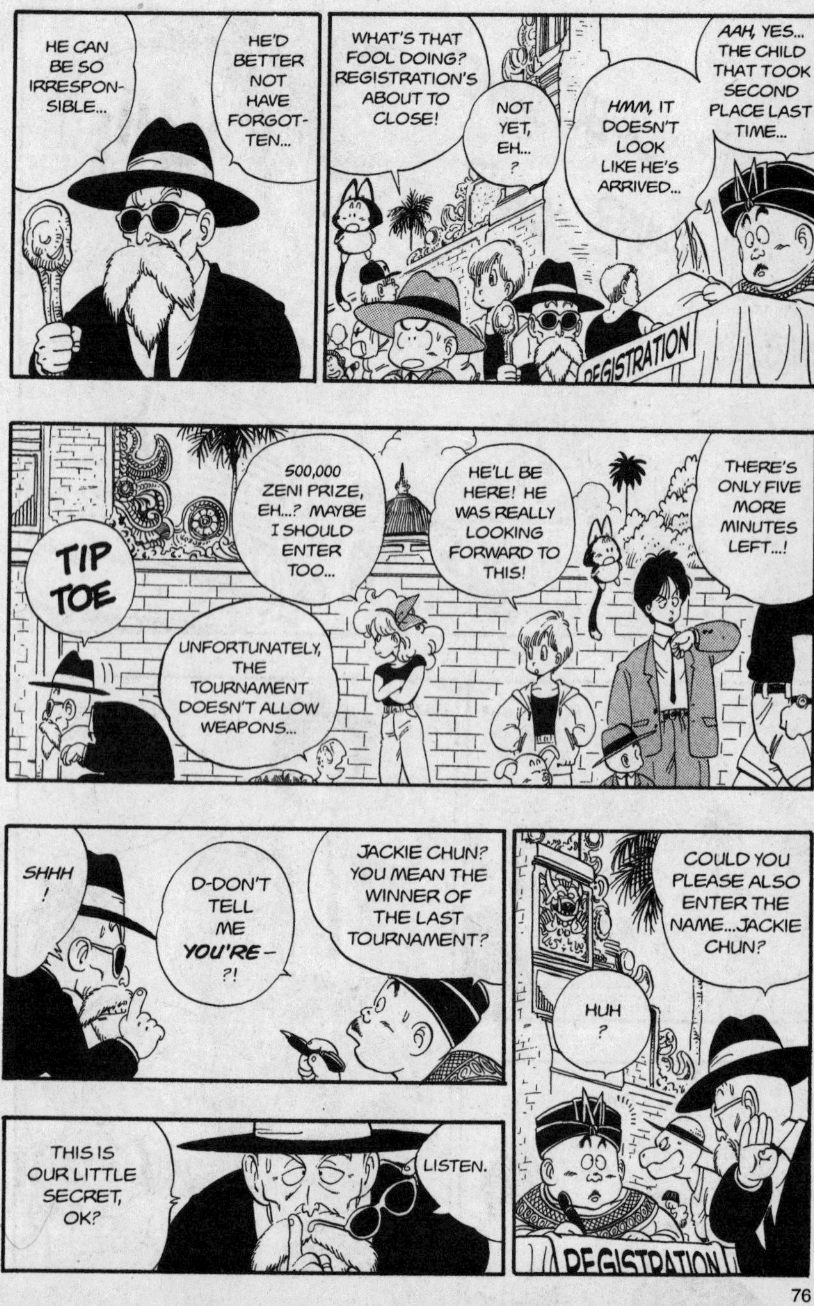
AAH, YES... THE CHILD THAT TOOK SECOND PLACE LAST TIME...
HMM, IT DOESN'T LOOK LIKE HE'S ARRIVED...
NOT YET, EH...?
WHAT'S THAT FOOL DOING? REGISTRATION'S ABOUT TO CLOSE!
REGISTRATION
HE'D BETTER NOT HAVE FORGOTTEN...
HE CAN BE SO IRRESPONSIBLE...
THERE'S ONLY FIVE MORE MINUTES LEFT...!
HE'LL BE HERE! HE WAS REALLY LOOKING FORWARD TO THIS!
500,000 ZENI PRIZE, EH...? MAYBE I SHOULD ENTER TOO...
UNFORTUNATELY, THE TOURNAMENT DOESN'T ALLOW WEAPONS...
TIP TOE
COULD YOU PLEASE ALSO ENTER THE NAME...JACKIE CHUN?
HUH?
REGISTRATION
JACKIE CHUN? YOU MEAN THE WINNER OF THE LAST TOURNAMENT?
D-DON'T TELL ME YOU'RE—?!
SHHH!
LISTEN.
THIS IS OUR LITTLE SECRET, OK?

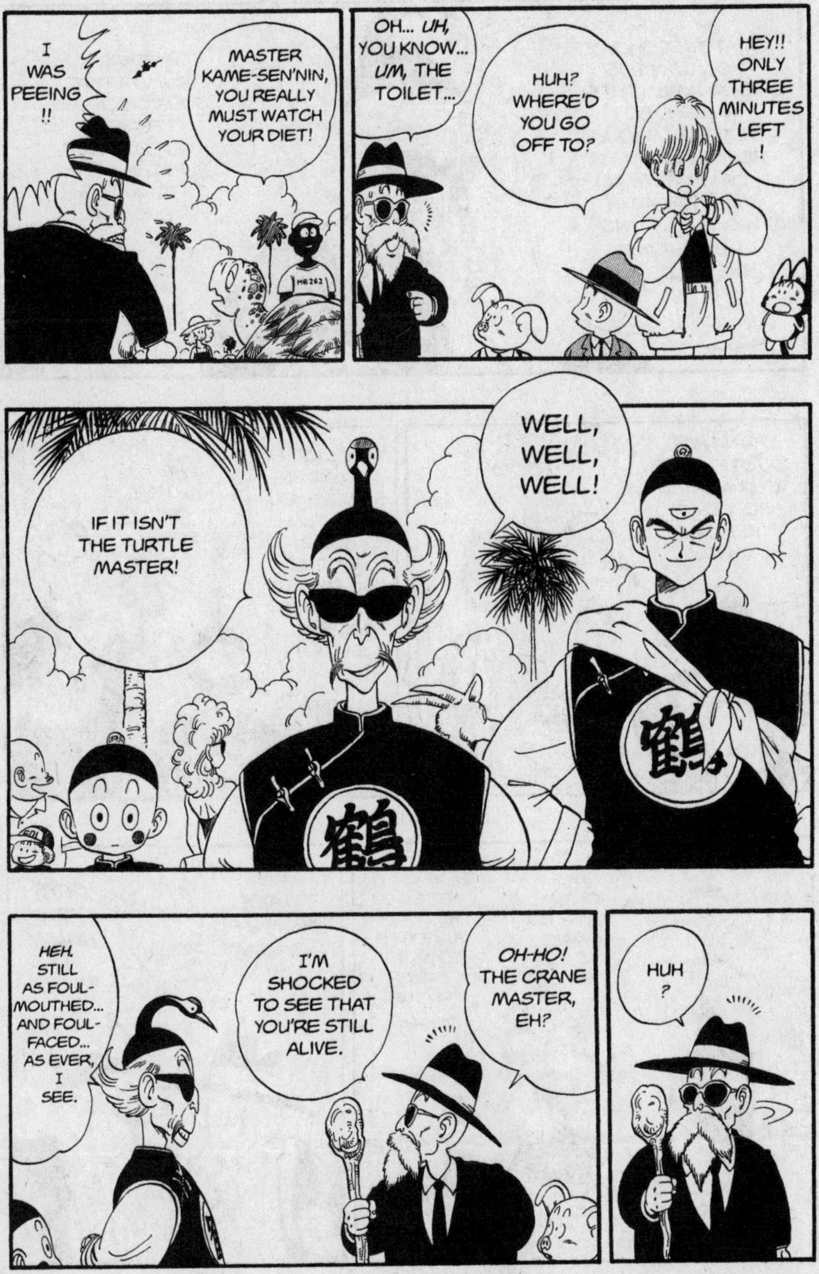
HEY!! ONLY THREE MINUTES LEFT!
HUH? WHERE'D YOU GO OFF TO?
OH... UH, YOU KNOW... UM, THE TOILET...
MASTER KAME-SEN'NIN, YOU REALLY MUST WATCH YOUR DIET!
I WAS PEEING!!
WELL, WELL, WELL!
IF IT ISN'T THE TURTLE MASTER!
HUH?
OH-HO! THE CRANE MASTER, EH?
I'M SHOCKED TO SEE THAT YOU'RE STILL ALIVE.
HEH. STILL AS FOUL-MOUTHED... AND FOUL-FACED... AS EVER, I SEE.

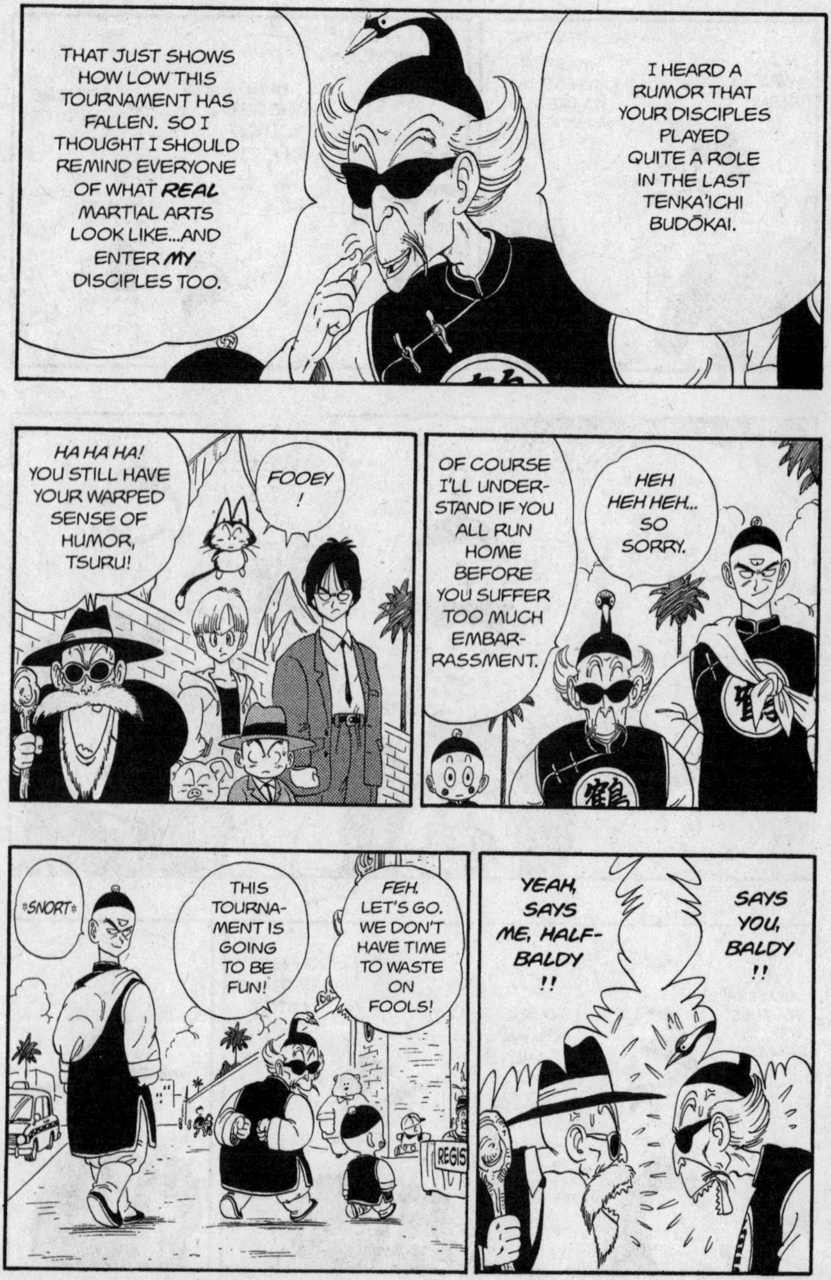
I HEARD A RUMOR THAT YOUR DISCIPLES PLAYED QUITE A ROLE IN THE LAST TENKA'ICHI BUDŌKAI.
THAT JUST SHOWS HOW LOW THIS TOURNAMENT HAS FALLEN. SO I THOUGHT I SHOULD REMIND EVERYONE OF WHAT **REAL** MARTIAL ARTS LOOK LIKE...AND ENTER ***MY*** DISCIPLES TOO.
HEH HEH HEH... SO SORRY.
OF COURSE I'LL UNDERSTAND IF YOU ALL RUN HOME BEFORE YOU SUFFER TOO MUCH EMBARRASSMENT.
FOOEY!
HA HA HA! YOU STILL HAVE YOUR WARPED SENSE OF HUMOR, TSURU!
SAYS YOU, BALDY!!
YEAH, SAYS ME, HALF-BALDY!!
FEH. LET'S GO. WE DON'T HAVE TIME TO WASTE ON FOOLS!
THIS TOURNAMENT IS GOING TO BE FUN!
REGIS
SNORT

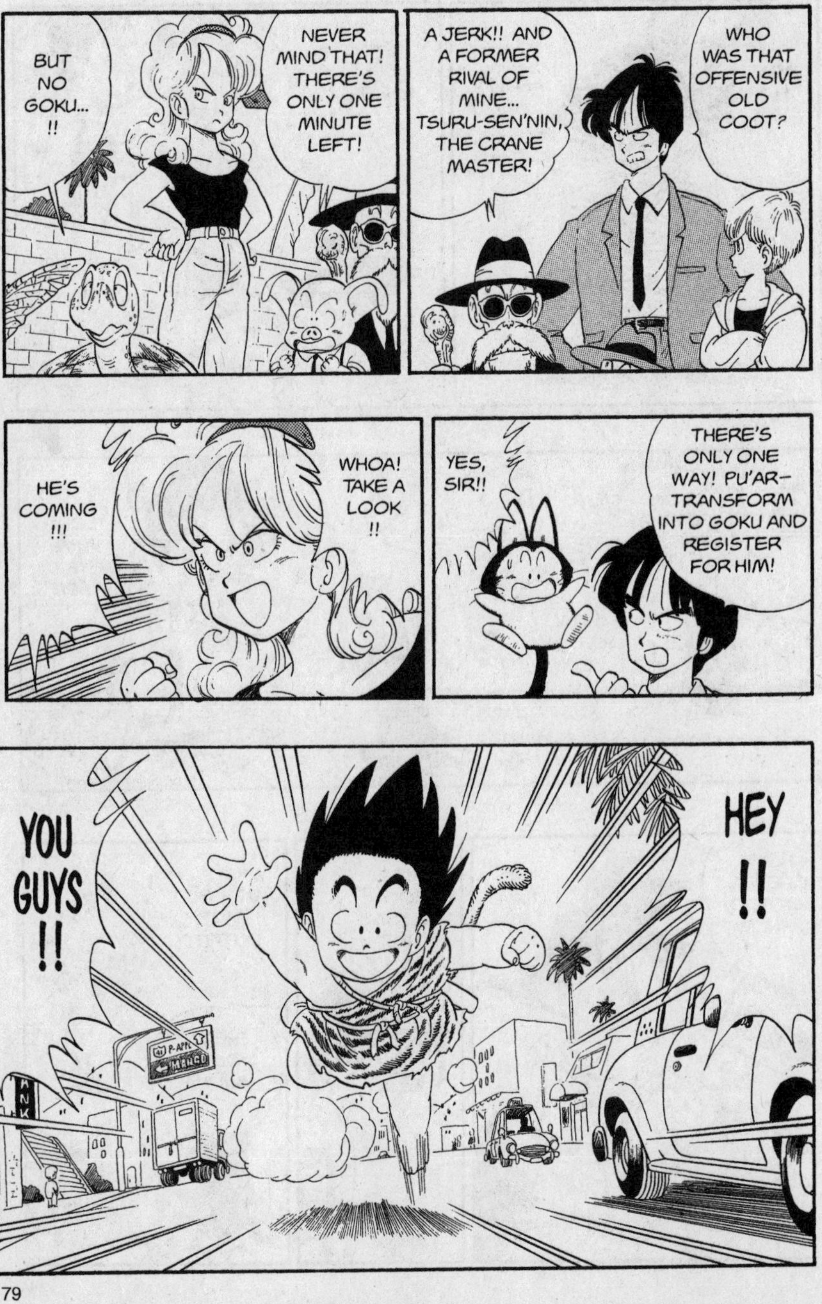
WHO WAS THAT OFFENSIVE OLD COOT?
A JERK!! AND A FORMER RIVAL OF MINE... TSURU-SEN'NIN, THE CRANE MASTER!
NEVER MIND THAT! THERE'S ONLY ONE MINUTE LEFT!
BUT NO GOKU... !!
THERE'S ONLY ONE WAY! PU'AR— TRANSFORM INTO GOKU AND REGISTER FOR HIM!
YES, SIR!!
WHOA! TAKE A LOOK !!
HE'S COMING !!!
HEY !!
YOU GUYS !!

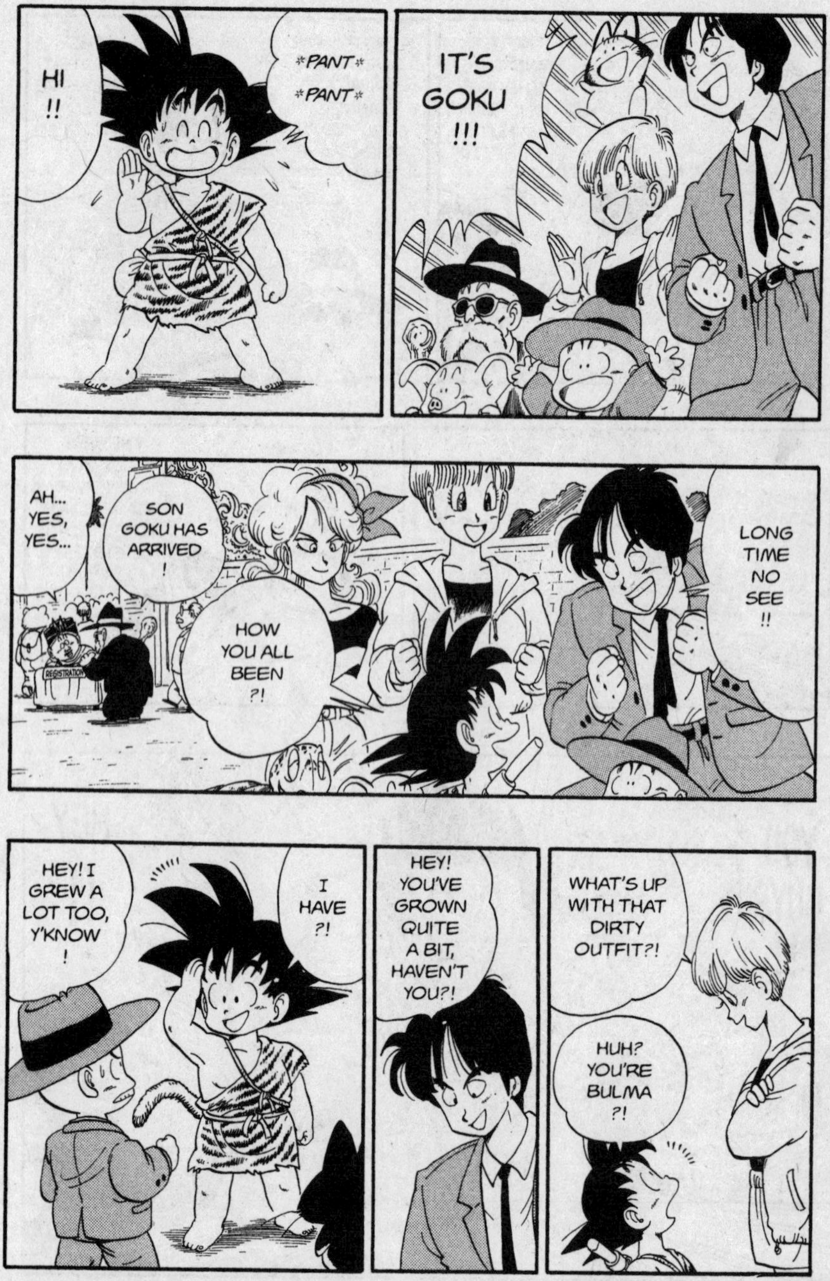
IT'S GOKU!!!
PANT *PANT*
HI!!
LONG TIME NO SEE!!
HOW YOU ALL BEEN?!
SON GOKU HAS ARRIVED!
AH... YES, YES...
WHAT'S UP WITH THAT DIRTY OUTFIT?!
HUH? YOU'RE BULMA?!
HEY! YOU'VE GROWN QUITE A BIT, HAVEN'T YOU?!
I HAVE?!
HEY! I GREW A LOT TOO, Y'KNOW!
REGISTRATION

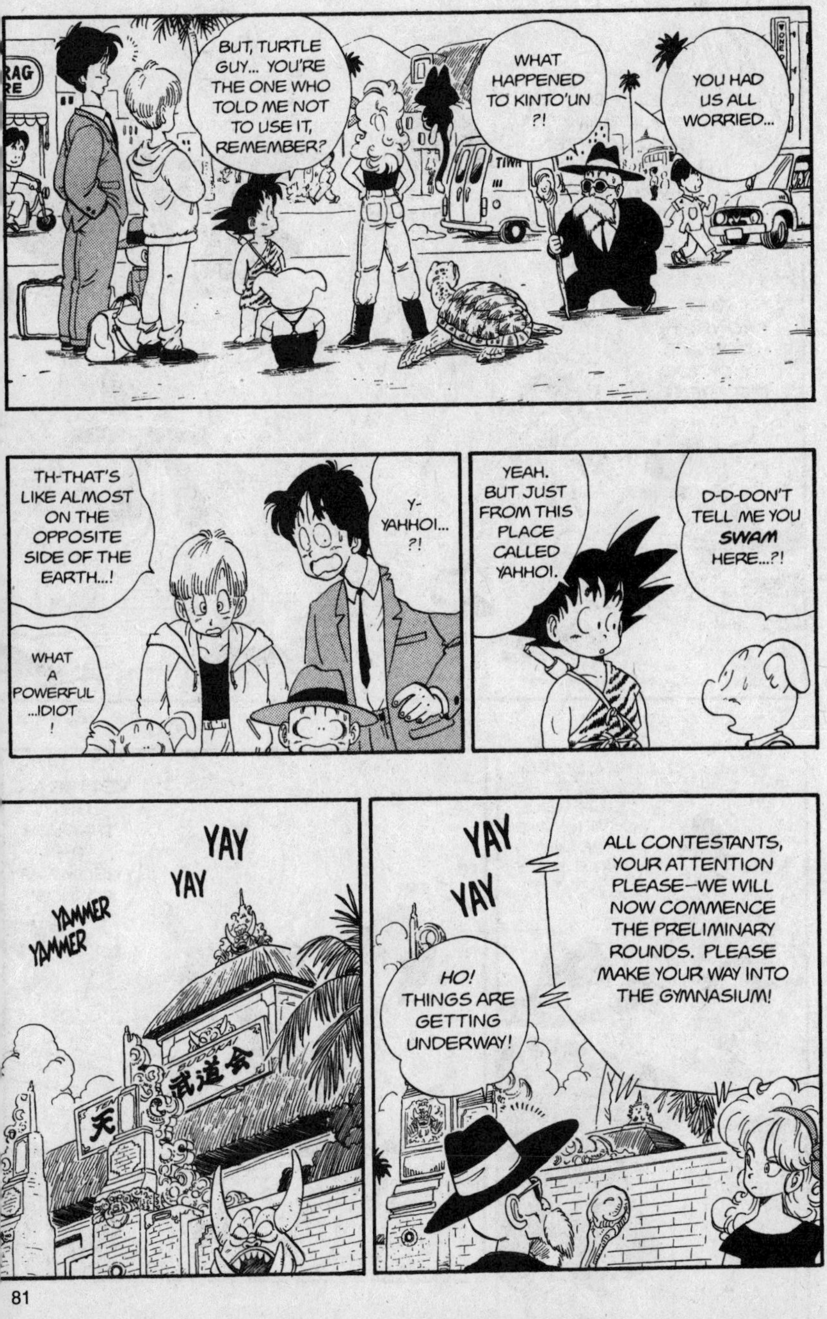
YOU HAD US ALL WORRIED...
WHAT HAPPENED TO KINTO'UN ?!
BUT, TURTLE GUY... YOU'RE THE ONE WHO TOLD ME NOT TO USE IT, REMEMBER?
D-D-DON'T TELL ME YOU SWAM HERE...?!
YEAH. BUT JUST FROM THIS PLACE CALLED YAHHOI.
Y-YAHHOI... ?!
TH-THAT'S LIKE ALMOST ON THE OPPOSITE SIDE OF THE EARTH...!
WHAT A POWERFUL ...IDIOT !
YAY
YAY
ALL CONTESTANTS, YOUR ATTENTION PLEASE—WE WILL NOW COMMENCE THE PRELIMINARY ROUNDS. PLEASE MAKE YOUR WAY INTO THE GYMNASIUM!
HO! THINGS ARE GETTING UNDERWAY!
YAY
YAY
YAMMER YAMMER
武道会
天

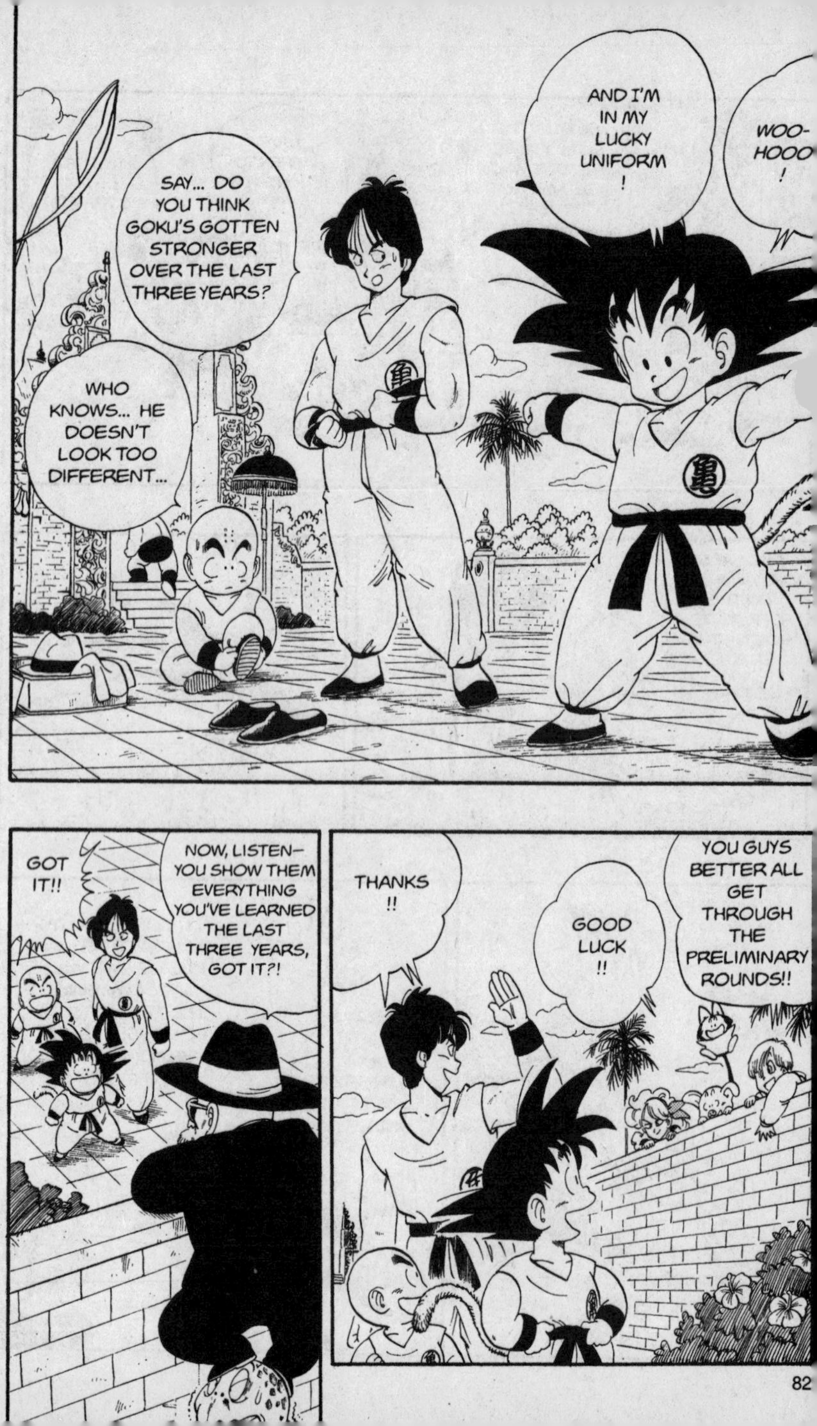
WOO-HOOO!
AND I'M IN MY LUCKY UNIFORM!
SAY... DO YOU THINK GOKU'S GOTTEN STRONGER OVER THE LAST THREE YEARS?
WHO KNOWS... HE DOESN'T LOOK TOO DIFFERENT...
YOU GUYS BETTER ALL GET THROUGH THE PRELIMINARY ROUNDS!!
GOOD LUCK!!
THANKS!!
NOW, LISTEN— YOU SHOW THEM EVERYTHING YOU'VE LEARNED THE LAST THREE YEARS, GOT IT?!
GOT IT!!

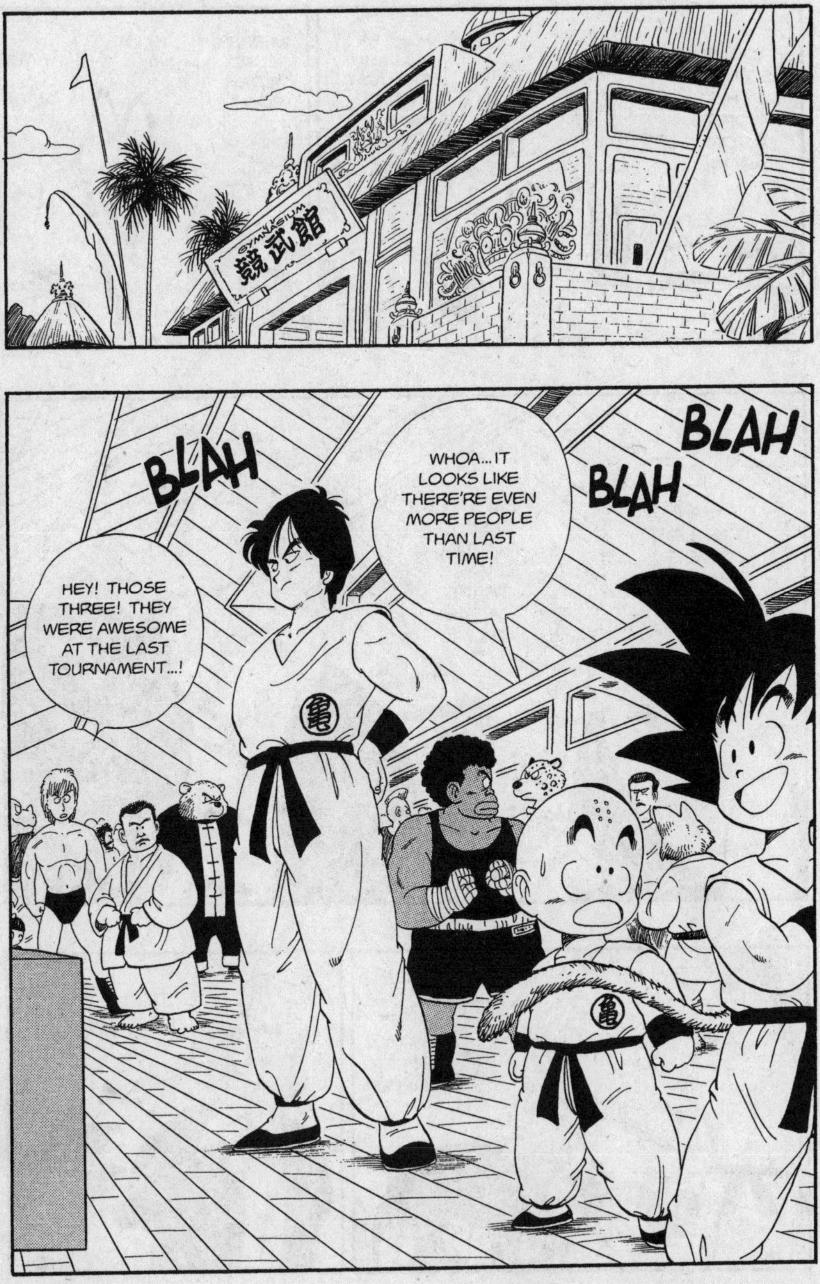
GYMNASIUM
競武館
BLAH
BLAH
WHOA... IT LOOKS LIKE THERE'RE EVEN MORE PEOPLE THAN LAST TIME!
BLAH
HEY! THOSE THREE! THEY WERE AWESOME AT THE LAST TOURNAMENT...!

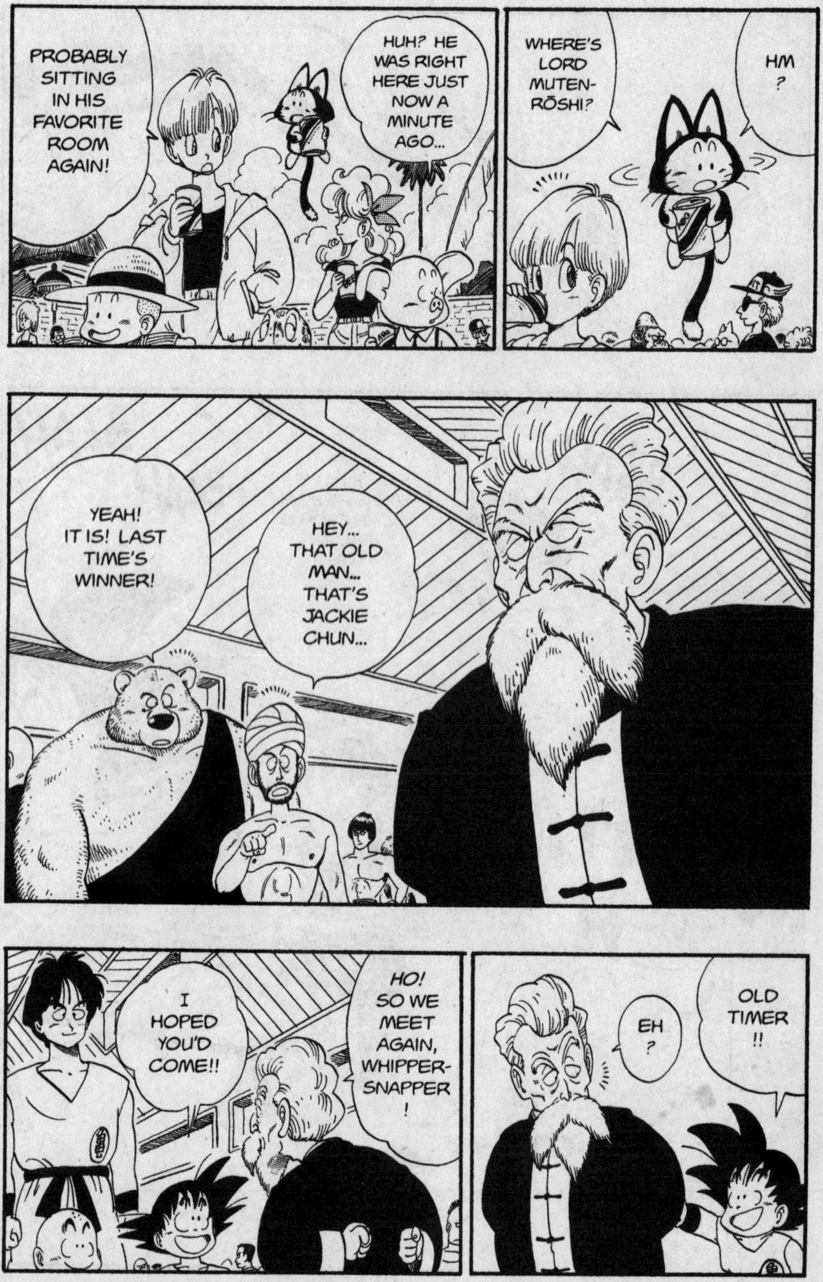
HM ?
WHERE'S LORD MUTEN-RŌSHI?
HUH? HE WAS RIGHT HERE JUST NOW A MINUTE AGO...
PROBABLY SITTING IN HIS FAVORITE ROOM AGAIN!
HEY... THAT OLD MAN... THAT'S JACKIE CHUN...
YEAH! IT IS! LAST TIME'S WINNER!
OLD TIMER !!
EH ?
HO! SO WE MEET AGAIN, WHIPPER-SNAPPER !
I HOPED YOU'D COME!!

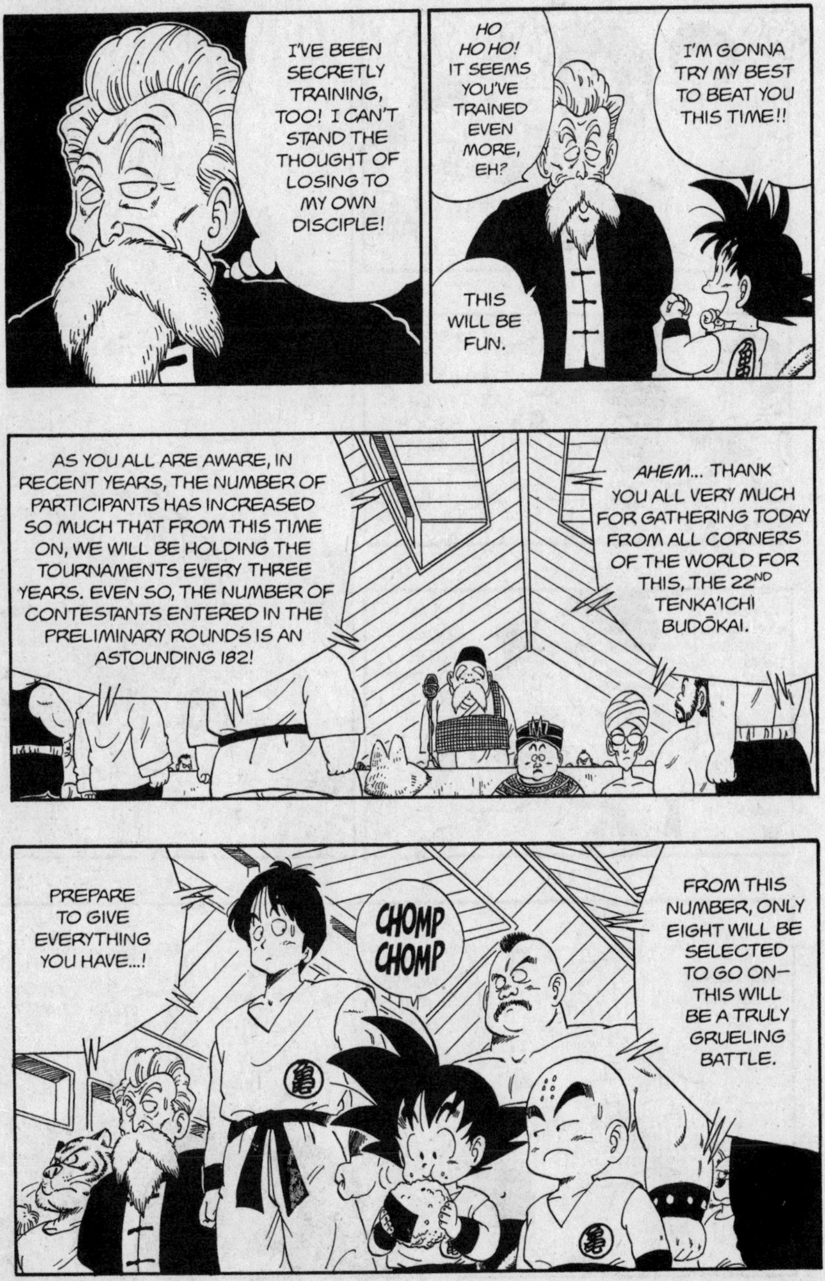
I'M GONNA TRY MY BEST TO BEAT YOU THIS TIME!!
HO HO HO! IT SEEMS YOU'VE TRAINED EVEN MORE, EH?
THIS WILL BE FUN.
I'VE BEEN SECRETLY TRAINING, TOO! I CAN'T STAND THE THOUGHT OF LOSING TO MY OWN DISCIPLE!
AHEM... THANK YOU ALL VERY MUCH FOR GATHERING TODAY FROM ALL CORNERS OF THE WORLD FOR THIS, THE 22ND TENKA'ICHI BUDŌKAI.
AS YOU ALL ARE AWARE, IN RECENT YEARS, THE NUMBER OF PARTICIPANTS HAS INCREASED SO MUCH THAT FROM THIS TIME ON, WE WILL BE HOLDING THE TOURNAMENTS EVERY THREE YEARS. EVEN SO, THE NUMBER OF CONTESTANTS ENTERED IN THE PRELIMINARY ROUNDS IS AN ASTOUNDING 182!
FROM THIS NUMBER, ONLY EIGHT WILL BE SELECTED TO GO ON— THIS WILL BE A TRULY GRUELING BATTLE.
CHOMP CHOMP
PREPARE TO GIVE EVERYTHING YOU HAVE...!

Tale 114
The Qualifying Rounds

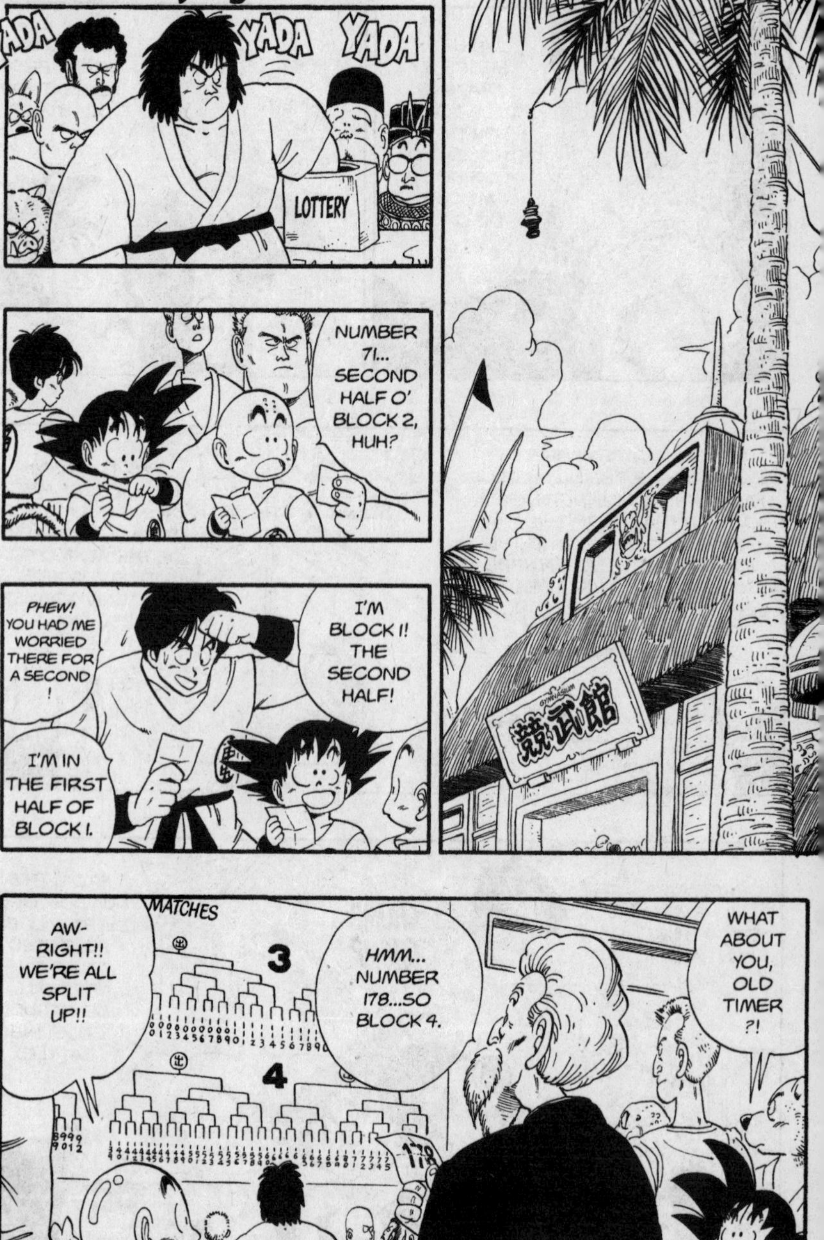

競武館
GYMNASIUM
YADA
YADA
YADA
LOTTERY
NUMBER 71... SECOND HALF O' BLOCK 2, HUH?
I'M BLOCK 1! THE SECOND HALF!
PHEW! YOU HAD ME WORRIED THERE FOR A SECOND!
I'M IN THE FIRST HALF OF BLOCK 1.
WHAT ABOUT YOU, OLD TIMER?!
HMM... NUMBER 178...SO BLOCK 4.
178
MATCHES
3
4
AW-RIGHT!! WE'RE ALL SPLIT UP!!

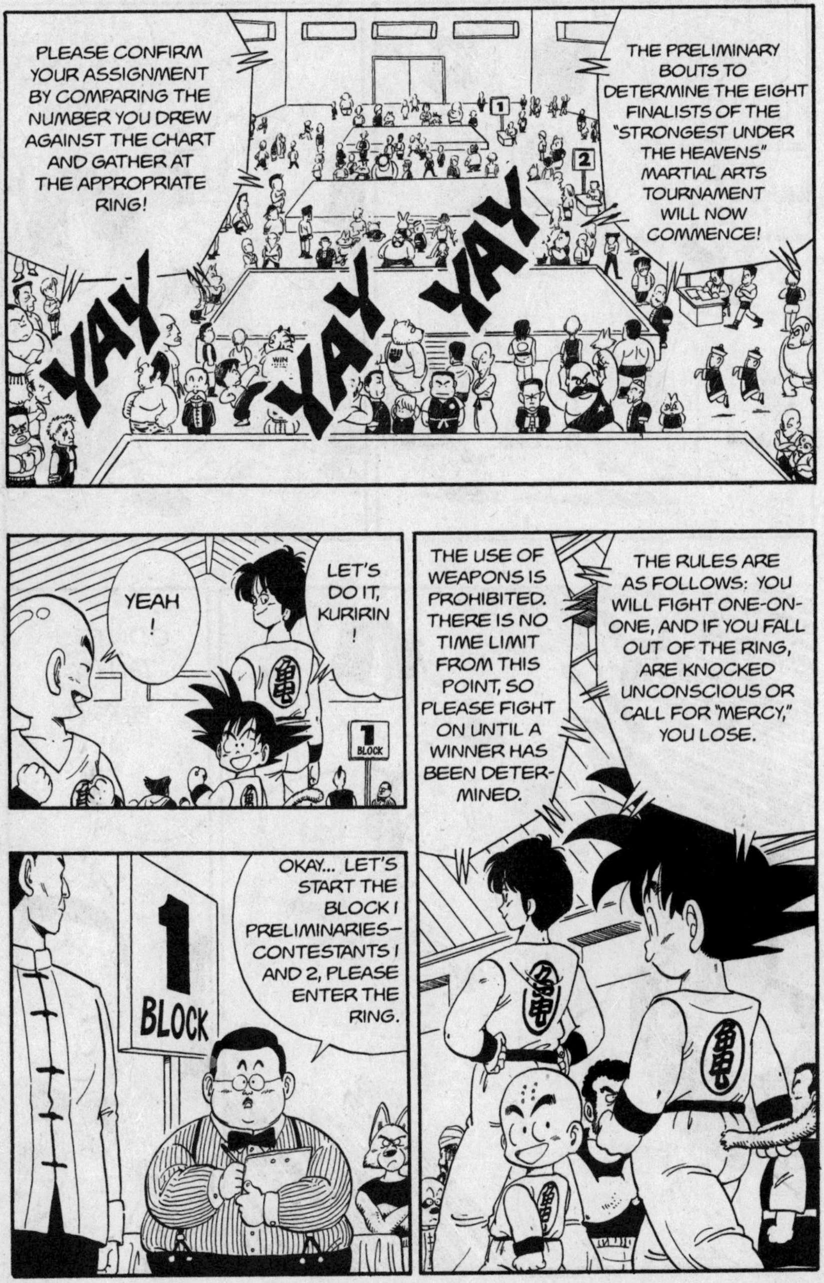
THE PRELIMINARY BOUTS TO DETERMINE THE EIGHT FINALISTS OF THE "STRONGEST UNDER THE HEAVENS" MARTIAL ARTS TOURNAMENT WILL NOW COMMENCE!
PLEASE CONFIRM YOUR ASSIGNMENT BY COMPARING THE NUMBER YOU DREW AGAINST THE CHART AND GATHER AT THE APPROPRIATE RING!
YAX YAX YAX
THE RULES ARE AS FOLLOWS: YOU WILL FIGHT ONE-ON-ONE, AND IF YOU FALL OUT OF THE RING, ARE KNOCKED UNCONSCIOUS OR CALL FOR "MERCY," YOU LOSE.
THE USE OF WEAPONS IS PROHIBITED. THERE IS NO TIME LIMIT FROM THIS POINT, SO PLEASE FIGHT ON UNTIL A WINNER HAS BEEN DETERMINED.
LET'S DO IT, KURIRIN!
YEAH!
1 BLOCK
OKAY... LET'S START THE BLOCK 1 PRELIMINARIES— CONTESTANTS 1 AND 2, PLEASE ENTER THE RING.
1 BLOCK

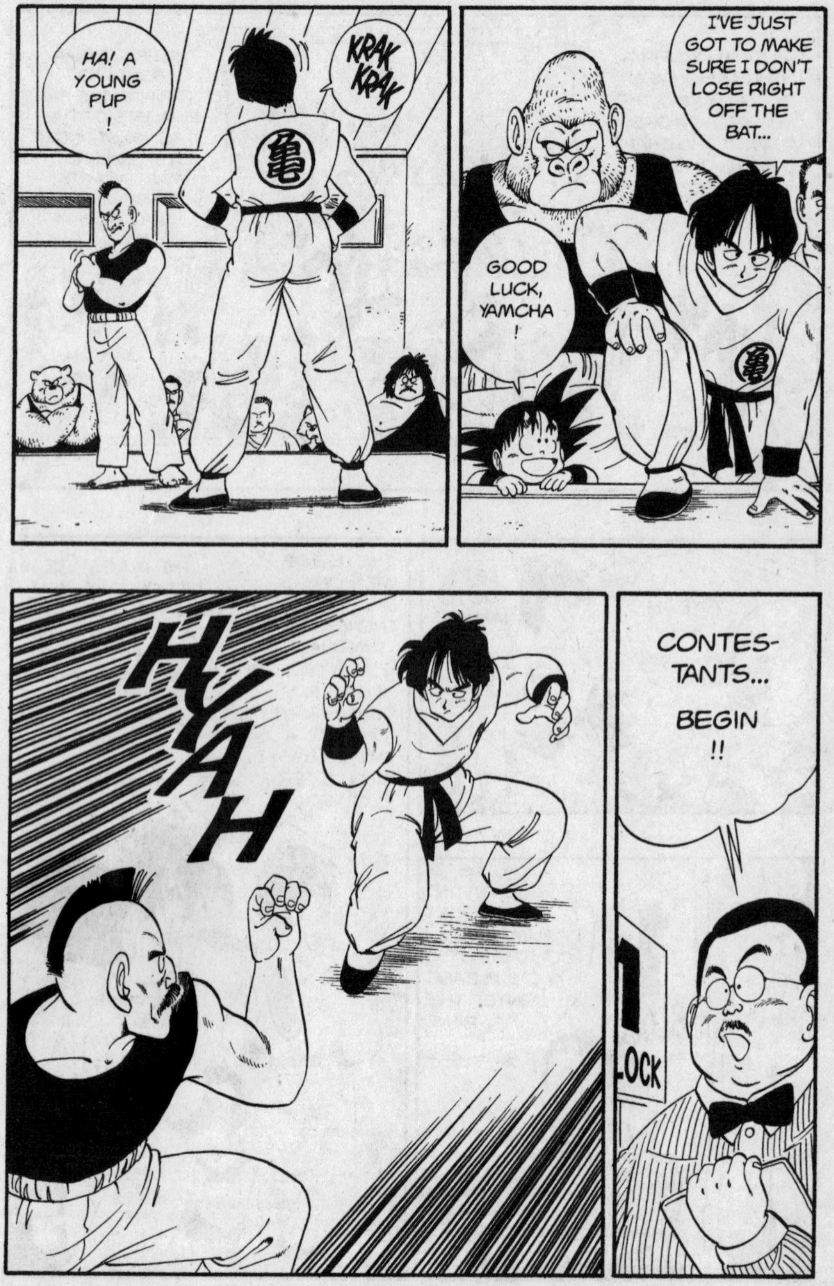
I'VE JUST GOT TO MAKE SURE I DON'T LOSE RIGHT OFF THE BAT...
GOOD LUCK, YAMCHA !
KRAK KRAK
HA! A YOUNG PUP !
CONTES- TANTS...
BEGIN !!
HYAH

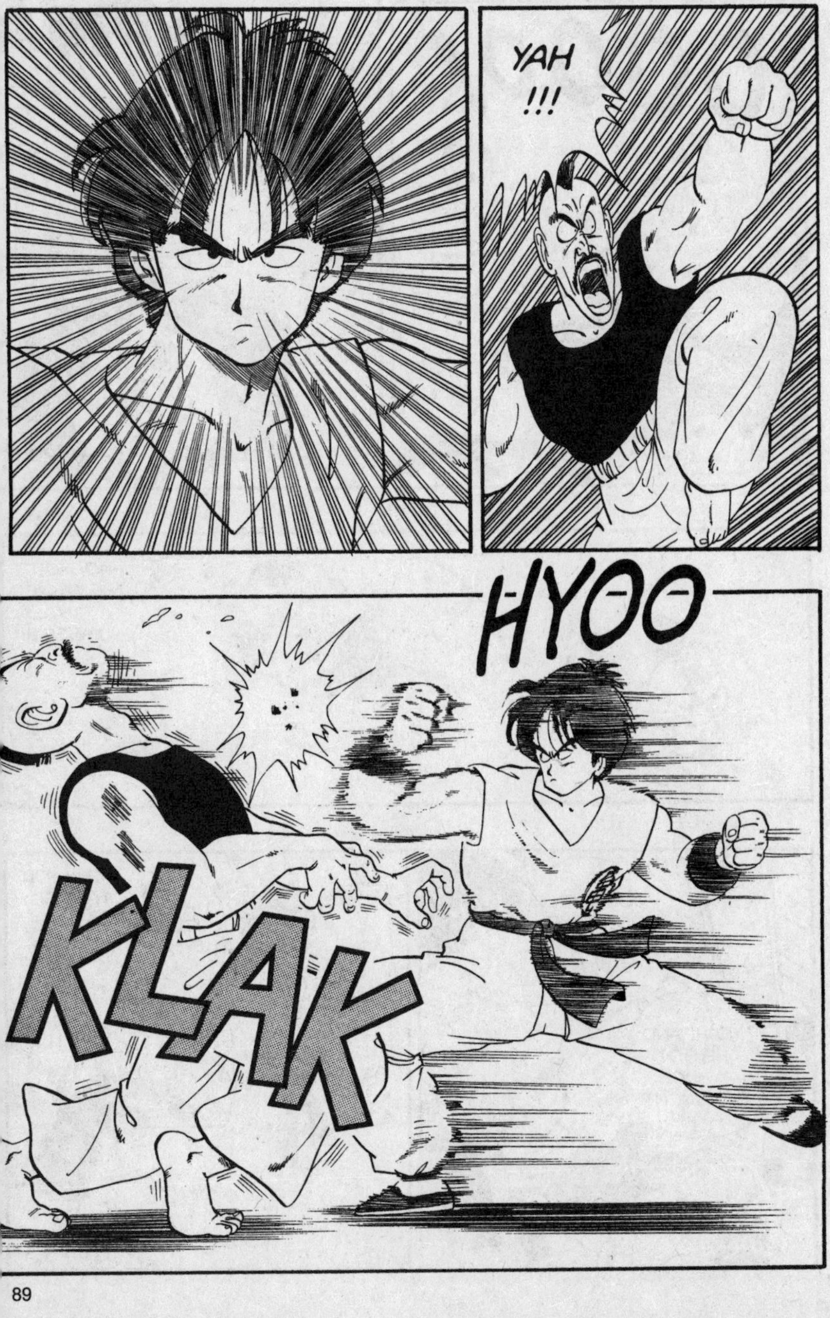
YAH
!!!
HYOO
KLAK

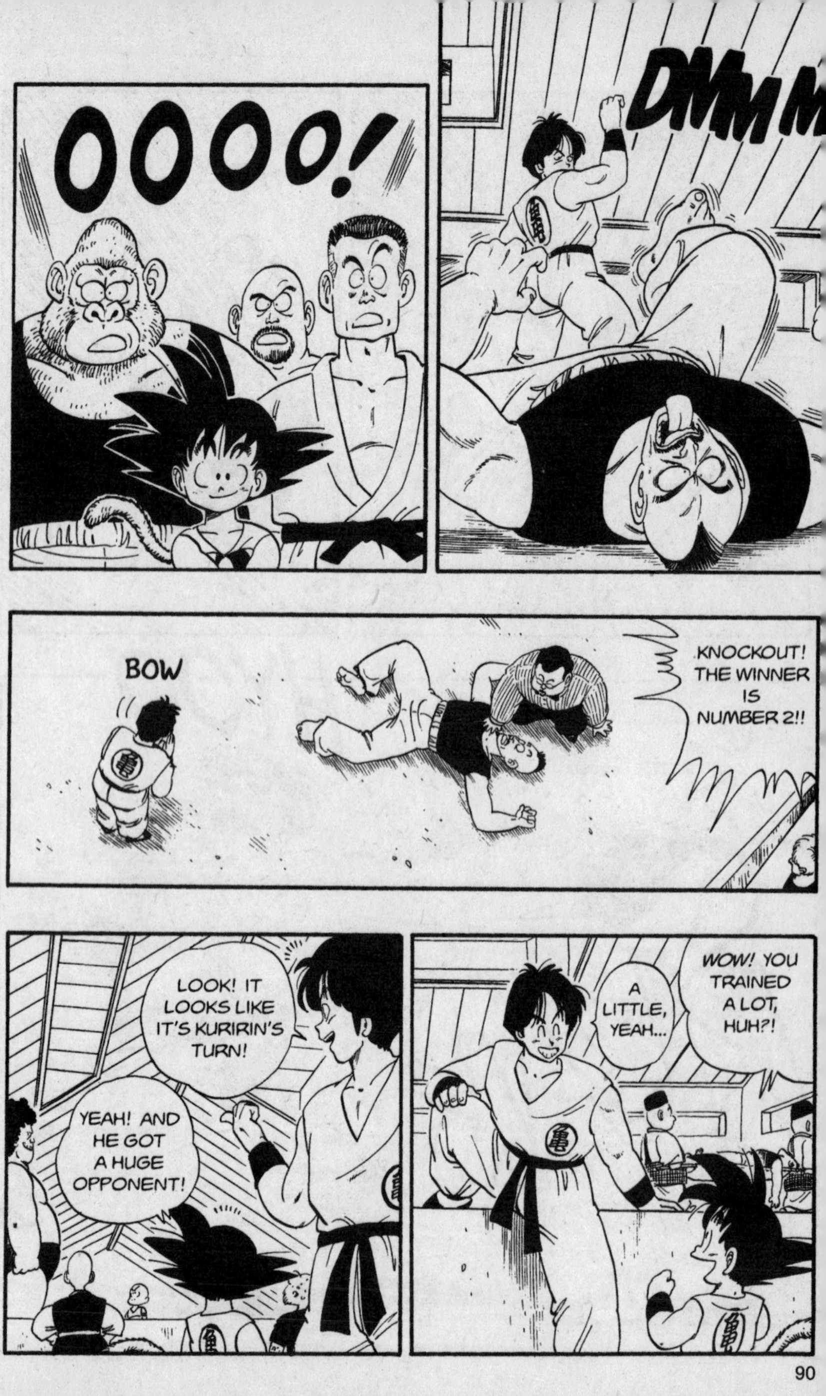
DMMM
OOOO!
KNOCKOUT! THE WINNER IS NUMBER 2!!
BOW
WOW! YOU TRAINED A LOT, HUH?!
A LITTLE, YEAH...
LOOK! IT LOOKS LIKE IT'S KURIRIN'S TURN!
YEAH! AND HE GOT A HUGE OPPONENT!

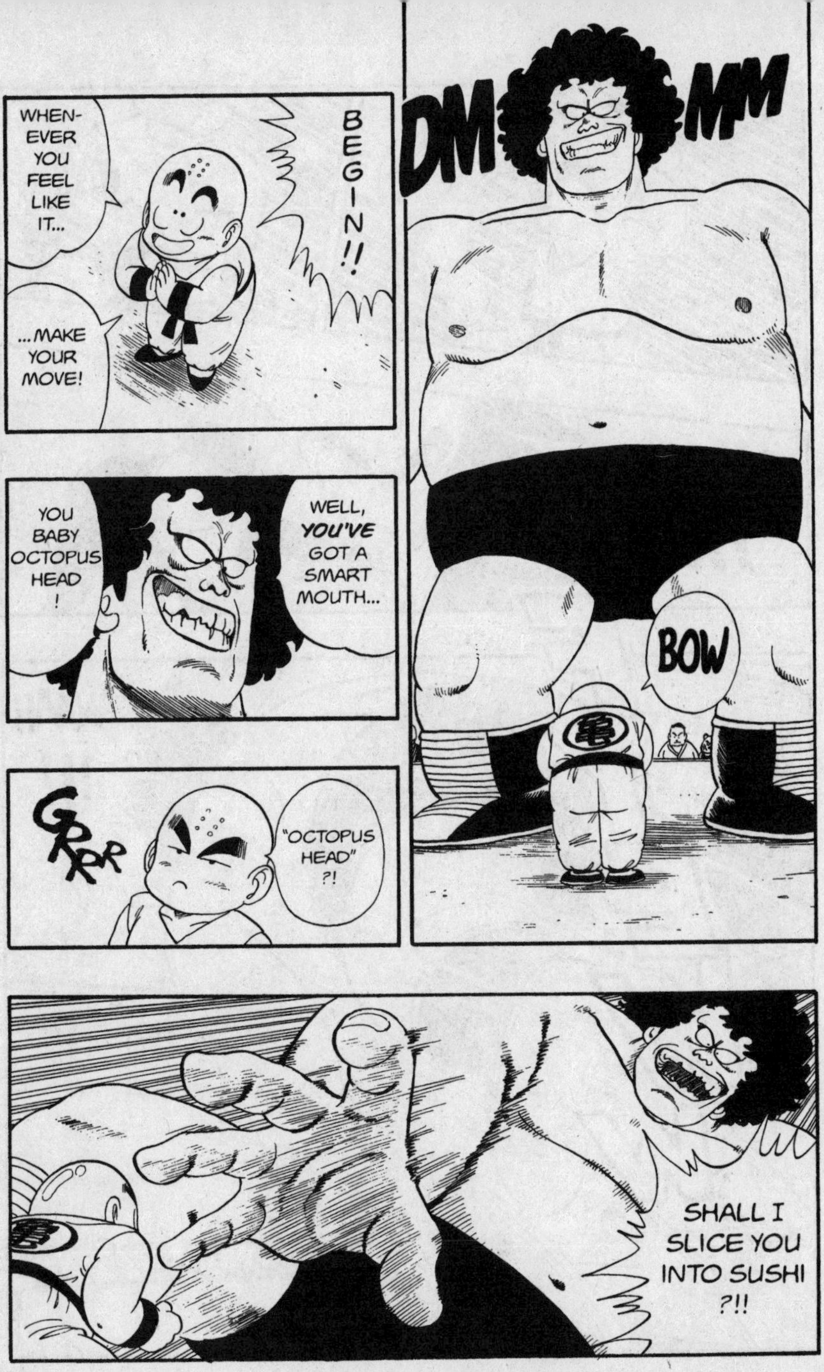
DMMMM
BOW
BEGIN!!
WHENEVER YOU FEEL LIKE IT...
...MAKE YOUR MOVE!
WELL, *YOU'VE* GOT A SMART MOUTH...
YOU BABY OCTOPUS HEAD!
"OCTOPUS HEAD"?!
GRRR
SHALL I SLICE YOU INTO SUSHI?!!

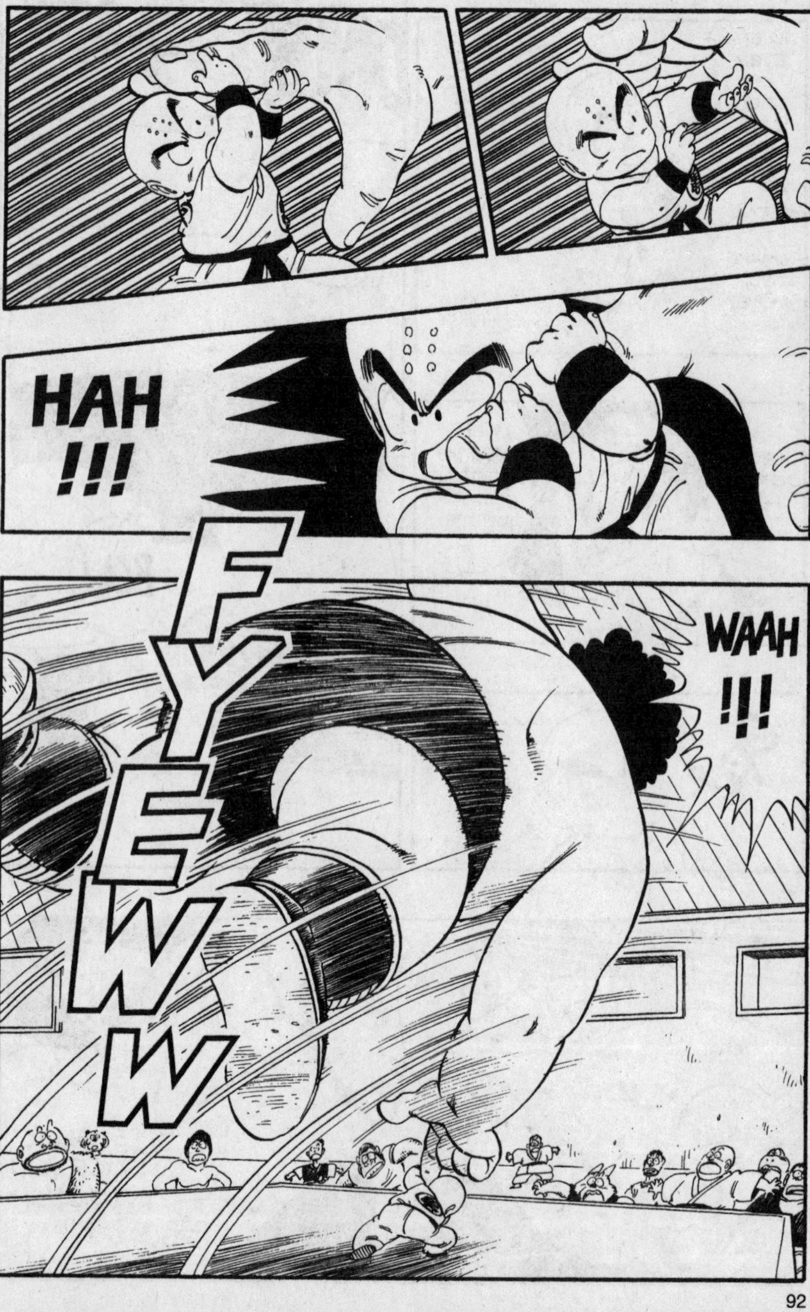
HAH !!!
WAAH !!!
FYEWW

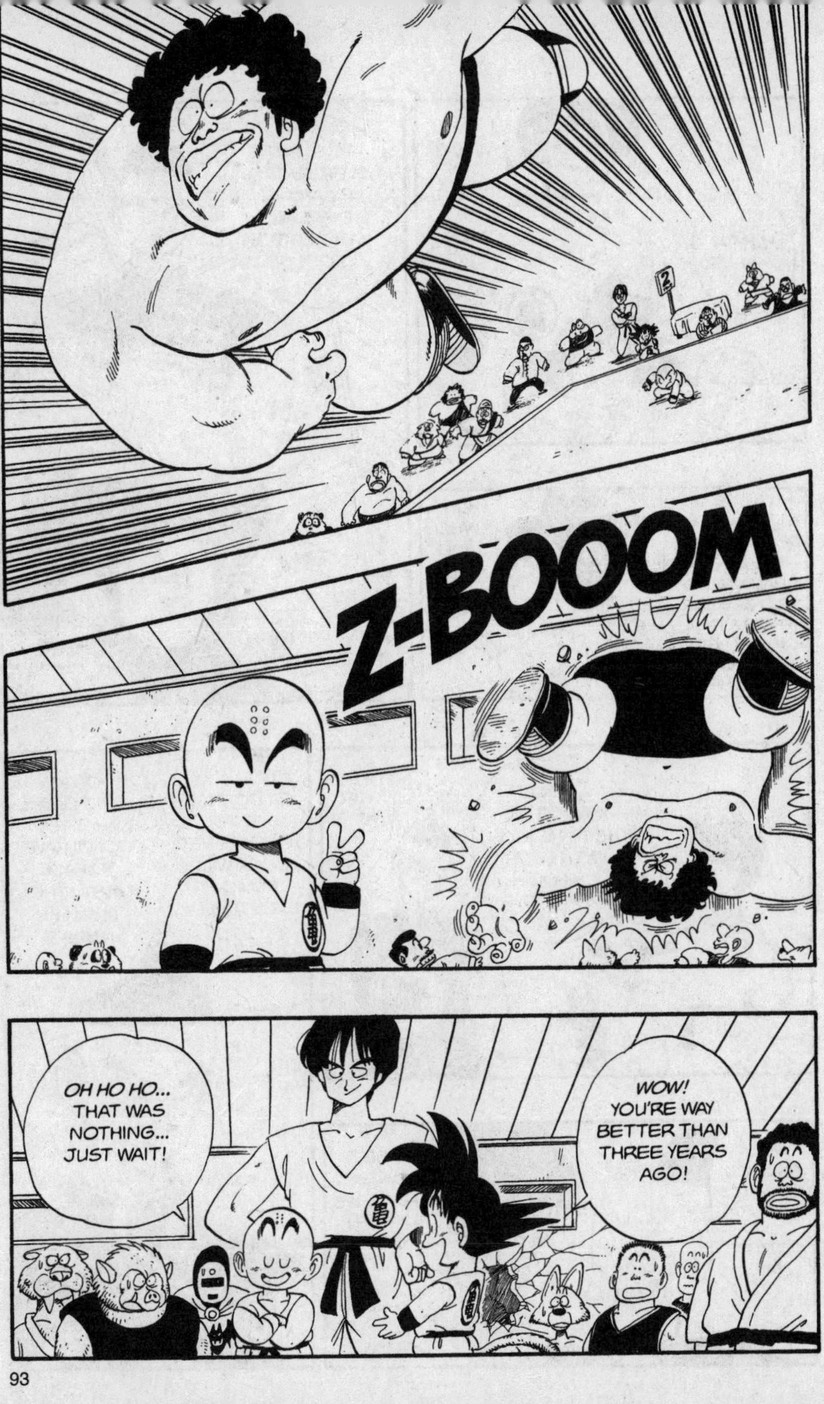
Z-BOOOM
WOW! YOU'RE WAY BETTER THAN THREE YEARS AGO!
OH HO HO... THAT WAS NOTHING... JUST WAIT!

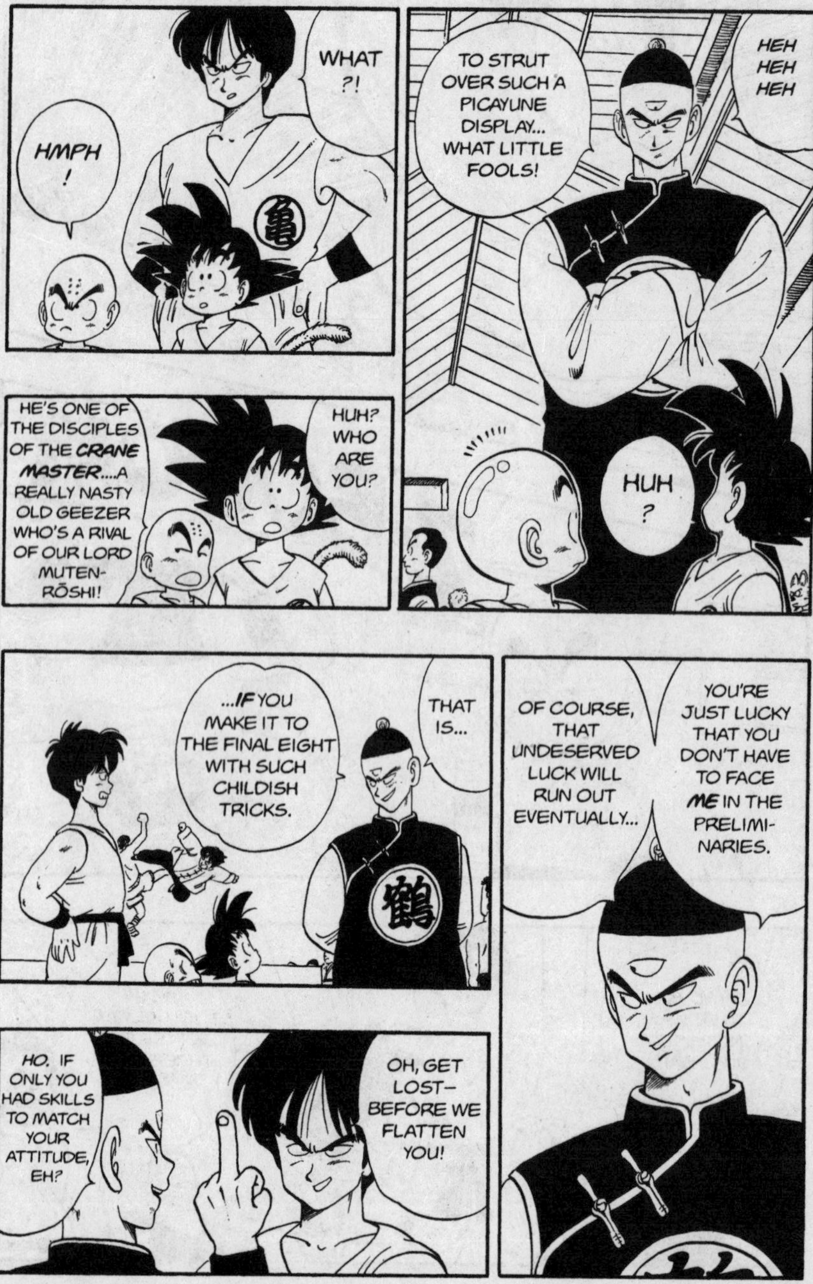
HEH HEH HEH
TO STRUT OVER SUCH A PICAYUNE DISPLAY... WHAT LITTLE FOOLS!
HUH ?
WHAT ?!
HMPH !
HUH? WHO ARE YOU?
HE'S ONE OF THE DISCIPLES OF THE CRANE MASTER....A REALLY NASTY OLD GEEZER WHO'S A RIVAL OF OUR LORD MUTEN-RŌSHI!
YOU'RE JUST LUCKY THAT YOU DON'T HAVE TO FACE ME IN THE PRELIMI-NARIES.
OF COURSE, THAT UNDESERVED LUCK WILL RUN OUT EVENTUALLY...
THAT IS...
...IF YOU MAKE IT TO THE FINAL EIGHT WITH SUCH CHILDISH TRICKS.
OH, GET LOST— BEFORE WE FLATTEN YOU!
HO. IF ONLY YOU HAD SKILLS TO MATCH YOUR ATTITUDE, EH?

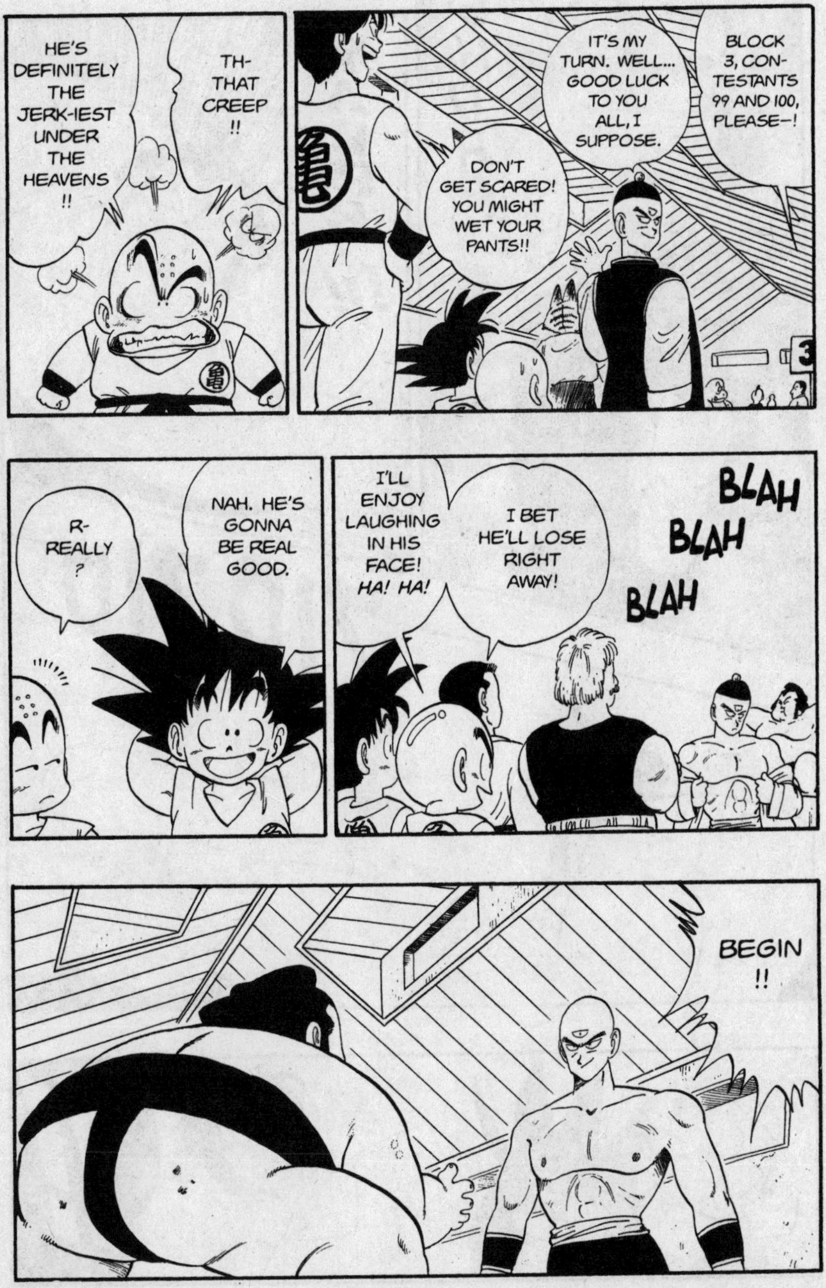

BLOCK 3, CONTESTANTS 99 AND 100, PLEASE–!
IT'S MY TURN. WELL... GOOD LUCK TO YOU ALL, I SUPPOSE.
DON'T GET SCARED! YOU MIGHT WET YOUR PANTS!!
TH-THAT CREEP!!
HE'S DEFINITELY THE JERK-IEST UNDER THE HEAVENS!!
BLAH BLAH BLAH
I BET HE'LL LOSE RIGHT AWAY!
I'LL ENJOY LAUGHING IN HIS FACE! *HA! HA!*
NAH. HE'S GONNA BE REAL GOOD.
R-REALLY?
BEGIN!!

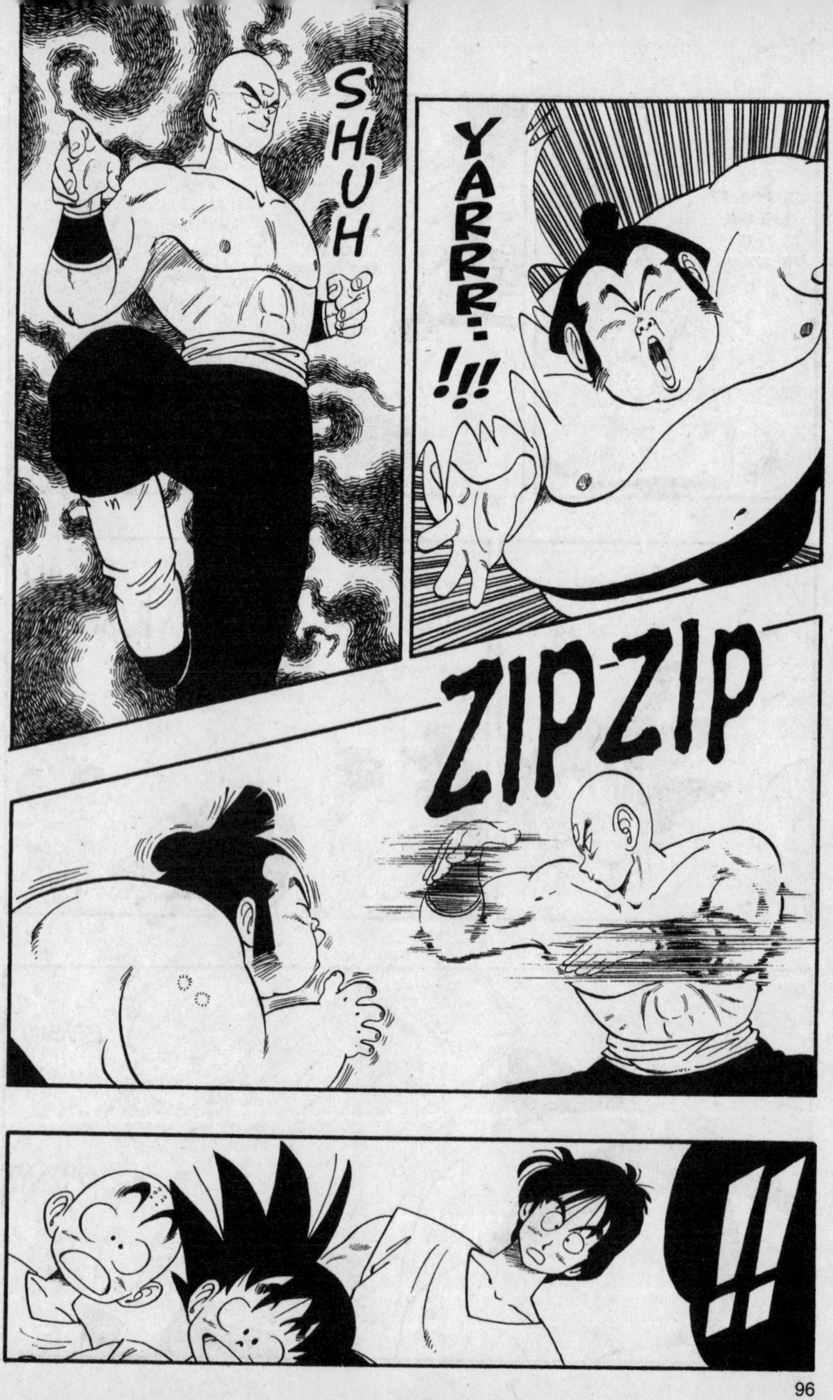
YARRR!!!
SHUH
ZIP ZIP
!!

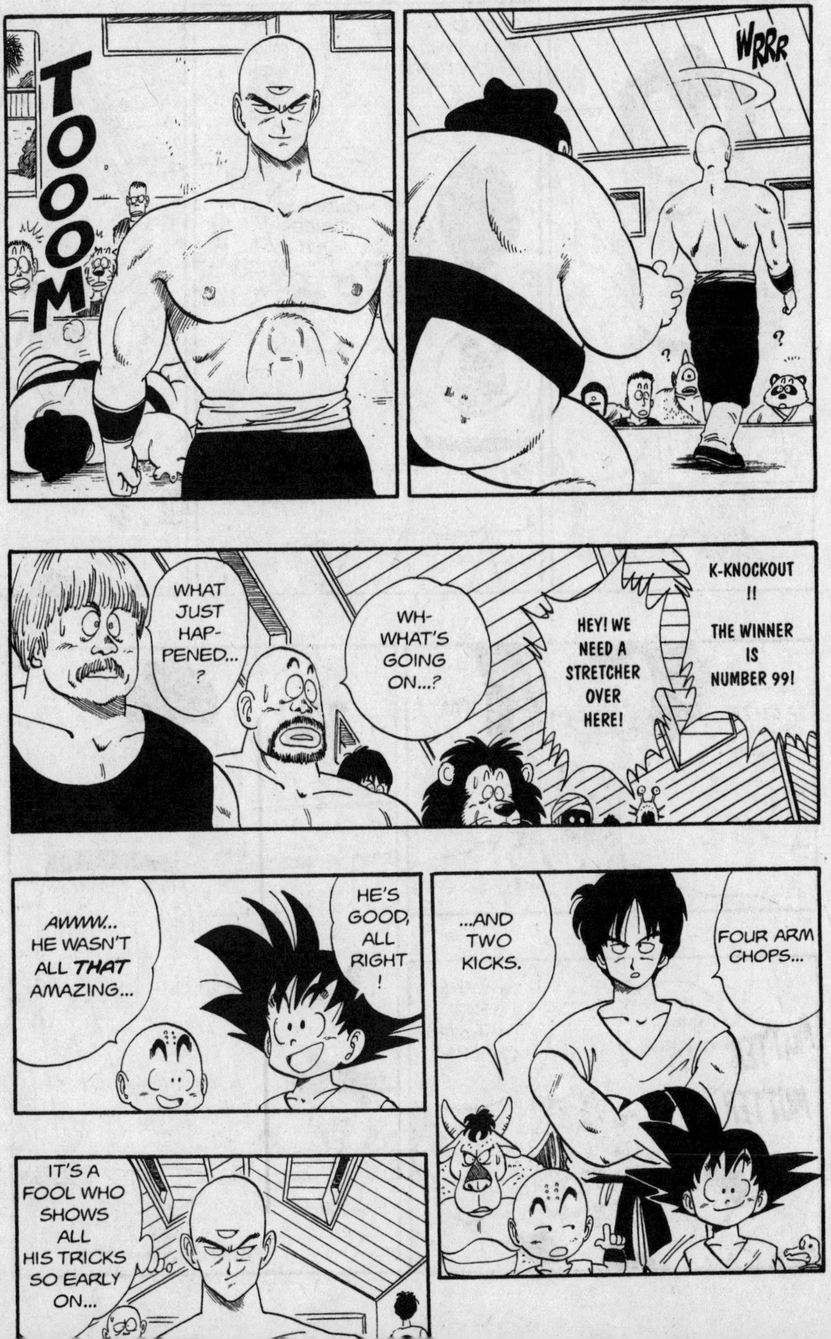
WRRR
TOOOM
K-KNOCKOUT!! THE WINNER IS NUMBER 99!
HEY! WE NEED A STRETCHER OVER HERE!
WH-WHAT'S GOING ON...?
WHAT JUST HAPPENED...?
FOUR ARM CHOPS...
...AND TWO KICKS.
HE'S GOOD, ALL RIGHT!
AWWW... HE WASN'T ALL THAT AMAZING...
IT'S A FOOL WHO SHOWS ALL HIS TRICKS SO EARLY ON...

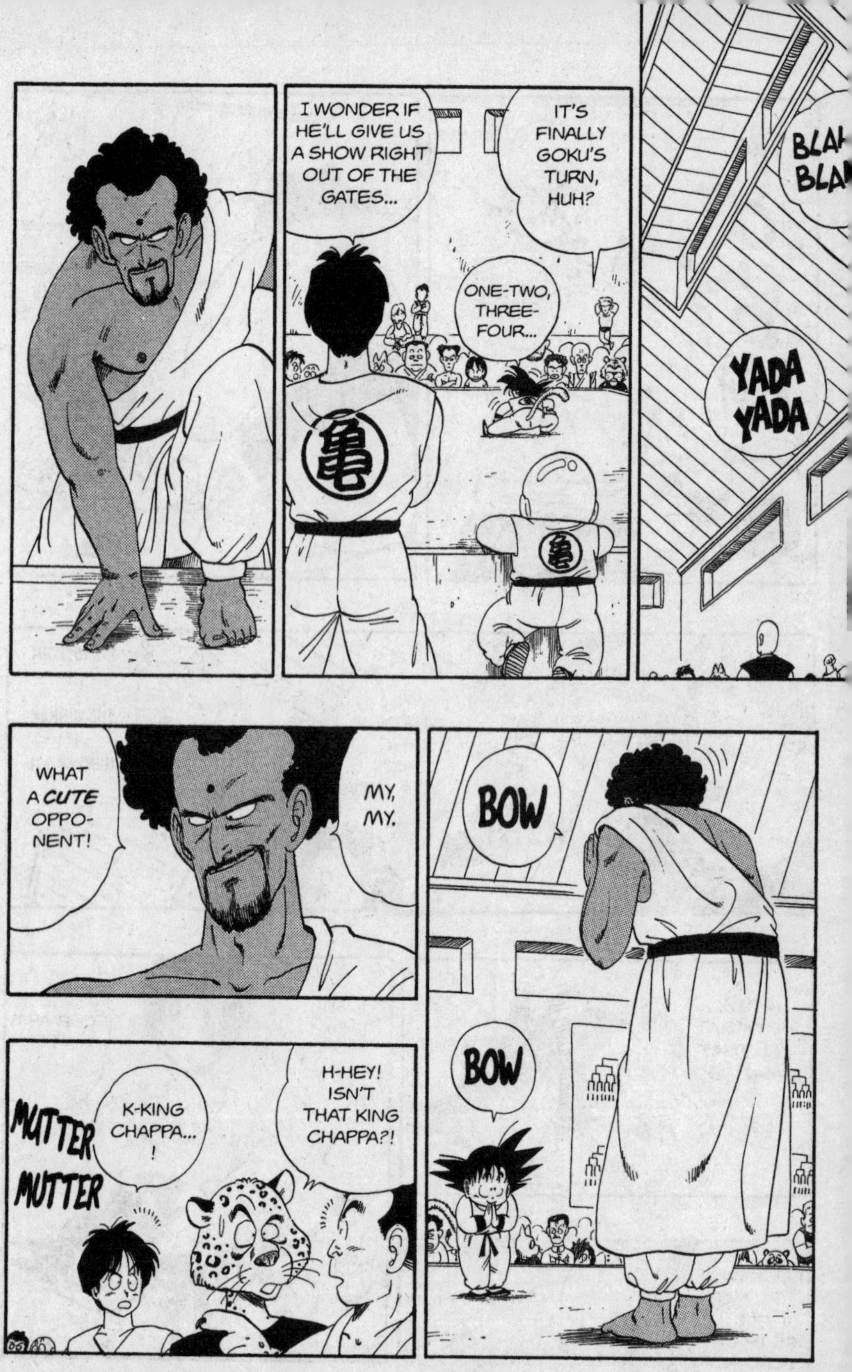
BLA BLA
YADA YADA
IT'S FINALLY GOKU'S TURN, HUH?
I WONDER IF HE'LL GIVE US A SHOW RIGHT OUT OF THE GATES...
ONE-TWO, THREE-FOUR...
BOW
BOW
MY, MY.
WHAT A *CUTE* OPPONENT!
H-HEY! ISN'T THAT KING CHAPPA?!
K-KING CHAPPA... !
MUTTER MUTTER

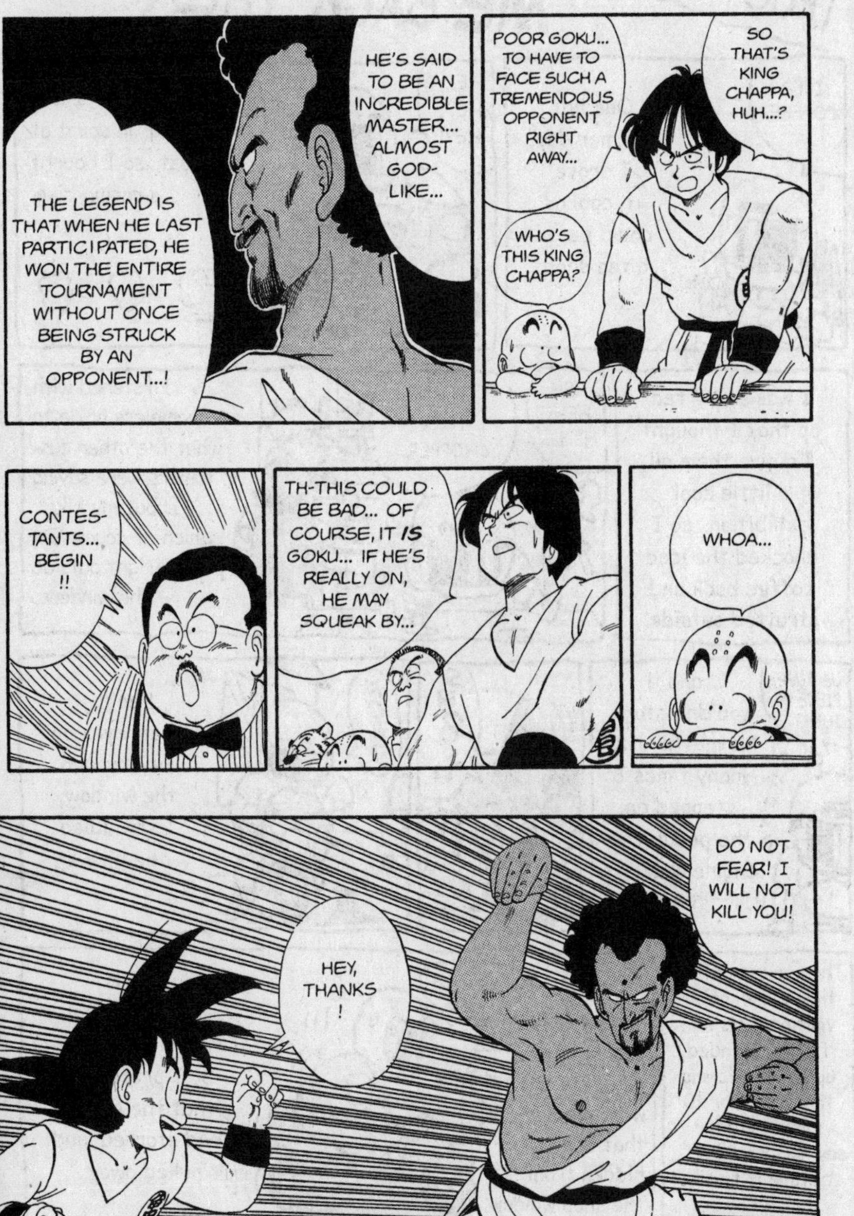
SO THAT'S KING CHAPPA, HUH...?
POOR GOKU... TO HAVE TO FACE SUCH A TREMENDOUS OPPONENT RIGHT AWAY...
WHO'S THIS KING CHAPPA?
HE'S SAID TO BE AN INCREDIBLE MASTER... ALMOST GOD-LIKE...
THE LEGEND IS THAT WHEN HE LAST PARTICIPATED, HE WON THE ENTIRE TOURNAMENT WITHOUT ONCE BEING STRUCK BY AN OPPONENT...!
WHOA...
TH-THIS COULD BE BAD... OF COURSE, IT *IS* GOKU... IF HE'S REALLY ON, HE MAY SQUEAK BY...
CONTESTANTS... BEGIN !!
DO NOT FEAR! I WILL NOT KILL YOU!
HEY, THANKS !

True Story — "ME BACK THEN"

By Akira Toriyama

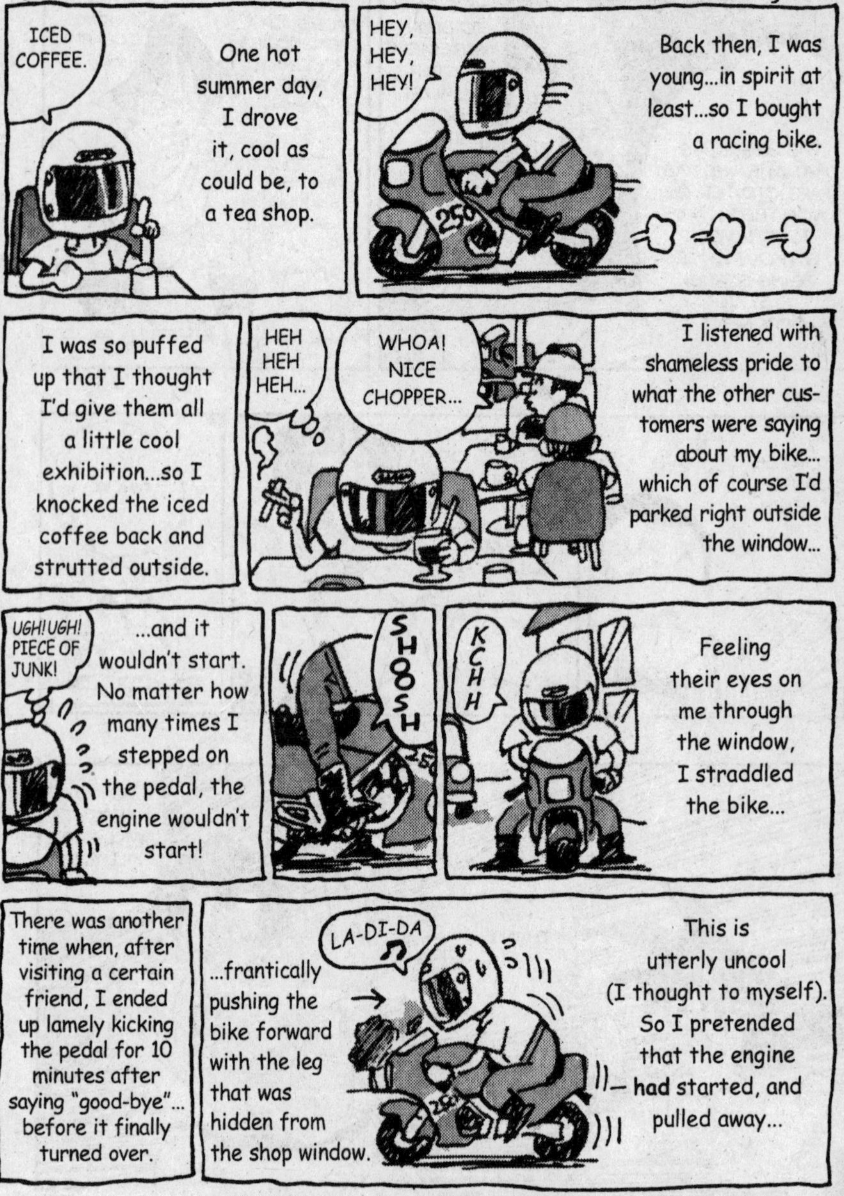
Back then, I was young...in spirit at least...so I bought a racing bike.
HEY, HEY, HEY!
One hot summer day, I drove it, cool as could be, to a tea shop.
ICED COFFEE.
I listened with shameless pride to what the other customers were saying about my bike... which of course I'd parked right outside the window...
WHOA! NICE CHOPPER...
HEH HEH HEH...
I was so puffed up that I thought I'd give them all a little cool exhibition...so I knocked the iced coffee back and strutted outside.
Feeling their eyes on me through the window, I straddled the bike...
KCHH
SHOOSH
...and it wouldn't start. No matter how many times I stepped on the pedal, the engine wouldn't start!
UGH!UGH! PIECE OF JUNK!
This is utterly uncool (I thought to myself). So I pretended that the engine **had** started, and pulled away...
LA-DI-DA
...frantically pushing the bike forward with the leg that was hidden from the shop window.
There was another time when, after visiting a certain friend, I ended up lamely kicking the pedal for 10 minutes after saying "good-bye"... before it finally turned over.

I don't have that bike anymore...
But I do have **another** flashy bike that starts more easily...

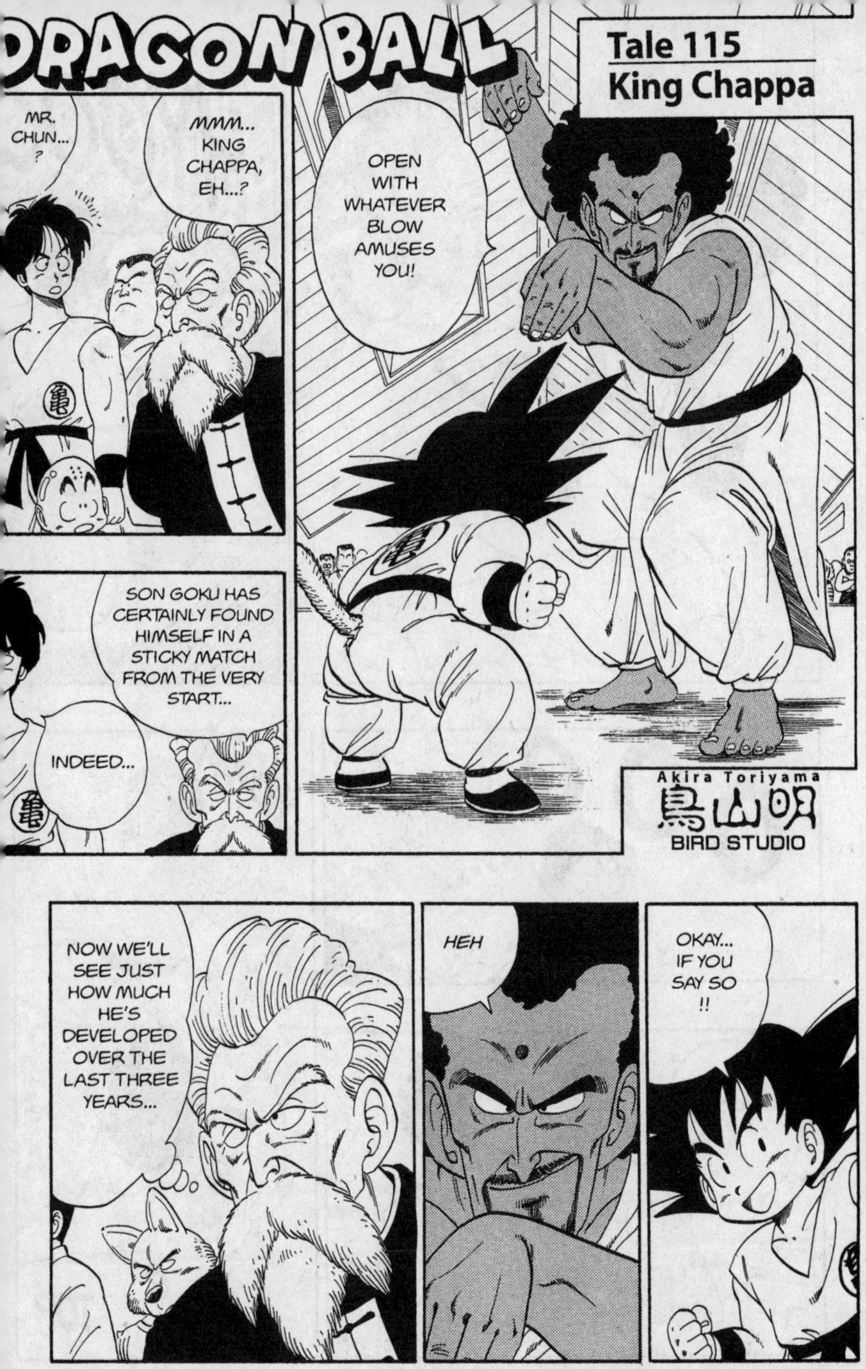
DRAGON BALL
Tale 115
King Chappa
OPEN WITH WHATEVER BLOW AMUSES YOU!
Akira Toriyama
鳥山明
BIRD STUDIO
MMM... KING CHAPPA, EH...?
MR. CHUN... ?
SON GOKU HAS CERTAINLY FOUND HIMSELF IN A STICKY MATCH FROM THE VERY START...
INDEED...
OKAY... IF YOU SAY SO !!
HEH
NOW WE'LL SEE JUST HOW MUCH HE'S DEVELOPED OVER THE LAST THREE YEARS...

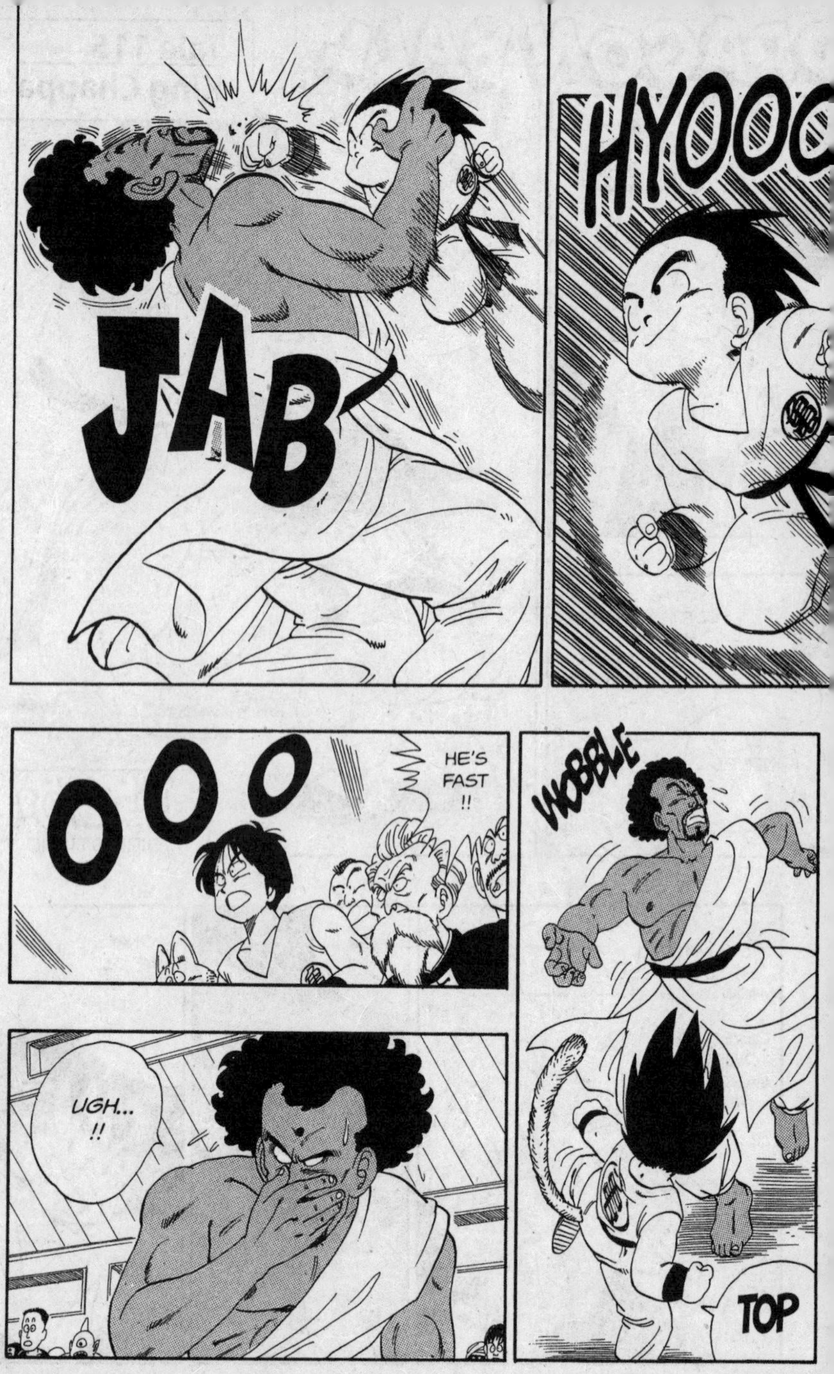
HYOOO
JAB
WOBBLE
TOP
OOO
HE'S FAST !!
UGH... !!

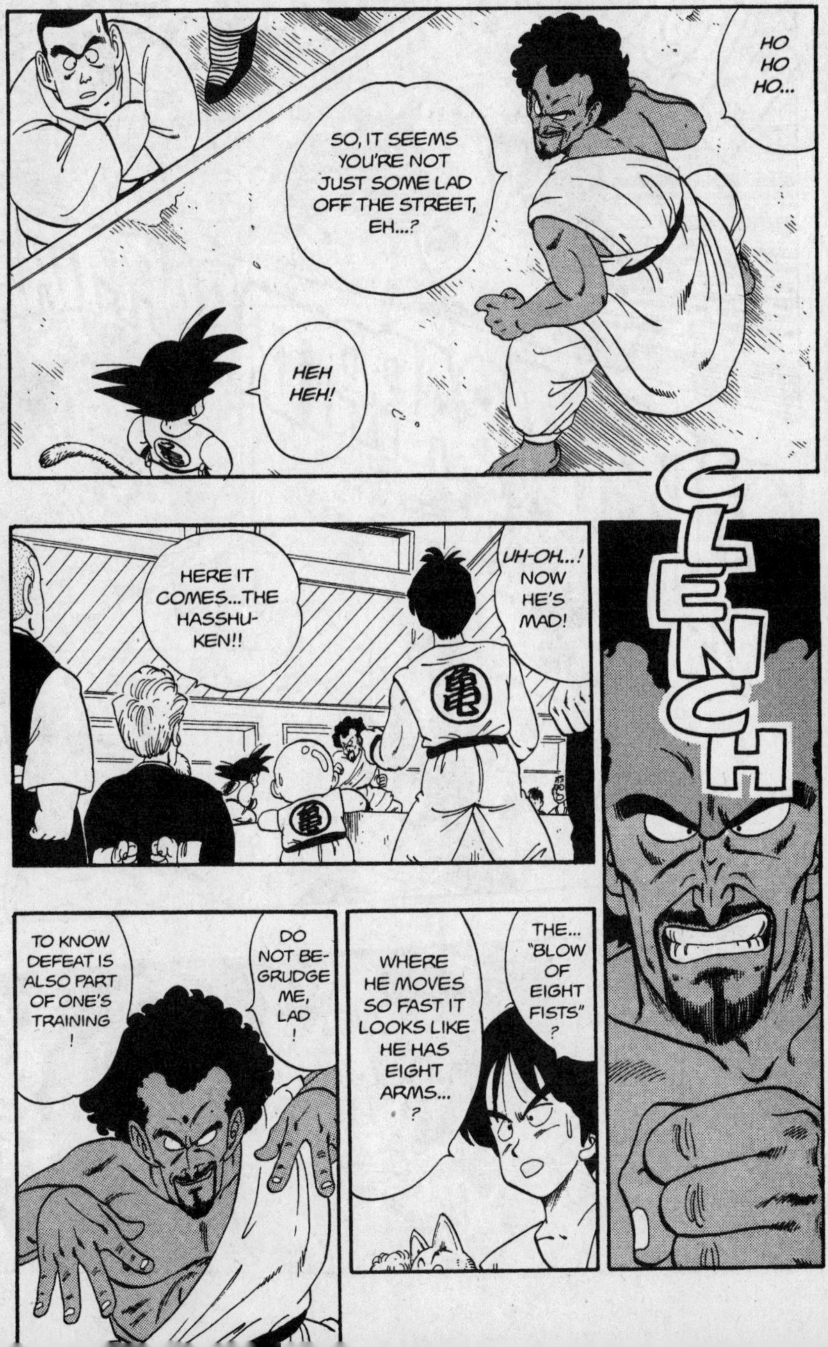
HO HO HO...
SO, IT SEEMS YOU'RE NOT JUST SOME LAD OFF THE STREET, EH...?
HEH HEH!
CLENCH
UH-OH...! NOW HE'S MAD!
HERE IT COMES...THE HASSHU-KEN!!
THE... "BLOW OF EIGHT FISTS"?
WHERE HE MOVES SO FAST IT LOOKS LIKE HE HAS EIGHT ARMS...?
DO NOT BE-GRUDGE ME, LAD!
TO KNOW DEFEAT IS ALSO PART OF ONE'S TRAINING!

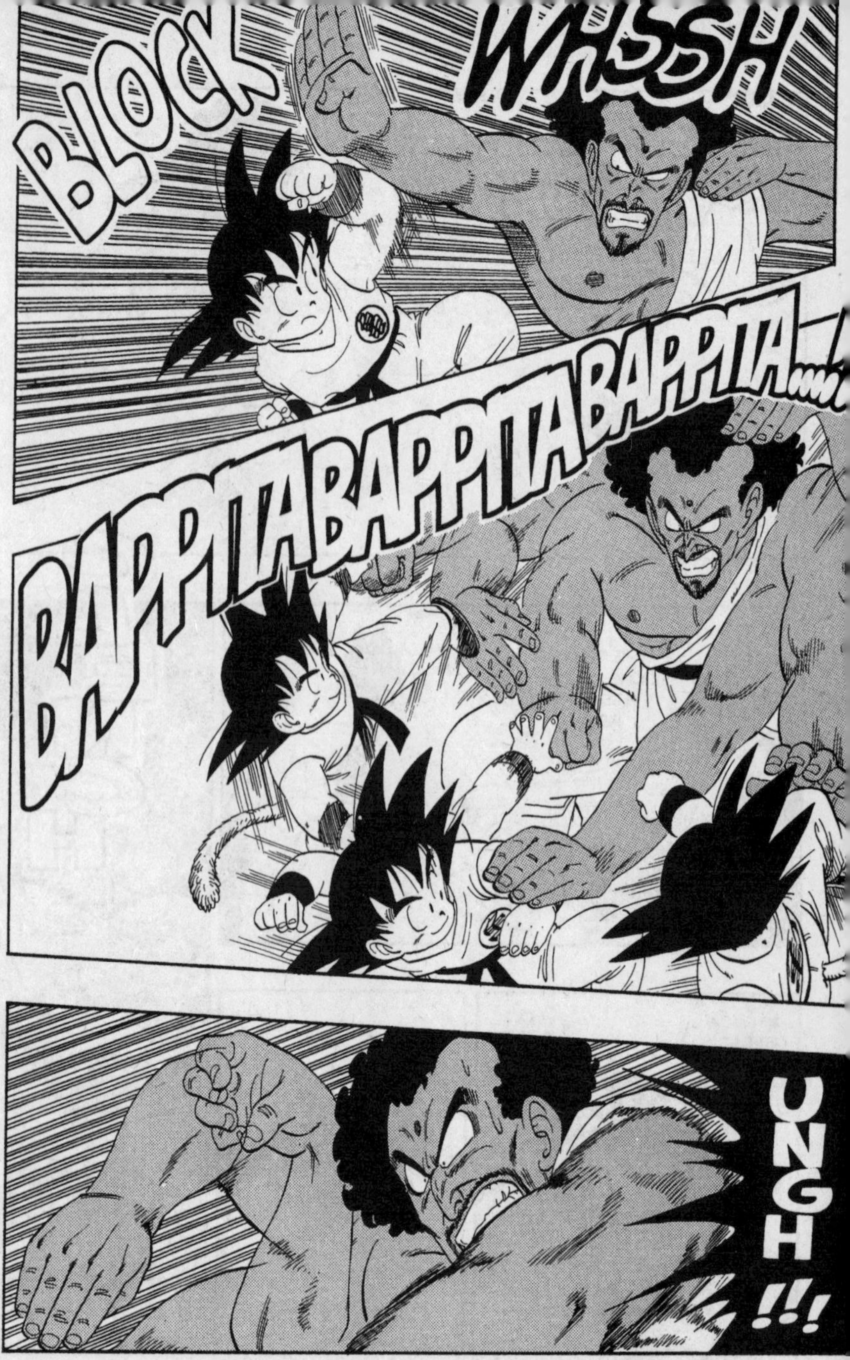
WHSSH
BLOCK
BAPPITABAPPITABAPPITA....!!
UNGH!!!

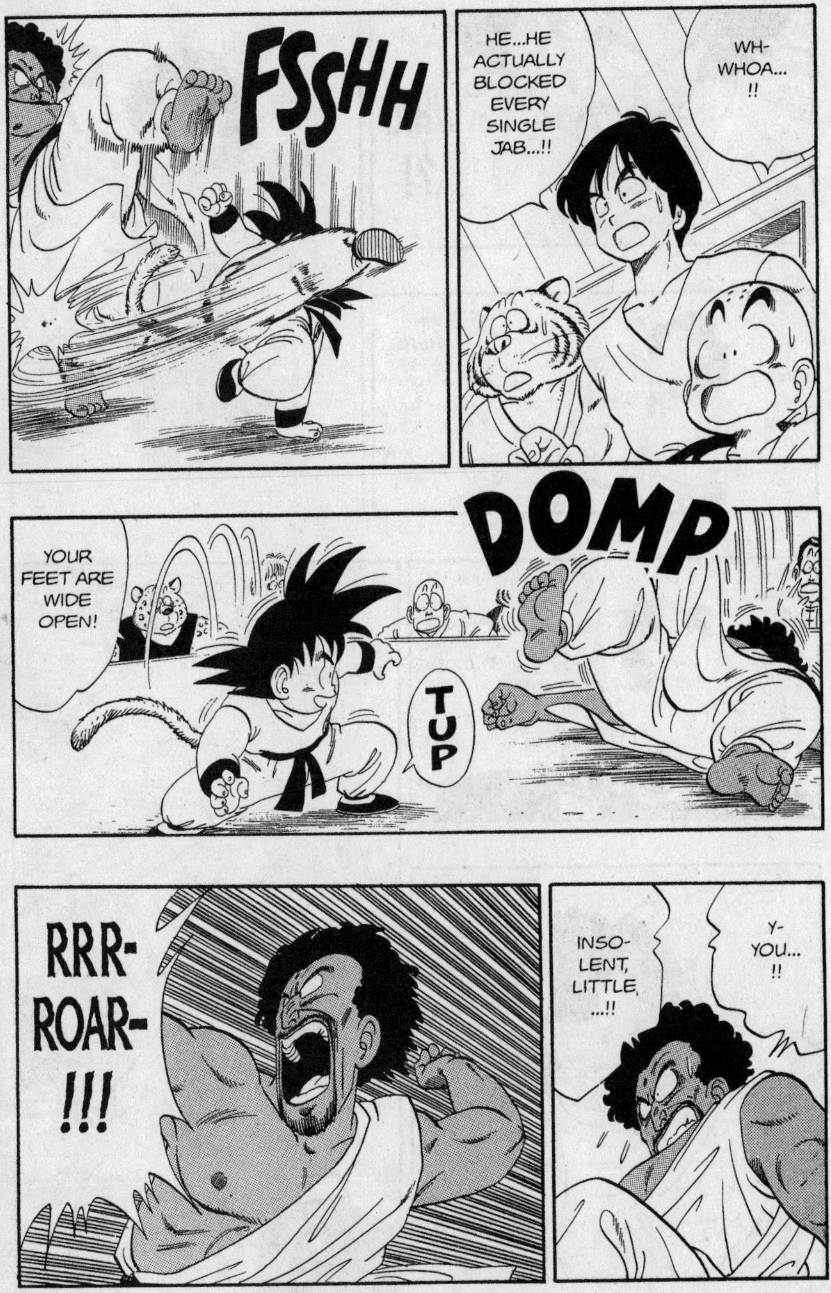
WH- WHOA... !!
HE...HE ACTUALLY BLOCKED EVERY SINGLE JAB...!!
FSSHH
DOMP
TUP
YOUR FEET ARE WIDE OPEN!
Y- YOU... !!
INSO- LENT, LITTLE, ...!!
RRR- ROAR- !!!

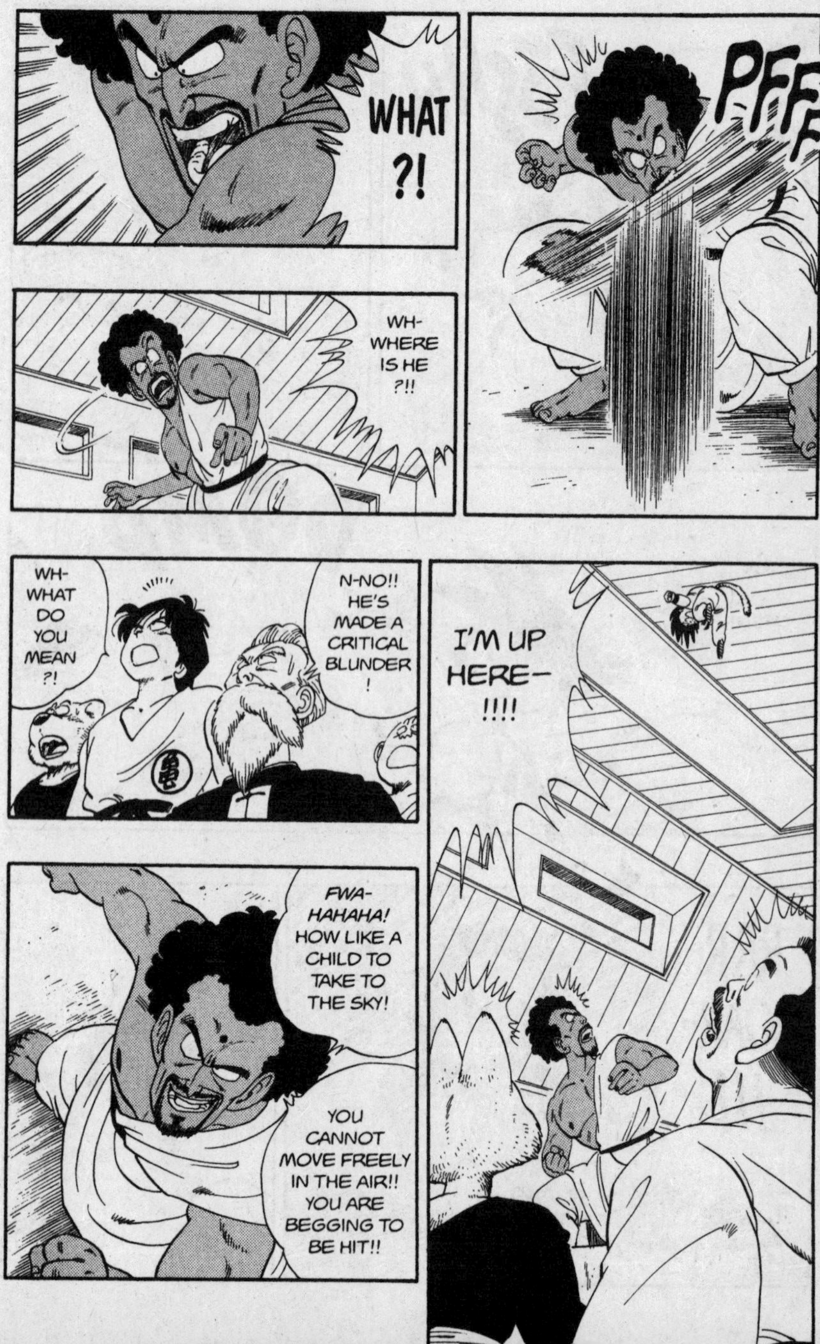
PFFF
WHAT ?!
WH- WHERE IS HE ?!!
I'M UP HERE- !!!!
N-NO!! HE'S MADE A CRITICAL BLUNDER !
WH- WHAT DO YOU MEAN ?!
FWA-HAHAHA! HOW LIKE A CHILD TO TAKE TO THE SKY!
YOU CANNOT MOVE FREELY IN THE AIR!! YOU ARE BEGGING TO BE HIT!!

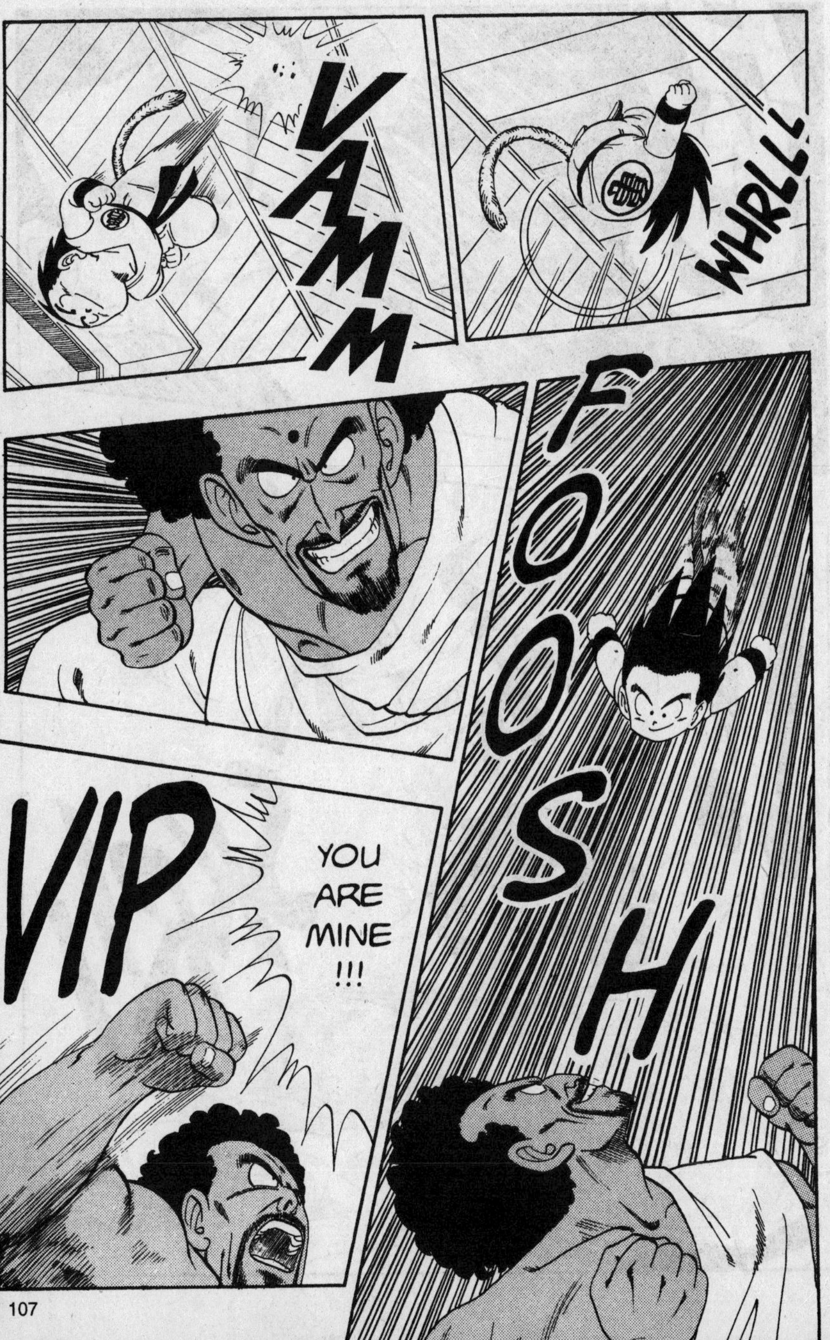
WHRLLL
VAMM
FOOSH
VIP
YOU ARE MINE !!!

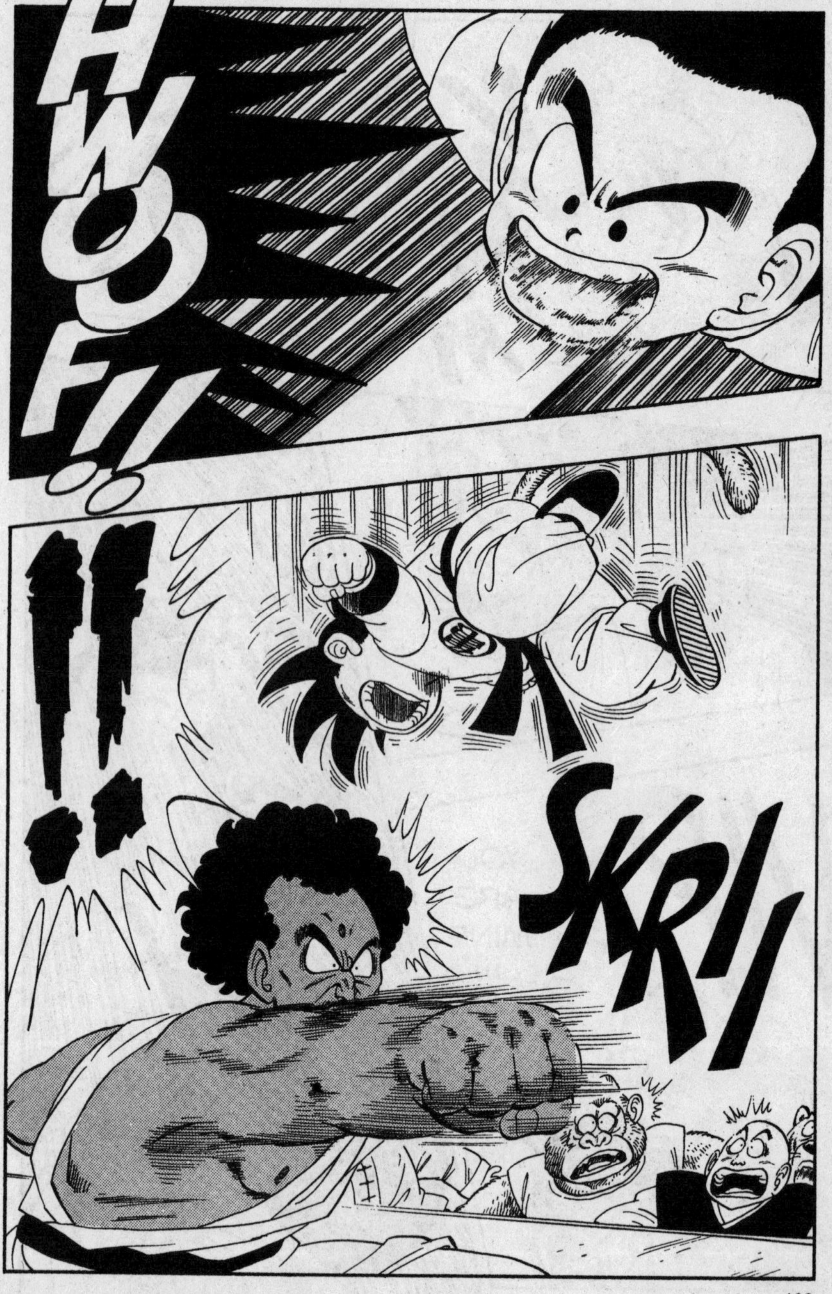
HWOOF!!
!!
SKRII

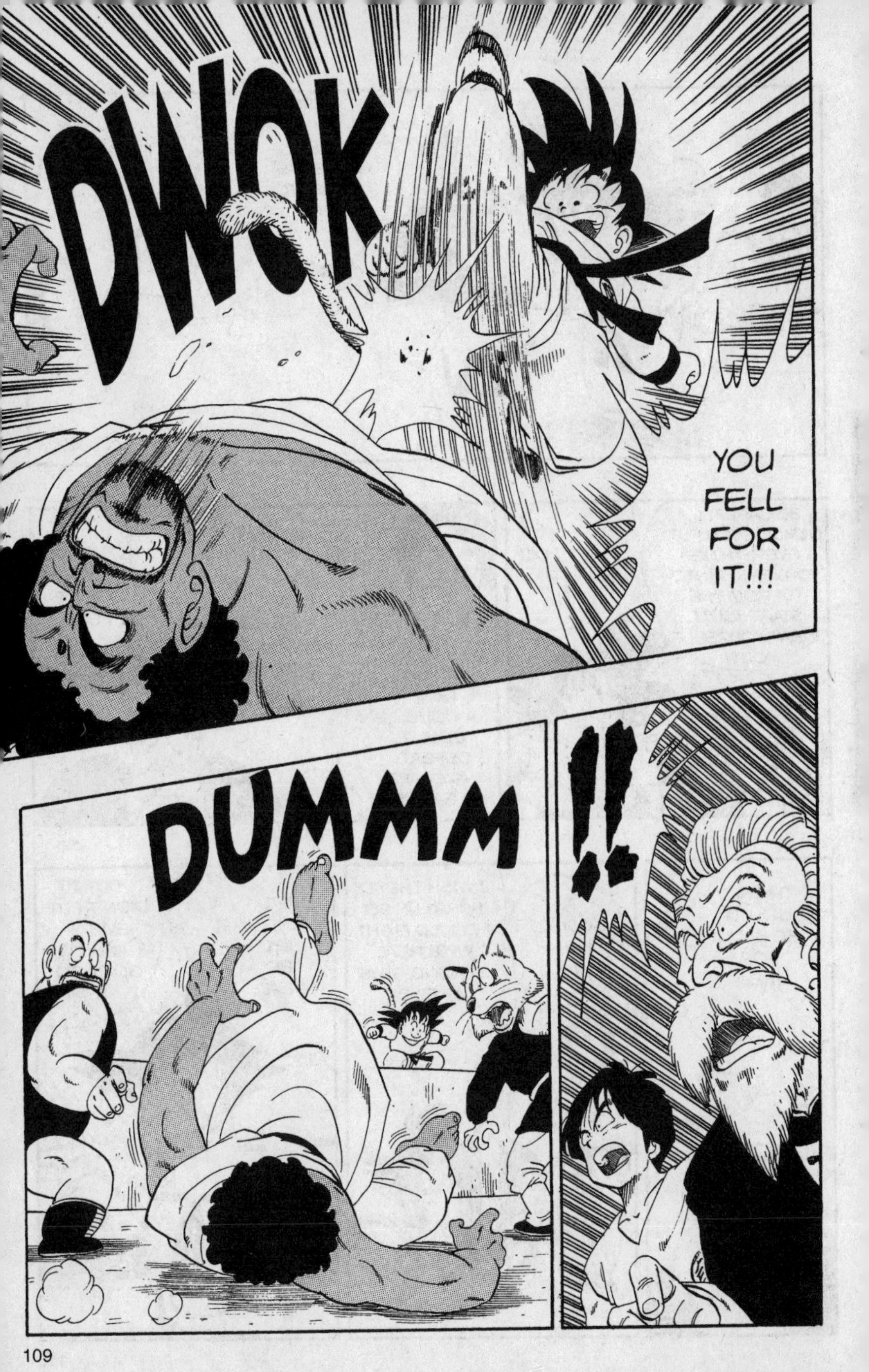
DWOK
YOU FELL FOR IT!!!
!!
DUMMM

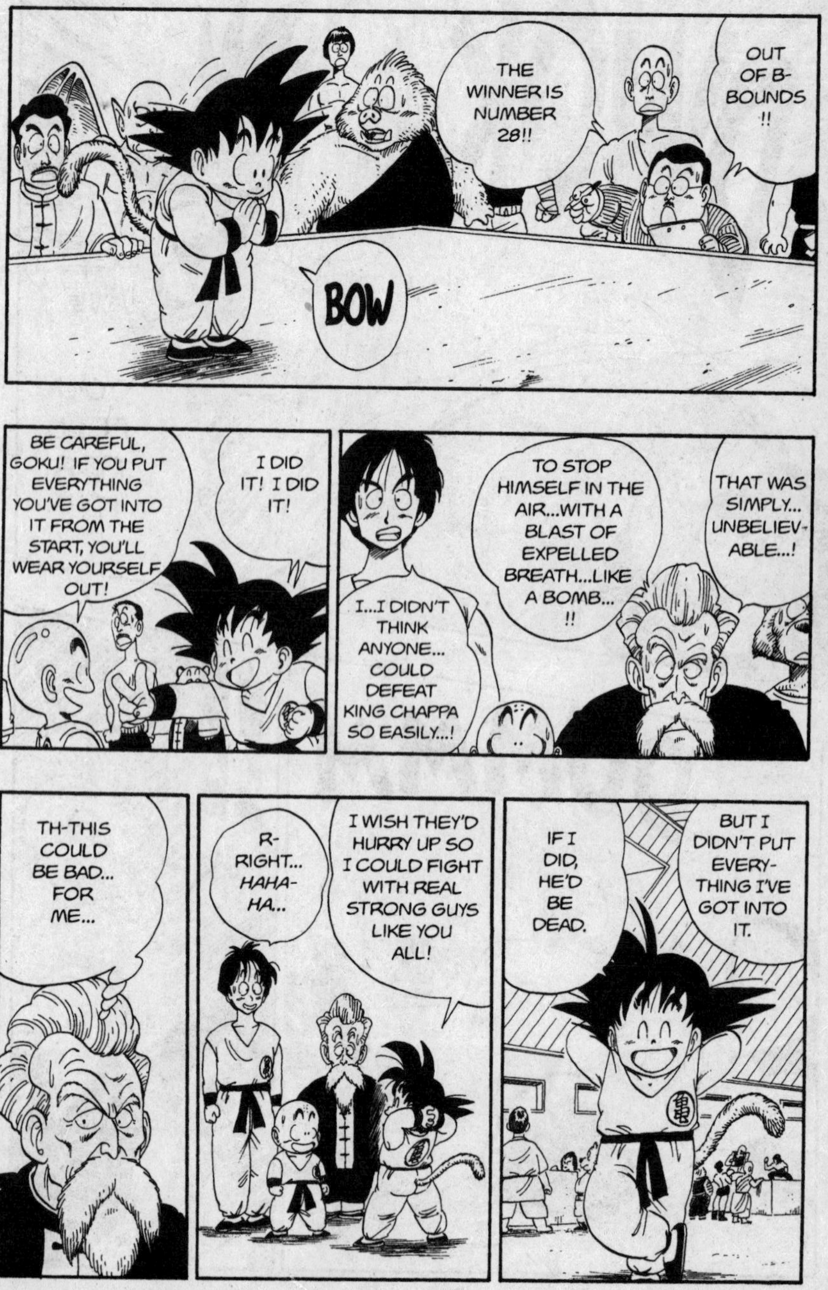
OUT OF B-BOUNDS !!
THE WINNER IS NUMBER 28!!
BOW
THAT WAS SIMPLY... UNBELIEV-ABLE...!
TO STOP HIMSELF IN THE AIR...WITH A BLAST OF EXPELLED BREATH...LIKE A BOMB... !!
I...I DIDN'T THINK ANYONE... COULD DEFEAT KING CHAPPA SO EASILY...!
I DID IT! I DID IT!
BE CAREFUL, GOKU! IF YOU PUT EVERYTHING YOU'VE GOT INTO IT FROM THE START, YOU'LL WEAR YOURSELF OUT!
BUT I DIDN'T PUT EVERY-THING I'VE GOT INTO IT.
IF I DID, HE'D BE DEAD.
I WISH THEY'D HURRY UP SO I COULD FIGHT WITH REAL STRONG GUYS LIKE YOU ALL!
R-RIGHT... *HAHA-HA...*
TH-THIS COULD BE BAD... FOR ME...

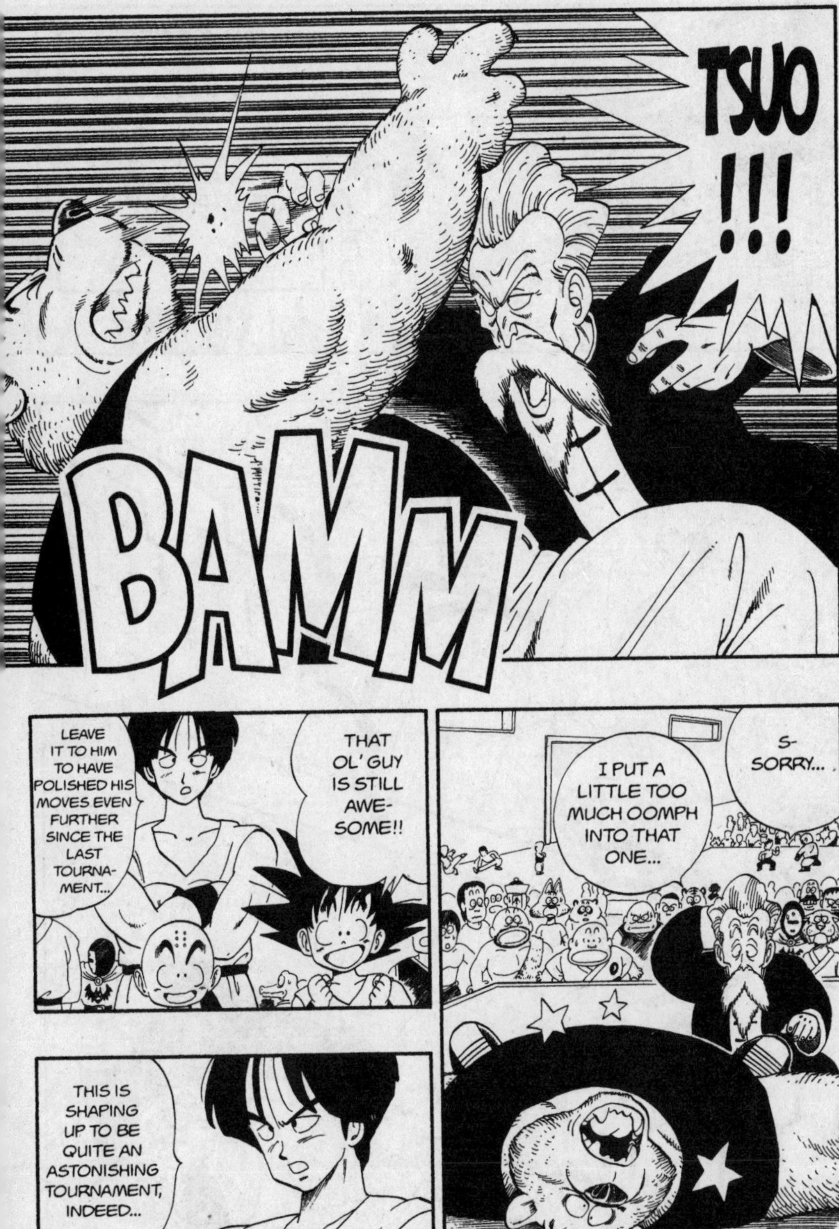
TSUO!!!
BAMM
S-SORRY...
I PUT A LITTLE TOO MUCH OOMPH INTO THAT ONE...
THAT OL' GUY IS STILL AWESOME!!
LEAVE IT TO HIM TO HAVE POLISHED HIS MOVES EVEN FURTHER SINCE THE LAST TOURNAMENT...
THIS IS SHAPING UP TO BE QUITE AN ASTONISHING TOURNAMENT, INDEED...

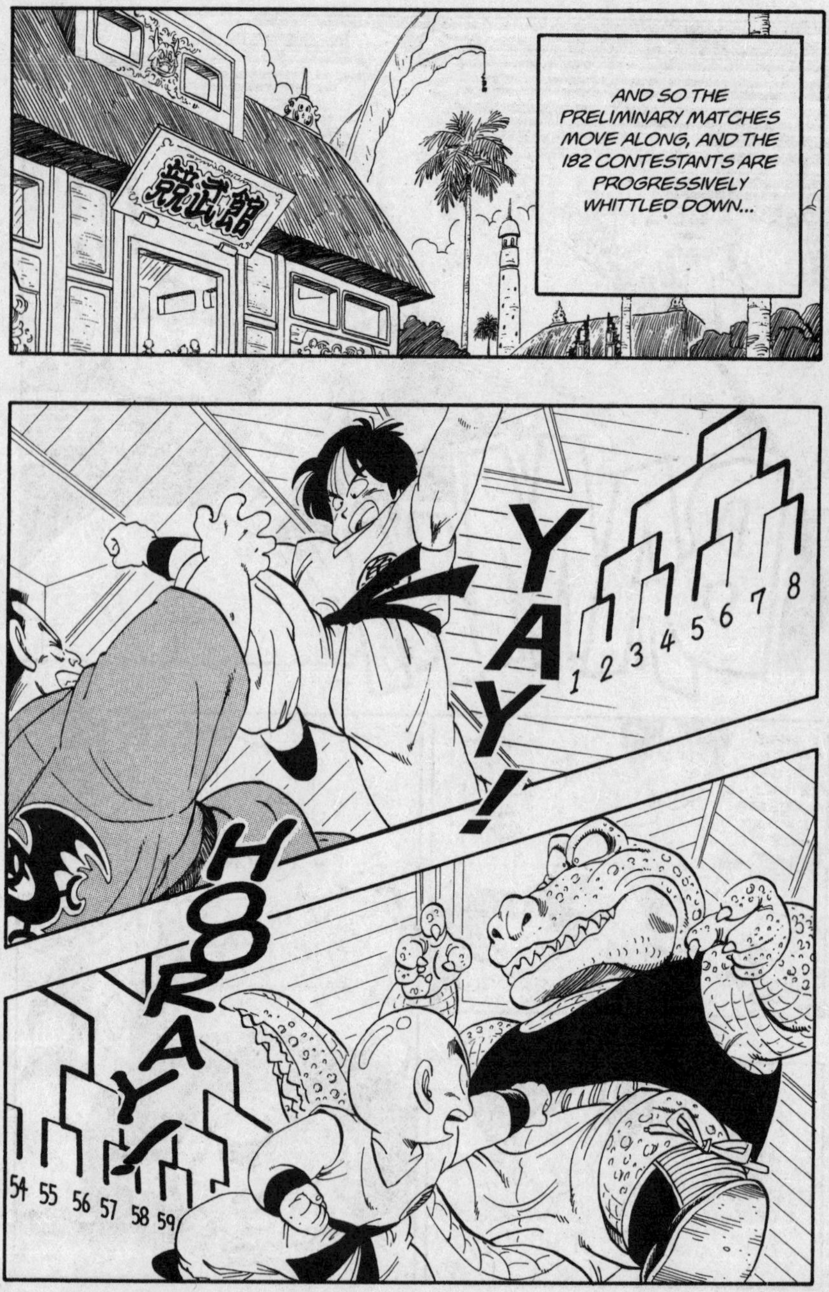
AND SO THE PRELIMINARY MATCHES MOVE ALONG, AND THE 182 CONTESTANTS ARE PROGRESSIVELY WHITTLED DOWN...
競武館
YAY!
1 2 3 4 5 6 7 8
HOORAY!
54 55 56 57 58 59

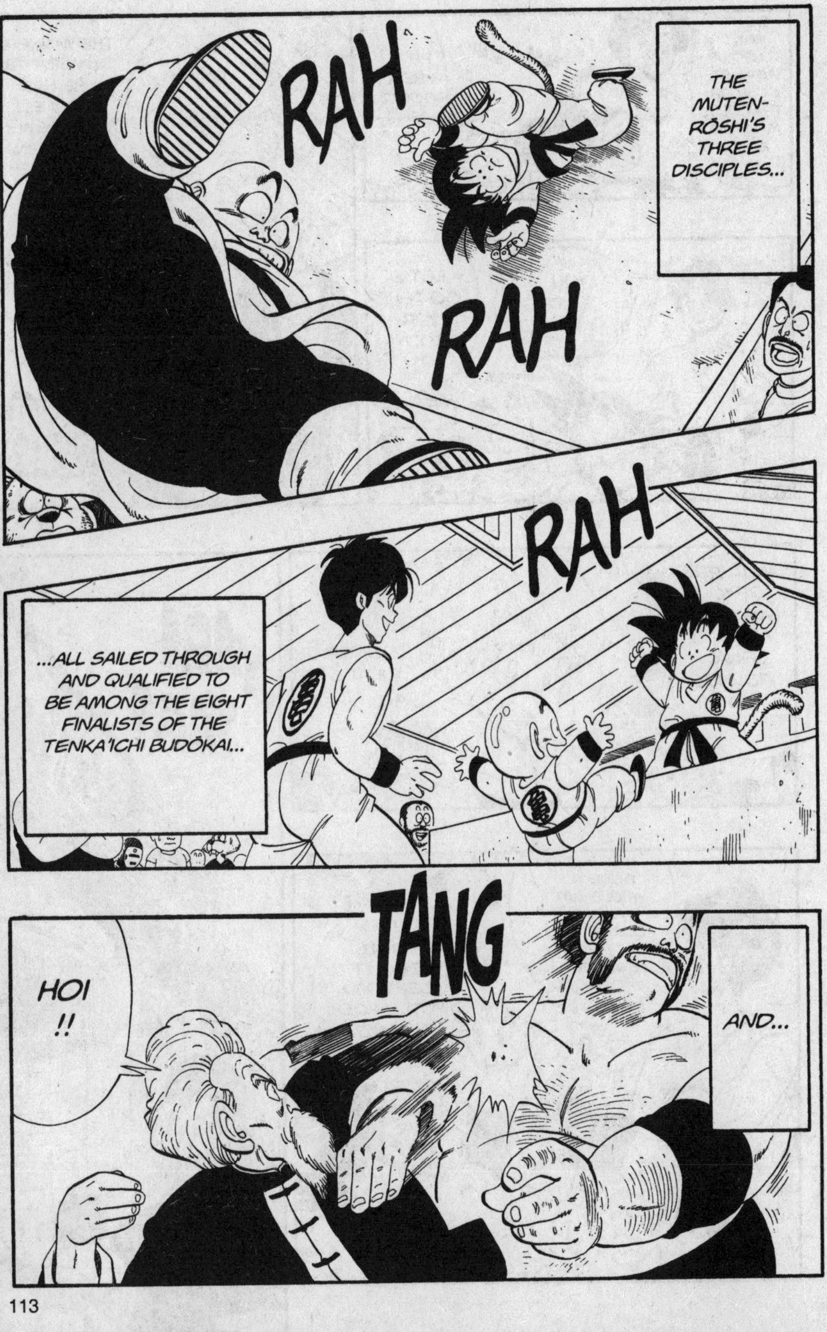
THE MUTEN-RŌSHI'S THREE DISCIPLES...
RAH
RAH
RAH
...ALL SAILED THROUGH AND QUALIFIED TO BE AMONG THE EIGHT FINALISTS OF THE TENKA'ICHI BUDŌKAI...
TANG
AND...
HOI !!

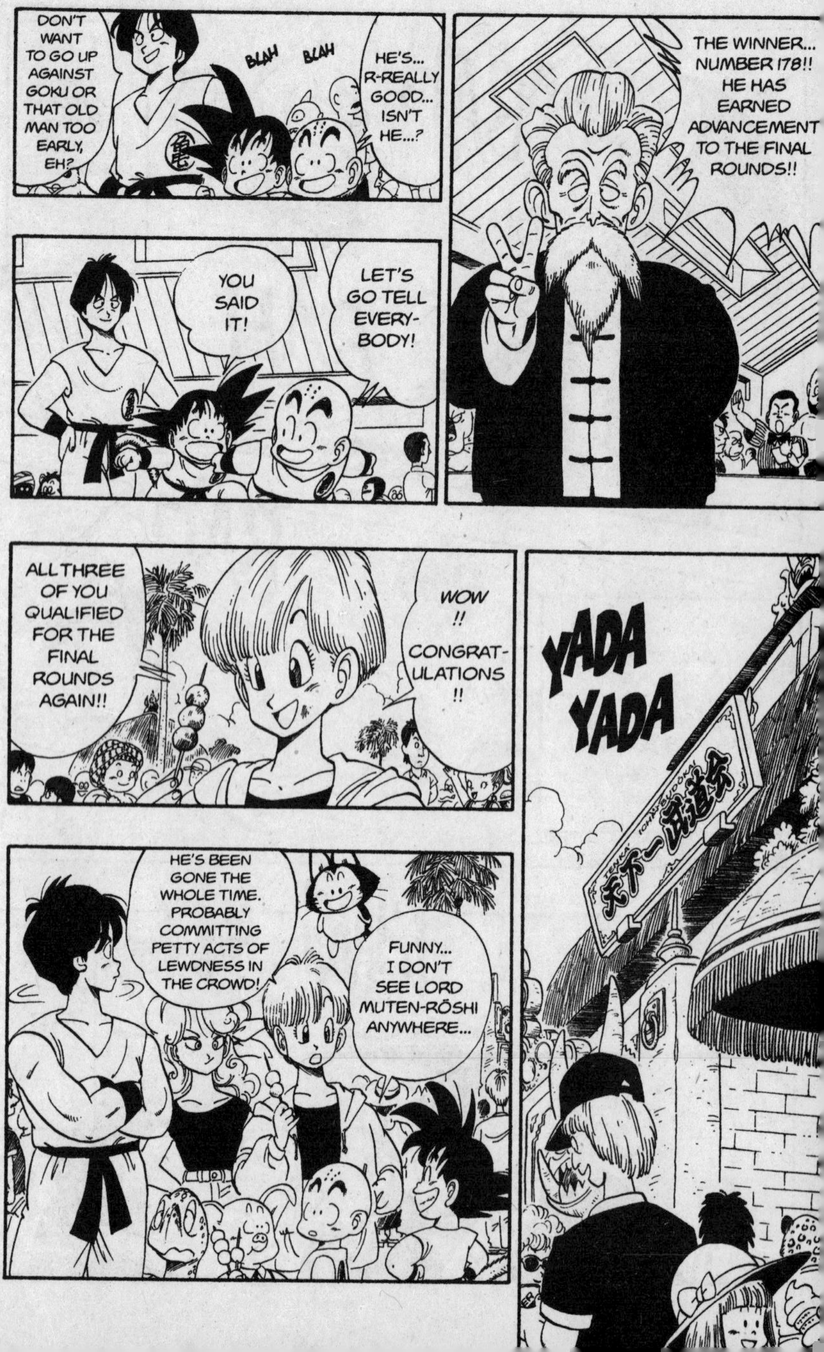
THE WINNER... NUMBER 178!! HE HAS EARNED ADVANCEMENT TO THE FINAL ROUNDS!!
HE'S... R-REALLY GOOD... ISN'T HE...?
BLAH BLAH
DON'T WANT TO GO UP AGAINST GOKU OR THAT OLD MAN TOO EARLY, EH?
LET'S GO TELL EVERY-BODY!
YOU SAID IT!
YADA YADA
天下一武道会
TENKA ICHI BUDOKAI
WOW!! CONGRAT-ULATIONS!!
ALL THREE OF YOU QUALIFIED FOR THE FINAL ROUNDS AGAIN!!
FUNNY... I DON'T SEE LORD MUTEN-RŌSHI ANYWHERE...
HE'S BEEN GONE THE WHOLE TIME. PROBABLY COMMITTING PETTY ACTS OF LEWDNESS IN THE CROWD!

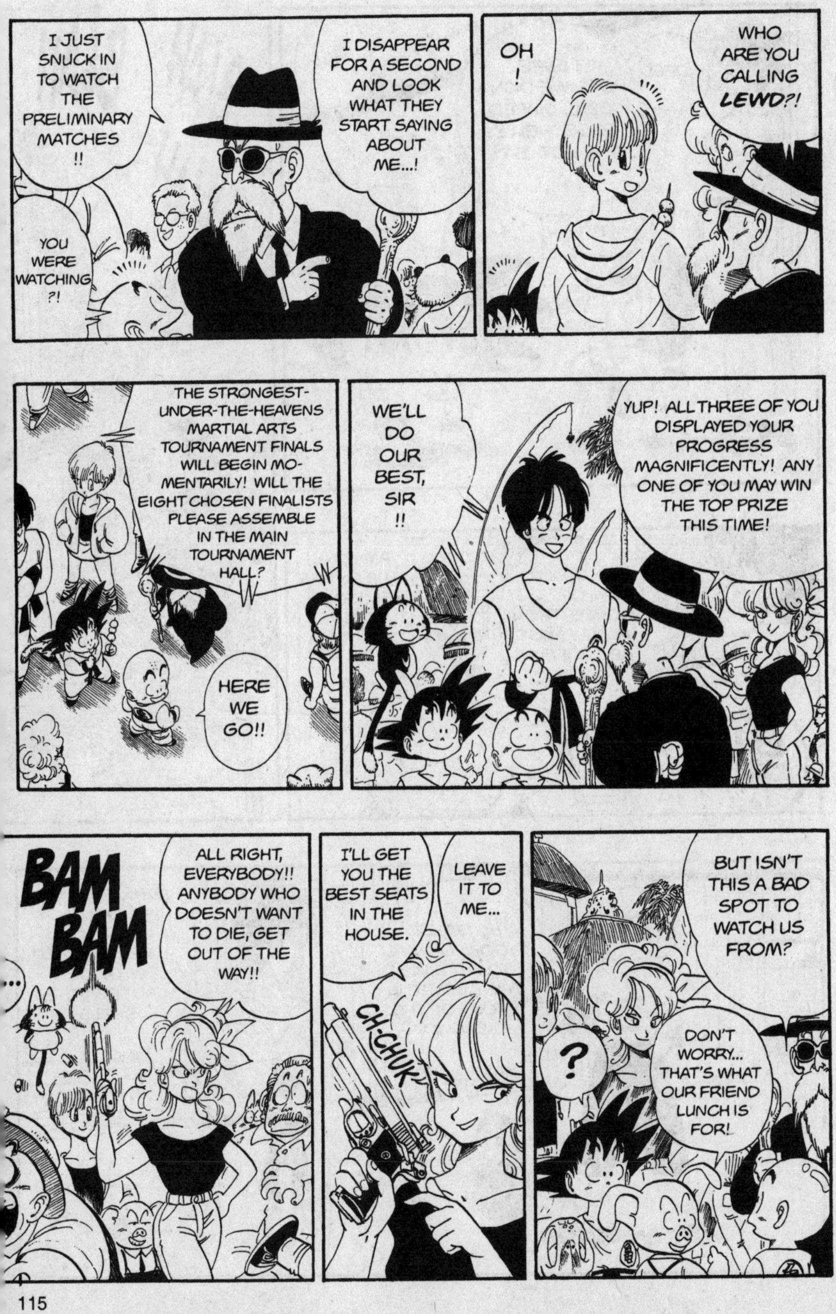
WHO ARE YOU CALLING LEWD?!
OH !
I DISAPPEAR FOR A SECOND AND LOOK WHAT THEY START SAYING ABOUT ME...!
I JUST SNUCK IN TO WATCH THE PRELIMINARY MATCHES !!
YOU WERE WATCHING ?!
YUP! ALL THREE OF YOU DISPLAYED YOUR PROGRESS MAGNIFICENTLY! ANY ONE OF YOU MAY WIN THE TOP PRIZE THIS TIME!
WE'LL DO OUR BEST, SIR !!
THE STRONGEST-UNDER-THE-HEAVENS MARTIAL ARTS TOURNAMENT FINALS WILL BEGIN MO-MENTARILY! WILL THE EIGHT CHOSEN FINALISTS PLEASE ASSEMBLE IN THE MAIN TOURNAMENT HALL?
HERE WE GO!!
BUT ISN'T THIS A BAD SPOT TO WATCH US FROM?
?
DON'T WORRY... THAT'S WHAT OUR FRIEND LUNCH IS FOR!
LEAVE IT TO ME...
I'LL GET YOU THE BEST SEATS IN THE HOUSE.
CH-CHUK
ALL RIGHT, EVERYBODY!! ANYBODY WHO DOESN'T WANT TO DIE, GET OUT OF THE WAY!!
BAM BAM
...

Tale 116 • The Doctored Lottery

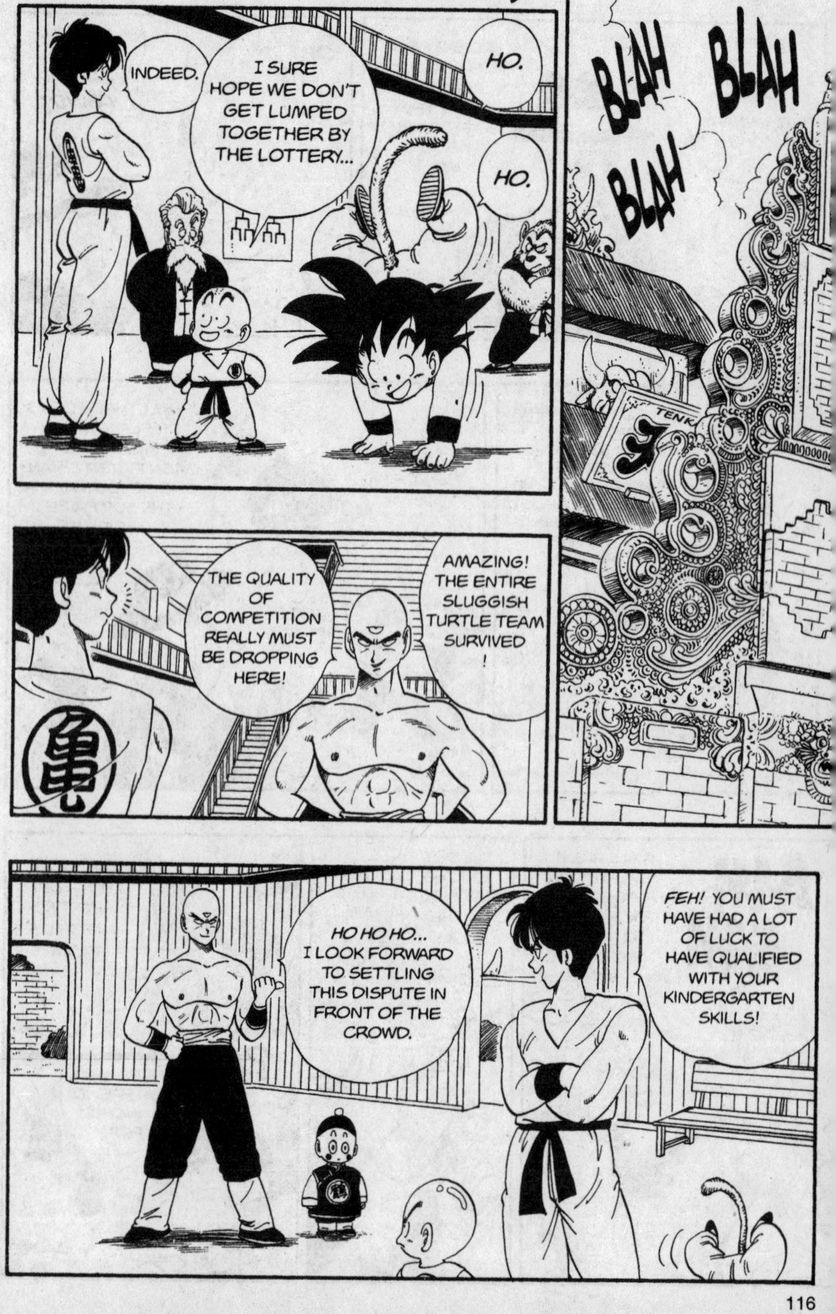
BLAH BLAH BLAH
HO.
HO.
I SURE HOPE WE DON'T GET LUMPED TOGETHER BY THE LOTTERY...
INDEED.
AMAZING! THE ENTIRE SLUGGISH TURTLE TEAM SURVIVED!
THE QUALITY OF COMPETITION REALLY MUST BE DROPPING HERE!
FEH! YOU MUST HAVE HAD A LOT OF LUCK TO HAVE QUALIFIED WITH YOUR KINDERGARTEN SKILLS!
HO HO HO... I LOOK FORWARD TO SETTLING THIS DISPUTE IN FRONT OF THE CROWD.

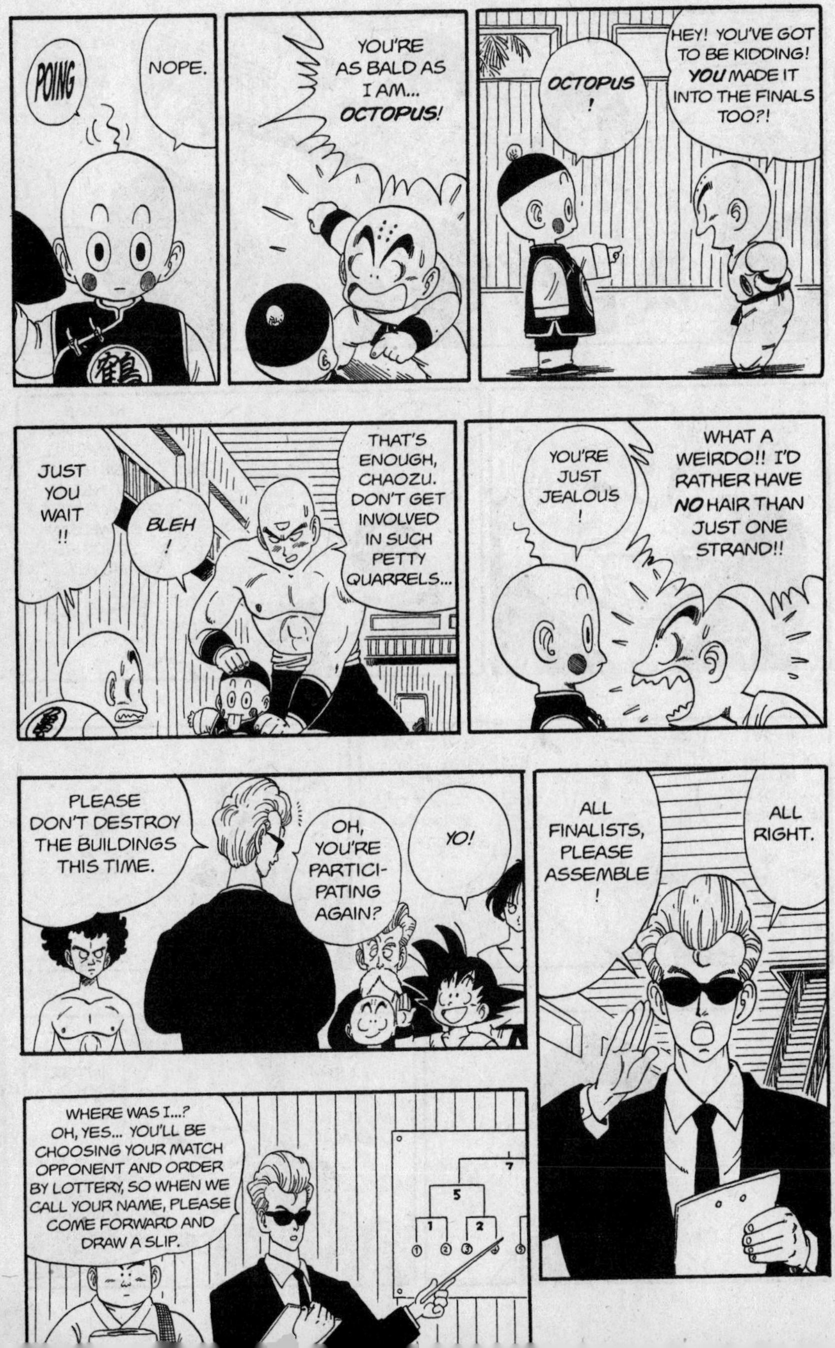
HEY! YOU'VE GOT TO BE KIDDING! ***YOU*** MADE IT INTO THE FINALS TOO?!
OCTOPUS!
YOU'RE AS BALD AS I AM... ***OCTOPUS!***
NOPE.
POING
WHAT A WEIRDO!! I'D RATHER HAVE ***NO*** HAIR THAN JUST ONE STRAND!!
YOU'RE JUST JEALOUS!
THAT'S ENOUGH, CHAOZU. DON'T GET INVOLVED IN SUCH PETTY QUARRELS...
BLEH!
JUST YOU WAIT!!
ALL RIGHT.
ALL FINALISTS, PLEASE ASSEMBLE!
YO!
OH, YOU'RE PARTICI-PATING AGAIN?
PLEASE DON'T DESTROY THE BUILDINGS THIS TIME.
WHERE WAS I...? OH, YES... YOU'LL BE CHOOSING YOUR MATCH OPPONENT AND ORDER BY LOTTERY, SO WHEN WE CALL YOUR NAME, PLEASE COME FORWARD AND DRAW A SLIP.

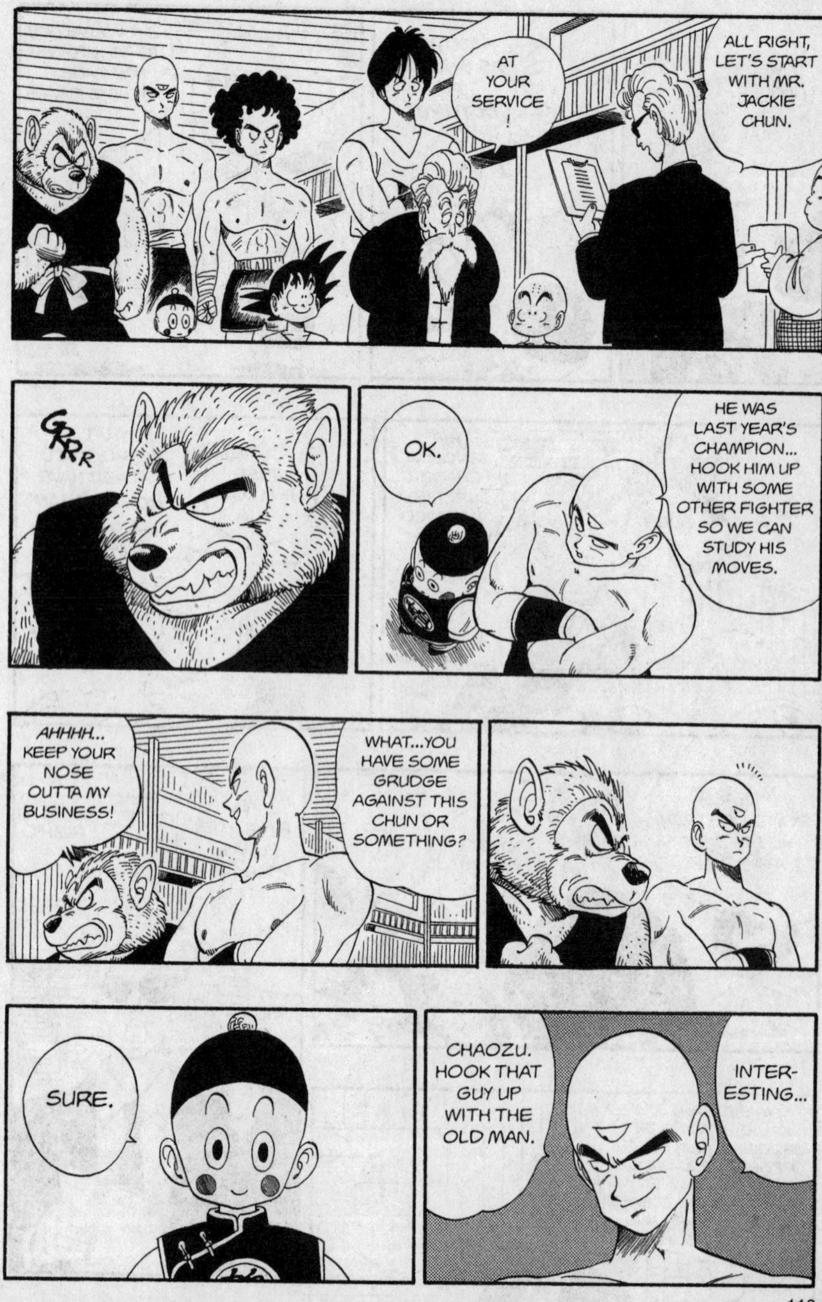
ALL RIGHT, LET'S START WITH MR. JACKIE CHUN.
AT YOUR SERVICE !
HE WAS LAST YEAR'S CHAMPION... HOOK HIM UP WITH SOME OTHER FIGHTER SO WE CAN STUDY HIS MOVES.
OK.
GRRR
WHAT...YOU HAVE SOME GRUDGE AGAINST THIS CHUN OR SOMETHING?
AHHHH... KEEP YOUR NOSE OUTTA MY BUSINESS!
INTER-ESTING...
CHAOZU. HOOK THAT GUY UP WITH THE OLD MAN.
SURE.

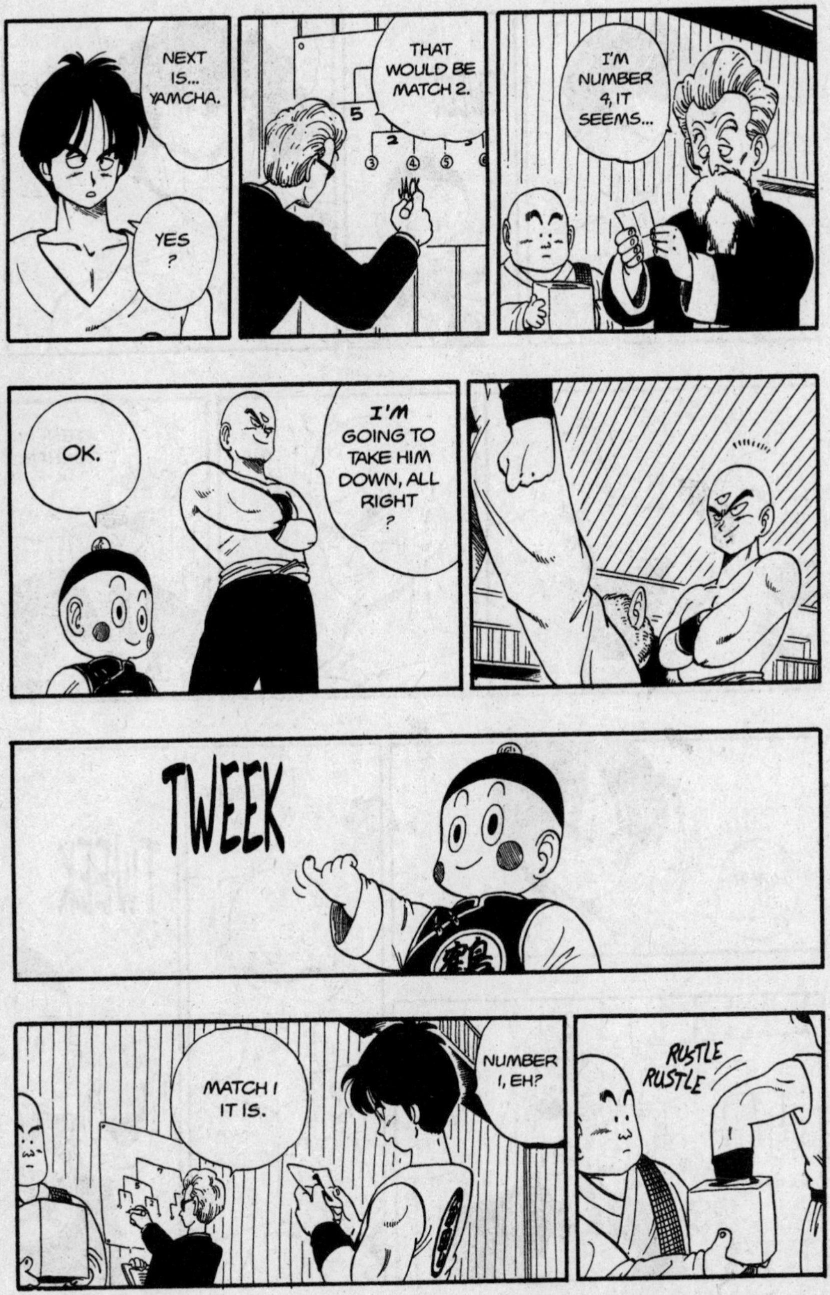
I'M NUMBER 4, IT SEEMS...
THAT WOULD BE MATCH 2.
NEXT IS... YAMCHA.
YES?
I'M GOING TO TAKE HIM DOWN, ALL RIGHT?
OK.
TWEEK
RUSTLE RUSTLE
NUMBER 1, EH?
MATCH 1 IT IS.

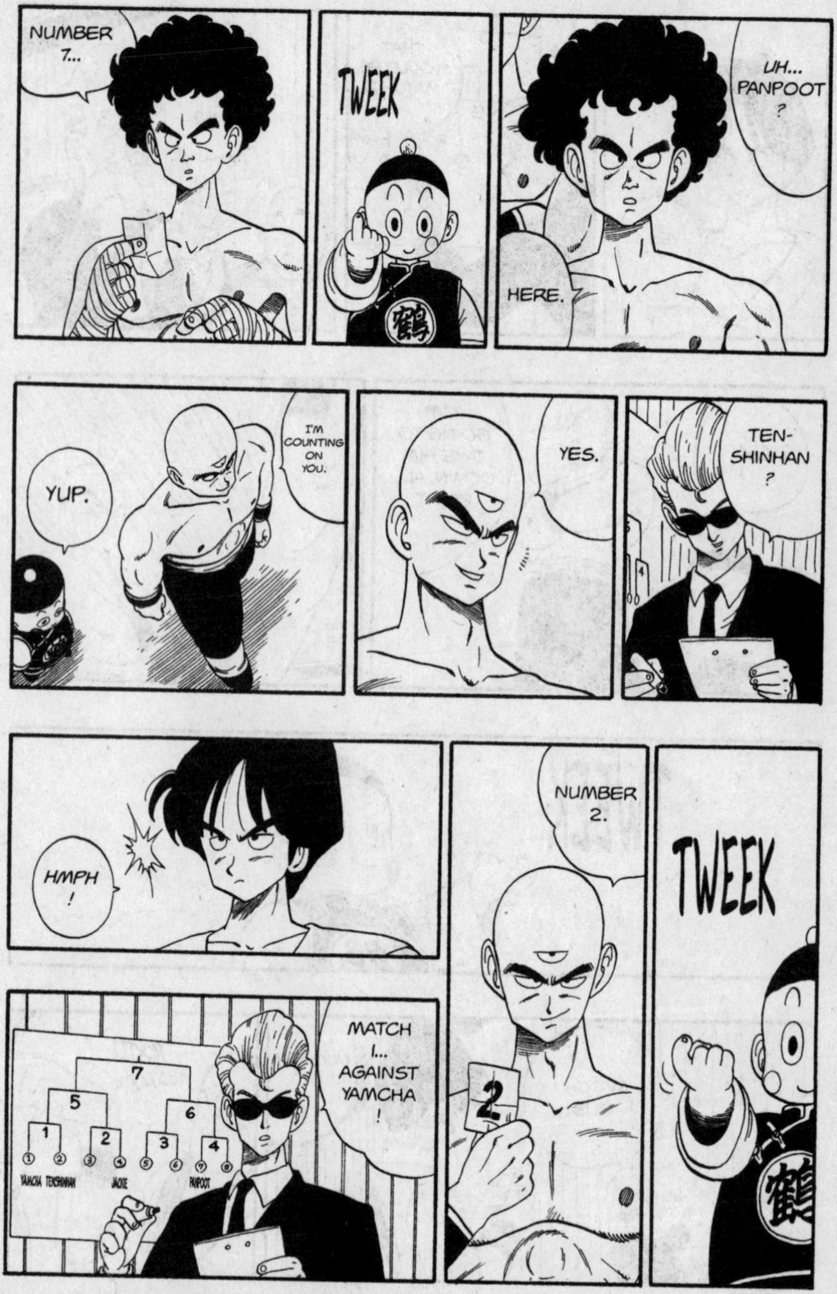
UH... PANPOOT ?
HERE.
TWEEK
NUMBER 7...
TEN-SHINHAN ?
YES.
I'M COUNTING ON YOU.
YUP.
TWEEK
NUMBER 2.
HMPH !
MATCH 1... AGAINST YAMCHA !
7
5
6
1
2
3
4
YAMCHA
TENSHINHAN
JACKIE
PANPOOT

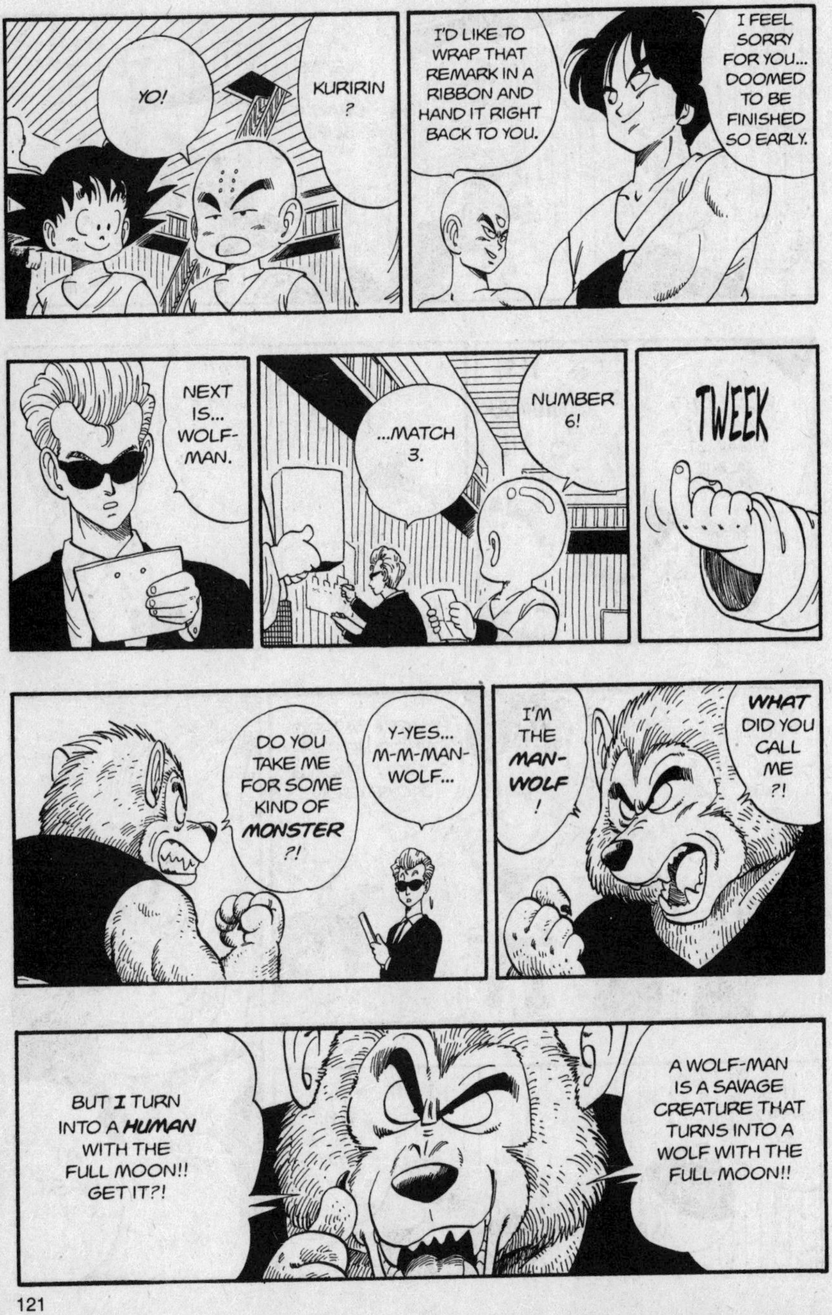
I FEEL SORRY FOR YOU... DOOMED TO BE FINISHED SO EARLY.
I'D LIKE TO WRAP THAT REMARK IN A RIBBON AND HAND IT RIGHT BACK TO YOU.
KURIRIN?
YO!
TWEEK
NUMBER 6!
...MATCH 3.
NEXT IS... WOLF-MAN.
WHAT DID YOU CALL ME?!
I'M THE MAN-WOLF!
Y-YES... M-M-MAN-WOLF...
DO YOU TAKE ME FOR SOME KIND OF MONSTER?!
A WOLF-MAN IS A SAVAGE CREATURE THAT TURNS INTO A WOLF WITH THE FULL MOON!!
BUT I TURN INTO A HUMAN WITH THE FULL MOON!! GET IT?!

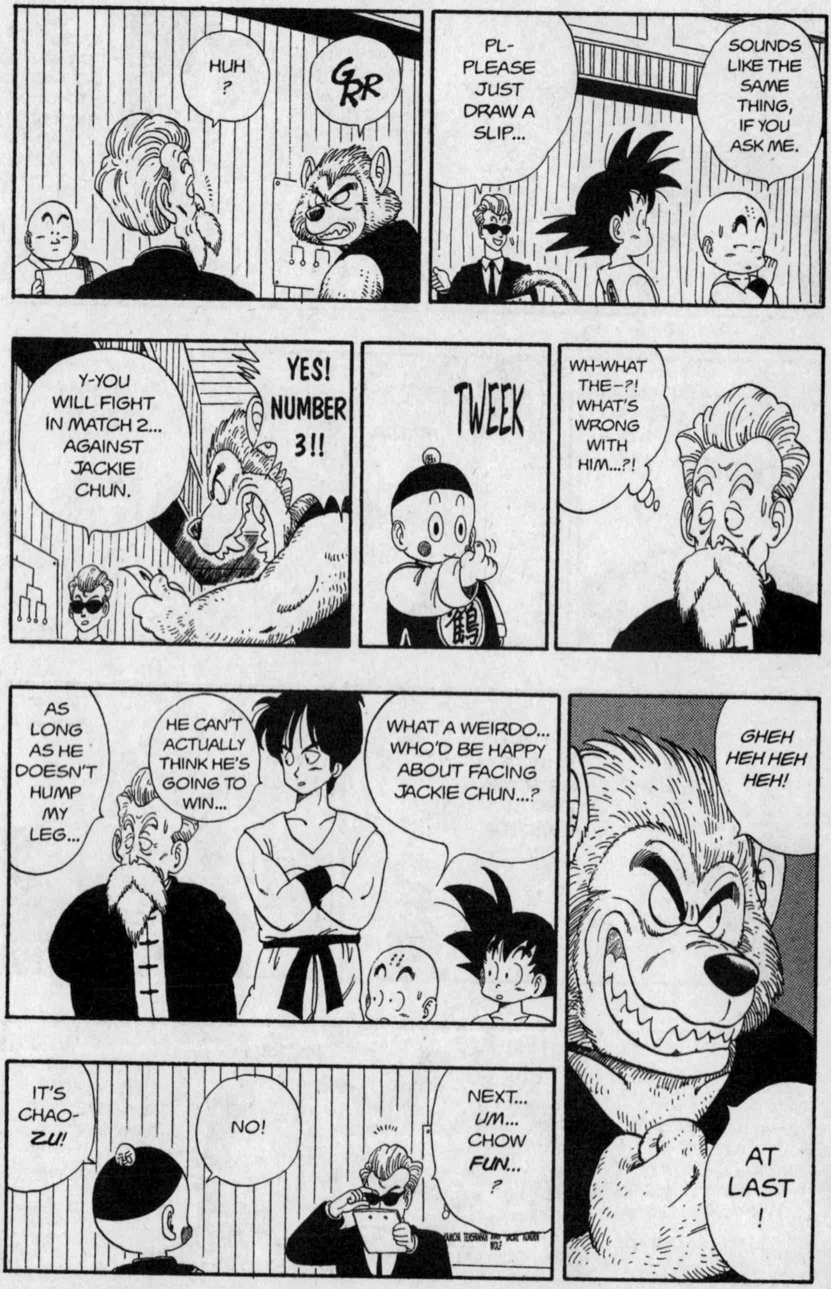
SOUNDS LIKE THE SAME THING, IF YOU ASK ME.
PL- PLEASE JUST DRAW A SLIP...
GRR
HUH ?
WH-WHAT THE–?! WHAT'S WRONG WITH HIM...?!
TWEEK
YES! NUMBER 3!!
Y-YOU WILL FIGHT IN MATCH 2... AGAINST JACKIE CHUN.
GHEH HEH HEH HEH!
AT LAST !
WHAT A WEIRDO... WHO'D BE HAPPY ABOUT FACING JACKIE CHUN...?
HE CAN'T ACTUALLY THINK HE'S GOING TO WIN...
AS LONG AS HE DOESN'T HUMP MY LEG...
NEXT... UM... CHOW FUN... ?
NO!
IT'S CHAO-ZU!

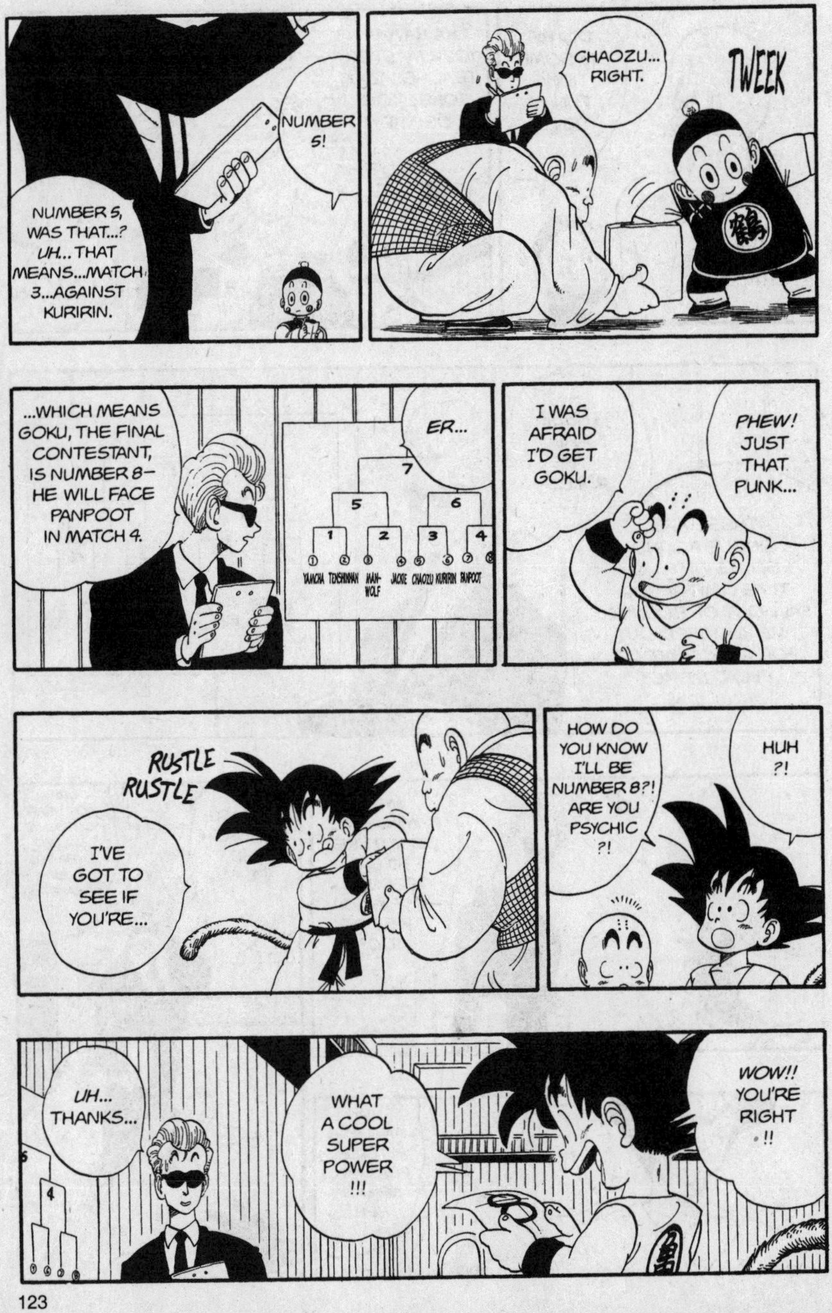
CHAOZU... RIGHT.
TWEEK
NUMBER 5!
NUMBER 5, WAS THAT...? UH... THAT MEANS...MATCH 3...AGAINST KURIRIN.
PHEW! JUST THAT PUNK...
I WAS AFRAID I'D GET GOKU.
ER...
...WHICH MEANS GOKU, THE FINAL CONTESTANT, IS NUMBER 8—HE WILL FACE PANPOOT IN MATCH 4.
7
5
6
1
2
3
4
YAMCHA TENSHINHAN MAN-WOLF JACKIE CHAOZU KURIRIN PANPOOT
HUH?!
HOW DO YOU KNOW I'LL BE NUMBER 8?! ARE YOU PSYCHIC?!
RUSTLE RUSTLE
I'VE GOT TO SEE IF YOU'RE...
WOW!! YOU'RE RIGHT!!
WHAT A COOL SUPER POWER!!!
UH... THANKS...

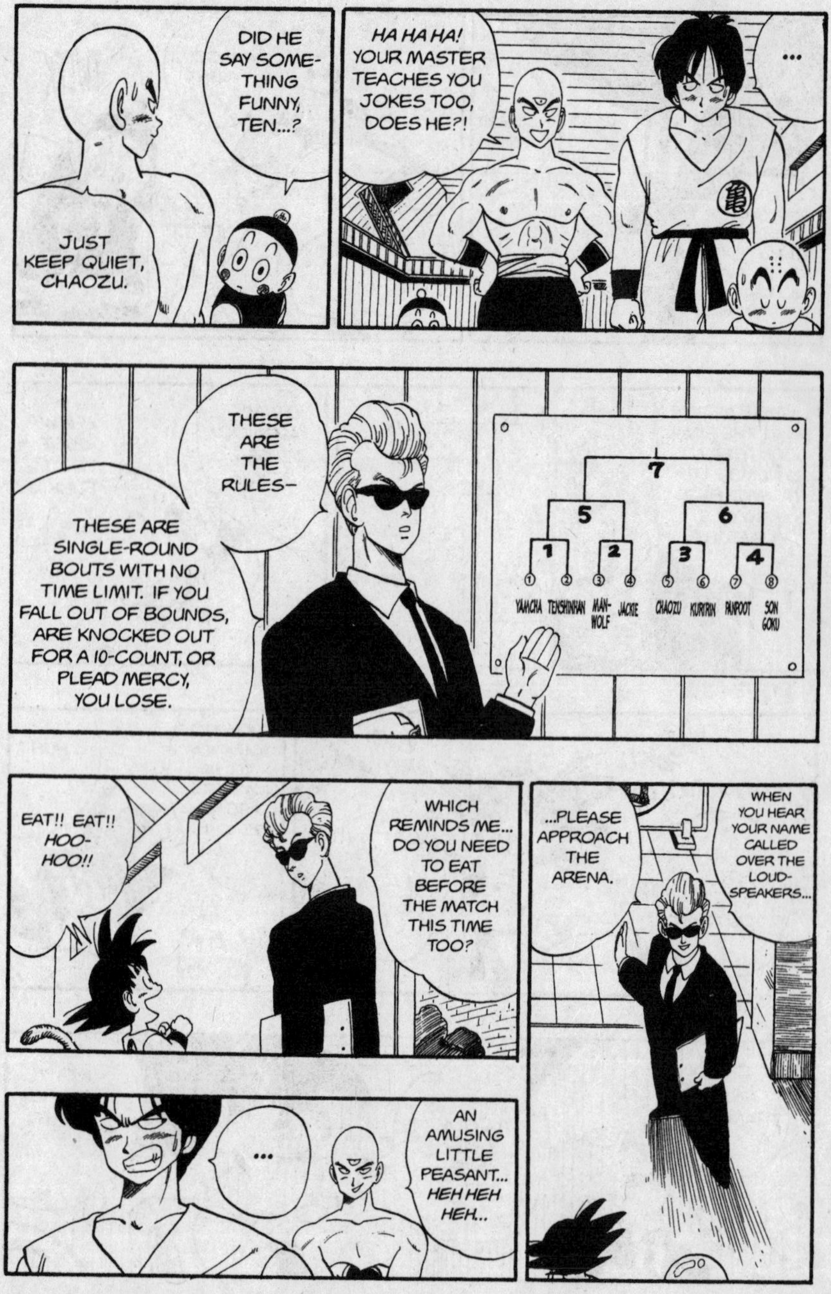

...
HA HA HA! YOUR MASTER TEACHES YOU JOKES TOO, DOES HE?!
DID HE SAY SOME-THING FUNNY, TEN...?
JUST KEEP QUIET, CHAOZU.
THESE ARE THE RULES—
THESE ARE SINGLE-ROUND BOUTS WITH NO TIME LIMIT. IF YOU FALL OUT OF BOUNDS, ARE KNOCKED OUT FOR A 10-COUNT, OR PLEAD MERCY, YOU LOSE.
7
5
6
1
2
3
4
① ② ③ ④ ⑤ ⑥ ⑦ ⑧
YAMCHA TENSHINHAN MAN-WOLF JACKIE CHAOZU KURIRIN PANPOOT SON GOKU
WHEN YOU HEAR YOUR NAME CALLED OVER THE LOUD-SPEAKERS...
...PLEASE APPROACH THE ARENA.
WHICH REMINDS ME... DO YOU NEED TO EAT BEFORE THE MATCH THIS TIME TOO?
EAT!! EAT!! HOO-HOO!!
AN AMUSING LITTLE PEASANT... HEH HEH HEH...
...

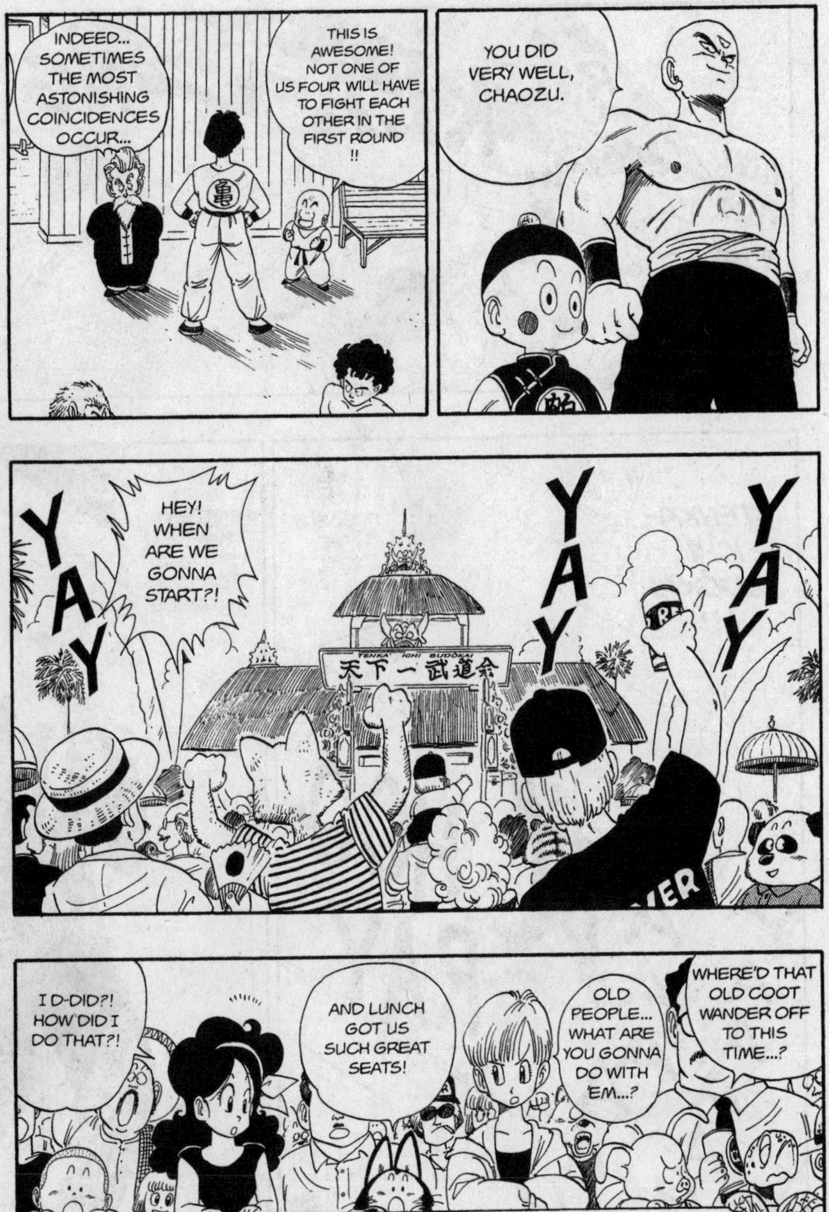
YOU DID VERY WELL, CHAOZU.
THIS IS AWESOME! NOT ONE OF US FOUR WILL HAVE TO FIGHT EACH OTHER IN THE FIRST ROUND !!
INDEED... SOMETIMES THE MOST ASTONISHING COINCIDENCES OCCUR...
YAY
YAY
天下一武道会
HEY! WHEN ARE WE GONNA START?!
YAY
WHERE'D THAT OLD COOT WANDER OFF TO THIS TIME...?
OLD PEOPLE... WHAT ARE YOU GONNA DO WITH 'EM...?
AND LUNCH GOT US SUCH GREAT SEATS!
I D-DID?! HOW DID I DO THAT?!

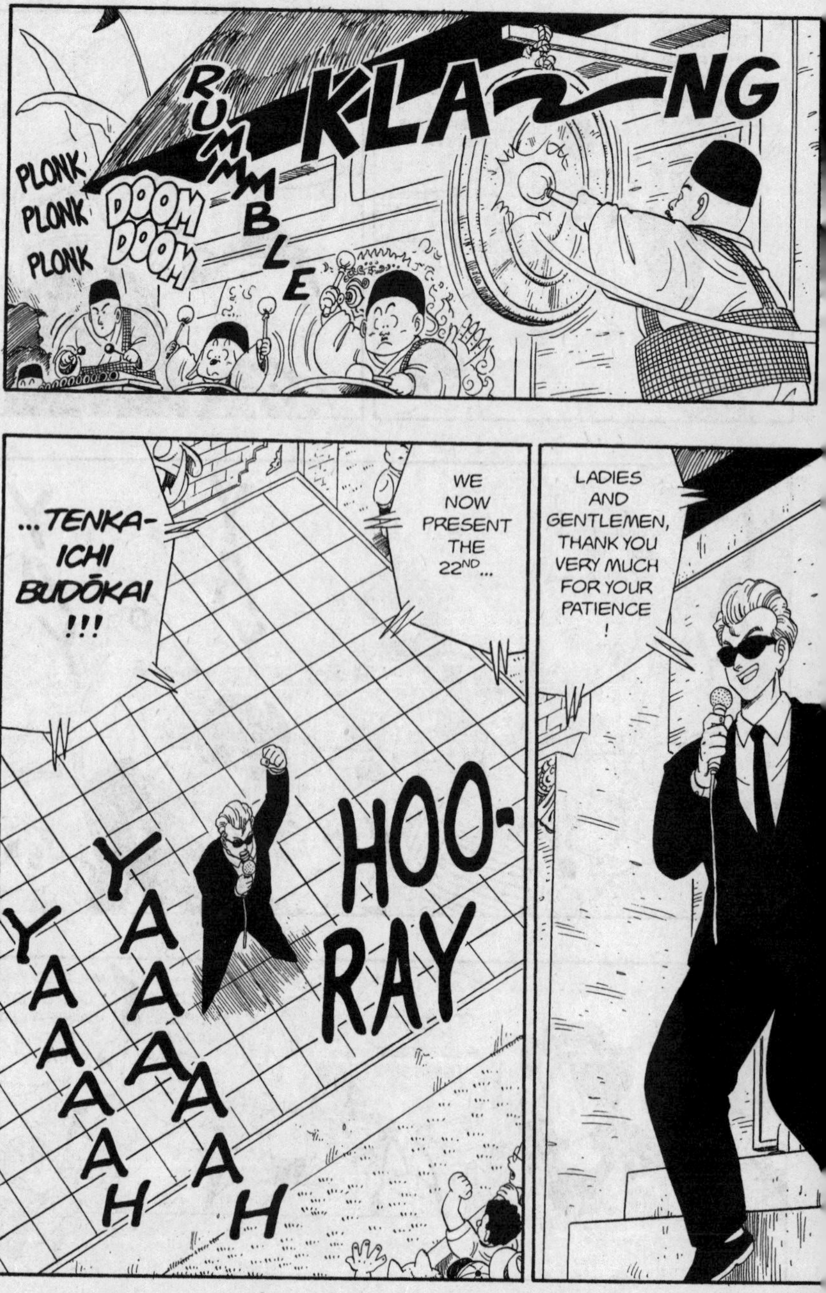
KLA——NG
RUMMMMBLE
DOOM DOOM
PLONK
PLONK
PLONK
LADIES AND GENTLEMEN, THANK YOU VERY MUCH FOR YOUR PATIENCE!
WE NOW PRESENT THE 22ND...
...TENKA-ICHI BUDŌKAI!!!
HOO-RAY
YAAAAAH
YAAAAAH

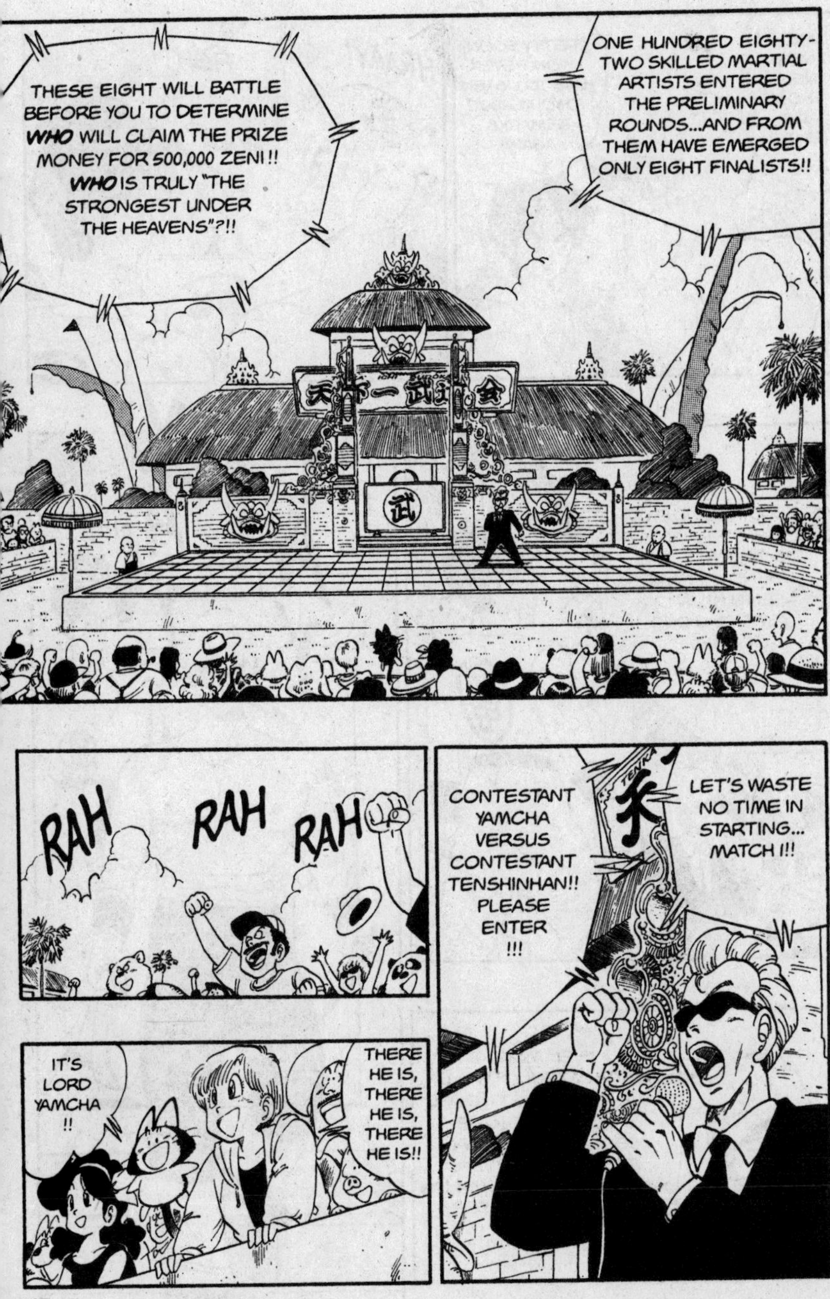
ONE HUNDRED EIGHTY-TWO SKILLED MARTIAL ARTISTS ENTERED THE PRELIMINARY ROUNDS...AND FROM THEM HAVE EMERGED ONLY EIGHT FINALISTS!!
THESE EIGHT WILL BATTLE BEFORE YOU TO DETERMINE WHO WILL CLAIM THE PRIZE MONEY FOR 500,000 ZENI!! WHO IS TRULY "THE STRONGEST UNDER THE HEAVENS"?!!
LET'S WASTE NO TIME IN STARTING... MATCH 1!!
CONTESTANT YAMCHA VERSUS CONTESTANT TENSHINHAN!! PLEASE ENTER !!!
RAH
RAH
RAH
THERE HE IS, THERE HE IS, THERE HE IS!!
IT'S LORD YAMCHA !!

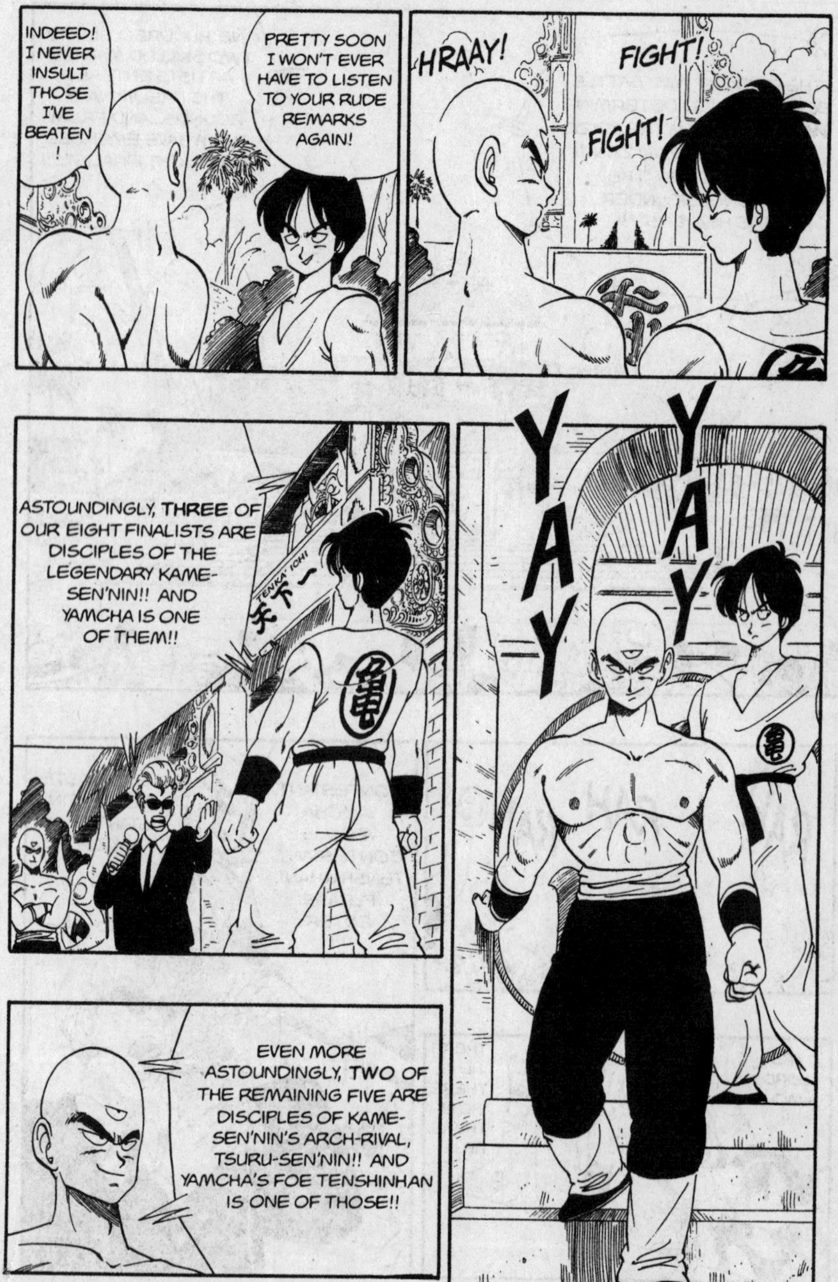

HRAAY!
FIGHT!
FIGHT!
PRETTY SOON I WON'T EVER HAVE TO LISTEN TO YOUR RUDE REMARKS AGAIN!
INDEED! I NEVER INSULT THOSE I'VE BEATEN!
YAY
YAY
ASTOUNDINGLY, THREE OF OUR EIGHT FINALISTS ARE DISCIPLES OF THE LEGENDARY KAME-SEN'NIN!! AND YAMCHA IS ONE OF THEM!!
TENKA' ICHI
天下一
EVEN MORE ASTOUNDINGLY, TWO OF THE REMAINING FIVE ARE DISCIPLES OF KAME-SEN'NIN'S ARCH-RIVAL, TSURU-SEN'NIN!! AND YAMCHA'S FOE TENSHINHAN IS ONE OF THOSE!!

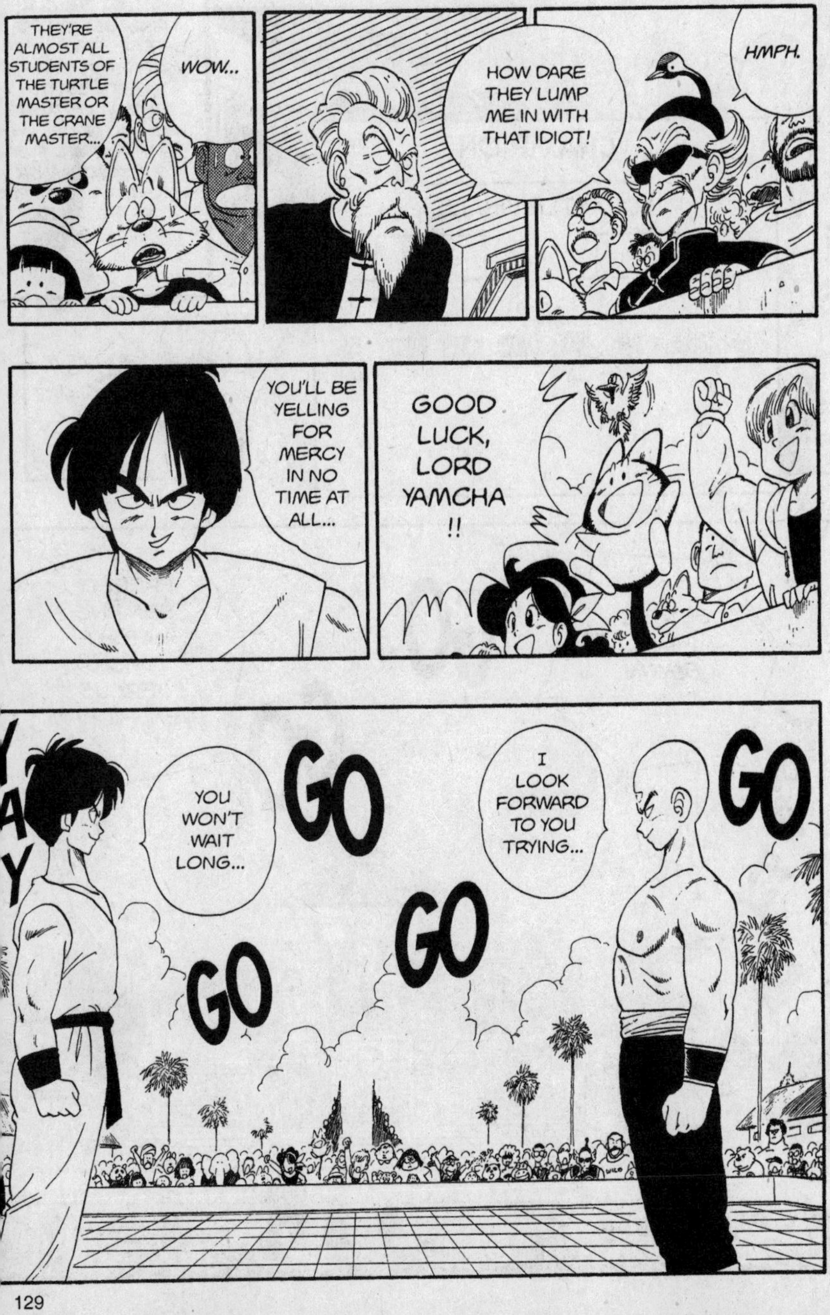
HMPH.
HOW DARE THEY LUMP ME IN WITH THAT IDIOT!
WOW...
THEY'RE ALMOST ALL STUDENTS OF THE TURTLE MASTER OR THE CRANE MASTER...
GOOD LUCK, LORD YAMCHA!!
YOU'LL BE YELLING FOR MERCY IN NO TIME AT ALL...
GO
I LOOK FORWARD TO YOU TRYING...
GO
GO
YOU WON'T WAIT LONG...
GO

Tale 117 • Yamcha's Kamehameha!

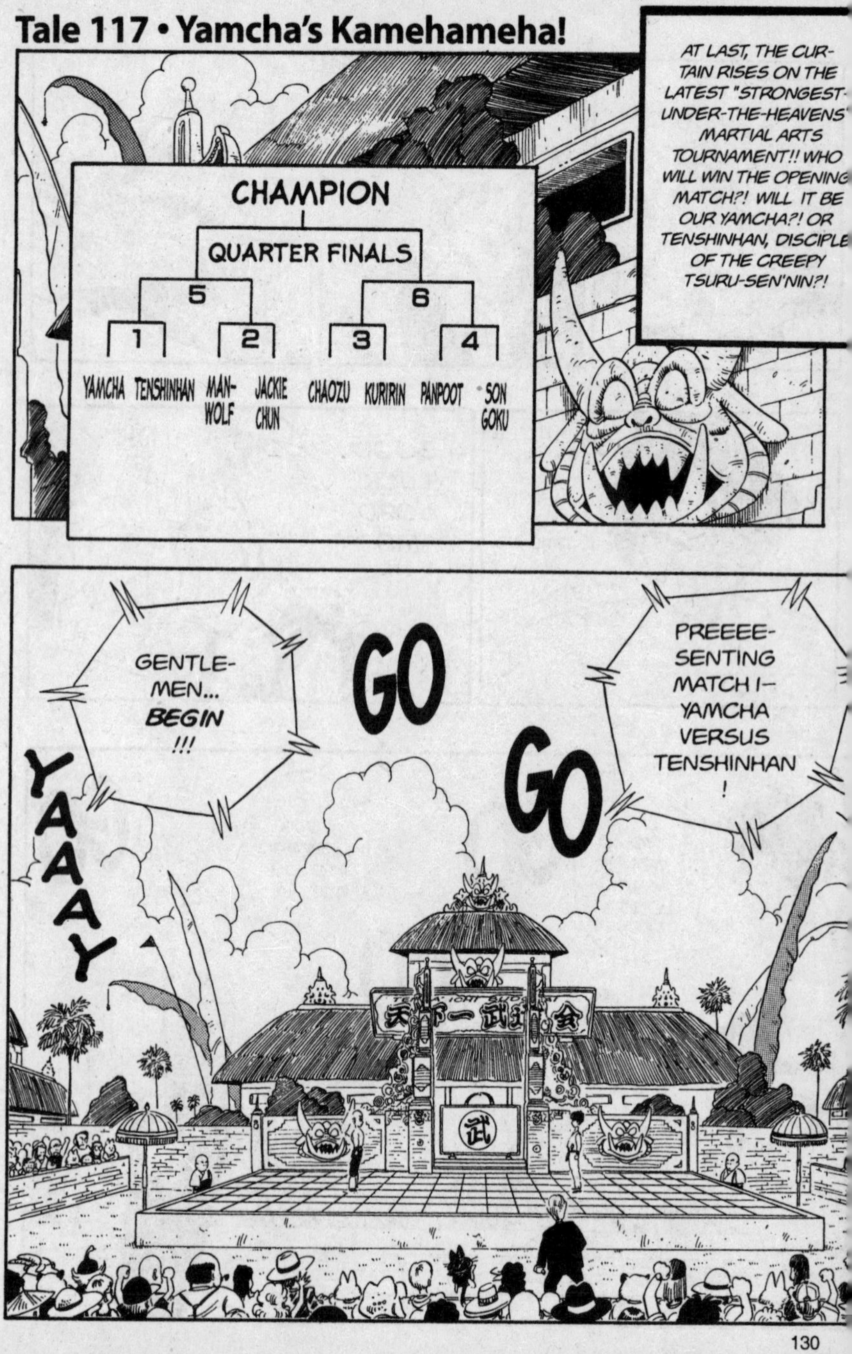

AT LAST, THE CURTAIN RISES ON THE LATEST "STRONGEST-UNDER-THE-HEAVENS" MARTIAL ARTS TOURNAMENT!! WHO WILL WIN THE OPENING MATCH?! WILL IT BE OUR YAMCHA?! OR TENSHINHAN, DISCIPLE OF THE CREEPY TSURU-SEN'NIN?!
CHAMPION
QUARTER FINALS
5
6
1
2
3
4
YAMCHA
TENSHINHAN
MAN-WOLF
JACKIE CHUN
CHAOZU
KURIRIN
PANPOOT
SON GOKU
PREEEE-SENTING MATCH I- YAMCHA VERSUS TENSHINHAN!
GO
GO
GENTLEMEN... BEGIN!!!
YAAAY

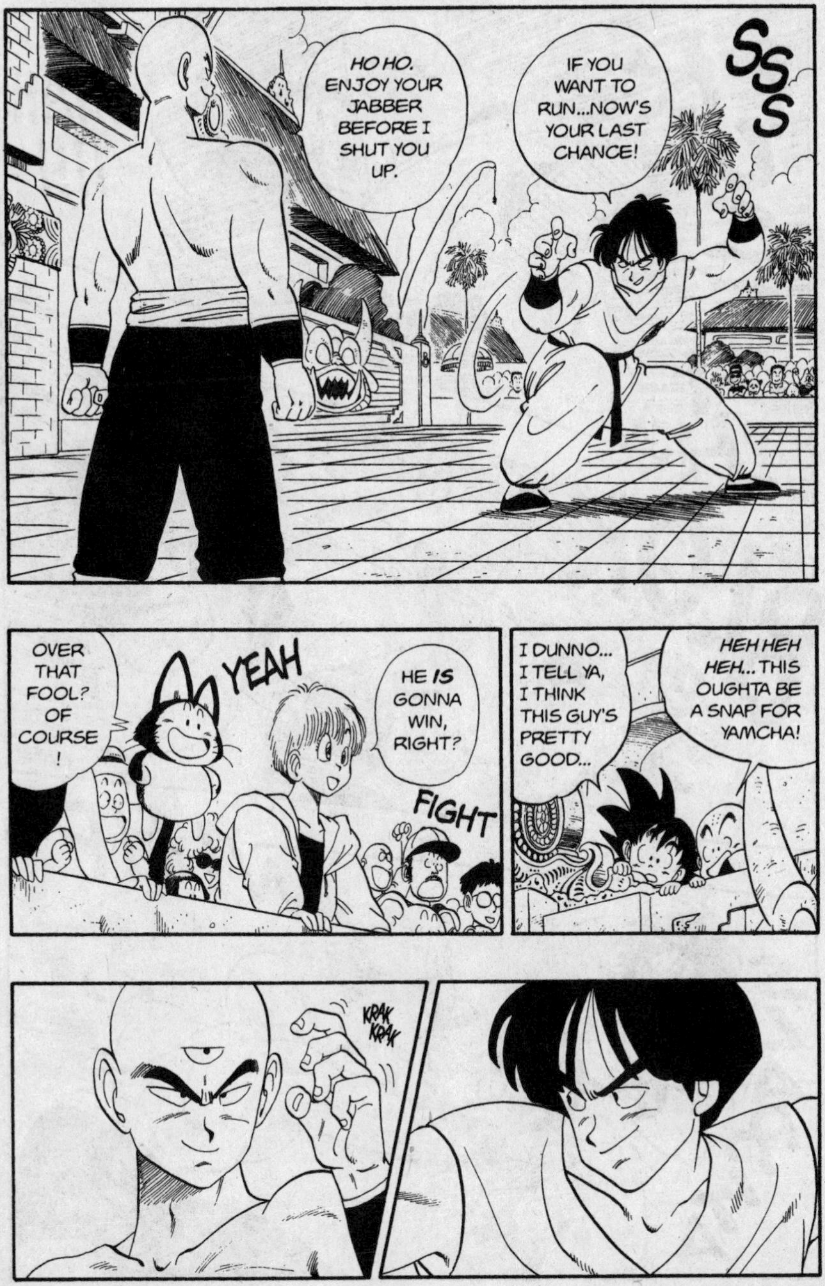
SSS
IF YOU WANT TO RUN...NOW'S YOUR LAST CHANCE!
HO HO. ENJOY YOUR JABBER BEFORE I SHUT YOU UP.
HEH HEH HEH... THIS OUGHTA BE A SNAP FOR YAMCHA!
I DUNNO... I TELL YA, I THINK THIS GUY'S PRETTY GOOD...
HE *IS* GONNA WIN, RIGHT?
YEAH
OVER THAT FOOL? OF COURSE!
FIGHT
KRAK KRAK

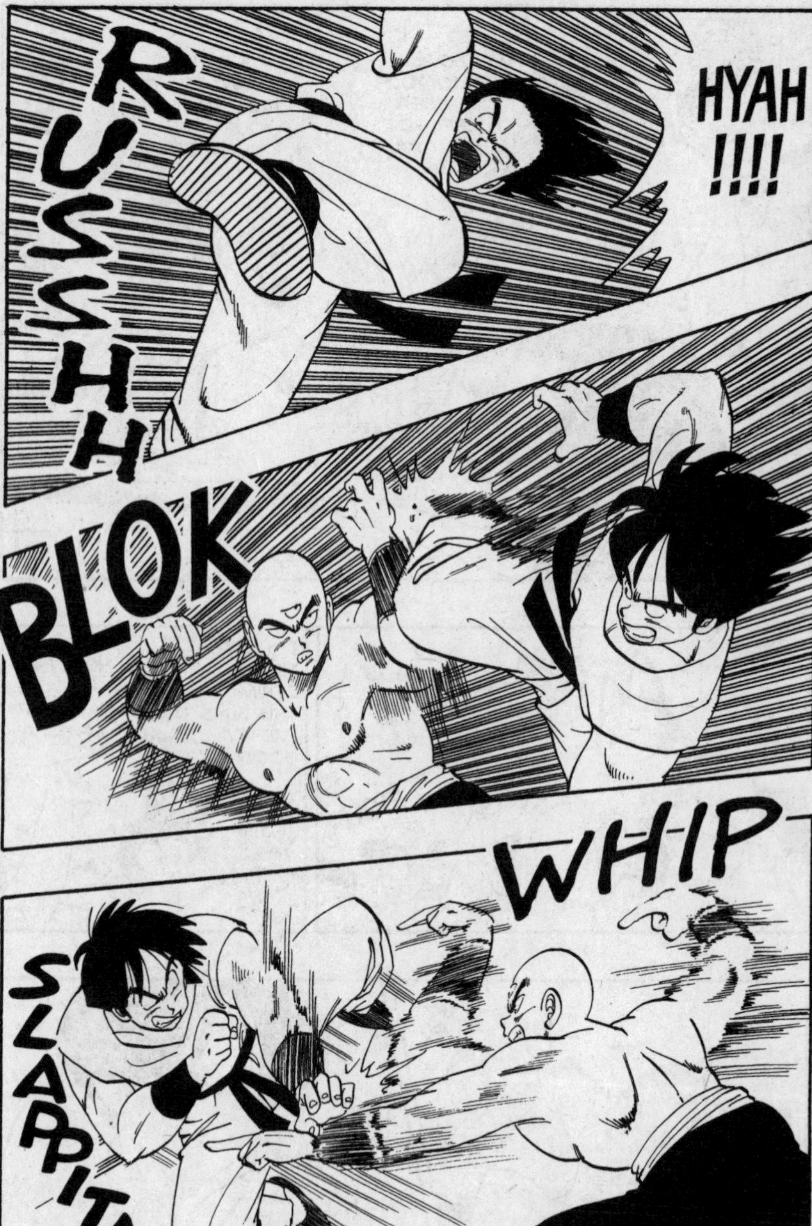
HYAH !!!!
RUSSHH
BLOK
WHIP
SLAPPITA

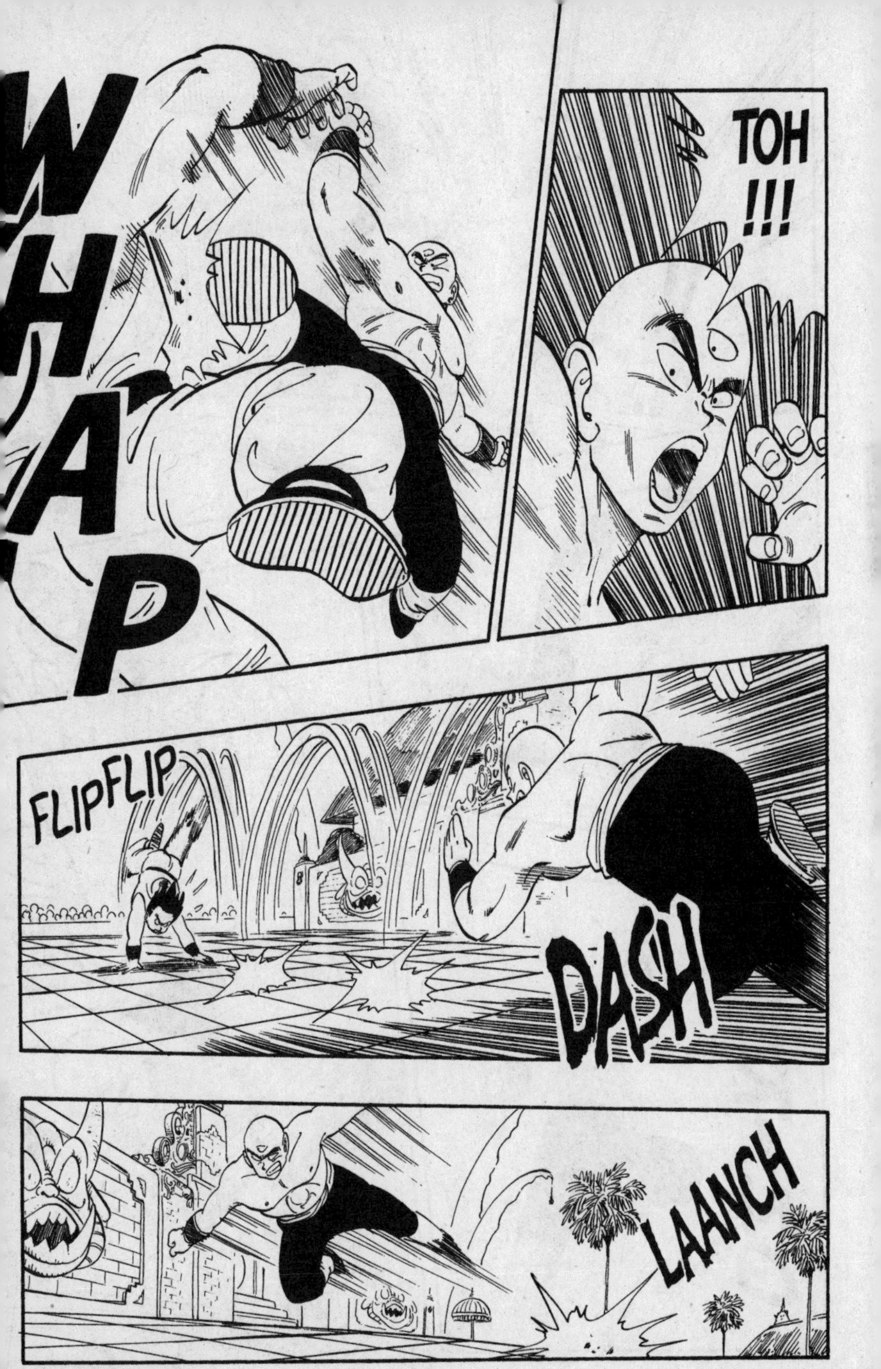
TOH !!!
WHAP
FLIPFLIP
DASH
LAANCH

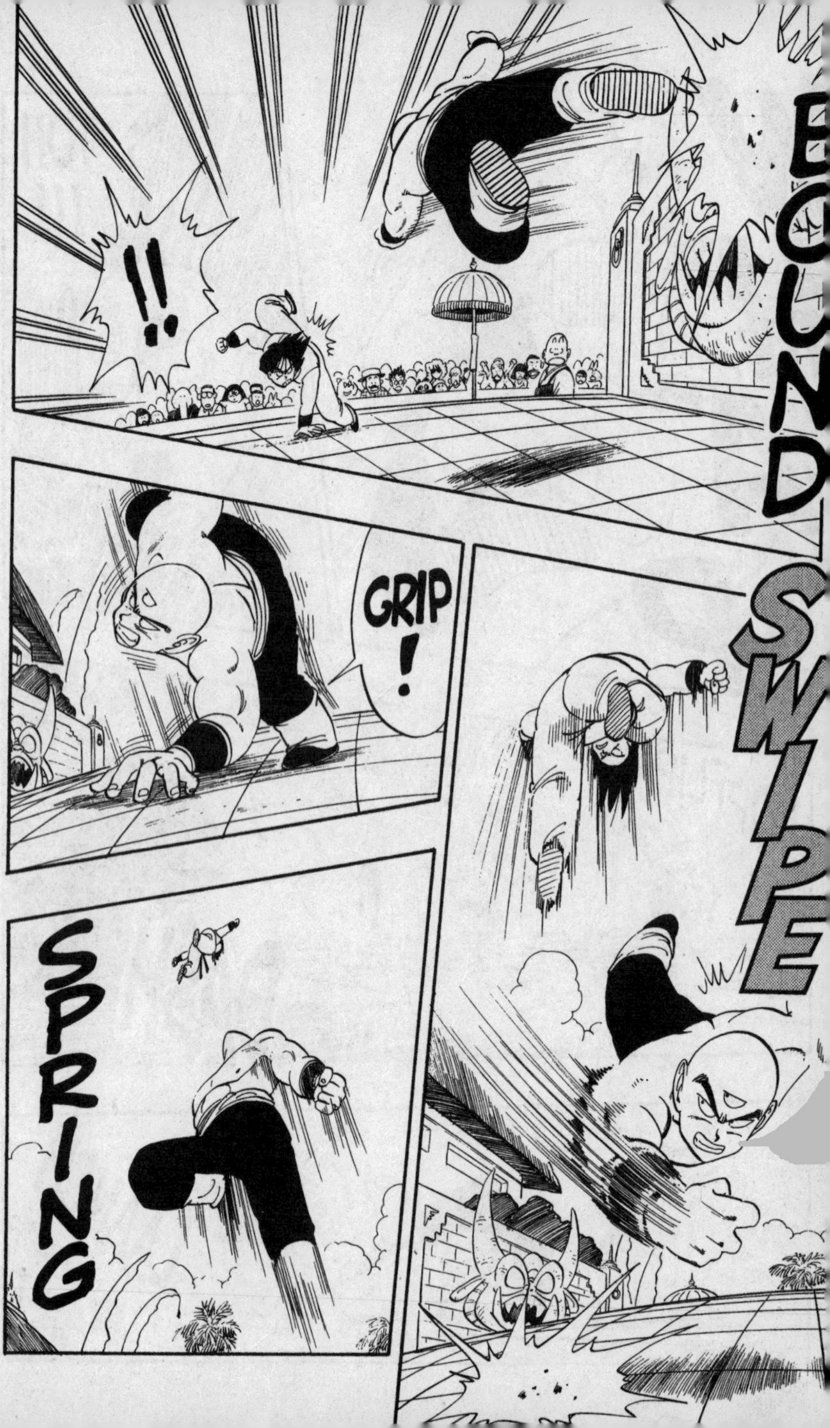
BOUND
!!
SWIPE
GRIP!
SPRING

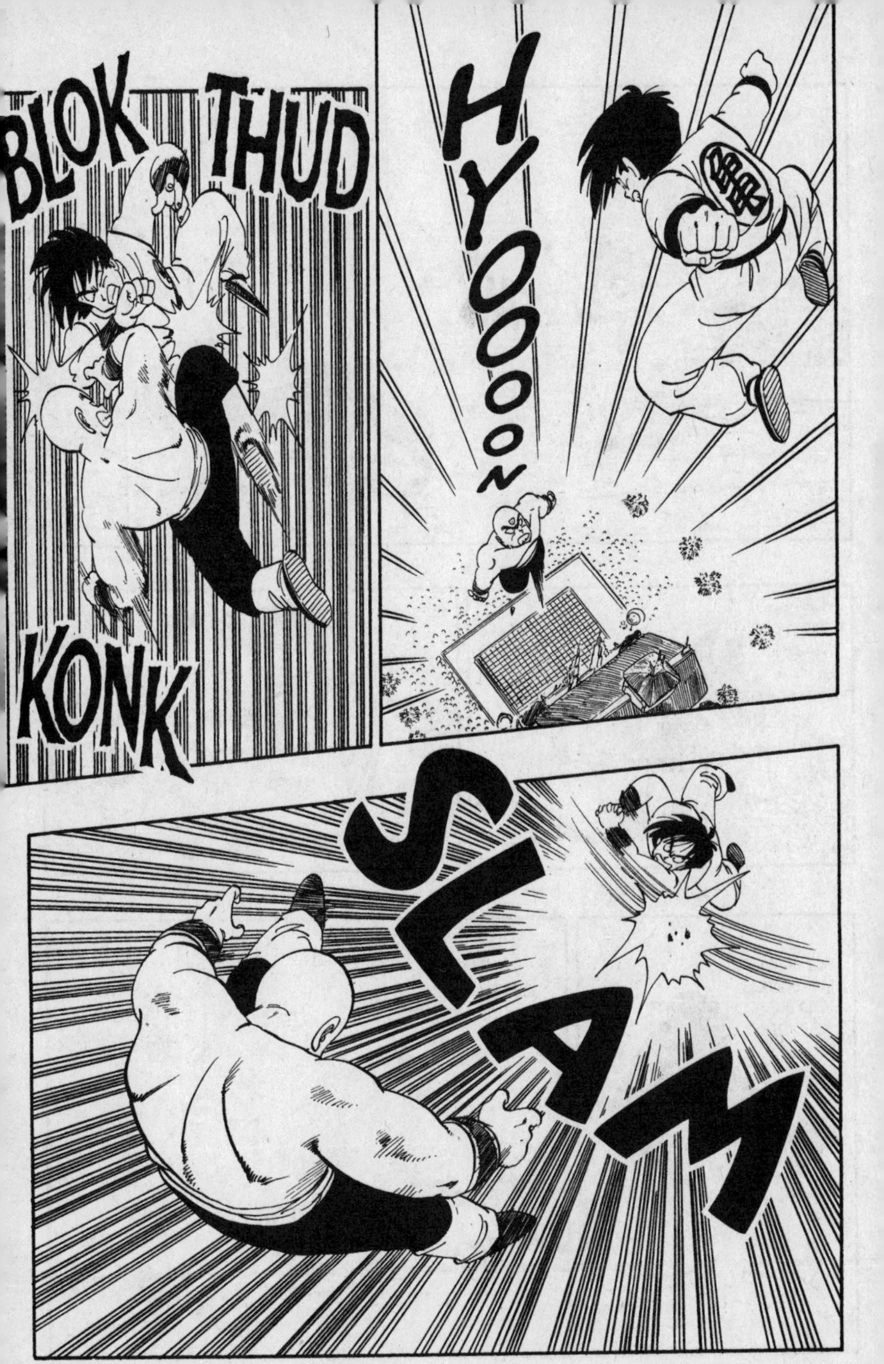
HYOOOOON
THUD
BLOK
KONK
SLAM

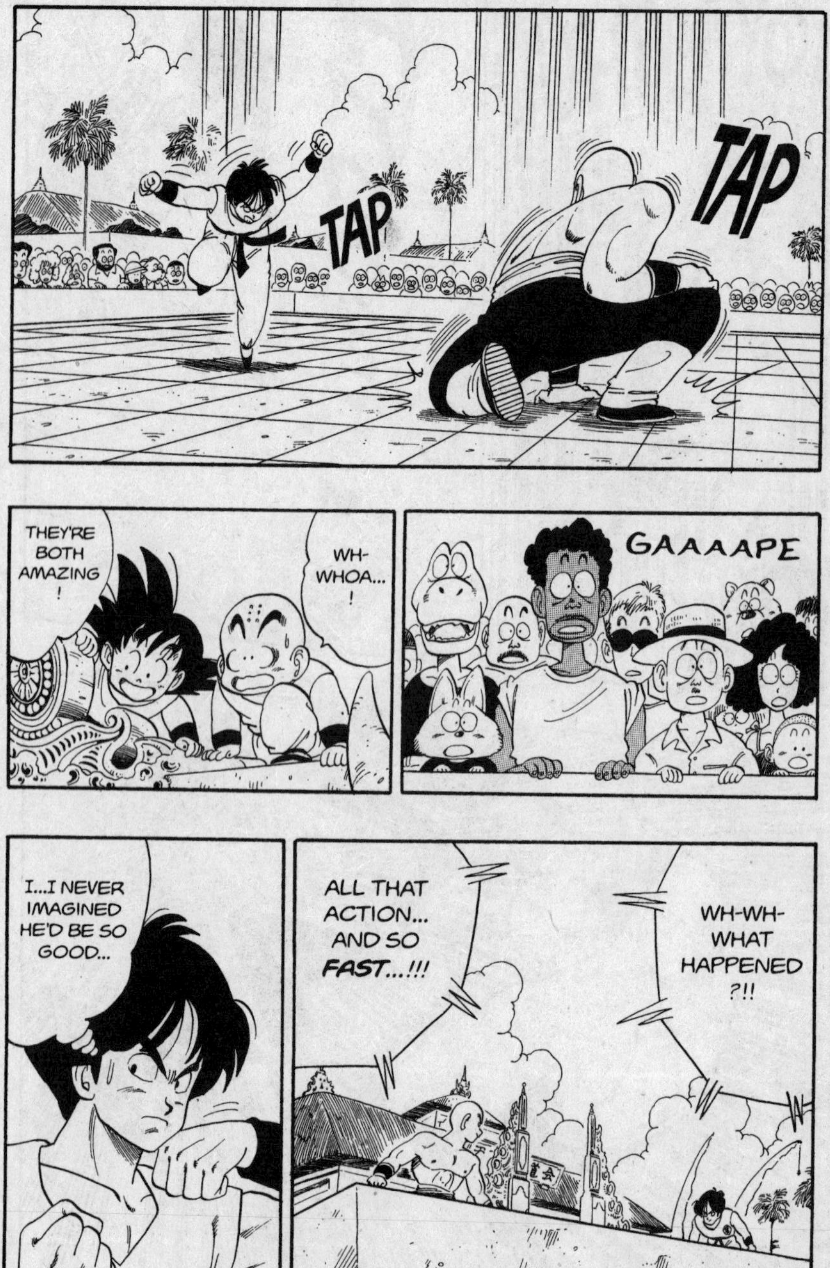
TAP
TAP
GAAAAPE
WH-WHOA...!
THEY'RE BOTH AMAZING!
WH-WH-WHAT HAPPENED?!!
ALL THAT ACTION... AND SO *FAST*...!!!
I...I NEVER IMAGINED HE'D BE SO GOOD...

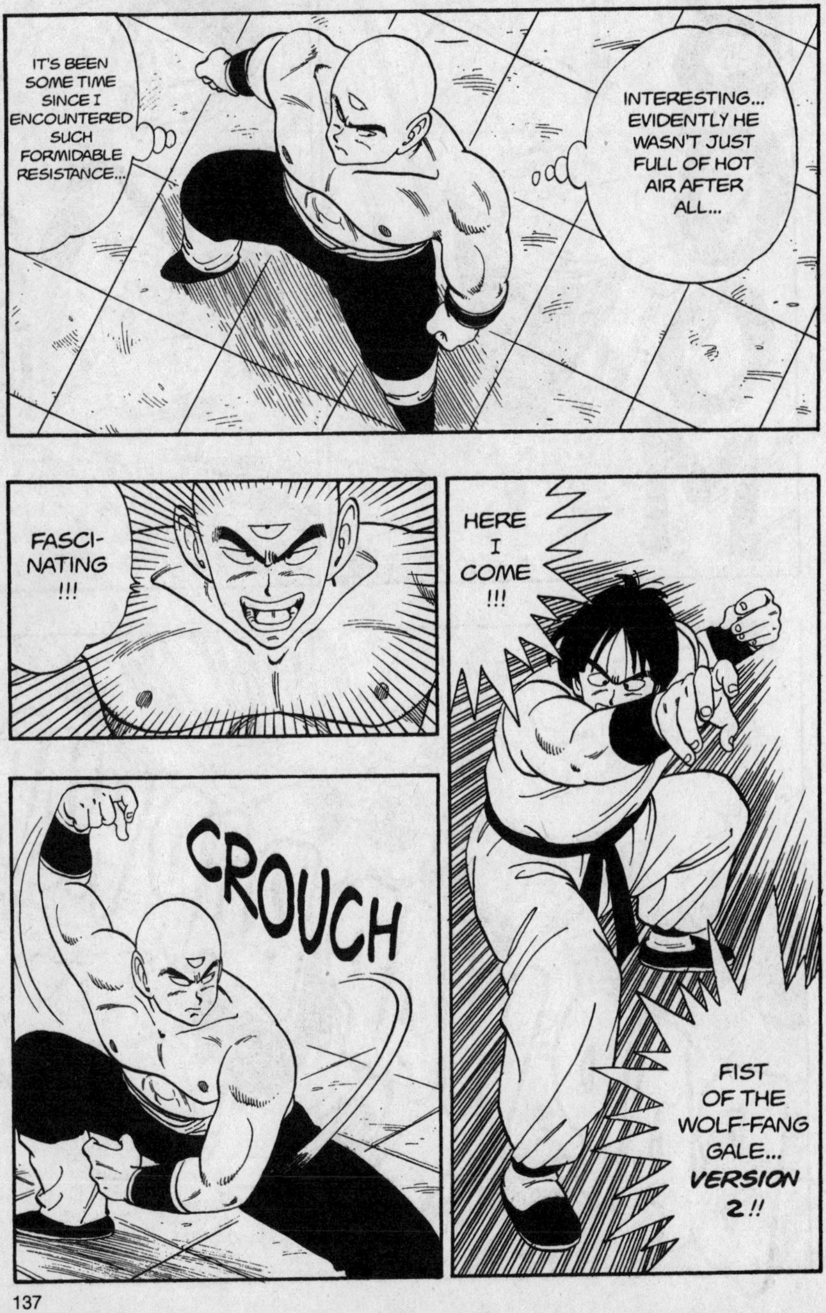
INTERESTING... EVIDENTLY HE WASN'T JUST FULL OF HOT AIR AFTER ALL...
IT'S BEEN SOME TIME SINCE I ENCOUNTERED SUCH FORMIDABLE RESISTANCE...
HERE I COME !!!
FIST OF THE WOLF-FANG GALE... **VERSION 2**!!
FASCI-NATING !!!
CROUCH

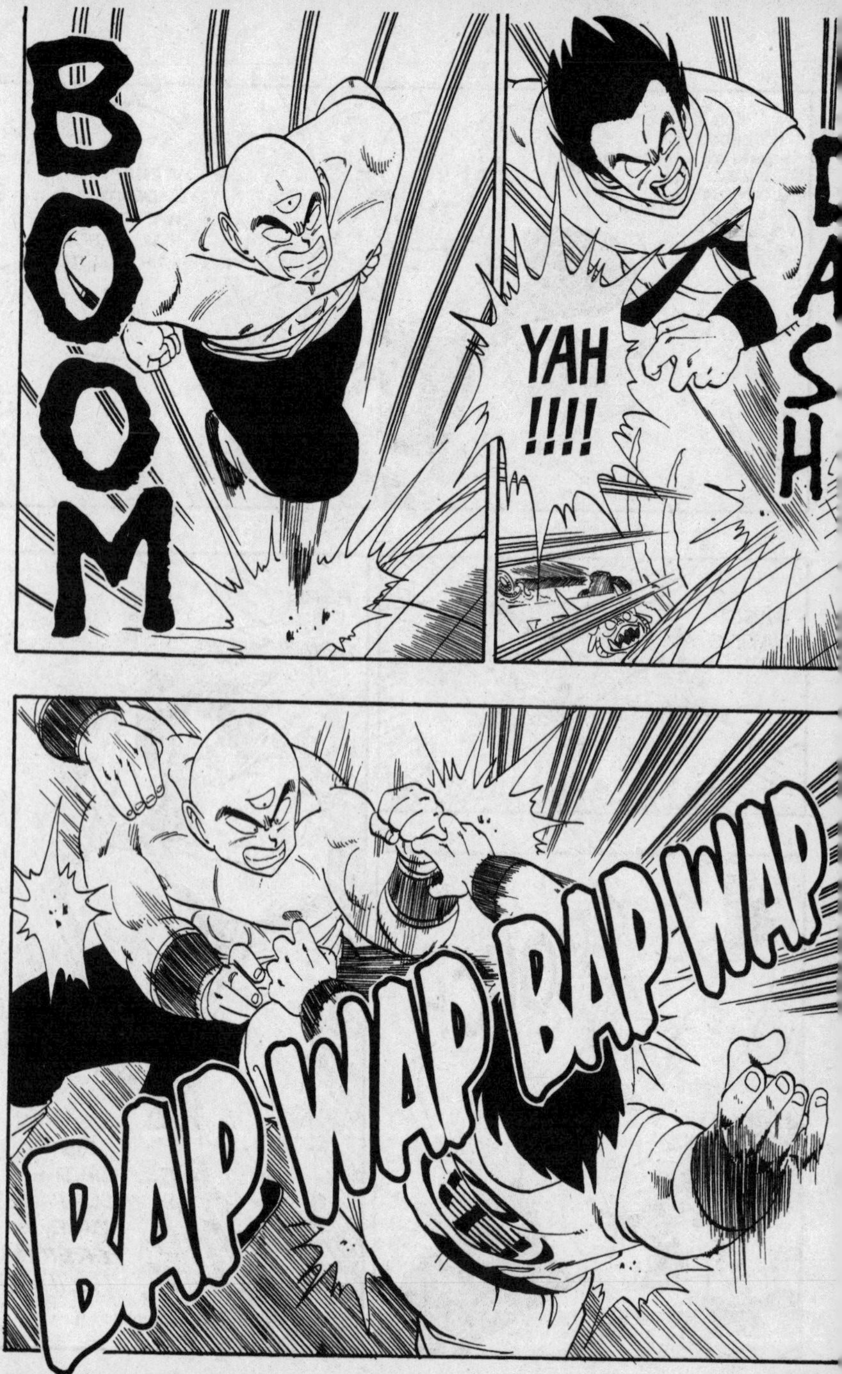
DASH
YAH !!!!
BOOM
BAP WAP BAP WAP

WHAK
KLUNK
SLAPPITA
KONK
SLAM
AARGH!!!

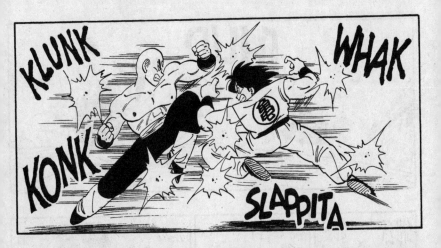

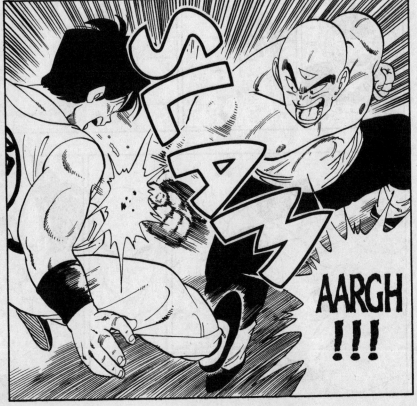

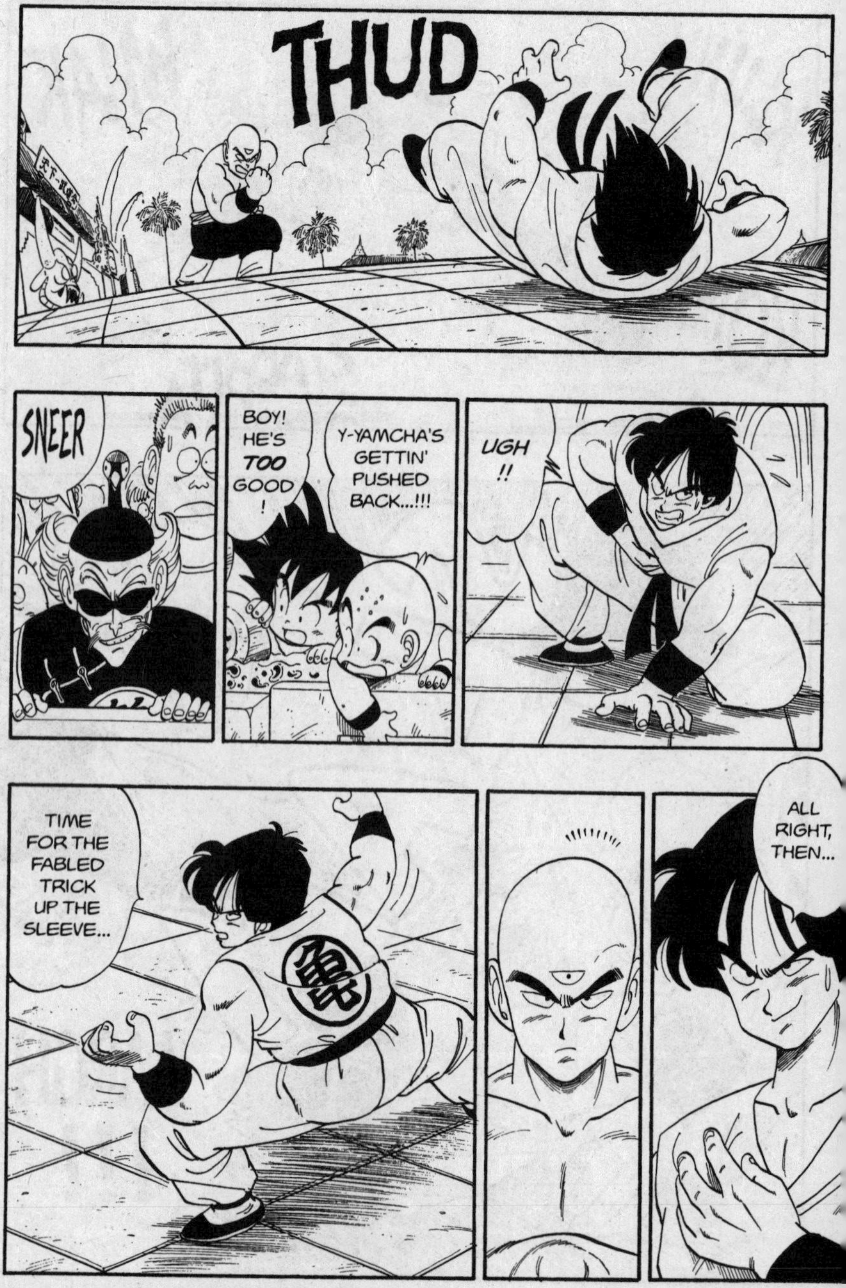
THUD
UGH !!
Y-YAMCHA'S GETTIN' PUSHED BACK...!!!
BOY! HE'S TOO GOOD!
SNEER
ALL RIGHT, THEN...
TIME FOR THE FABLED TRICK UP THE SLEEVE...

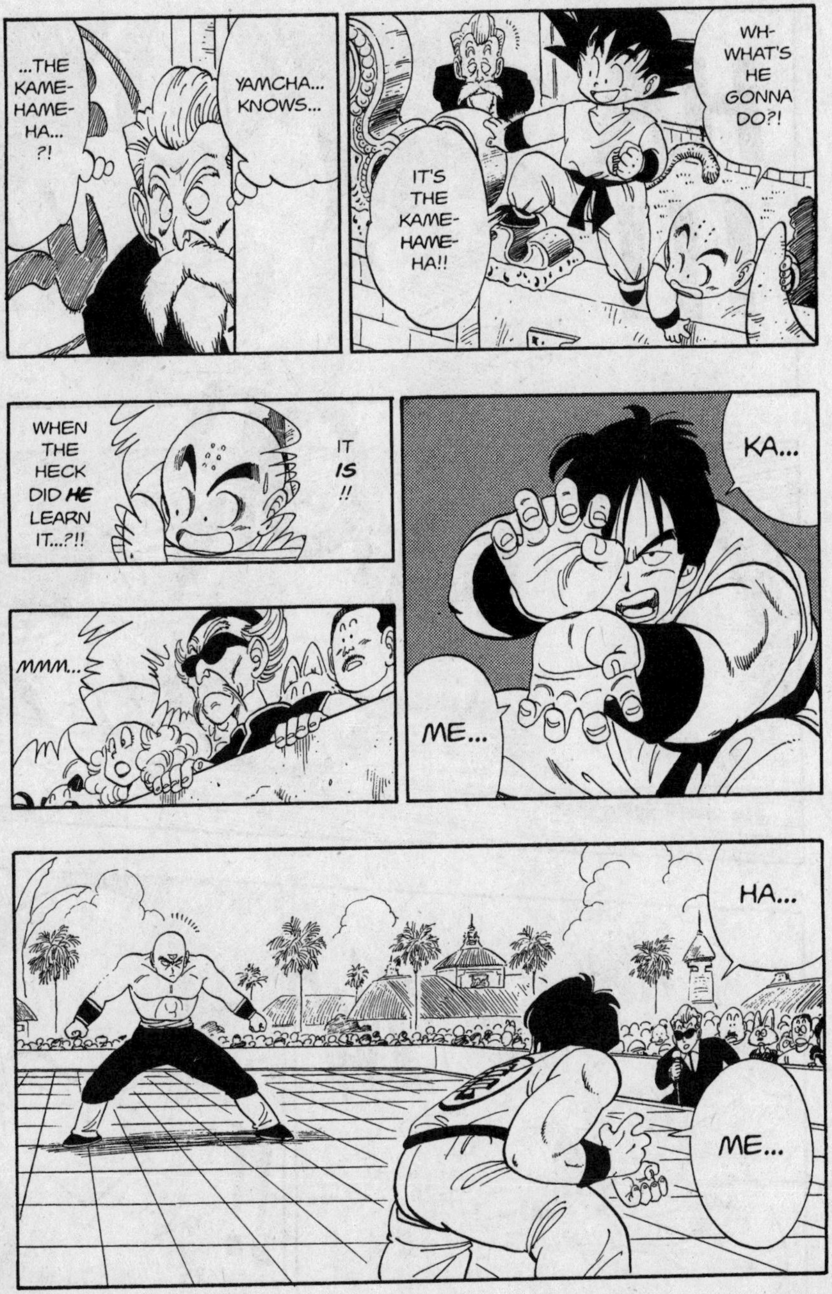
WH-WHAT'S HE GONNA DO?!
IT'S THE KAME-HAME-HA!!
YAMCHA... KNOWS...
...THE KAME-HAME-HA...?!
KA...
ME...
IT IS!!
WHEN THE HECK DID HE LEARN IT...?!!
MMM...
HA...
ME...

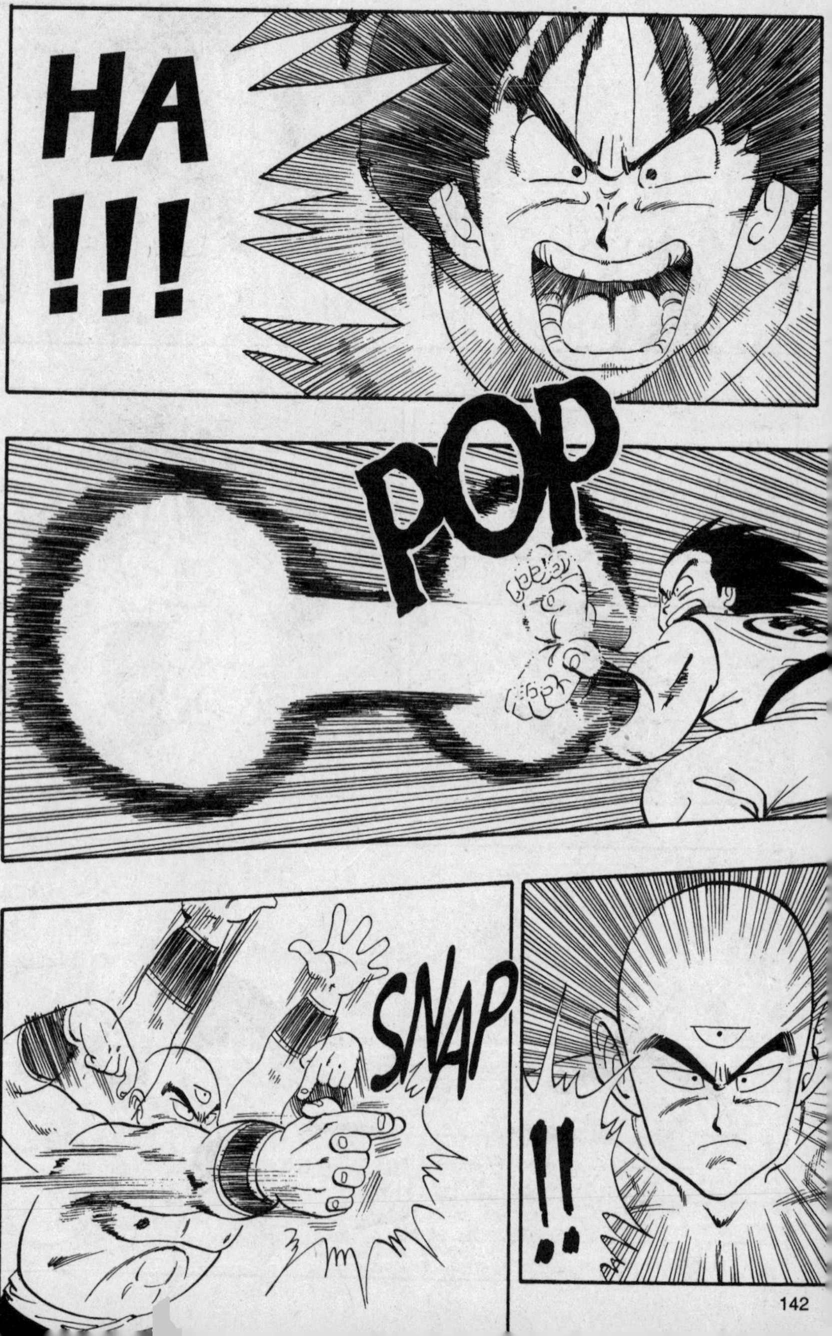
HA !!!
POP
!!
SNAP

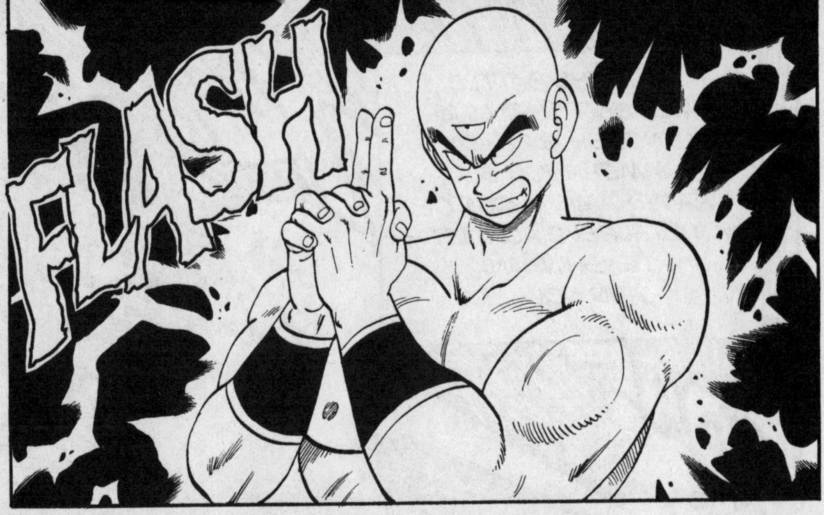
FLASH
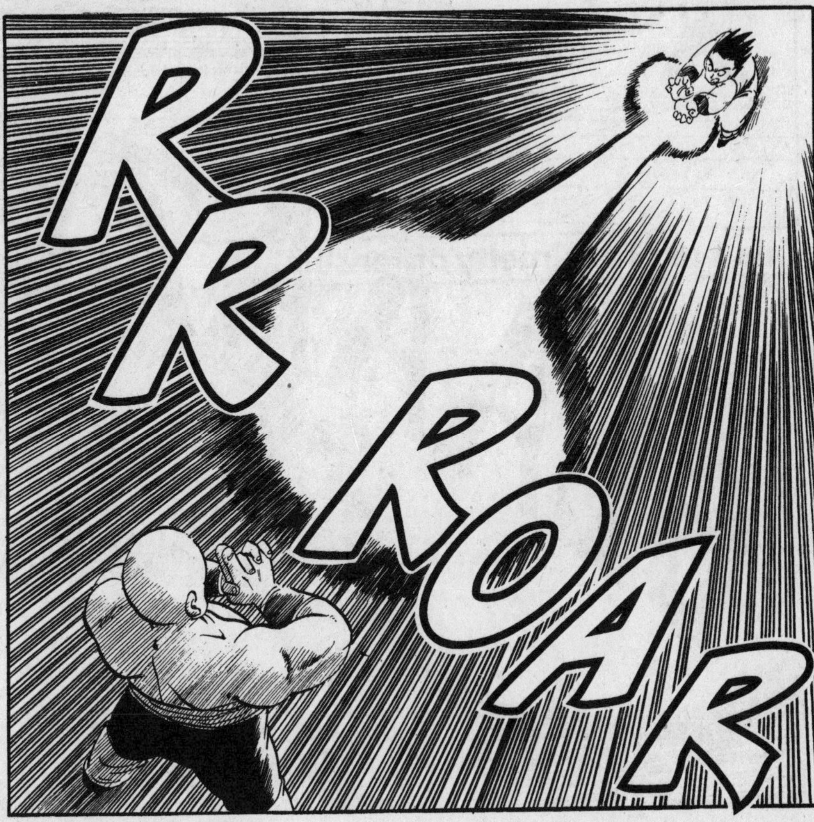
RRROAR

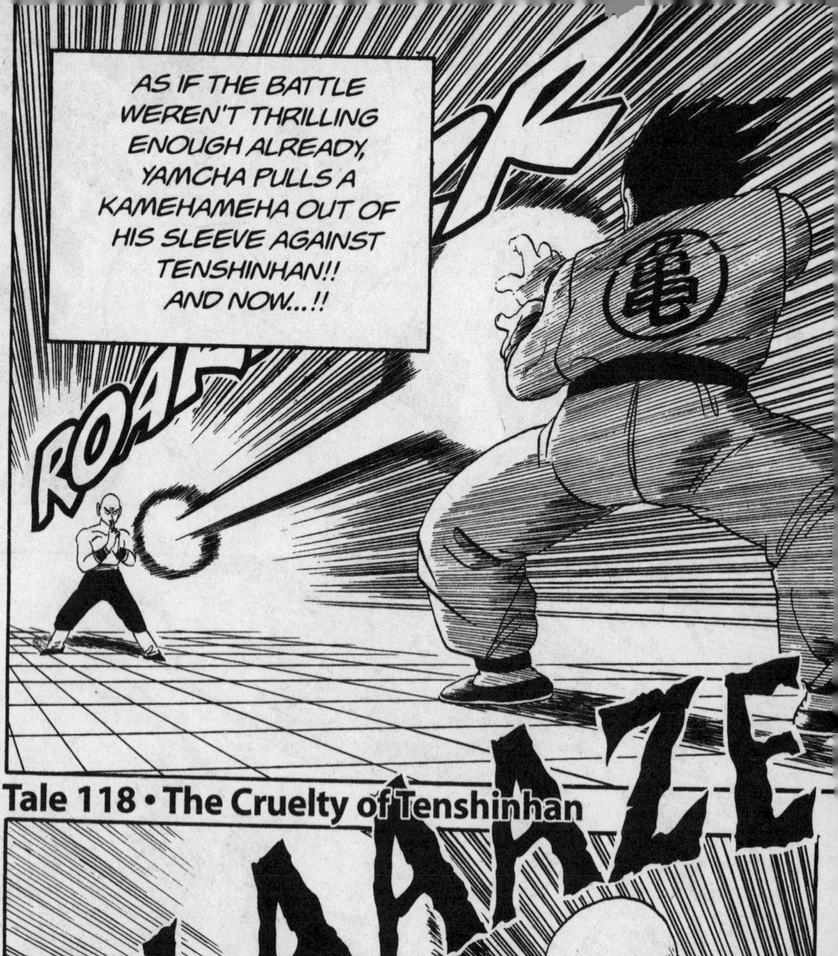
AS IF THE BATTLE WEREN'T THRILLING ENOUGH ALREADY, YAMCHA PULLS A KAMEHAMEHA OUT OF HIS SLEEVE AGAINST TENSHINHAN!! AND NOW...!!
ROA

Tale 118 • The Cruelty of Tenshinhan

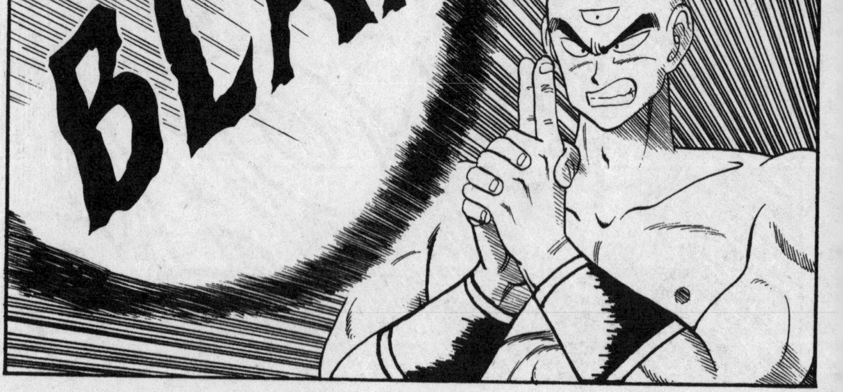
BLAAAZE

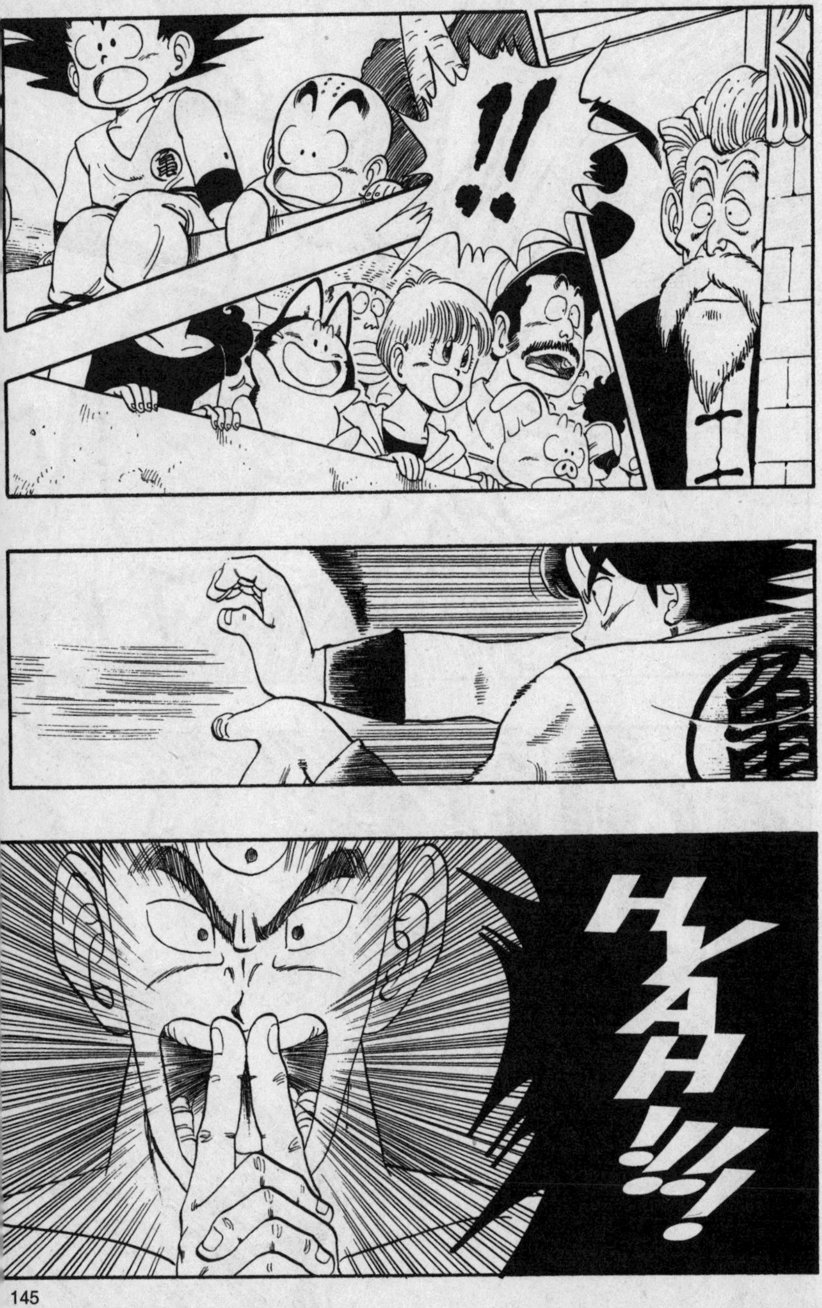
!!
HYAH!!!

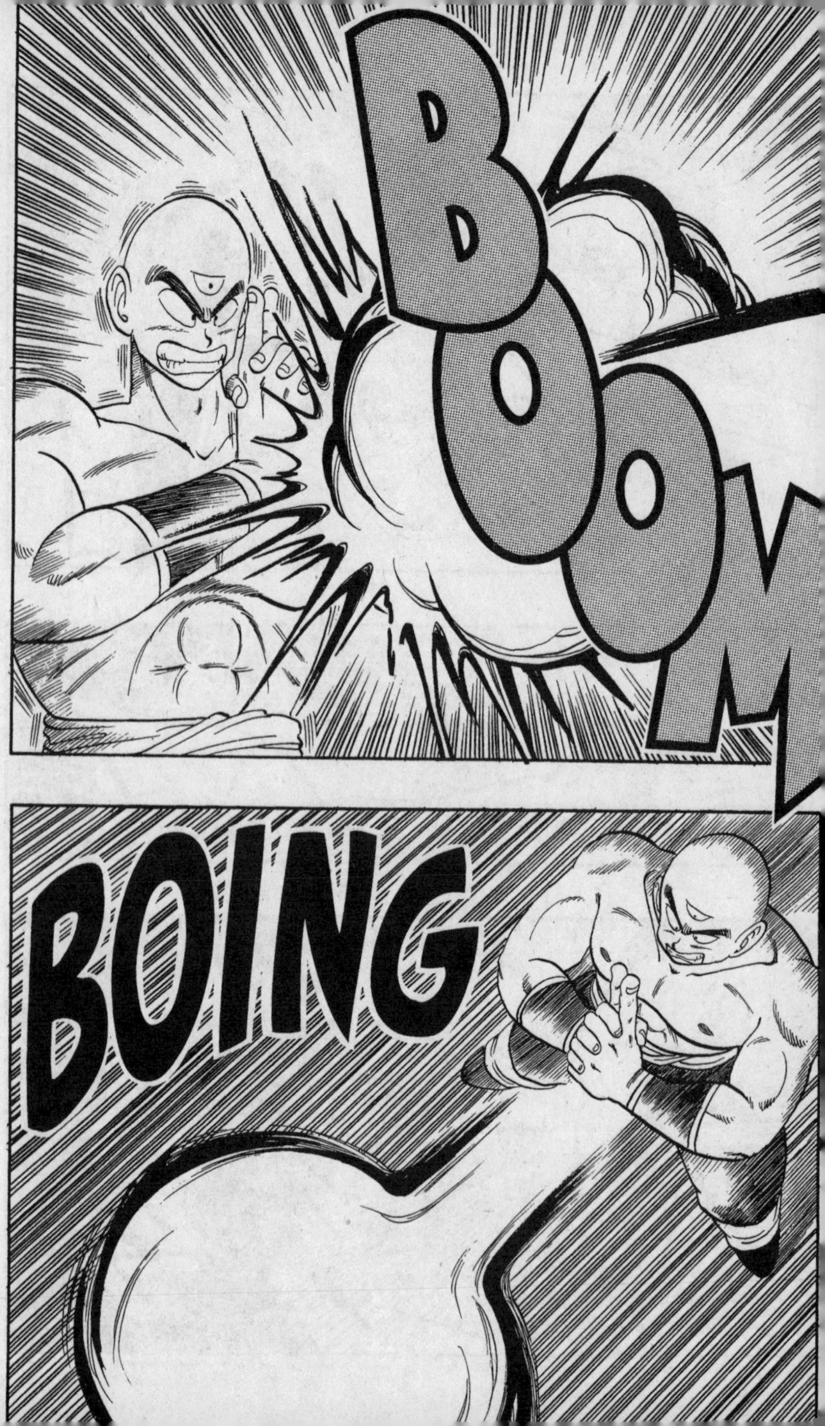
BOOOM
BOING

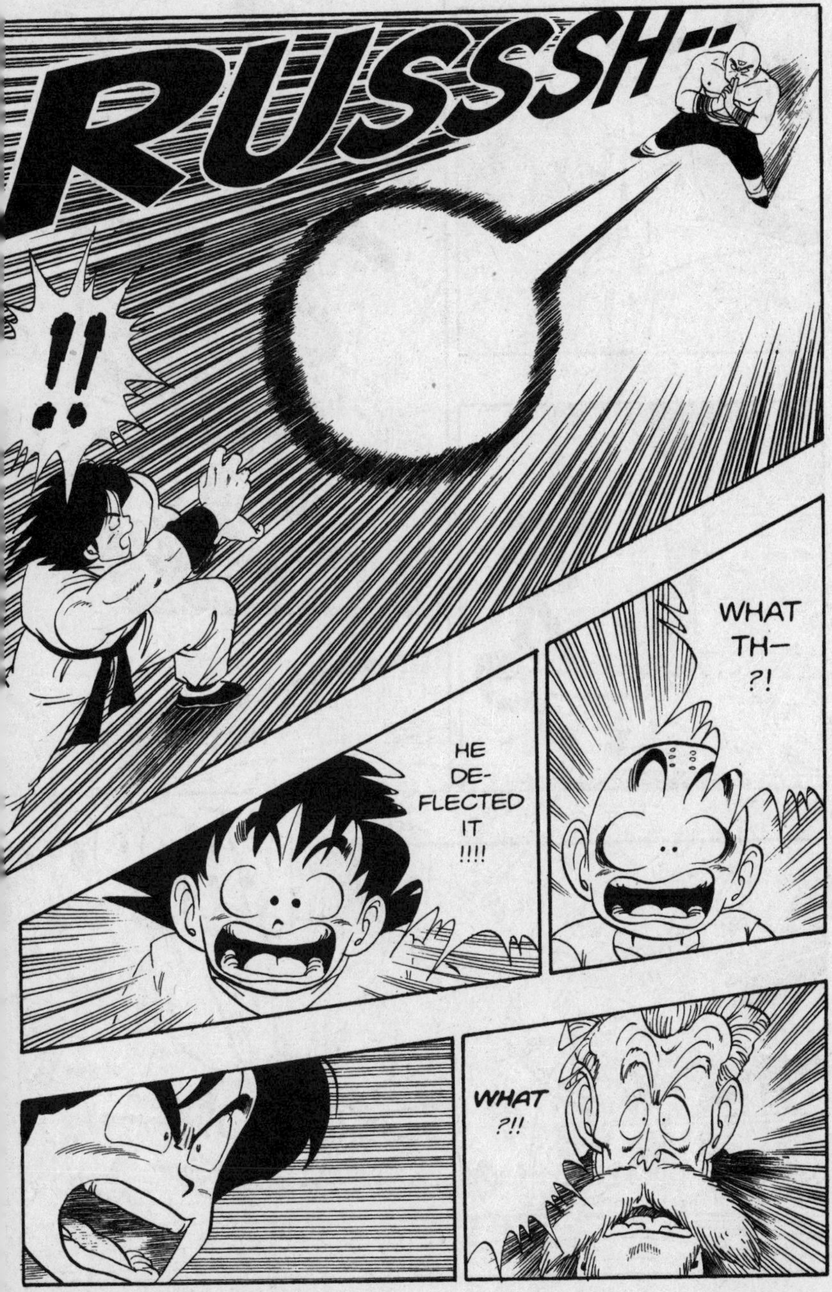
RUSSSH-
!!
WHAT TH— ?!
HE DE-FLECTED IT !!!!
WHAT ?!!

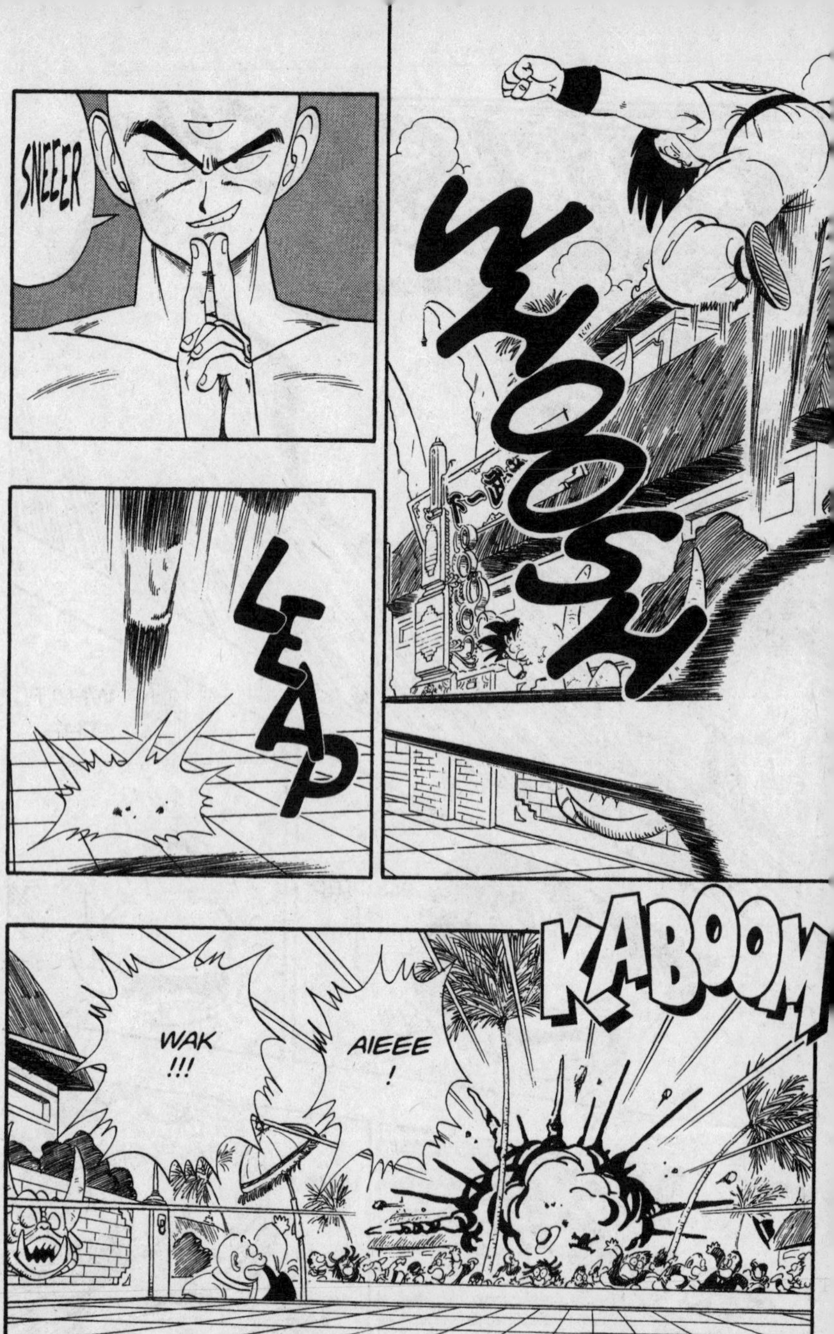
WHOOSH
SNEEER
LEAP
KABOOM
AIEEE !
WAK !!!

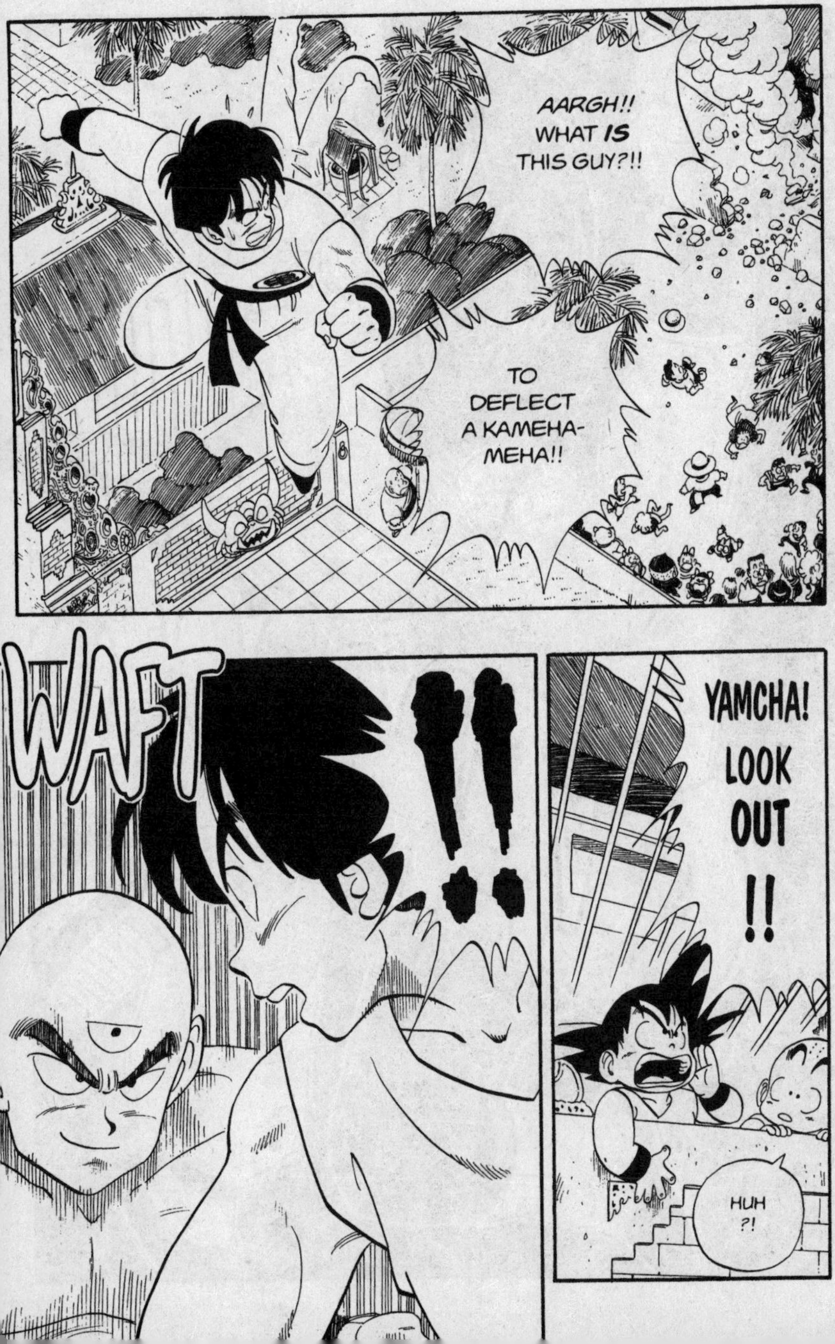
AARGH!! WHAT *IS* THIS GUY?!!
TO DEFLECT A KAMEHA-MEHA!!
YAMCHA! LOOK OUT !!
HUH ?!
WAFT
!!

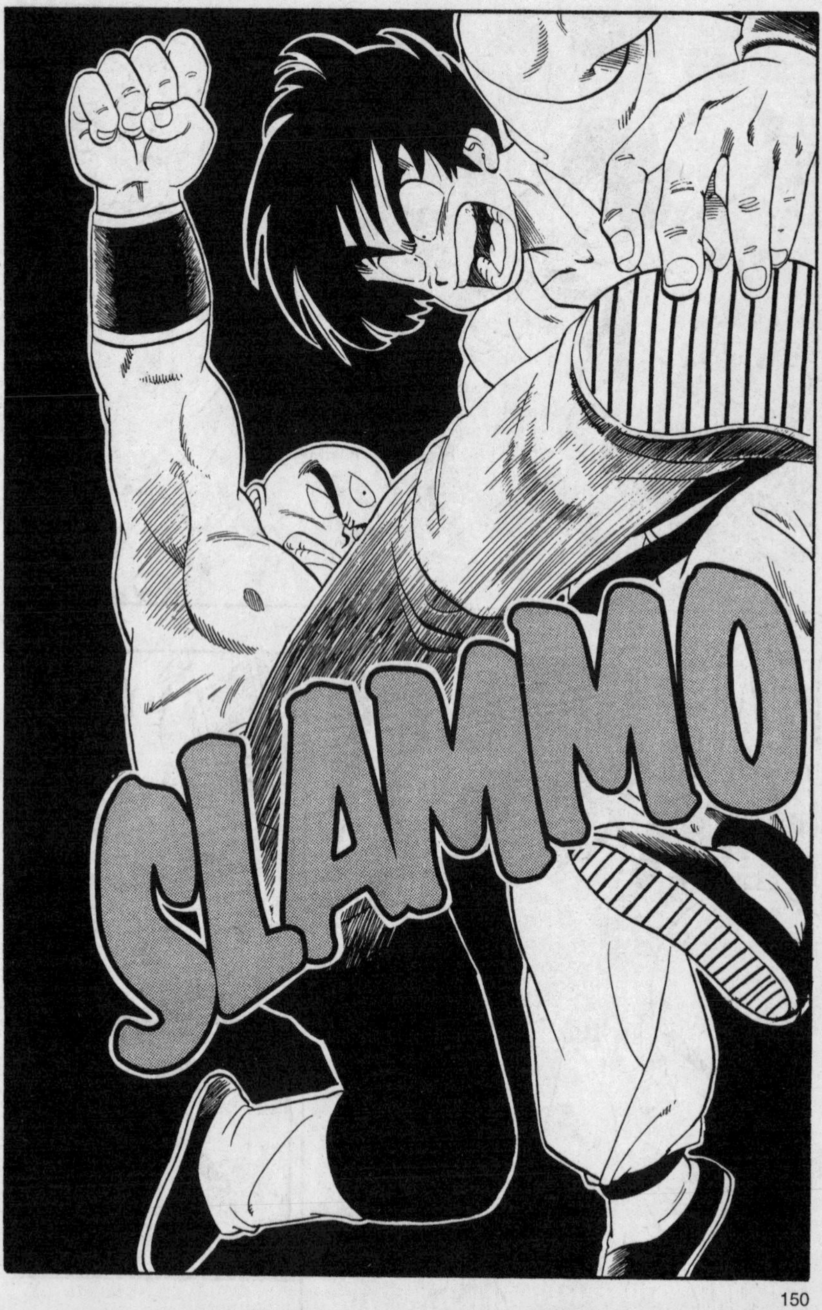
SLAMMO

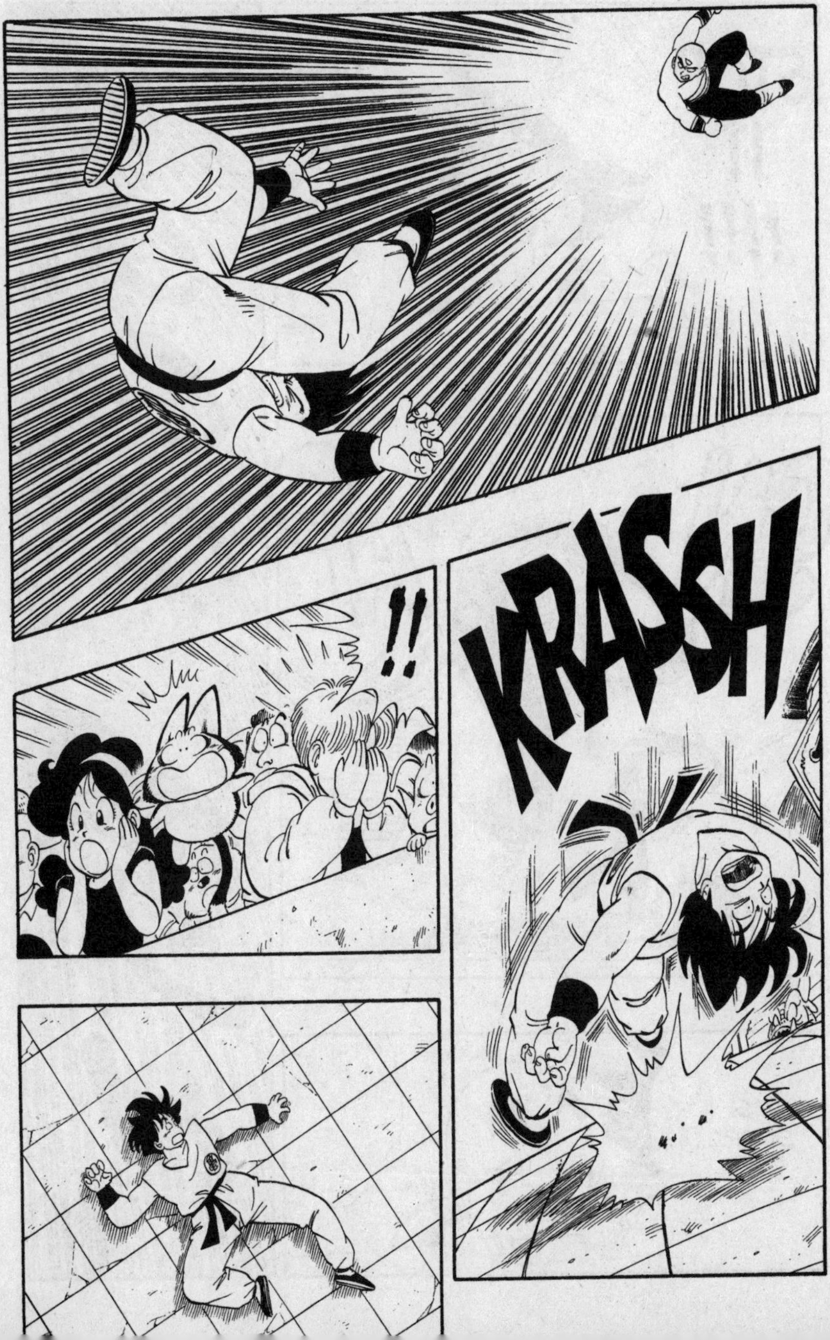
KRASSH
!!

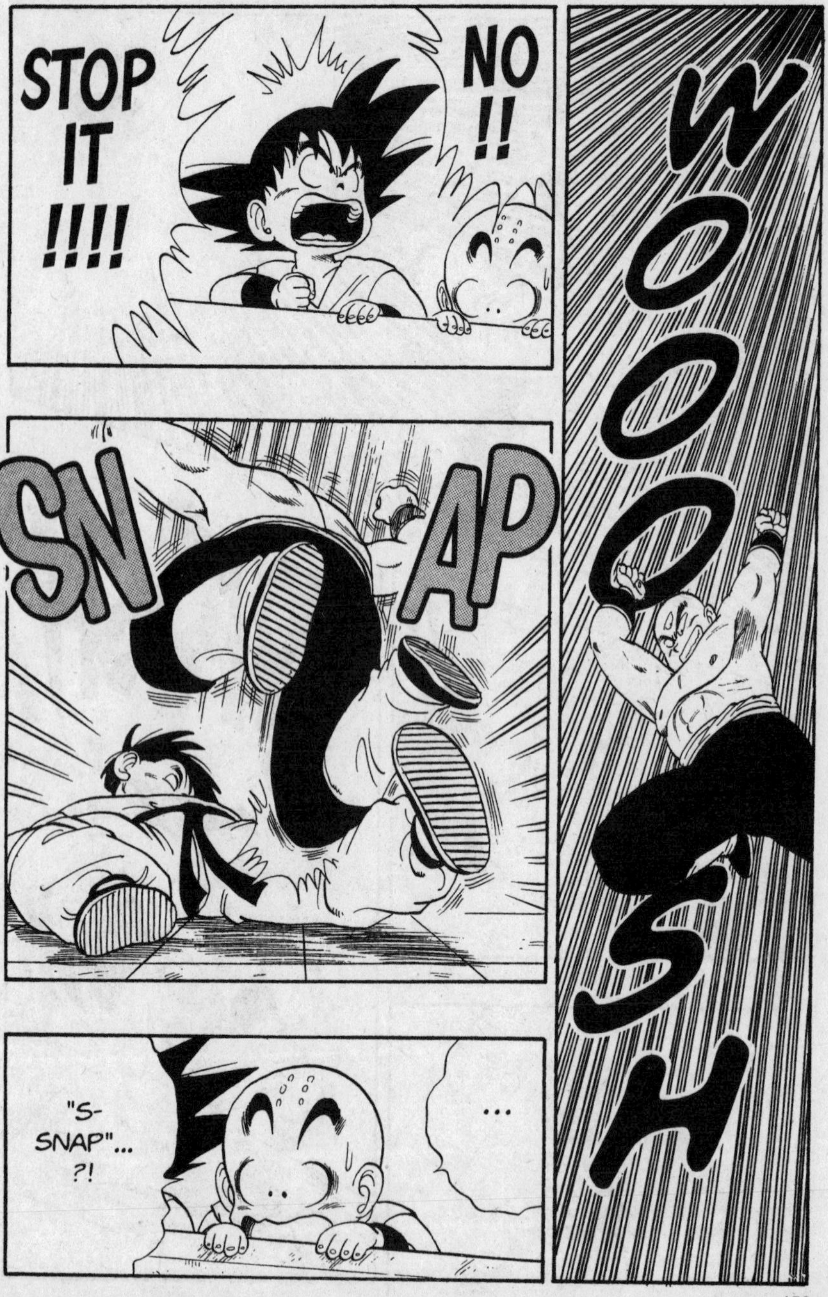
WOOOSH
NO !!
STOP IT !!!!
SNAP
...
"S-SNAP"... ?!

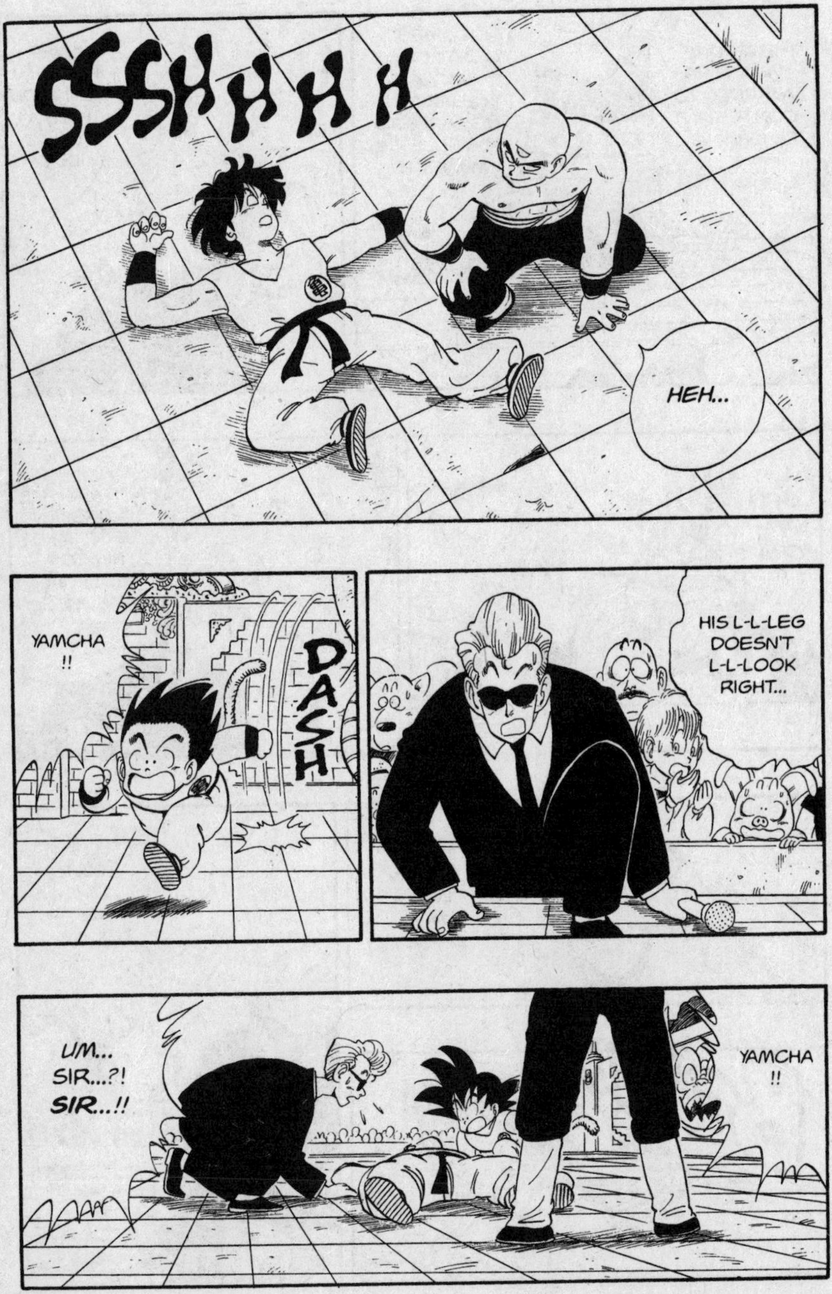
SSSHHHH
HEH...
HIS L-L-LEG DOESN'T L-L-LOOK RIGHT...
YAMCHA !!
DASH
YAMCHA !!
UM... SIR...?! SIR...!!

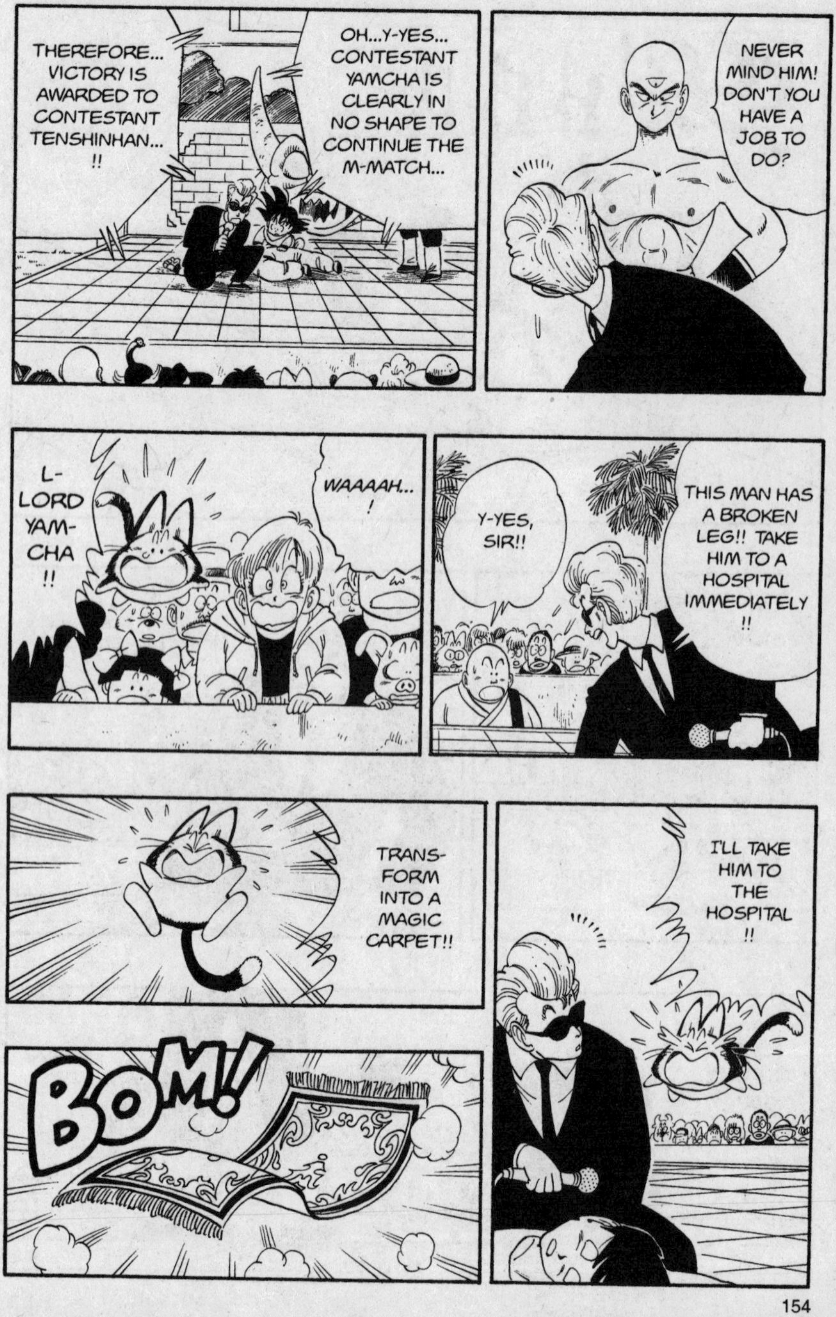
NEVER MIND HIM! DON'T YOU HAVE A JOB TO DO?
OH...Y-YES... CONTESTANT YAMCHA IS CLEARLY IN NO SHAPE TO CONTINUE THE M-MATCH...
THEREFORE... VICTORY IS AWARDED TO CONTESTANT TENSHINHAN... !!
THIS MAN HAS A BROKEN LEG!! TAKE HIM TO A HOSPITAL IMMEDIATELY !!
Y-YES, SIR!!
WAAAAH... !
L-LORD YAMCHA !!
I'LL TAKE HIM TO THE HOSPITAL !!
TRANSFORM INTO A MAGIC CARPET!!
BOM!

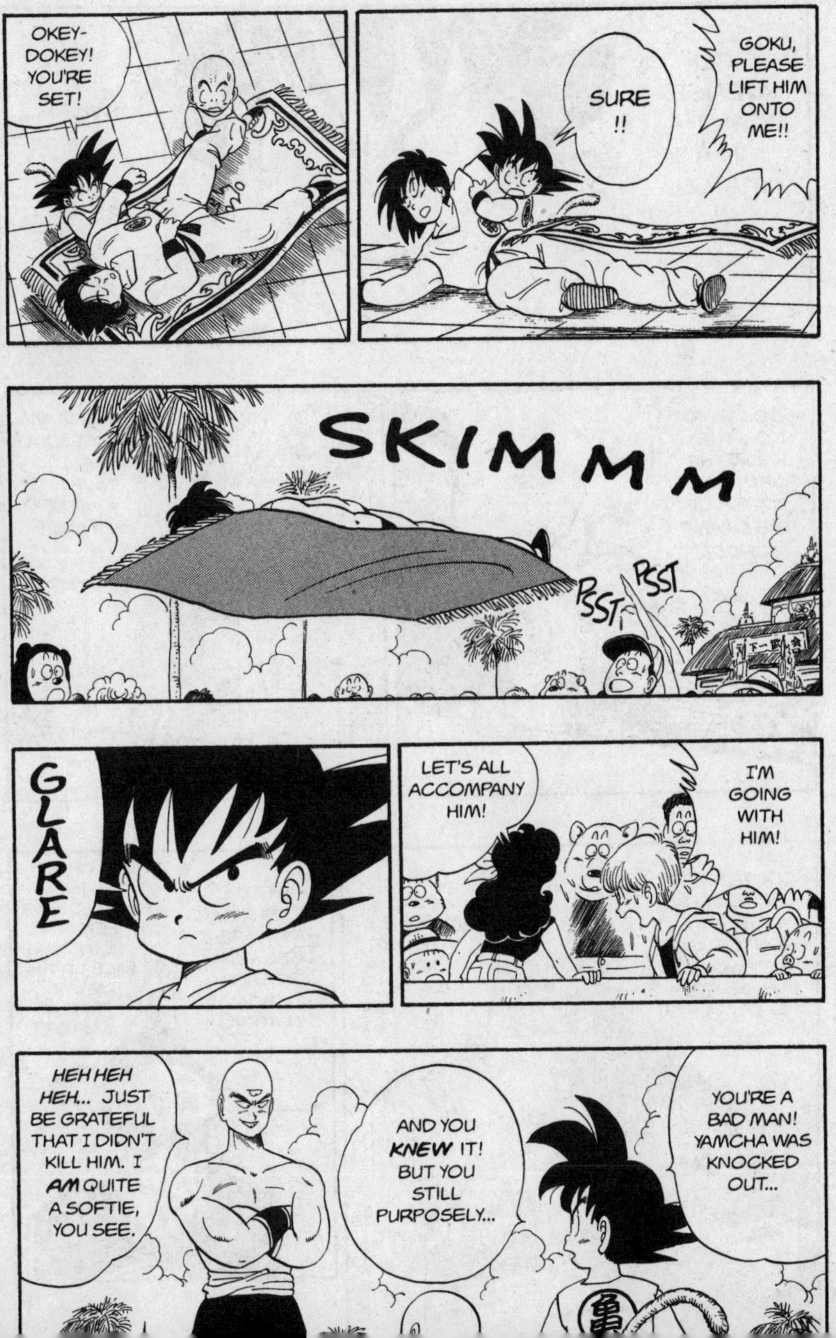
GOKU, PLEASE LIFT HIM ONTO ME!!
SURE!!
OKEY-DOKEY! YOU'RE SET!
SKIMMMM
PSST
PSST
I'M GOING WITH HIM!
LET'S ALL ACCOMPANY HIM!
GLARE
YOU'RE A BAD MAN! YAMCHA WAS KNOCKED OUT...
AND YOU *KNEW* IT! BUT YOU STILL PURPOSELY...
HEH HEH HEH... JUST BE GRATEFUL THAT I DIDN'T KILL HIM. I *AM* QUITE A SOFTIE, YOU SEE.

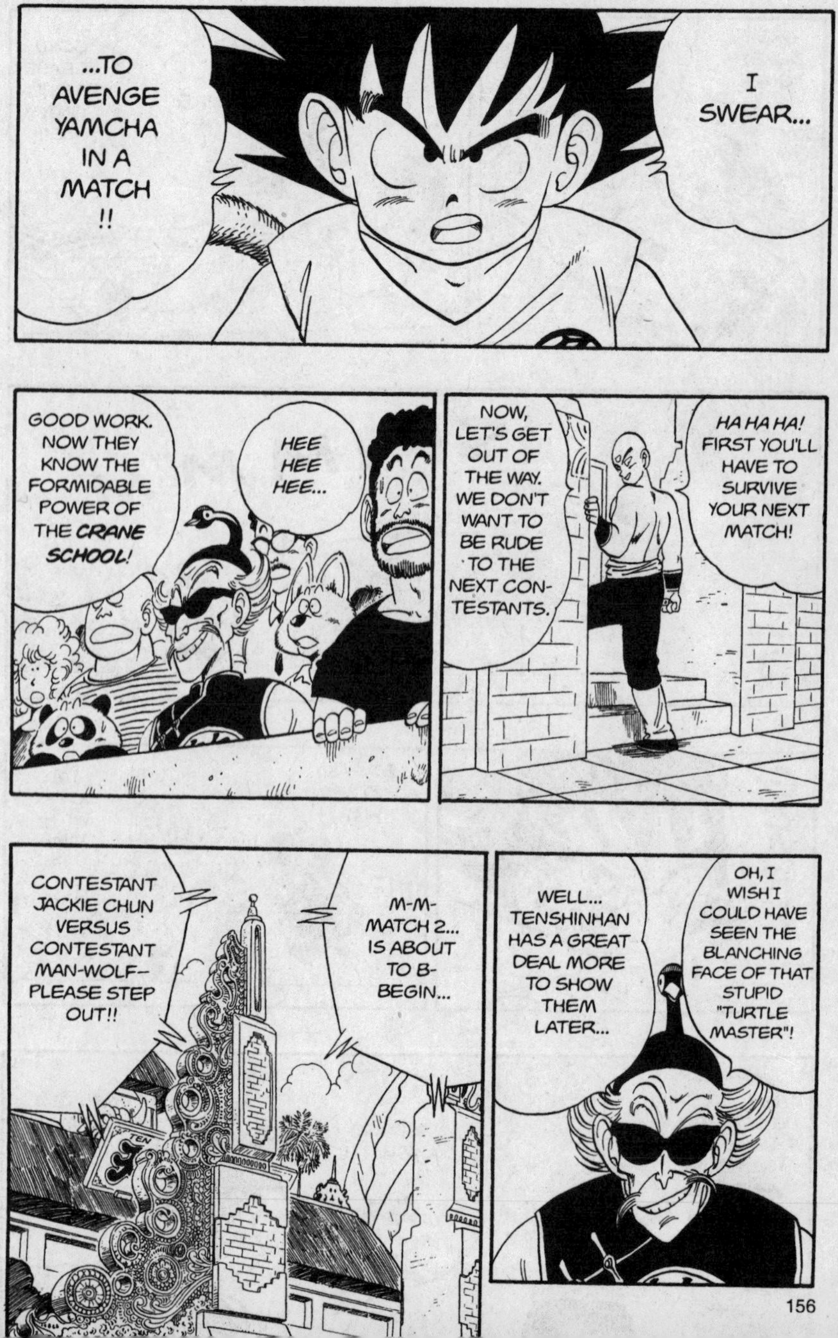

I SWEAR...
...TO AVENGE YAMCHA IN A MATCH !!
HA HA HA! FIRST YOU'LL HAVE TO SURVIVE YOUR NEXT MATCH!
NOW, LET'S GET OUT OF THE WAY. WE DON'T WANT TO BE RUDE TO THE NEXT CONTESTANTS.
HEE HEE HEE...
GOOD WORK. NOW THEY KNOW THE FORMIDABLE POWER OF THE CRANE SCHOOL!
OH, I WISH I COULD HAVE SEEN THE BLANCHING FACE OF THAT STUPID "TURTLE MASTER"!
WELL... TENSHINHAN HAS A GREAT DEAL MORE TO SHOW THEM LATER...
M-M-MATCH 2... IS ABOUT TO B-BEGIN...
CONTESTANT JACKIE CHUN VERSUS CONTESTANT MAN-WOLF-PLEASE STEP OUT!!

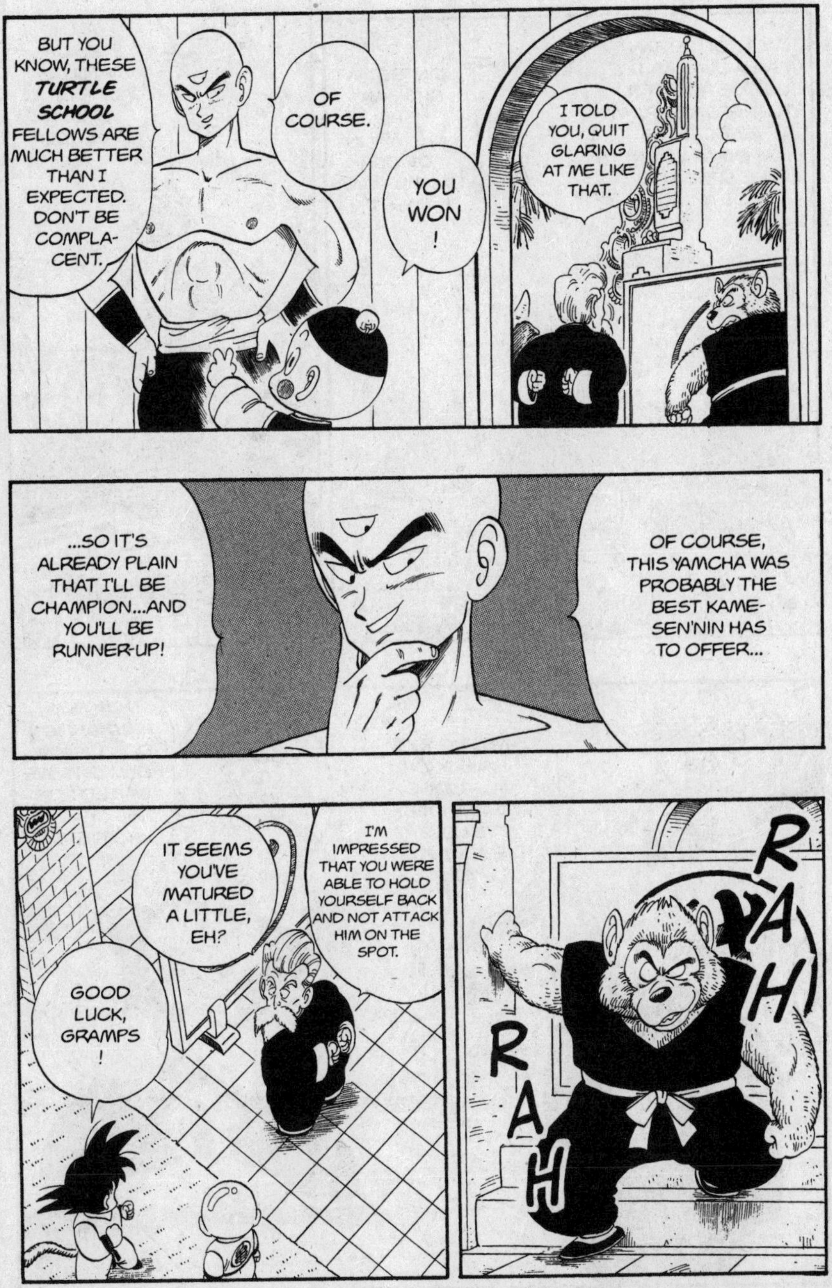
I TOLD YOU, QUIT GLARING AT ME LIKE THAT.
YOU WON!
OF COURSE.
BUT YOU KNOW, THESE **TURTLE SCHOOL** FELLOWS ARE MUCH BETTER THAN I EXPECTED. DON'T BE COMPLACENT.
OF COURSE, THIS YAMCHA WAS PROBABLY THE BEST KAME-SEN'NIN HAS TO OFFER...
...SO IT'S ALREADY PLAIN THAT I'LL BE CHAMPION...AND YOU'LL BE RUNNER-UP!
RAH
RAH
I'M IMPRESSED THAT YOU WERE ABLE TO HOLD YOURSELF BACK AND NOT ATTACK HIM ON THE SPOT.
IT SEEMS YOU'VE MATURED A LITTLE, EH?
GOOD LUCK, GRAMPS!

Tale 119
The Full Moon Grudge

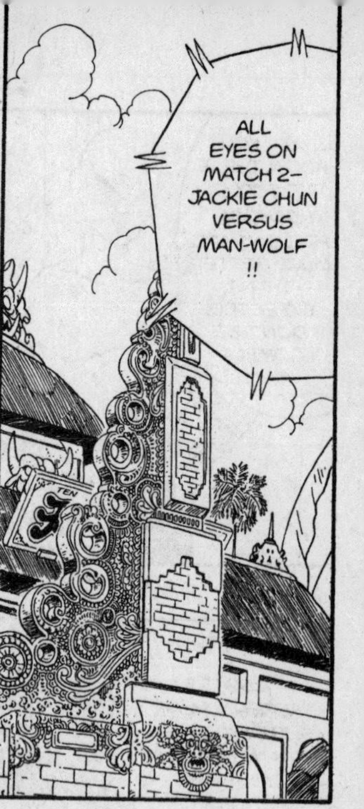
ALL EYES ON MATCH 2—JACKIE CHUN VERSUS MAN-WOLF!!

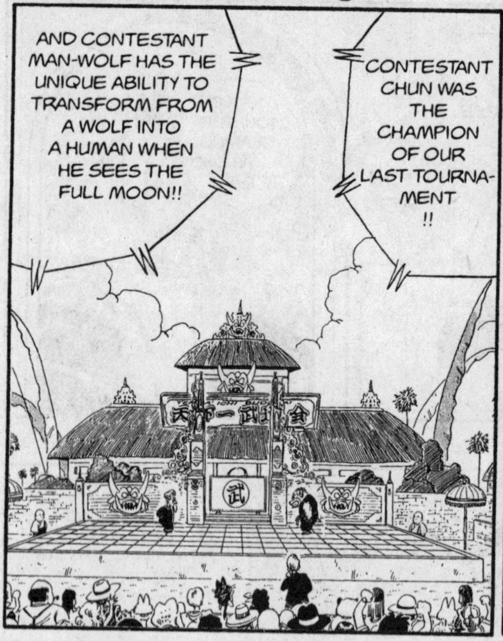
CONTESTANT CHUN WAS THE CHAMPION OF OUR LAST TOURNAMENT!!
AND CONTESTANT MAN-WOLF HAS THE UNIQUE ABILITY TO TRANSFORM FROM A WOLF INTO A HUMAN WHEN HE SEES THE FULL MOON!!

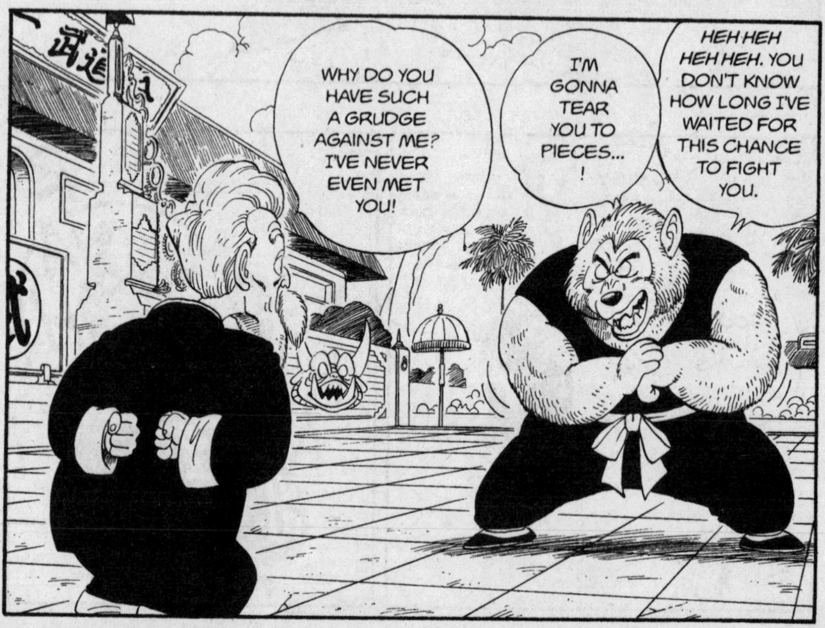
HEH HEH HEH HEH. YOU DON'T KNOW HOW LONG I'VE WAITED FOR THIS CHANCE TO FIGHT YOU.
I'M GONNA TEAR YOU TO PIECES...!
WHY DO YOU HAVE SUCH A GRUDGE AGAINST ME? I'VE NEVER EVEN MET YOU!

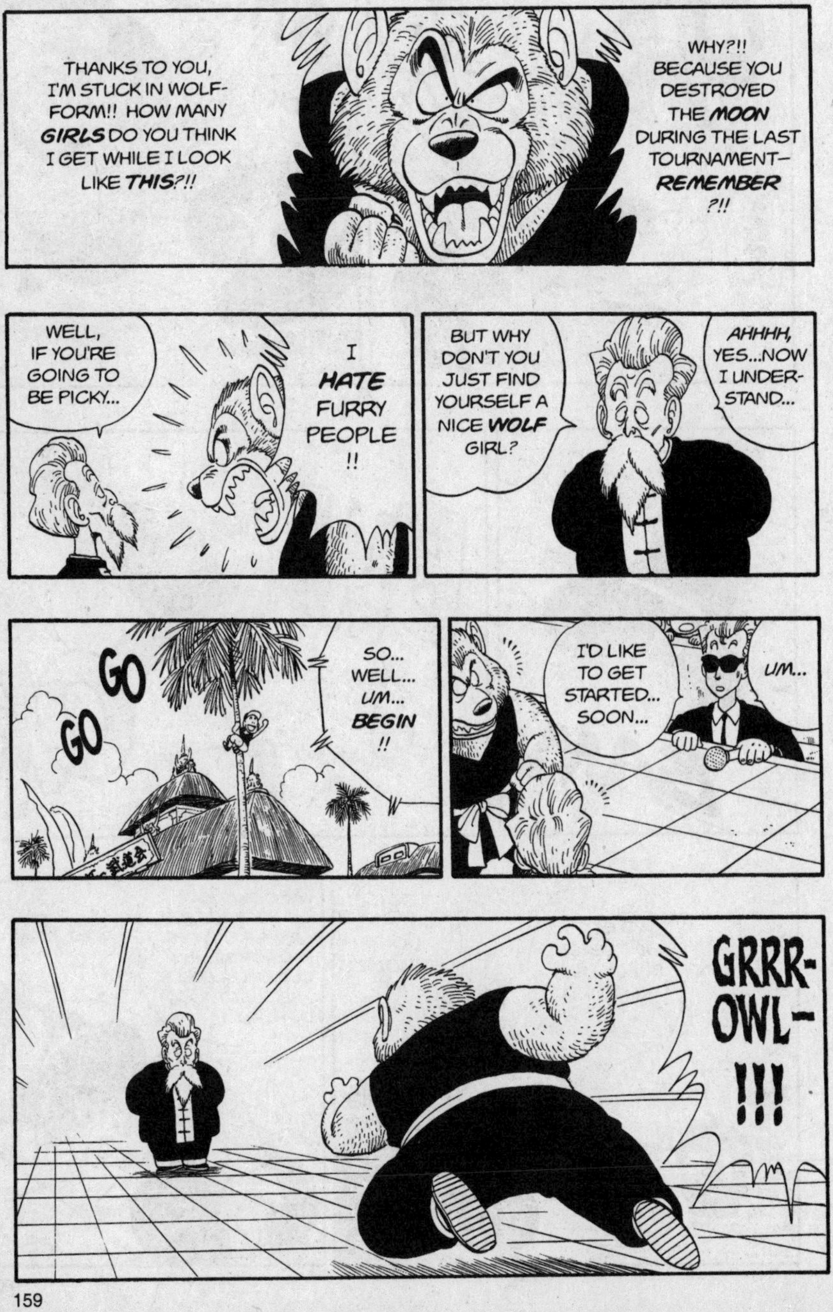
WHY?!! BECAUSE YOU DESTROYED THE ***MOON*** DURING THE LAST TOURNAMENT—***REMEMBER***?!!
THANKS TO YOU, I'M STUCK IN WOLF-FORM!! HOW MANY ***GIRLS*** DO YOU THINK I GET WHILE I LOOK LIKE ***THIS***?!!
AHHHH, YES...NOW I UNDER-STAND...
BUT WHY DON'T YOU JUST FIND YOURSELF A NICE ***WOLF*** GIRL?
I ***HATE*** FURRY PEOPLE!!
WELL, IF YOU'RE GOING TO BE PICKY...
UM...
I'D LIKE TO GET STARTED... SOON...
SO... WELL... UM... ***BEGIN***!!
GO
GO
GRRR-OWL-!!!

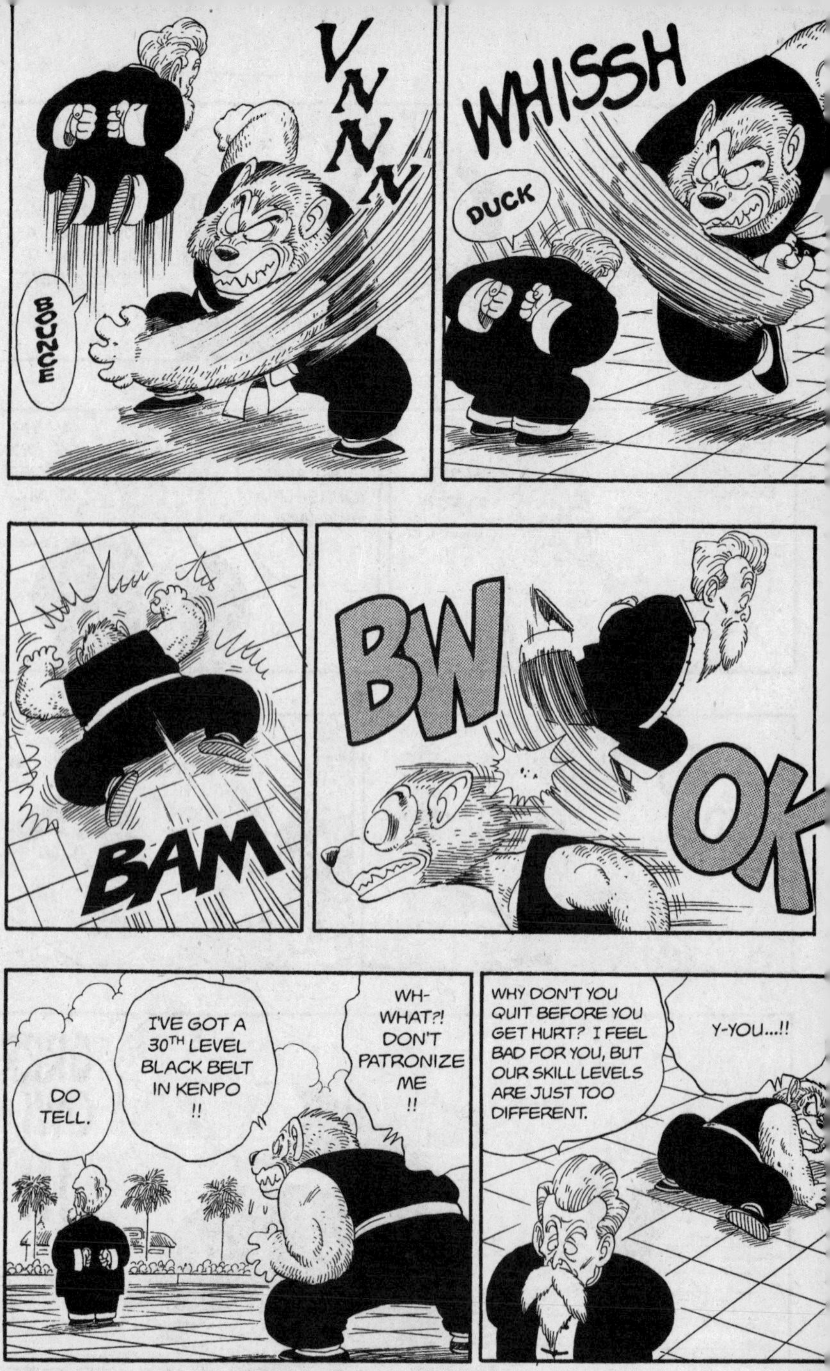
WHISSH
DUCK
VNNN
BOUNCE
BWOK
BAM
Y-YOU...!!
WHY DON'T YOU QUIT BEFORE YOU GET HURT? I FEEL BAD FOR YOU, BUT OUR SKILL LEVELS ARE JUST TOO DIFFERENT.
WH- WHAT?! DON'T PATRONIZE ME !!
I'VE GOT A 30TH LEVEL BLACK BELT IN KENPO !!
DO TELL.

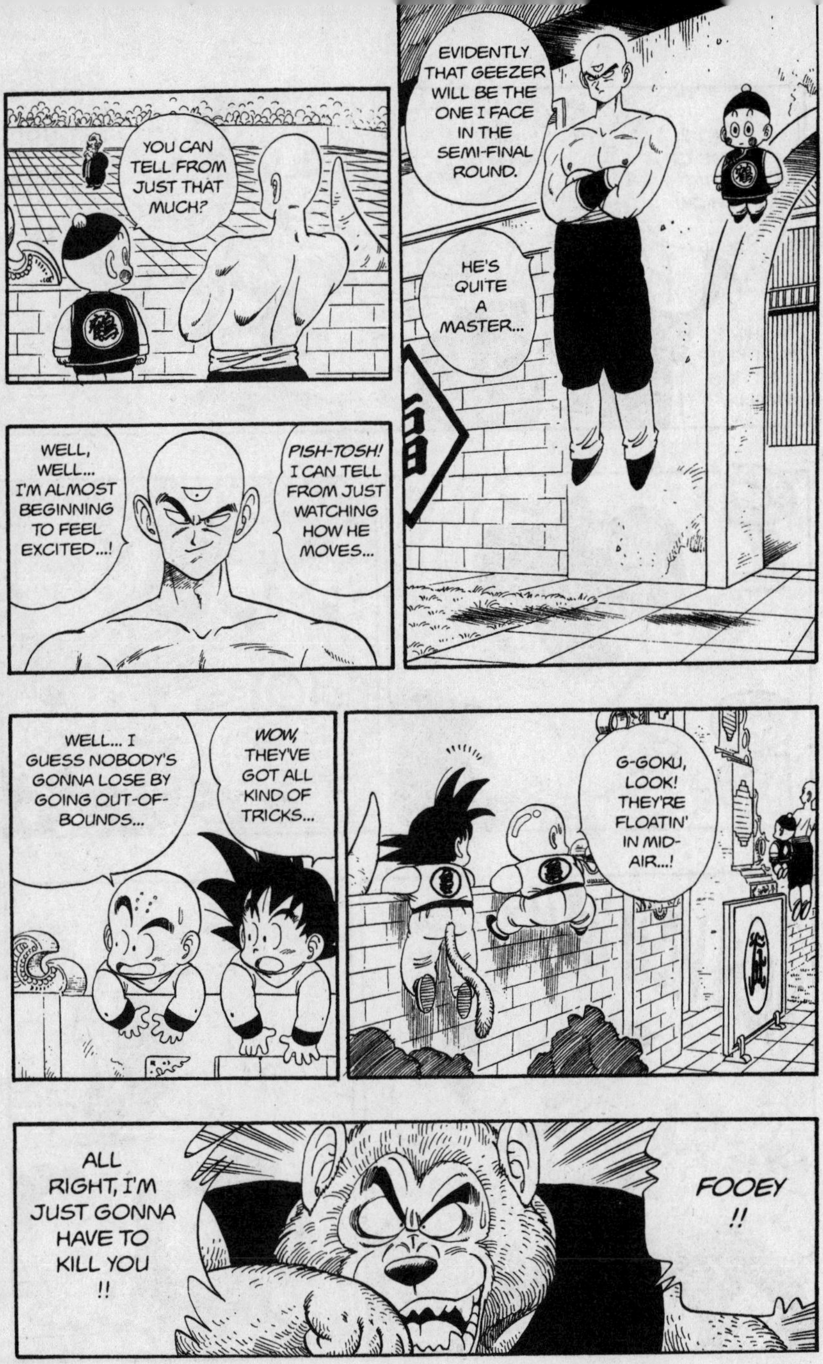
EVIDENTLY THAT GEEZER WILL BE THE ONE I FACE IN THE SEMI-FINAL ROUND.
HE'S QUITE A MASTER...
YOU CAN TELL FROM JUST THAT MUCH?
PISH-TOSH! I CAN TELL FROM JUST WATCHING HOW HE MOVES...
WELL, WELL... I'M ALMOST BEGINNING TO FEEL EXCITED...!
G-GOKU, LOOK! THEY'RE FLOATIN' IN MID-AIR...!
WOW, THEY'VE GOT ALL KIND OF TRICKS...
WELL... I GUESS NOBODY'S GONNA LOSE BY GOING OUT-OF-BOUNDS...
FOOEY !!
ALL RIGHT, I'M JUST GONNA HAVE TO KILL YOU !!

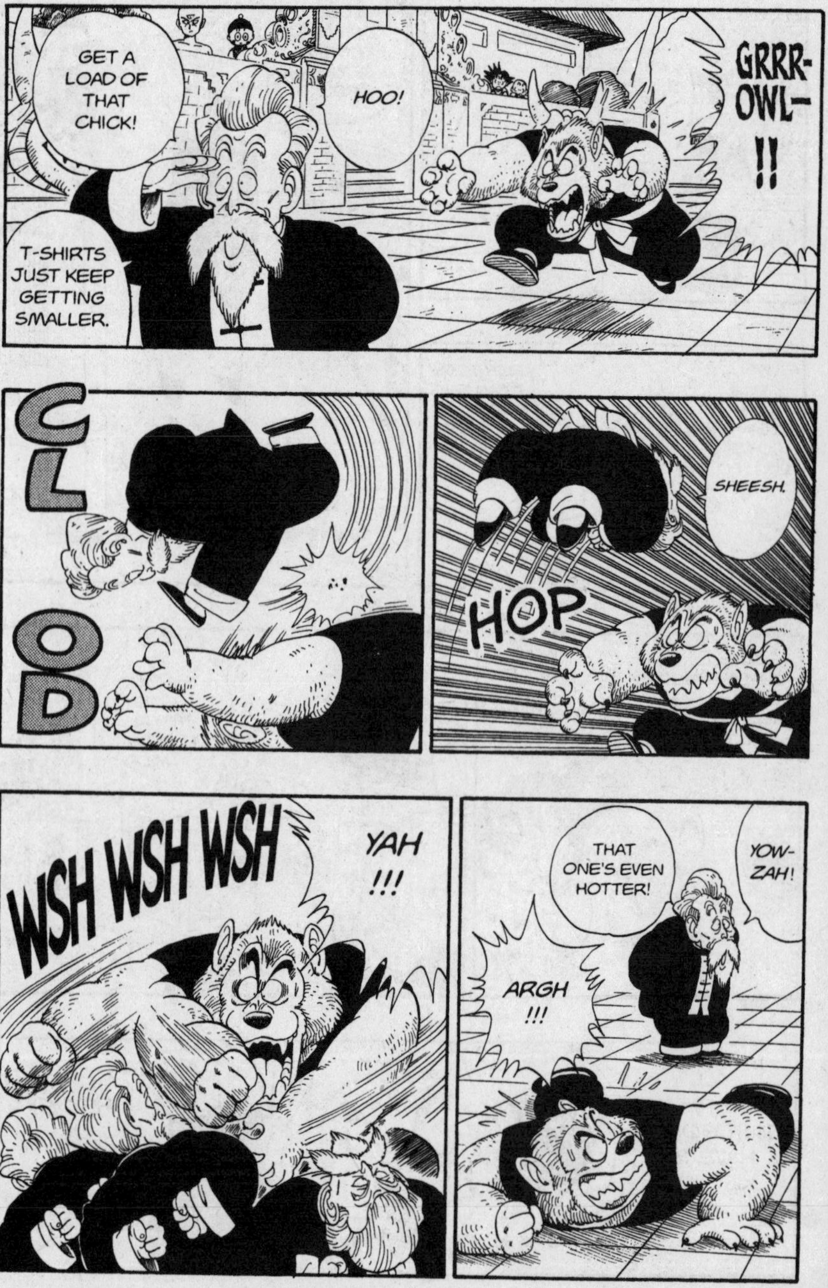
GRRR-OWL-!!
HOO!
GET A LOAD OF THAT CHICK!
T-SHIRTS JUST KEEP GETTING SMALLER.
SHEESH.
HOP
CLOD
YOW-ZAH!
THAT ONE'S EVEN HOTTER!
ARGH !!!
YAH !!!
WSH WSH WSH

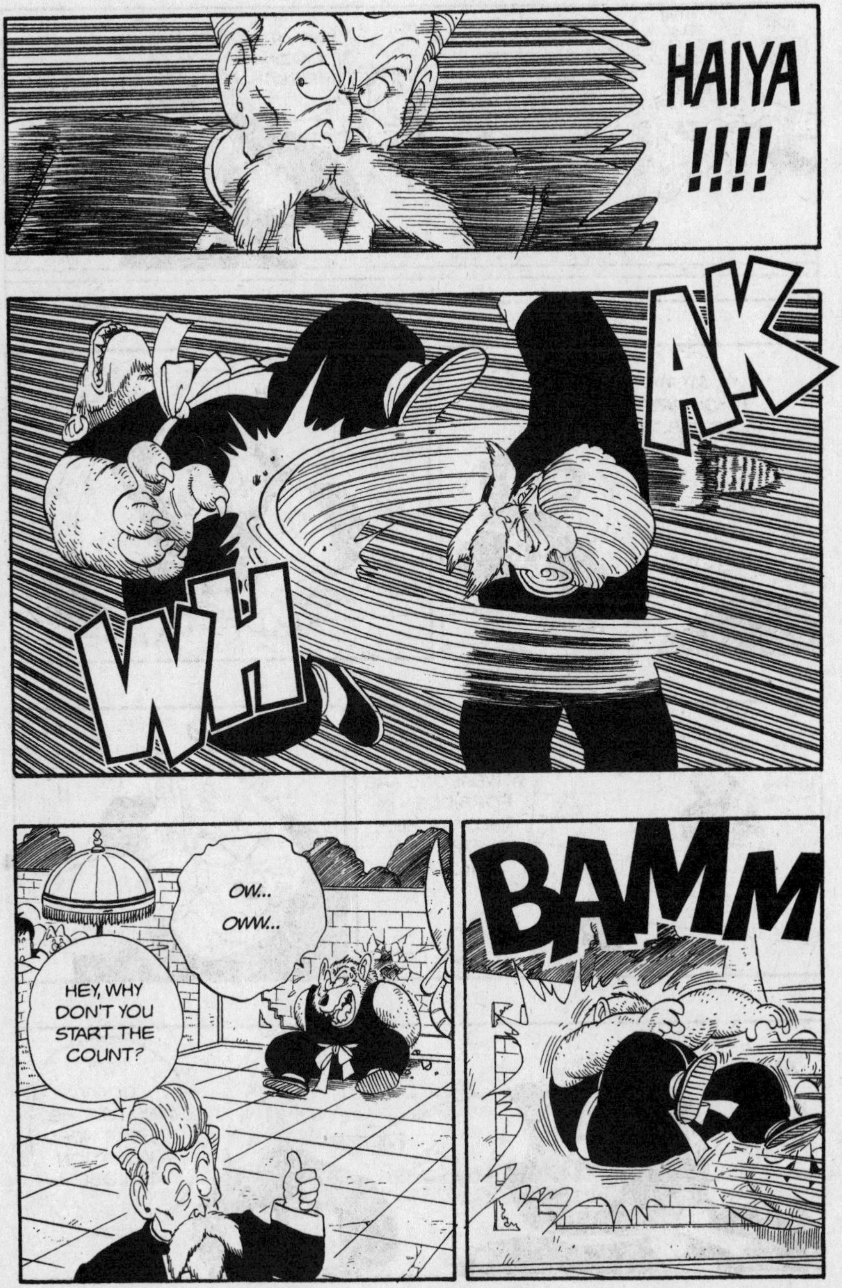

HAIYA !!!!
AK
WH
BAMM
OW... OWW...
HEY, WHY DON'T YOU START THE COUNT?

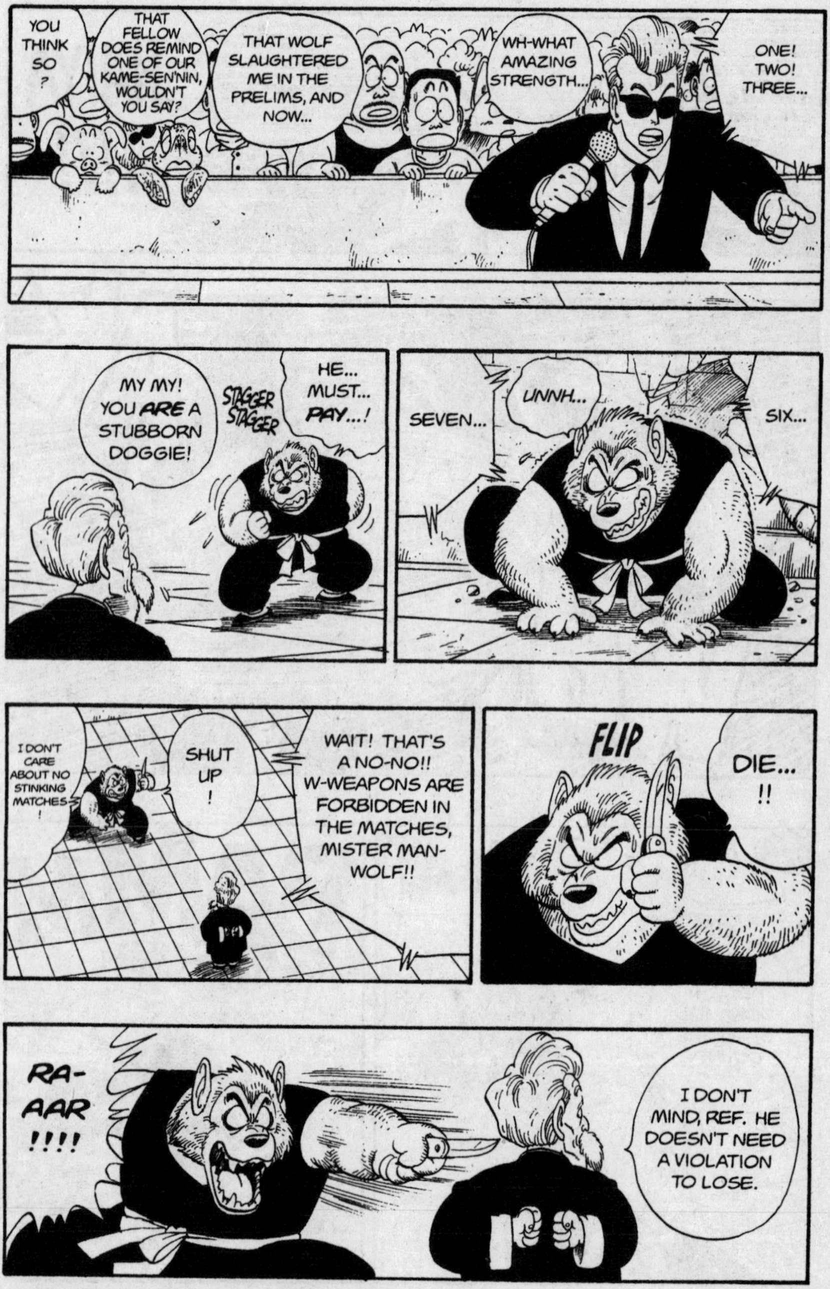
ONE! TWO! THREE...
WH-WHAT AMAZING STRENGTH...
THAT WOLF SLAUGHTERED ME IN THE PRELIMS, AND NOW...
THAT FELLOW DOES REMIND ONE OF OUR KAME-SEN'NIN, WOULDN'T YOU SAY?
YOU THINK SO?
SIX...
UNNH...
SEVEN...
HE... MUST... PAY...!
STAGGER STAGGER
MY MY! YOU ARE A STUBBORN DOGGIE!
DIE...!!
FLIP
WAIT! THAT'S A NO-NO!! W-WEAPONS ARE FORBIDDEN IN THE MATCHES, MISTER MAN-WOLF!!
SHUT UP!
I DON'T CARE ABOUT NO STINKING MATCHES!
I DON'T MIND, REF. HE DOESN'T NEED A VIOLATION TO LOSE.
RA-AAR!!!!

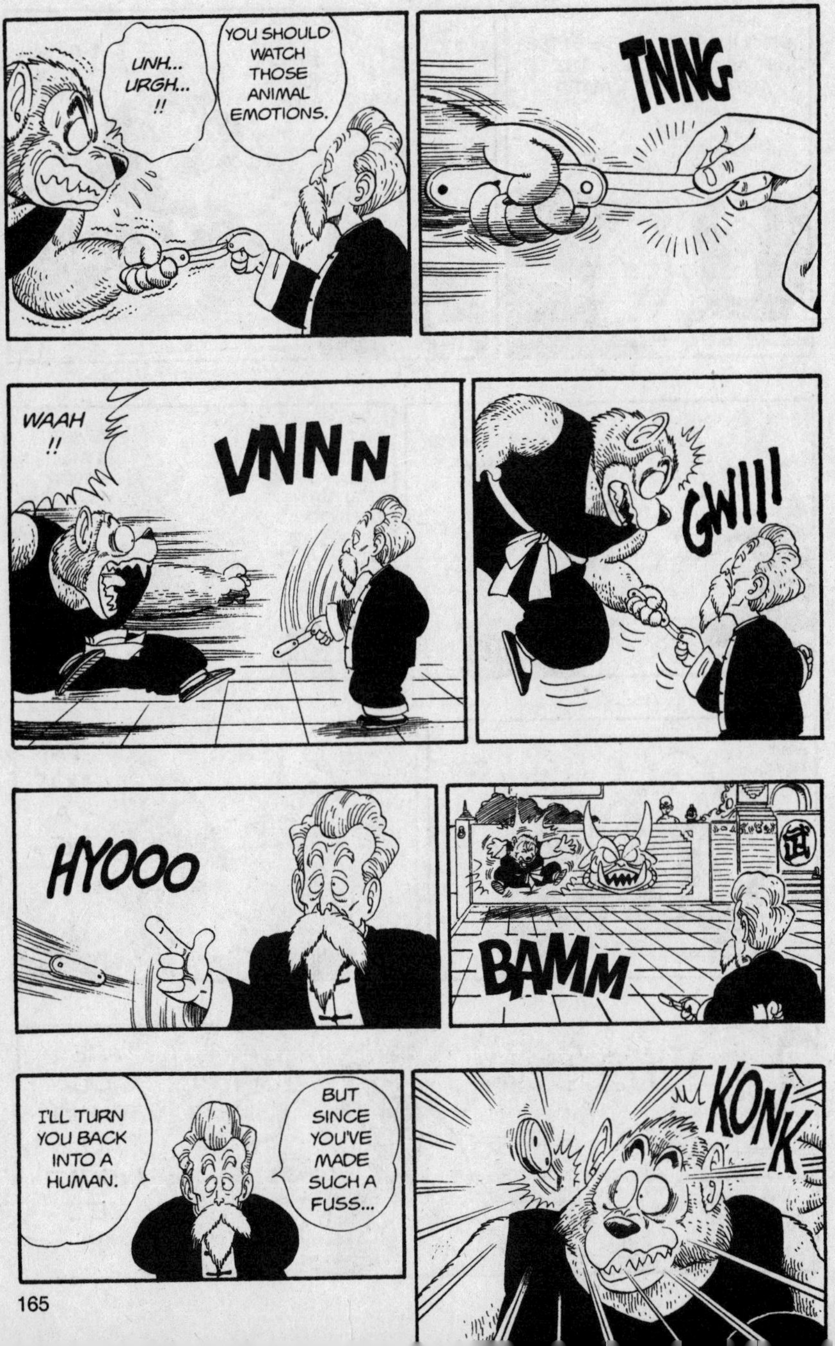
TNNG
YOU SHOULD WATCH THOSE ANIMAL EMOTIONS.
UNH... URGH... !!
GWIII
VNNN
WAAH !!
BAMM
HYOOO
KONK
BUT SINCE YOU'VE MADE SUCH A FUSS...
I'LL TURN YOU BACK INTO A HUMAN.

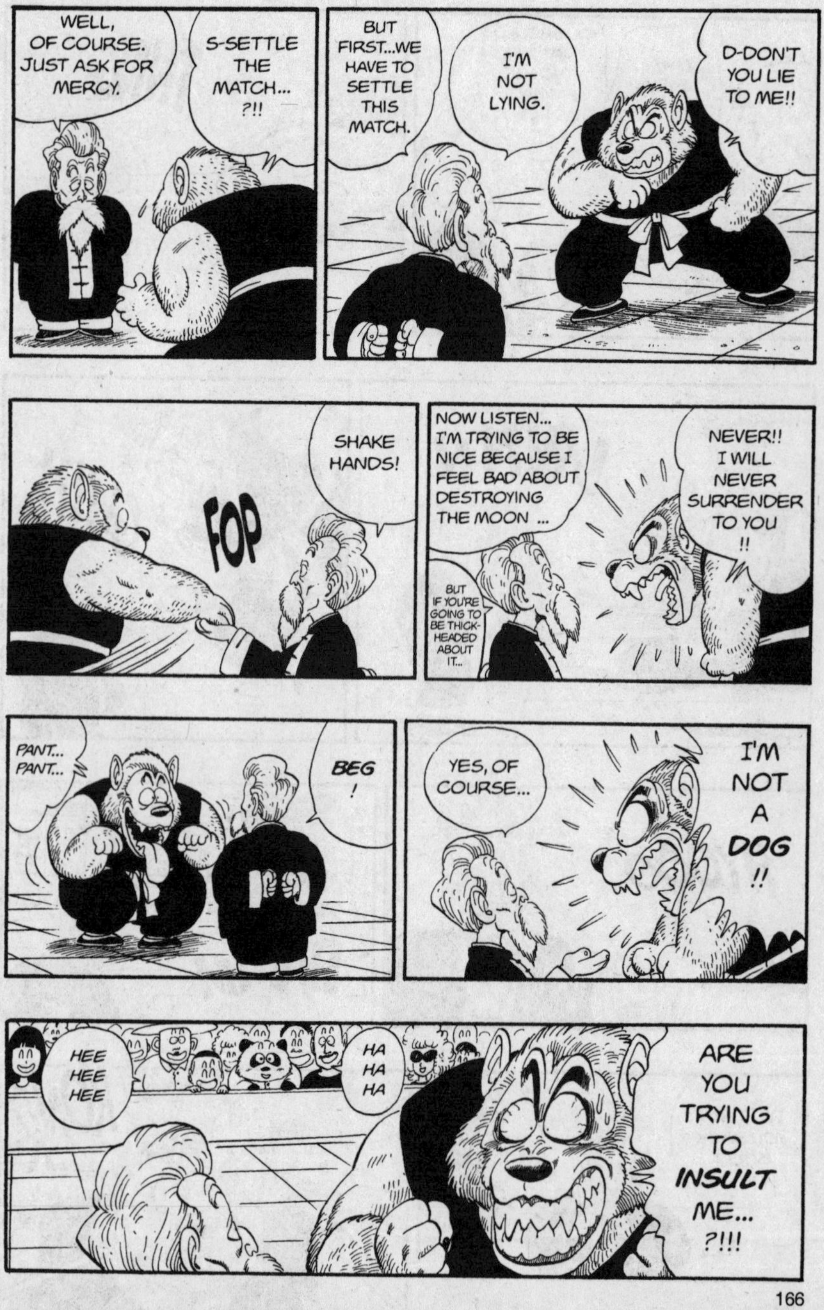
D-DON'T YOU LIE TO ME!!
I'M NOT LYING.
BUT FIRST...WE HAVE TO SETTLE THIS MATCH.
S-SETTLE THE MATCH... ?!!
WELL, OF COURSE. JUST ASK FOR MERCY.
NEVER!! I WILL NEVER SURRENDER TO YOU !!
NOW LISTEN... I'M TRYING TO BE NICE BECAUSE I FEEL BAD ABOUT DESTROYING THE MOON ...
BUT IF YOU'RE GOING TO BE THICK-HEADED ABOUT IT...
SHAKE HANDS!
FOP
I'M NOT A DOG !!
YES, OF COURSE...
BEG !
PANT... PANT...
ARE YOU TRYING TO INSULT ME... ?!!!
HA HA HA
HEE HEE HEE

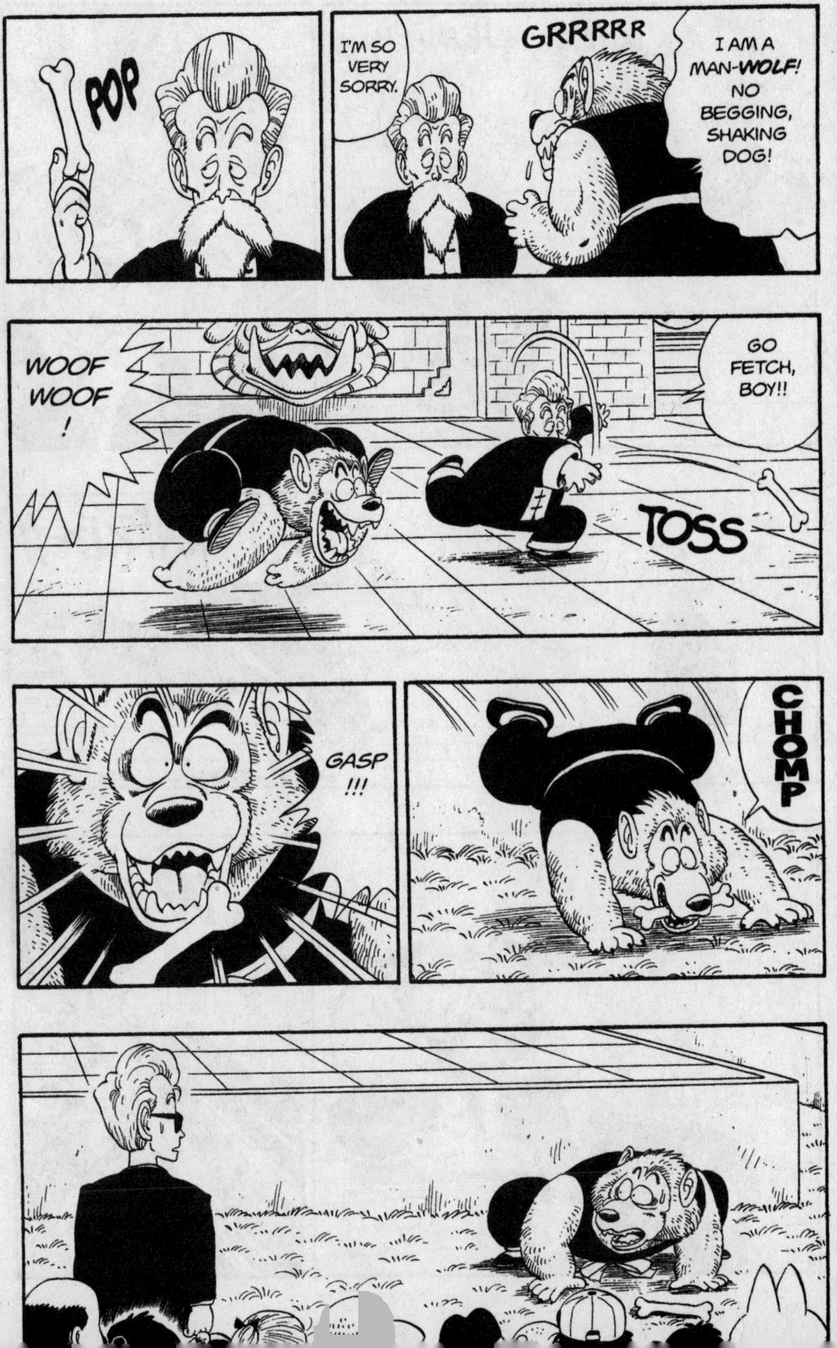
I AM A MAN-WOLF! NO BEGGING, SHAKING DOG!
GRRRRR
I'M SO VERY SORRY.
POP
GO FETCH, BOY!!
TOSS
WOOF WOOF!
CHOMP
GASP!!!

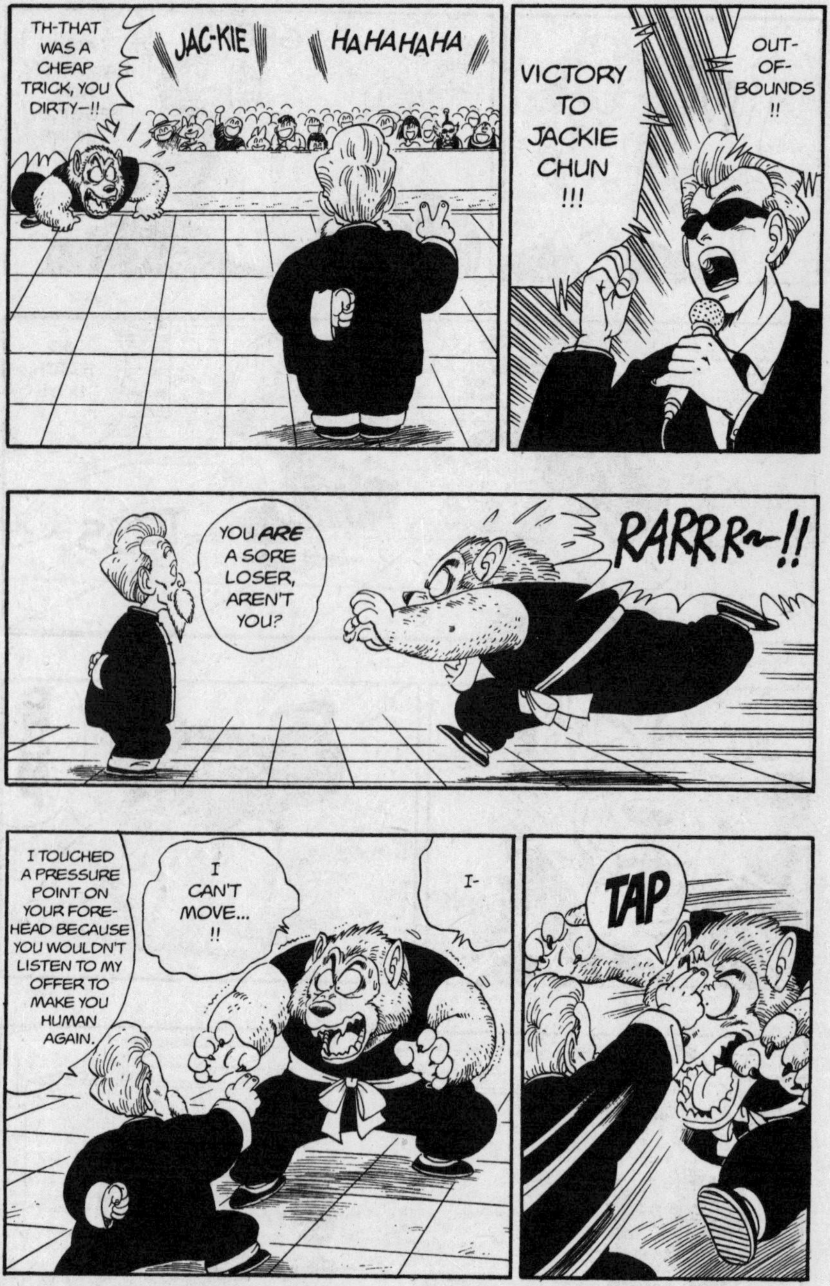
OUT-OF-BOUNDS !!
VICTORY TO JACKIE CHUN !!!
HAHAHAHA
JAC-KIE
TH-THAT WAS A CHEAP TRICK, YOU DIRTY—!!
RARRR~!!
YOU *ARE* A SORE LOSER, AREN'T YOU?
TAP
I-
I CAN'T MOVE... !!
I TOUCHED A PRESSURE POINT ON YOUR FORE-HEAD BECAUSE YOU WOULDN'T LISTEN TO MY OFFER TO MAKE YOU HUMAN AGAIN.

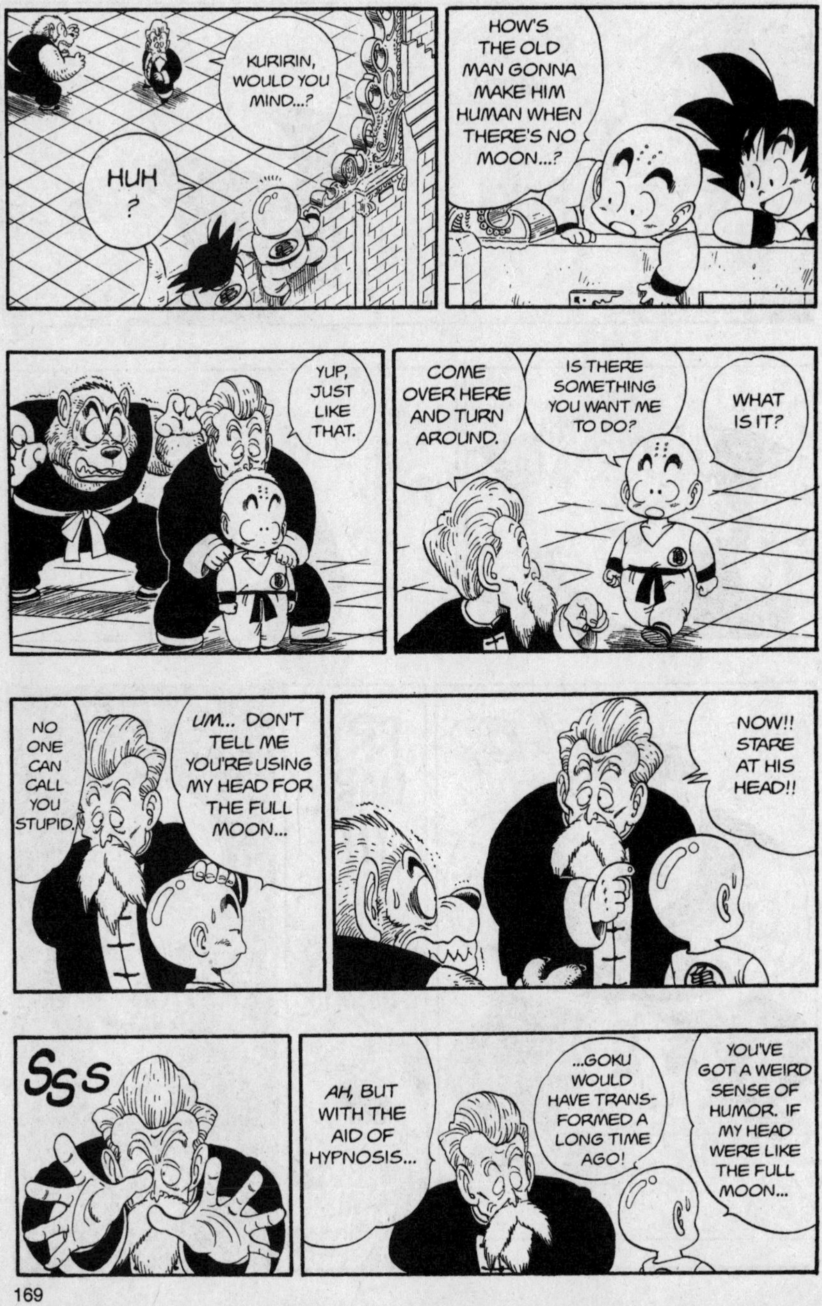
HOW'S THE OLD MAN GONNA MAKE HIM HUMAN WHEN THERE'S NO MOON...?
KURIRIN, WOULD YOU MIND...?
HUH ?
WHAT IS IT?
IS THERE SOMETHING YOU WANT ME TO DO?
COME OVER HERE AND TURN AROUND.
YUP, JUST LIKE THAT.
NOW!! STARE AT HIS HEAD!!
UM... DON'T TELL ME YOU'RE USING MY HEAD FOR THE FULL MOON...
NO ONE CAN CALL YOU STUPID.
YOU'VE GOT A WEIRD SENSE OF HUMOR. IF MY HEAD WERE LIKE THE FULL MOON...
...GOKU WOULD HAVE TRANS-FORMED A LONG TIME AGO!
AH, BUT WITH THE AID OF HYPNOSIS...
SSS

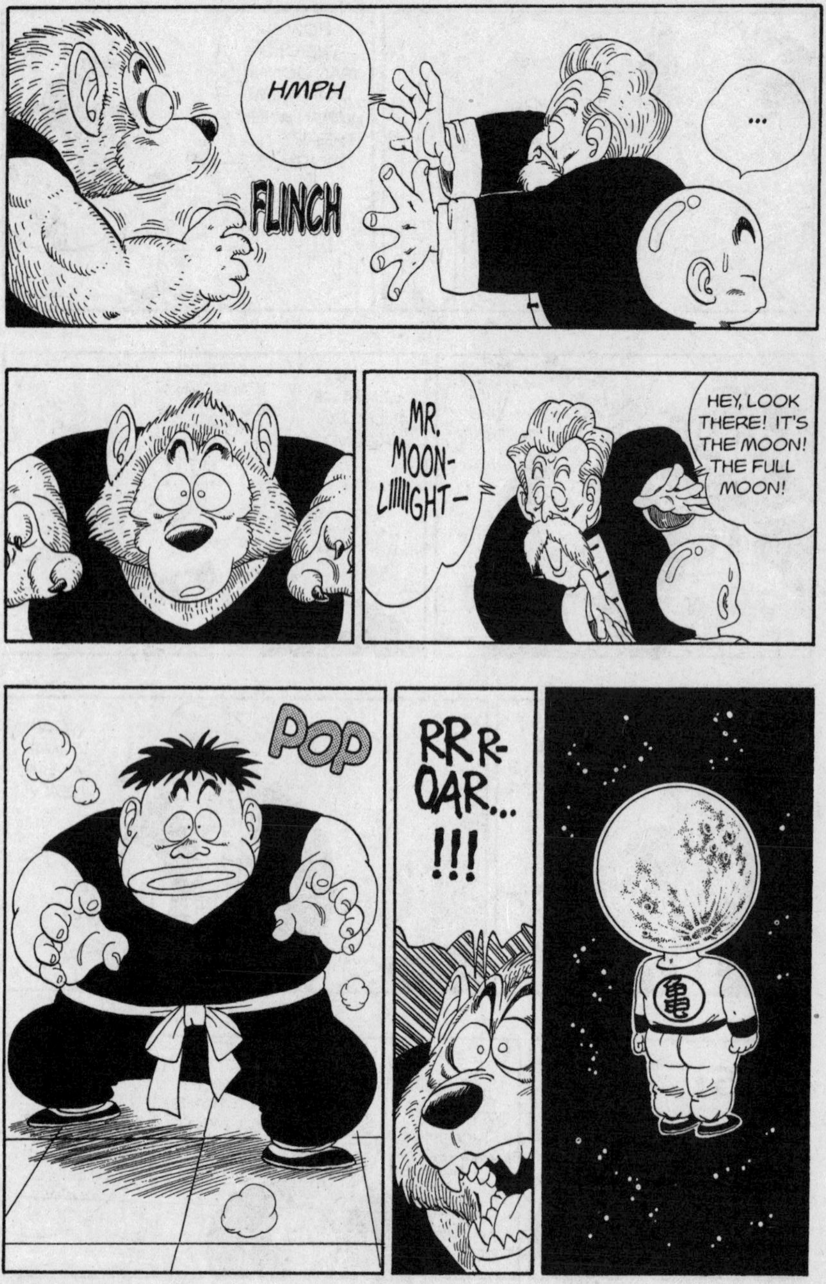
...
HMPH
FLINCH
HEY, LOOK THERE! IT'S THE MOON! THE FULL MOON!
MR. MOON-LIIIIIGHT—
RRR-OAR...
!!!
POP

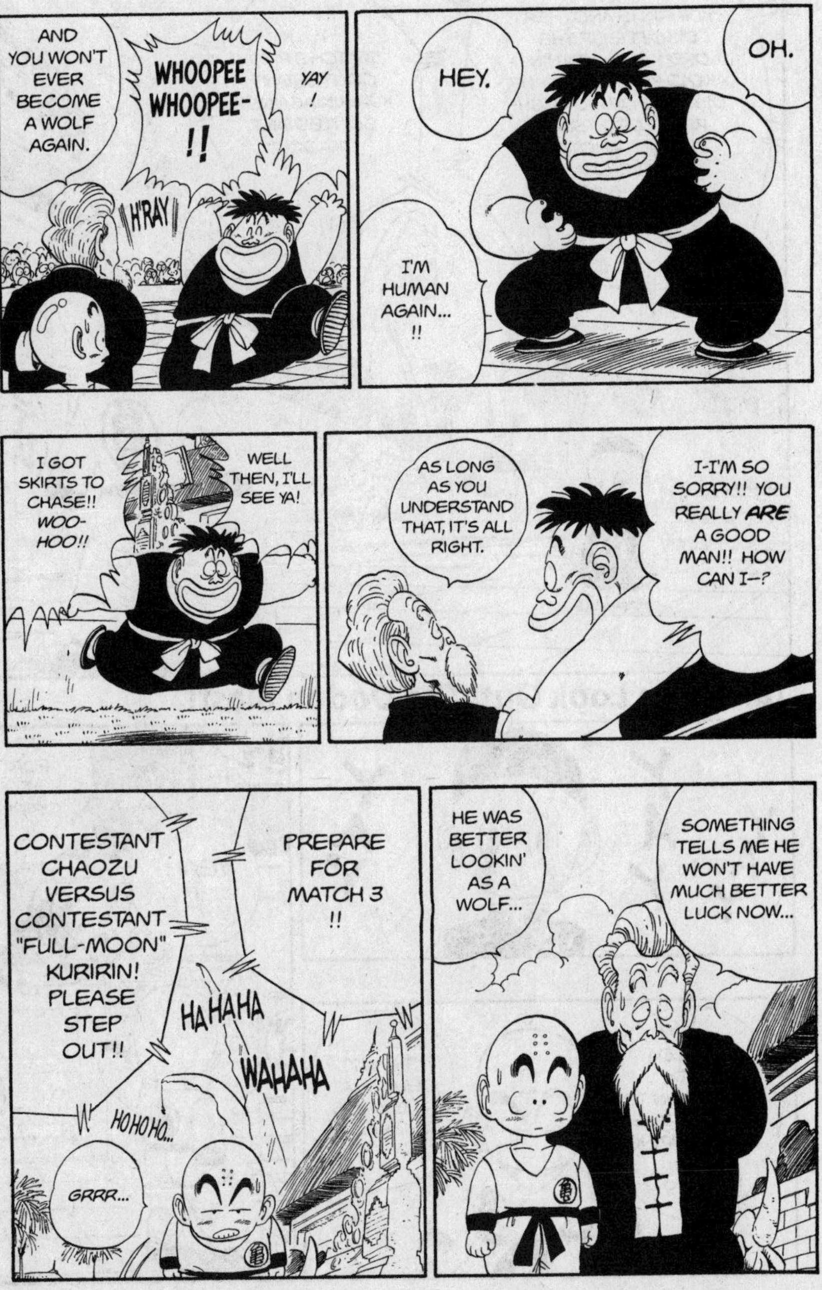
OH.
HEY.
I'M HUMAN AGAIN... !!
YAY!
WHOOPEE WHOOPEE-!!
AND YOU WON'T EVER BECOME A WOLF AGAIN.
H'RAY
I-I'M SO SORRY!! YOU REALLY **ARE** A GOOD MAN!! HOW CAN I--?
AS LONG AS YOU UNDERSTAND THAT, IT'S ALL RIGHT.
WELL THEN, I'LL SEE YA!
I GOT SKIRTS TO CHASE!! WOO-HOO!!
SOMETHING TELLS ME HE WON'T HAVE MUCH BETTER LUCK NOW...
HE WAS BETTER LOOKIN' AS A WOLF...
PREPARE FOR MATCH 3 !!
CONTESTANT CHAOZU VERSUS CONTESTANT "FULL-MOON" KURIRIN! PLEASE STEP OUT!!
HAHAHA
WAHAHA
HOHOHO...
GRRR...

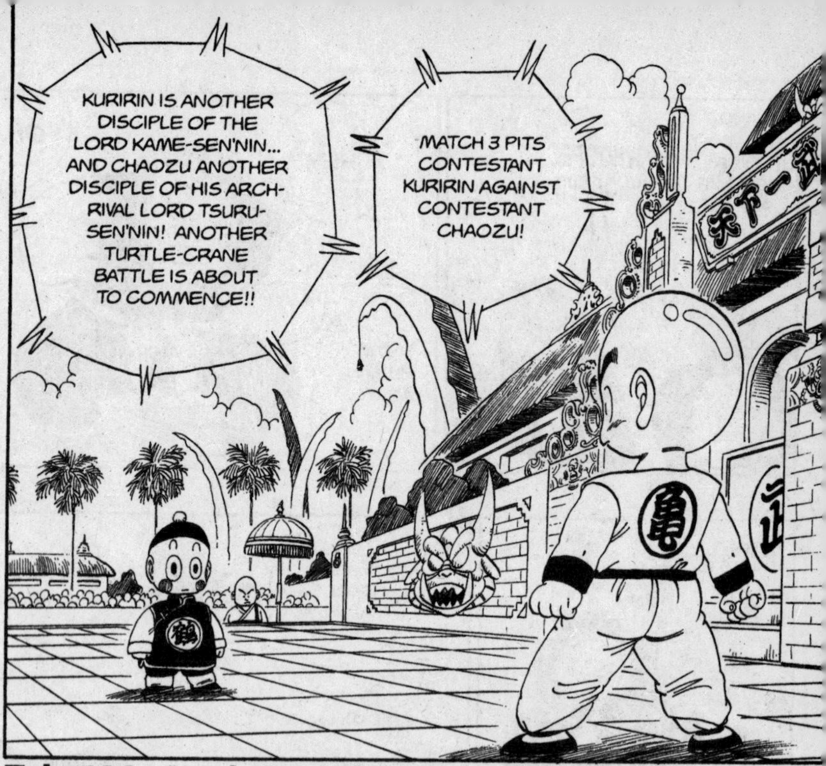
MATCH 3 PITS CONTESTANT KURIRIN AGAINST CONTESTANT CHAOZU!
KURIRIN IS ANOTHER DISCIPLE OF THE LORD KAME-SEN'NIN... AND CHAOZU ANOTHER DISCIPLE OF HIS ARCH-RIVAL LORD TSURU-SEN'NIN! ANOTHER TURTLE-CRANE BATTLE IS ABOUT TO COMMENCE!!

Tale 120 • Look Out! The Dodon Blast!

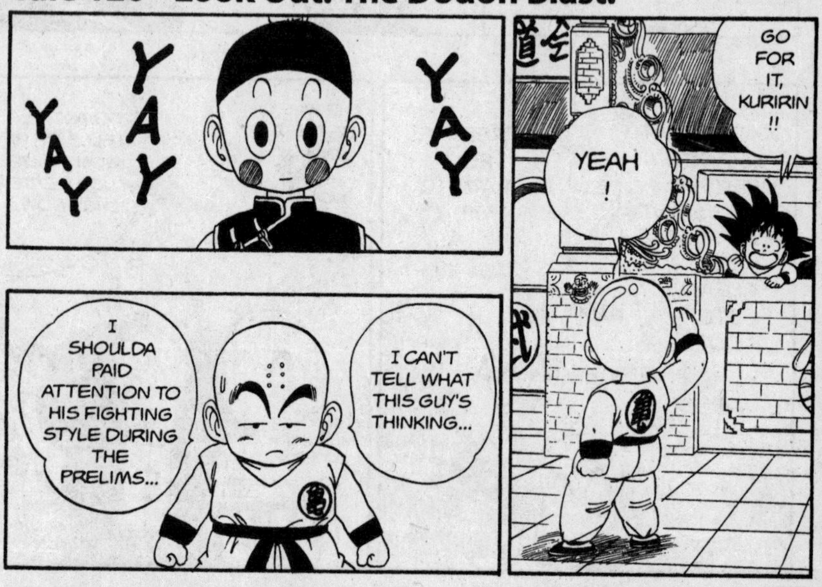
GO FOR IT, KURIRIN!!
YEAH!
YAY
YAY
YAY
I CAN'T TELL WHAT THIS GUY'S THINKING...
I SHOULDA PAID ATTENTION TO HIS FIGHTING STYLE DURING THE PRELIMS...

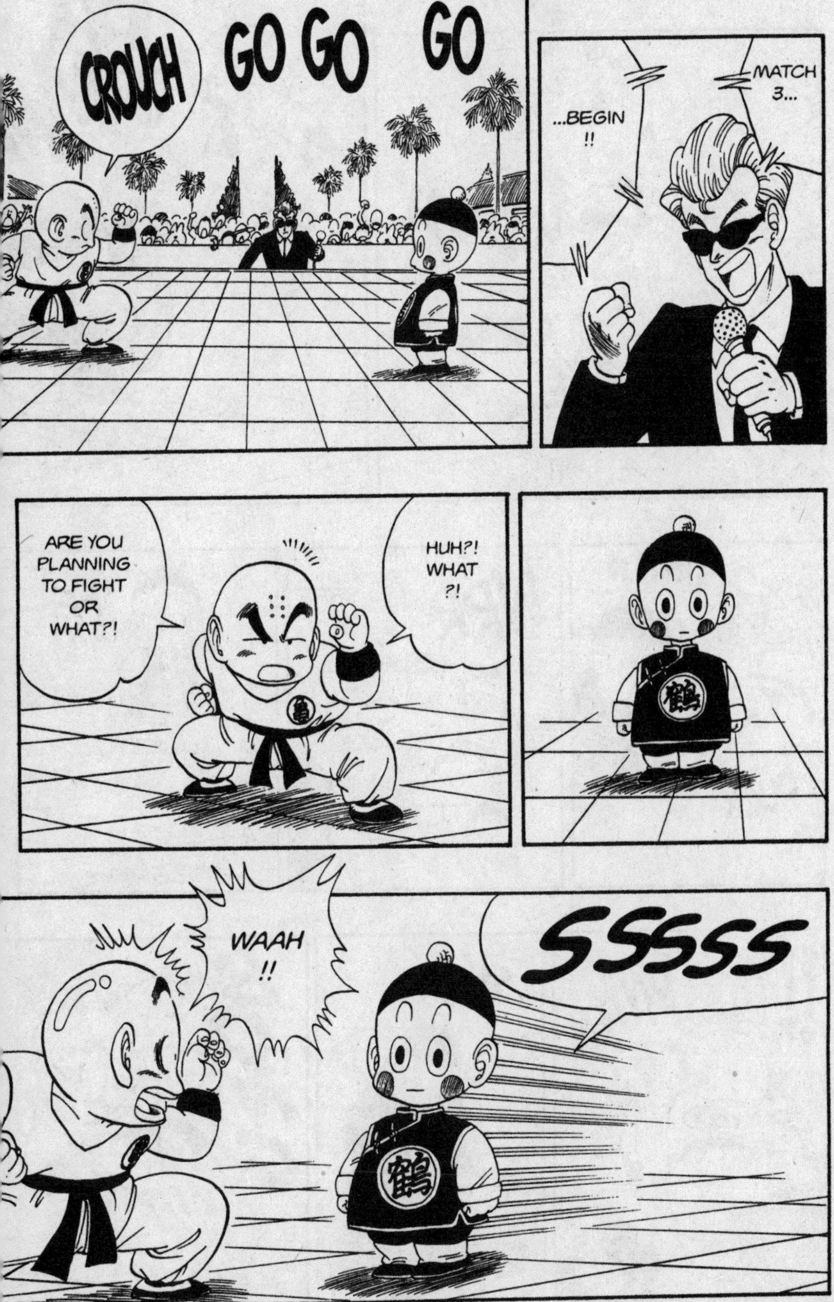
MATCH 3...
...BEGIN !!
GO GO GO
CROUCH
HUH?! WHAT ?!
ARE YOU PLANNING TO FIGHT OR WHAT?!
SSSSS
WAAH !!

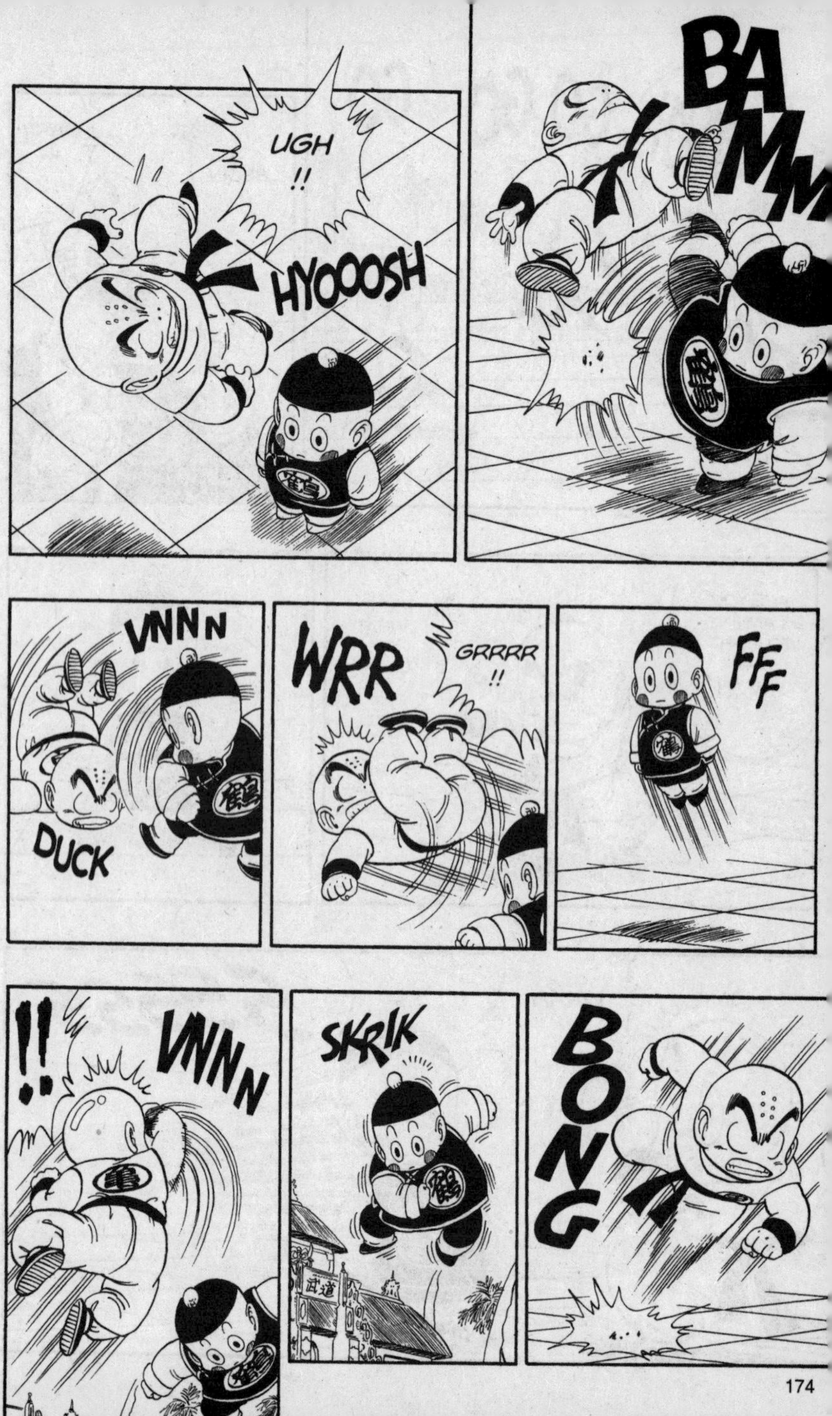
BAMMM
UGH !!
HYOOOSH
FFF
WRR
GRRRR !!
VNNn
DUCK
BONG
SKRIK
!!
VNNn

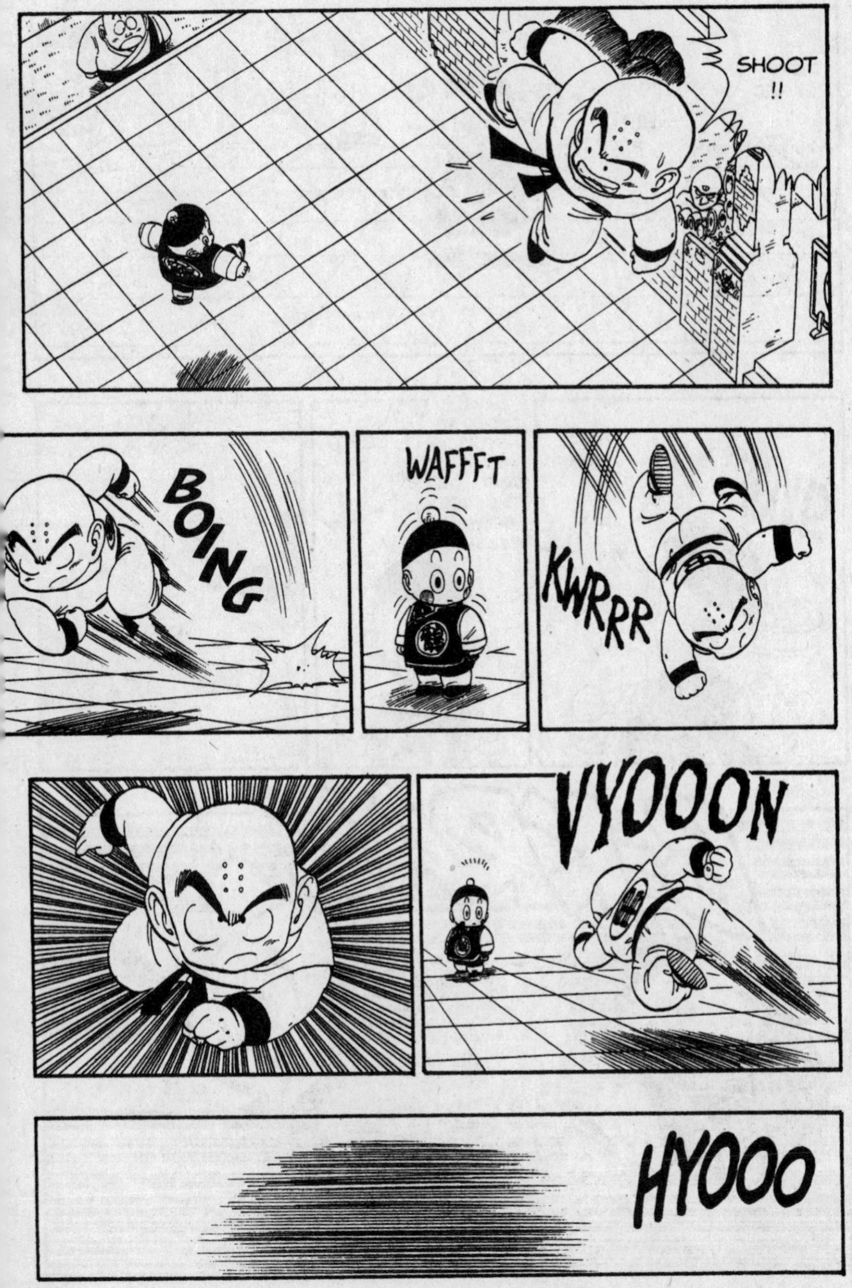
SHOOT !!
KWRRR
WAFFFT
BOING
VYOOON
HYOOO

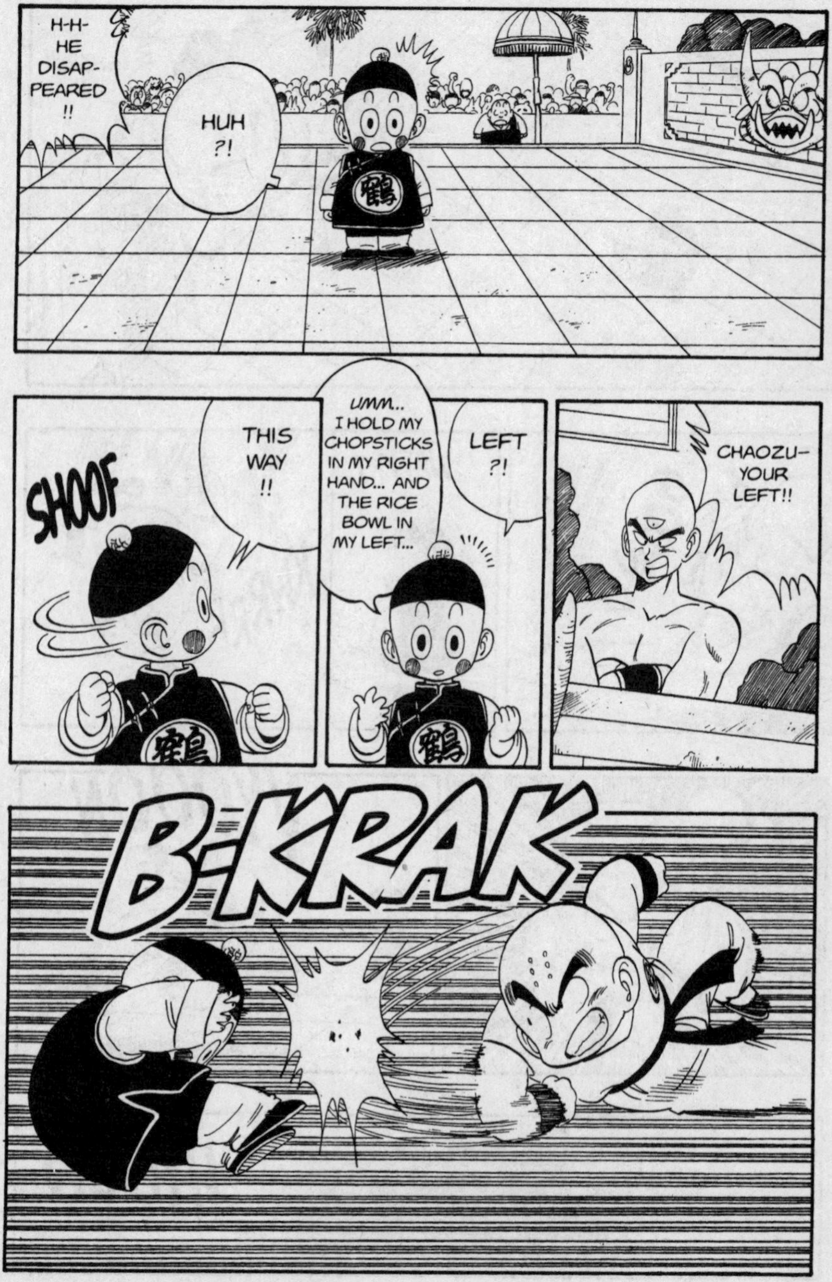
HUH ?!
H-H-HE DISAPPEARED !!
CHAOZU-YOUR LEFT!!
LEFT ?!
UMM... I HOLD MY CHOPSTICKS IN MY RIGHT HAND... AND THE RICE BOWL IN MY LEFT...
THIS WAY !!
SHOOF
B-KRAK

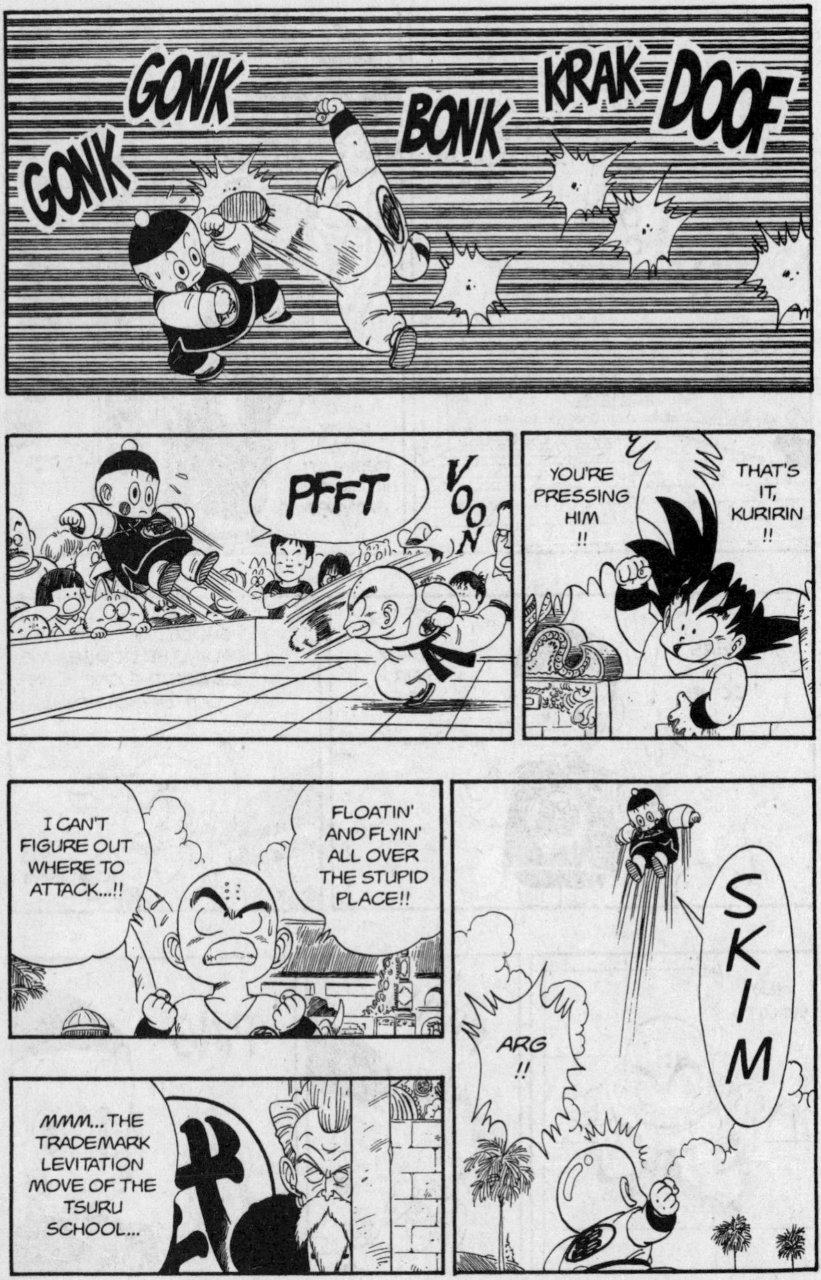
GONK
GONK
BONK
KRAK
DOOF
THAT'S IT, KURIRIN!!
YOU'RE PRESSING HIM!!
VOON
PFFT
SKIM
ARG!!
FLOATIN' AND FLYIN' ALL OVER THE STUPID PLACE!!
I CAN'T FIGURE OUT WHERE TO ATTACK...!!
MMM... THE TRADEMARK LEVITATION MOVE OF THE TSURU SCHOOL...

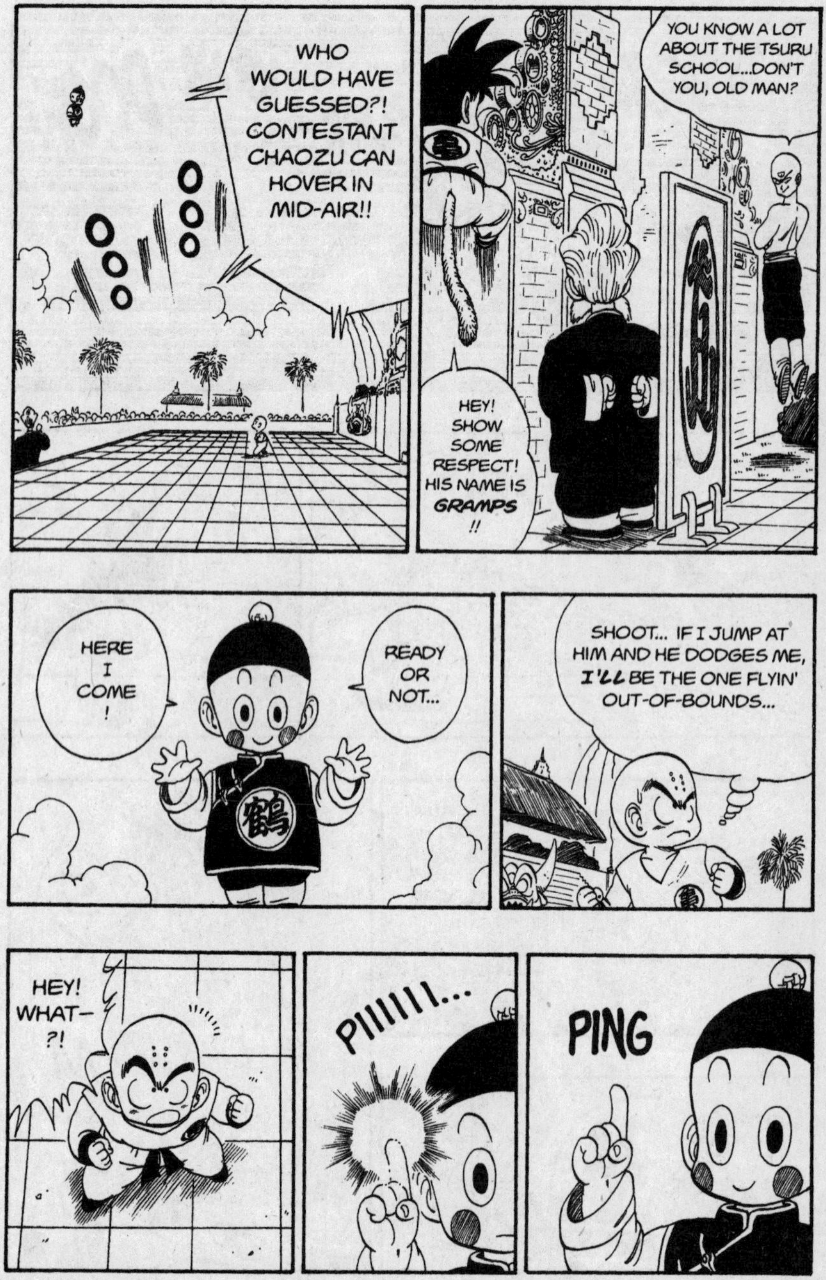

YOU KNOW A LOT ABOUT THE TSURU SCHOOL...DON'T YOU, OLD MAN?
HEY! SHOW SOME RESPECT! HIS NAME IS GRAMPS!!
WHO WOULD HAVE GUESSED?! CONTESTANT CHAOZU CAN HOVER IN MID-AIR!!
SHOOT... IF I JUMP AT HIM AND HE DODGES ME, I'LL BE THE ONE FLYIN' OUT-OF-BOUNDS...
READY OR NOT...
HERE I COME!
PING
PIIIIII...
HEY! WHAT—?!

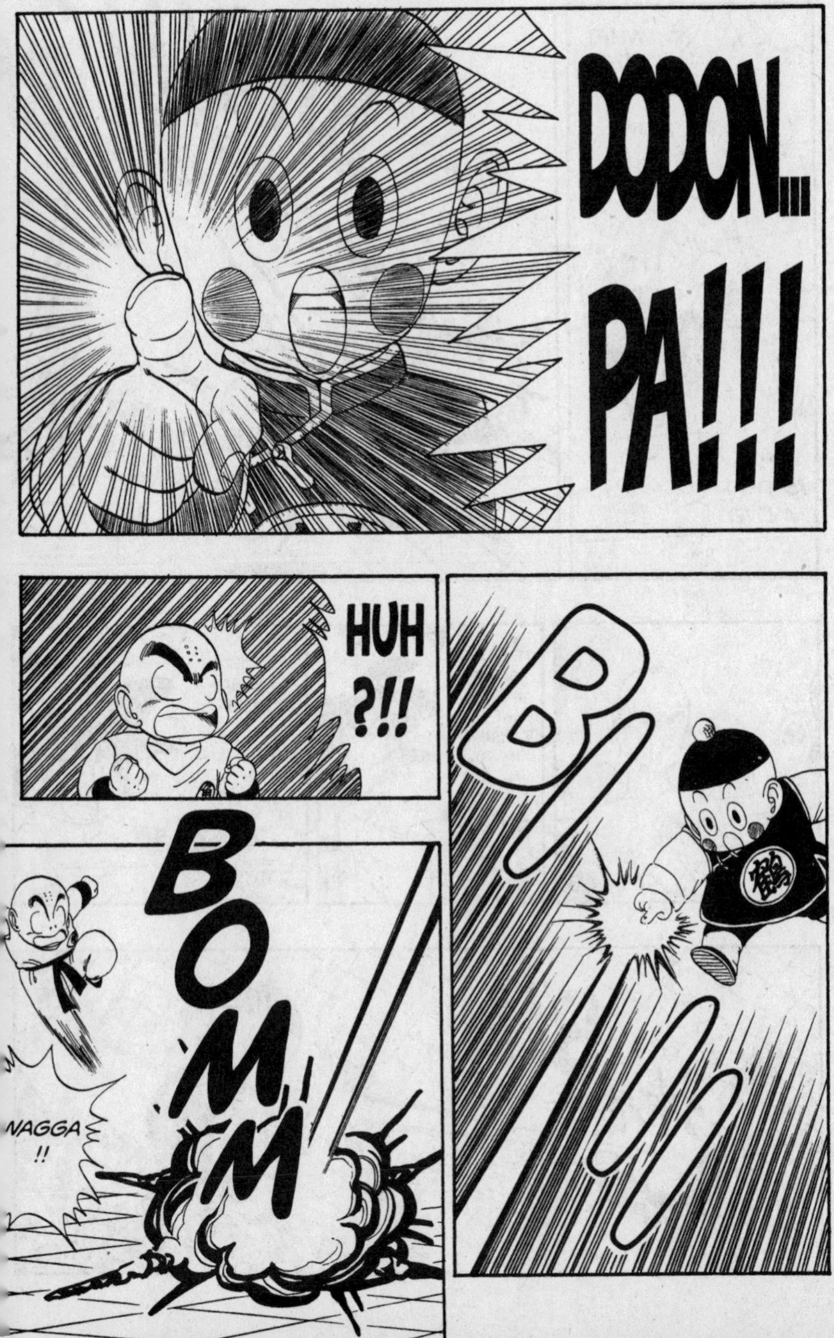
DODON... PA!!!
BIJUUU
HUH ?!!
BOMMM
NAGGA !!

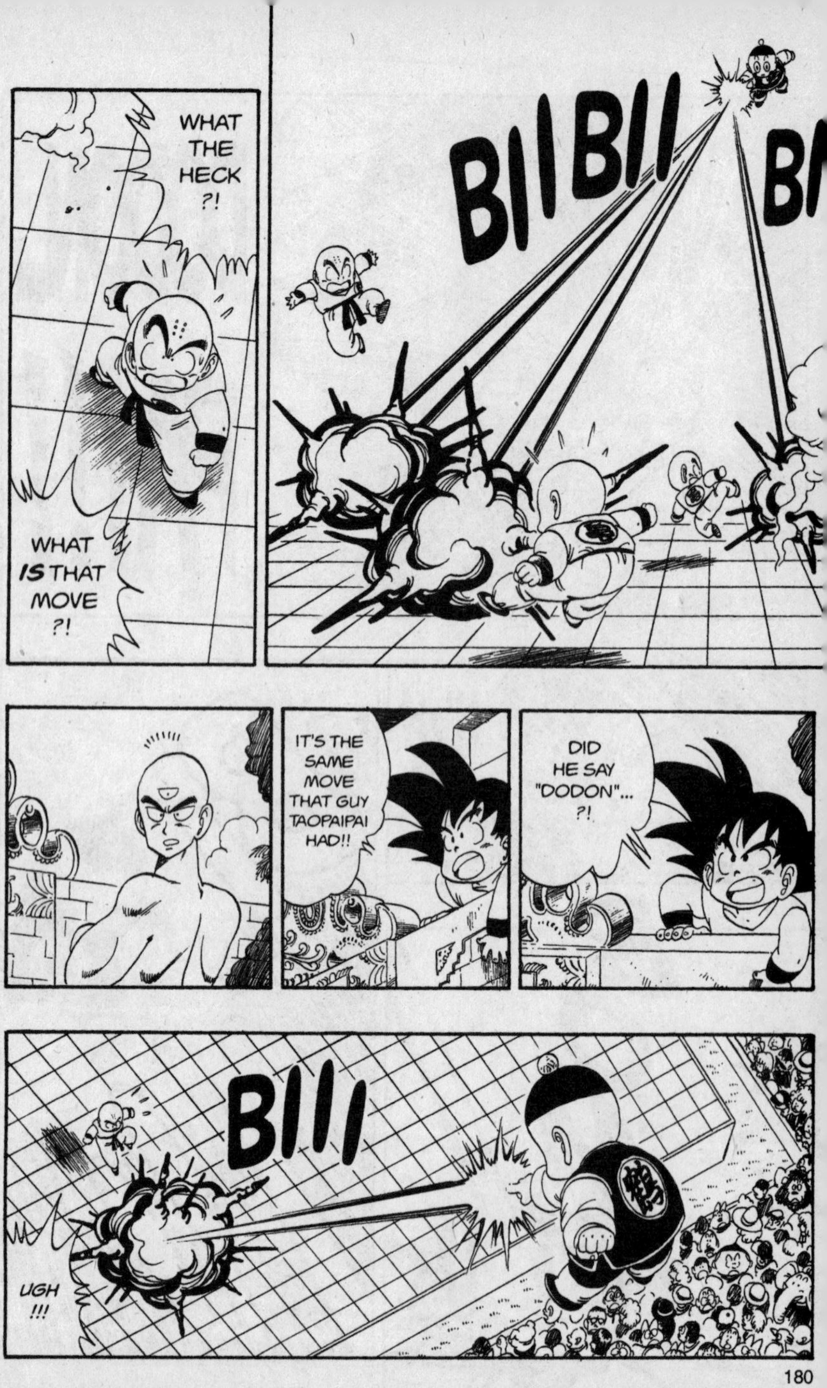
BIIBII
BI
WHAT THE HECK ?!
WHAT IS THAT MOVE ?!
DID HE SAY "DODON"... ?!
IT'S THE SAME MOVE THAT GUY TAOPAIPAI HAD!!
BIII
UGH !!!

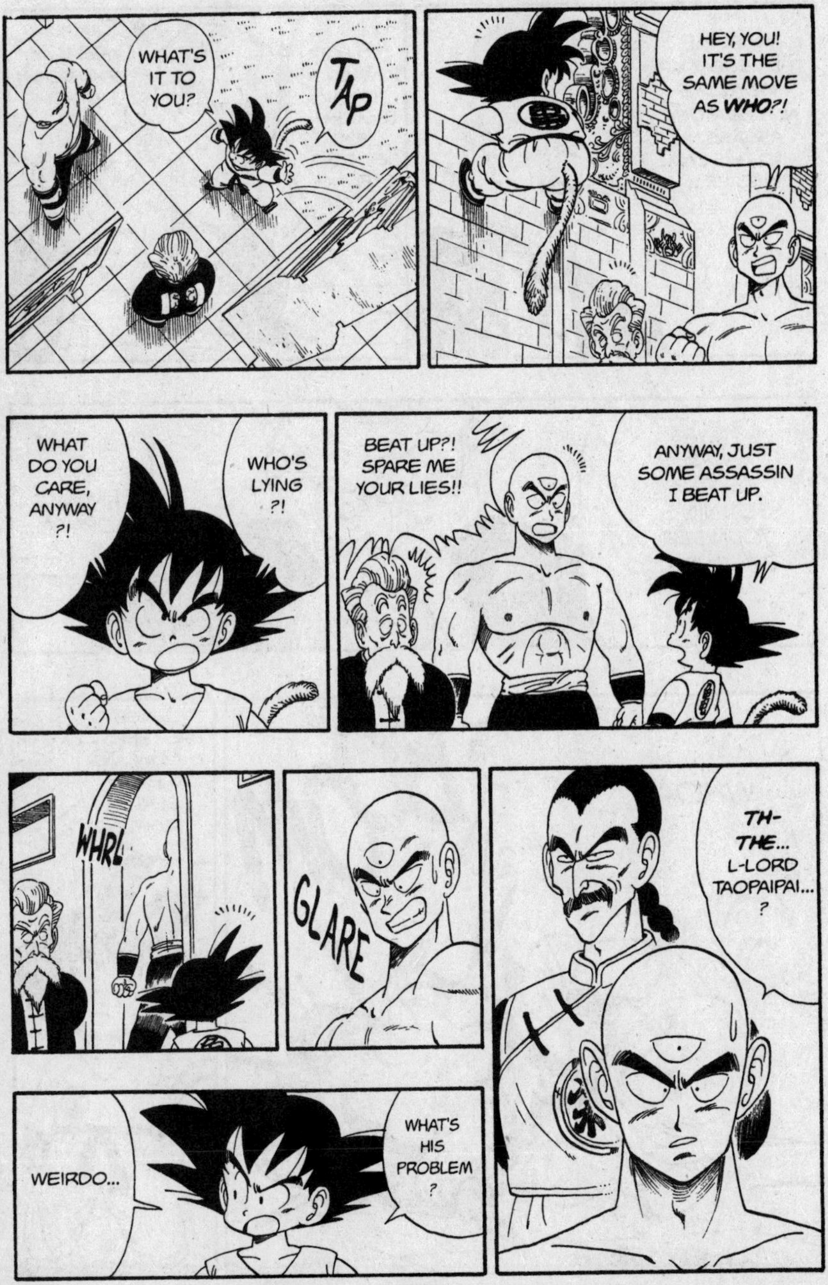

HEY, YOU! IT'S THE SAME MOVE AS **WHO**?!
TAP
WHAT'S IT TO YOU?
ANYWAY, JUST SOME ASSASSIN I BEAT UP.
BEAT UP?! SPARE ME YOUR LIES!!
WHO'S LYING ?!
WHAT DO YOU CARE, ANYWAY ?!
TH-THE... L-LORD TAOPAIPAI... ?
GLARE
WHRL
WHAT'S HIS PROBLEM ?
WEIRDO...

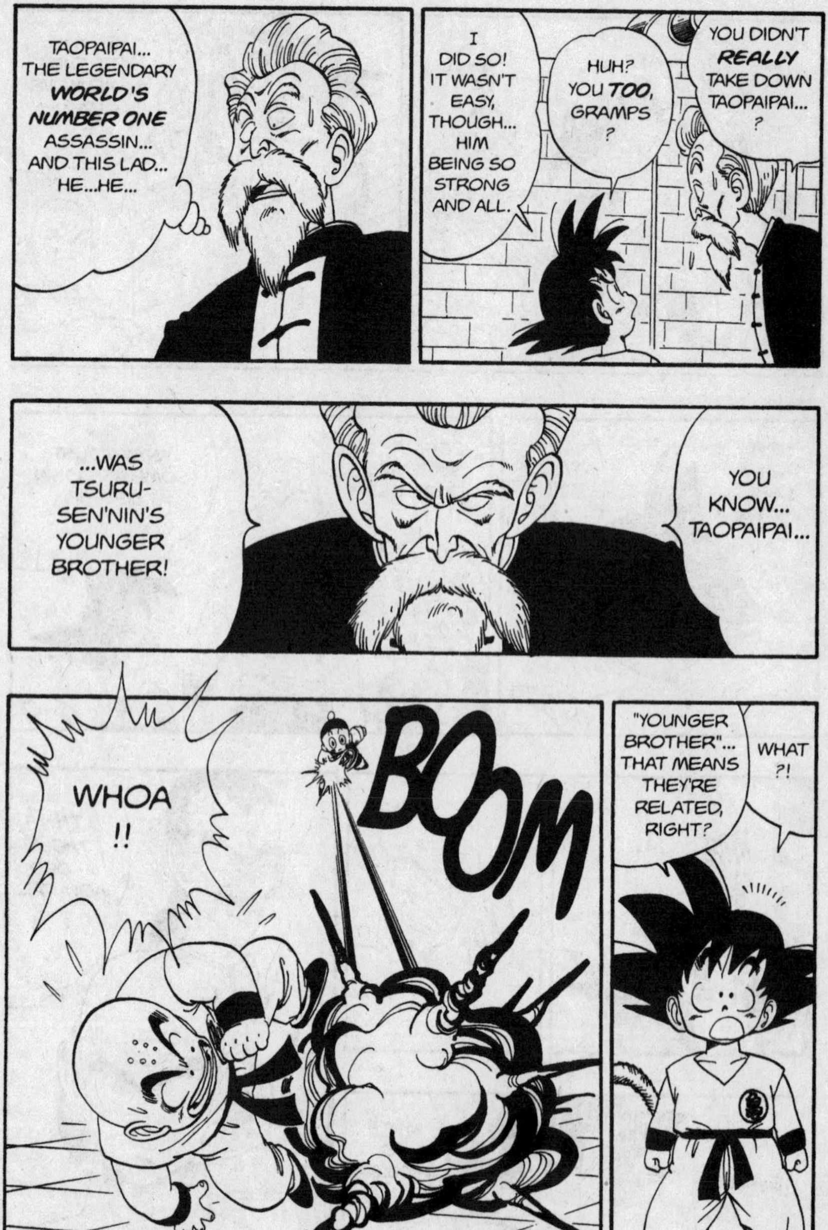
YOU DIDN'T **REALLY** TAKE DOWN TAOPAIPAI...?
HUH? YOU **TOO**, GRAMPS?
I DID SO! IT WASN'T EASY, THOUGH... HIM BEING SO STRONG AND ALL.
TAOPAIPAI... THE LEGENDARY **WORLD'S NUMBER ONE** ASSASSIN... AND THIS LAD... HE...HE...
YOU KNOW... TAOPAIPAI...
...WAS TSURU-SEN'NIN'S YOUNGER BROTHER!
WHAT?!
"YOUNGER BROTHER"... THAT MEANS THEY'RE RELATED, RIGHT?
BOOM
WHOA!!

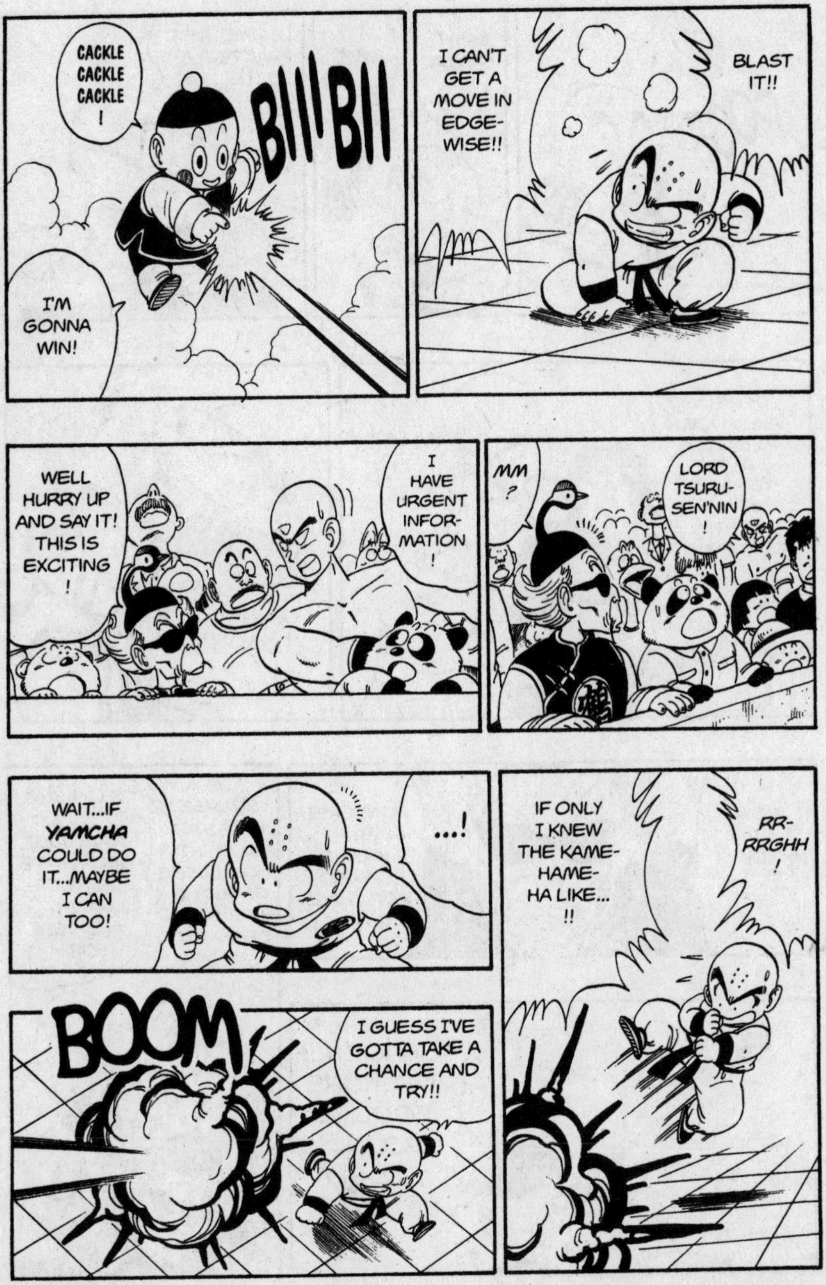
BLAST IT!!
I CAN'T GET A MOVE IN EDGE-WISE!!
CACKLE CACKLE CACKLE !
BIIBII
I'M GONNA WIN!
LORD TSURU-SEN'NIN !
MM ?
I HAVE URGENT INFOR-MATION !
WELL HURRY UP AND SAY IT! THIS IS EXCITING !
RR-RRGHH !
IF ONLY I KNEW THE KAME-HAME-HA LIKE... !!
...!
WAIT...IF YAMCHA COULD DO IT...MAYBE I CAN TOO!
I GUESS I'VE GOTTA TAKE A CHANCE AND TRY!!
BOOM

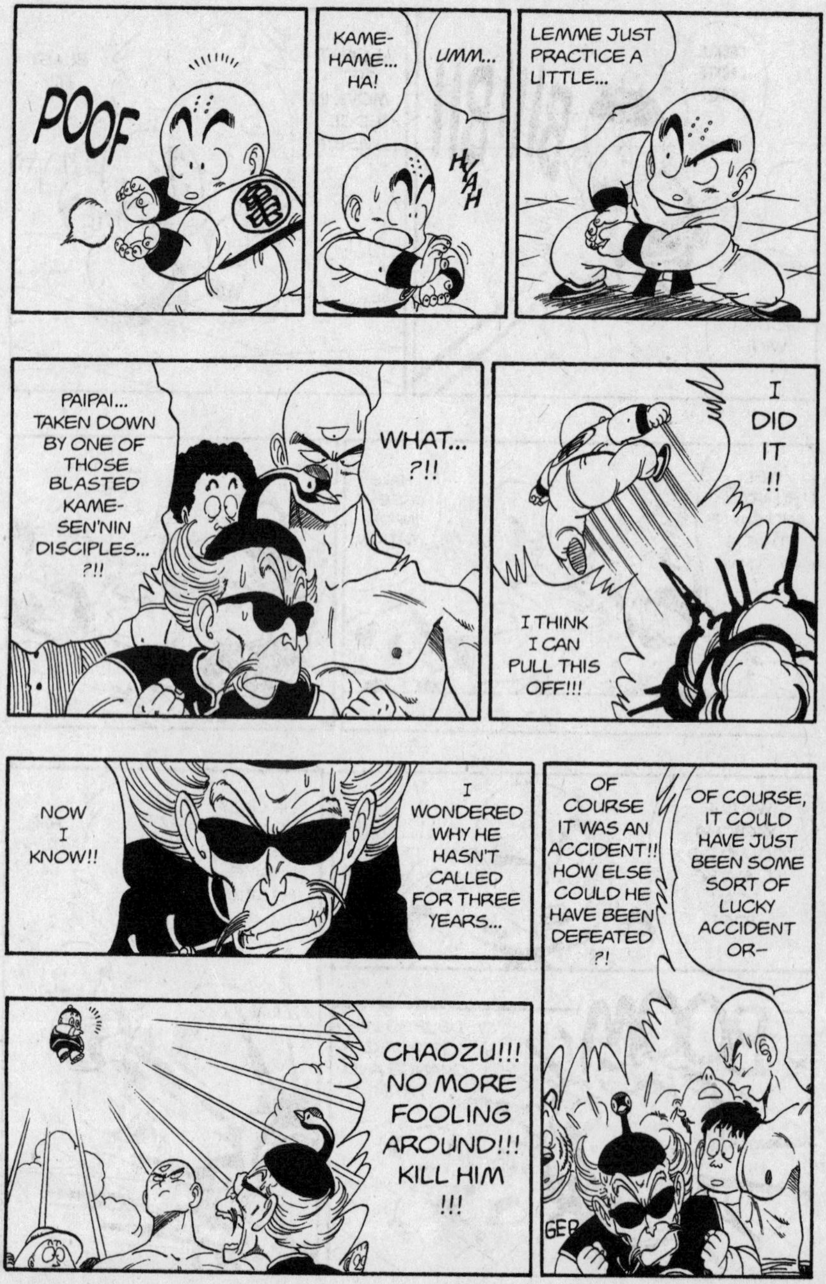

LEMME JUST PRACTICE A LITTLE...
UMM...
KAME-HAME... HA!
HYAAH
POOF
I DID IT !!
I THINK I CAN PULL THIS OFF!!!
WHAT...?!!
PAIPAI... TAKEN DOWN BY ONE OF THOSE BLASTED KAME-SEN'NIN DISCIPLES...?!!
OF COURSE, IT COULD HAVE JUST BEEN SOME SORT OF LUCKY ACCIDENT OR–
OF COURSE IT WAS AN ACCIDENT!! HOW ELSE COULD HE HAVE BEEN DEFEATED ?!
GEP
I WONDERED WHY HE HASN'T CALLED FOR THREE YEARS...
NOW I KNOW!!
CHAOZU!!! NO MORE FOOLING AROUND!!! KILL HIM !!!

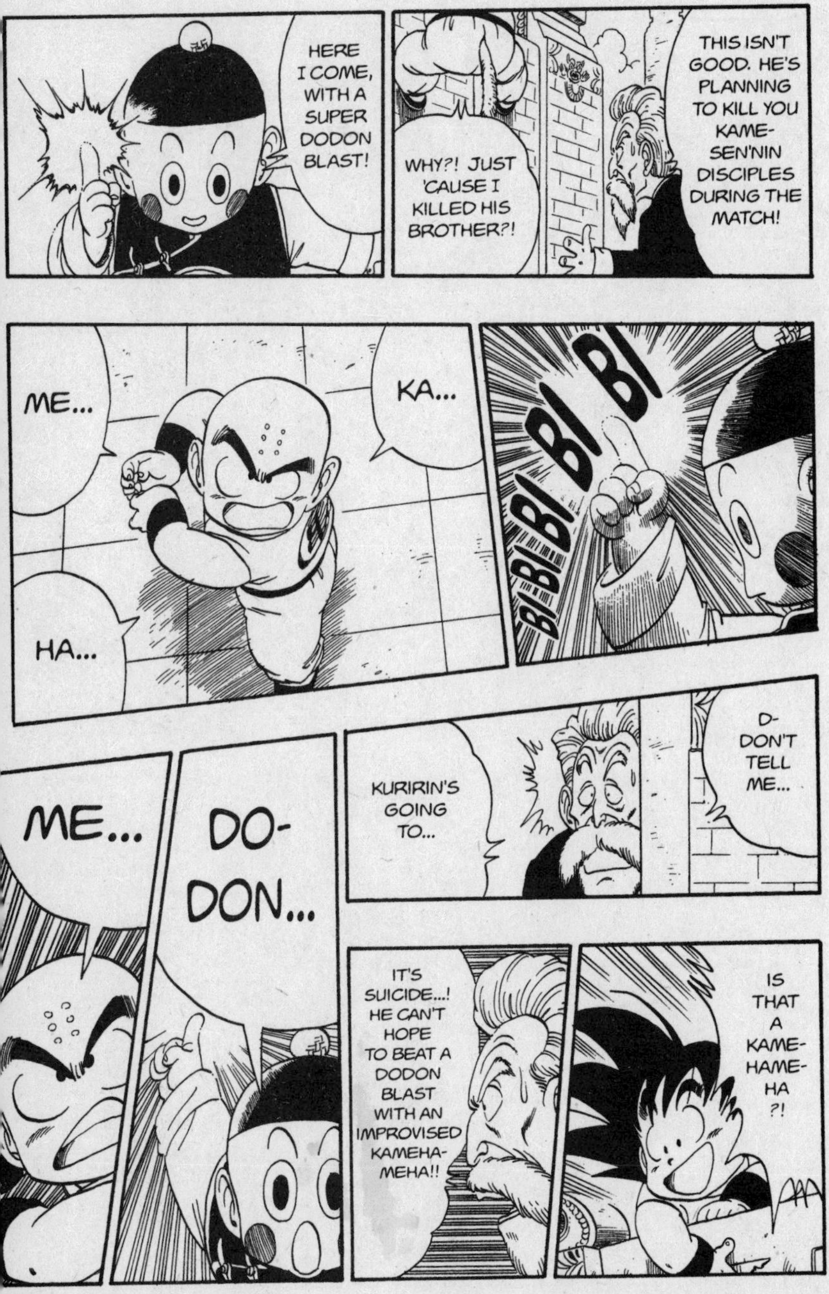
THIS ISN'T GOOD. HE'S PLANNING TO KILL YOU KAME-SEN'NIN DISCIPLES DURING THE MATCH!
WHY?! JUST 'CAUSE I KILLED HIS BROTHER?!
HERE I COME, WITH A SUPER DODON BLAST!
BI BI BI BI BI BI
KA...
ME...
HA...
D-DON'T TELL ME...
KURIRIN'S GOING TO...
IS THAT A KAME-HAME-HA?!
IT'S SUICIDE...! HE CAN'T HOPE TO BEAT A DODON BLAST WITH AN IMPROVISED KAMEHA-MEHA!!
DO-DON...
ME...

Dragonball

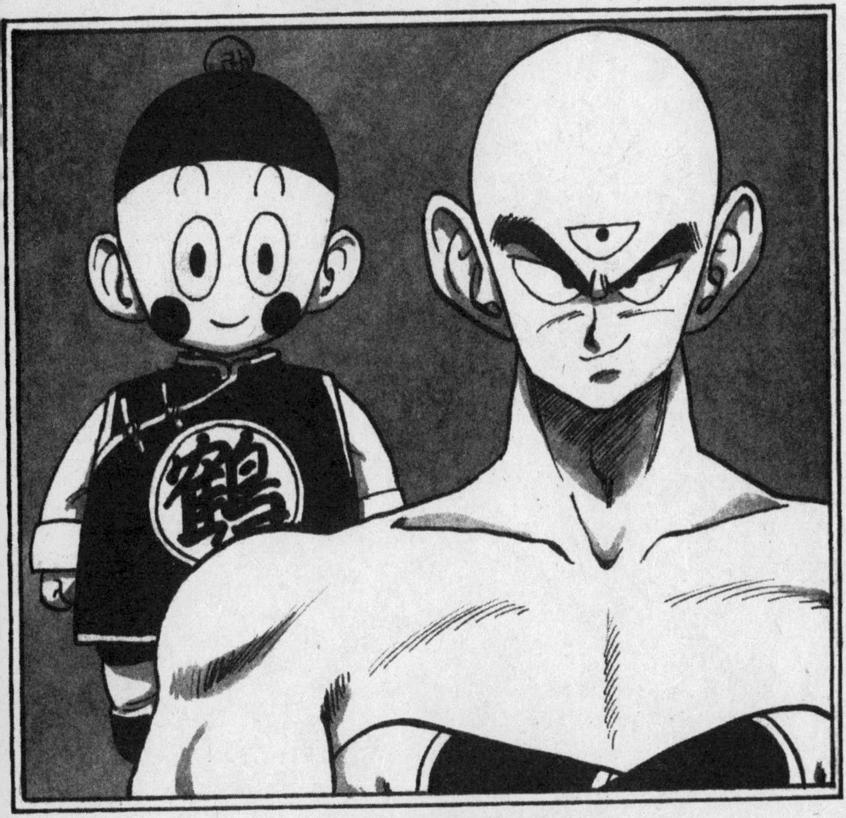

VOLUME 11

THE EYES OF TENSHINHAN

Tale 121
Kuririn's Master Plan

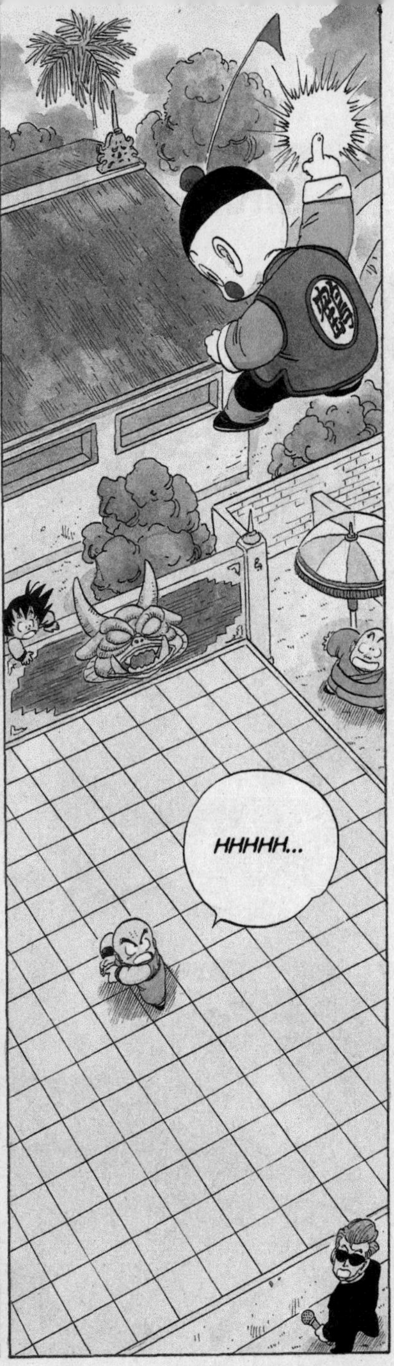
HHHHH...

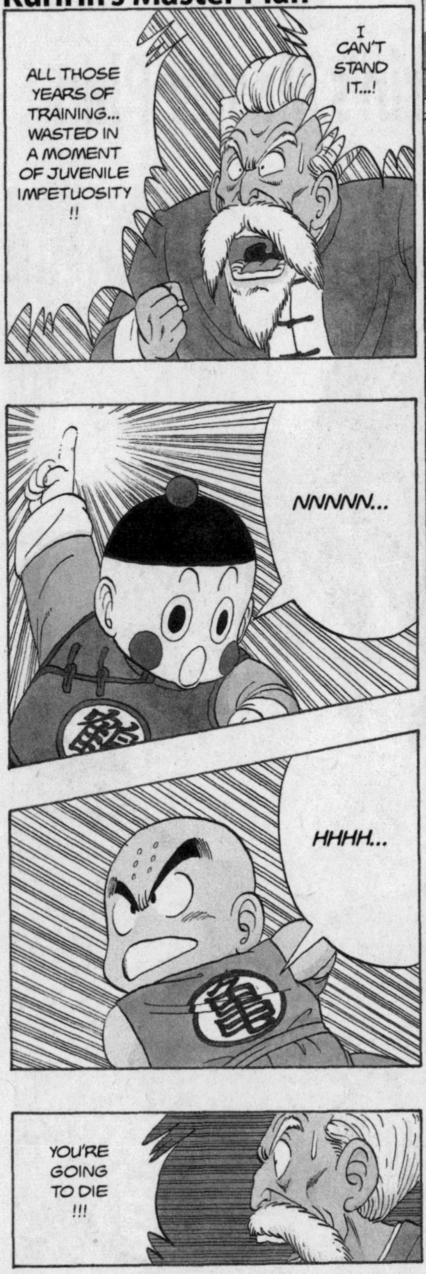
I CAN'T STAND IT...!
ALL THOSE YEARS OF TRAINING... WASTED IN A MOMENT OF JUVENILE IMPETUOSITY !!
NNNNN...
HHHH...
YOU'RE GOING TO DIE !!!

Tale 121 · Kuririn's Master Plan

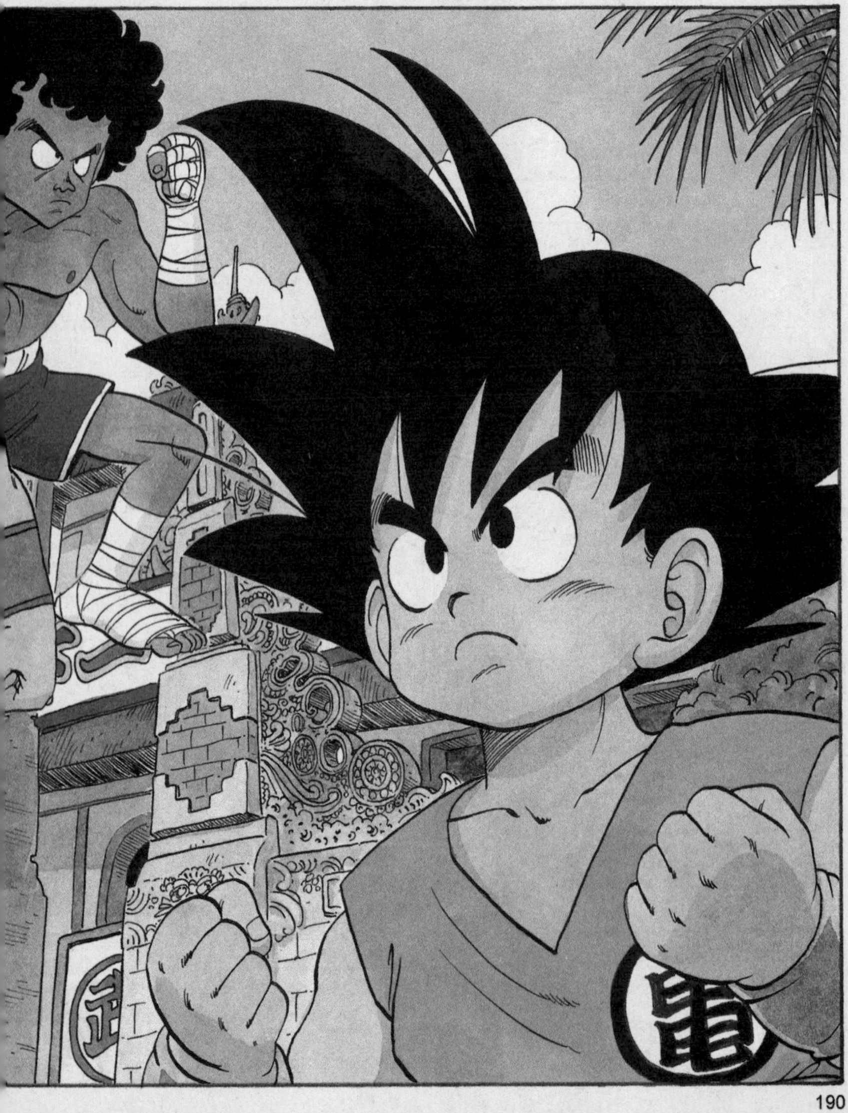

ドラゴンボール

DRAGON BALL

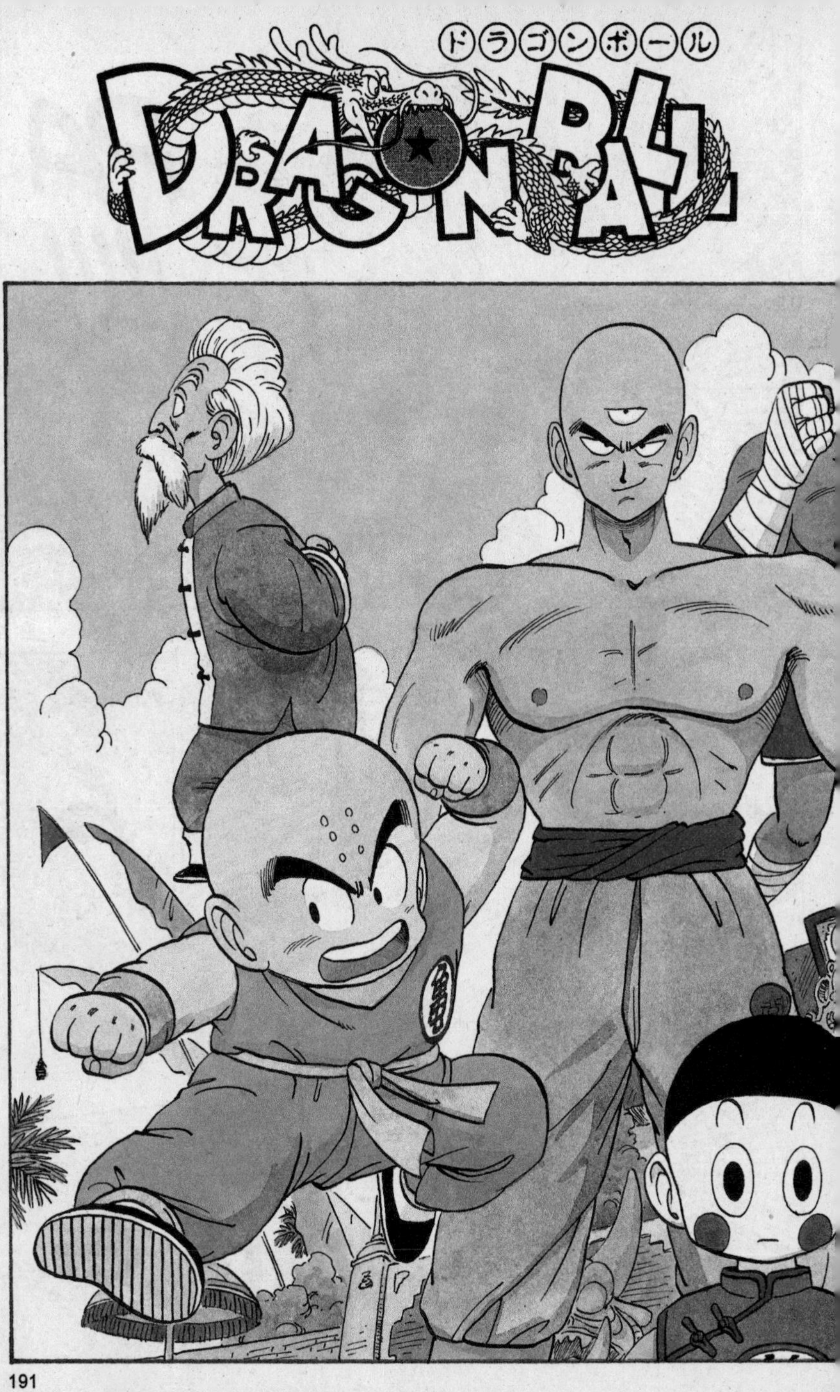

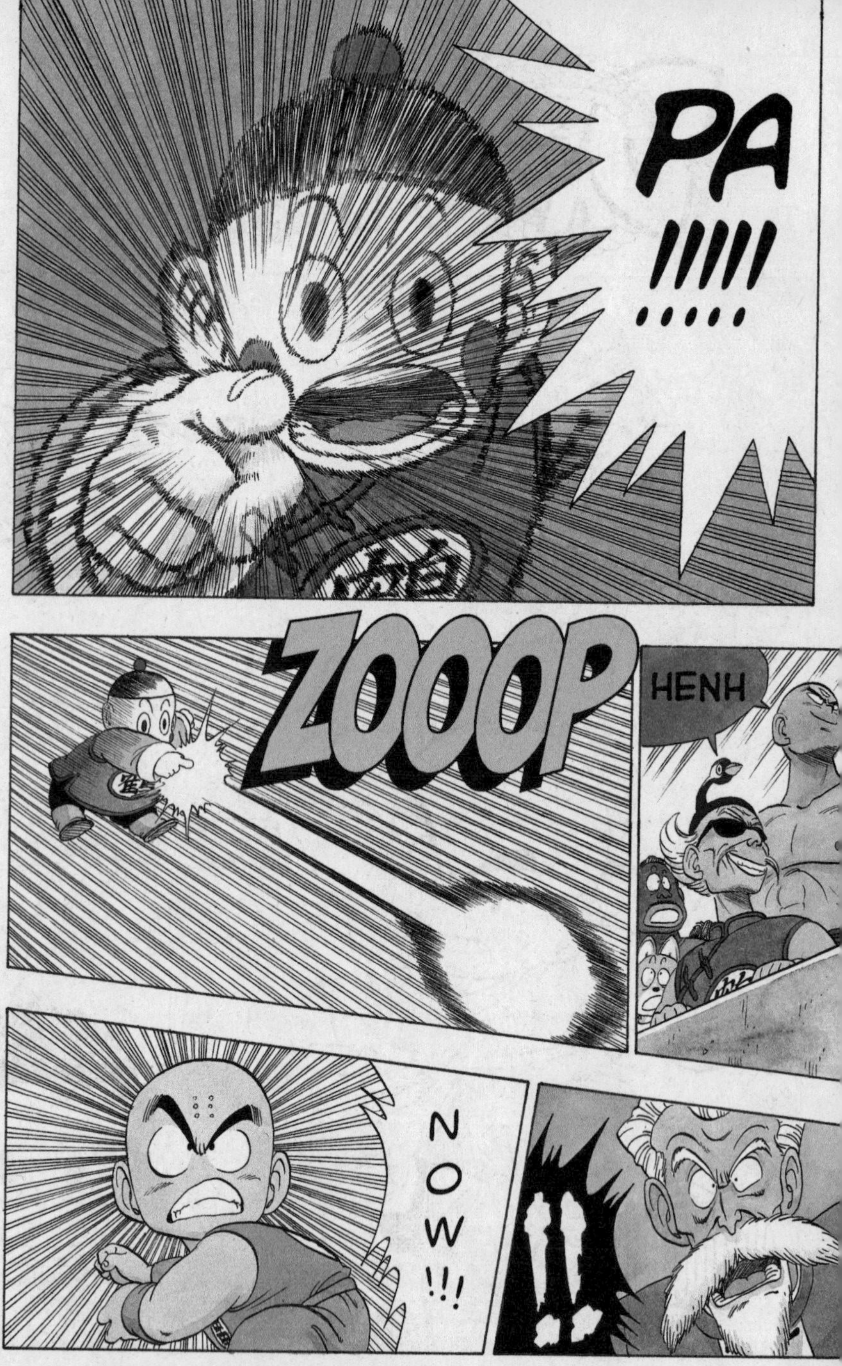
PA!!!!!!......
HENH
ZOOOP
!!
NOW!!!

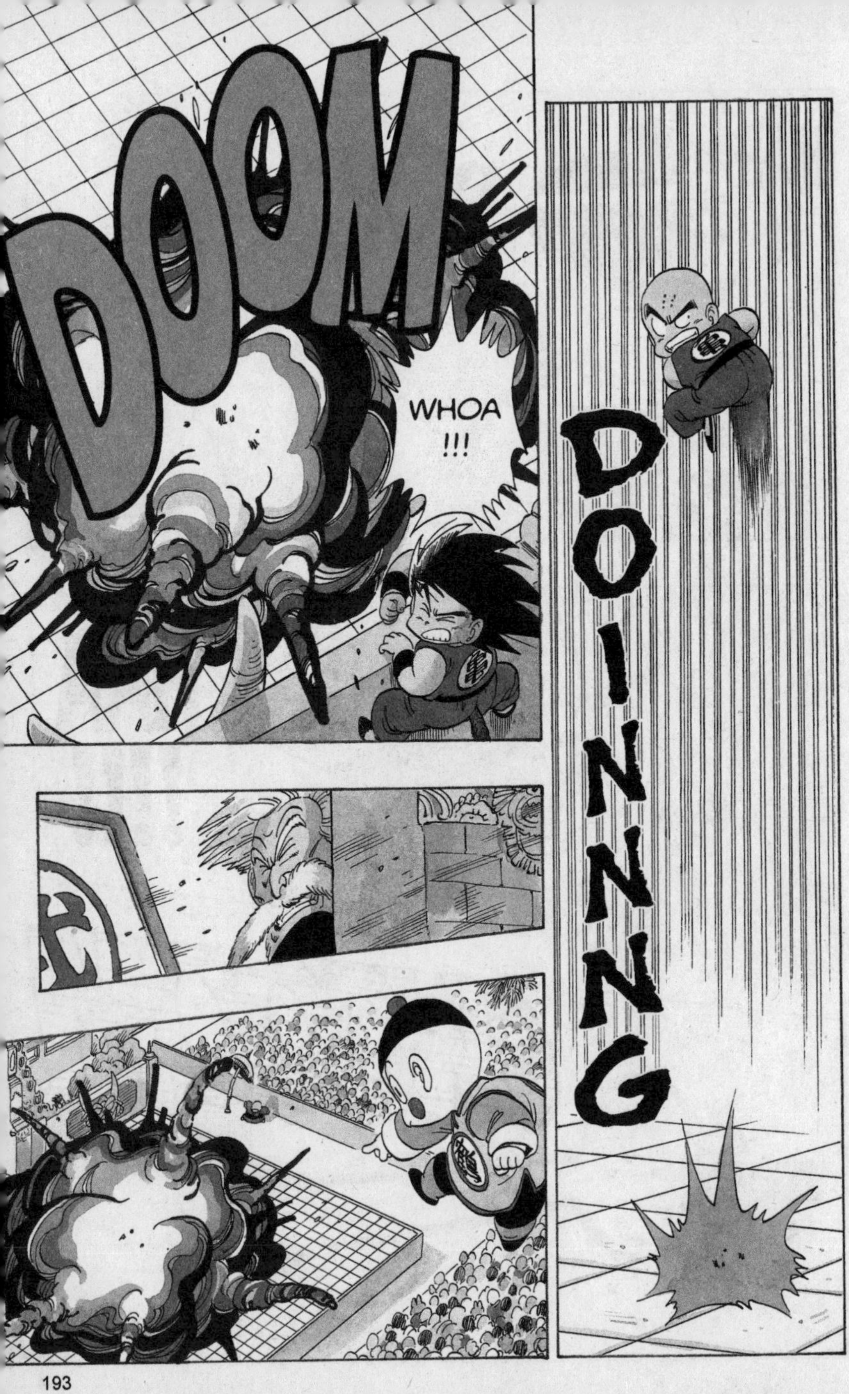
DOINNNG
DOOM
WHOA !!!

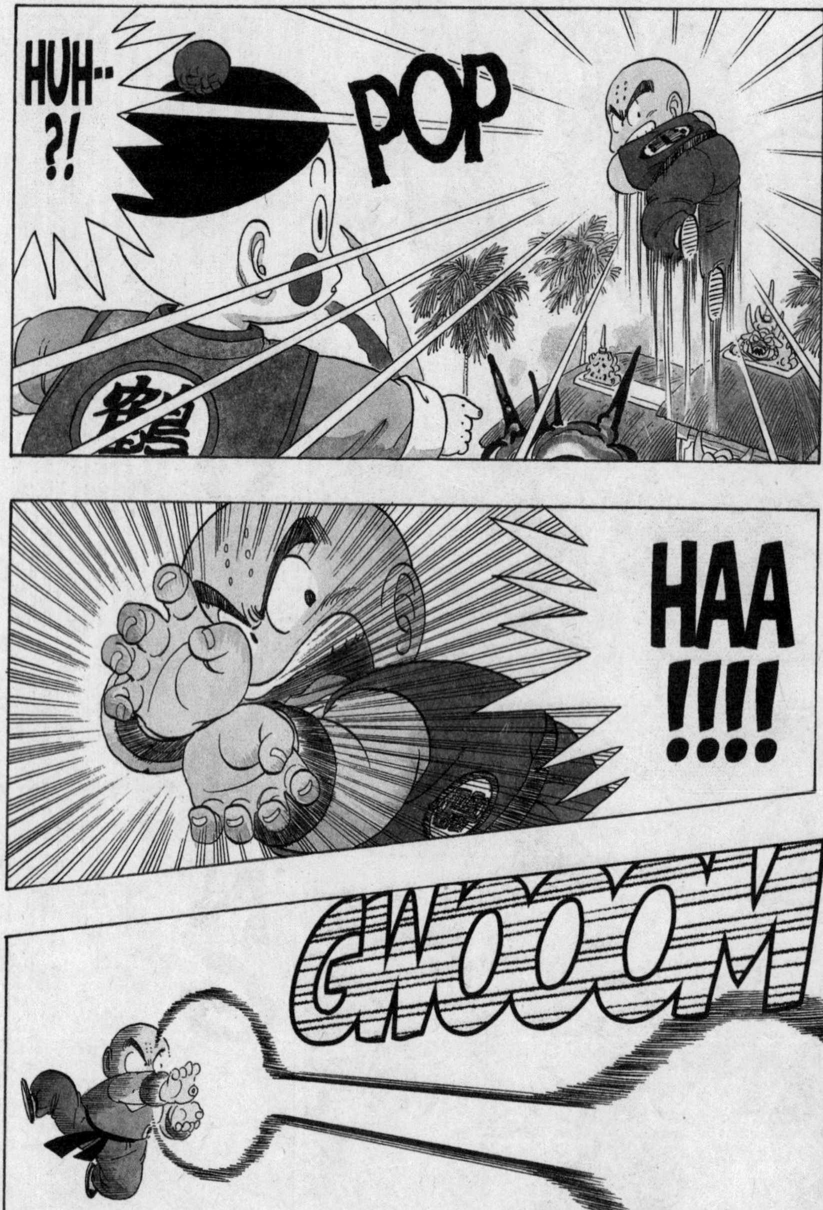
POP
HUH-- ?!
HAA !!!!
GWOOOM

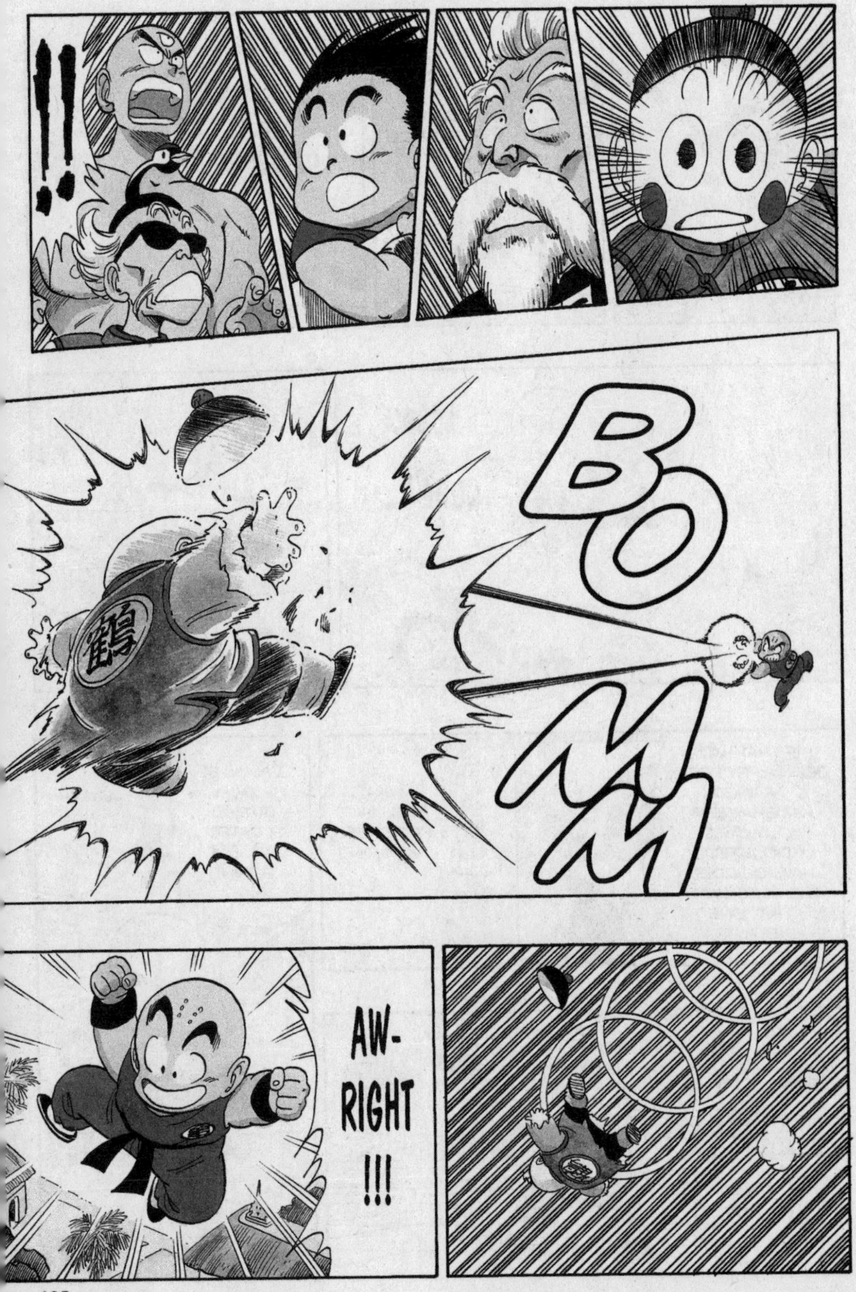
!!
BOMMM
AW-RIGHT!!!

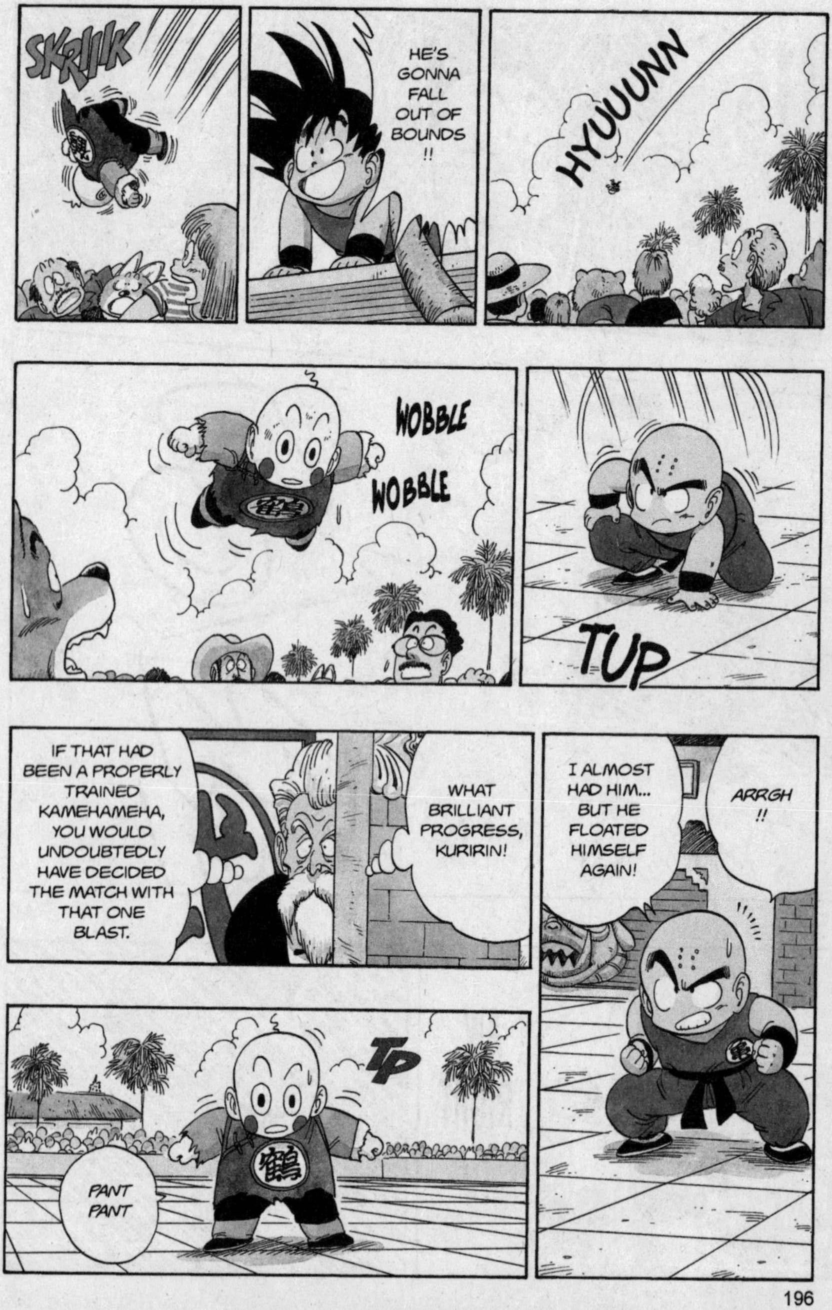
HYUUUNN
HE'S GONNA FALL OUT OF BOUNDS !!
SKRIIIK
TUP
WOBBLE
WOBBLE
ARRGH !!
I ALMOST HAD HIM... BUT HE FLOATED HIMSELF AGAIN!
WHAT BRILLIANT PROGRESS, KURIRIN!
IF THAT HAD BEEN A PROPERLY TRAINED KAMEHAMEHA, YOU WOULD UNDOUBTEDLY HAVE DECIDED THE MATCH WITH THAT ONE BLAST.
TP
PANT PANT

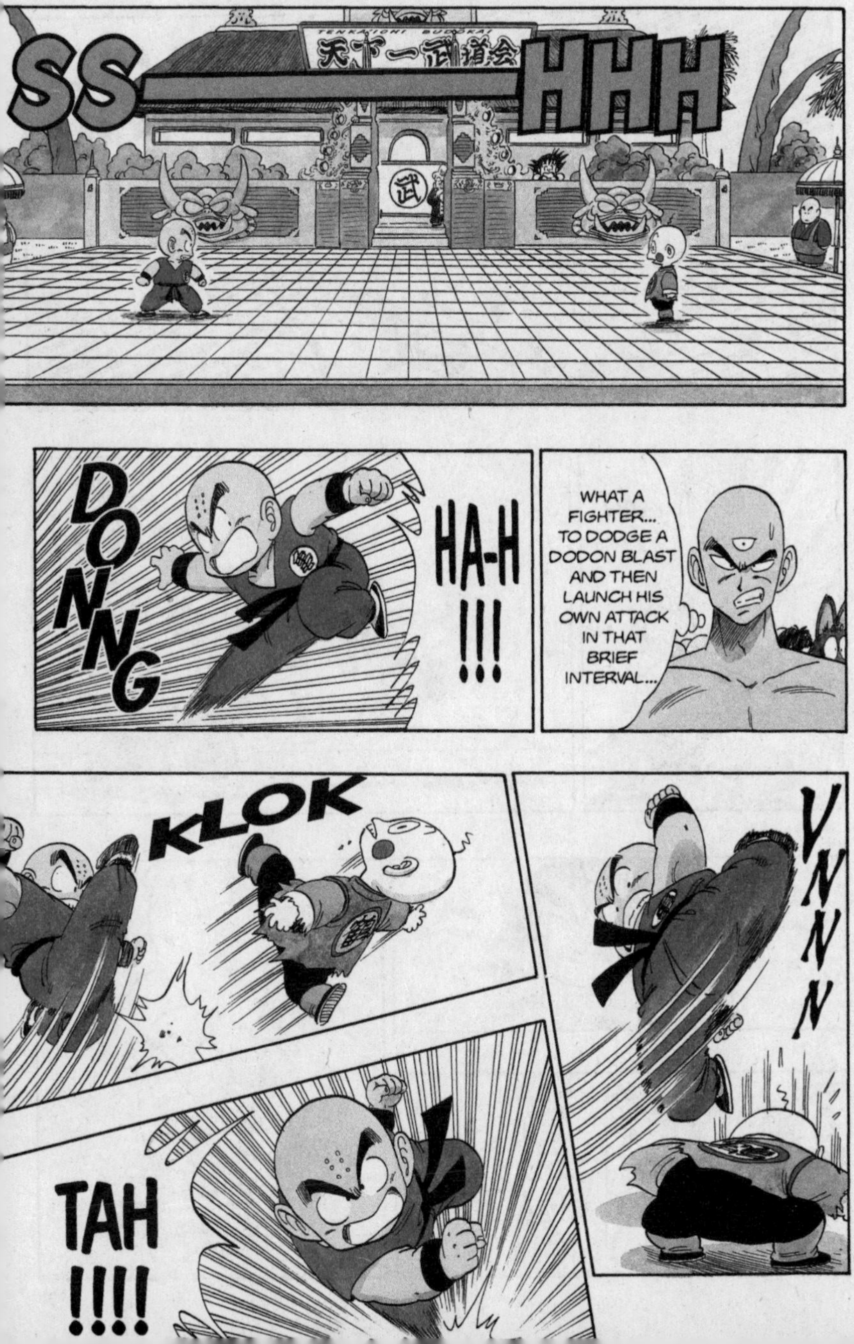

SS—HHH
TENKAICHI BUDOKAI
天下一武道会
WHAT A FIGHTER... TO DODGE A DODON BLAST AND THEN LAUNCH HIS OWN ATTACK IN THAT BRIEF INTERVAL...
HA-H!!!
DONNG
VNNN
KLOK
TAH!!!!

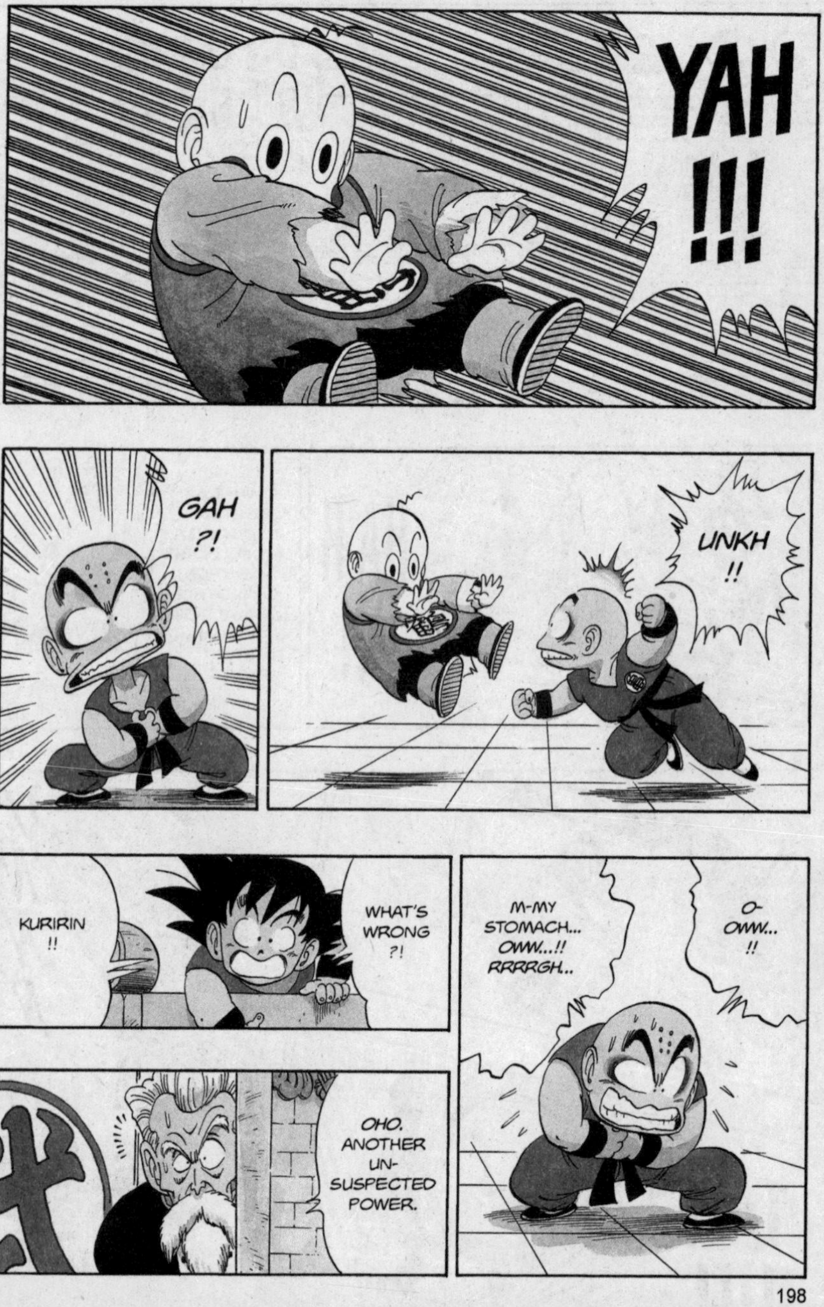
YAH !!!
UNKH !!
GAH ?!
O-OWW... !!
M-MY STOMACH... OWW...!! RRRRGH...
WHAT'S WRONG ?!
KURIRIN !!
OHO. ANOTHER UN-SUSPECTED POWER.

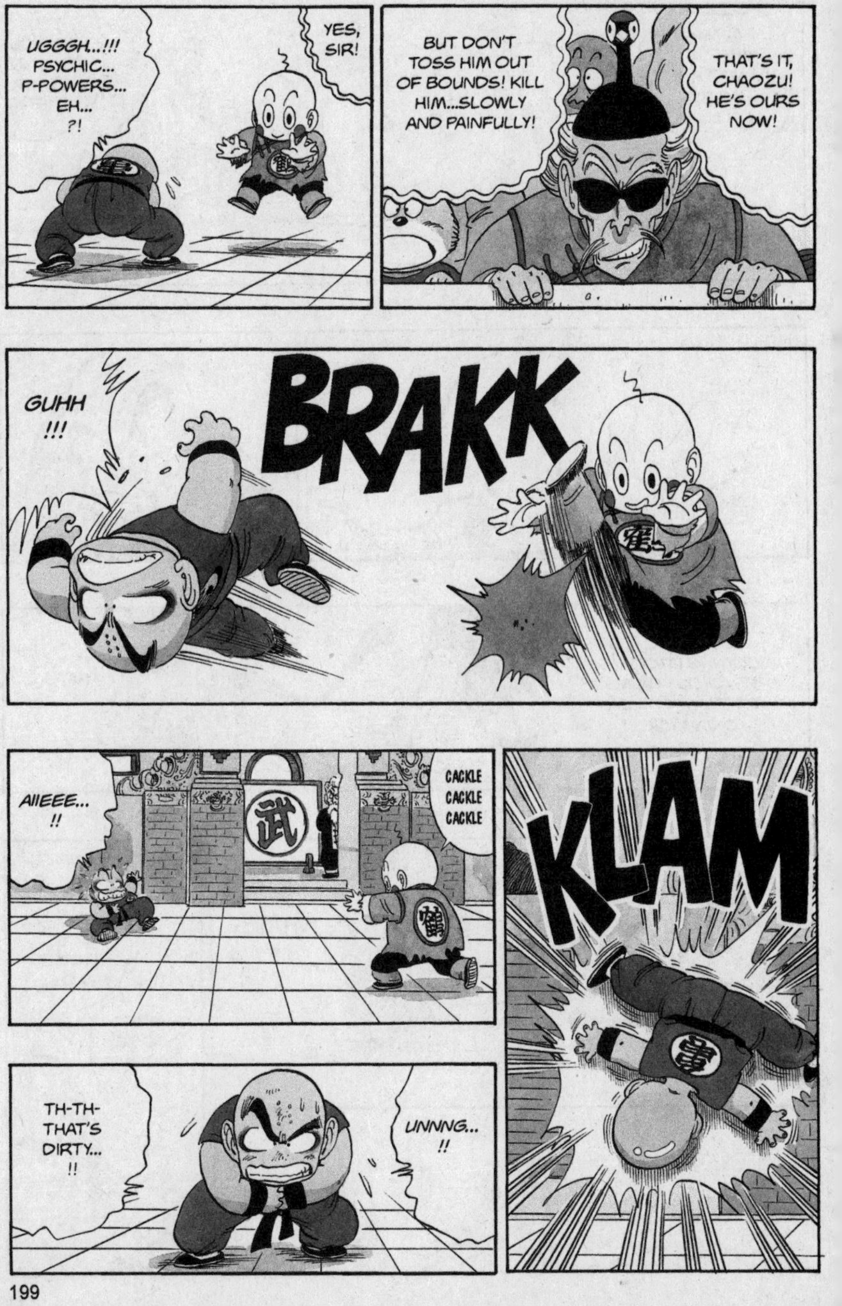
THAT'S IT, CHAOZU! HE'S OURS NOW!
BUT DON'T TOSS HIM OUT OF BOUNDS! KILL HIM...SLOWLY AND PAINFULLY!
YES, SIR!
UGGGH...!!! PSYCHIC... P-POWERS... EH... ?!
BRAKK
GUHH !!!
KLAM
CACKLE CACKLE CACKLE
AIIEEE... !!
UNNNG... !!
TH-TH-THAT'S DIRTY... !!

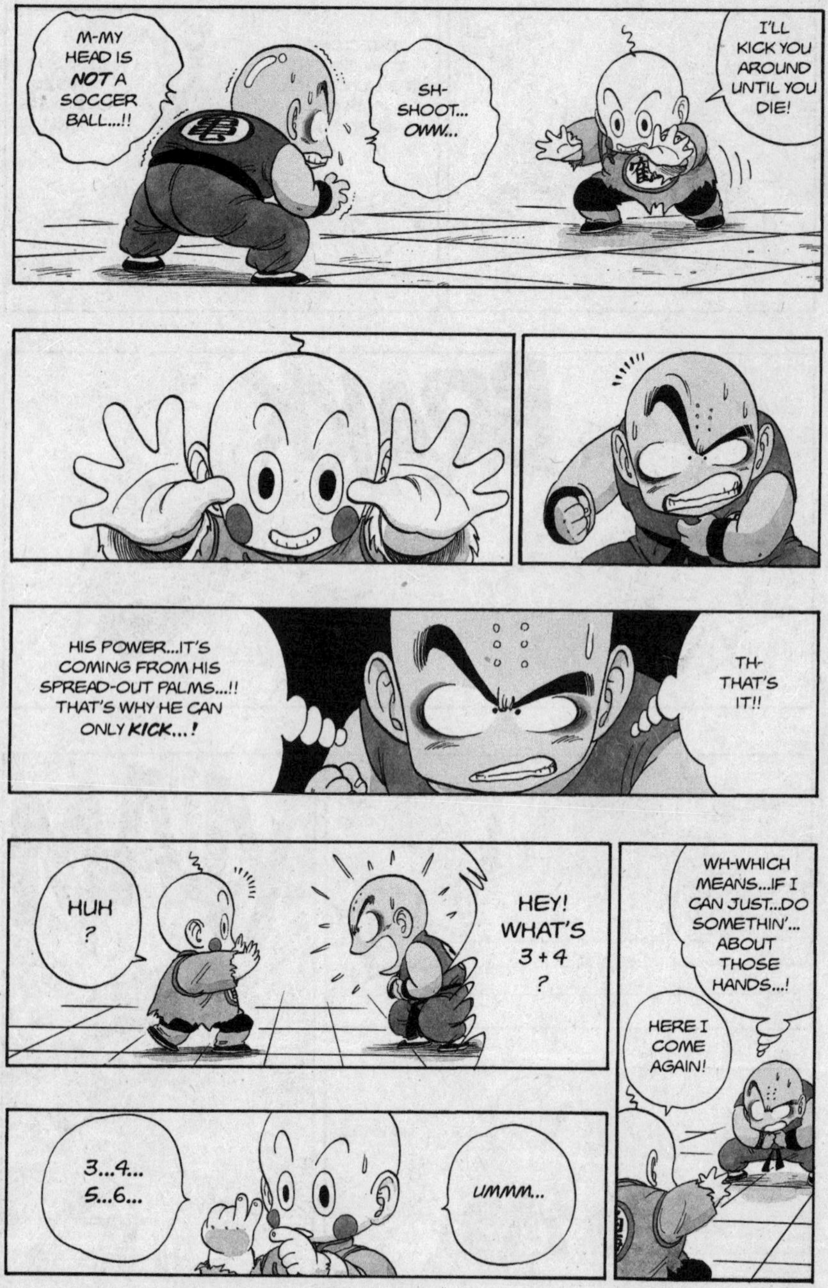
I'LL KICK YOU AROUND UNTIL YOU DIE!
SH- SHOOT... OWW...
M-MY HEAD IS NOT A SOCCER BALL...!!
TH- THAT'S IT!!
HIS POWER...IT'S COMING FROM HIS SPREAD-OUT PALMS...!! THAT'S WHY HE CAN ONLY KICK...!
WH-WHICH MEANS...IF I CAN JUST...DO SOMETHIN'... ABOUT THOSE HANDS...!
HERE I COME AGAIN!
HEY! WHAT'S 3 + 4 ?
HUH ?
UMMM...
3...4... 5...6...

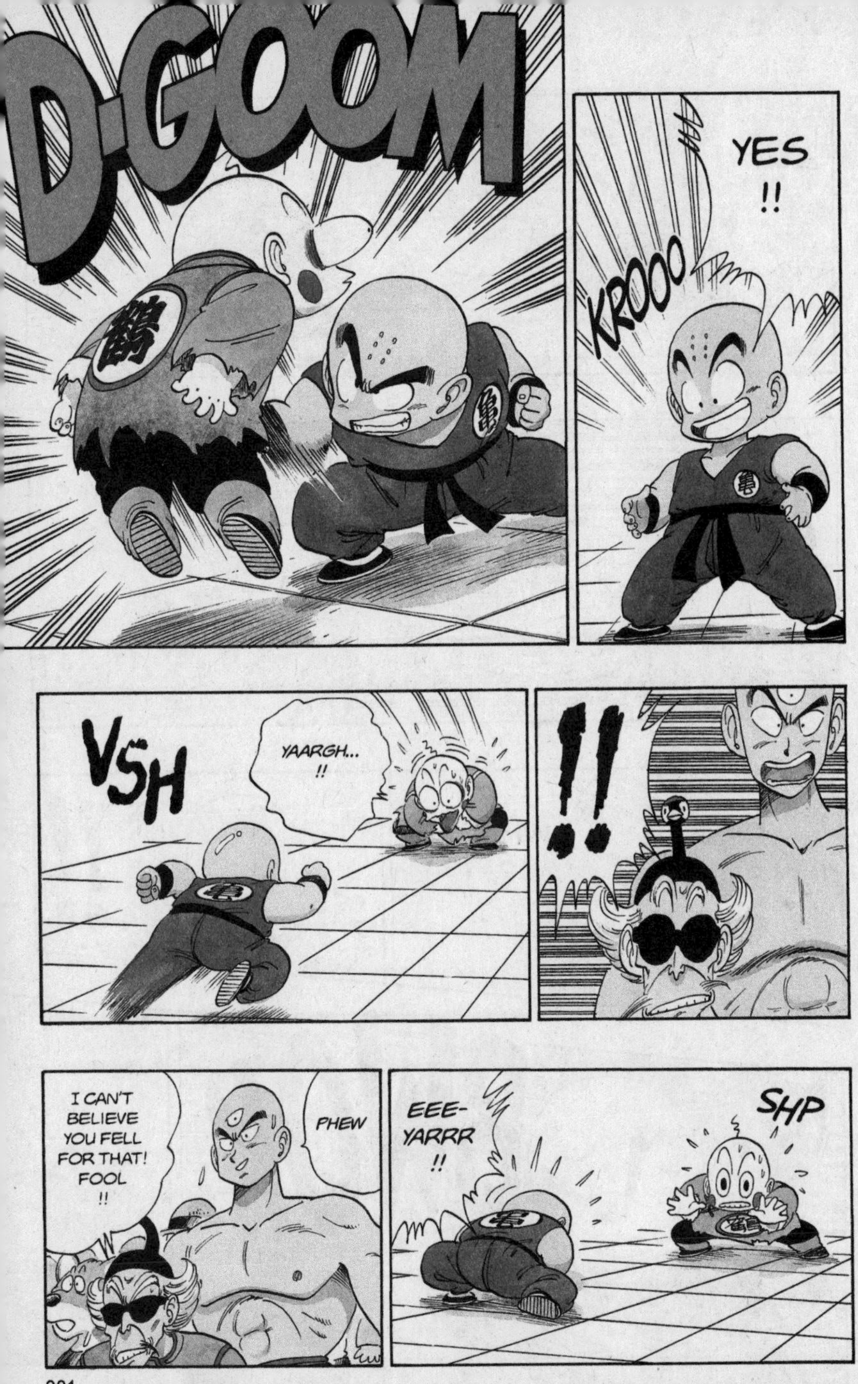
YES !!
KROOO
D-GOOM
!!
YAARGH... !!
VSH
SHP
EEE-YARRR !!
PHEW
I CAN'T BELIEVE YOU FELL FOR THAT! FOOL !!

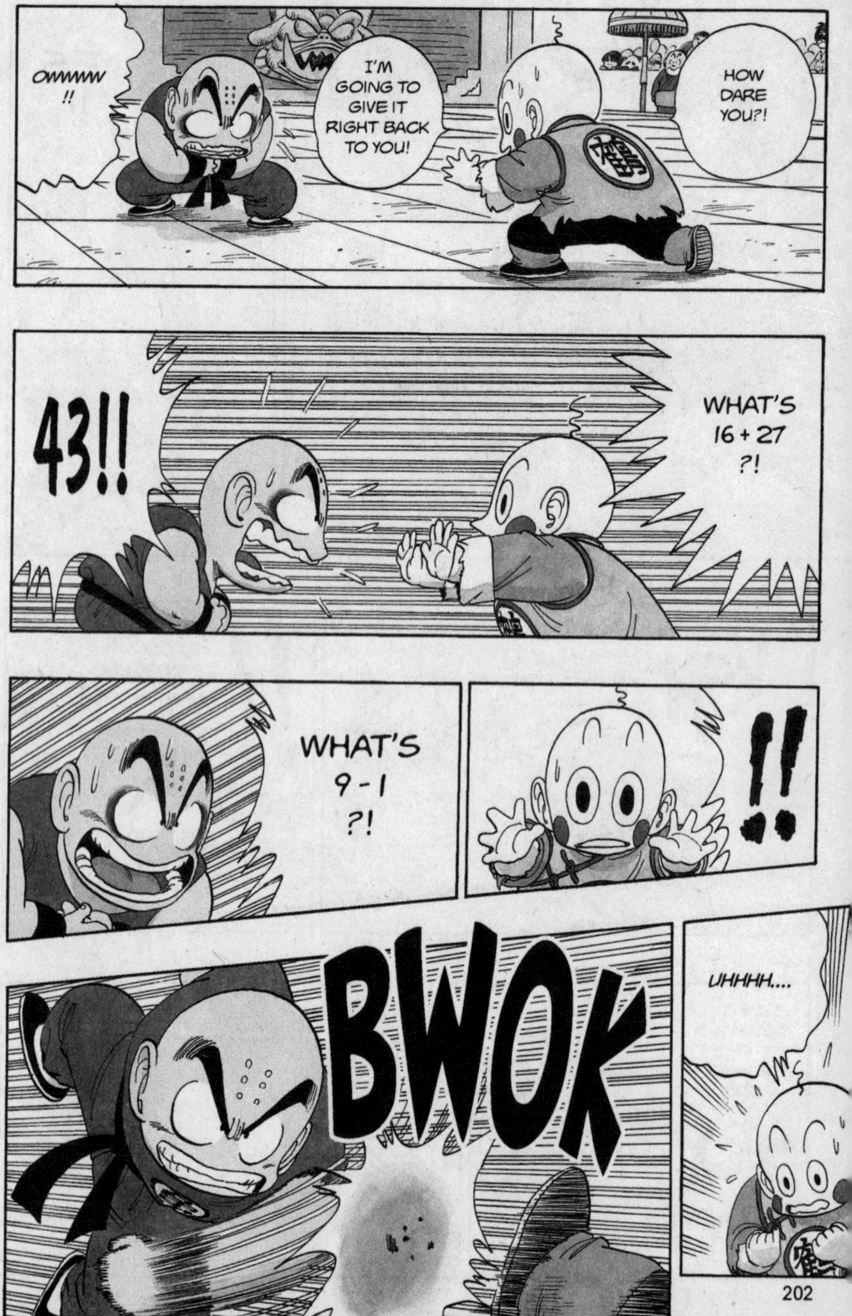
HOW DARE YOU?!
I'M GOING TO GIVE IT RIGHT BACK TO YOU!
OWWWW !!
WHAT'S 16 + 27 ?!
43!!
!!
WHAT'S 9 - 1 ?!
UHHHH....
BWOK

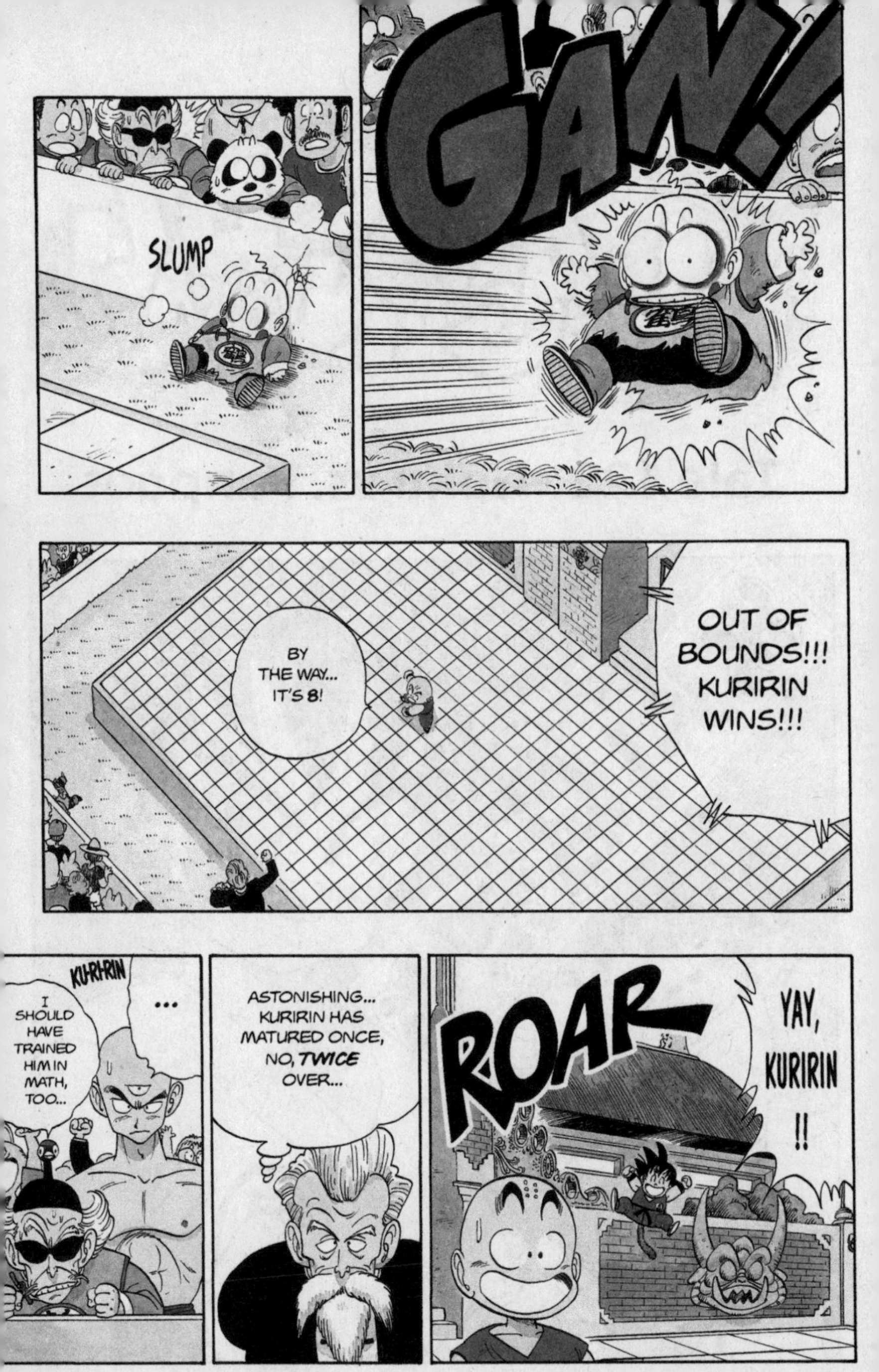
GAN!
SLUMP
OUT OF BOUNDS!!! KURIRIN WINS!!!
BY THE WAY... IT'S 8!
YAY, KURIRIN !!
ROAR
ASTONISHING... KURIRIN HAS MATURED ONCE, NO, TWICE OVER...
...
KU-RI-RIN
I SHOULD HAVE TRAINED HIM IN MATH, TOO...

Tale 122 · Goku vs. Panpoot

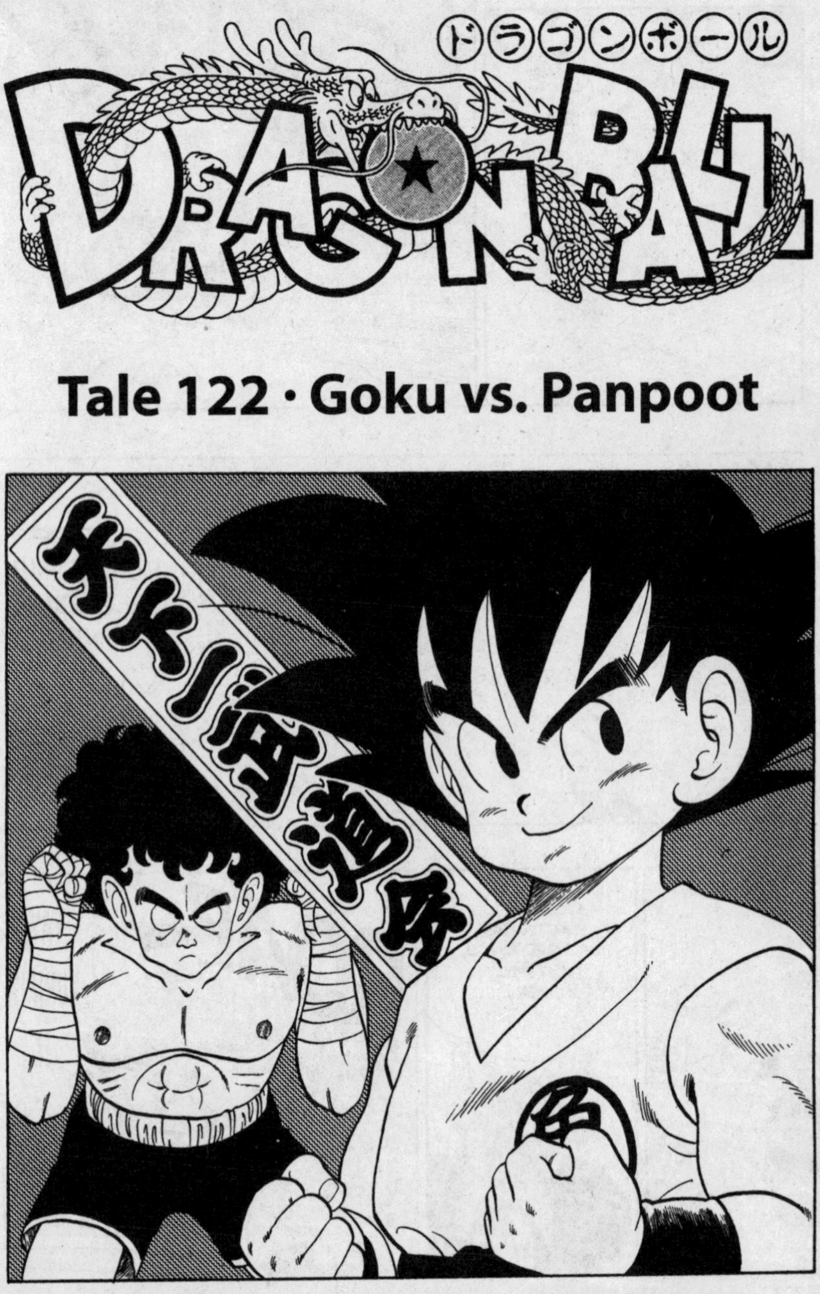

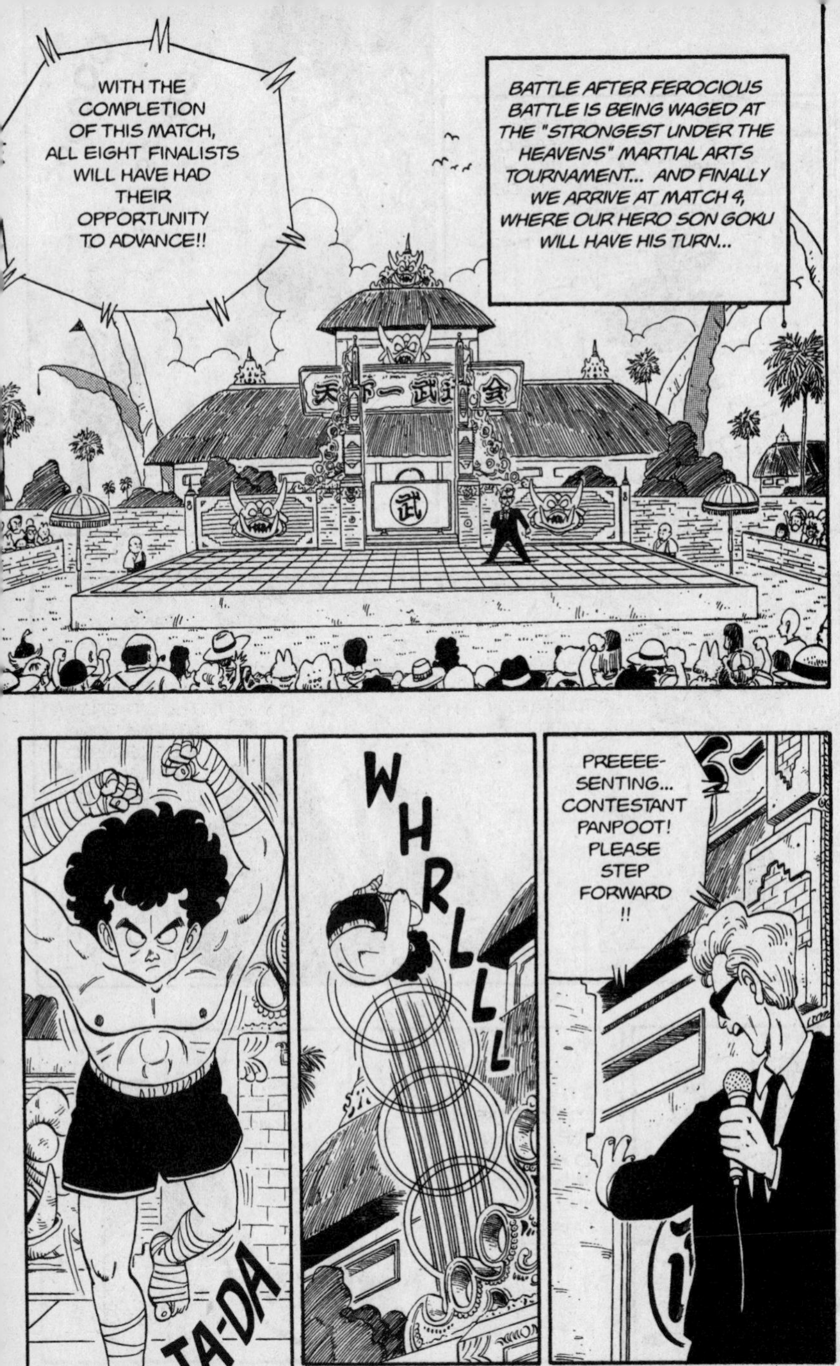
BATTLE AFTER FEROCIOUS BATTLE IS BEING WAGED AT THE "STRONGEST UNDER THE HEAVENS" MARTIAL ARTS TOURNAMENT... AND FINALLY WE ARRIVE AT MATCH 4, WHERE OUR HERO SON GOKU WILL HAVE HIS TURN...
WITH THE COMPLETION OF THIS MATCH, ALL EIGHT FINALISTS WILL HAVE HAD THEIR OPPORTUNITY TO ADVANCE!!
PREEEE-SENTING... CONTESTANT PANPOOT! PLEASE STEP FORWARD !!
WHRLLLL
TA-DA

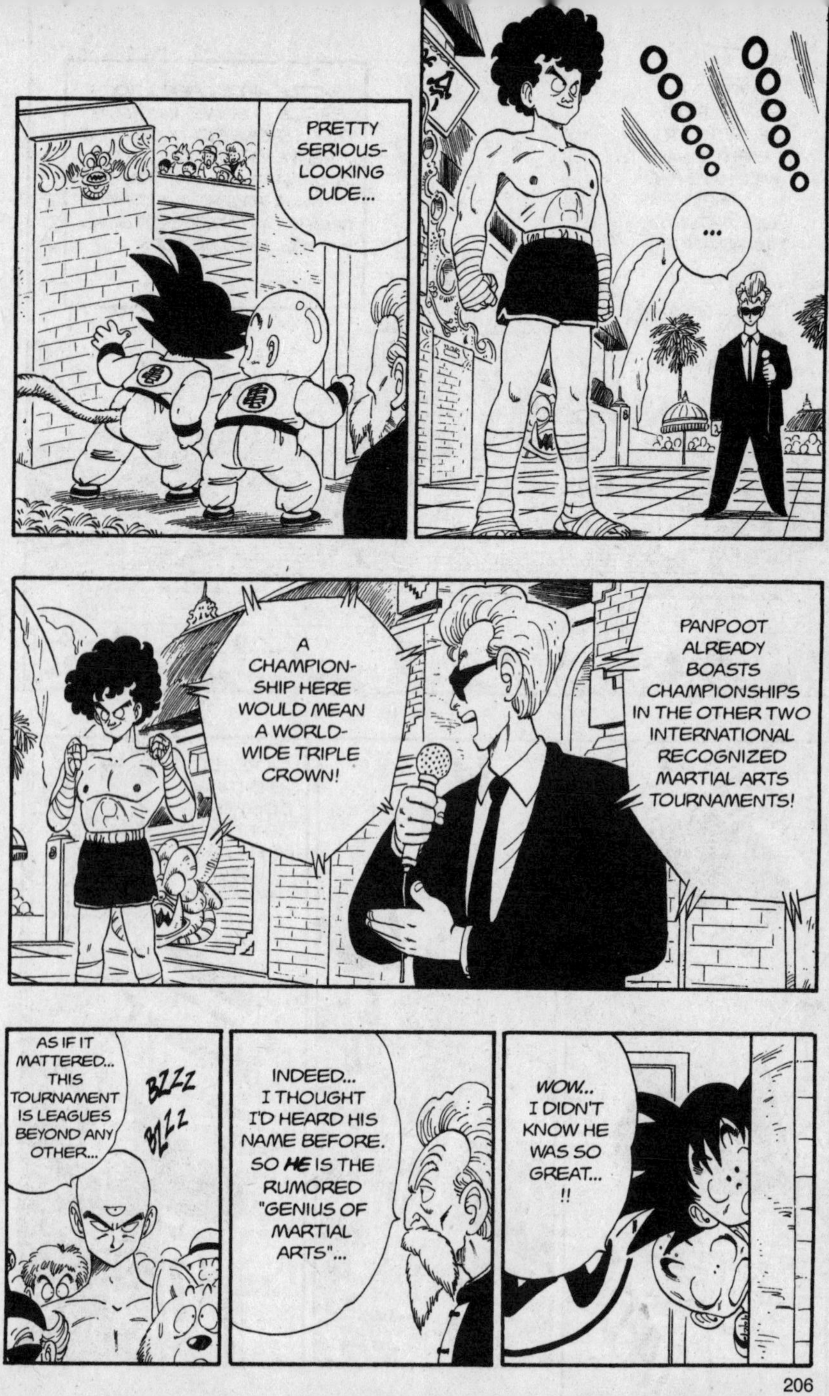
OOOOOO
OOOOOO
...
PRETTY SERIOUS-LOOKING DUDE...
PANPOOT ALREADY BOASTS CHAMPIONSHIPS IN THE OTHER TWO INTERNATIONAL RECOGNIZED MARTIAL ARTS TOURNAMENTS!
A CHAMPIONSHIP HERE WOULD MEAN A WORLD-WIDE TRIPLE CROWN!
WOW... I DIDN'T KNOW HE WAS SO GREAT...
!!
INDEED... I THOUGHT I'D HEARD HIS NAME BEFORE. SO ***HE*** IS THE RUMORED "GENIUS OF MARTIAL ARTS"...
AS IF IT MATTERED... THIS TOURNAMENT IS LEAGUES BEYOND ANY OTHER...
BZZZ
BZZZ

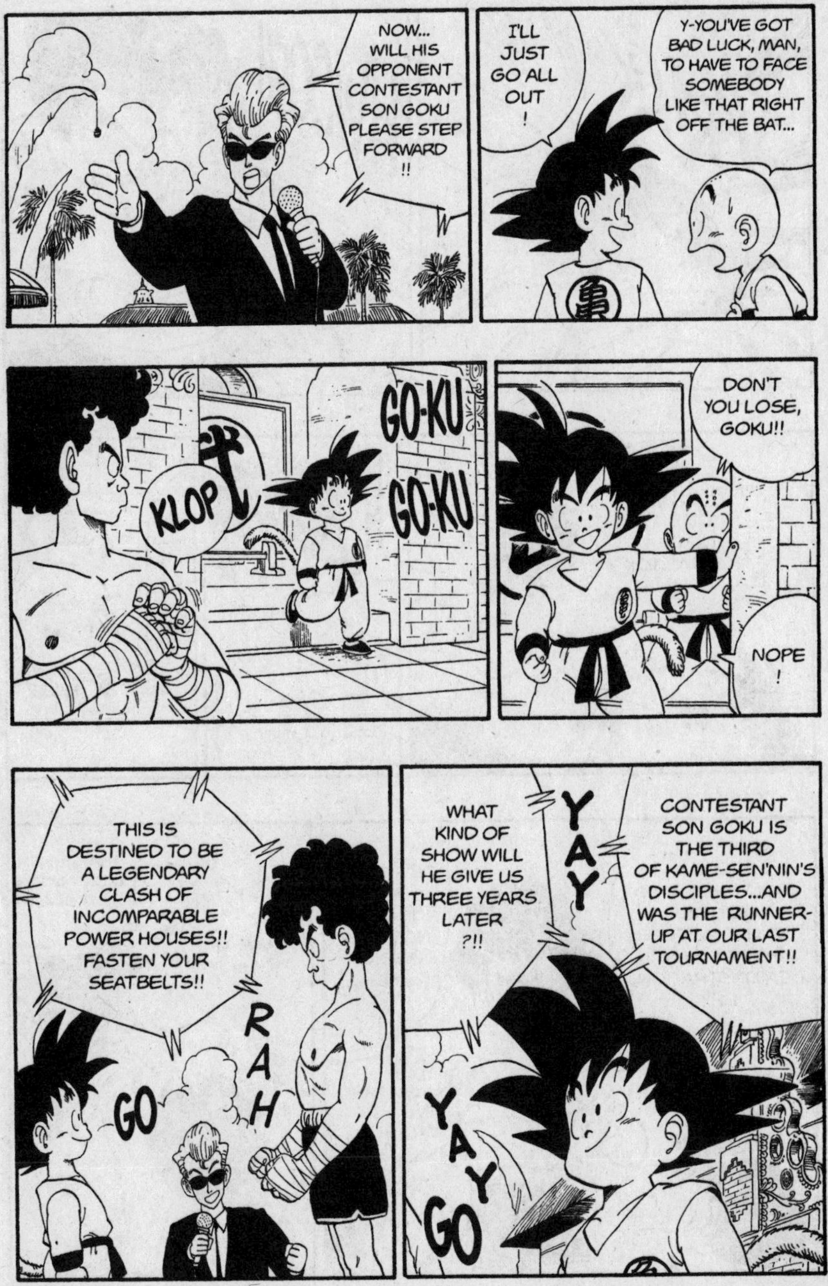
Y-YOU'VE GOT BAD LUCK, MAN, TO HAVE TO FACE SOMEBODY LIKE THAT RIGHT OFF THE BAT...
I'LL JUST GO ALL OUT!
NOW... WILL HIS OPPONENT CONTESTANT SON GOKU PLEASE STEP FORWARD!!
DON'T YOU LOSE, GOKU!!
NOPE!
GO-KU
GO-KU
KLOP
CONTESTANT SON GOKU IS THE THIRD OF KAME-SEN'NIN'S DISCIPLES...AND WAS THE RUNNER-UP AT OUR LAST TOURNAMENT!!
WHAT KIND OF SHOW WILL HE GIVE US THREE YEARS LATER?!!
YAY
YAY
YAY
GO
THIS IS DESTINED TO BE A LEGENDARY CLASH OF INCOMPARABLE POWER HOUSES!! FASTEN YOUR SEATBELTS!!
RAH
GO

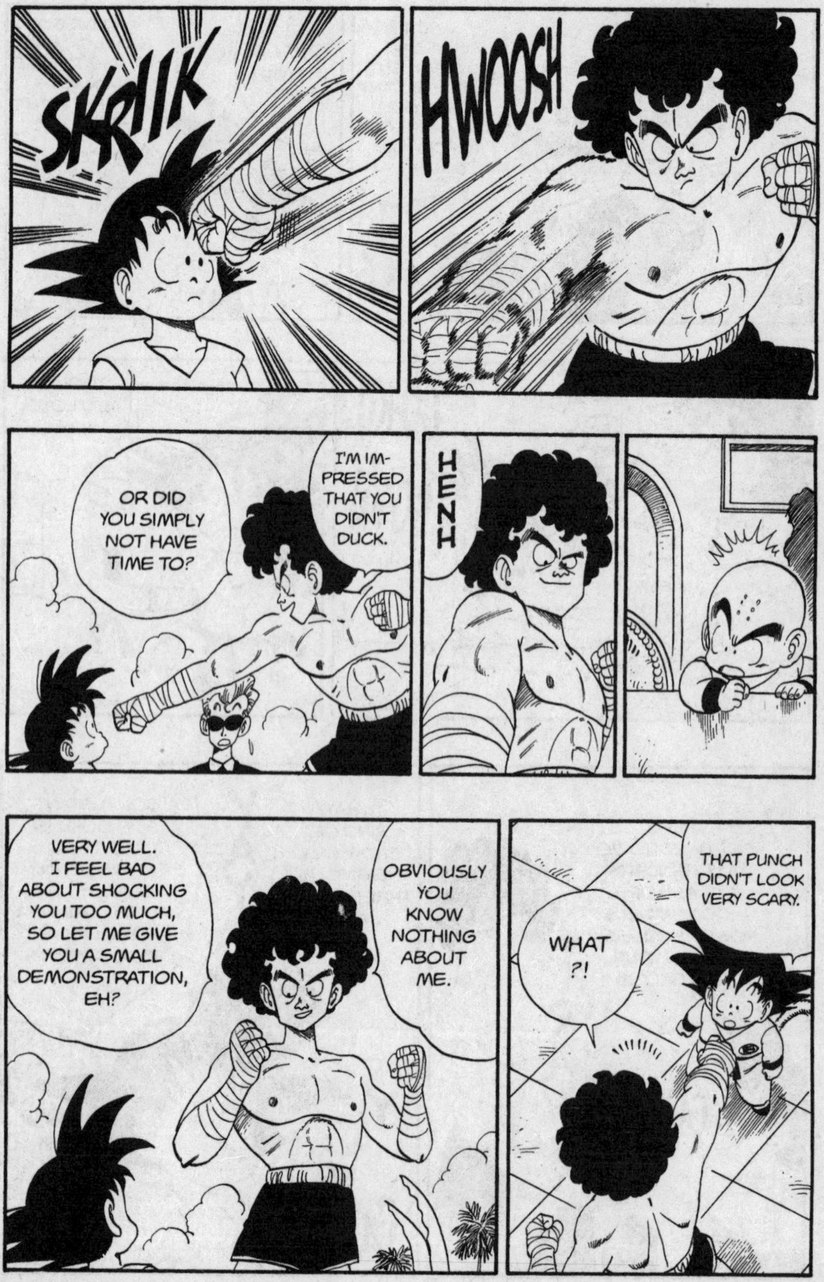
HWOOSH
SKRIIK
HENH
I'M IMPRESSED THAT YOU DIDN'T DUCK.
OR DID YOU SIMPLY NOT HAVE TIME TO?
THAT PUNCH DIDN'T LOOK VERY SCARY.
WHAT ?!
OBVIOUSLY YOU KNOW NOTHING ABOUT ME.
VERY WELL. I FEEL BAD ABOUT SHOCKING YOU TOO MUCH, SO LET ME GIVE YOU A SMALL DEMONSTRATION, EH?

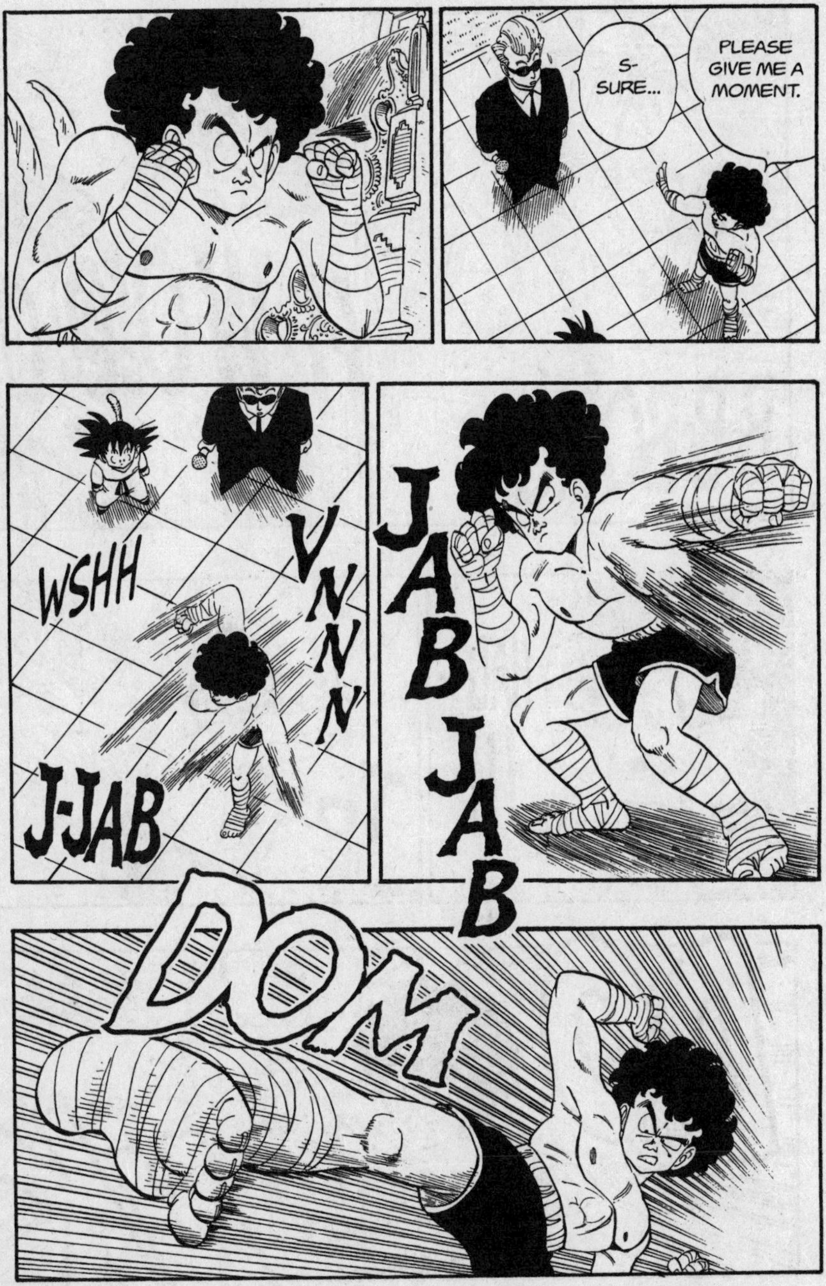
PLEASE GIVE ME A MOMENT.
S-SURE...
JAB JAB
VNNN
WSHH
J-JAB
DOM

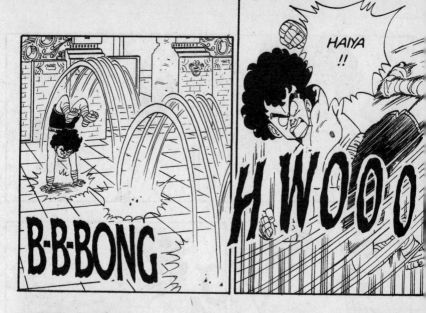

B-B-BONG

HAIYA !!

HWOOOO

HAO—!!!

TP

DO

NK

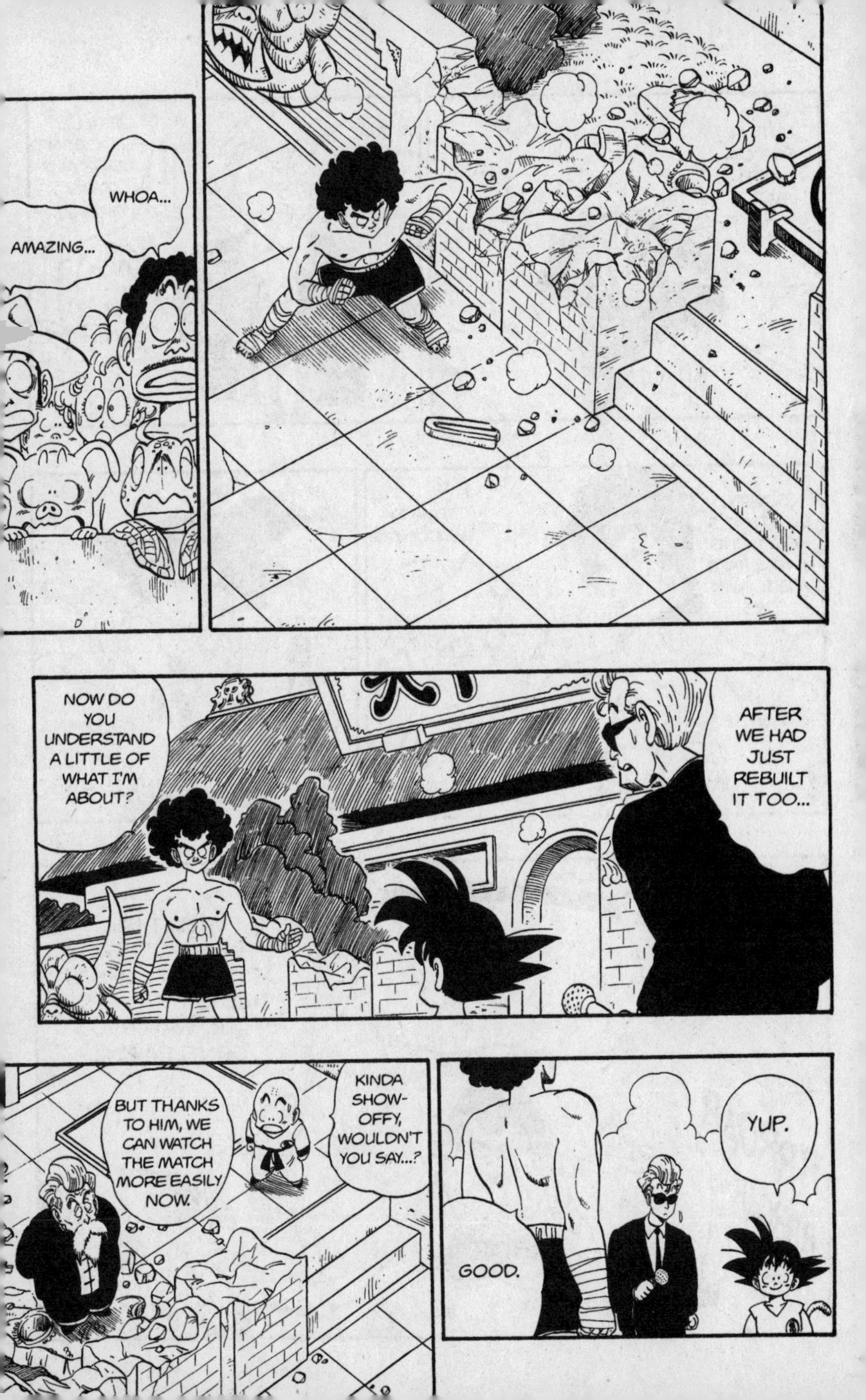
WHOA...
AMAZING...
AFTER WE HAD JUST REBUILT IT TOO...
NOW DO YOU UNDERSTAND A LITTLE OF WHAT I'M ABOUT?
YUP.
GOOD.
KINDA SHOW-OFFY, WOULDN'T YOU SAY...?
BUT THANKS TO HIM, WE CAN WATCH THE MATCH MORE EASILY NOW.

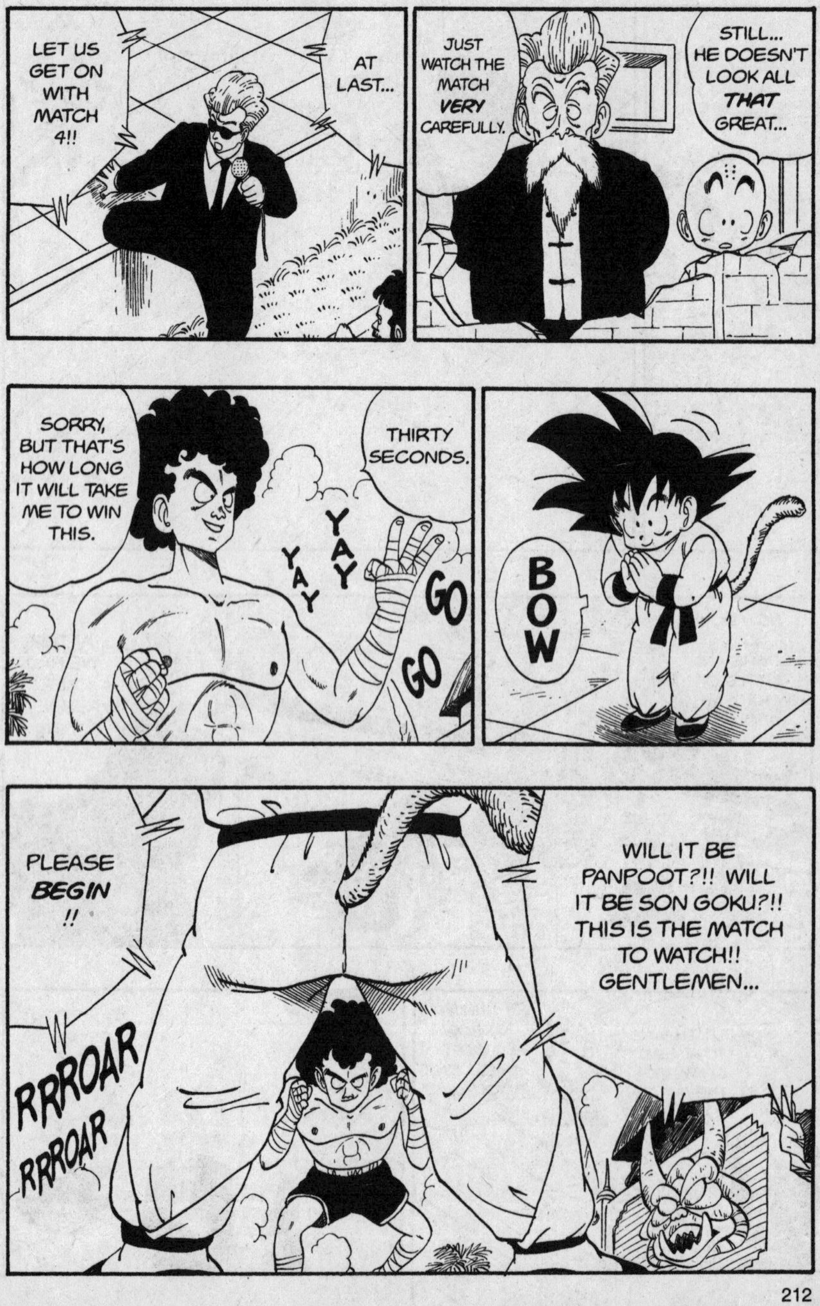
STILL... HE DOESN'T LOOK ALL THAT GREAT...
JUST WATCH THE MATCH VERY CAREFULLY.
AT LAST...
LET US GET ON WITH MATCH 4!!
BOW
BOW
THIRTY SECONDS.
SORRY, BUT THAT'S HOW LONG IT WILL TAKE ME TO WIN THIS.
YAY
YAY
GO
GO
WILL IT BE PANPOOT?!! WILL IT BE SON GOKU?!! THIS IS THE MATCH TO WATCH!! GENTLEMEN...
PLEASE BEGIN !!
RRROAR
RRROAR

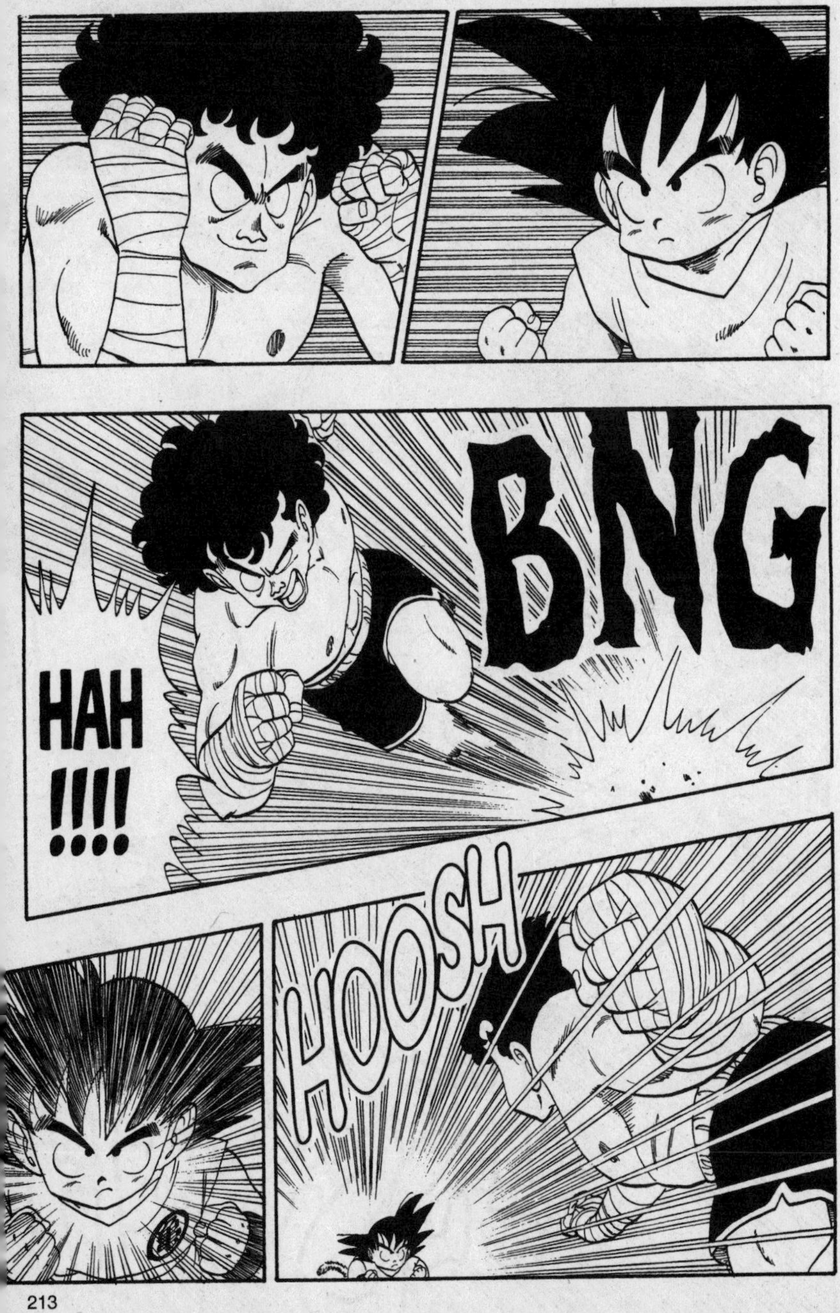
BNG
HAH !!!!
HOOSH

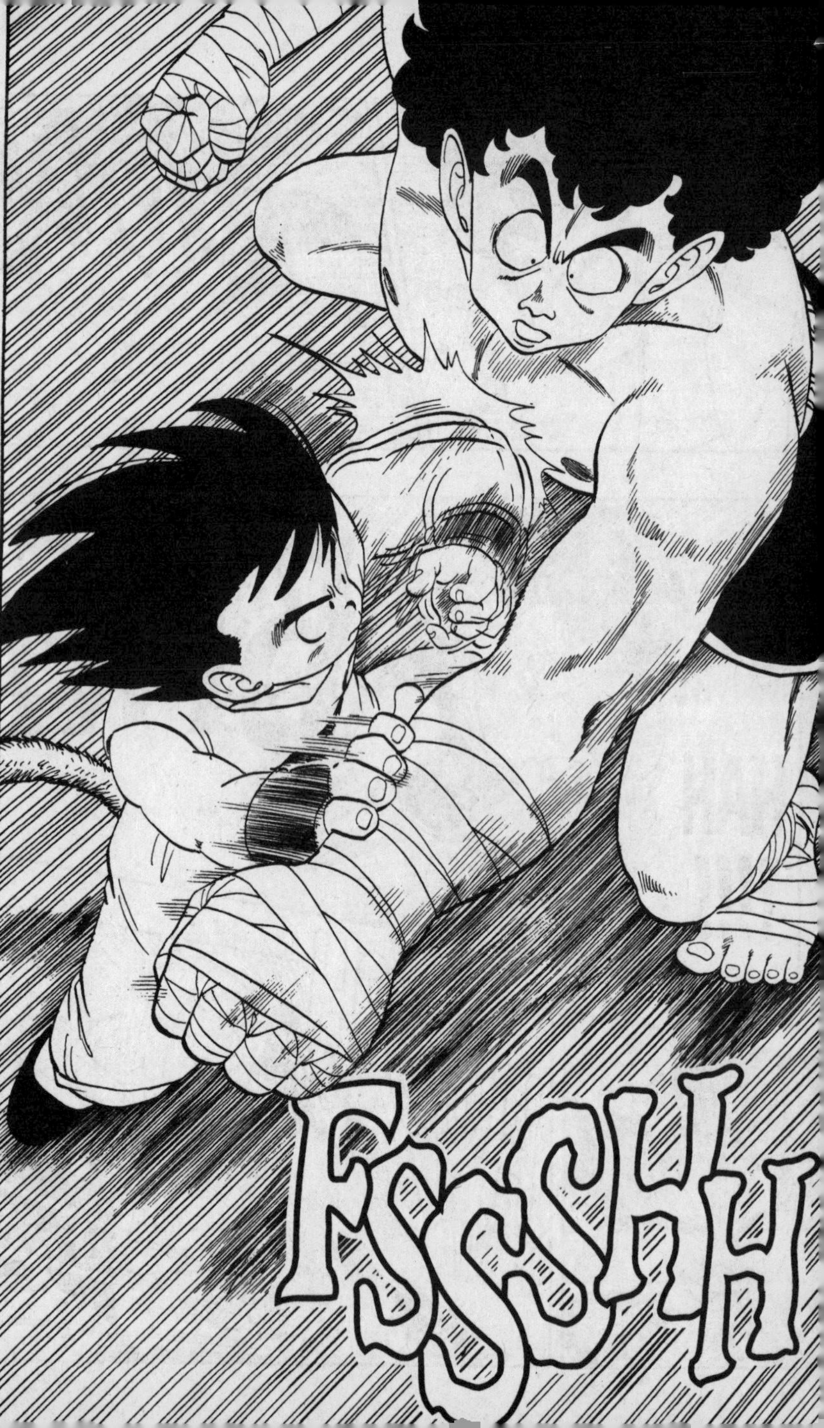
FSSSH

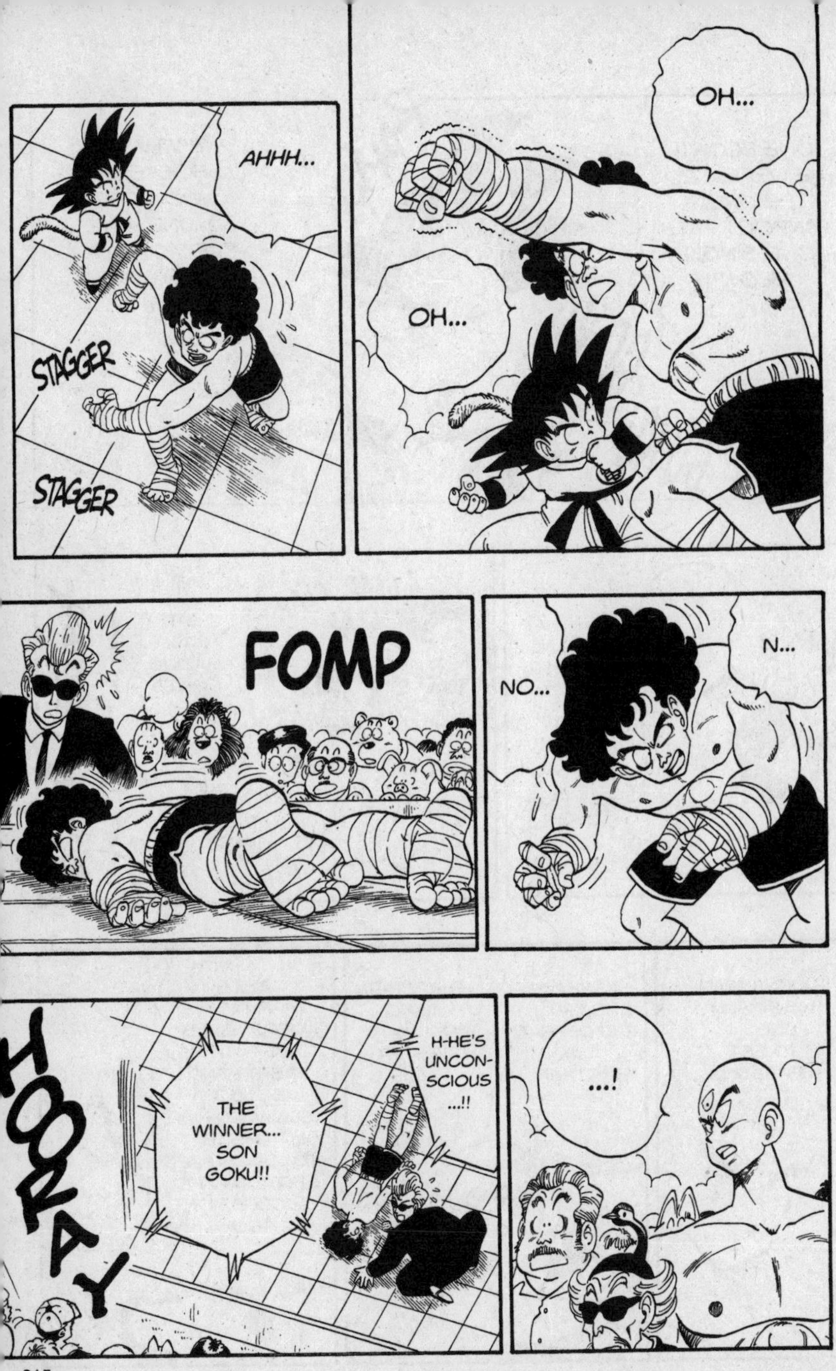

OH...
OH...
AHHH...
STAGGER
STAGGER
N...
NO...
FOMP
...!
H-HE'S UNCONSCIOUS ...!!
THE WINNER... SON GOKU!!
HOORAY

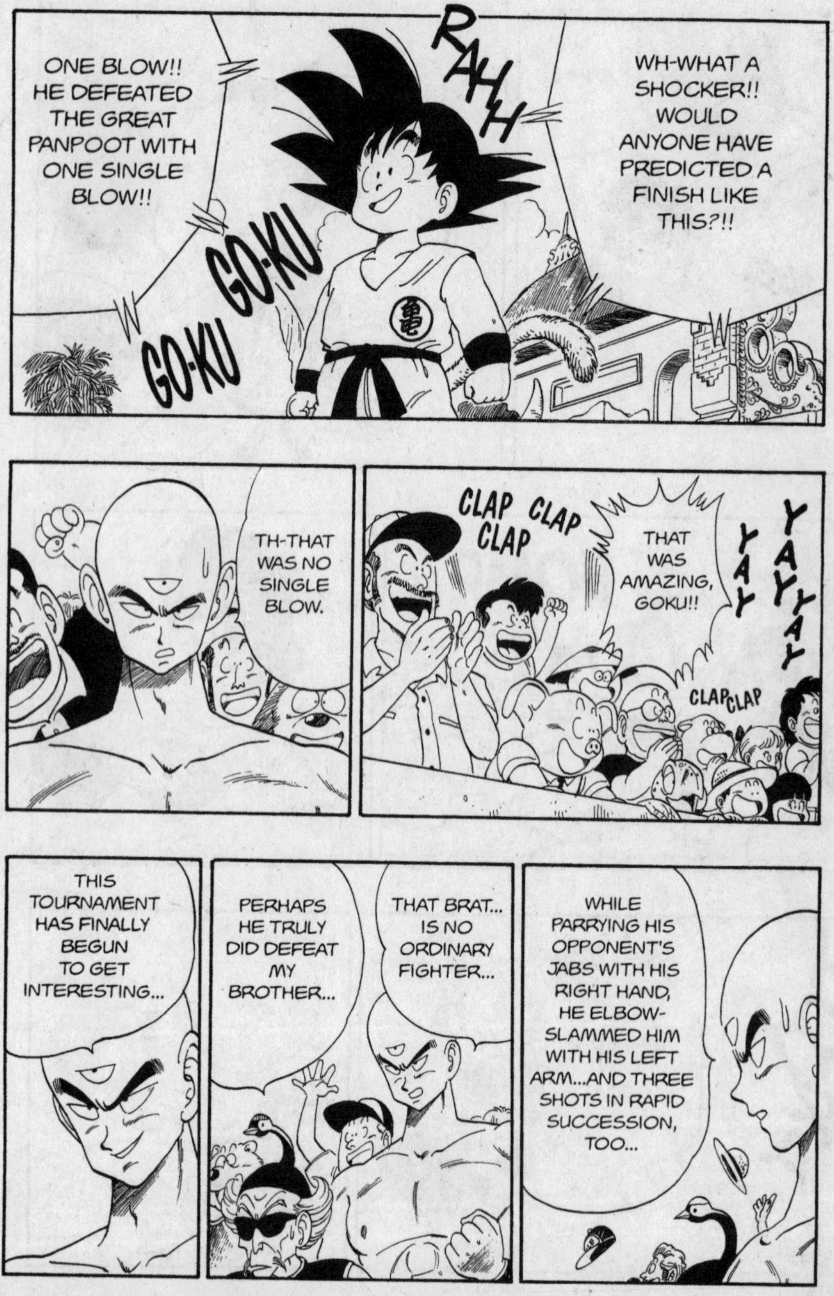
WH-WHAT A SHOCKER!! WOULD ANYONE HAVE PREDICTED A FINISH LIKE THIS?!!
RAHH
ONE BLOW!! HE DEFEATED THE GREAT PANPOOT WITH ONE SINGLE BLOW!!
GO-KU
GO-KU
YAY YAY YAY
THAT WAS AMAZING, GOKU!!
CLAP CLAP CLAP
CLAP CLAP
TH-THAT WAS NO SINGLE BLOW.
WHILE PARRYING HIS OPPONENT'S JABS WITH HIS RIGHT HAND, HE ELBOW-SLAMMED HIM WITH HIS LEFT ARM...AND THREE SHOTS IN RAPID SUCCESSION, TOO...
THAT BRAT... IS NO ORDINARY FIGHTER...
PERHAPS HE TRULY DID DEFEAT MY BROTHER...
THIS TOURNAMENT HAS FINALLY BEGUN TO GET INTERESTING...

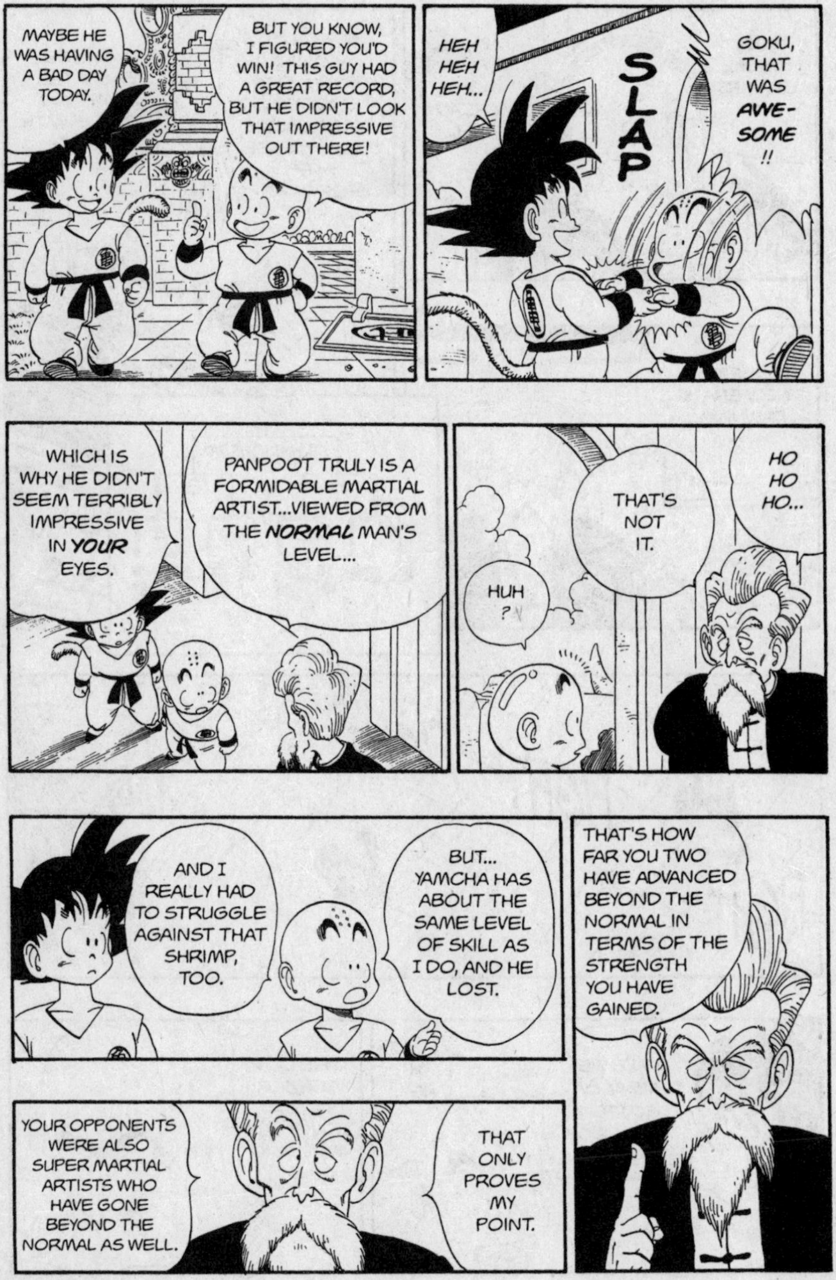
GOKU, THAT WAS AWESOME!!
SLAP
HEH HEH HEH...
BUT YOU KNOW, I FIGURED YOU'D WIN! THIS GUY HAD A GREAT RECORD, BUT HE DIDN'T LOOK THAT IMPRESSIVE OUT THERE!
MAYBE HE WAS HAVING A BAD DAY TODAY.
HO HO HO...
THAT'S NOT IT.
HUH?
PANPOOT TRULY IS A FORMIDABLE MARTIAL ARTIST...VIEWED FROM THE NORMAL MAN'S LEVEL...
WHICH IS WHY HE DIDN'T SEEM TERRIBLY IMPRESSIVE IN YOUR EYES.
THAT'S HOW FAR YOU TWO HAVE ADVANCED BEYOND THE NORMAL IN TERMS OF THE STRENGTH YOU HAVE GAINED.
BUT... YAMCHA HAS ABOUT THE SAME LEVEL OF SKILL AS I DO, AND HE LOST.
AND I REALLY HAD TO STRUGGLE AGAINST THAT SHRIMP, TOO.
THAT ONLY PROVES MY POINT.
YOUR OPPONENTS WERE ALSO SUPER MARTIAL ARTISTS WHO HAVE GONE BEYOND THE NORMAL AS WELL.

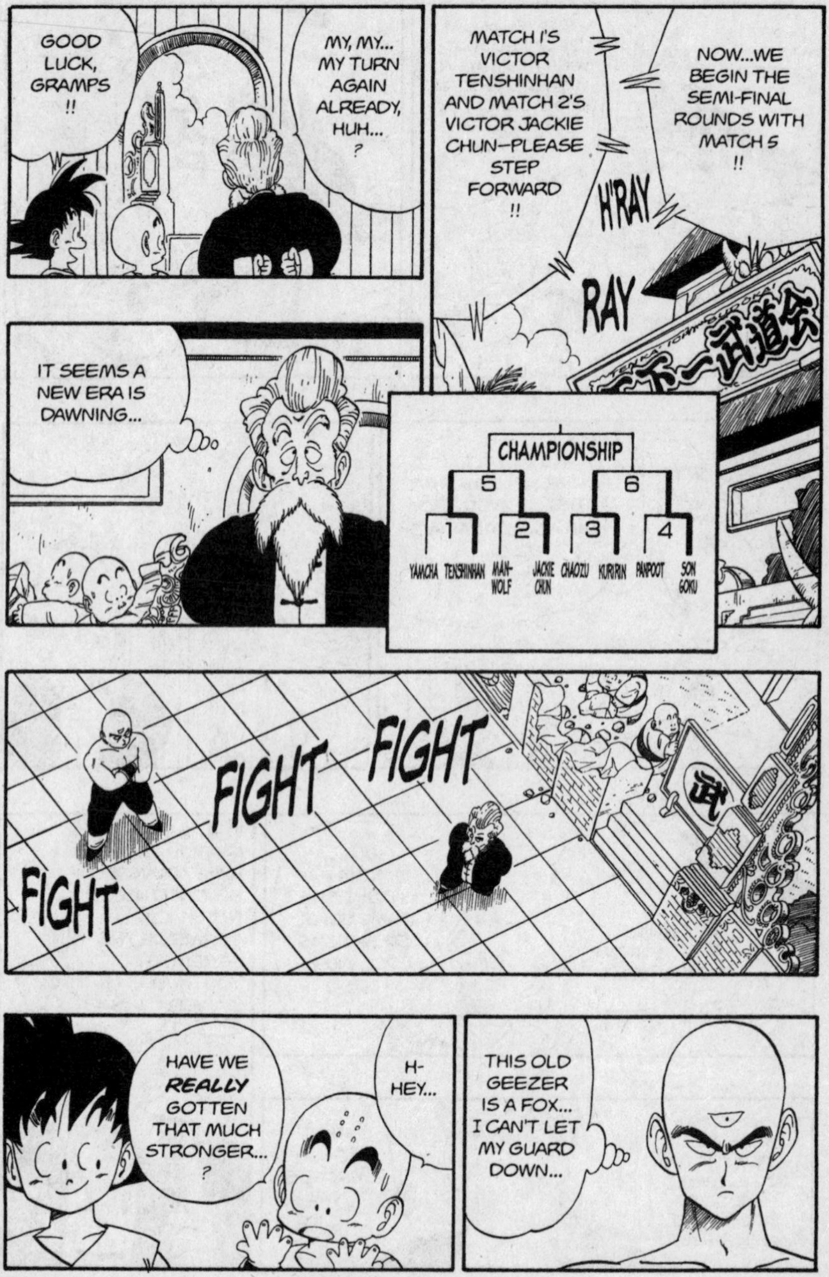
NOW...WE BEGIN THE SEMI-FINAL ROUNDS WITH MATCH 5!!
MATCH 1'S VICTOR TENSHINHAN AND MATCH 2'S VICTOR JACKIE CHUN—PLEASE STEP FORWARD!!
H'RAY
RAY
MY, MY... MY TURN AGAIN ALREADY, HUH...?
GOOD LUCK, GRAMPS!!
IT SEEMS A NEW ERA IS DAWNING...
CHAMPIONSHIP
5
6
1
2
3
4
YAMCHA
TENSHINHAN
MAN-WOLF
JACKIE CHUN
CHAOZU
KURIRIN
PANPOOT
SON GOKU
FIGHT
FIGHT
FIGHT
THIS OLD GEEZER IS A FOX... I CAN'T LET MY GUARD DOWN...
H-HEY...
HAVE WE *REALLY* GOTTEN THAT MUCH STRONGER...?

Tale 123 · Tenshinhan vs. Jackie Chun

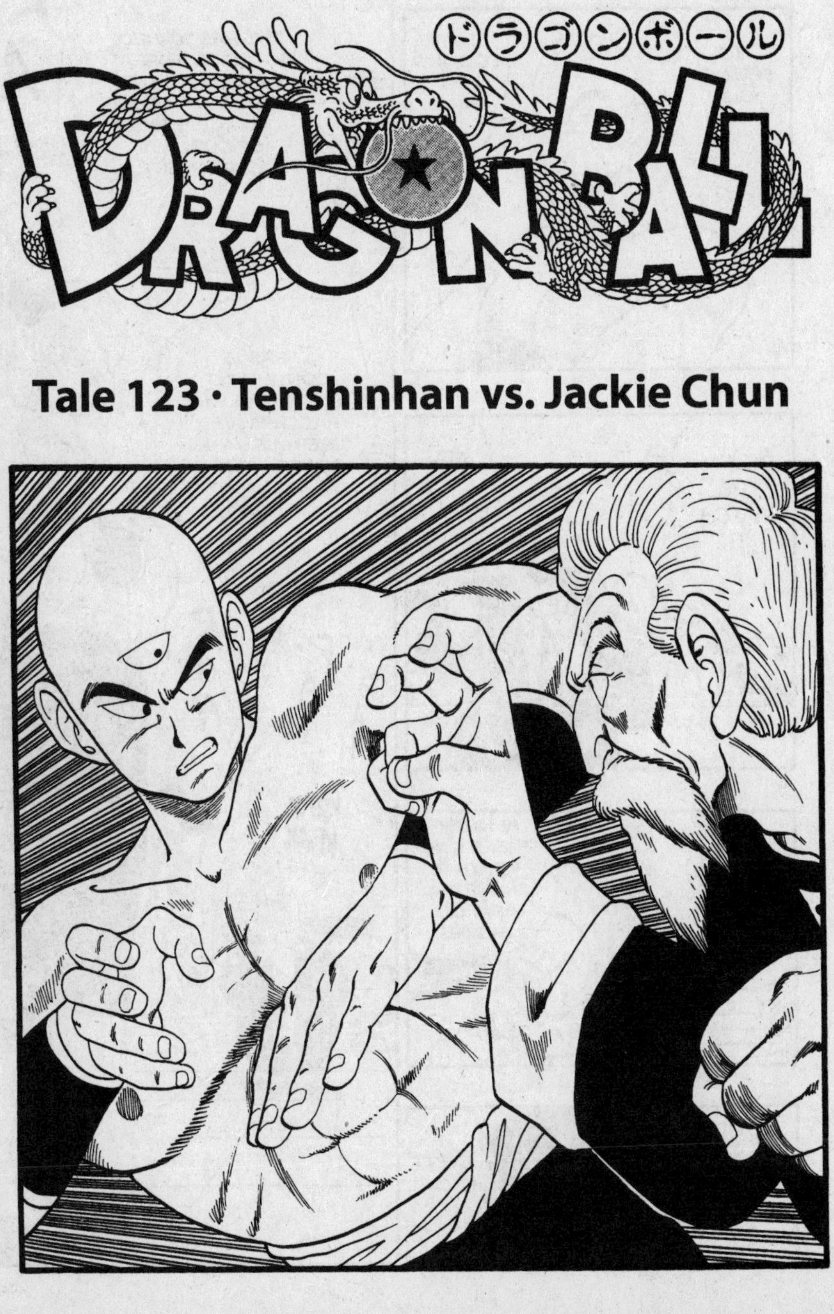

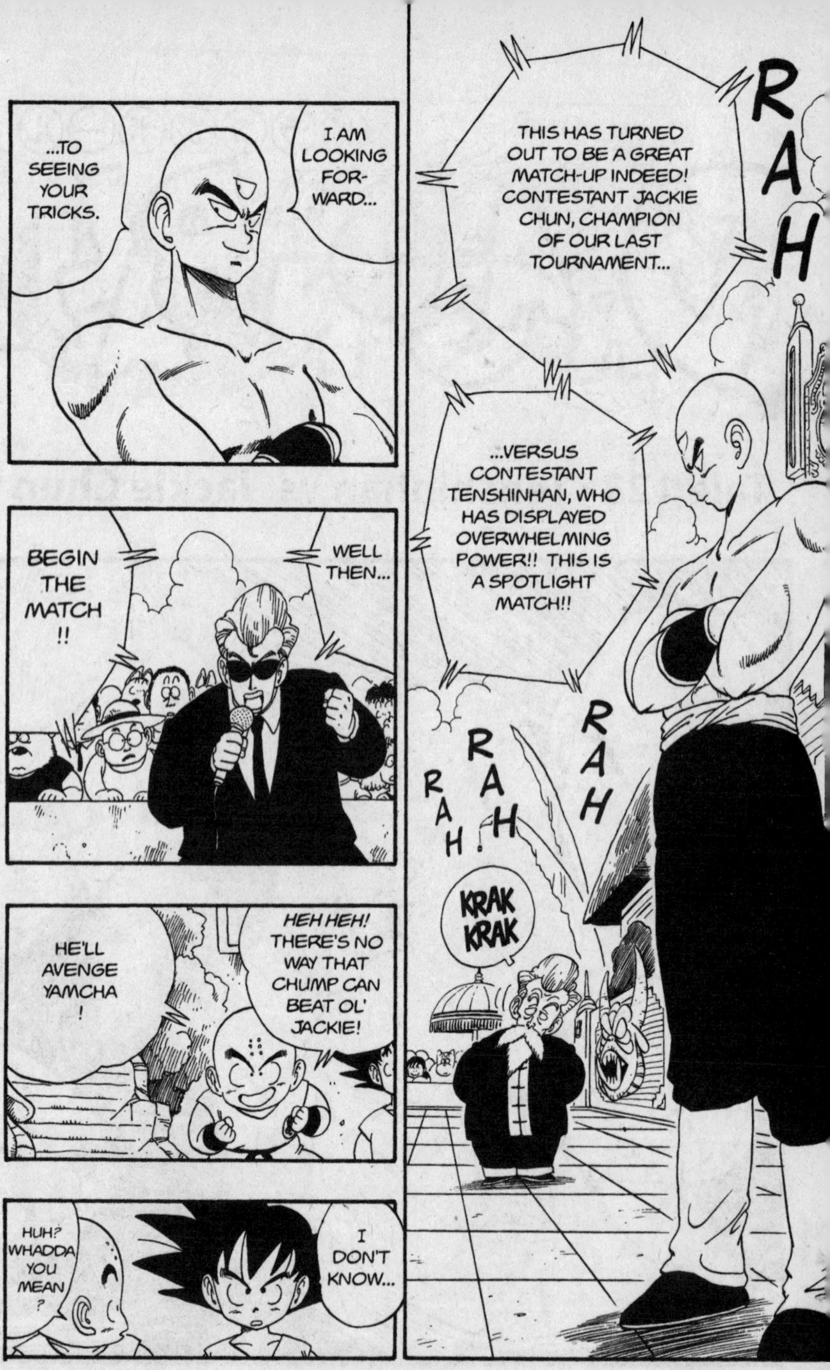
RAH
THIS HAS TURNED OUT TO BE A GREAT MATCH-UP INDEED! CONTESTANT JACKIE CHUN, CHAMPION OF OUR LAST TOURNAMENT...
...VERSUS CONTESTANT TENSHINHAN, WHO HAS DISPLAYED OVERWHELMING POWER!! THIS IS A SPOTLIGHT MATCH!!
RAH
RAH
RAH
KRAK KRAK
I AM LOOKING FOR-WARD...
...TO SEEING YOUR TRICKS.
WELL THEN...
BEGIN THE MATCH!!
HEH HEH! THERE'S NO WAY THAT CHUMP CAN BEAT OL' JACKIE!
HE'LL AVENGE YAMCHA!
I DON'T KNOW...
HUH? WHADDA YOU MEAN?

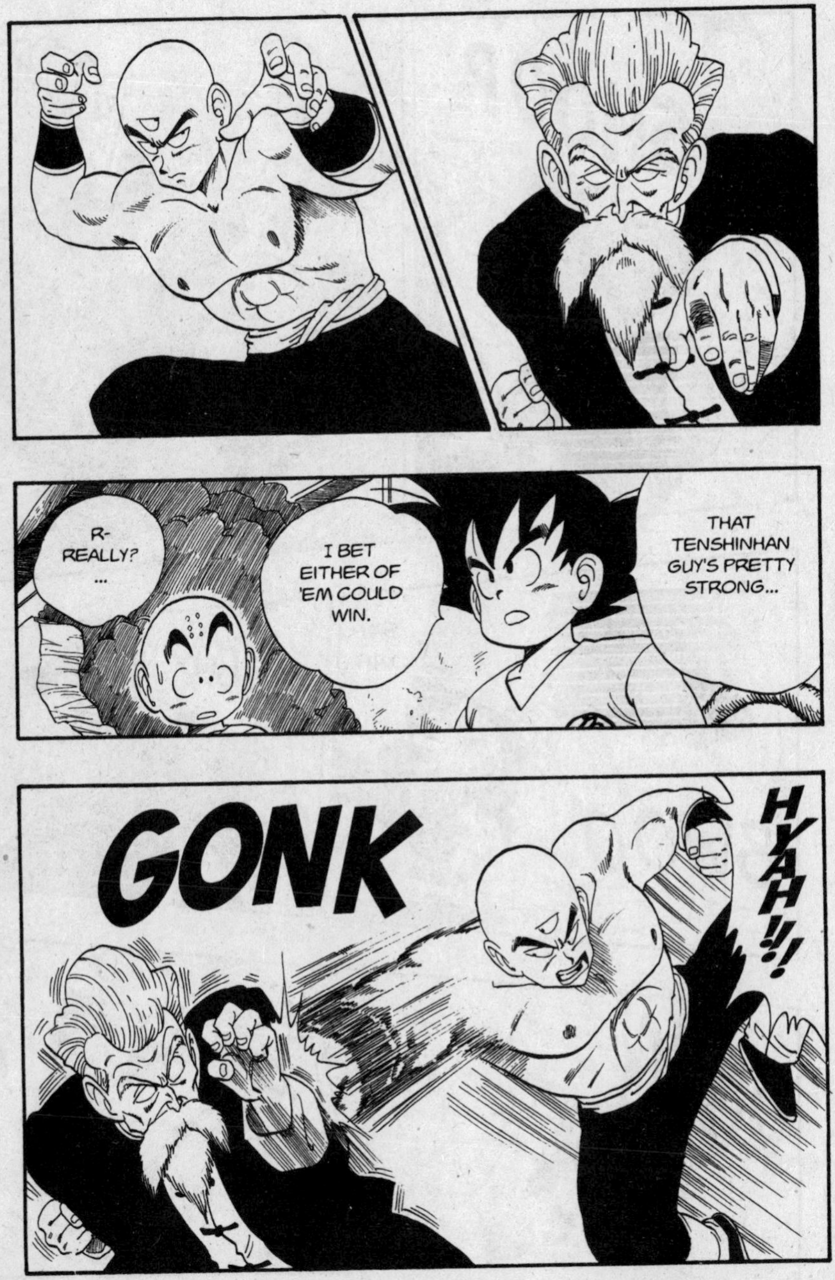

THAT TENSHINHAN GUY'S PRETTY STRONG...
I BET EITHER OF 'EM COULD WIN.
R- REALLY? ...
HYAH!!!
GONK

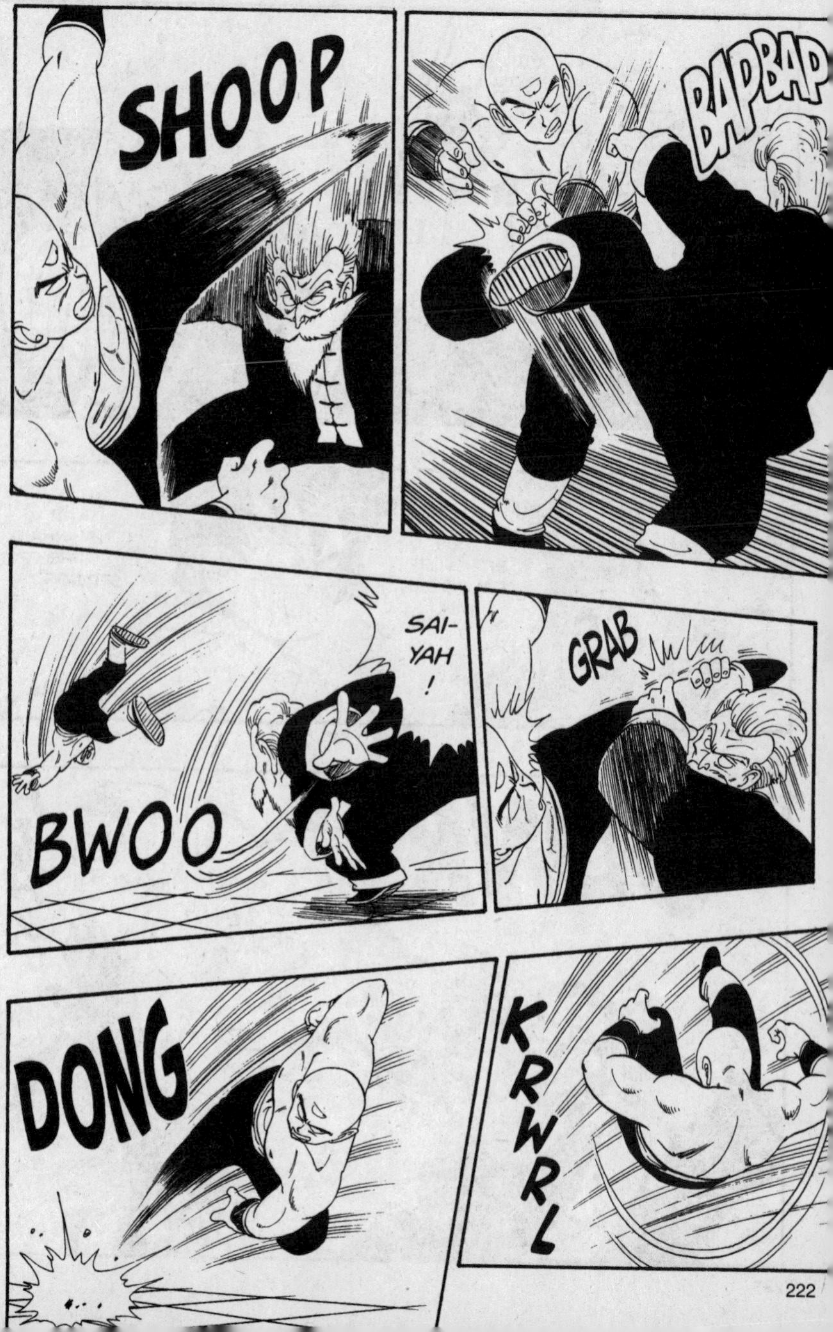
BAPBAP
SHOOP
GRAB
SAI-YAH!
BWOO
KRWRL
DONG

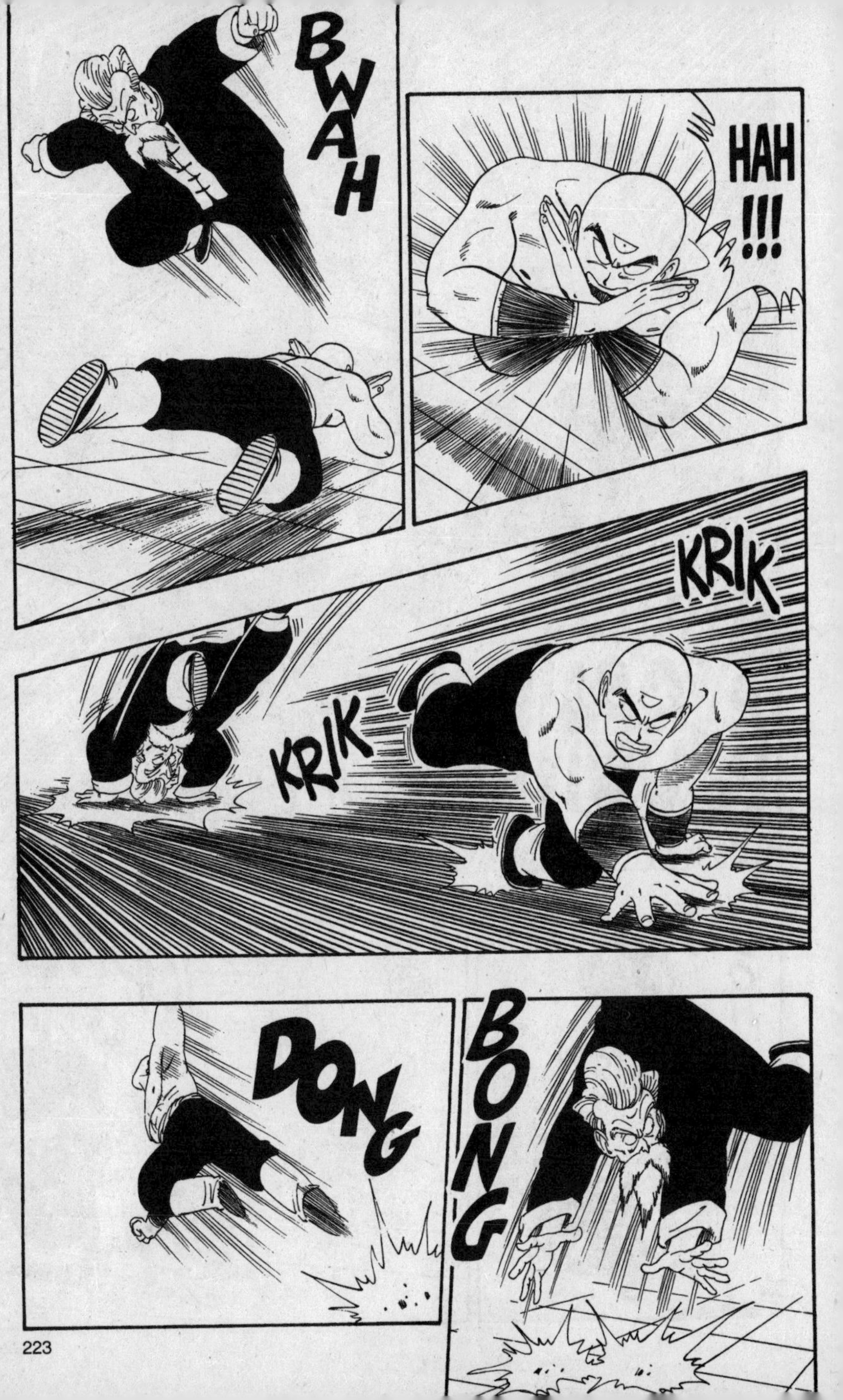
HAH !!!
BWAH
KRIK
KRIK
BONG
DONG

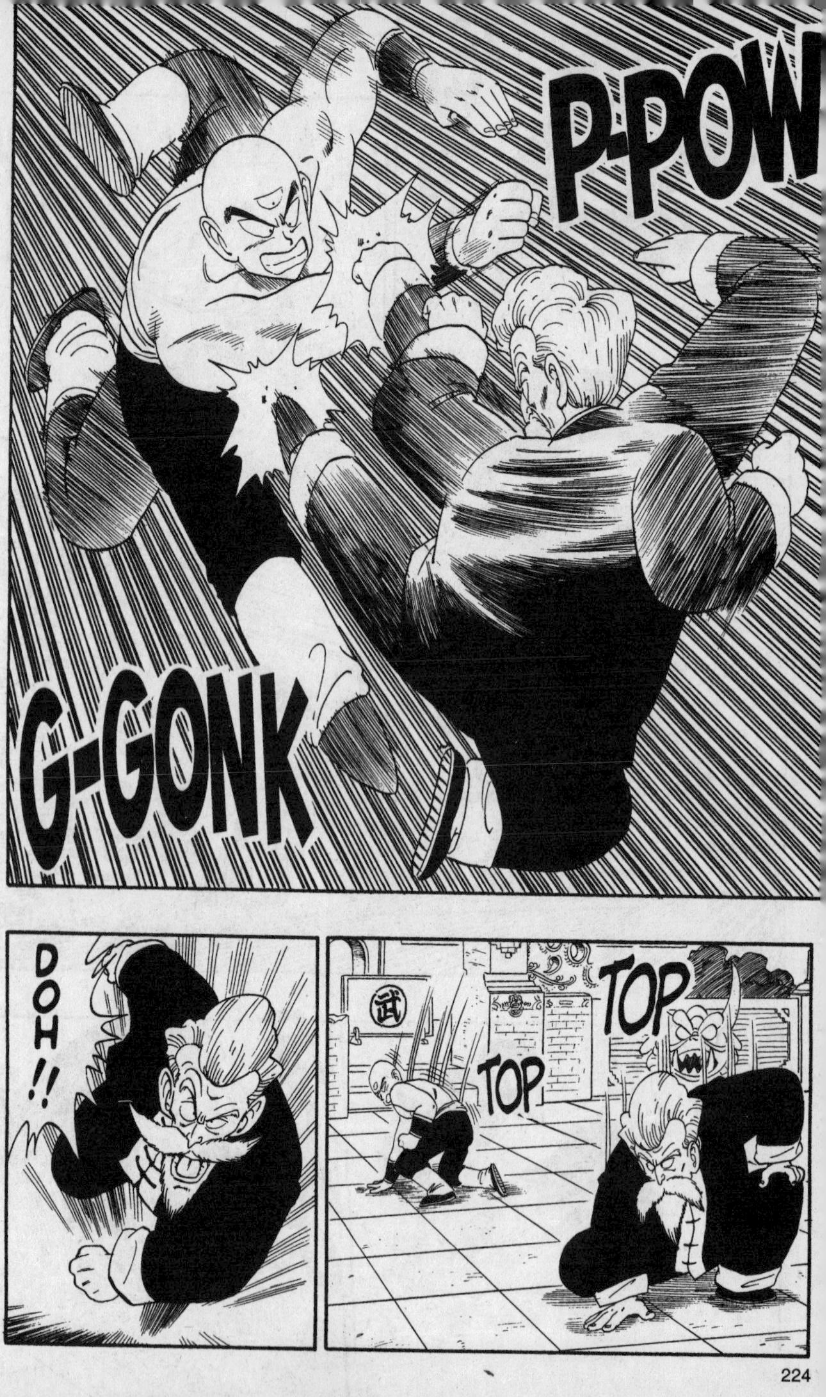
P-POW
G-GONK
TOP
TOP
武
DOH!!

HYOOO HYOOO

BAP BAP BAP

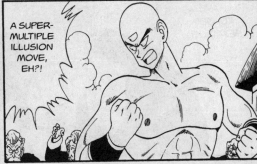

A SUPER-MULTIPLE ILLUSION MOVE, EH?!

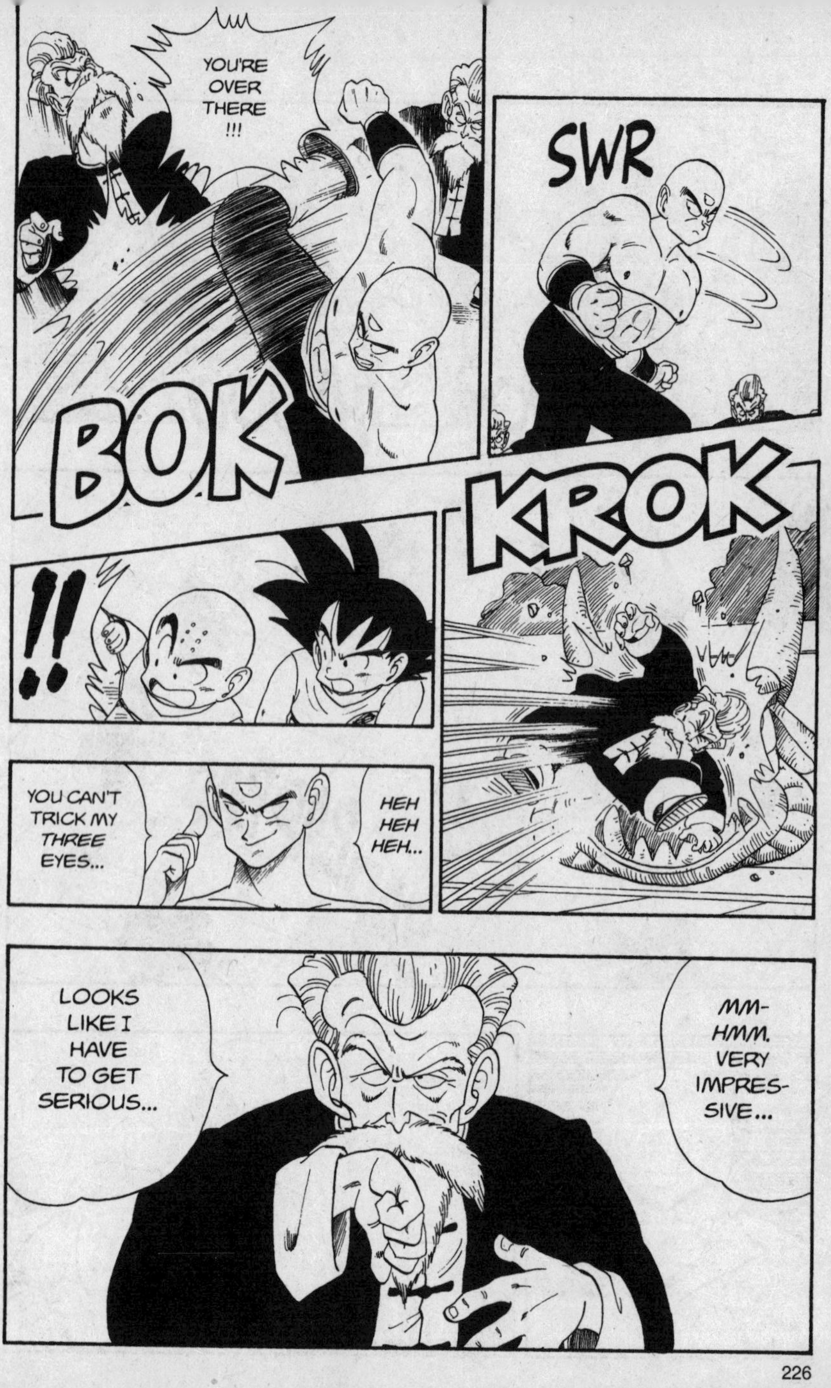
SWR
YOU'RE OVER THERE!!!
BOK
KROK
!!
HEH HEH HEH...
YOU CAN'T TRICK MY THREE EYES...
MM-HMM. VERY IMPRESSIVE...
LOOKS LIKE I HAVE TO GET SERIOUS...

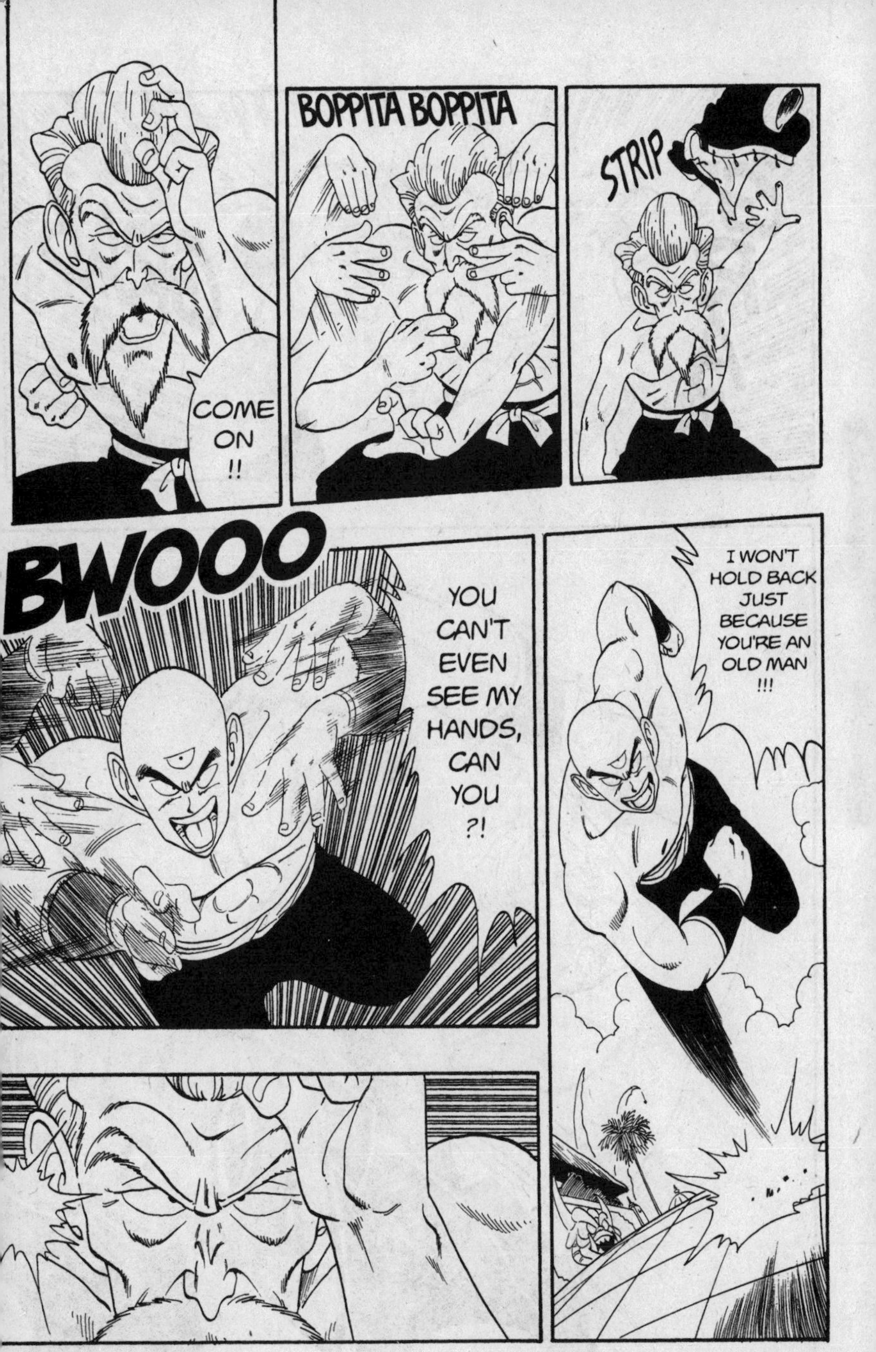
STRIP
BOPPITA BOPPITA
COME ON !!
I WON'T HOLD BACK JUST BECAUSE YOU'RE AN OLD MAN !!!
BWOOO
YOU CAN'T EVEN SEE MY HANDS, CAN YOU ?!

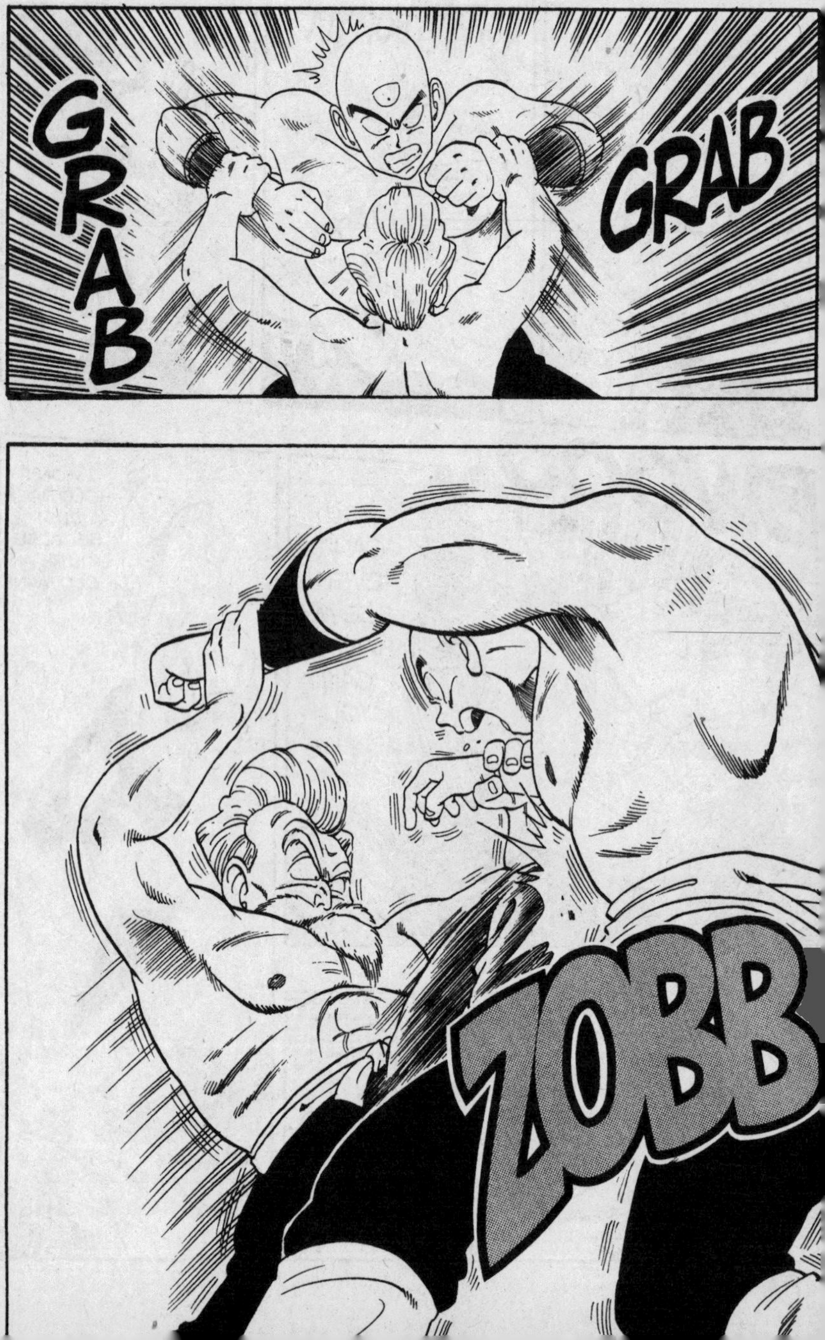
GRAB
GRAB
ZOBB

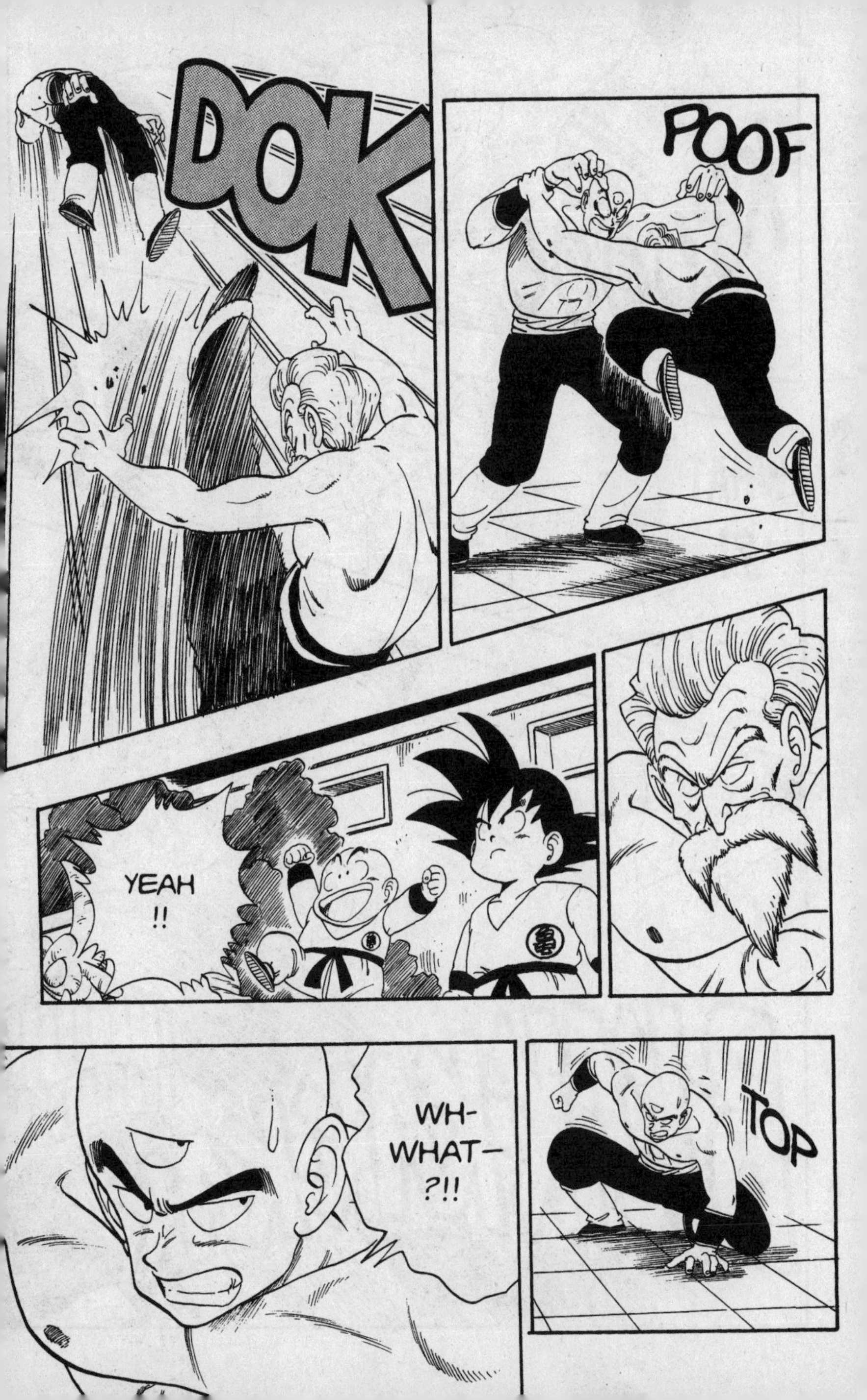
POOF
DOK
YEAH !!
TOP
WH- WHAT- ?!!

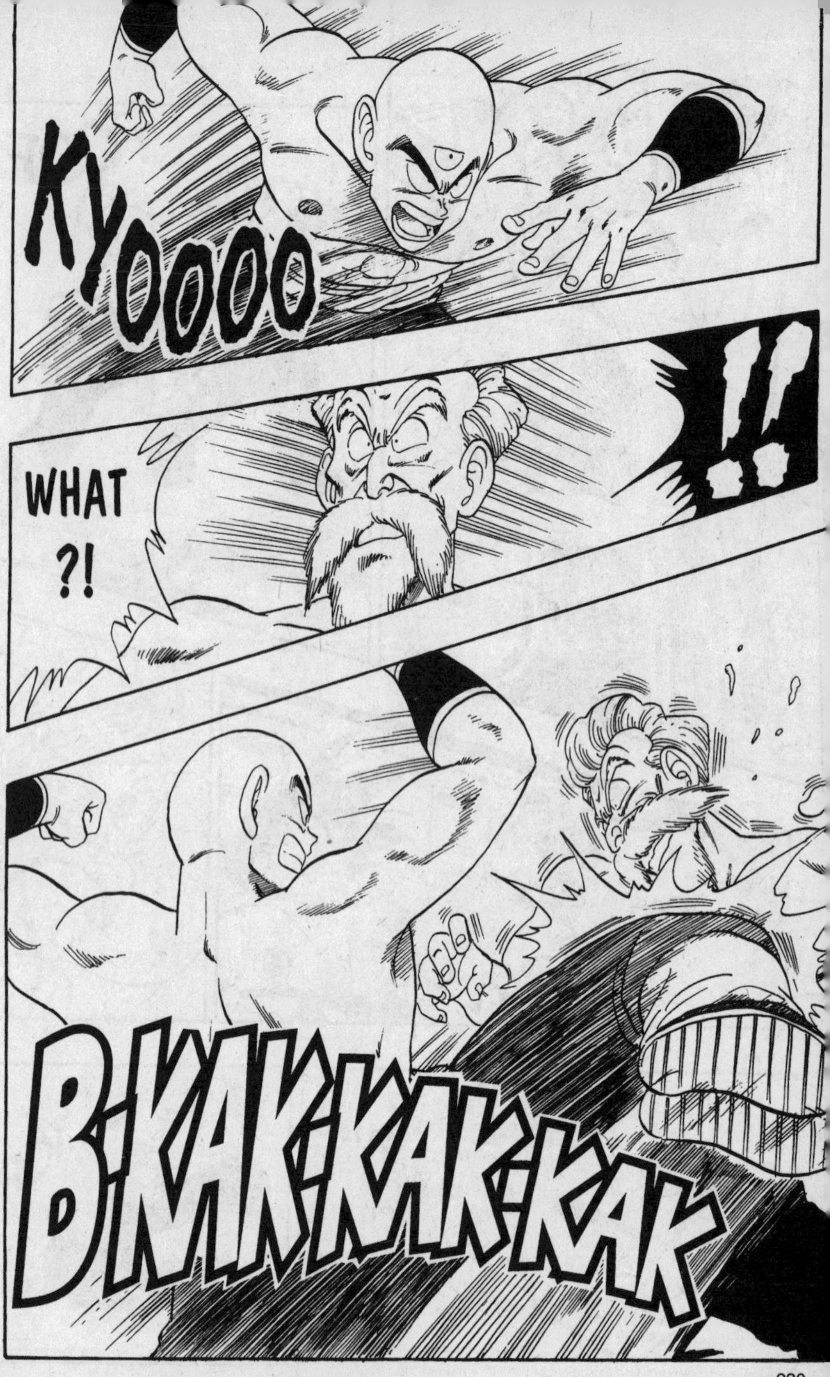
KYOOOO
!!
WHAT ?!
B-KAK-KAK-KAK-KAK

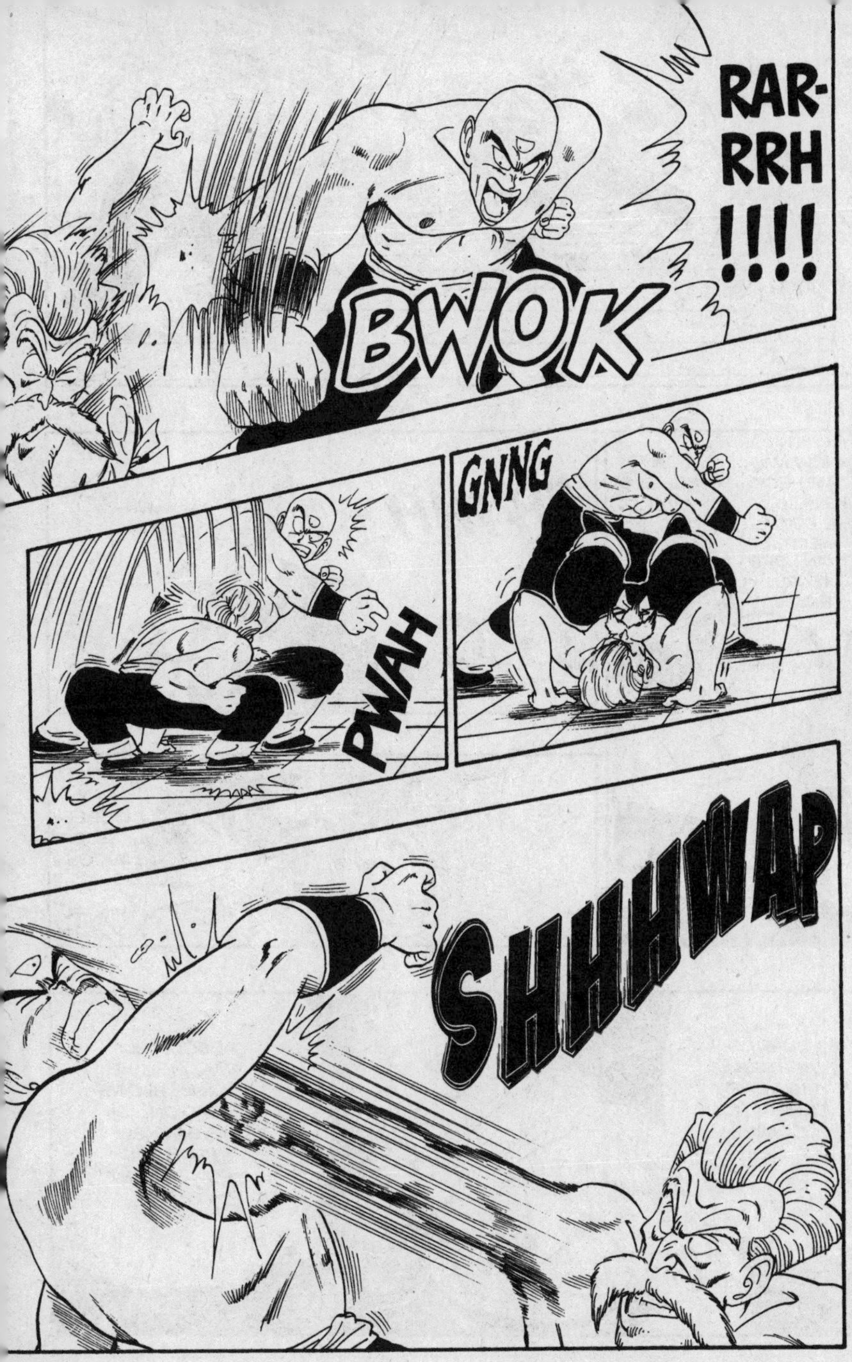
RAR-RRH!!!!
BWOK
GNNG
PWAH
SHHHWAP

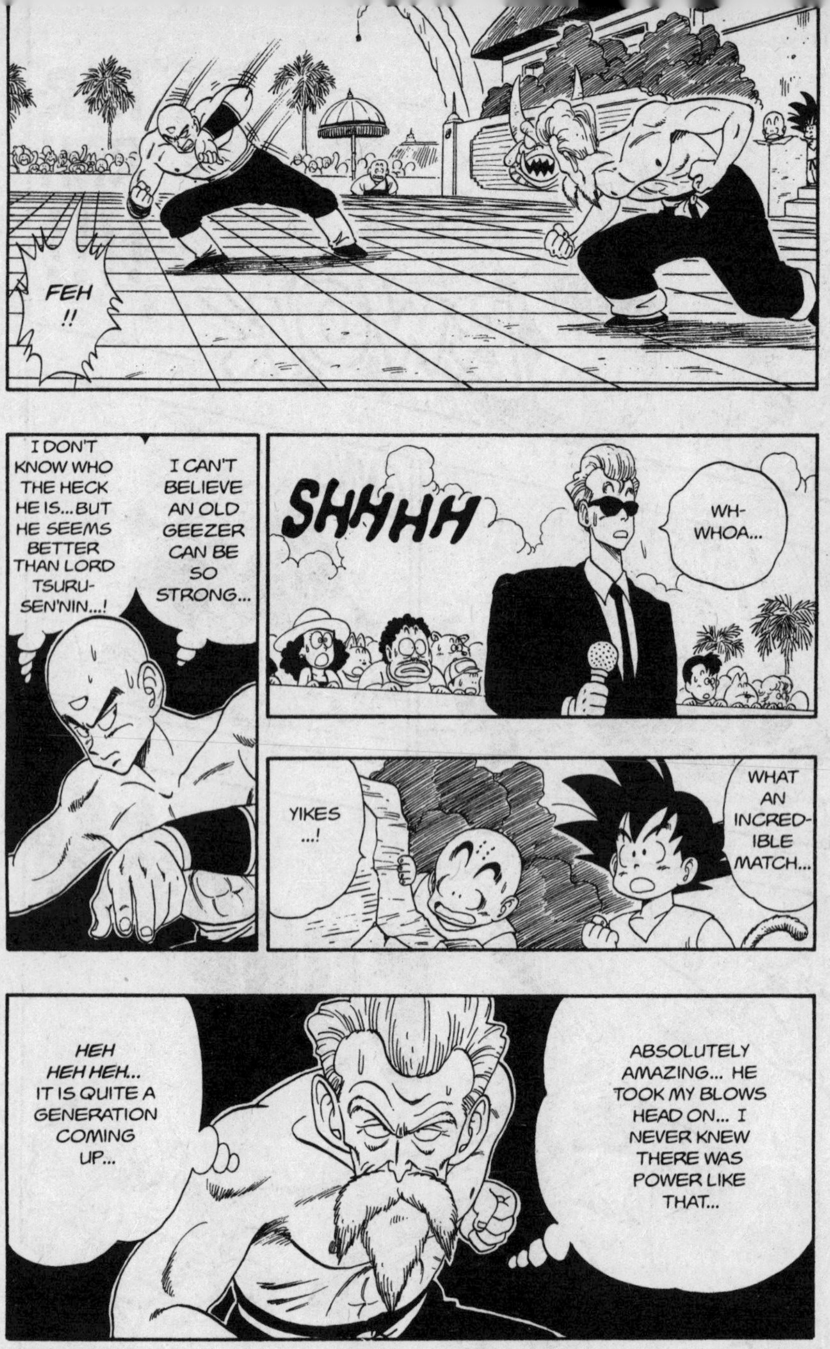
FEH !!
WH- WHOA...
SHHHH
WHAT AN INCRED-IBLE MATCH...
YIKES ...!
I CAN'T BELIEVE AN OLD GEEZER CAN BE SO STRONG...
I DON'T KNOW WHO THE HECK HE IS...BUT HE SEEMS BETTER THAN LORD TSURU-SEN'NIN...!
ABSOLUTELY AMAZING... HE TOOK MY BLOWS HEAD ON... I NEVER KNEW THERE WAS POWER LIKE THAT...
HEH HEH HEH... IT IS QUITE A GENERATION COMING UP...

Tale 124
Young Tenshinhan

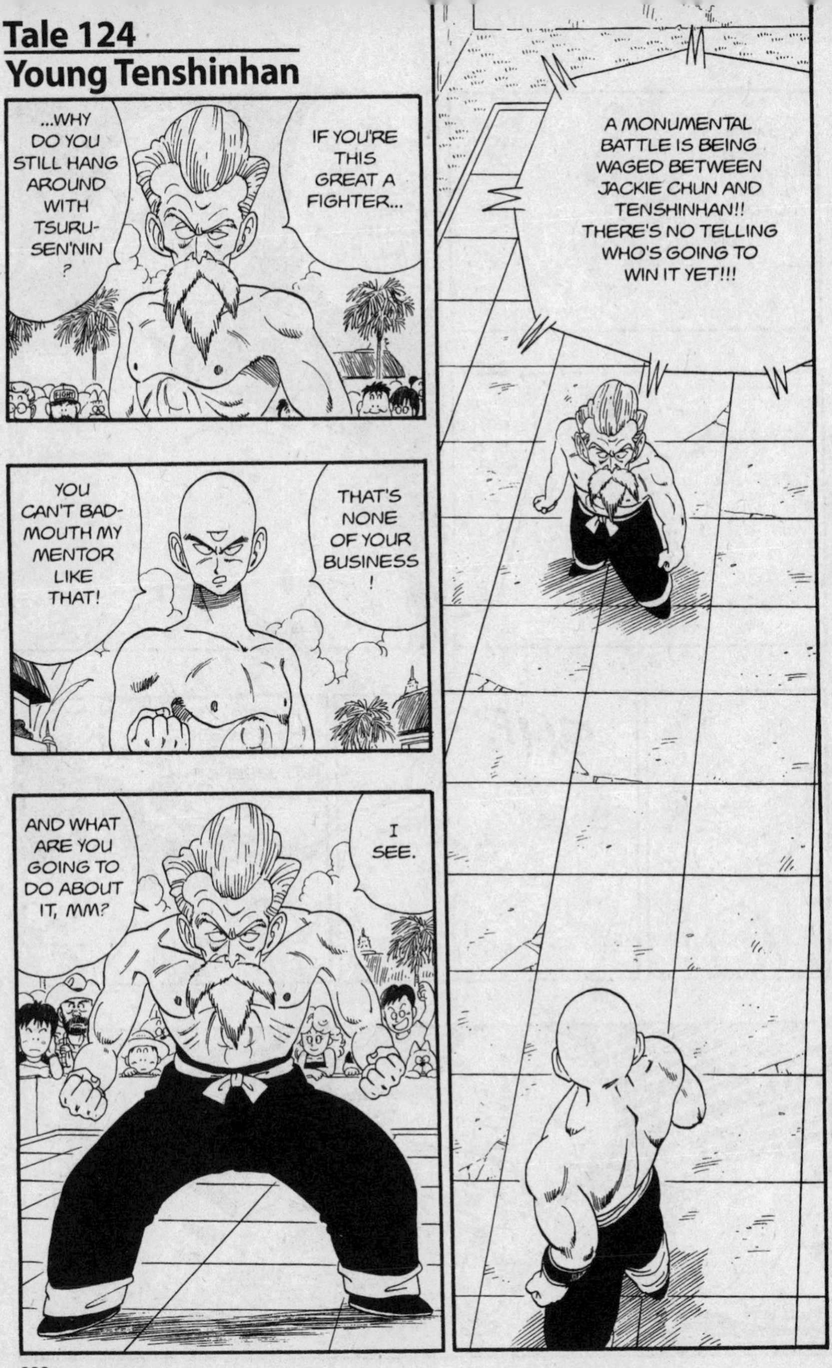
A MONUMENTAL BATTLE IS BEING WAGED BETWEEN JACKIE CHUN AND TENSHINHAN!! THERE'S NO TELLING WHO'S GOING TO WIN IT YET!!!
IF YOU'RE THIS GREAT A FIGHTER...
...WHY DO YOU STILL HANG AROUND WITH TSURU-SEN'NIN?
THAT'S NONE OF YOUR BUSINESS!
YOU CAN'T BAD-MOUTH MY MENTOR LIKE THAT!
I SEE.
AND WHAT ARE YOU GOING TO DO ABOUT IT, MM?

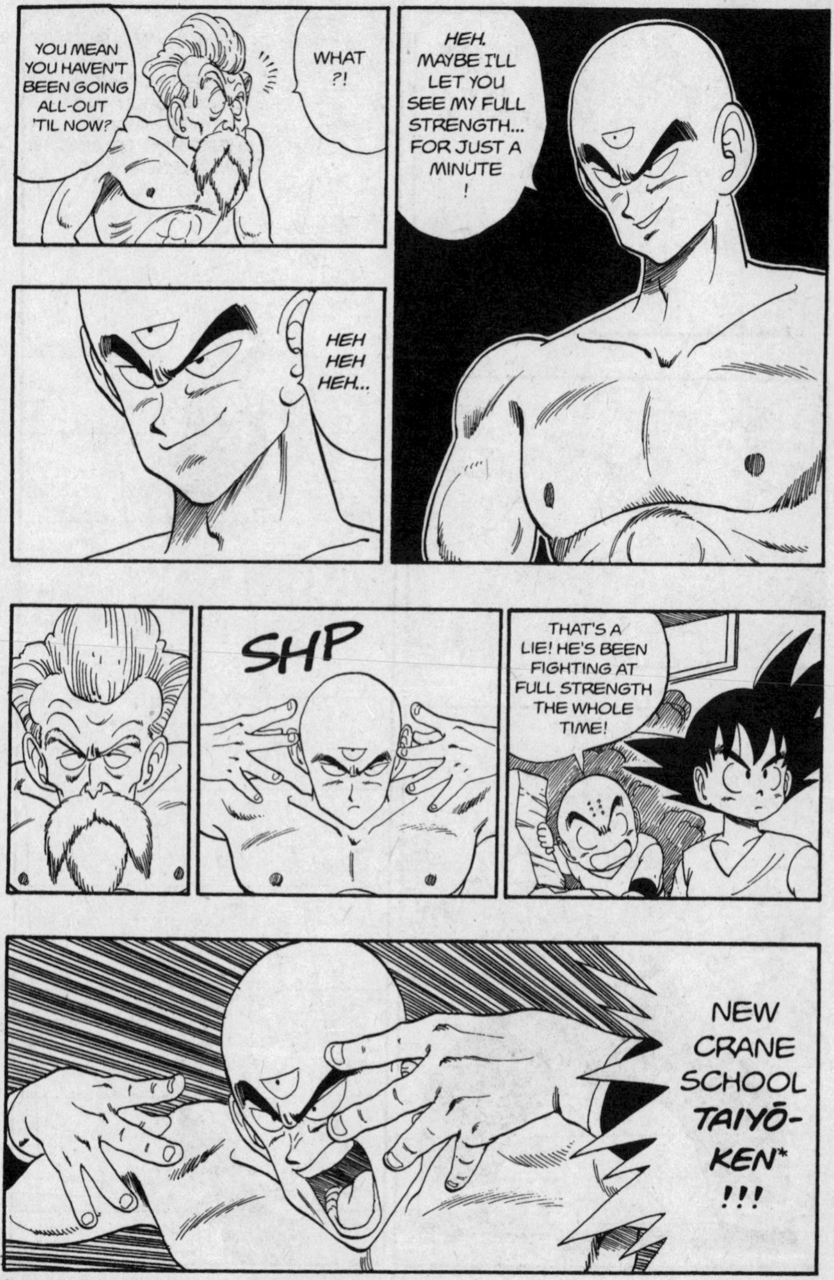
HEH. MAYBE I'LL LET YOU SEE MY FULL STRENGTH... FOR JUST A MINUTE !
WHAT ?!
YOU MEAN YOU HAVEN'T BEEN GOING ALL-OUT 'TIL NOW?
HEH HEH HEH...
THAT'S A LIE! HE'S BEEN FIGHTING AT FULL STRENGTH THE WHOLE TIME!
SHP
NEW CRANE SCHOOL TAIYŌ-KEN* !!!

*A.K.A. "FIST OF THE SUN"

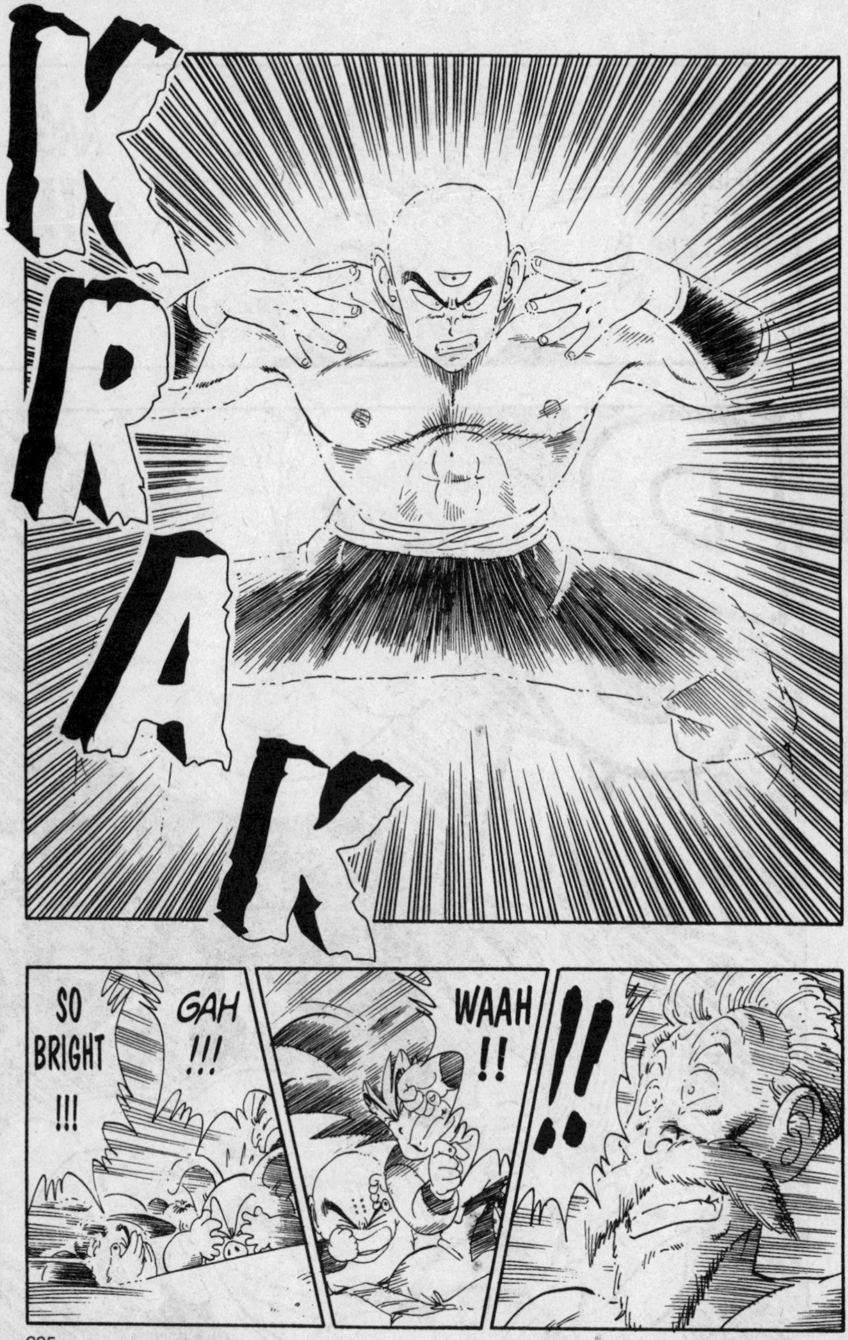
KRAK
!!
WAAH !!
GAH !!!
SO BRIGHT !!!

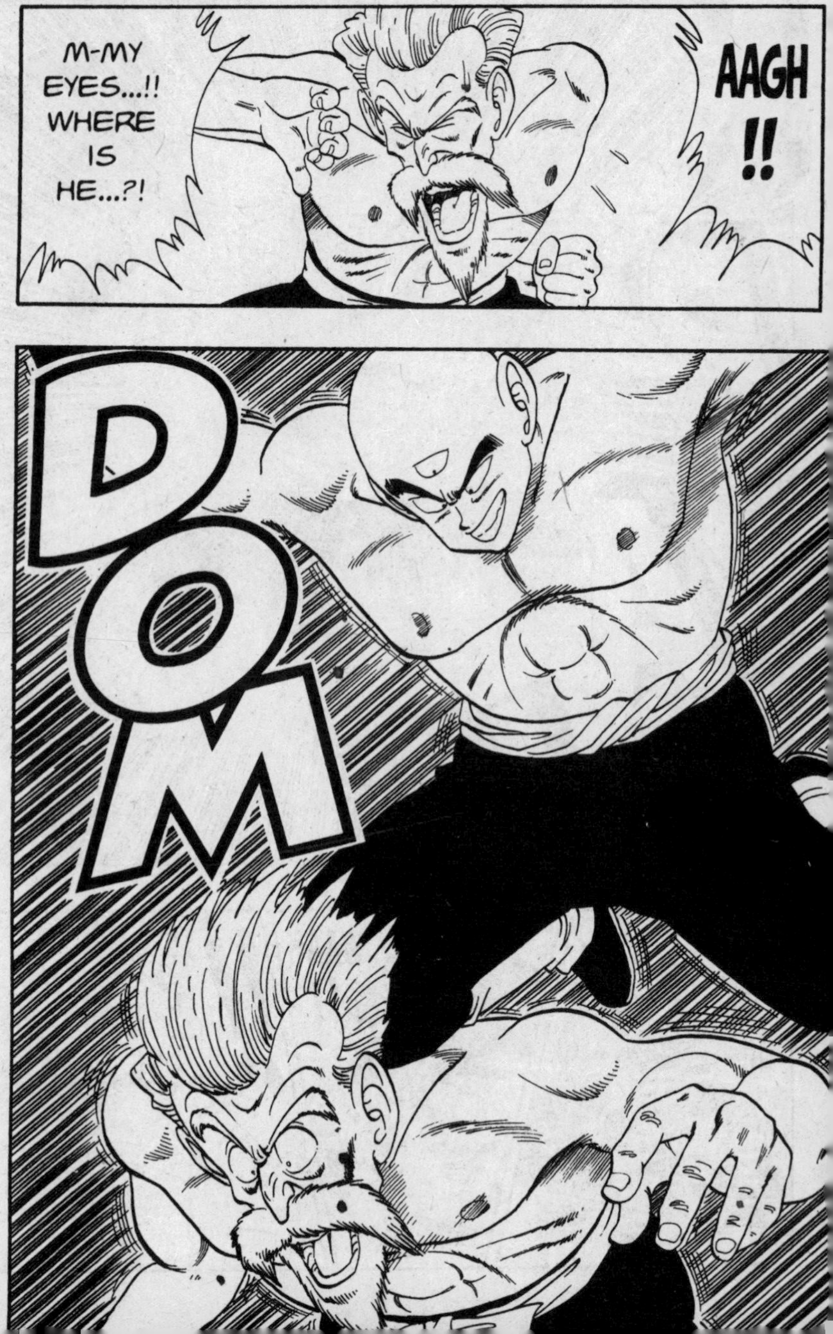
AAGH !!
M-MY EYES...!! WHERE IS HE...?!
DOM

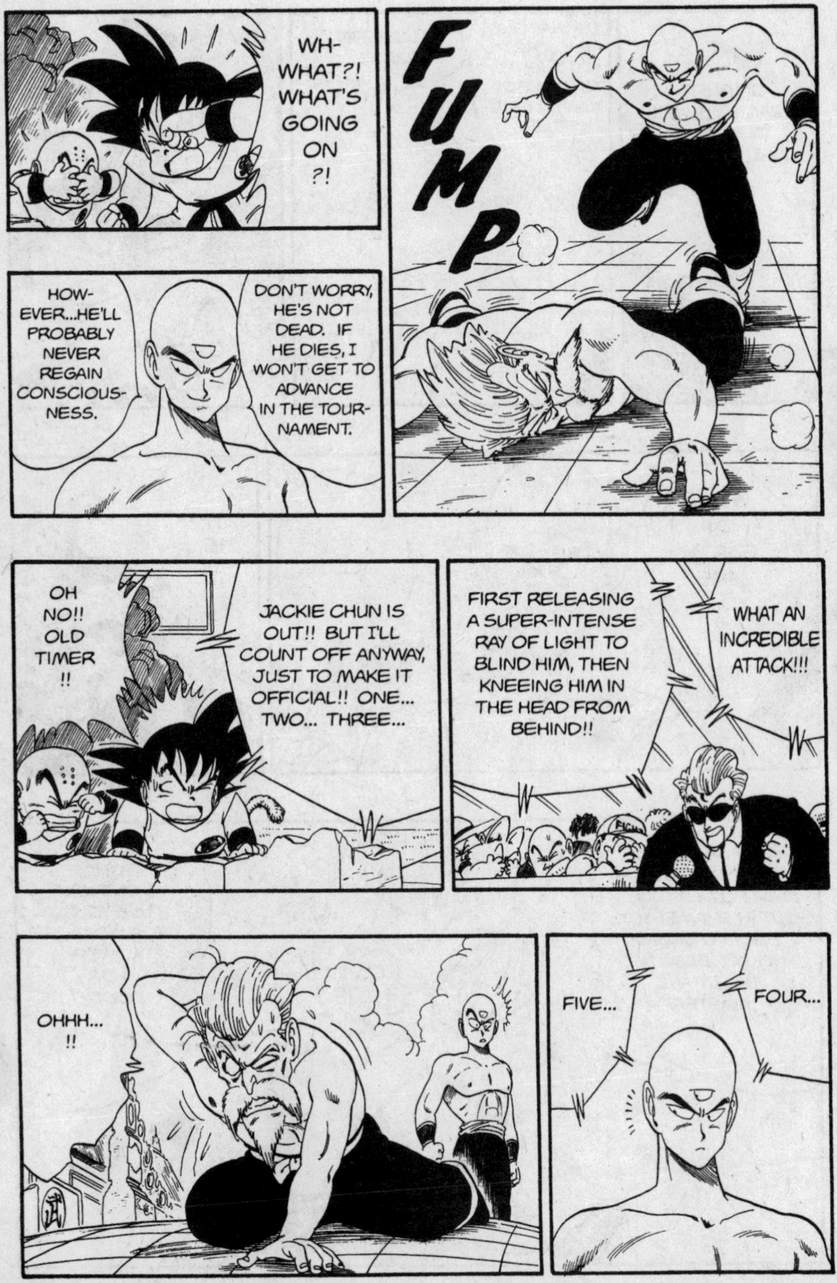
FUMP
WH- WHAT?! WHAT'S GOING ON ?!
DON'T WORRY, HE'S NOT DEAD. IF HE DIES, I WON'T GET TO ADVANCE IN THE TOURNAMENT.
HOWEVER...HE'LL PROBABLY NEVER REGAIN CONSCIOUSNESS.
WHAT AN INCREDIBLE ATTACK!!!
FIRST RELEASING A SUPER-INTENSE RAY OF LIGHT TO BLIND HIM, THEN KNEEING HIM IN THE HEAD FROM BEHIND!!
JACKIE CHUN IS OUT!! BUT I'LL COUNT OFF ANYWAY, JUST TO MAKE IT OFFICIAL!! ONE... TWO... THREE...
OH NO!! OLD TIMER !!
FOUR...
FIVE...
OHHH... !!

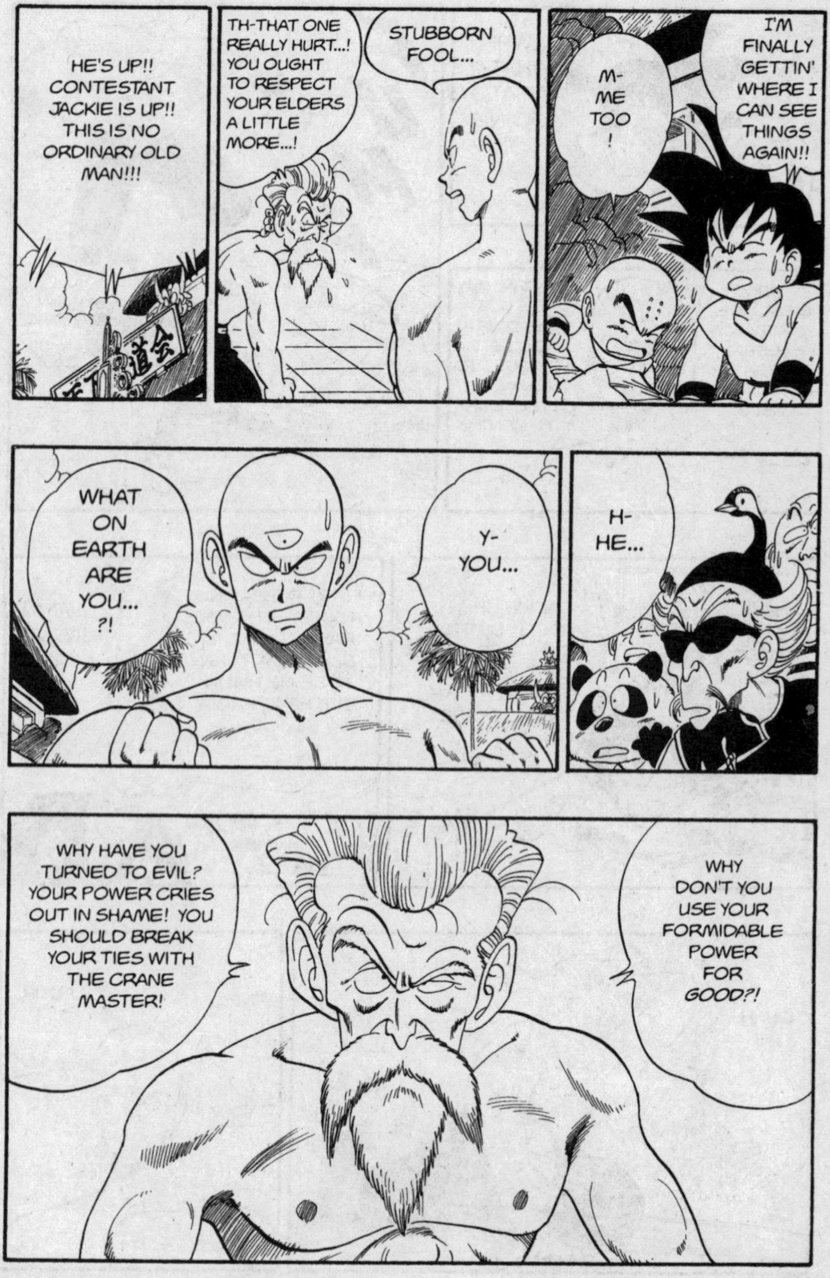
I'M FINALLY GETTIN' WHERE I CAN SEE THINGS AGAIN!!
M-ME TOO!
STUBBORN FOOL...
TH-THAT ONE REALLY HURT...! YOU OUGHT TO RESPECT YOUR ELDERS A LITTLE MORE...!
HE'S UP!! CONTESTANT JACKIE IS UP!! THIS IS NO ORDINARY OLD MAN!!!
H-HE...
Y-YOU...
WHAT ON EARTH ARE YOU...?!
WHY DON'T YOU USE YOUR FORMIDABLE POWER FOR GOOD?!
WHY HAVE YOU TURNED TO EVIL? YOUR POWER CRIES OUT IN SHAME! YOU SHOULD BREAK YOUR TIES WITH THE CRANE MASTER!

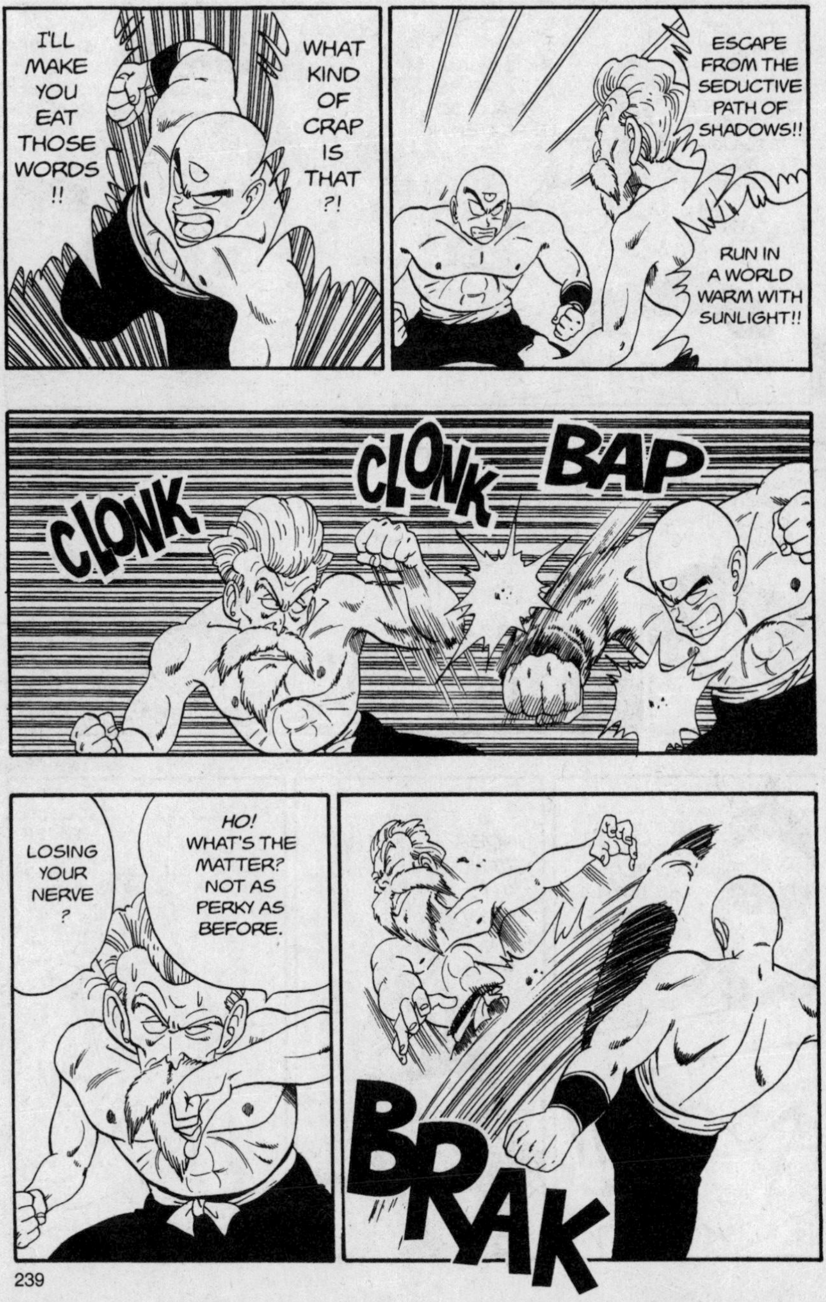
ESCAPE FROM THE SEDUCTIVE PATH OF SHADOWS!!
RUN IN A WORLD WARM WITH SUNLIGHT!!
WHAT KIND OF CRAP IS THAT?!
I'LL MAKE YOU EAT THOSE WORDS!!
BAP
CLONK
CLONK
BRAK
HO! WHAT'S THE MATTER? NOT AS PERKY AS BEFORE.
LOSING YOUR NERVE?

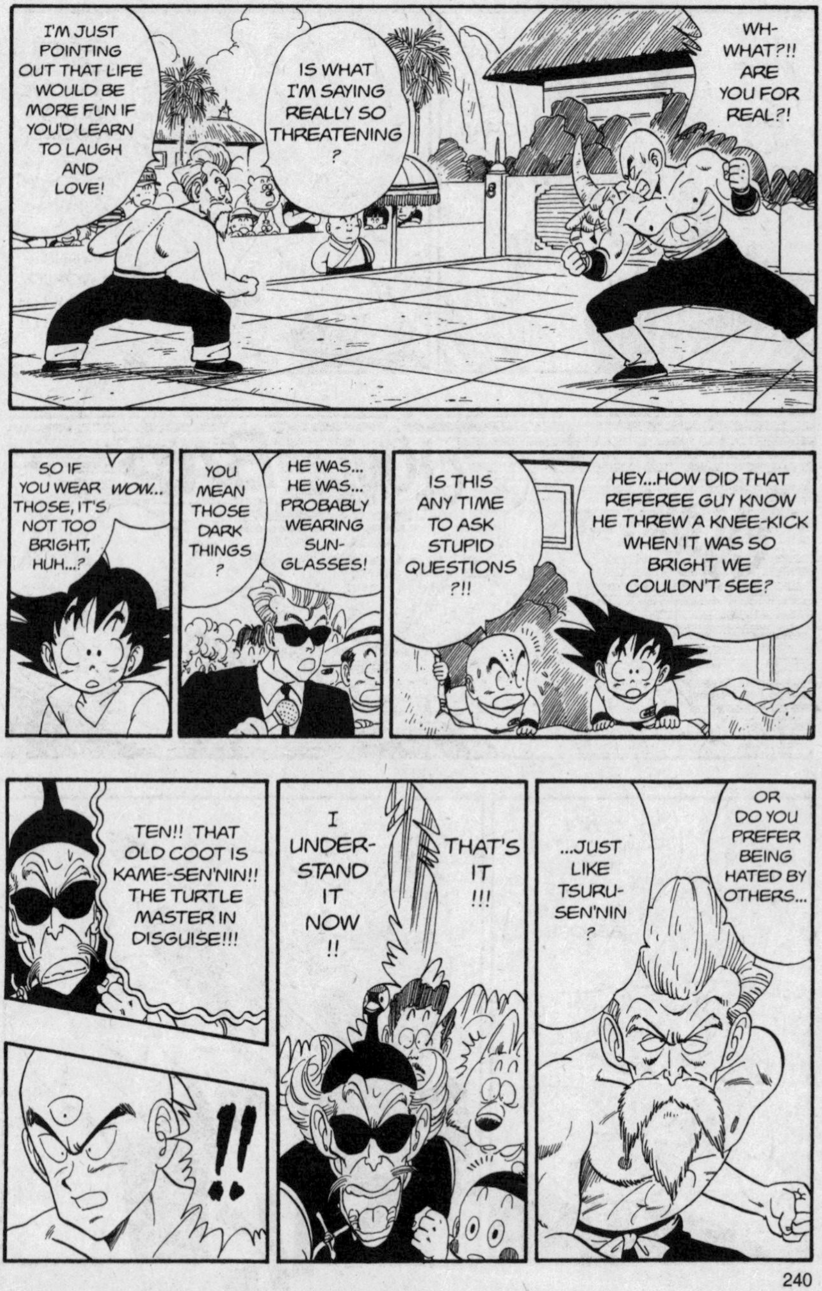
WH- WHAT?!! ARE YOU FOR REAL?!
IS WHAT I'M SAYING REALLY SO THREATENING?
I'M JUST POINTING OUT THAT LIFE WOULD BE MORE FUN IF YOU'D LEARN TO LAUGH AND LOVE!
HEY...HOW DID THAT REFEREE GUY KNOW HE THREW A KNEE-KICK WHEN IT WAS SO BRIGHT WE COULDN'T SEE?
IS THIS ANY TIME TO ASK STUPID QUESTIONS?!!
HE WAS... HE WAS... PROBABLY WEARING SUN-GLASSES!
YOU MEAN THOSE DARK THINGS?
WOW...
SO IF YOU WEAR THOSE, IT'S NOT TOO BRIGHT, HUH...?
OR DO YOU PREFER BEING HATED BY OTHERS...
...JUST LIKE TSURU-SEN'NIN?
THAT'S IT!!!
I UNDER-STAND IT NOW!!
TEN!! THAT OLD COOT IS KAME-SEN'NIN!! THE TURTLE MASTER IN DISGUISE!!!
!!

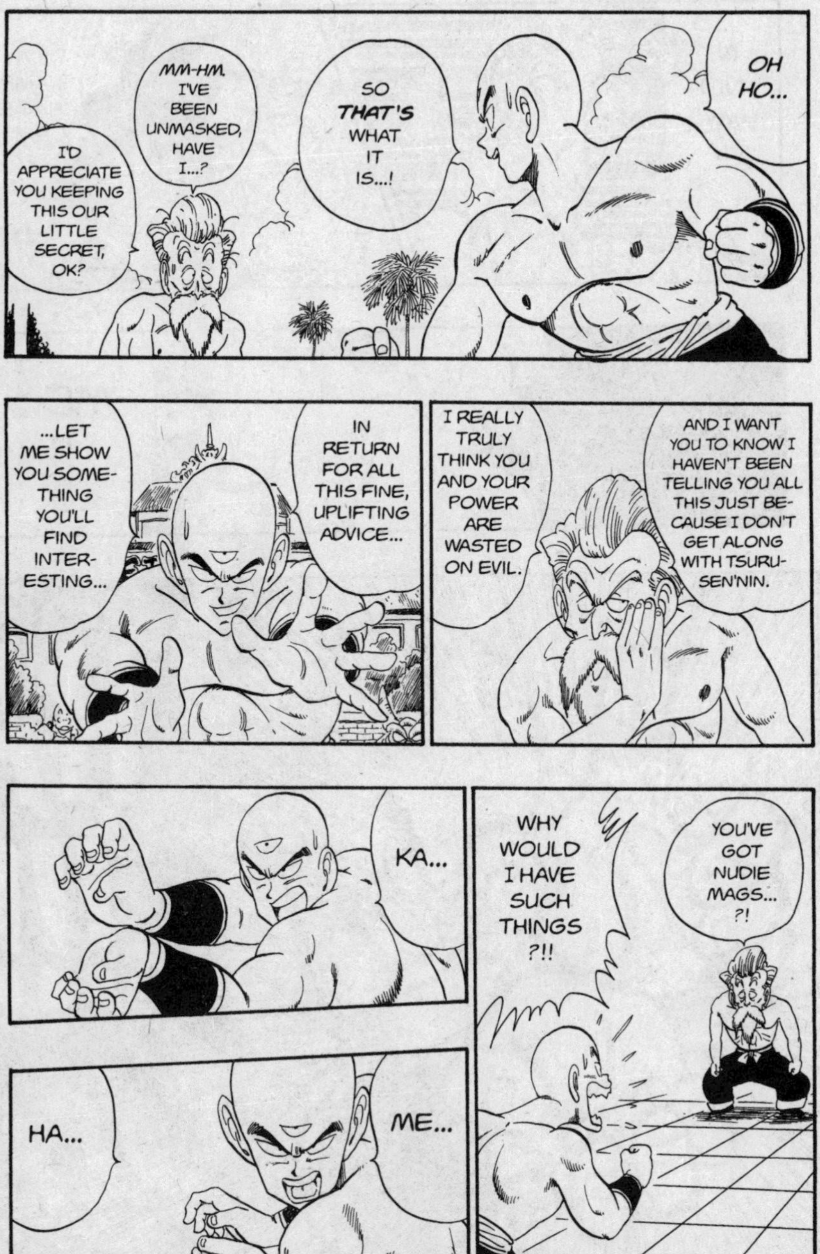
OH HO...
SO THAT'S WHAT IT IS...!
MM-HM. I'VE BEEN UNMASKED, HAVE I...?
I'D APPRECIATE YOU KEEPING THIS OUR LITTLE SECRET, OK?
AND I WANT YOU TO KNOW I HAVEN'T BEEN TELLING YOU ALL THIS JUST BECAUSE I DON'T GET ALONG WITH TSURU-SEN'NIN.
I REALLY TRULY THINK YOU AND YOUR POWER ARE WASTED ON EVIL.
IN RETURN FOR ALL THIS FINE, UPLIFTING ADVICE...
...LET ME SHOW YOU SOMETHING YOU'LL FIND INTERESTING...
YOU'VE GOT NUDIE MAGS...?!
WHY WOULD I HAVE SUCH THINGS?!!
KA...
ME...
HA...

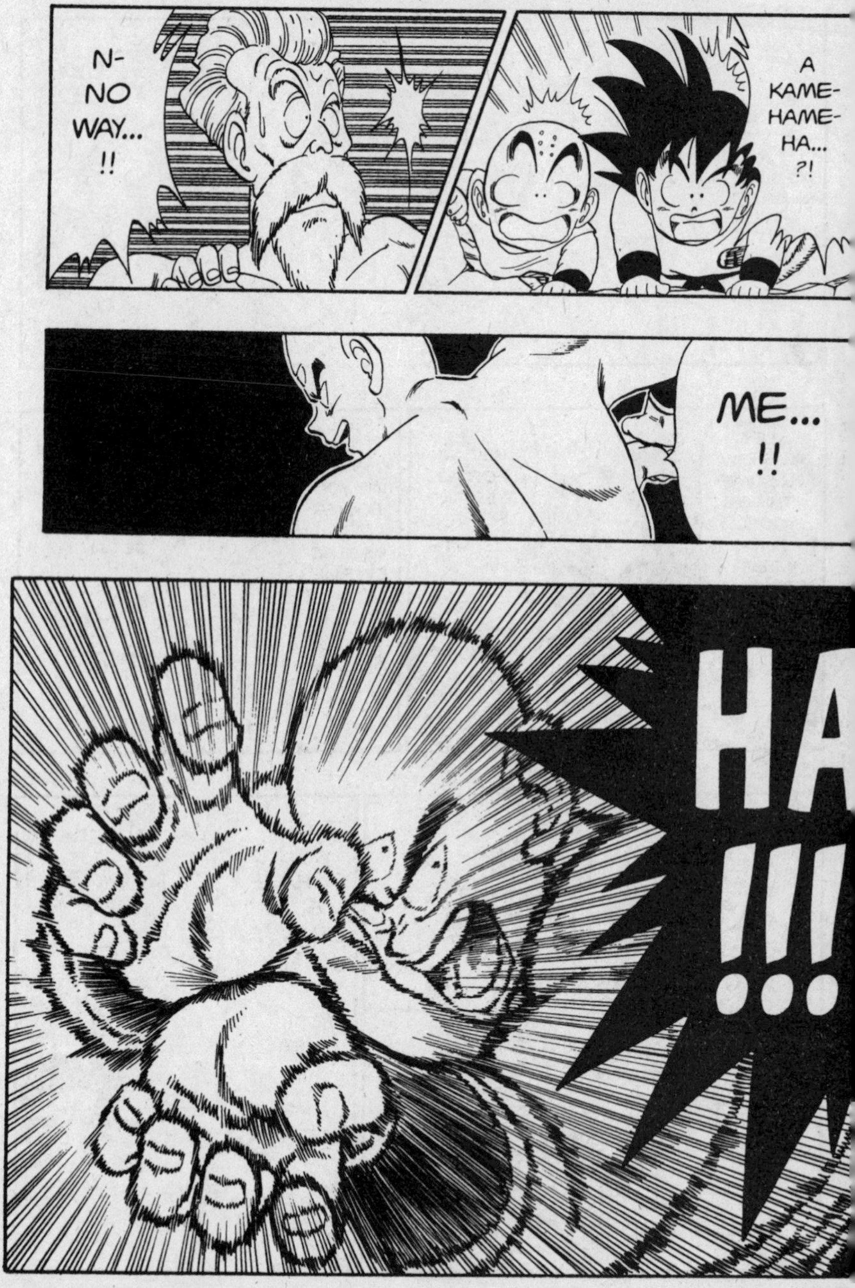
A KAME-HAME-HA...?!
N-NO WAY...!!
ME...!!
HA!!!

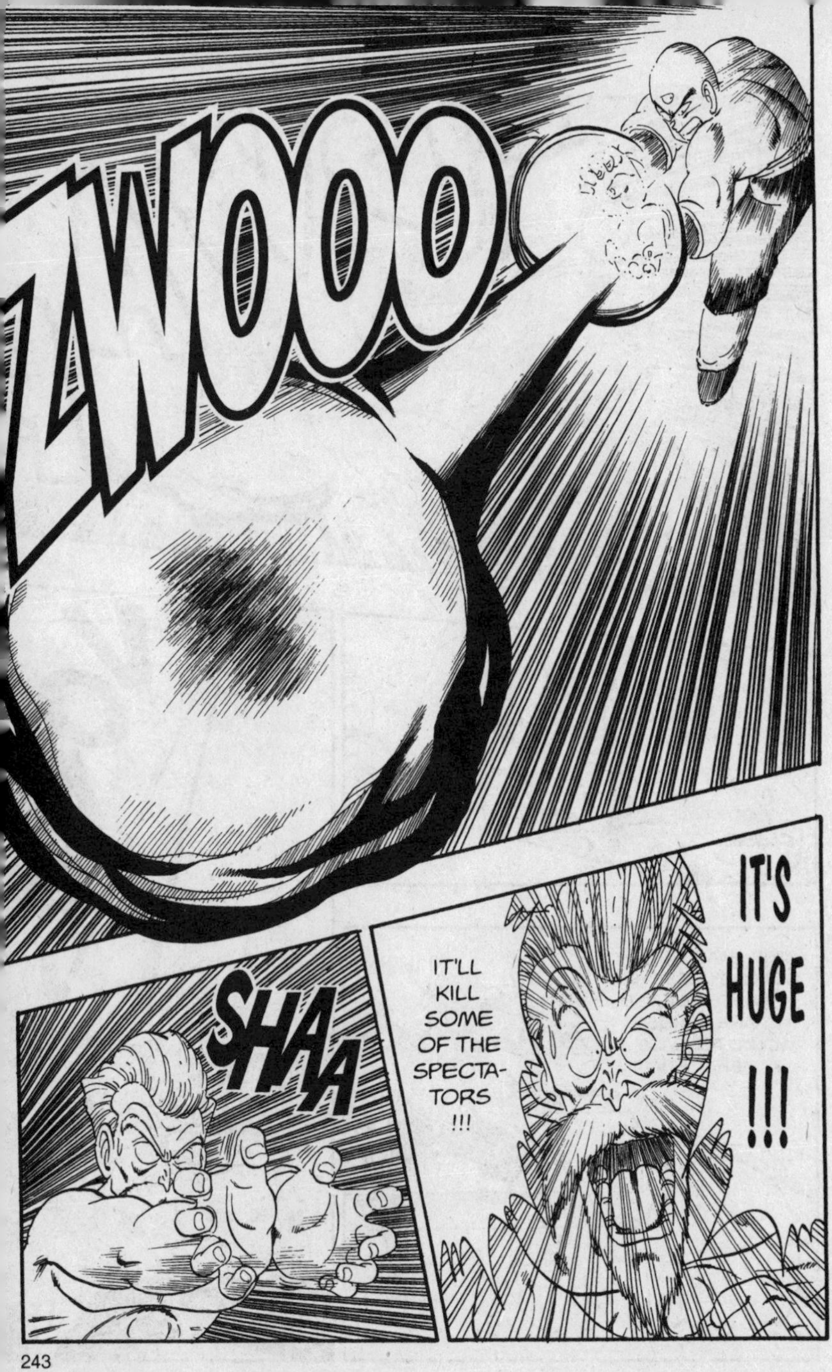
ZWOOO
IT'S HUGE !!!
IT'LL KILL SOME OF THE SPECTATORS !!!
SHAA

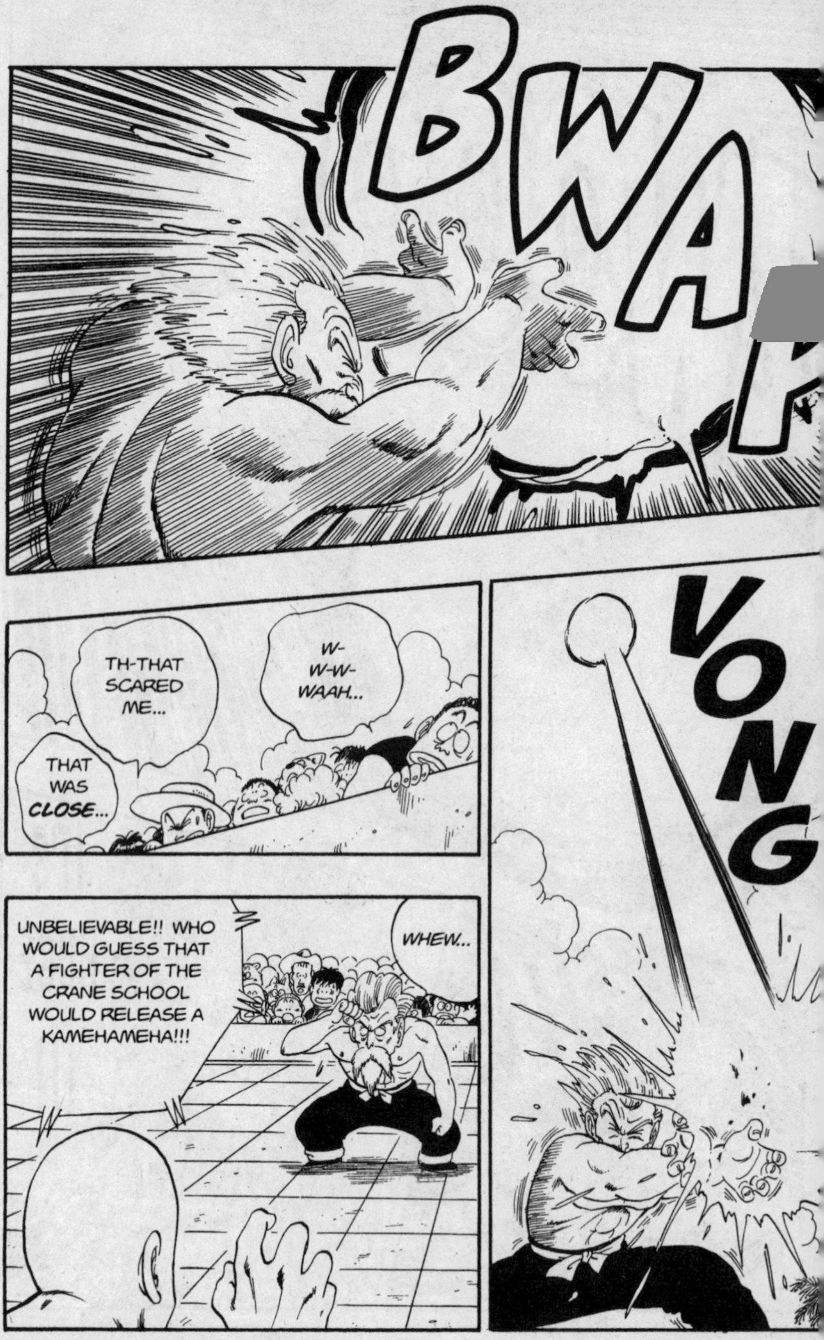
BWAP
VONG
W-W-W-WAAH...
TH-THAT SCARED ME...
THAT WAS CLOSE...
WHEW...
UNBELIEVABLE!! WHO WOULD GUESS THAT A FIGHTER OF THE CRANE SCHOOL WOULD RELEASE A KAMEHAMEHA!!!

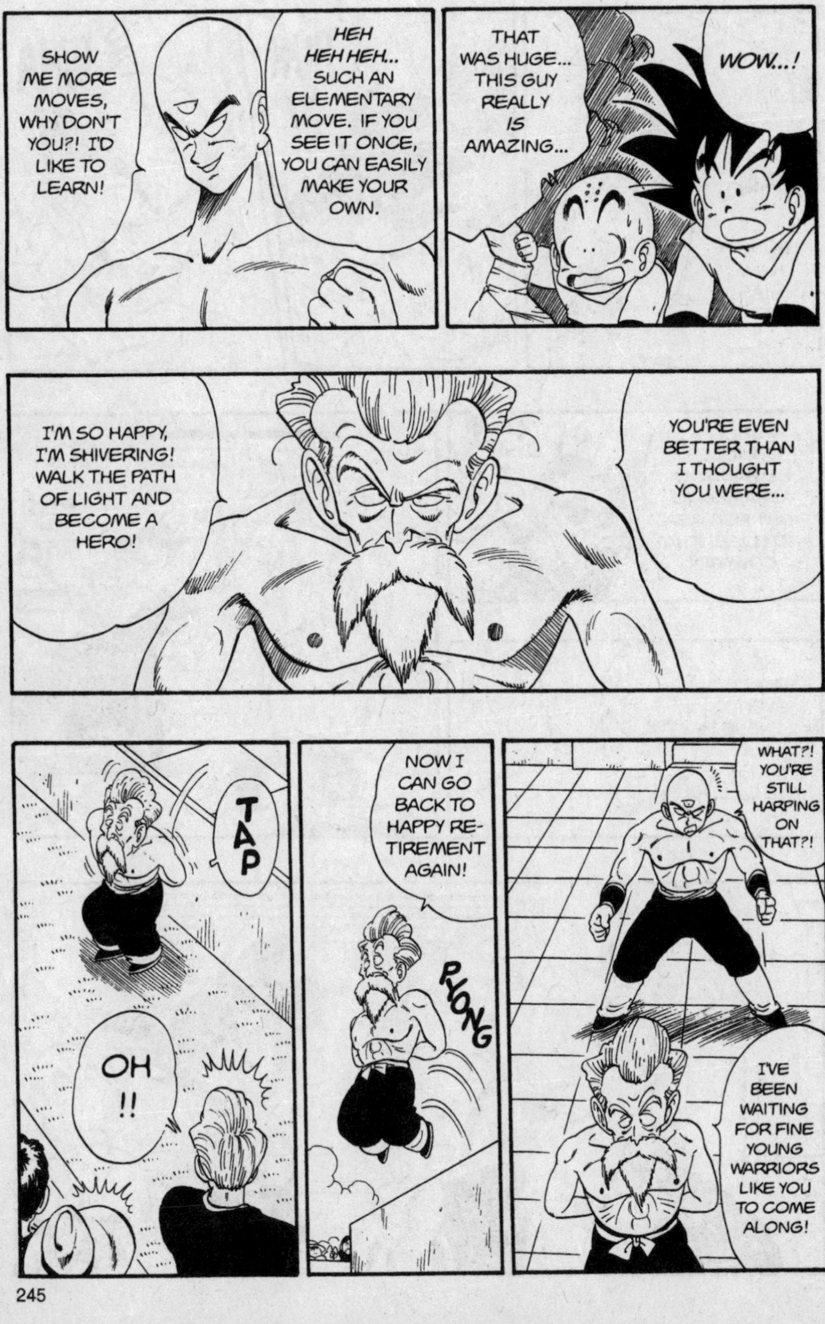
WOW...!
THAT WAS HUGE... THIS GUY REALLY IS AMAZING...
HEH HEH HEH... SUCH AN ELEMENTARY MOVE. IF YOU SEE IT ONCE, YOU CAN EASILY MAKE YOUR OWN.
SHOW ME MORE MOVES, WHY DON'T YOU?! I'D LIKE TO LEARN!
YOU'RE EVEN BETTER THAN I THOUGHT YOU WERE...
I'M SO HAPPY, I'M SHIVERING! WALK THE PATH OF LIGHT AND BECOME A HERO!
WHAT?! YOU'RE STILL HARPING ON THAT?!
I'VE BEEN WAITING FOR FINE YOUNG WARRIORS LIKE YOU TO COME ALONG!
NOW I CAN GO BACK TO HAPPY RE-TIREMENT AGAIN!
PYONG
TAP
OH !!

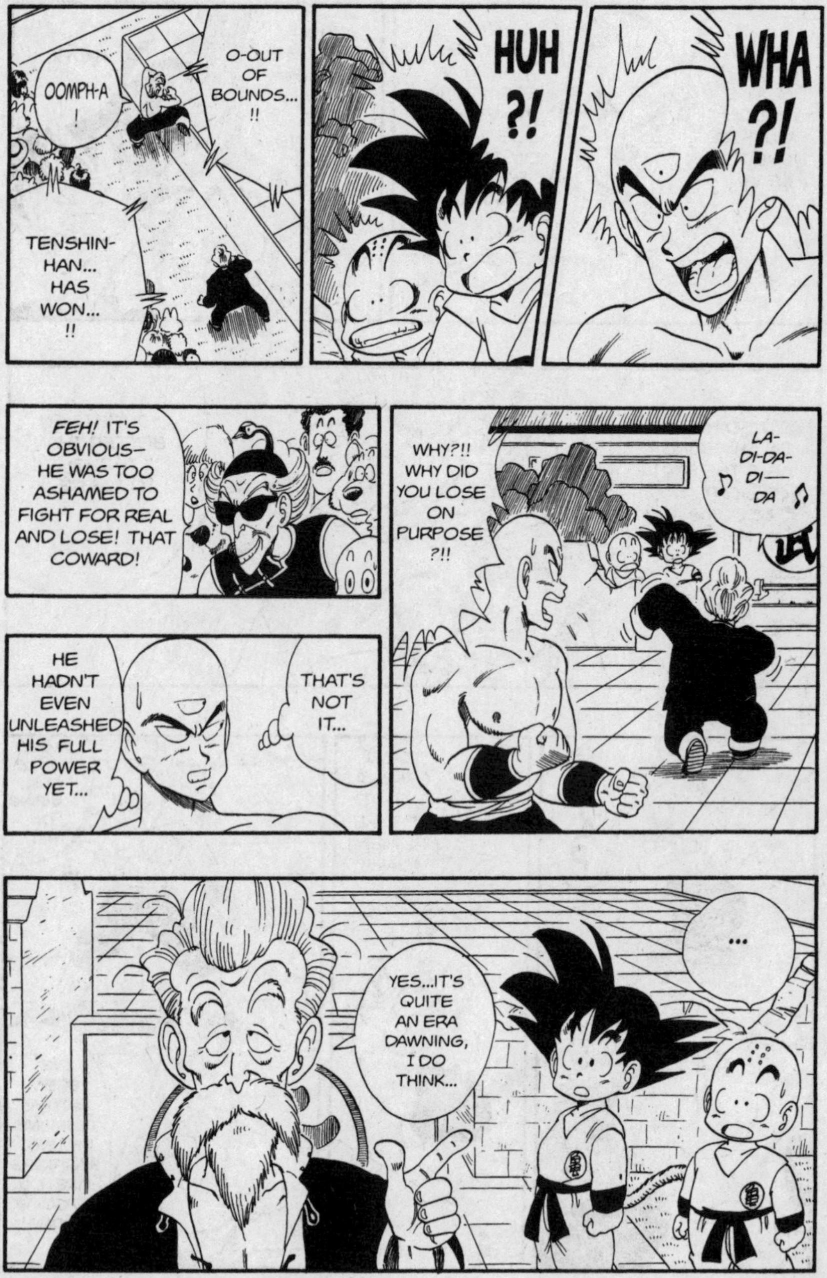
WHA ?!
HUH ?!
O-OUT OF BOUNDS... !!
OOMPH-A !
TENSHIN-HAN... HAS WON... !!
LA-DI-DA-DI—DA
WHY?!! WHY DID YOU LOSE ON PURPOSE ?!!
FEH! IT'S OBVIOUS— HE WAS TOO ASHAMED TO FIGHT FOR REAL AND LOSE! THAT COWARD!
THAT'S NOT IT...
HE HADN'T EVEN UNLEASHED HIS FULL POWER YET...
...
YES...IT'S QUITE AN ERA DAWNING, I DO THINK...

Tale 125 · Goku vs. Kuririn

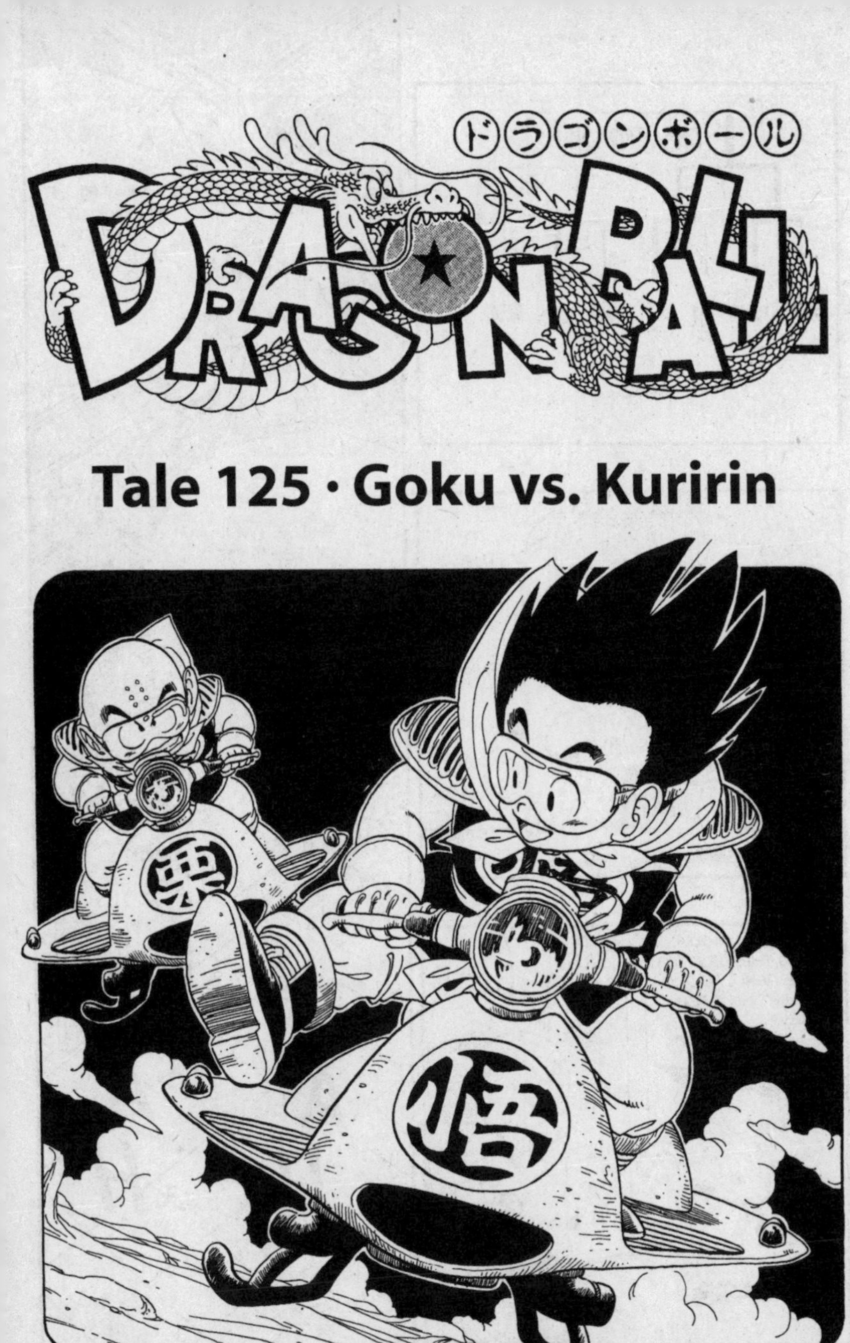

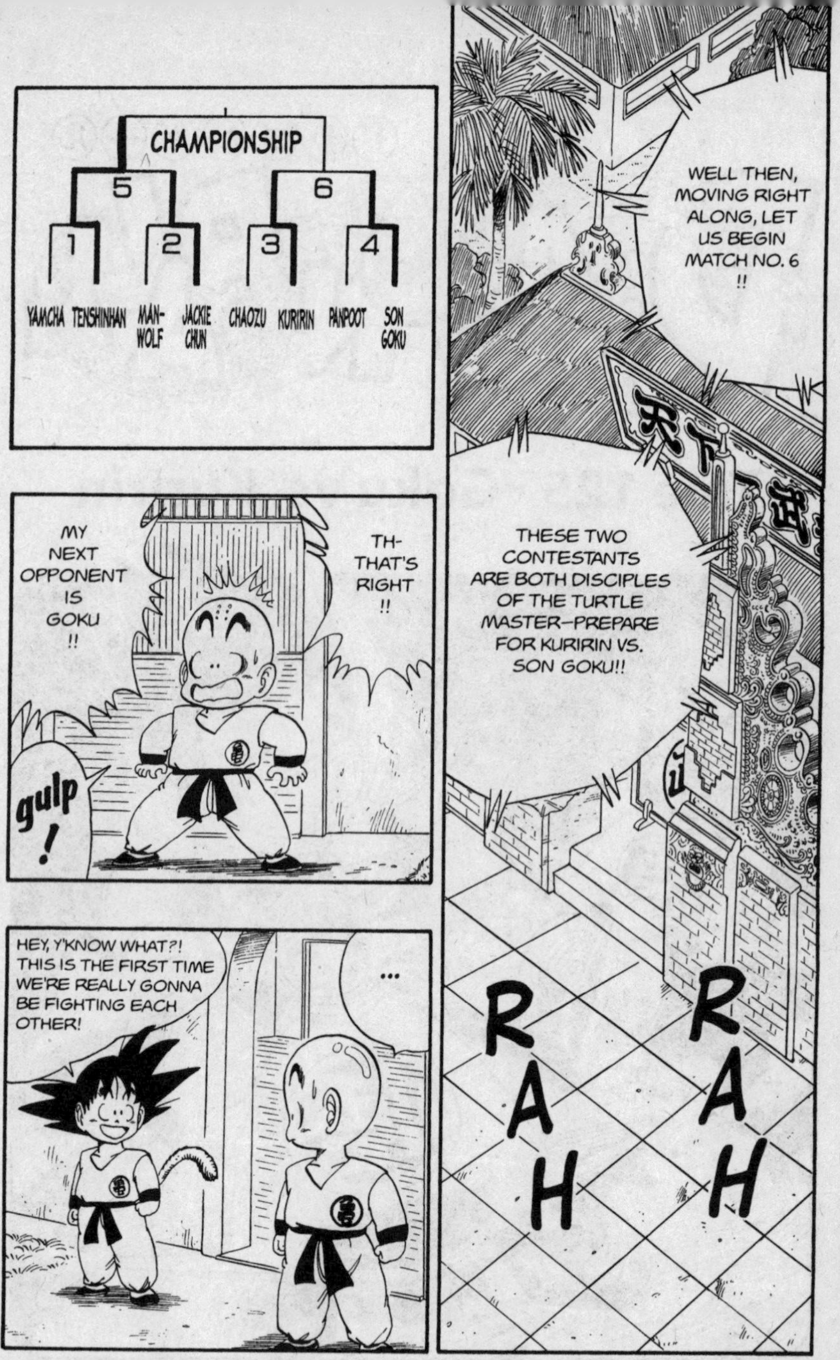

WELL THEN, MOVING RIGHT ALONG, LET US BEGIN MATCH NO. 6 !!
THESE TWO CONTESTANTS ARE BOTH DISCIPLES OF THE TURTLE MASTER–PREPARE FOR KURIRIN VS. SON GOKU!!
RAH RAH
CHAMPIONSHIP
5
6
1
2
3
4
YAMCHA
TENSHINHAN
MAN-WOLF
JACKIE CHUN
CHAOZU
KURIRIN
PANPOOT
SON GOKU
TH- THAT'S RIGHT !!
MY NEXT OPPONENT IS GOKU !!
gulp !
...
HEY, Y'KNOW WHAT?! THIS IS THE FIRST TIME WE'RE REALLY GONNA BE FIGHTING EACH OTHER!

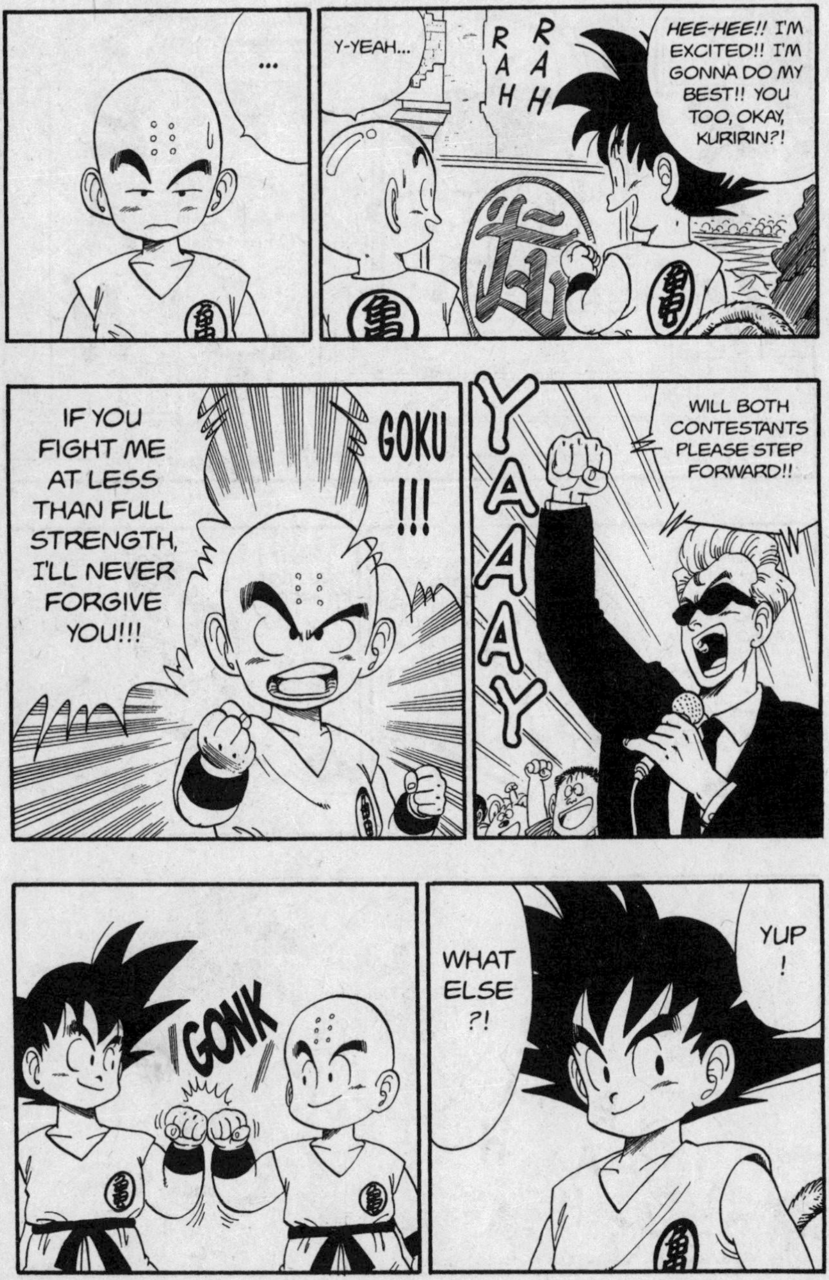
HEE-HEE!! I'M EXCITED!! I'M GONNA DO MY BEST!! YOU TOO, OKAY, KURIRIN?!
RAH RAH
Y-YEAH...
...
WILL BOTH CONTESTANTS PLEASE STEP FORWARD!!
YAAAAY
GOKU !!!
IF YOU FIGHT ME AT LESS THAN FULL STRENGTH, I'LL NEVER FORGIVE YOU!!!
YUP !
WHAT ELSE ?!
GONK

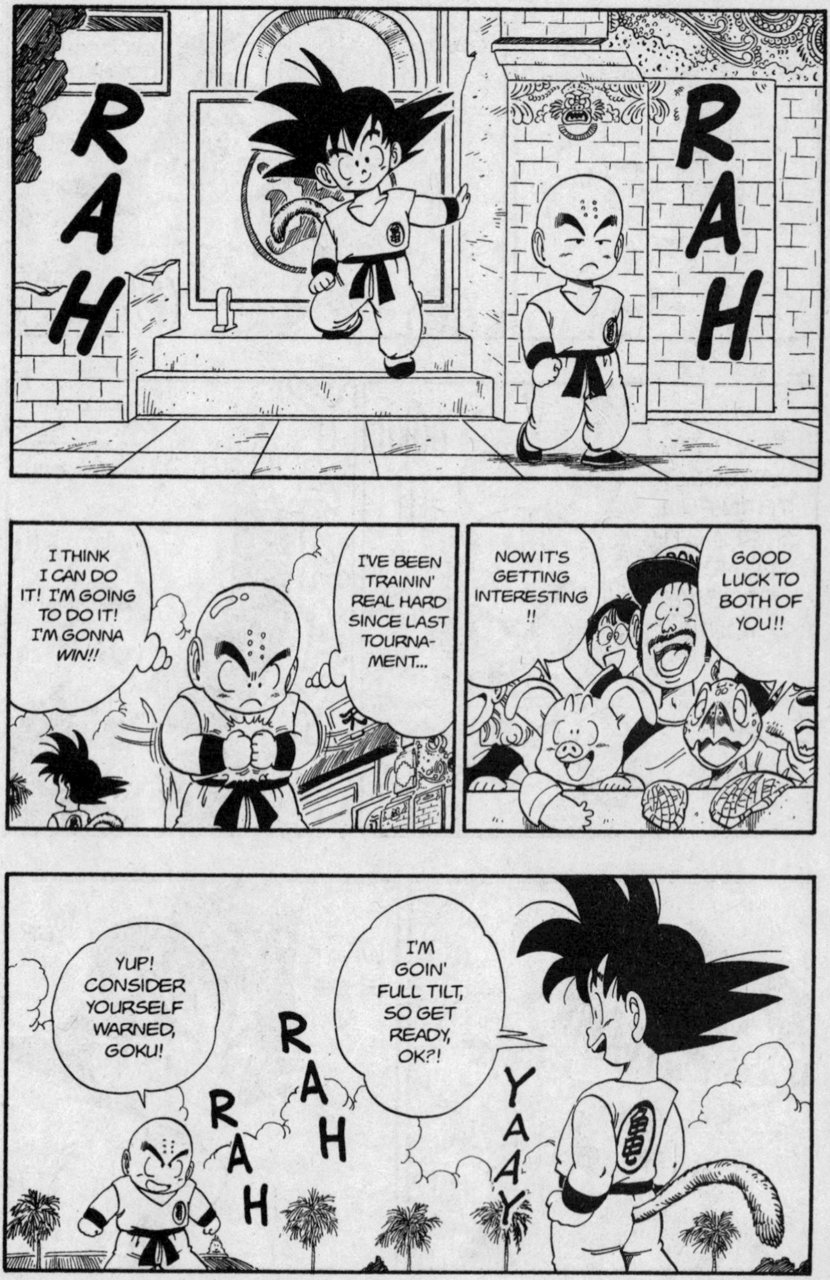
RAH
RAH
GOOD LUCK TO BOTH OF YOU!!
NOW IT'S GETTING INTERESTING!!
I'VE BEEN TRAININ' REAL HARD SINCE LAST TOURNAMENT...
I THINK I CAN DO IT! I'M GOING TO DO IT! I'M GONNA WIN!!
I'M GOIN' FULL TILT, SO GET READY, OK?!
YAAAY
RAH
RAH
YUP! CONSIDER YOURSELF WARNED, GOKU!

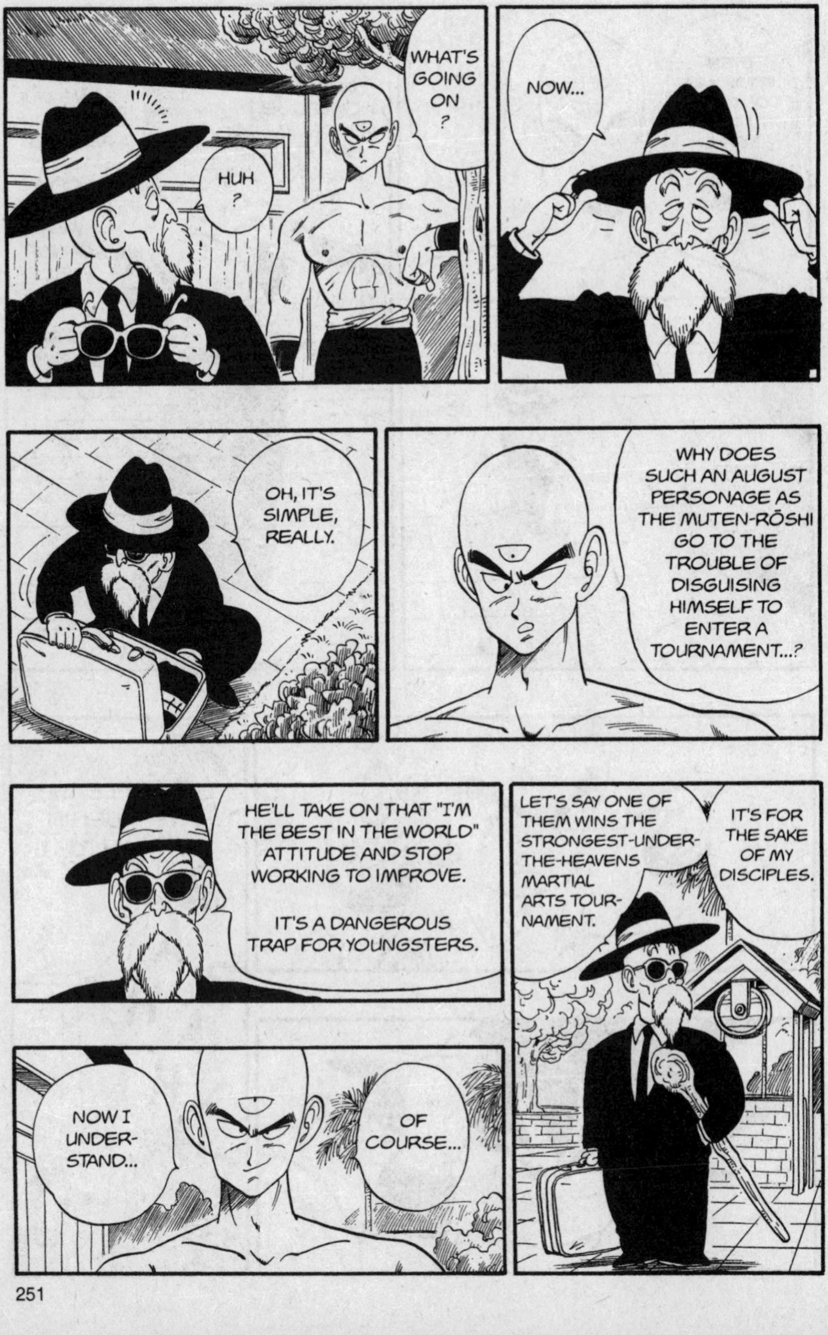
NOW...
WHAT'S GOING ON ?
HUH ?
WHY DOES SUCH AN AUGUST PERSONAGE AS THE MUTEN-RŌSHI GO TO THE TROUBLE OF DISGUISING HIMSELF TO ENTER A TOURNAMENT...?
OH, IT'S SIMPLE, REALLY.
IT'S FOR THE SAKE OF MY DISCIPLES.
LET'S SAY ONE OF THEM WINS THE STRONGEST-UNDER-THE-HEAVENS MARTIAL ARTS TOURNAMENT.
HE'LL TAKE ON THAT "I'M THE BEST IN THE WORLD" ATTITUDE AND STOP WORKING TO IMPROVE.
IT'S A DANGEROUS TRAP FOR YOUNGSTERS.
OF COURSE...
NOW I UNDERSTAND...

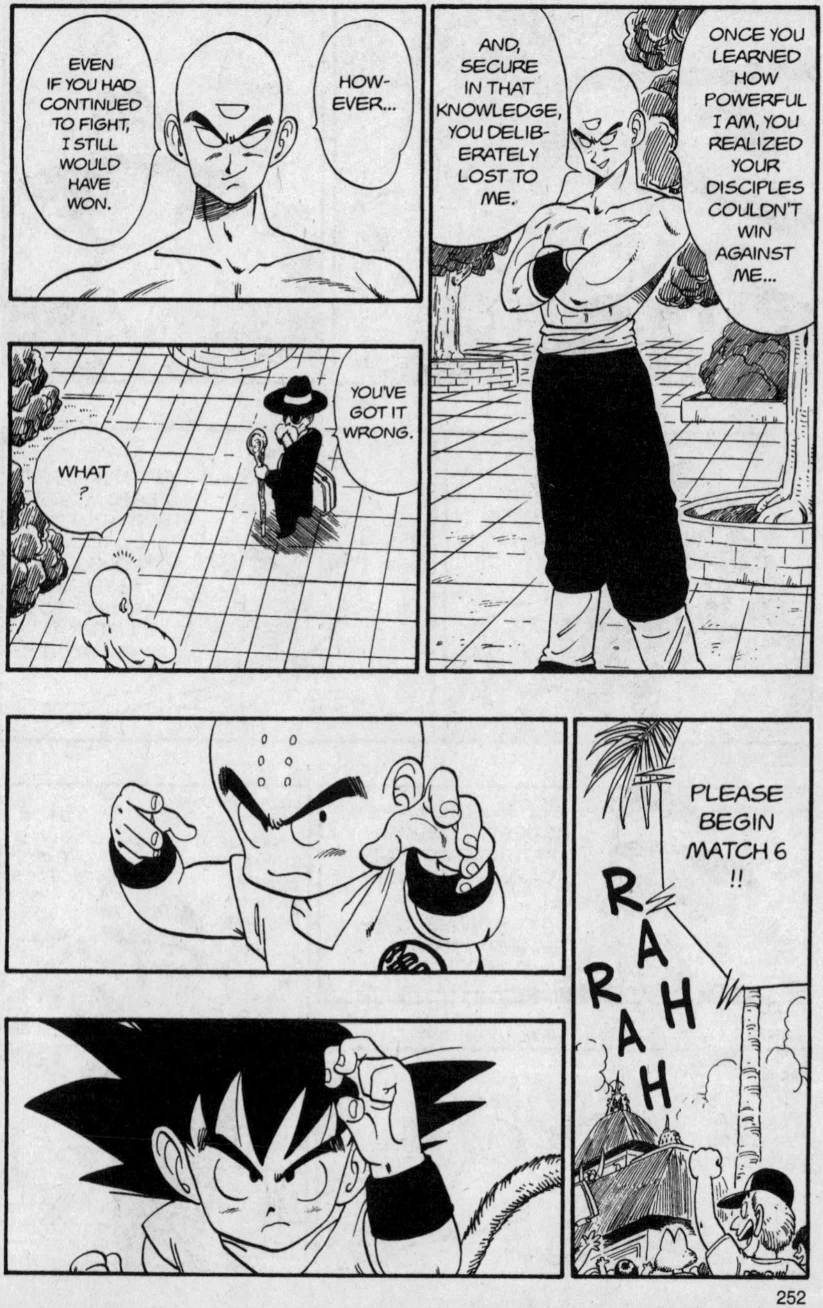
ONCE YOU LEARNED HOW POWERFUL I AM, YOU REALIZED YOUR DISCIPLES COULDN'T WIN AGAINST ME...
AND, SECURE IN THAT KNOWLEDGE, YOU DELIBERATELY LOST TO ME.
HOW-EVER...
EVEN IF YOU HAD CONTINUED TO FIGHT, I STILL WOULD HAVE WON.
YOU'VE GOT IT WRONG.
WHAT?
PLEASE BEGIN MATCH 6 !!
RAH RAH

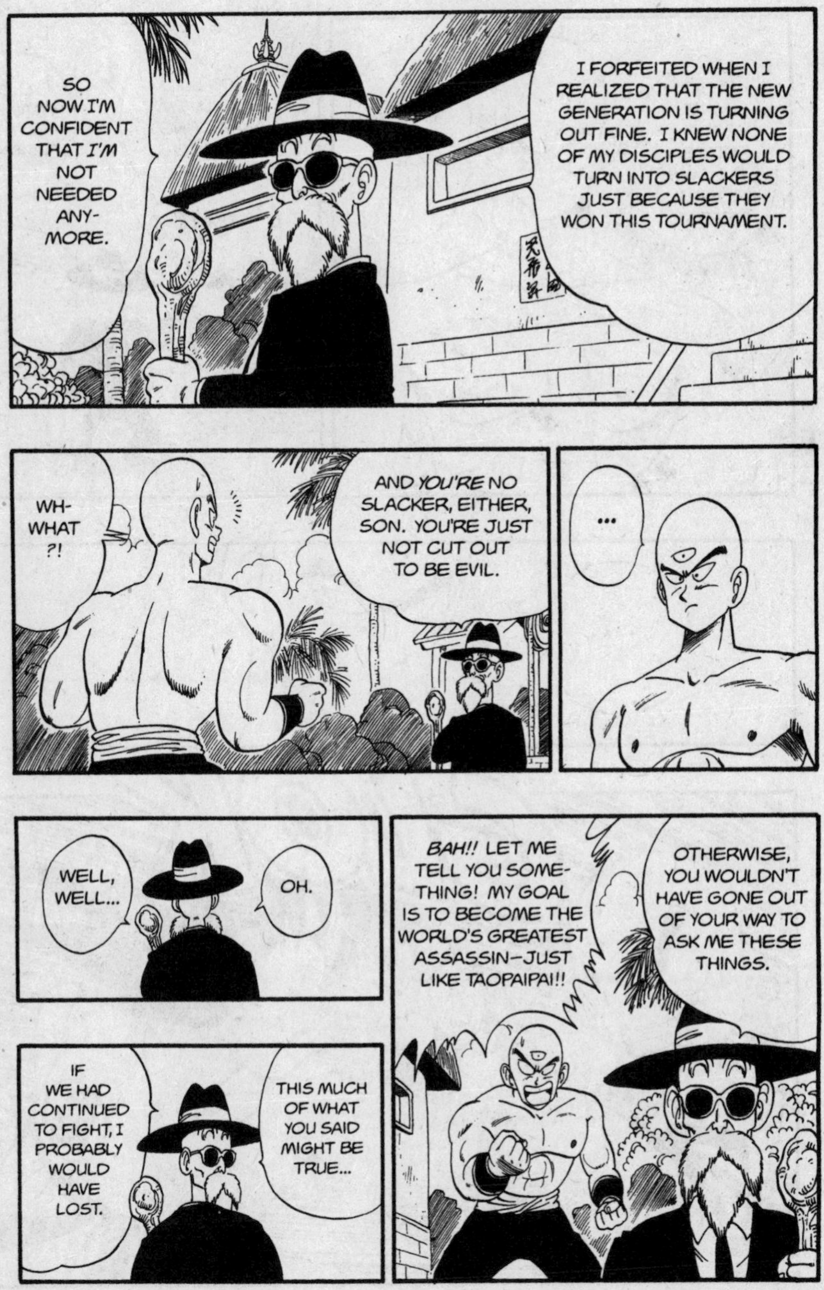
I FORFEITED WHEN I REALIZED THAT THE NEW GENERATION IS TURNING OUT FINE. I KNEW NONE OF MY DISCIPLES WOULD TURN INTO SLACKERS JUST BECAUSE THEY WON THIS TOURNAMENT.
SO NOW I'M CONFIDENT THAT *I'M* NOT NEEDED ANYMORE.
...
AND *YOU'RE* NO SLACKER, EITHER, SON. YOU'RE JUST NOT CUT OUT TO BE EVIL.
WH-WHAT?!
OTHERWISE, YOU WOULDN'T HAVE GONE OUT OF YOUR WAY TO ASK ME THESE THINGS.
BAH!! LET ME TELL YOU SOMETHING! MY GOAL IS TO BECOME THE WORLD'S GREATEST ASSASSIN—JUST LIKE TAOPAIPAI!!
OH.
WELL, WELL...
THIS MUCH OF WHAT YOU SAID MIGHT BE TRUE...
IF WE HAD CONTINUED TO FIGHT, I PROBABLY WOULD HAVE LOST.

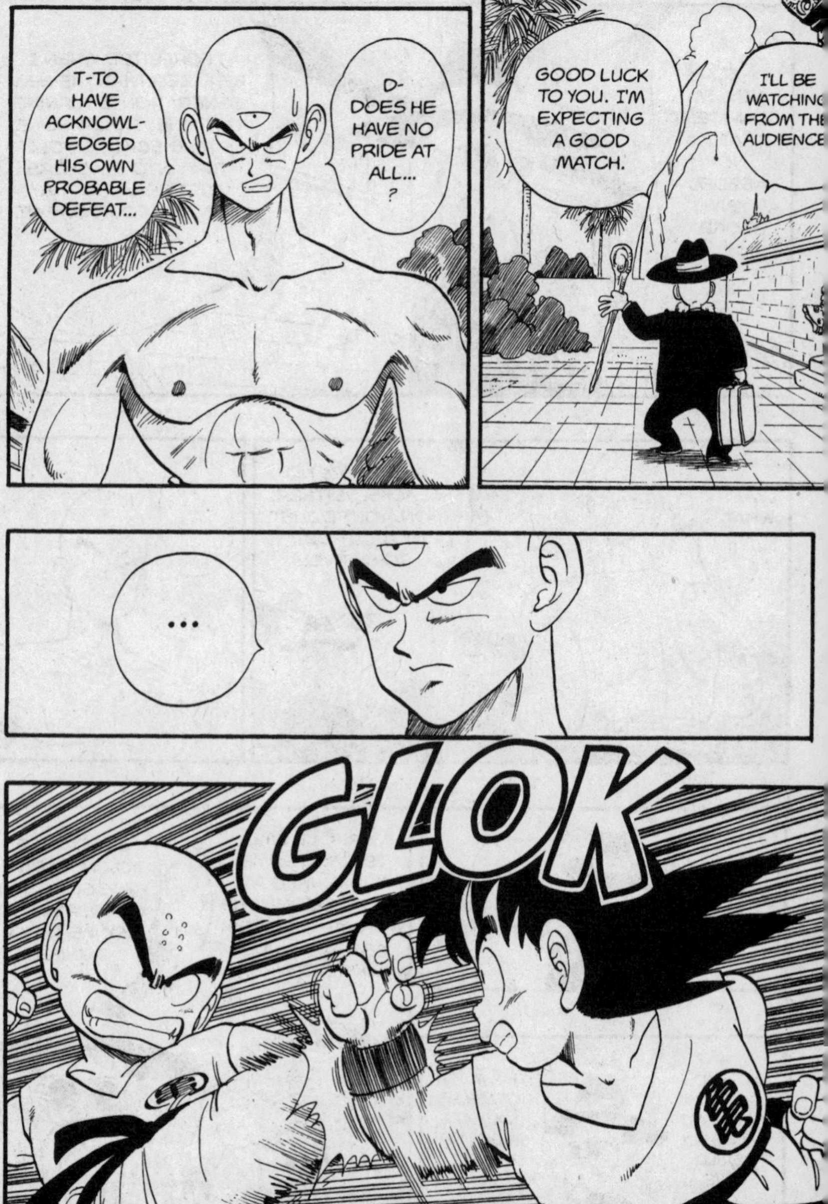
I'LL BE WATCHING FROM THE AUDIENCE
GOOD LUCK TO YOU. I'M EXPECTING A GOOD MATCH.
D-DOES HE HAVE NO PRIDE AT ALL...?
T-TO HAVE ACKNOWLEDGED HIS OWN PROBABLE DEFEAT...
...
GLOK

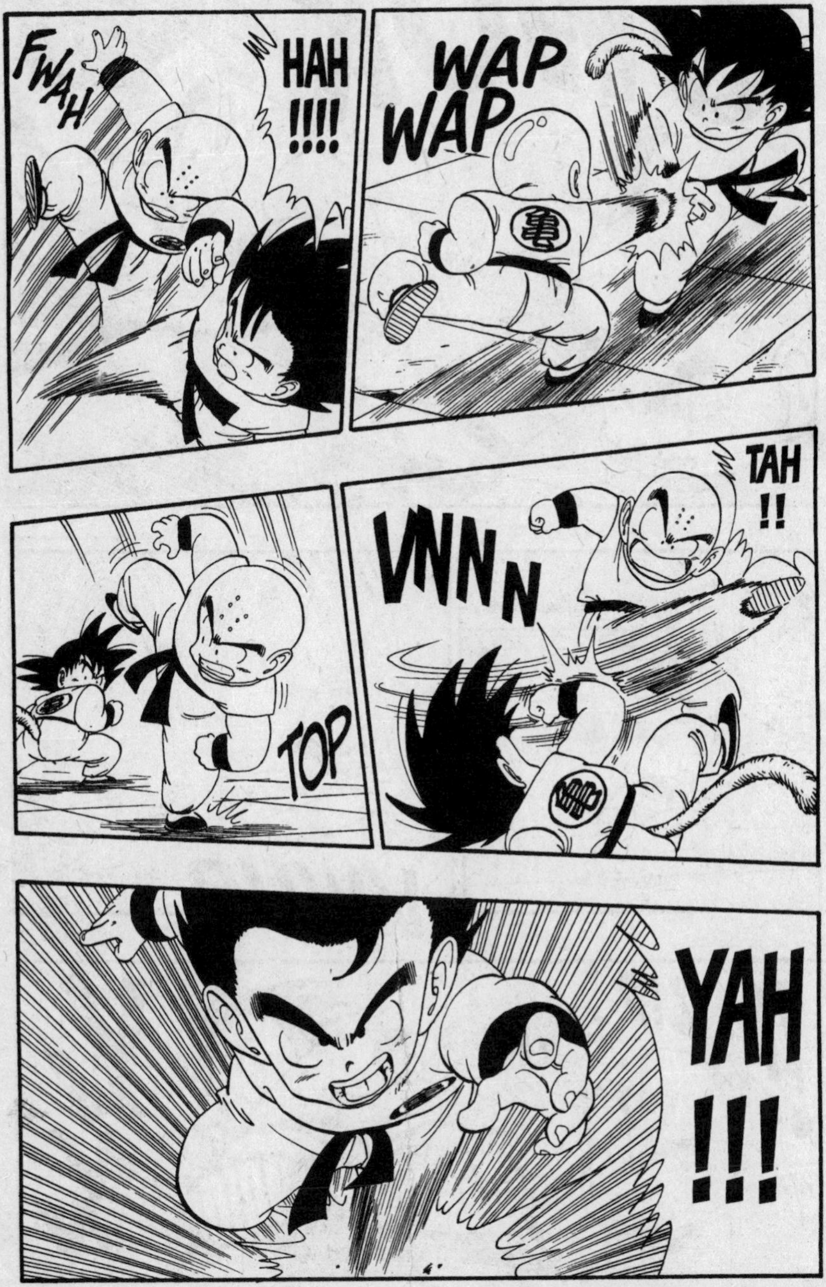
WAP
WAP
HAH
!!!!
FWAH
TAH
!!
VNNN
TOP
YAH
!!!

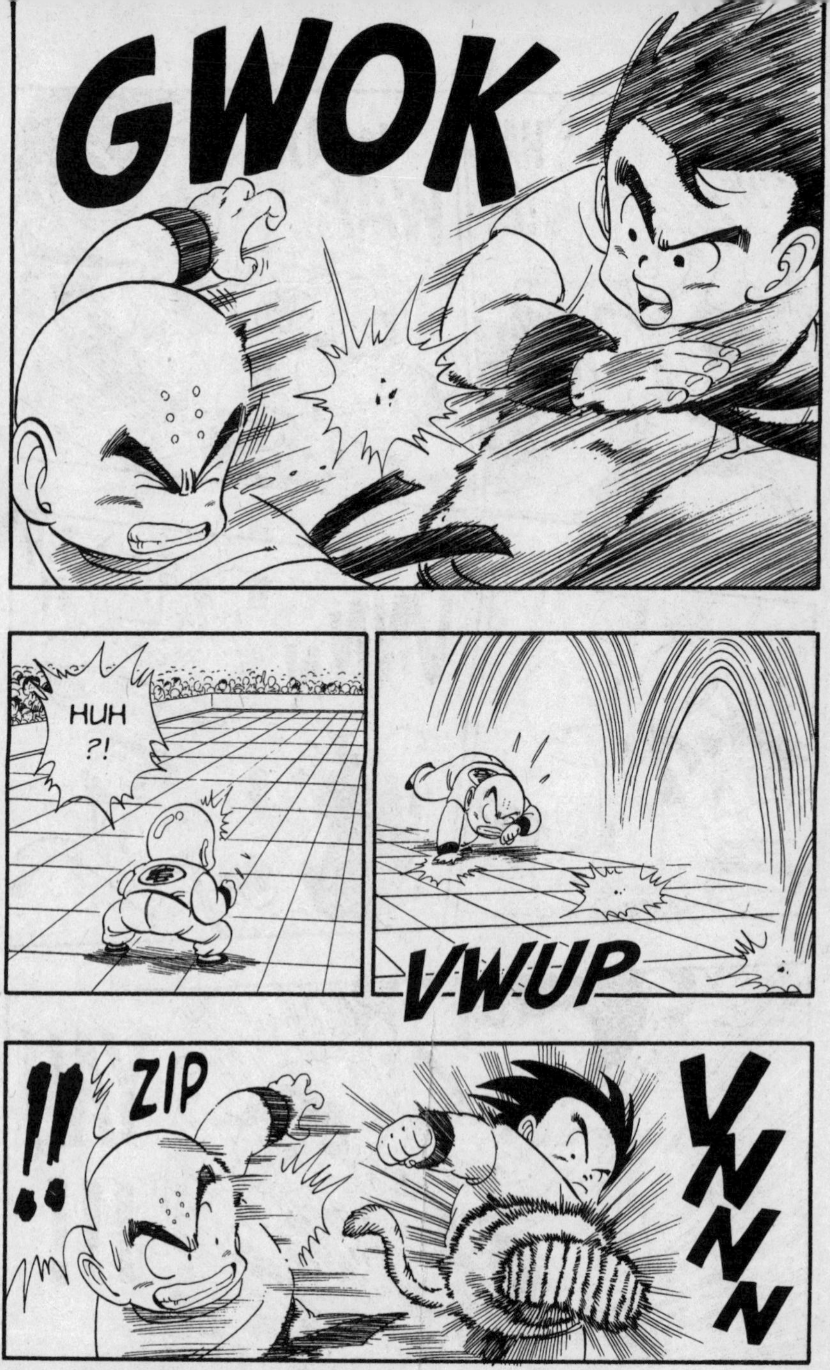
GWOK
VWUP
HUH ?!
YNNN
ZIP
!!

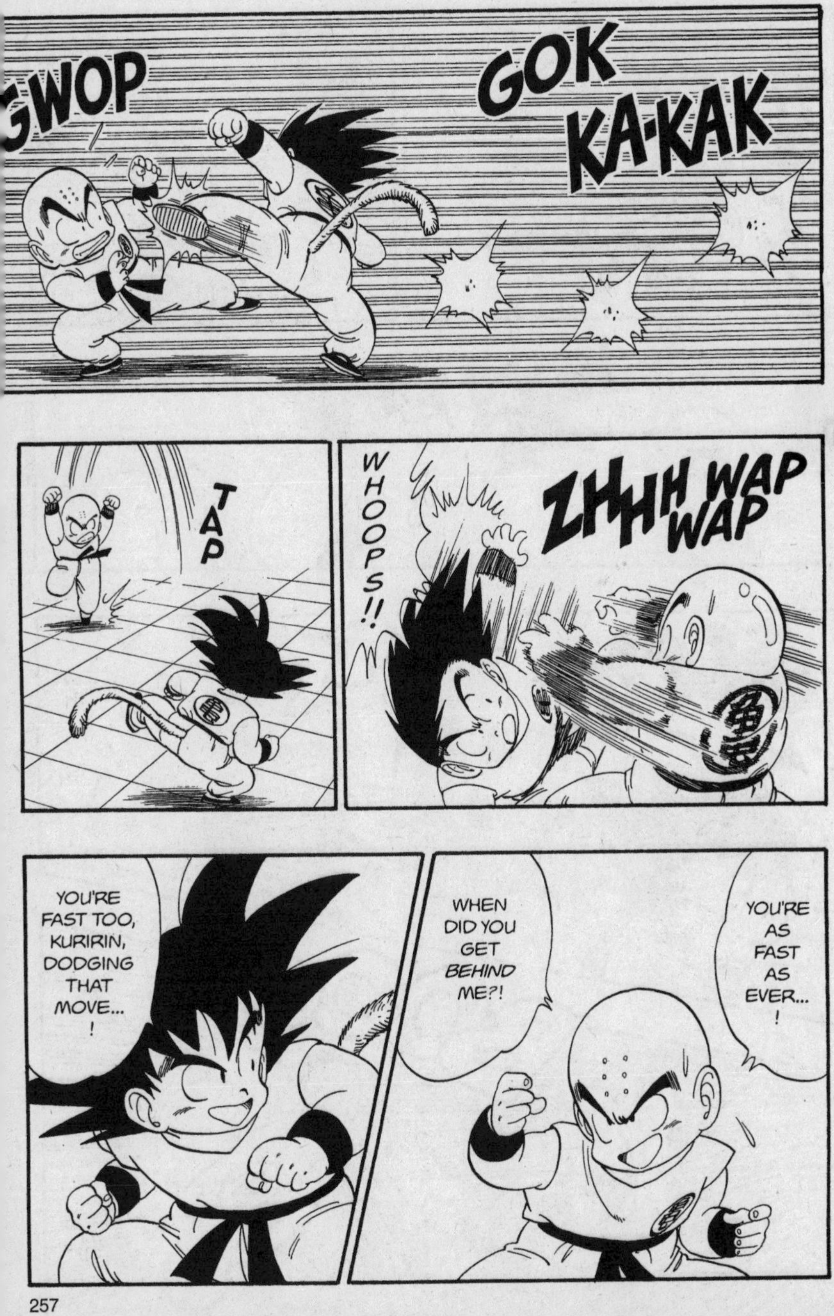
GOK
KA-KAK
GWOP
ZHHH WAP WAP
WHOOPS!!
TAP
YOU'RE AS FAST AS EVER... !
WHEN DID YOU GET BEHIND ME?!
YOU'RE FAST TOO, KURIRIN, DODGING THAT MOVE... !

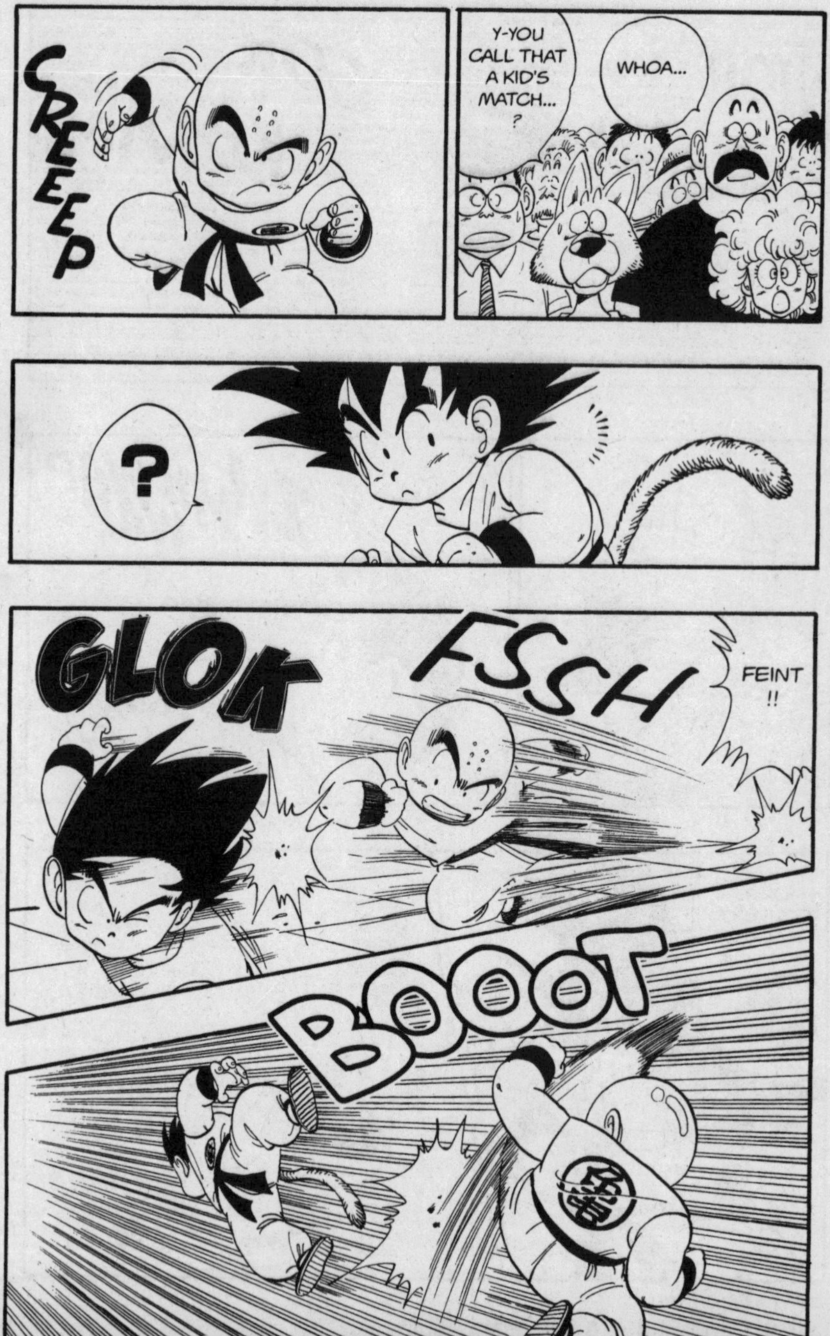
WHOA...
Y-YOU CALL THAT A KID'S MATCH...?
CREEEP
?
FEINT!!
FSSH
GLOK
BOOOT

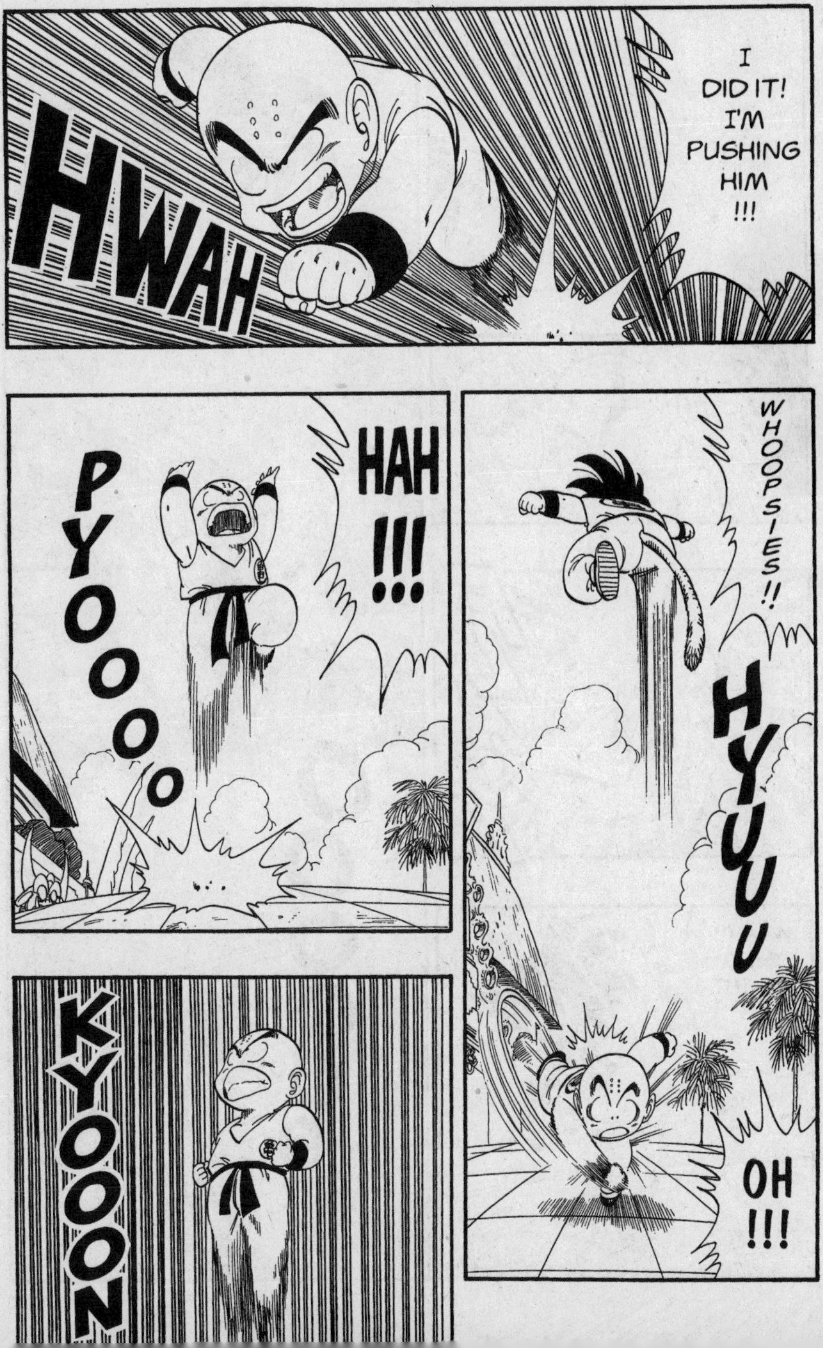
I DID IT! I'M PUSHING HIM!!!
HWAH
WHOOPSIES!!
HYUUU
OH!!!
HAH!!!
PYOOOO
KYOOON

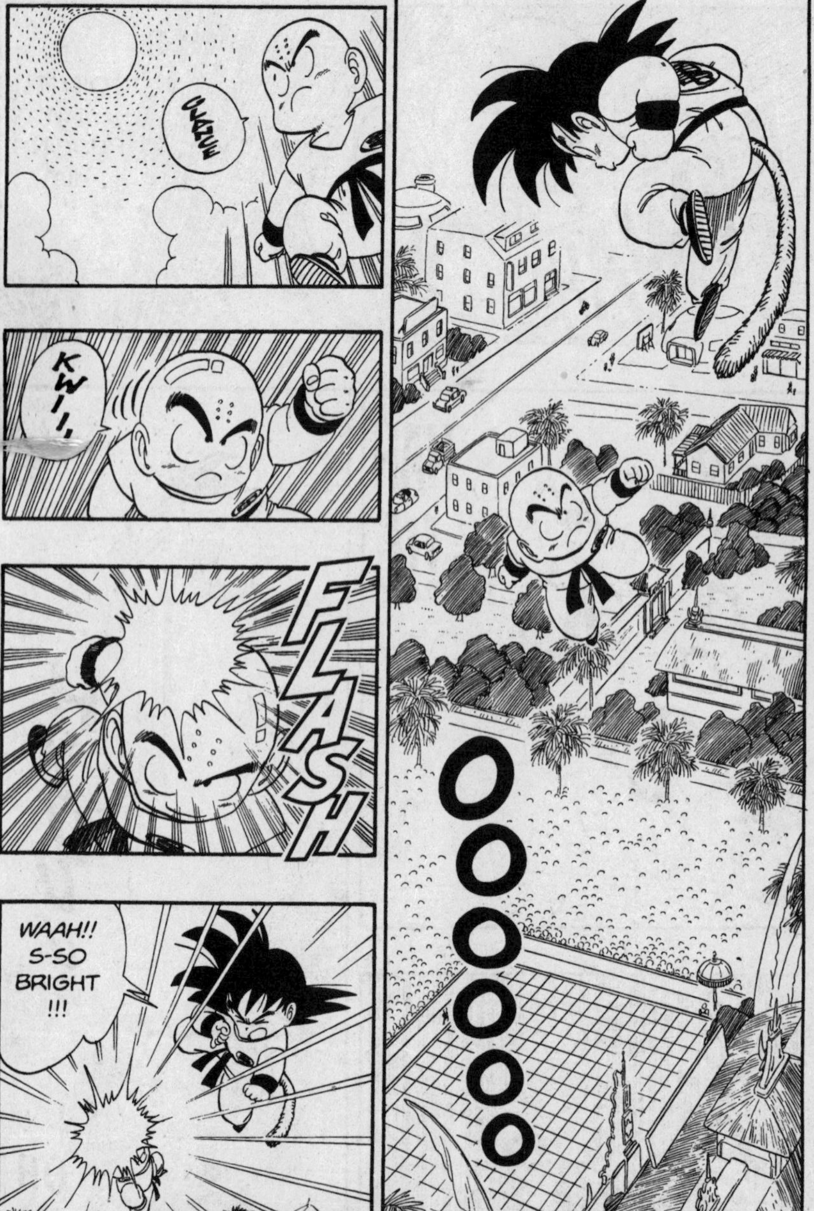

OOOOOO
GLANCE
KWI!!
FLASH
WAAH!! S-SO BRIGHT !!!

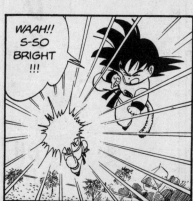

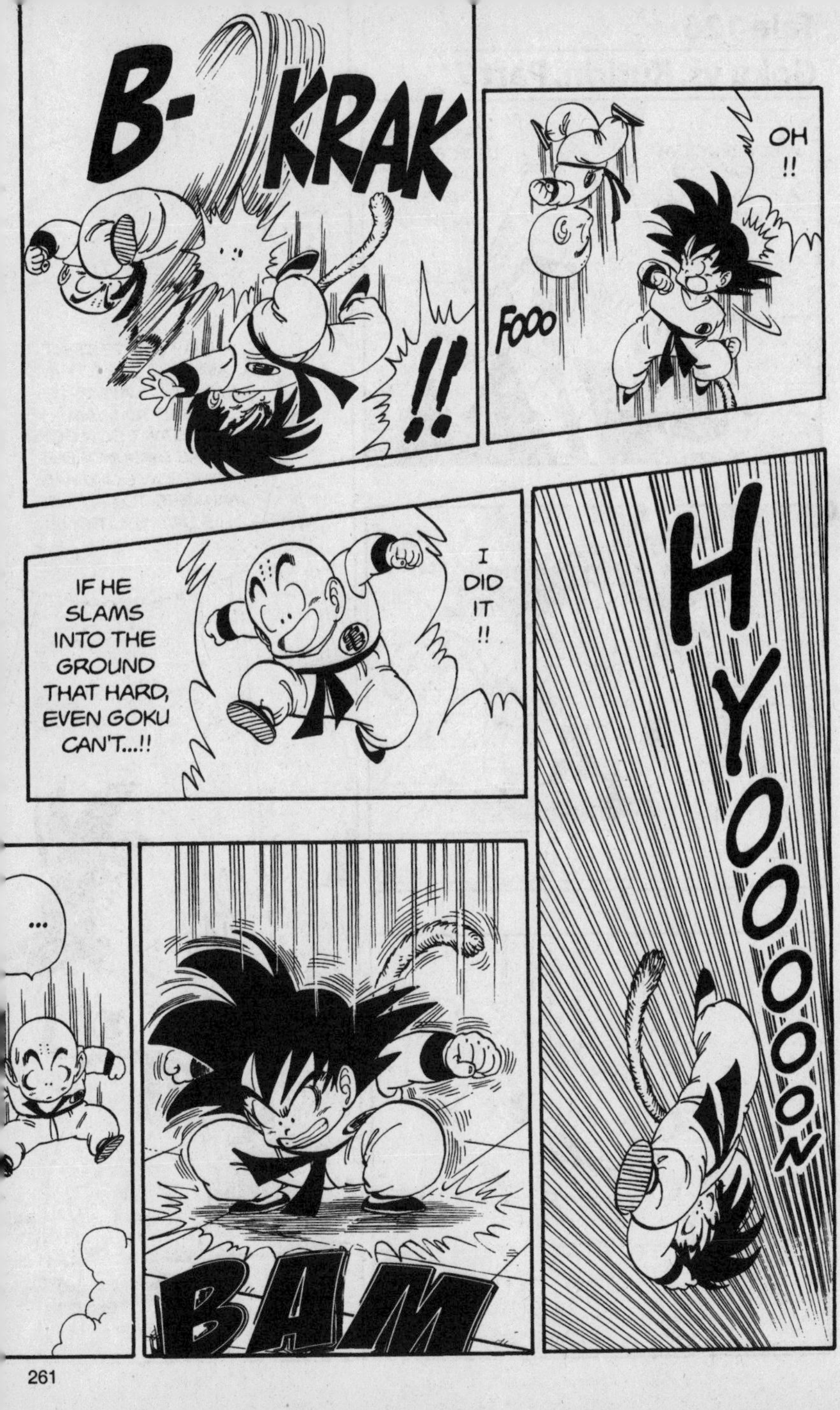
OH !!
FOOO
B- KRAK
!!
HYOOOOOON
I DID IT !!
IF HE SLAMS INTO THE GROUND THAT HARD, EVEN GOKU CAN'T...!!
BAM
...

Tale 126
Goku vs. Kuririn, Part 2

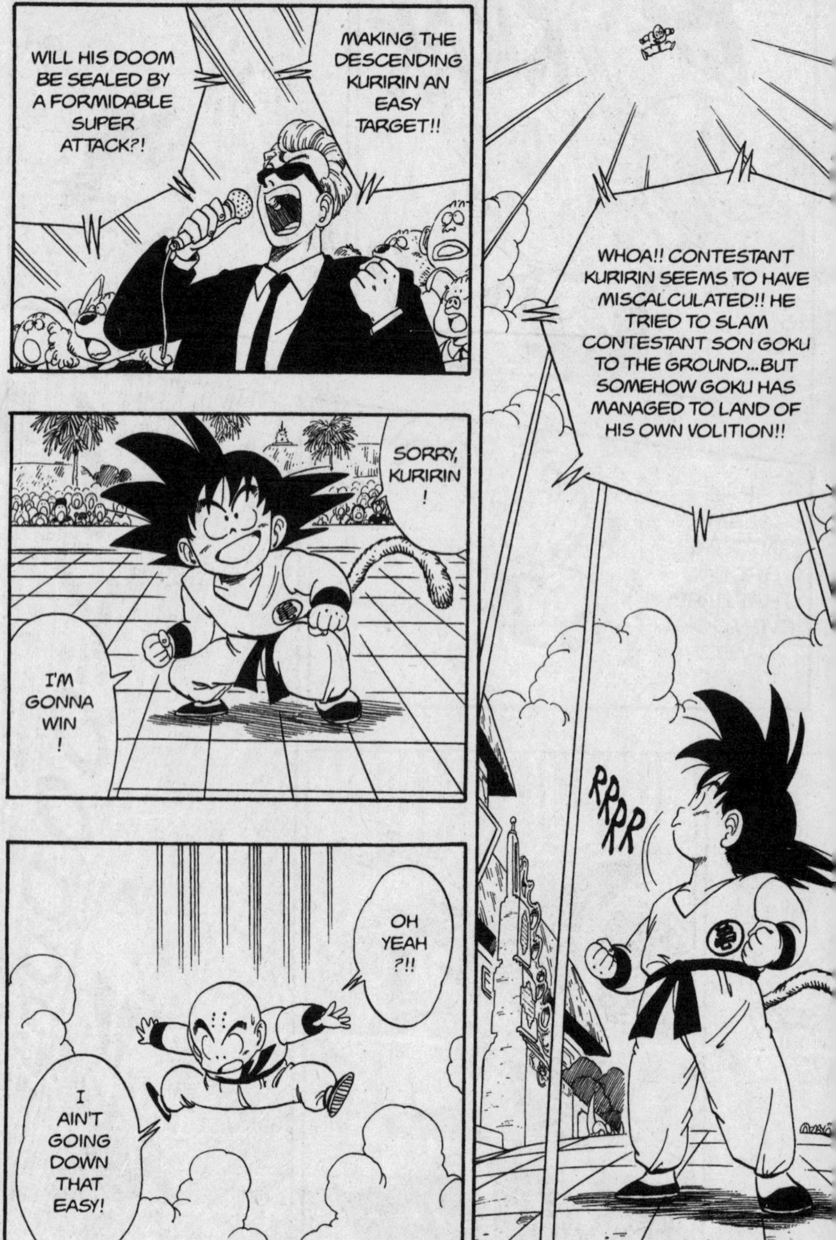
WHOA!! CONTESTANT KURIRIN SEEMS TO HAVE MISCALCULATED!! HE TRIED TO SLAM CONTESTANT SON GOKU TO THE GROUND...BUT SOMEHOW GOKU HAS MANAGED TO LAND OF HIS OWN VOLITION!!
RRRR
MAKING THE DESCENDING KURIRIN AN EASY TARGET!!
WILL HIS DOOM BE SEALED BY A FORMIDABLE SUPER ATTACK?!
SORRY, KURIRIN!
I'M GONNA WIN!
OH YEAH?!!
I AIN'T GOING DOWN THAT EASY!

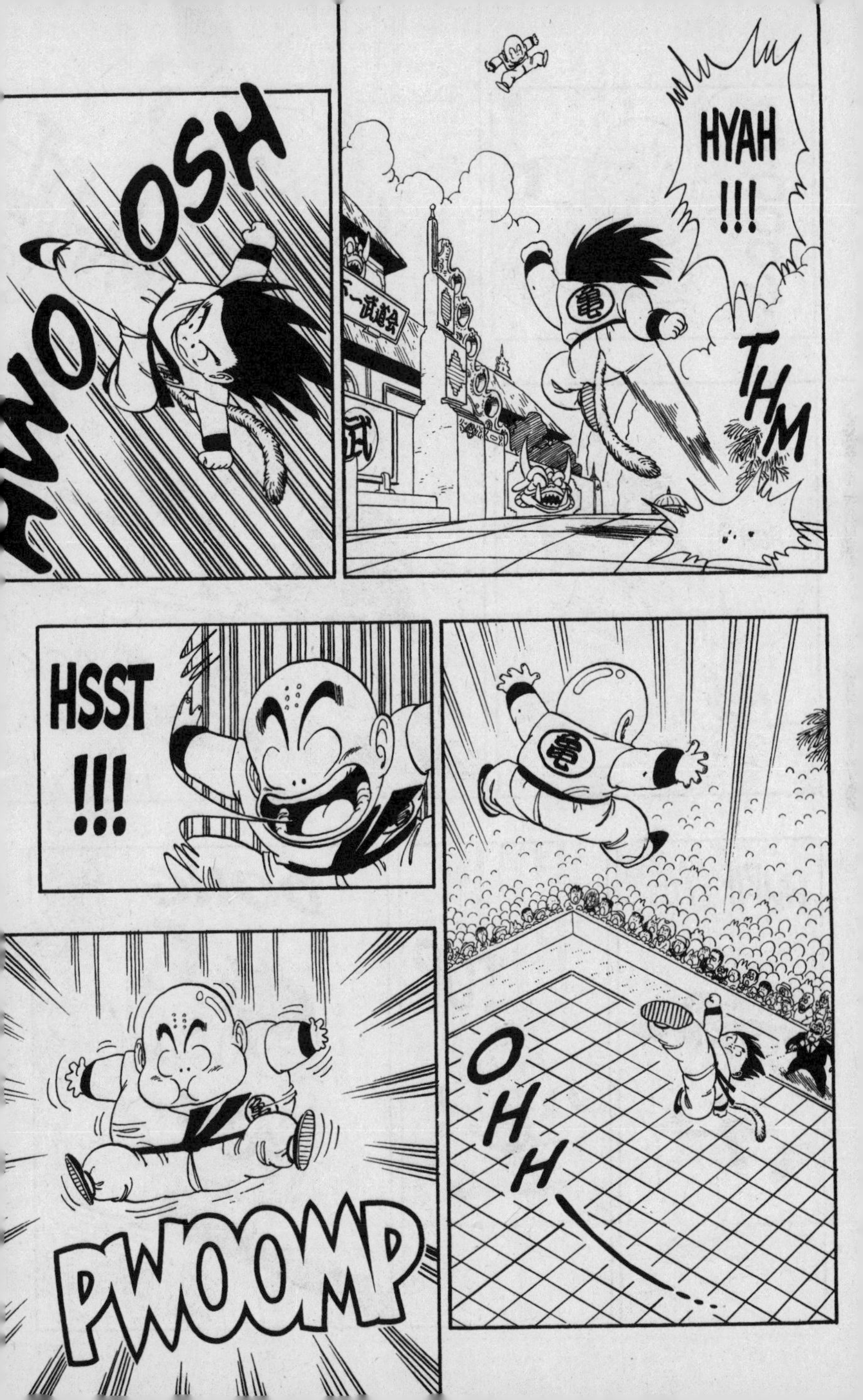
HYAH
!!!
THM
WHOOSH
OHH
HSST
!!!
PWOOMP

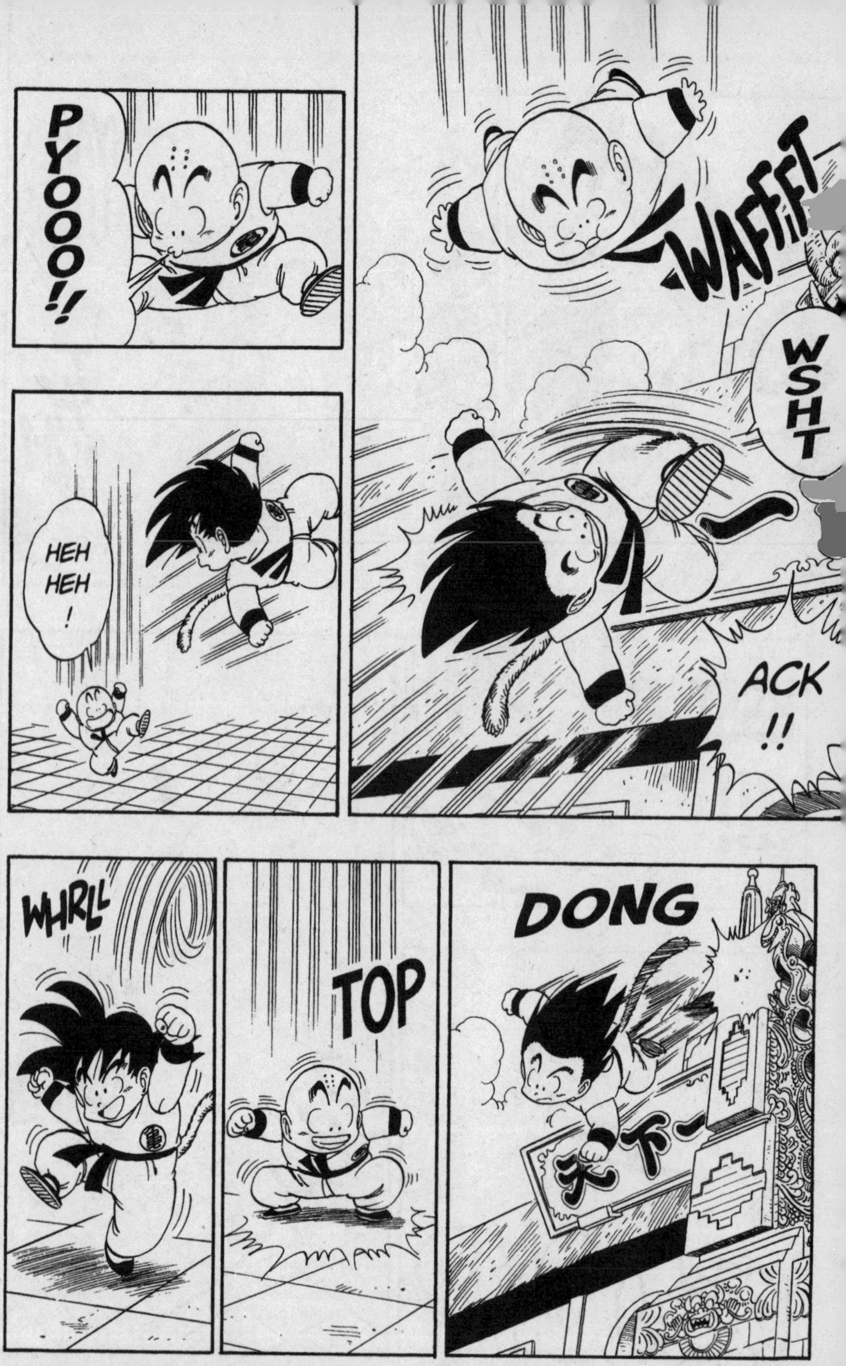
WAFFFT
WSHT
ACK!!
PYOOOO!!
HEH HEH!
DONG
TOP
WHRLL

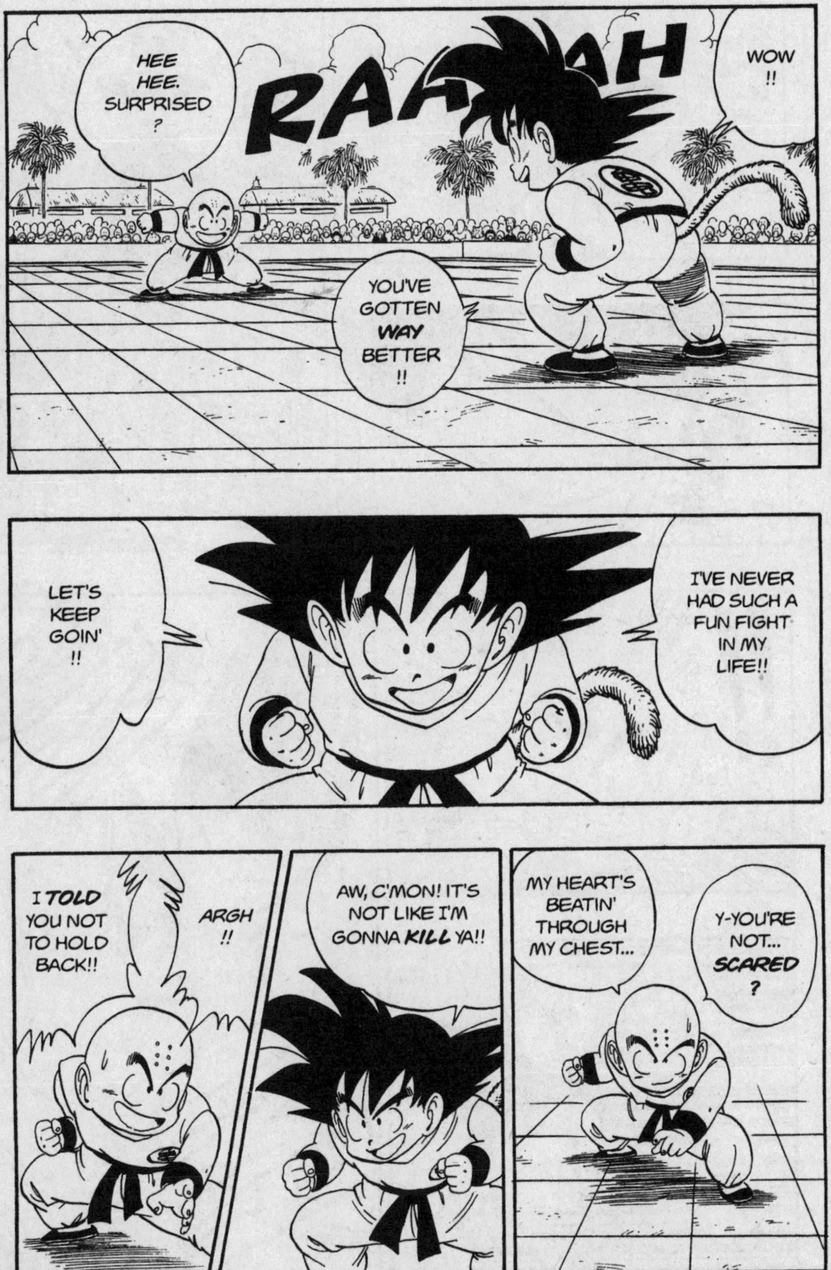
WOW !!
RAAAH
HEE HEE. SURPRISED ?
YOU'VE GOTTEN WAY BETTER !!
I'VE NEVER HAD SUCH A FUN FIGHT IN MY LIFE!!
LET'S KEEP GOIN' !!
Y-YOU'RE NOT... SCARED ?
MY HEART'S BEATIN' THROUGH MY CHEST...
AW, C'MON! IT'S NOT LIKE I'M GONNA KILL YA!!
ARGH !!
I TOLD YOU NOT TO HOLD BACK!!

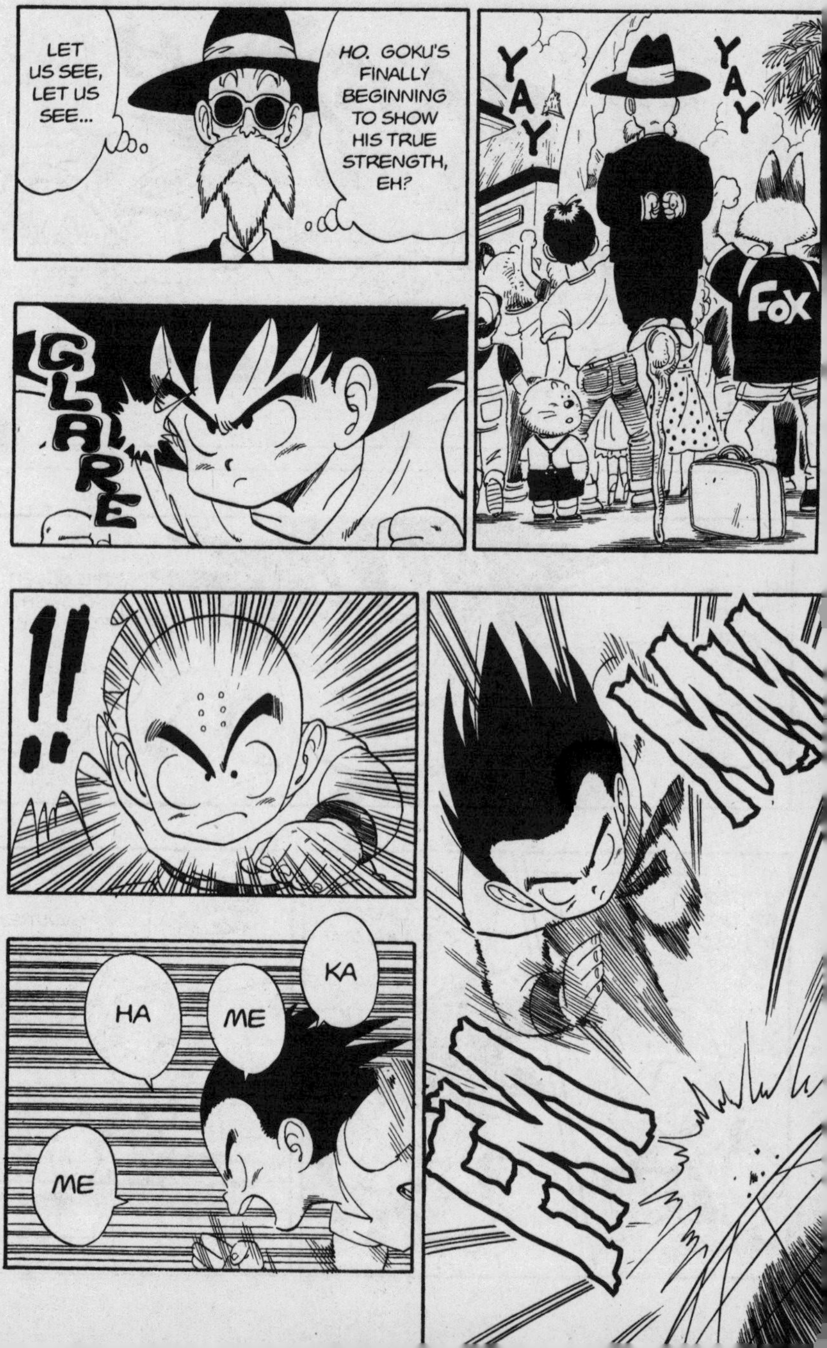
YAY
YAY
FOX
HO. GOKU'S FINALLY BEGINNING TO SHOW HIS TRUE STRENGTH, EH?
LET US SEE, LET US SEE...
GLARE
!!
KA
ME
HA
ME

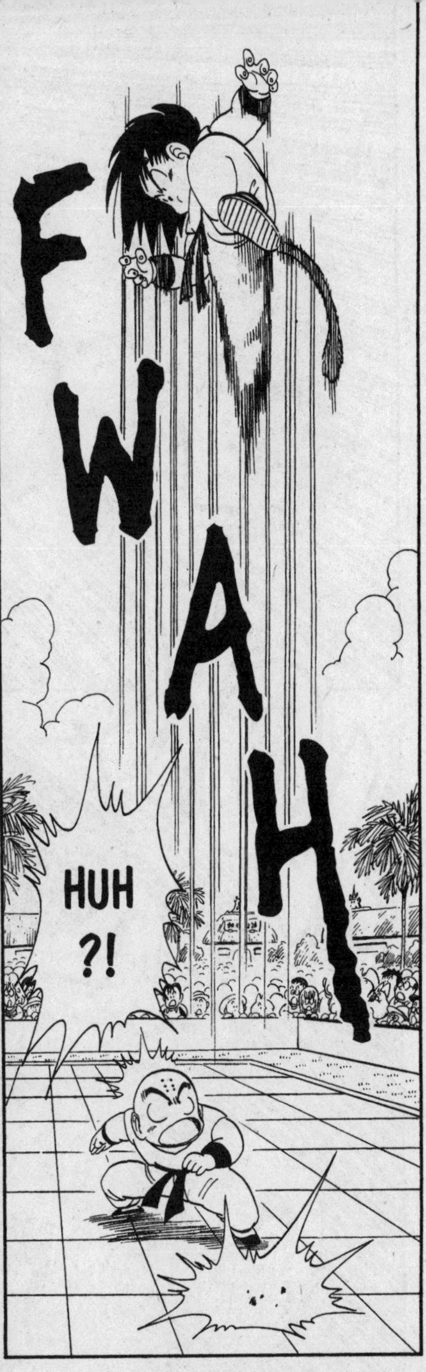
FWAH
HUH ?!

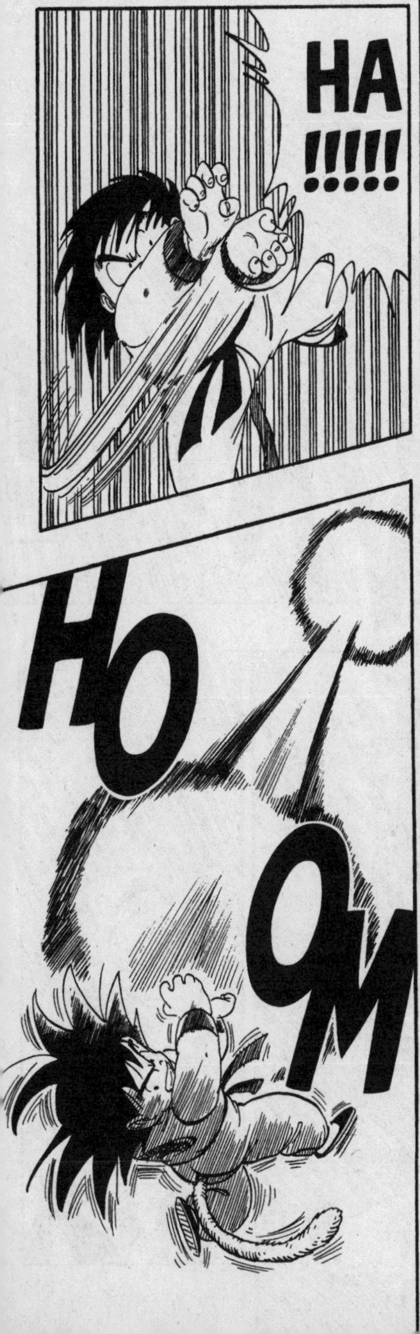
HA !!!!!
HOOM

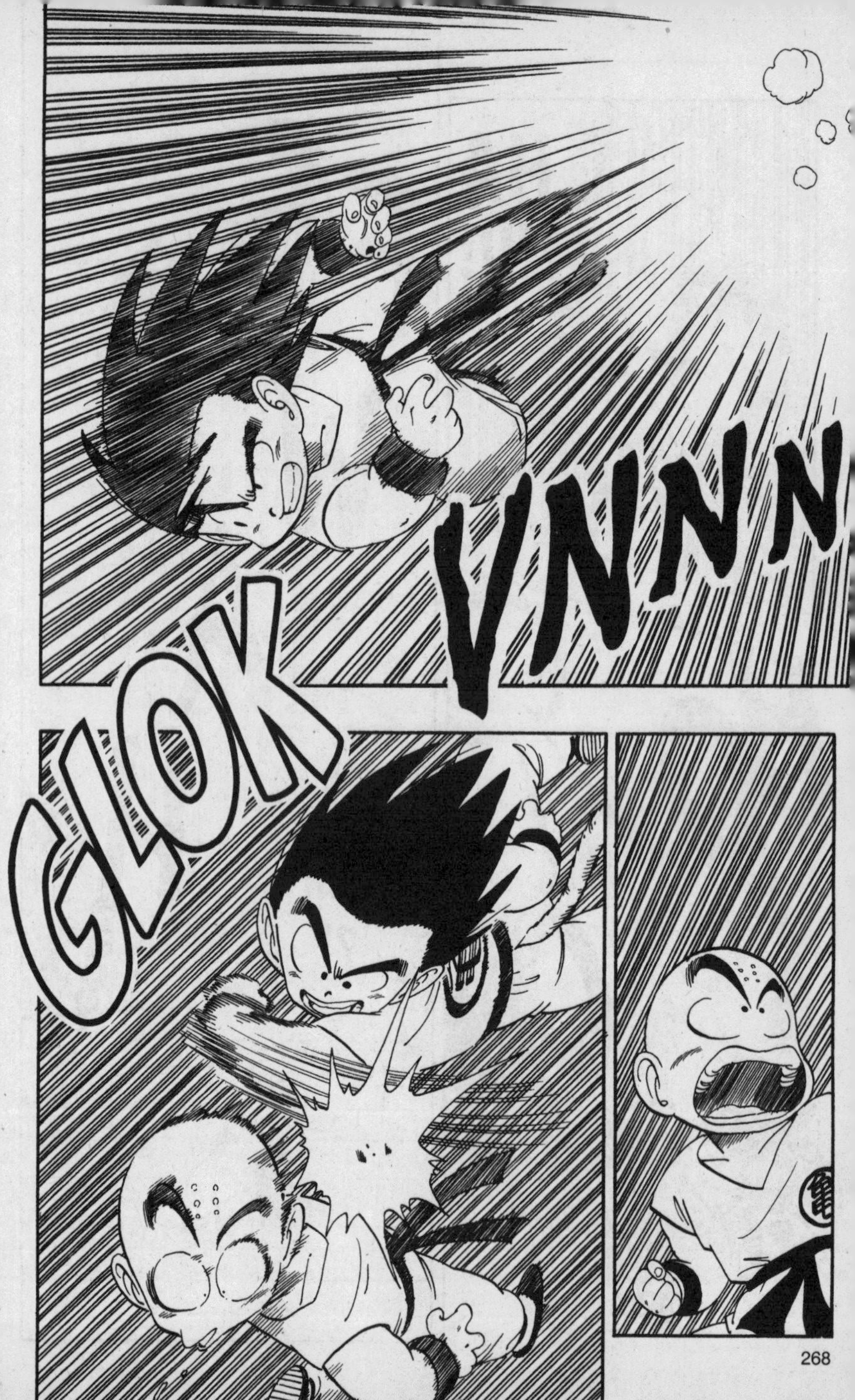
VNNN
CLOK

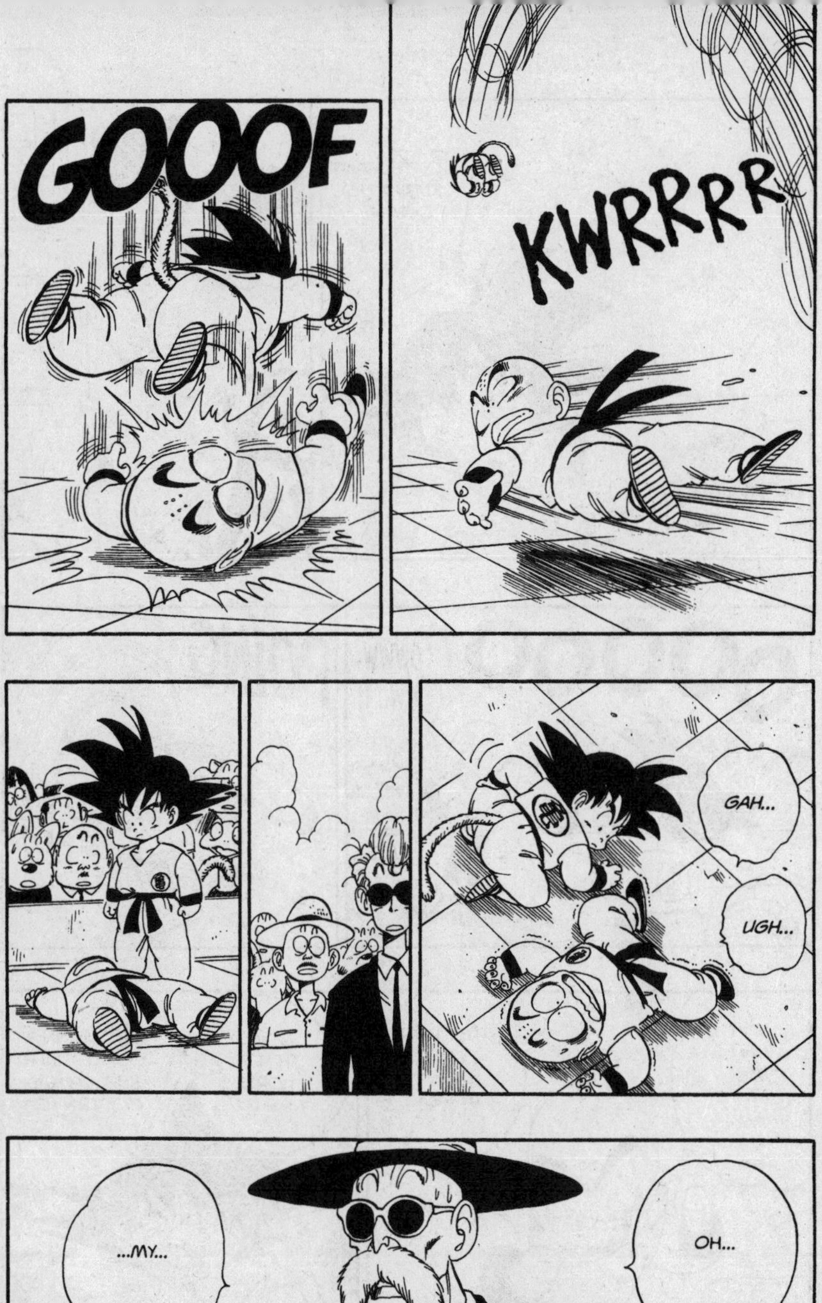
KWRRRR
GOOOF
GAH...
UGH...
OH...
...MY...

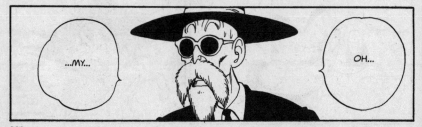

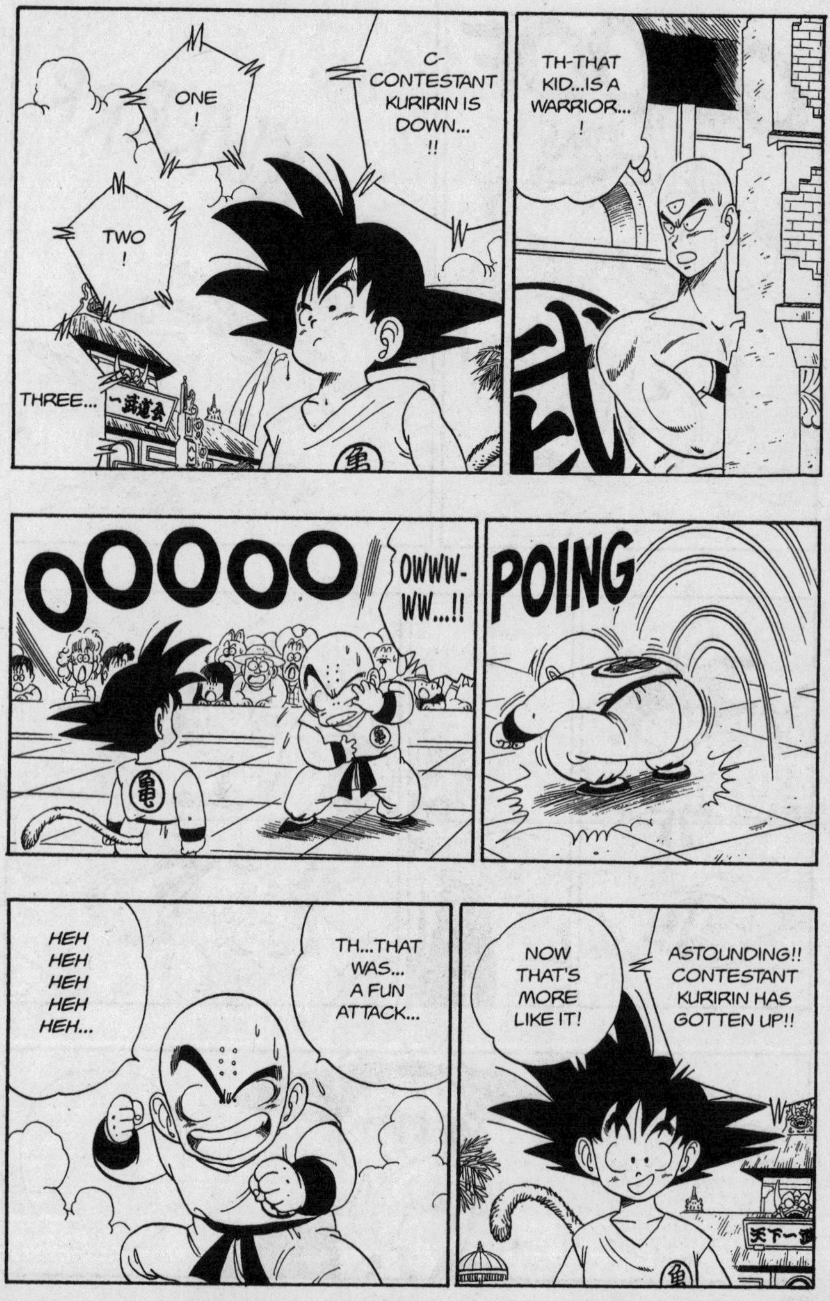
TH-THAT KID...IS A WARRIOR...!
C-CONTESTANT KURIRIN IS DOWN...!!
ONE!
TWO!
THREE...
POING
OWWW-WW...!!
OOOOO
ASTOUNDING!! CONTESTANT KURIRIN HAS GOTTEN UP!!
NOW THAT'S MORE LIKE IT!
TH...THAT WAS... A FUN ATTACK...
HEH HEH HEH HEH HEH...

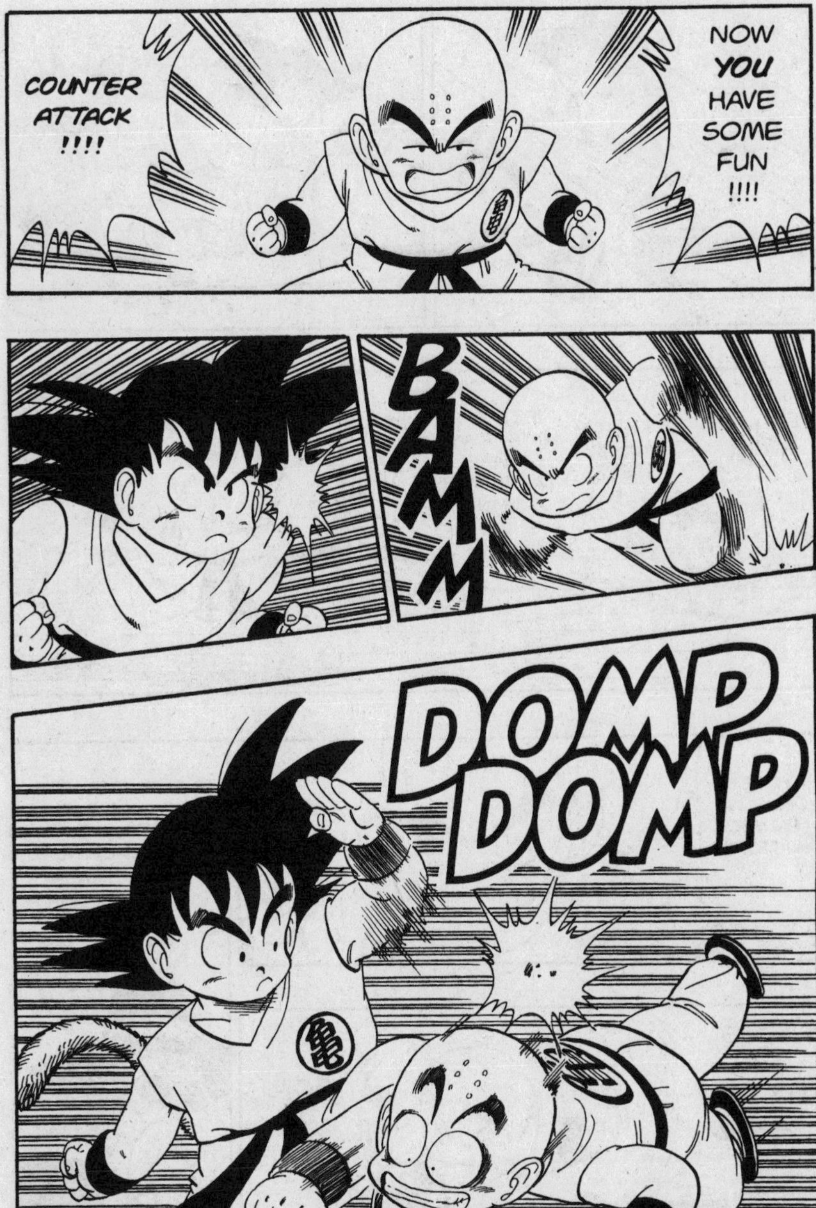
NOW YOU HAVE SOME FUN !!!!
COUNTER ATTACK !!!!
BAMM
DOMP DOMP

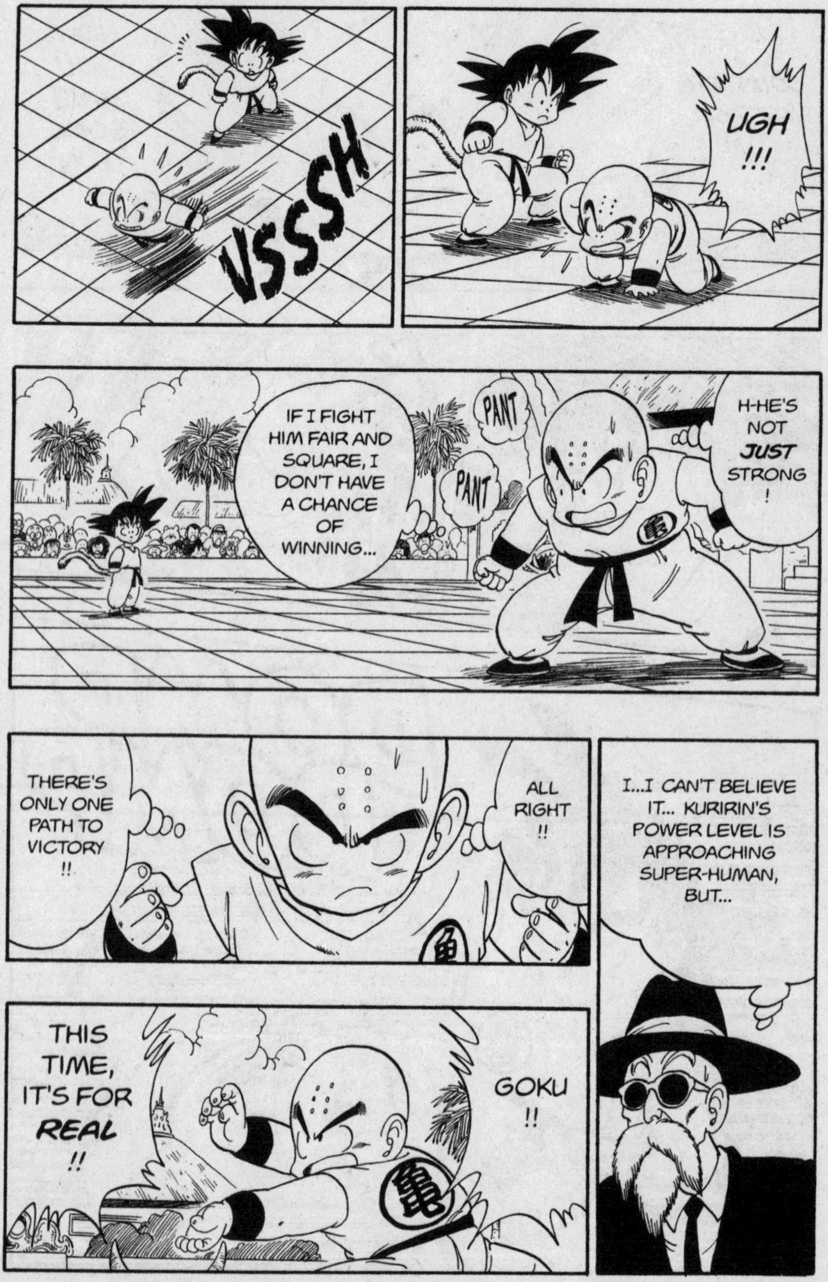
UGH !!!
VSSSH
H-HE'S NOT JUST STRONG !
PANT
PANT
IF I FIGHT HIM FAIR AND SQUARE, I DON'T HAVE A CHANCE OF WINNING...
I...I CAN'T BELIEVE IT... KURIRIN'S POWER LEVEL IS APPROACHING SUPER-HUMAN, BUT...
ALL RIGHT !!
THERE'S ONLY ONE PATH TO VICTORY !!
GOKU !!
THIS TIME, IT'S FOR REAL !!

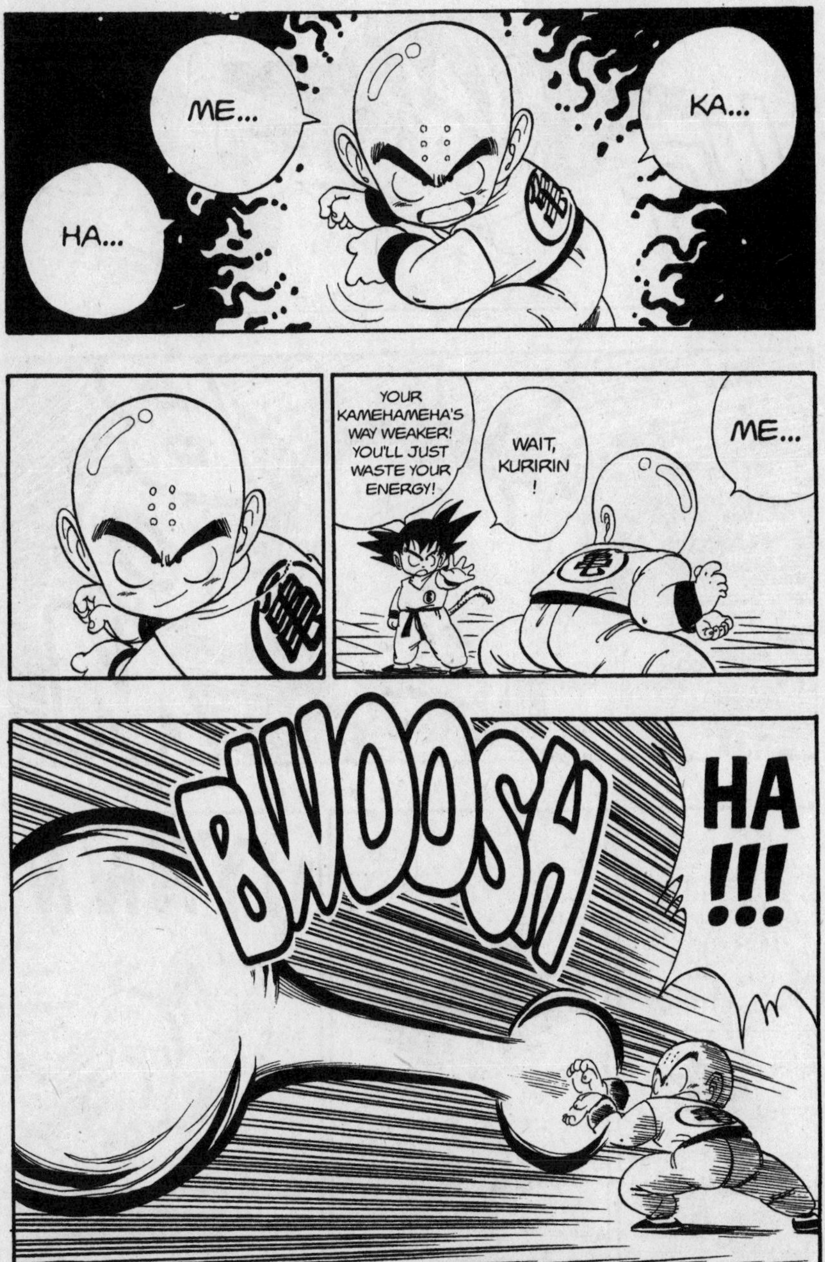
KA...
ME...
HA...
ME...
WAIT, KURIRIN!
YOUR KAMEHAMEHA'S WAY WEAKER! YOU'LL JUST WASTE YOUR ENERGY!
HA!!!
BWOOSH

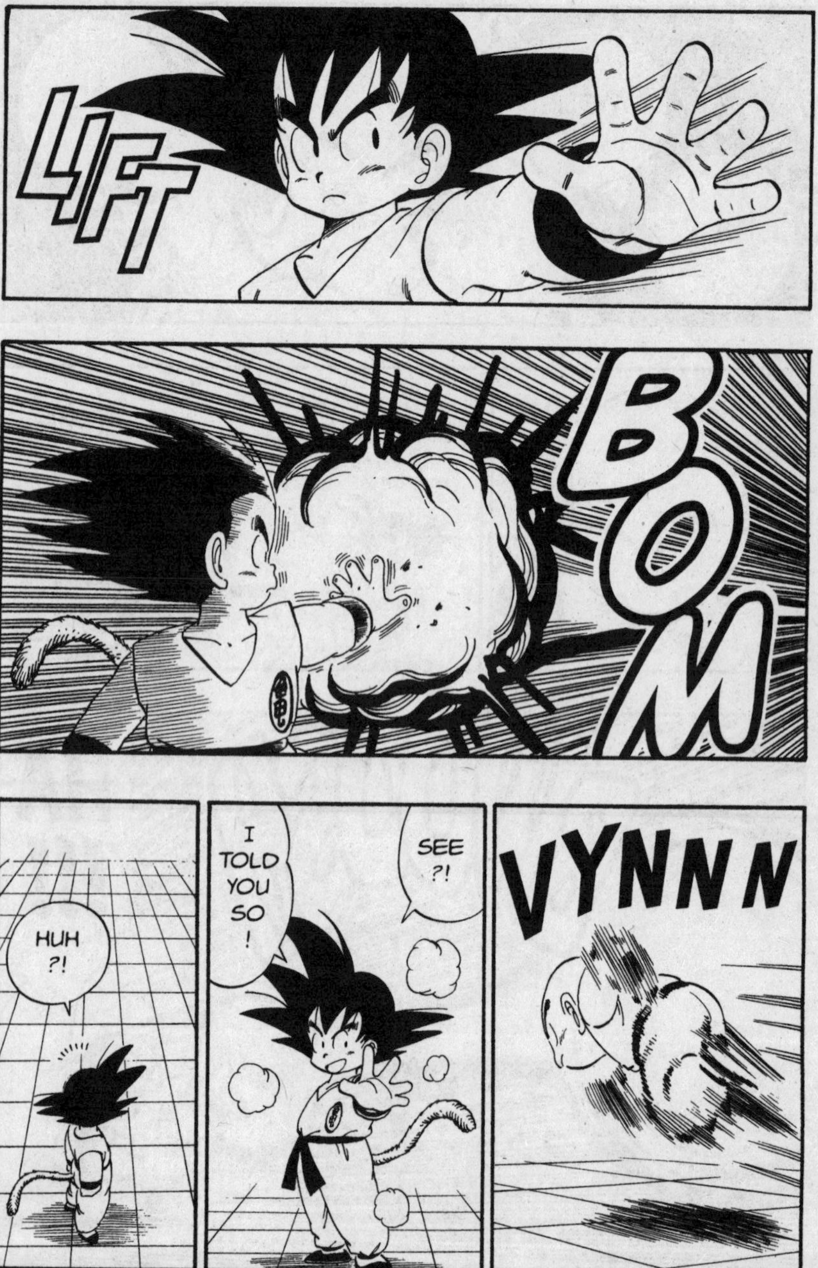
LIFT
BOM
VYNNN
SEE ?!
I TOLD YOU SO !
HUH ?!

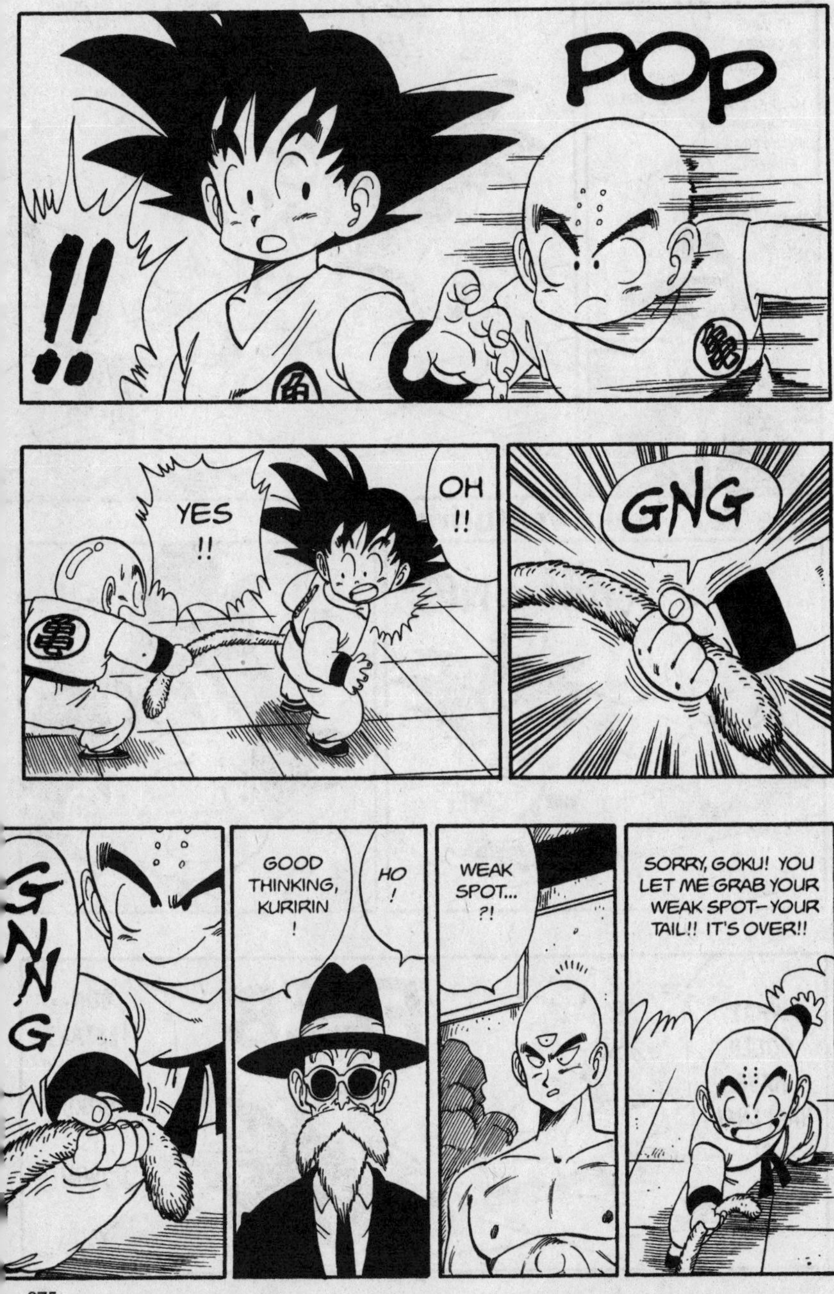
POP
!!
GNG
OH !!
YES !!
SORRY, GOKU! YOU LET ME GRAB YOUR WEAK SPOT—YOUR TAIL!! IT'S OVER!!
WEAK SPOT... ?!
HO !
GOOD THINKING, KURIRIN !
GNNG

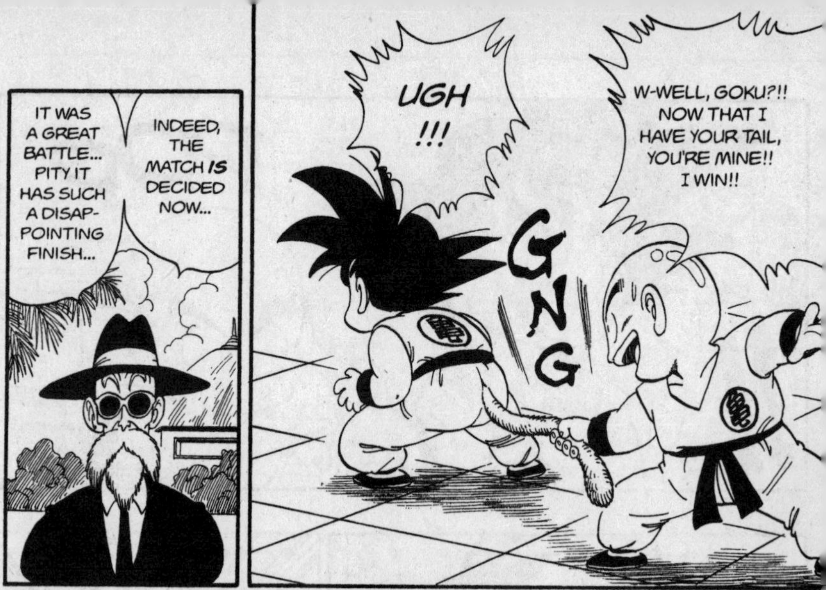
W-WELL, GOKU?!! NOW THAT I HAVE YOUR TAIL, YOU'RE MINE!! I WIN!!
UGH !!!
GNG
INDEED, THE MATCH IS DECIDED NOW...
IT WAS A GREAT BATTLE... PITY IT HAS SUCH A DISAP-POINTING FINISH...

Tale 127 • Goku vs. Kuririn, Part 3

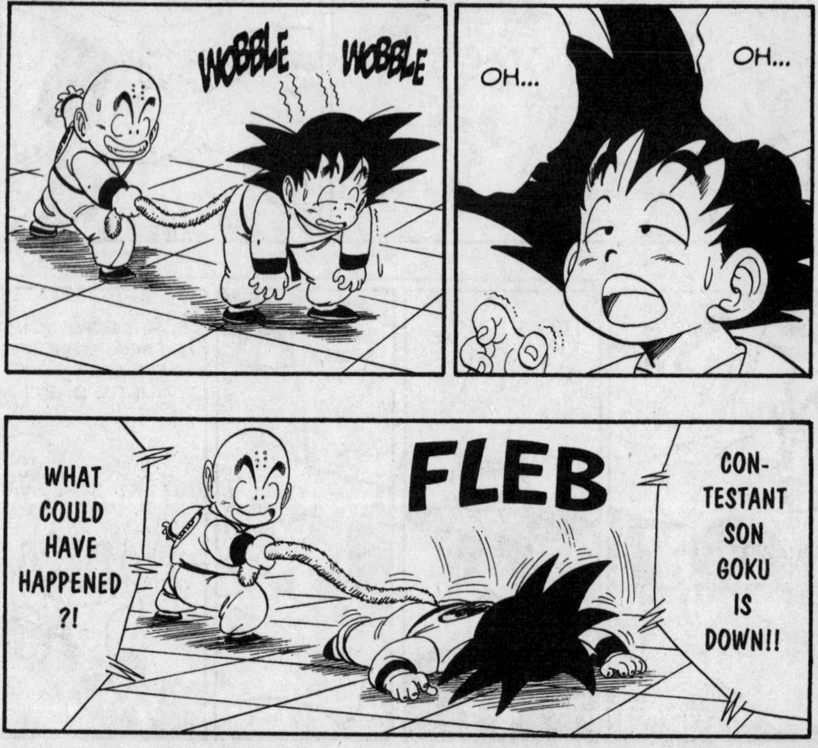
OH...
OH...
WOBBLE
WOBBLE
CON-TESTANT SON GOKU IS DOWN!!
FLEB
WHAT COULD HAVE HAPPENED ?!

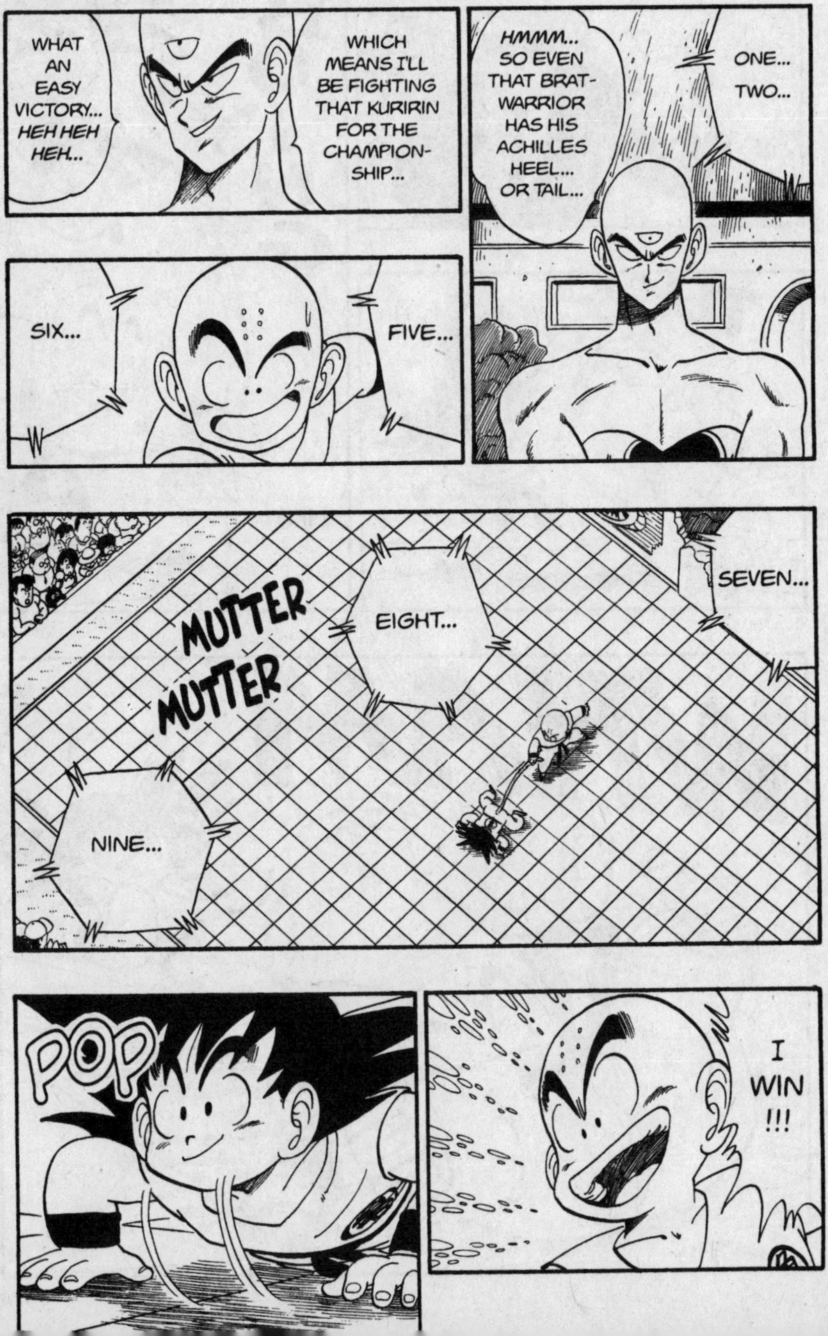
ONE... TWO...
HMMM... SO EVEN THAT BRAT-WARRIOR HAS HIS ACHILLES HEEL... OR TAIL...
WHICH MEANS I'LL BE FIGHTING THAT KURIRIN FOR THE CHAMPIONSHIP...
WHAT AN EASY VICTORY... HEH HEH HEH...
FIVE...
SIX...
SEVEN...
EIGHT...
MUTTER MUTTER
NINE...
I WIN !!!
POP

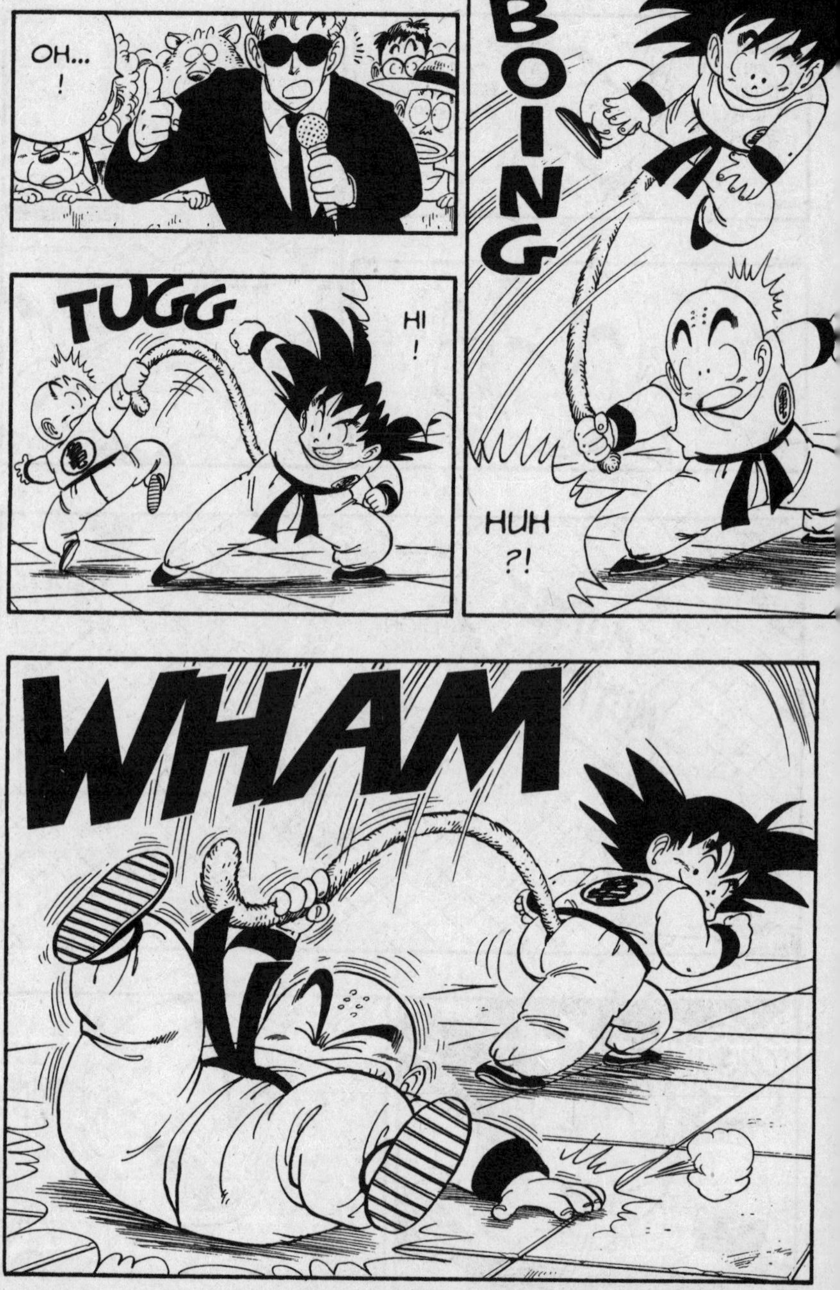
BOING
HUH ?!
OH... !
TUGG
HI !
WHAM

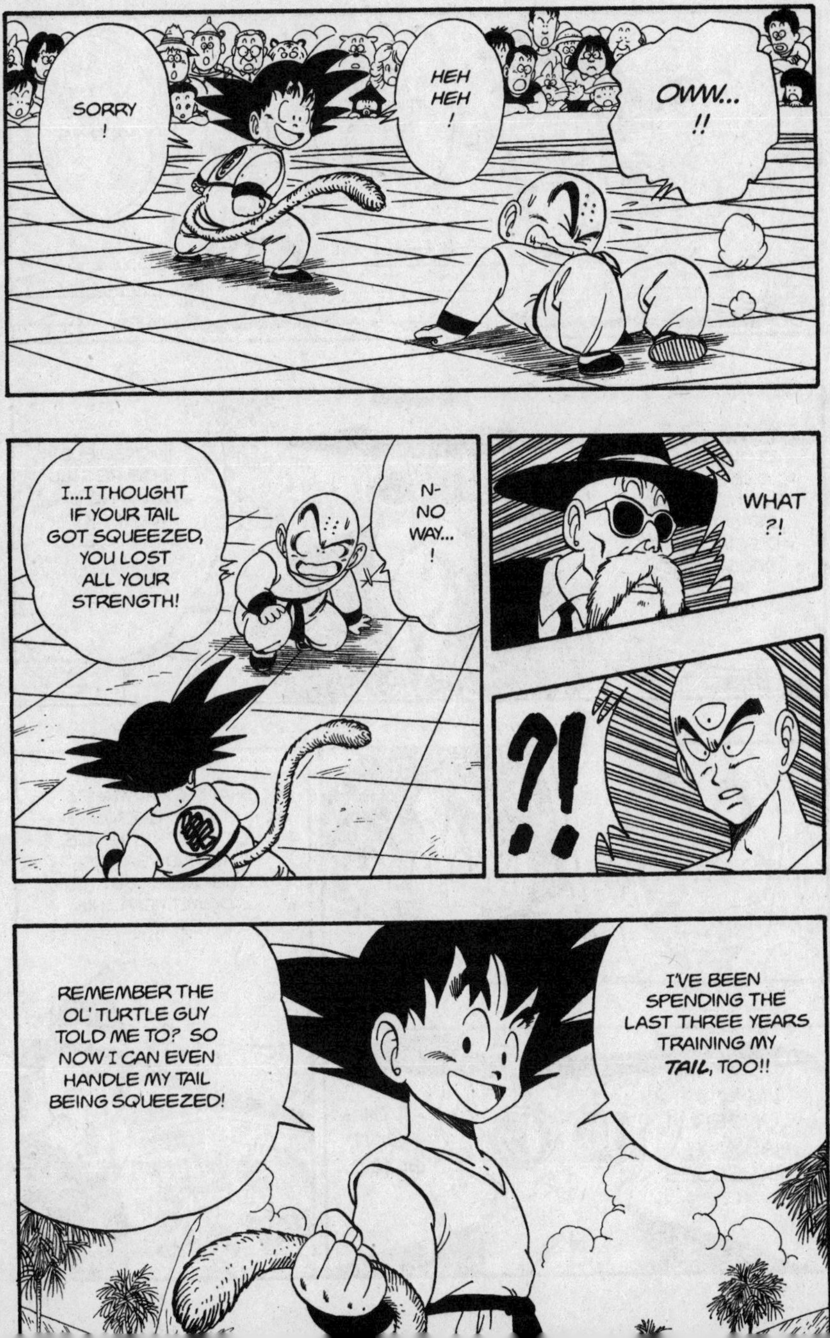
OWW... !!
HEH HEH !
SORRY !
WHAT ?!
?!!
N- NO WAY... !
I...I THOUGHT IF YOUR TAIL GOT SQUEEZED, YOU LOST ALL YOUR STRENGTH!
I'VE BEEN SPENDING THE LAST THREE YEARS TRAINING MY *TAIL*, TOO!!
REMEMBER THE OL' TURTLE GUY TOLD ME TO? SO NOW I CAN EVEN HANDLE MY TAIL BEING SQUEEZED!

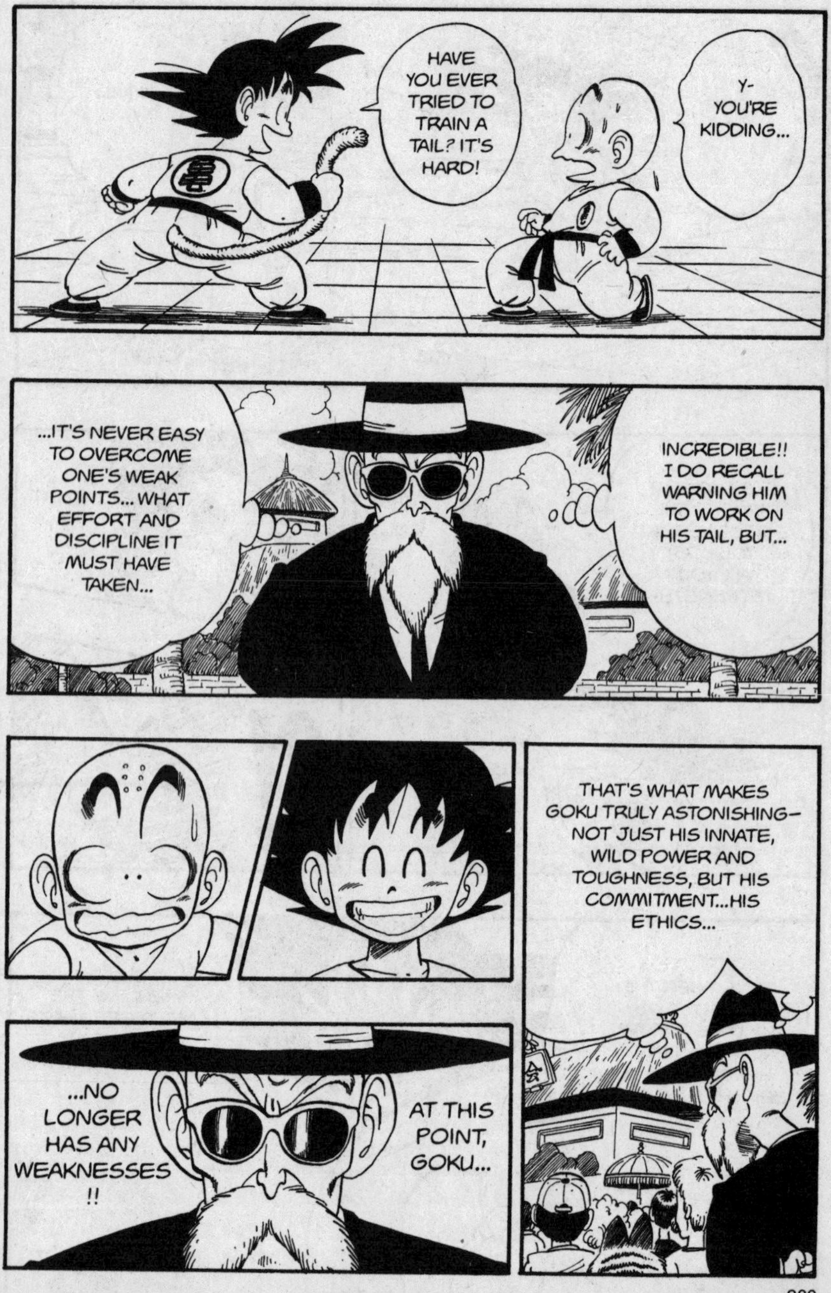
Y- YOU'RE KIDDING...
HAVE YOU EVER TRIED TO TRAIN A TAIL? IT'S HARD!
INCREDIBLE!! I DO RECALL WARNING HIM TO WORK ON HIS TAIL, BUT...
...IT'S NEVER EASY TO OVERCOME ONE'S WEAK POINTS... WHAT EFFORT AND DISCIPLINE IT MUST HAVE TAKEN...
THAT'S WHAT MAKES GOKU TRULY ASTONISHING– NOT JUST HIS INNATE, WILD POWER AND TOUGHNESS, BUT HIS COMMITMENT...HIS ETHICS...
AT THIS POINT, GOKU...
...NO LONGER HAS ANY WEAKNESSES !!

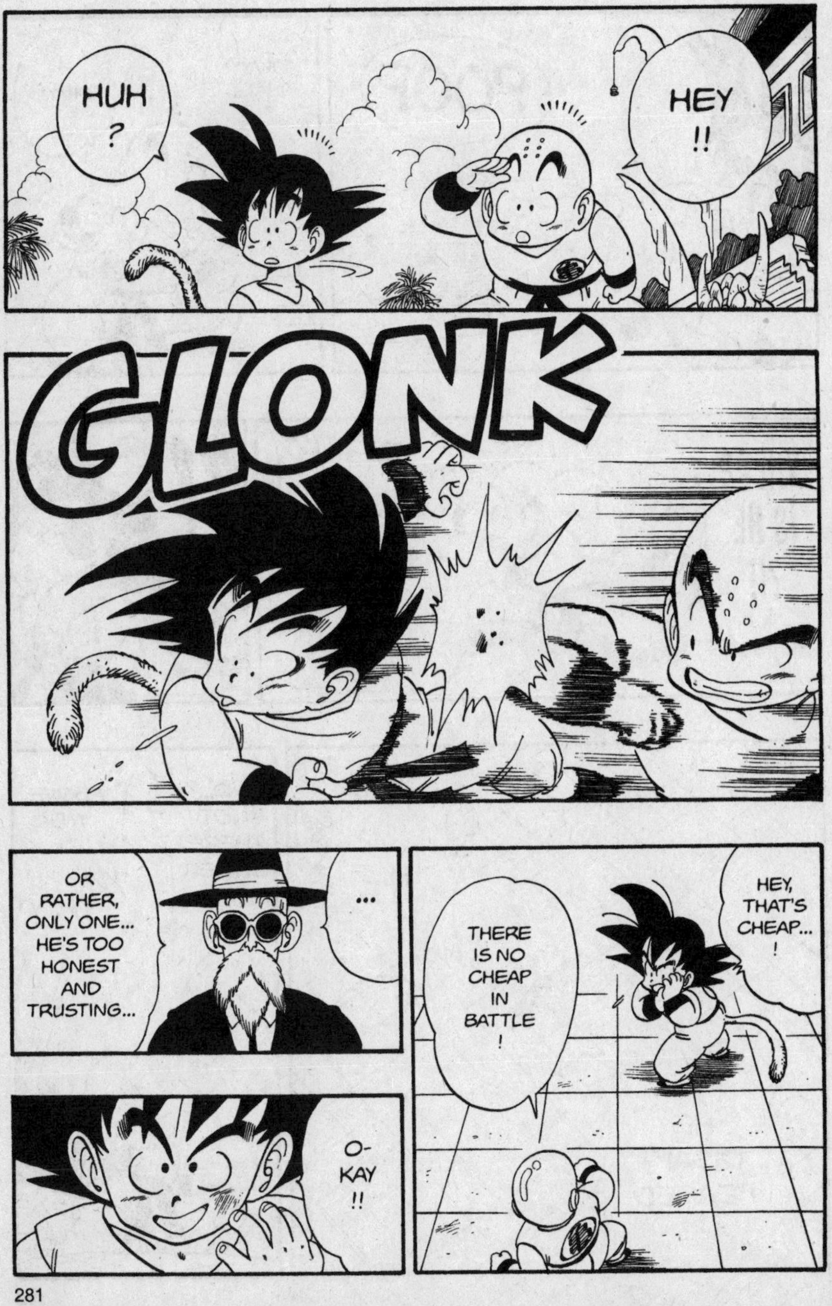
HEY !!
HUH ?
GLONK
HEY, THAT'S CHEAP... !
THERE IS NO CHEAP IN BATTLE !
...
OR RATHER, ONLY ONE... HE'S TOO HONEST AND TRUSTING...
O-KAY !!

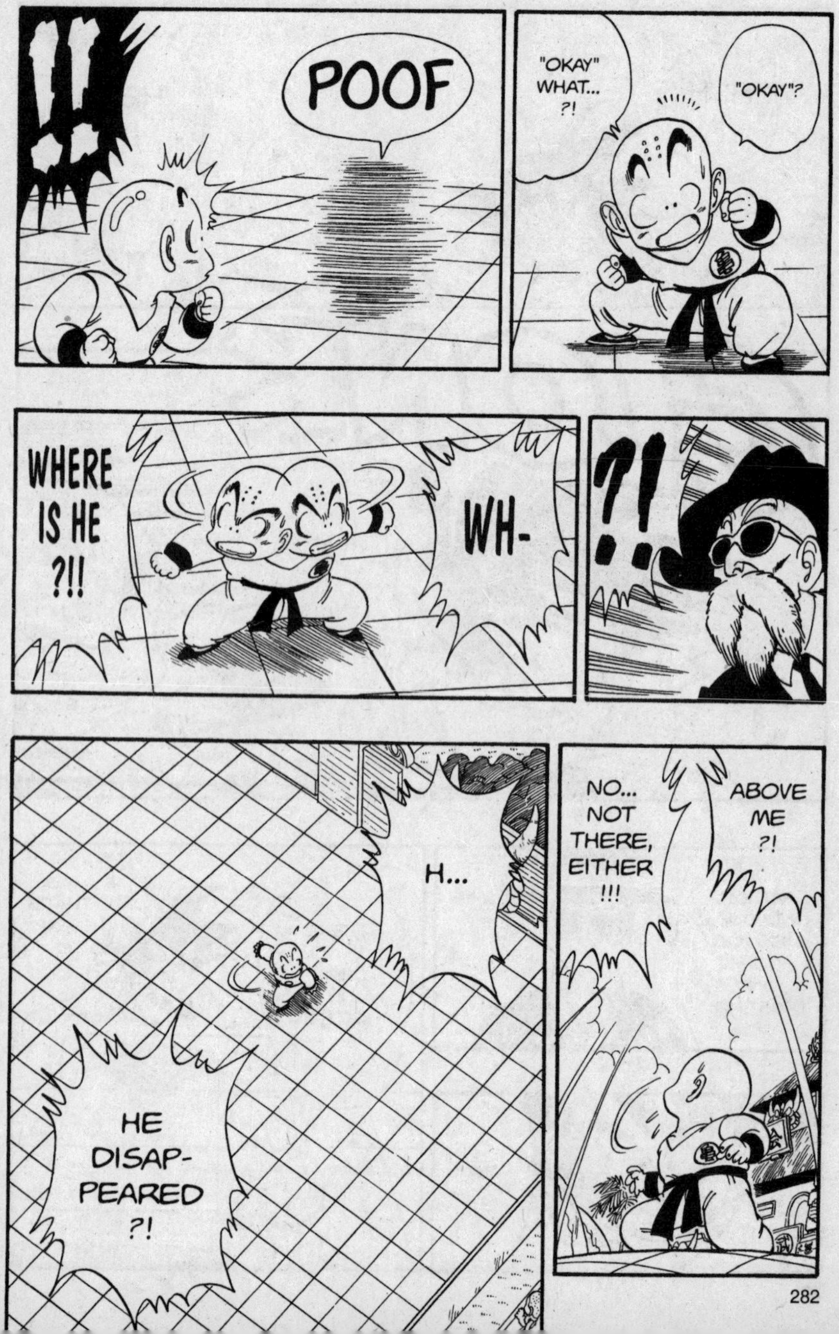
"OKAY"?
"OKAY" WHAT... ?!
POOF
!!
?!!
WH-
WHERE IS HE ?!!
ABOVE ME ?!
NO... NOT THERE, EITHER !!!
H...
HE DISAP-PEARED ?!

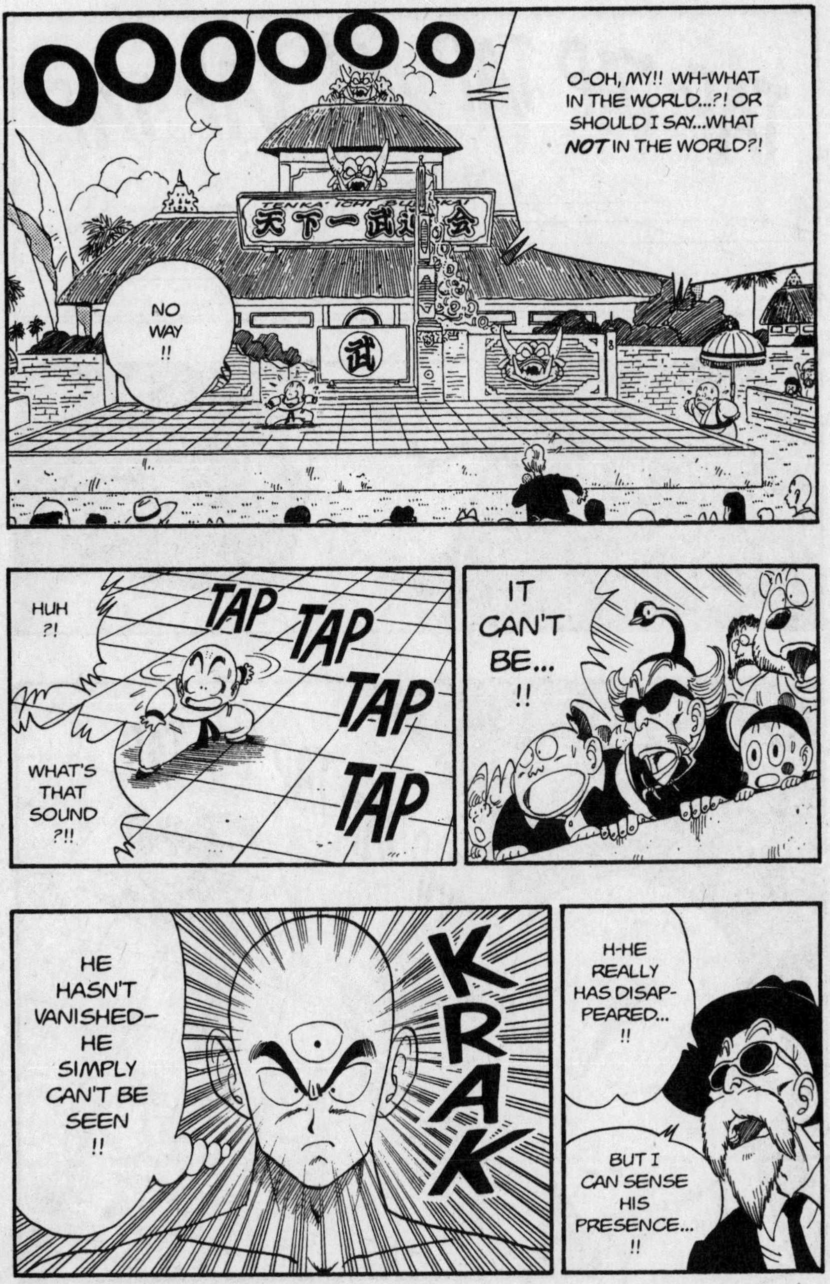
OOOOOO
O-OH, MY!! WH-WHAT IN THE WORLD...?! OR SHOULD I SAY...WHAT *NOT* IN THE WORLD?!
NO WAY !!
IT CAN'T BE... !!
HUH ?!
TAP TAP TAP TAP
WHAT'S THAT SOUND ?!!
H-HE REALLY HAS DISAP-PEARED... !!
BUT I CAN SENSE HIS PRESENCE... !!
KRAK
HE HASN'T VANISHED— HE SIMPLY CAN'T BE SEEN !!

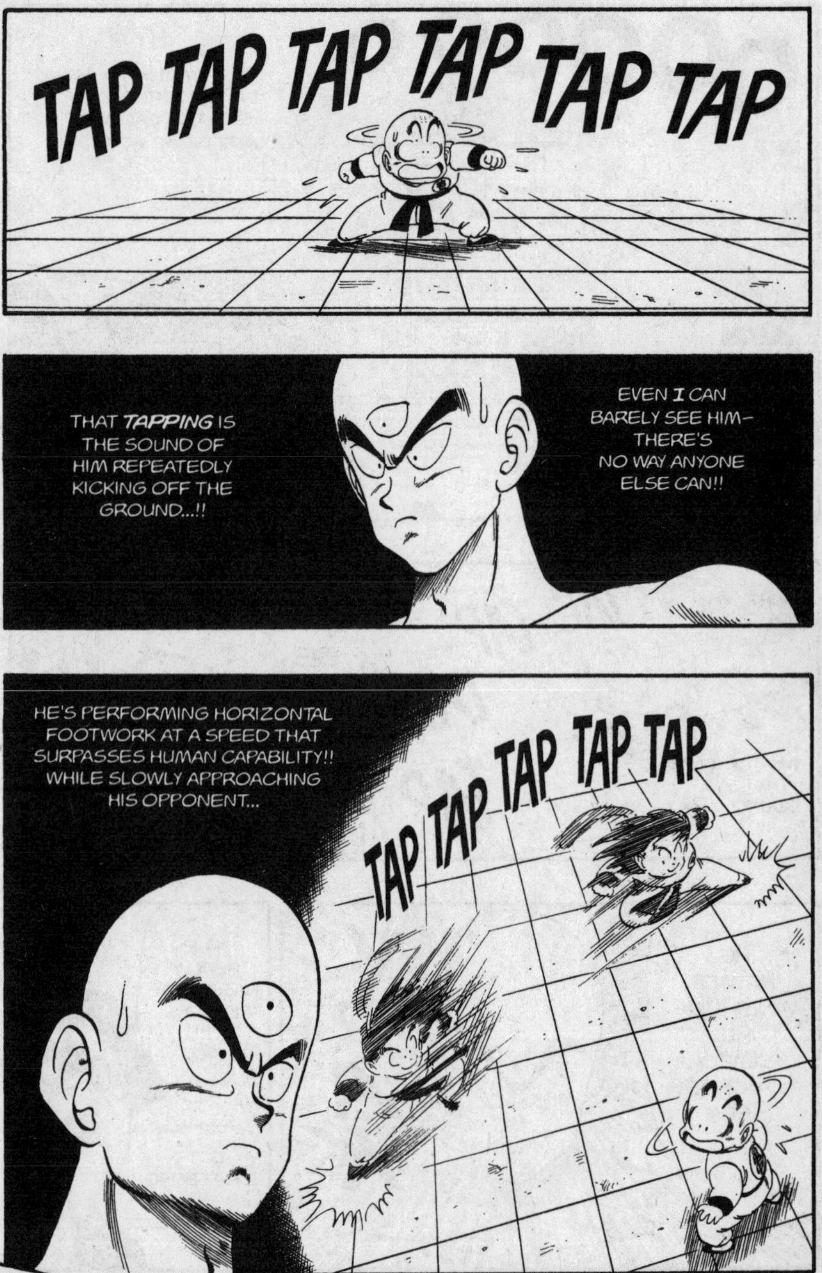
TAP TAP TAP TAP TAP TAP
EVEN I CAN BARELY SEE HIM— THERE'S NO WAY ANYONE ELSE CAN!!
THAT *TAPPING* IS THE SOUND OF HIM REPEATEDLY KICKING OFF THE GROUND...!!
HE'S PERFORMING HORIZONTAL FOOTWORK AT A SPEED THAT SURPASSES HUMAN CAPABILITY!! WHILE SLOWLY APPROACHING HIS OPPONENT...
TAP TAP TAP TAP TAP

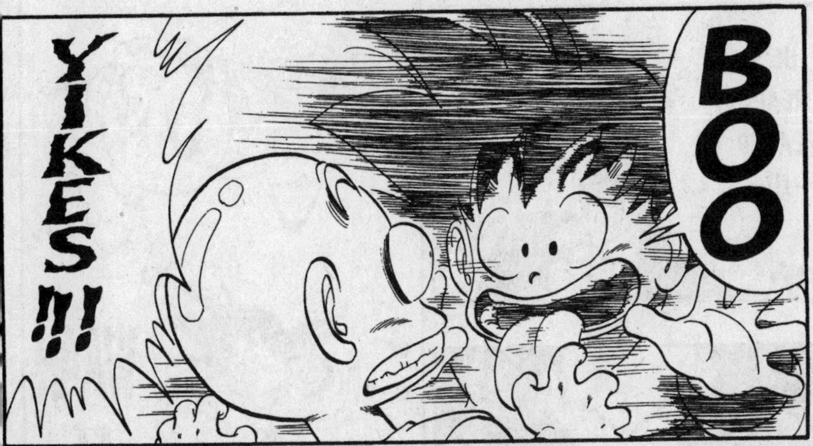
BOO
YIKES!?!

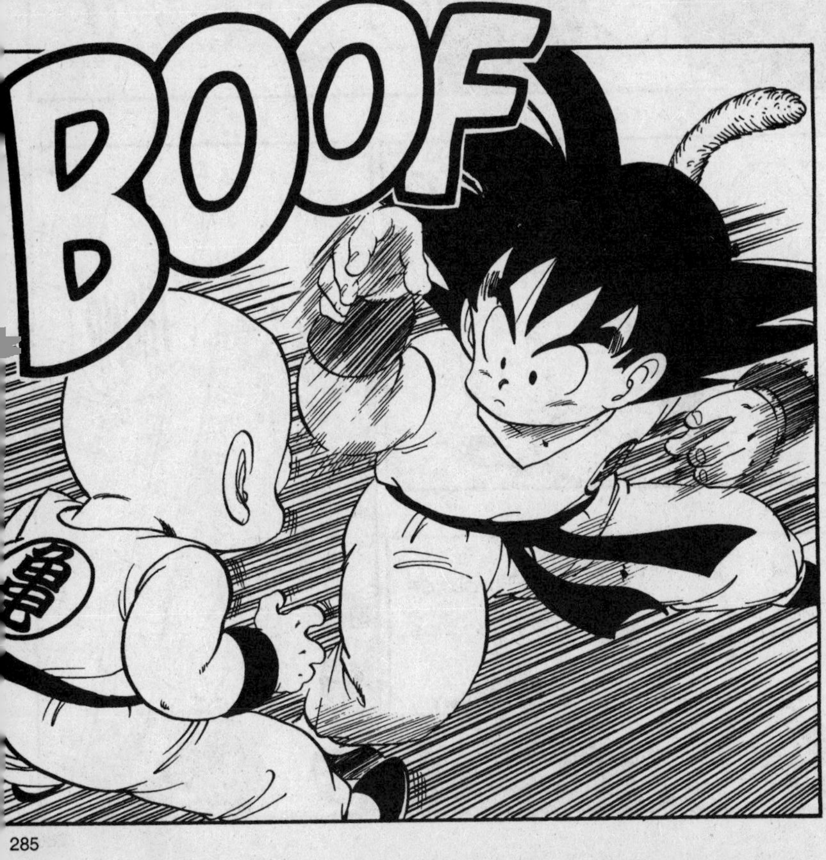
BOOF

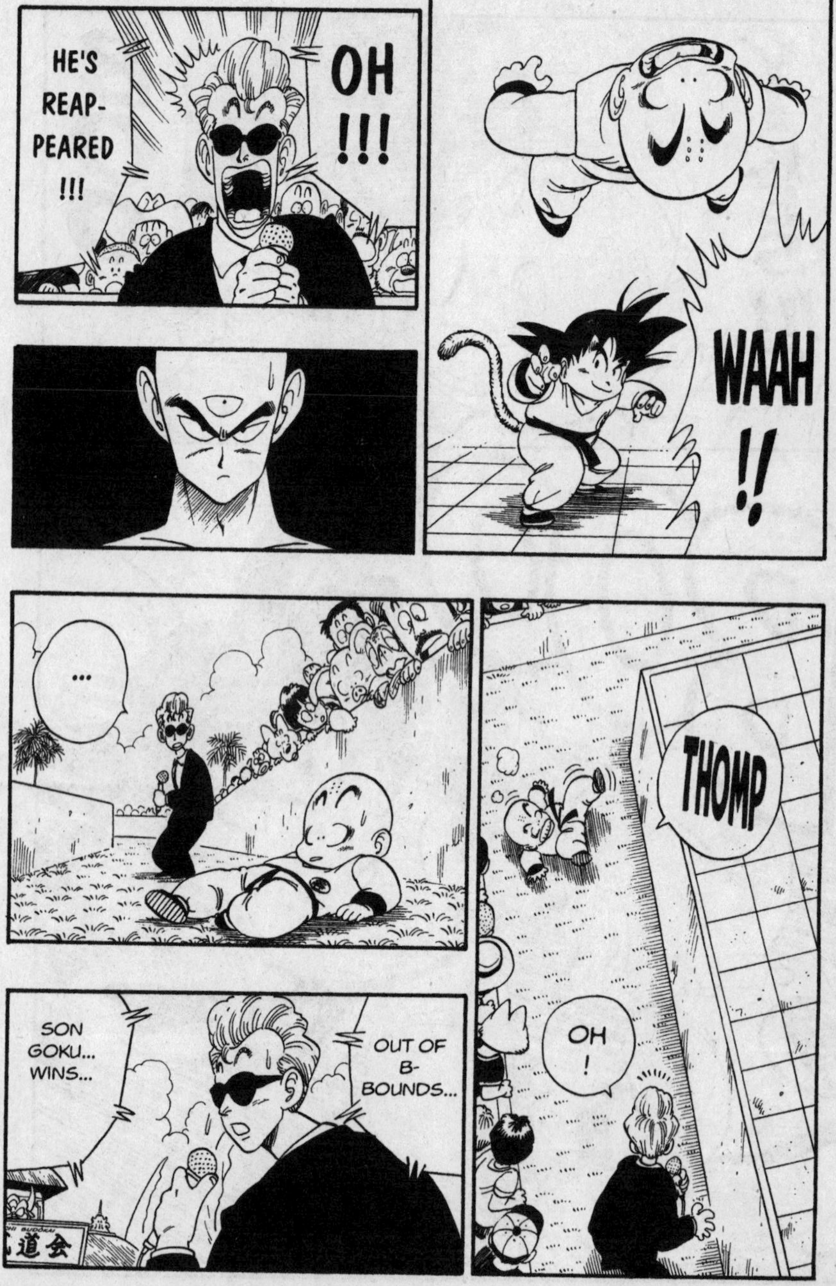
WAAH !!
OH !!!
HE'S REAP-PEARED !!!
THOMP
OH !
...
OUT OF B-BOUNDS...
SON GOKU... WINS...

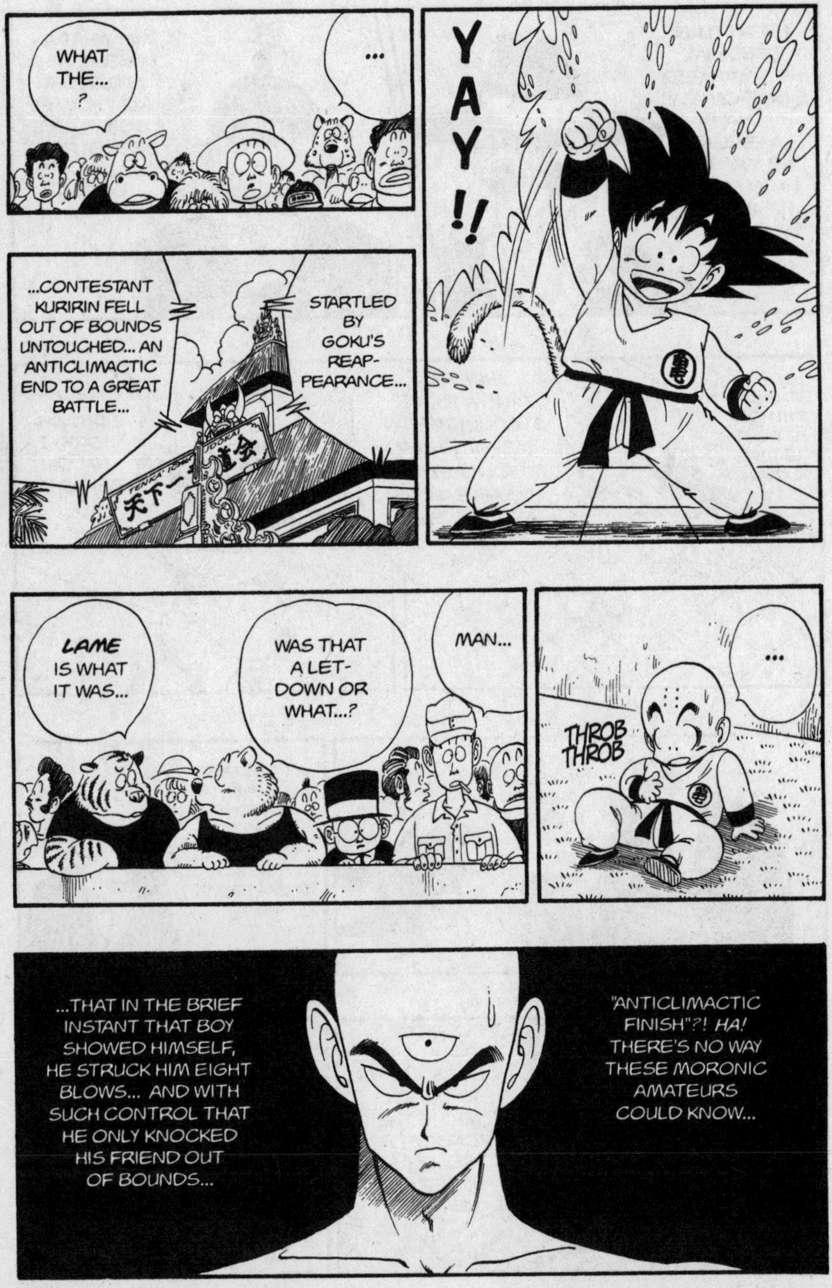
YAY!!
...
WHAT THE...?
STARTLED BY GOKU'S REAP-PEARANCE...
...CONTESTANT KURIRIN FELL OUT OF BOUNDS UNTOUCHED... AN ANTICLIMACTIC END TO A GREAT BATTLE...
...
THROB THROB
MAN...
WAS THAT A LET-DOWN OR WHAT...?
LAME IS WHAT IT WAS...
"ANTICLIMACTIC FINISH"?! *HA!* THERE'S NO WAY THESE MORONIC AMATEURS COULD KNOW...
...THAT IN THE BRIEF INSTANT THAT BOY SHOWED HIMSELF, HE STRUCK HIM EIGHT BLOWS... AND WITH SUCH CONTROL THAT HE ONLY KNOCKED HIS FRIEND OUT OF BOUNDS...

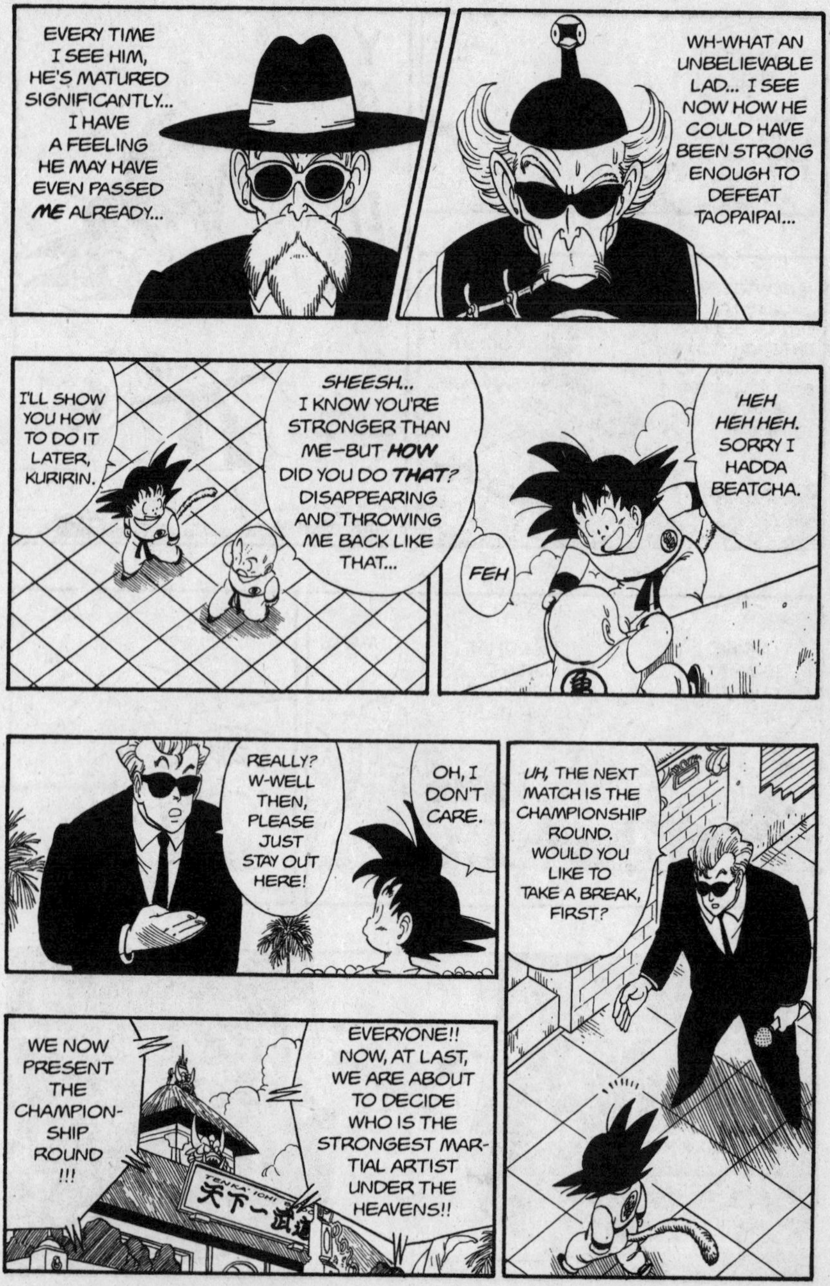
WH-WHAT AN UNBELIEVABLE LAD... I SEE NOW HOW HE COULD HAVE BEEN STRONG ENOUGH TO DEFEAT TAOPAIPAI...
EVERY TIME I SEE HIM, HE'S MATURED SIGNIFICANTLY... I HAVE A FEELING HE MAY HAVE EVEN PASSED *ME* ALREADY...
HEH HEH HEH. SORRY I HADDA BEATCHA.
FEH
SHEESH... I KNOW YOU'RE STRONGER THAN ME—BUT ***HOW*** DID YOU DO ***THAT***? DISAPPEARING AND THROWING ME BACK LIKE THAT...
I'LL SHOW YOU HOW TO DO IT LATER, KURIRIN.
UH, THE NEXT MATCH IS THE CHAMPIONSHIP ROUND. WOULD YOU LIKE TO TAKE A BREAK, FIRST?
OH, I DON'T CARE.
REALLY? W-WELL THEN, PLEASE JUST STAY OUT HERE!
EVERYONE!! NOW, AT LAST, WE ARE ABOUT TO DECIDE WHO IS THE STRONGEST MARTIAL ARTIST UNDER THE HEAVENS!!
WE NOW PRESENT THE CHAMPIONSHIP ROUND !!!

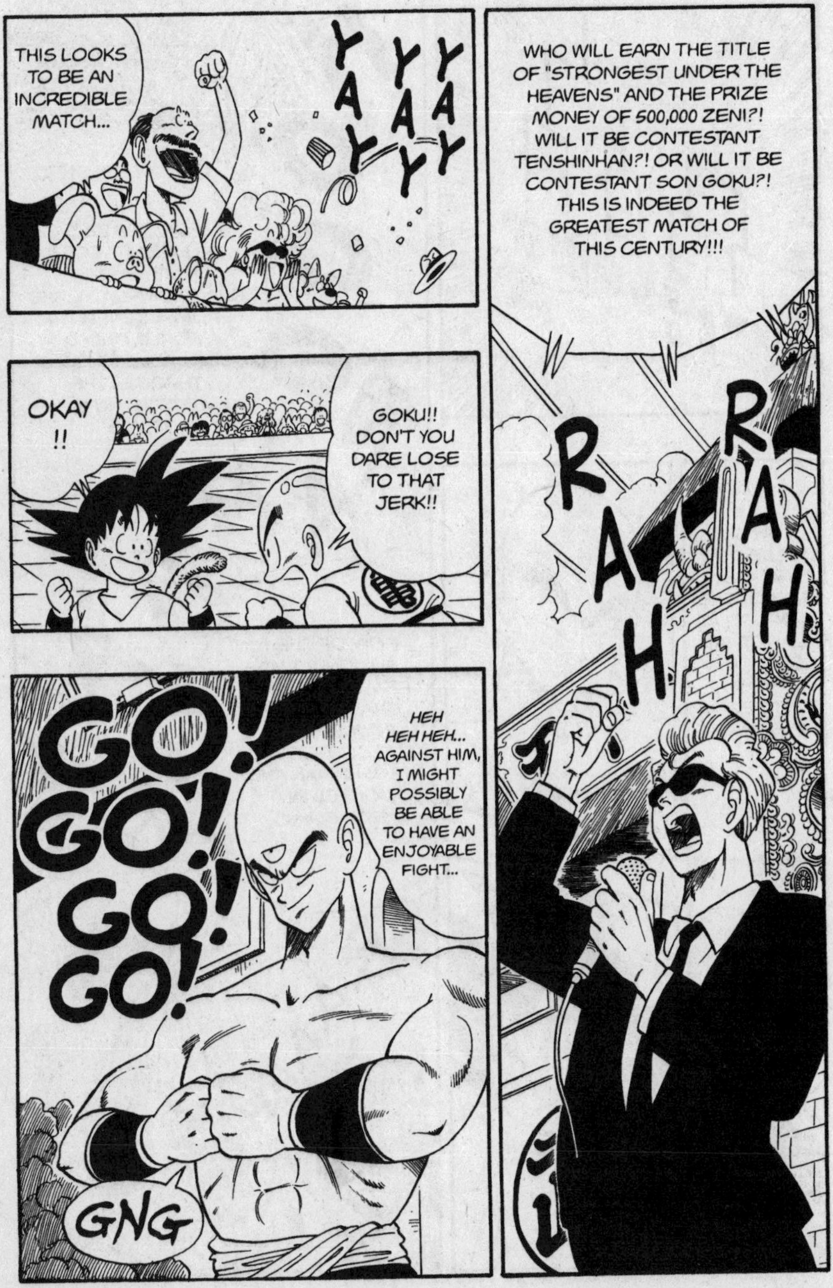
WHO WILL EARN THE TITLE OF "STRONGEST UNDER THE HEAVENS" AND THE PRIZE MONEY OF 500,000 ZENI?! WILL IT BE CONTESTANT TENSHINHAN?! OR WILL IT BE CONTESTANT SON GOKU?! THIS IS INDEED THE GREATEST MATCH OF THIS CENTURY!!!
RAH
RAH
YAY
YAY
YAY
THIS LOOKS TO BE AN INCREDIBLE MATCH...
GOKU!! DON'T YOU DARE LOSE TO THAT JERK!!
OKAY !!
HEH HEH HEH... AGAINST HIM, I MIGHT POSSIBLY BE ABLE TO HAVE AN ENJOYABLE FIGHT...
GO! GO! GO! GO!
GNG

Tale 128
Goku vs. Tenshinhan

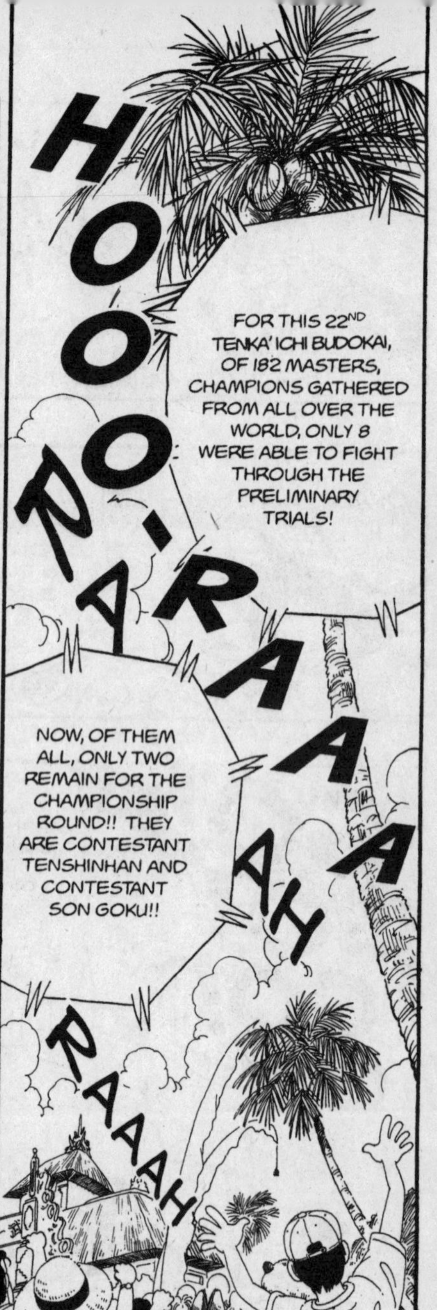
HOOOOOORAAAAAAA
FOR THIS 22ND TENKA'ICHI BUDOKAI, OF 182 MASTERS, CHAMPIONS GATHERED FROM ALL OVER THE WORLD, ONLY 8 WERE ABLE TO FIGHT THROUGH THE PRELIMINARY TRIALS!
NOW, OF THEM ALL, ONLY TWO REMAIN FOR THE CHAMPIONSHIP ROUND!! THEY ARE CONTESTANT TENSHINHAN AND CONTESTANT SON GOKU!!
RAAH
RAAAAH
PENNZOIL

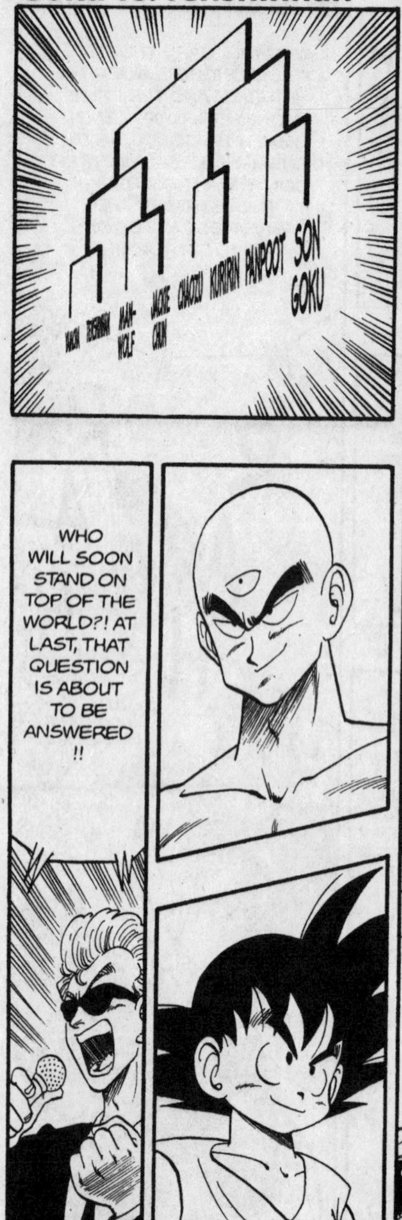
YAMCHA
TENSHINHAN
MAN-WOLF
JACKIE CHUN
CHAOZU
KURIRIN
PANPOOT
SON GOKU
WHO WILL SOON STAND ON TOP OF THE WORLD?! AT LAST, THAT QUESTION IS ABOUT TO BE ANSWERED !!

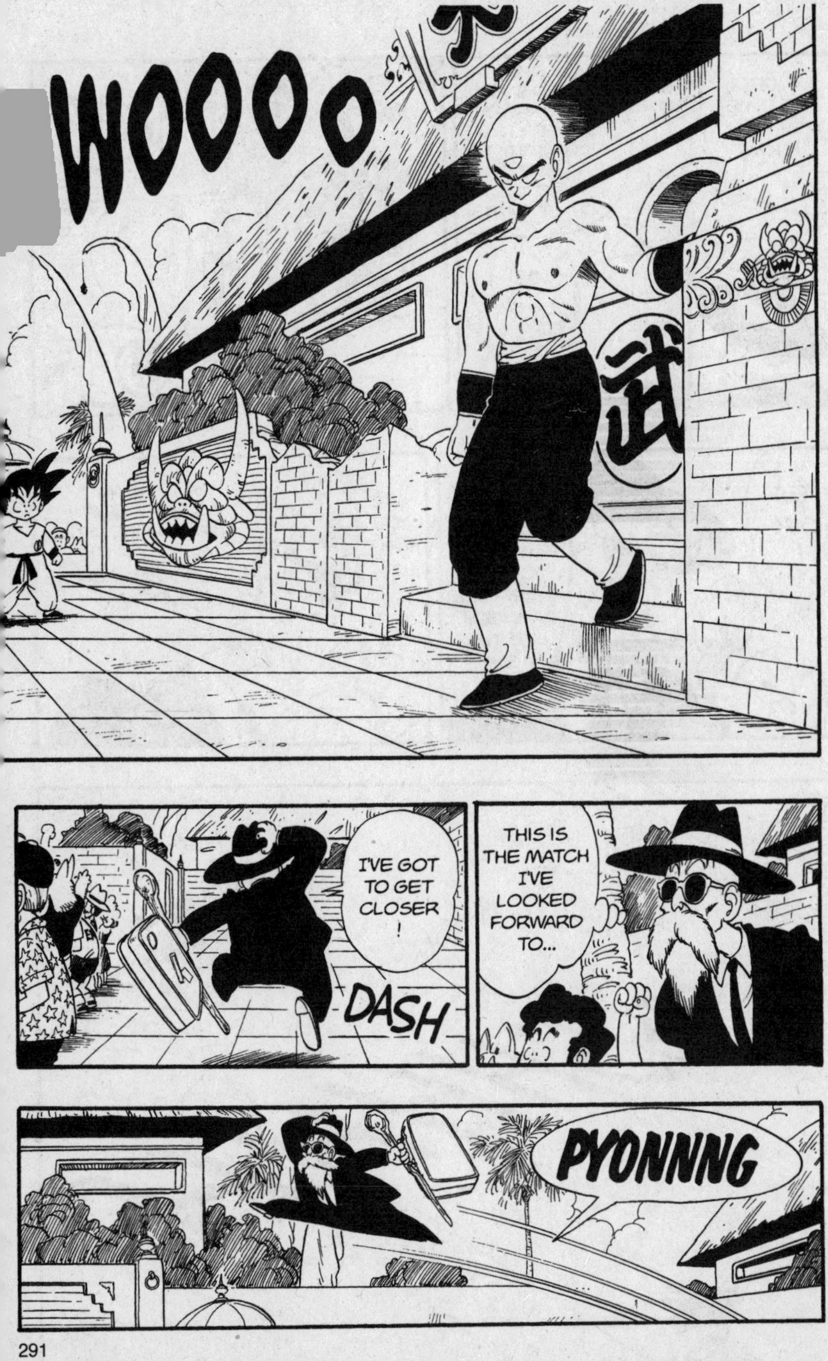
WOOOO
THIS IS THE MATCH I'VE LOOKED FORWARD TO...
I'VE GOT TO GET CLOSER !
DASH
PYONNNG

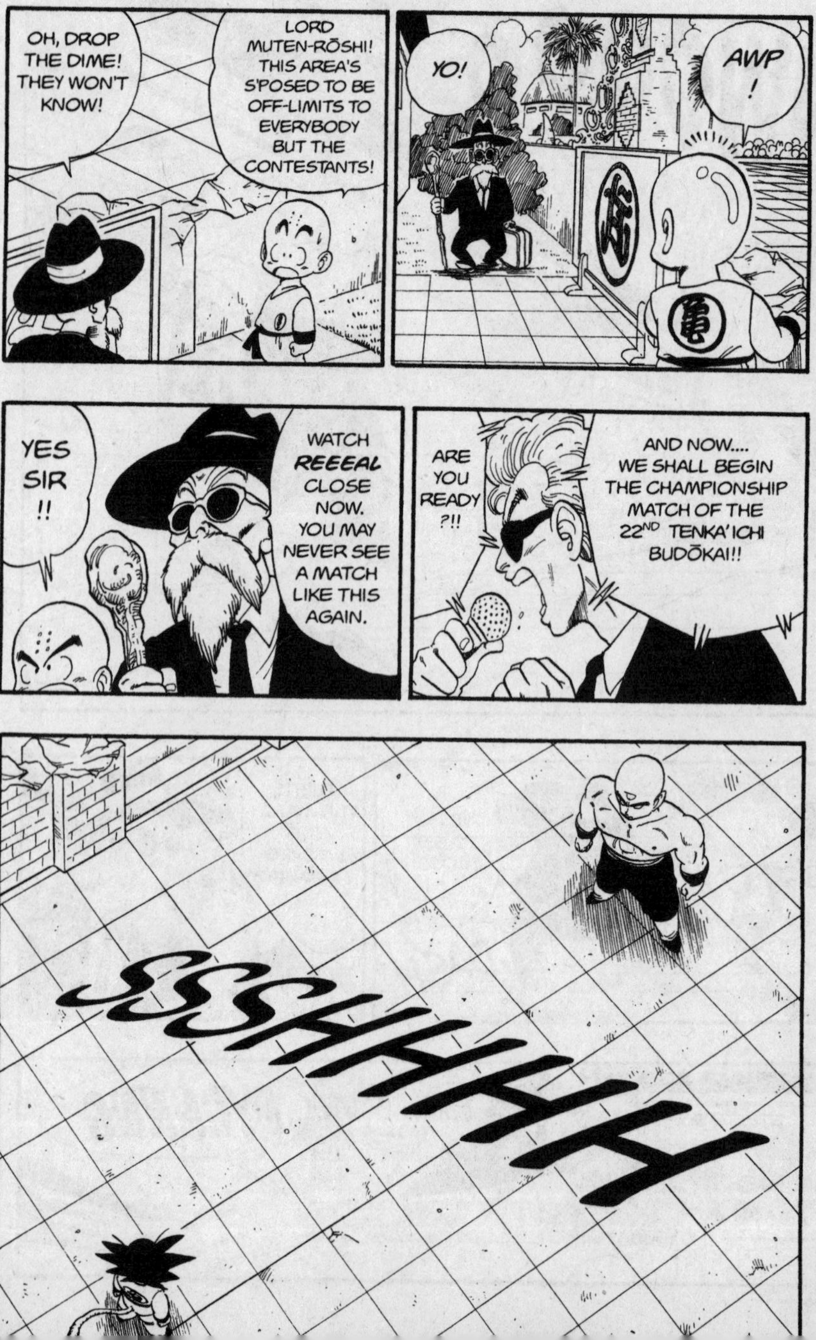
AWP!
YO!
LORD MUTEN-RŌSHI! THIS AREA'S S'POSED TO BE OFF-LIMITS TO EVERYBODY BUT THE CONTESTANTS!
OH, DROP THE DIME! THEY WON'T KNOW!
AND NOW.... WE SHALL BEGIN THE CHAMPIONSHIP MATCH OF THE 22ND TENKA'ICHI BUDŌKAI!!
ARE YOU READY?!!
WATCH REEEAL CLOSE NOW. YOU MAY NEVER SEE A MATCH LIKE THIS AGAIN.
YES SIR!!
SSHHHH

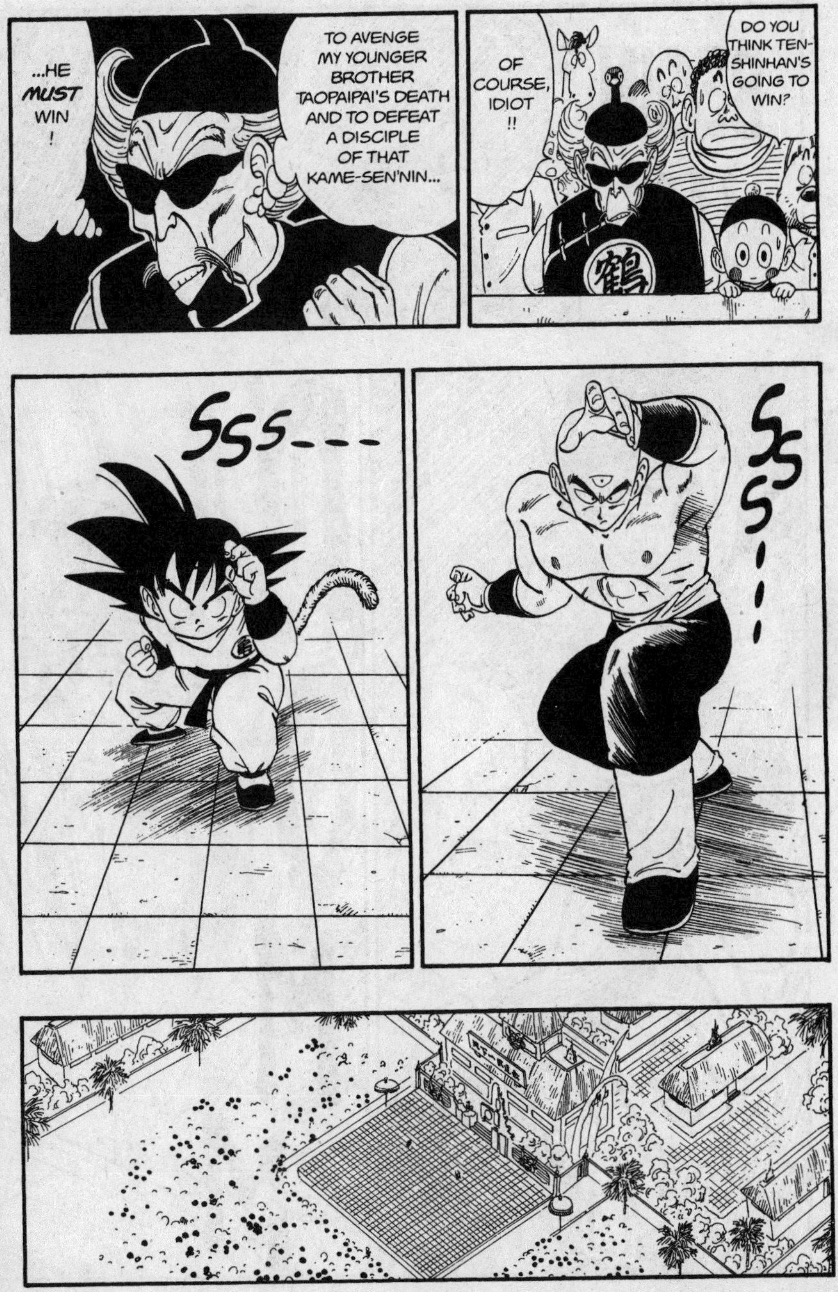

DO YOU THINK TEN-SHINHAN'S GOING TO WIN?
OF COURSE, IDIOT !!
TO AVENGE MY YOUNGER BROTHER TAOPAIPAI'S DEATH AND TO DEFEAT A DISCIPLE OF THAT KAME-SEN'NIN...
...HE *MUST* WIN !
SSS---
SSS---

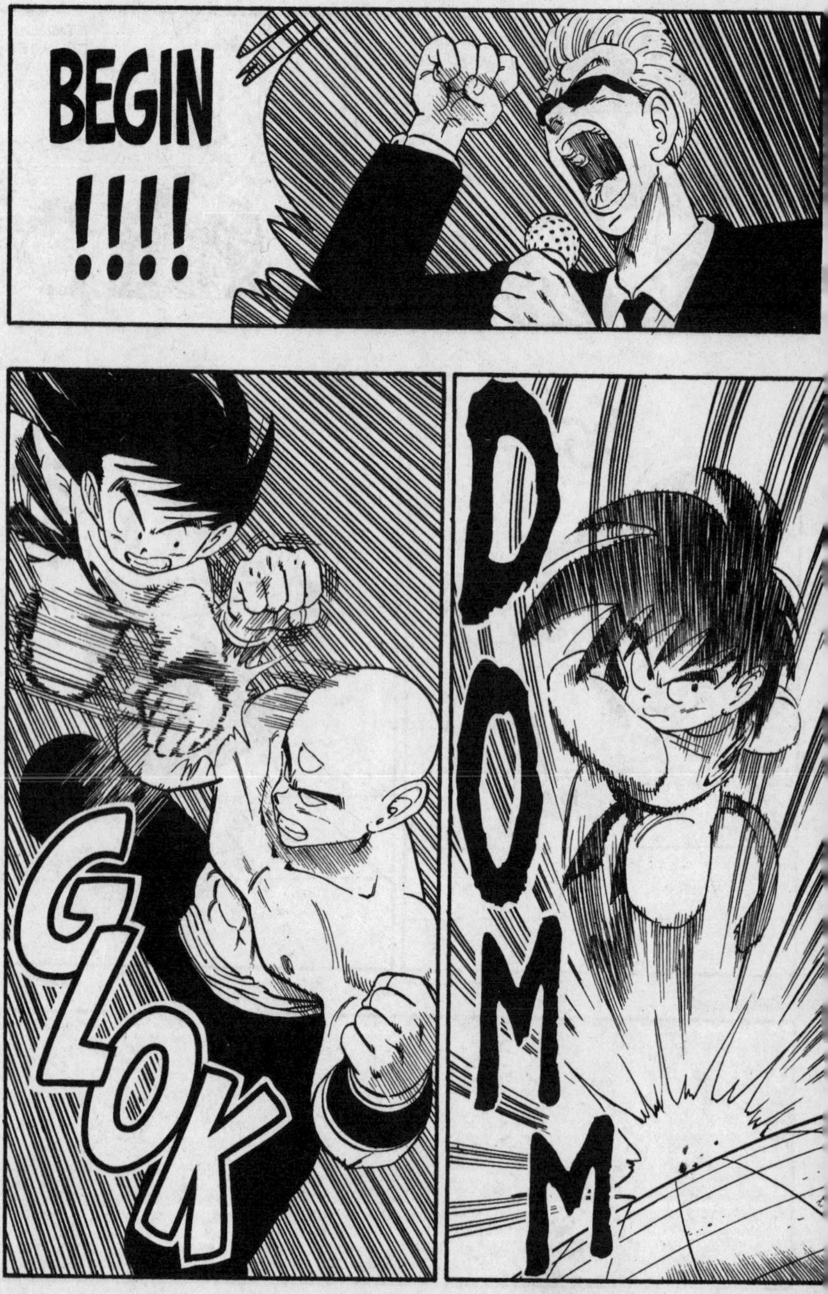
BEGIN!!!!
DOMMM
GLOK

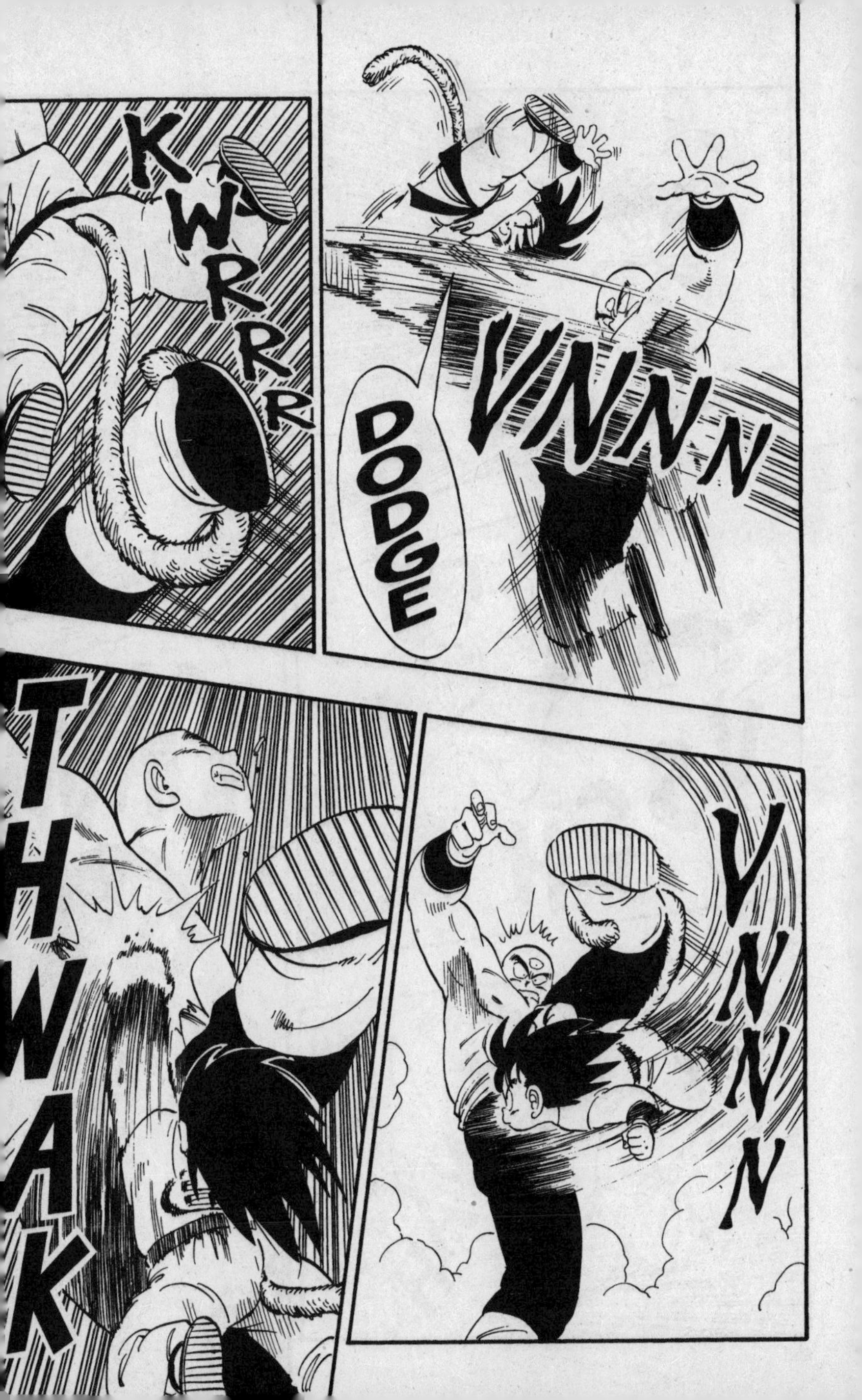
VNNNN
DODGE
KWRRRR
VNNNN
THWAK

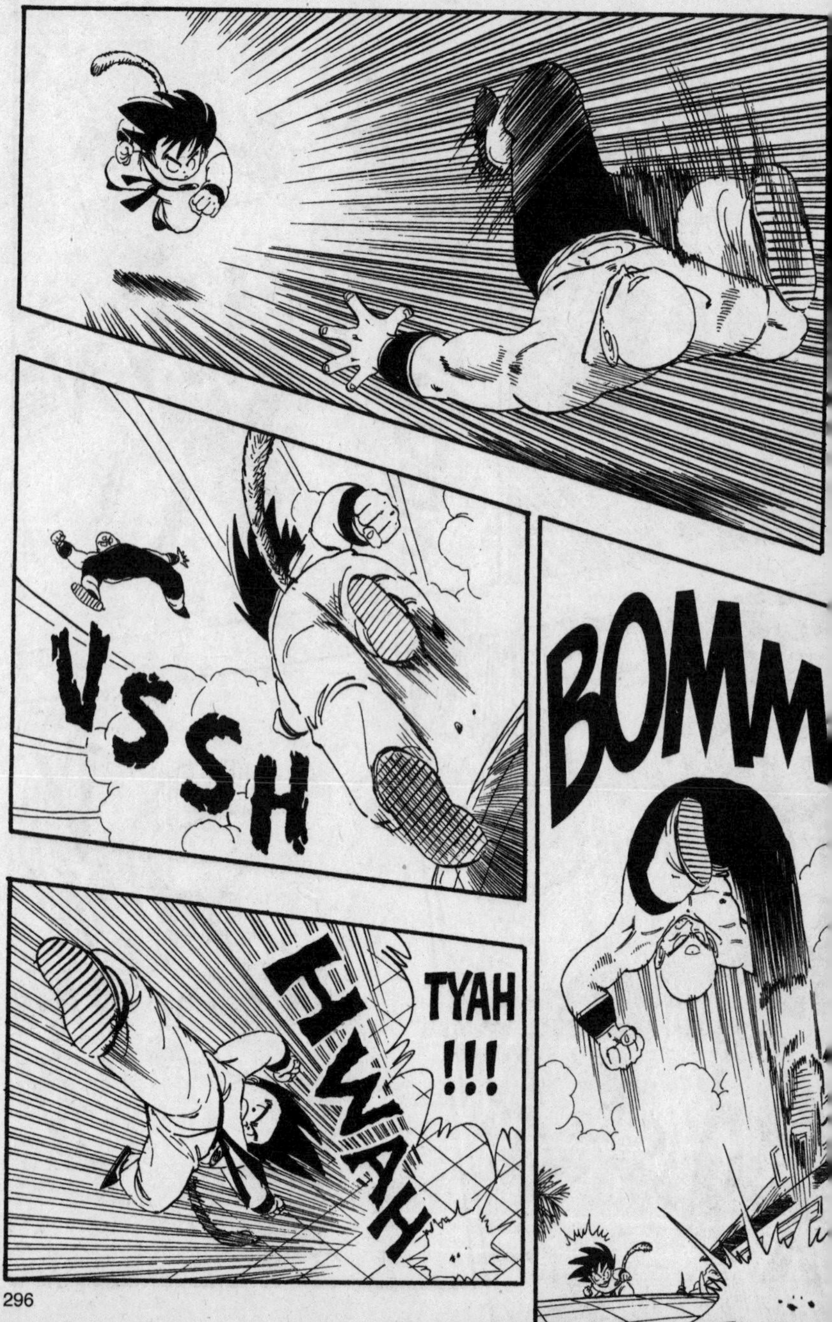
BOMM
VSSH
TYAH
!!!
HWAH

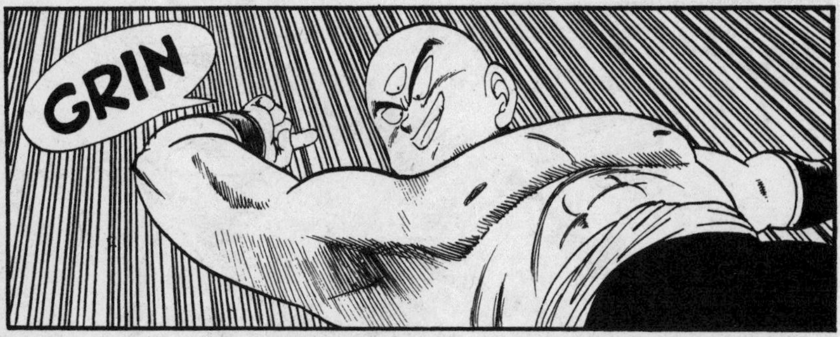
GRIN

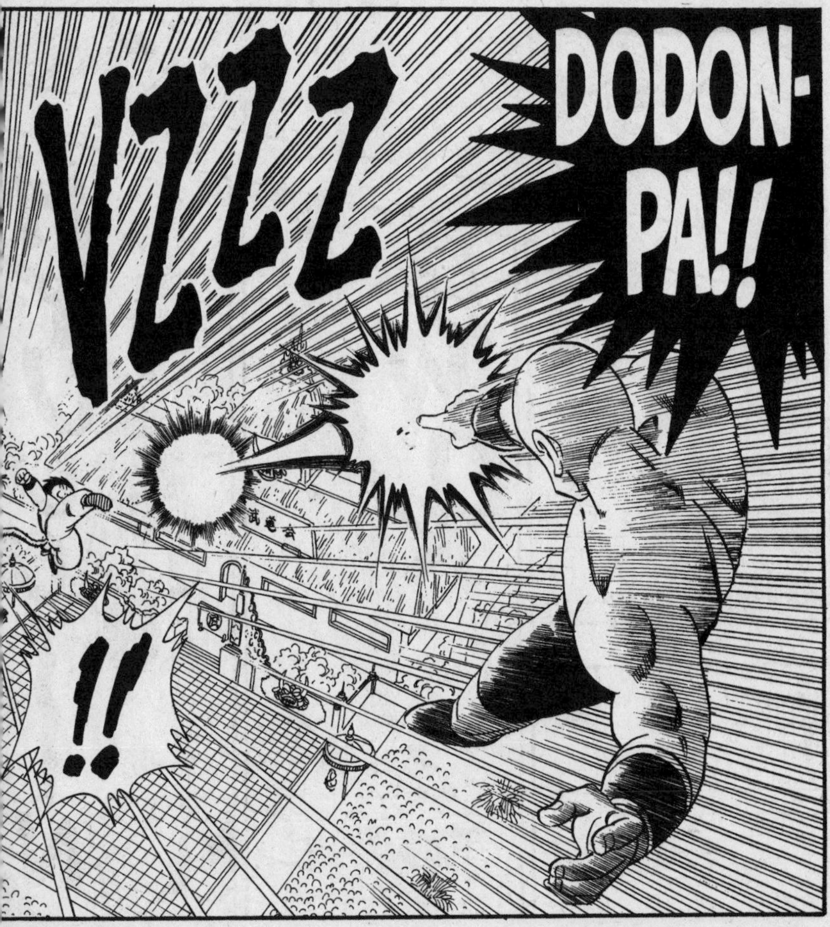
DODON-PA!!
VZZZ
!!

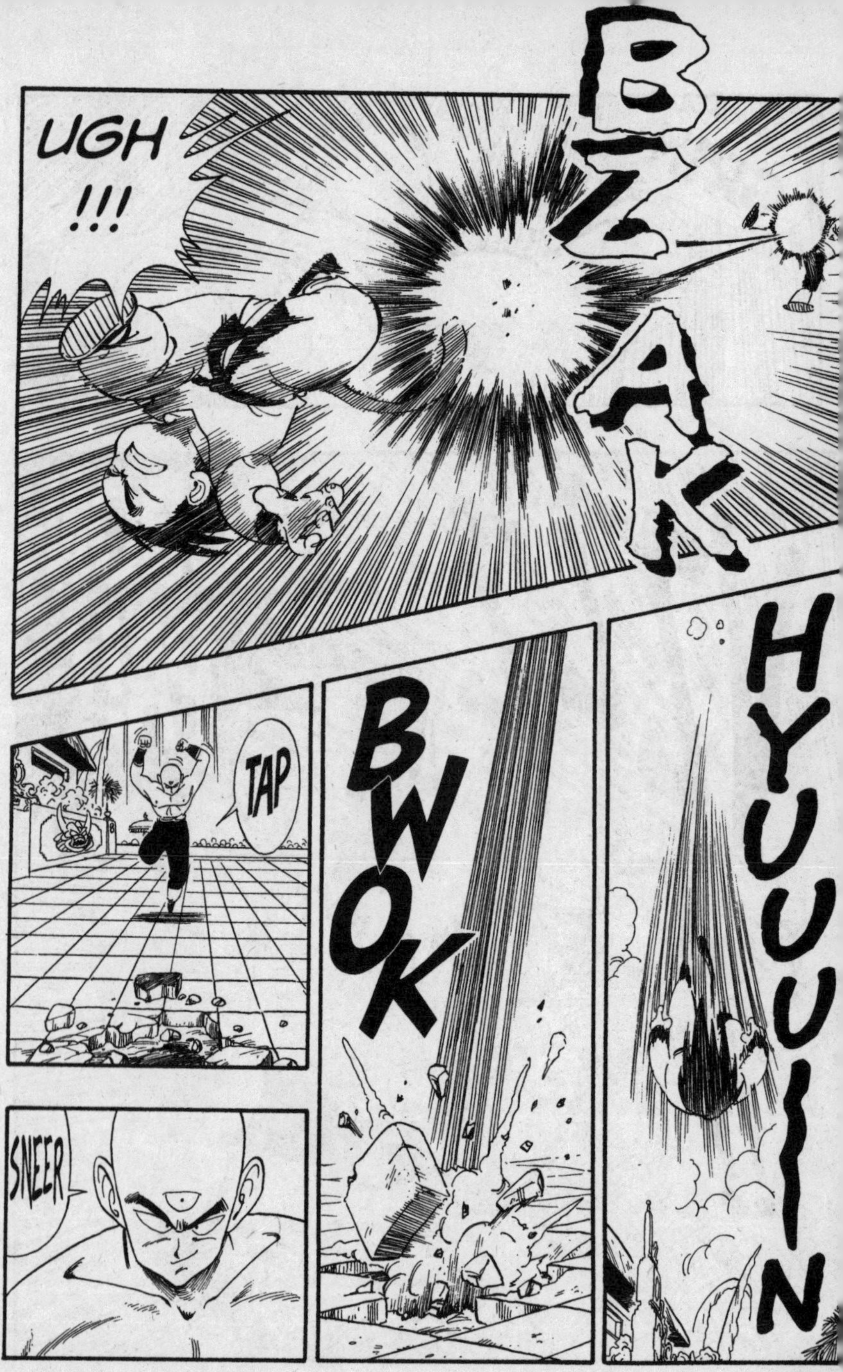
BZAK
UGH !!!
HYUUUIIN
BWOK
TAP
SNEER

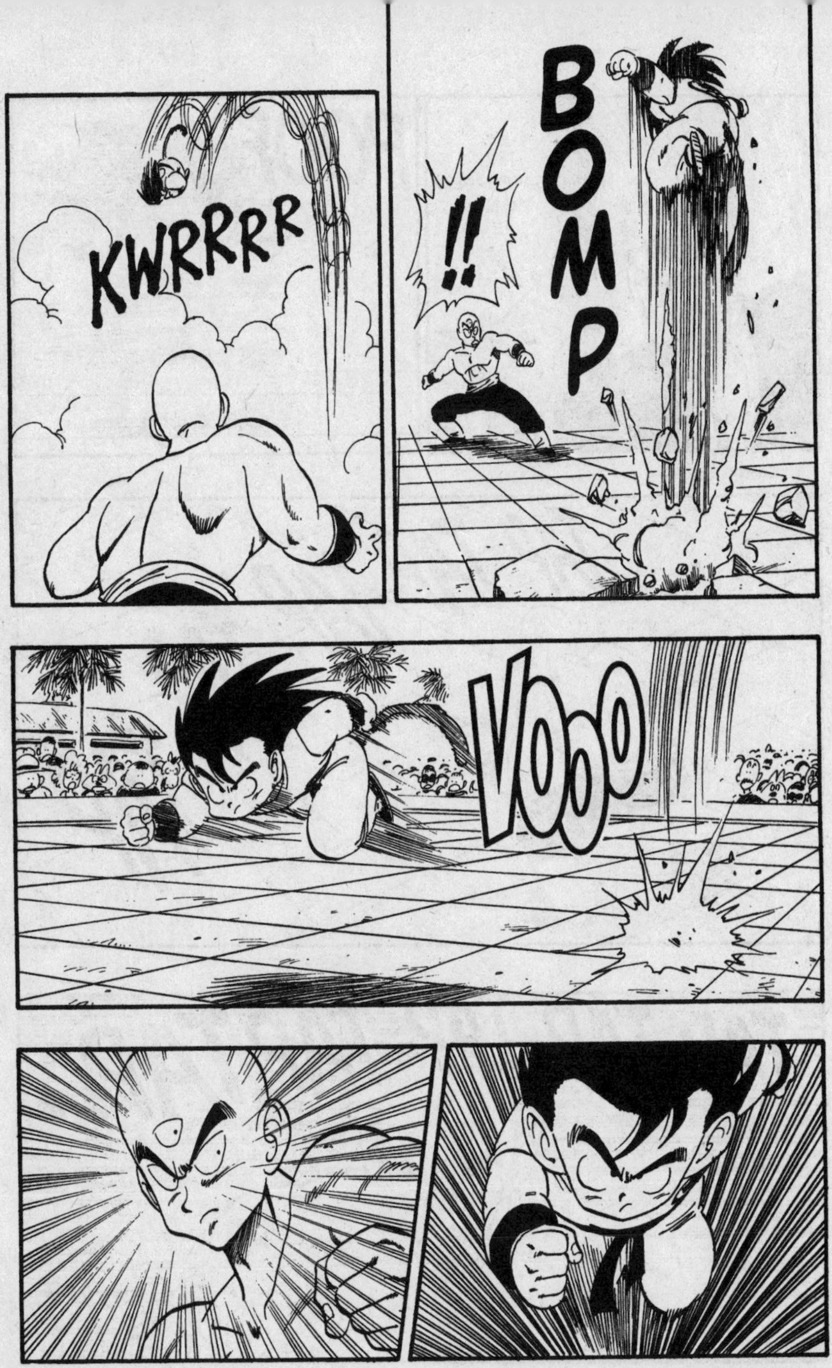

BOMP
!!
KWRRRR
VOOO

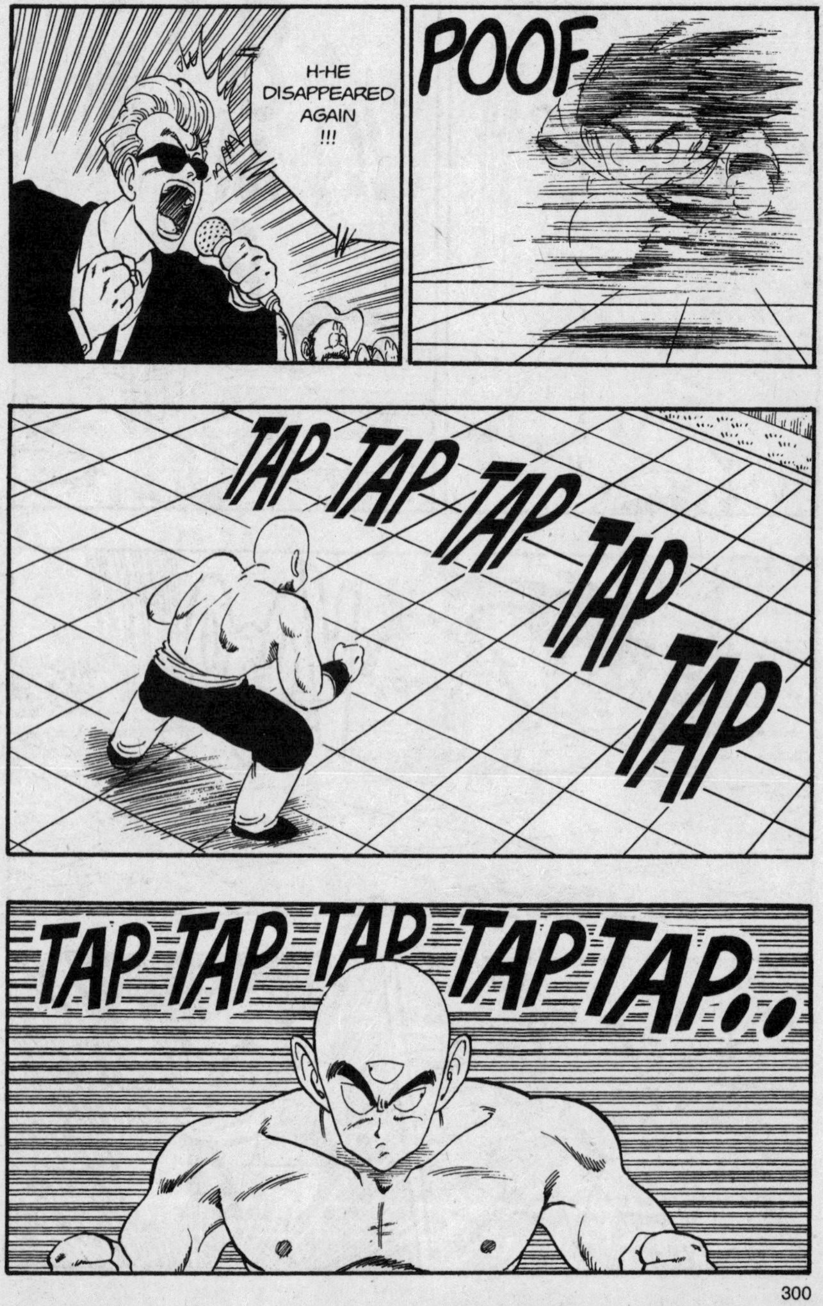
POOF
H-HE DISAPPEARED AGAIN !!!
TAP TAP TAP TAP TAP
TAP TAP TAP TAP TAP..

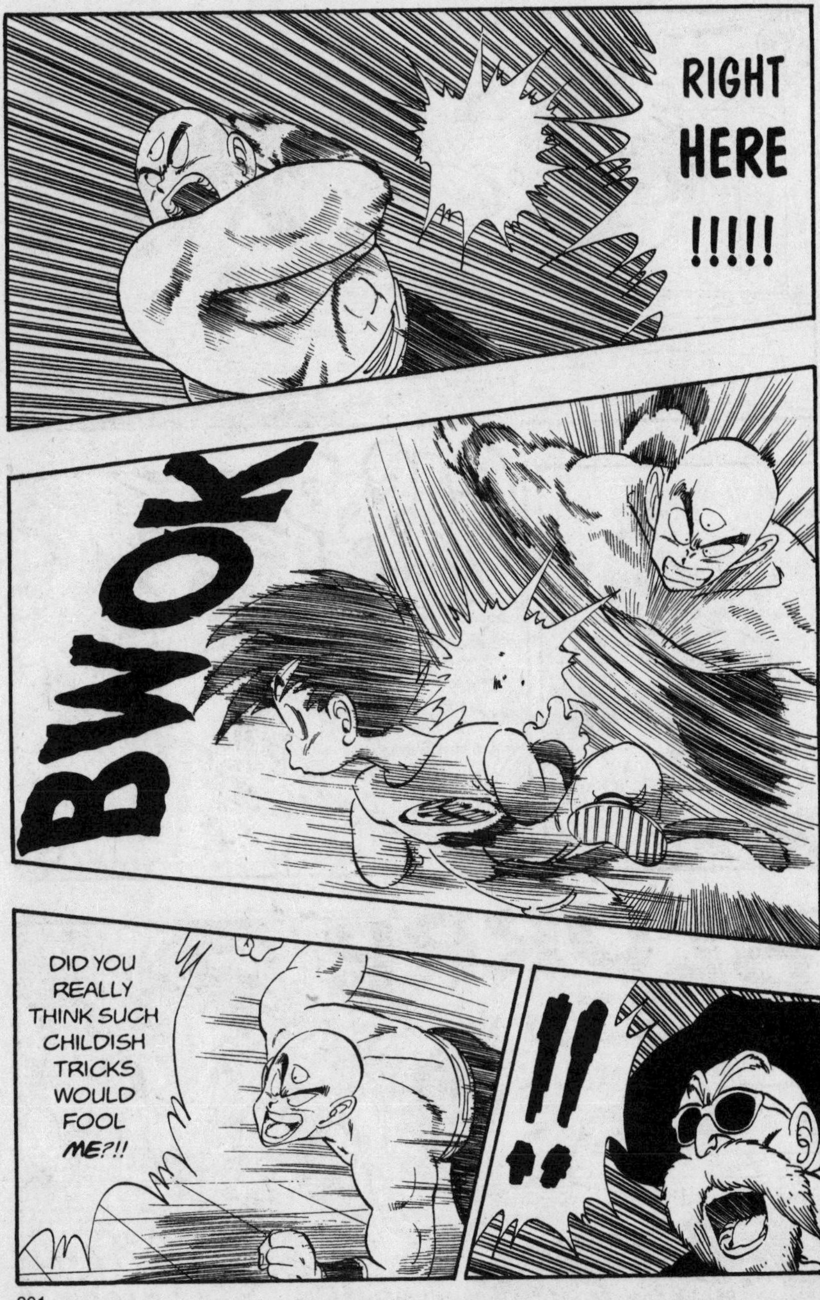
RIGHT HERE !!!!!
BWOK
!!
DID YOU REALLY THINK SUCH CHILDISH TRICKS WOULD FOOL *ME*?!!

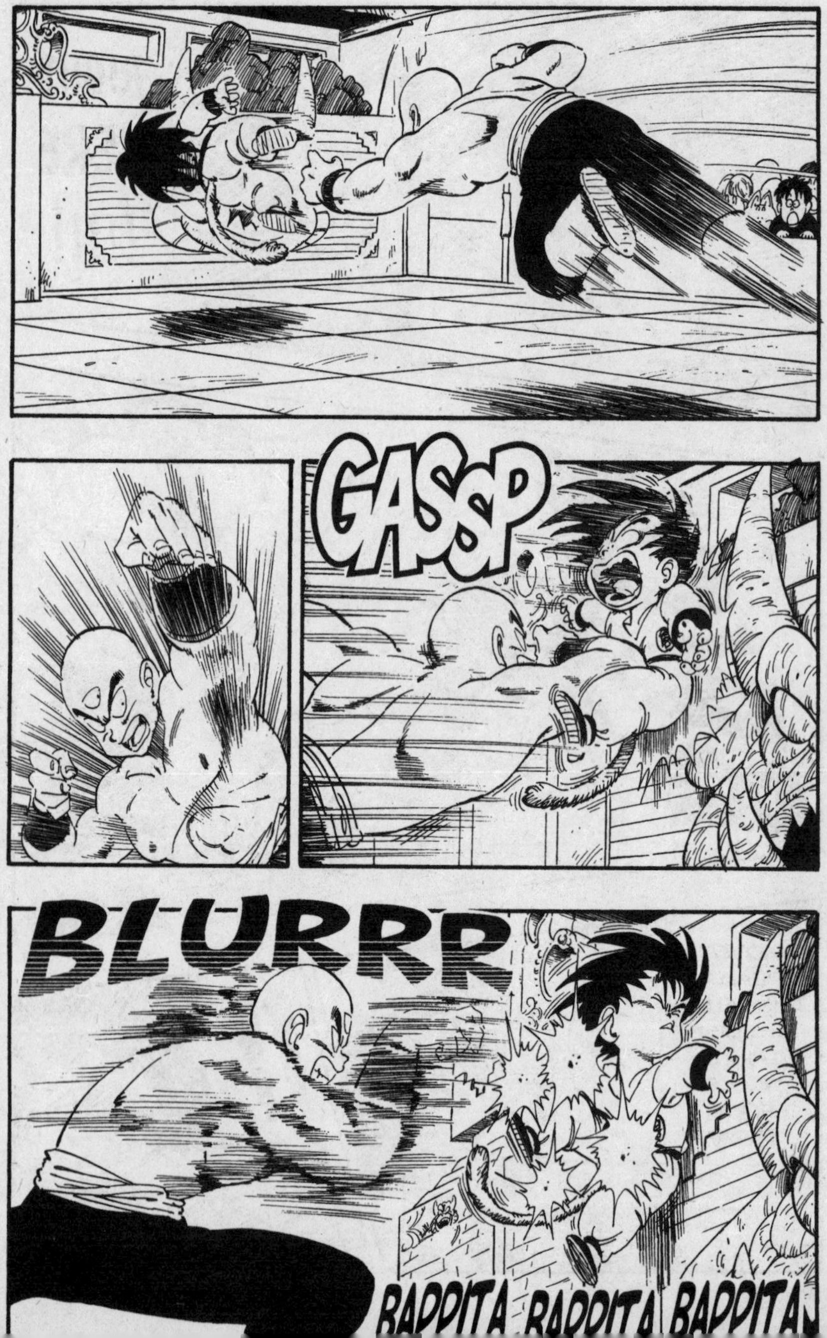
GASSP
BLURRR
BADDITA BADDITA BADDITA

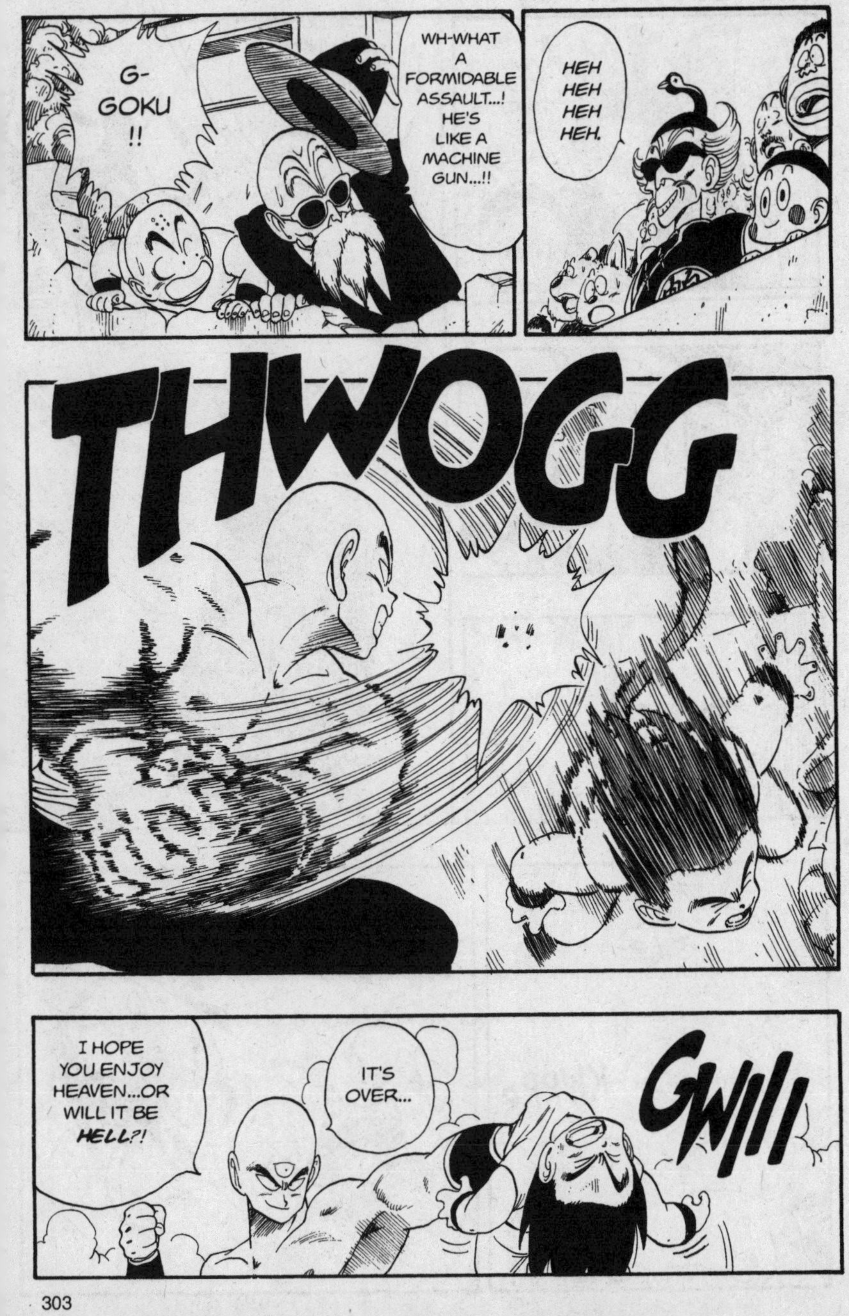
HEH HEH HEH HEH.
WH-WHAT A FORMIDABLE ASSAULT...! HE'S LIKE A MACHINE GUN...!!
G-GOKU !!
THWOGG
GWIII
IT'S OVER...
I HOPE YOU ENJOY HEAVEN...OR WILL IT BE **HELL**?!

Tale 129
The Volleyball Play

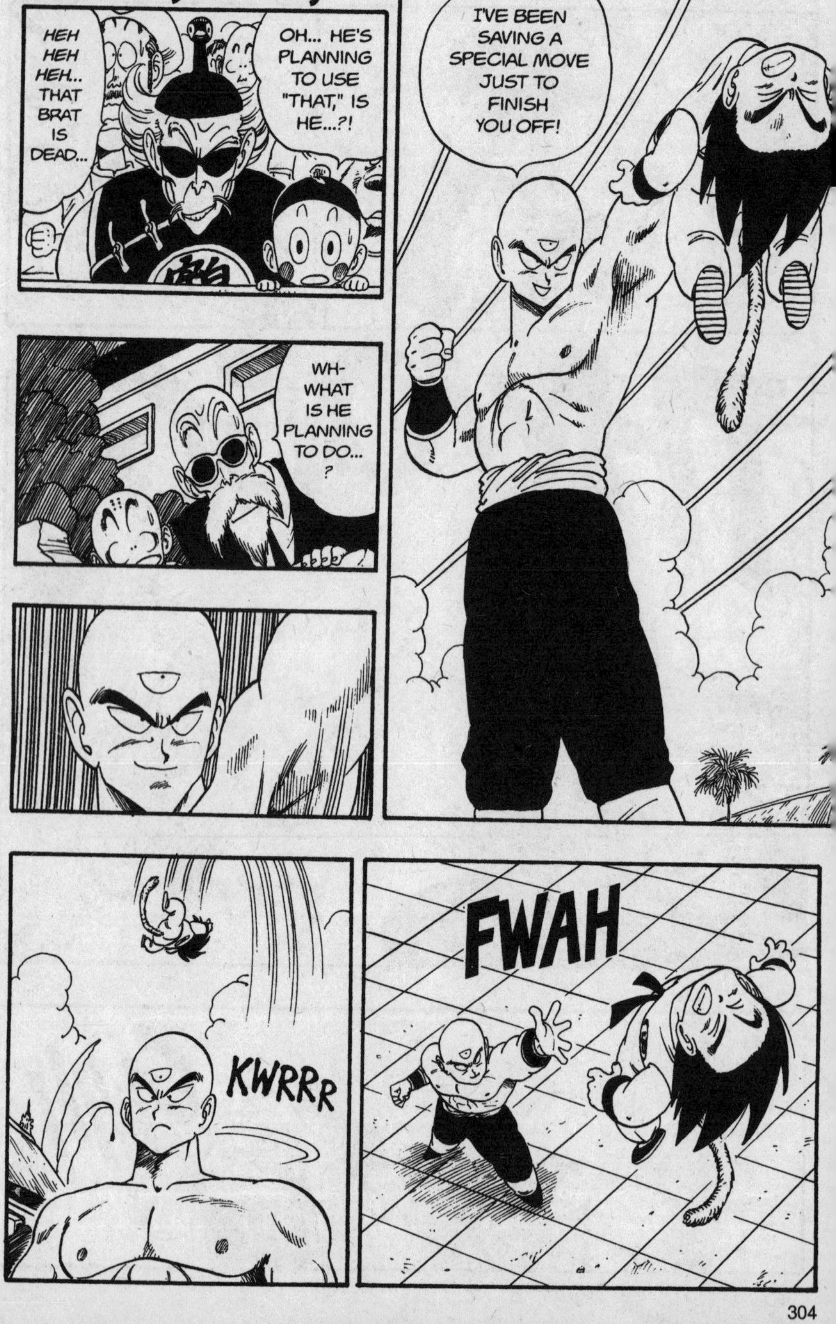
I'VE BEEN SAVING A SPECIAL MOVE JUST TO FINISH YOU OFF!
OH... HE'S PLANNING TO USE "THAT," IS HE...?!
HEH HEH HEH... THAT BRAT IS DEAD...
WH-WHAT IS HE PLANNING TO DO...?
FWAH
KWRRR

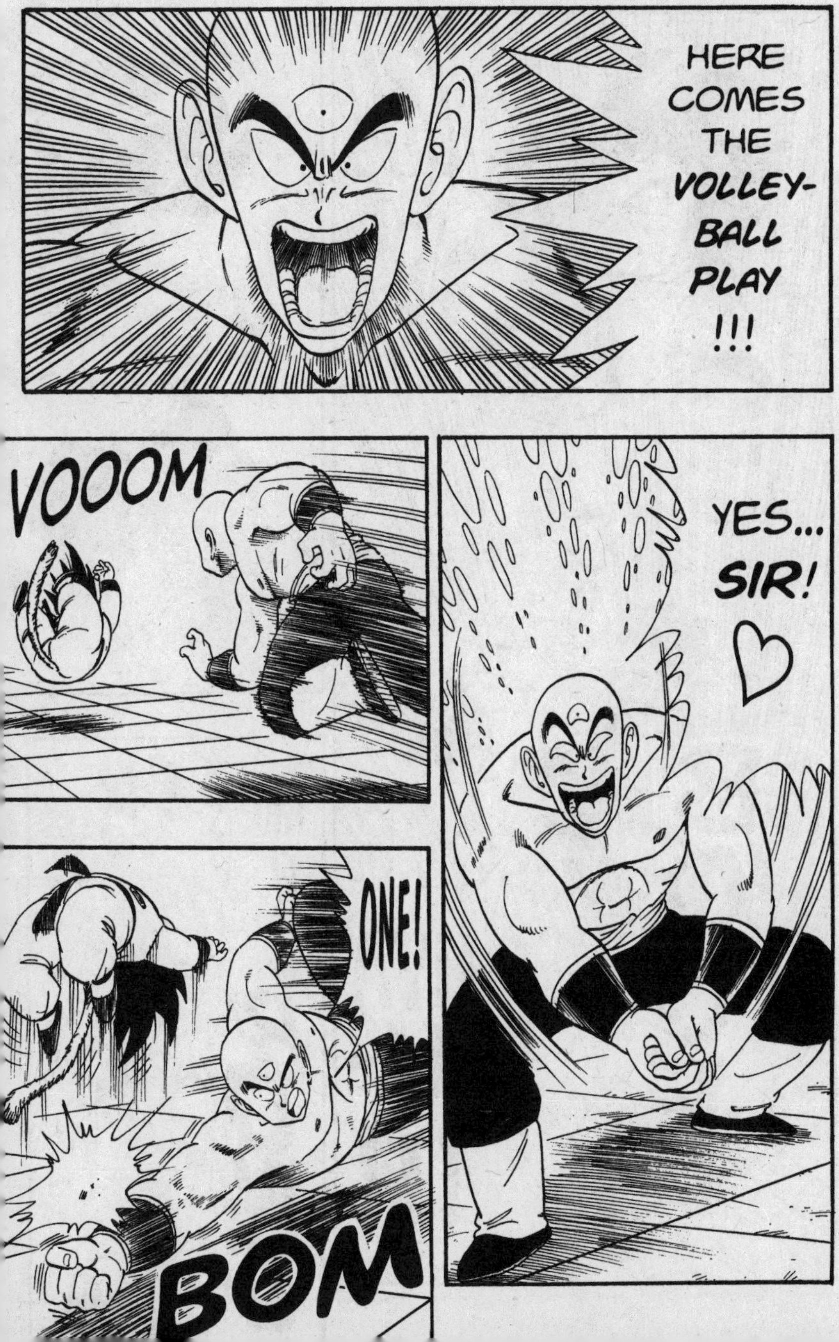
HERE COMES THE VOLLEY-BALL PLAY!!!
YES... SIR! ♥
VOOOM
ONE!
BOM

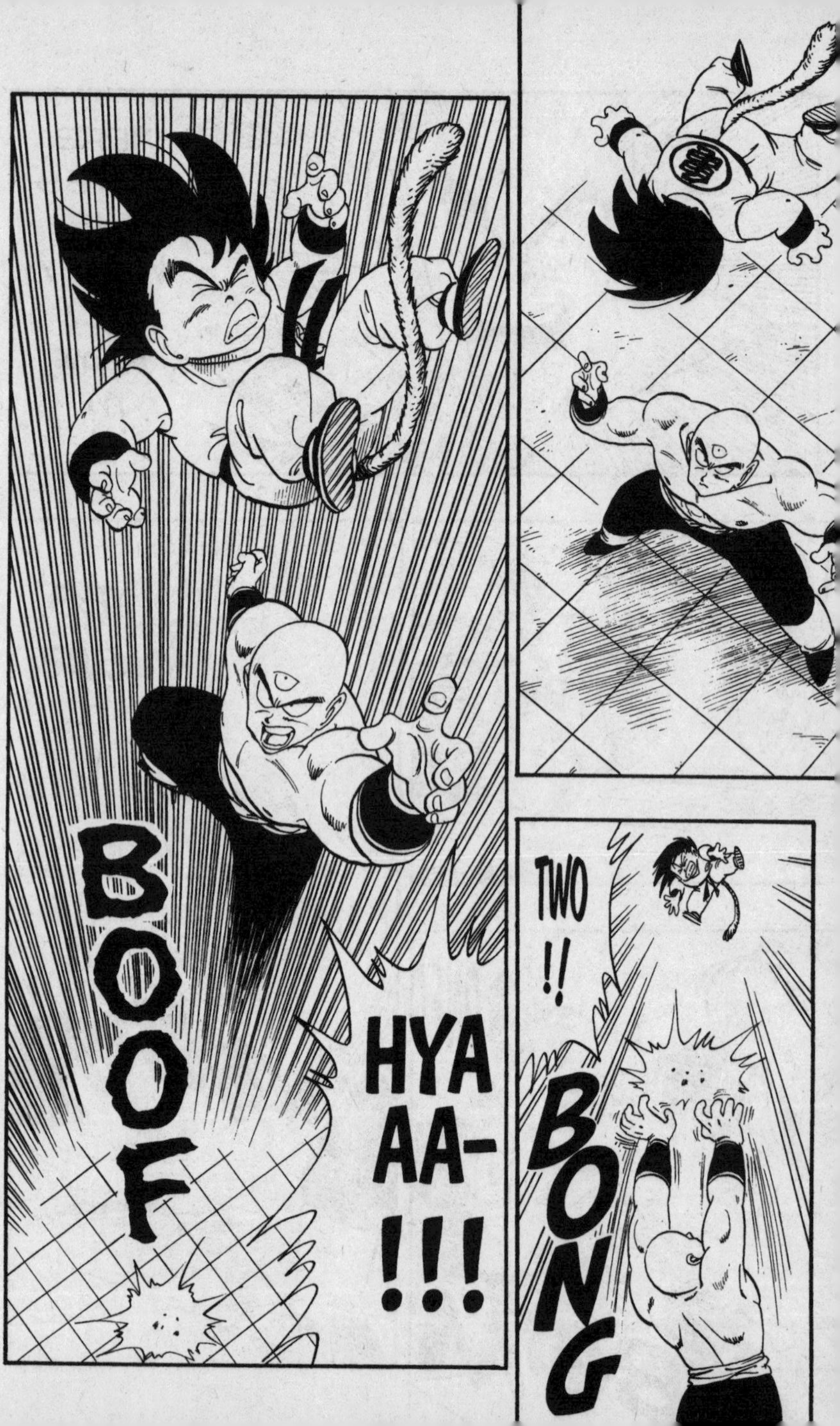
TWO!!
BONG
HYAAA-!!!
BOOF

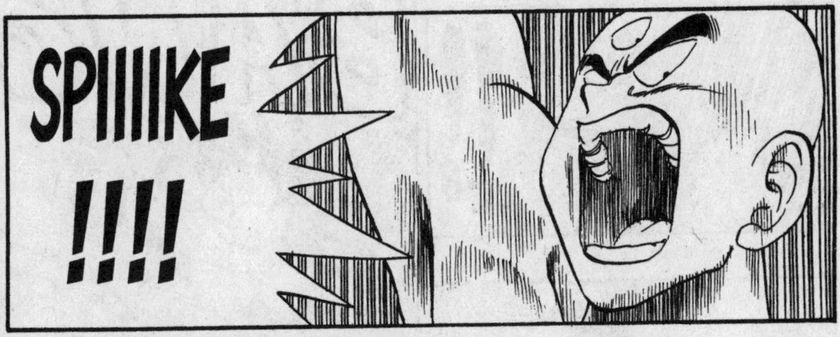
SPIIIIKE
!!!!
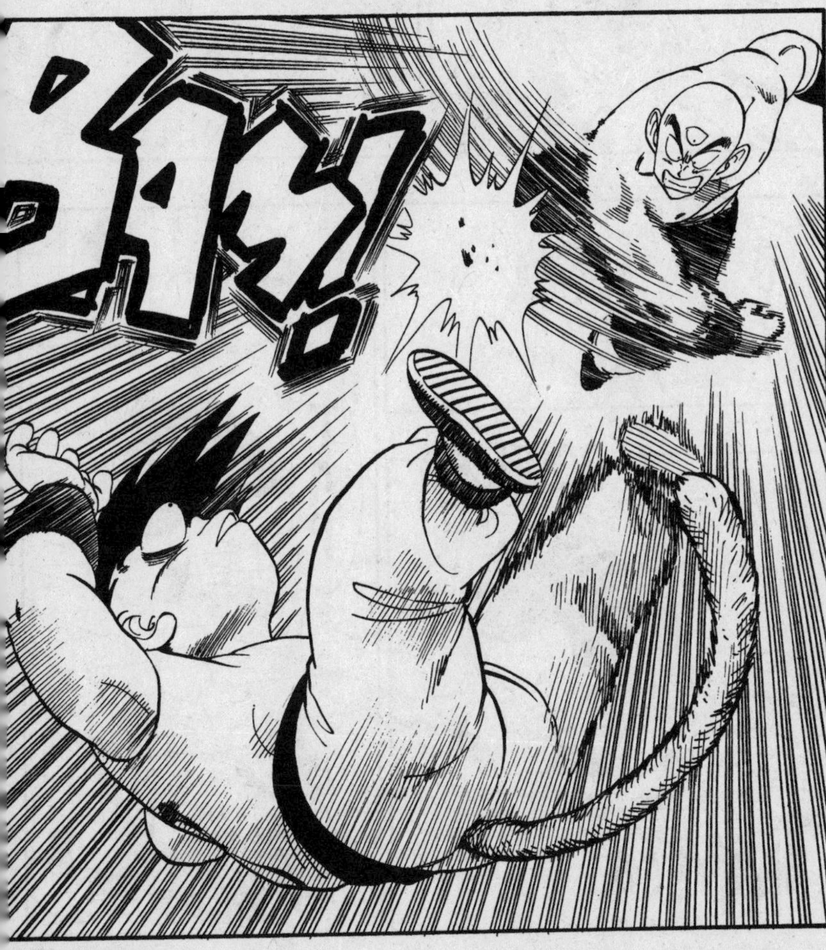

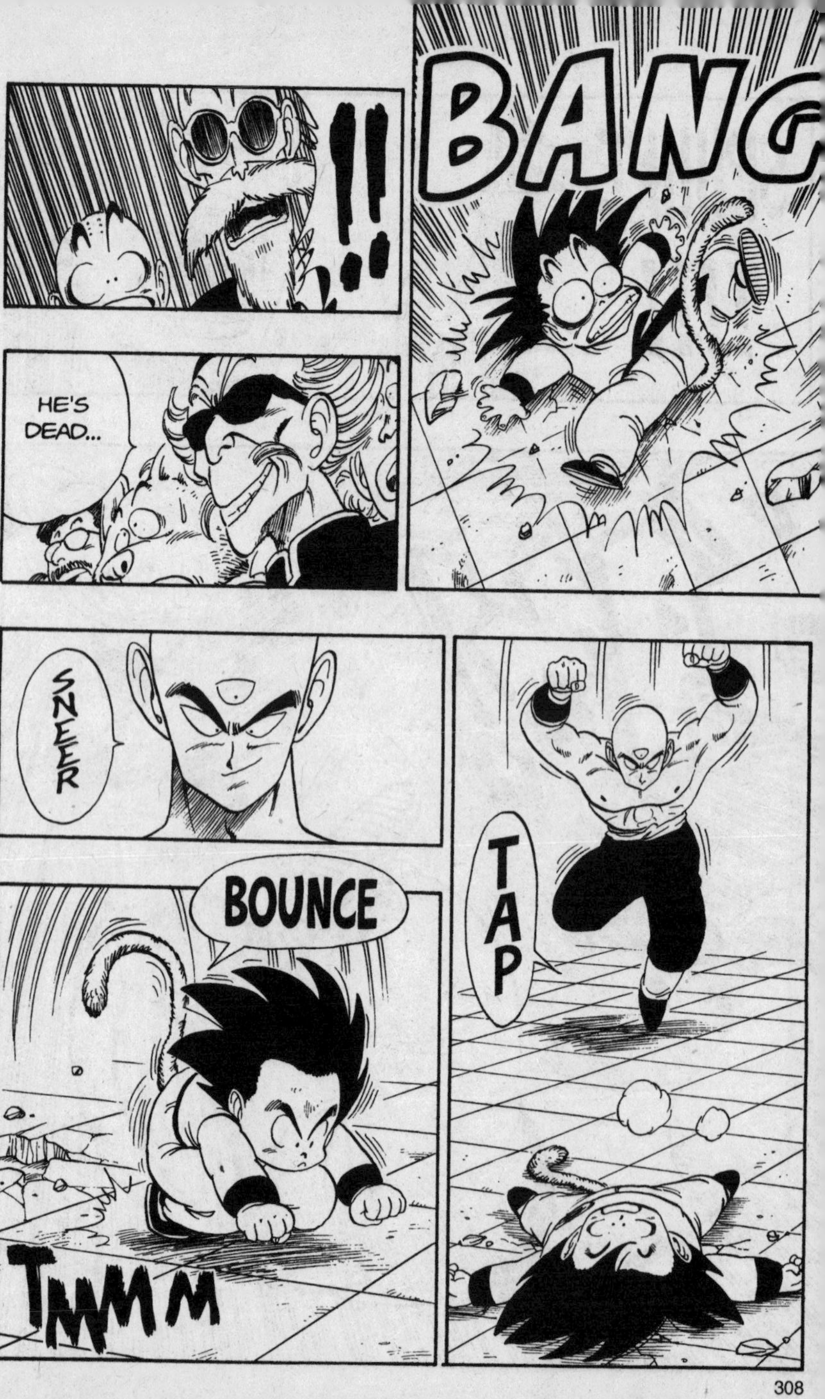
BANG
!!
HE'S DEAD...
TAP
SNEER
BOUNCE
TMMM

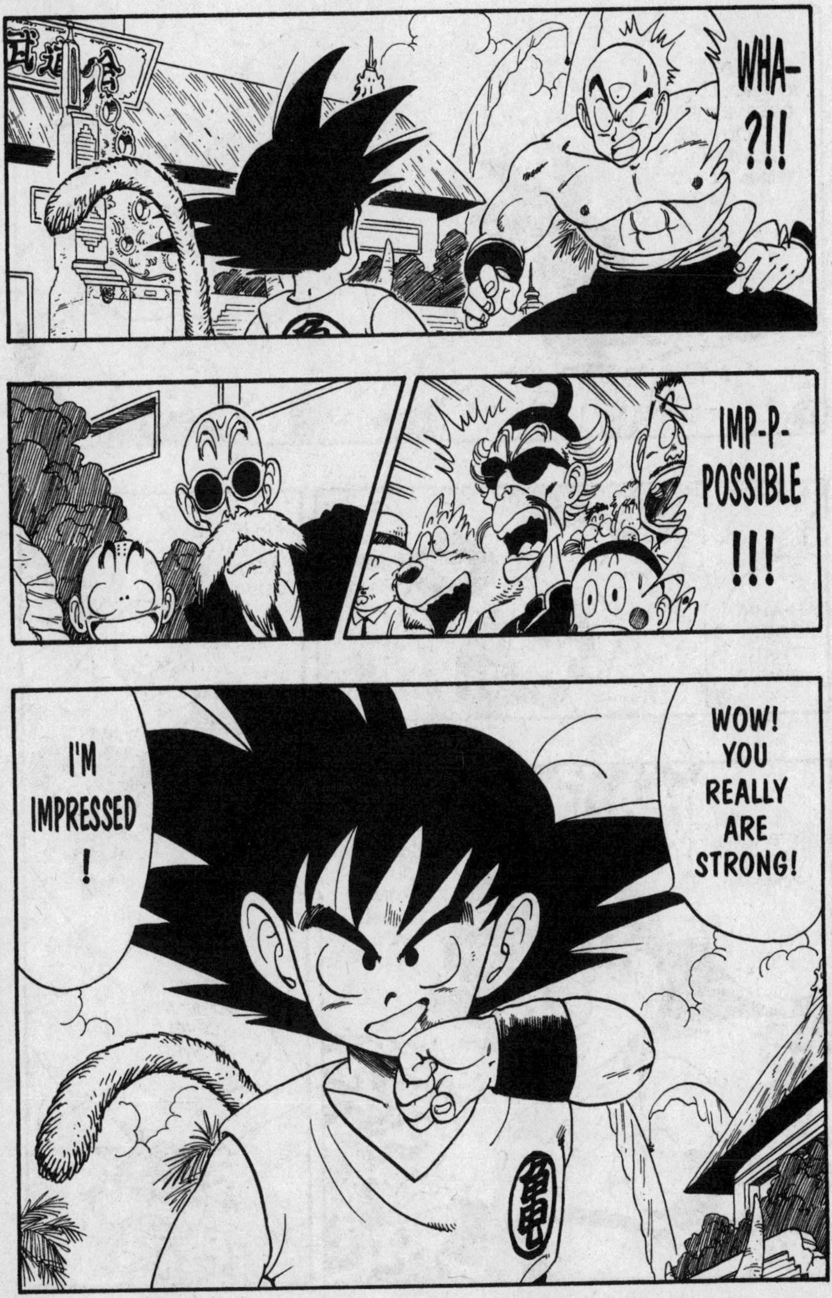
WHA-?!!
IMP-P-POSSIBLE!!!
WOW! YOU REALLY ARE STRONG!
I'M IMPRESSED!

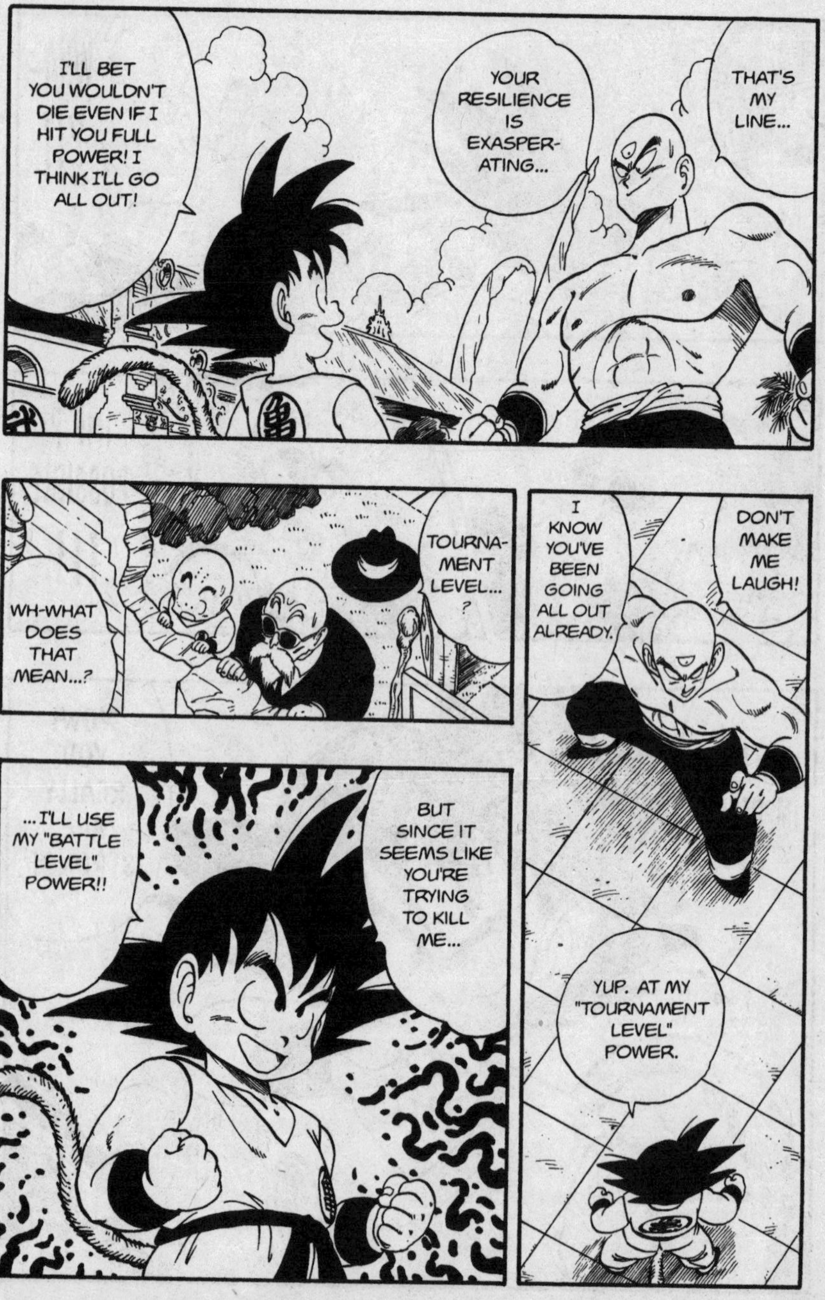
THAT'S MY LINE...
YOUR RESILIENCE IS EXASPER-ATING...
I'LL BET YOU WOULDN'T DIE EVEN IF I HIT YOU FULL POWER! I THINK I'LL GO ALL OUT!
DON'T MAKE ME LAUGH!
I KNOW YOU'VE BEEN GOING ALL OUT ALREADY.
YUP. AT MY "TOURNAMENT LEVEL" POWER.
TOURNA-MENT LEVEL...?
WH-WHAT DOES THAT MEAN...?
BUT SINCE IT SEEMS LIKE YOU'RE TRYING TO KILL ME...
...I'LL USE MY "BATTLE LEVEL" POWER!!

"BATTLE LEVEL"...? YOU'RE TELLING ME YOU HAVE A WHOLE OTHER LEVEL OF POWER...?

FOOEY! SPARE ME THE CHILDISH FANTASIES!

HERE I COME! BATTLE— ENGAGE!!

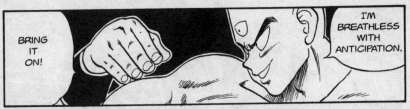

BRING IT ON!

I'M BREATHLESS WITH ANTICIPATION.

HNAH

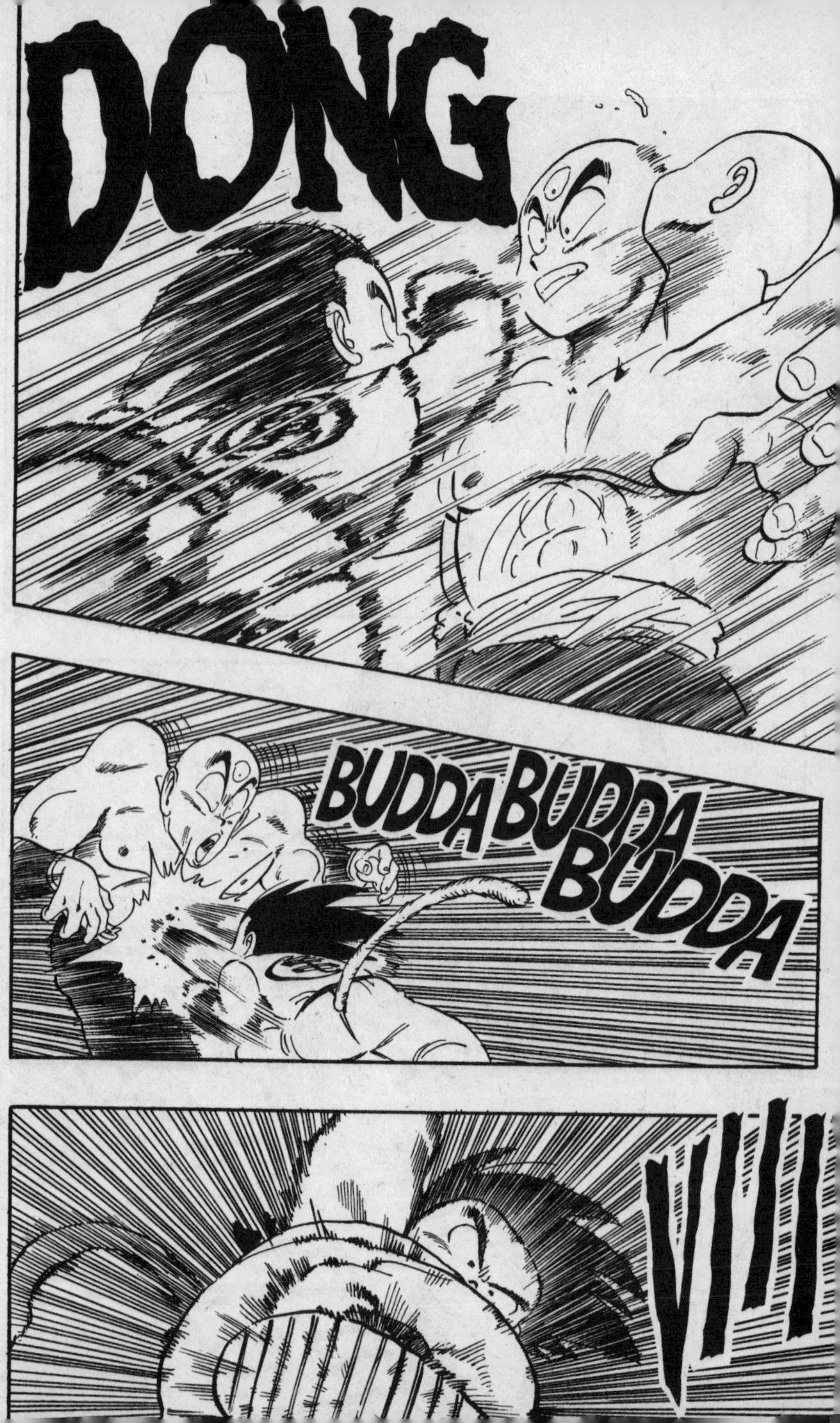
DONG
BUDDA BUDDA BUDDA BUDDA
VIII

BOF
天下一武道会
BAMMM

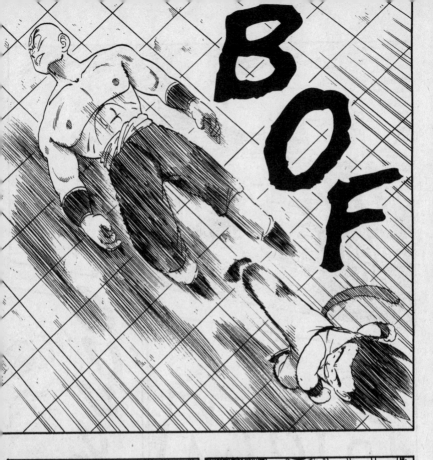

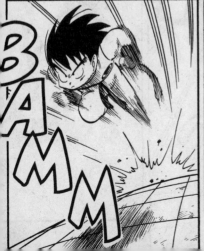

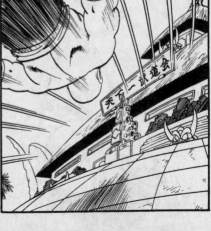

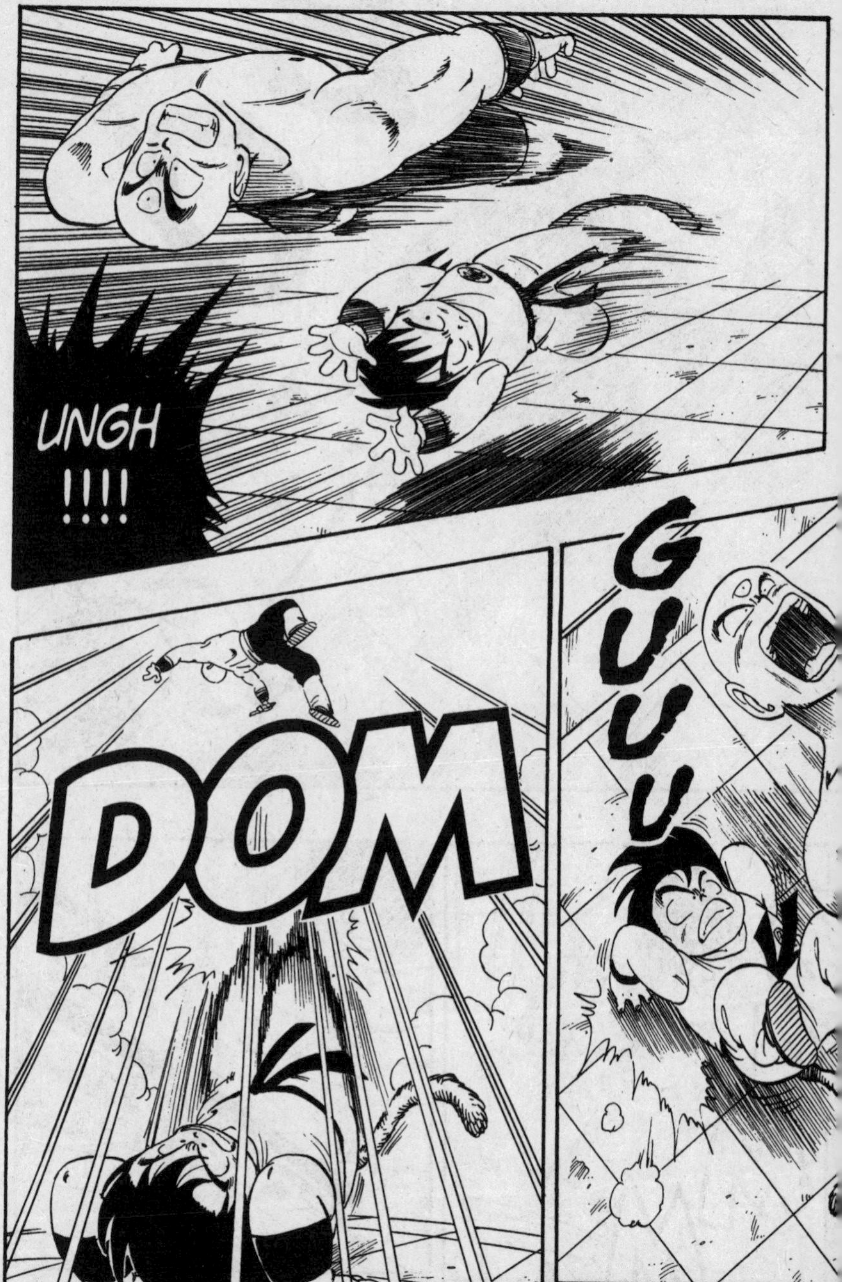
UNGH
!!!!
GUUU
DOM

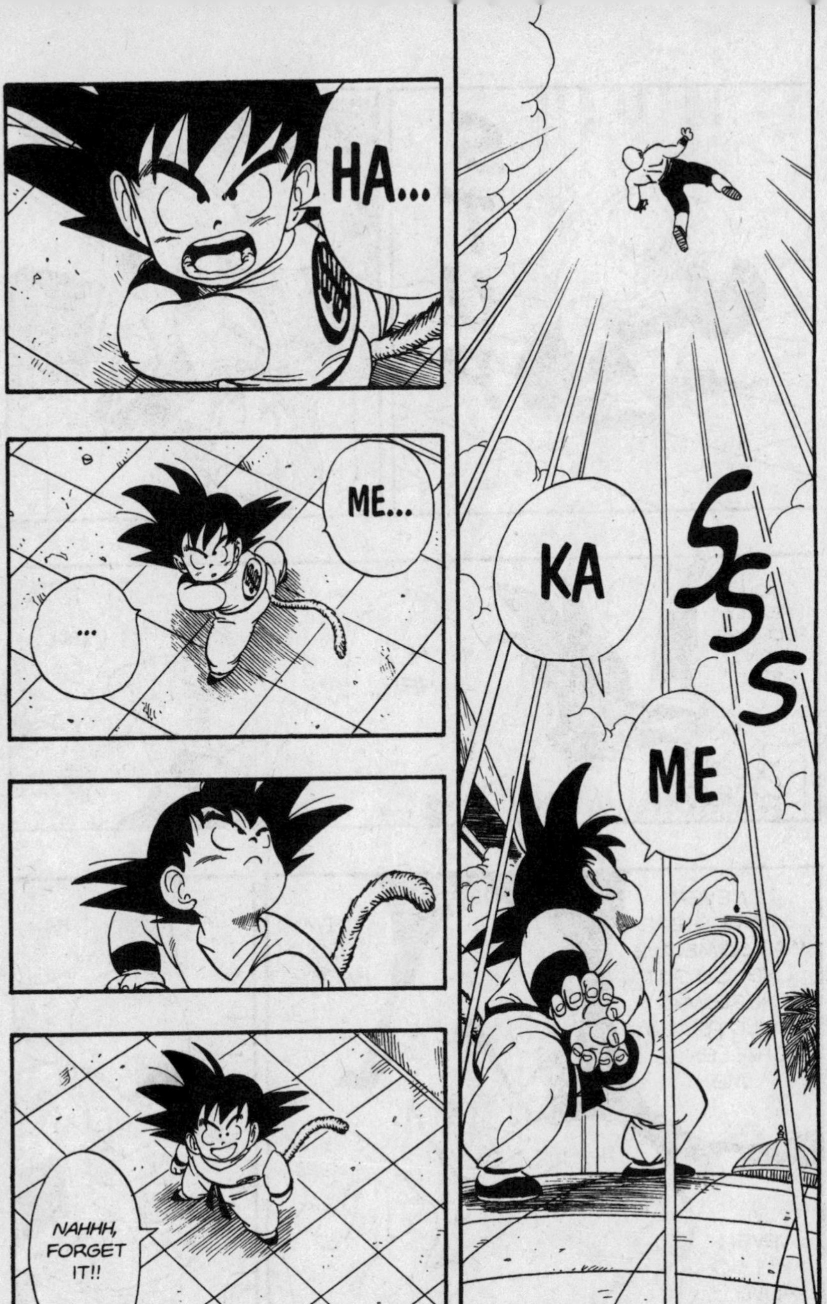
KA
SSS
ME
HA...
ME...
...
NAHHH, FORGET IT!!

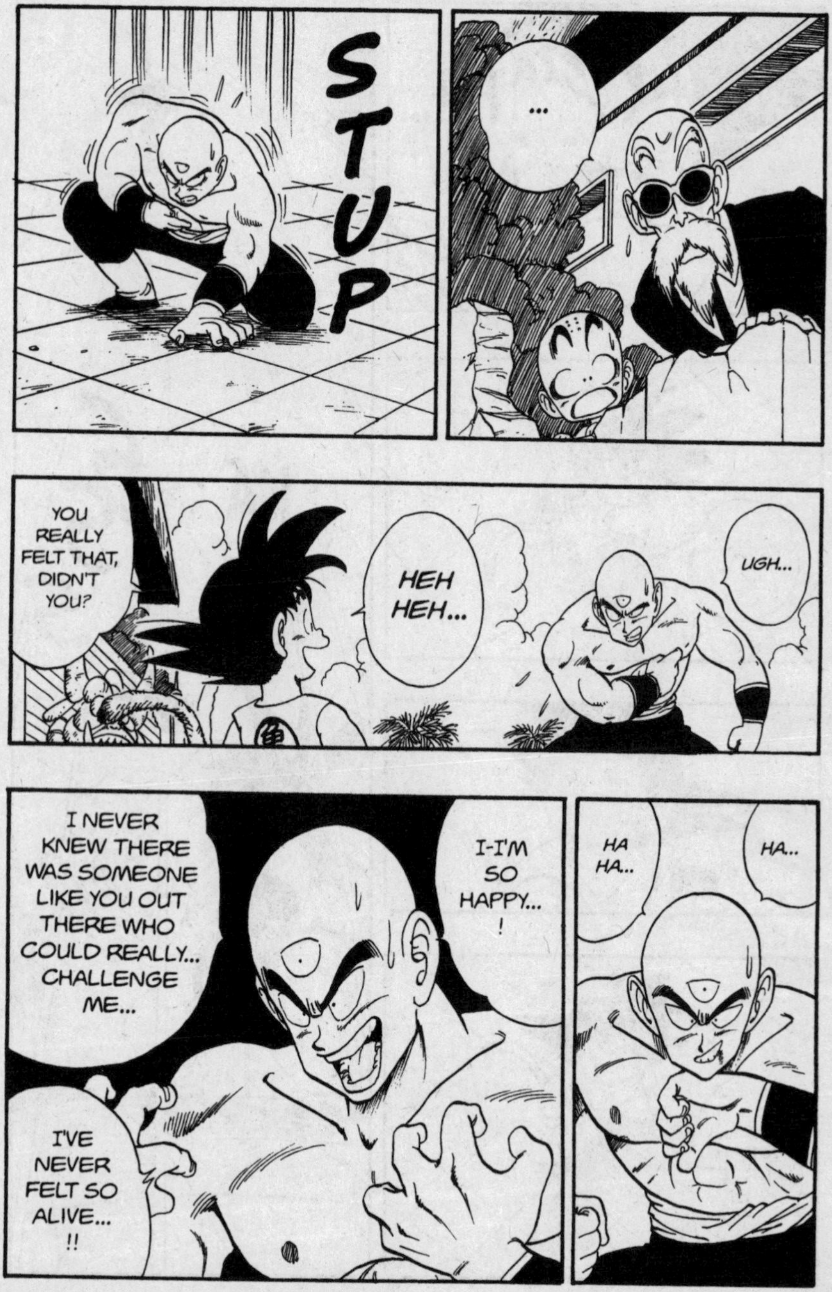
...
STUP
UGH...
HEH HEH...
YOU REALLY FELT THAT, DIDN'T YOU?
HA...
HA HA...
I-I'M SO HAPPY...!
I NEVER KNEW THERE WAS SOMEONE LIKE YOU OUT THERE WHO COULD REALLY... CHALLENGE ME...
I'VE NEVER FELT SO ALIVE...!!

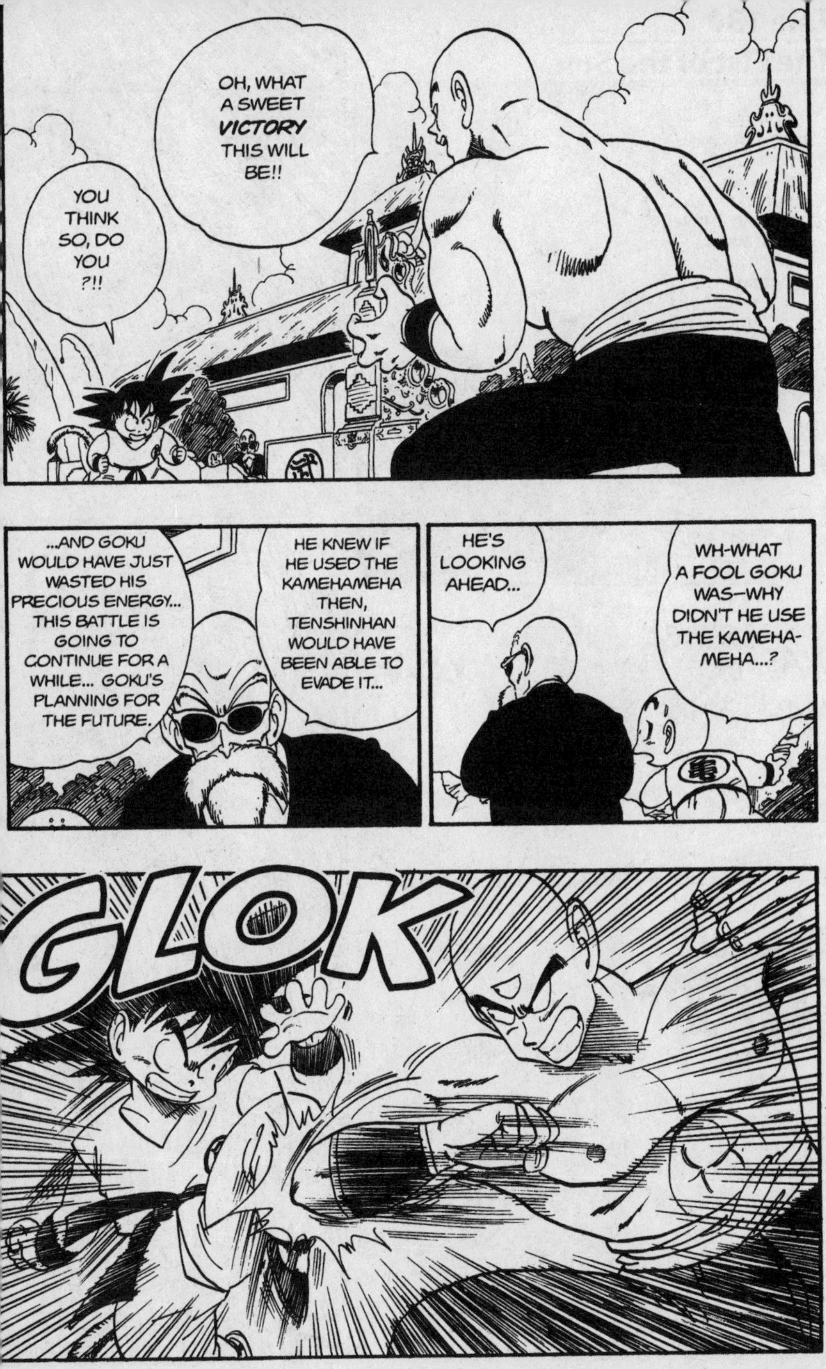
OH, WHAT A SWEET **VICTORY** THIS WILL BE!!
YOU THINK SO, DO YOU ?!!
WH-WHAT A FOOL GOKU WAS—WHY DIDN'T HE USE THE KAMEHA-MEHA...?
HE'S LOOKING AHEAD...
HE KNEW IF HE USED THE KAMEHAMEHA THEN, TENSHINHAN WOULD HAVE BEEN ABLE TO EVADE IT...
...AND GOKU WOULD HAVE JUST WASTED HIS PRECIOUS ENERGY... THIS BATTLE IS GOING TO CONTINUE FOR A WHILE... GOKU'S PLANNING FOR THE FUTURE.
GLOK

Tale 130
The Fist of the Sun

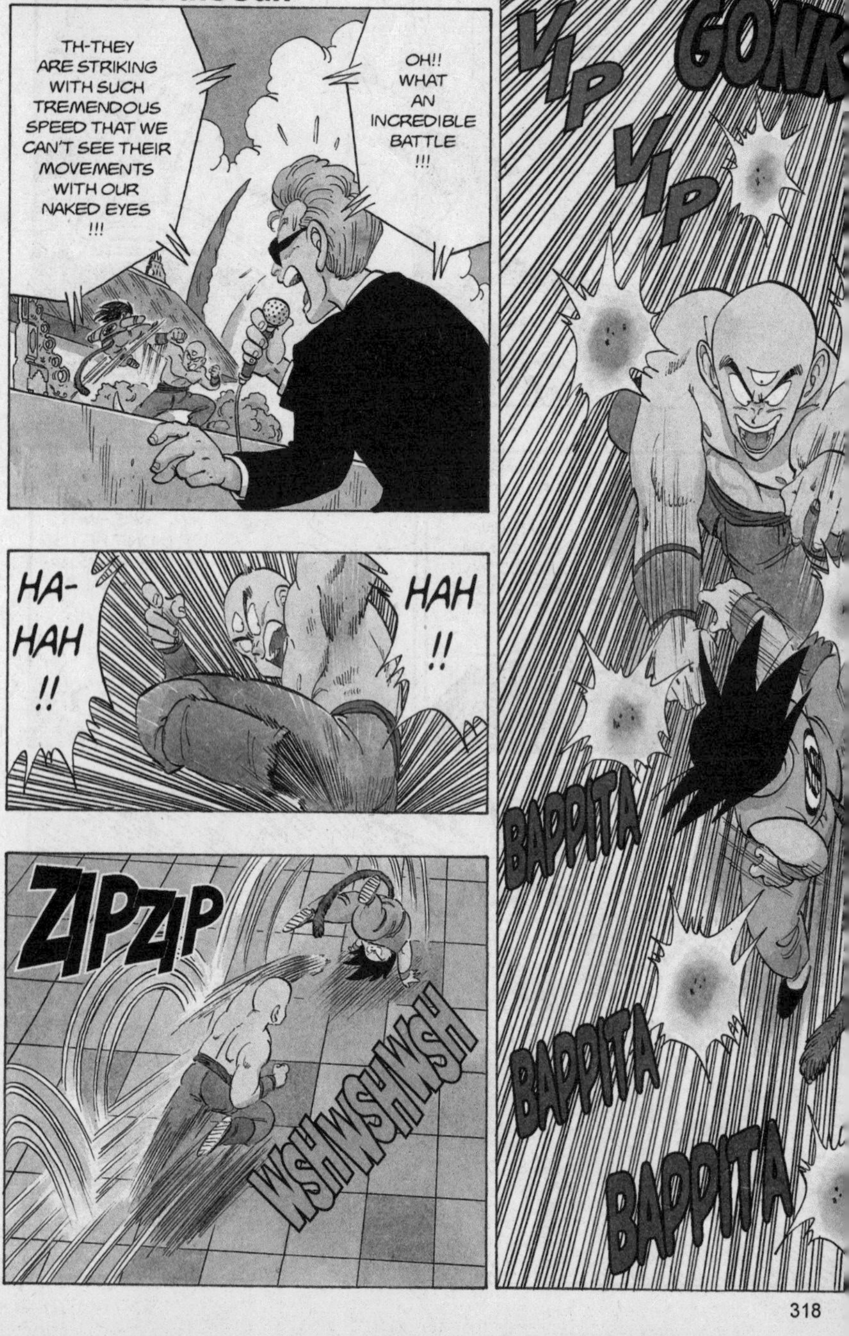
VIP
GONK
VIP
VIP
BAPPITA
BAPPITA
BAPPITA
OH!! WHAT AN INCREDIBLE BATTLE !!!
TH-THEY ARE STRIKING WITH SUCH TREMENDOUS SPEED THAT WE CAN'T SEE THEIR MOVEMENTS WITH OUR NAKED EYES !!!
HAH !!
HA-HAH !!
ZIPZAP
WSHWSHWSH

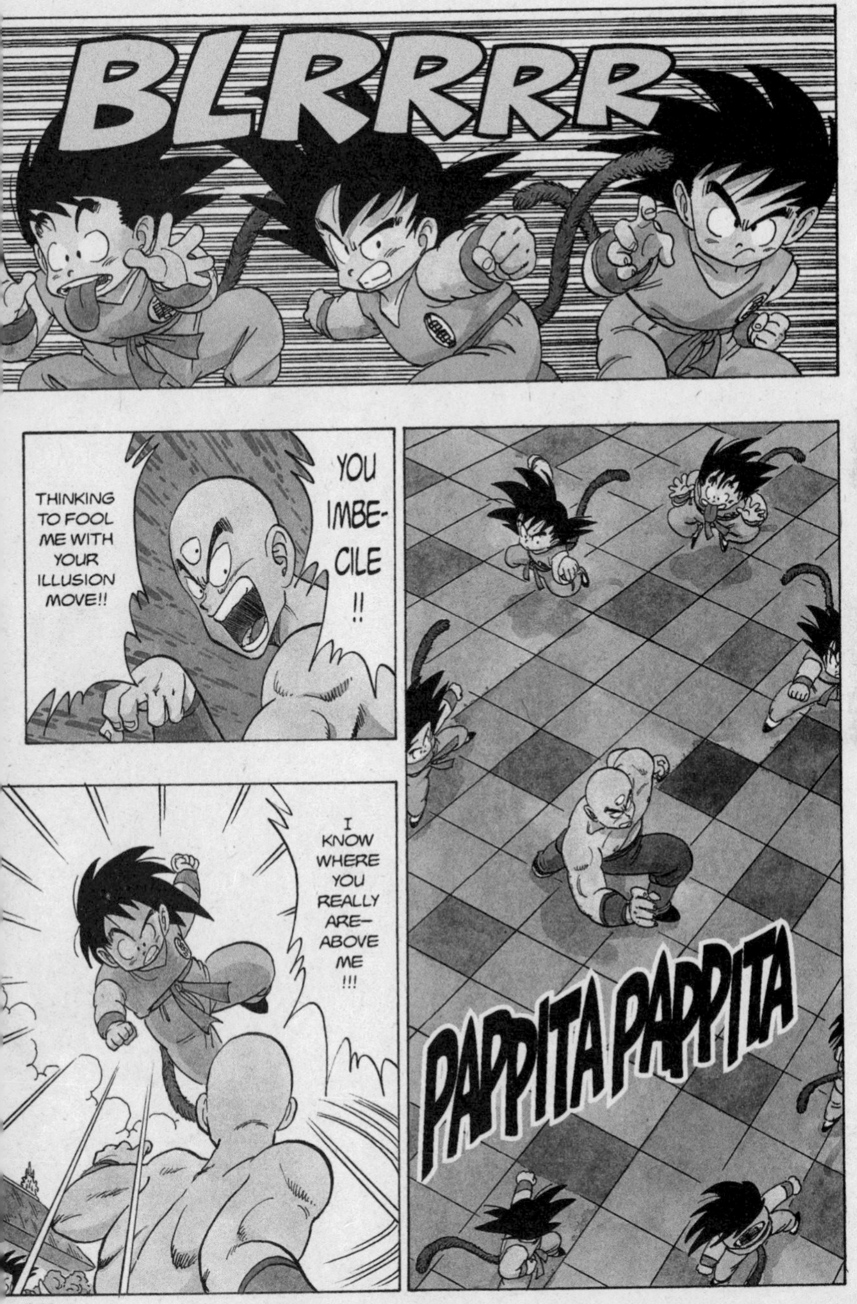
BLRRRR
PAPPITA PAPPITA
YOU IMBE-CILE !!
THINKING TO FOOL ME WITH YOUR ILLUSION MOVE!!
I KNOW WHERE YOU REALLY ARE— ABOVE ME !!!

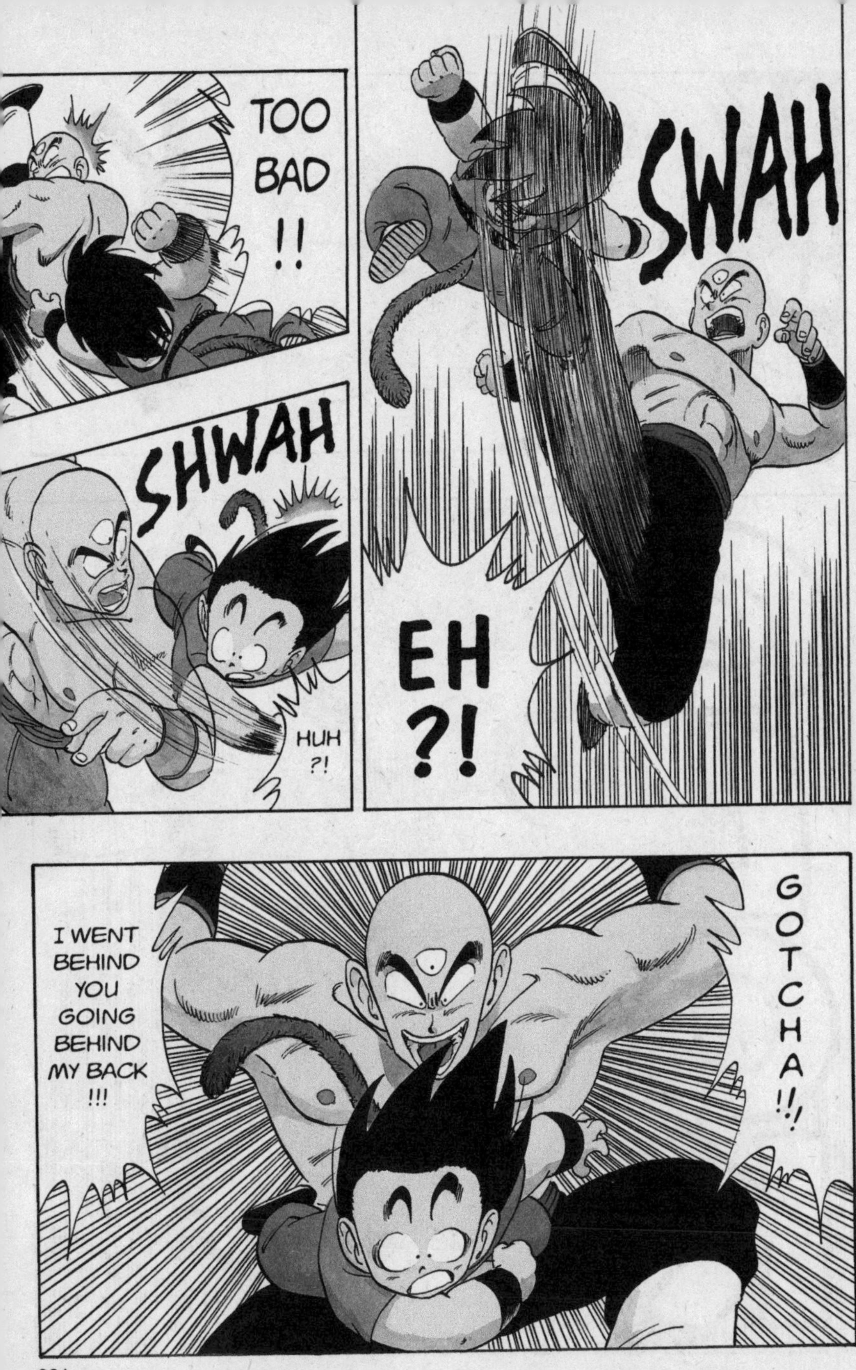
SWAH
EH ?!
TOO BAD !!
SHWAH
HUH ?!
GOTCHA!!!
I WENT BEHIND YOU GOING BEHIND MY BACK !!!

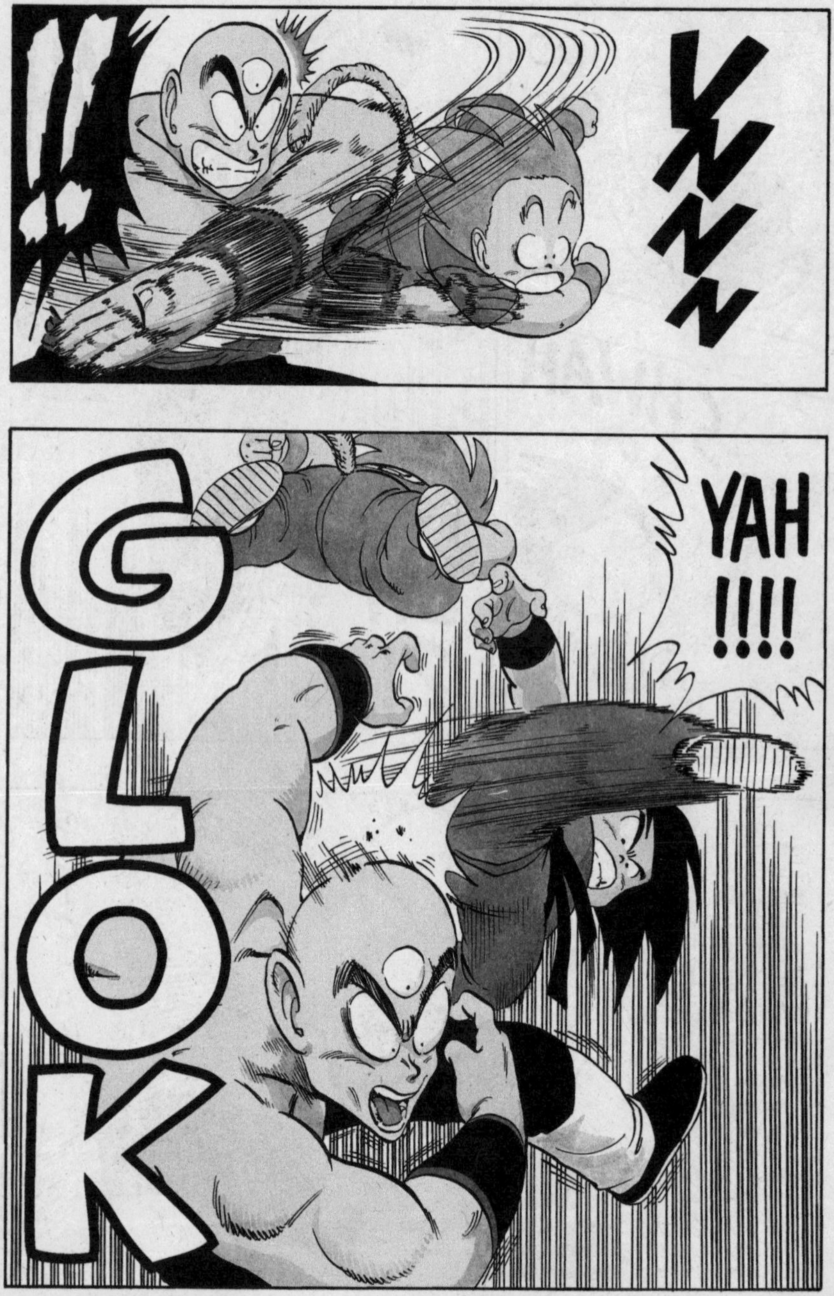
!!
VNNN
YAH !!!!
GLOK

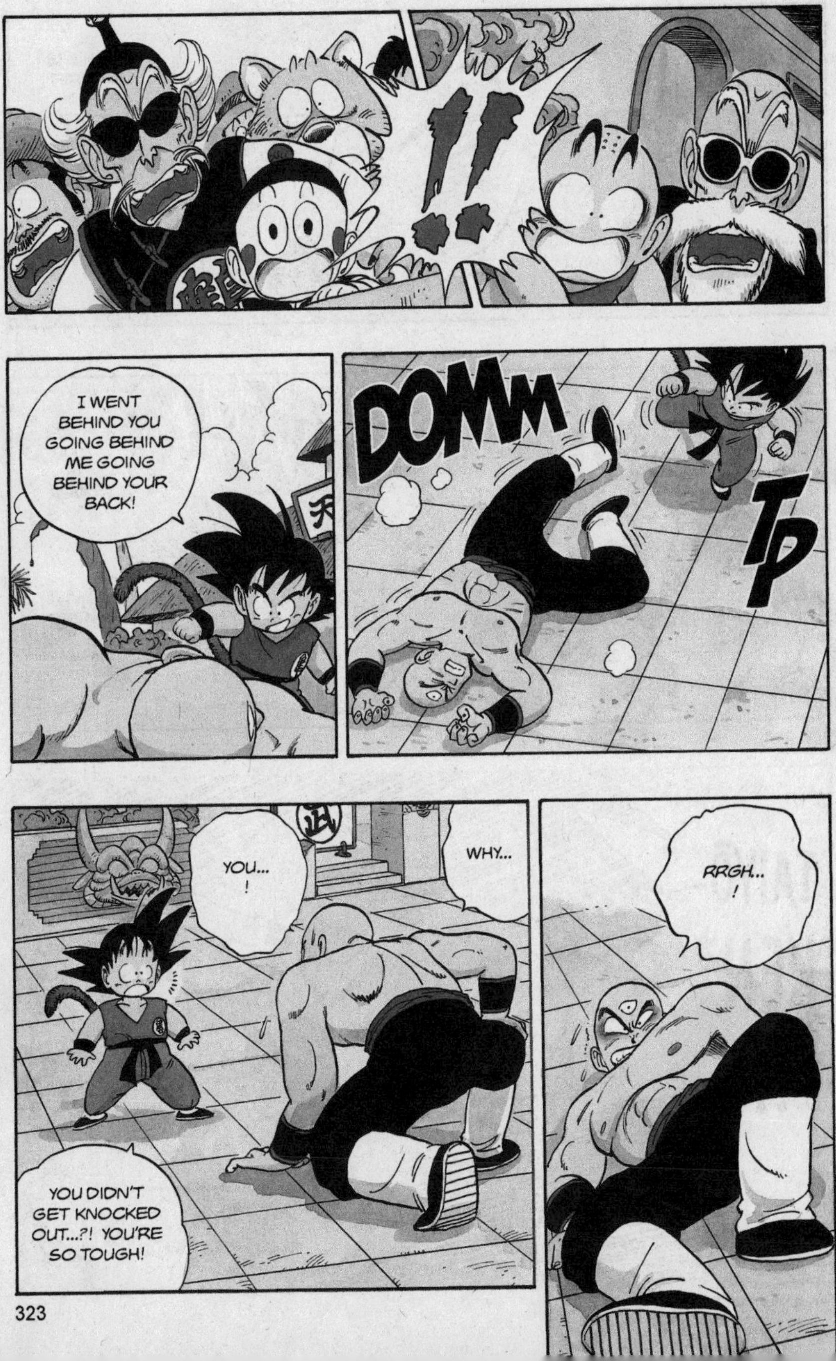
!!
DOMM
TP
I WENT BEHIND YOU GOING BEHIND ME GOING BEHIND YOUR BACK!
RRGH... !
WHY...
YOU... !
YOU DIDN'T GET KNOCKED OUT...?! YOU'RE SO TOUGH!

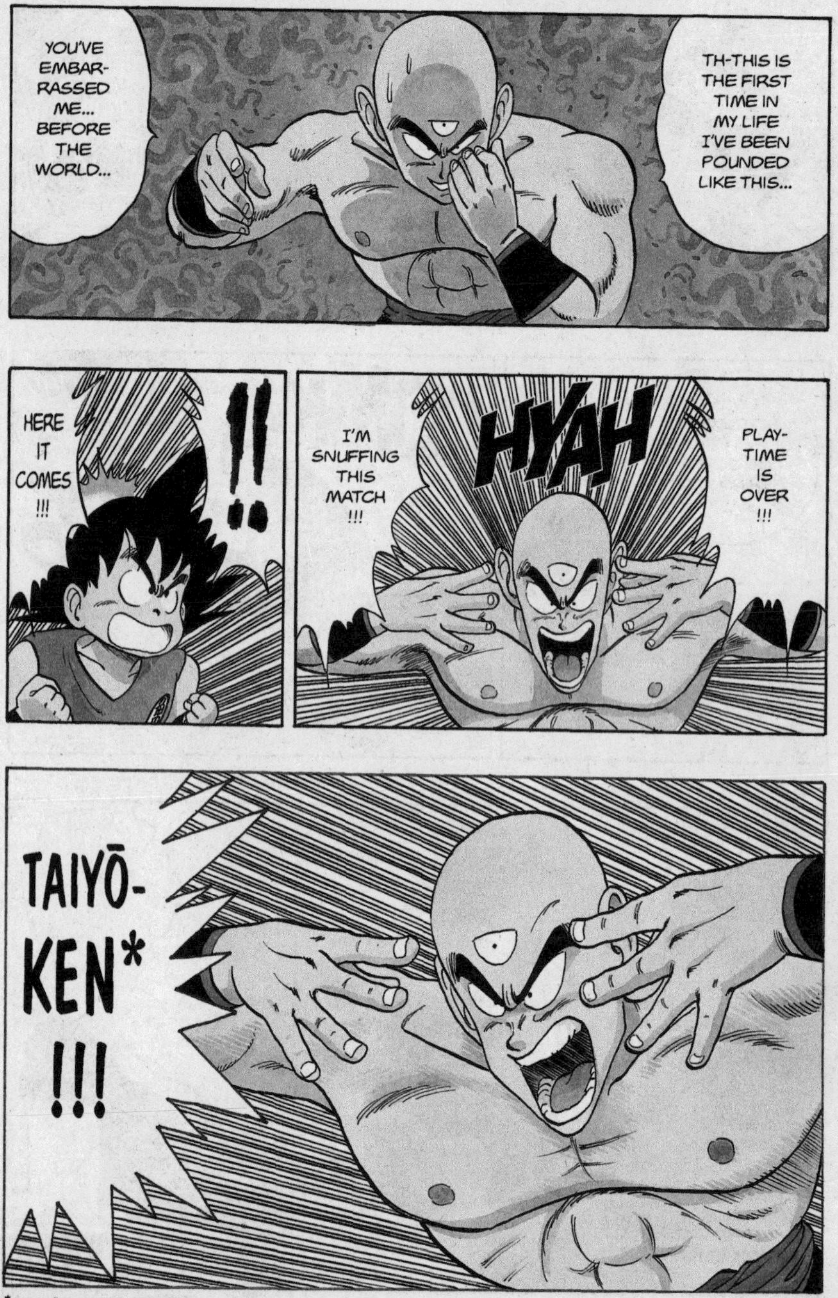
TH-THIS IS THE FIRST TIME IN MY LIFE I'VE BEEN POUNDED LIKE THIS...
YOU'VE EMBAR-RASSED ME... BEFORE THE WORLD...
PLAY-TIME IS OVER!!!
HYAH
I'M SNUFFING THIS MATCH!!!
!!
HERE IT COMES!!!
TAIYŌ-KEN*!!!

*A.K.A "FIST OF THE SUN"

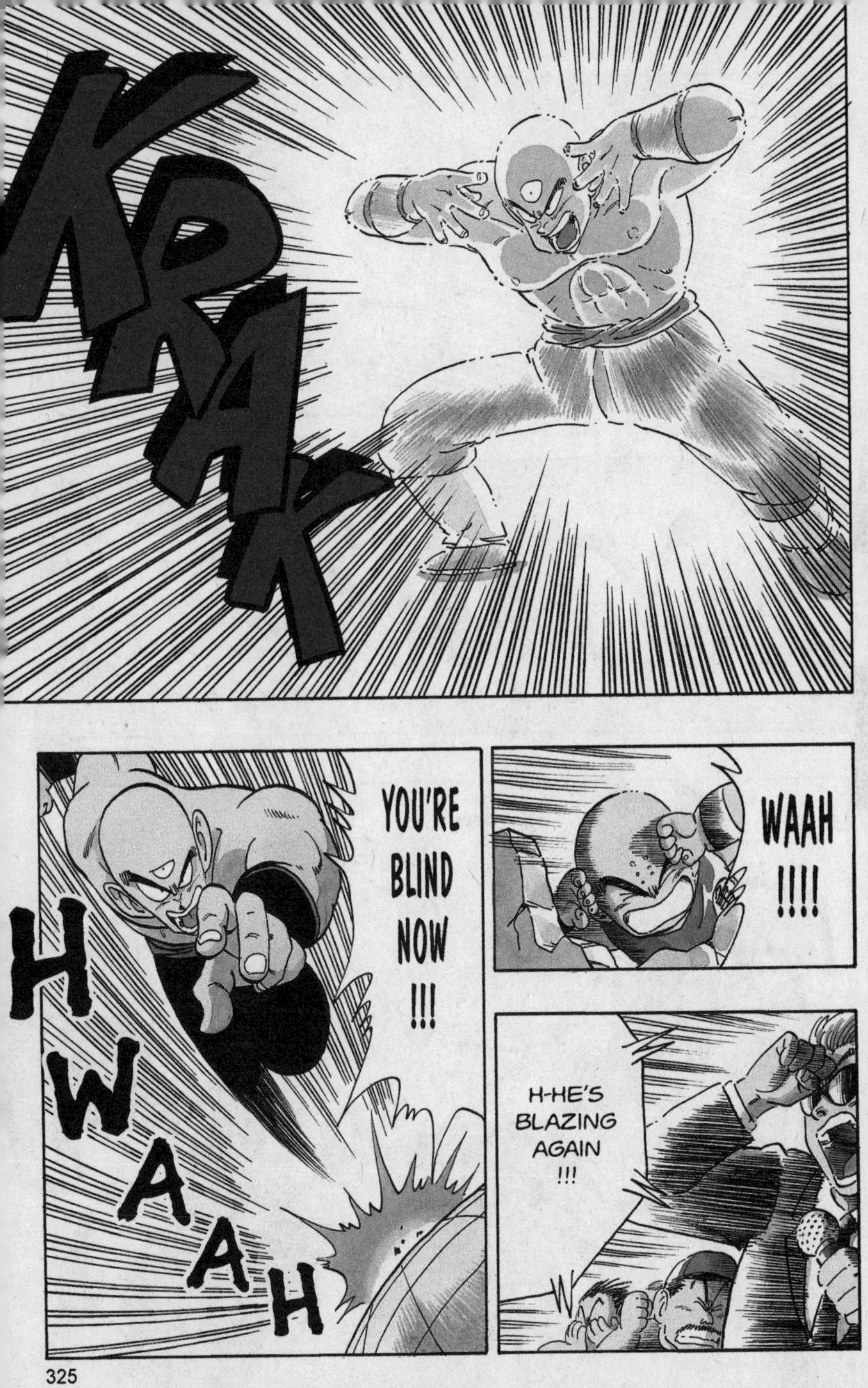
KRAAAK
WAAH !!!!
H-HE'S BLAZING AGAIN !!!
YOU'RE BLIND NOW !!!
HWAAAH

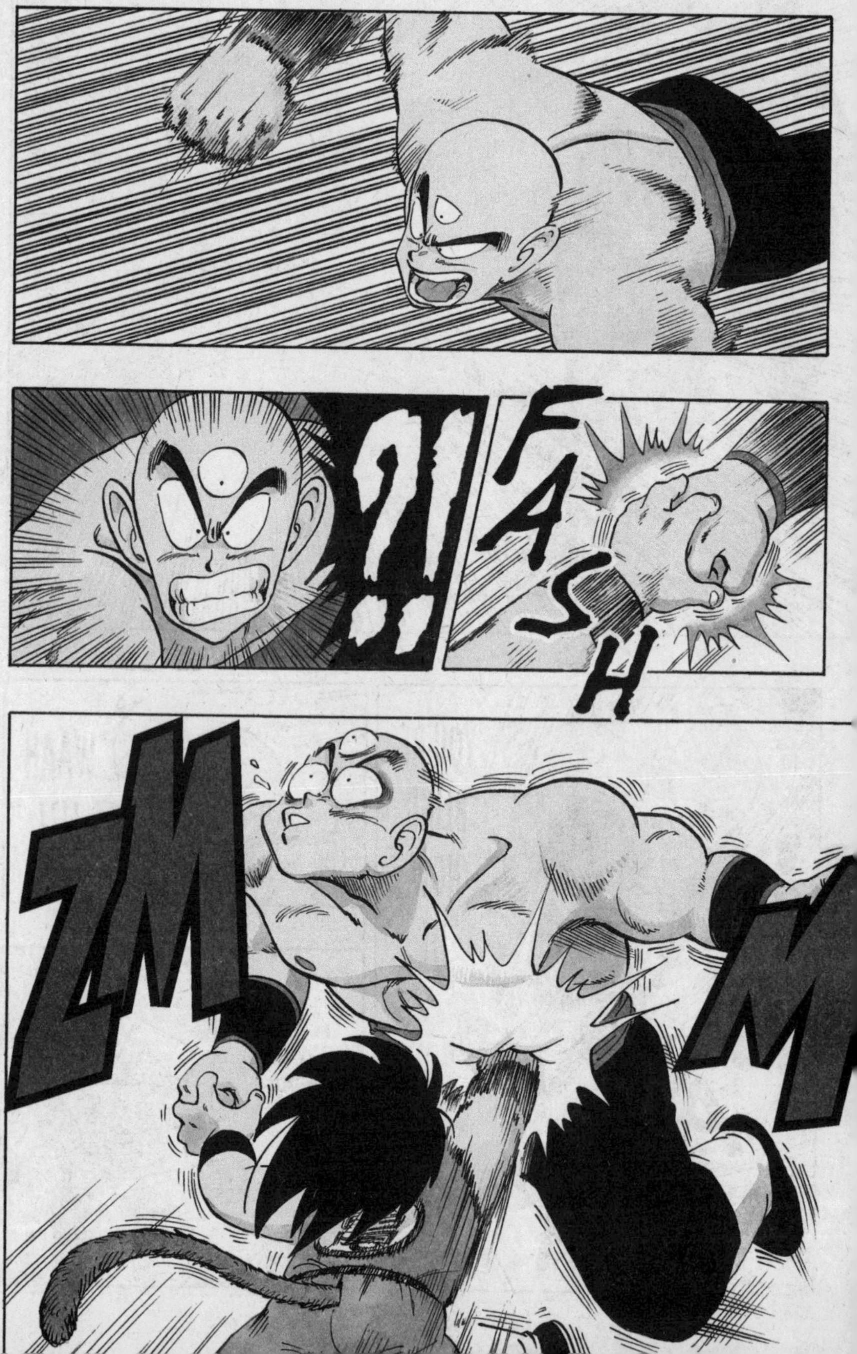
FASH
?!
ZMM

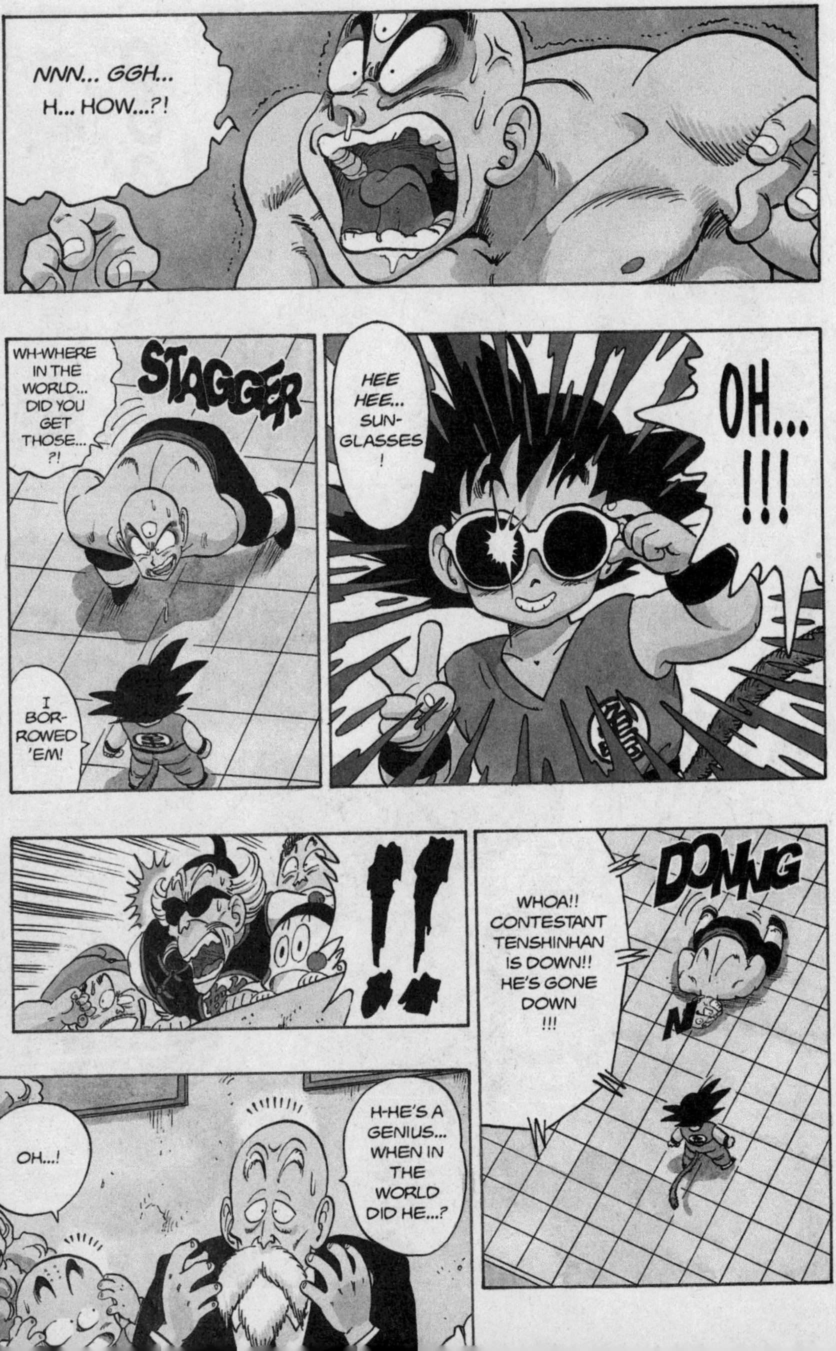
NNN... GGH... H... HOW...?!
OH... !!!
HEE HEE... SUN-GLASSES!
STAGGER
WH-WHERE IN THE WORLD... DID YOU GET THOSE...?!
I BOR-ROWED 'EM!
DONNG
WHOA!! CONTESTANT TENSHINHAN IS DOWN!! HE'S GONE DOWN!!!
!!
H-HE'S A GENIUS... WHEN IN THE WORLD DID HE...?
OH...!

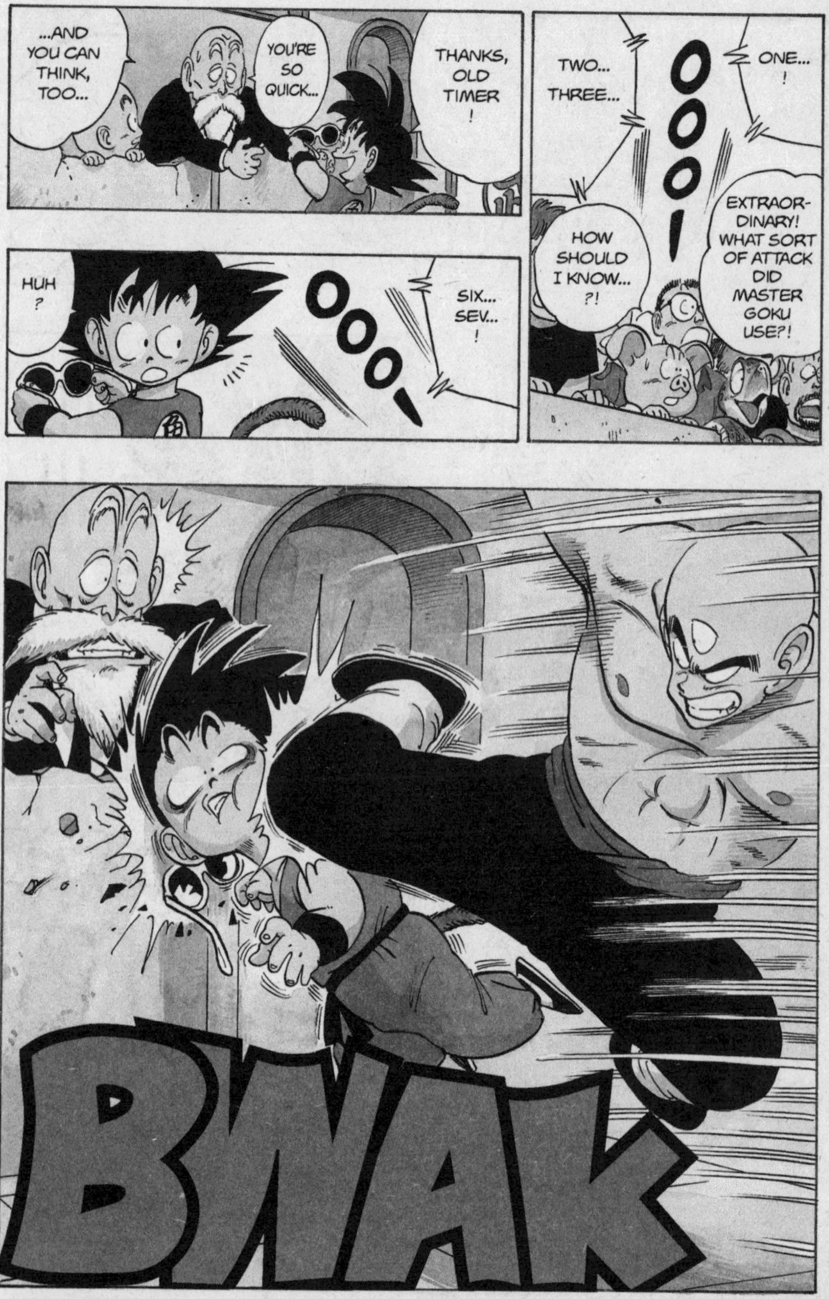

ONE...!
OOOOI
TWO... THREE...
EXTRAOR-DINARY! WHAT SORT OF ATTACK DID MASTER GOKU USE?!
HOW SHOULD I KNOW...?!
THANKS, OLD TIMER!
YOU'RE SO QUICK...
...AND YOU CAN THINK, TOO...
SIX... SEV...!
OOOI
HUH?
BWAK

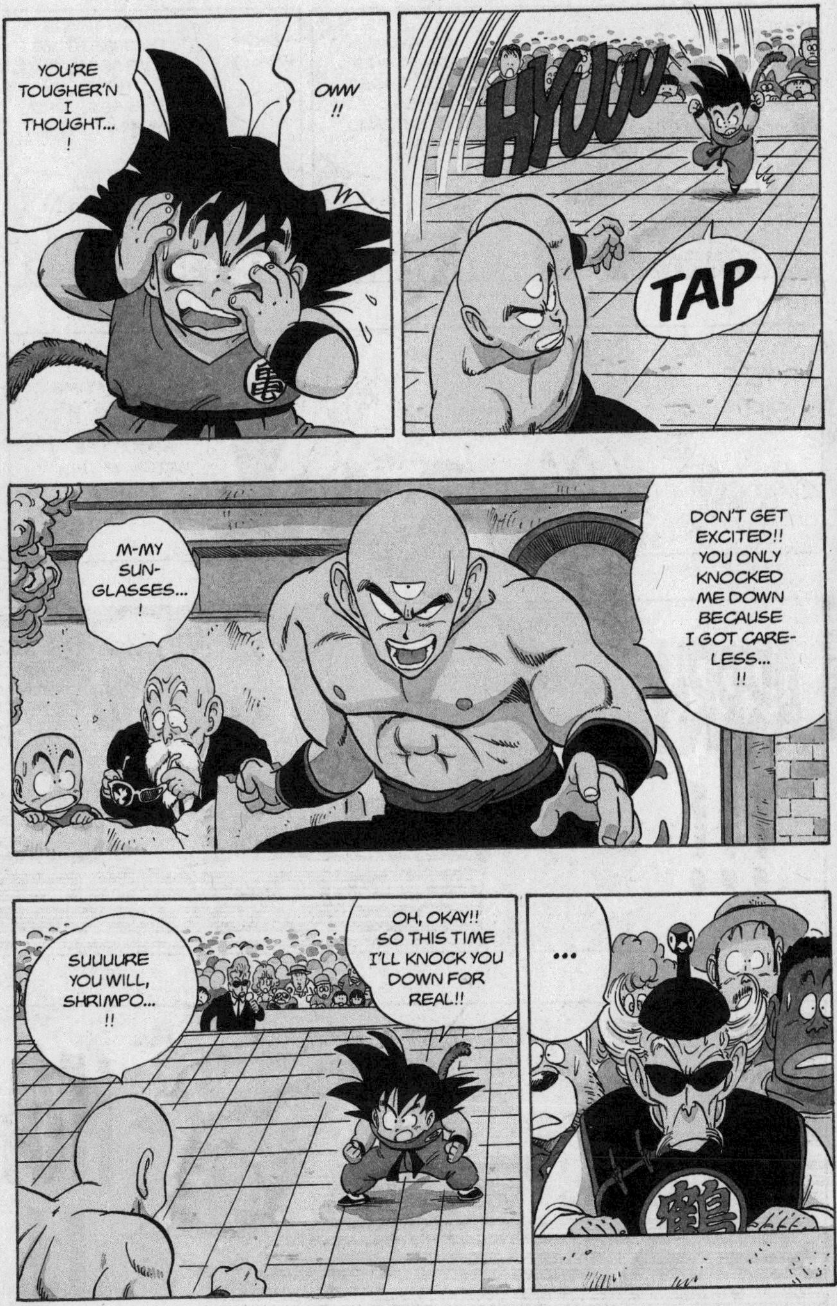
HYUUU
TAP
OWW !!
YOU'RE TOUGHER'N I THOUGHT... !
DON'T GET EXCITED!! YOU ONLY KNOCKED ME DOWN BECAUSE I GOT CARE-LESS... !!
M-MY SUN-GLASSES... !
...
OH, OKAY!! SO THIS TIME I'LL KNOCK YOU DOWN FOR REAL!!
SUUUURE YOU WILL, SHRIMPO... !!

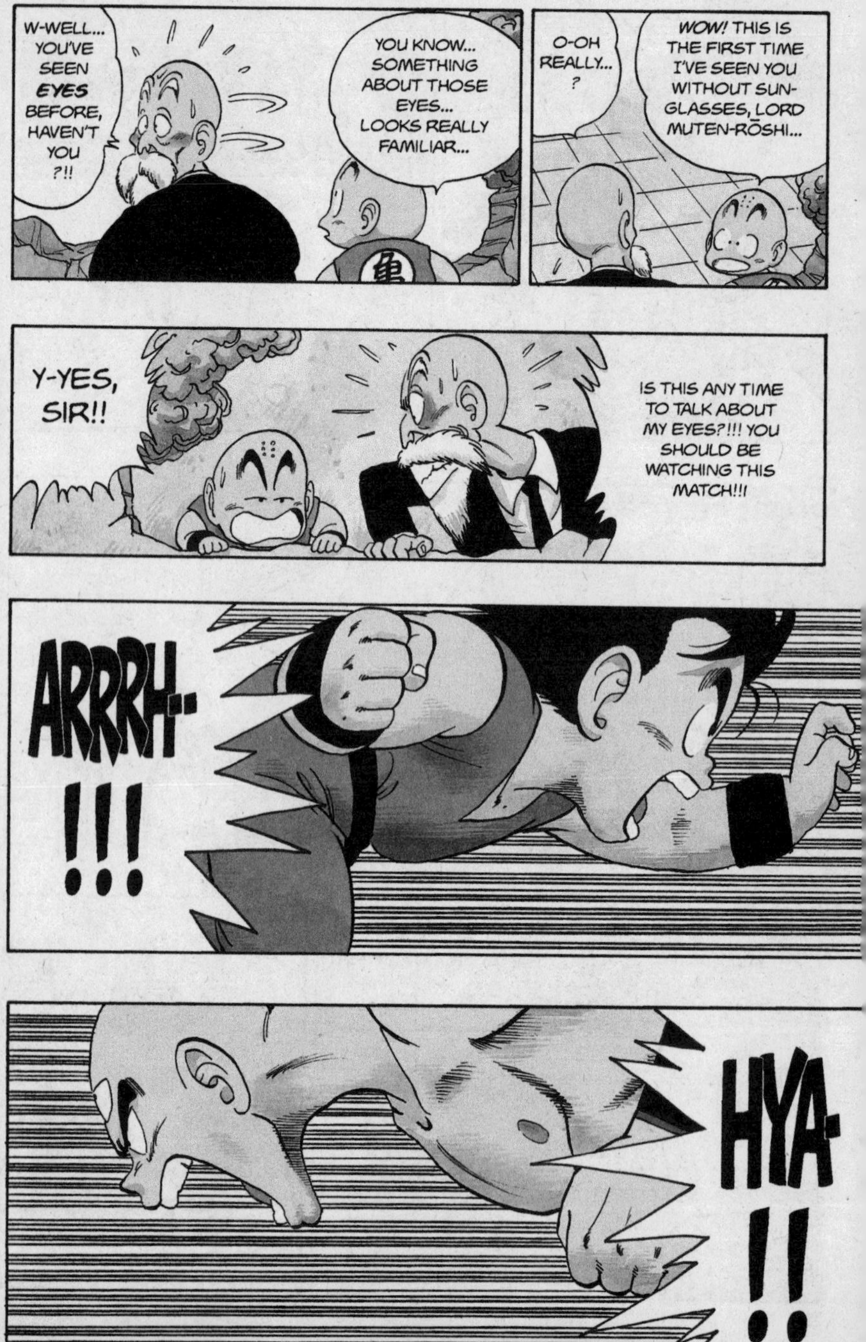
WOW! THIS IS THE FIRST TIME I'VE SEEN YOU WITHOUT SUN-GLASSES, LORD MUTEN-RŌSHI...
O-OH REALLY... ?
YOU KNOW... SOMETHING ABOUT THOSE EYES... LOOKS REALLY FAMILIAR...
W-WELL... YOU'VE SEEN EYES BEFORE, HAVEN'T YOU ?!!
IS THIS ANY TIME TO TALK ABOUT MY EYES?!!! YOU SHOULD BE WATCHING THIS MATCH!!!
Y-YES, SIR!!
ARRRH-!!!
HYA-!!

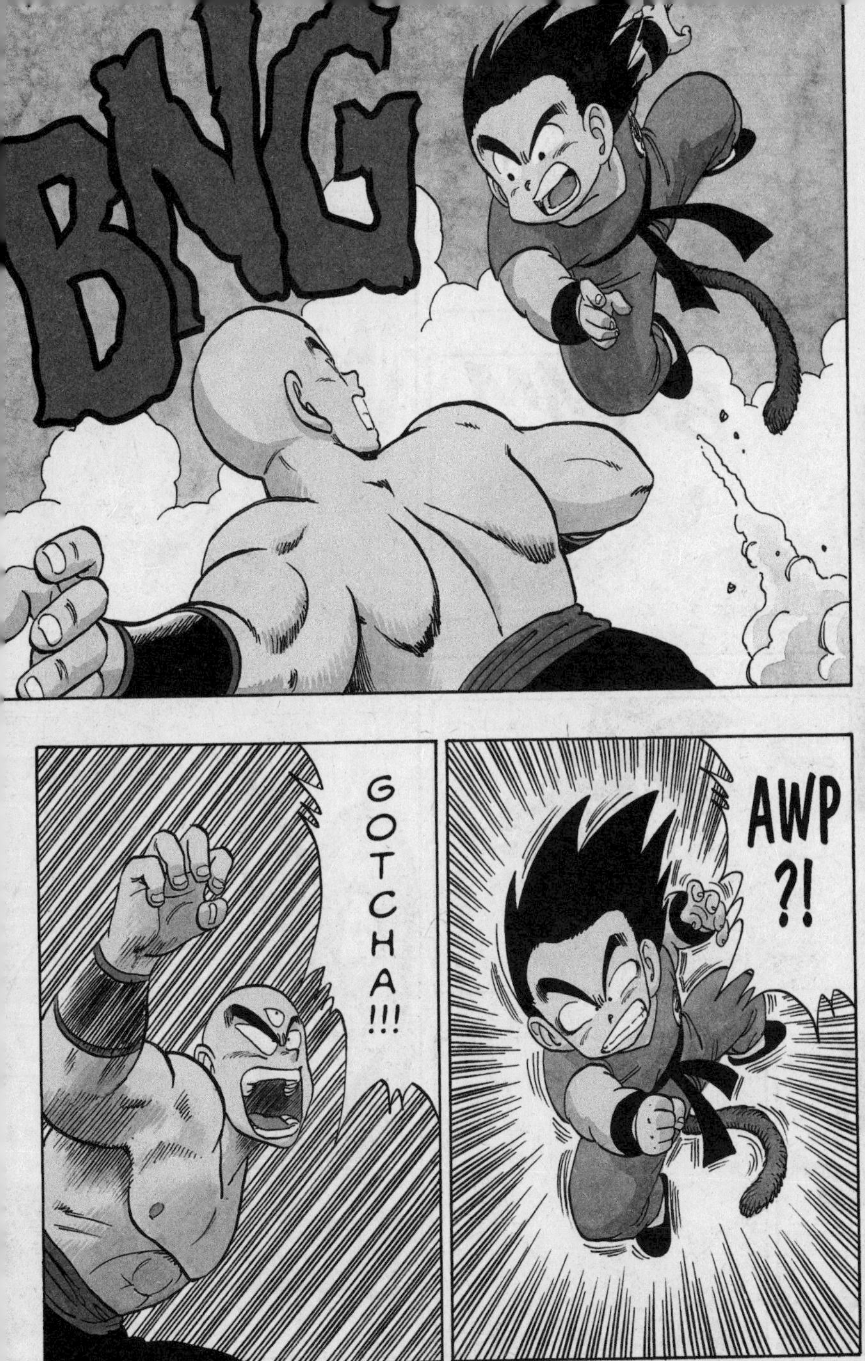
BNG
AWP ?!
GOTCHA!!!

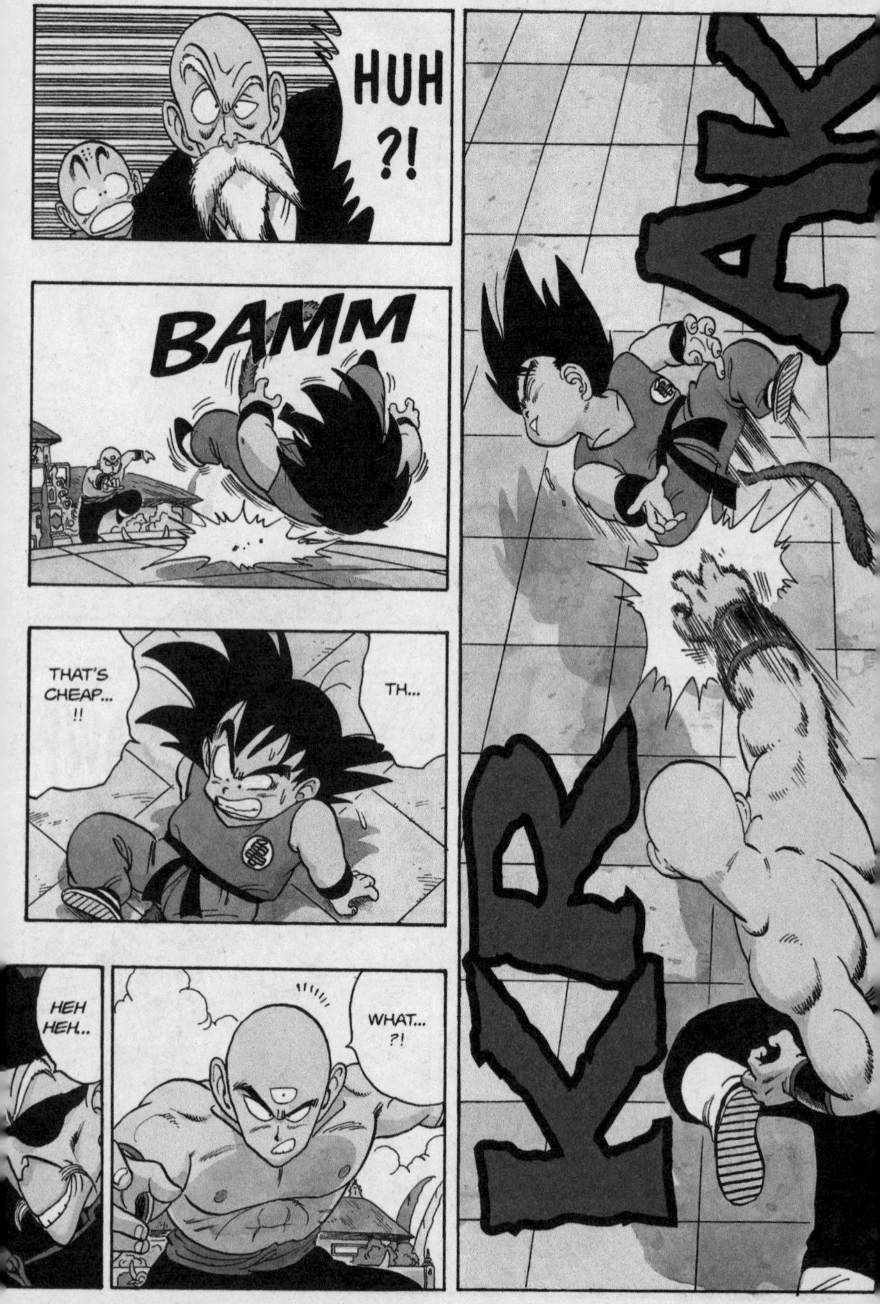
KRAK
HUH ?!
BAMM
TH...
THAT'S CHEAP... !!
WHAT... ?!
HEH HEH..

Tale 131 • Tsuru-Sen'nin

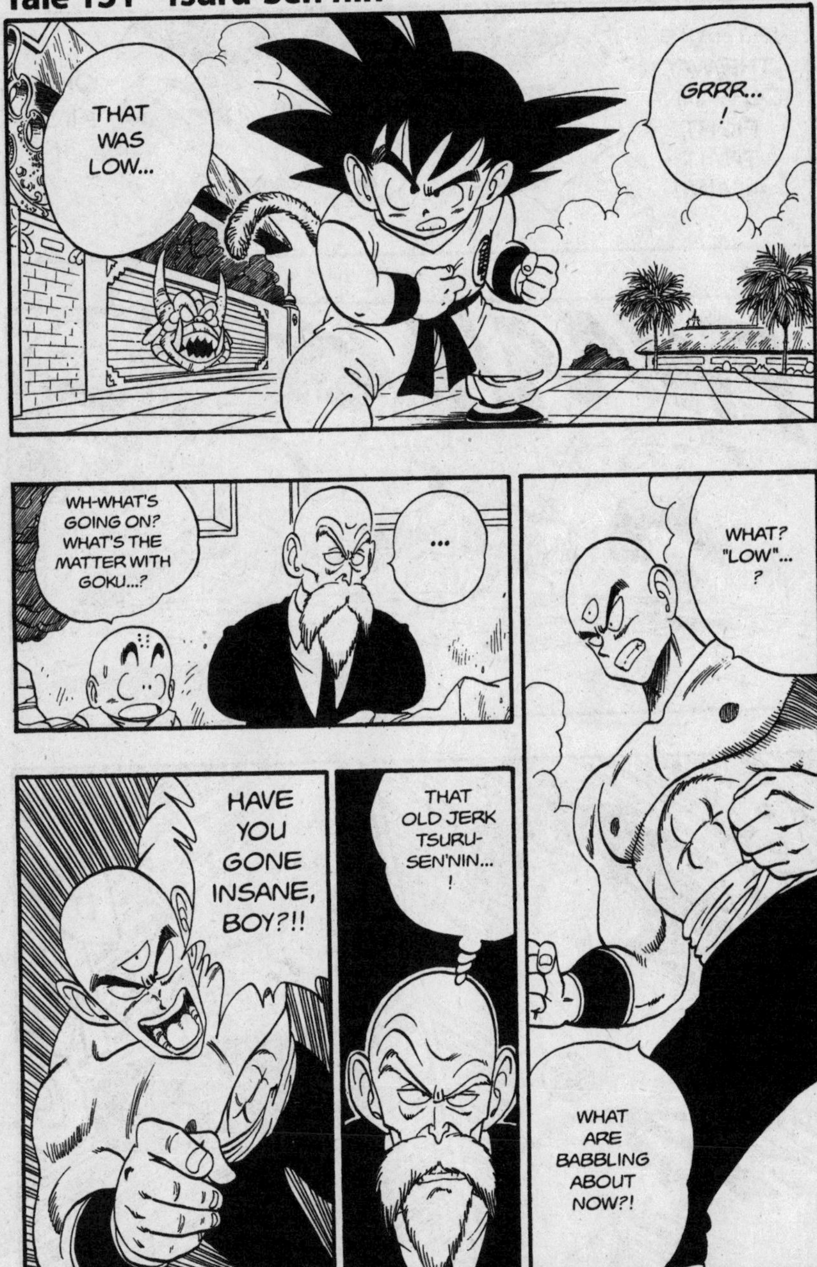
GRRR... !
THAT WAS LOW...
WHAT? "LOW"... ?
WHAT ARE BABBLING ABOUT NOW?!
...
WH-WHAT'S GOING ON? WHAT'S THE MATTER WITH GOKU...?
THAT OLD JERK TSURU-SEN'NIN... !
HAVE YOU GONE INSANE, BOY?!!

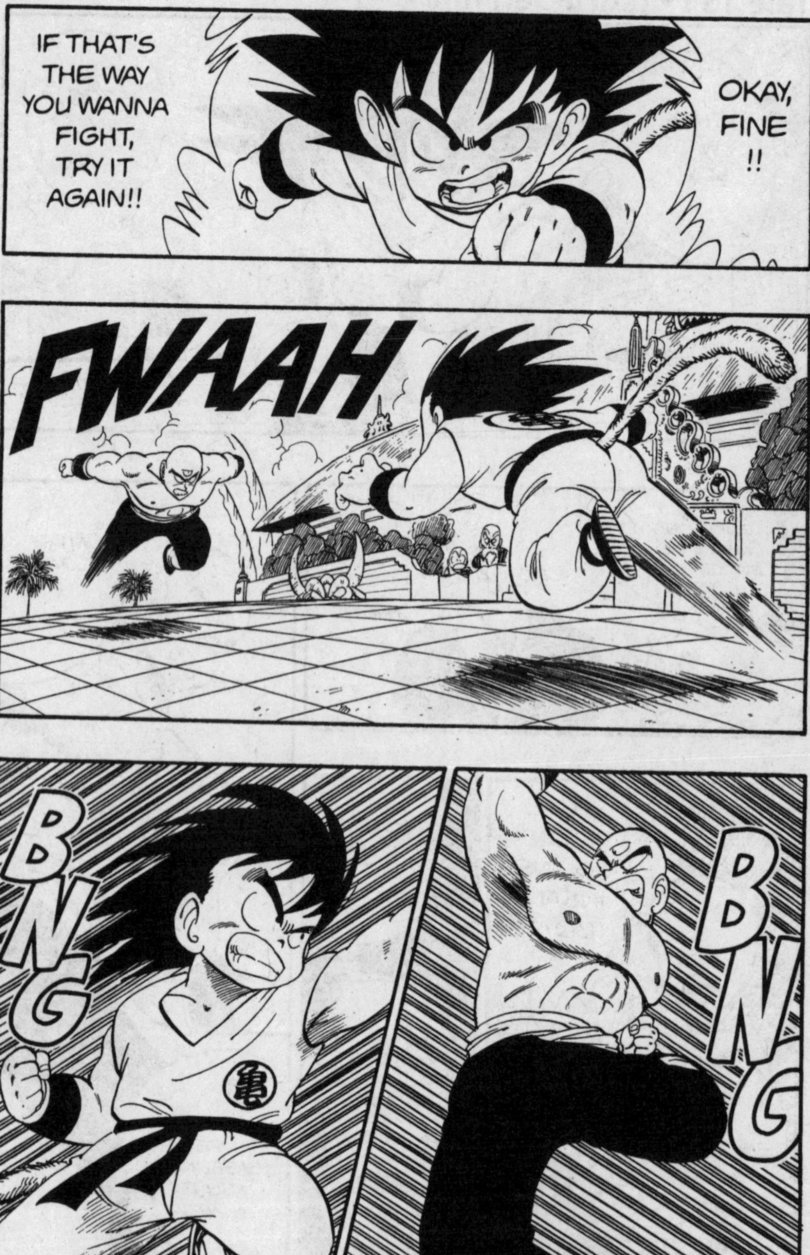
OKAY, FINE !!
IF THAT'S THE WAY YOU WANNA FIGHT, TRY IT AGAIN!!
FWAAH
BNG
BNG

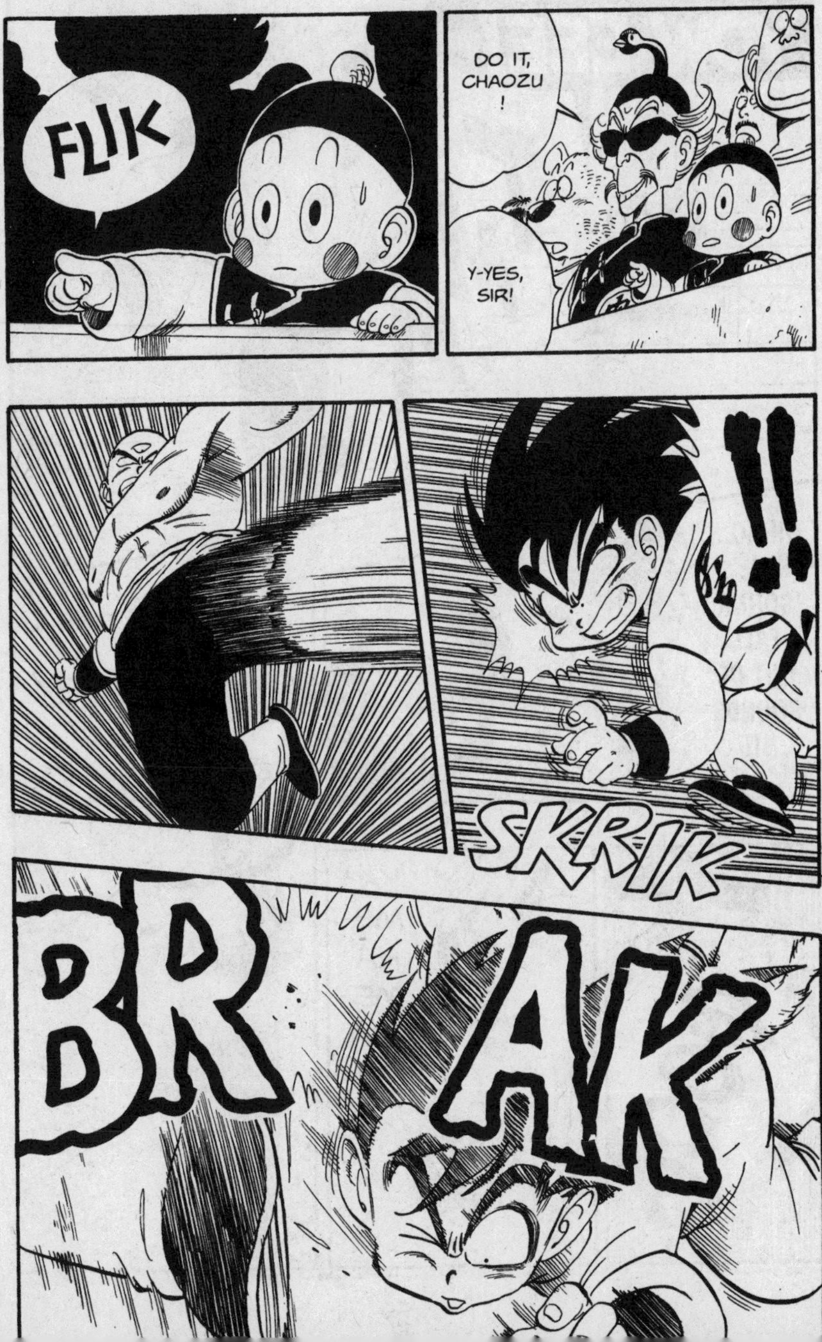
DO IT, CHAOZU!
Y-YES, SIR!
FLIK
!!
SKRIK
BRAK

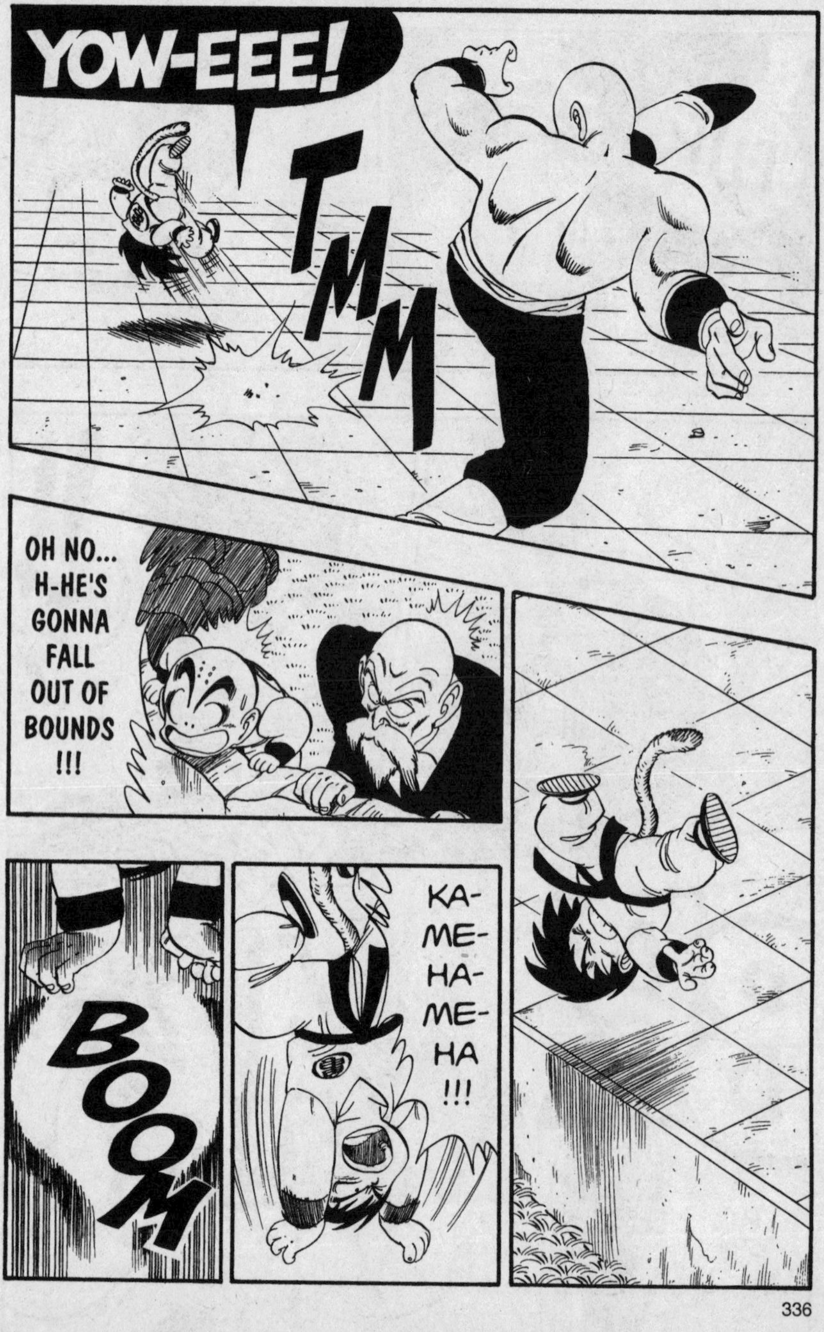
YOW-EEE!
TMM
OH NO... H-HE'S GONNA FALL OUT OF BOUNDS !!!
KA-ME-HA-ME-HA !!!
BOOM

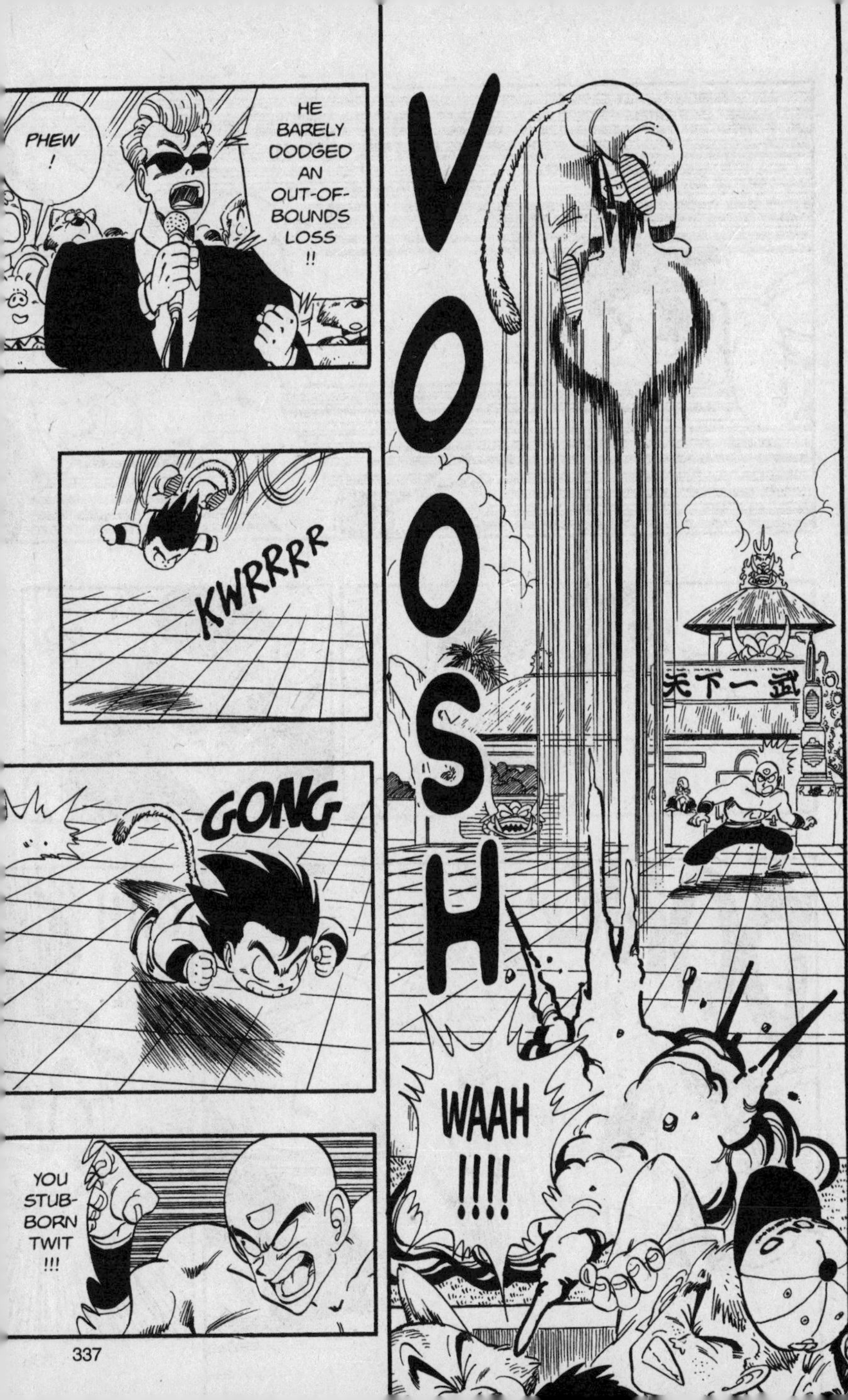
VOOOSH
WAAH !!!!
PHEW !
HE BARELY DODGED AN OUT-OF-BOUNDS LOSS !!
KWRRRR
GONG
YOU STUBBORN TWIT !!!

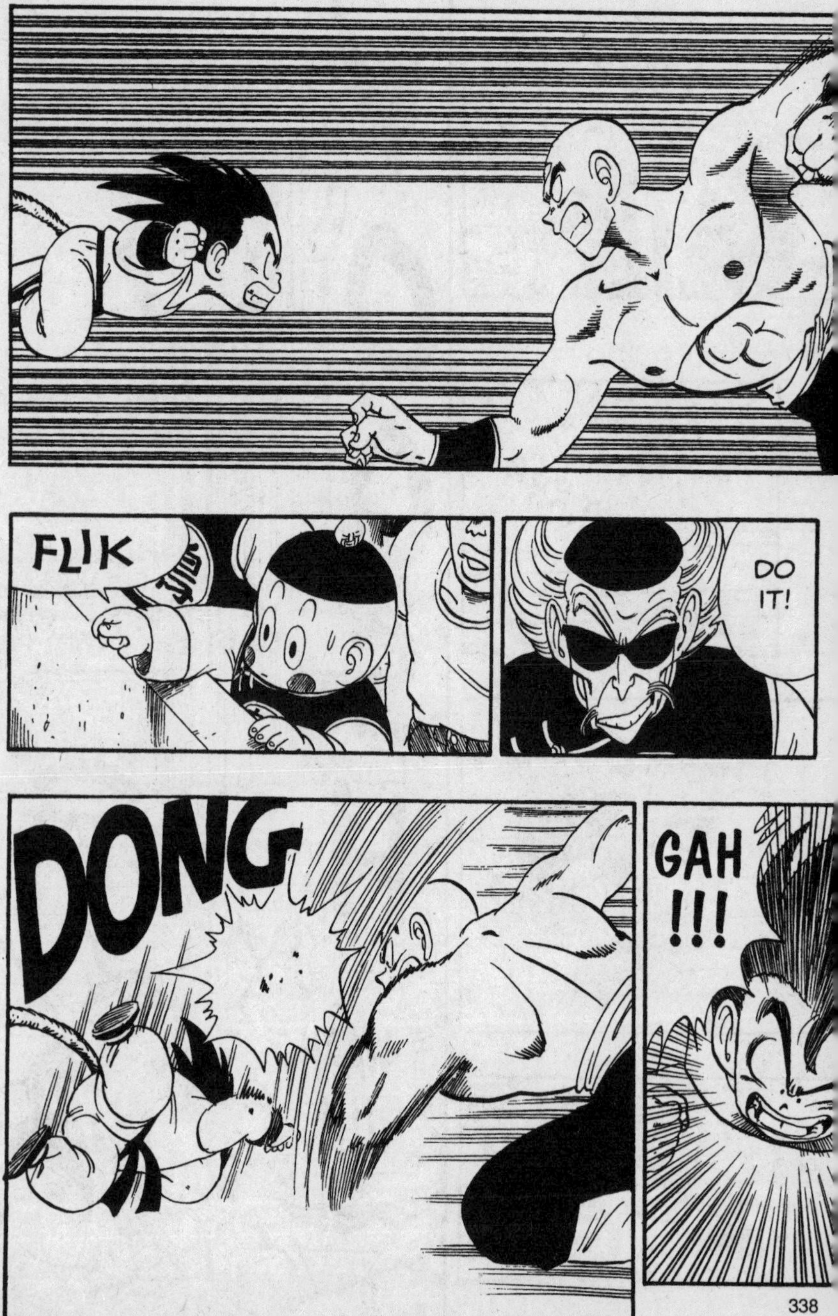
DO IT!
FLIK
GAH!!!
DONG

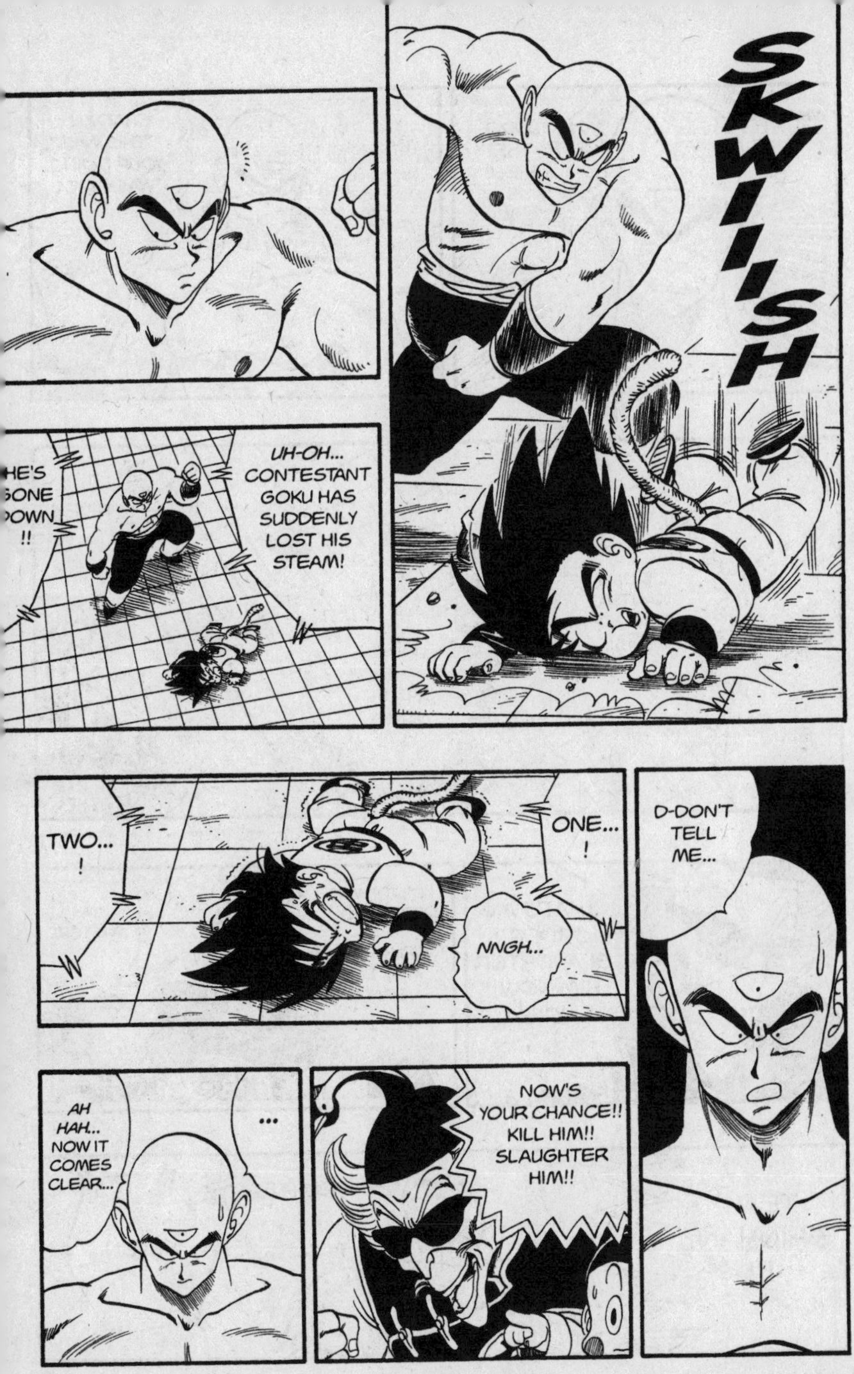
SKWIIISH
UH-OH... CONTESTANT GOKU HAS SUDDENLY LOST HIS STEAM!
HE'S GONE DOWN !!
D-DON'T TELL ME...
ONE... !
NNGH...
TWO... !
NOW'S YOUR CHANCE!! KILL HIM!! SLAUGHTER HIM!!
...
AH HAH... NOW IT COMES CLEAR...

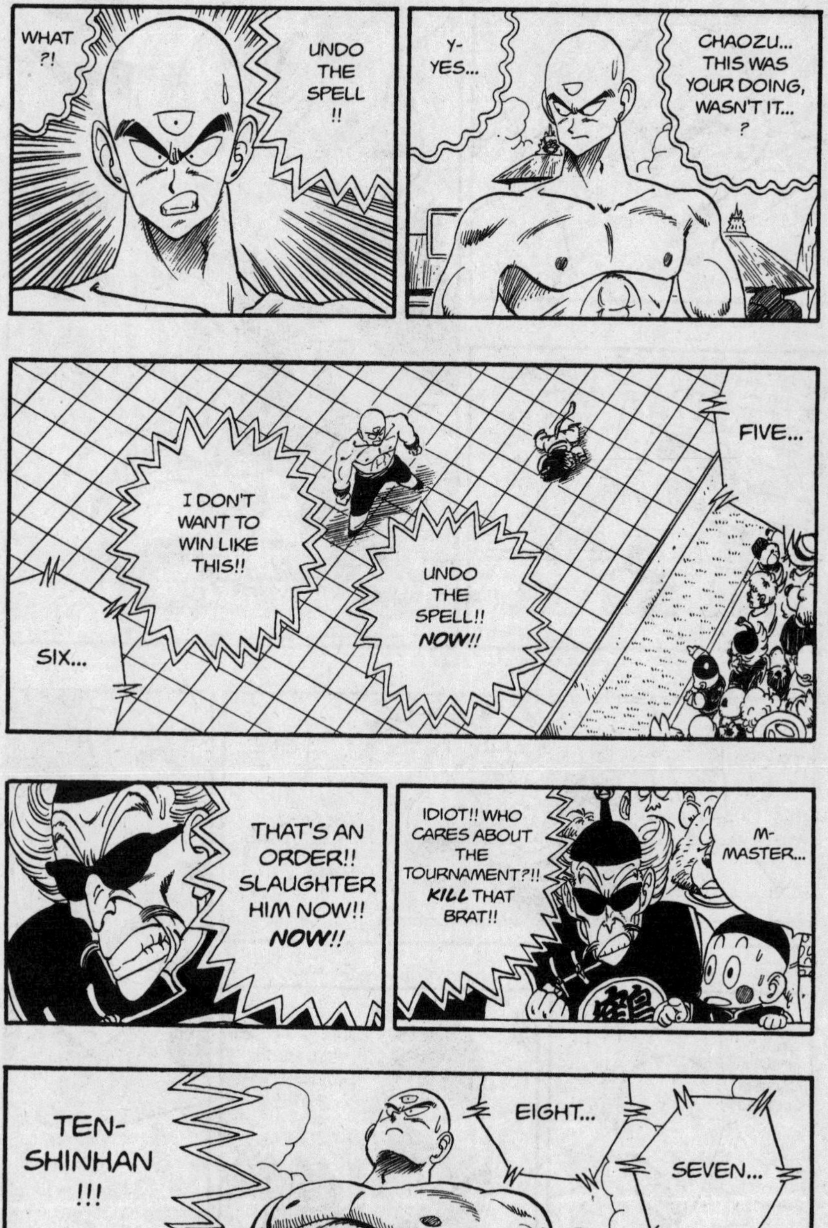
CHAOZU... THIS WAS YOUR DOING, WASN'T IT...?
Y-YES...
WHAT?!
UNDO THE SPELL!!
FIVE...
I DON'T WANT TO WIN LIKE THIS!!
UNDO THE SPELL!! *NOW!!*
SIX...
M-MASTER...
IDIOT!! WHO CARES ABOUT THE TOURNAMENT?!! *KILL* THAT BRAT!!
THAT'S AN ORDER!! SLAUGHTER HIM NOW!! *NOW!!*
SEVEN...
EIGHT...
TEN-SHINHAN!!!

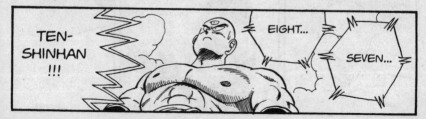

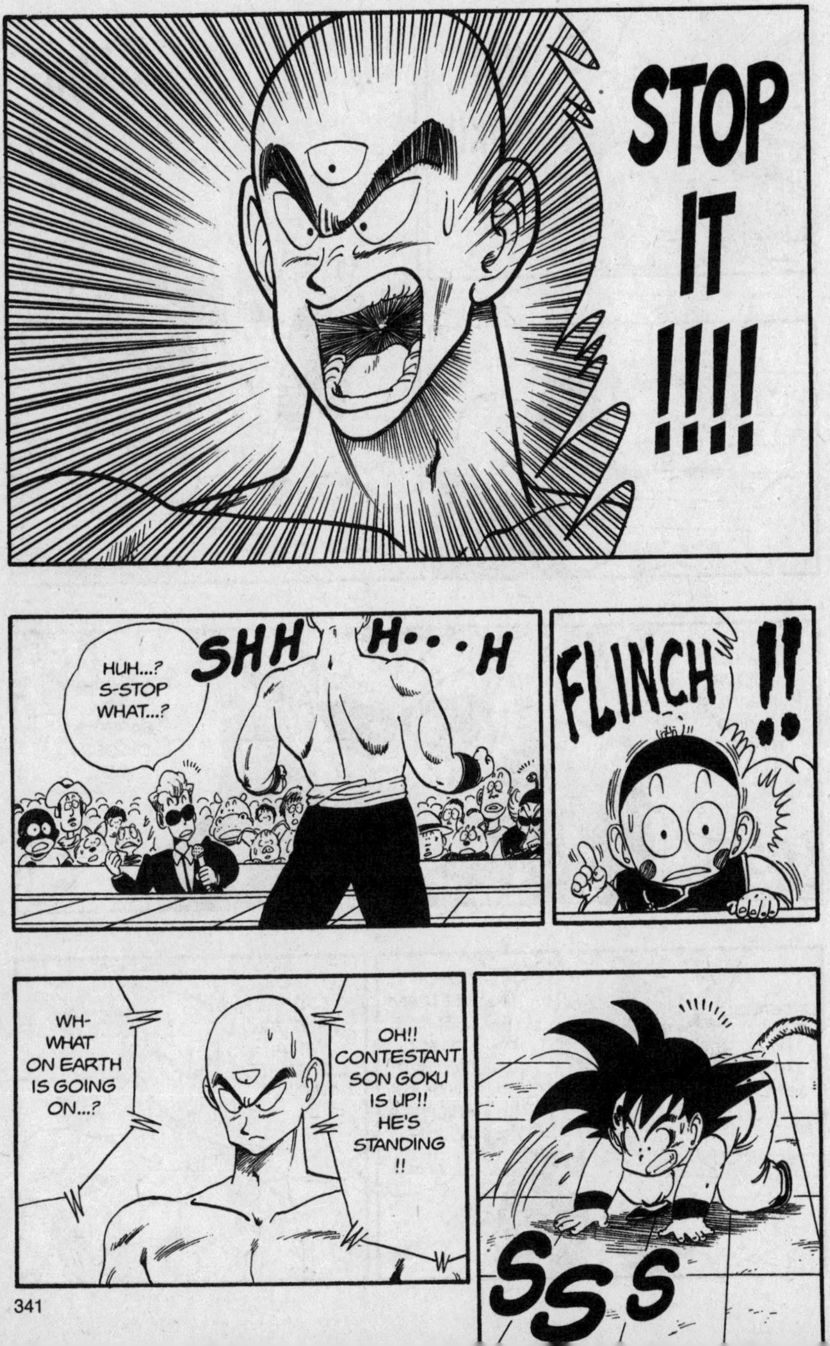
STOP IT!!!!
FLINCH!!
SHHH...H
HUH...? S-STOP WHAT...?
SSS
OH!! CONTESTANT SON GOKU IS UP!! HE'S STANDING!!
WH-WHAT ON EARTH IS GOING ON...?

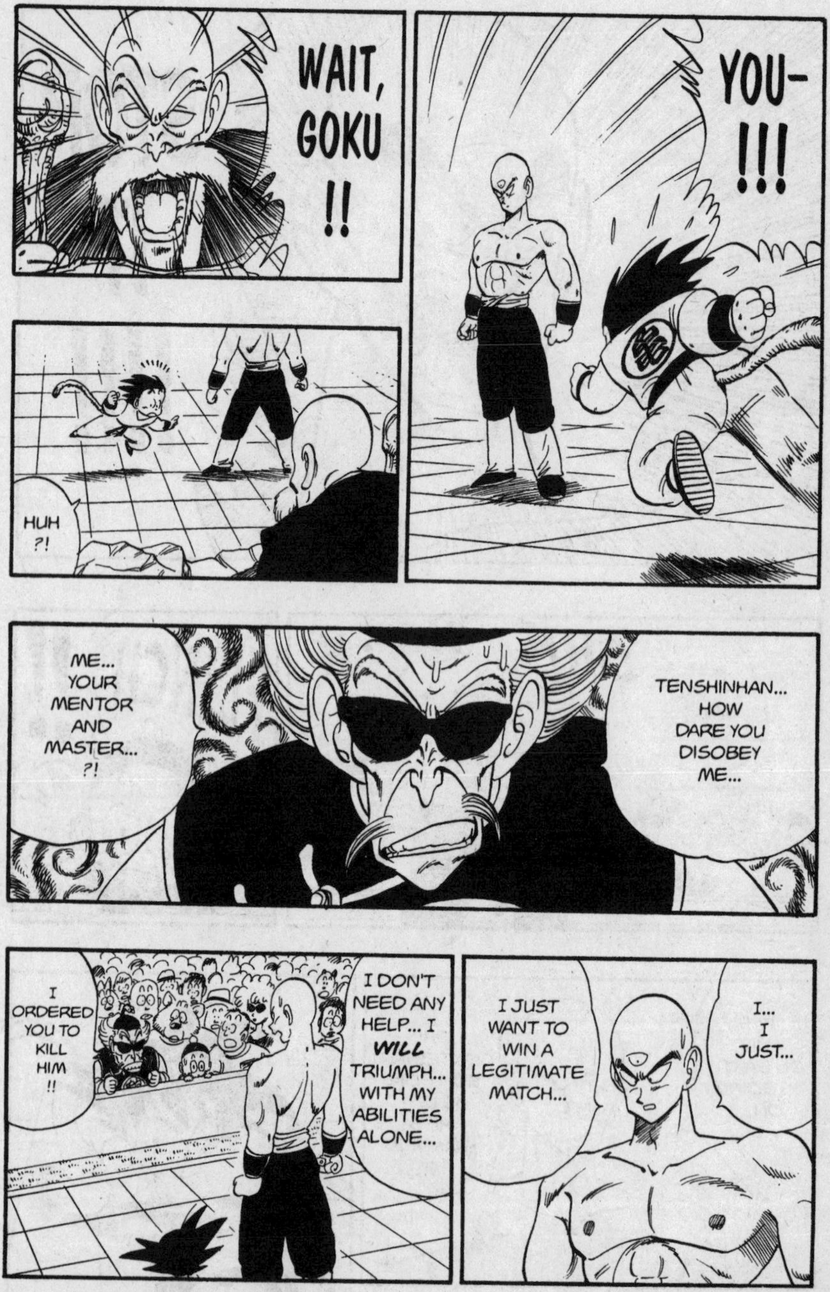

YOU- !!!
WAIT, GOKU !!
HUH ?!
TENSHINHAN... HOW DARE YOU DISOBEY ME...
ME... YOUR MENTOR AND MASTER... ?!
I... I JUST...
I JUST WANT TO WIN A LEGITIMATE MATCH...
I DON'T NEED ANY HELP... I *WILL* TRIUMPH... WITH MY ABILITIES ALONE...
I ORDERED YOU TO KILL HIM !!

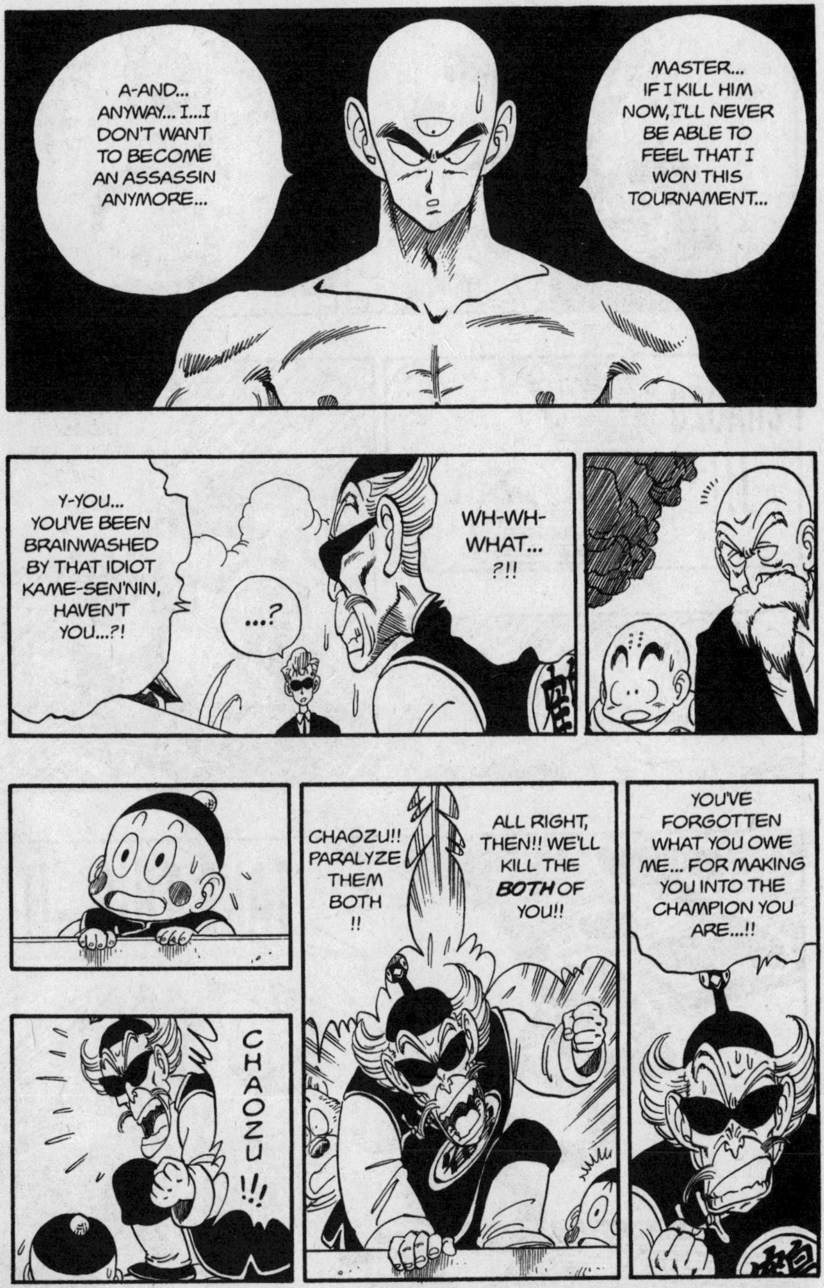
MASTER... IF I KILL HIM NOW, I'LL NEVER BE ABLE TO FEEL THAT I WON THIS TOURNAMENT...
A-AND... ANYWAY... I...I DON'T WANT TO BECOME AN ASSASSIN ANYMORE...
WH-WH-WHAT... ?!!
...?
Y-YOU... YOU'VE BEEN BRAINWASHED BY THAT IDIOT KAME-SEN'NIN, HAVEN'T YOU...?!
YOU'VE FORGOTTEN WHAT YOU OWE ME... FOR MAKING YOU INTO THE CHAMPION YOU ARE...!!
ALL RIGHT, THEN!! WE'LL KILL THE BOTH OF YOU!!
CHAOZU!! PARALYZE THEM BOTH !!
CHAOZU !!!

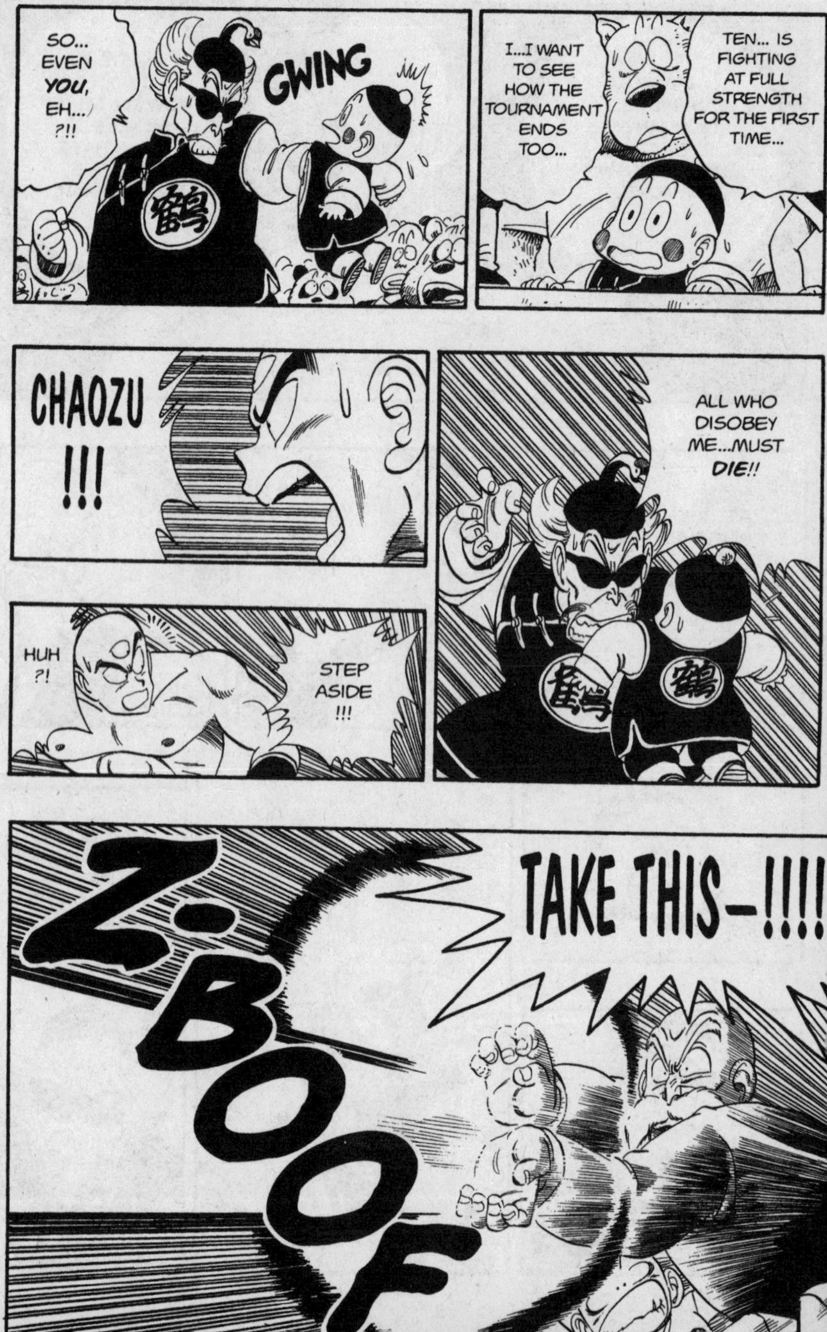
TEN... IS FIGHTING AT FULL STRENGTH FOR THE FIRST TIME...
I...I WANT TO SEE HOW THE TOURNAMENT ENDS TOO...
GWING
SO... EVEN YOU, EH... ?!!
ALL WHO DISOBEY ME...MUST DIE!!
CHAOZU !!!
STEP ASIDE !!!
HUH ?!
TAKE THIS-!!!!
Z-BOOF

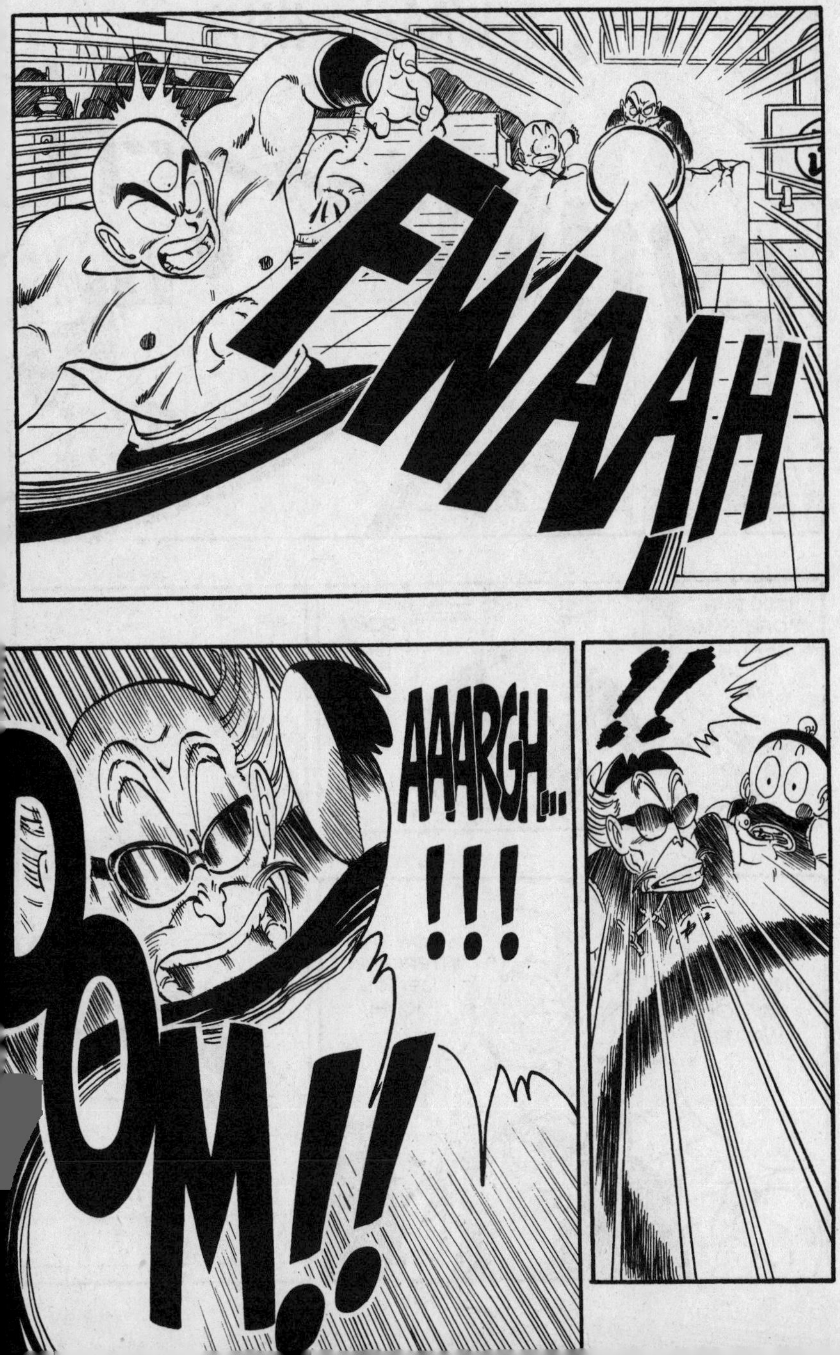
FWAAH
!!
AAARGH...!!!
OOM!!

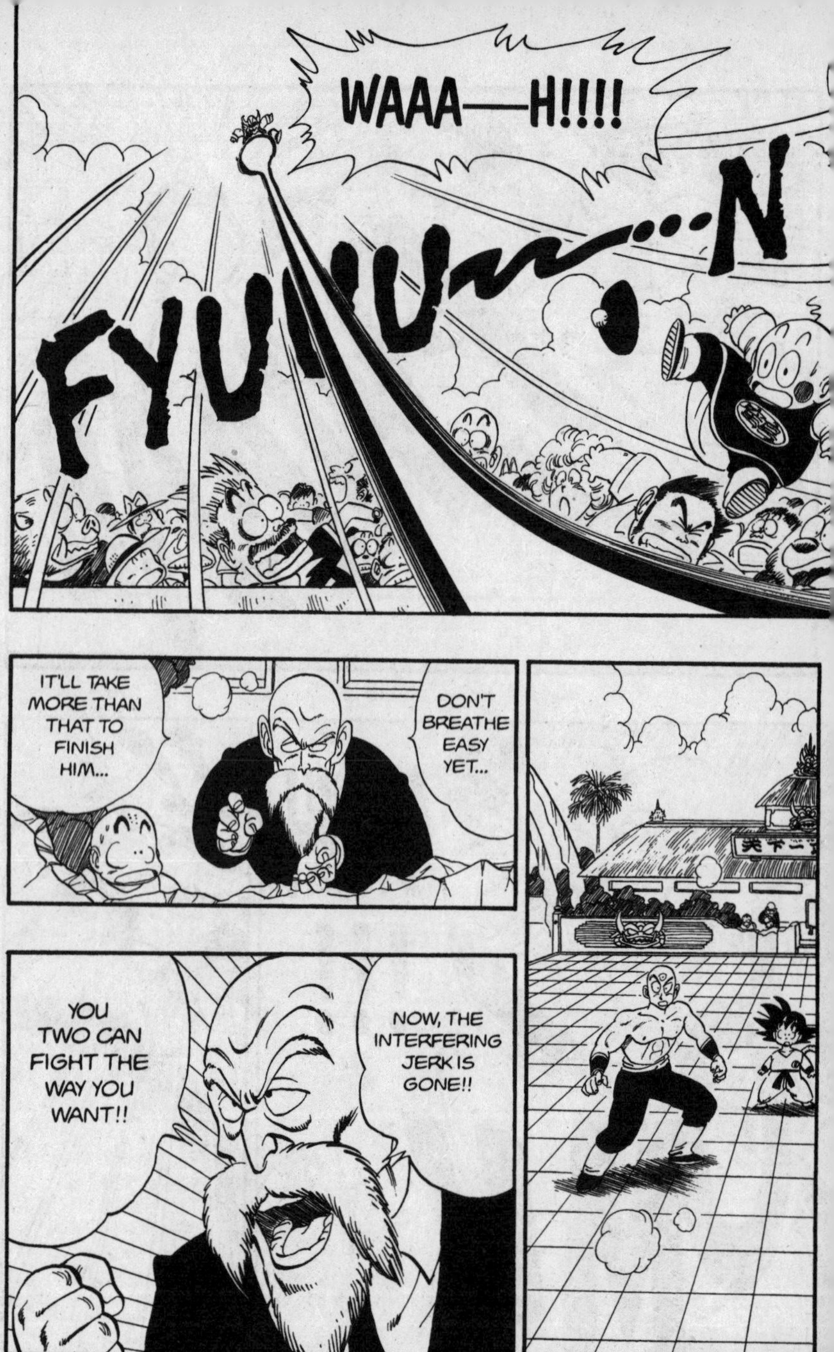
WAAA—H!!!!
FYUUUU...N
DON'T BREATHE EASY YET...
IT'LL TAKE MORE THAN THAT TO FINISH HIM...
NOW, THE INTERFERING JERK IS GONE!!
YOU TWO CAN FIGHT THE WAY YOU WANT!!

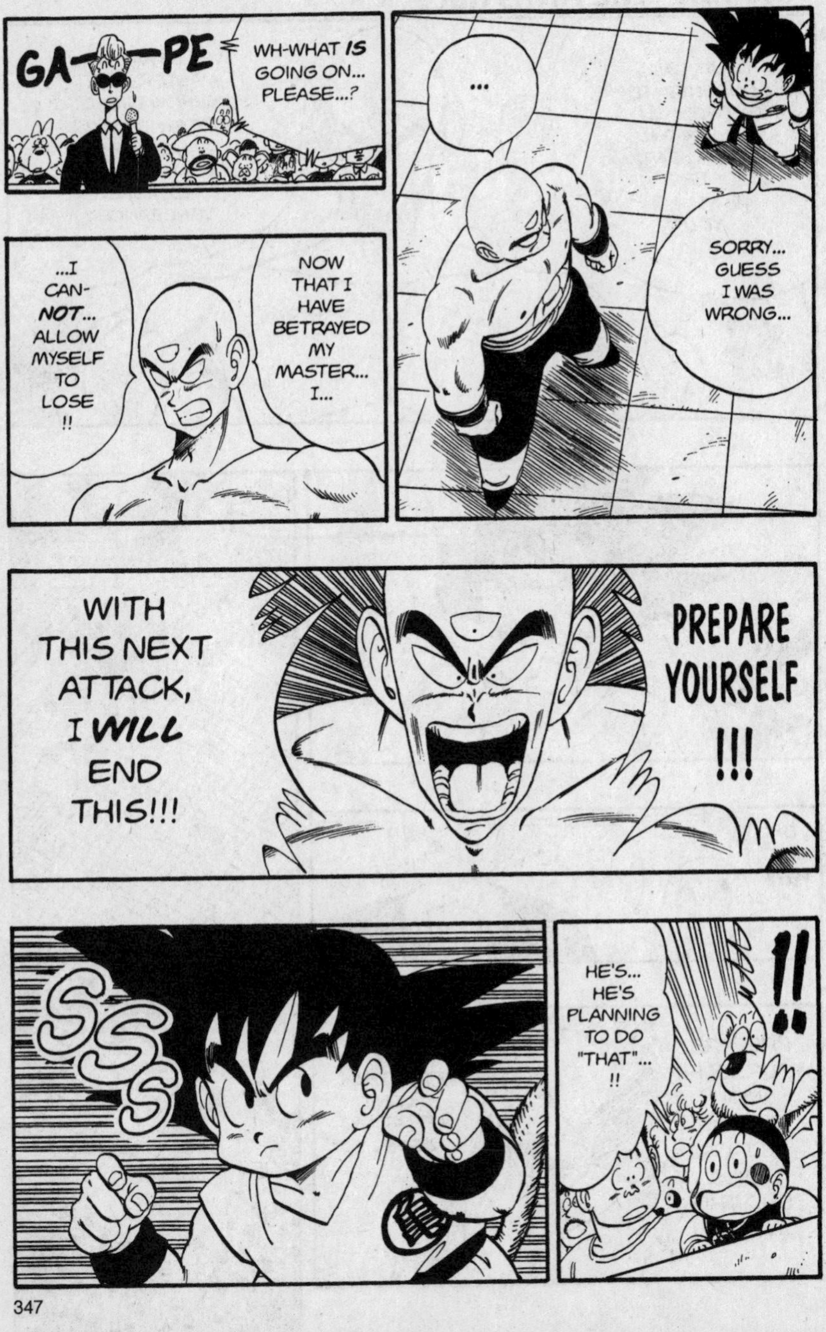
...
SORRY... GUESS I WAS WRONG...
GA—PE
WH-WHAT IS GOING ON... PLEASE...?
NOW THAT I HAVE BETRAYED MY MASTER... I...
...I CAN-NOT... ALLOW MYSELF TO LOSE !!
PREPARE YOURSELF !!!
WITH THIS NEXT ATTACK, I WILL END THIS!!!
!!
HE'S... HE'S PLANNING TO DO "THAT"... !!
SSS

Tale 132 • The Arms Race

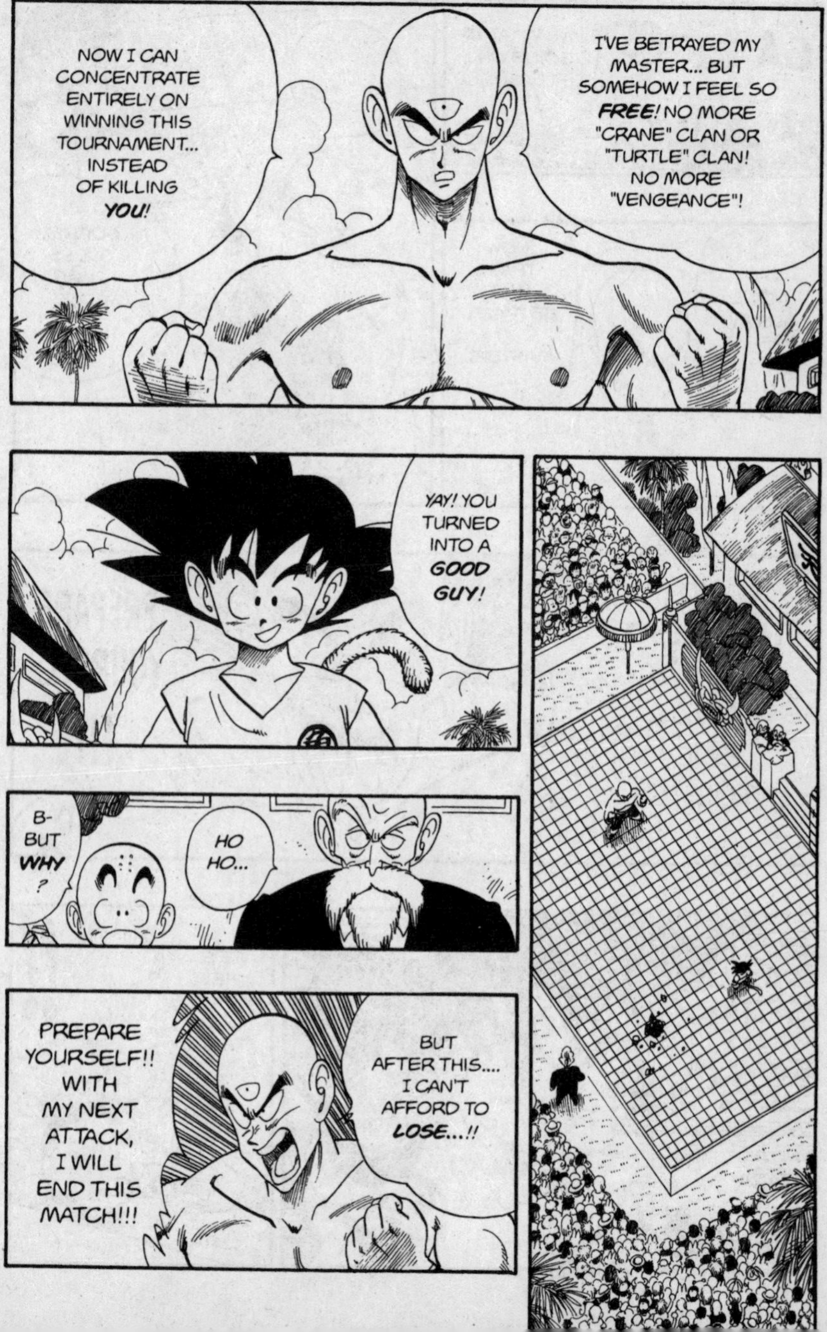

I'VE BETRAYED MY MASTER... BUT SOMEHOW I FEEL SO **FREE**! NO MORE "CRANE" CLAN OR "TURTLE" CLAN! NO MORE "VENGEANCE"!
NOW I CAN CONCENTRATE ENTIRELY ON WINNING THIS TOURNAMENT... INSTEAD OF KILLING **YOU**!
YAY! YOU TURNED INTO A **GOOD GUY**!
HO HO...
B-BUT **WHY**?
BUT AFTER THIS.... I CAN'T AFFORD TO **LOSE**...!!
PREPARE YOURSELF!! WITH MY NEXT ATTACK, I WILL END THIS MATCH!!!

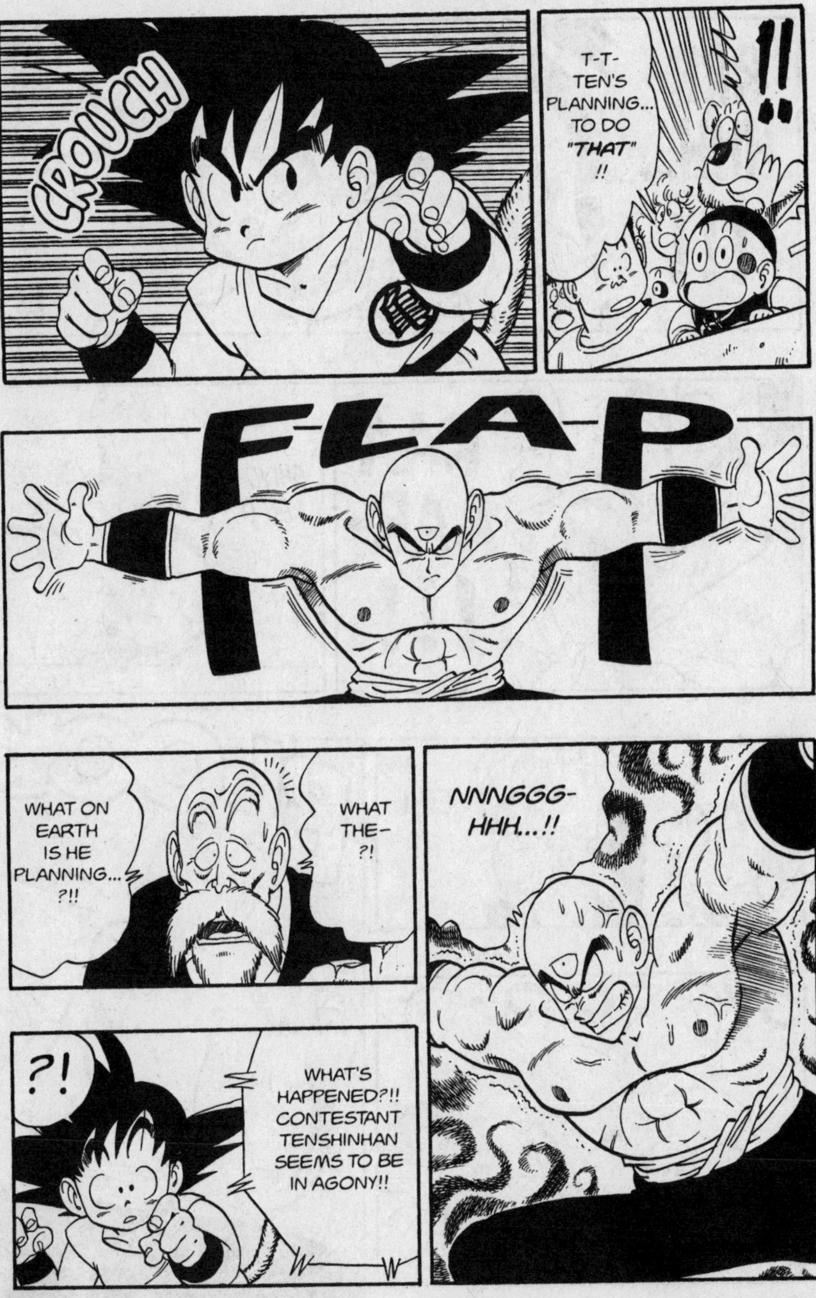
!!
T-T-TEN'S PLANNING... TO DO "THAT" !!
CROUCH
FLAP
NNNGGG-HHH...!!
WHAT THE-?!
WHAT ON EARTH IS HE PLANNING...?!!
WHAT'S HAPPENED?!! CONTESTANT TENSHINHAN SEEMS TO BE IN AGONY!!
?!

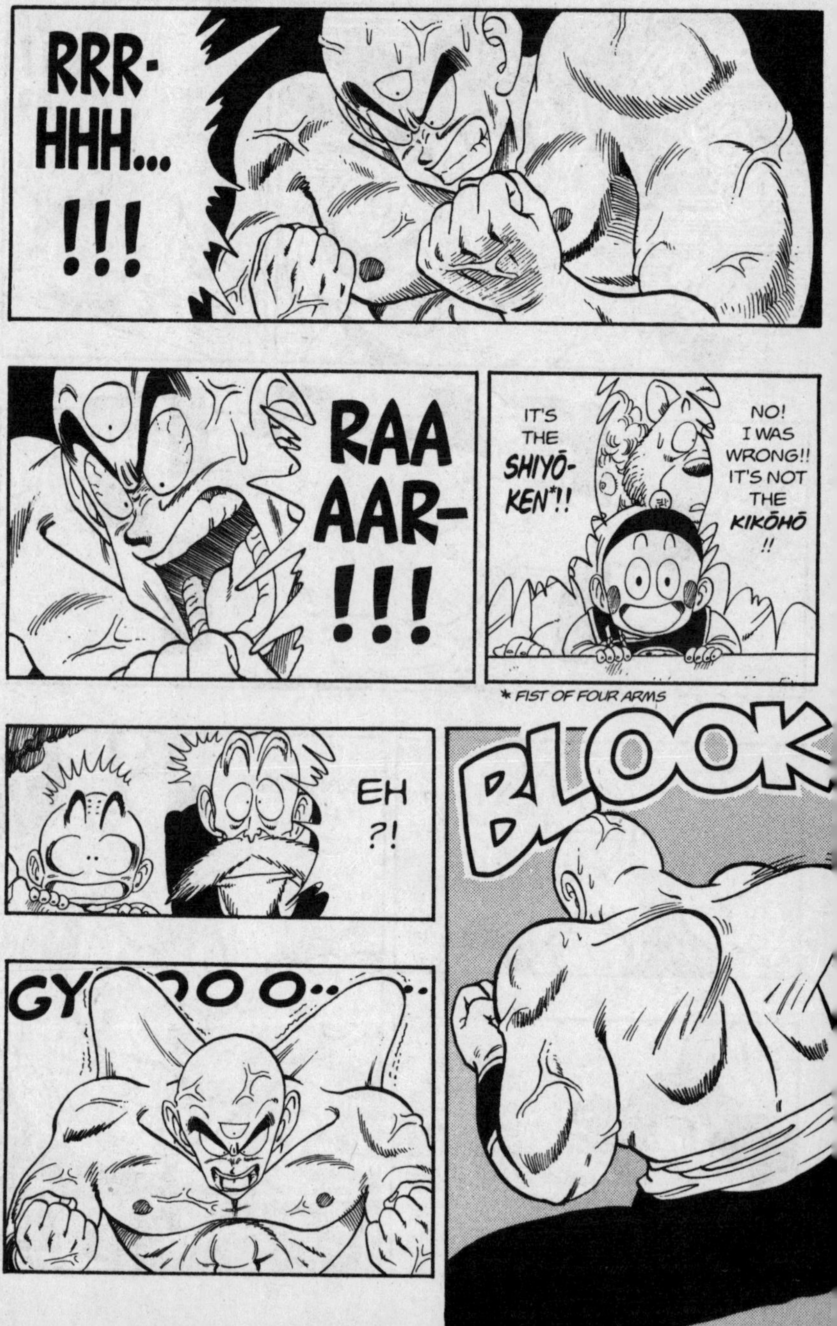
RRR-HHH... !!!
NO! I WAS WRONG!! IT'S NOT THE KIKŌHŌ!!
IT'S THE SHIYŌ-KEN*!!
RAAAAR-!!!
* FIST OF FOUR ARMS
BLOOK
EH ?!
GY OO O.. ..

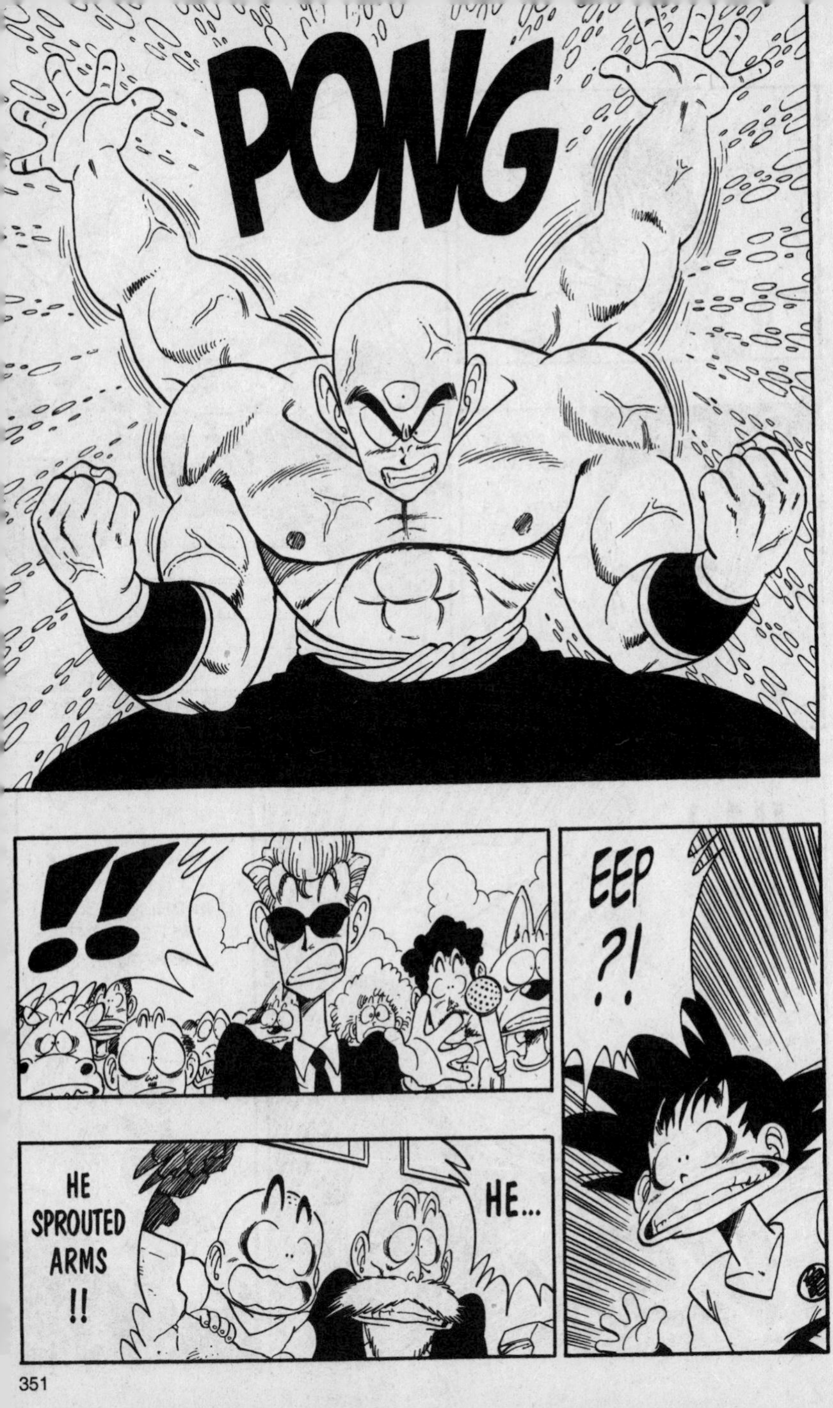
PONG
EEP ?!
!!
HE...
HE SPROUTED ARMS !!

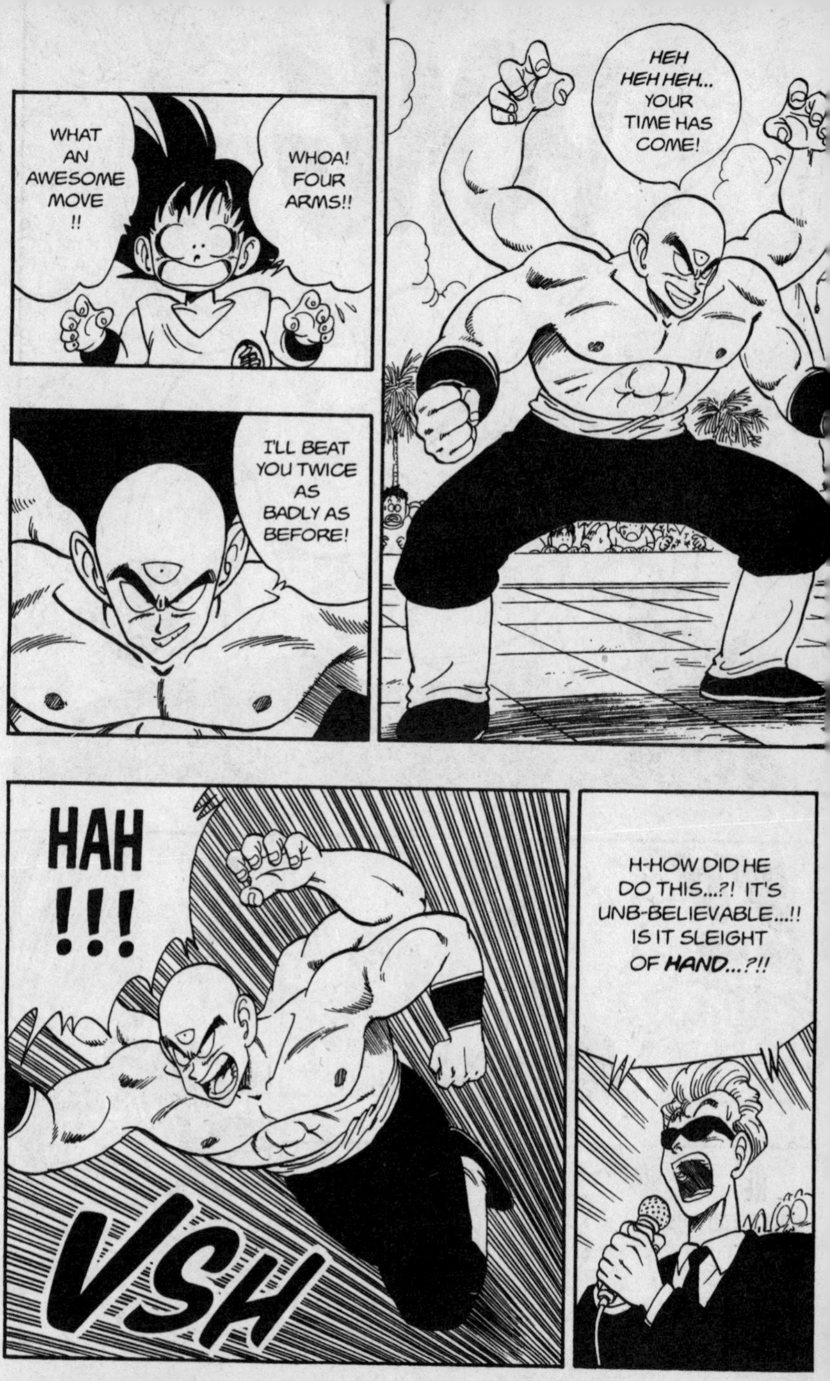
HEH HEH HEH... YOUR TIME HAS COME!
WHOA! FOUR ARMS!!
WHAT AN AWESOME MOVE !!
I'LL BEAT YOU TWICE AS BADLY AS BEFORE!
H-HOW DID HE DO THIS...?! IT'S UNB-BELIEVABLE...!! IS IT SLEIGHT OF HAND...?!!
HAH !!!
VSH

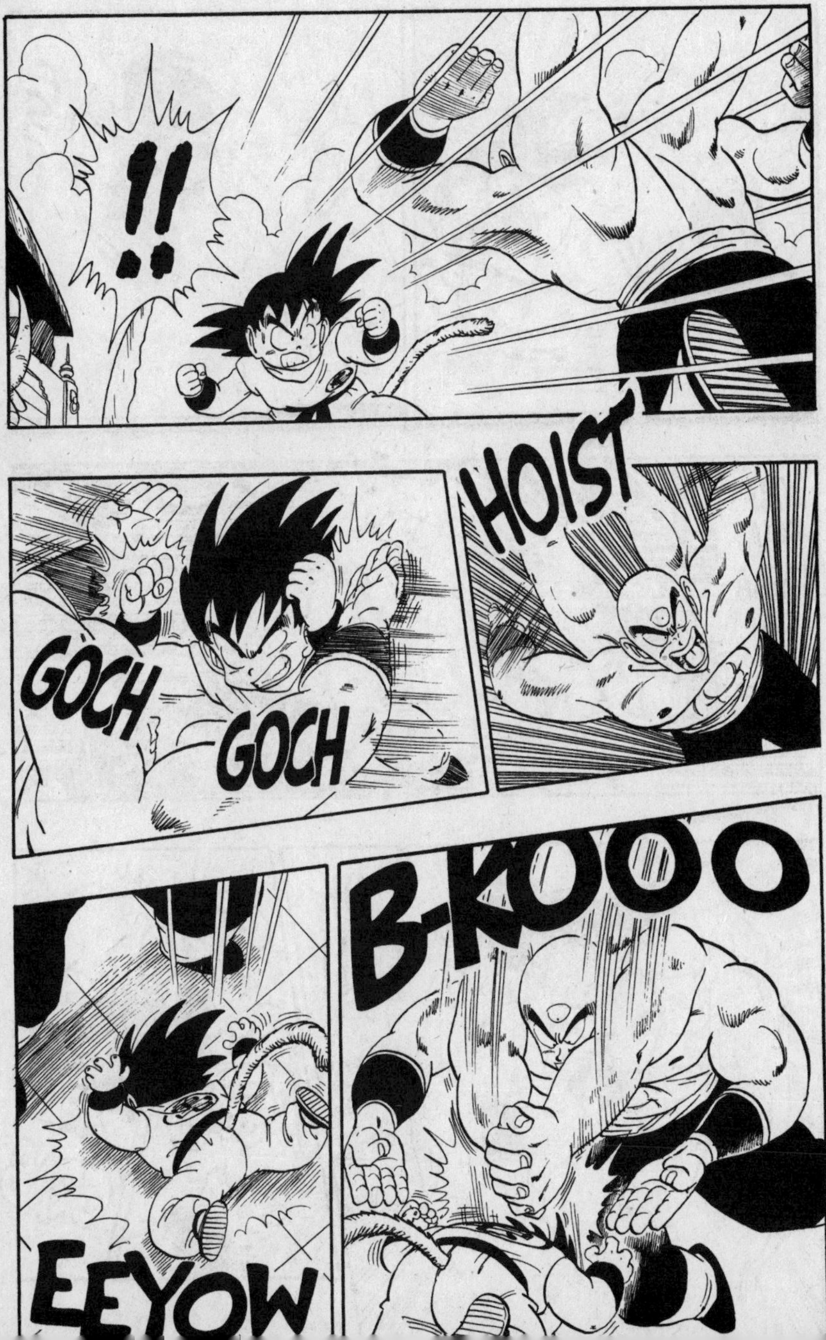
!!
HOIST
GOCH
GOCH
B-KOOO
EEYOW

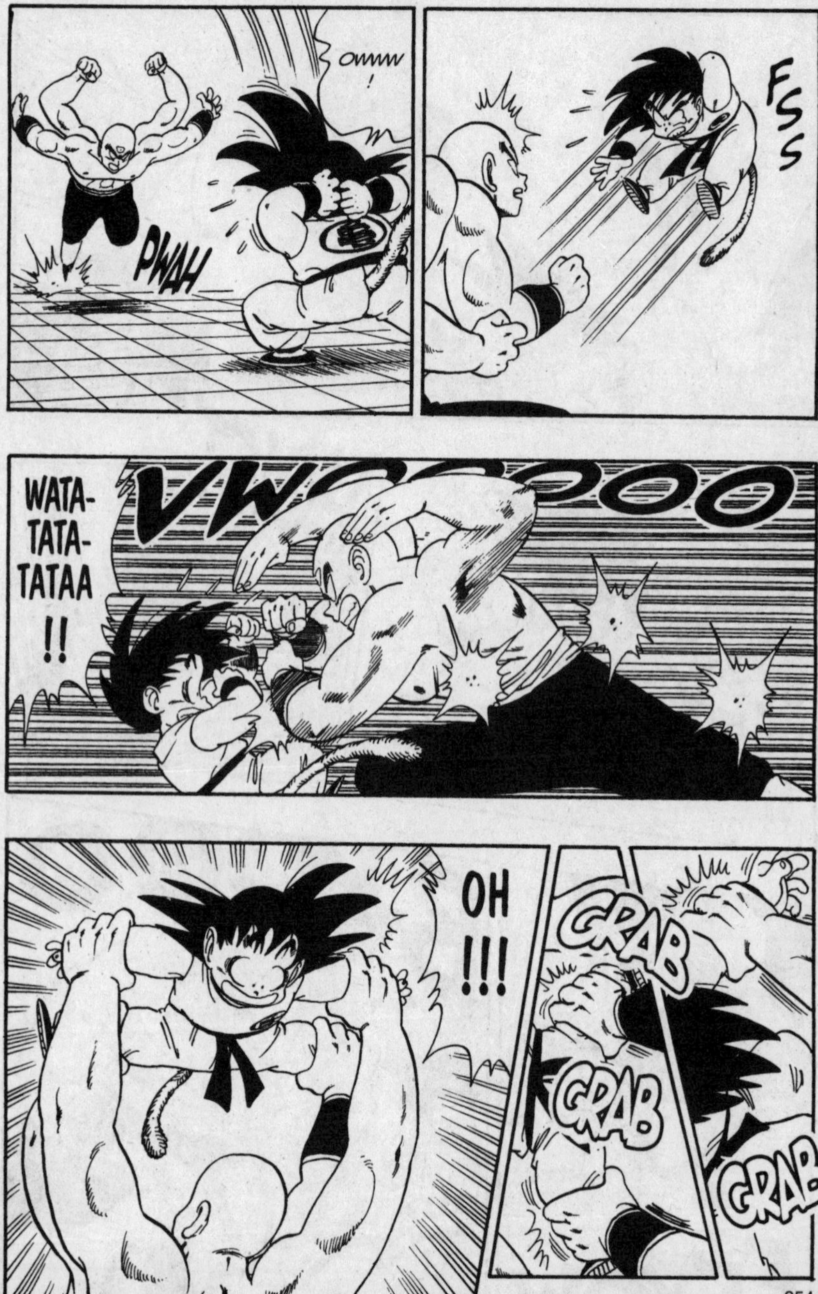
FSS
OWWW!
PWAH
VWOOOOO
WATA-TATA-TATAA!!
GRAB
GRAB
GRAB
OH!!!

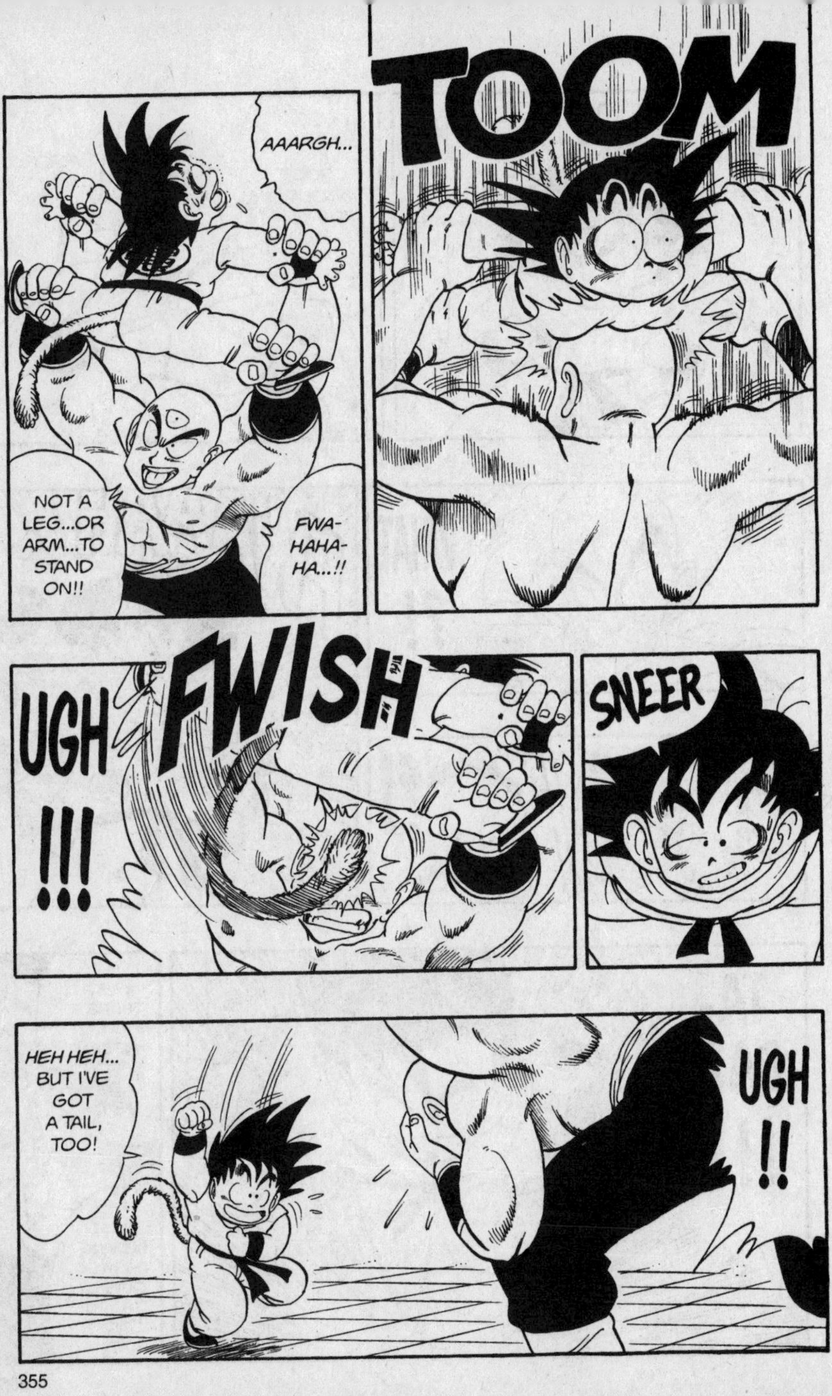
TOOM
AAARGH...
FWA-HAHA-HA...!!
NOT A LEG...OR ARM...TO STAND ON!!
SNEER
FWISH
UGH!!!
UGH!!
HEH HEH... BUT I'VE GOT A TAIL, TOO!

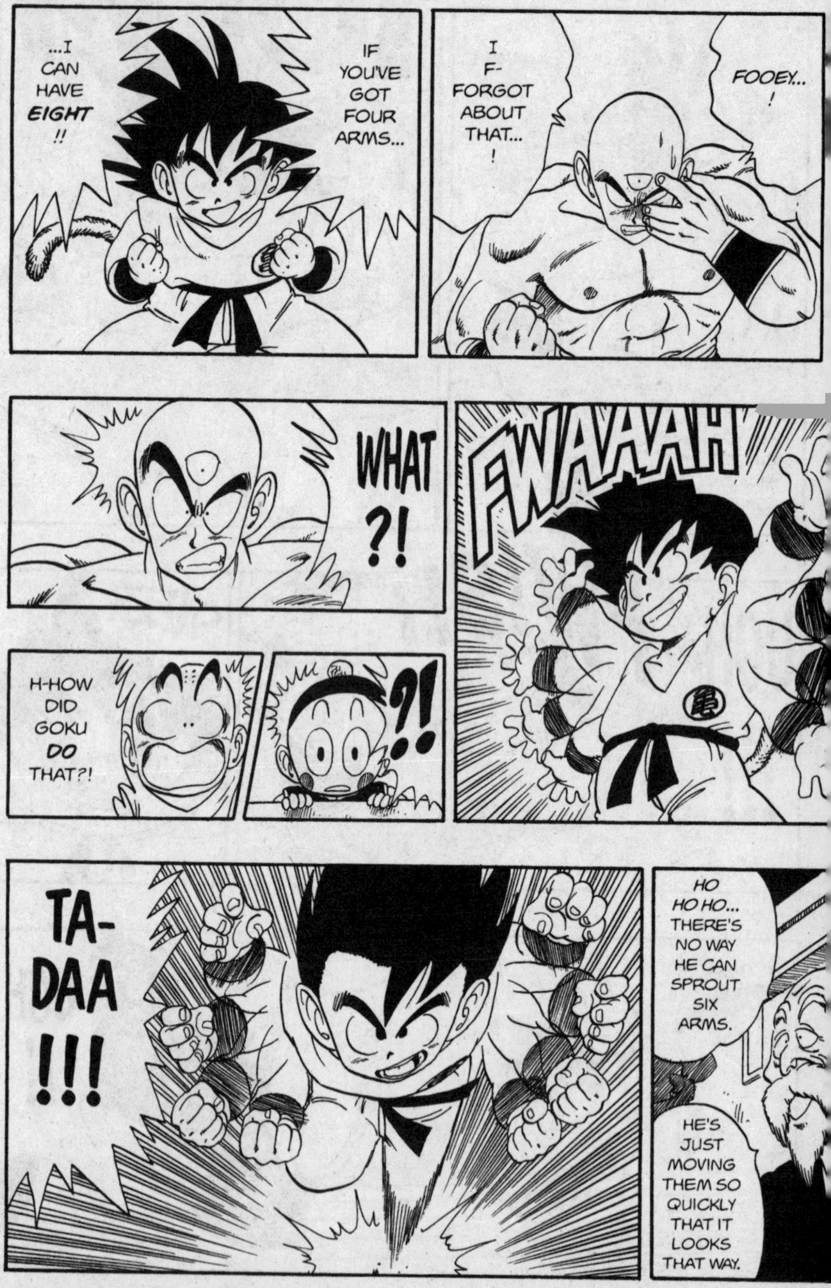
FOOEY...!
I F-FORGOT ABOUT THAT...!
IF YOU'VE GOT FOUR ARMS...
...I CAN HAVE EIGHT!!
FWAAAH
WHAT?!
?!
H-HOW DID GOKU DO THAT?!
HO HO HO... THERE'S NO WAY HE CAN SPROUT SIX ARMS.
HE'S JUST MOVING THEM SO QUICKLY THAT IT LOOKS THAT WAY.
TA-DAA!!!

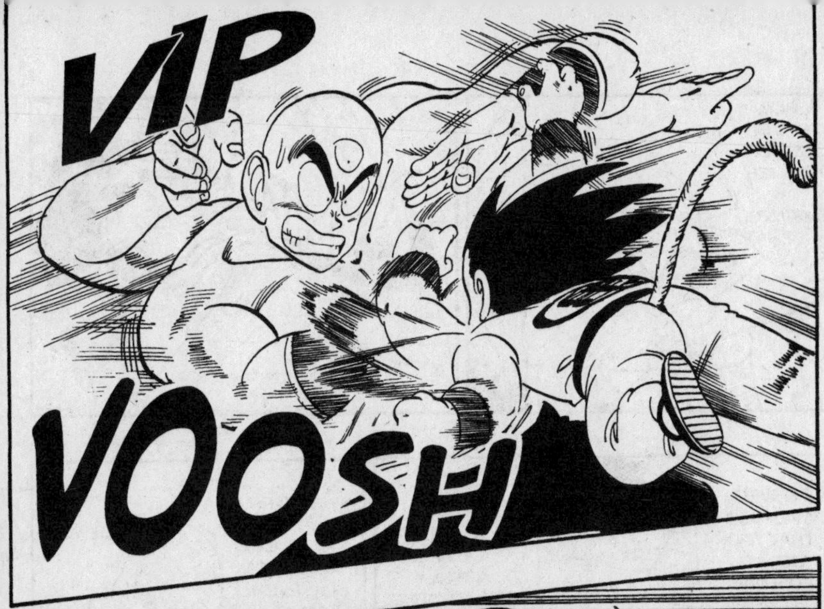
VIP
VOOSH
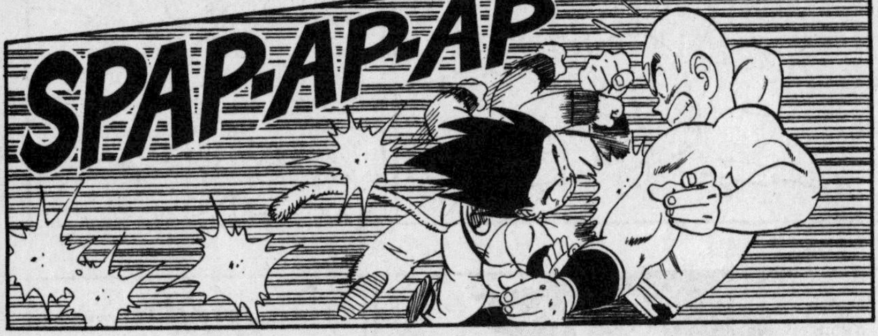
SPAP-AP-AP
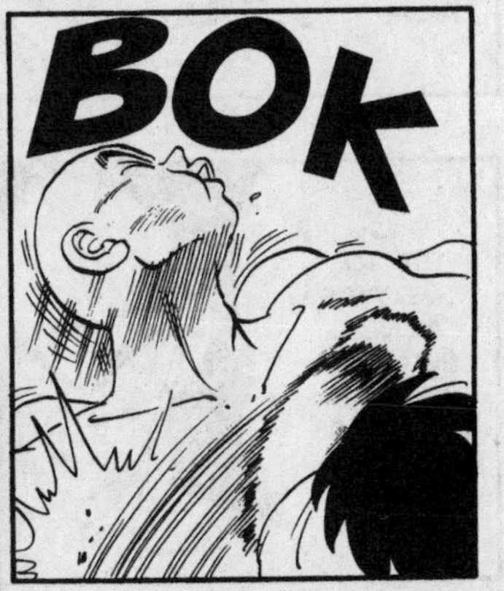
BOK
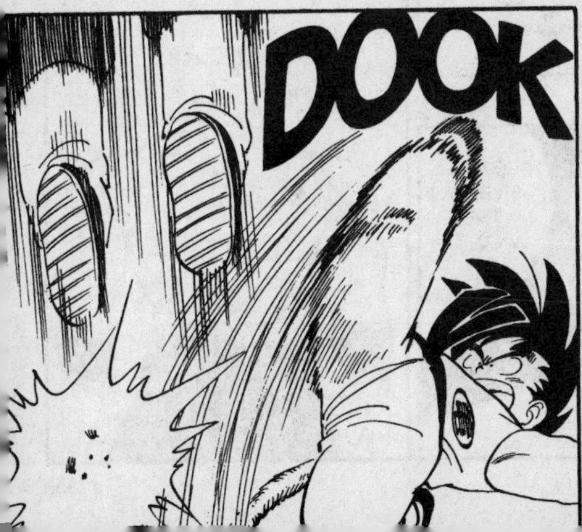
DOOK

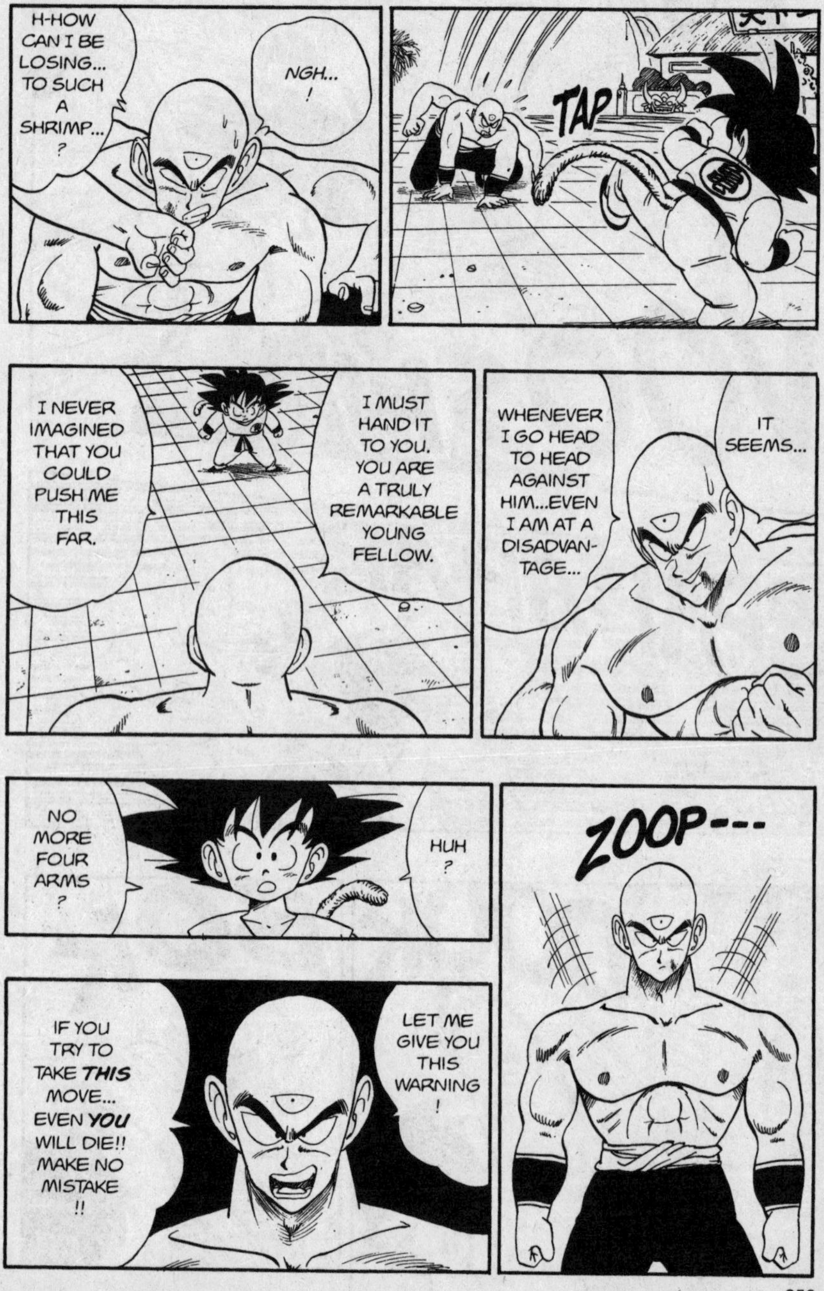
TAP
NGH... !
H-HOW CAN I BE LOSING... TO SUCH A SHRIMP... ?
IT SEEMS...
WHENEVER I GO HEAD TO HEAD AGAINST HIM...EVEN I AM AT A DISADVANTAGE...
I MUST HAND IT TO YOU. YOU ARE A TRULY REMARKABLE YOUNG FELLOW.
I NEVER IMAGINED THAT YOU COULD PUSH ME THIS FAR.
ZOOP---
HUH ?
NO MORE FOUR ARMS ?
LET ME GIVE YOU THIS WARNING !
IF YOU TRY TO TAKE THIS MOVE... EVEN YOU WILL DIE!! MAKE NO MISTAKE !!

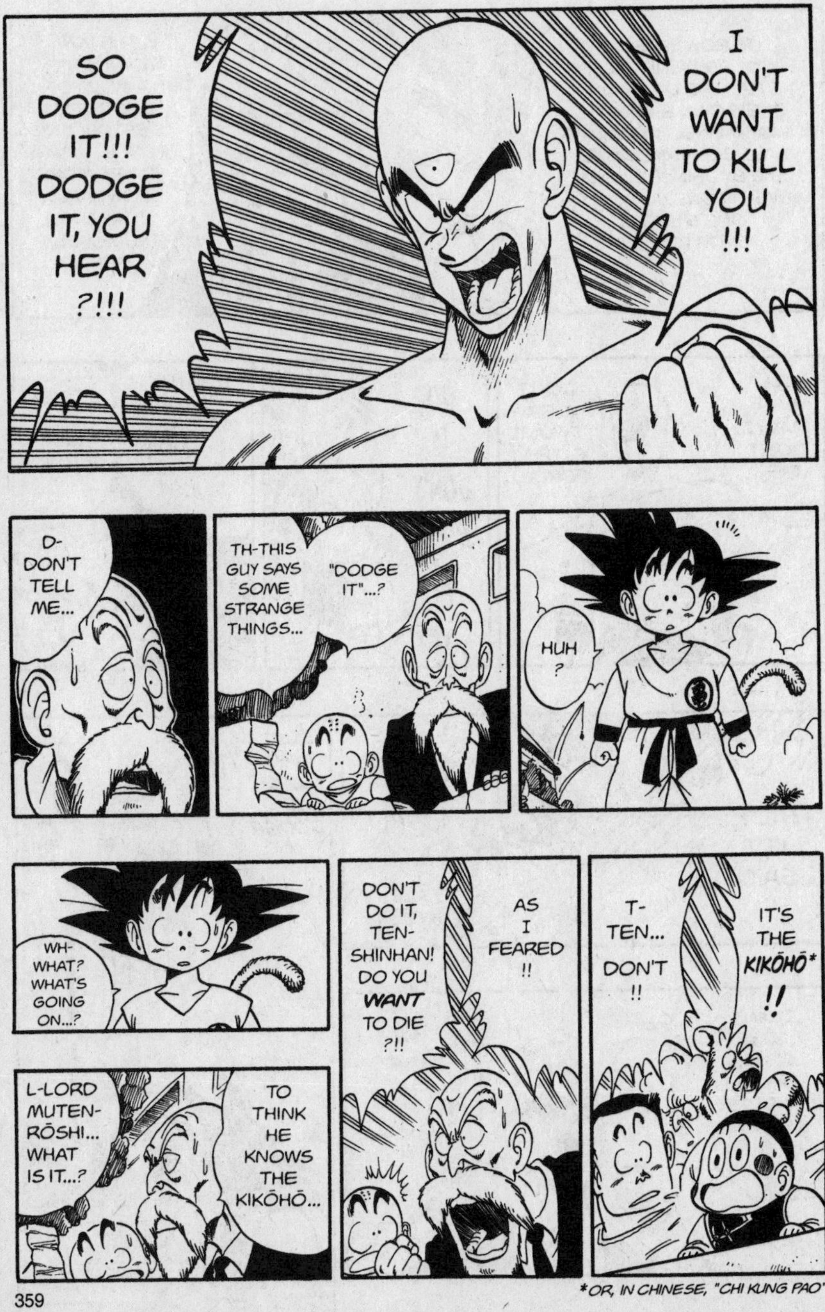
I DON'T WANT TO KILL YOU!!!
SO DODGE IT!!! DODGE IT, YOU HEAR?!!!
HUH?
"DODGE IT"...?
TH-THIS GUY SAYS SOME STRANGE THINGS...
D-DON'T TELL ME...
IT'S THE *KIKŌHŌ**!!
T-TEN... DON'T!!
AS I FEARED!!
DON'T DO IT, TEN-SHINHAN! DO YOU *WANT* TO DIE?!!
WH-WHAT? WHAT'S GOING ON...?
TO THINK HE KNOWS THE KIKŌHŌ...
L-LORD MUTEN-RŌSHI... WHAT IS IT...?

**OR, IN CHINESE, "CHI KUNG PAO"*

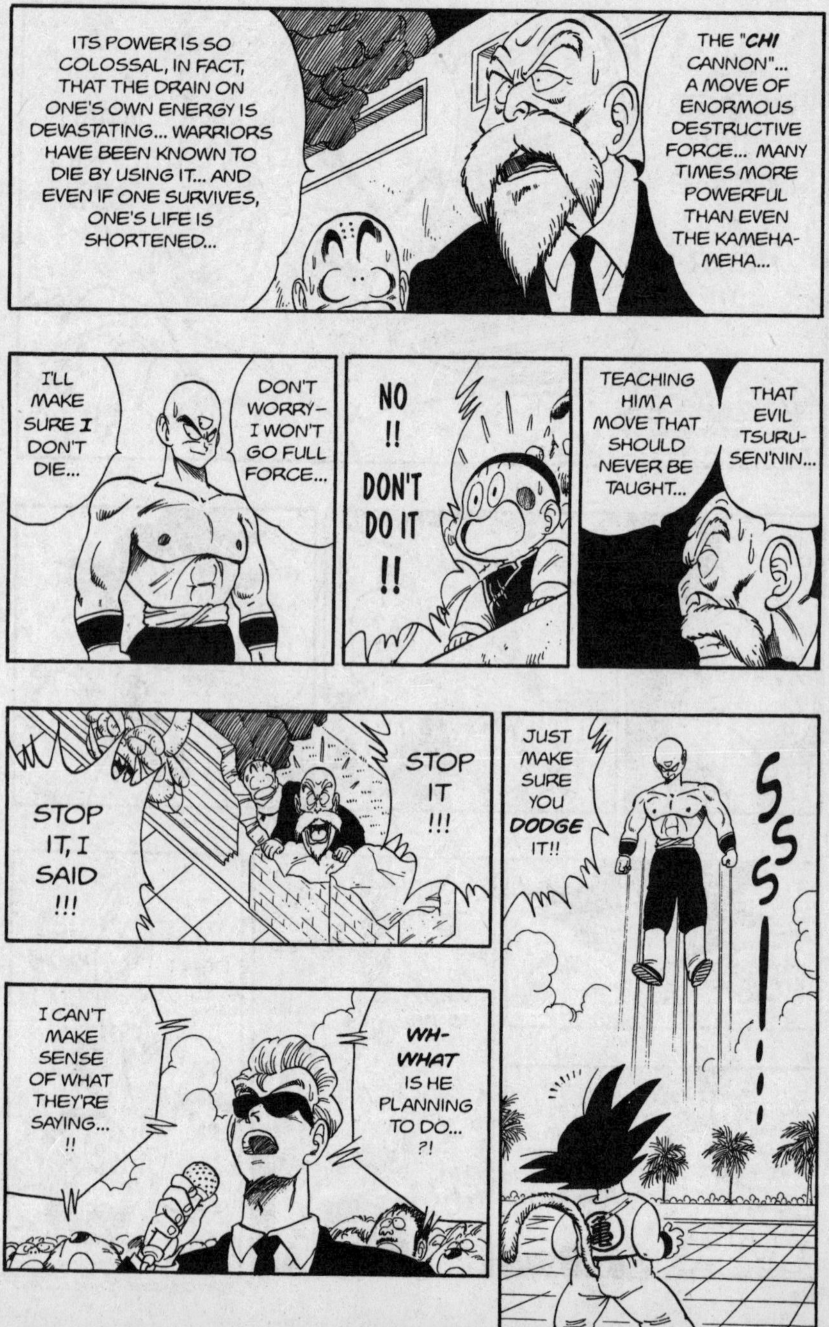
THE "CHI CANNON"... A MOVE OF ENORMOUS DESTRUCTIVE FORCE... MANY TIMES MORE POWERFUL THAN EVEN THE KAMEHA-MEHA...
ITS POWER IS SO COLOSSAL, IN FACT, THAT THE DRAIN ON ONE'S OWN ENERGY IS DEVASTATING... WARRIORS HAVE BEEN KNOWN TO DIE BY USING IT... AND EVEN IF ONE SURVIVES, ONE'S LIFE IS SHORTENED...
THAT EVIL TSURU-SEN'NIN...
TEACHING HIM A MOVE THAT SHOULD NEVER BE TAUGHT...
NO !! DON'T DO IT !!
DON'T WORRY- I WON'T GO FULL FORCE...
I'LL MAKE SURE I DON'T DIE...
JUST MAKE SURE YOU DODGE IT!!
SSS
STOP IT !!!
STOP IT, I SAID !!!
WH-WHAT IS HE PLANNING TO DO... ?!
I CAN'T MAKE SENSE OF WHAT THEY'RE SAYING... !!

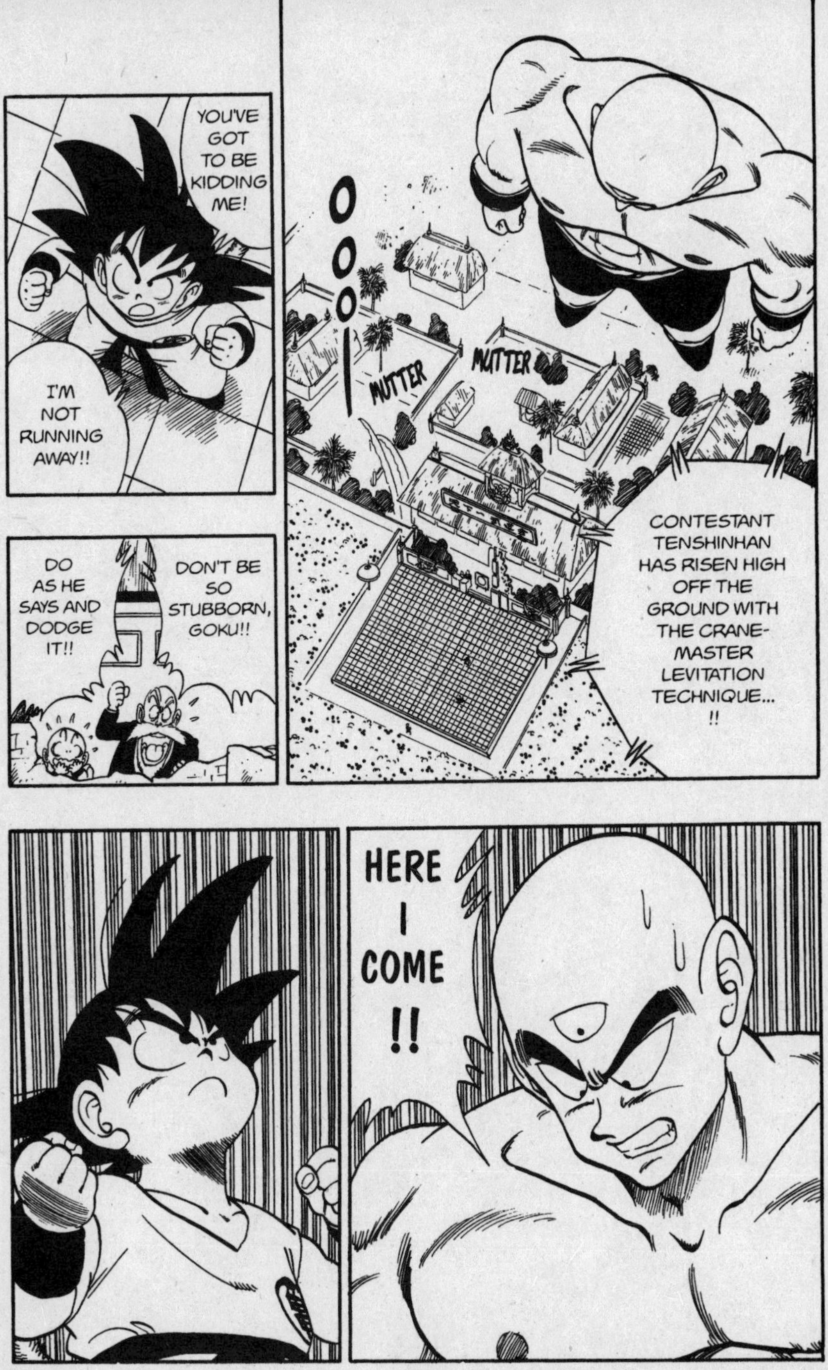
OOO!
MUTTER
MUTTER
CONTESTANT TENSHINHAN HAS RISEN HIGH OFF THE GROUND WITH THE CRANE-MASTER LEVITATION TECHNIQUE... !!
YOU'VE GOT TO BE KIDDING ME!
I'M NOT RUNNING AWAY!!
DON'T BE SO STUBBORN, GOKU!!
DO AS HE SAYS AND DODGE IT!!
HERE I COME !!

Dragonball

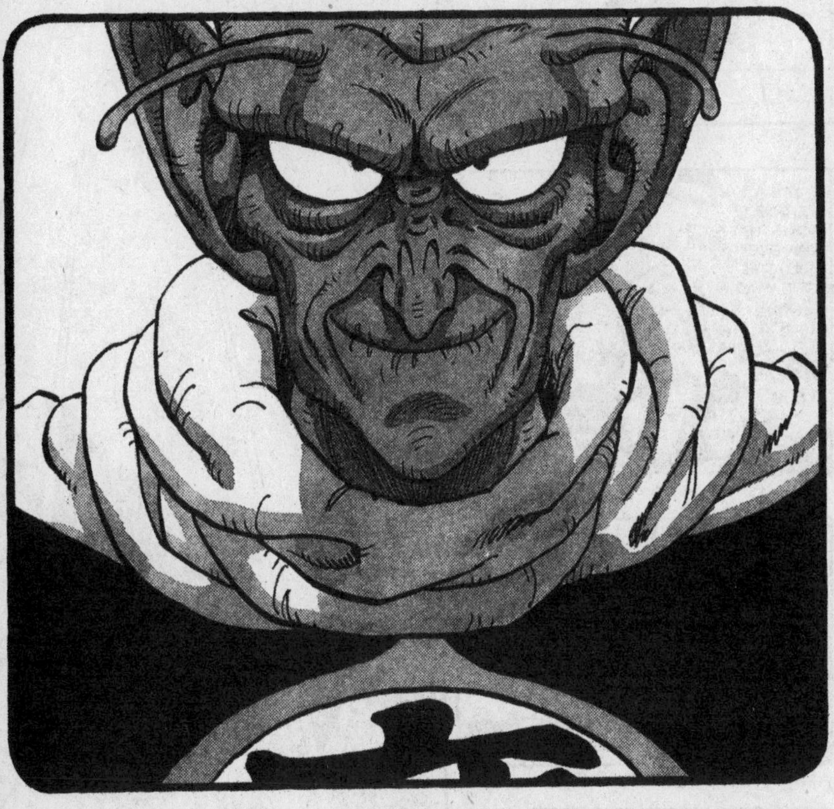

VOLUME 12

THE DEMON KING PICCOLO

Tale 133
Desperation Move

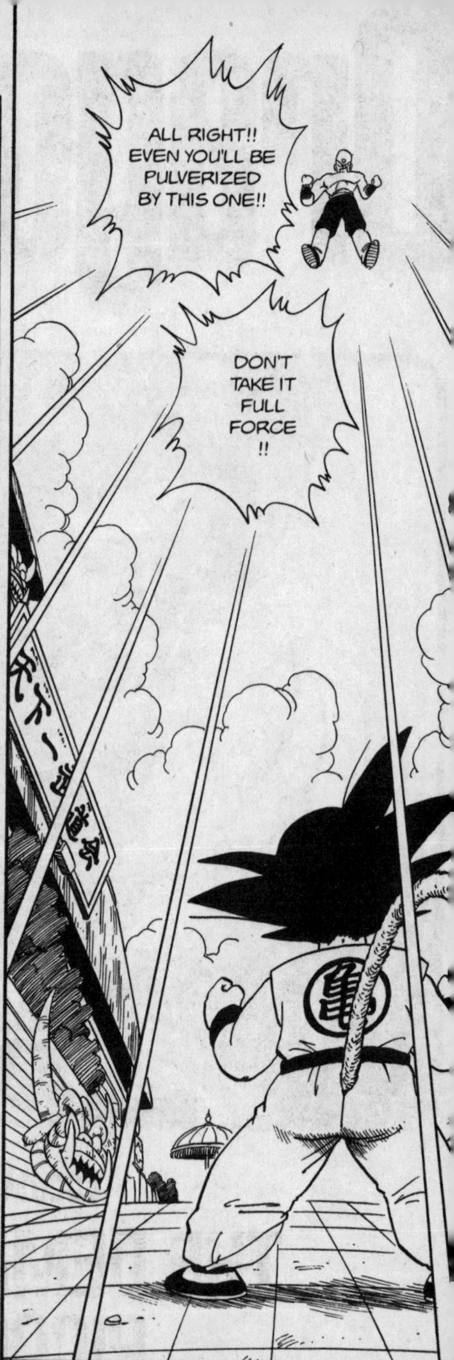
ALL RIGHT!! EVEN YOU'LL BE PULVERIZED BY THIS ONE!!
DON'T TAKE IT FULL FORCE !!

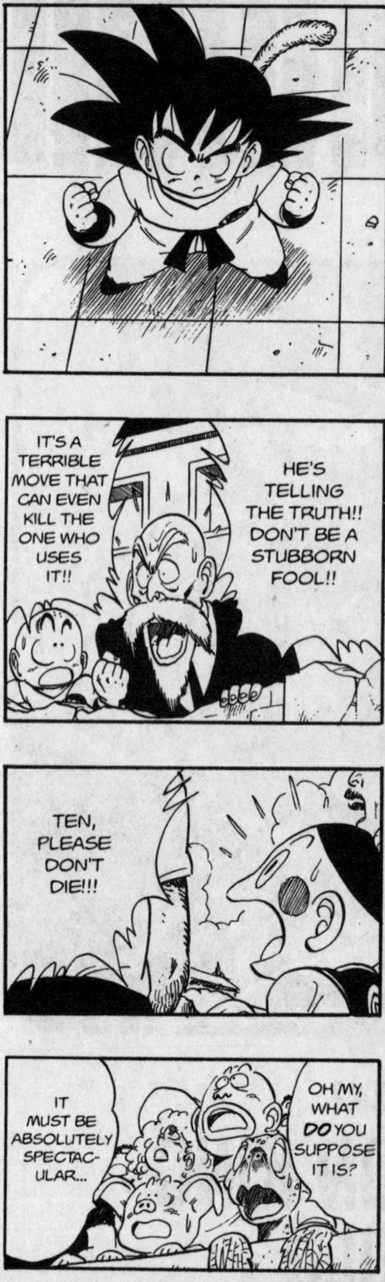
HE'S TELLING THE TRUTH!! DON'T BE A STUBBORN FOOL!!
IT'S A TERRIBLE MOVE THAT CAN EVEN KILL THE ONE WHO USES IT!!
TEN, PLEASE DON'T DIE!!!
OH MY, WHAT DO YOU SUPPOSE IT IS?
IT MUST BE ABSOLUTELY SPECTAC-ULAR...

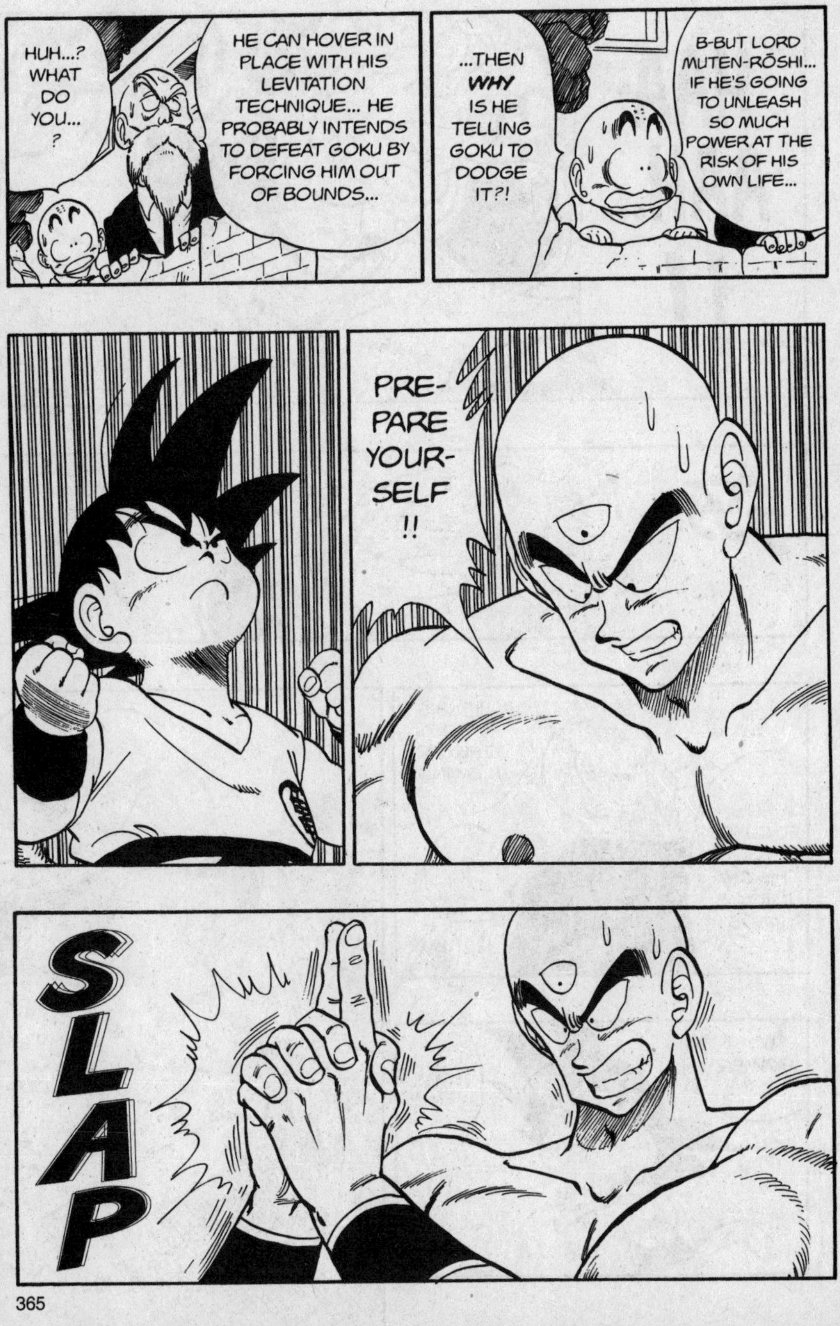
B-BUT LORD MUTEN-RŌSHI... IF HE'S GOING TO UNLEASH SO MUCH POWER AT THE RISK OF HIS OWN LIFE...
...THEN **WHY** IS HE TELLING GOKU TO DODGE IT?!
HE CAN HOVER IN PLACE WITH HIS LEVITATION TECHNIQUE... HE PROBABLY INTENDS TO DEFEAT GOKU BY FORCING HIM OUT OF BOUNDS...
HUH...? WHAT DO YOU... ?
PRE-PARE YOUR-SELF !!
SLAP

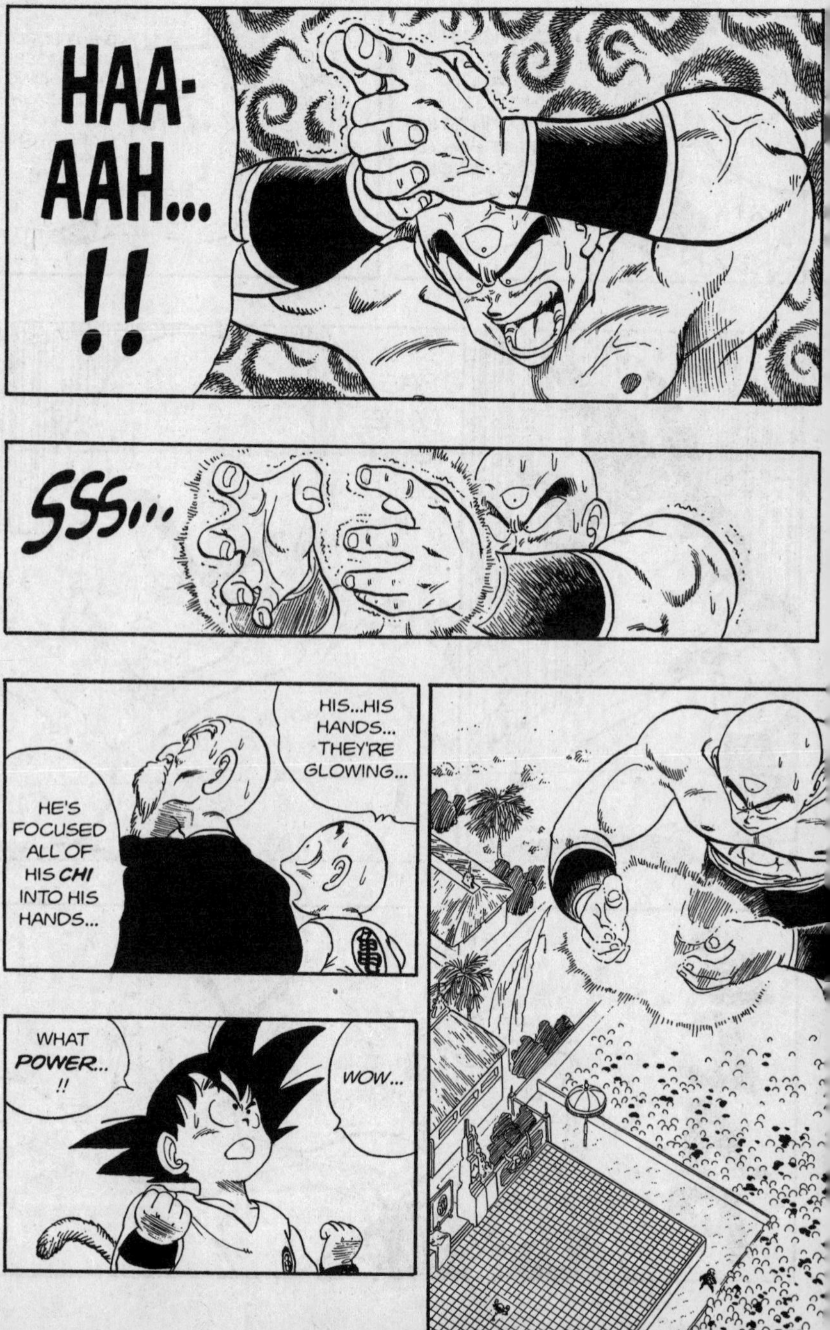
HAA-AAH...!!
SSS...
HIS...HIS HANDS... THEY'RE GLOWING...
HE'S FOCUSED ALL OF HIS CHI INTO HIS HANDS...
WOW...
WHAT POWER...!!

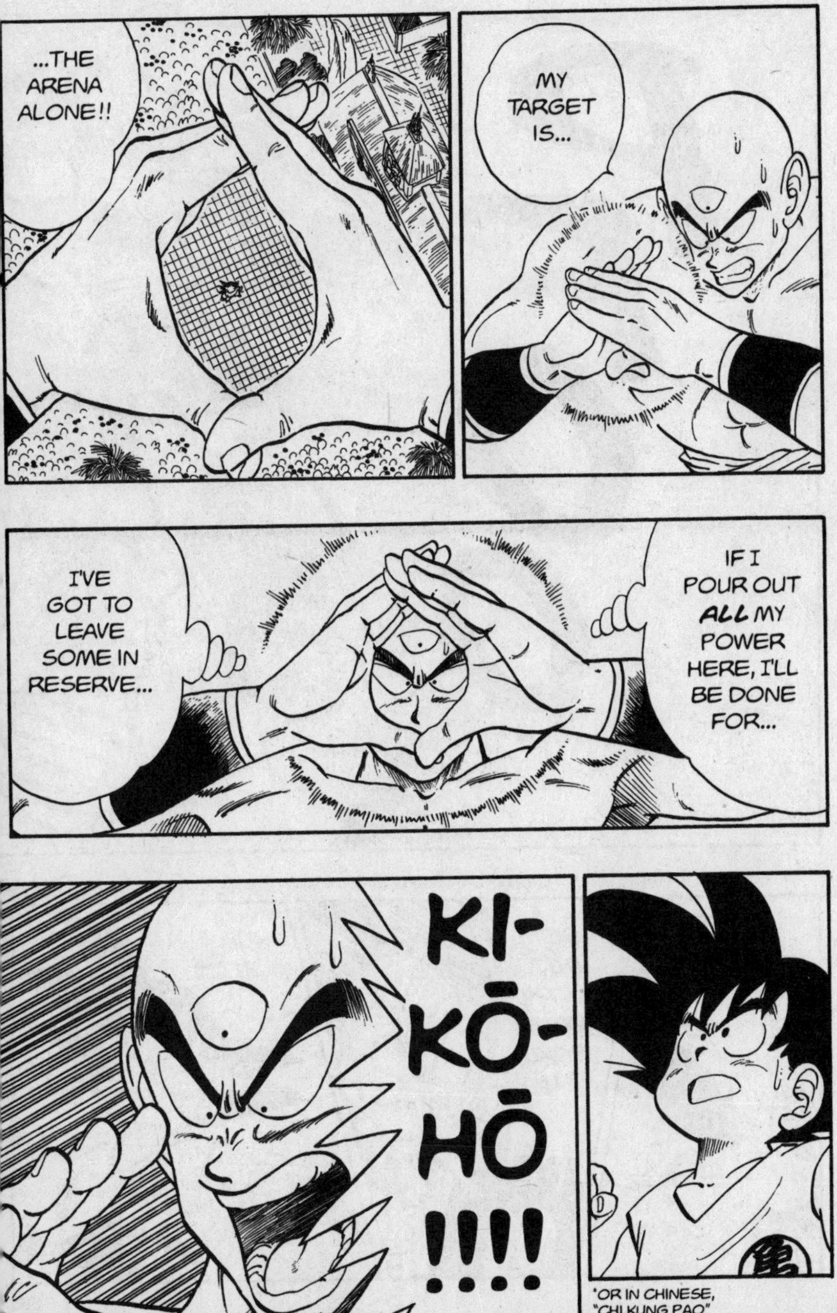
MY TARGET IS...
...THE ARENA ALONE!!
IF I POUR OUT ALL MY POWER HERE, I'LL BE DONE FOR...
I'VE GOT TO LEAVE SOME IN RESERVE...
KI-KŌ-HŌ!!!!

*OR IN CHINESE, "CHI KUNG PAO"

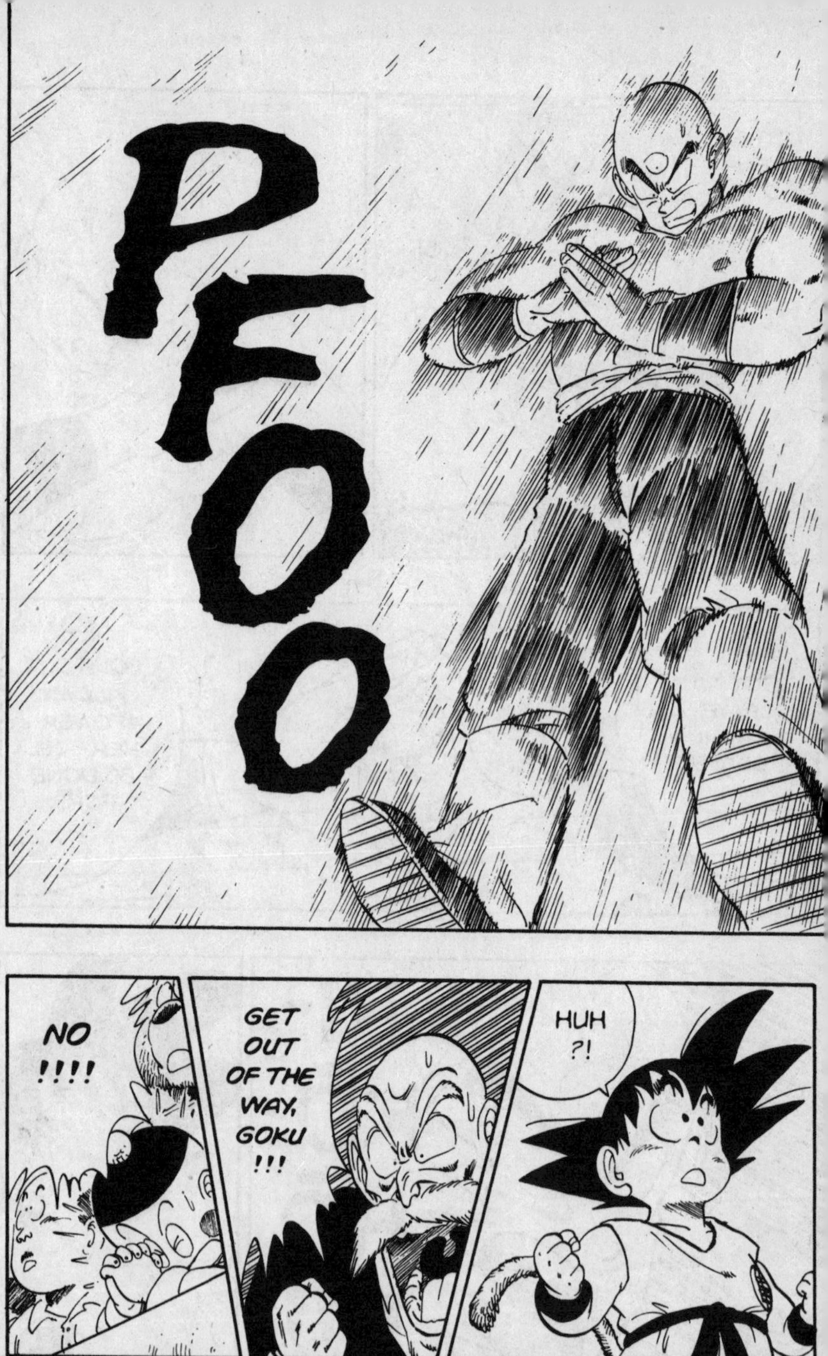
PFOO
HUH ?!
GET OUT OF THE WAY, GOKU !!!
NO !!!!

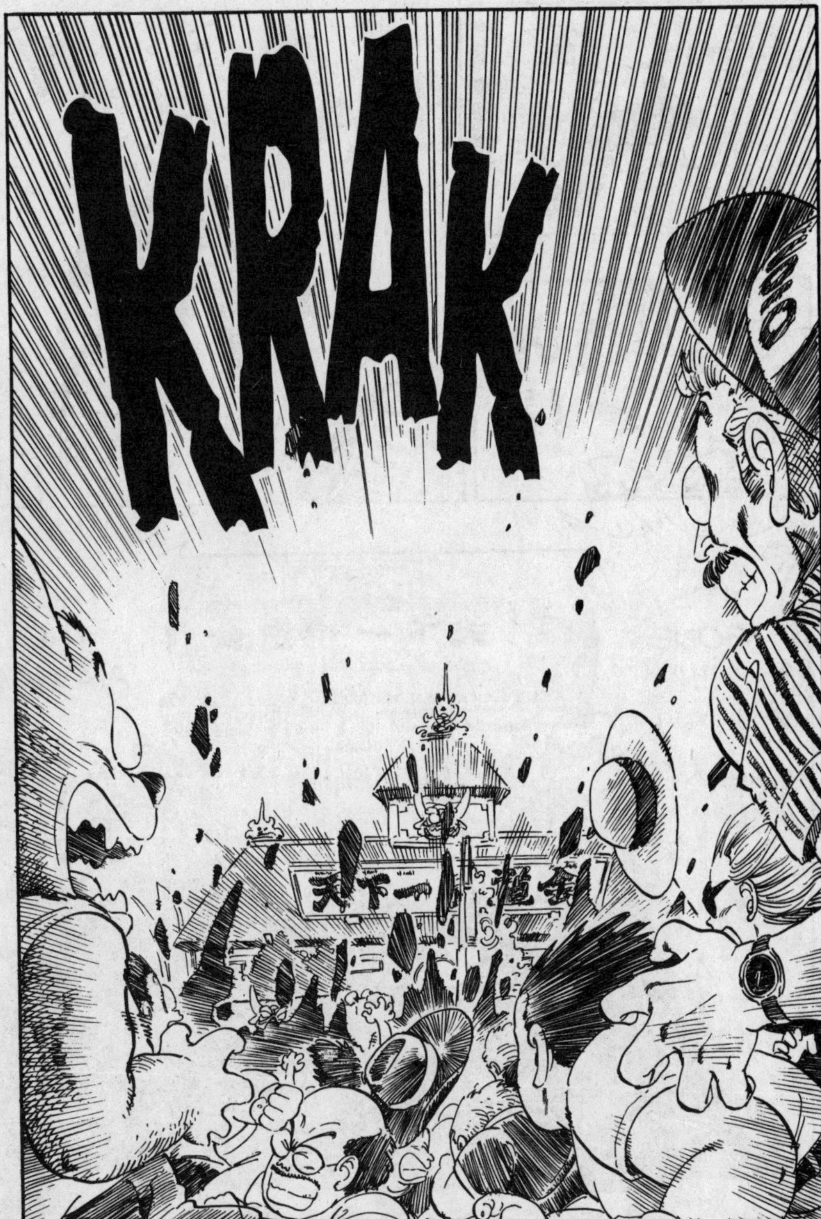
KRAK

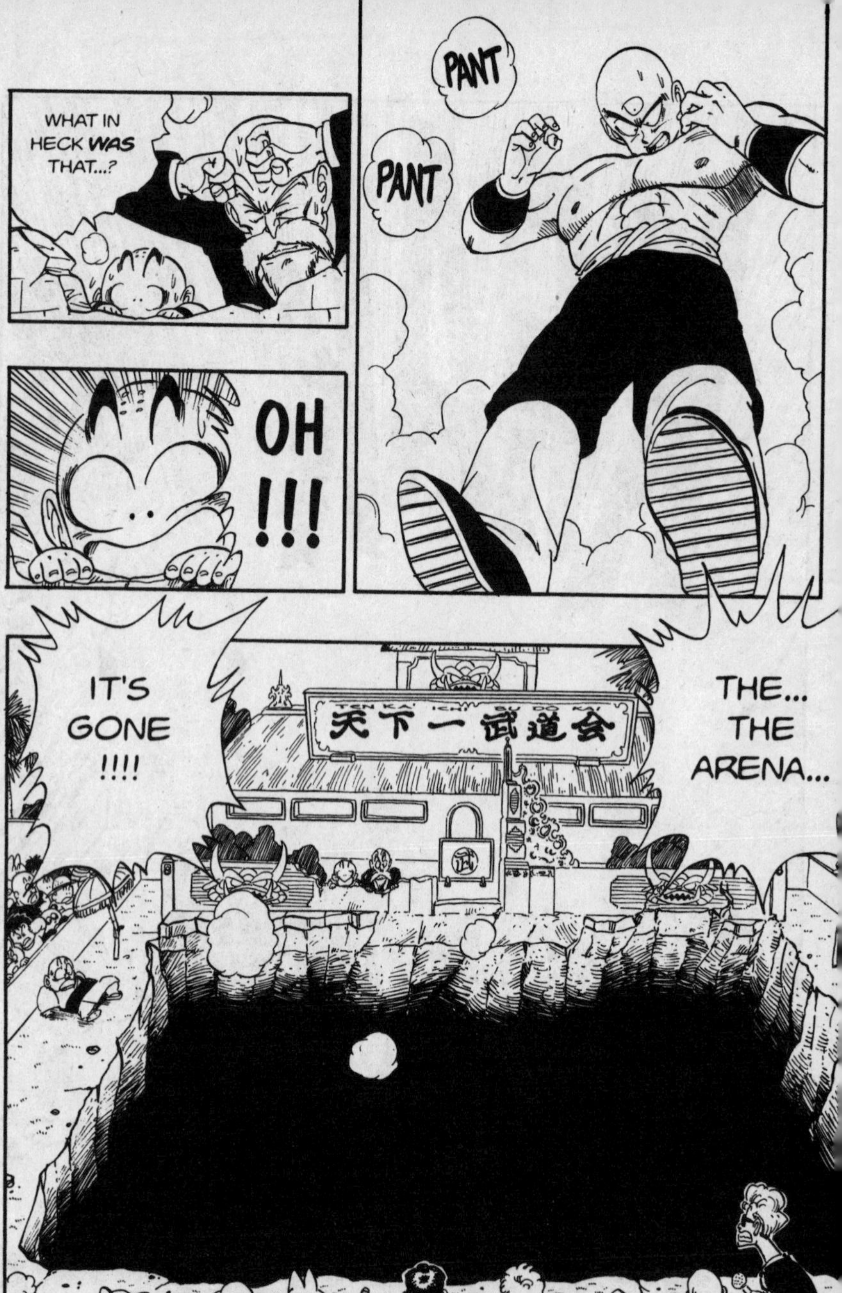
PANT
PANT
WHAT IN HECK WAS THAT...?
OH !!!
THE... THE ARENA...
IT'S GONE !!!!
天下一武道会

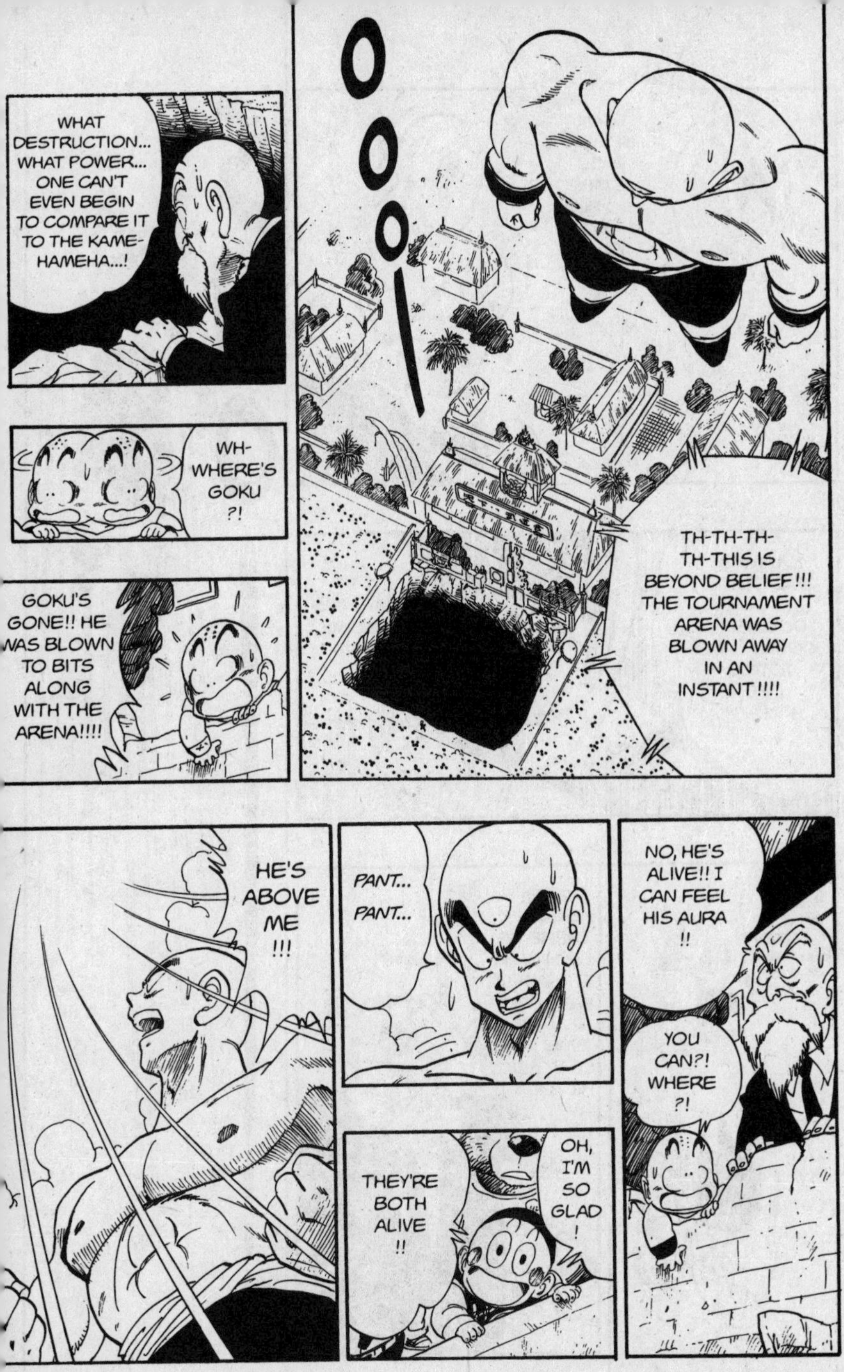
OOOO!
TH-TH-TH-TH-THIS IS BEYOND BELIEF!!! THE TOURNAMENT ARENA WAS BLOWN AWAY IN AN INSTANT!!!!
WHAT DESTRUCTION... WHAT POWER... ONE CAN'T EVEN BEGIN TO COMPARE IT TO THE KAME-HAMEHA...!
WH-WHERE'S GOKU ?!
GOKU'S GONE!! HE WAS BLOWN TO BITS ALONG WITH THE ARENA!!!!
NO, HE'S ALIVE!! I CAN FEEL HIS AURA !!
YOU CAN?! WHERE ?!
PANT... PANT...
HE'S ABOVE ME !!!
OH, I'M SO GLAD !
THEY'RE BOTH ALIVE !!

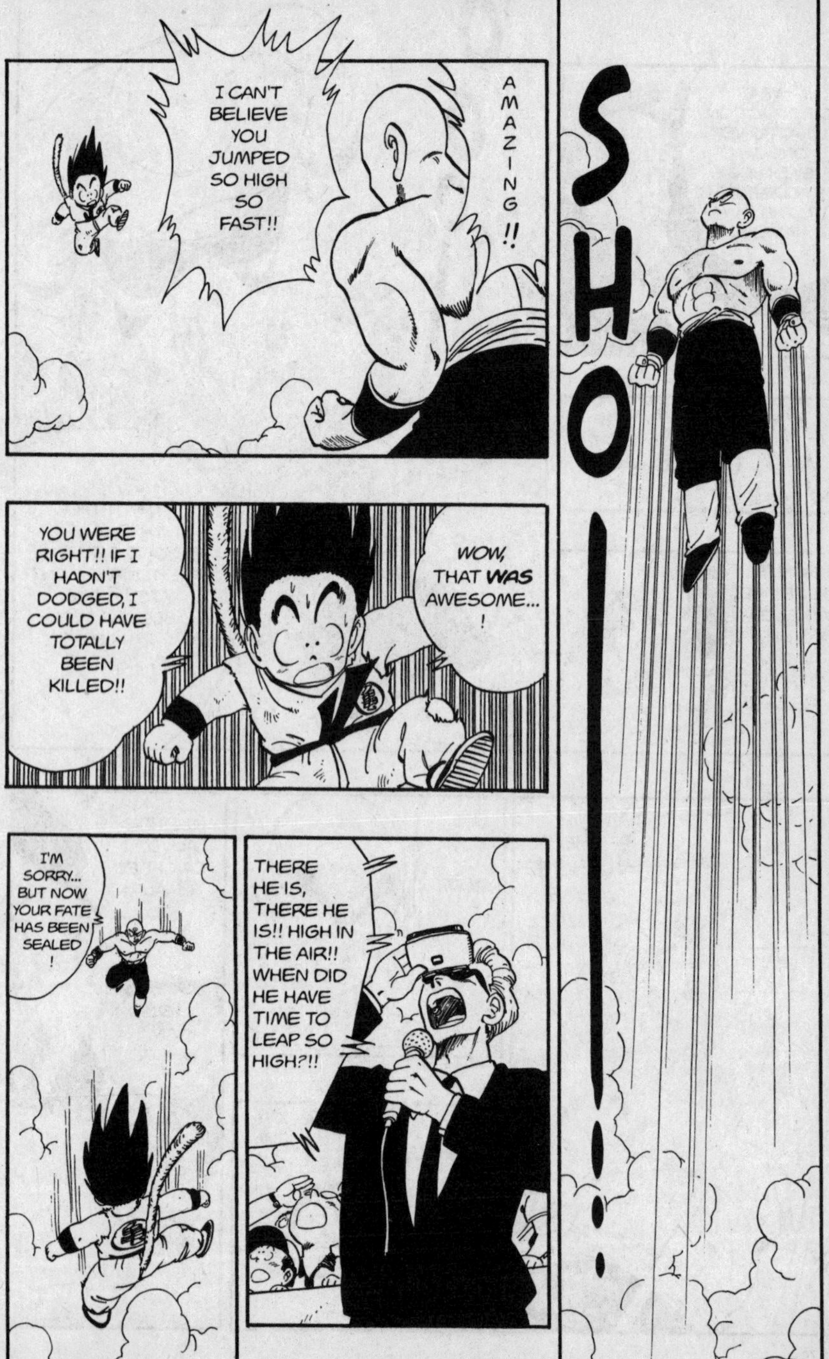
SHOOO...!!
AMAZING!!
I CAN'T BELIEVE YOU JUMPED SO HIGH SO FAST!!
WOW, THAT WAS AWESOME...!
YOU WERE RIGHT!! IF I HADN'T DODGED, I COULD HAVE TOTALLY BEEN KILLED!!
THERE HE IS, THERE HE IS!! HIGH IN THE AIR!! WHEN DID HE HAVE TIME TO LEAP SO HIGH?!!
I'M SORRY... BUT NOW YOUR FATE HAS BEEN SEALED!

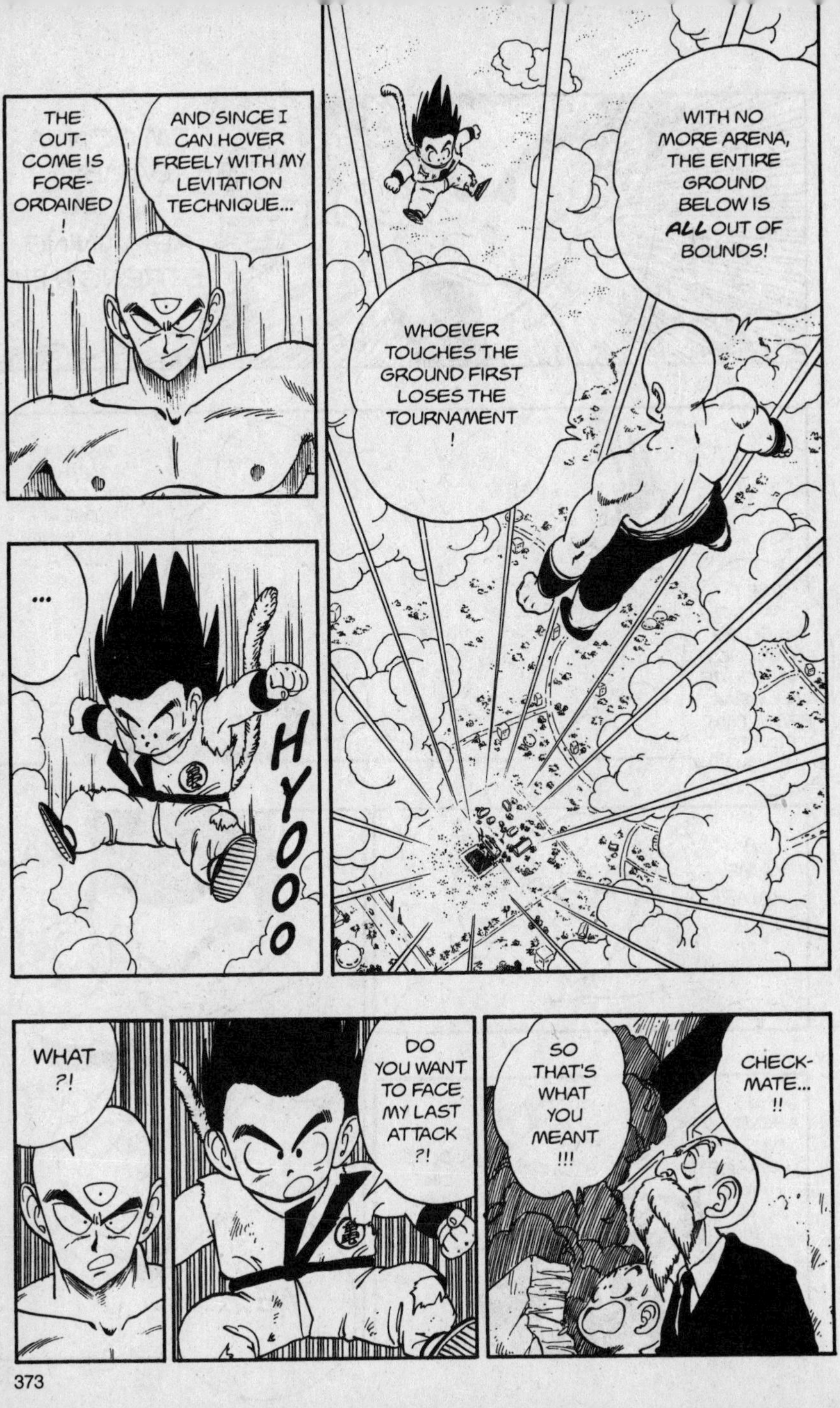
WITH NO MORE ARENA, THE ENTIRE GROUND BELOW IS **ALL** OUT OF BOUNDS!
WHOEVER TOUCHES THE GROUND FIRST LOSES THE TOURNAMENT!
AND SINCE I CAN HOVER FREELY WITH MY LEVITATION TECHNIQUE...
THE OUT-COME IS FORE-ORDAINED!
...
HYOOO
CHECK-MATE...!!
SO THAT'S WHAT YOU MEANT!!!
DO YOU WANT TO FACE MY LAST ATTACK?!
WHAT?!

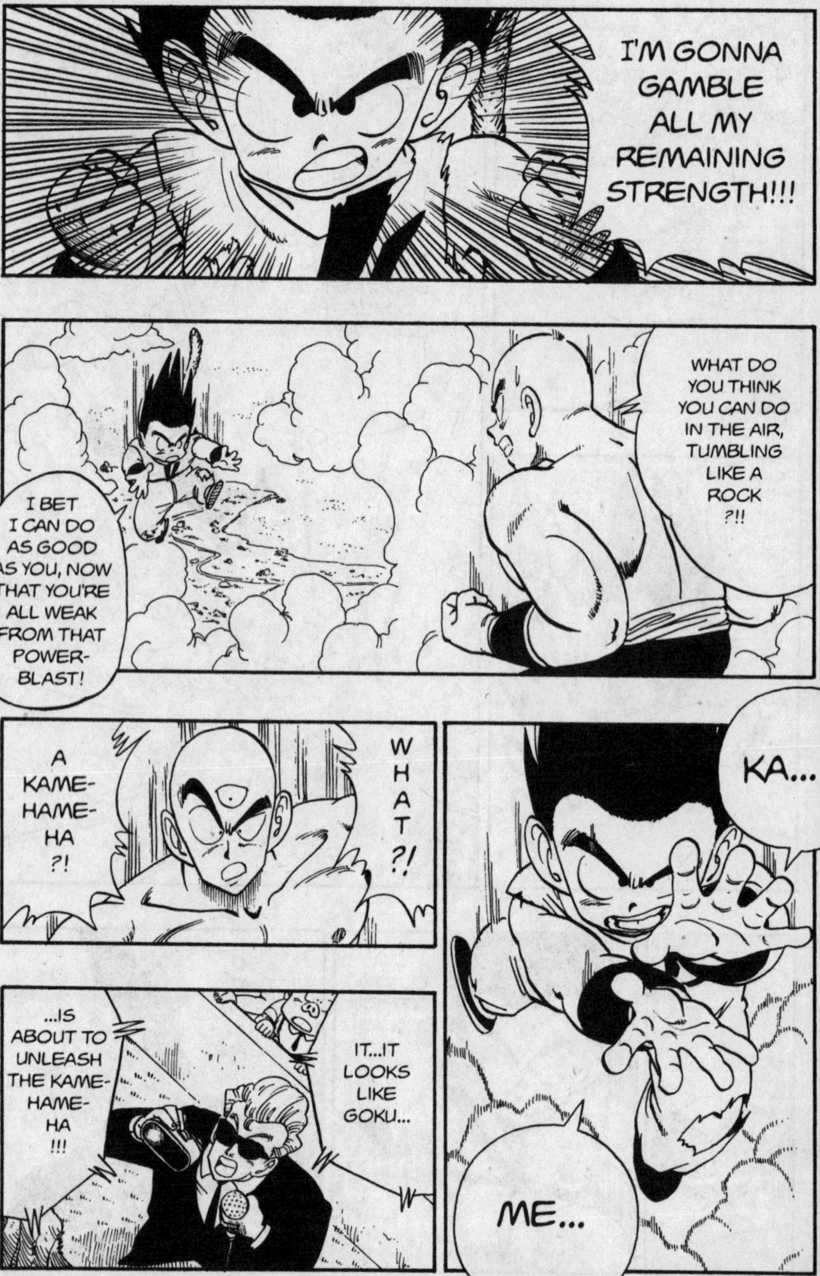
I'M GONNA GAMBLE ALL MY REMAINING STRENGTH!!!
WHAT DO YOU THINK YOU CAN DO IN THE AIR, TUMBLING LIKE A ROCK ?!!
I BET I CAN DO AS GOOD AS YOU, NOW THAT YOU'RE ALL WEAK FROM THAT POWER-BLAST!
KA...
ME...
WHAT ?!
A KAME-HAME-HA ?!
IT...IT LOOKS LIKE GOKU...
...IS ABOUT TO UNLEASH THE KAME-HAME-HA !!!

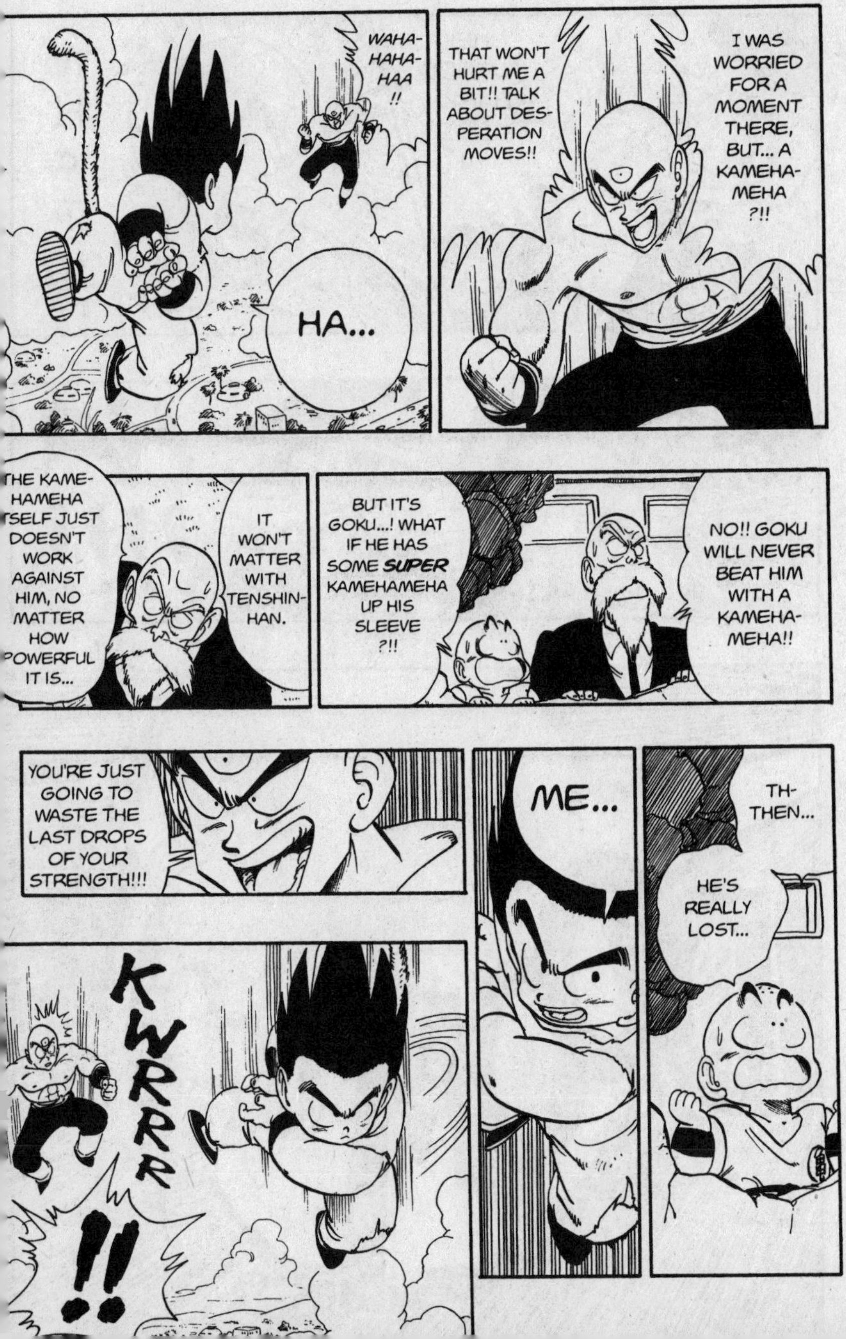
I WAS WORRIED FOR A MOMENT THERE, BUT... A KAMEHAMEHA ?!!
THAT WON'T HURT ME A BIT!! TALK ABOUT DESPERATION MOVES!!
WAHAHAHAHAA!!
HA...
NO!! GOKU WILL NEVER BEAT HIM WITH A KAMEHAMEHA!!
BUT IT'S GOKU...! WHAT IF HE HAS SOME **SUPER** KAMEHAMEHA UP HIS SLEEVE ?!!
IT WON'T MATTER WITH TENSHINHAN.
THE KAMEHAMEHA ITSELF JUST DOESN'T WORK AGAINST HIM, NO MATTER HOW POWERFUL IT IS...
TH-THEN...
HE'S REALLY LOST...
ME...
YOU'RE JUST GOING TO WASTE THE LAST DROPS OF YOUR STRENGTH!!!
KWRRR!!

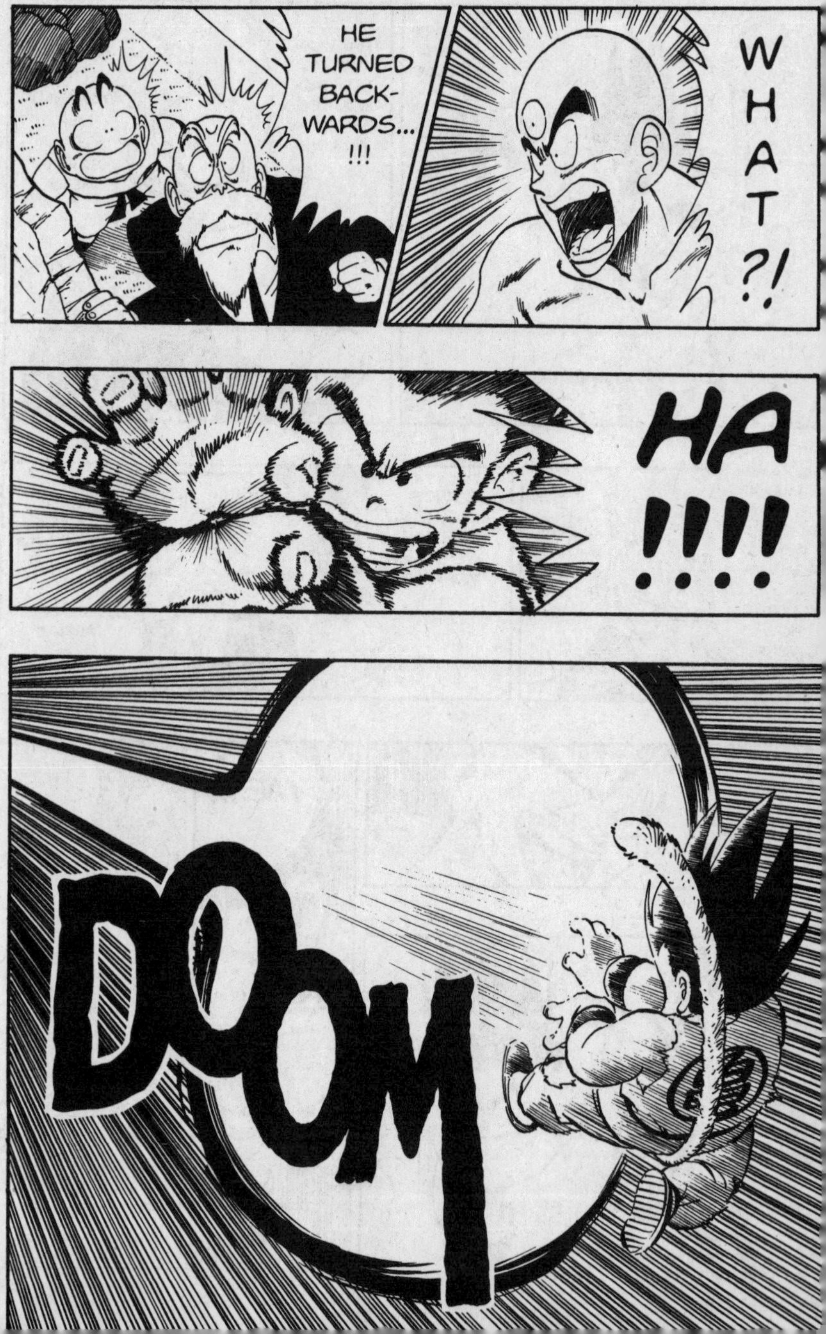
WHAT ?!
HE TURNED BACK-WARDS... !!!
HA !!!!
DOOM

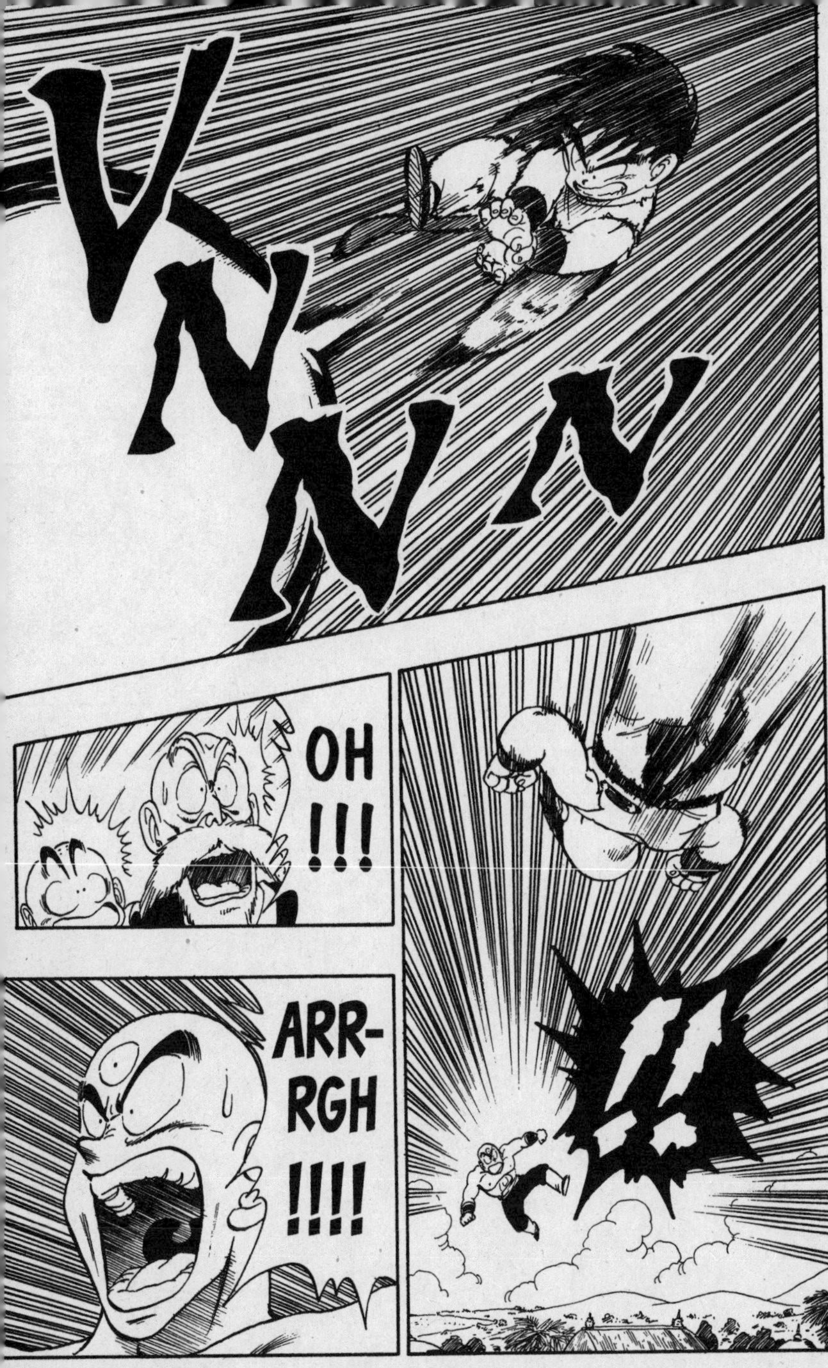
OH
!!!
ARR-
RGH
!!!!

Tale 134 · Up in the Air

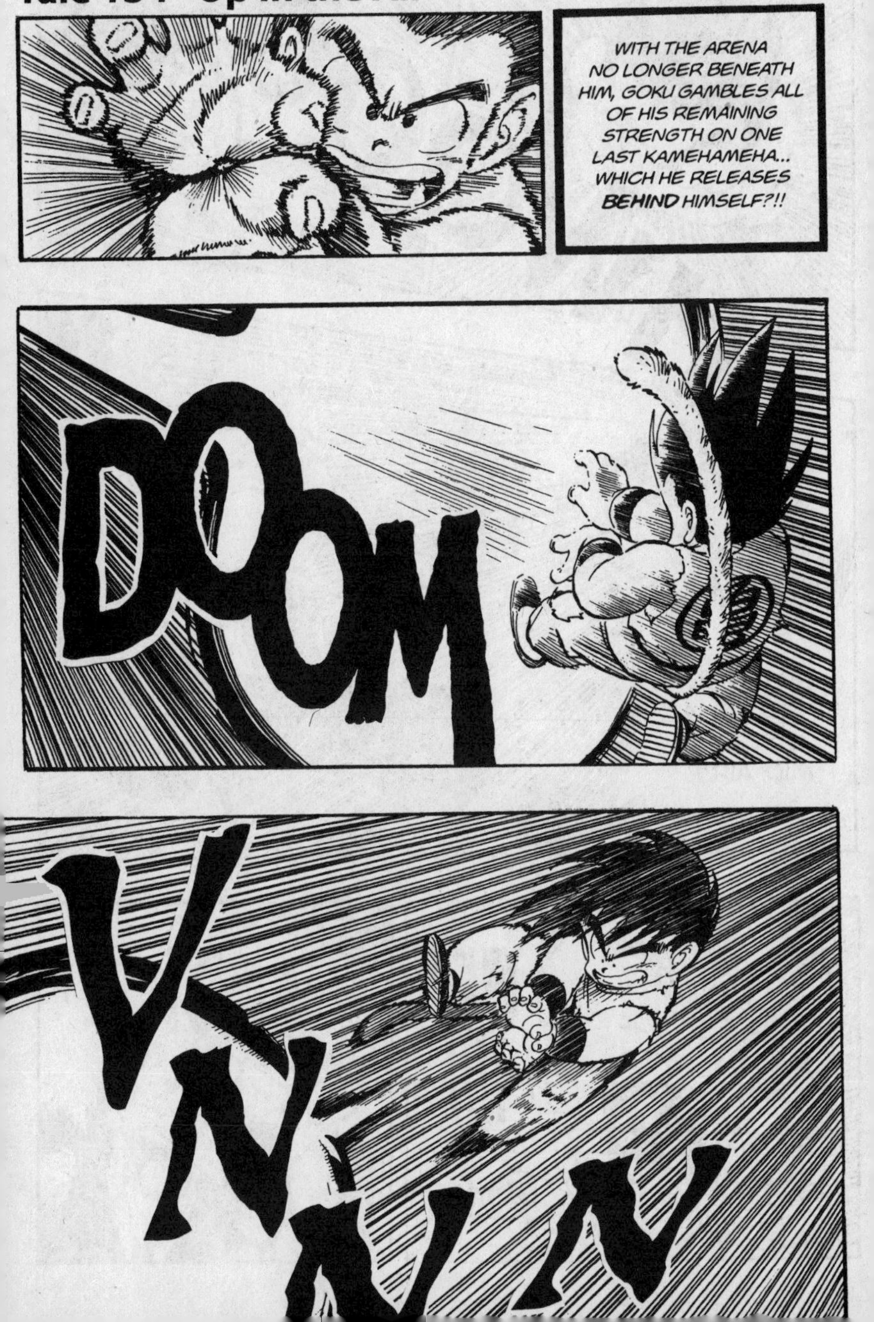
WITH THE ARENA NO LONGER BENEATH HIM, GOKU GAMBLES ALL OF HIS REMAINING STRENGTH ON ONE LAST KAMEHAMEHA... WHICH HE RELEASES **BEHIND** HIMSELF?!!
DOOM

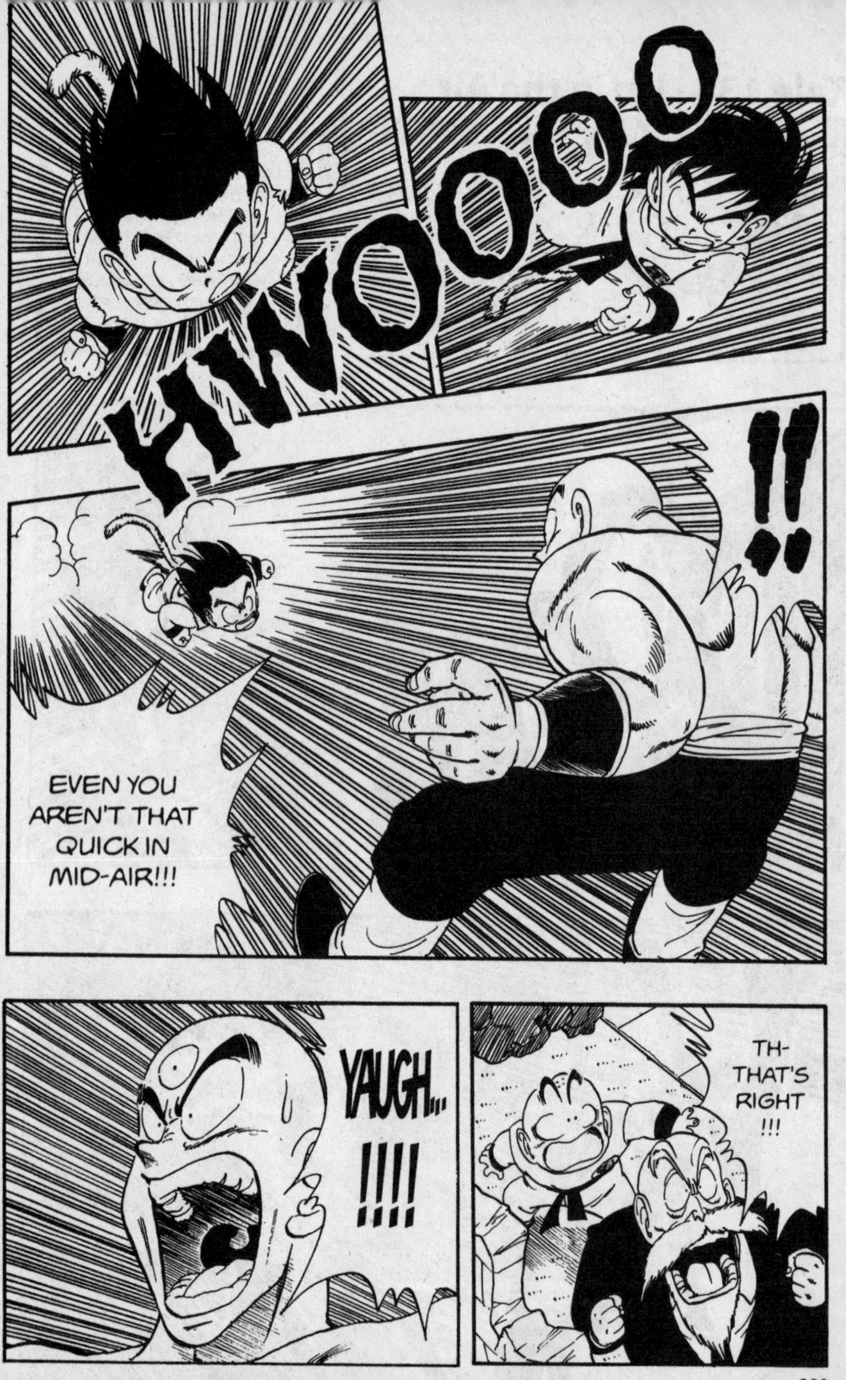
HWOOOOOO
!!
EVEN YOU AREN'T THAT QUICK IN MID-AIR!!!
TH- THAT'S RIGHT !!!
YAUGH... !!!!

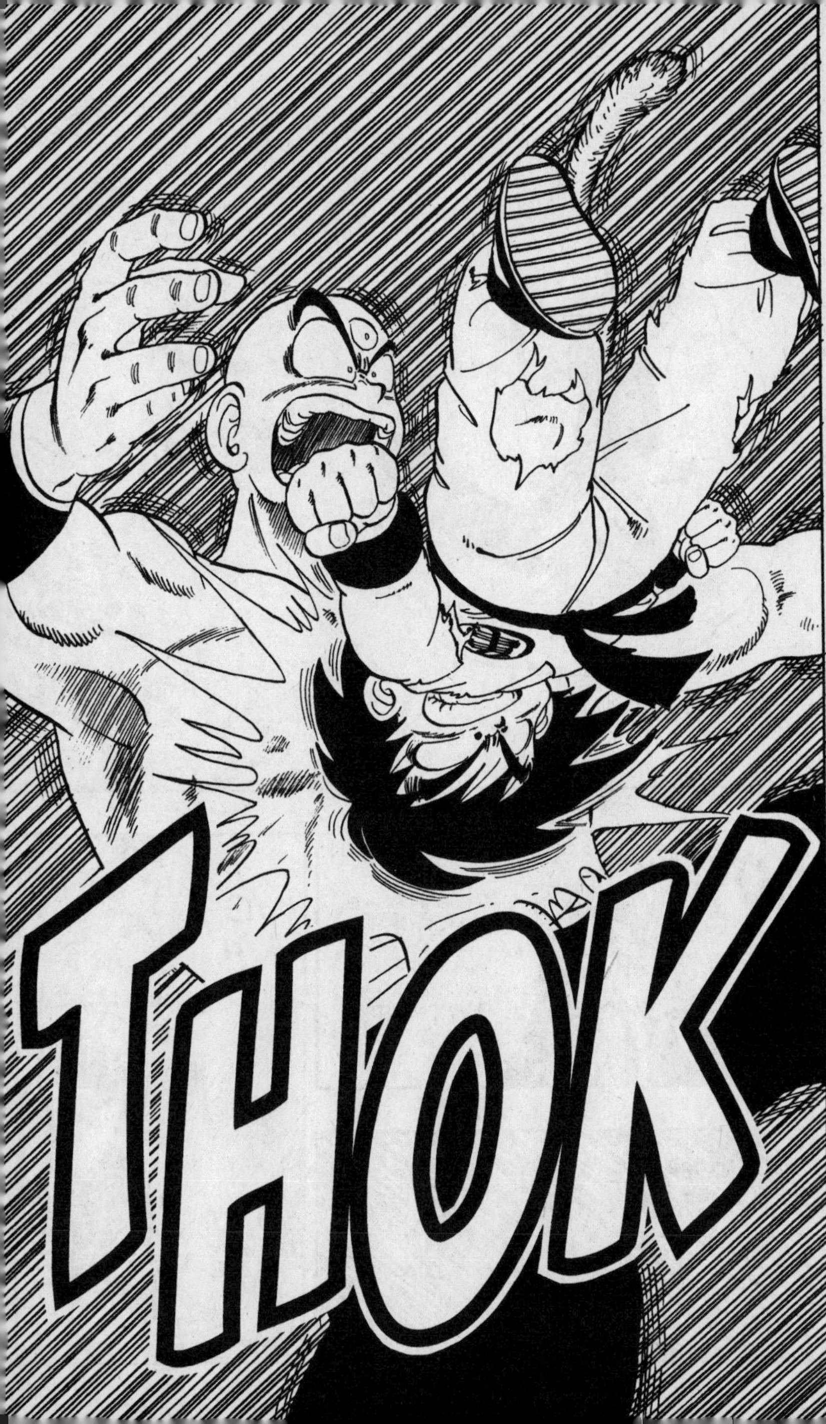
THOK

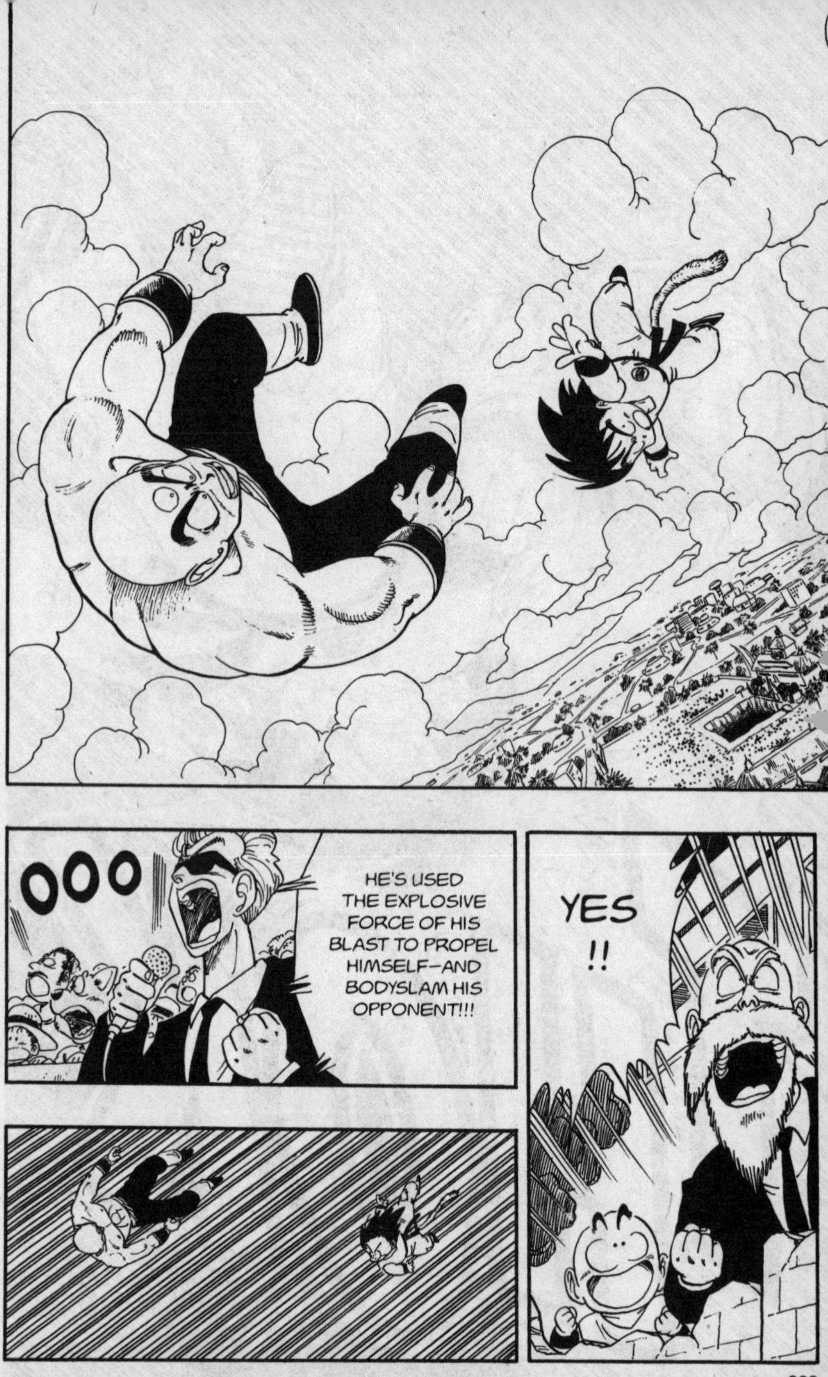
YES
!!
HE'S USED THE EXPLOSIVE FORCE OF HIS BLAST TO PROPEL HIMSELF—AND BODYSLAM HIS OPPONENT!!!
OOO

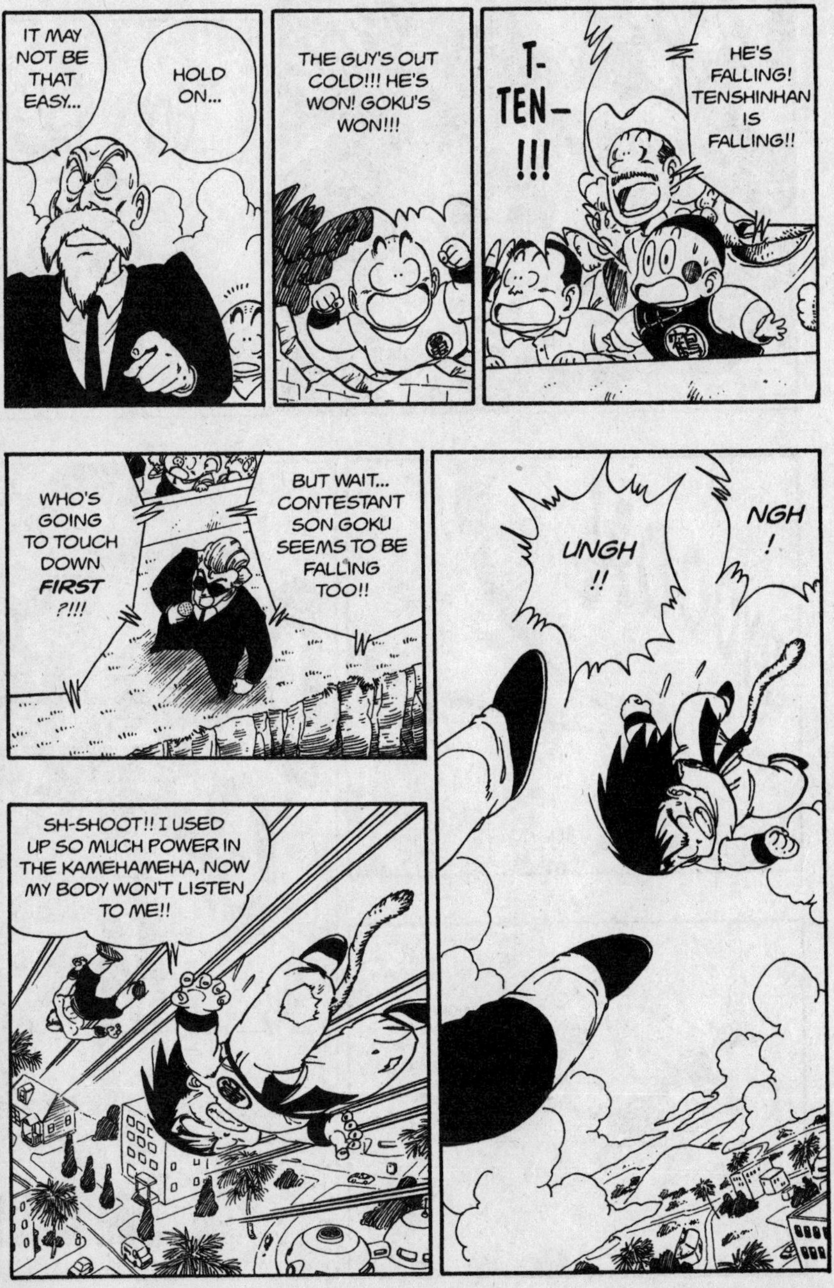
HE'S FALLING! TENSHINHAN IS FALLING!!
T-TEN—!!!
THE GUY'S OUT COLD!!! HE'S WON! GOKU'S WON!!!
HOLD ON...
IT MAY NOT BE THAT EASY...
NGH!
UNGH!!
BUT WAIT... CONTESTANT SON GOKU SEEMS TO BE FALLING TOO!!
WHO'S GOING TO TOUCH DOWN **FIRST**?!!!
SH-SHOOT!! I USED UP SO MUCH POWER IN THE KAMEHAMEHA, NOW MY BODY WON'T LISTEN TO ME!!

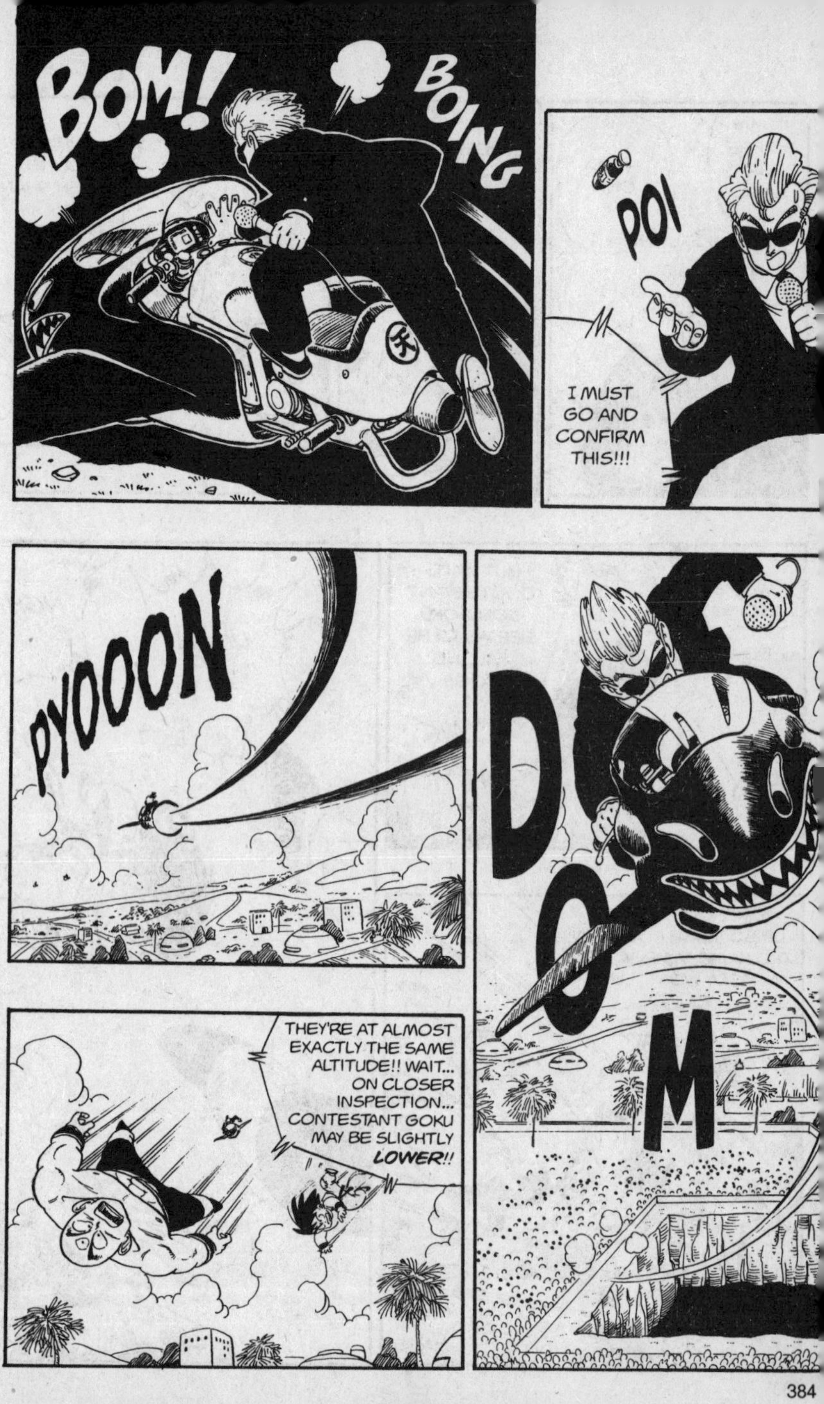
POI
I MUST GO AND CONFIRM THIS!!!
BOM!
BOING
DOM
PYOOON
THEY'RE AT ALMOST EXACTLY THE SAME ALTITUDE!! WAIT... ON CLOSER INSPECTION... CONTESTANT GOKU MAY BE SLIGHTLY LOWER!!

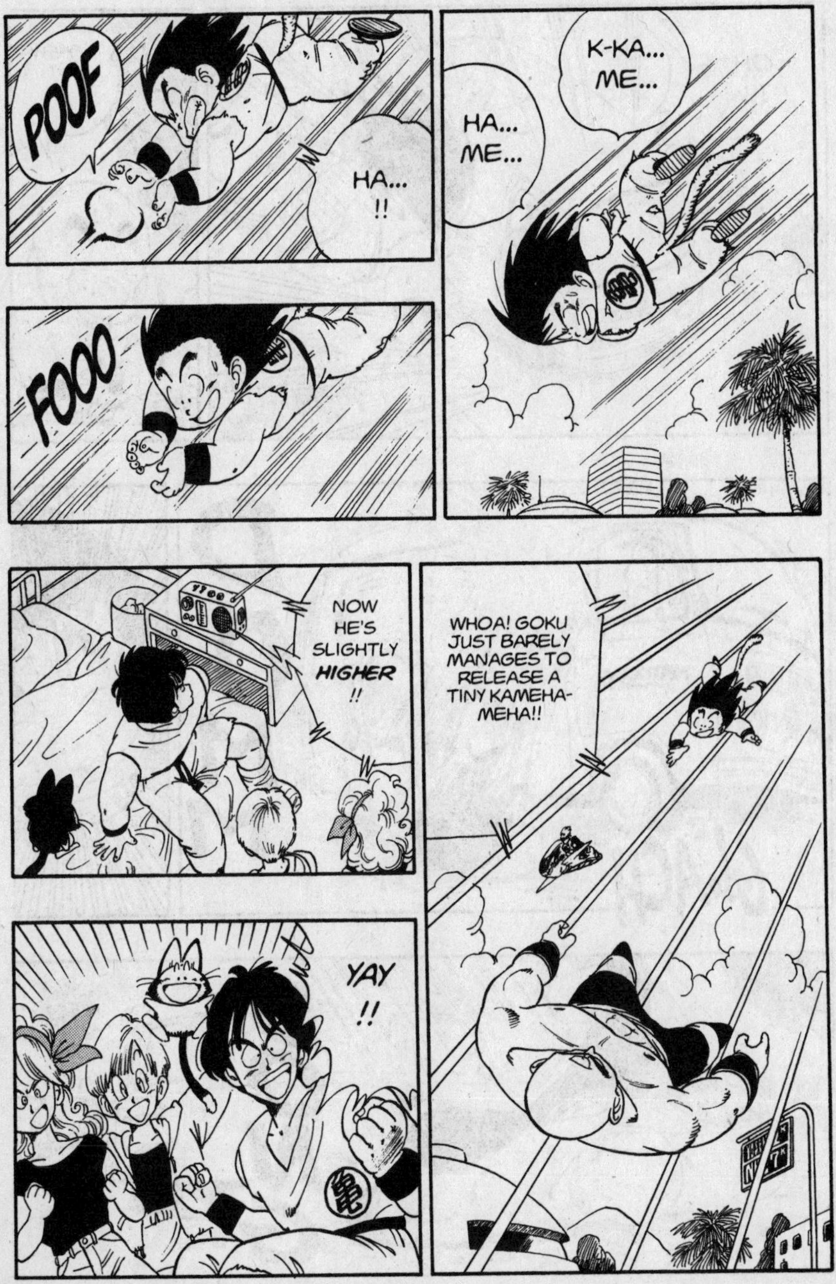
K-KA... ME...
HA... ME...
HA... !!
POOF
FOOO
WHOA! GOKU JUST BARELY MANAGES TO RELEASE A TINY KAMEHA-MEHA!!
NOW HE'S SLIGHTLY ***HIGHER*** !!
YAY !!

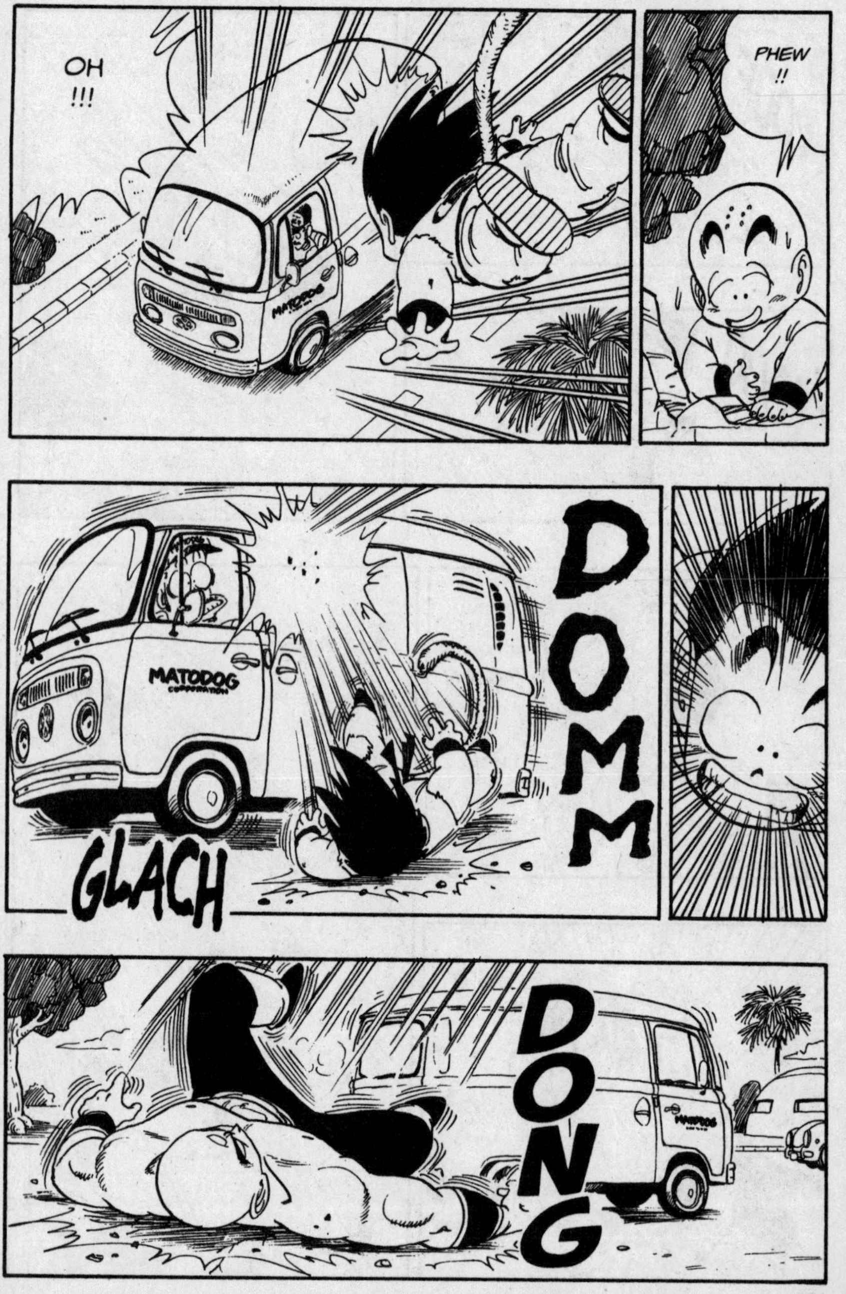
PHEW !!
OH !!!
DOMM
GLACH
DONG

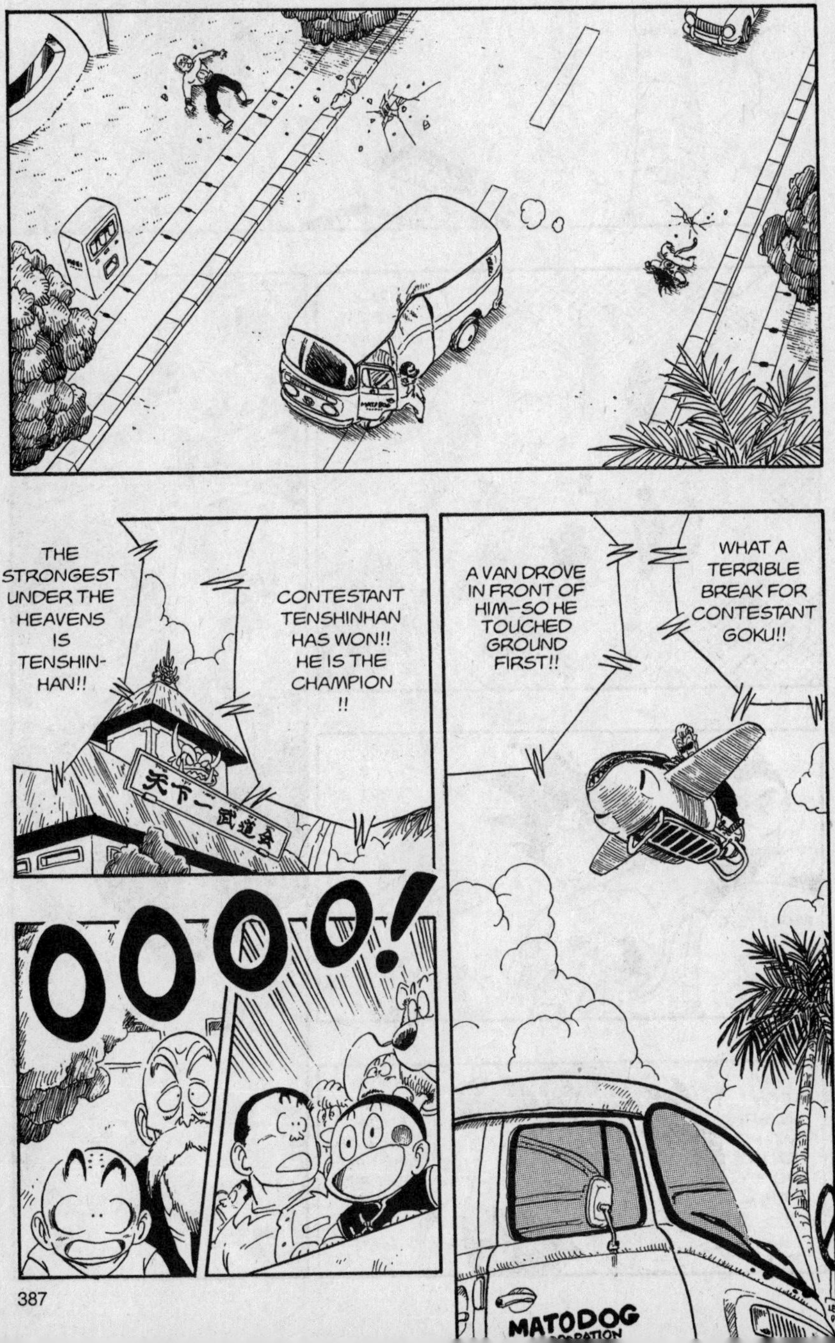
WHAT A TERRIBLE BREAK FOR CONTESTANT GOKU!!
A VAN DROVE IN FRONT OF HIM—SO HE TOUCHED GROUND FIRST!!
MATODOG
CONTESTANT TENSHINHAN HAS WON!! HE IS THE CHAMPION!!
THE STRONGEST UNDER THE HEAVENS IS TENSHINHAN!!
天下一武道会
OOOOO!

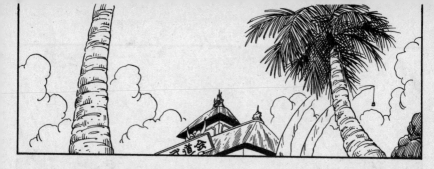

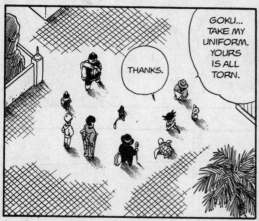

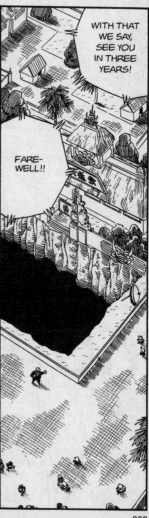

WITH THAT WE SAY, SEE YOU IN THREE YEARS!
FARE-WELL!!
GOKU... TAKE MY UNIFORM. YOURS IS ALL TORN.
THANKS.
MAN... THAT WAS *SO* CLOSE...
WHATEVER... LOSING CLOSE IS STILL LOSING...
YOU KNOW... IF YOU'D LIKE HALF THE PRIZE MONEY...
NAW! I DON'T UNDER-STAND HOW TO USE MONEY ANYHOW.

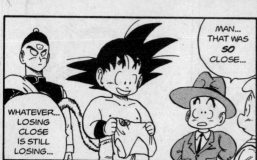

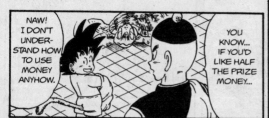

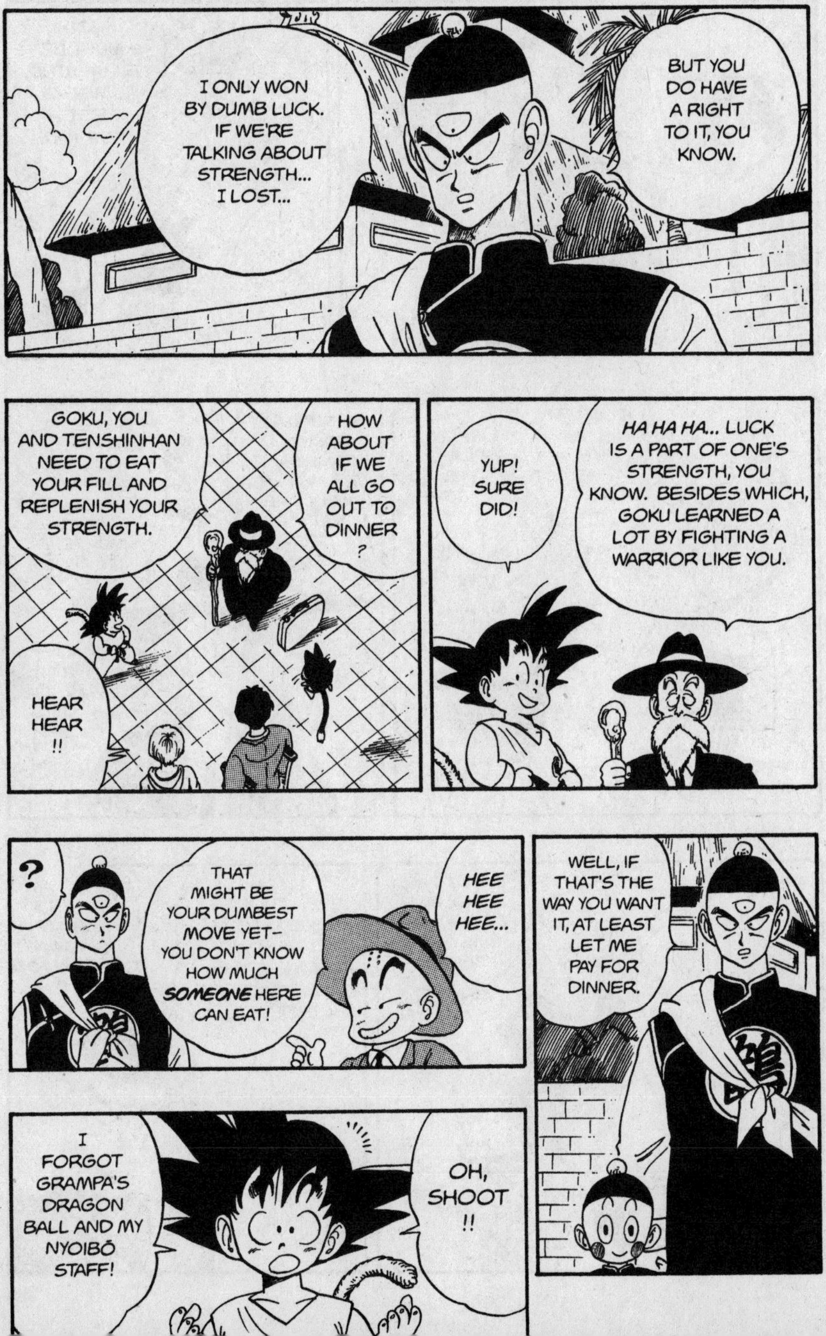
BUT YOU DO HAVE A RIGHT TO IT, YOU KNOW.
I ONLY WON BY DUMB LUCK. IF WE'RE TALKING ABOUT STRENGTH... I LOST...
HA HA HA... LUCK IS A PART OF ONE'S STRENGTH, YOU KNOW. BESIDES WHICH, GOKU LEARNED A LOT BY FIGHTING A WARRIOR LIKE YOU.
YUP! SURE DID!
HOW ABOUT IF WE ALL GO OUT TO DINNER?
GOKU, YOU AND TENSHINHAN NEED TO EAT YOUR FILL AND REPLENISH YOUR STRENGTH.
HEAR HEAR !!
WELL, IF THAT'S THE WAY YOU WANT IT, AT LEAST LET ME PAY FOR DINNER.
HEE HEE HEE...
THAT MIGHT BE YOUR DUMBEST MOVE YET— YOU DON'T KNOW HOW MUCH ***SOMEONE*** HERE CAN EAT!
?
OH, SHOOT !!
I FORGOT GRAMPA'S DRAGON BALL AND MY NYOIBŌ STAFF!

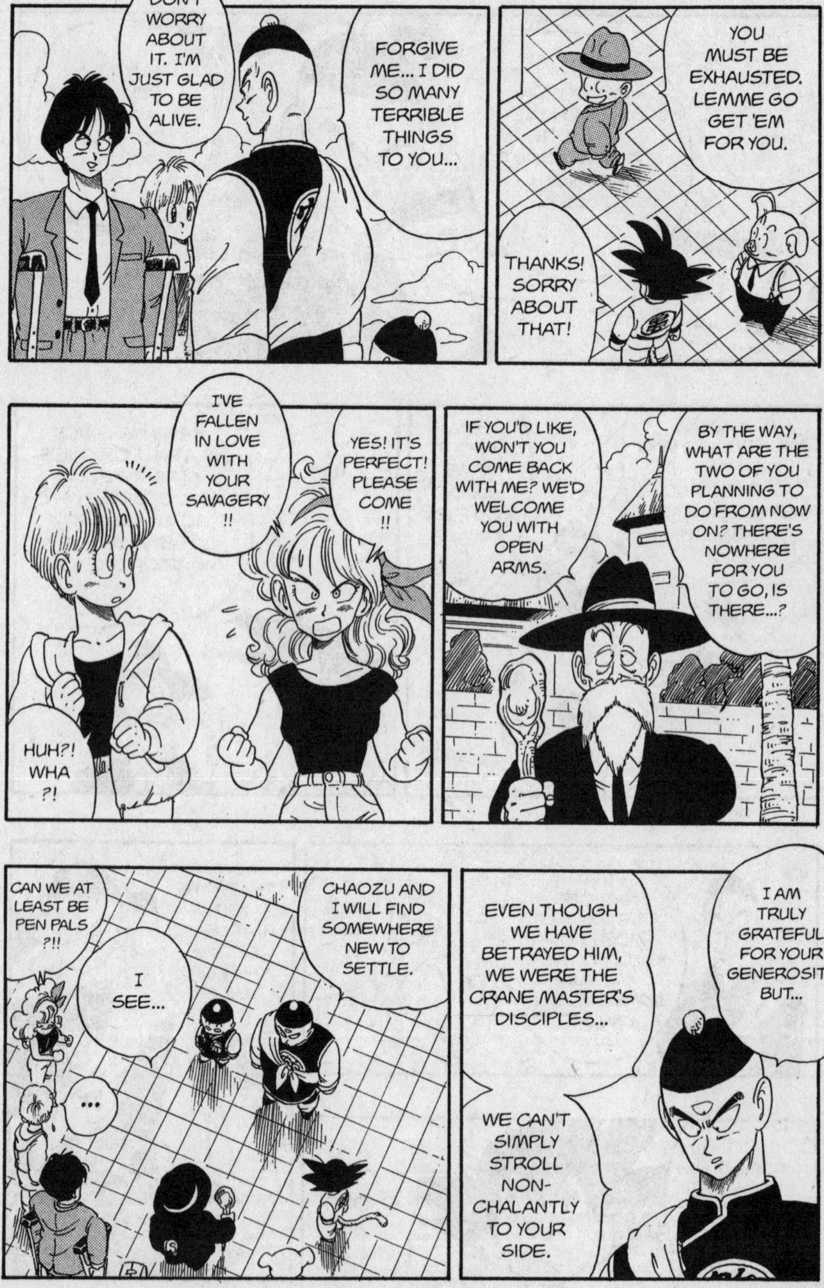

YOU MUST BE EXHAUSTED. LEMME GO GET 'EM FOR YOU.
THANKS! SORRY ABOUT THAT!
FORGIVE ME... I DID SO MANY TERRIBLE THINGS TO YOU...
DON'T WORRY ABOUT IT. I'M JUST GLAD TO BE ALIVE.
BY THE WAY, WHAT ARE THE TWO OF YOU PLANNING TO DO FROM NOW ON? THERE'S NOWHERE FOR YOU TO GO, IS THERE...?
IF YOU'D LIKE, WON'T YOU COME BACK WITH ME? WE'D WELCOME YOU WITH OPEN ARMS.
YES! IT'S PERFECT! PLEASE COME!!
I'VE FALLEN IN LOVE WITH YOUR SAVAGERY!!
HUH?! WHA?!
I AM TRULY GRATEFUL FOR YOUR GENEROSITY, BUT...
EVEN THOUGH WE HAVE BETRAYED HIM, WE WERE THE CRANE MASTER'S DISCIPLES...
WE CAN'T SIMPLY STROLL NON-CHALANTLY TO YOUR SIDE.
CHAOZU AND I WILL FIND SOMEWHERE NEW TO SETTLE.
I SEE...
CAN WE AT LEAST BE PEN PALS?!!
...

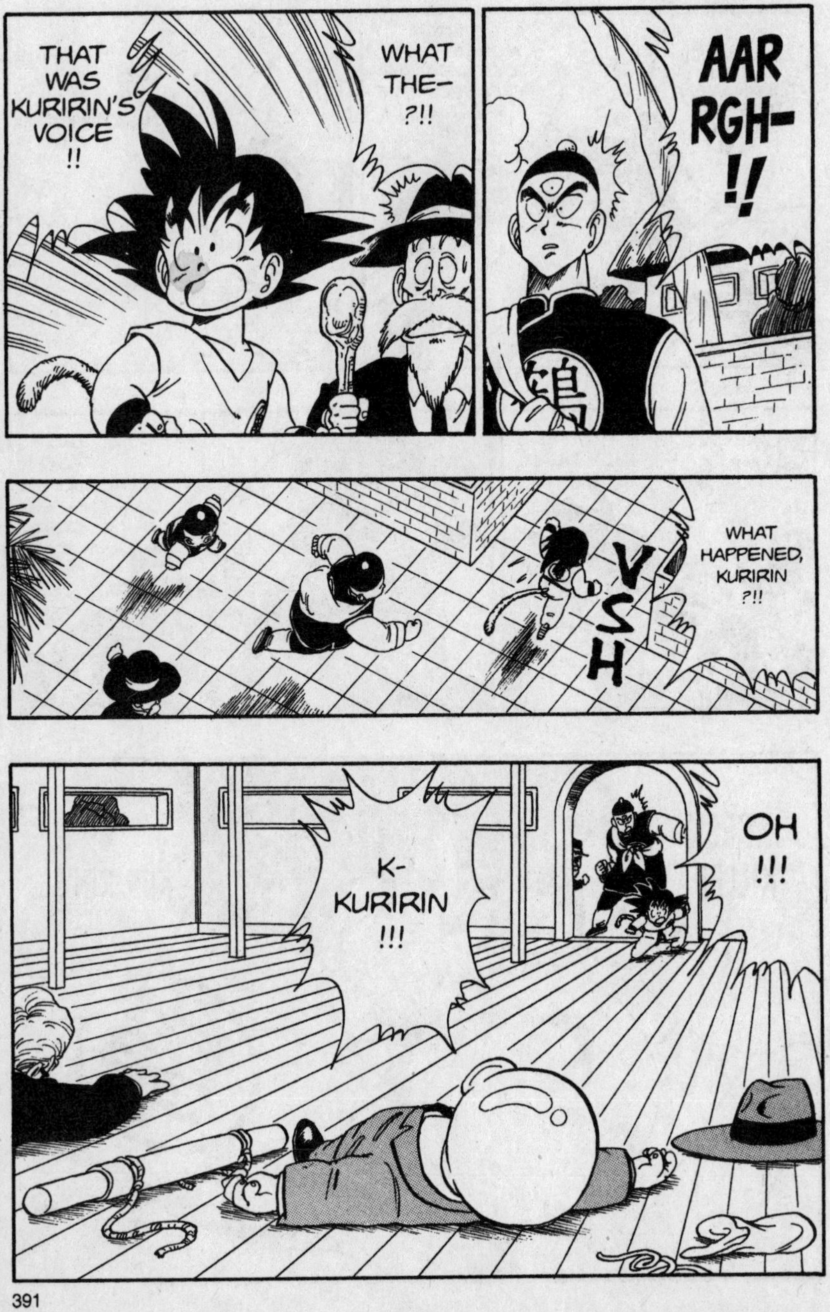
AAR RGH-!!
WHAT THE-?!!
THAT WAS KURIRIN'S VOICE!!
WHAT HAPPENED, KURIRIN?!!
VSH
OH!!!
K-KURIRIN!!!

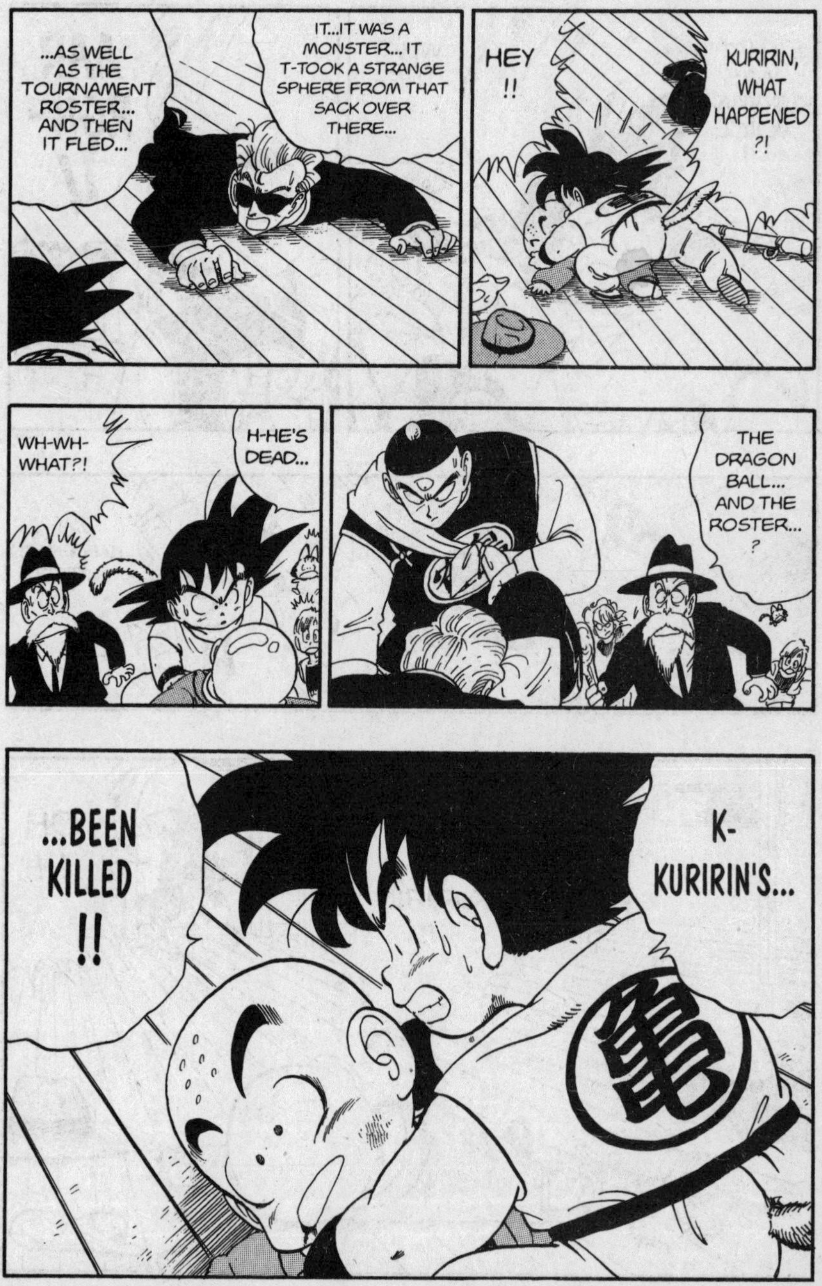
KURIRIN, WHAT HAPPENED ?!
HEY !!
IT...IT WAS A MONSTER... IT T-TOOK A STRANGE SPHERE FROM THAT SACK OVER THERE...
...AS WELL AS THE TOURNAMENT ROSTER... AND THEN IT FLED...
THE DRAGON BALL... AND THE ROSTER... ?
H-HE'S DEAD...
WH-WH-WHAT?!
K-KURIRIN'S...
...BEEN KILLED !!

Tale 135 · The Death of Kuririn

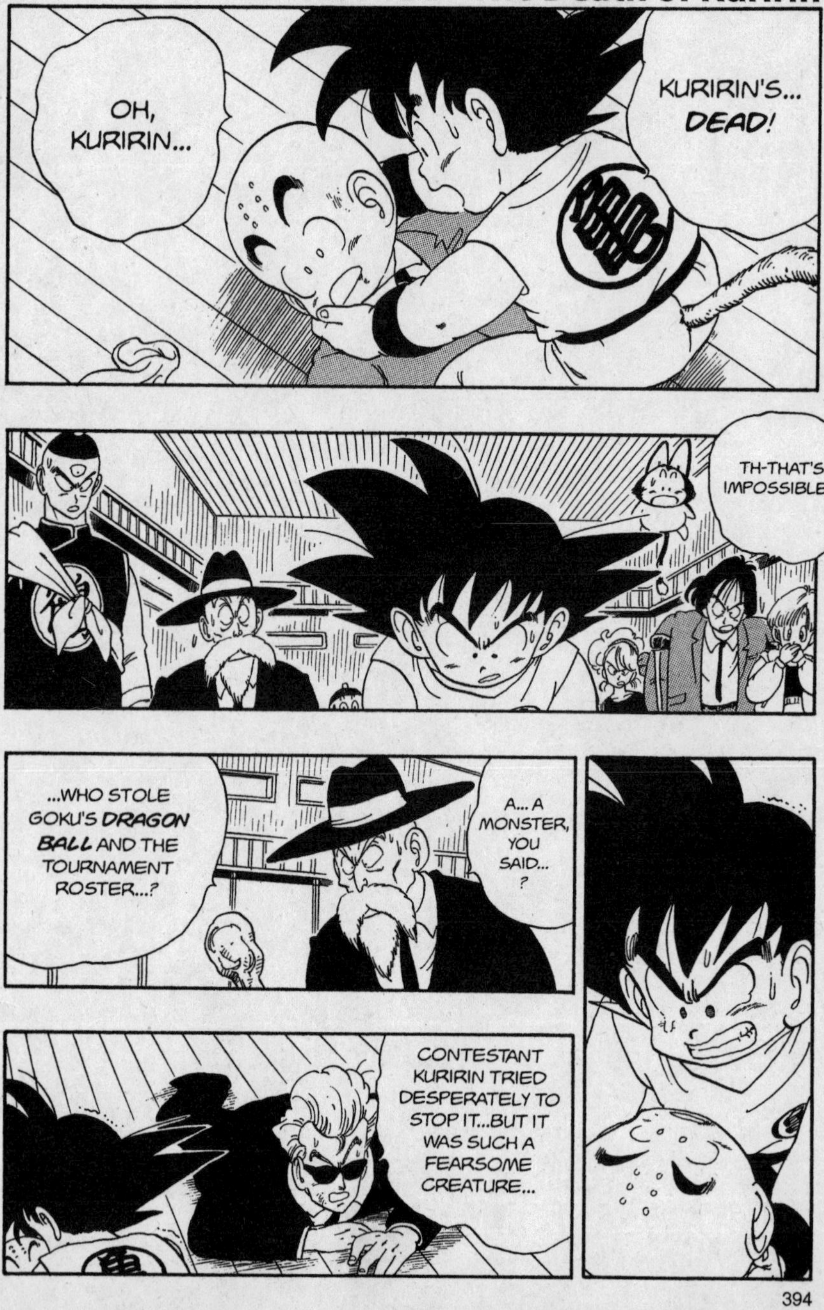
KURIRIN'S... *DEAD!*
OH, KURIRIN...
TH-THAT'S IMPOSSIBLE...
A... A MONSTER, YOU SAID... ?
...WHO STOLE GOKU'S *DRAGON BALL* AND THE TOURNAMENT ROSTER...?
CONTESTANT KURIRIN TRIED DESPERATELY TO STOP IT...BUT IT WAS SUCH A FEARSOME CREATURE...

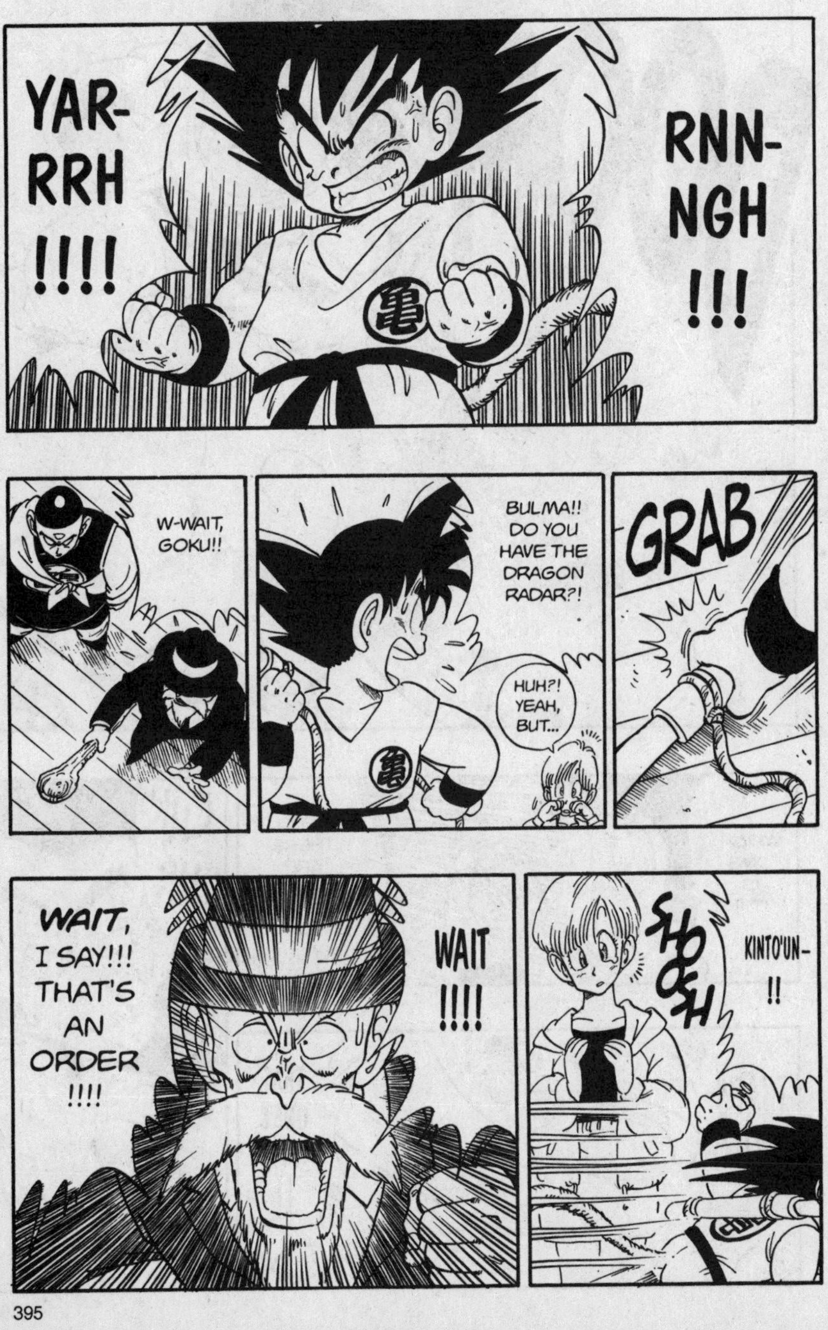
RNN-NGH!!!
YARR-RRH!!!!
GRAB
BULMA!! DO YOU HAVE THE DRAGON RADAR?!
HUH?! YEAH, BUT...
W-WAIT, GOKU!!
KINTO'UN-!!
SHOOSH
WAIT!!!!
WAIT, I SAY!!! THAT'S AN ORDER!!!!

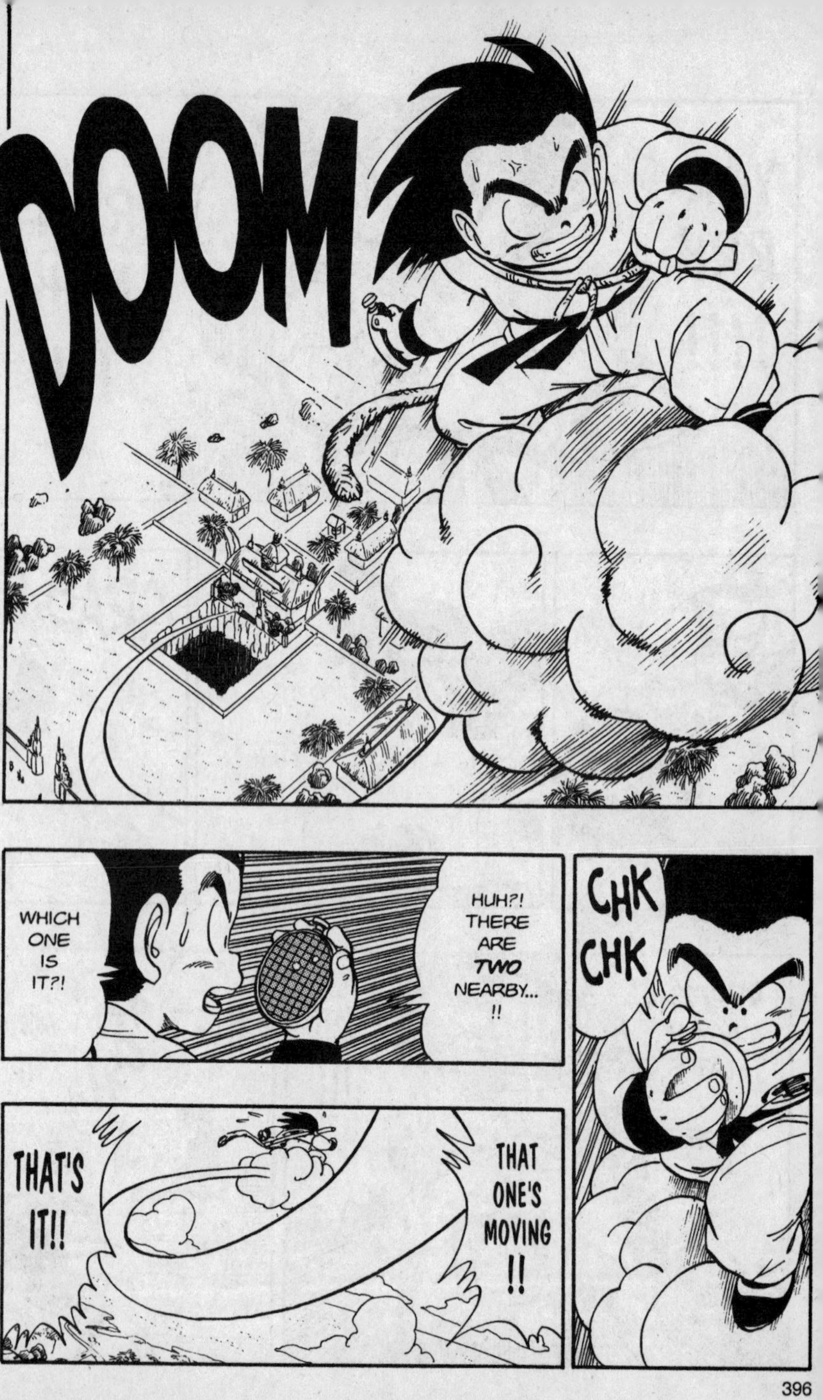
DOOM
CHK CHK
HUH?! THERE ARE *TWO* NEARBY... !!
WHICH ONE IS IT?!
THAT ONE'S MOVING !!
THAT'S IT!!

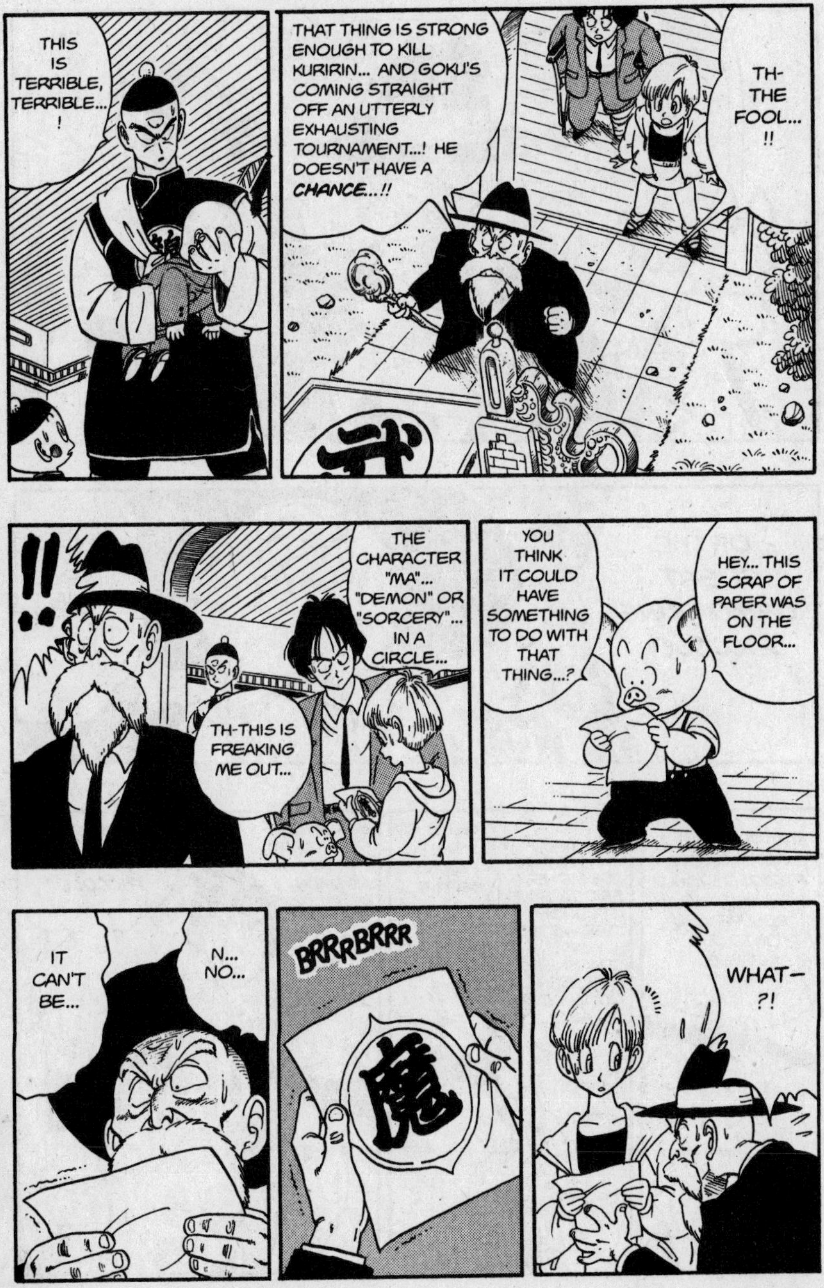

TH-THE FOOL... !!
THAT THING IS STRONG ENOUGH TO KILL KURIRIN... AND GOKU'S COMING STRAIGHT OFF AN UTTERLY EXHAUSTING TOURNAMENT...! HE DOESN'T HAVE A ***CHANCE...!!***
THIS IS TERRIBLE, TERRIBLE... !
HEY... THIS SCRAP OF PAPER WAS ON THE FLOOR...
YOU THINK IT COULD HAVE SOMETHING TO DO WITH THAT THING...?
THE CHARACTER "MA"... "DEMON" OR "SORCERY"... IN A CIRCLE...
!!
TH-THIS IS FREAKING ME OUT...
WHAT—?!
BRRRBRRR
魔
N... NO...
IT CAN'T BE...

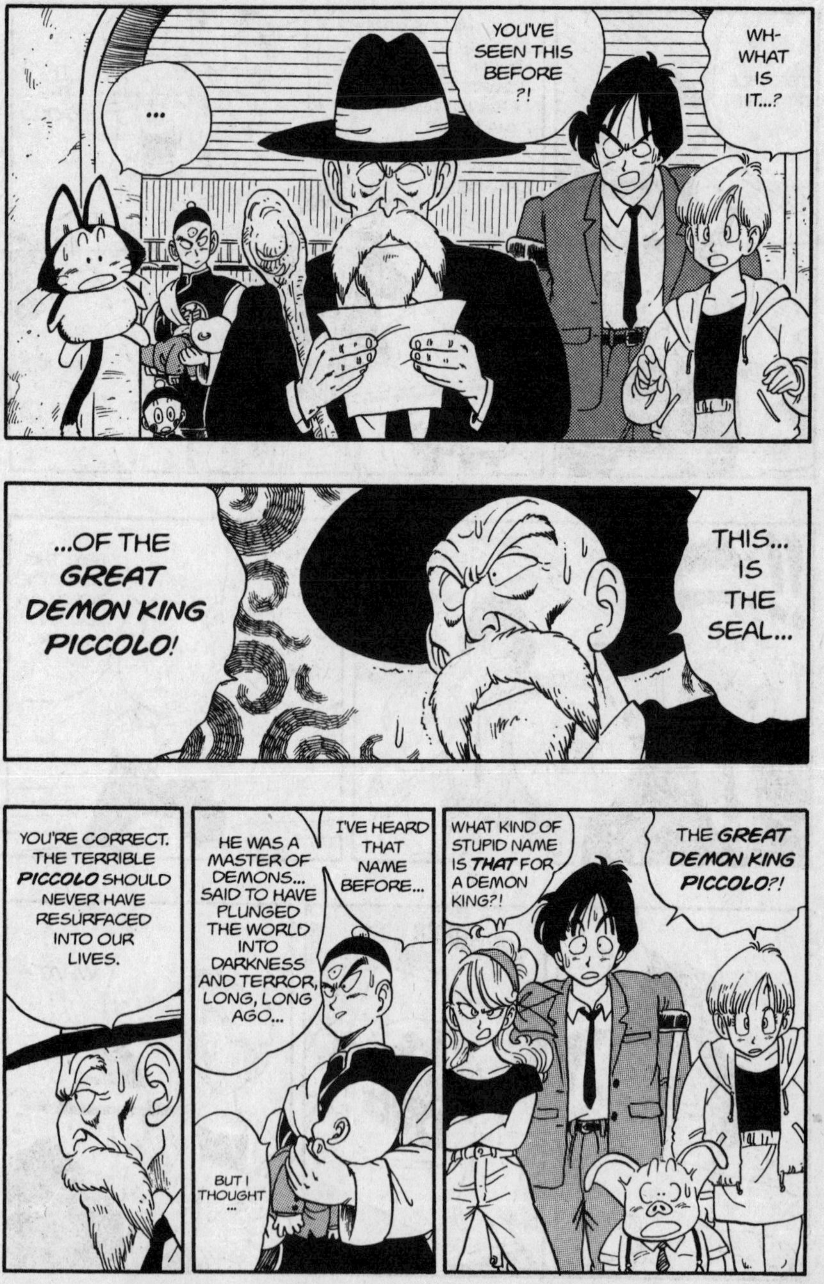

WH- WHAT IS IT...?
YOU'VE SEEN THIS BEFORE ?!
...
THIS... IS THE SEAL...
...OF THE GREAT DEMON KING PICCOLO!
THE GREAT DEMON KING PICCOLO?!
WHAT KIND OF STUPID NAME IS THAT FOR A DEMON KING?!
I'VE HEARD THAT NAME BEFORE...
HE WAS A MASTER OF DEMONS... SAID TO HAVE PLUNGED THE WORLD INTO DARKNESS AND TERROR, LONG, LONG AGO...
BUT I THOUGHT ...
YOU'RE CORRECT. THE TERRIBLE PICCOLO SHOULD NEVER HAVE RESURFACED INTO OUR LIVES.

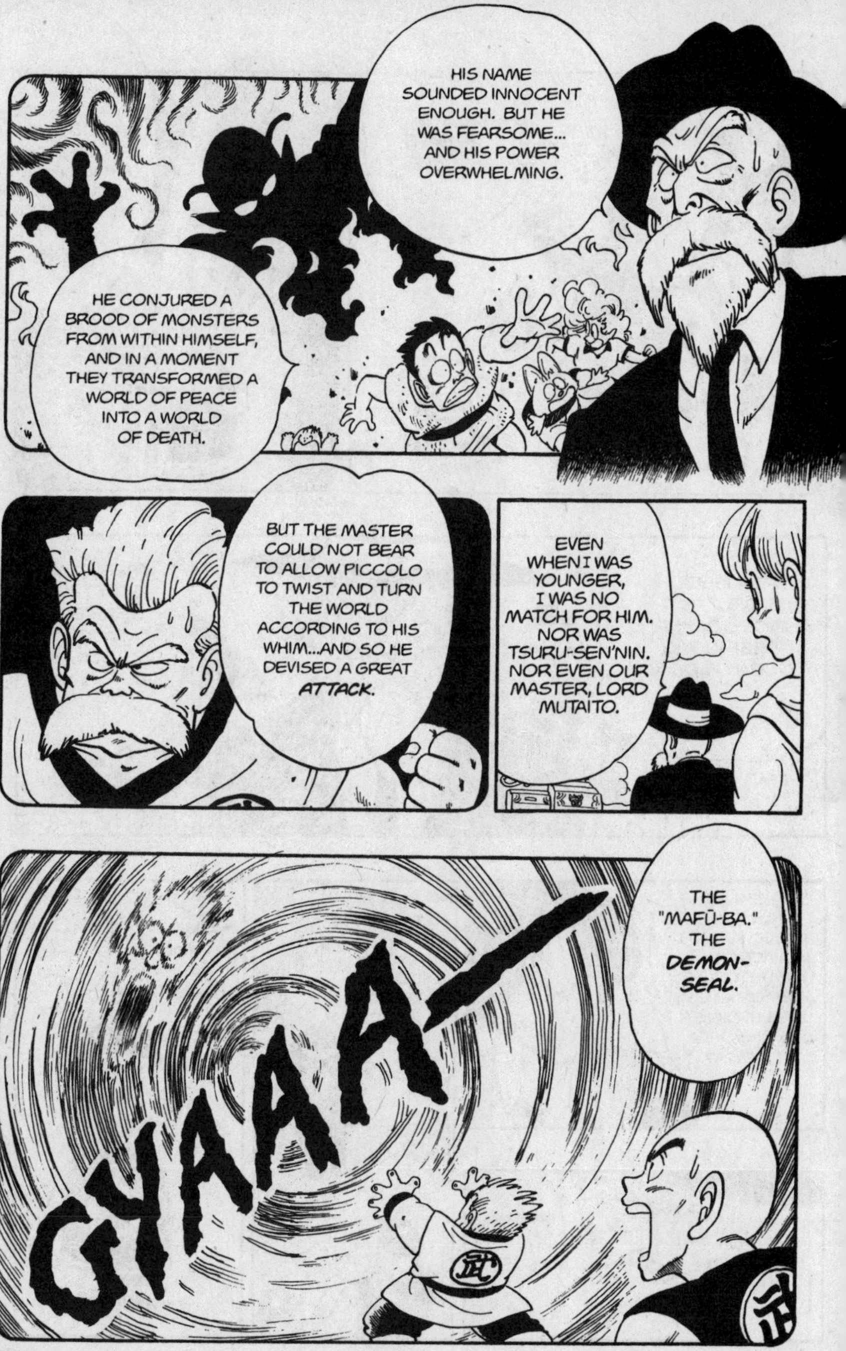
HIS NAME SOUNDED INNOCENT ENOUGH. BUT HE WAS FEARSOME... AND HIS POWER OVERWHELMING.
HE CONJURED A BROOD OF MONSTERS FROM WITHIN HIMSELF, AND IN A MOMENT THEY TRANSFORMED A WORLD OF PEACE INTO A WORLD OF DEATH.
EVEN WHEN I WAS YOUNGER, I WAS NO MATCH FOR HIM. NOR WAS TSURU-SEN'NIN. NOR EVEN OUR MASTER, LORD MUTAITO.
BUT THE MASTER COULD NOT BEAR TO ALLOW PICCOLO TO TWIST AND TURN THE WORLD ACCORDING TO HIS WHIM...AND SO HE DEVISED A GREAT ATTACK.
THE "MAFŪ-BA." THE DEMON-SEAL.
GYAAA

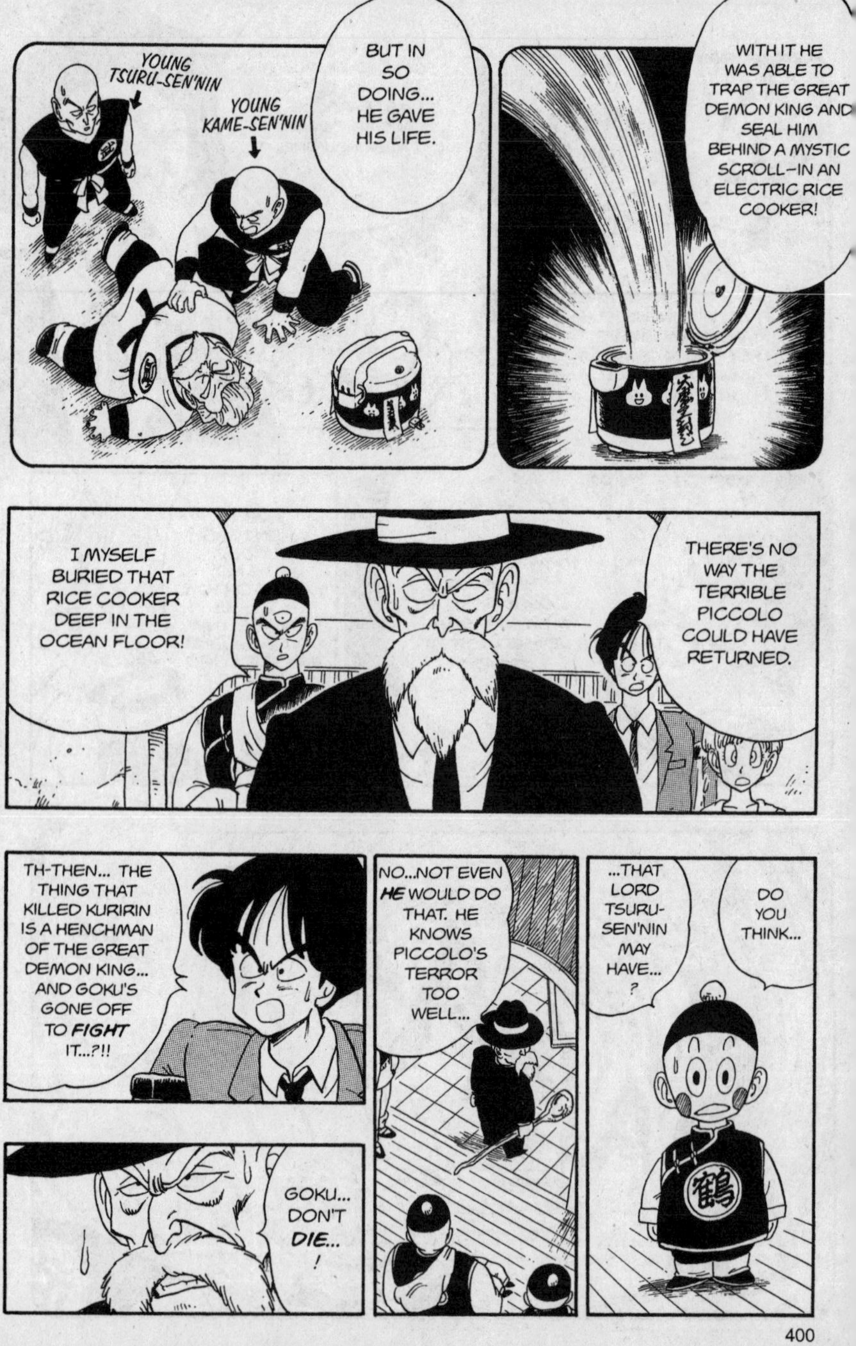
WITH IT HE WAS ABLE TO TRAP THE GREAT DEMON KING AND SEAL HIM BEHIND A MYSTIC SCROLL—IN AN ELECTRIC RICE COOKER!
BUT IN SO DOING... HE GAVE HIS LIFE.
YOUNG TSURU-SEN'NIN
YOUNG KAME-SEN'NIN
THERE'S NO WAY THE TERRIBLE PICCOLO COULD HAVE RETURNED.
I MYSELF BURIED THAT RICE COOKER DEEP IN THE OCEAN FLOOR!
DO YOU THINK...
...THAT LORD TSURU-SEN'NIN MAY HAVE...?
NO...NOT EVEN *HE* WOULD DO THAT. HE KNOWS PICCOLO'S TERROR TOO WELL...
TH-THEN... THE THING THAT KILLED KURIRIN IS A HENCHMAN OF THE GREAT DEMON KING... AND GOKU'S GONE OFF TO *FIGHT* IT...?!!
GOKU... DON'T *DIE*...!

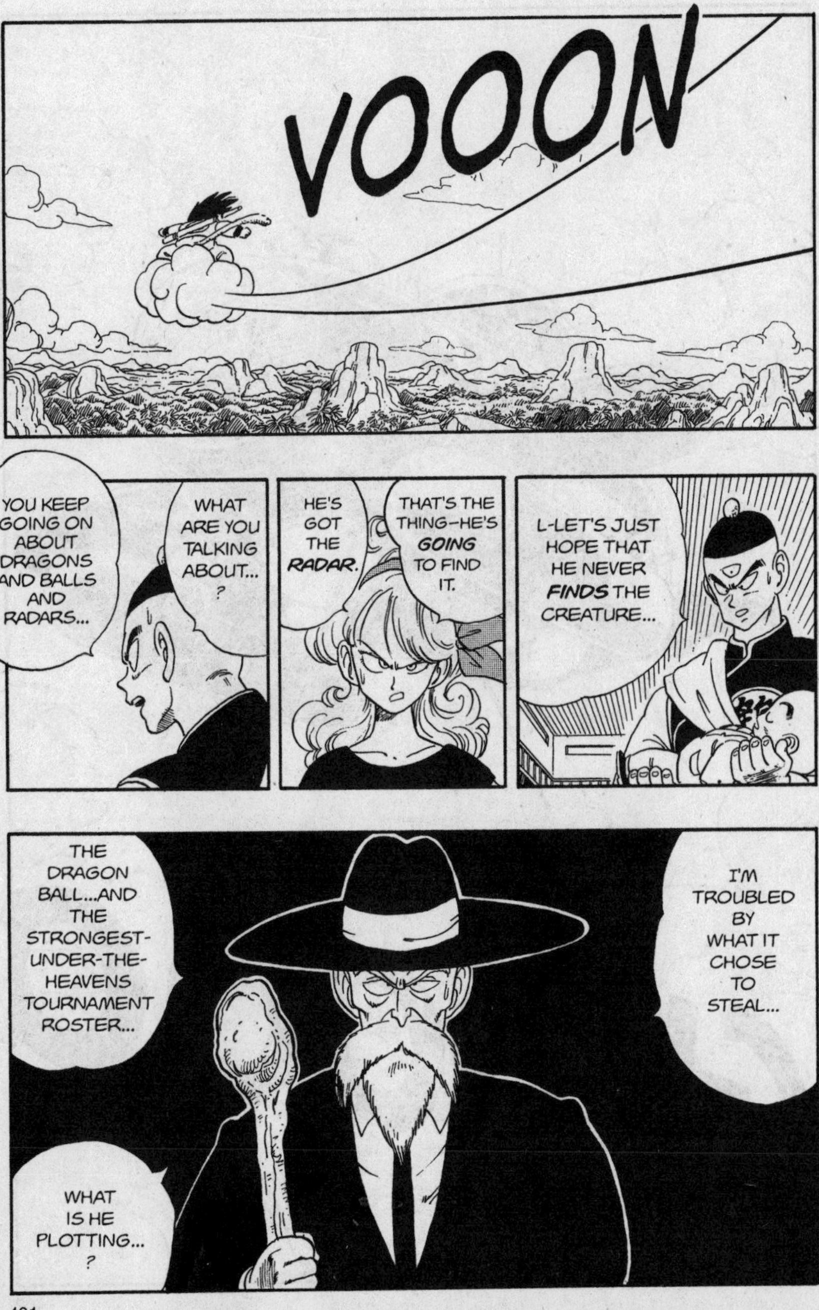
VOOON
L-LET'S JUST HOPE THAT HE NEVER FINDS THE CREATURE...
THAT'S THE THING—HE'S GOING TO FIND IT.
HE'S GOT THE RADAR.
WHAT ARE YOU TALKING ABOUT...?
YOU KEEP GOING ON ABOUT DRAGONS AND BALLS AND RADARS...
I'M TROUBLED BY WHAT IT CHOSE TO STEAL...
THE DRAGON BALL...AND THE STRONGEST-UNDER-THE-HEAVENS TOURNAMENT ROSTER...
WHAT IS HE PLOTTING...?

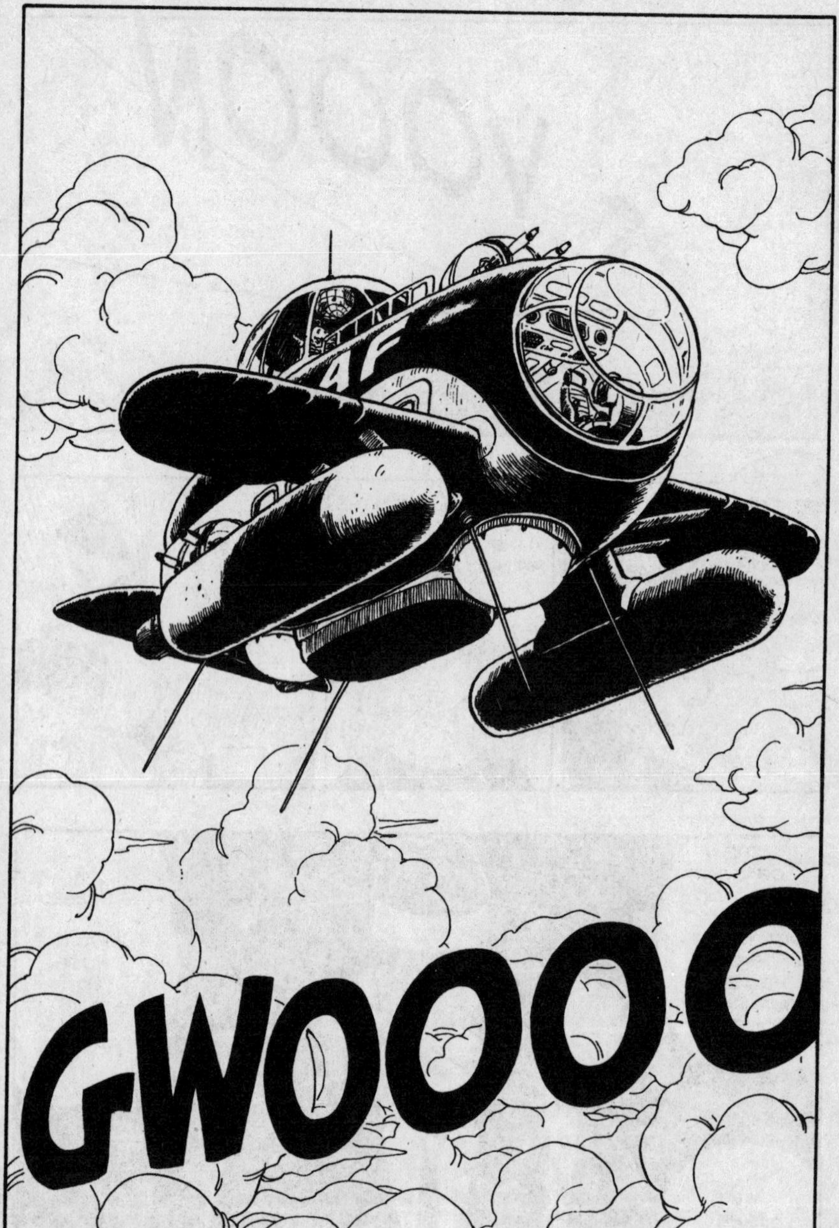
4F
GWOOOO

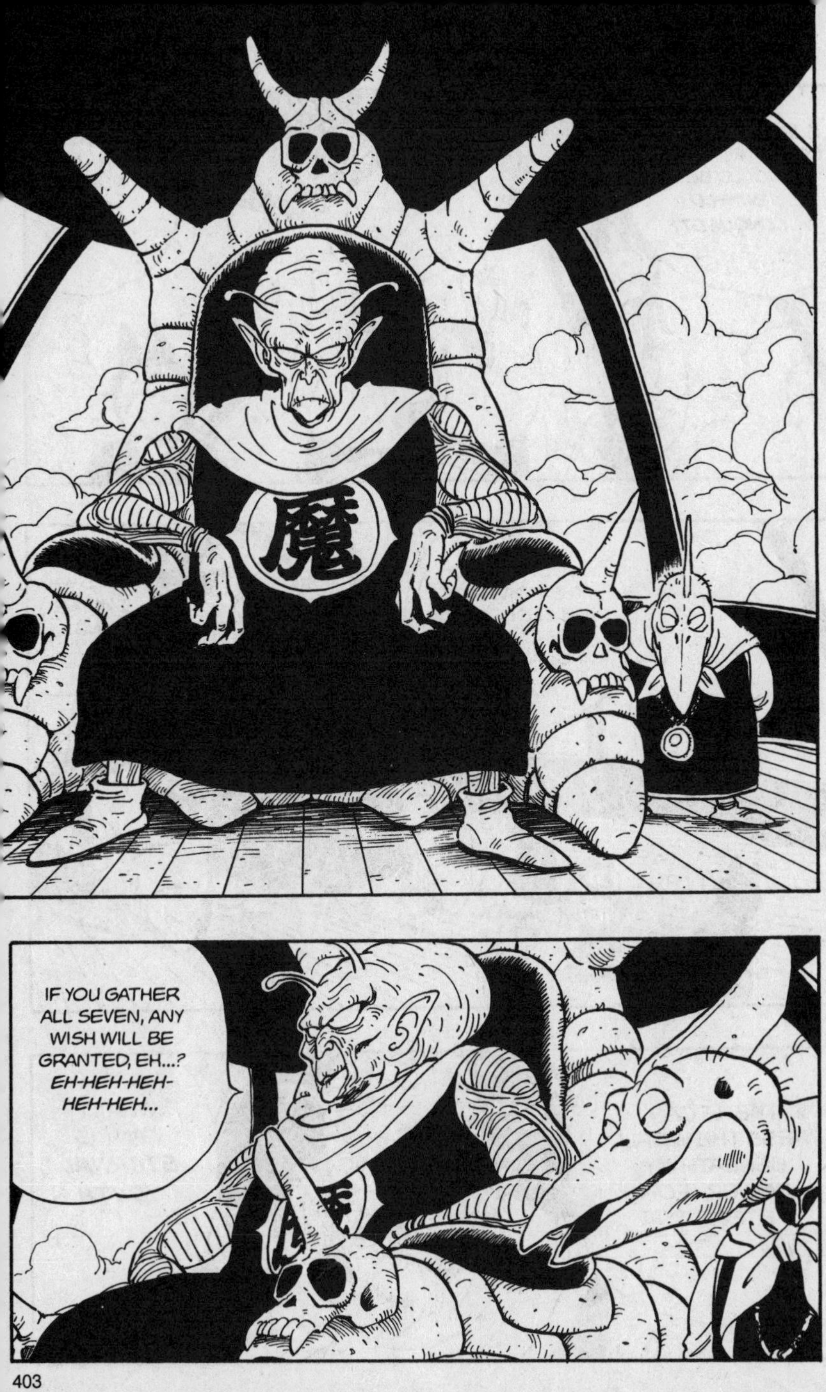
IF YOU GATHER ALL SEVEN, ANY WISH WILL BE GRANTED, EH...? EH-HEH-HEH-HEH-HEH...

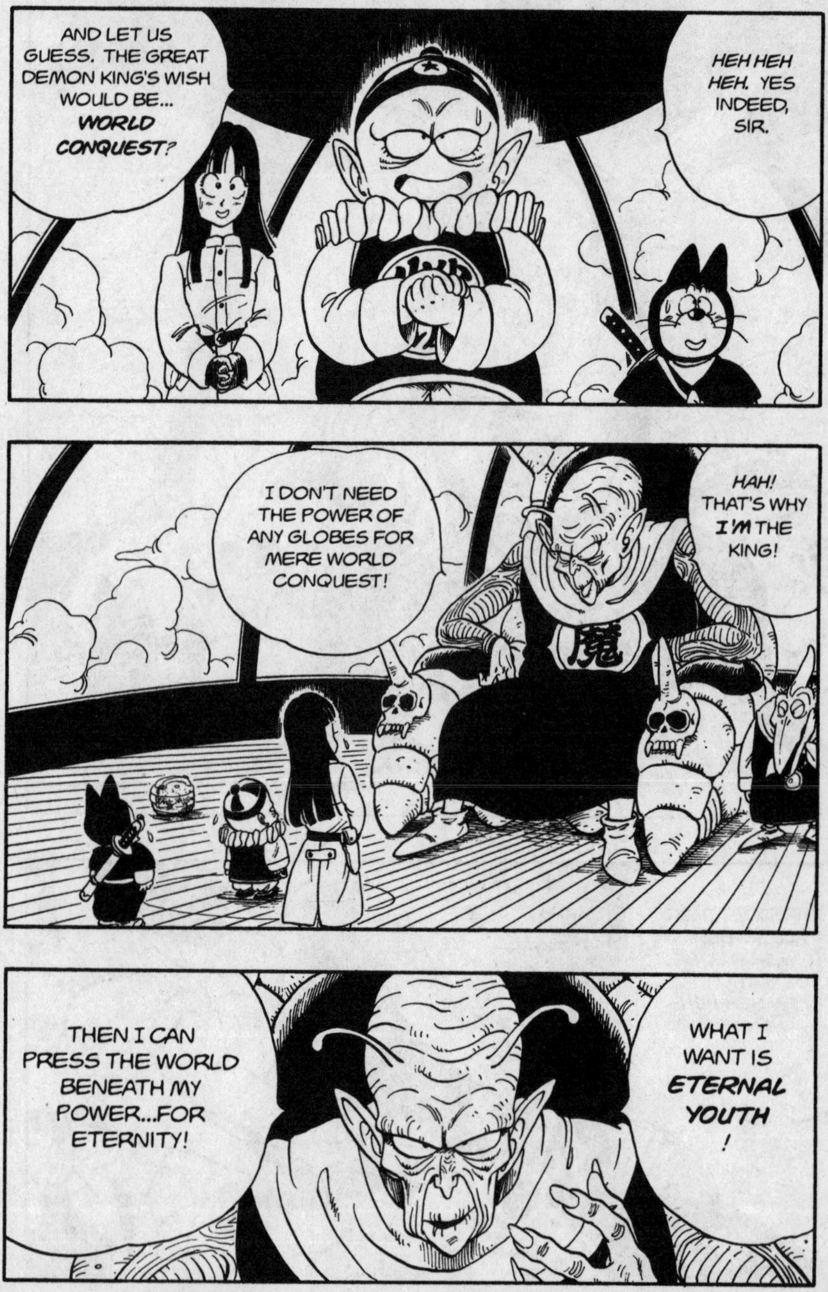
HEH HEH HEH. YES INDEED, SIR.
AND LET US GUESS. THE GREAT DEMON KING'S WISH WOULD BE... **WORLD CONQUEST**?
HAH! THAT'S WHY ***I'M*** THE KING!
I DON'T NEED THE POWER OF ANY GLOBES FOR MERE WORLD CONQUEST!
WHAT I WANT IS **ETERNAL YOUTH**!
THEN I CAN PRESS THE WORLD BENEATH MY POWER...FOR ETERNITY!

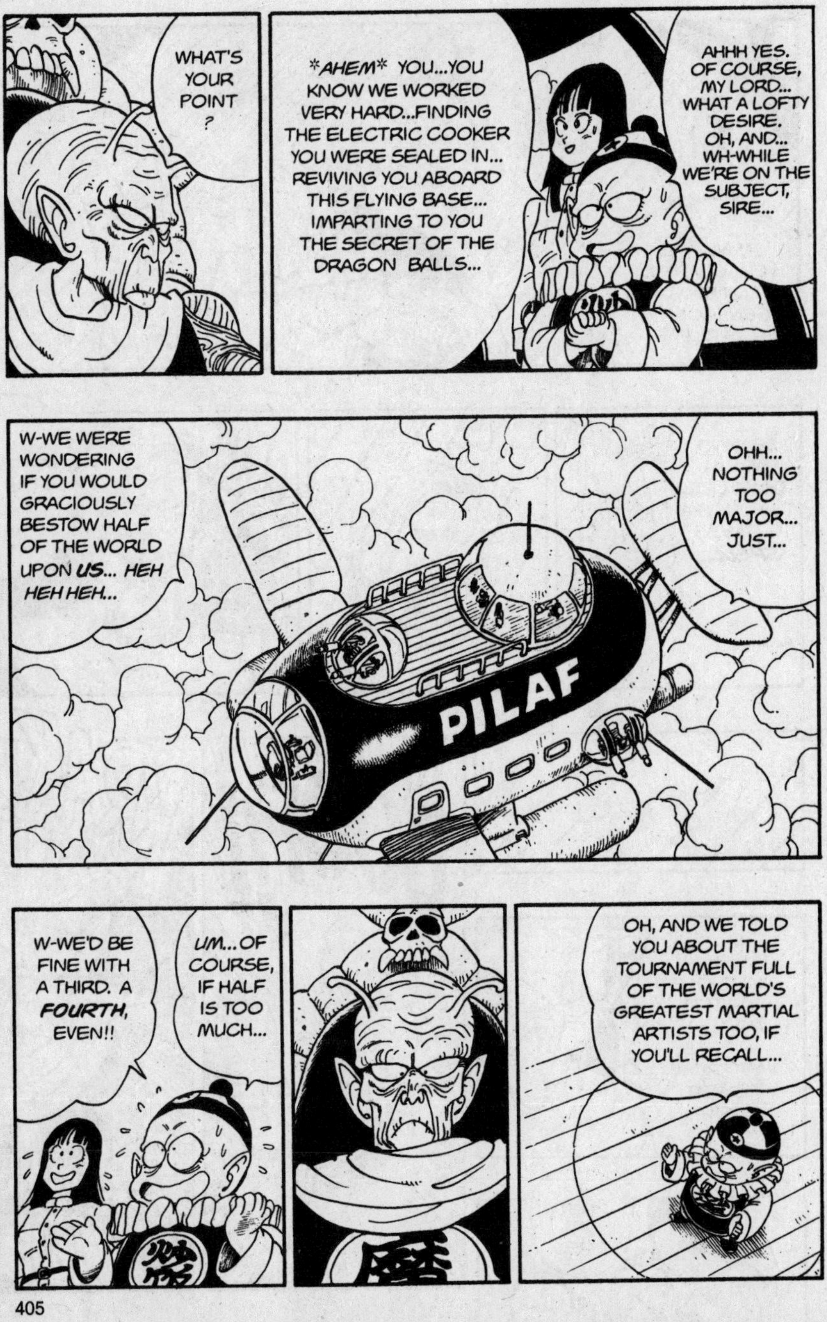
AHHH YES. OF COURSE, MY LORD... WHAT A LOFTY DESIRE. OH, AND... WH-WHILE WE'RE ON THE SUBJECT, SIRE...
AHEM YOU...YOU KNOW WE WORKED VERY HARD...FINDING THE ELECTRIC COOKER YOU WERE SEALED IN... REVIVING YOU ABOARD THIS FLYING BASE... IMPARTING TO YOU THE SECRET OF THE DRAGON BALLS...
WHAT'S YOUR POINT ?
OHH... NOTHING TOO MAJOR... JUST...
W-WE WERE WONDERING IF YOU WOULD GRACIOUSLY BESTOW HALF OF THE WORLD UPON *US*... *HEH HEH HEH...*
PILAF
OH, AND WE TOLD YOU ABOUT THE TOURNAMENT FULL OF THE WORLD'S GREATEST MARTIAL ARTISTS TOO, IF YOU'LL RECALL...
UM...OF COURSE, IF HALF IS TOO MUCH...
W-WE'D BE FINE WITH A THIRD. A ***FOURTH***, EVEN!!

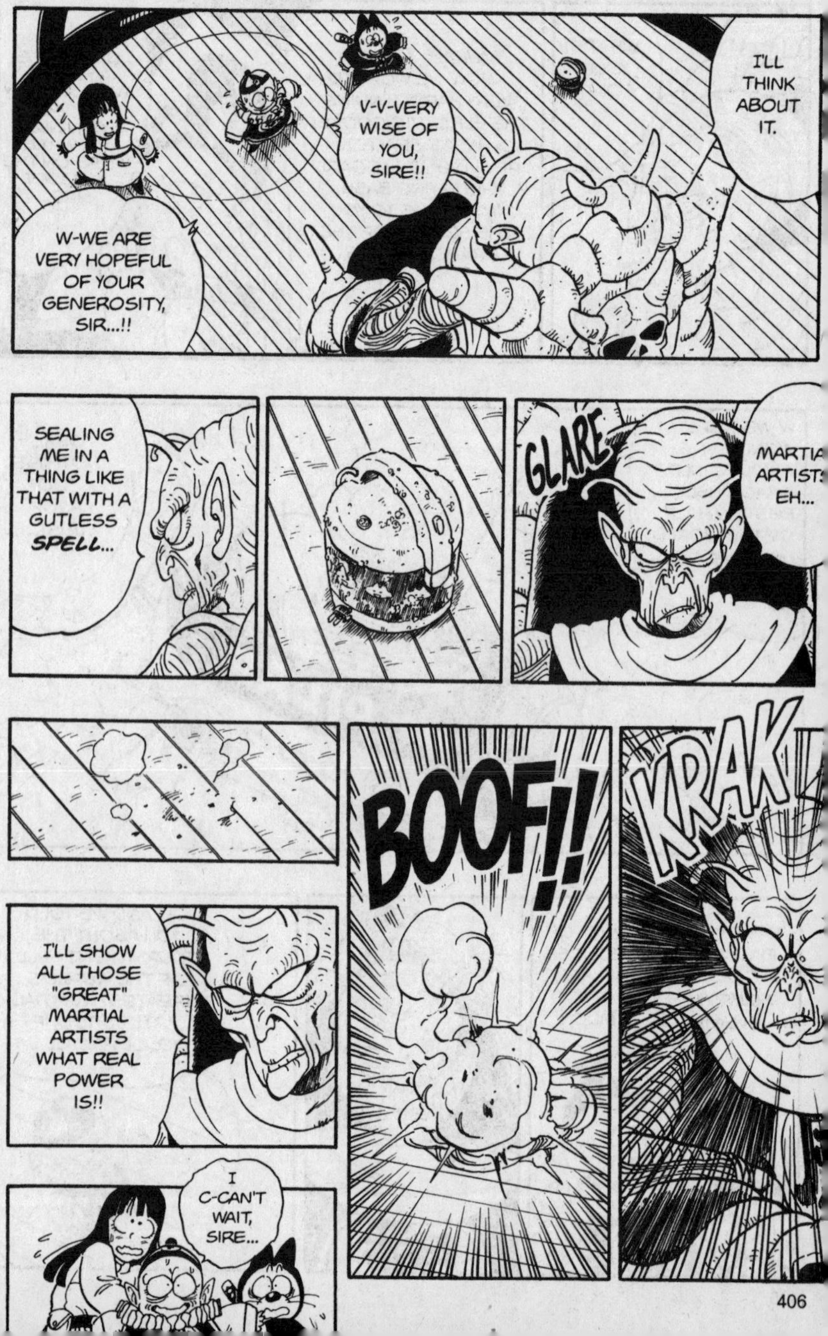
I'LL THINK ABOUT IT.
V-V-VERY WISE OF YOU, SIRE!!
W-WE ARE VERY HOPEFUL OF YOUR GENEROSITY, SIR...!!
MARTIA ARTIST EH...
GLARE
SEALING ME IN A THING LIKE THAT WITH A GUTLESS SPELL...
KRAK
BOOF!!
I'LL SHOW ALL THOSE "GREAT" MARTIAL ARTISTS WHAT REAL POWER IS!!
I C-CAN'T WAIT, SIRE...

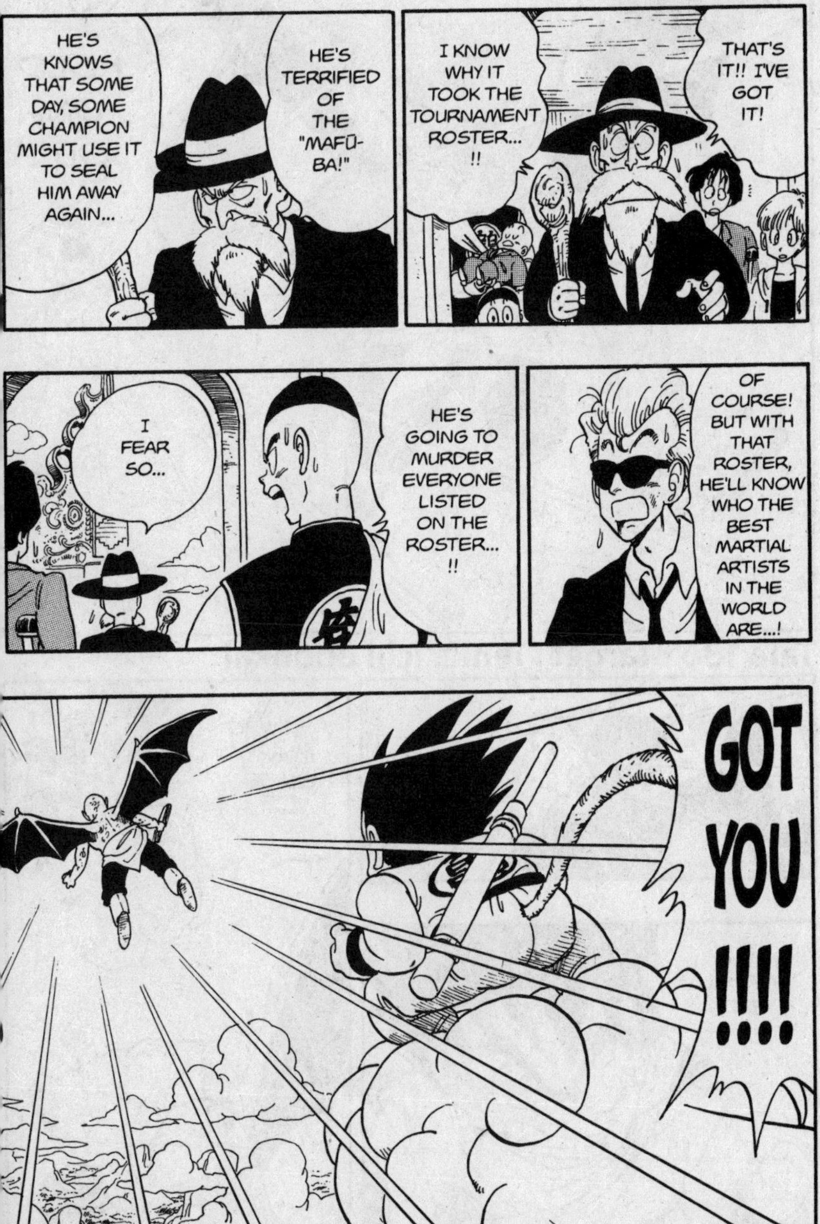
THAT'S IT!! I'VE GOT IT!
I KNOW WHY IT TOOK THE TOURNAMENT ROSTER... !!
HE'S TERRIFIED OF THE "MAFŪ-BA!"
HE'S KNOWS THAT SOME DAY, SOME CHAMPION MIGHT USE IT TO SEAL HIM AWAY AGAIN...
OF COURSE! BUT WITH THAT ROSTER, HE'LL KNOW WHO THE BEST MARTIAL ARTISTS IN THE WORLD ARE...!
HE'S GOING TO MURDER EVERYONE LISTED ON THE ROSTER... !!
I FEAR SO...
GOT YOU !!!!

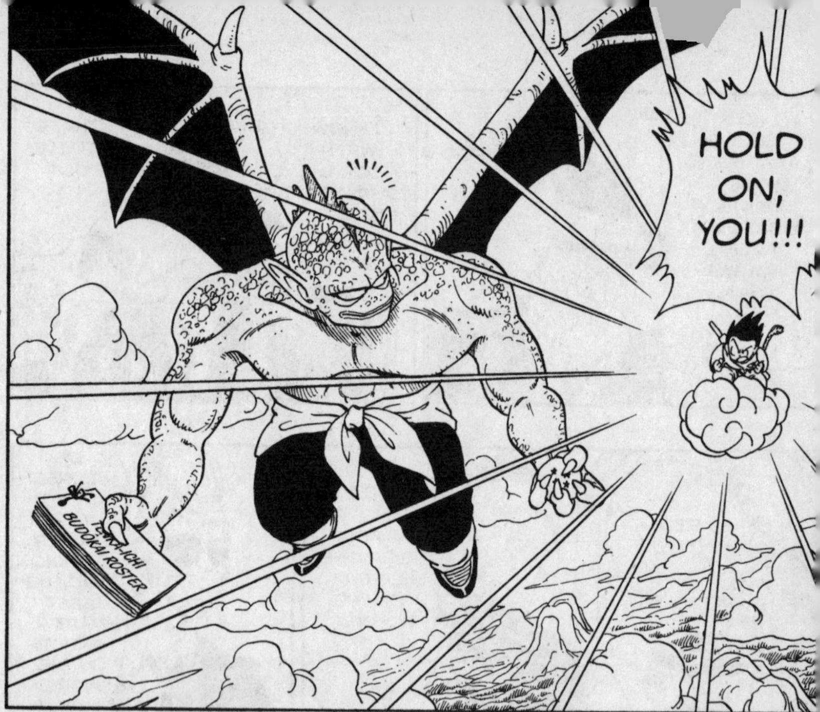
HOLD ON, YOU!!!
TENKA'ICHI BUDOKAI ROSTER

Tale 136 • Target : Tenka'ichi Budōkai

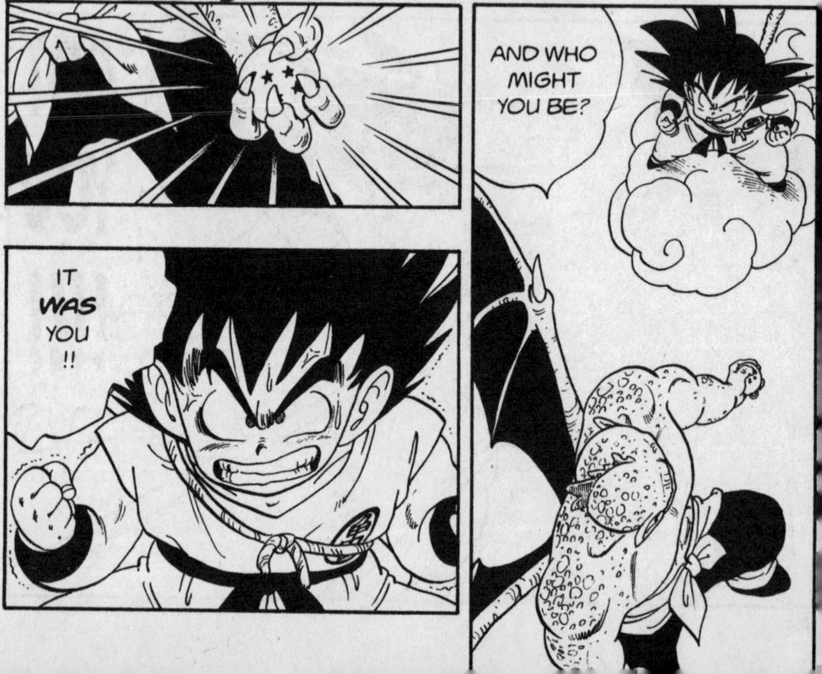
AND WHO MIGHT YOU BE?
IT WAS YOU!!

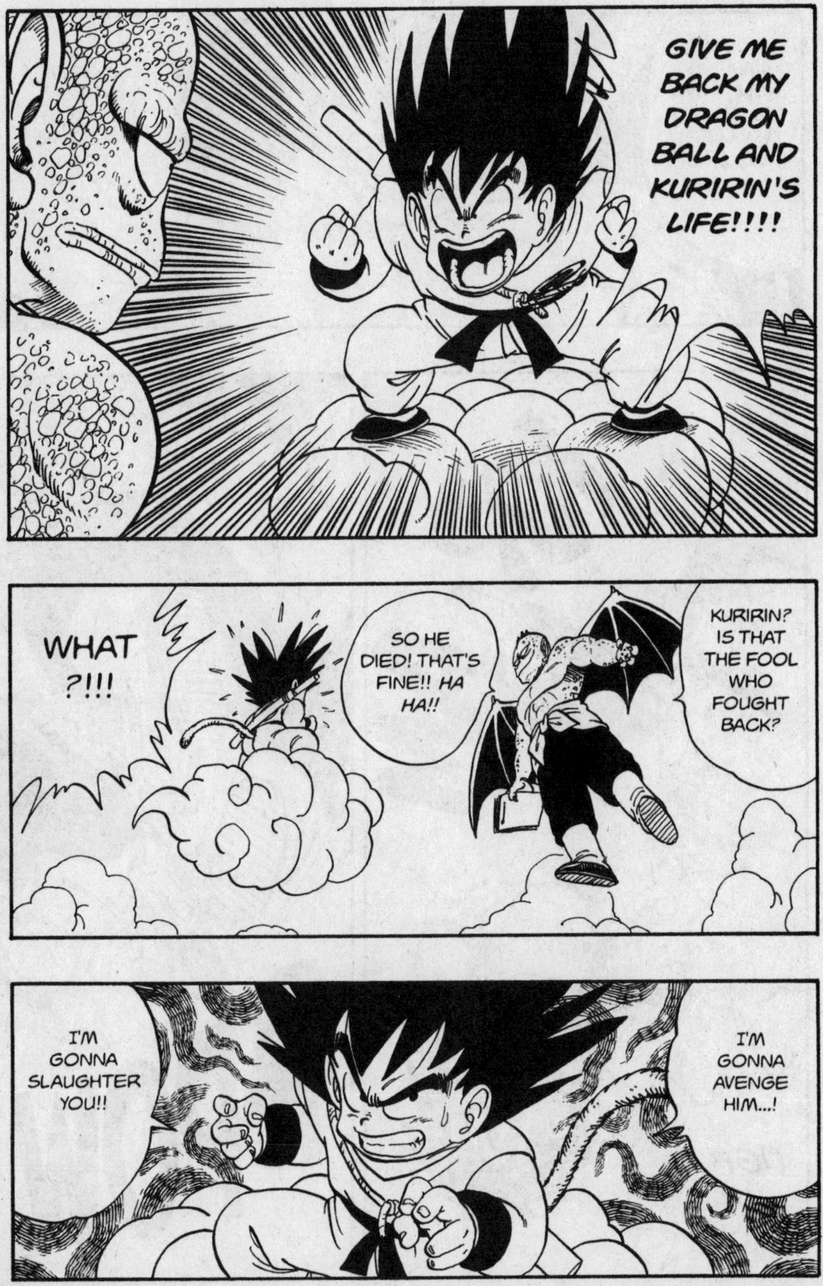
GIVE ME BACK MY DRAGON BALL AND KURIRIN'S LIFE!!!!
KURIRIN? IS THAT THE FOOL WHO FOUGHT BACK?
SO HE DIED! THAT'S FINE!! HA HA!!
WHAT?!!!
I'M GONNA AVENGE HIM...!
I'M GONNA SLAUGHTER YOU!!

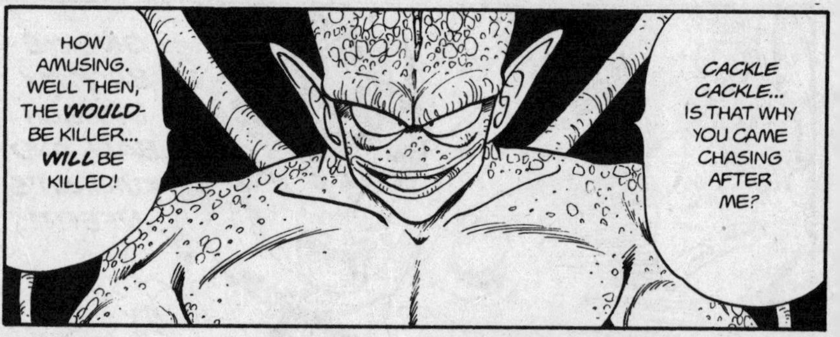
CACKLE CACKLE... IS THAT WHY YOU CAME CHASING AFTER ME?
HOW AMUSING. WELL THEN, THE *WOULD*-BE KILLER... *WILL* BE KILLED!
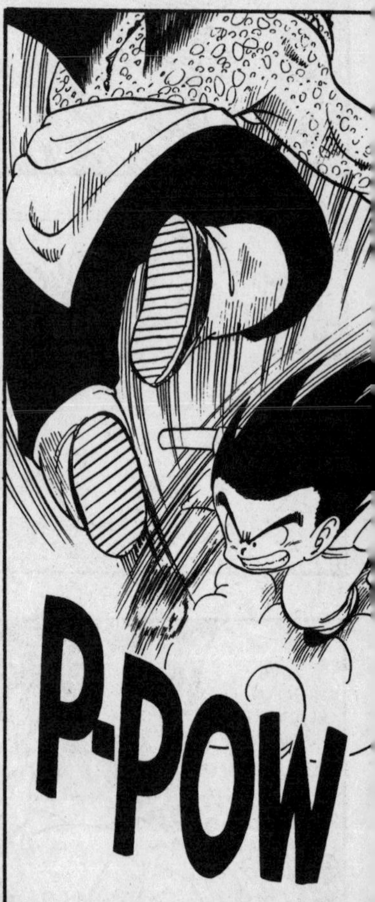
P-POW
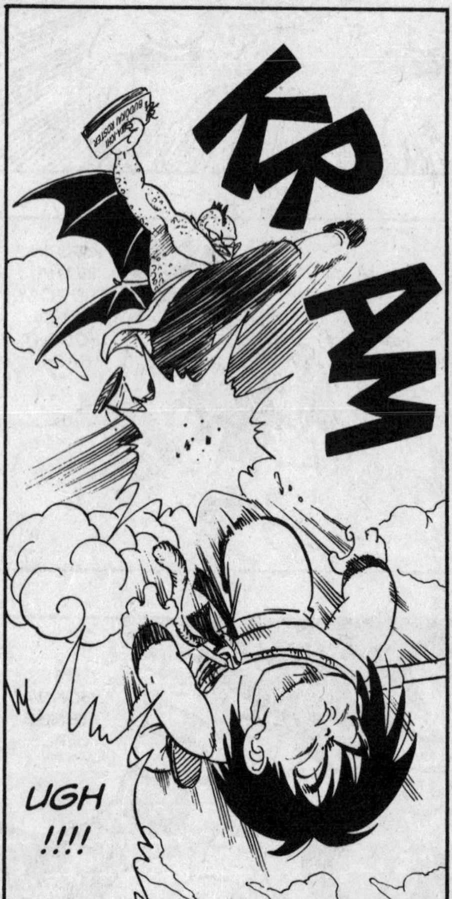
KRAM
UGH !!!!

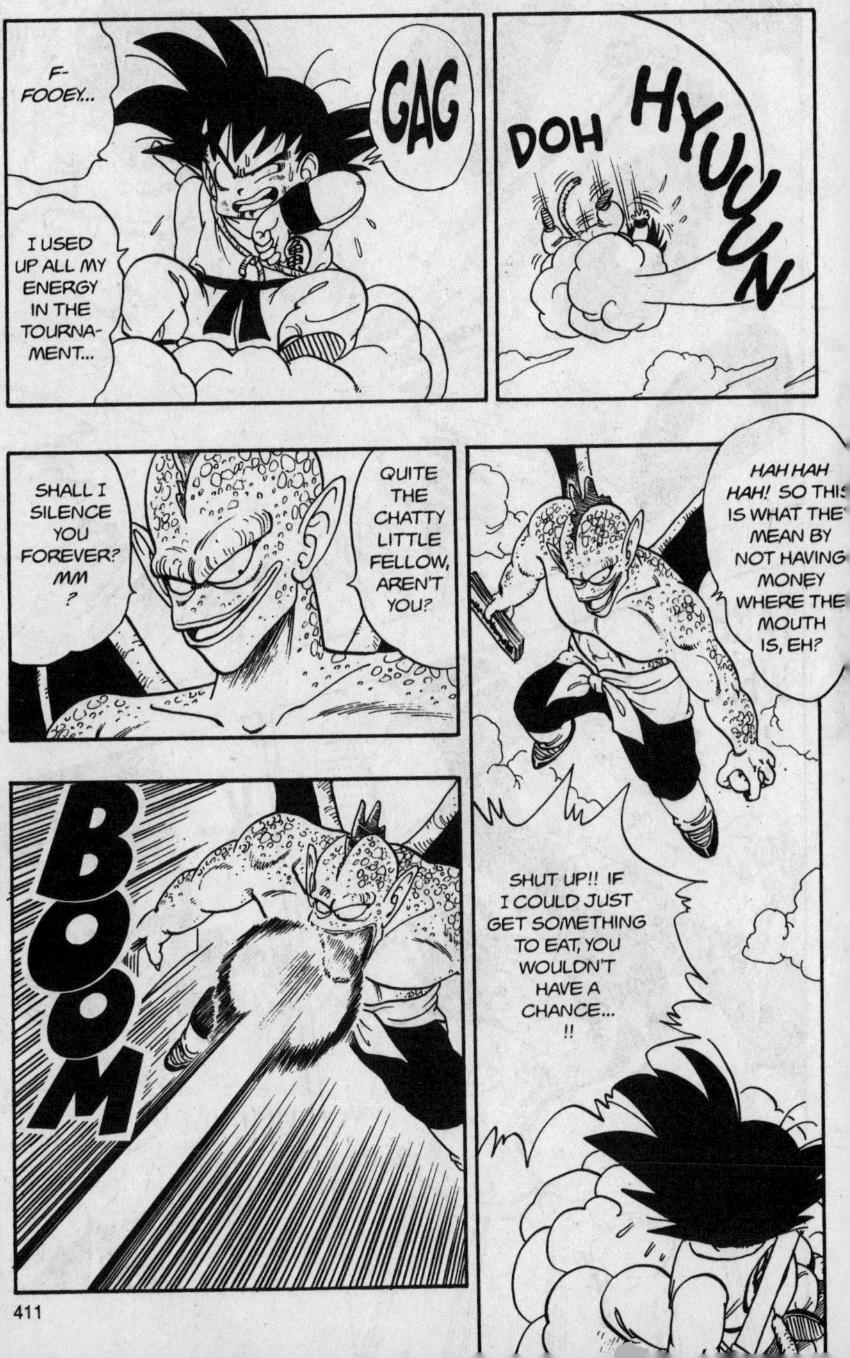
DOH HYUUUN
GAG
F- FOOEY...
I USED UP ALL MY ENERGY IN THE TOURNA- MENT...
HAH HAH HAH! SO THI IS WHAT THE MEAN BY NOT HAVING MONEY WHERE THE MOUTH IS, EH?
SHUT UP!! IF I COULD JUST GET SOMETHING TO EAT, YOU WOULDN'T HAVE A CHANCE...
!!
QUITE THE CHATTY LITTLE FELLOW, AREN'T YOU?
SHALL I SILENCE YOU FOREVER? MM ?
BOOM

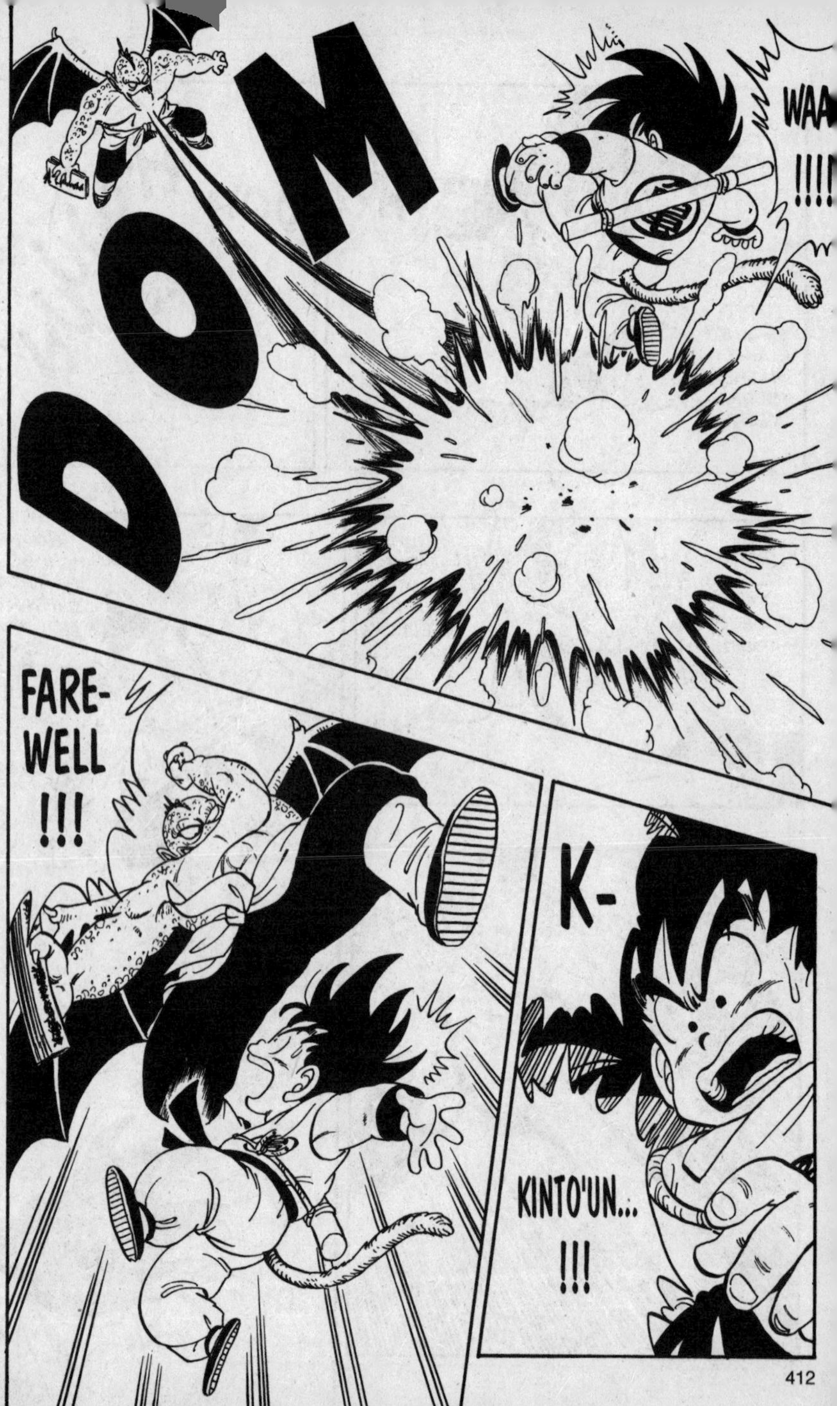
WAA !!!!
DOM
FARE-WELL !!!
K-
KINTO'UN... !!!

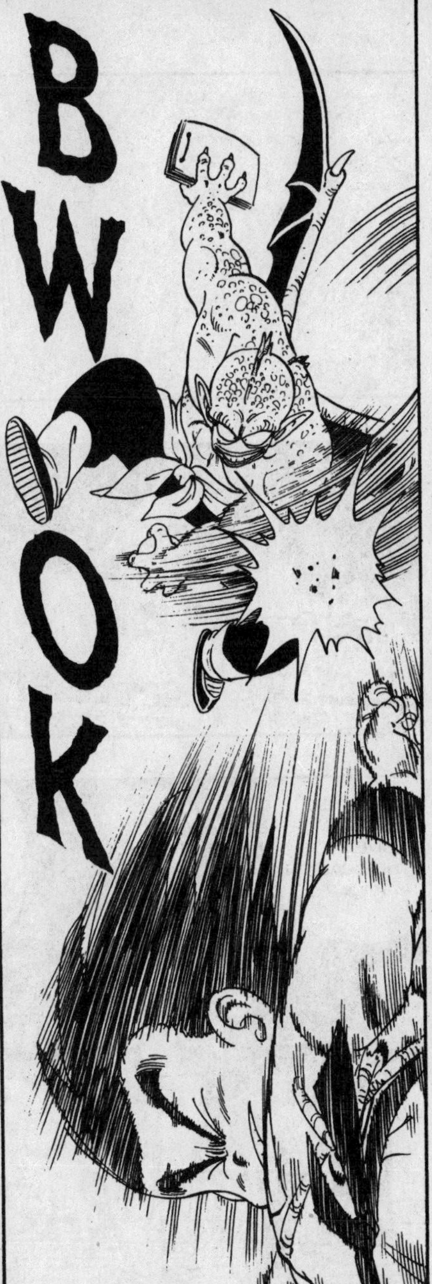
BWOK

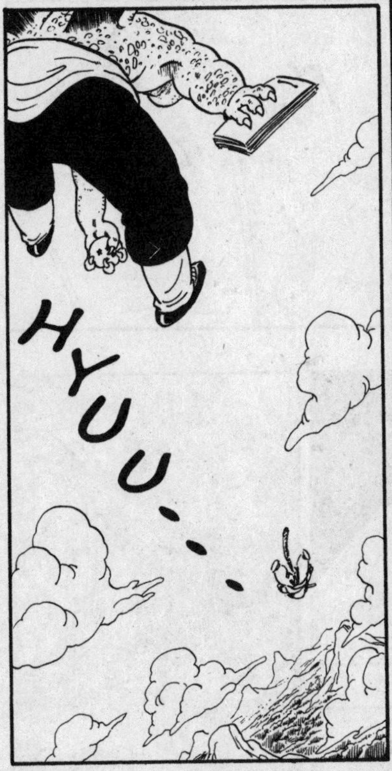
HYUU...

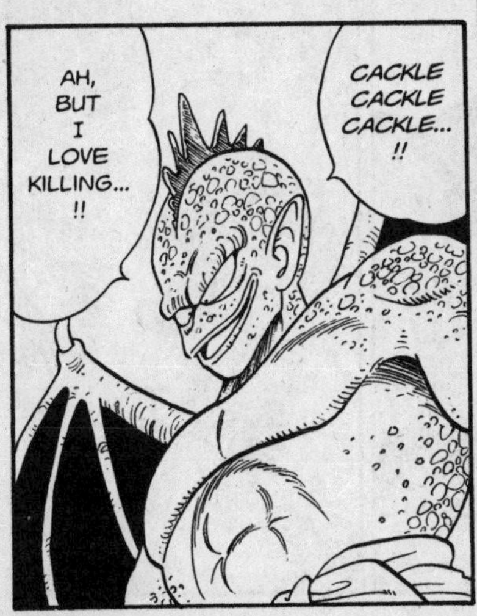
CACKLE CACKLE CACKLE... !!
AH, BUT I LOVE KILLING... !!

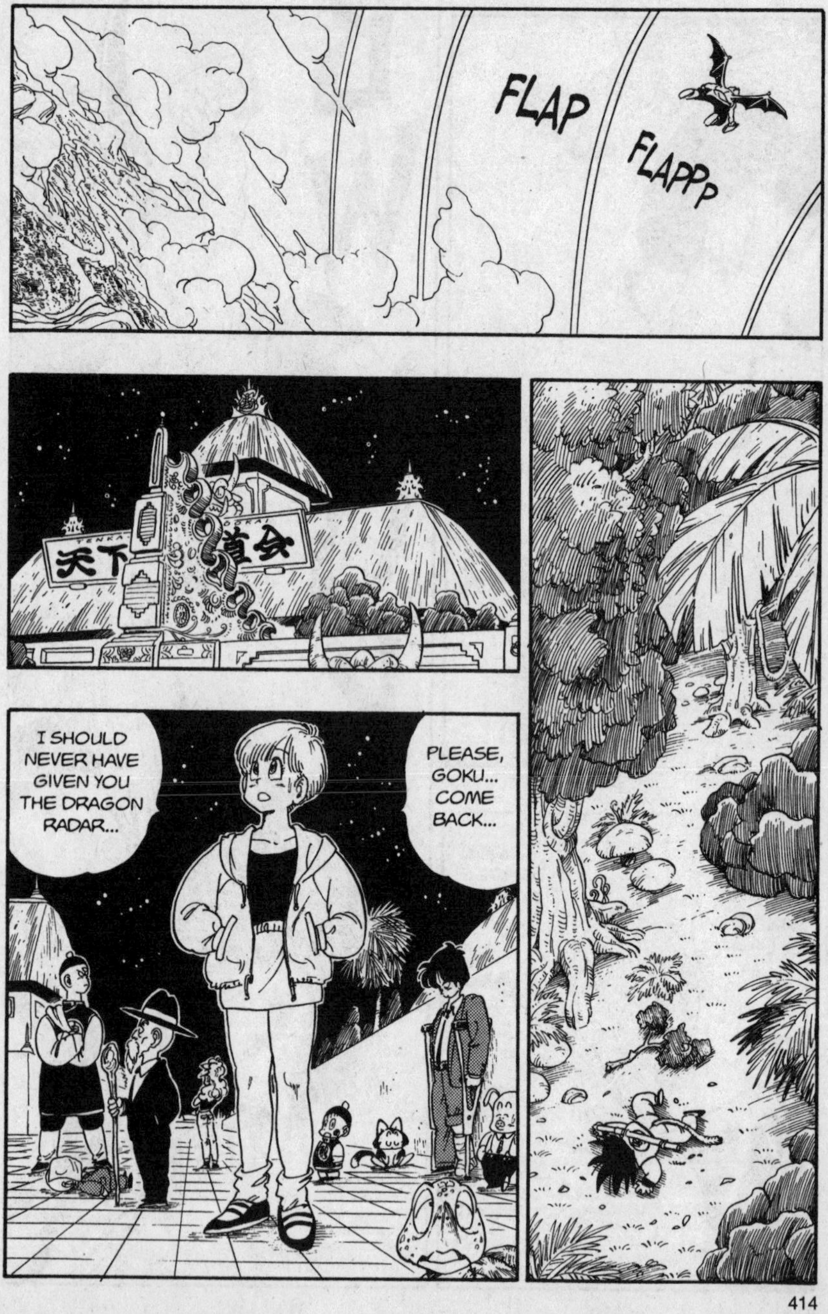
FLAP
FLAPPP
PLEASE, GOKU... COME BACK...
I SHOULD NEVER HAVE GIVEN YOU THE DRAGON RADAR...

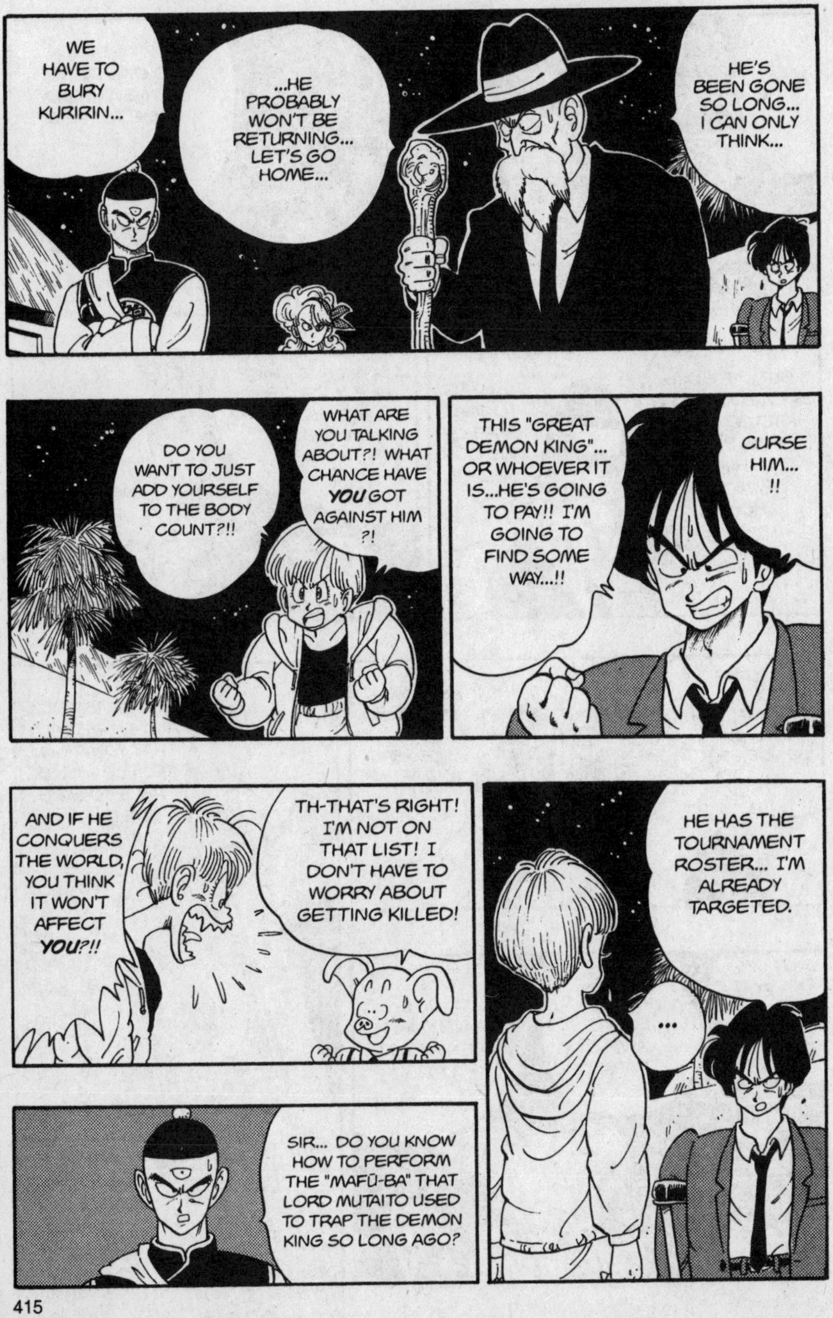
HE'S BEEN GONE SO LONG... I CAN ONLY THINK...
...HE PROBABLY WON'T BE RETURNING... LET'S GO HOME...
WE HAVE TO BURY KURIRIN...
CURSE HIM... !!
THIS "GREAT DEMON KING"... OR WHOEVER IT IS...HE'S GOING TO PAY!! I'M GOING TO FIND SOME WAY...!!
WHAT ARE YOU TALKING ABOUT?! WHAT CHANCE HAVE **YOU** GOT AGAINST HIM ?!
DO YOU WANT TO JUST ADD YOURSELF TO THE BODY COUNT?!!
HE HAS THE TOURNAMENT ROSTER... I'M ALREADY TARGETED.
...
TH-THAT'S RIGHT! I'M NOT ON THAT LIST! I DON'T HAVE TO WORRY ABOUT GETTING KILLED!
AND IF HE CONQUERS THE WORLD, YOU THINK IT WON'T AFFECT **YOU**?!!
SIR... DO YOU KNOW HOW TO PERFORM THE "MAFŪ-BA" THAT LORD MUTAITO USED TO TRAP THE DEMON KING SO LONG AGO?

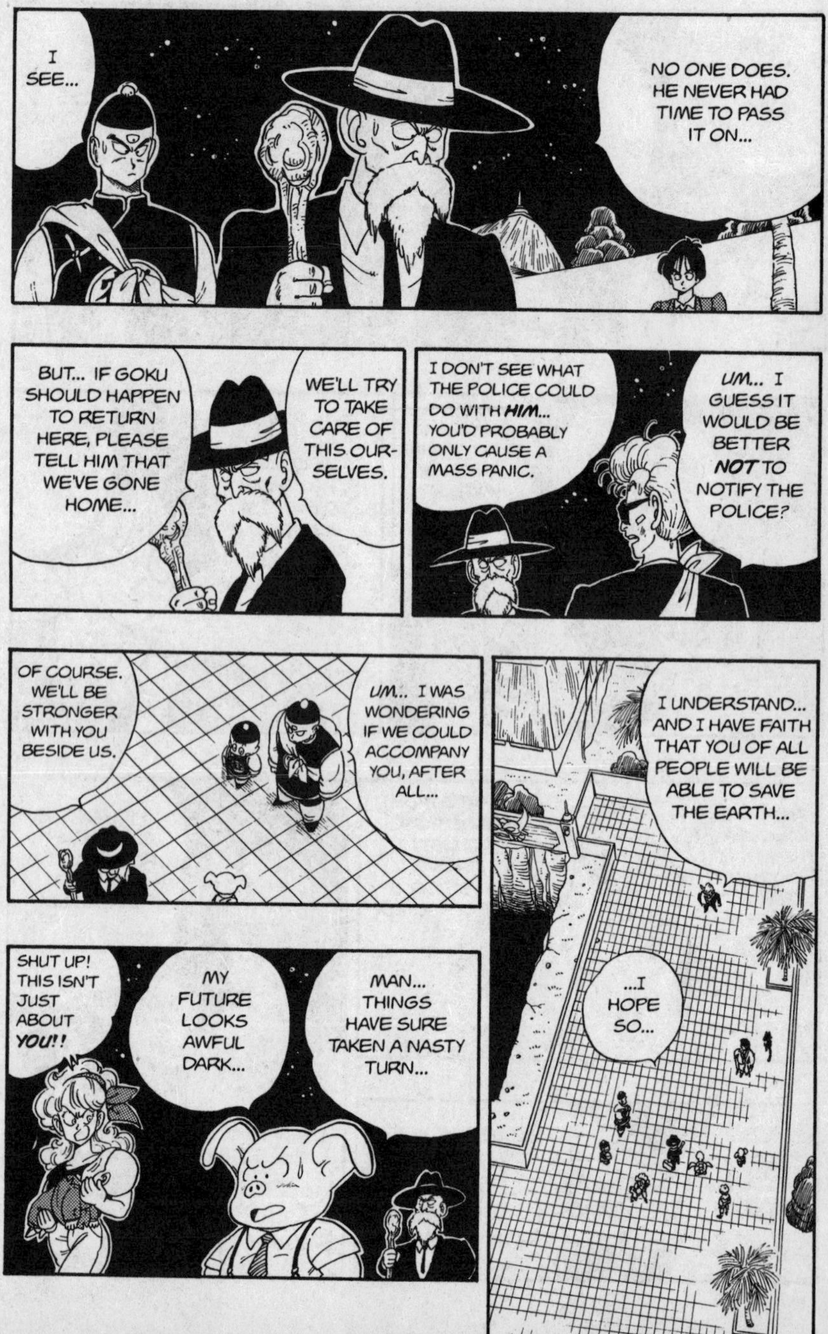
NO ONE DOES. HE NEVER HAD TIME TO PASS IT ON...
I SEE...
UM... I GUESS IT WOULD BE BETTER NOT TO NOTIFY THE POLICE?
I DON'T SEE WHAT THE POLICE COULD DO WITH HIM... YOU'D PROBABLY ONLY CAUSE A MASS PANIC.
WE'LL TRY TO TAKE CARE OF THIS OURSELVES.
BUT... IF GOKU SHOULD HAPPEN TO RETURN HERE, PLEASE TELL HIM THAT WE'VE GONE HOME...
I UNDERSTAND... AND I HAVE FAITH THAT YOU OF ALL PEOPLE WILL BE ABLE TO SAVE THE EARTH...
...I HOPE SO...
UM... I WAS WONDERING IF WE COULD ACCOMPANY YOU, AFTER ALL...
OF COURSE. WE'LL BE STRONGER WITH YOU BESIDE US.
MAN... THINGS HAVE SURE TAKEN A NASTY TURN...
MY FUTURE LOOKS AWFUL DARK...
SHUT UP! THIS ISN'T JUST ABOUT YOU!!

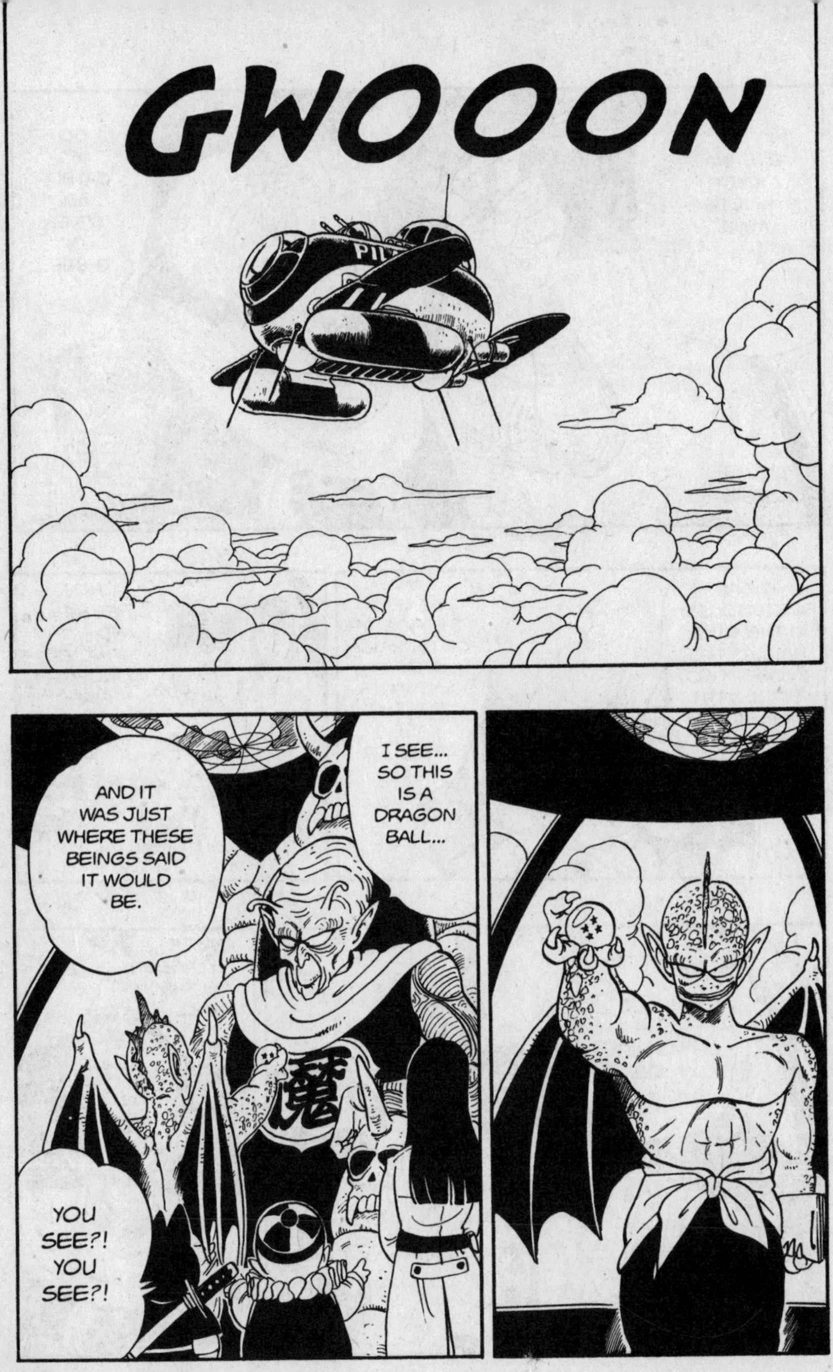
GWOOON
PILA
I SEE... SO THIS IS A DRAGON BALL...
AND IT WAS JUST WHERE THESE BEINGS SAID IT WOULD BE.
YOU SEE?! YOU SEE?!

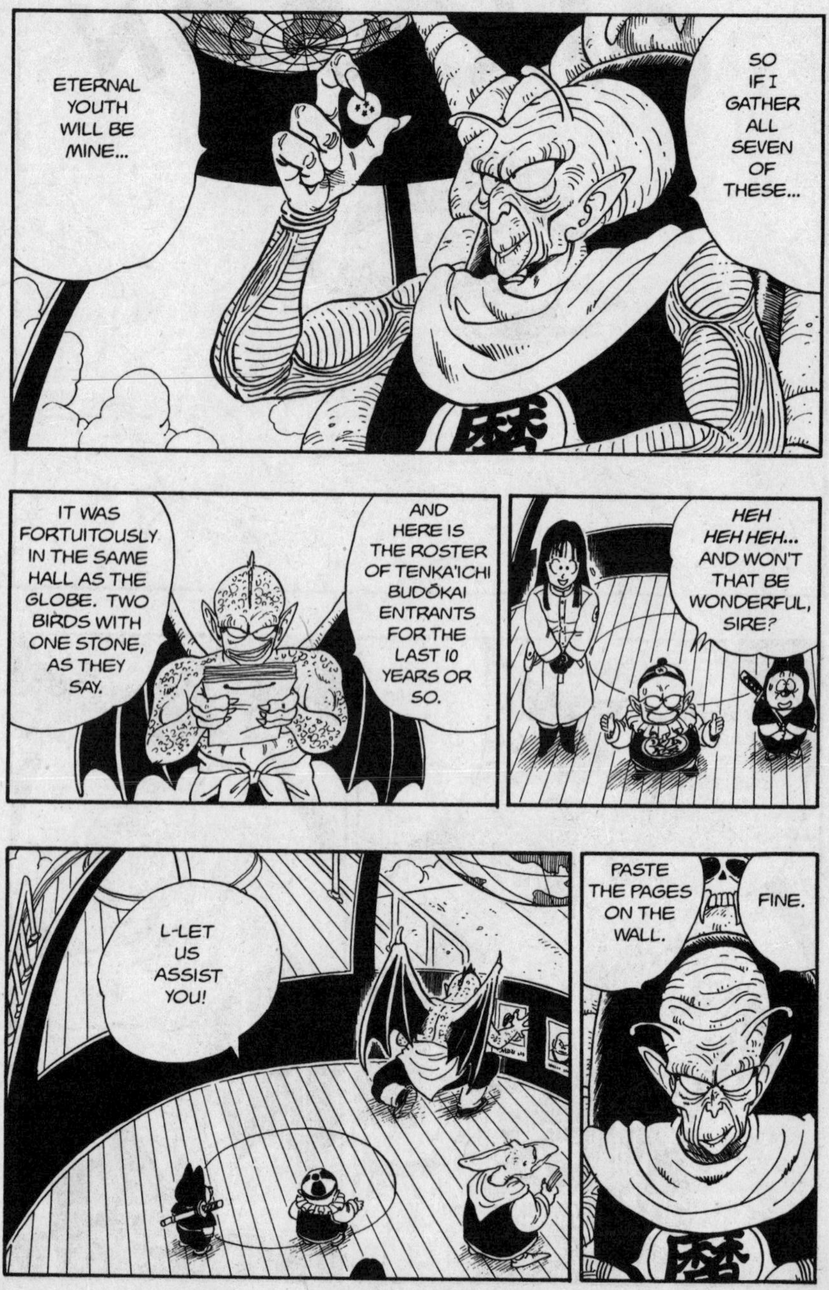
SO IF I GATHER ALL SEVEN OF THESE...
ETERNAL YOUTH WILL BE MINE...
HEH HEH HEH... AND WON'T THAT BE WONDERFUL, SIRE?
AND HERE IS THE ROSTER OF TENKA'ICHI BUDŌKAI ENTRANTS FOR THE LAST 10 YEARS OR SO.
IT WAS FORTUITOUSLY IN THE SAME HALL AS THE GLOBE. TWO BIRDS WITH ONE STONE, AS THEY SAY.
FINE.
PASTE THE PAGES ON THE WALL.
L-LET US ASSIST YOU!

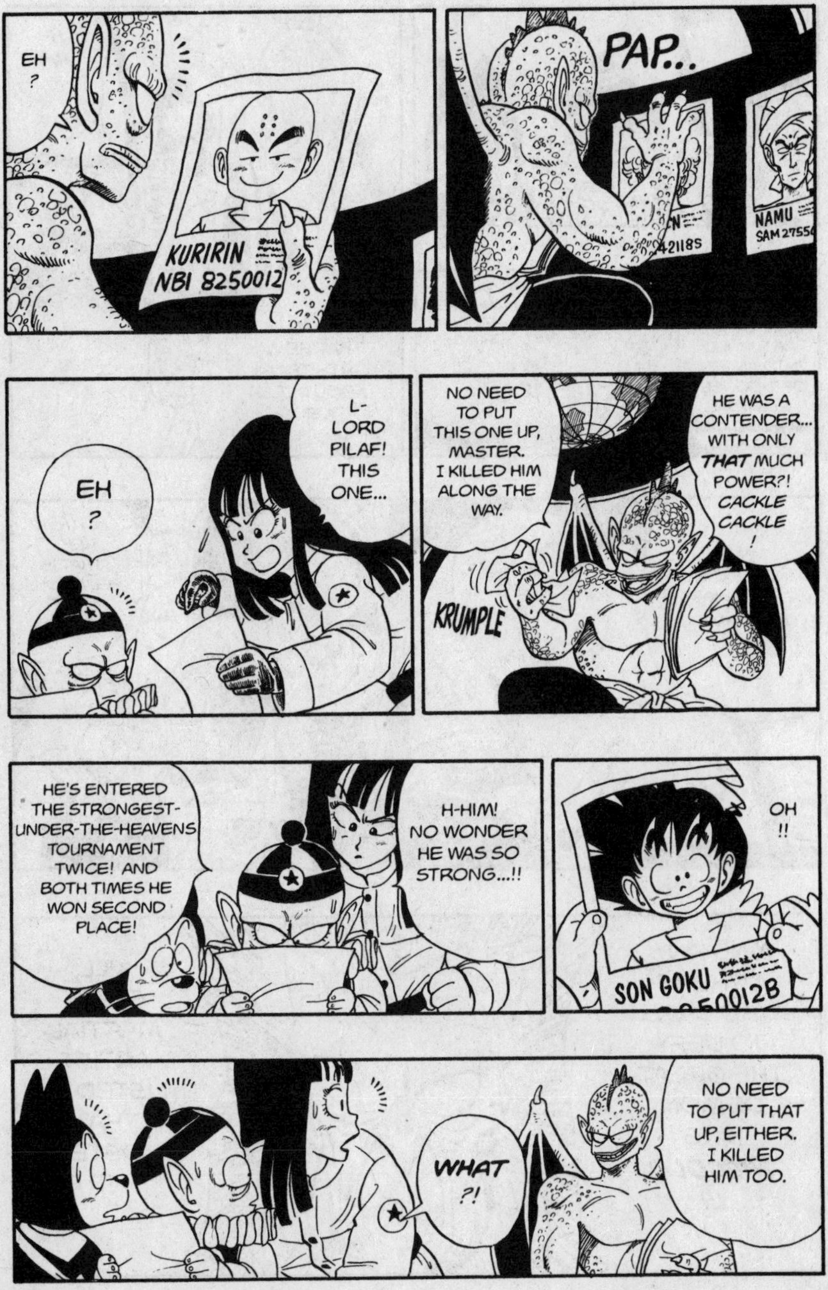
PAP...
NAMU
EH ?
KURIRIN
NBI 8250012
HE WAS A CONTENDER... WITH ONLY THAT MUCH POWER?! CACKLE CACKLE !
NO NEED TO PUT THIS ONE UP, MASTER. I KILLED HIM ALONG THE WAY.
KRUMPLE
L-LORD PILAF! THIS ONE...
EH ?
OH !!
SON GOKU
H-HIM! NO WONDER HE WAS SO STRONG...!!
HE'S ENTERED THE STRONGEST-UNDER-THE-HEAVENS TOURNAMENT TWICE! AND BOTH TIMES HE WON SECOND PLACE!
NO NEED TO PUT THAT UP, EITHER. I KILLED HIM TOO.
WHAT ?!

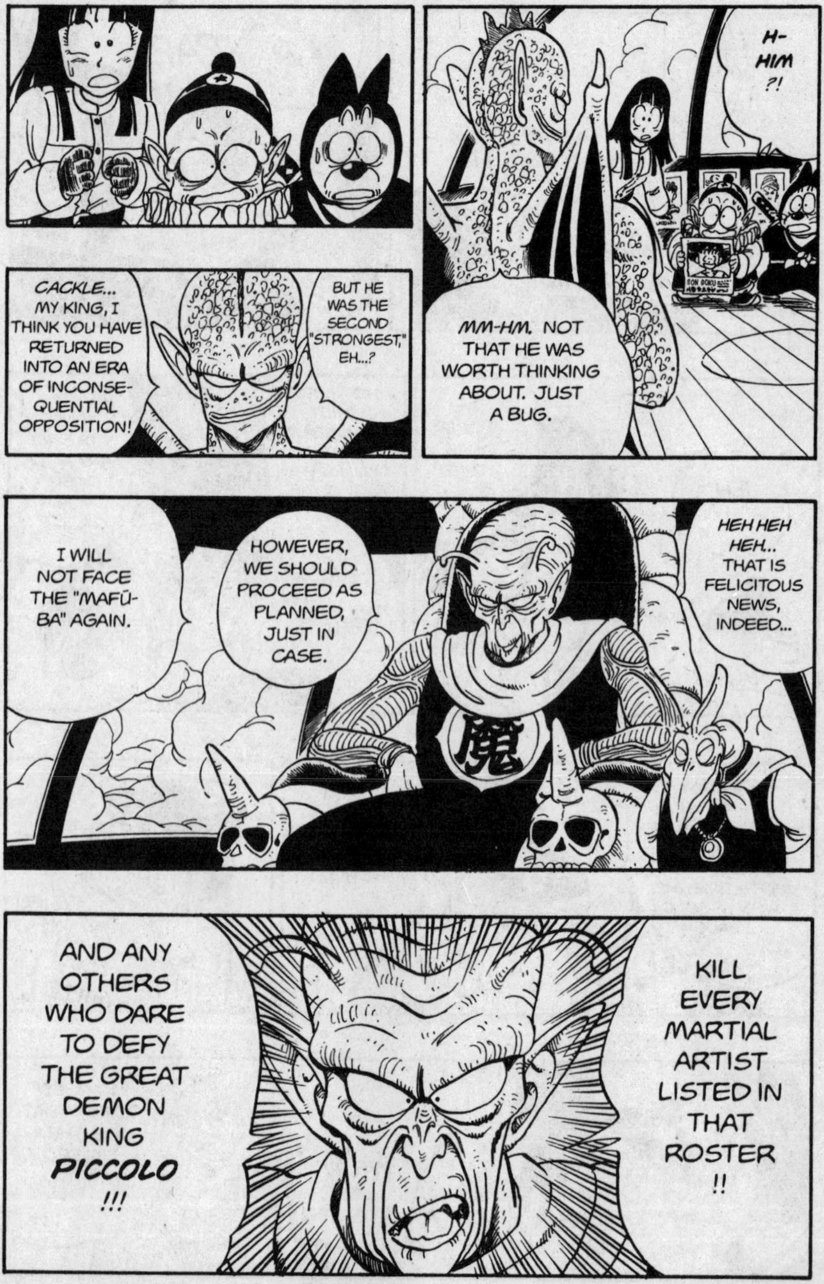
H-HIM ?!
MM-HM. NOT THAT HE WAS WORTH THINKING ABOUT. JUST A BUG.
BUT HE WAS THE SECOND "STRONGEST," EH...?
CACKLE... MY KING, I THINK YOU HAVE RETURNED INTO AN ERA OF INCONSE-QUENTIAL OPPOSITION!
HEH HEH HEH... THAT IS FELICITOUS NEWS, INDEED...
HOWEVER, WE SHOULD PROCEED AS PLANNED, JUST IN CASE.
I WILL NOT FACE THE "MAFŪ-BA" AGAIN.
KILL EVERY MARTIAL ARTIST LISTED IN THAT ROSTER !!
AND ANY OTHERS WHO DARE TO DEFY THE GREAT DEMON KING PICCOLO !!!

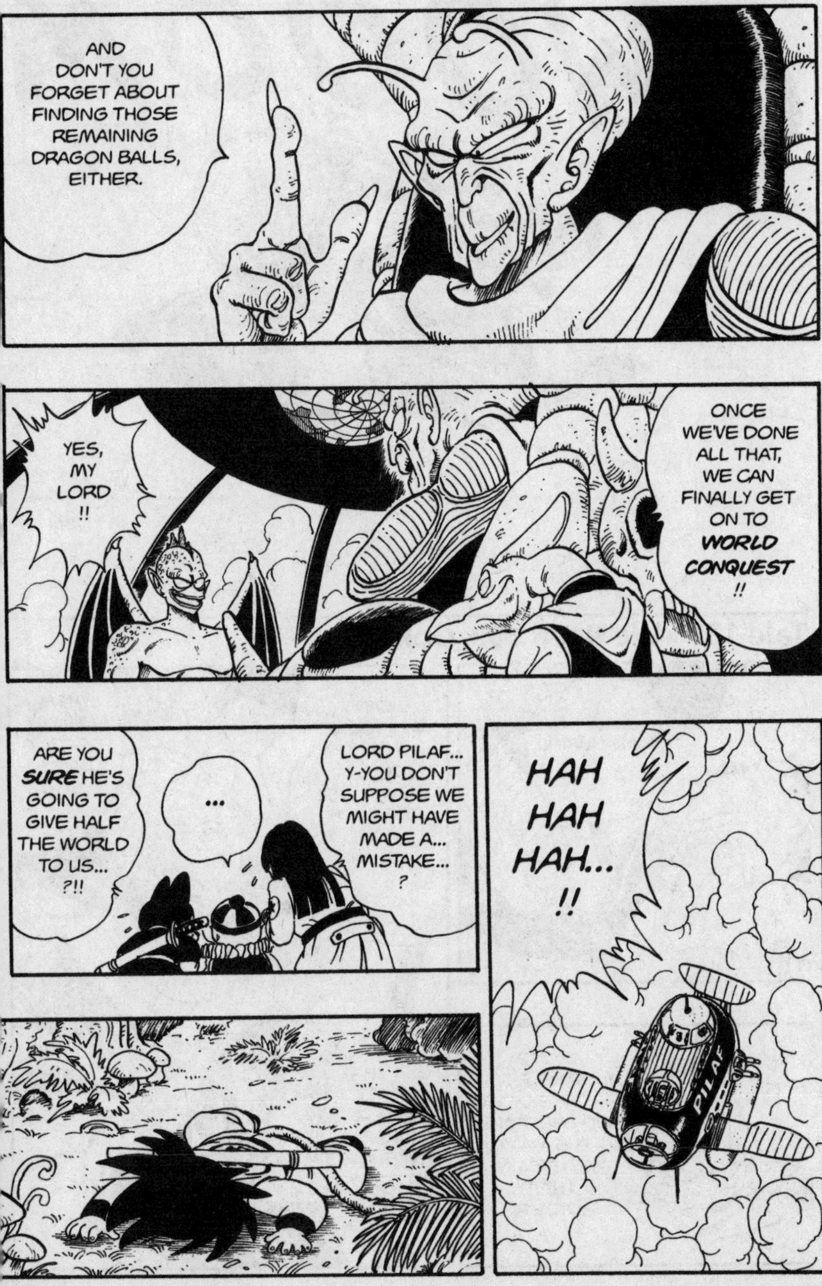
AND DON'T YOU FORGET ABOUT FINDING THOSE REMAINING DRAGON BALLS, EITHER.
ONCE WE'VE DONE ALL THAT, WE CAN FINALLY GET ON TO **WORLD CONQUEST** !!
YES, MY LORD !!
HAH HAH HAH... !!
LORD PILAF... Y-YOU DON'T SUPPOSE WE MIGHT HAVE MADE A... MISTAKE... ?
...
ARE YOU **SURE** HE'S GOING TO GIVE HALF THE WORLD TO US... ?!!
PILAF

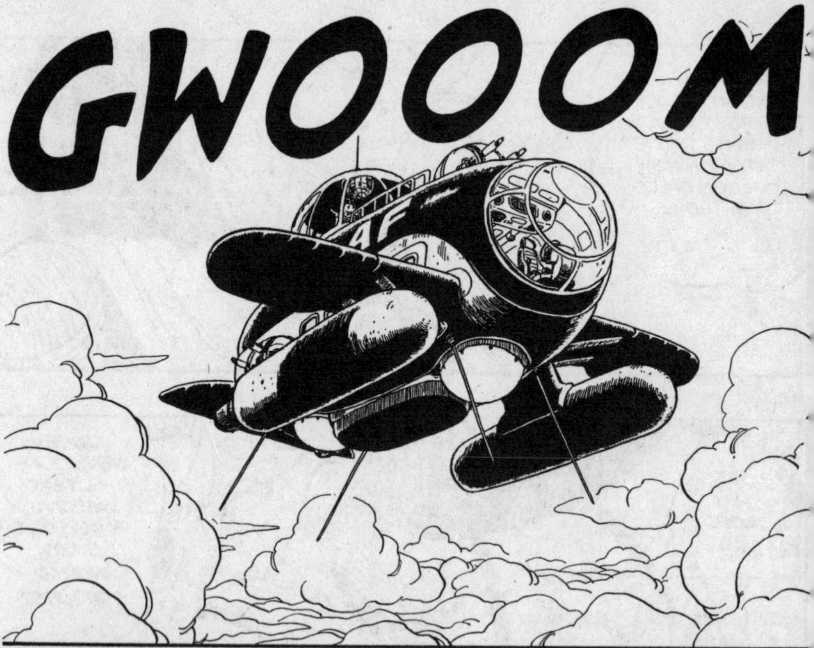
GWOOOM

Tale 137 • We Need You, Goku!

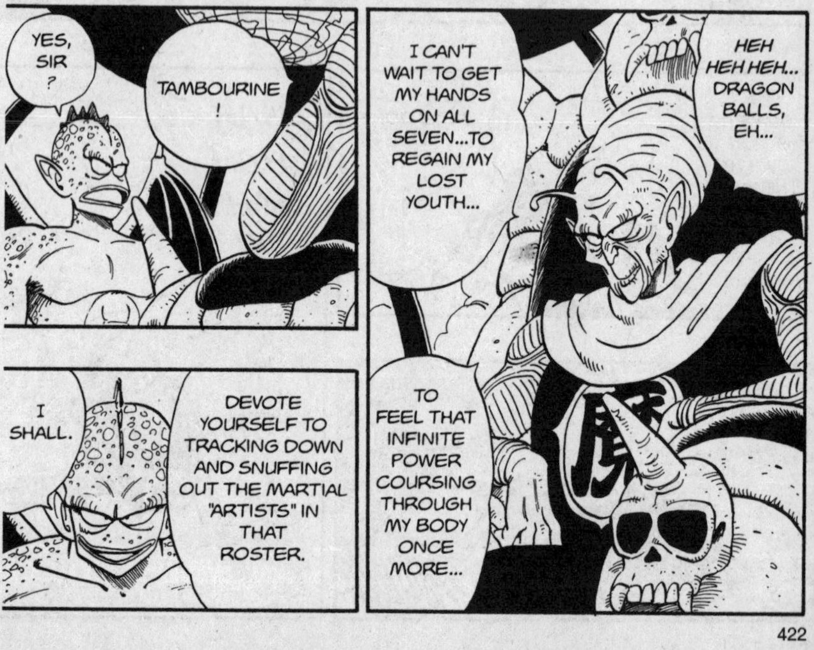
HEH HEH HEH... DRAGON BALLS, EH...
I CAN'T WAIT TO GET MY HANDS ON ALL SEVEN...TO REGAIN MY LOST YOUTH...
TO FEEL THAT INFINITE POWER COURSING THROUGH MY BODY ONCE MORE...
TAMBOURINE!
YES, SIR?
DEVOTE YOURSELF TO TRACKING DOWN AND SNUFFING OUT THE MARTIAL "ARTISTS" IN THAT ROSTER.
I SHALL.

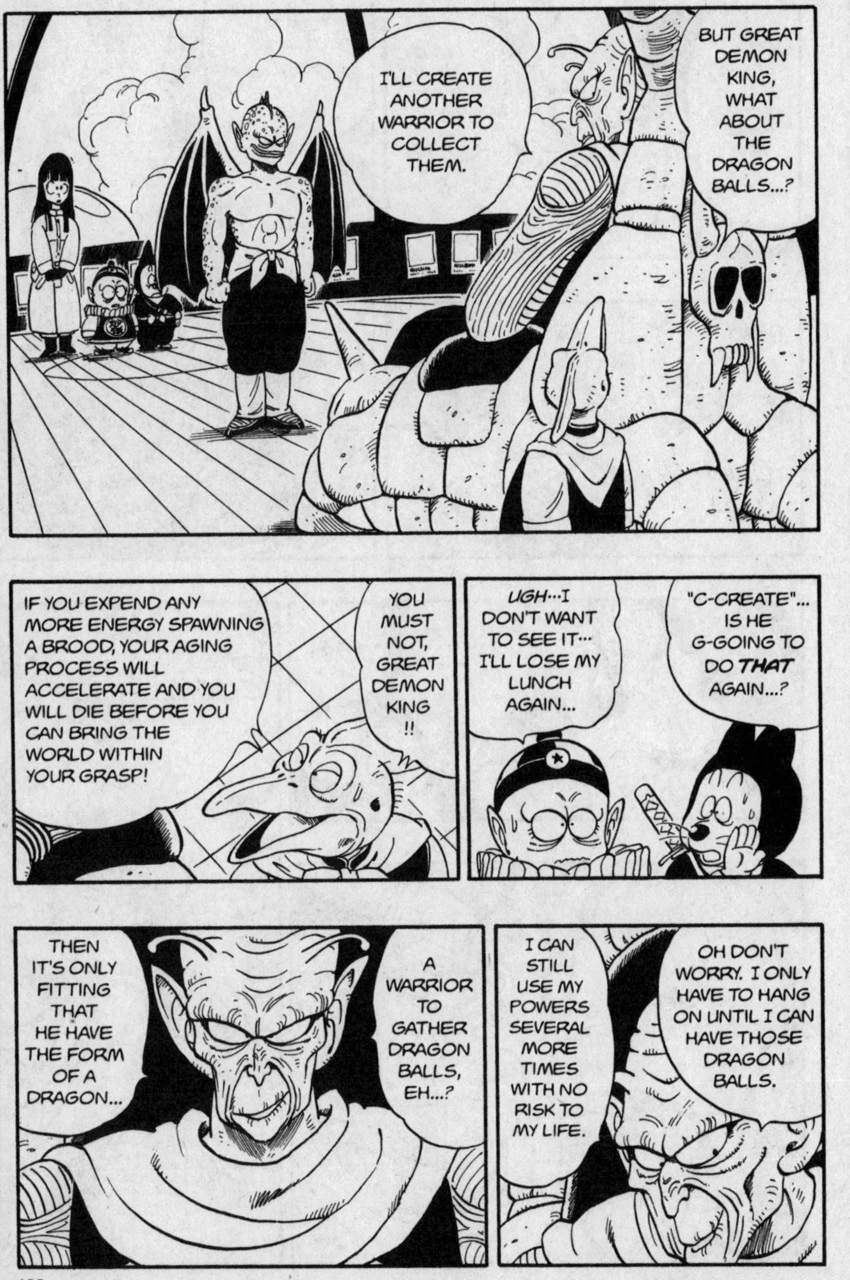
BUT GREAT DEMON KING, WHAT ABOUT THE DRAGON BALLS...?
I'LL CREATE ANOTHER WARRIOR TO COLLECT THEM.
"C-CREATE"... IS HE G-GOING TO DO *THAT* AGAIN...?
UGH...I DON'T WANT TO SEE IT... I'LL LOSE MY LUNCH AGAIN...
YOU MUST NOT, GREAT DEMON KING !!
IF YOU EXPEND ANY MORE ENERGY SPAWNING A BROOD, YOUR AGING PROCESS WILL ACCELERATE AND YOU WILL DIE BEFORE YOU CAN BRING THE WORLD WITHIN YOUR GRASP!
OH DON'T WORRY. I ONLY HAVE TO HANG ON UNTIL I CAN HAVE THOSE DRAGON BALLS.
I CAN STILL USE MY POWERS SEVERAL MORE TIMES WITH NO RISK TO MY LIFE.
A WARRIOR TO GATHER DRAGON BALLS, EH...?
THEN IT'S ONLY FITTING THAT HE HAVE THE FORM OF A DRAGON...

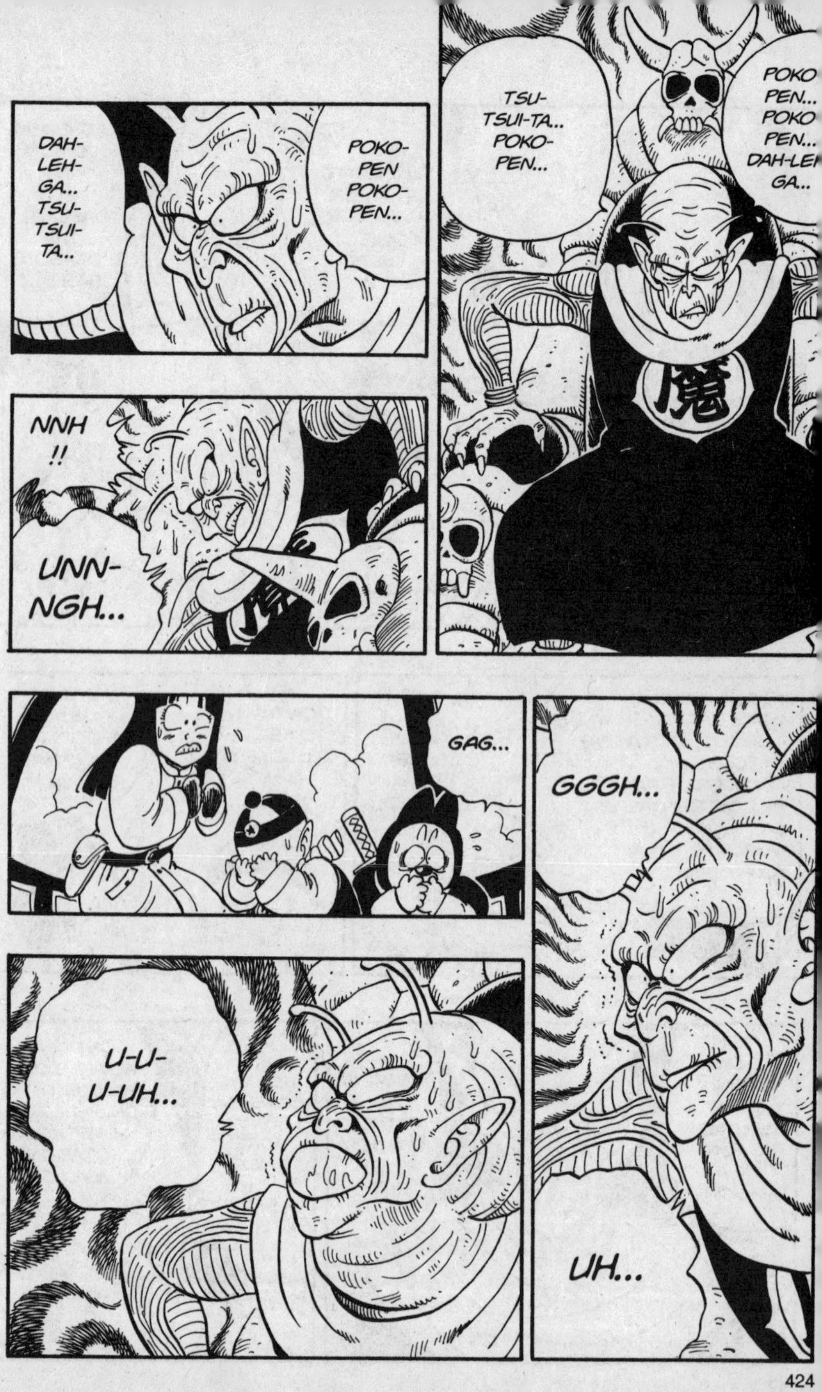
POKO PEN... POKO PEN... DAH-LE GA...
TSU-TSUI-TA... POKO-PEN...
POKO-PEN POKO-PEN...
DAH-LEH-GA... TSU-TSUI-TA...
NNH !!
UNN-NGH...
GGGH...
UH...
GAG...
U-U-U-UH...

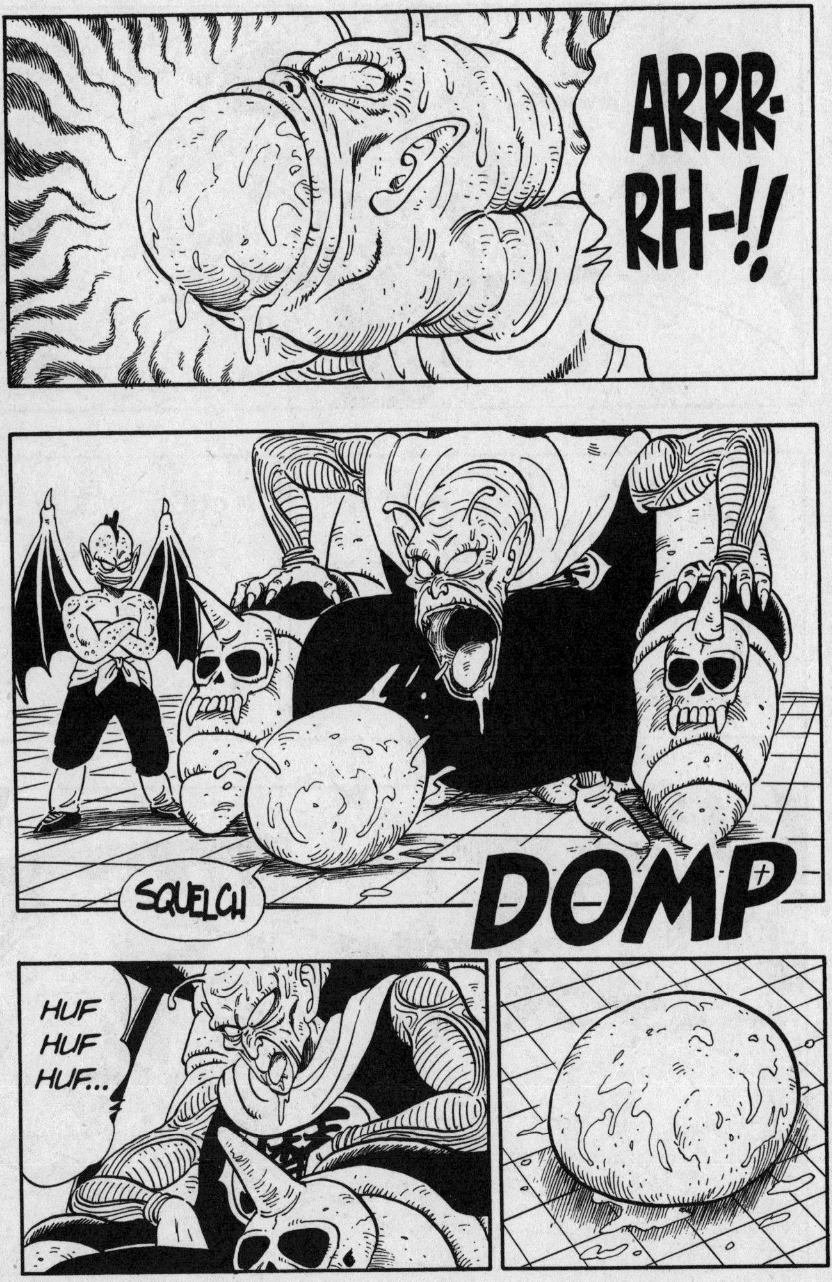
ARRRR-RH-!!
DOMP
SQUELCH
HUF HUF HUF...

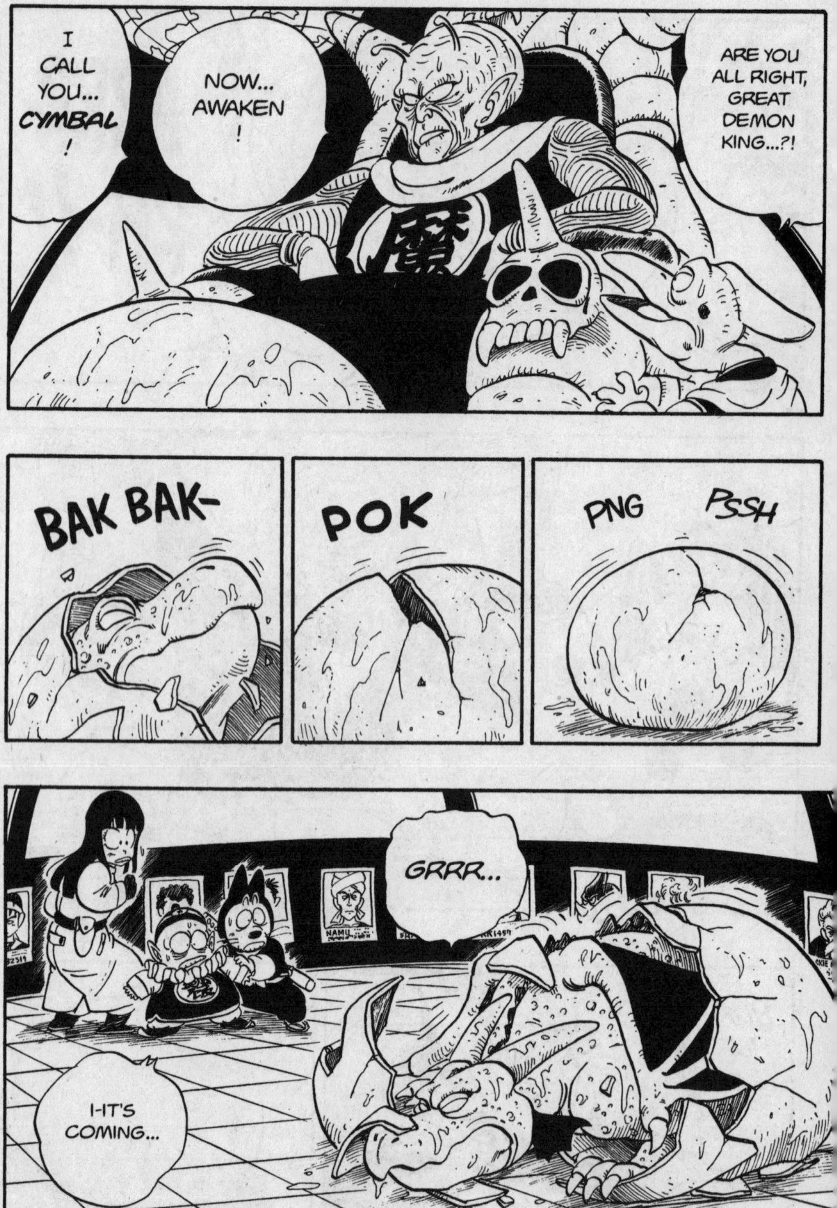
ARE YOU ALL RIGHT, GREAT DEMON KING...?!
NOW... AWAKEN!
I CALL YOU... CYMBAL!
PSSH
PNG
POK
BAK BAK-
GRRR...
I-IT'S COMING...

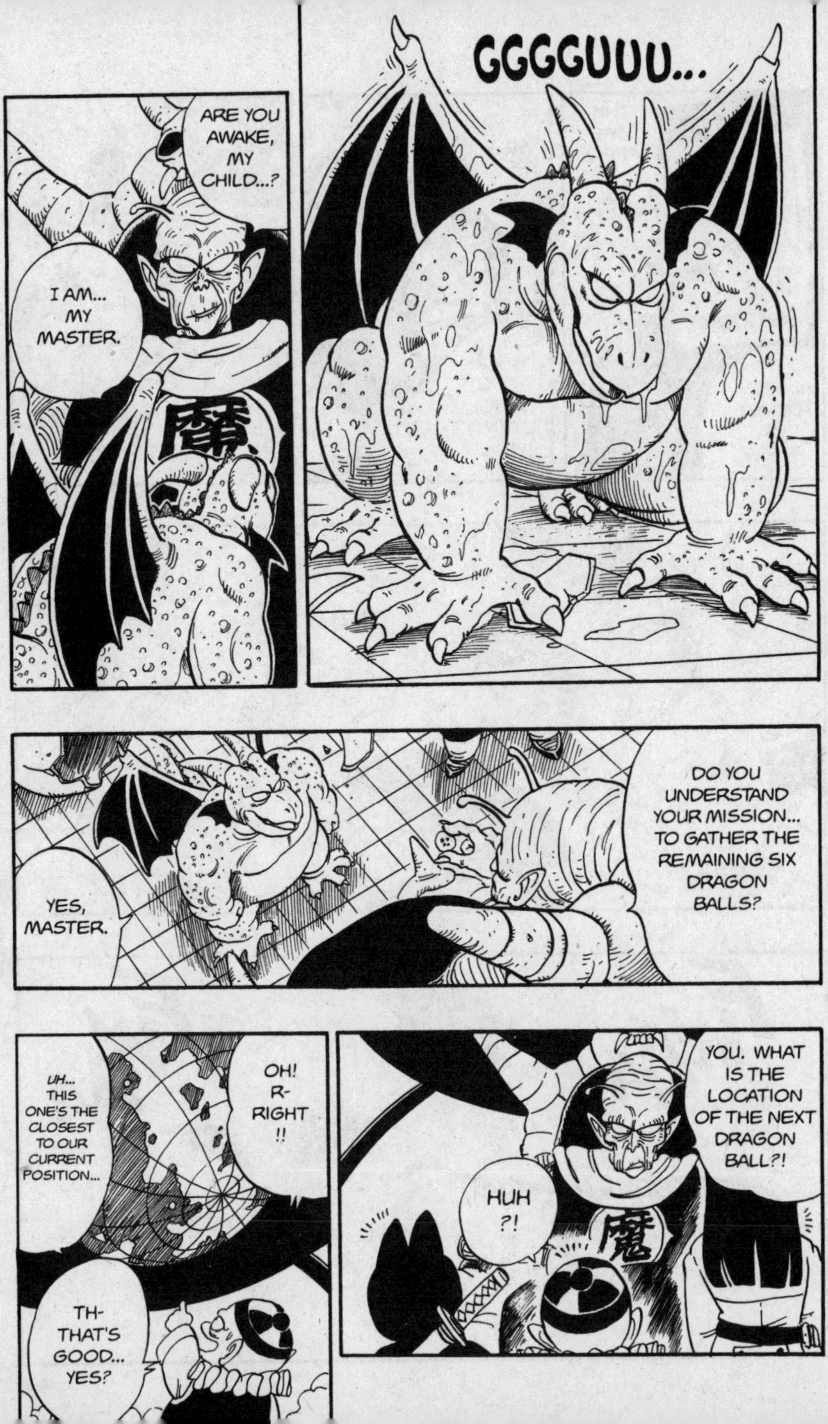
GGGGUUU...
ARE YOU AWAKE, MY CHILD...?
I AM... MY MASTER.
DO YOU UNDERSTAND YOUR MISSION... TO GATHER THE REMAINING SIX DRAGON BALLS?
YES, MASTER.
YOU. WHAT IS THE LOCATION OF THE NEXT DRAGON BALL?!
HUH ?!
OH! R-RIGHT !!
UH... THIS ONE'S THE CLOSEST TO OUR CURRENT POSITION...
TH-THAT'S GOOD... YES?

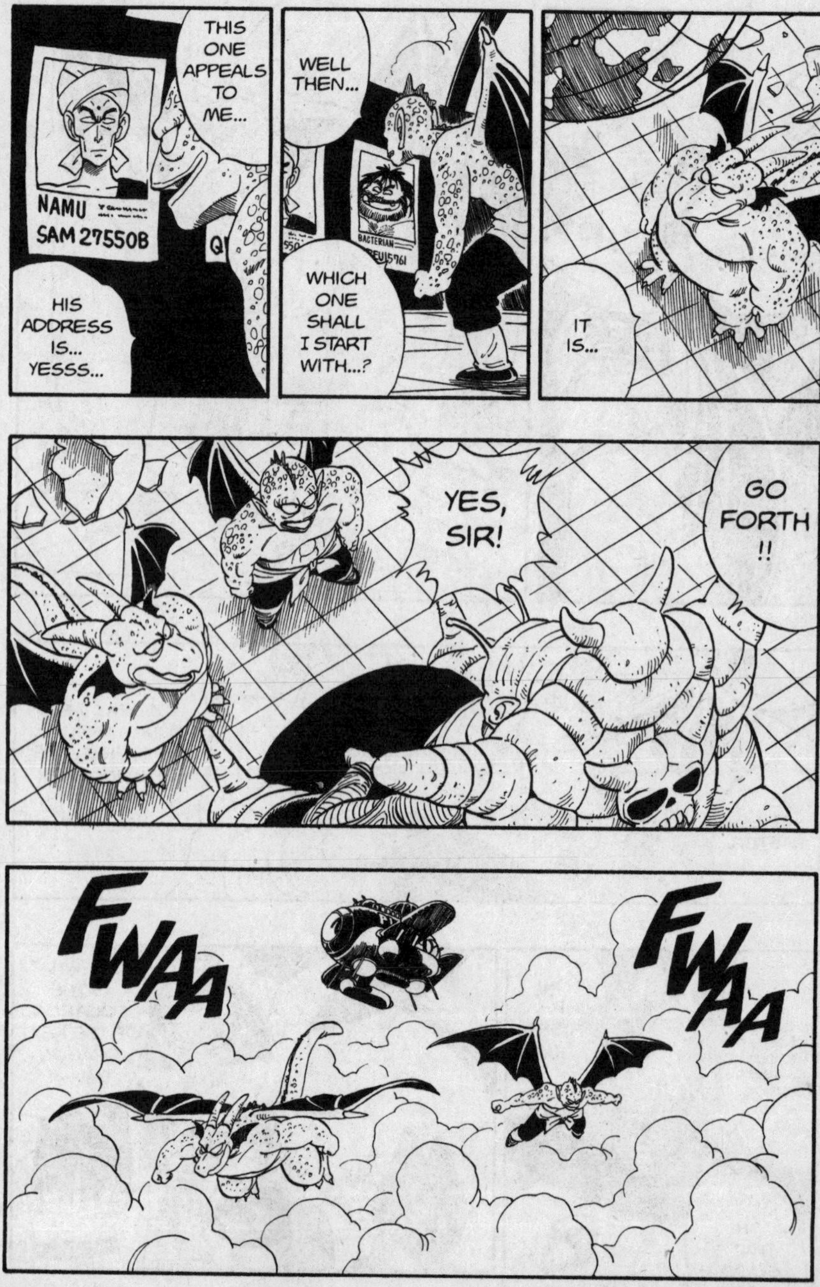
IT IS...
WELL THEN...
WHICH ONE SHALL I START WITH...?
BACTERIAN
THIS ONE APPEALS TO ME...
NAMU
SAM 27550B
HIS ADDRESS IS... YESSS...
GO FORTH !!
YES, SIR!
FWAA
FWAA

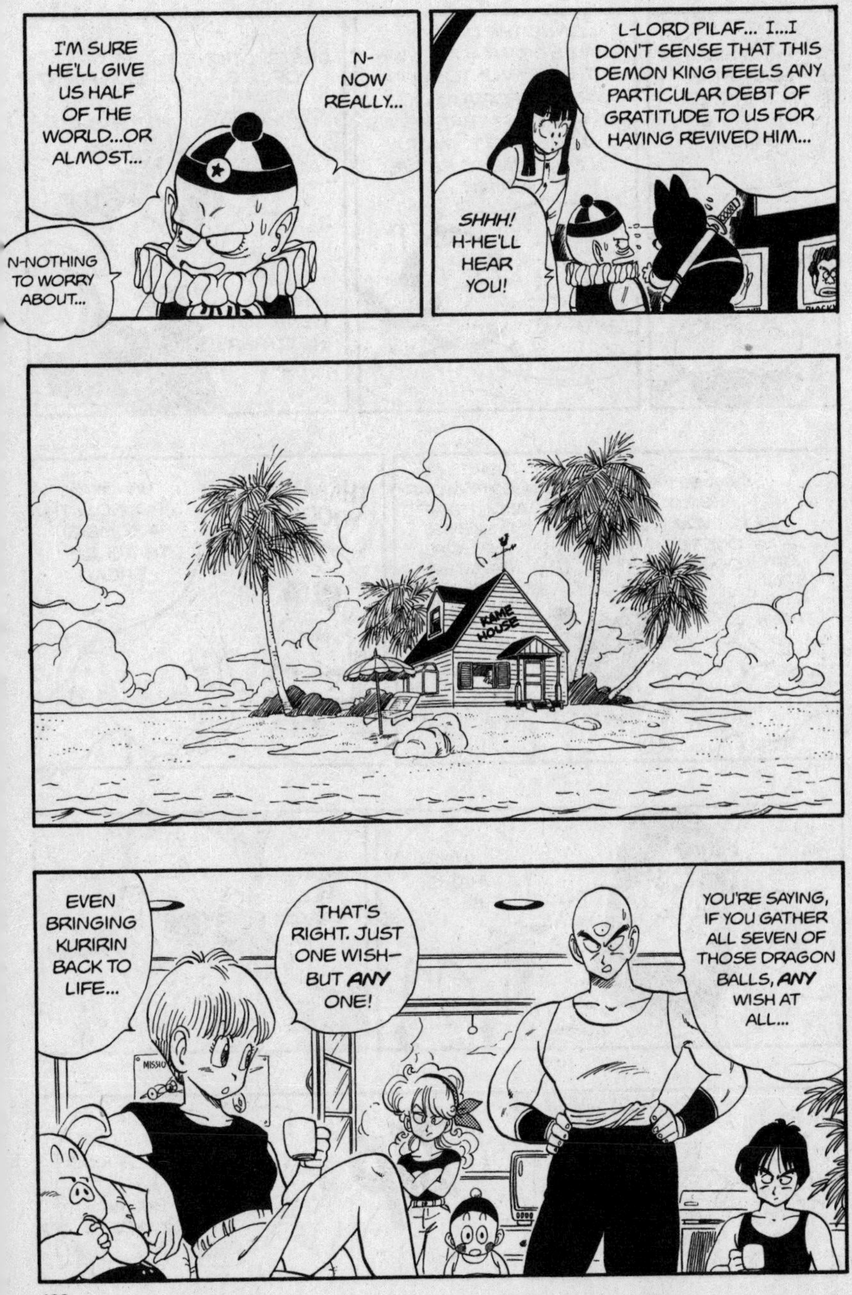
L-LORD PILAF... I...I DON'T SENSE THAT THIS DEMON KING FEELS ANY PARTICULAR DEBT OF GRATITUDE TO US FOR HAVING REVIVED HIM...
SHHH! H-HE'LL HEAR YOU!
N- NOW REALLY...
I'M SURE HE'LL GIVE US HALF OF THE WORLD...OR ALMOST...
N-NOTHING TO WORRY ABOUT...
KAME HOUSE
YOU'RE SAYING, IF YOU GATHER ALL SEVEN OF THOSE DRAGON BALLS, ANY WISH AT ALL...
THAT'S RIGHT. JUST ONE WISH-BUT ANY ONE!
EVEN BRINGING KURIRIN BACK TO LIFE...

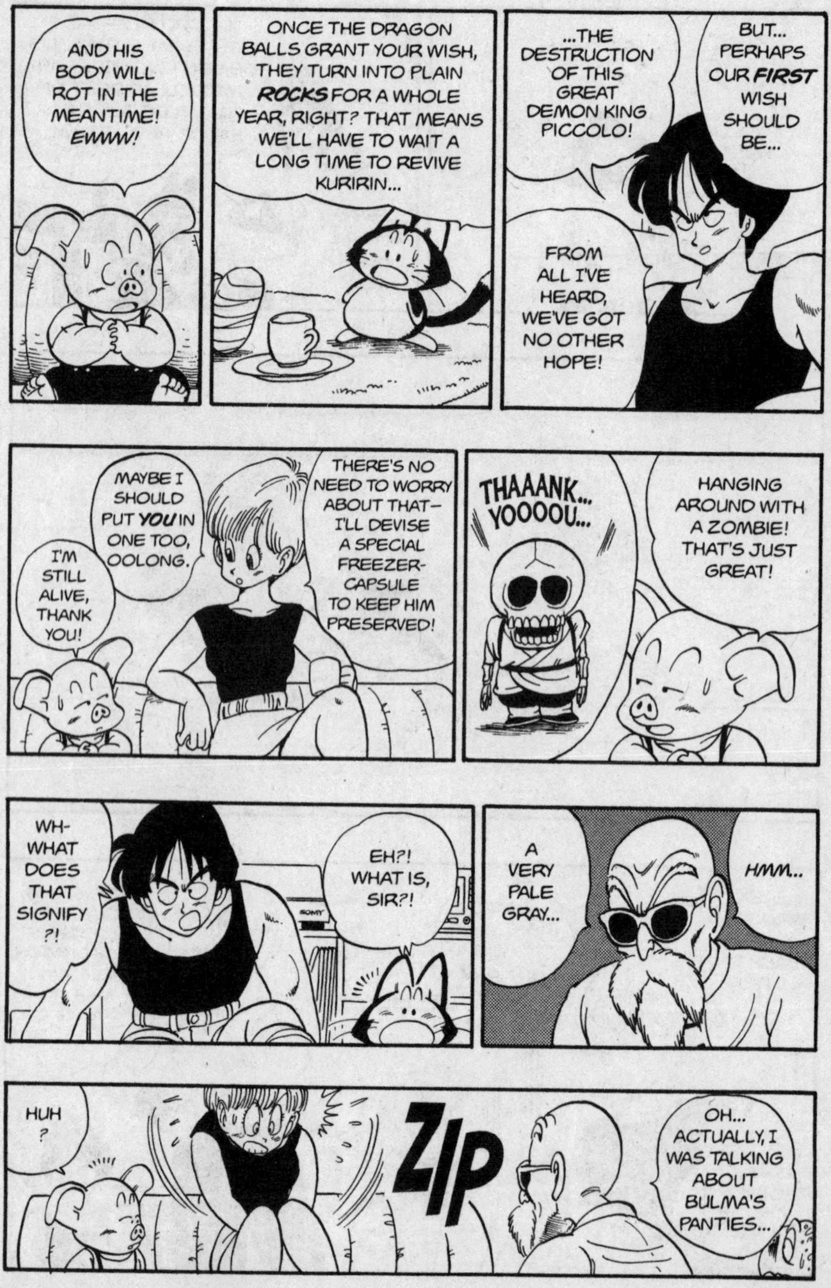
BUT... PERHAPS OUR FIRST WISH SHOULD BE...
...THE DESTRUCTION OF THIS GREAT DEMON KING PICCOLO!
FROM ALL I'VE HEARD, WE'VE GOT NO OTHER HOPE!
ONCE THE DRAGON BALLS GRANT YOUR WISH, THEY TURN INTO PLAIN ROCKS FOR A WHOLE YEAR, RIGHT? THAT MEANS WE'LL HAVE TO WAIT A LONG TIME TO REVIVE KURIRIN...
AND HIS BODY WILL ROT IN THE MEANTIME! EWWW!
HANGING AROUND WITH A ZOMBIE! THAT'S JUST GREAT!
THAAANK... YOOOOU...
THERE'S NO NEED TO WORRY ABOUT THAT— I'LL DEVISE A SPECIAL FREEZER-CAPSULE TO KEEP HIM PRESERVED!
MAYBE I SHOULD PUT YOU IN ONE TOO, OOLONG.
I'M STILL ALIVE, THANK YOU!
HMM...
A VERY PALE GRAY...
EH?! WHAT IS, SIR?!
WH- WHAT DOES THAT SIGNIFY ?!
OH... ACTUALLY, I WAS TALKING ABOUT BULMA'S PANTIES...
ZIP
HUH ?

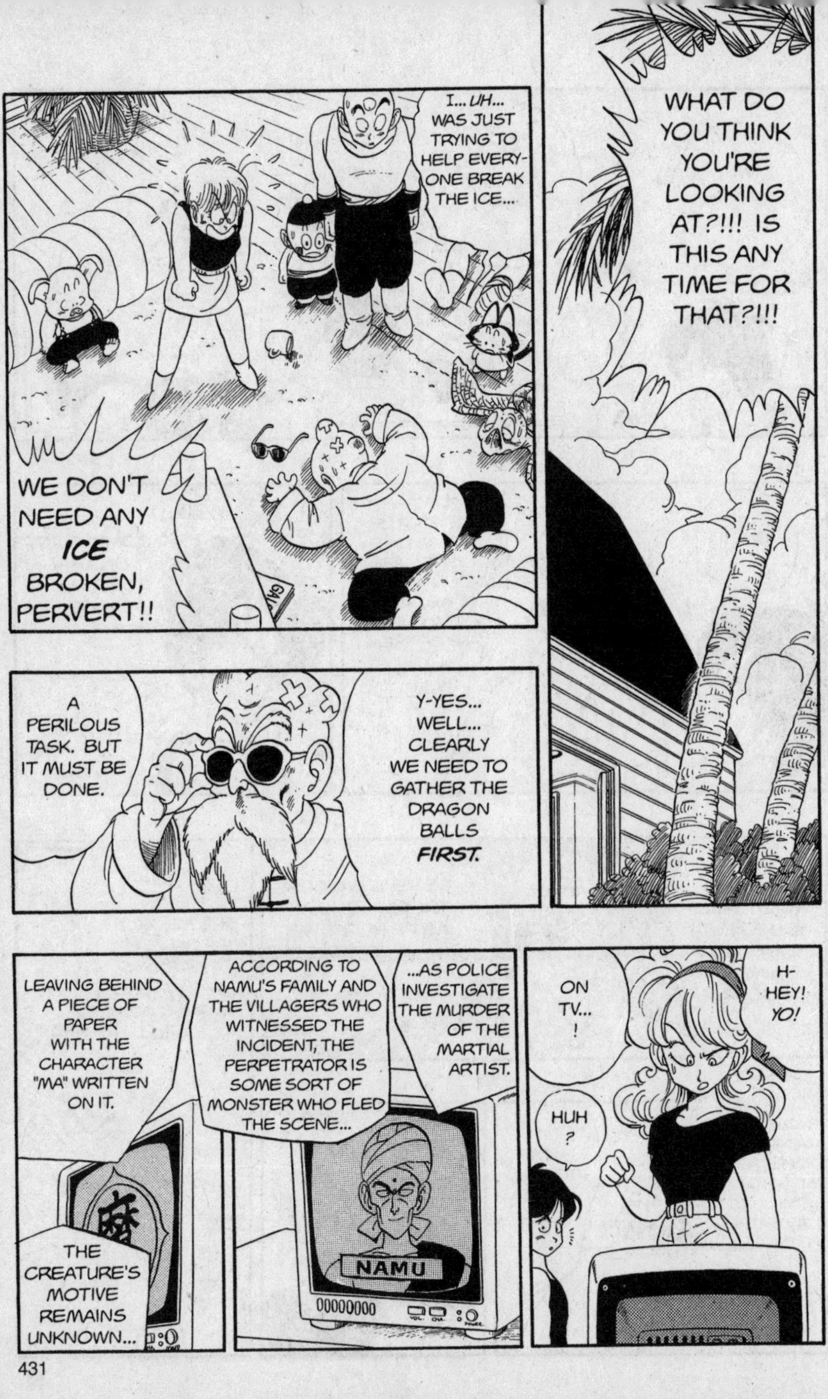
WHAT DO YOU THINK YOU'RE LOOKING AT?!!! IS THIS ANY TIME FOR THAT?!!!
I... UH... WAS JUST TRYING TO HELP EVERYONE BREAK THE ICE...
WE DON'T NEED ANY ICE BROKEN, PERVERT!!
Y-YES... WELL... CLEARLY WE NEED TO GATHER THE DRAGON BALLS FIRST.
A PERILOUS TASK. BUT IT MUST BE DONE.
H- HEY! YO!
ON TV... !
HUH ?
...AS POLICE INVESTIGATE THE MURDER OF THE MARTIAL ARTIST.
ACCORDING TO NAMU'S FAMILY AND THE VILLAGERS WHO WITNESSED THE INCIDENT, THE PERPETRATOR IS SOME SORT OF MONSTER WHO FLED THE SCENE...
NAMU
LEAVING BEHIND A PIECE OF PAPER WITH THE CHARACTER "MA" WRITTEN ON IT.
THE CREATURE'S MOTIVE REMAINS UNKNOWN...

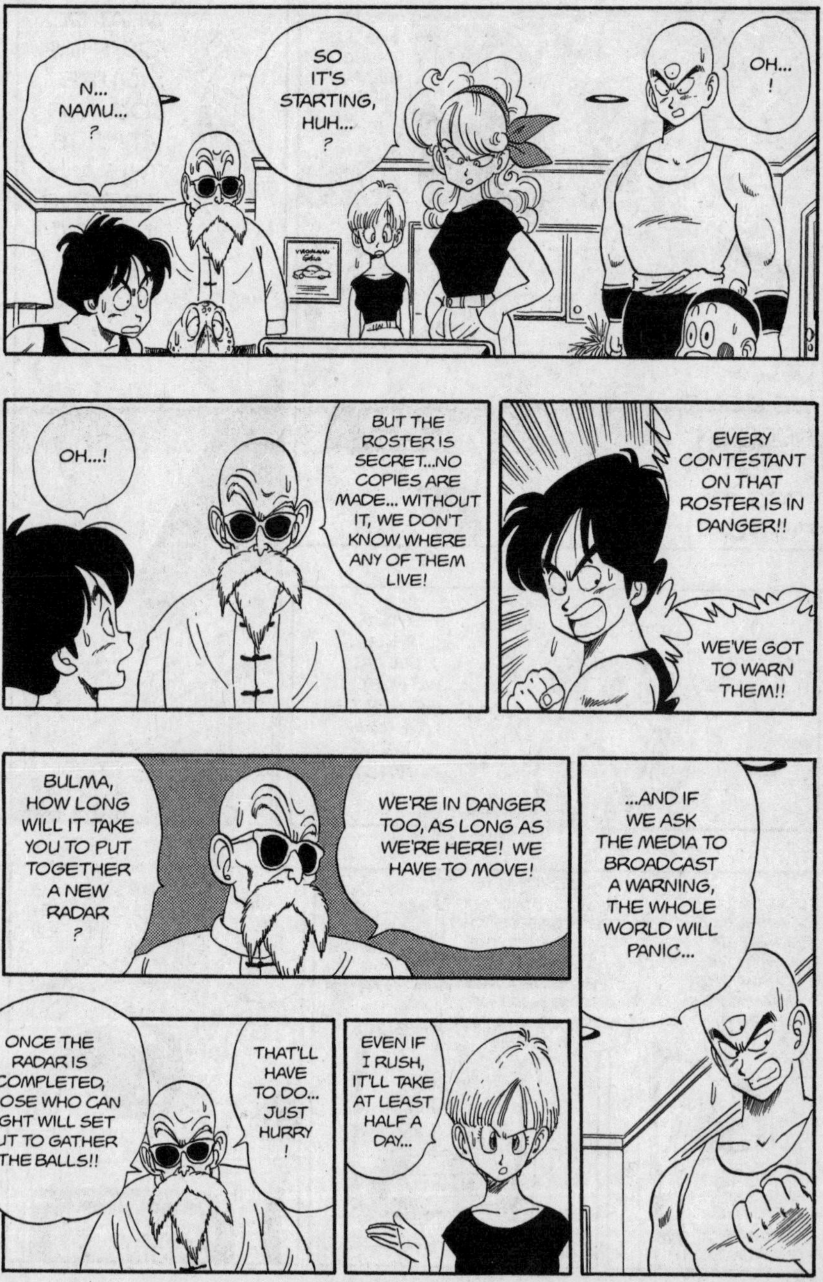
OH... !
SO IT'S STARTING, HUH... ?
N... NAMU... ?
EVERY CONTESTANT ON THAT ROSTER IS IN DANGER!!
WE'VE GOT TO WARN THEM!!
BUT THE ROSTER IS SECRET...NO COPIES ARE MADE... WITHOUT IT, WE DON'T KNOW WHERE ANY OF THEM LIVE!
OH...!
...AND IF WE ASK THE MEDIA TO BROADCAST A WARNING, THE WHOLE WORLD WILL PANIC...
WE'RE IN DANGER TOO, AS LONG AS WE'RE HERE! WE HAVE TO MOVE!
BULMA, HOW LONG WILL IT TAKE YOU TO PUT TOGETHER A NEW RADAR ?
EVEN IF I RUSH, IT'LL TAKE AT LEAST HALF A DAY...
THAT'LL HAVE TO DO... JUST HURRY !
ONCE THE RADAR IS COMPLETED, THOSE WHO CAN FIGHT WILL SET OUT TO GATHER THE BALLS!!

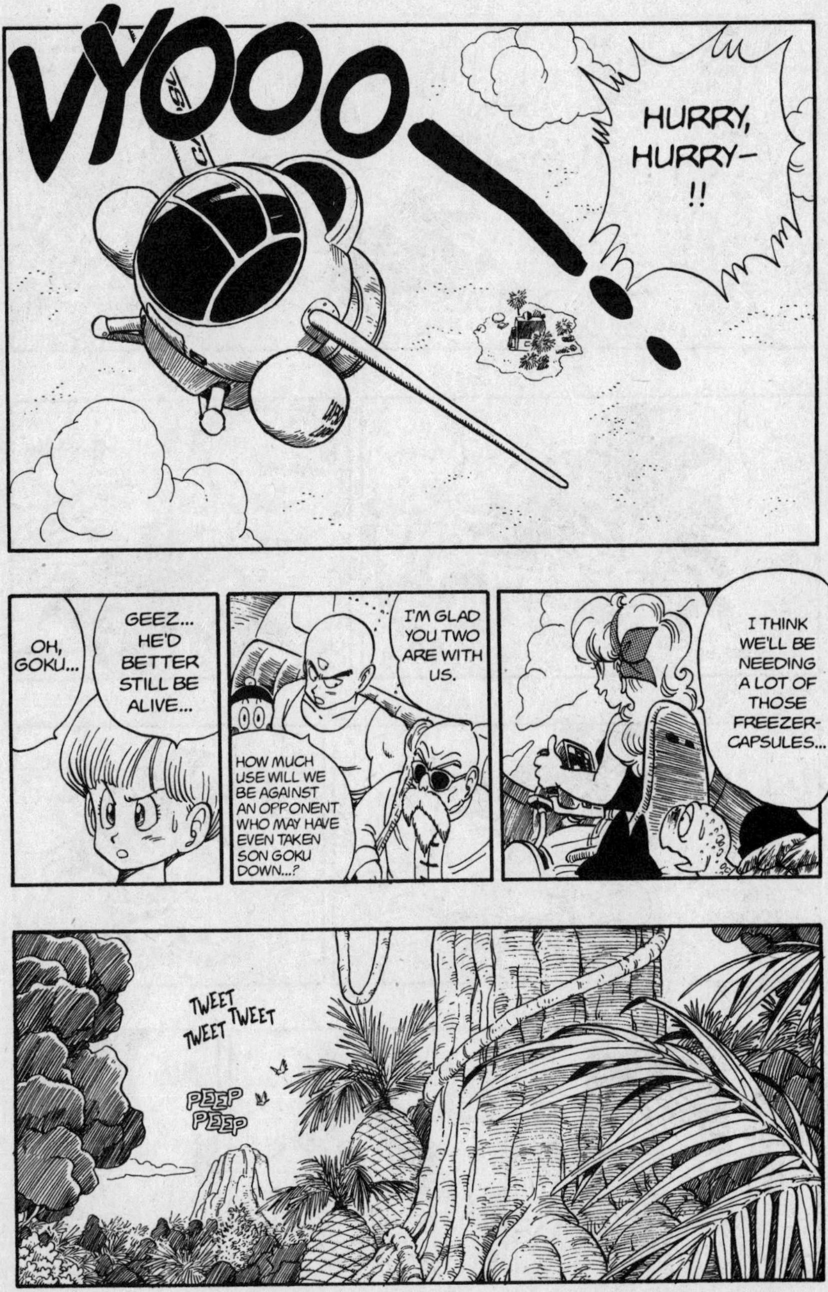
HURRY, HURRY—!!
VYOOO
I THINK WE'LL BE NEEDING A LOT OF THOSE FREEZER-CAPSULES...
I'M GLAD YOU TWO ARE WITH US.
HOW MUCH USE WILL WE BE AGAINST AN OPPONENT WHO MAY HAVE EVEN TAKEN SON GOKU DOWN...?
GEEZ... HE'D BETTER STILL BE ALIVE...
OH, GOKU...
TWEET TWEET TWEET
PEEP PEEP

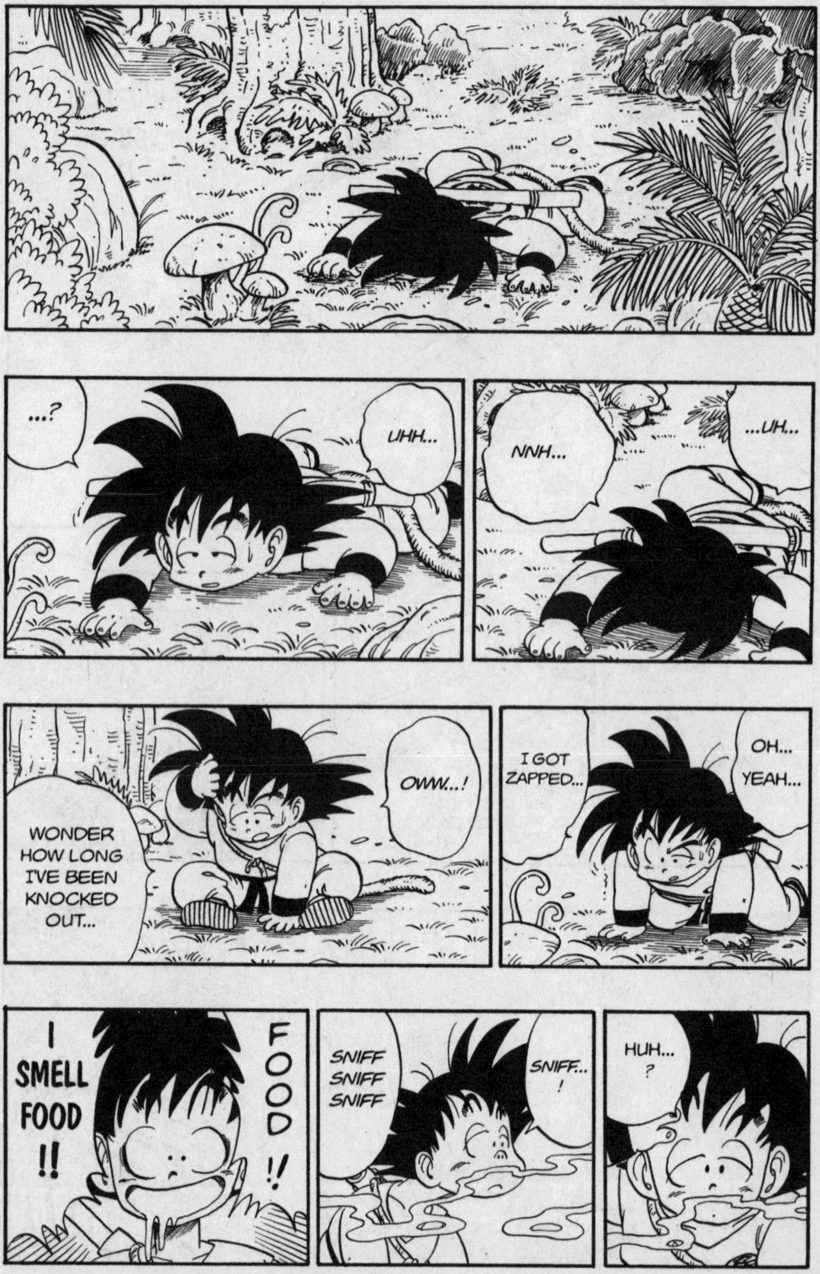
...UH...
NNH...
UHH...
...?
OH... YEAH...
I GOT ZAPPED...
OWW...!
WONDER HOW LONG I'VE BEEN KNOCKED OUT...
HUH... ?
SNIFF... !
SNIFF SNIFF SNIFF
FOOD !!
I SMELL FOOD !!

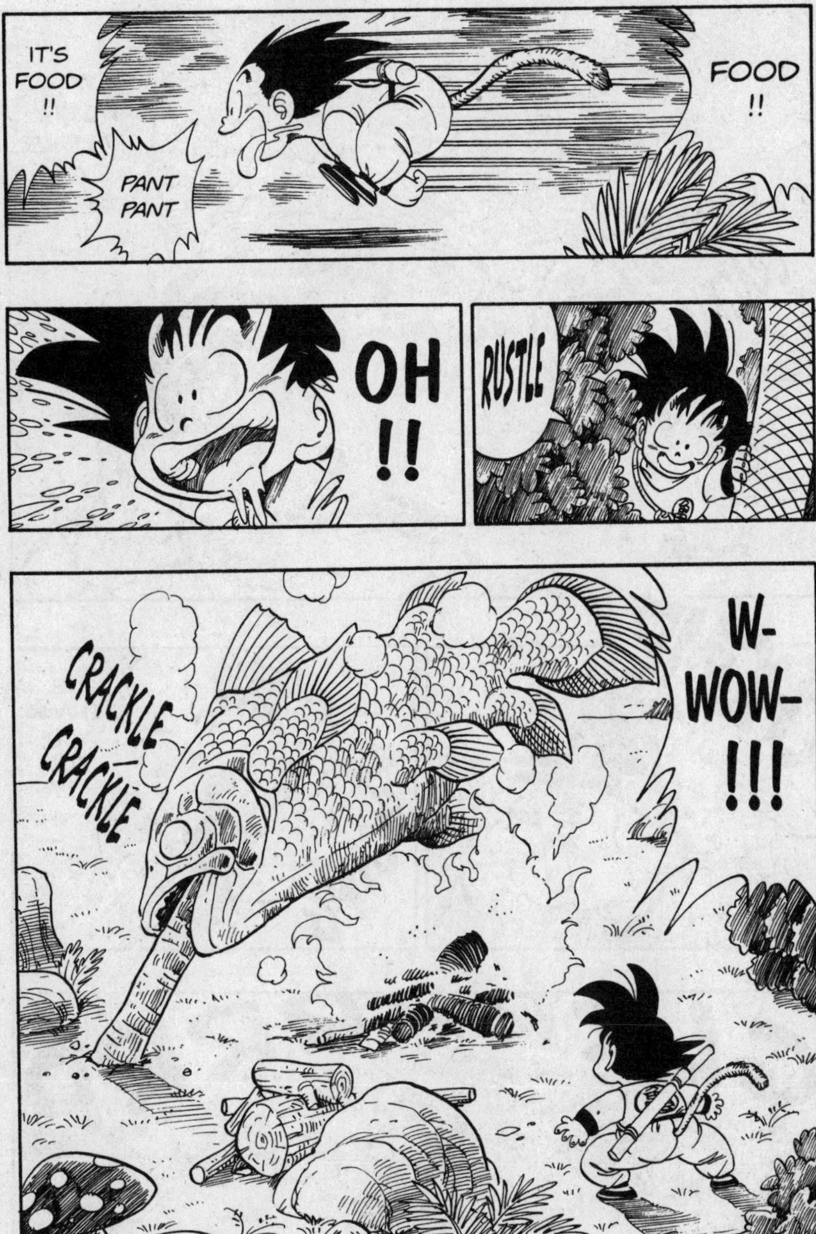
IT'S FOOD !!
PANT PANT
FOOD !!
OH !!
RUSTLE
CRACKLE CRACKLE
W-WOW-!!!

Tale 138 · The Weirdo with the Ball

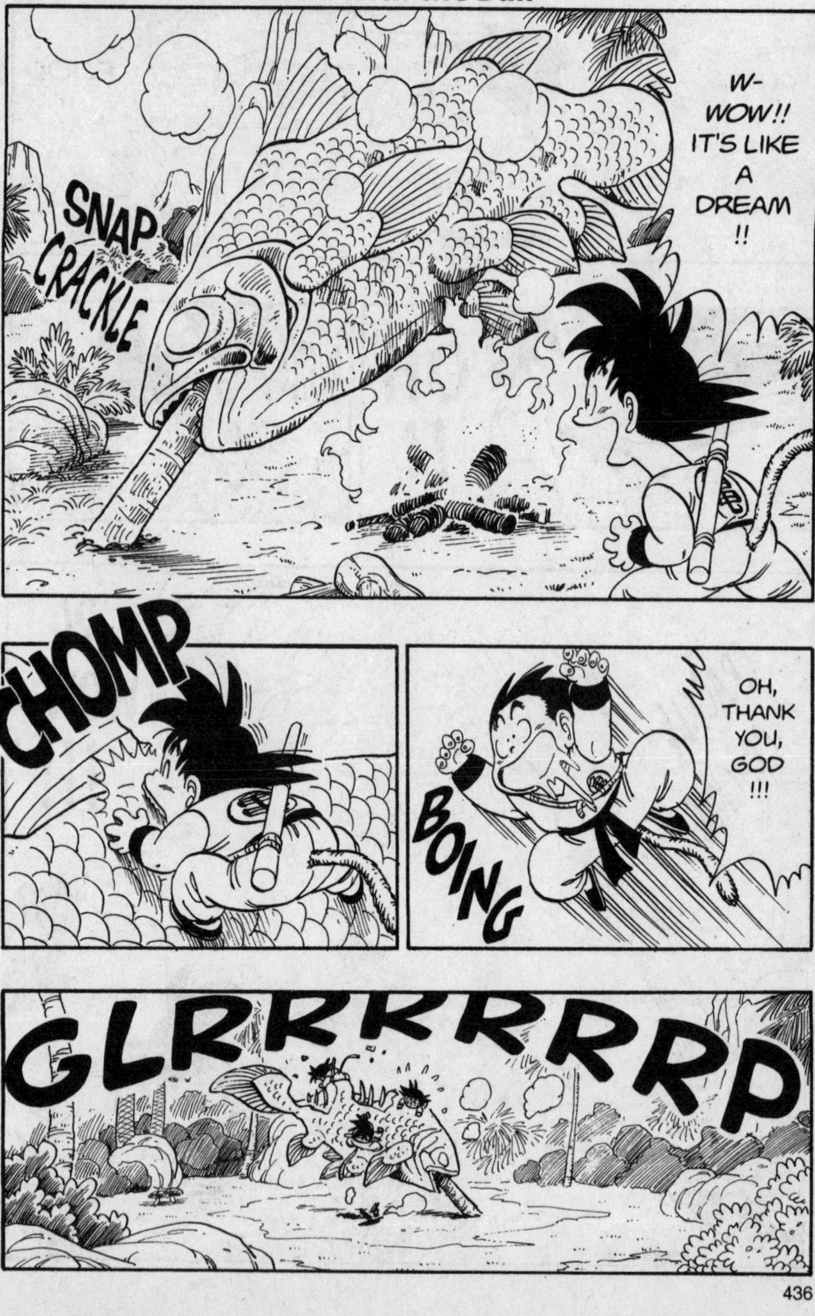
W-WOW!! IT'S LIKE A DREAM !!
SNAP
CRACKLE
OH, THANK YOU, GOD !!!
BOING
CHOMP
GLRRRRRRP

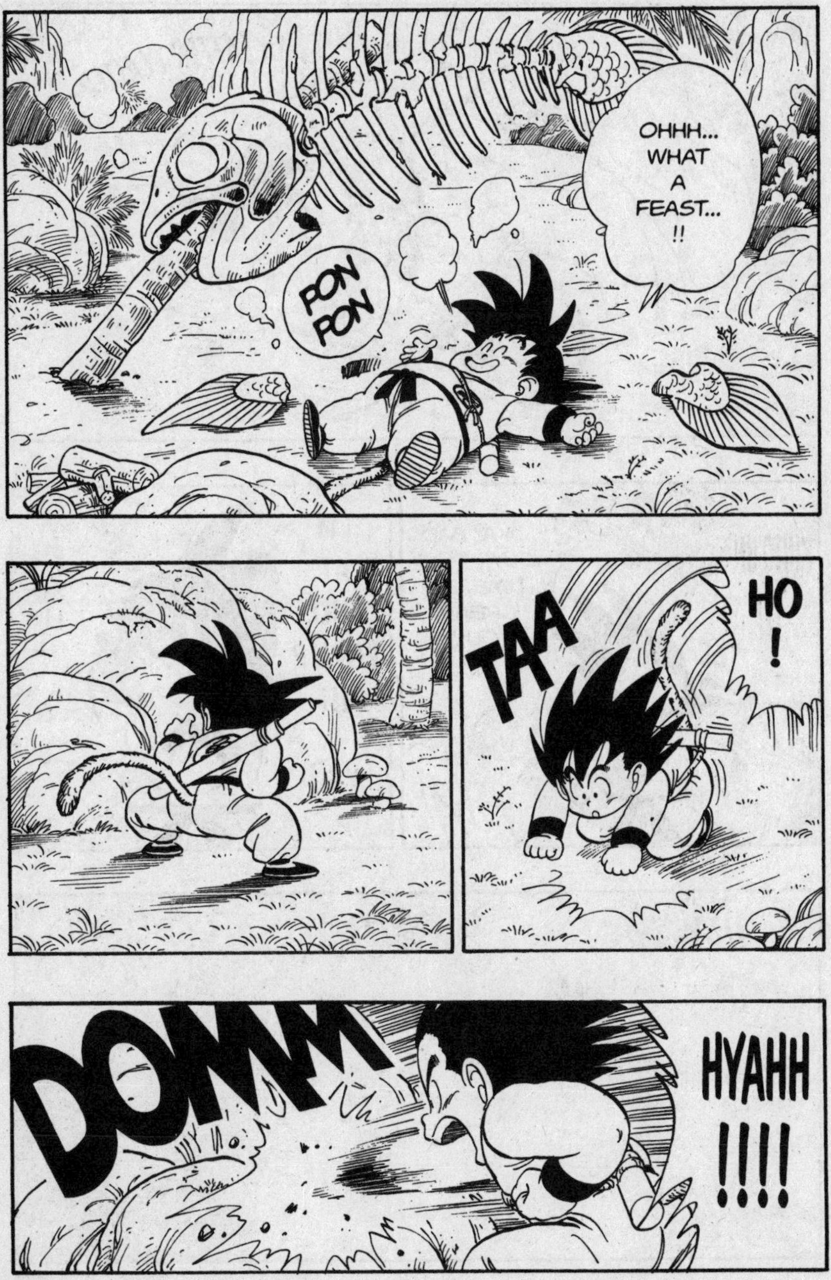
OHHH... WHAT A FEAST... !!
PON PON
HO!
TAA
HYAHH!!!!
DOMM

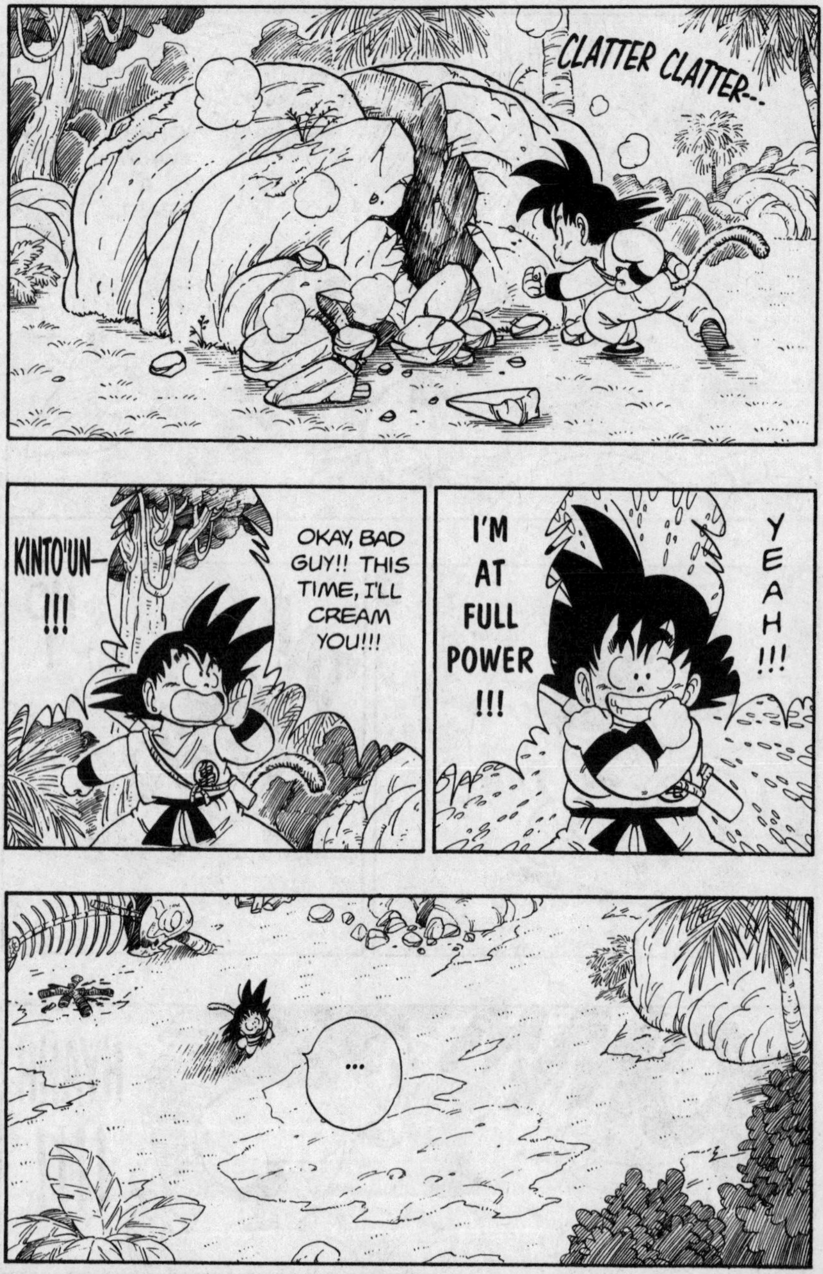
CLATTER CLATTER---
YEAH!!!
I'M AT FULL POWER!!!
OKAY, BAD GUY!! THIS TIME, I'LL CREAM YOU!!!
KINTO'UN— !!!
...

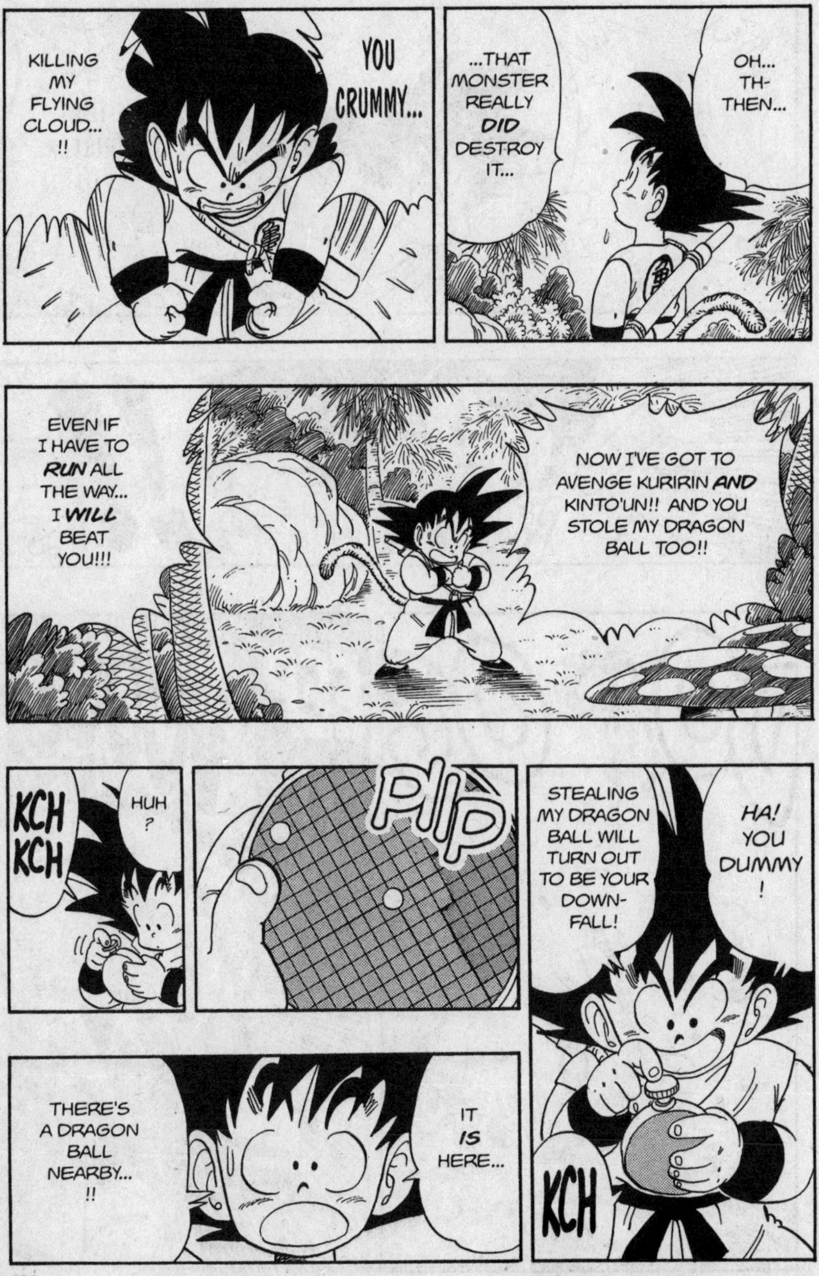
OH... TH- THEN...
...THAT MONSTER REALLY DID DESTROY IT...
YOU CRUMMY...
KILLING MY FLYING CLOUD... !!
NOW I'VE GOT TO AVENGE KURIRIN AND KINTO'UN!! AND YOU STOLE MY DRAGON BALL TOO!!
EVEN IF I HAVE TO RUN ALL THE WAY... I WILL BEAT YOU!!!
HA! YOU DUMMY!
STEALING MY DRAGON BALL WILL TURN OUT TO BE YOUR DOWN-FALL!
KCH
PIP
HUH ?
KCH KCH
IT IS HERE...
THERE'S A DRAGON BALL NEARBY... !!

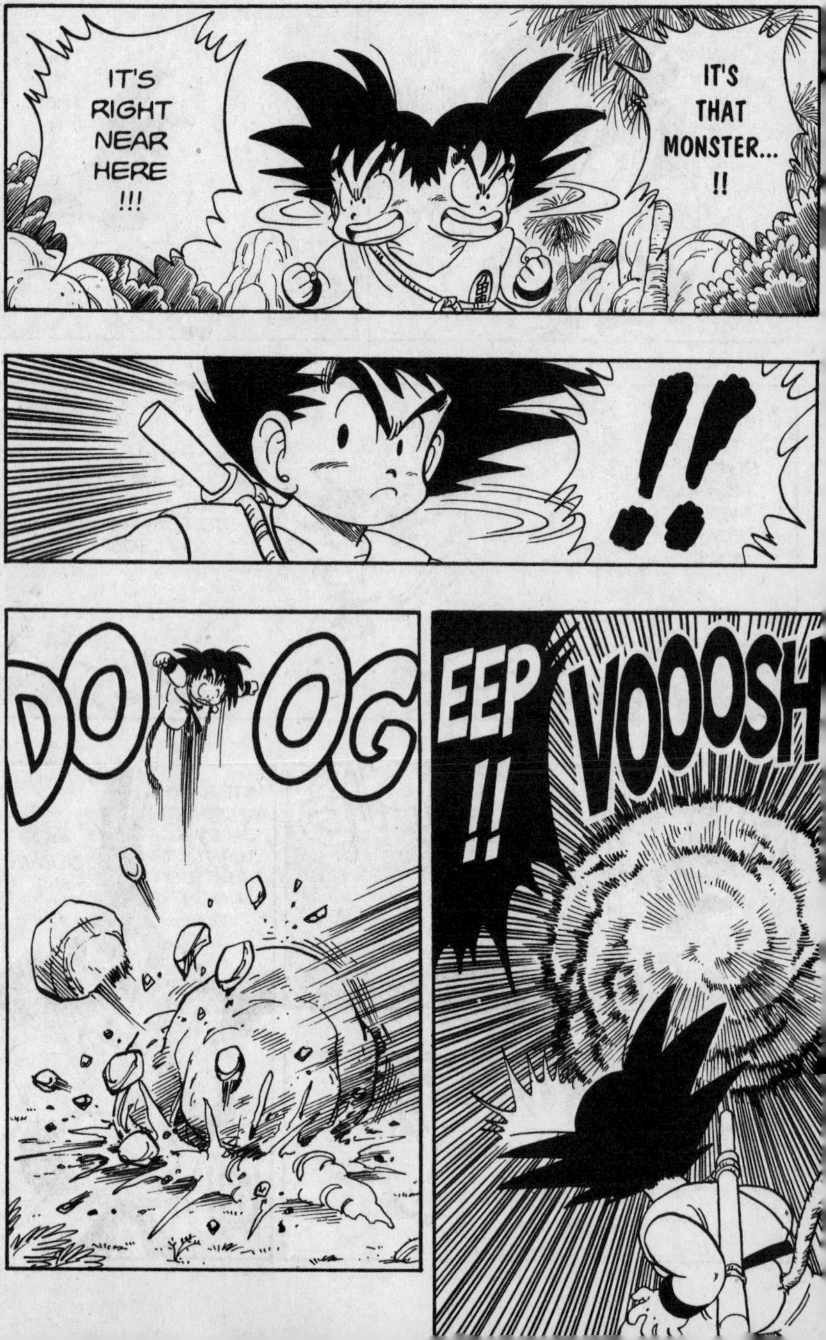
IT'S THAT MONSTER... !!
IT'S RIGHT NEAR HERE !!!
!!
VOOOSH
EEP !!
DO OG

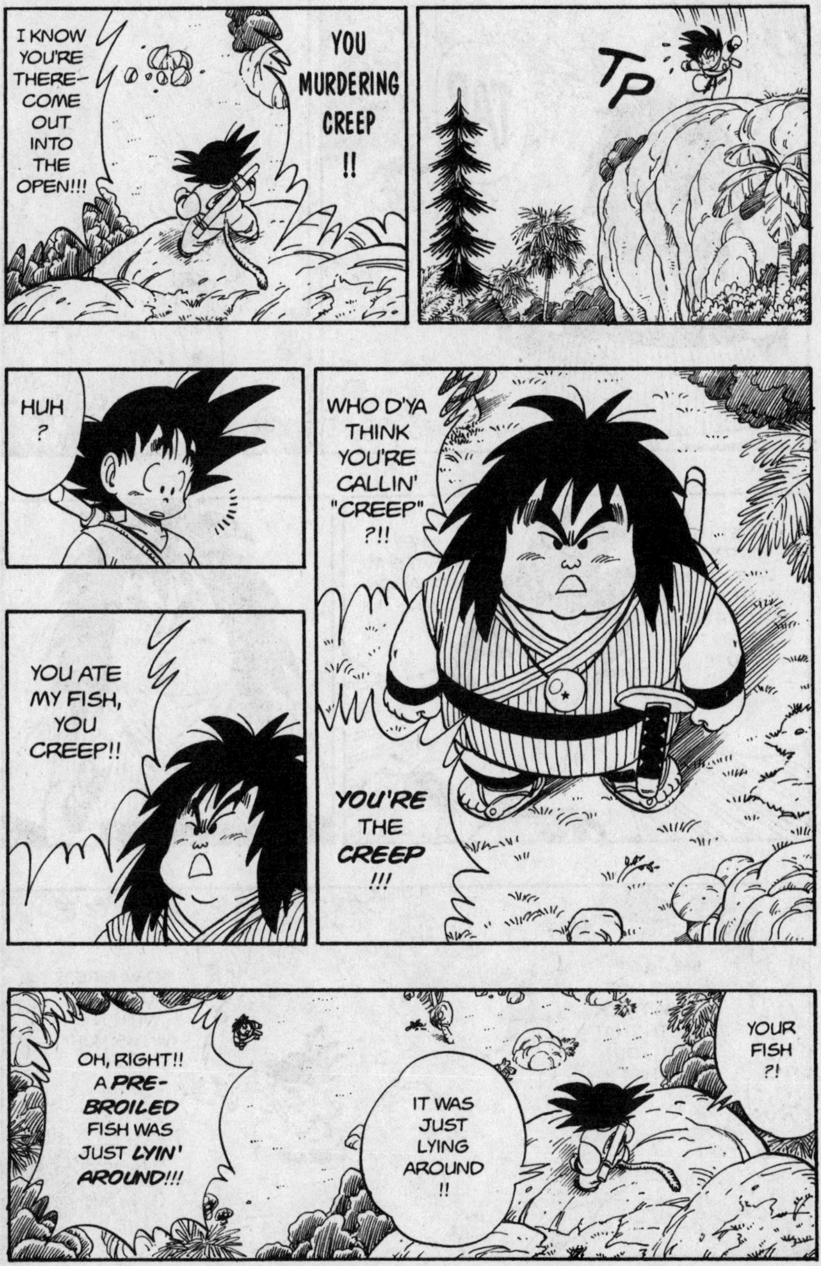
TP
YOU MURDERING CREEP !!
I KNOW YOU'RE THERE—COME OUT INTO THE OPEN!!!
WHO D'YA THINK YOU'RE CALLIN' "CREEP" ?!!
YOU'RE THE CREEP !!!
HUH ?
YOU ATE MY FISH, YOU CREEP!!
YOUR FISH ?!
IT WAS JUST LYING AROUND !!
OH, RIGHT!! A PRE-BROILED FISH WAS JUST LYIN' AROUND!!!

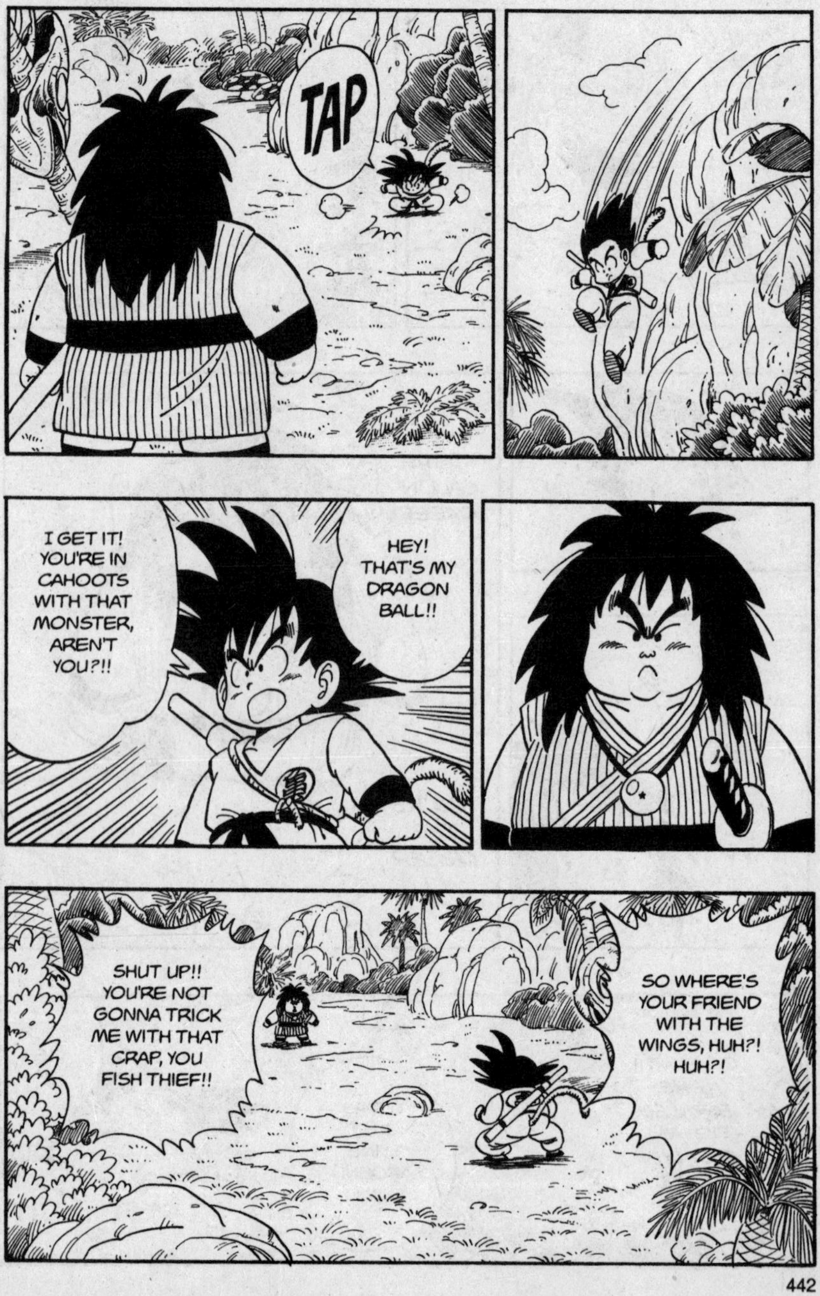
TAP
HEY! THAT'S MY DRAGON BALL!!
I GET IT! YOU'RE IN CAHOOTS WITH THAT MONSTER, AREN'T YOU?!!
SO WHERE'S YOUR FRIEND WITH THE WINGS, HUH?! HUH?!
SHUT UP!! YOU'RE NOT GONNA TRICK ME WITH THAT CRAP, YOU FISH THIEF!!

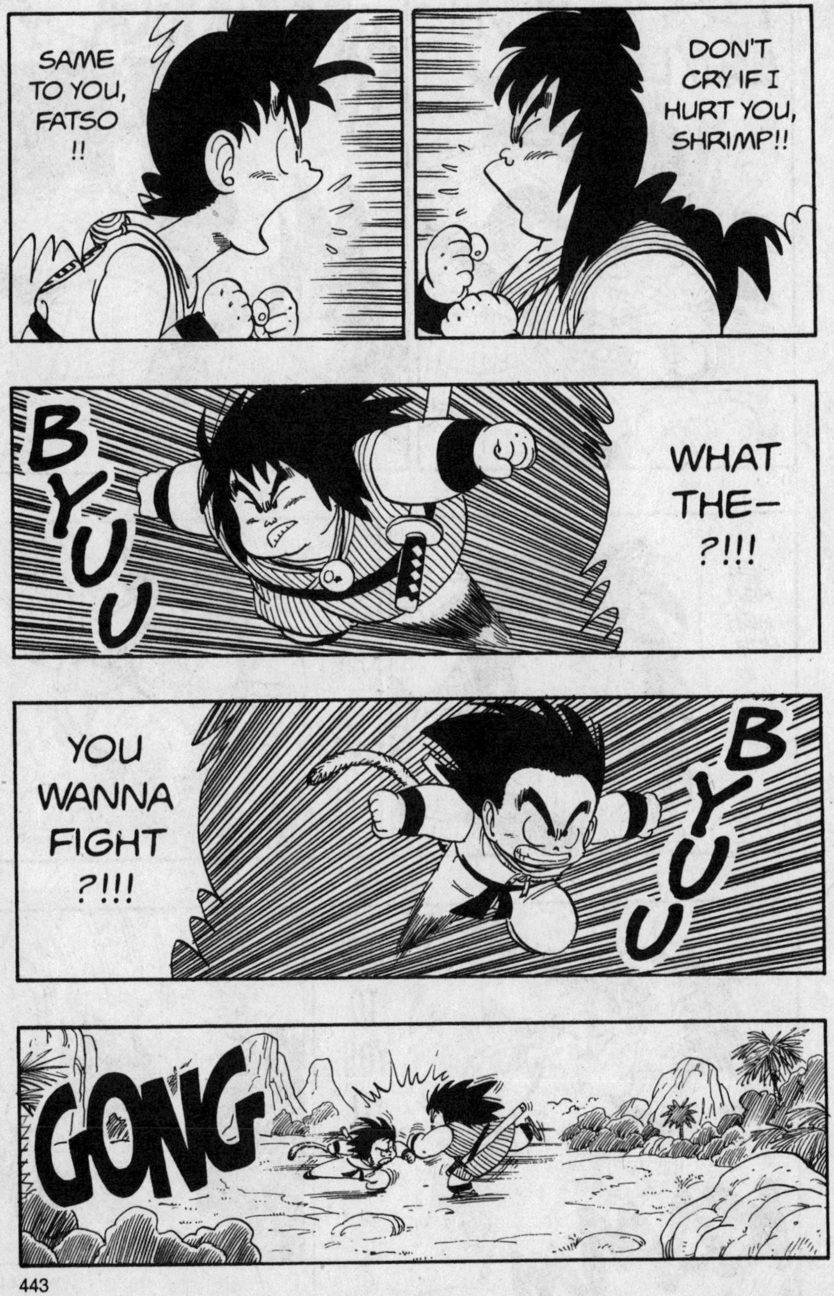
DON'T CRY IF I HURT YOU, SHRIMP!!
SAME TO YOU, FATSO !!
WHAT THE— ?!!!
BYUU
BYUU
YOU WANNA FIGHT ?!!!
GONG

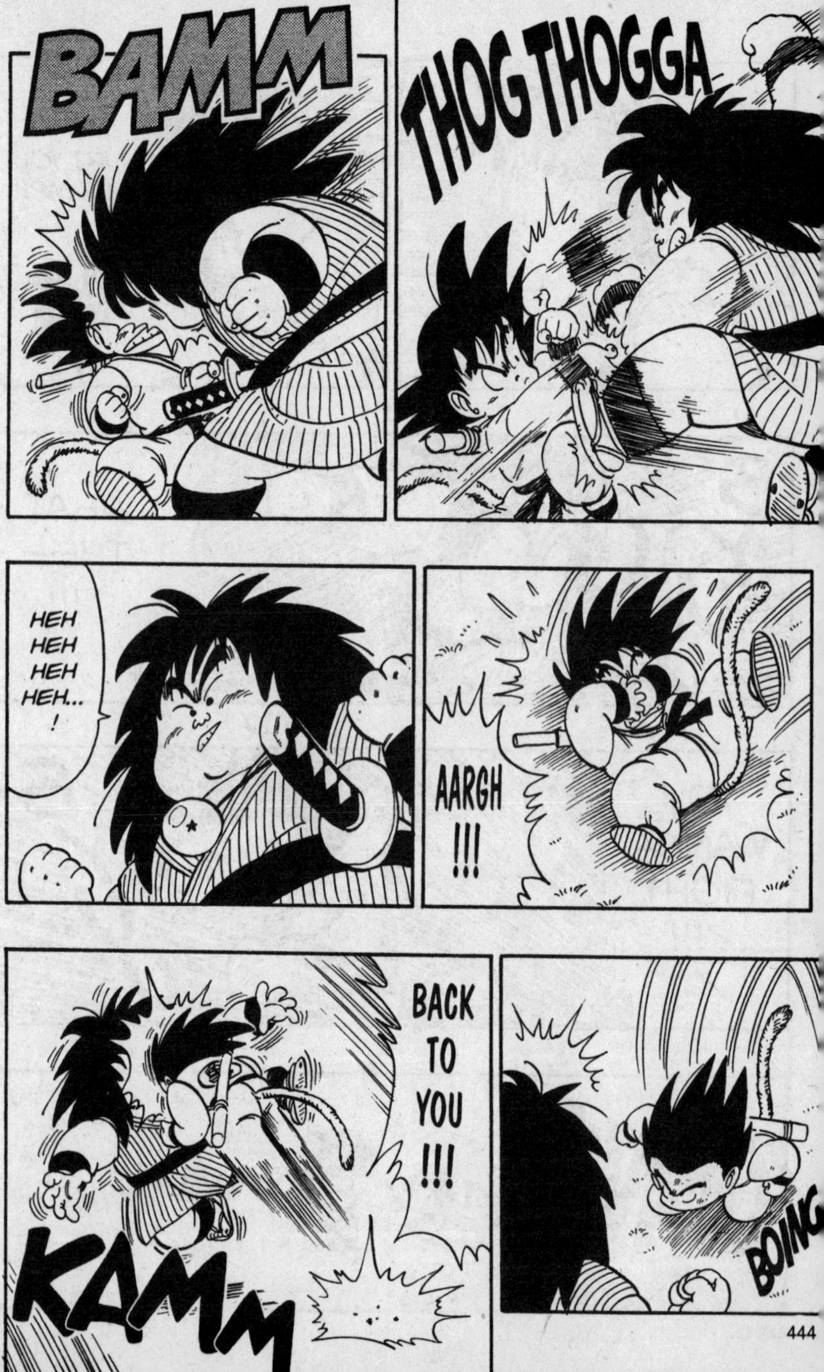

THOG THOGGA
BAMM
AARGH !!!
HEH HEH HEH HEH... !
BOING
BACK TO YOU !!!
KAMM

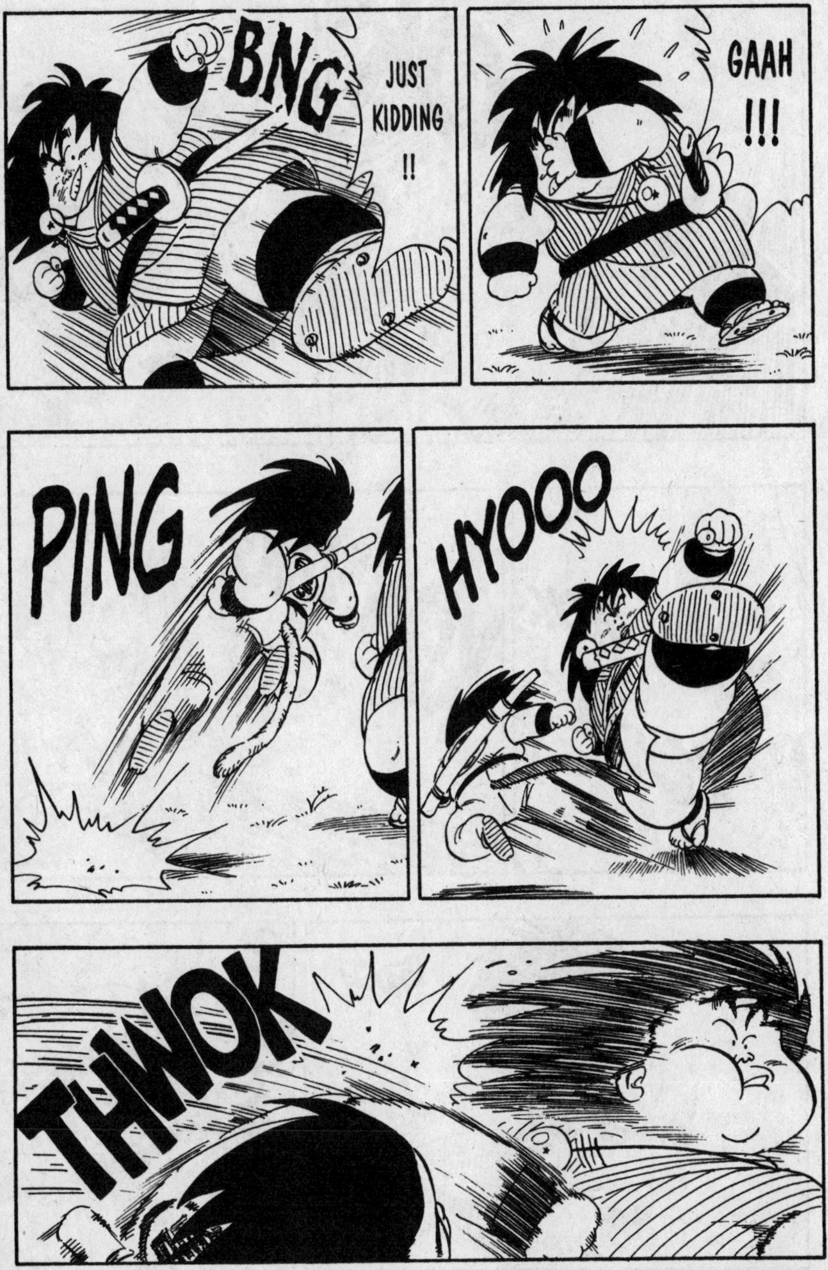
GAAH !!!
BNG
JUST KIDDING !!
HYOOO
PING
THWOK

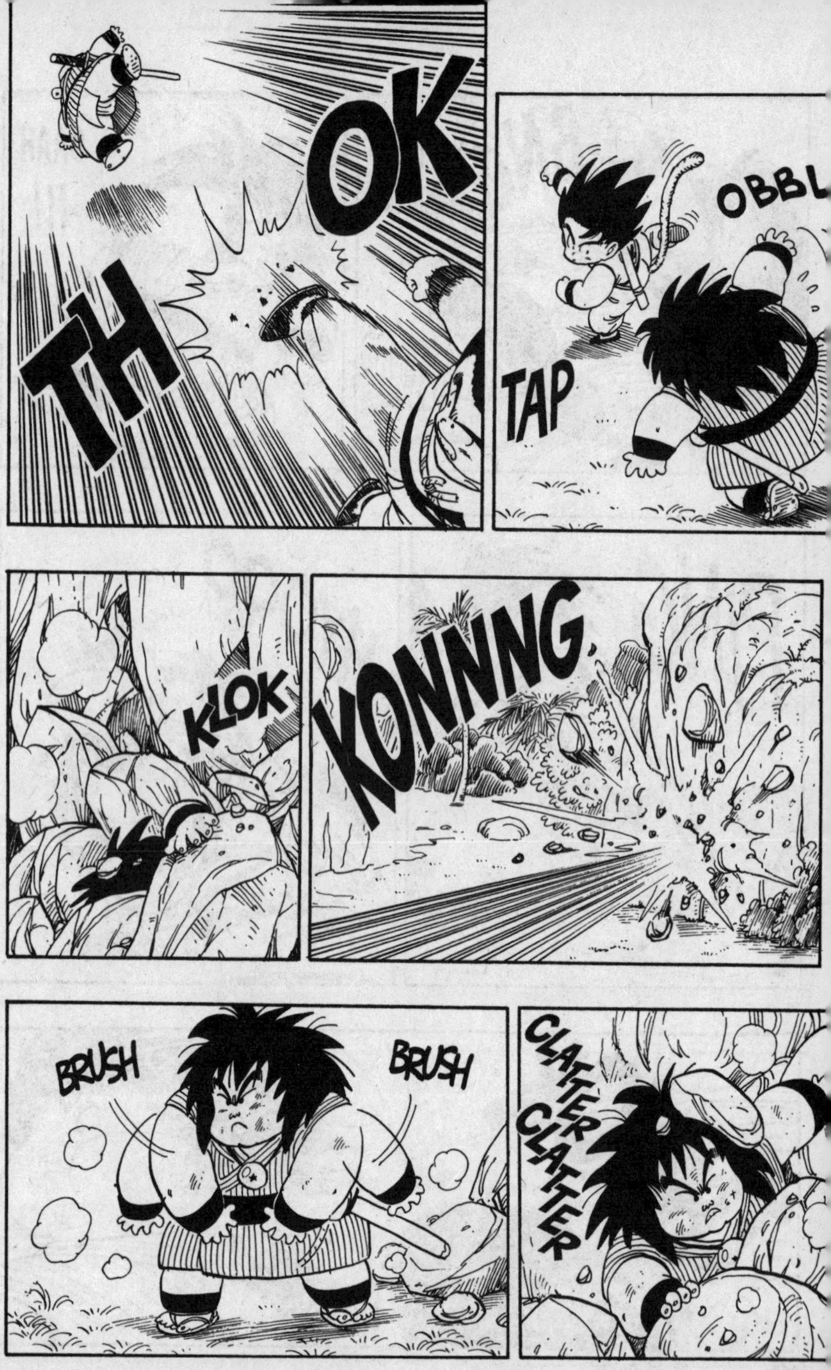
OBBL
TAP
THOK
KONNNG
KLOK
CLATTER CLATTER
BRUSH
BRUSH

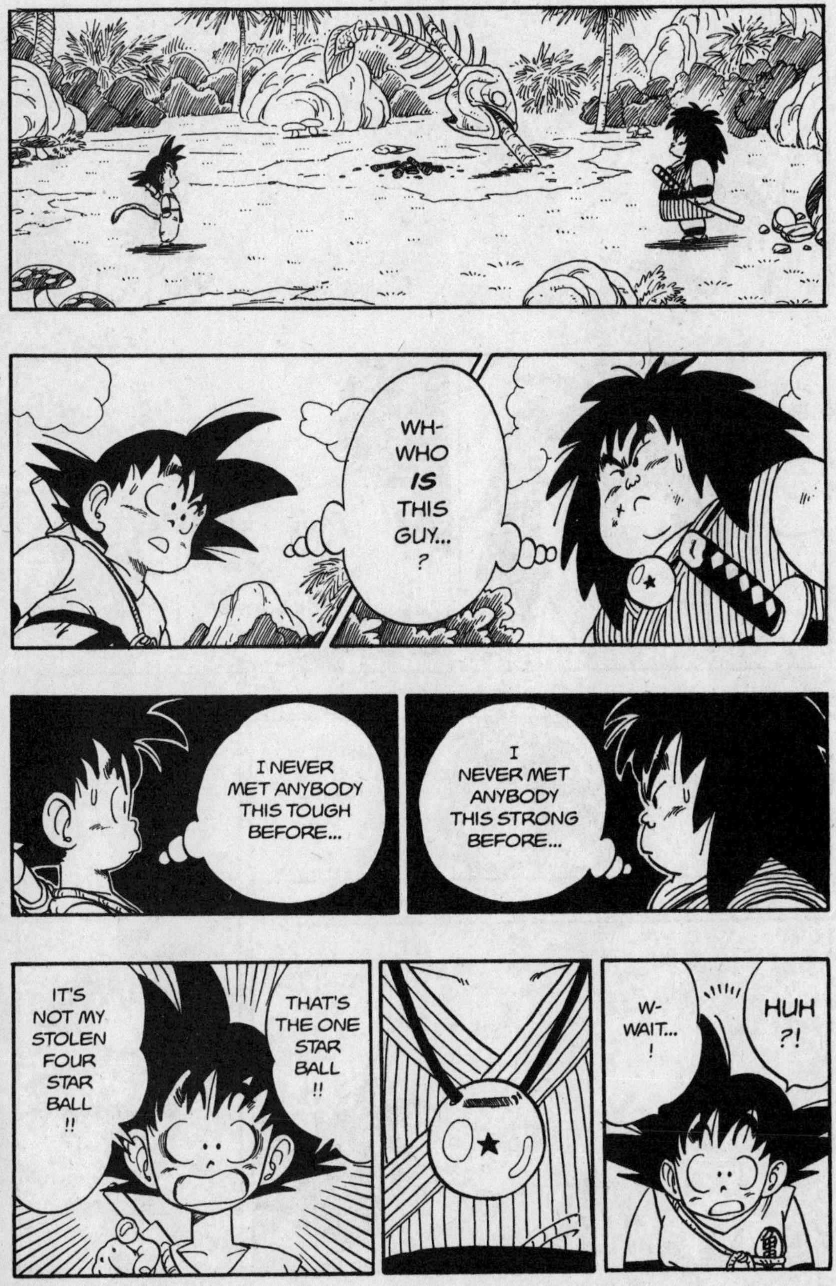
WH-WHO IS THIS GUY...?
I NEVER MET ANYBODY THIS STRONG BEFORE...
I NEVER MET ANYBODY THIS TOUGH BEFORE...
HUH?!
W-WAIT...!
THAT'S THE ONE STAR BALL!!
IT'S NOT MY STOLEN FOUR STAR BALL!!

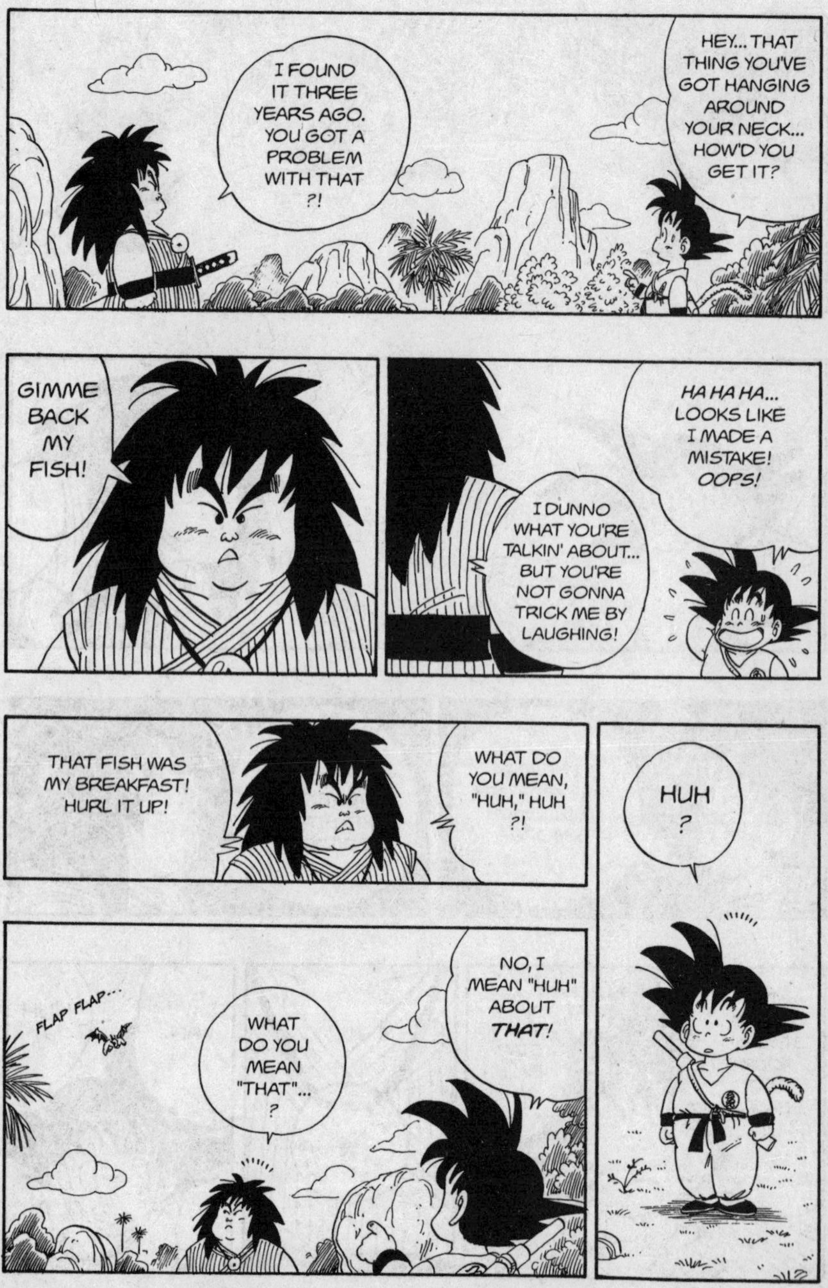
HEY... THAT THING YOU'VE GOT HANGING AROUND YOUR NECK... HOW'D YOU GET IT?
I FOUND IT THREE YEARS AGO. YOU GOT A PROBLEM WITH THAT ?!
HA HA HA... LOOKS LIKE I MADE A MISTAKE! OOPS!
I DUNNO WHAT YOU'RE TALKIN' ABOUT... BUT YOU'RE NOT GONNA TRICK ME BY LAUGHING!
GIMME BACK MY FISH!
HUH ?
WHAT DO YOU MEAN, "HUH," HUH ?!
THAT FISH WAS MY BREAKFAST! HURL IT UP!
NO, I MEAN "HUH" ABOUT THAT!
WHAT DO YOU MEAN "THAT"... ?
FLAP FLAP...

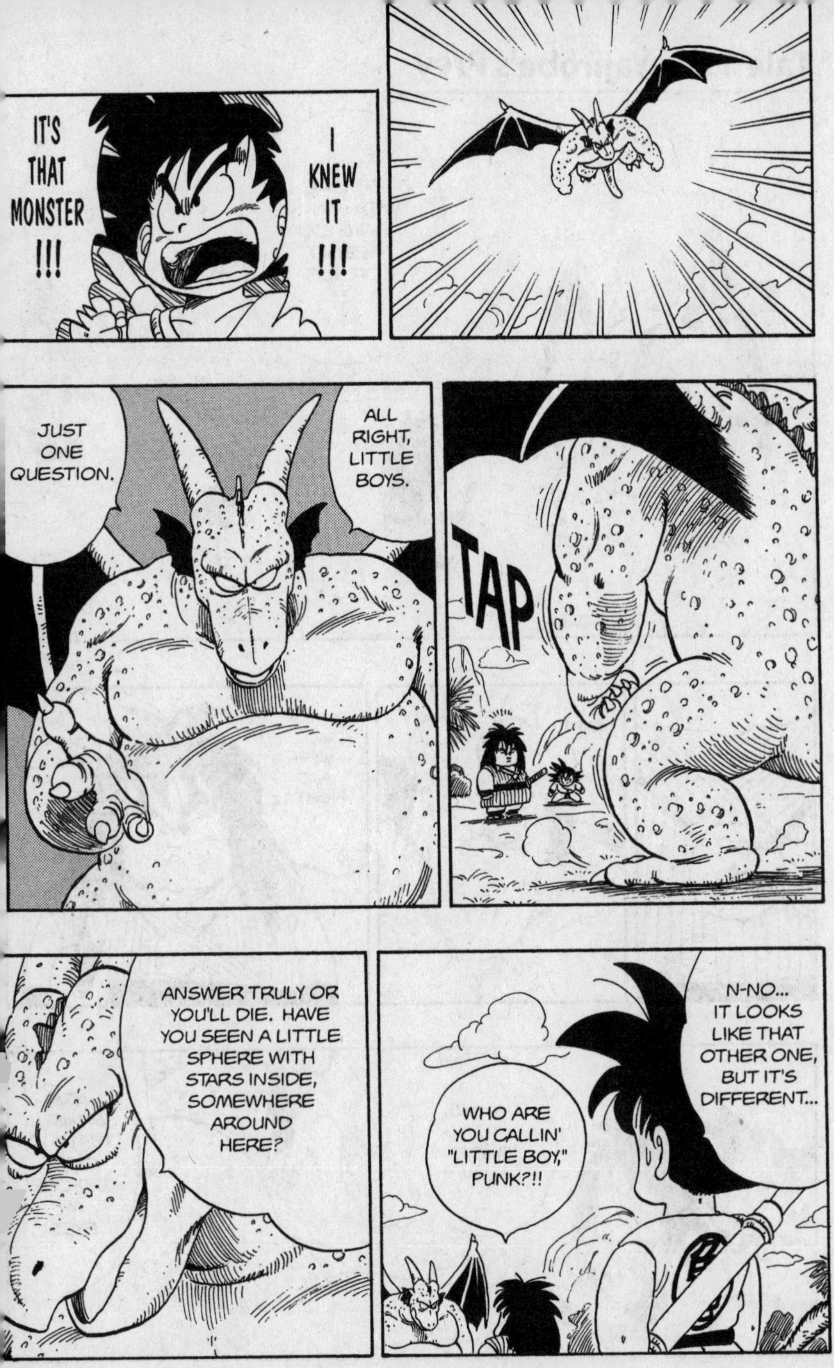
I KNEW IT !!!
IT'S THAT MONSTER !!!
TAP
ALL RIGHT, LITTLE BOYS.
JUST ONE QUESTION.
N-NO... IT LOOKS LIKE THAT OTHER ONE, BUT IT'S DIFFERENT...
WHO ARE YOU CALLIN' "LITTLE BOY," PUNK?!!
ANSWER TRULY OR YOU'LL DIE. HAVE YOU SEEN A LITTLE SPHERE WITH STARS INSIDE, SOMEWHERE AROUND HERE?

Tale 139 • Yajirobe's Prey

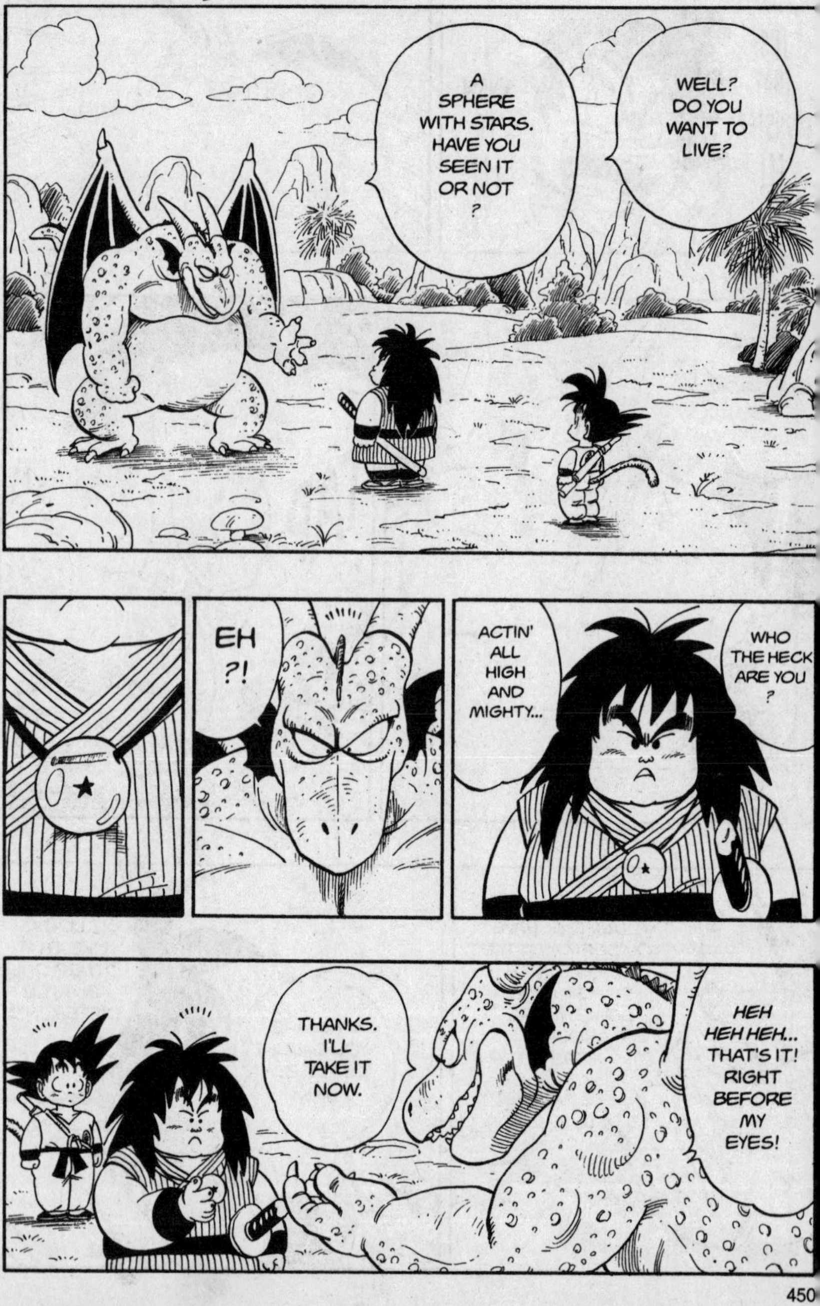
WELL? DO YOU WANT TO LIVE?
A SPHERE WITH STARS. HAVE YOU SEEN IT OR NOT ?
WHO THE HECK ARE YOU ?
ACTIN' ALL HIGH AND MIGHTY...
EH ?!
HEH HEH HEH... THAT'S IT! RIGHT BEFORE MY EYES!
THANKS. I'LL TAKE IT NOW.

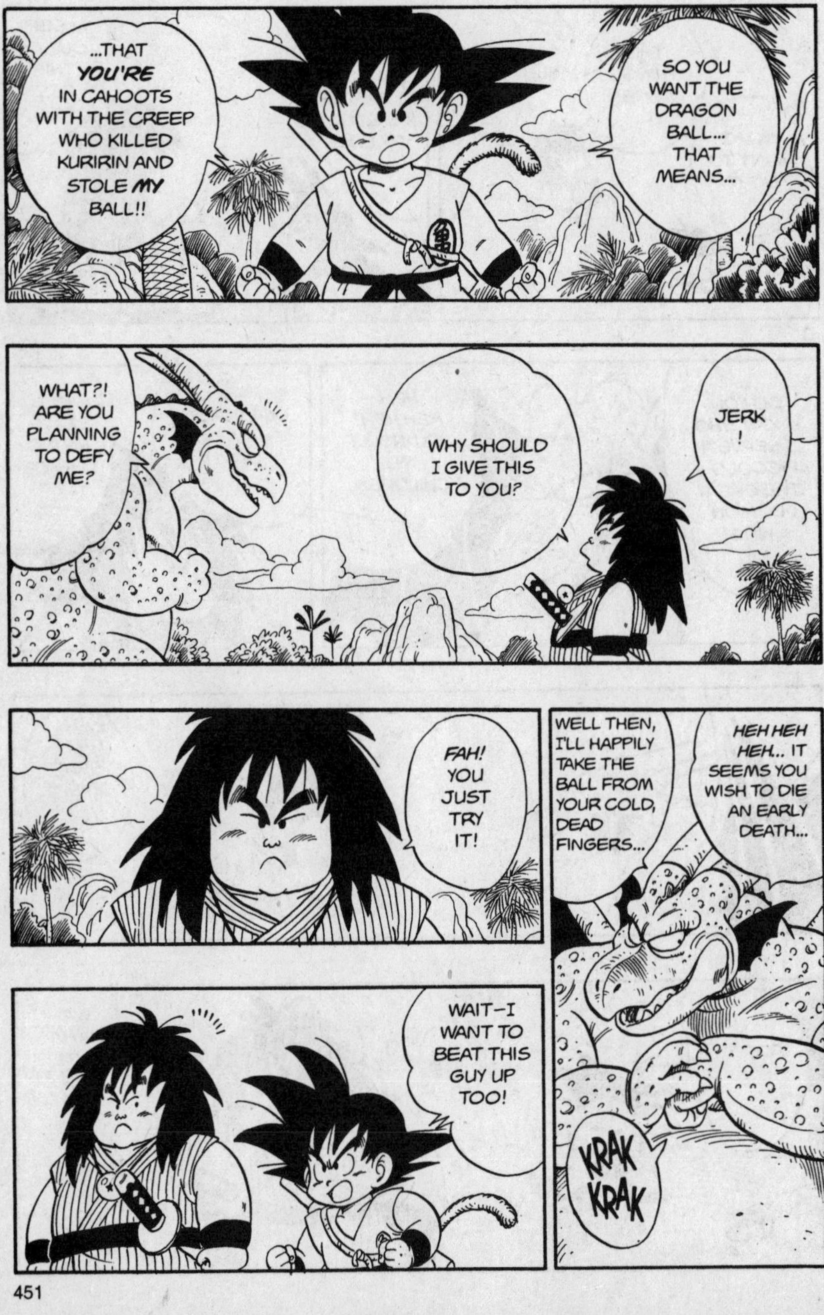
SO YOU WANT THE DRAGON BALL... THAT MEANS...
...THAT *YOU'RE* IN CAHOOTS WITH THE CREEP WHO KILLED KURIRIN AND STOLE *MY* BALL!!
JERK!
WHY SHOULD I GIVE THIS TO YOU?
WHAT?! ARE YOU PLANNING TO DEFY ME?
HEH HEH HEH... IT SEEMS YOU WISH TO DIE AN EARLY DEATH...
WELL THEN, I'LL HAPPILY TAKE THE BALL FROM YOUR COLD, DEAD FINGERS...
KRAK KRAK
FAH! YOU JUST TRY IT!
WAIT—I WANT TO BEAT THIS GUY UP TOO!

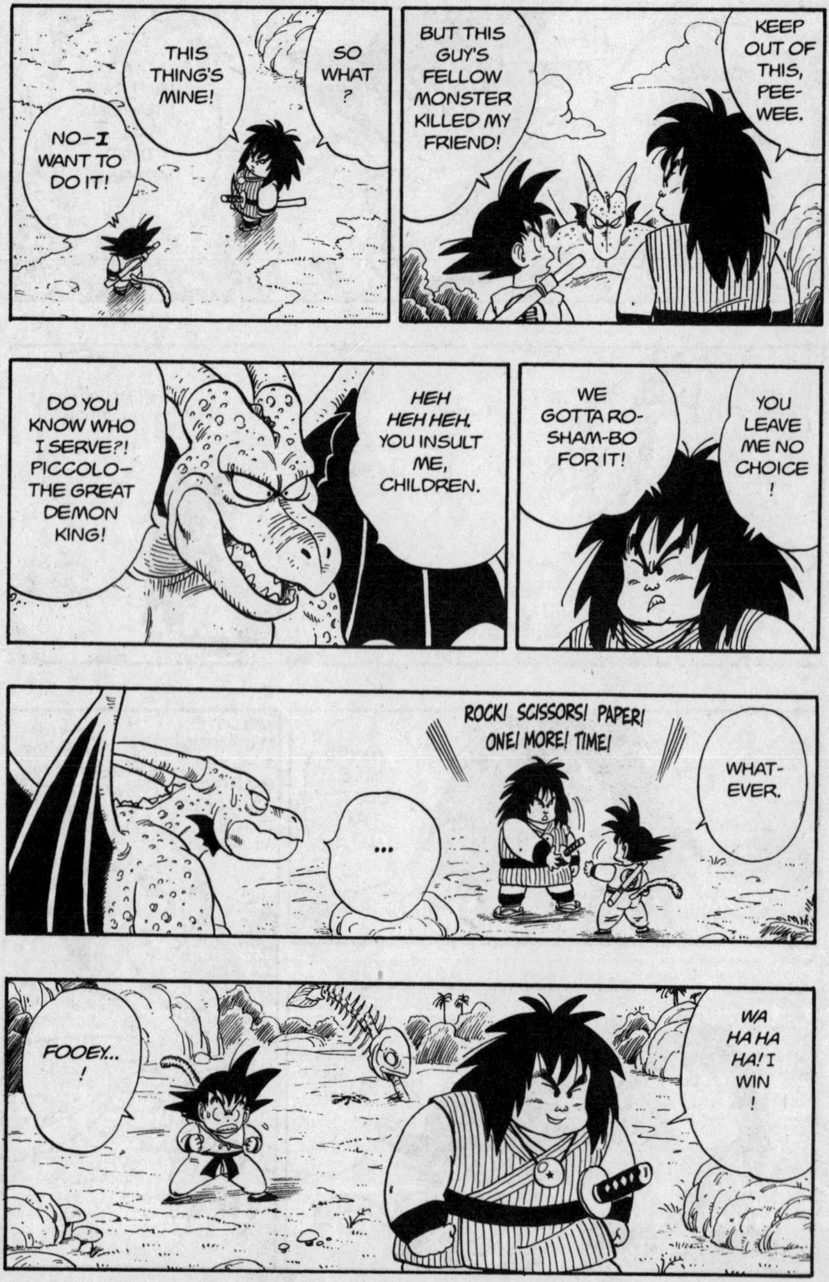
KEEP OUT OF THIS, PEE-WEE.
BUT THIS GUY'S FELLOW MONSTER KILLED MY FRIEND!
SO WHAT?
THIS THING'S MINE!
NO—I WANT TO DO IT!
YOU LEAVE ME NO CHOICE!
WE GOTTA RO-SHAM-BO FOR IT!
HEH HEH HEH. YOU INSULT ME, CHILDREN.
DO YOU KNOW WHO I SERVE?! PICCOLO—THE GREAT DEMON KING!
WHAT-EVER.
ROCK! SCISSORS! PAPER! ONE! MORE! TIME!
...
WA HA HA HA! I WIN!
FOOEY...!

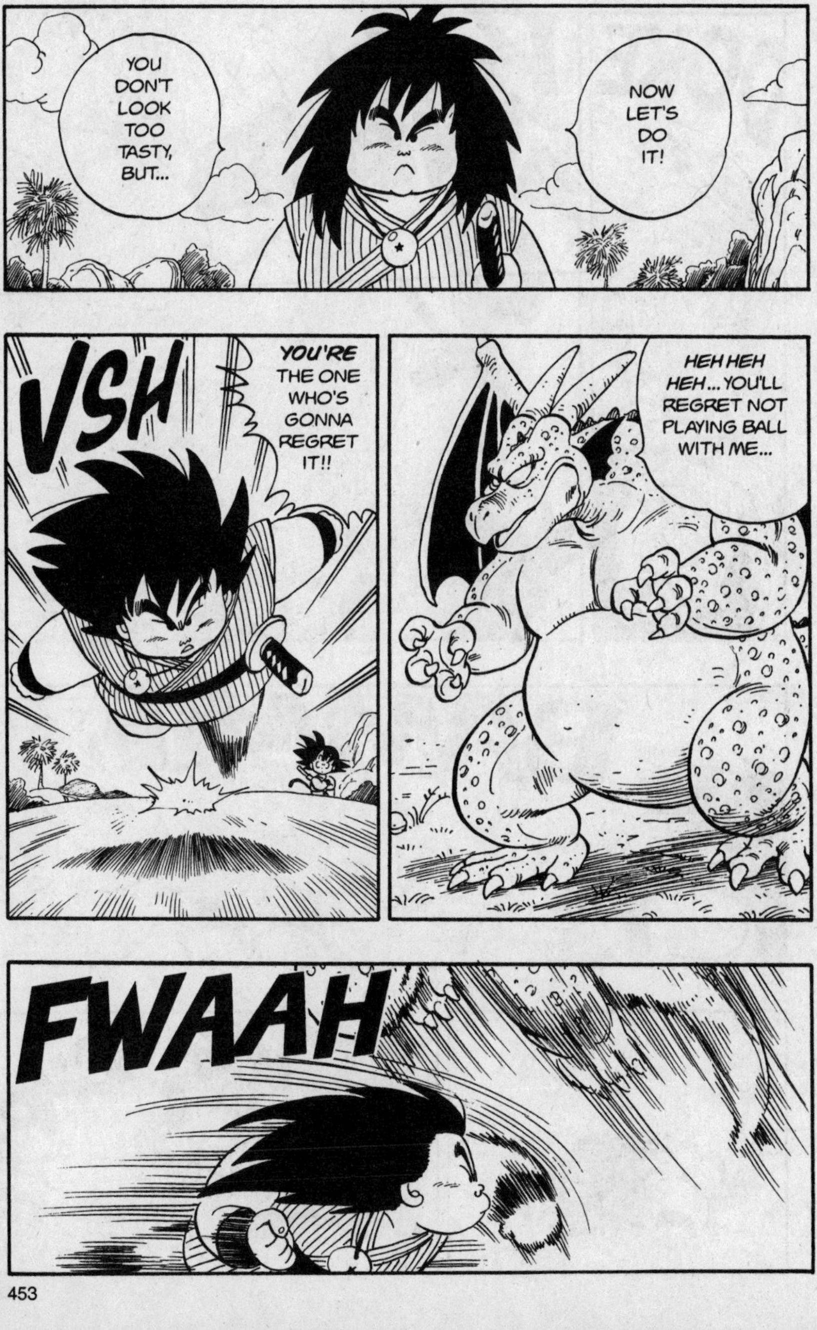
NOW LET'S DO IT!
YOU DON'T LOOK TOO TASTY, BUT...
HEH HEH HEH... YOU'LL REGRET NOT PLAYING BALL WITH ME...
YOU'RE THE ONE WHO'S GONNA REGRET IT!!
VSH
FWAAH

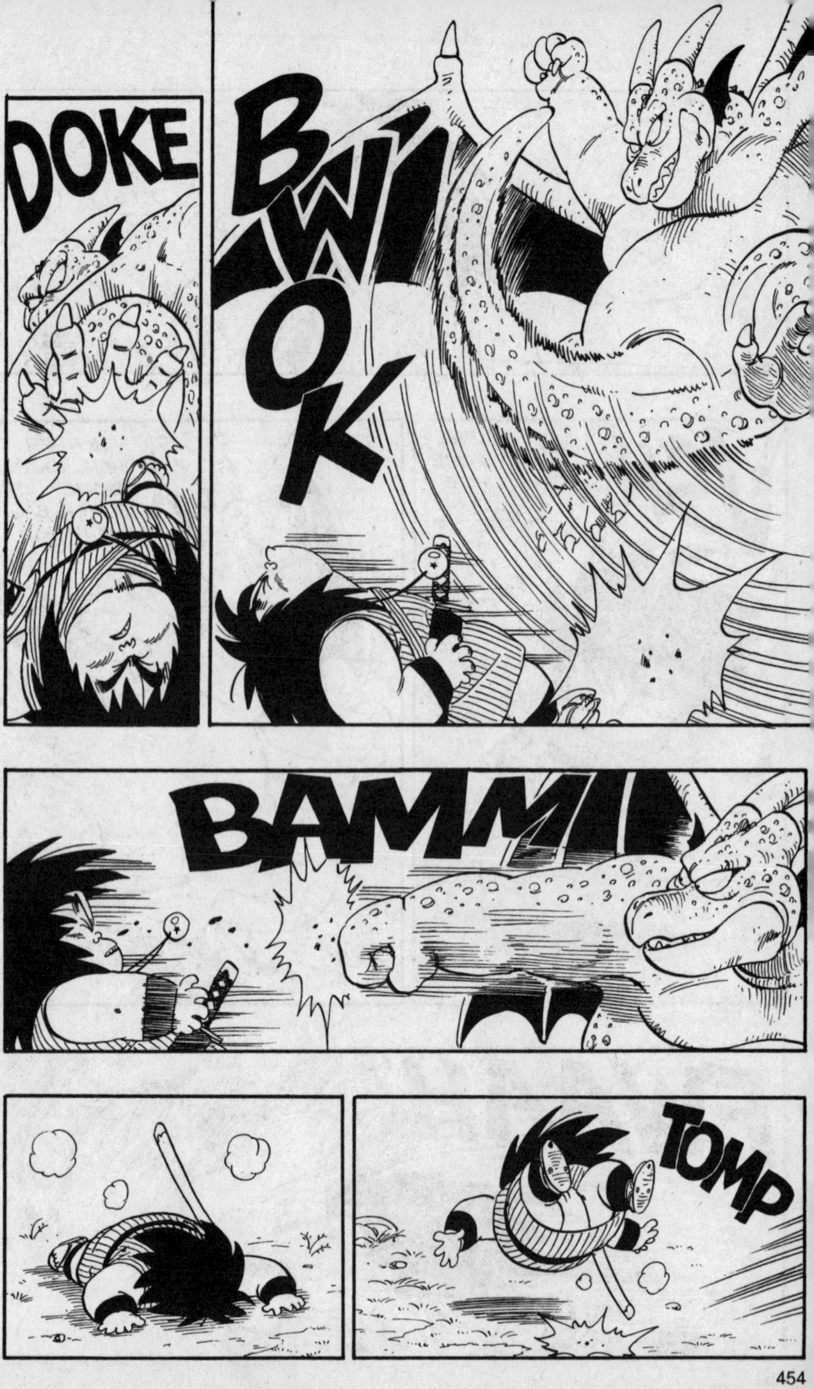
BWOK
DOKE
BAMM
TOMP

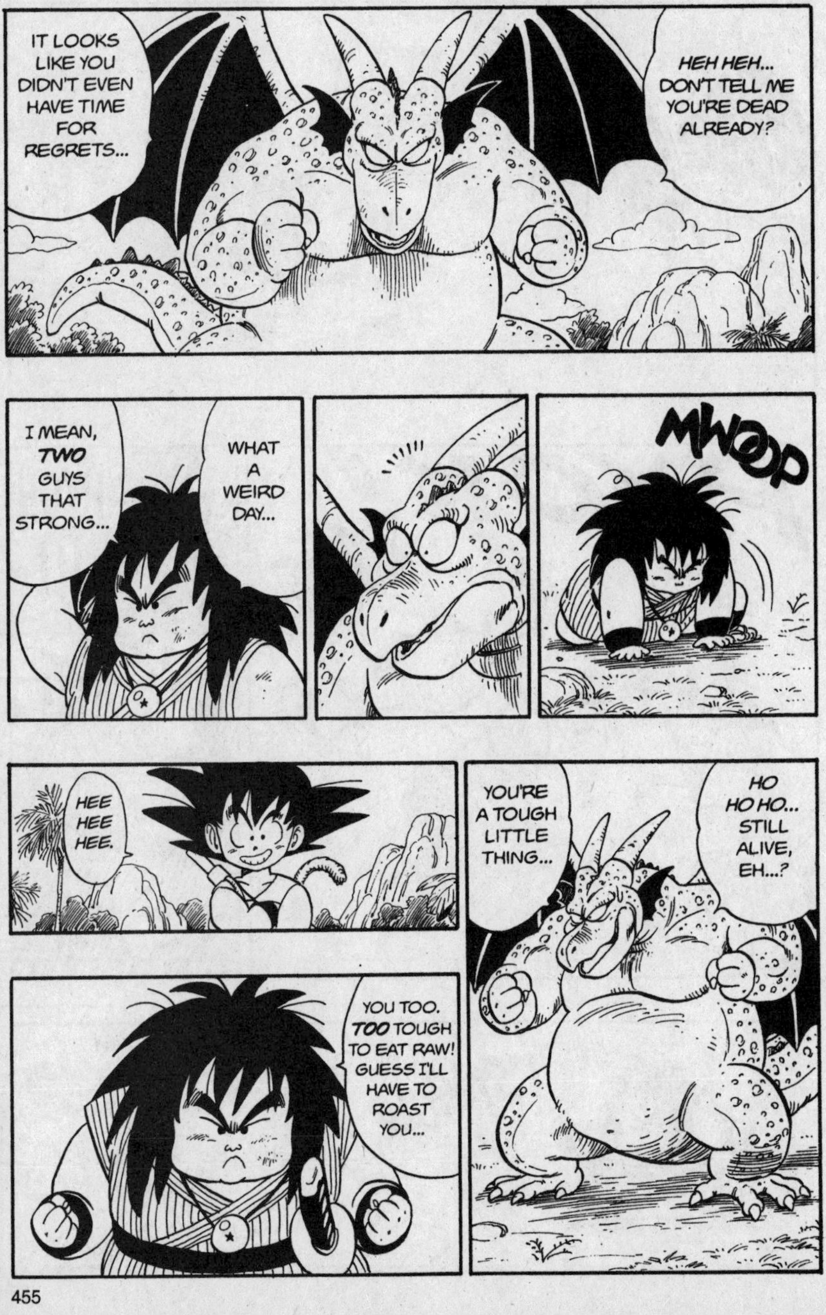
HEH HEH... DON'T TELL ME YOU'RE DEAD ALREADY?
IT LOOKS LIKE YOU DIDN'T EVEN HAVE TIME FOR REGRETS...
MWOOP
WHAT A WEIRD DAY...
I MEAN, **TWO** GUYS THAT STRONG...
HO HO HO... STILL ALIVE, EH...?
YOU'RE A TOUGH LITTLE THING...
HEE HEE HEE.
YOU TOO. **TOO** TOUGH TO EAT RAW! GUESS I'LL HAVE TO ROAST YOU...

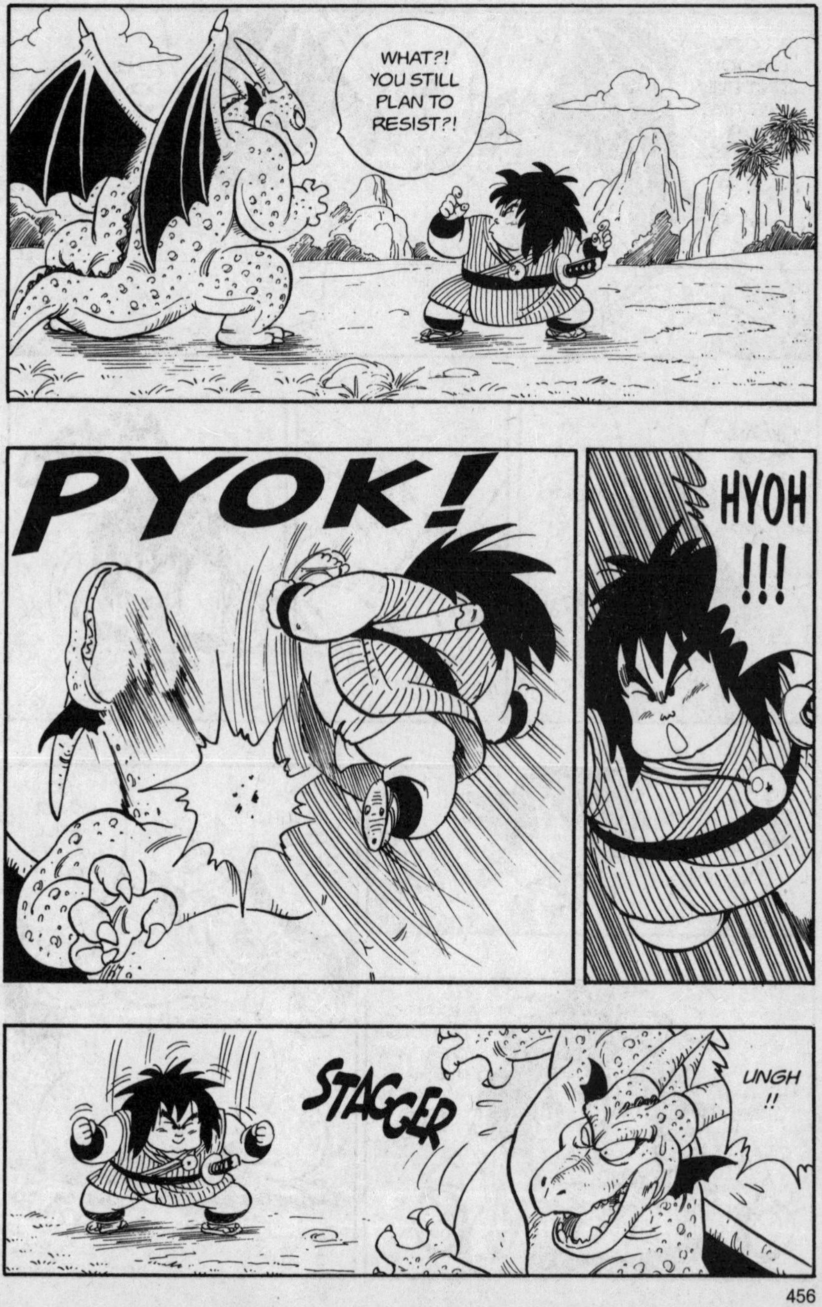
WHAT?! YOU STILL PLAN TO RESIST?!
HYOH !!!
PYOK!
UNGH !!
STAGGER

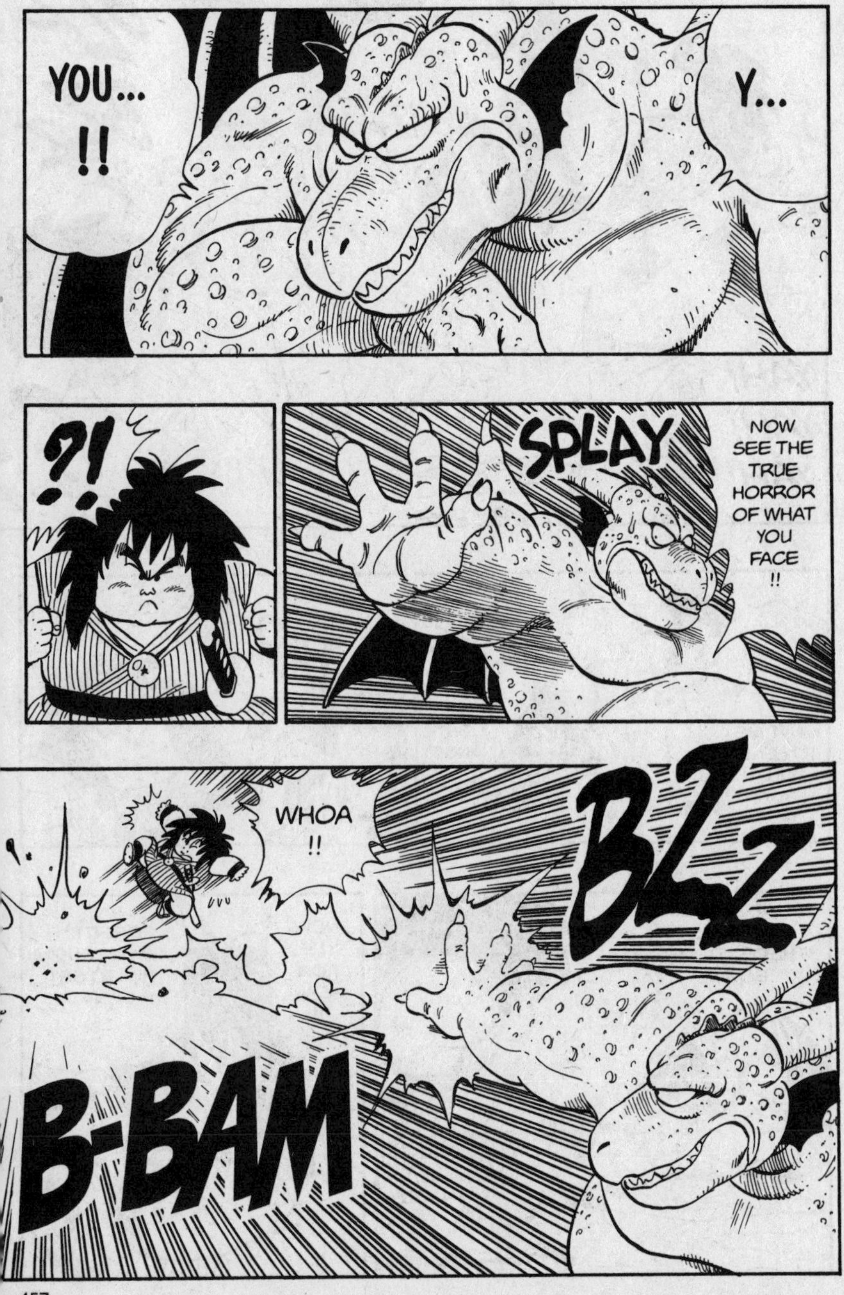
Y...
YOU... !!
SPLAY
NOW SEE THE TRUE HORROR OF WHAT YOU FACE !!
?!
BZZ
WHOA !!
B-BAM

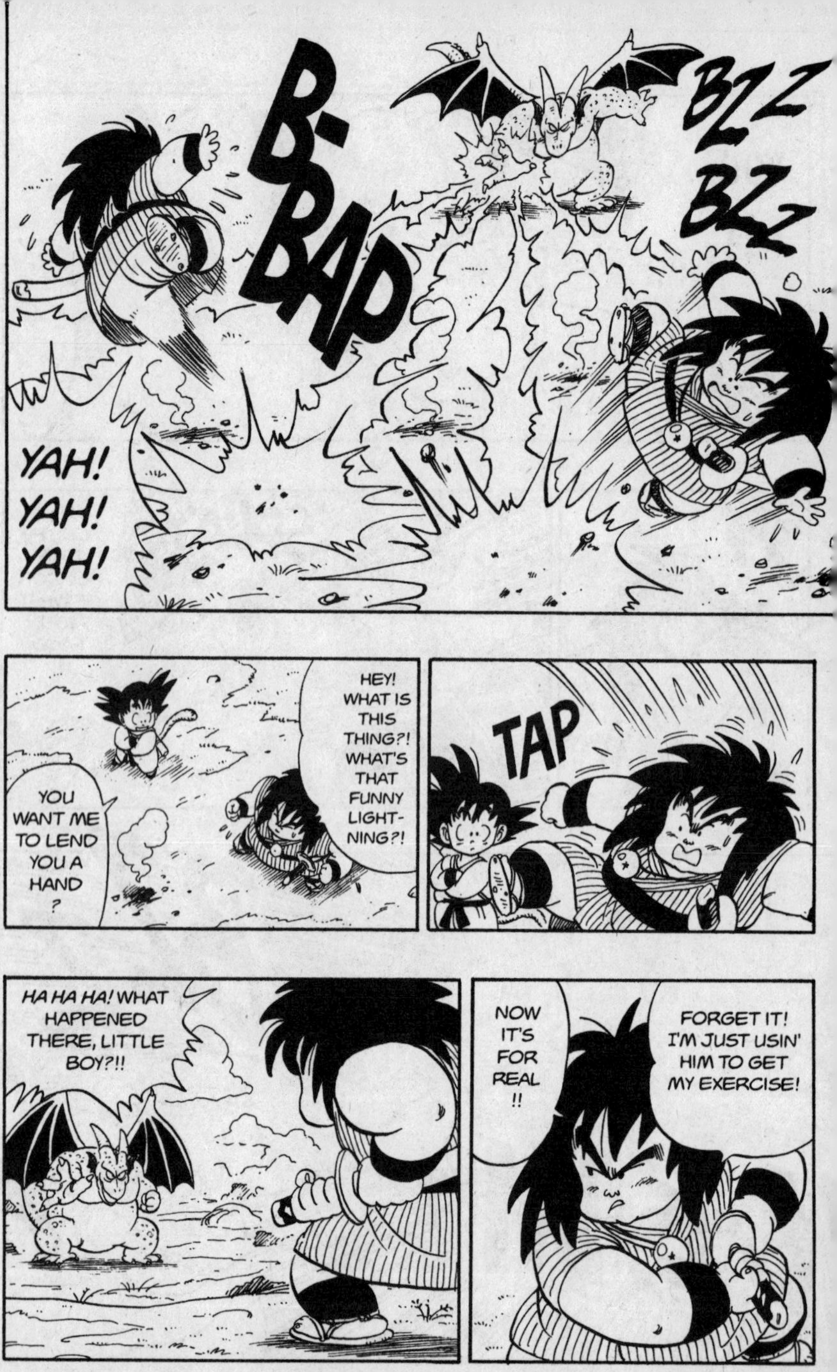
BZZ BZZ
B-BAP
YAH! YAH! YAH!
TAP
HEY! WHAT IS THIS THING?! WHAT'S THAT FUNNY LIGHTNING?!
YOU WANT ME TO LEND YOU A HAND?
FORGET IT! I'M JUST USIN' HIM TO GET MY EXERCISE!
NOW IT'S FOR REAL!!
HA HA HA! WHAT HAPPENED THERE, LITTLE BOY?!!

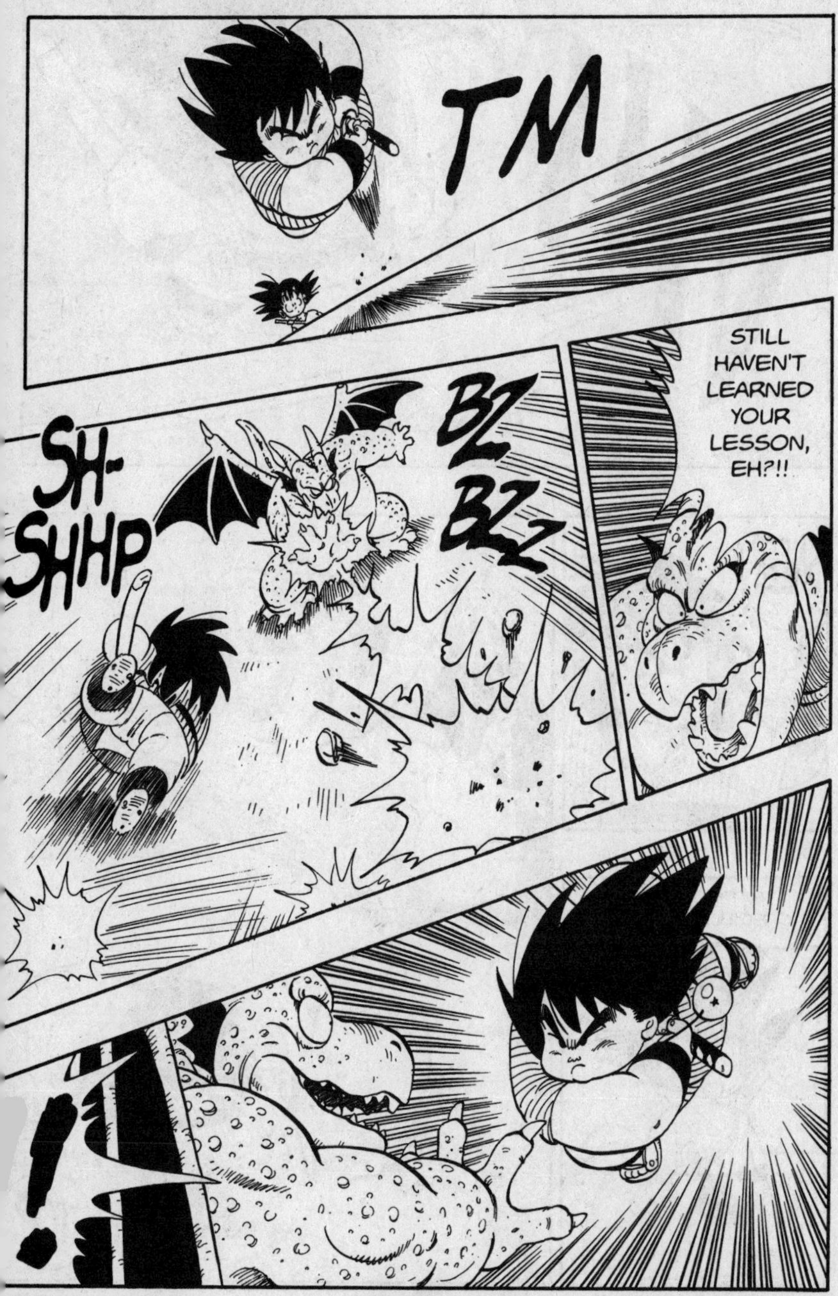
TM
STILL HAVEN'T LEARNED YOUR LESSON, EH?!!
BZ BZZ
SH-SHHP
!

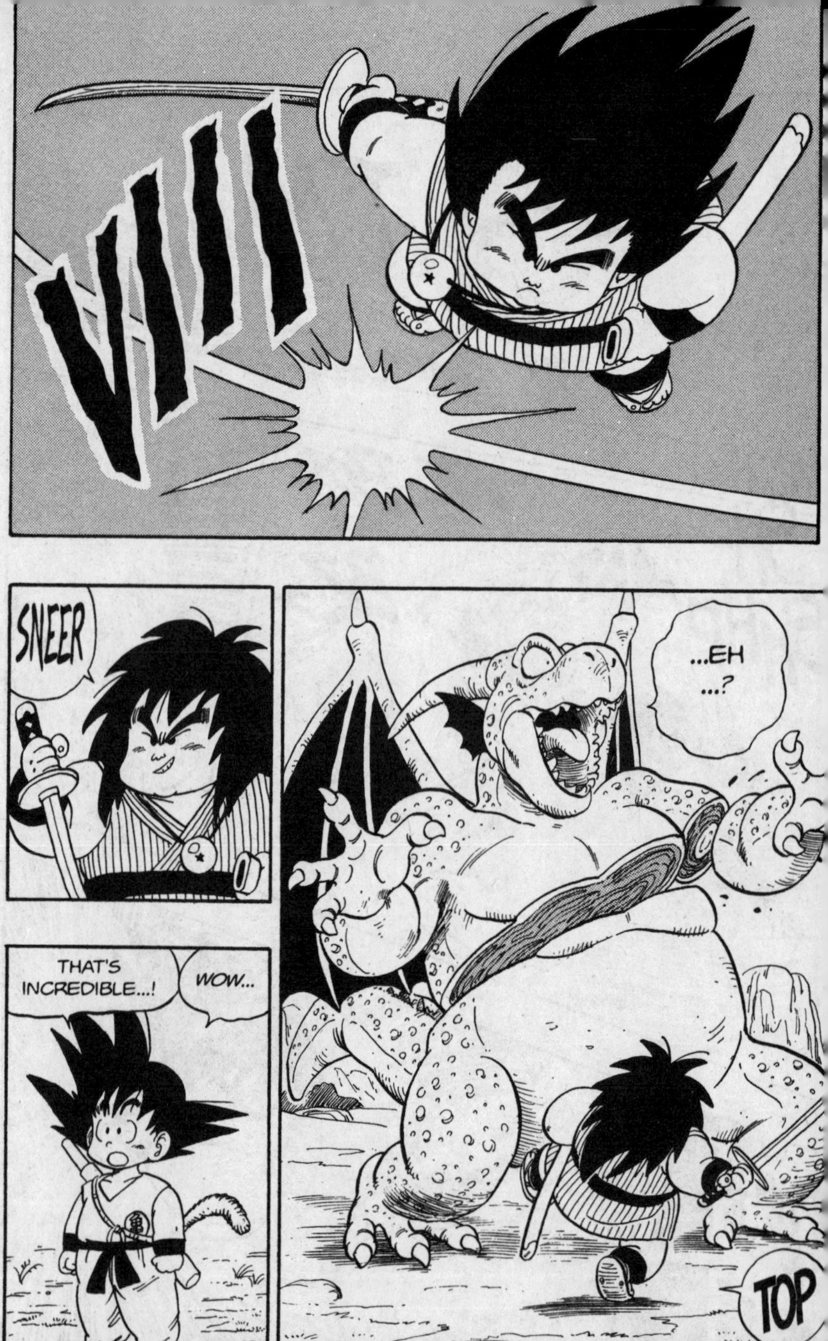
VIII
...EH ...?
TOP
SNEER
WOW...
THAT'S INCREDIBLE...!

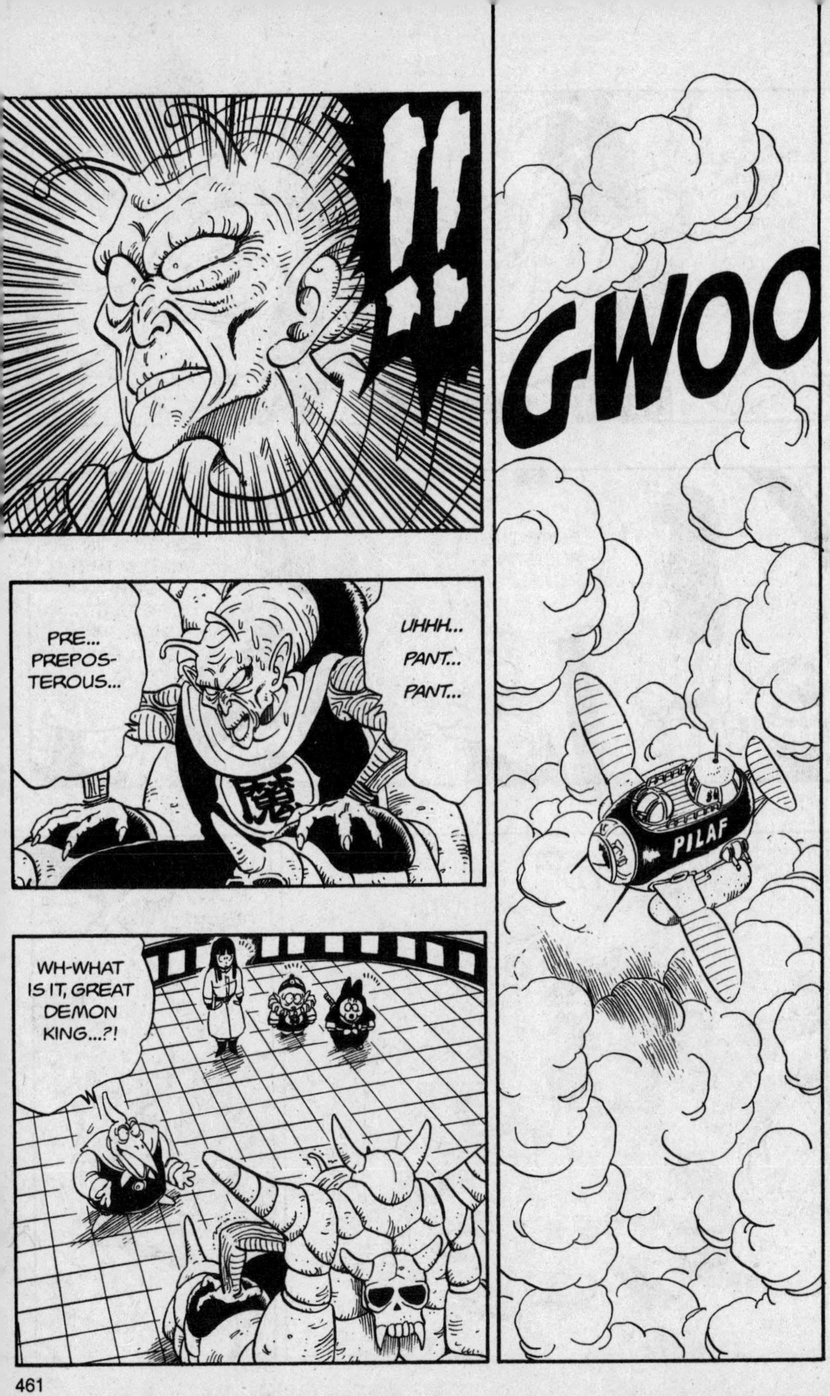
GWOO
PILAF
UHHH... PANT... PANT...
PRE... PREPOSTEROUS...
WH-WHAT IS IT, GREAT DEMON KING...?!

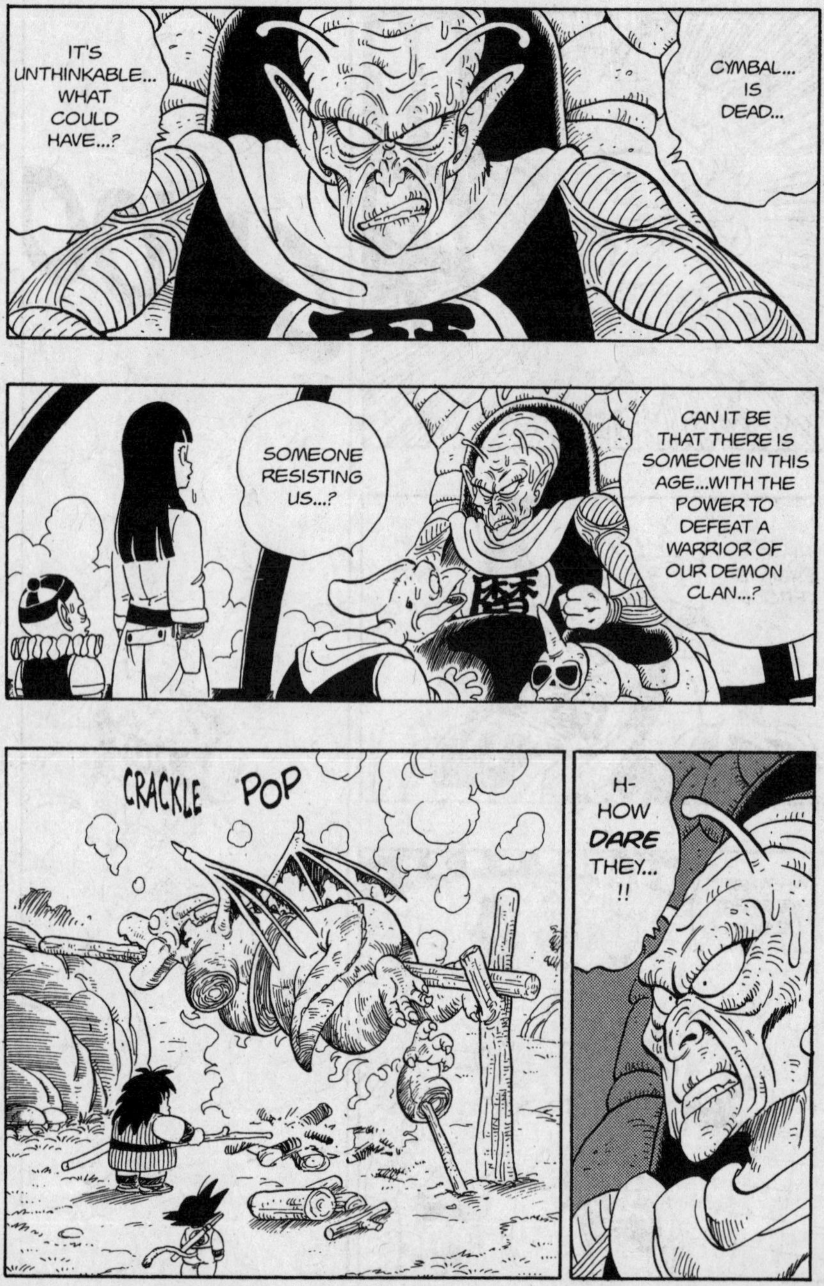
CYMBAL... IS DEAD...
IT'S UNTHINKABLE... WHAT COULD HAVE...?
CAN IT BE THAT THERE IS SOMEONE IN THIS AGE...WITH THE POWER TO DEFEAT A WARRIOR OF OUR DEMON CLAN...?
SOMEONE RESISTING US...?
H- HOW DARE THEY... !!
CRACKLE
POP

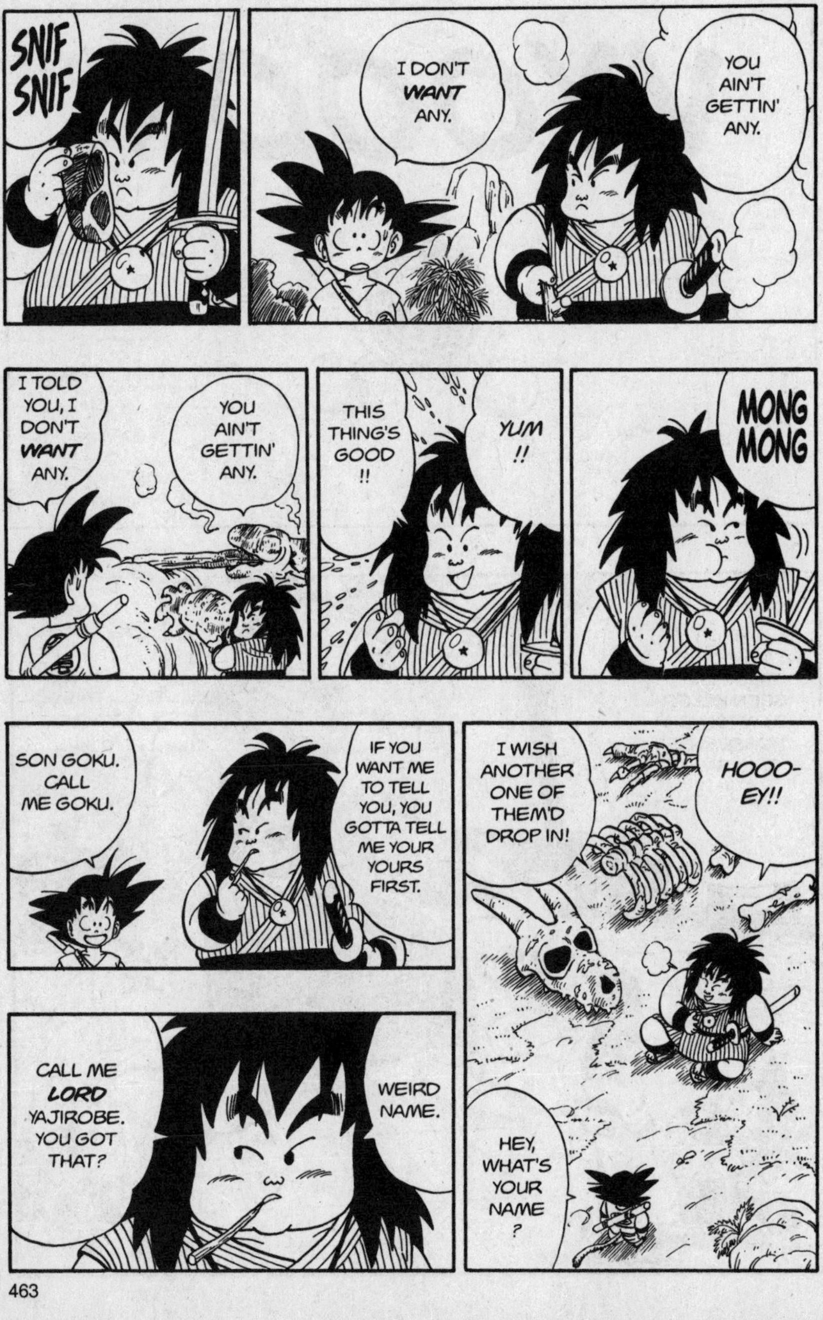
YOU AIN'T GETTIN' ANY.
I DON'T WANT ANY.
SNIF SNIF
MONG MONG
YUM!!
THIS THING'S GOOD!!
YOU AIN'T GETTIN' ANY.
I TOLD YOU, I DON'T WANT ANY.
HOOOEY!!
I WISH ANOTHER ONE OF THEM'D DROP IN!
HEY, WHAT'S YOUR NAME?
IF YOU WANT ME TO TELL YOU, YOU GOTTA TELL ME YOUR YOURS FIRST.
SON GOKU. CALL ME GOKU.
WEIRD NAME.
CALL ME LORD YAJIROBE. YOU GOT THAT?

Tale 140 • The Martial Artist Hunters

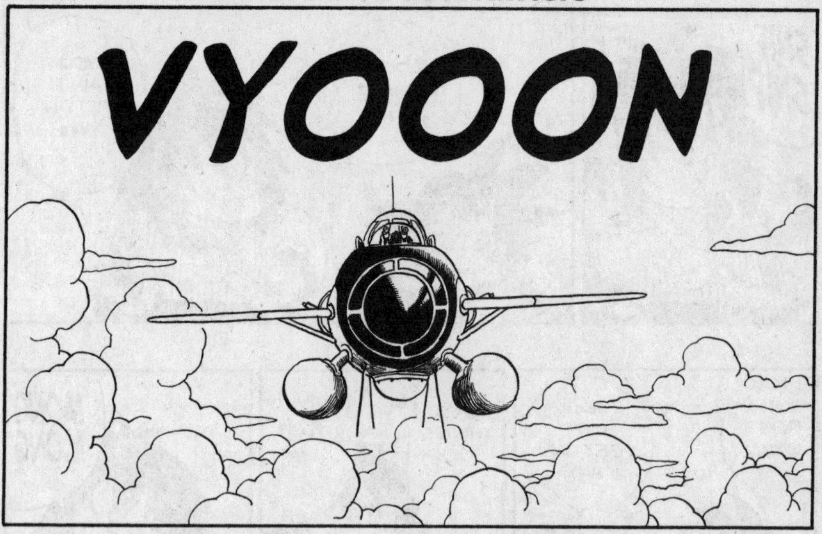
VYOOON

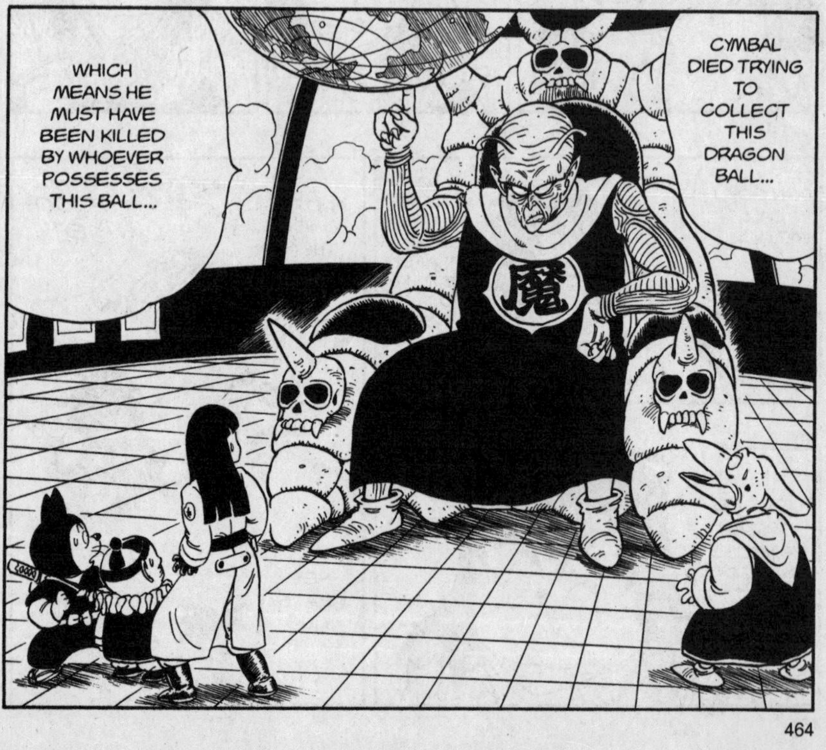
CYMBAL DIED TRYING TO COLLECT THIS DRAGON BALL...
WHICH MEANS HE MUST HAVE BEEN KILLED BY WHOEVER POSSESSES THIS BALL...

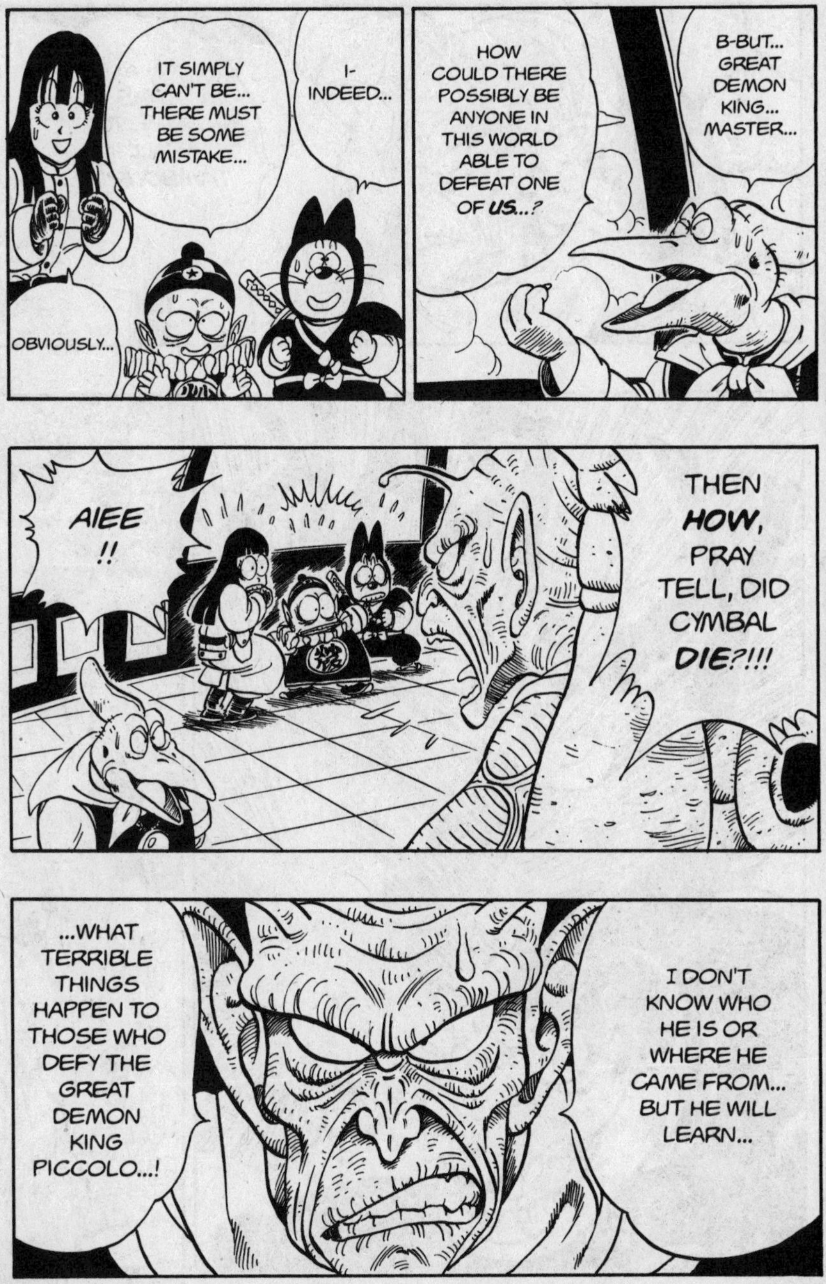
B-BUT... GREAT DEMON KING... MASTER...
HOW COULD THERE POSSIBLY BE ANYONE IN THIS WORLD ABLE TO DEFEAT ONE OF *US*...?
I- INDEED...
IT SIMPLY CAN'T BE... THERE MUST BE SOME MISTAKE...
OBVIOUSLY...
THEN *HOW*, PRAY TELL, DID CYMBAL *DIE*?!!!
AIEE !!
I DON'T KNOW WHO HE IS OR WHERE HE CAME FROM... BUT HE WILL LEARN...
...WHAT TERRIBLE THINGS HAPPEN TO THOSE WHO DEFY THE GREAT DEMON KING PICCOLO...!

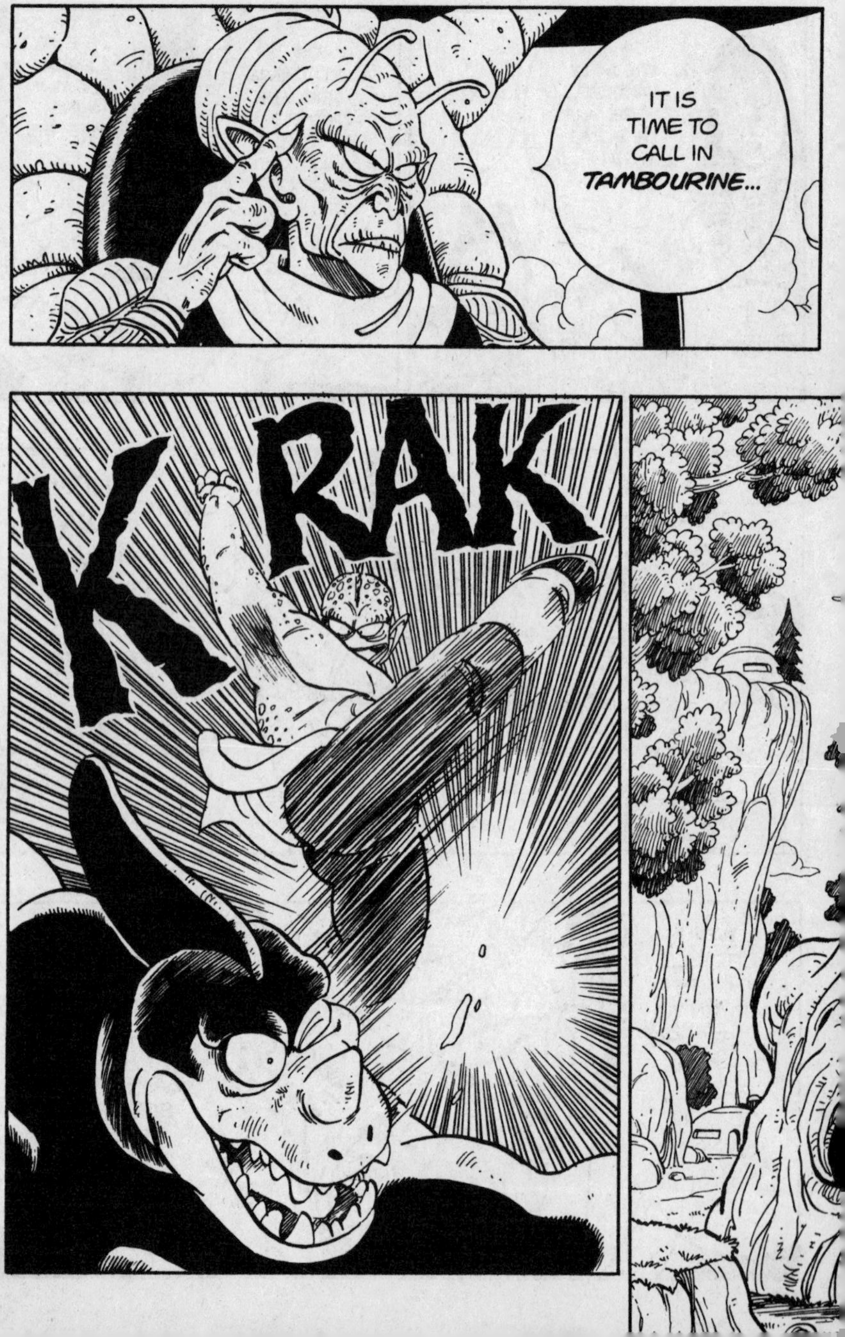
IT IS TIME TO CALL IN TAMBOURINE...
KRAK

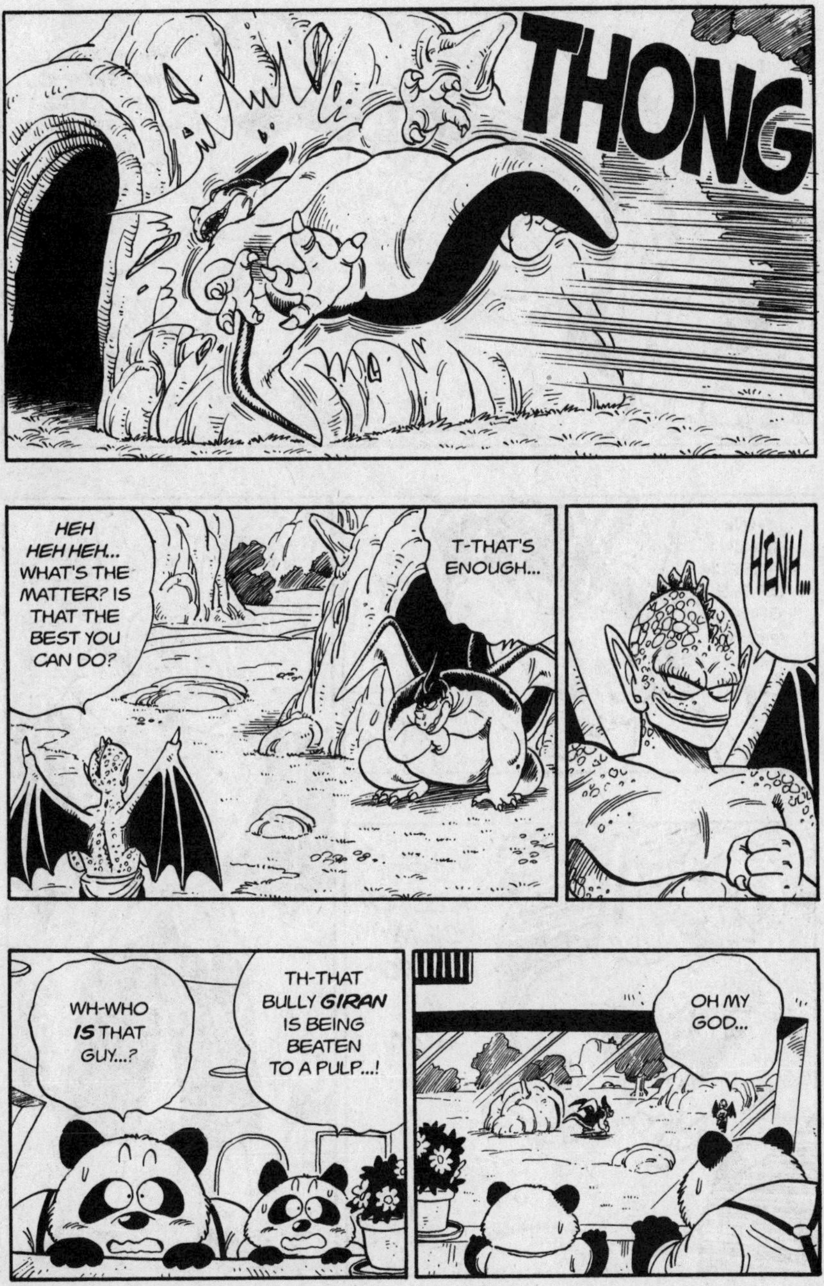
THONG
HENH...
T-THAT'S ENOUGH...
HEH HEH HEH... WHAT'S THE MATTER? IS THAT THE BEST YOU CAN DO?
OH MY GOD...
TH-THAT BULLY GIRAN IS BEING BEATEN TO A PULP...!
WH-WHO IS THAT GUY...?

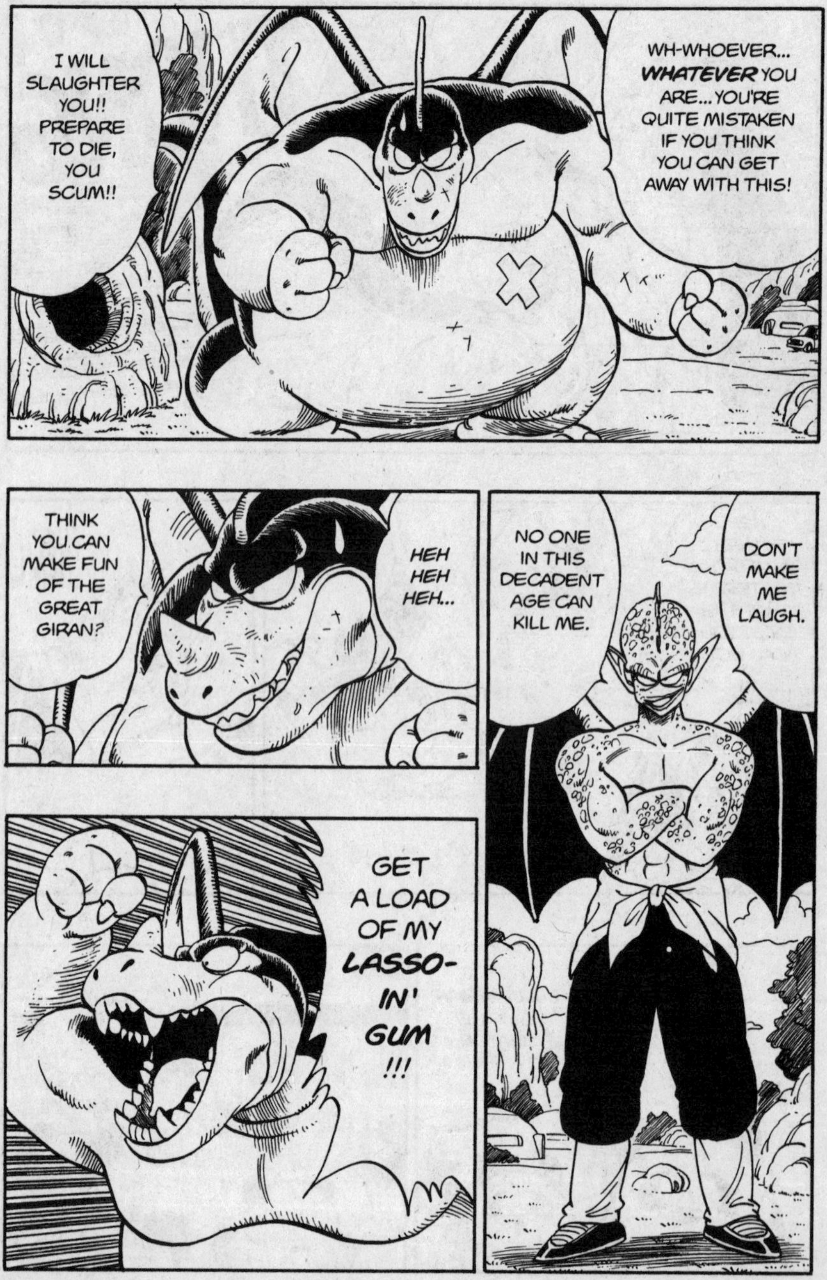
WH-WHOEVER... ***WHATEVER*** YOU ARE... YOU'RE QUITE MISTAKEN IF YOU THINK YOU CAN GET AWAY WITH THIS!
I WILL SLAUGHTER YOU!! PREPARE TO DIE, YOU SCUM!!
DON'T MAKE ME LAUGH.
NO ONE IN THIS DECADENT AGE CAN KILL ME.
HEH HEH HEH...
THINK YOU CAN MAKE FUN OF THE GREAT GIRAN?
GET A LOAD OF MY ***LASSO-IN' GUM*** !!!

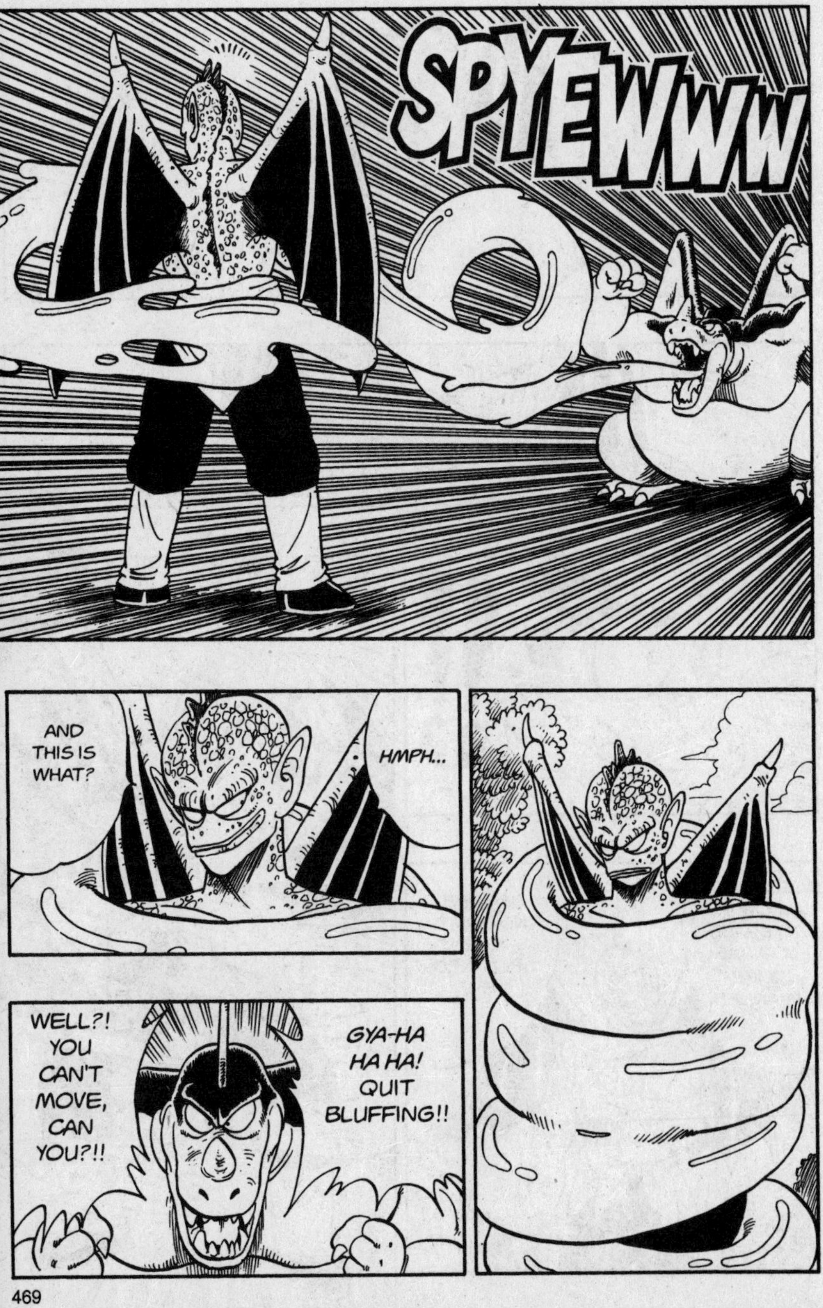
SPYEWWW
HMPH...
AND THIS IS WHAT?
GYA-HA HA HA! QUIT BLUFFING!!
WELL?! YOU CAN'T MOVE, CAN YOU?!!

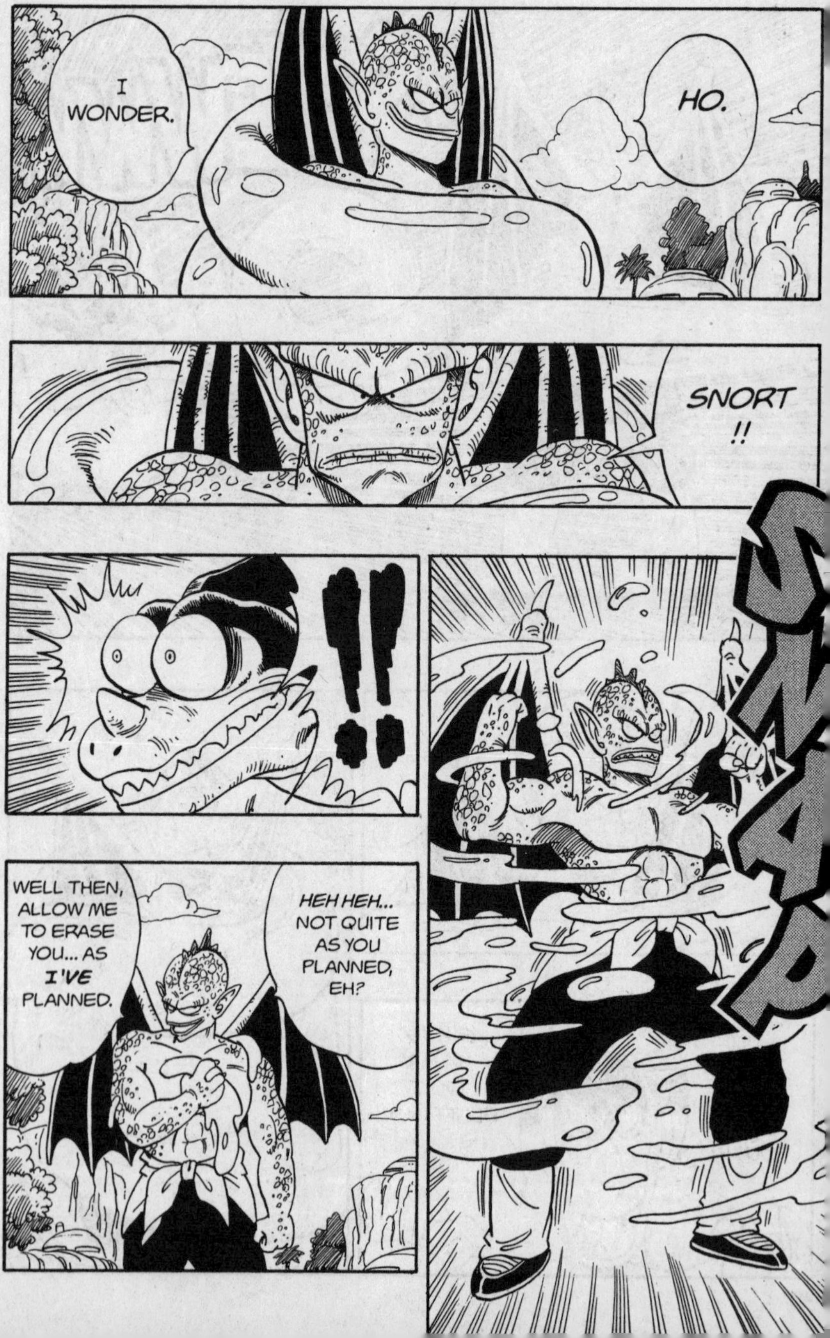
HO.
I WONDER.
SNORT !!
SNAP
!!
HEH HEH... NOT QUITE AS YOU PLANNED, EH?
WELL THEN, ALLOW ME TO ERASE YOU... AS *I'VE* PLANNED.

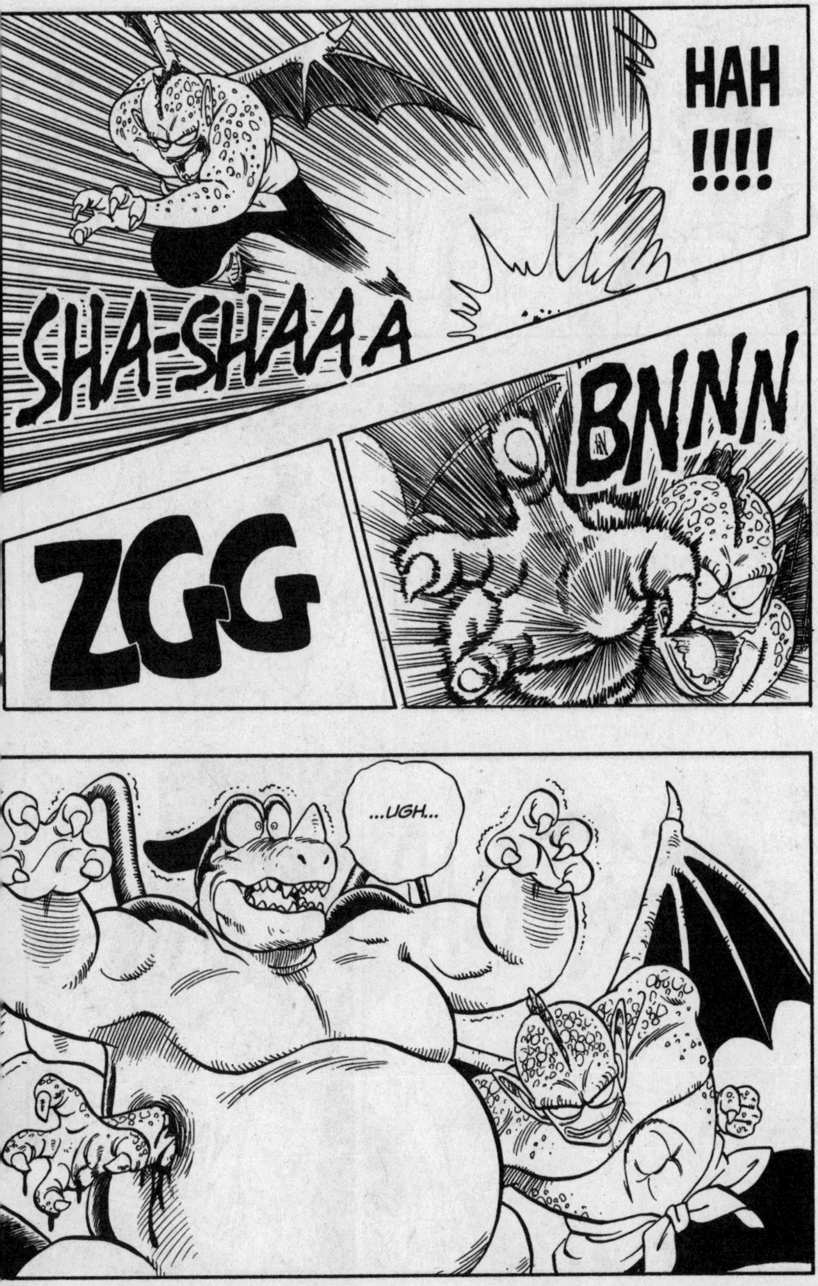
HAH !!!!
SHA-SHAAAA
BNNN
ZGG
...UGH...

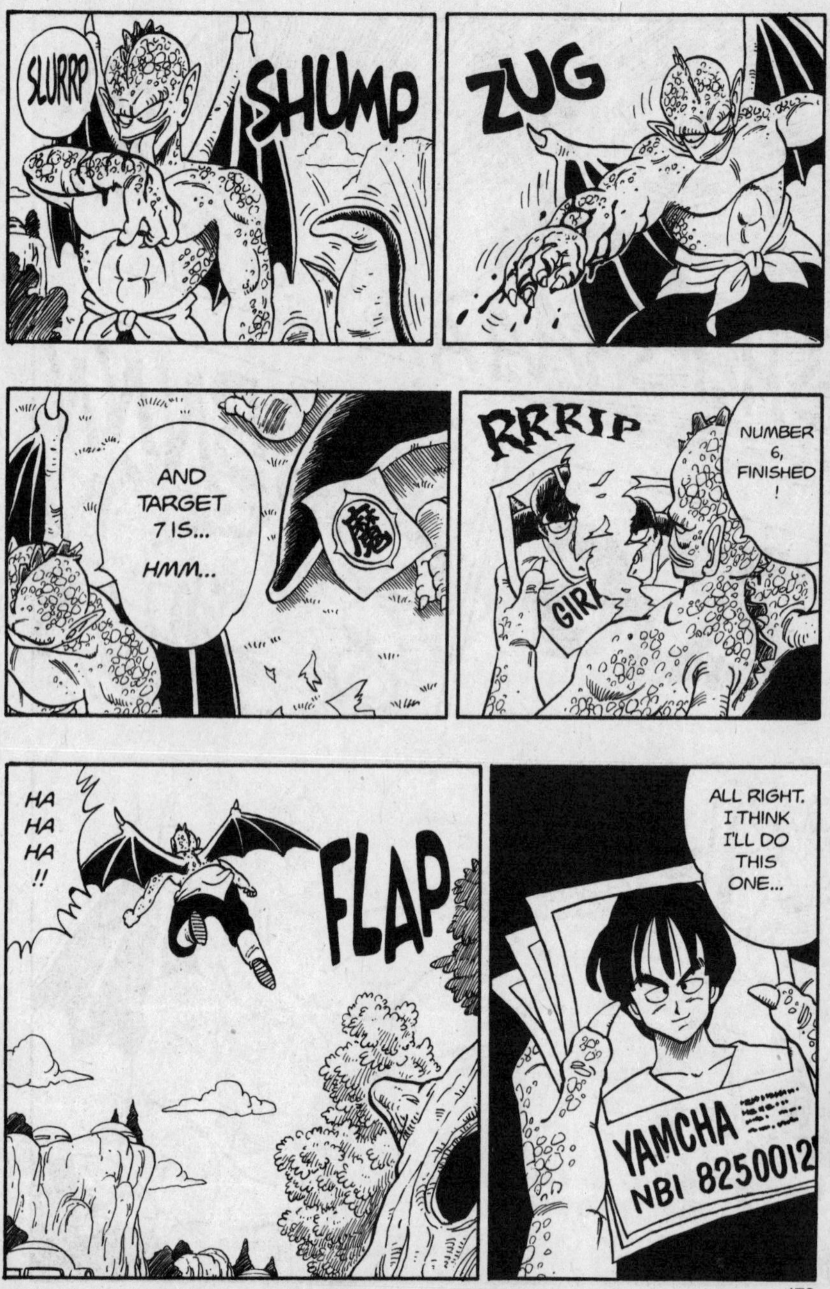
ZUG
SHUMP
SLURRP
RRRIP
NUMBER 6, FINISHED!
AND TARGET 7 IS... HMM...
魔
ALL RIGHT. I THINK I'LL DO THIS ONE...
YAMCHA
NBI
FLAP
HA HA HA!!

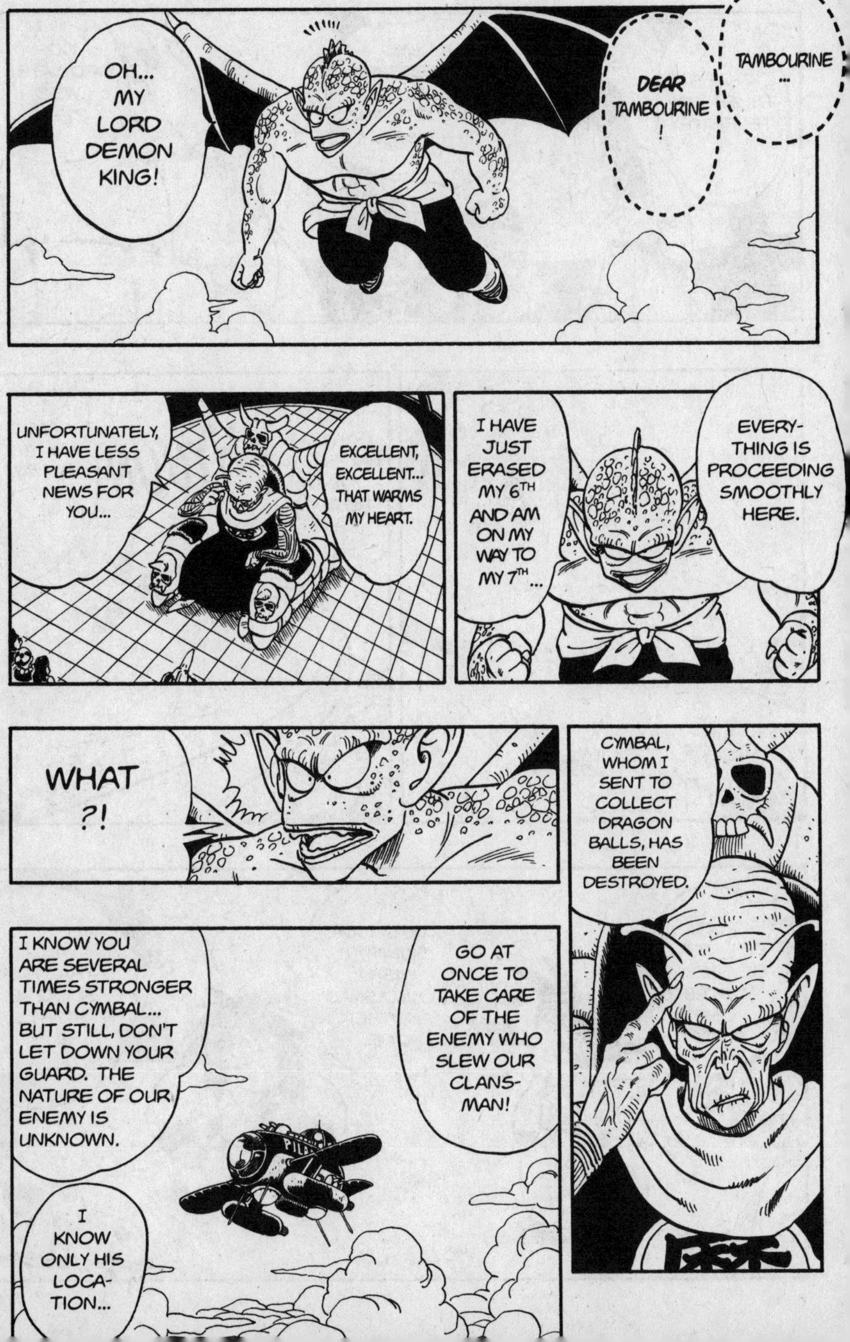
TAMBOURINE ...
DEAR TAMBOURINE !
OH... MY LORD DEMON KING!
EVERY-THING IS PROCEEDING SMOOTHLY HERE.
I HAVE JUST ERASED MY 6TH AND AM ON MY WAY TO MY 7TH...
EXCELLENT, EXCELLENT... THAT WARMS MY HEART.
UNFORTUNATELY, I HAVE LESS PLEASANT NEWS FOR YOU...
CYMBAL, WHOM I SENT TO COLLECT DRAGON BALLS, HAS BEEN DESTROYED.
WHAT ?!
GO AT ONCE TO TAKE CARE OF THE ENEMY WHO SLEW OUR CLANS-MAN!
I KNOW YOU ARE SEVERAL TIMES STRONGER THAN CYMBAL... BUT STILL, DON'T LET DOWN YOUR GUARD. THE NATURE OF OUR ENEMY IS UNKNOWN.
I KNOW ONLY HIS LOCA-TION...

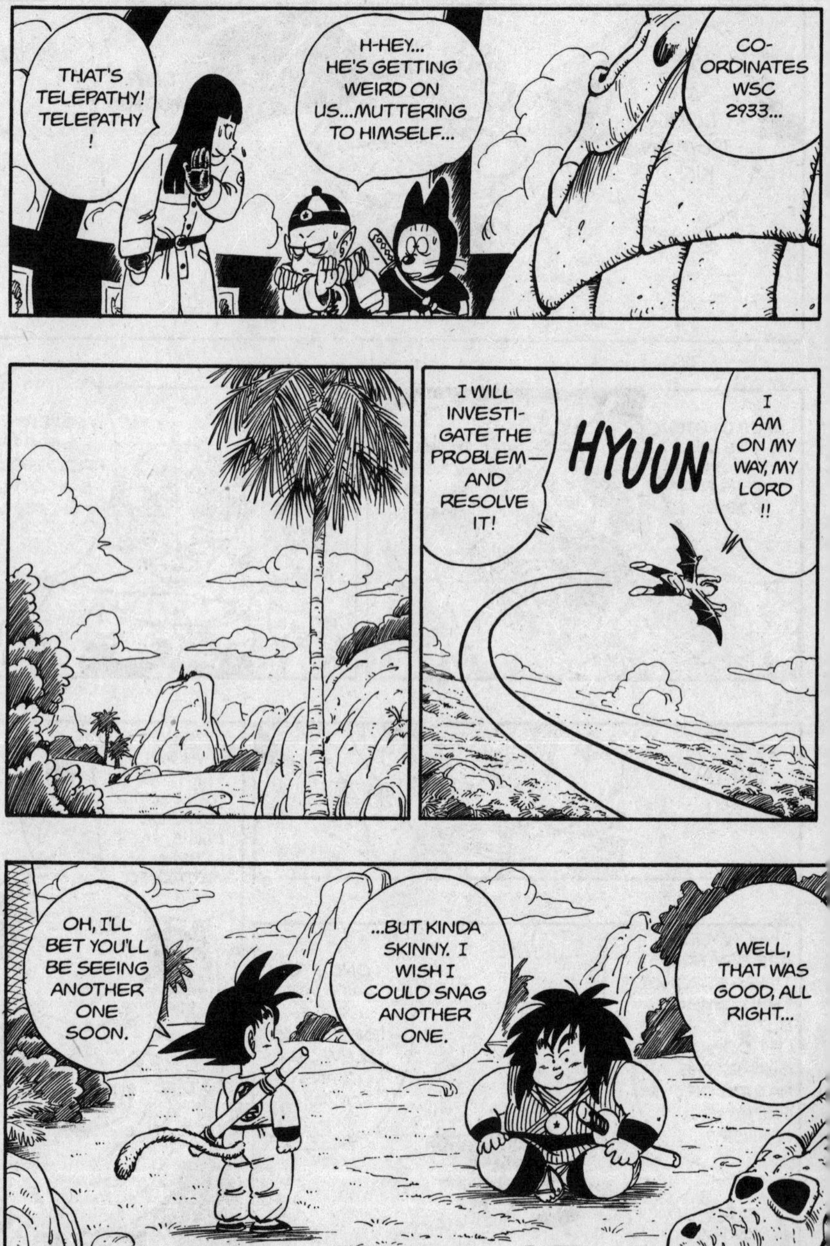
CO-ORDINATES WSC 2933...
H-HEY... HE'S GETTING WEIRD ON US...MUTTERING TO HIMSELF...
THAT'S TELEPATHY! TELEPATHY!
I AM ON MY WAY, MY LORD!!
HYUUN
I WILL INVESTIGATE THE PROBLEM—AND RESOLVE IT!
WELL, THAT WAS GOOD, ALL RIGHT...
...BUT KINDA SKINNY. I WISH I COULD SNAG ANOTHER ONE.
OH, I'LL BET YOU'LL BE SEEING ANOTHER ONE SOON.

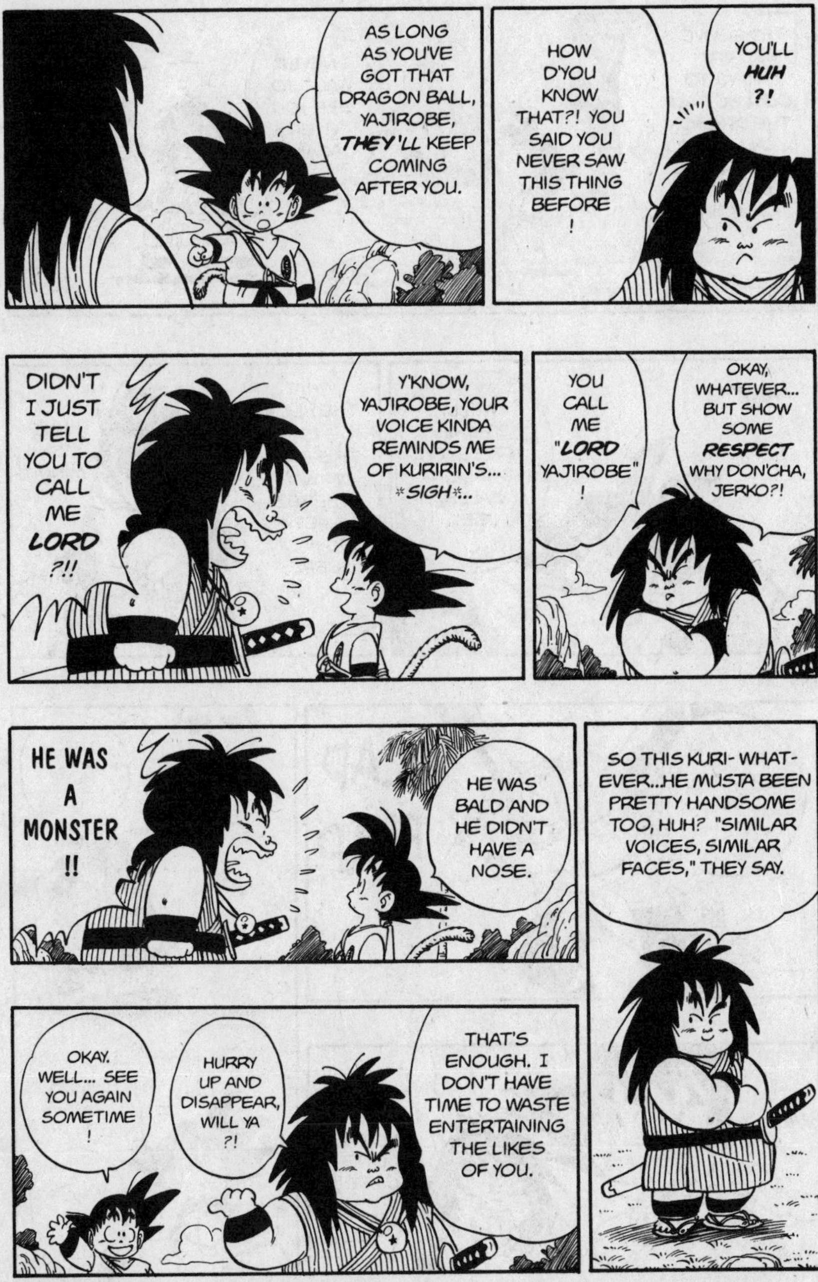
YOU'LL **HUH** ?!
HOW D'YOU KNOW THAT?! YOU SAID YOU NEVER SAW THIS THING BEFORE !
AS LONG AS YOU'VE GOT THAT DRAGON BALL, YAJIROBE, ***THEY'LL*** KEEP COMING AFTER YOU.
OKAY, WHATEVER... BUT SHOW SOME ***RESPECT*** WHY DON'CHA, JERKO?!
YOU CALL ME "***LORD*** YAJIROBE" !
Y'KNOW, YAJIROBE, YOUR VOICE KINDA REMINDS ME OF KURIRIN'S... *SIGH*...
DIDN'T I JUST TELL YOU TO CALL ME ***LORD*** ?!!
SO THIS KURI-WHAT-EVER...HE MUSTA BEEN PRETTY HANDSOME TOO, HUH? "SIMILAR VOICES, SIMILAR FACES," THEY SAY.
HE WAS BALD AND HE DIDN'T HAVE A NOSE.
HE WAS A MONSTER !!
THAT'S ENOUGH. I DON'T HAVE TIME TO WASTE ENTERTAINING THE LIKES OF YOU.
HURRY UP AND DISAPPEAR, WILL YA ?!
OKAY. WELL... SEE YOU AGAIN SOMETIME !

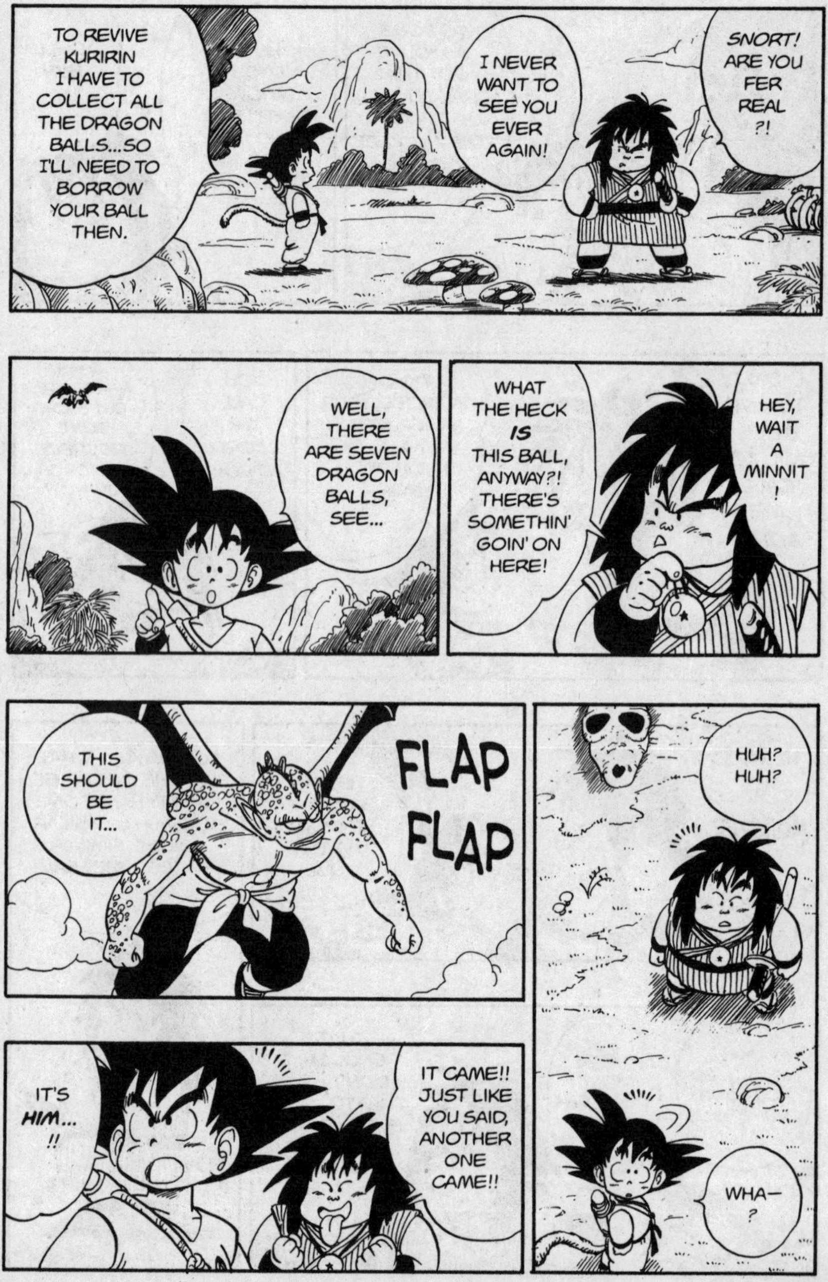
SNORT! ARE YOU FER REAL ?!
I NEVER WANT TO SEE YOU EVER AGAIN!
TO REVIVE KURIRIN I HAVE TO COLLECT ALL THE DRAGON BALLS...SO I'LL NEED TO BORROW YOUR BALL THEN.
HEY, WAIT A MINNIT !
WHAT THE HECK ***IS*** THIS BALL, ANYWAY?! THERE'S SOMETHIN' GOIN' ON HERE!
WELL, THERE ARE SEVEN DRAGON BALLS, SEE...
HUH? HUH?
WHA— ?
FLAP FLAP
THIS SHOULD BE IT...
IT CAME!! JUST LIKE YOU SAID, ANOTHER ONE CAME!!
IT'S ***HIM***... !!

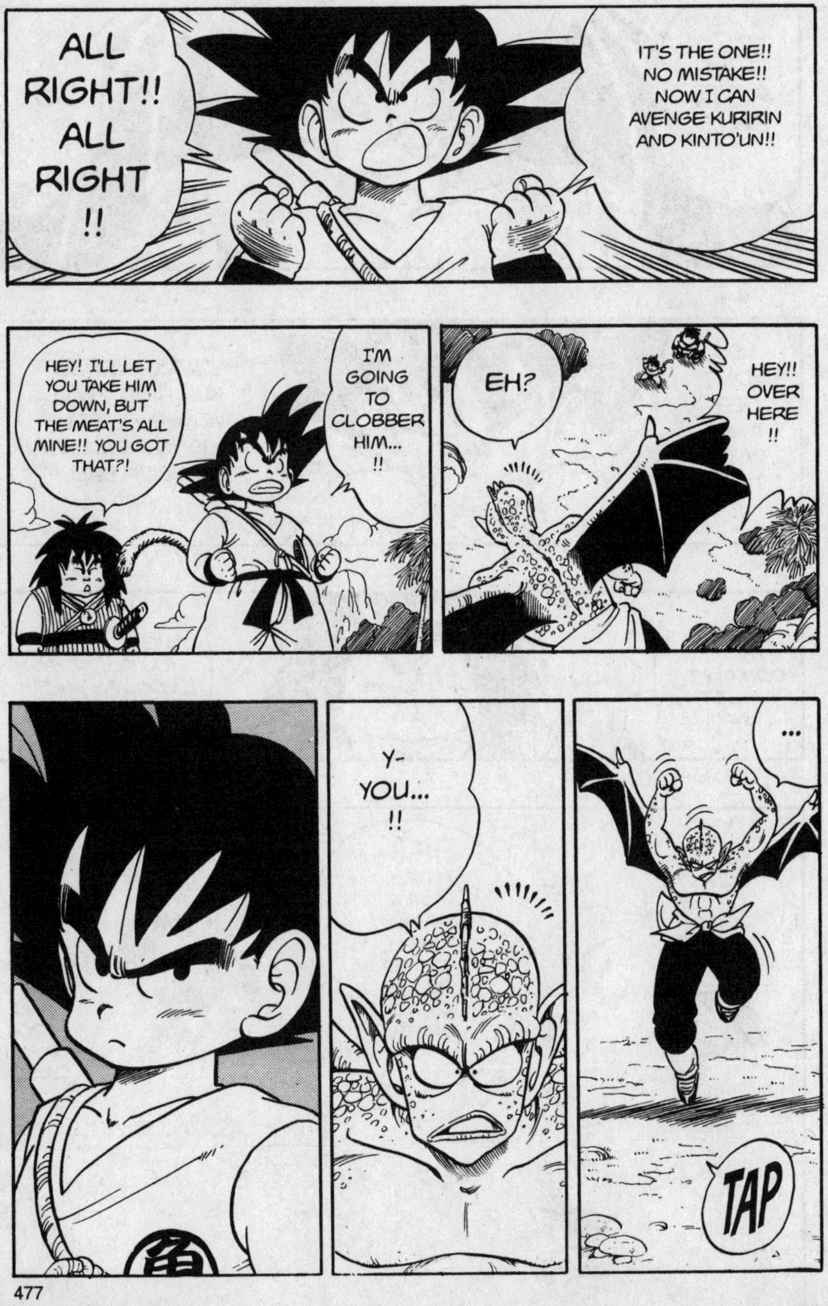

IT'S THE ONE!! NO MISTAKE!! NOW I CAN AVENGE KURIRIN AND KINTO'UN!!
ALL RIGHT!! ALL RIGHT !!
HEY!! OVER HERE !!
EH?
I'M GOING TO CLOBBER HIM... !!
HEY! I'LL LET YOU TAKE HIM DOWN, BUT THE MEAT'S ALL MINE!! YOU GOT THAT?!
...
TAP
Y- YOU... !!

Tale 141 • Goku vs. Tambourine

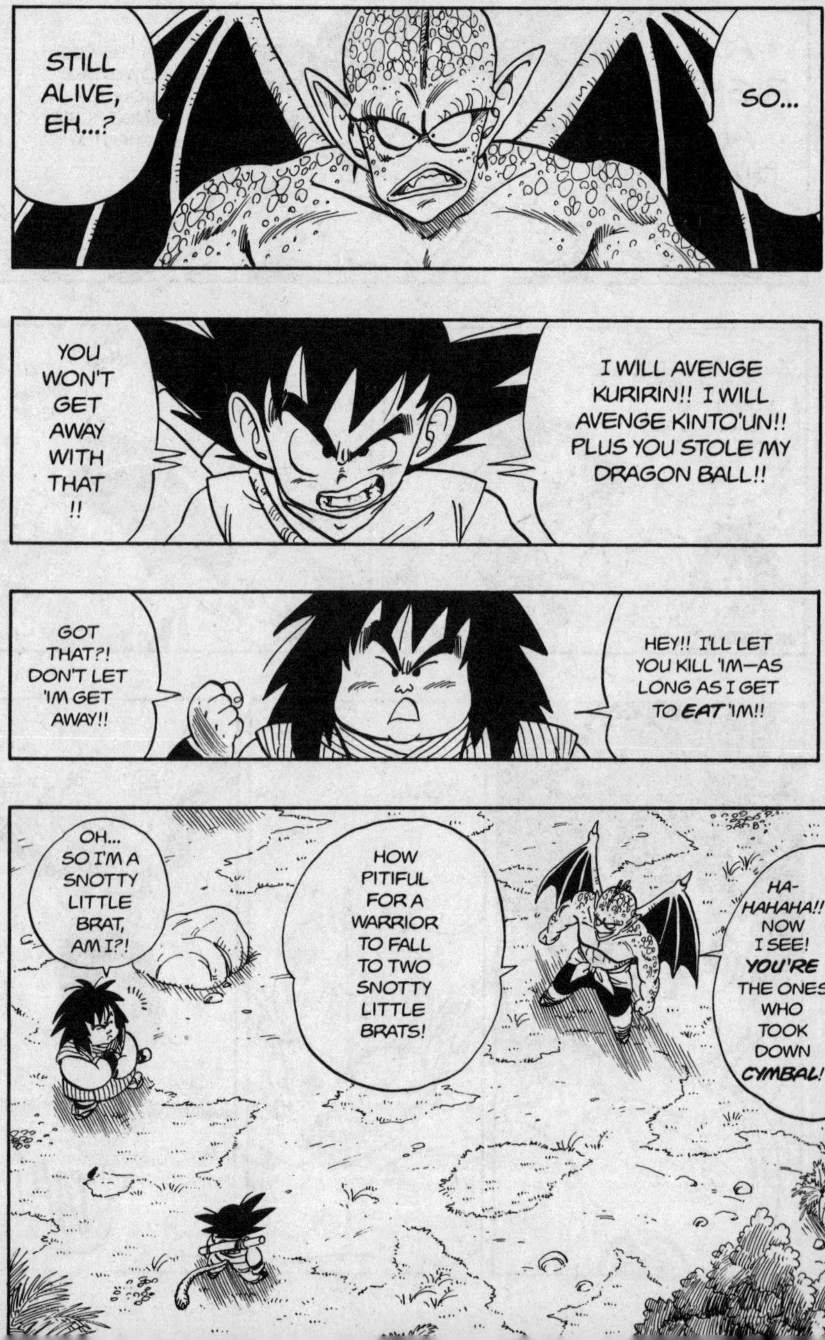
SO...
STILL ALIVE, EH...?
I WILL AVENGE KURIRIN!! I WILL AVENGE KINTO'UN!! PLUS YOU STOLE MY DRAGON BALL!!
YOU WON'T GET AWAY WITH THAT!!
HEY!! I'LL LET YOU KILL 'IM—AS LONG AS I GET TO *EAT* 'IM!!
GOT THAT?! DON'T LET 'IM GET AWAY!!
HA-HAHAHA!! NOW I SEE! *YOU'RE* THE ONES WHO TOOK DOWN *CYMBAL!*
HOW PITIFUL FOR A WARRIOR TO FALL TO TWO SNOTTY LITTLE BRATS!
OH... SO I'M A SNOTTY LITTLE BRAT, AM I?!

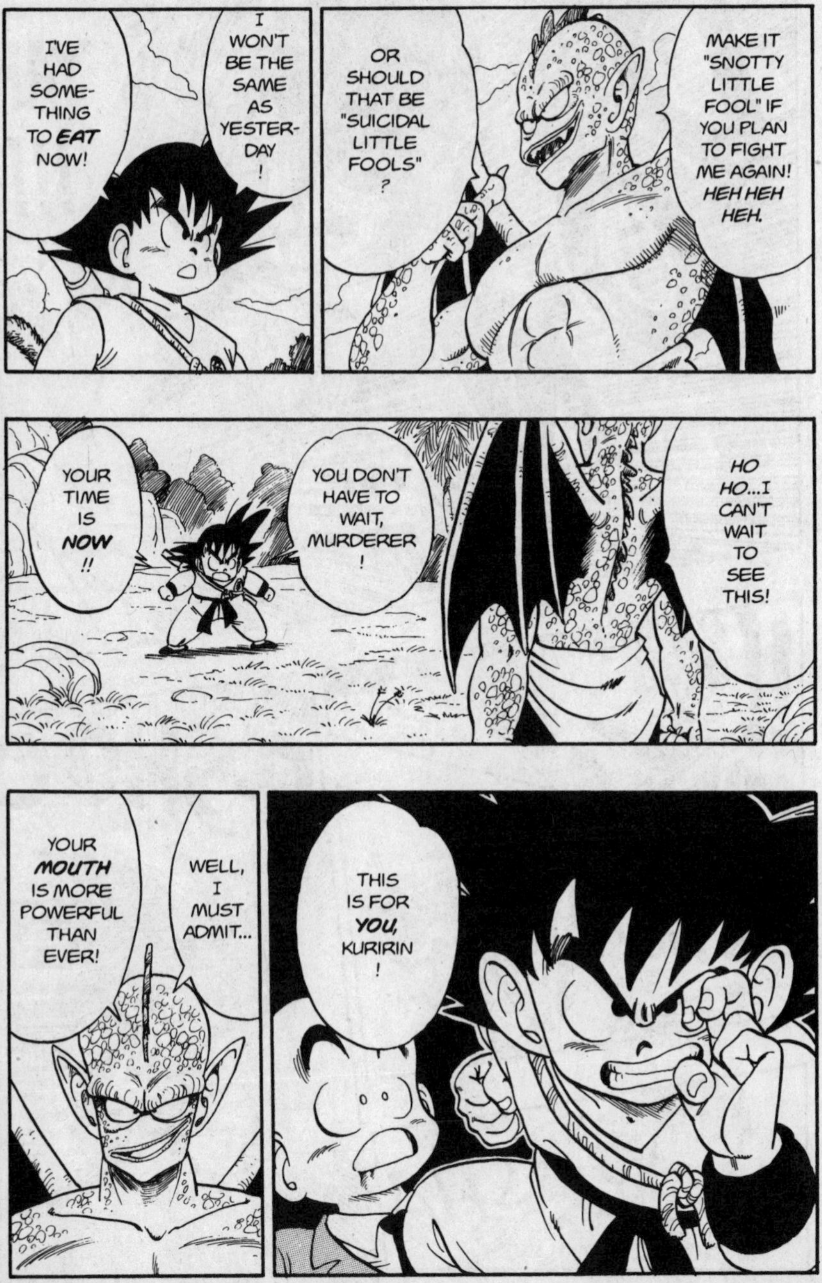
MAKE IT "SNOTTY LITTLE FOOL" IF YOU PLAN TO FIGHT ME AGAIN! HEH HEH HEH.
OR SHOULD THAT BE "SUICIDAL LITTLE FOOLS"?
I WON'T BE THE SAME AS YESTERDAY!
I'VE HAD SOMETHING TO EAT NOW!
HO HO...I CAN'T WAIT TO SEE THIS!
YOU DON'T HAVE TO WAIT, MURDERER!
YOUR TIME IS NOW!!
THIS IS FOR YOU, KURIRIN!
WELL, I MUST ADMIT...
YOUR MOUTH IS MORE POWERFUL THAN EVER!

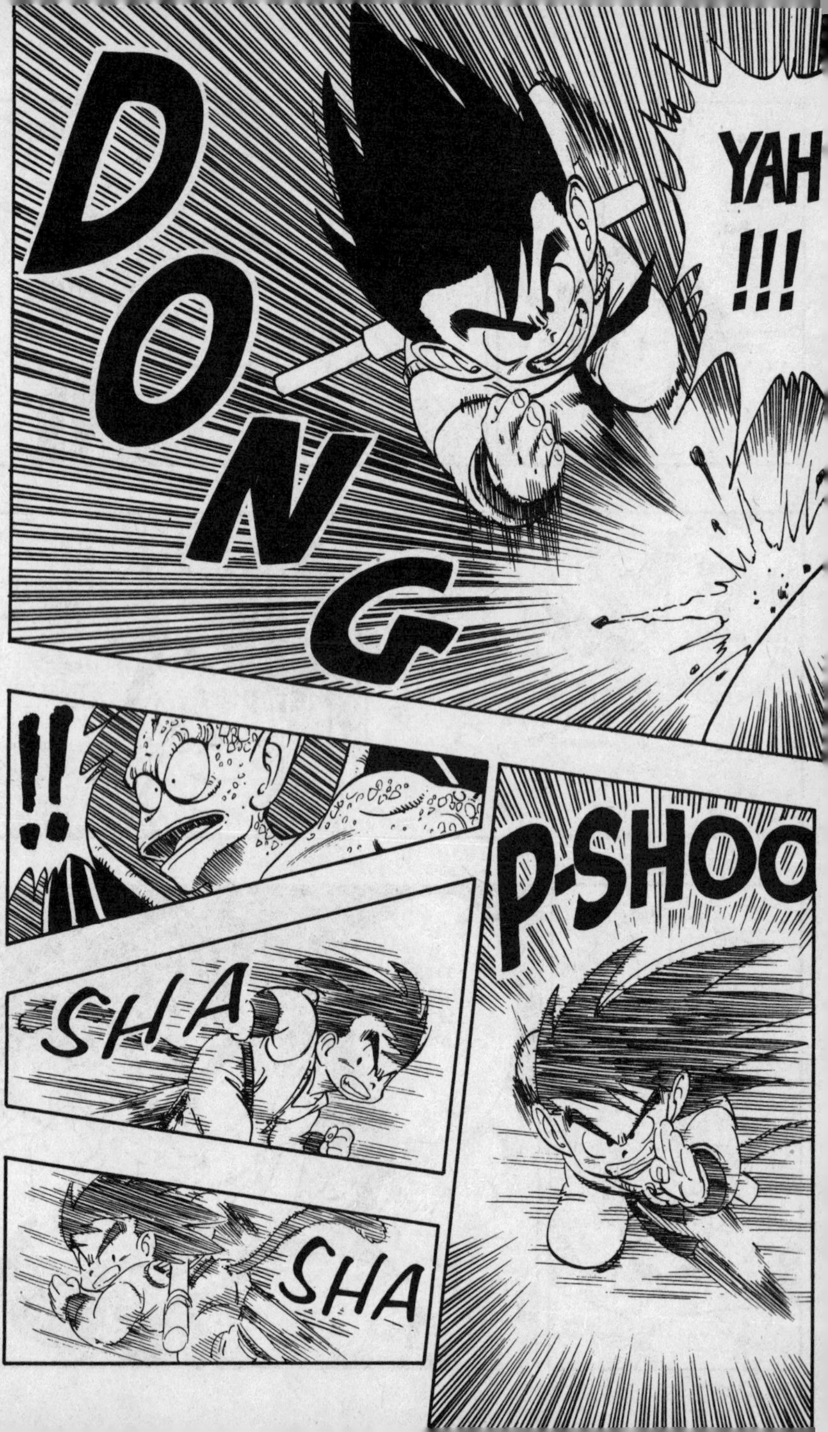
YAH!!!
DONG
P-SHOO
!!
SHA
SHA

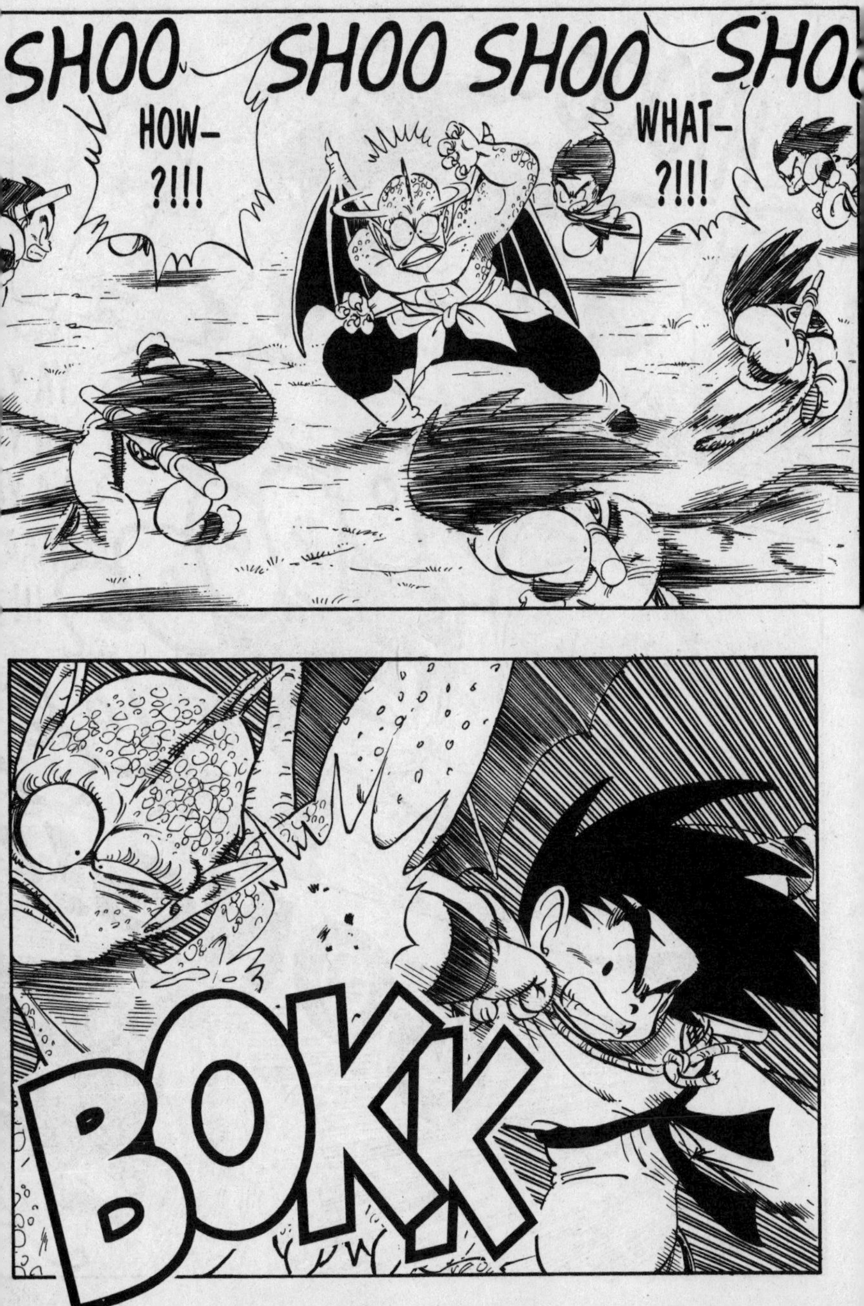
SHOO SHOO SHOO SHO
WHAT- ?!!!
HOW- ?!!!
BOKK

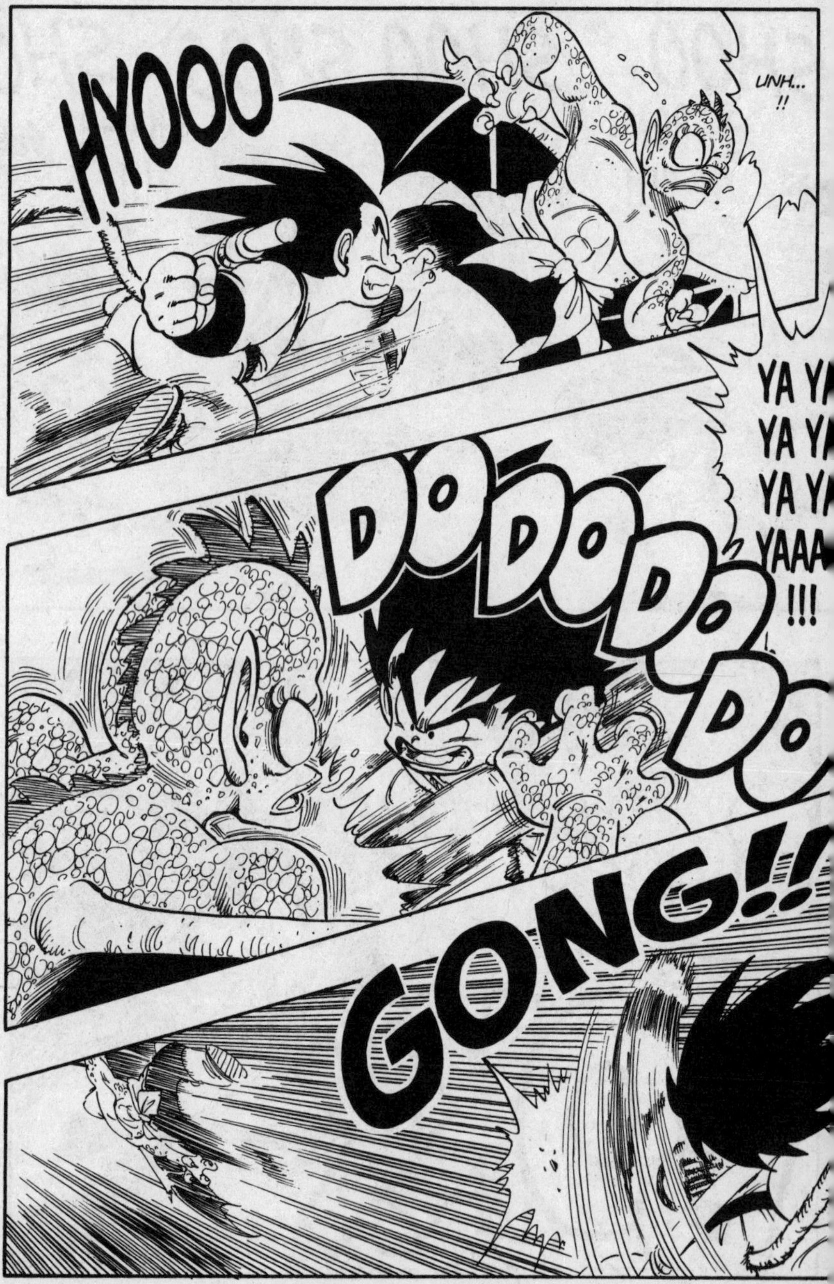
UNH... !!
HYOOO
YA YA YA YA YA YA YAAA !!!
DO DO DO DO DO
GONG!!

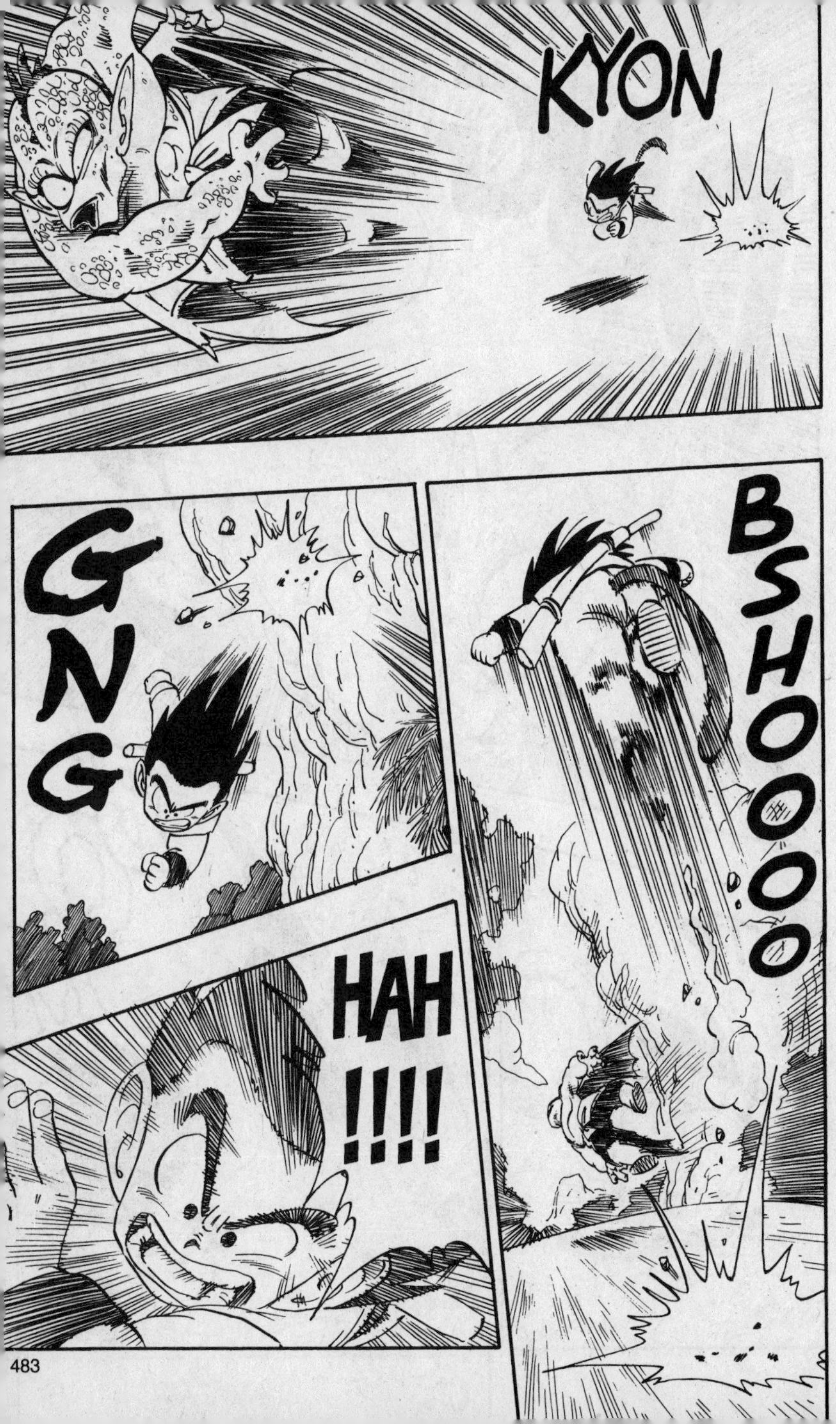
KYON
BSHOOOOO
GNG
HAH
!!!!

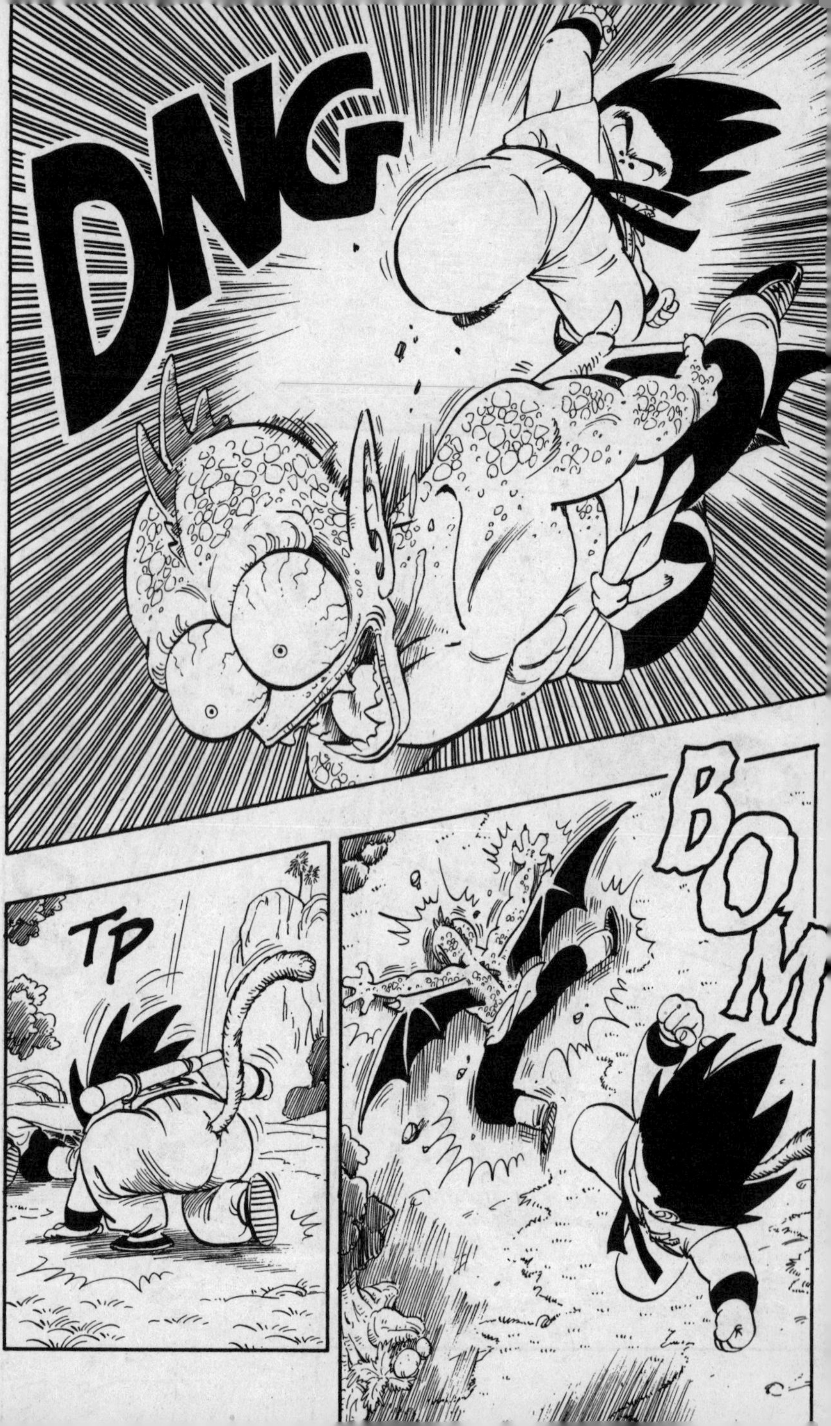
DNG
BOM
TP

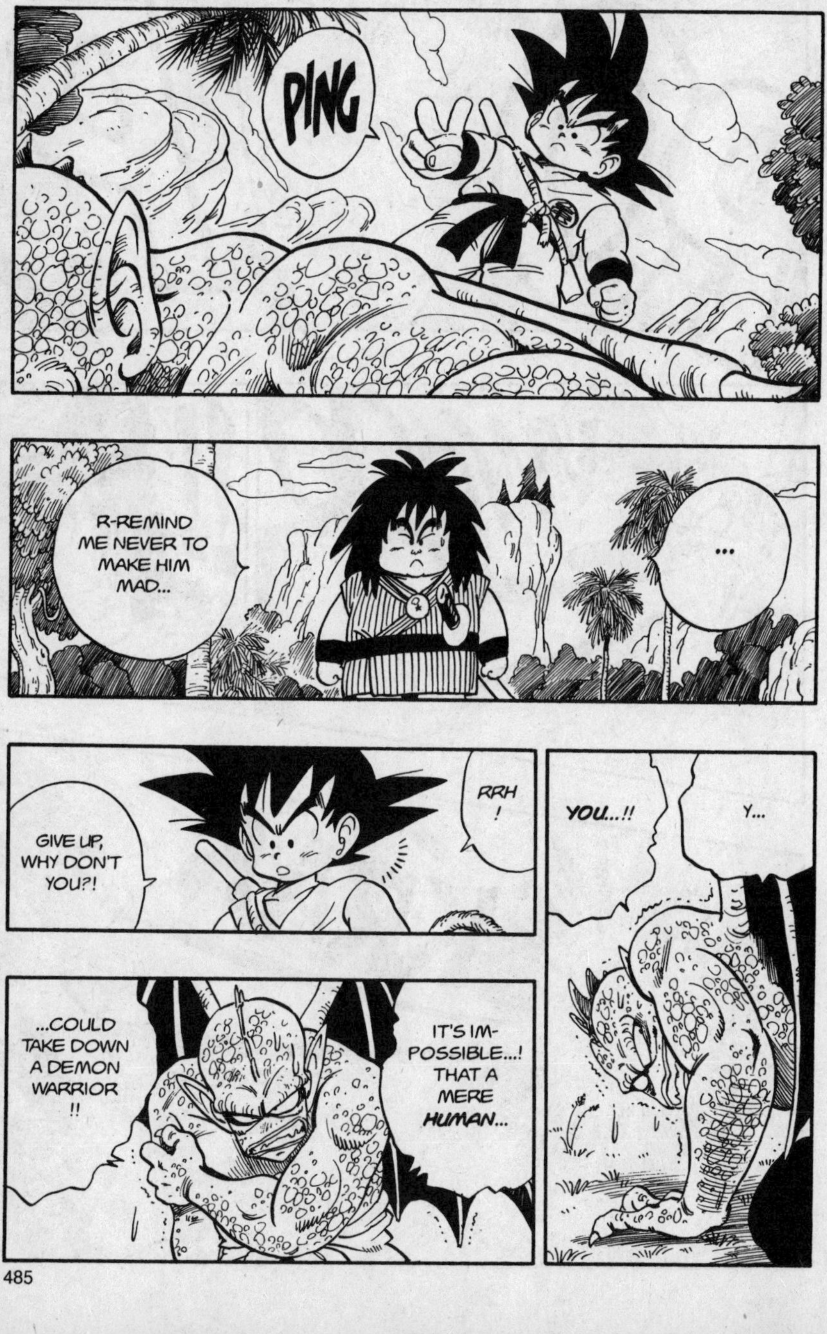
PING
...
R-REMIND ME NEVER TO MAKE HIM MAD...
Y...
YOU...!!
RRH !
GIVE UP, WHY DON'T YOU?!
IT'S IM-POSSIBLE...! THAT A MERE *HUMAN*...
...COULD TAKE DOWN A DEMON WARRIOR !!

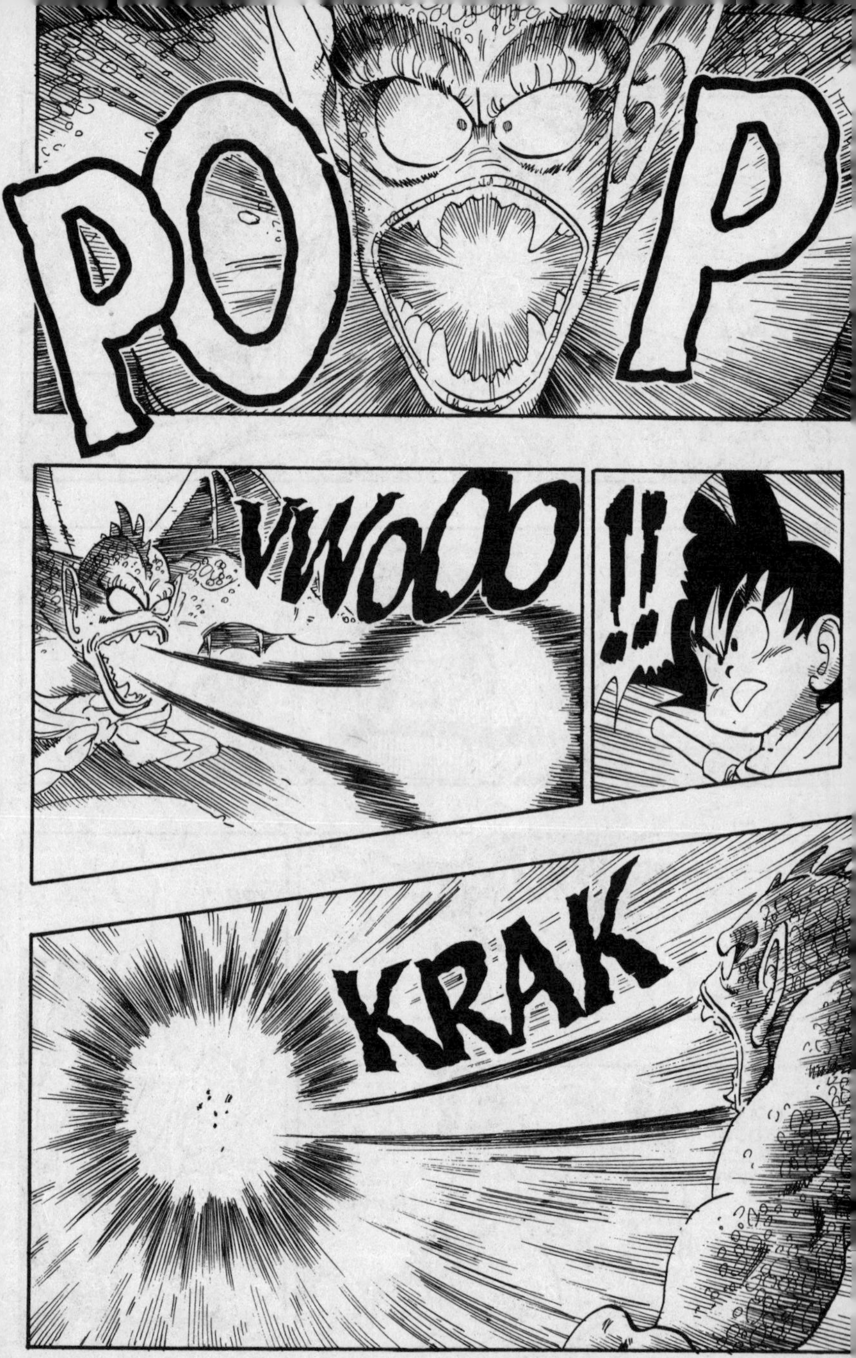
POOP
!!
VWOOO
KRAK

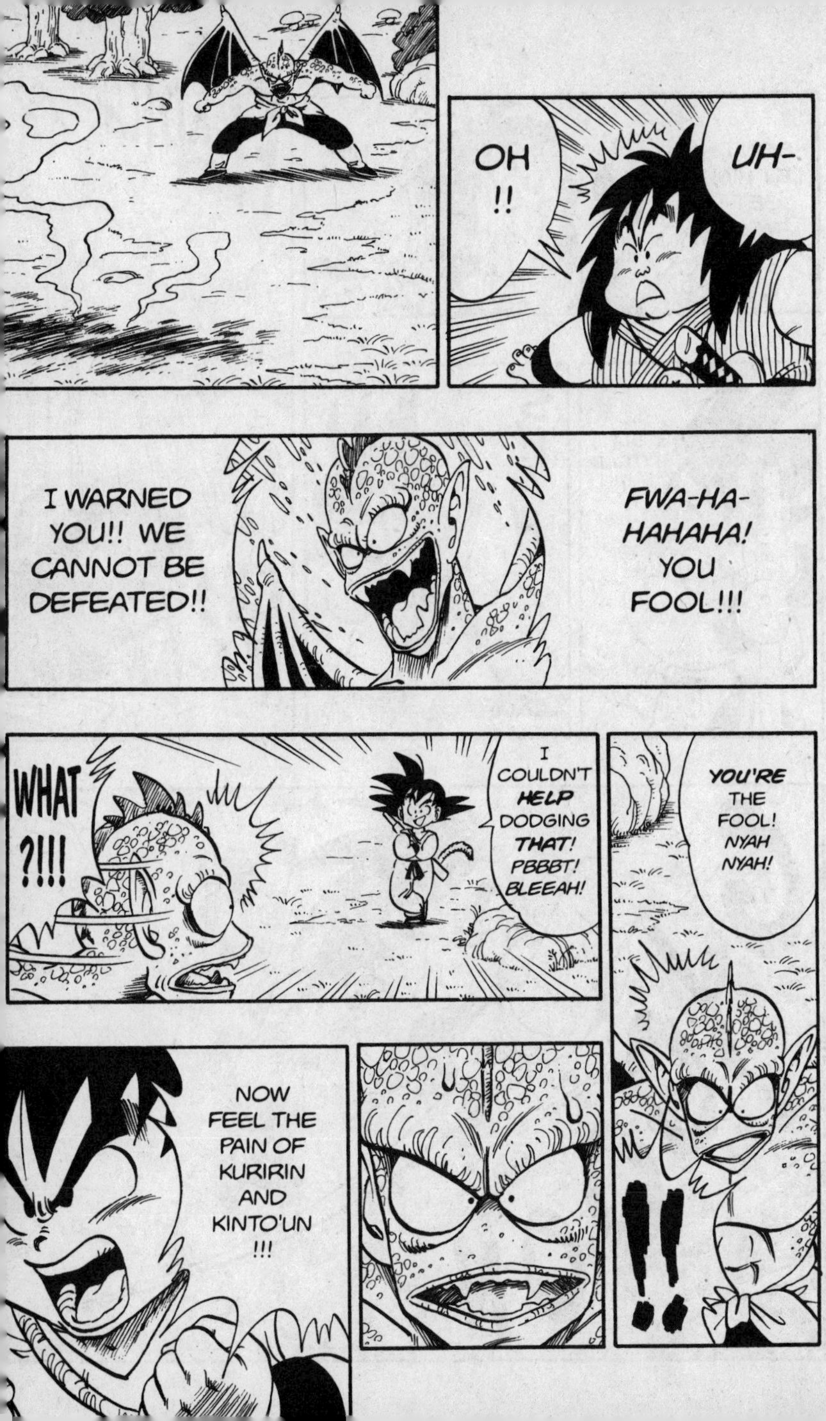
UH-
OH !!
FWA-HA-HAHAHA! YOU FOOL!!!
I WARNED YOU!! WE CANNOT BE DEFEATED!!
YOU'RE THE FOOL! NYAH NYAH!
!!
I COULDN'T HELP DODGING THAT! PBBBT! BLEEAH!
WHAT ?!!!
NOW FEEL THE PAIN OF KURIRIN AND KINTO'UN !!!

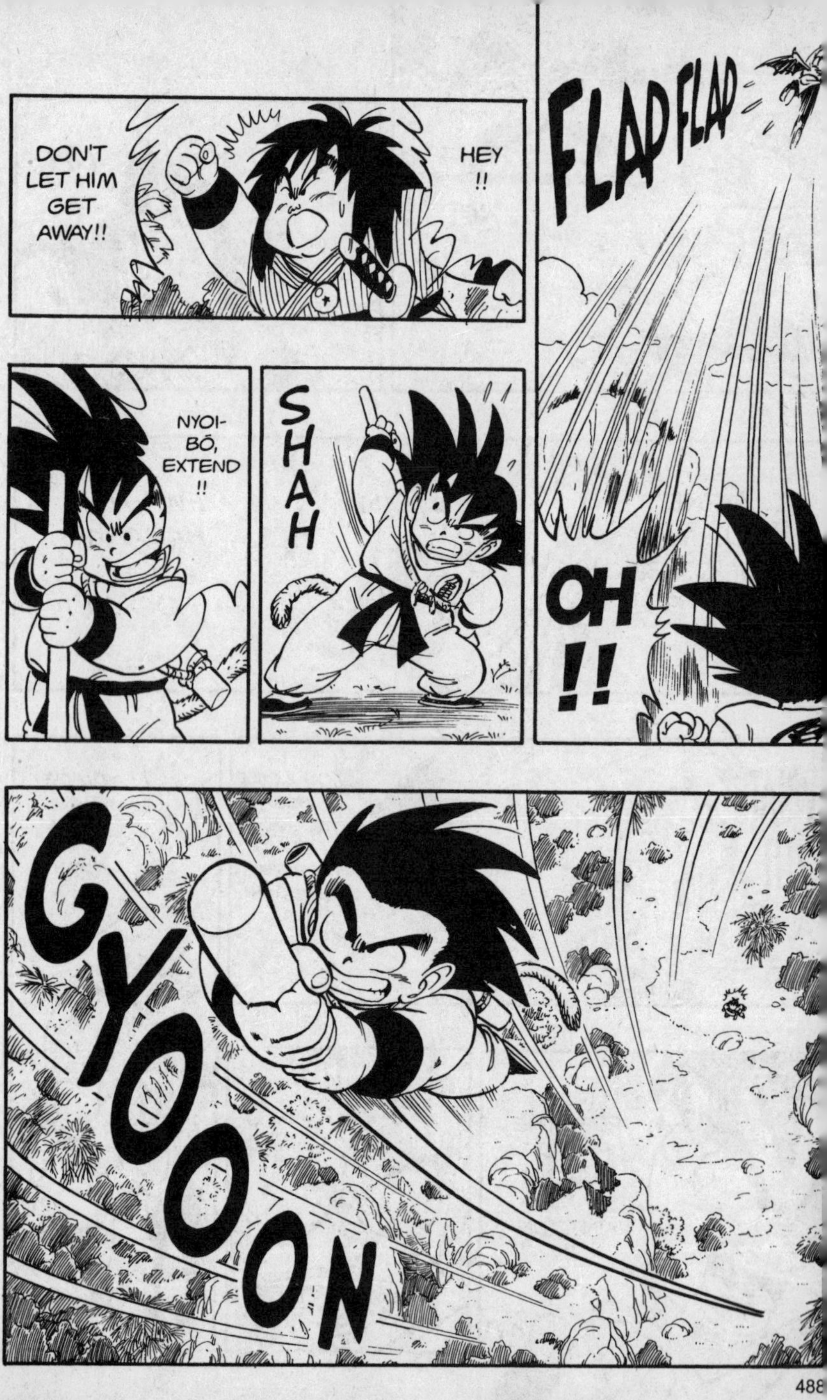
FLAP FLAP
OH!!
HEY!!
DON'T LET HIM GET AWAY!!
SHAH
NYOI-BŌ, EXTEND!!
GYOOOON

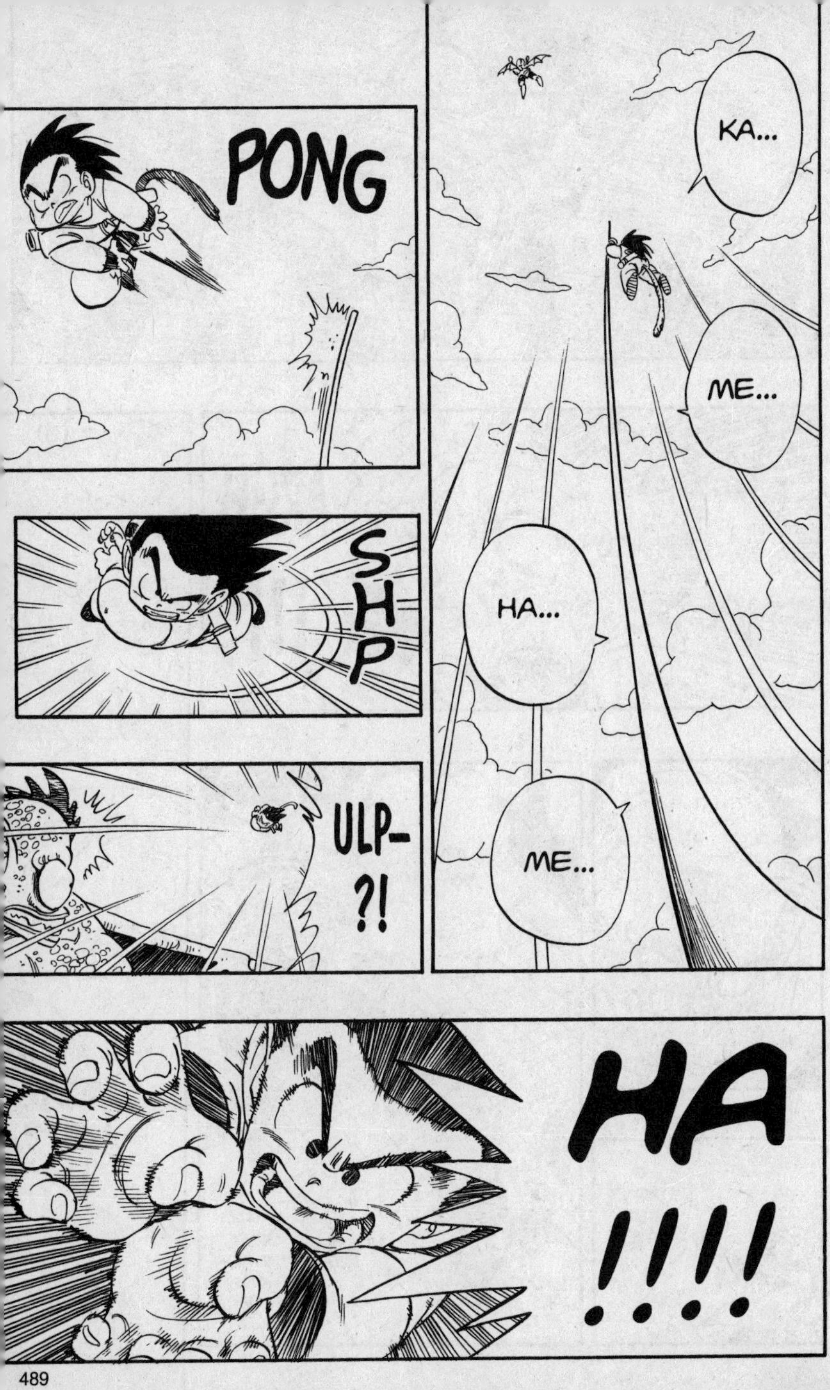
KA...
ME...
HA...
ME...
PONG
SHP
ULP-
?!
HA
!!!!

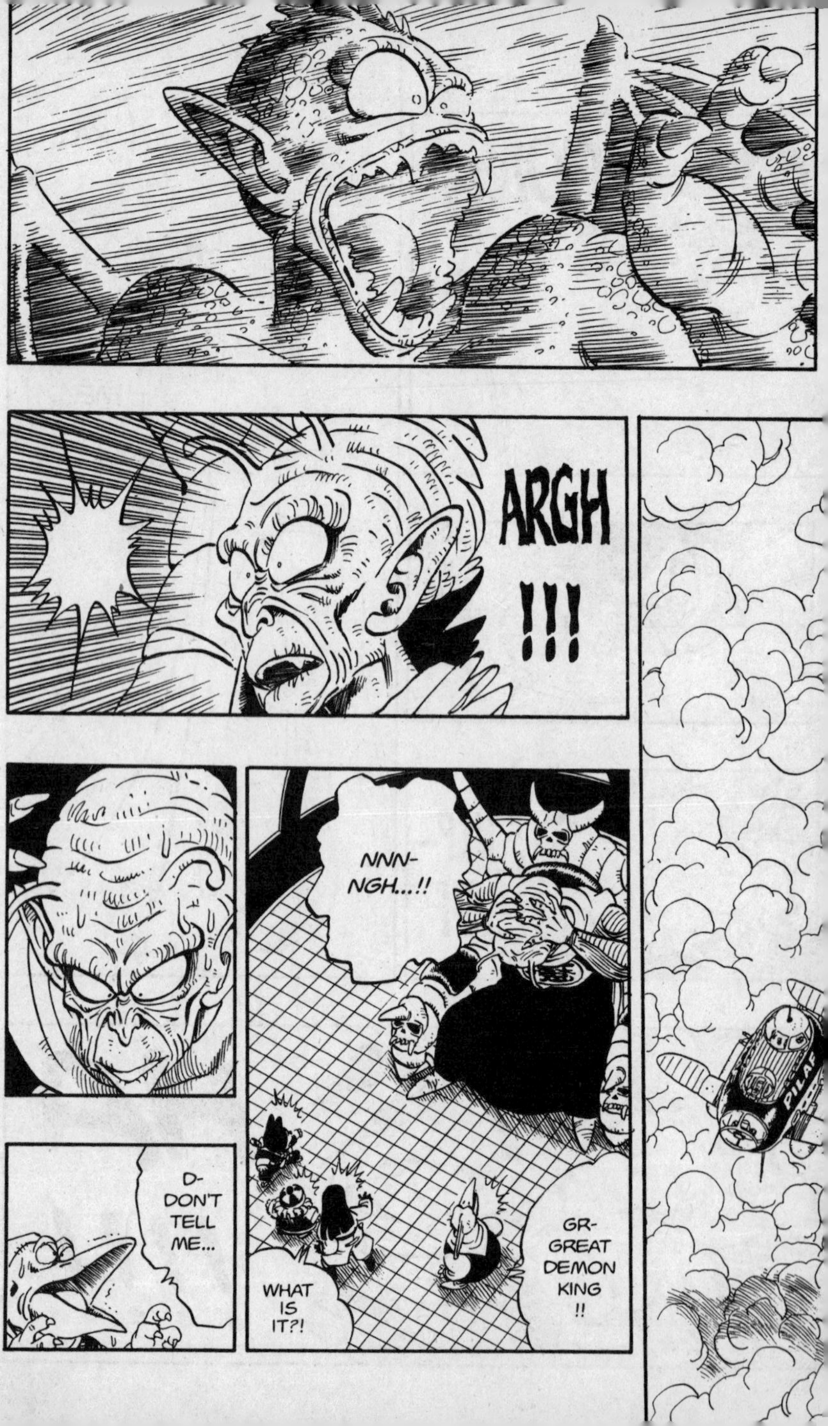
PILAF
ARGH!!!
NNN-NGH...!!
GR-GREAT DEMON KING!!
WHAT IS IT?!
D-DON'T TELL ME...

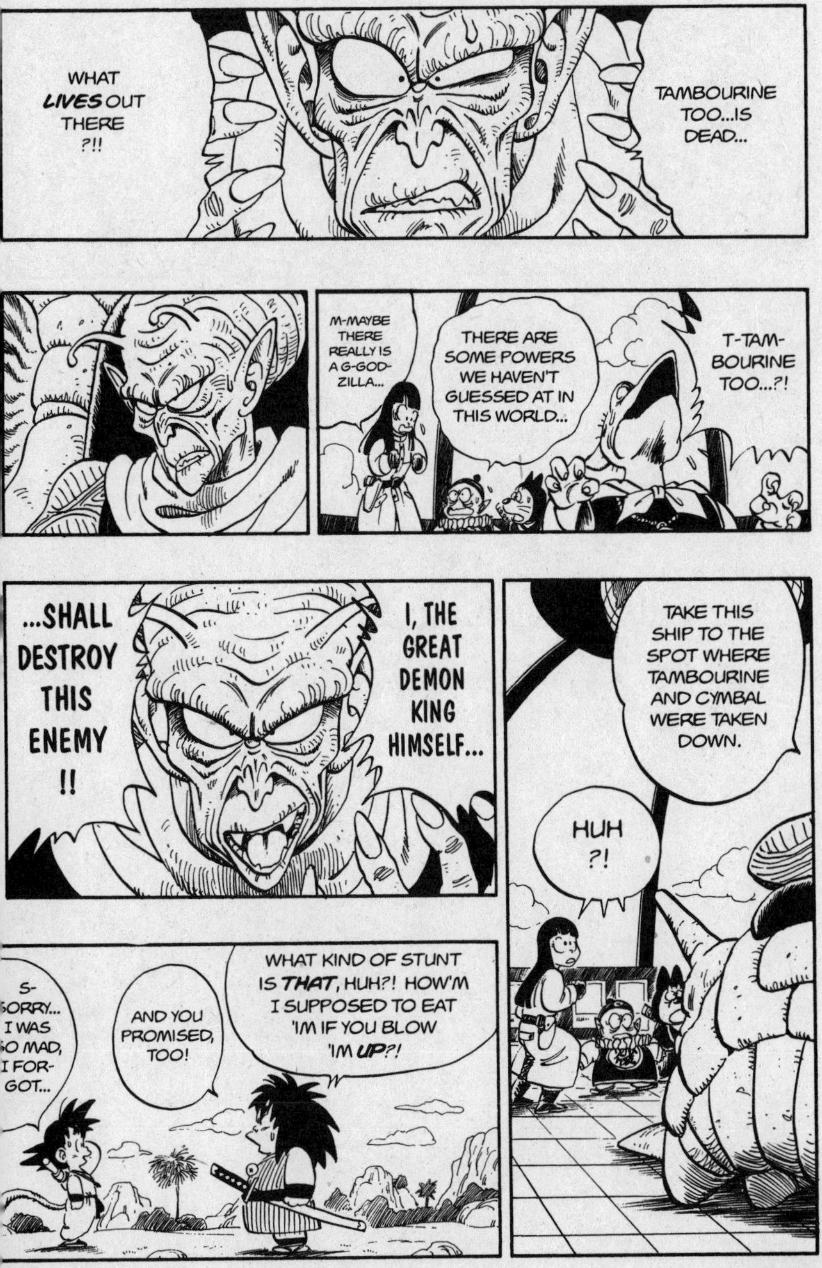
TAMBOURINE TOO...IS DEAD...
WHAT *LIVES* OUT THERE ?!!
T-TAMBOURINE TOO...?!
THERE ARE SOME POWERS WE HAVEN'T GUESSED AT IN THIS WORLD...
M-MAYBE THERE REALLY IS A G-GODZILLA...
TAKE THIS SHIP TO THE SPOT WHERE TAMBOURINE AND CYMBAL WERE TAKEN DOWN.
HUH ?!
I, THE GREAT DEMON KING HIMSELF...
...SHALL DESTROY THIS ENEMY !!
WHAT KIND OF STUNT IS *THAT*, HUH?! HOW'M I SUPPOSED TO EAT 'IM IF YOU BLOW 'IM *UP*?!
AND YOU PROMISED, TOO!
S-SORRY... I WAS SO MAD, I FOR-GOT...

Tale 142 · Piccolo Descends!

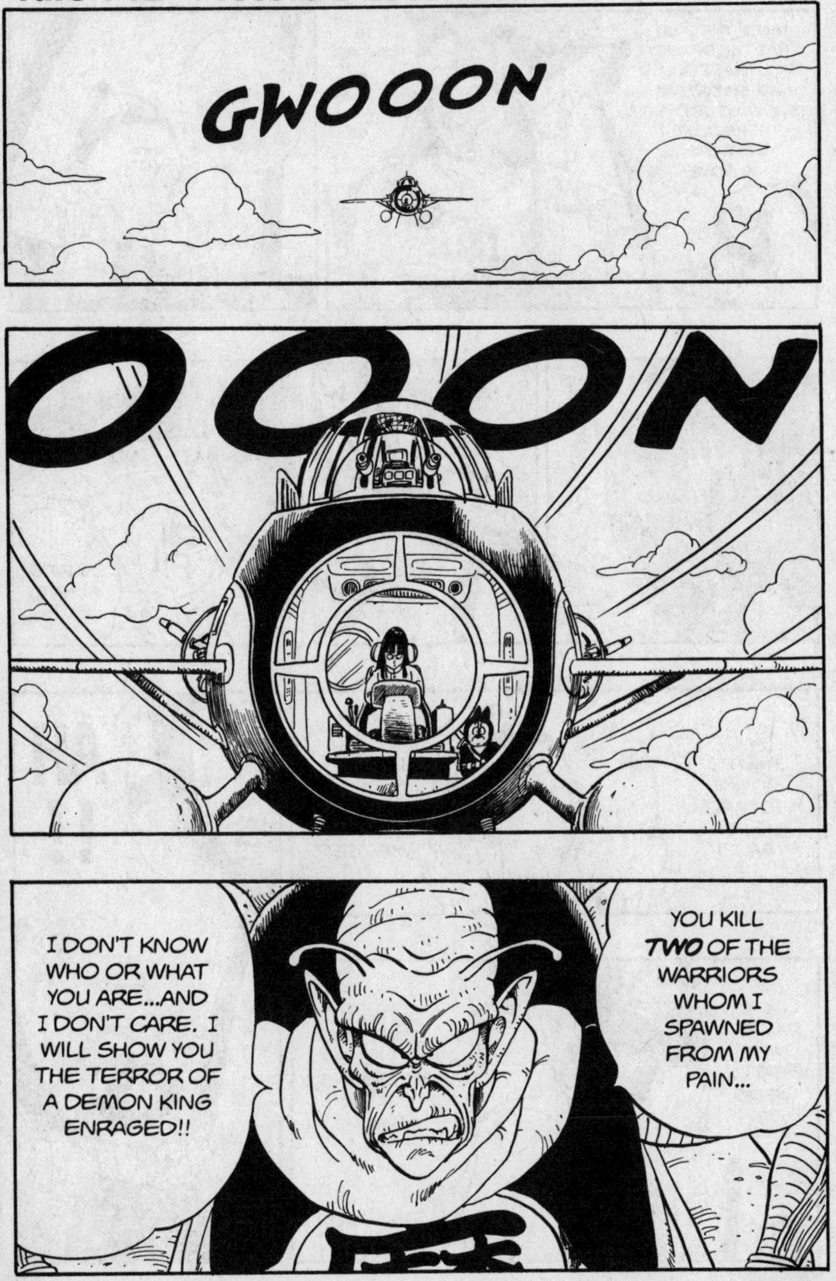
GWOOON
OOON
YOU KILL **TWO** OF THE WARRIORS WHOM I SPAWNED FROM MY PAIN...
I DON'T KNOW WHO OR WHAT YOU ARE...AND I DON'T CARE. I WILL SHOW YOU THE TERROR OF A DEMON KING ENRAGED!!

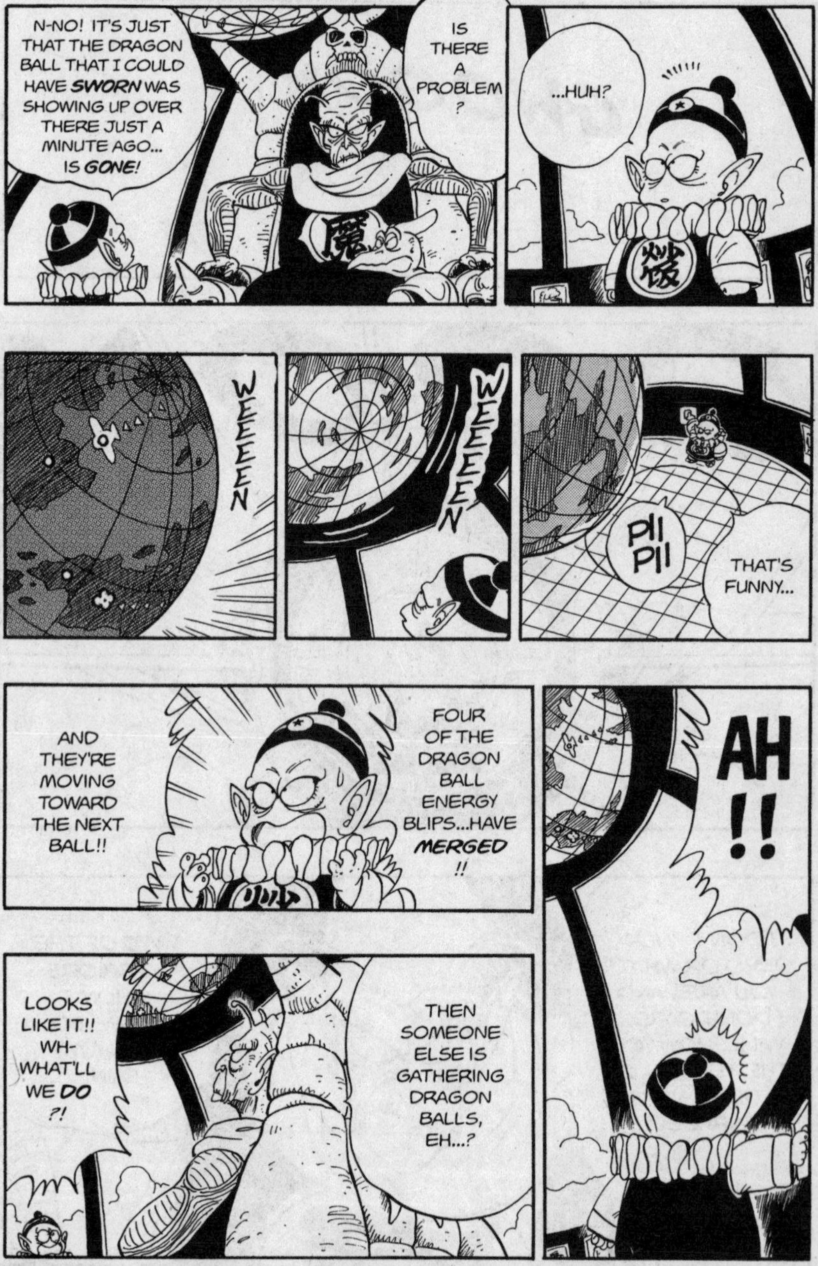
...HUH?
IS THERE A PROBLEM?
N-NO! IT'S JUST THAT THE DRAGON BALL THAT I COULD HAVE *SWORN* WAS SHOWING UP OVER THERE JUST A MINUTE AGO... IS *GONE*!
PII PII
THAT'S FUNNY...
WEEEEEN
WEEEEEN
AH!!
FOUR OF THE DRAGON BALL ENERGY BLIPS...HAVE *MERGED*!!
AND THEY'RE MOVING TOWARD THE NEXT BALL!!
THEN SOMEONE ELSE IS GATHERING DRAGON BALLS, EH...?
LOOKS LIKE IT!! WH-WHAT'LL WE *DO*?!

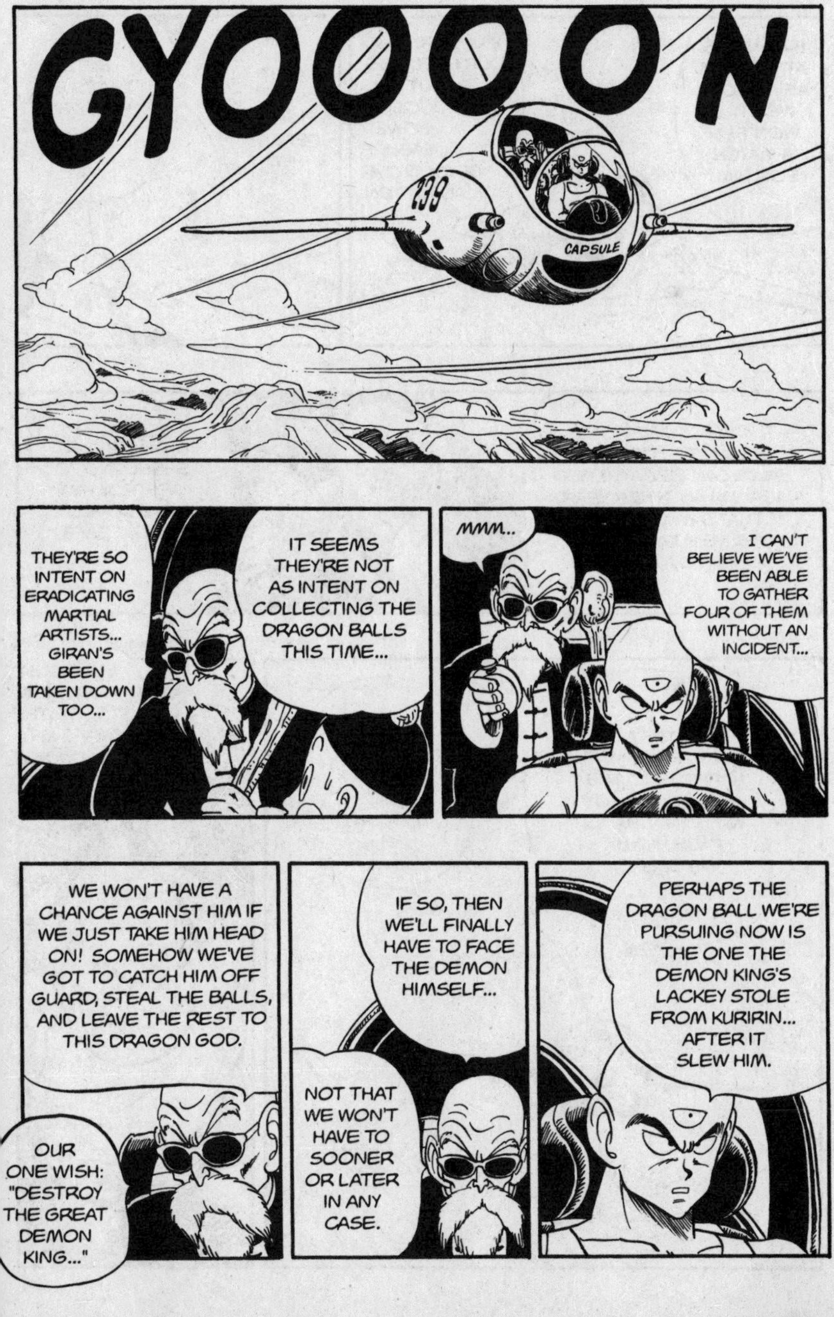

GYOOOON
CAPSULE
239
I CAN'T BELIEVE WE'VE BEEN ABLE TO GATHER FOUR OF THEM WITHOUT AN INCIDENT...
MMM...
IT SEEMS THEY'RE NOT AS INTENT ON COLLECTING THE DRAGON BALLS THIS TIME...
THEY'RE SO INTENT ON ERADICATING MARTIAL ARTISTS... GIRAN'S BEEN TAKEN DOWN TOO...
PERHAPS THE DRAGON BALL WE'RE PURSUING NOW IS THE ONE THE DEMON KING'S LACKEY STOLE FROM KURIRIN... AFTER IT SLEW HIM.
IF SO, THEN WE'LL FINALLY HAVE TO FACE THE DEMON HIMSELF...
NOT THAT WE WON'T HAVE TO SOONER OR LATER IN ANY CASE.
WE WON'T HAVE A CHANCE AGAINST HIM IF WE JUST TAKE HIM HEAD ON! SOMEHOW WE'VE GOT TO CATCH HIM OFF GUARD, STEAL THE BALLS, AND LEAVE THE REST TO THIS DRAGON GOD.
OUR ONE WISH: "DESTROY THE GREAT DEMON KING..."

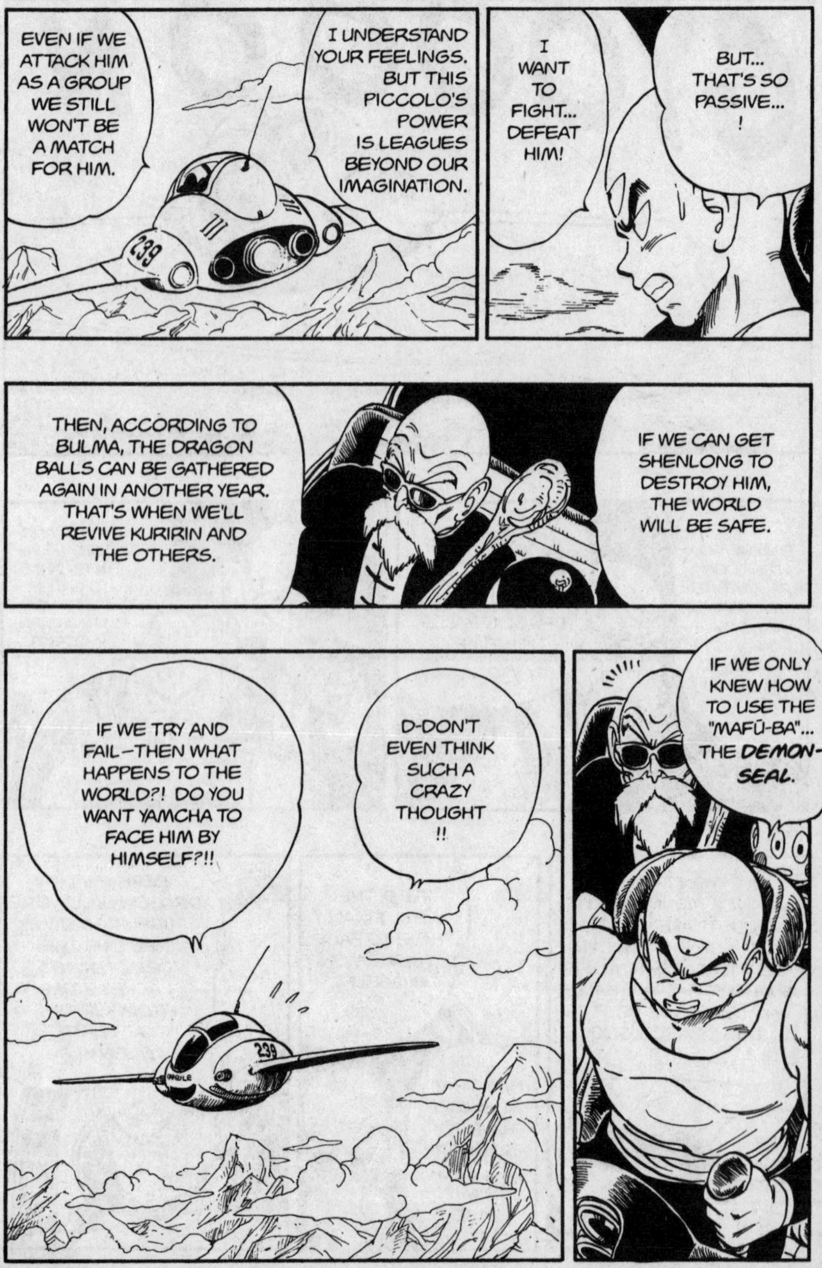
BUT... THAT'S SO PASSIVE...!
I WANT TO FIGHT... DEFEAT HIM!
I UNDERSTAND YOUR FEELINGS. BUT THIS PICCOLO'S POWER IS LEAGUES BEYOND OUR IMAGINATION.
EVEN IF WE ATTACK HIM AS A GROUP WE STILL WON'T BE A MATCH FOR HIM.
IF WE CAN GET SHENLONG TO DESTROY HIM, THE WORLD WILL BE SAFE.
THEN, ACCORDING TO BULMA, THE DRAGON BALLS CAN BE GATHERED AGAIN IN ANOTHER YEAR. THAT'S WHEN WE'LL REVIVE KURIRIN AND THE OTHERS.
IF WE ONLY KNEW HOW TO USE THE "MAFŪ-BA"... THE ***DEMON-SEAL.***
D-DON'T EVEN THINK SUCH A CRAZY THOUGHT!!
IF WE TRY AND FAIL—THEN WHAT HAPPENS TO THE WORLD?! DO YOU WANT YAMCHA TO FACE HIM BY HIMSELF?!!

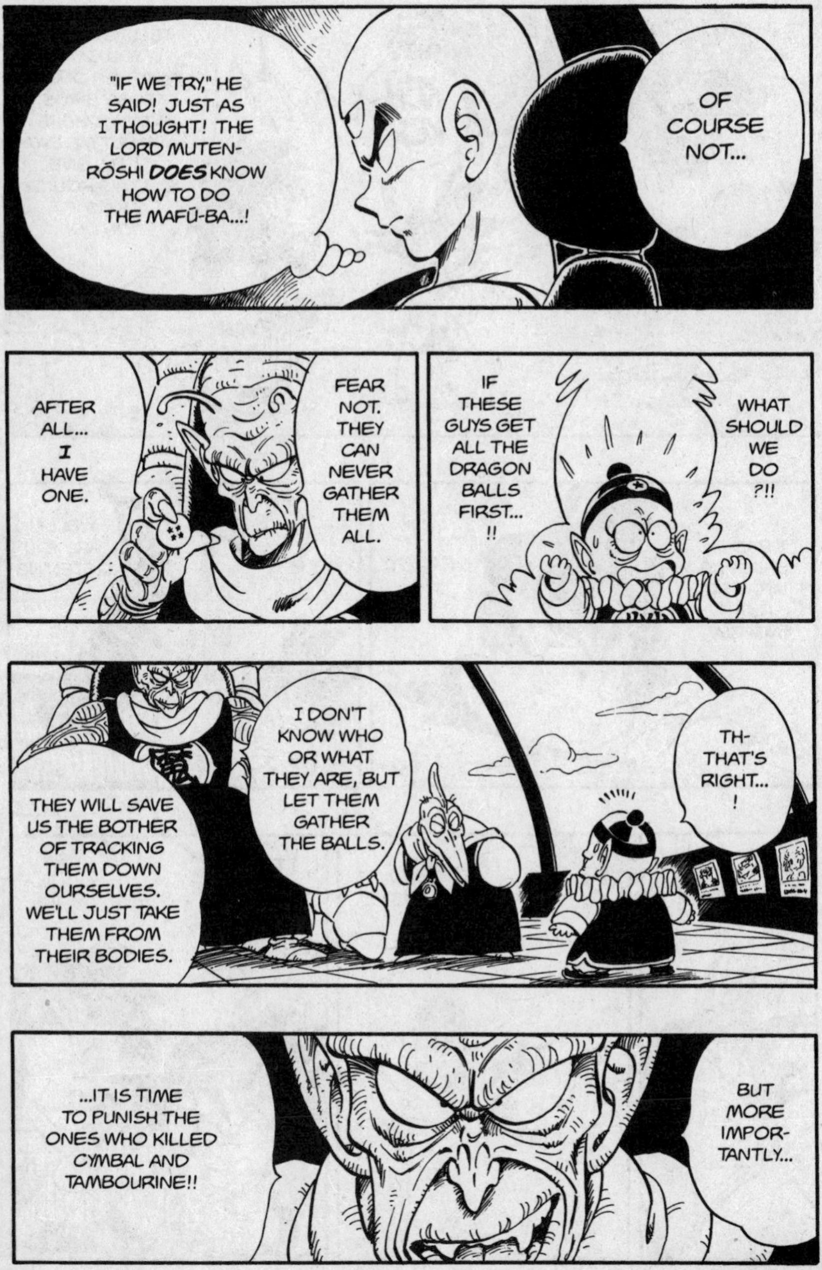
OF COURSE NOT...
"IF WE TRY," HE SAID! JUST AS I THOUGHT! THE LORD MUTEN-RŌSHI **DOES** KNOW HOW TO DO THE MAFŪ-BA...!
WHAT SHOULD WE DO?!!
IF THESE GUYS GET ALL THE DRAGON BALLS FIRST...!!
FEAR NOT. THEY CAN NEVER GATHER THEM ALL.
AFTER ALL... I HAVE ONE.
TH-THAT'S RIGHT...!
I DON'T KNOW WHO OR WHAT THEY ARE, BUT LET THEM GATHER THE BALLS.
THEY WILL SAVE US THE BOTHER OF TRACKING THEM DOWN OURSELVES. WE'LL JUST TAKE THEM FROM THEIR BODIES.
BUT MORE IMPOR-TANTLY...
...IT IS TIME TO PUNISH THE ONES WHO KILLED CYMBAL AND TAMBOURINE!!

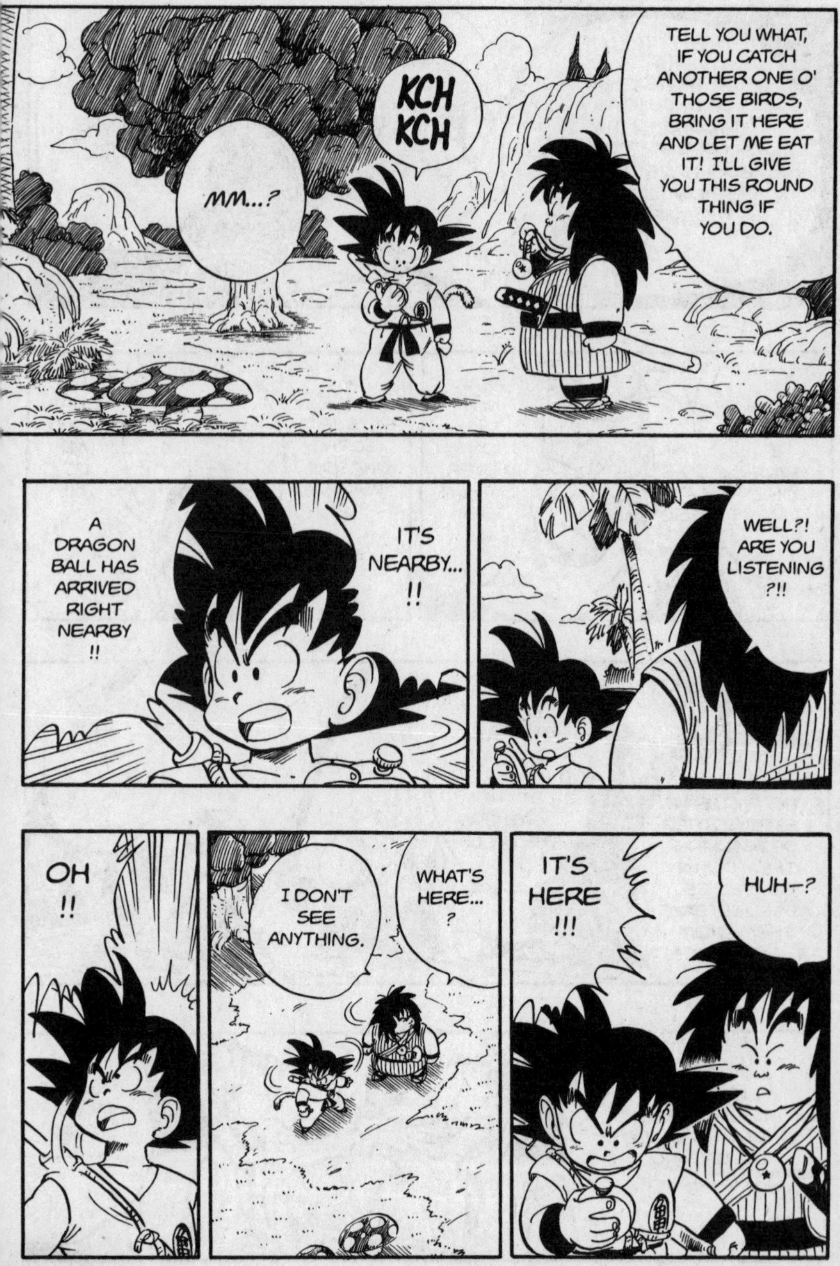
TELL YOU WHAT, IF YOU CATCH ANOTHER ONE O' THOSE BIRDS, BRING IT HERE AND LET ME EAT IT! I'LL GIVE YOU THIS ROUND THING IF YOU DO.
KCH KCH
MM...?
WELL?! ARE YOU LISTENING ?!!
IT'S NEARBY... !!
A DRAGON BALL HAS ARRIVED RIGHT NEARBY !!
HUH–?
IT'S HERE !!!
WHAT'S HERE... ?
I DON'T SEE ANYTHING.
OH !!

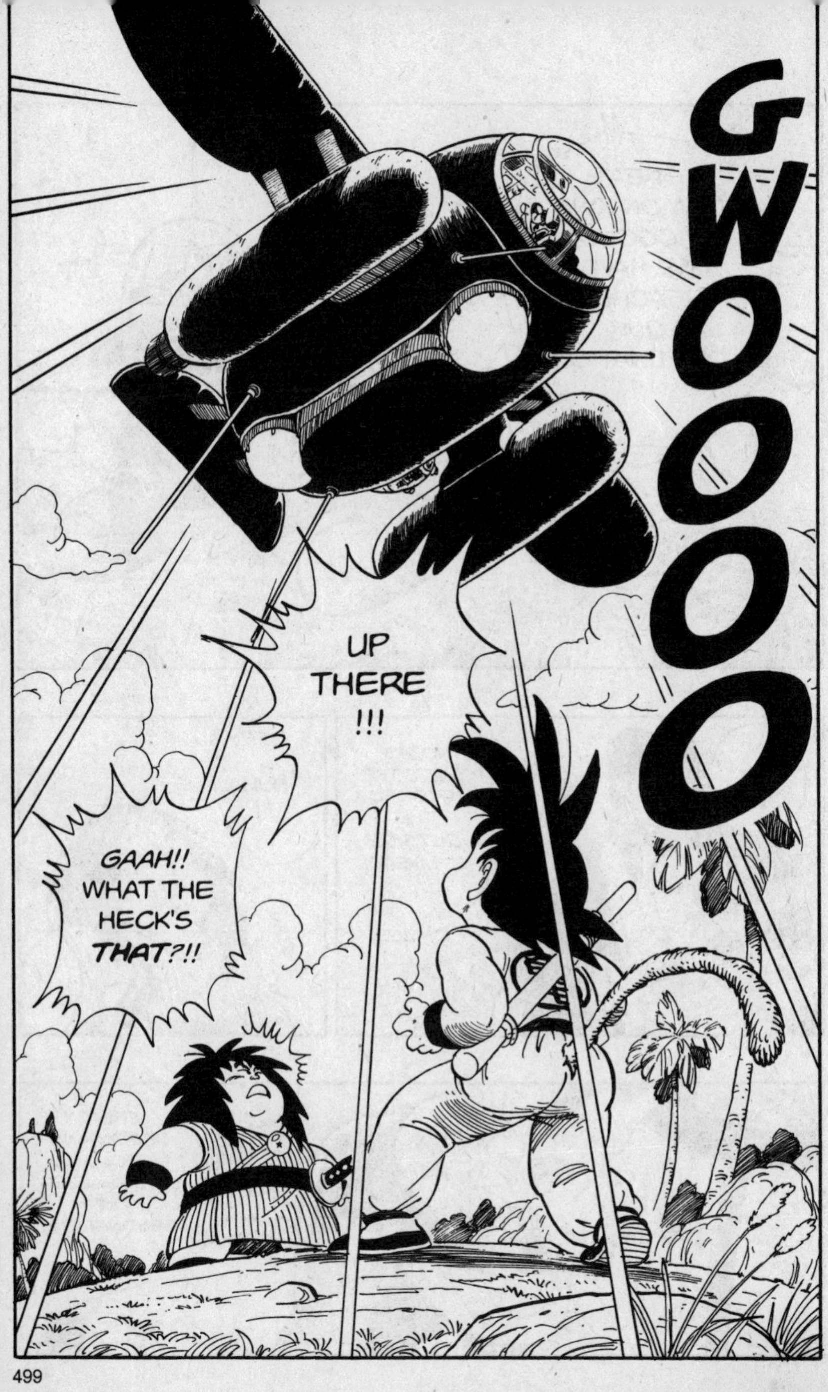
GWOOOOO
UP THERE !!!
GAAH!! WHAT THE HECK'S *THAT*?!!

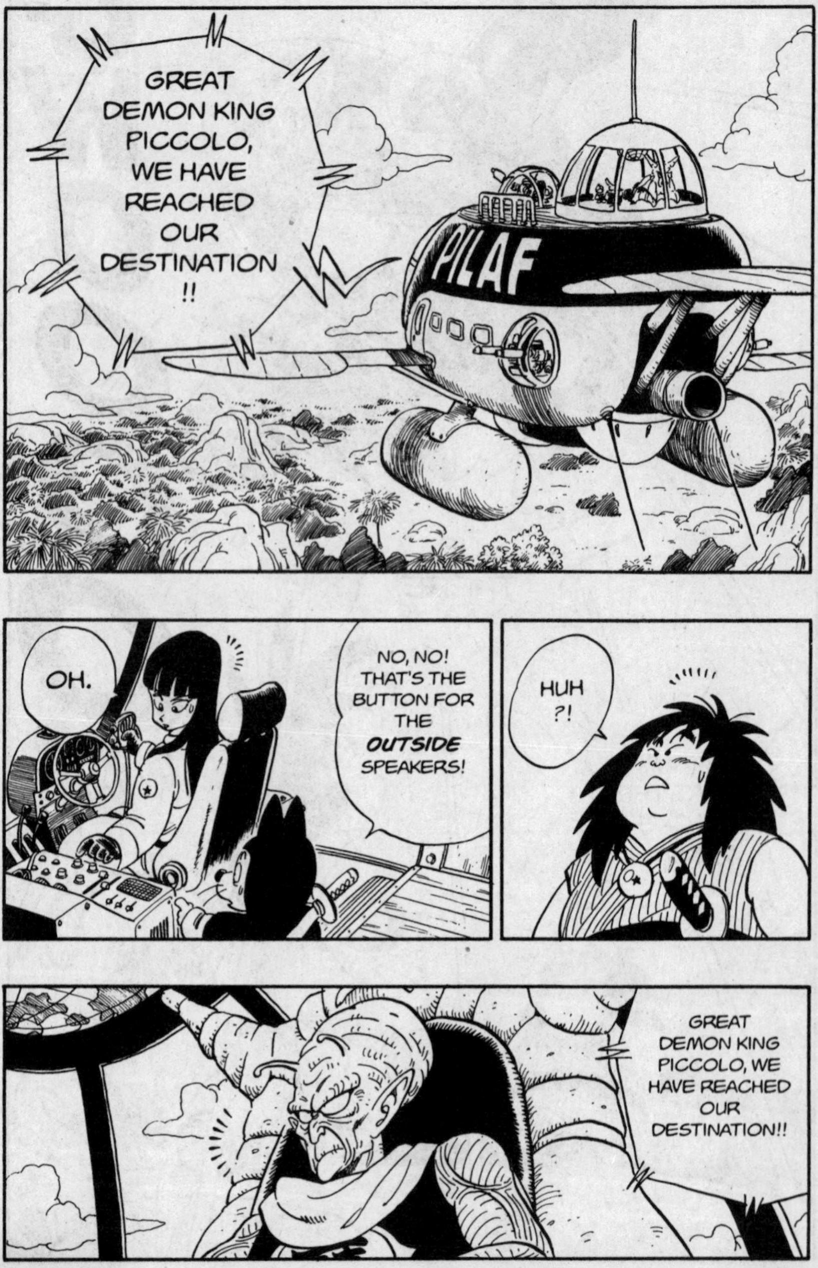
GREAT DEMON KING PICCOLO, WE HAVE REACHED OUR DESTINATION !!
PILAF
HUH ?!
NO, NO! THAT'S THE BUTTON FOR THE ***OUTSIDE*** SPEAKERS!
OH.
GREAT DEMON KING PICCOLO, WE HAVE REACHED OUR DESTINATION!!

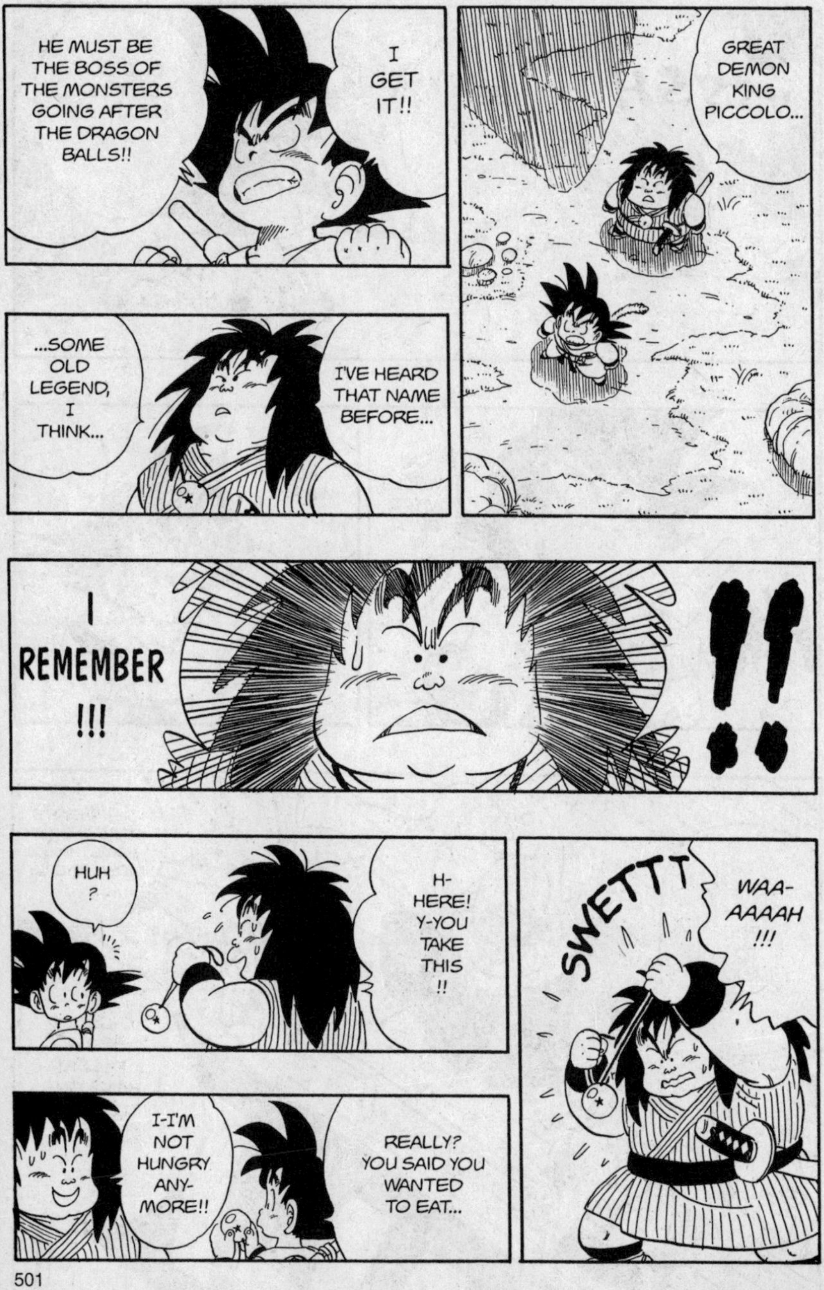
GREAT DEMON KING PICCOLO...
I GET IT!!
HE MUST BE THE BOSS OF THE MONSTERS GOING AFTER THE DRAGON BALLS!!
I'VE HEARD THAT NAME BEFORE...
...SOME OLD LEGEND, I THINK...
!!
I REMEMBER!!!
SWETTT
WAA-AAAAH!!!
H-HERE! Y-YOU TAKE THIS!!
HUH?
REALLY? YOU SAID YOU WANTED TO EAT...
I-I'M NOT HUNGRY ANY-MORE!!

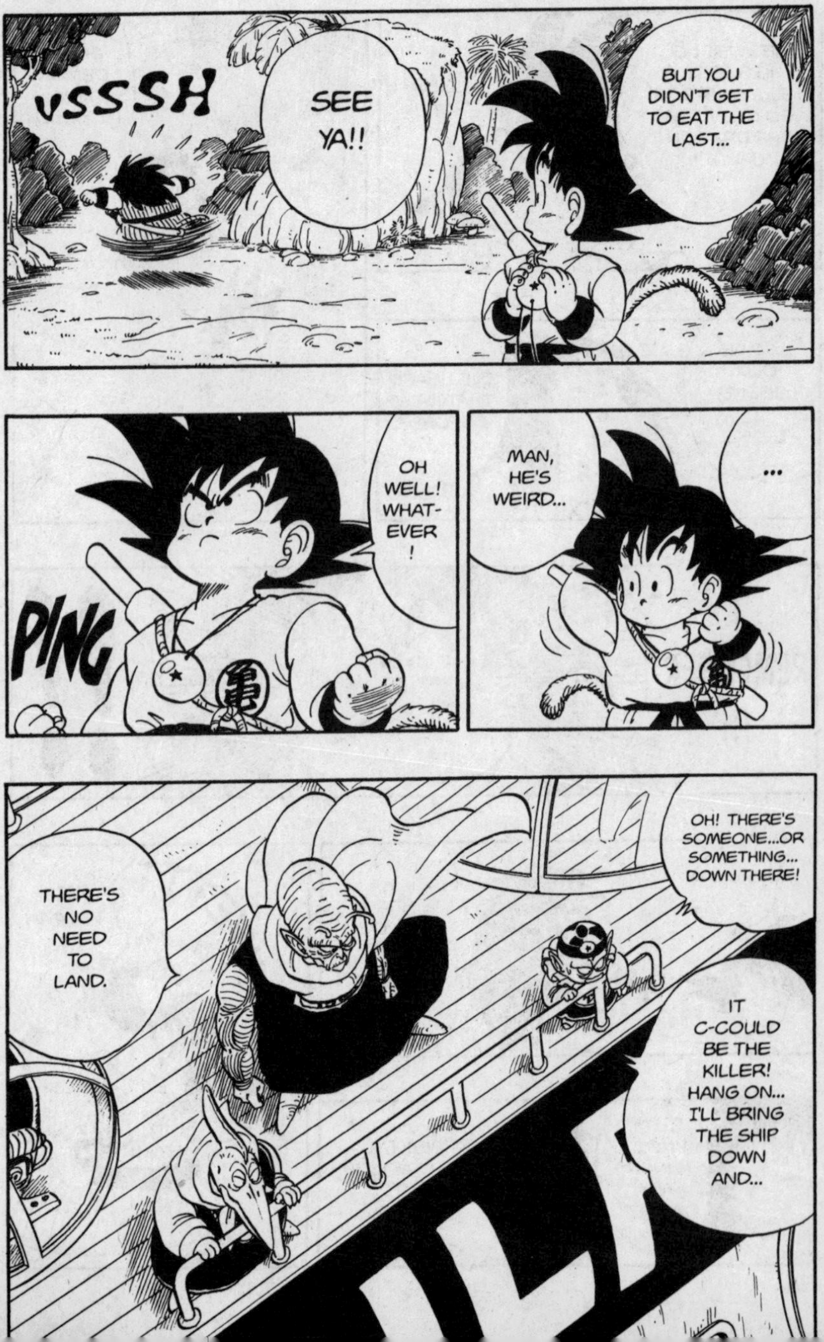
BUT YOU DIDN'T GET TO EAT THE LAST...
SEE YA!!
VSSSH
...
MAN, HE'S WEIRD...
OH WELL! WHATEVER!
PING
OH! THERE'S SOMEONE...OR SOMETHING... DOWN THERE!
IT C-COULD BE THE KILLER! HANG ON... I'LL BRING THE SHIP DOWN AND...
THERE'S NO NEED TO LAND.

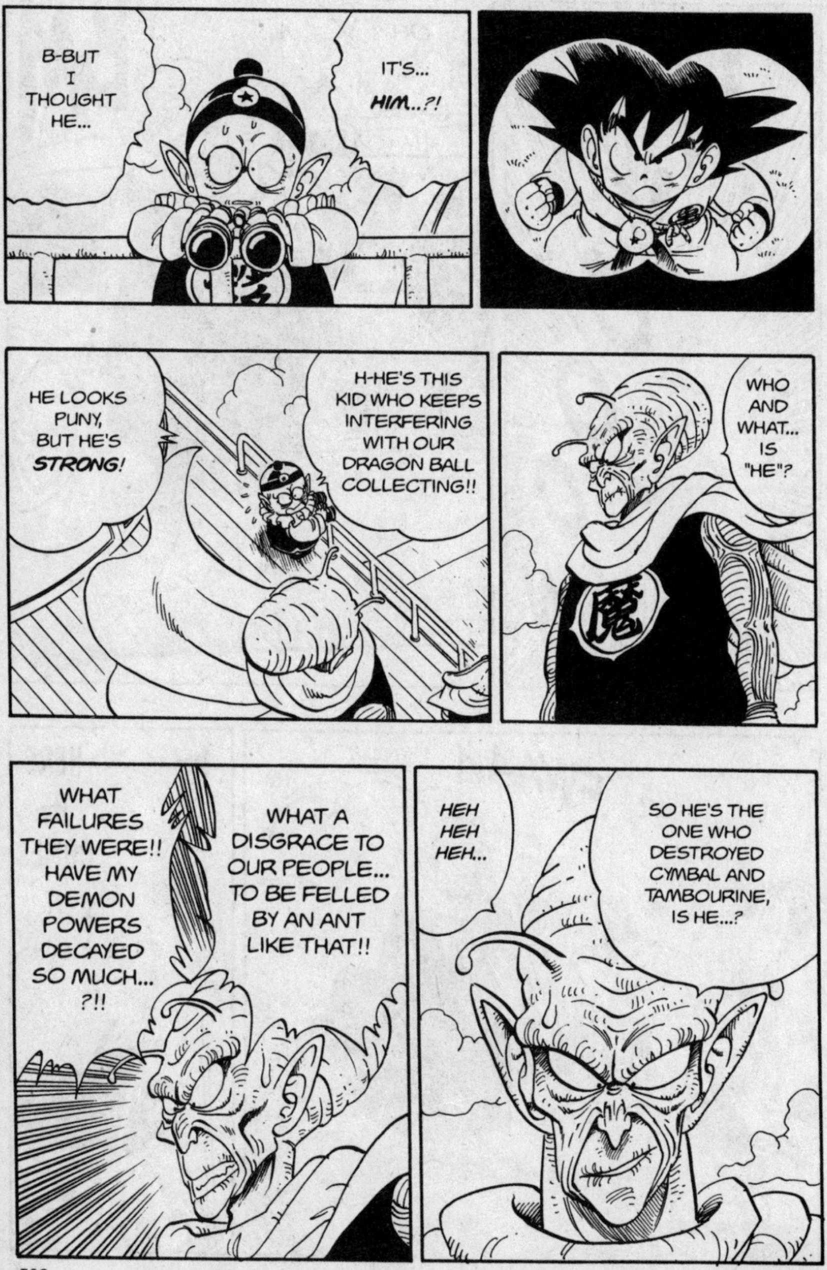
IT'S... HIM...?!
B-BUT I THOUGHT HE...
WHO AND WHAT... IS "HE"?
H-HE'S THIS KID WHO KEEPS INTERFERING WITH OUR DRAGON BALL COLLECTING!!
HE LOOKS PUNY, BUT HE'S STRONG!
SO HE'S THE ONE WHO DESTROYED CYMBAL AND TAMBOURINE, IS HE...?
HEH HEH HEH...
WHAT A DISGRACE TO OUR PEOPLE... TO BE FELLED BY AN ANT LIKE THAT!!
WHAT FAILURES THEY WERE!! HAVE MY DEMON POWERS DECAYED SO MUCH...?!!

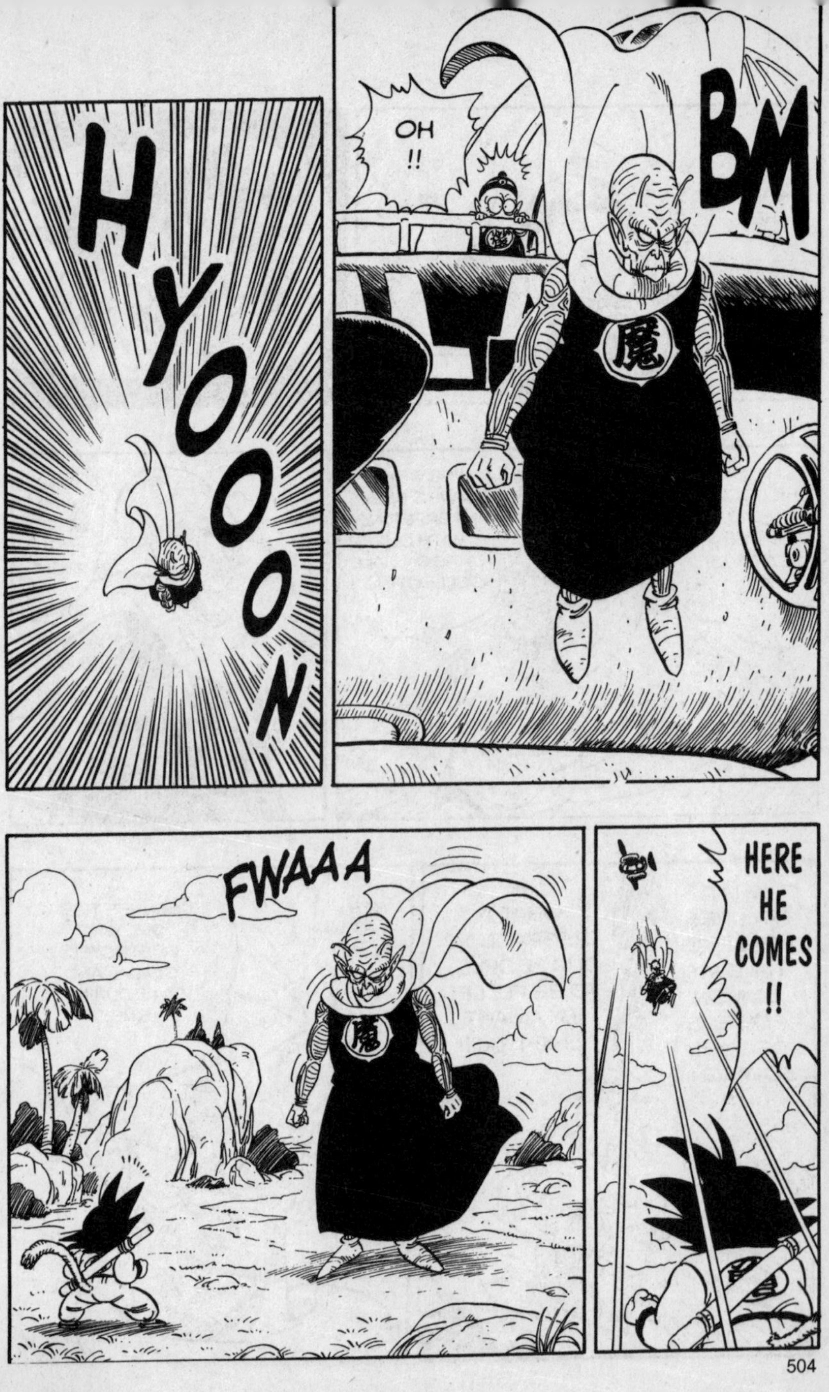
OH !!
BM
HYOOON
HERE HE COMES !!
FWAAA

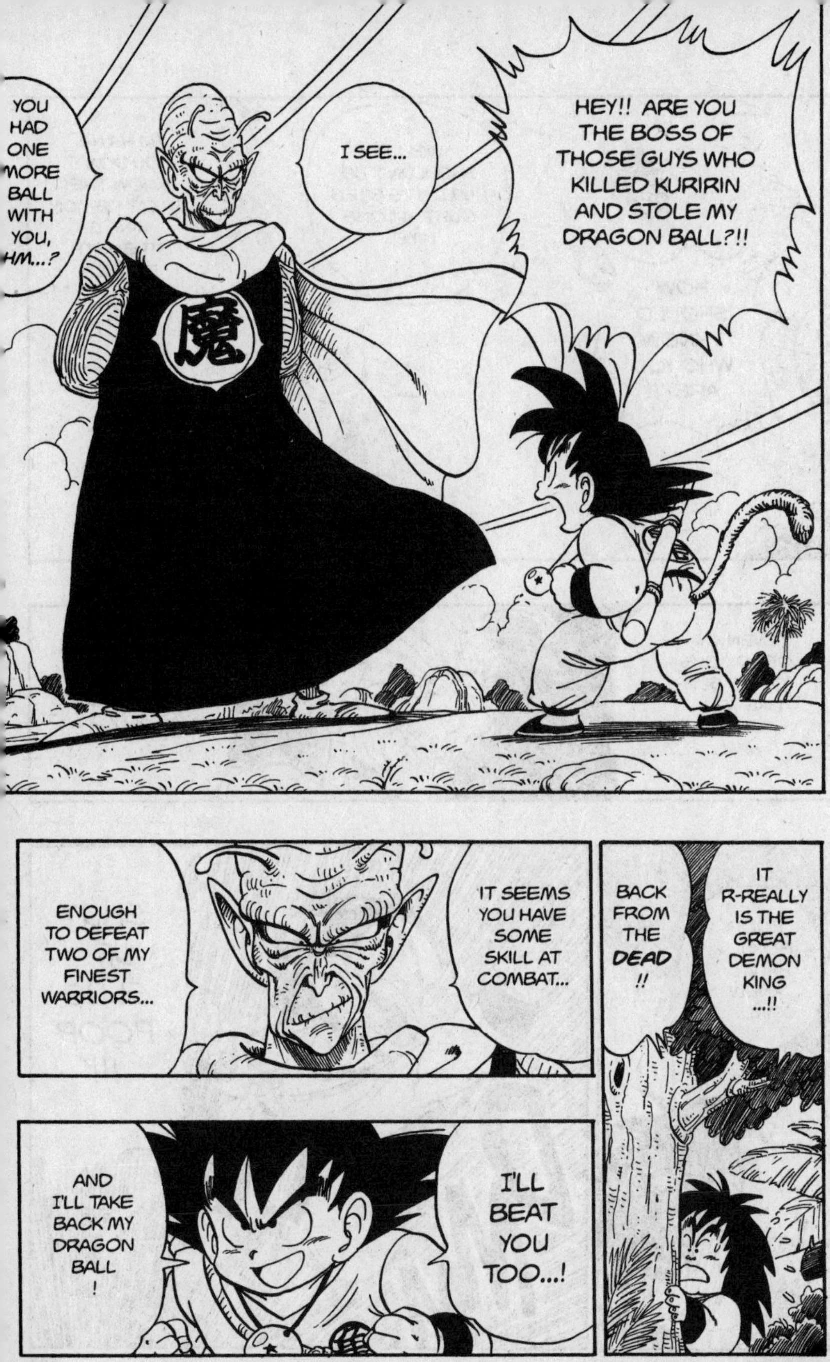

HEY!! ARE YOU THE BOSS OF THOSE GUYS WHO KILLED KURIRIN AND STOLE MY DRAGON BALL?!!
I SEE...
YOU HAD ONE MORE BALL WITH YOU, HM...?
魔
IT R-REALLY IS THE GREAT DEMON KING ...!!
BACK FROM THE *DEAD* !!
IT SEEMS YOU HAVE SOME SKILL AT COMBAT...
ENOUGH TO DEFEAT TWO OF MY FINEST WARRIORS...
I'LL BEAT YOU TOO...!
AND I'LL TAKE BACK MY DRAGON BALL !

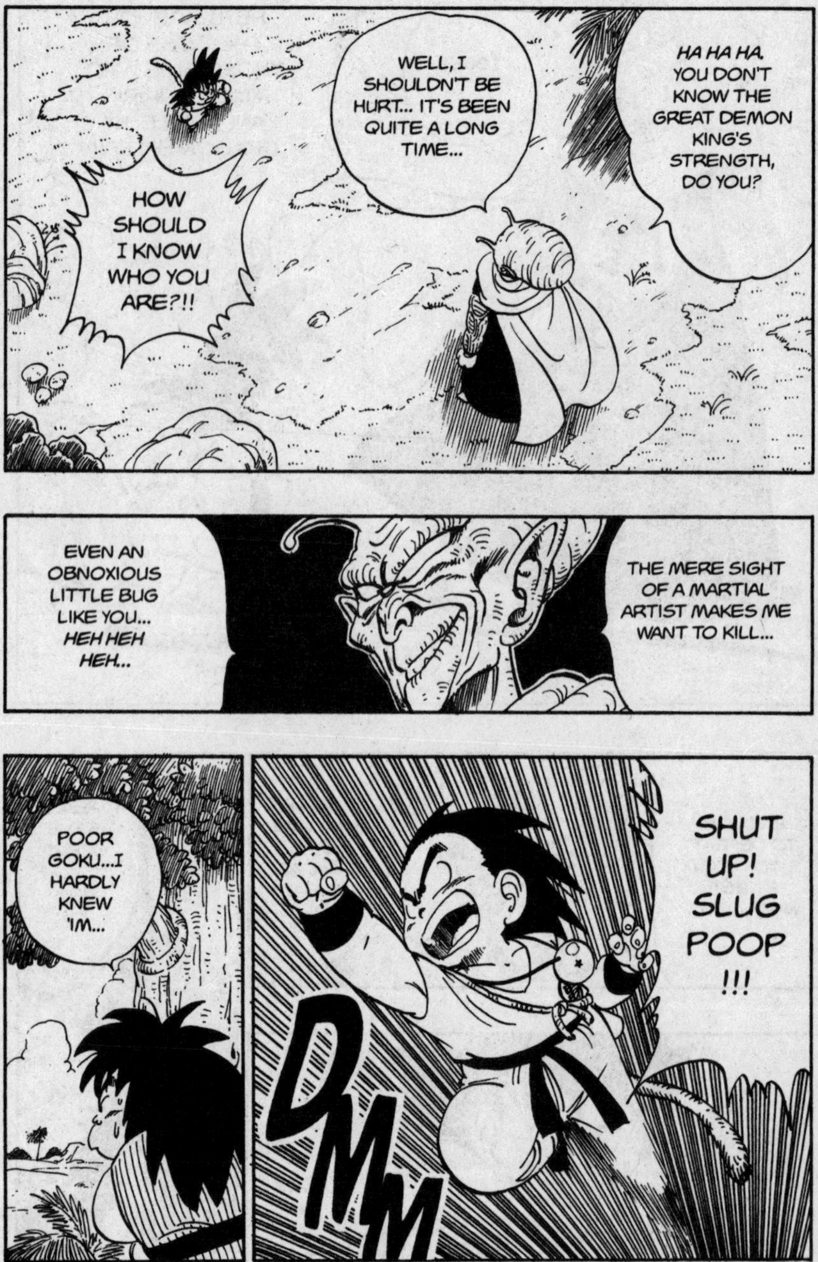
HA HA HA. YOU DON'T KNOW THE GREAT DEMON KING'S STRENGTH, DO YOU?
WELL, I SHOULDN'T BE HURT... IT'S BEEN QUITE A LONG TIME...
HOW SHOULD I KNOW WHO YOU ARE?!!
THE MERE SIGHT OF A MARTIAL ARTIST MAKES ME WANT TO KILL...
EVEN AN OBNOXIOUS LITTLE BUG LIKE YOU... HEH HEH HEH...
SHUT UP! SLUG POOP!!!
DMM
POOR GOKU...I HARDLY KNEW 'IM...

Tale 143 · Goku vs. The Demon King

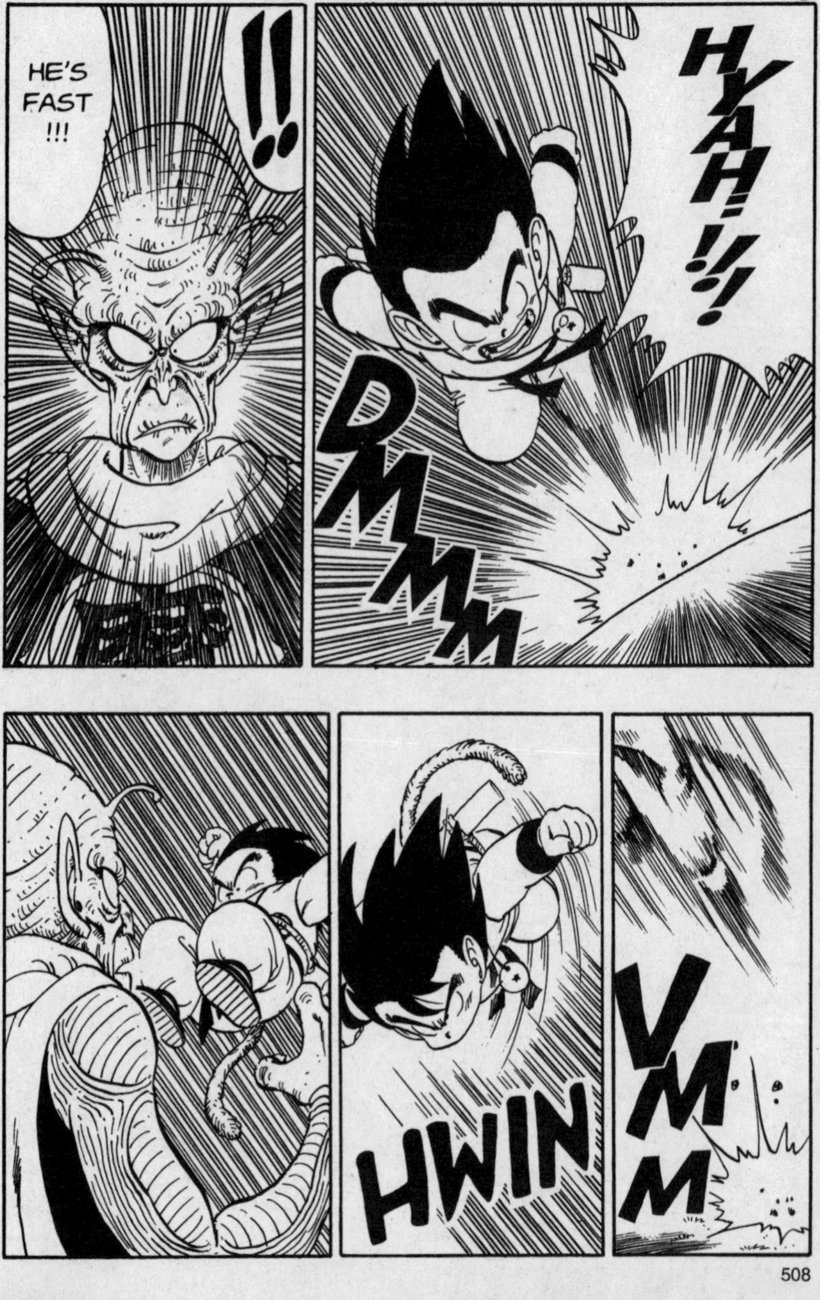
HYAH!!!
DMMMM
!!
HE'S FAST !!!
VMMM
HWIN

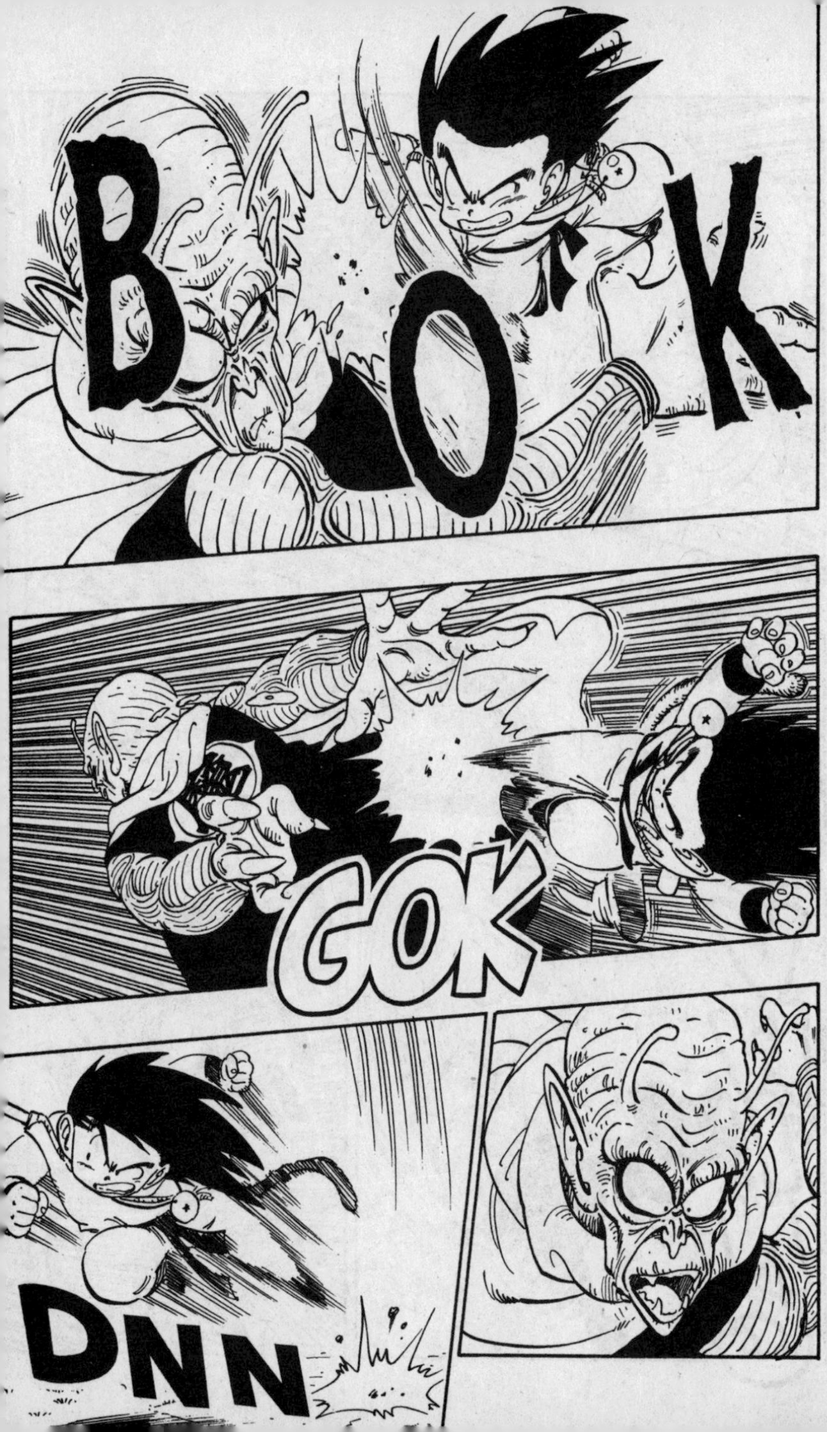
BOOK
GOK
DNN

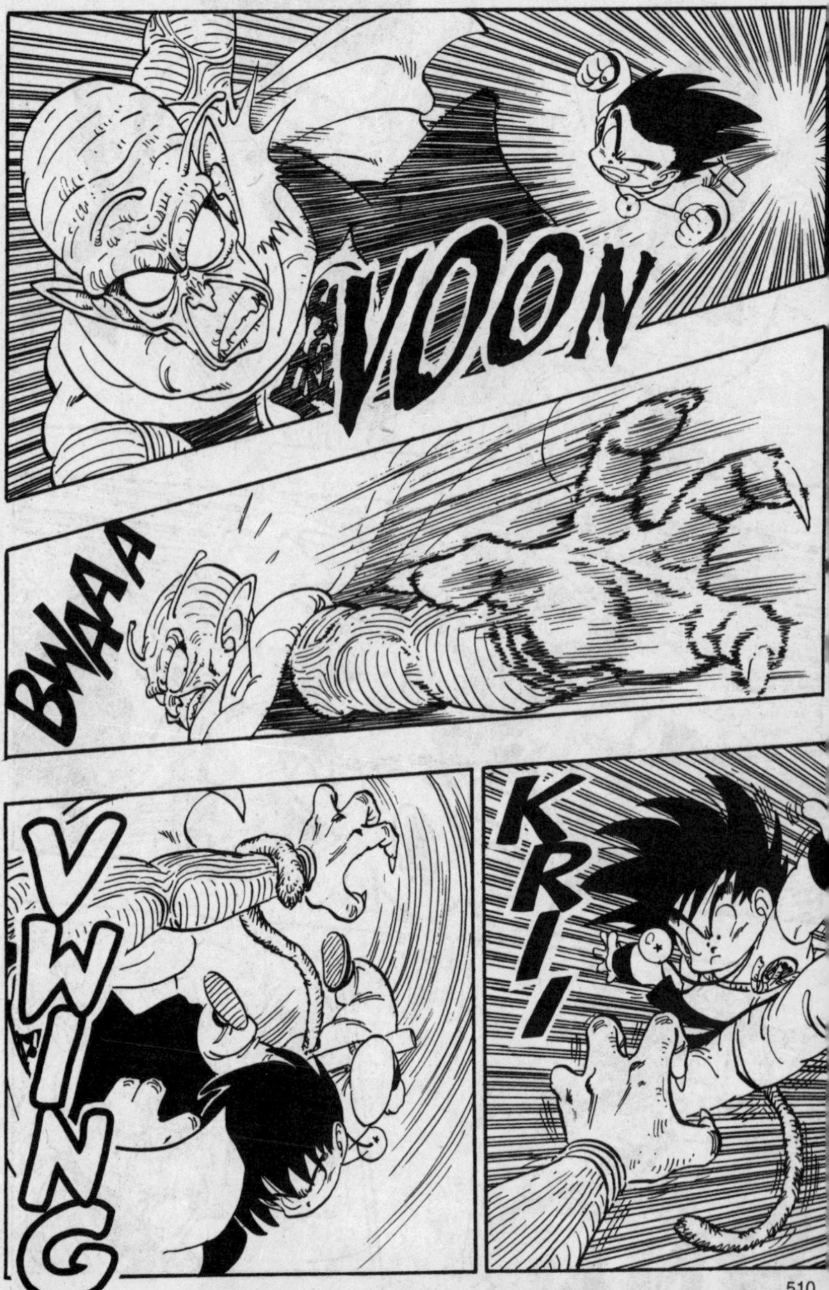
VOON
BWAAA
KRII
VWING

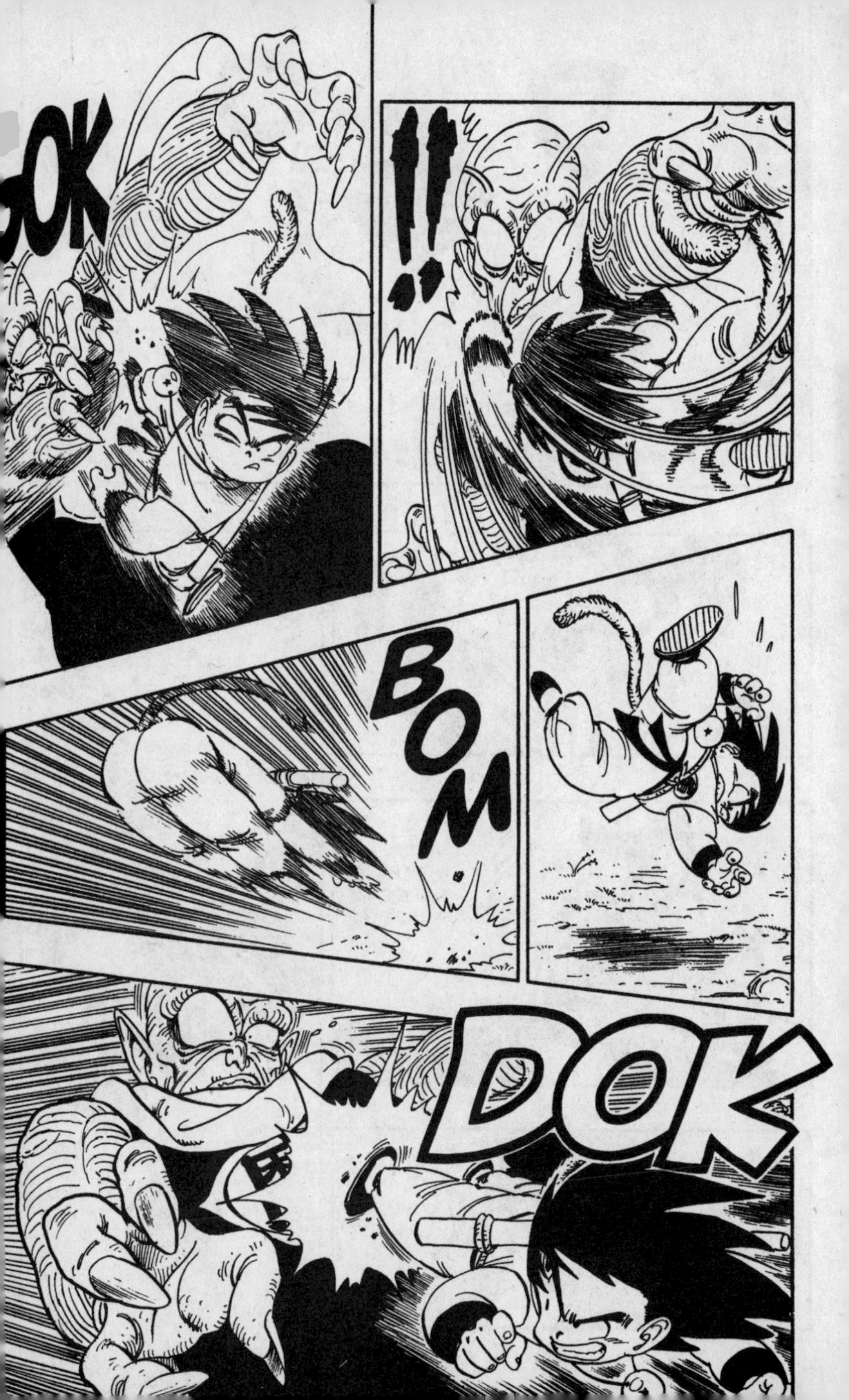

!!
OK
BOM
DOK

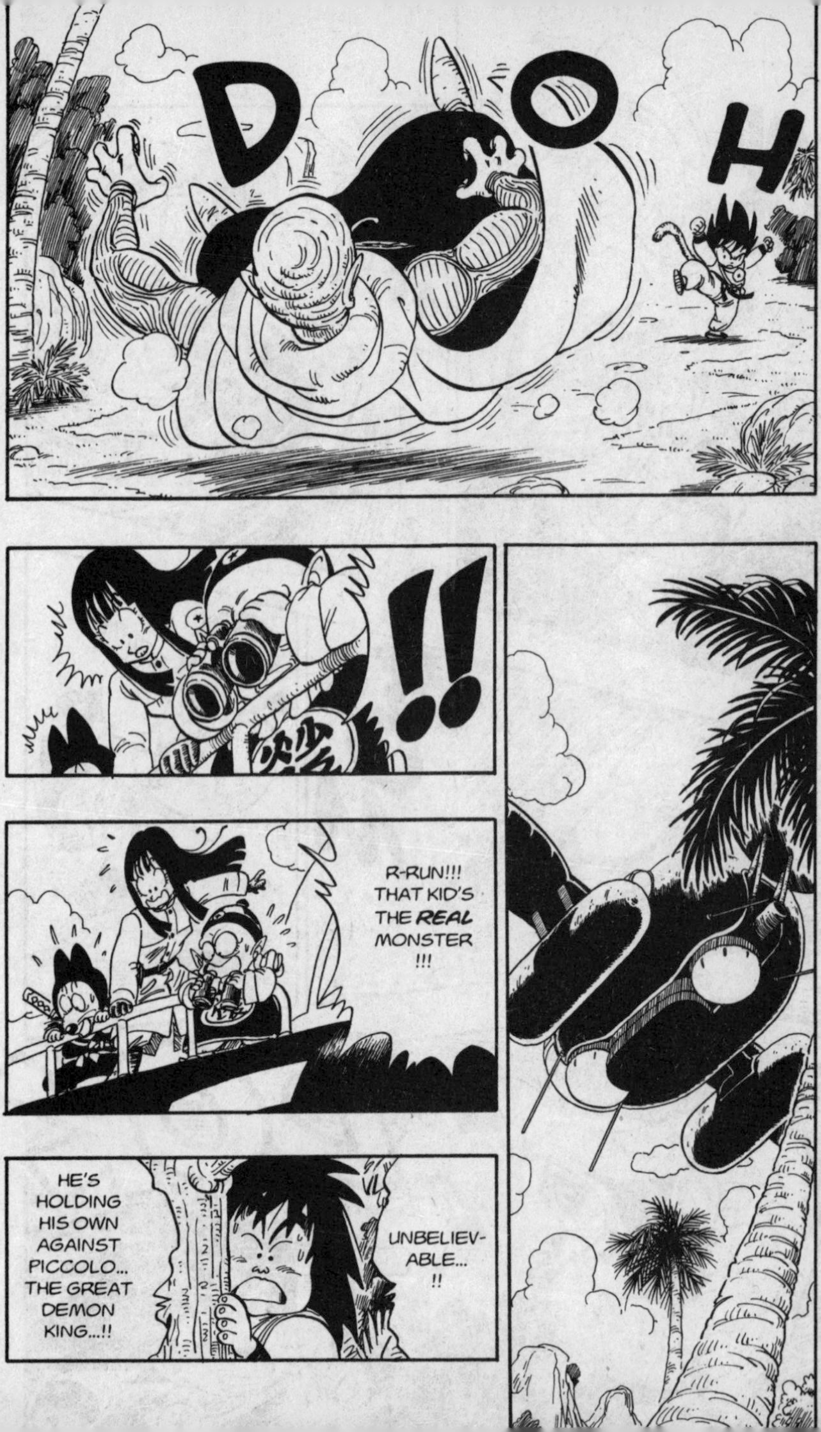
DOH
!!
R-RUN!!! THAT KID'S THE ***REAL*** MONSTER !!!
UNBELIEV-ABLE... !!
HE'S HOLDING HIS OWN AGAINST PICCOLO... THE GREAT DEMON KING...!!

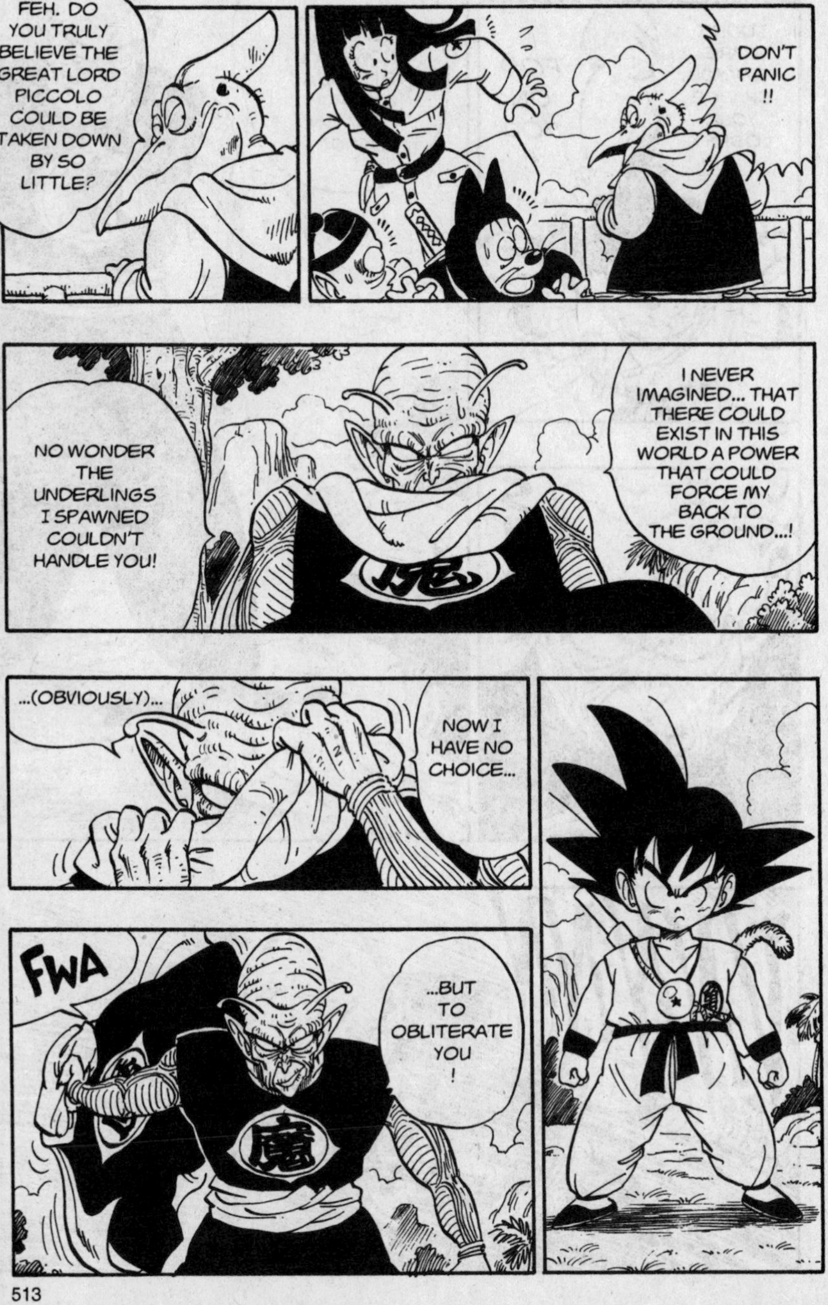
DON'T PANIC !!
FEH. DO YOU TRULY BELIEVE THE GREAT LORD PICCOLO COULD BE TAKEN DOWN BY SO LITTLE?
I NEVER IMAGINED... THAT THERE COULD EXIST IN THIS WORLD A POWER THAT COULD FORCE MY BACK TO THE GROUND...!
NO WONDER THE UNDERLINGS I SPAWNED COULDN'T HANDLE YOU!
...(OBVIOUSLY)...
NOW I HAVE NO CHOICE...
...BUT TO OBLITERATE YOU !
FWA

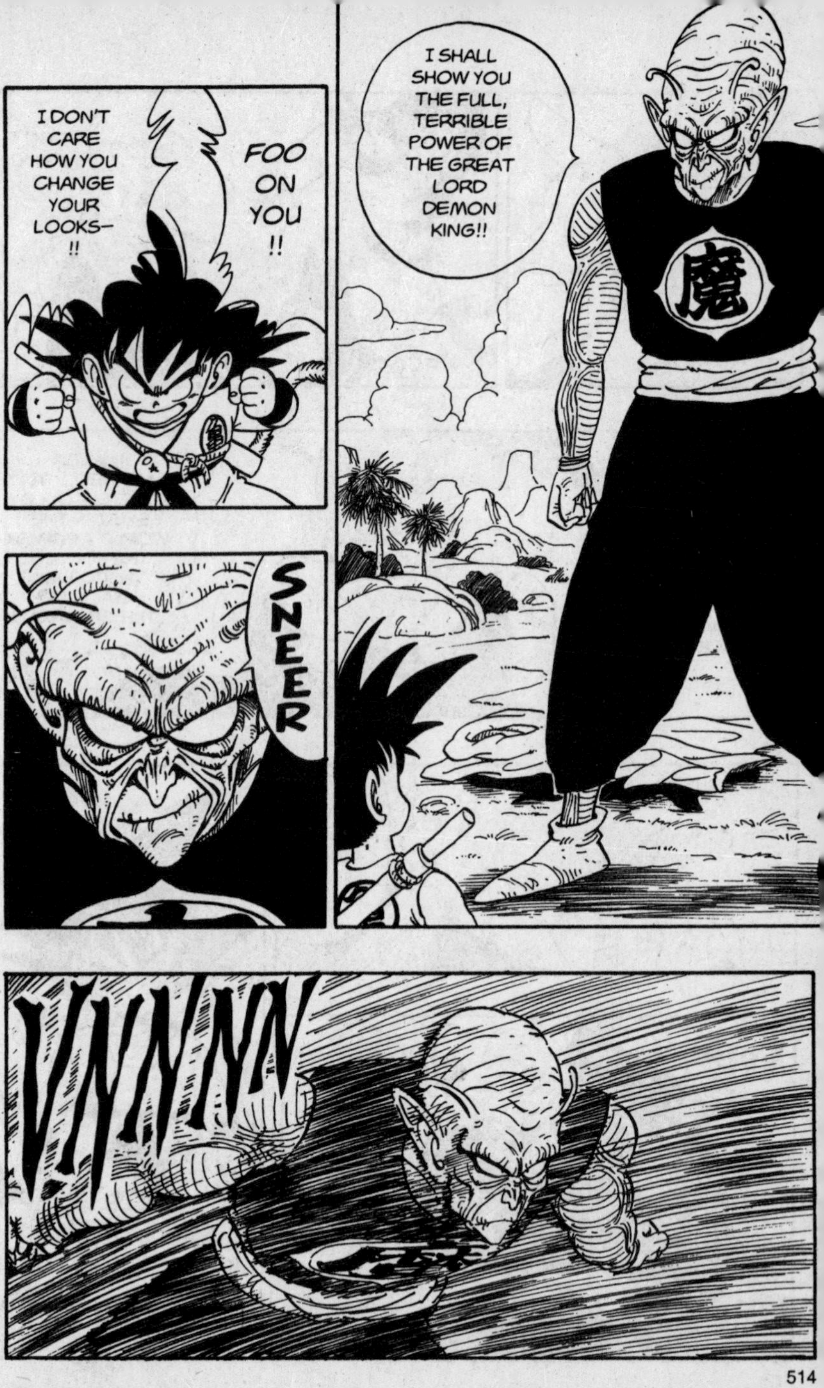
I SHALL SHOW YOU THE FULL, TERRIBLE POWER OF THE GREAT LORD DEMON KING!!
I DON'T CARE HOW YOU CHANGE YOUR LOOKS— !!
FOO ON YOU !!
SNEER
VNNNN

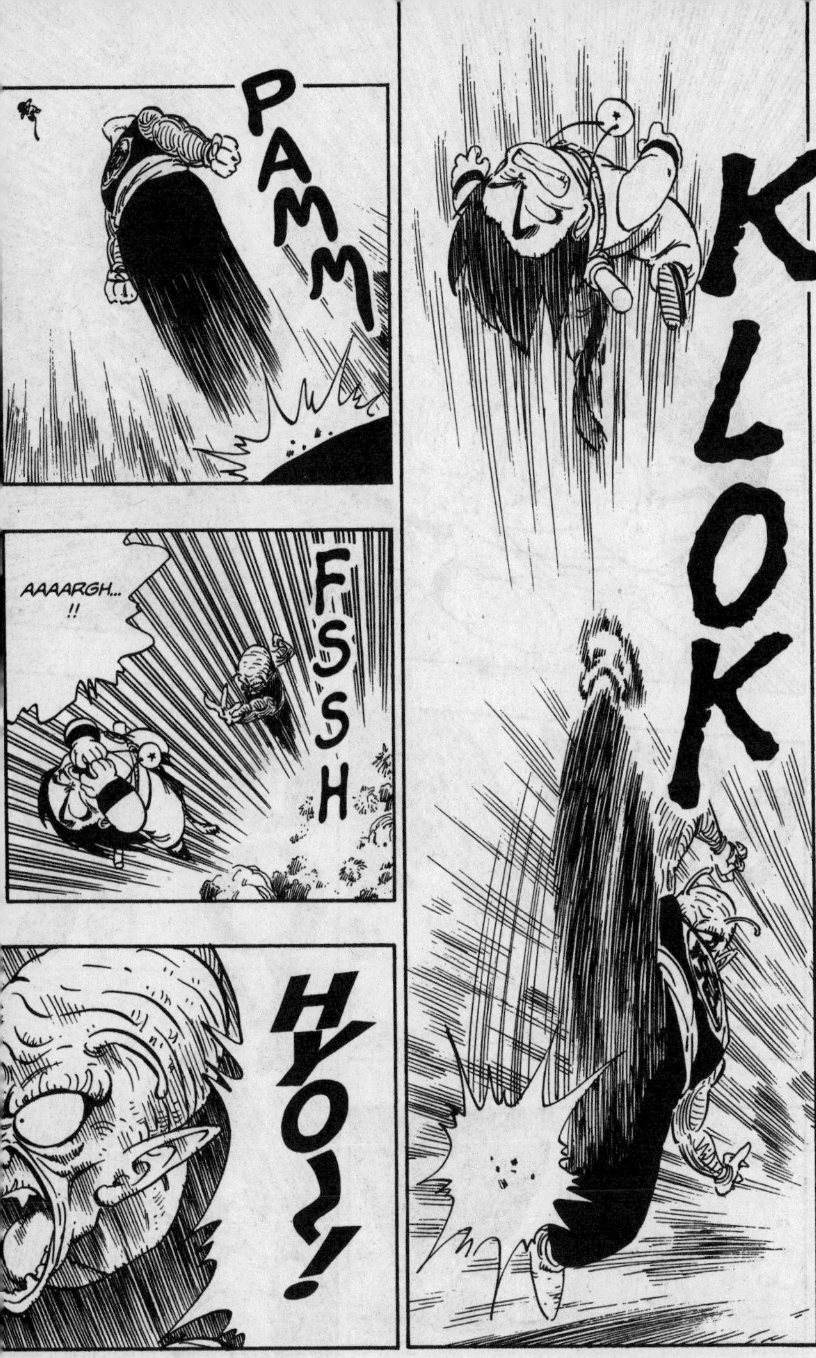
KLOK
PAMM
AAAARGH... !!
FSSH
HYO~!

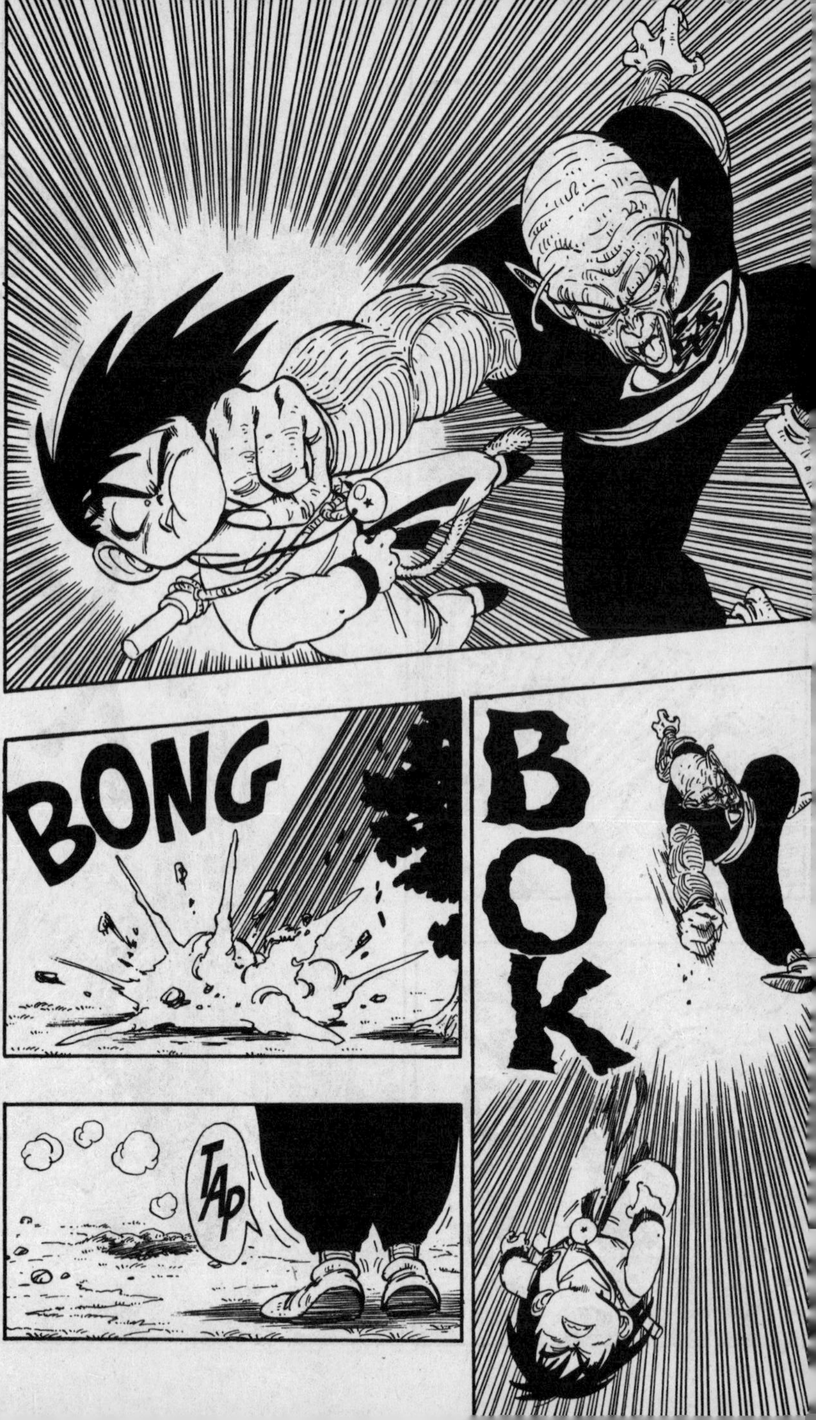
BOK
BONG
TAP

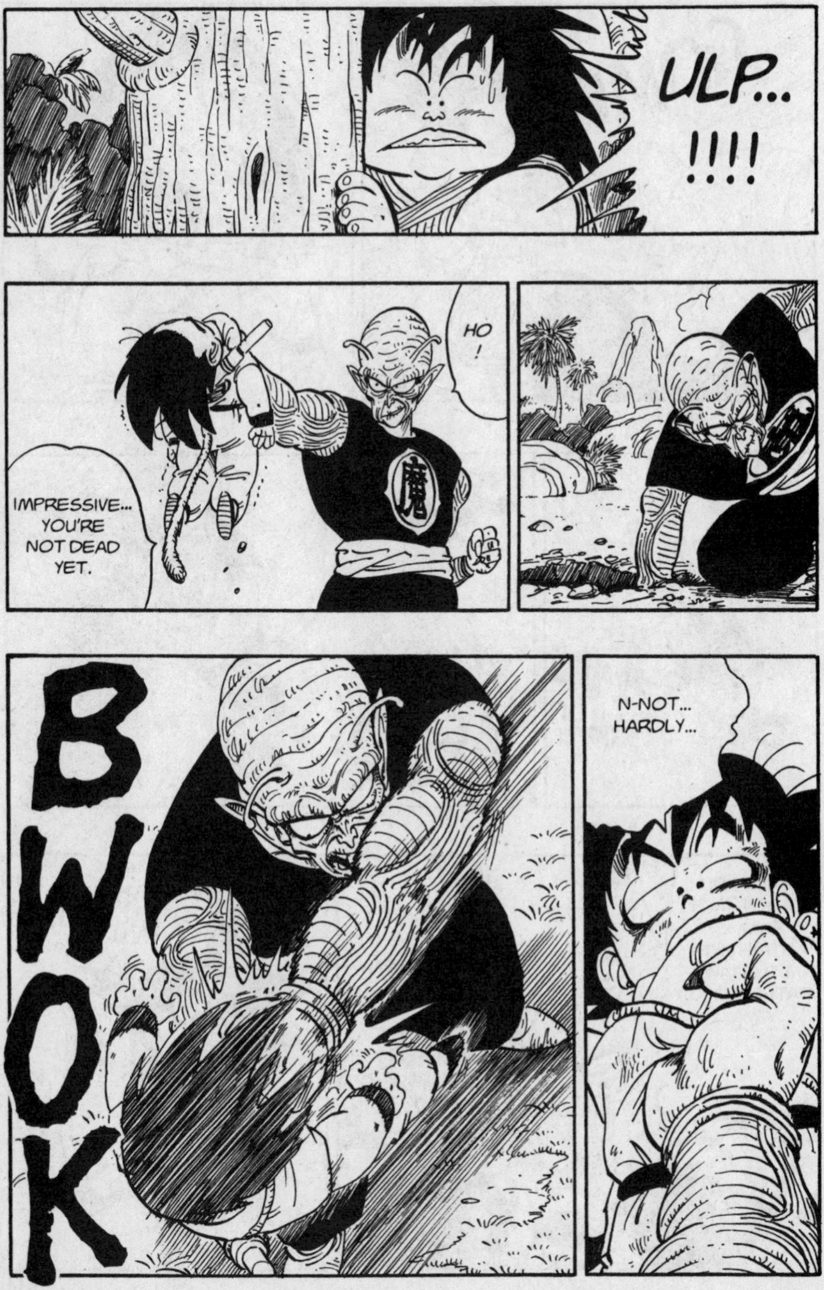
ULP...
!!!!
HO!
IMPRESSIVE... YOU'RE NOT DEAD YET.
N-NOT... HARDLY...
BWOK

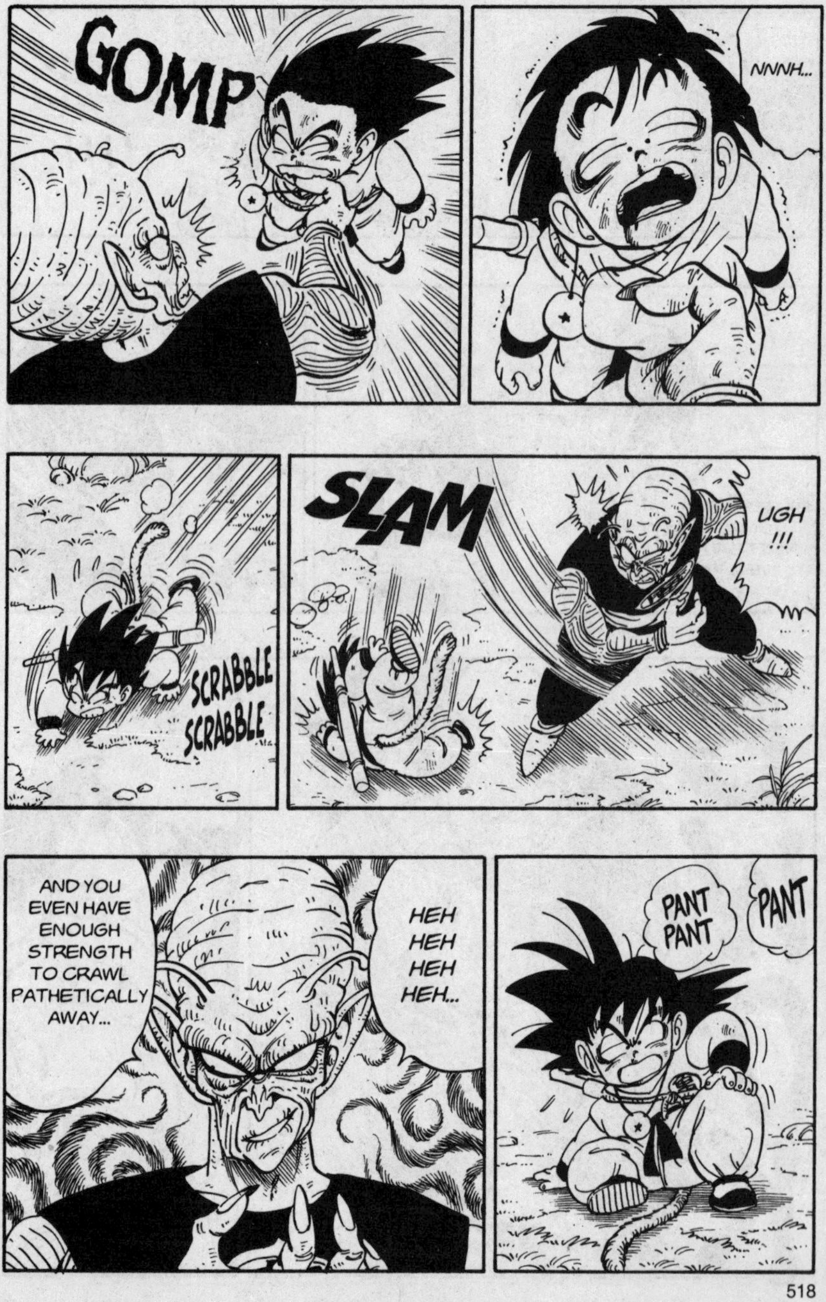
NNNH...
GOMP
UGH !!!
SLAM
SCRABBLE SCRABBLE
PANT
PANT PANT
HEH HEH HEH HEH...
AND YOU EVEN HAVE ENOUGH STRENGTH TO CRAWL PATHETICALLY AWAY...

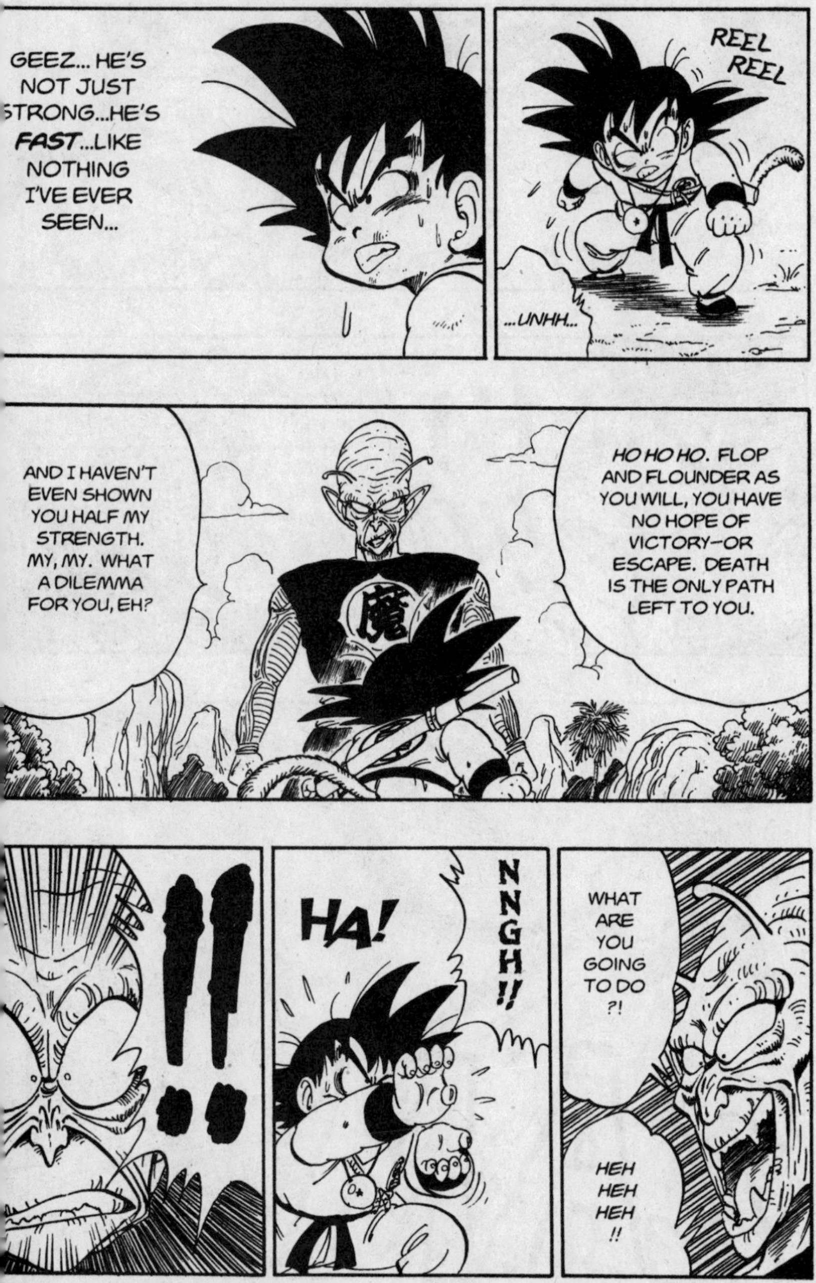
REEL REEL
...UNHH...
GEEZ... HE'S NOT JUST STRONG...HE'S ***FAST***...LIKE NOTHING I'VE EVER SEEN...
HO HO HO. FLOP AND FLOUNDER AS YOU WILL, YOU HAVE NO HOPE OF VICTORY—OR ESCAPE. DEATH IS THE ONLY PATH LEFT TO YOU.
AND I HAVEN'T EVEN SHOWN YOU HALF MY STRENGTH. MY, MY. WHAT A DILEMMA FOR YOU, EH?
WHAT ARE YOU GOING TO DO ?!
HEH HEH HEH !!
NNGH!!
HA!
!!

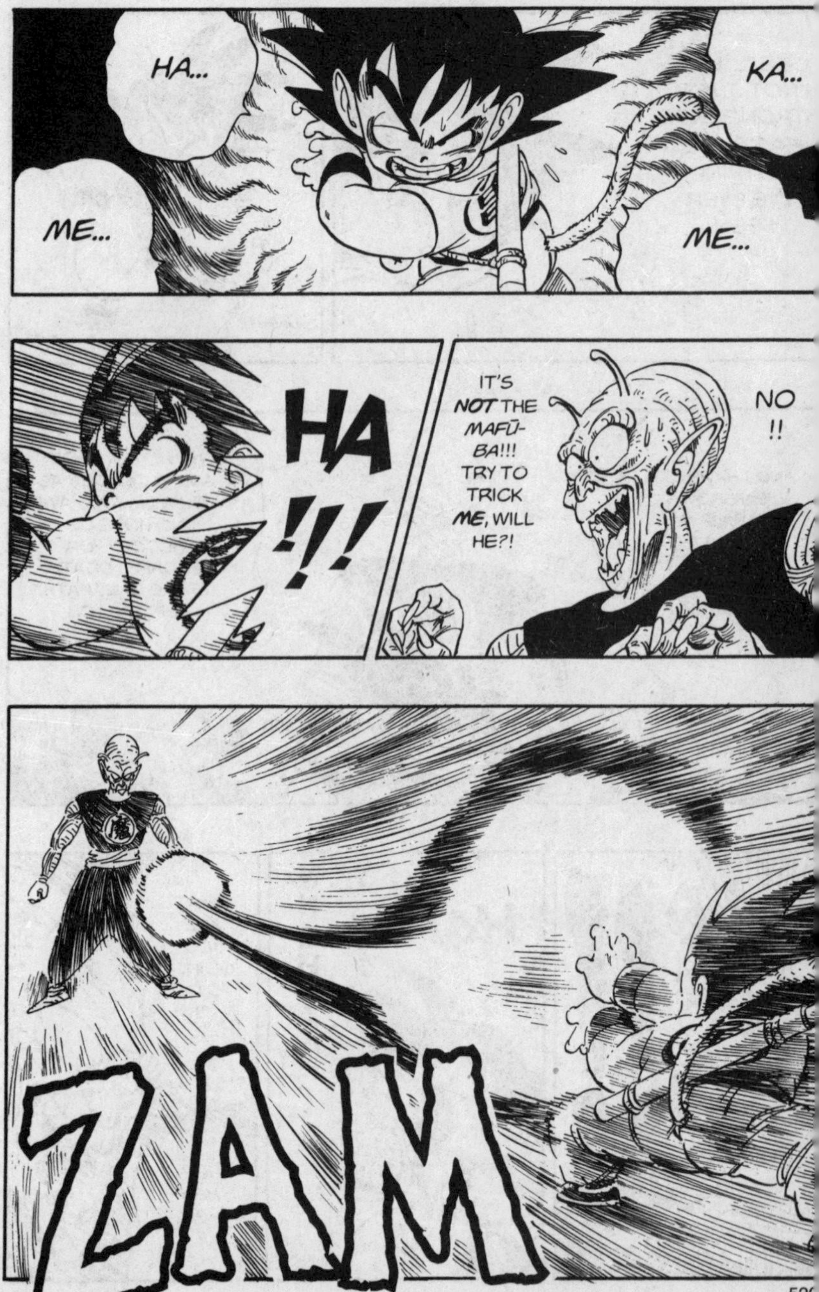
KA...
ME...
HA...
ME...
NO !!
IT'S *NOT* THE *MAFŪBA*!!! TRY TO TRICK *ME*, WILL HE?!
HA !!!
ZAM

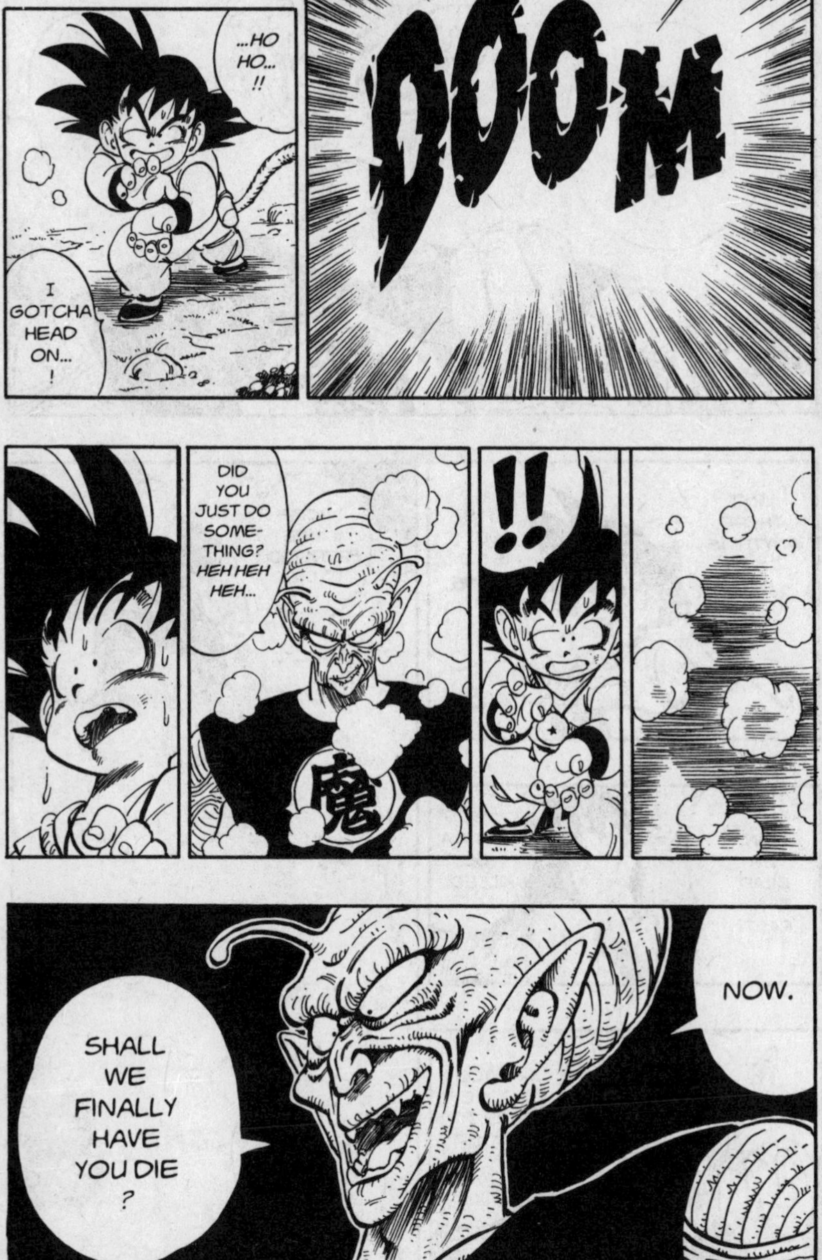
DOOM
...HO HO... !!
I GOTCHA HEAD ON... !
!!
DID YOU JUST DO SOMETHING? HEH HEH HEH...
NOW.
SHALL WE FINALLY HAVE YOU DIE ?

Tale 144 • Goku...Loses?

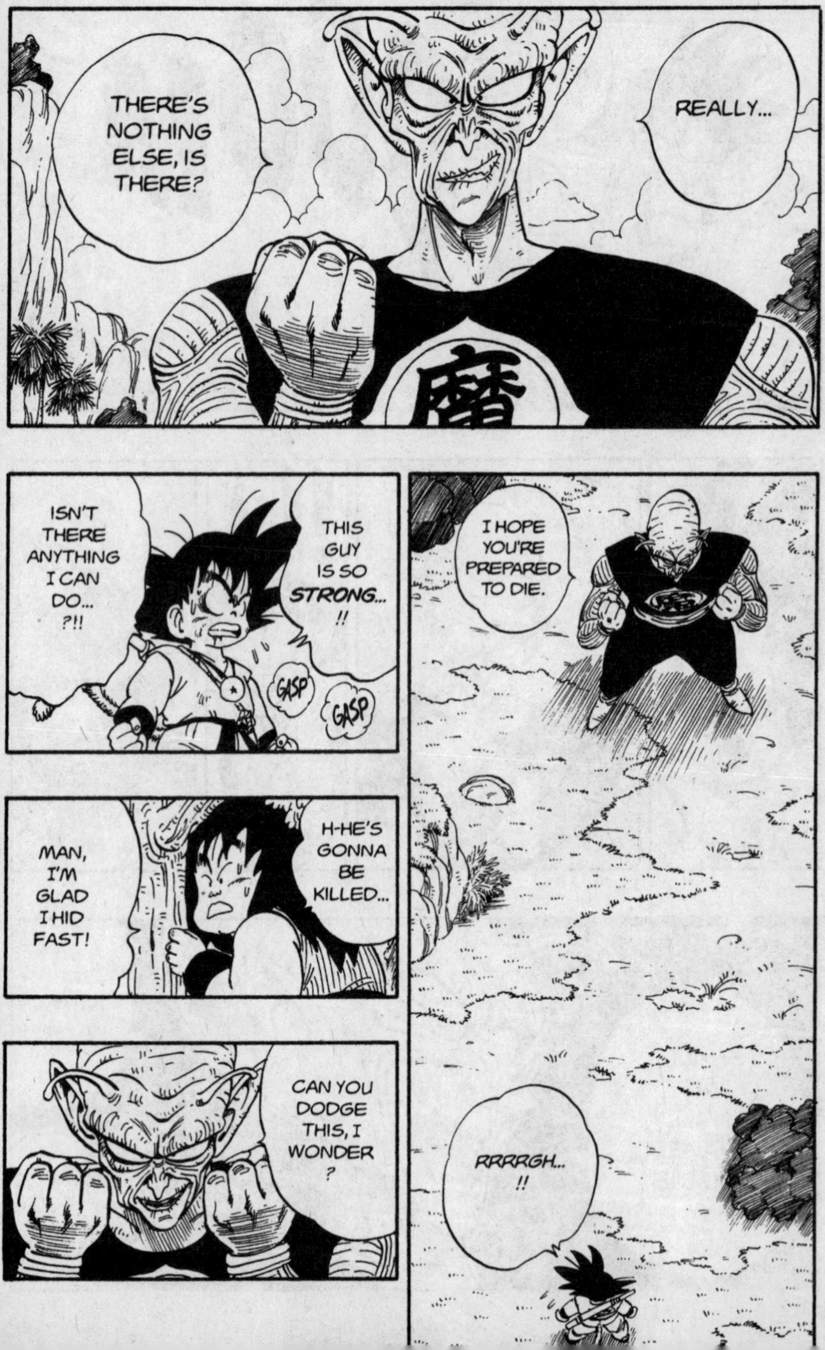
REALLY...
THERE'S NOTHING ELSE, IS THERE?
I HOPE YOU'RE PREPARED TO DIE.
RRRRGH... !!
THIS GUY IS SO *STRONG...* !!
ISN'T THERE ANYTHING I CAN DO... ?!!
GASP
GASP
H-HE'S GONNA BE KILLED...
MAN, I'M GLAD I HID FAST!
CAN YOU DODGE THIS, I WONDER ?

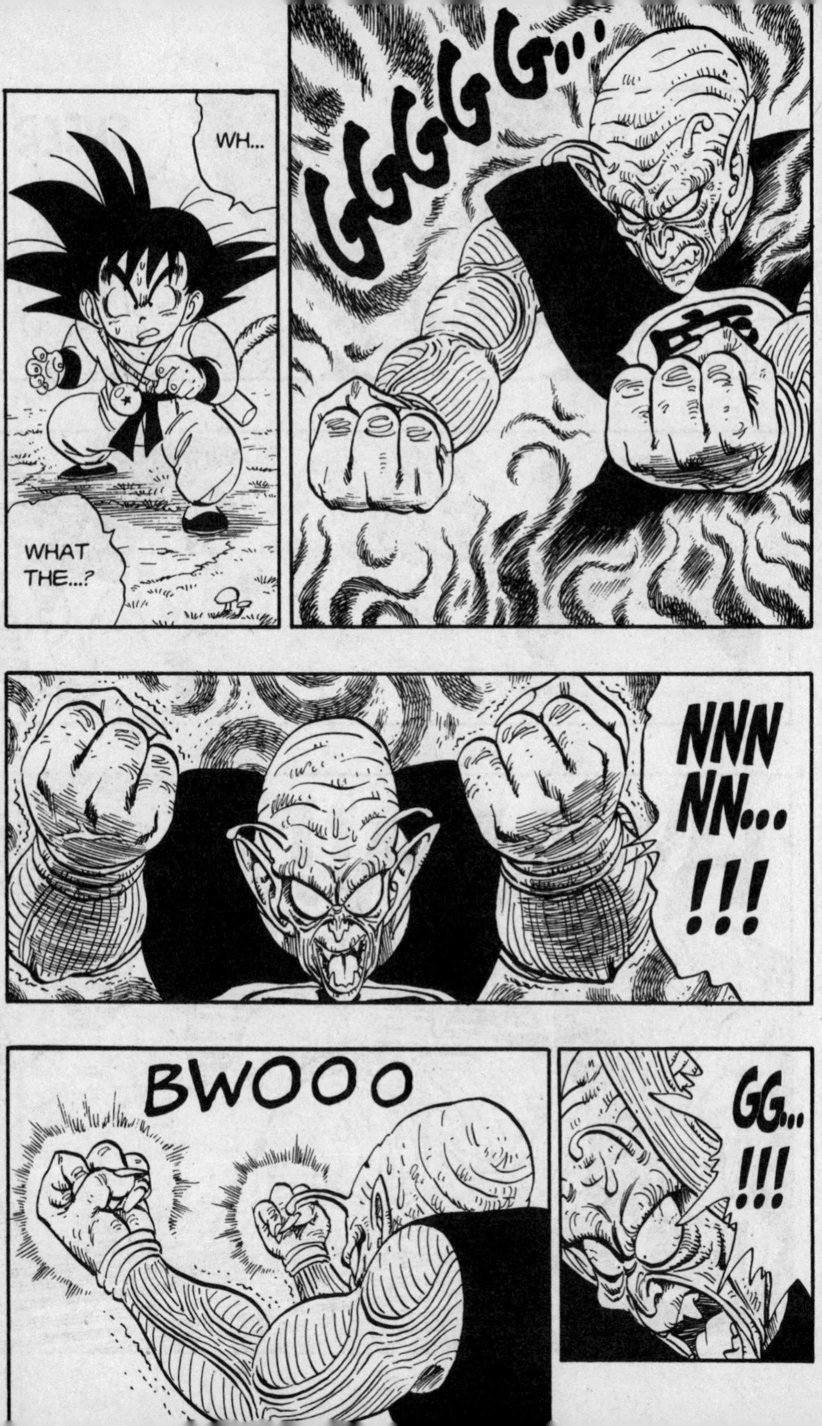
GGGG...
WH...
WHAT THE...?
NNN NN...!!!
GG...!!!
BWOOO

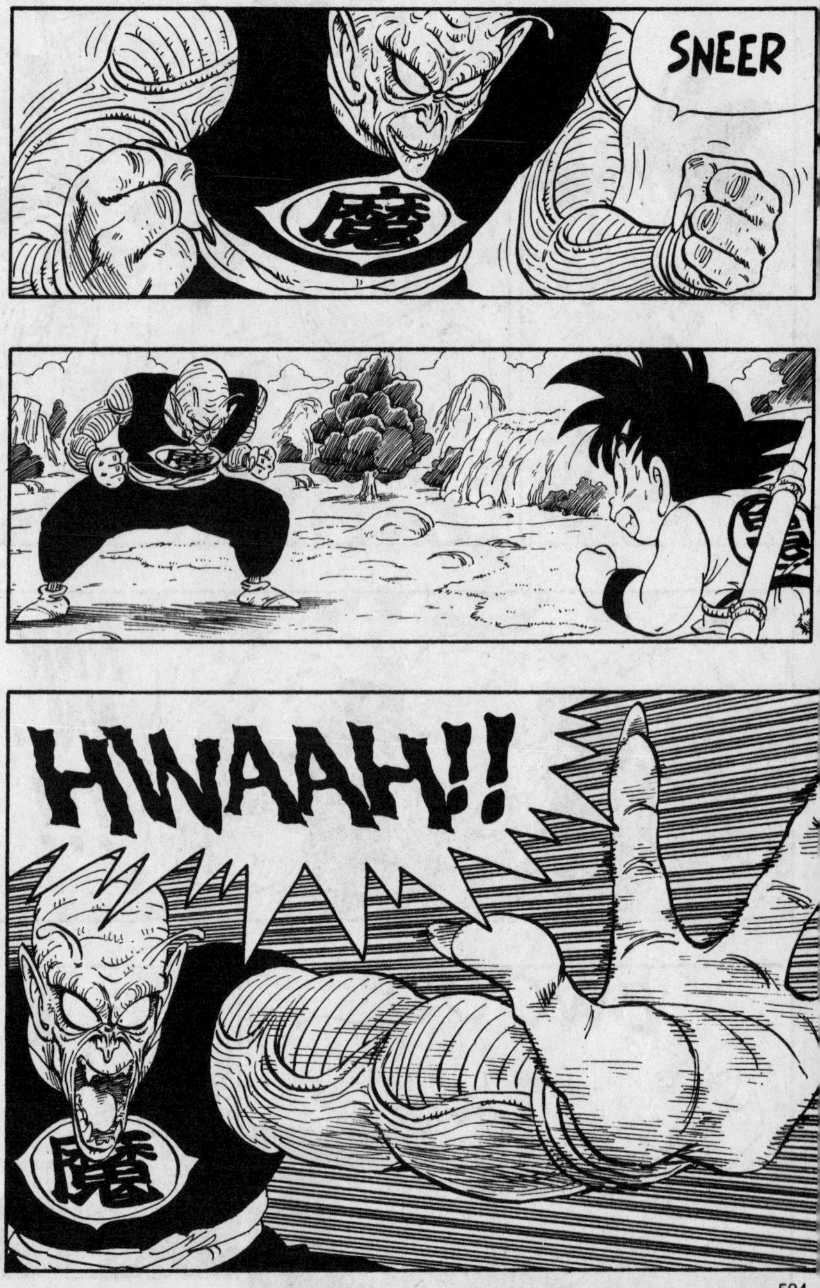
SNEER
HWAAH!!

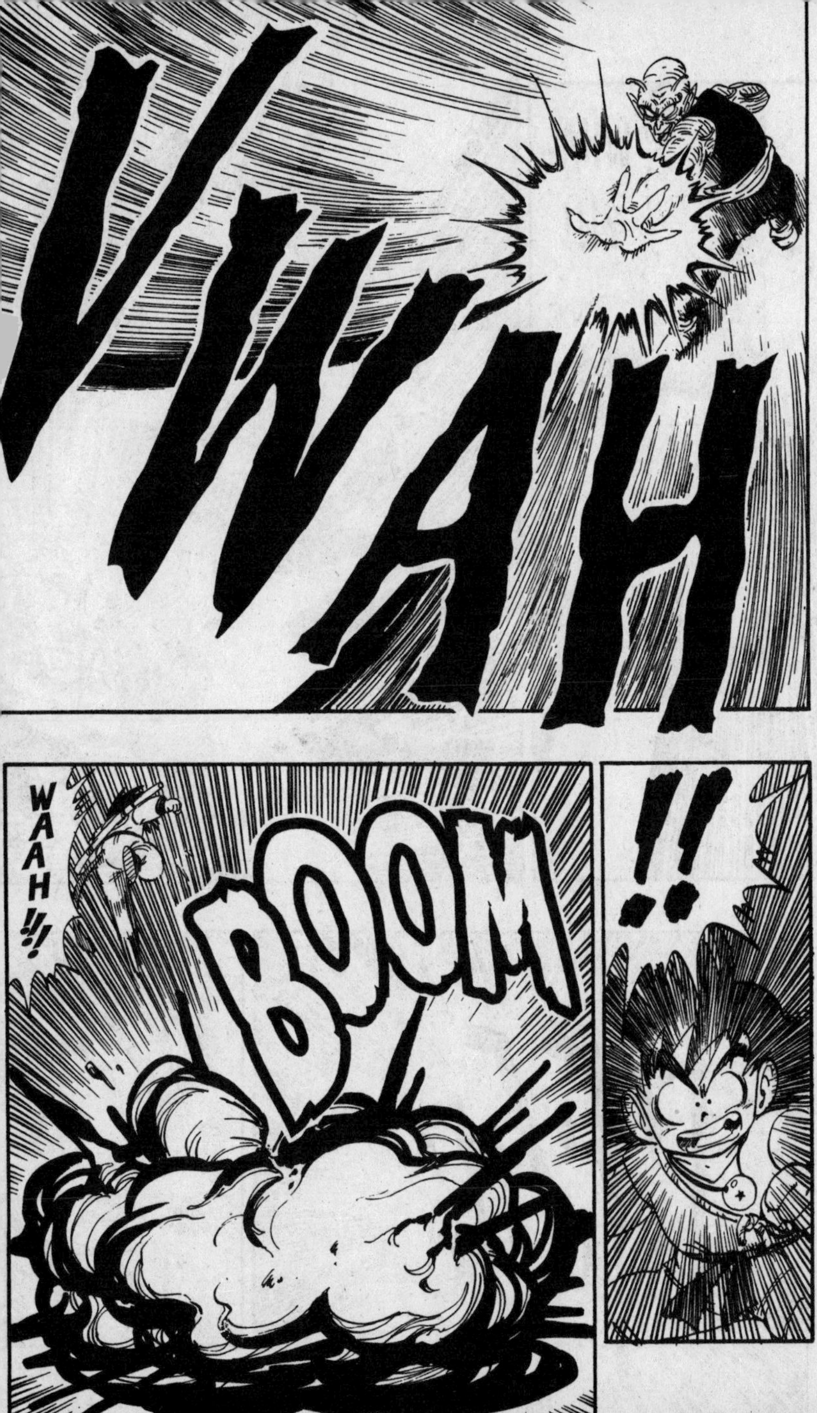
WAAH
!!
WAAH!!!
BOOM

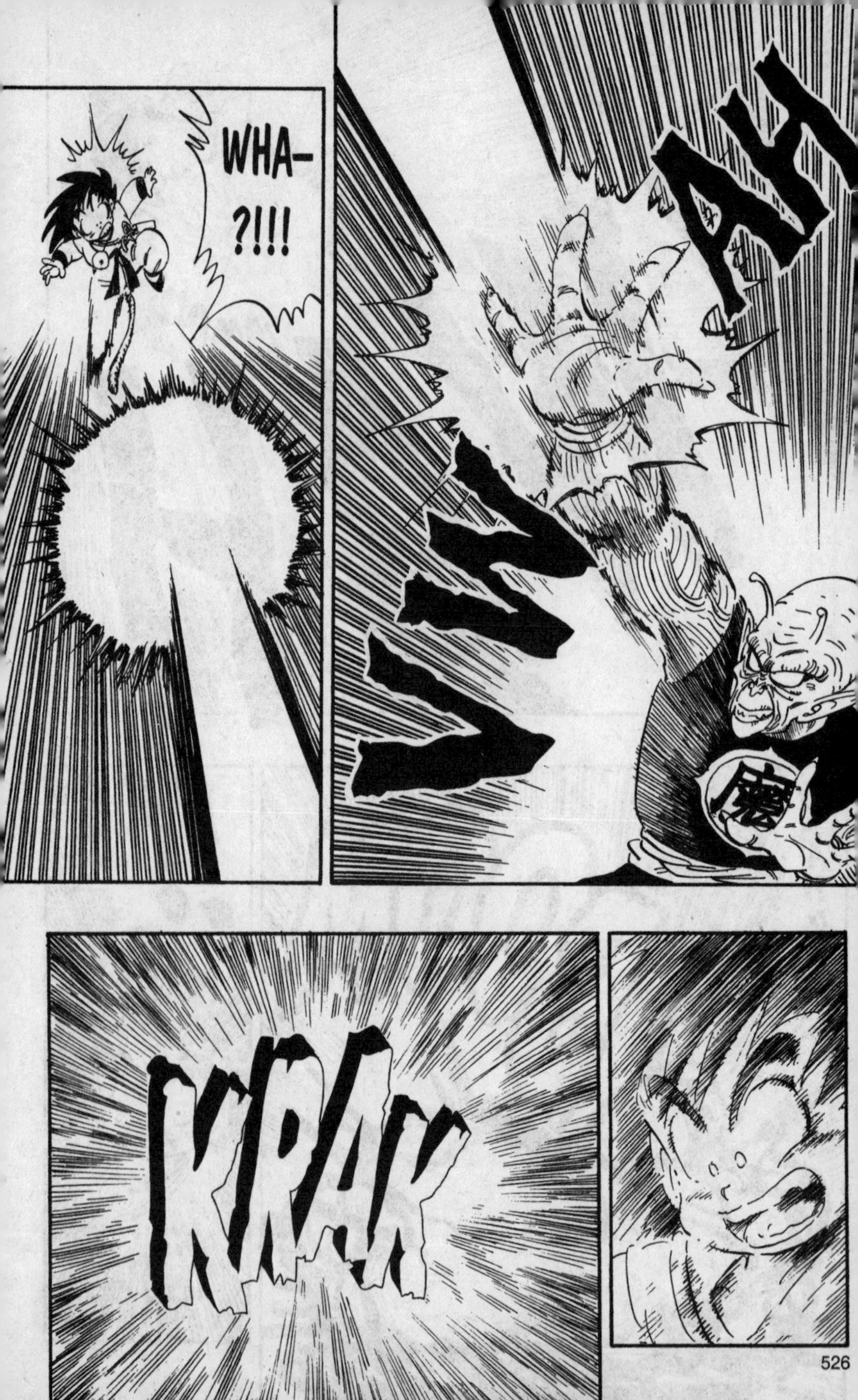
AH
WHA- ?!!!
KRAK

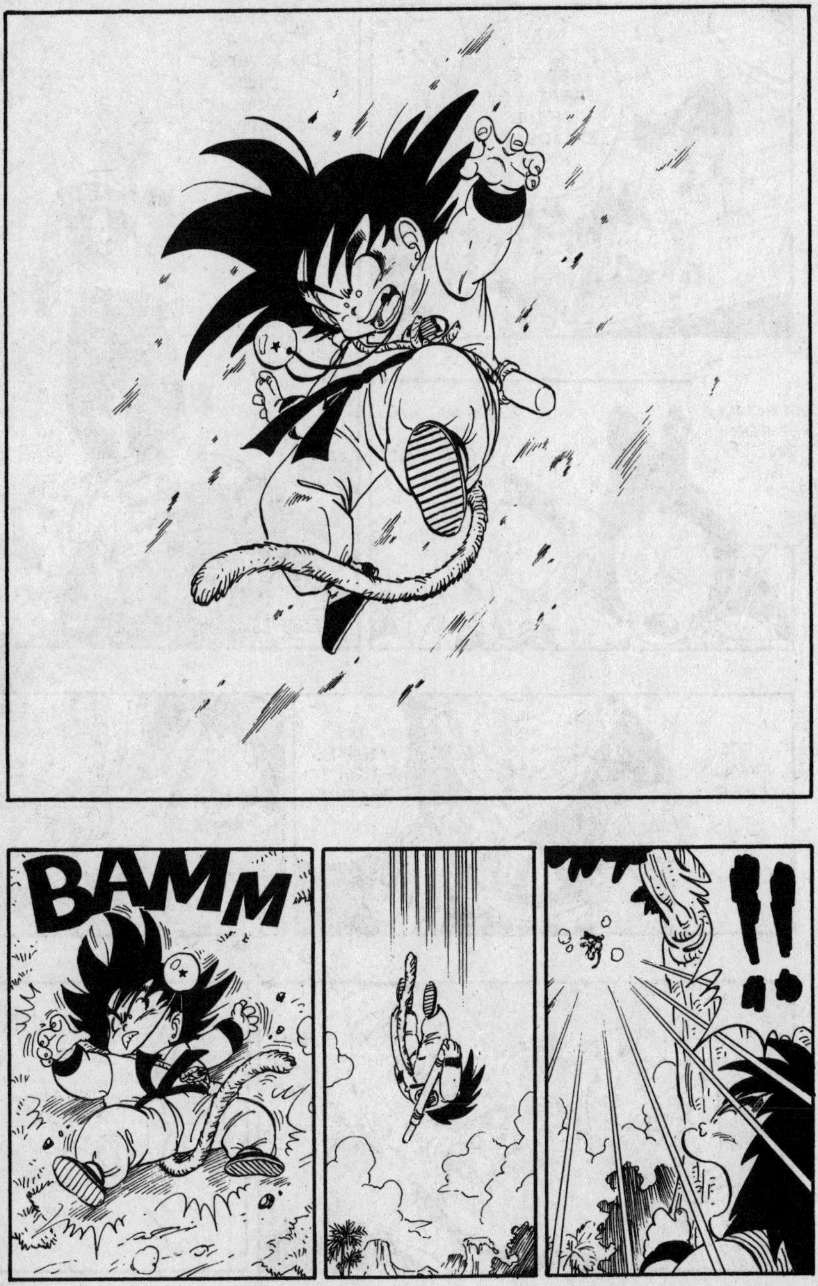
!!
BAMM

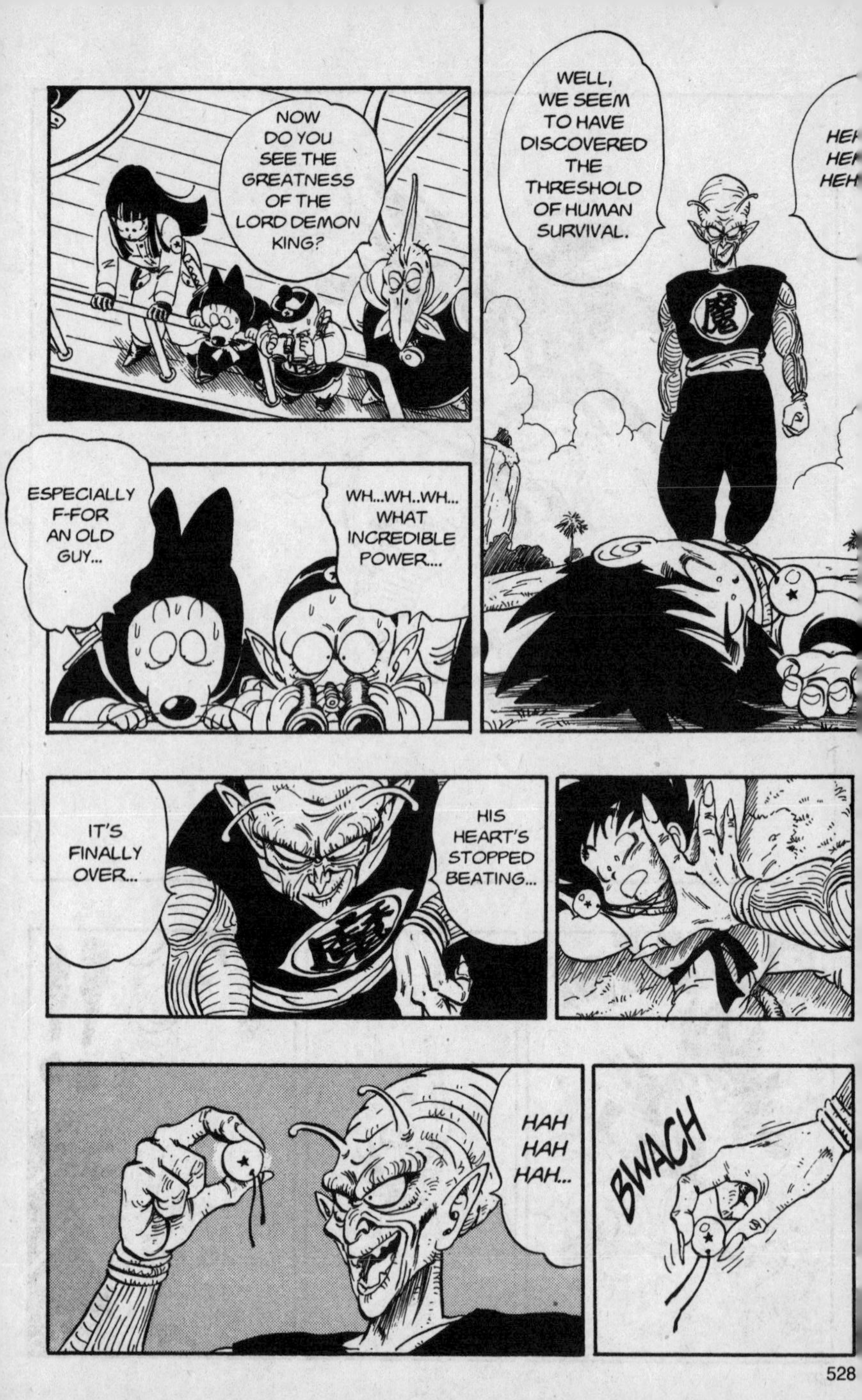
HE HE HEH
WELL, WE SEEM TO HAVE DISCOVERED THE THRESHOLD OF HUMAN SURVIVAL.
NOW DO YOU SEE THE GREATNESS OF THE LORD DEMON KING?
WH...WH..WH... WHAT INCREDIBLE POWER...
ESPECIALLY F-FOR AN OLD GUY...
HIS HEART'S STOPPED BEATING...
IT'S FINALLY OVER...
BWACH
HAH HAH HAH...

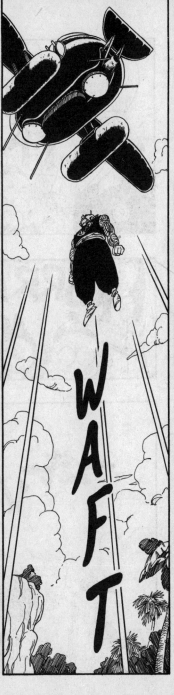

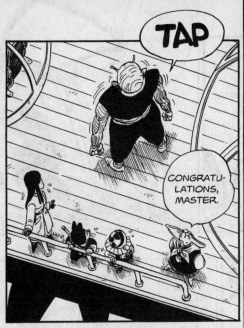

WAFT
TAP
CONGRATULATIONS, MASTER.
YOU DID MENTION THAT SOME GROUP WAS GATHERING THE REMAINING DRAGON BALLS, DID YOU NOT?
LET'S GO TAKE THEM!
THE REJUVENATION OF THE LORD PICCOLO IS NOW ONLY A MATTER OF TIME!

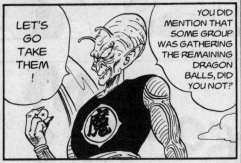

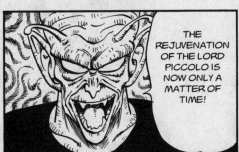

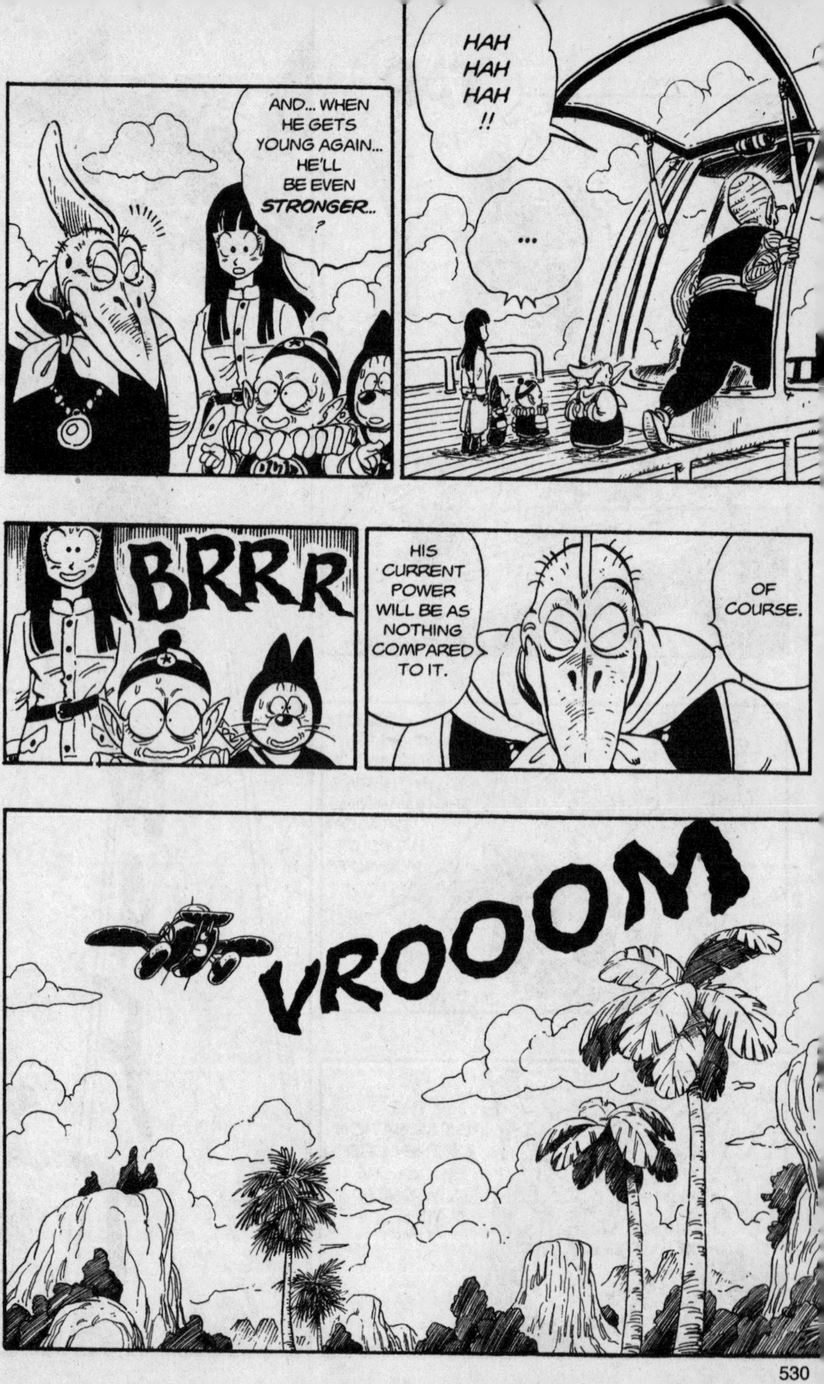

HAH HAH HAH !!
...
AND... WHEN HE GETS YOUNG AGAIN... HE'LL BE EVEN STRONGER... ?
OF COURSE.
HIS CURRENT POWER WILL BE AS NOTHING COMPARED TO IT.
BRRR
VROOOM

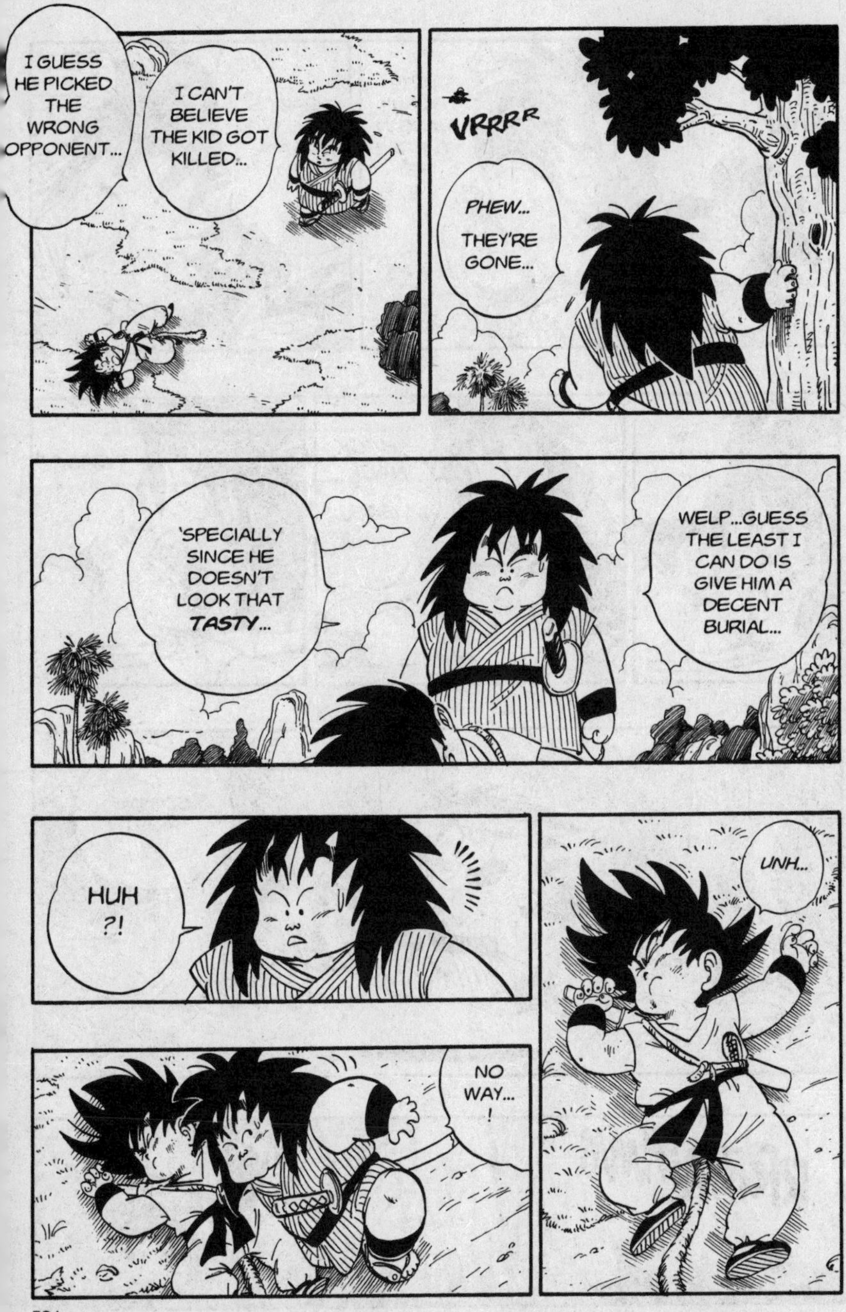
VRRRR
PHEW... THEY'RE GONE...
I CAN'T BELIEVE THE KID GOT KILLED...
I GUESS HE PICKED THE WRONG OPPONENT...
WELP...GUESS THE LEAST I CAN DO IS GIVE HIM A DECENT BURIAL...
'SPECIALLY SINCE HE DOESN'T LOOK THAT *TASTY*...
UNH...
HUH ?!
NO WAY... !

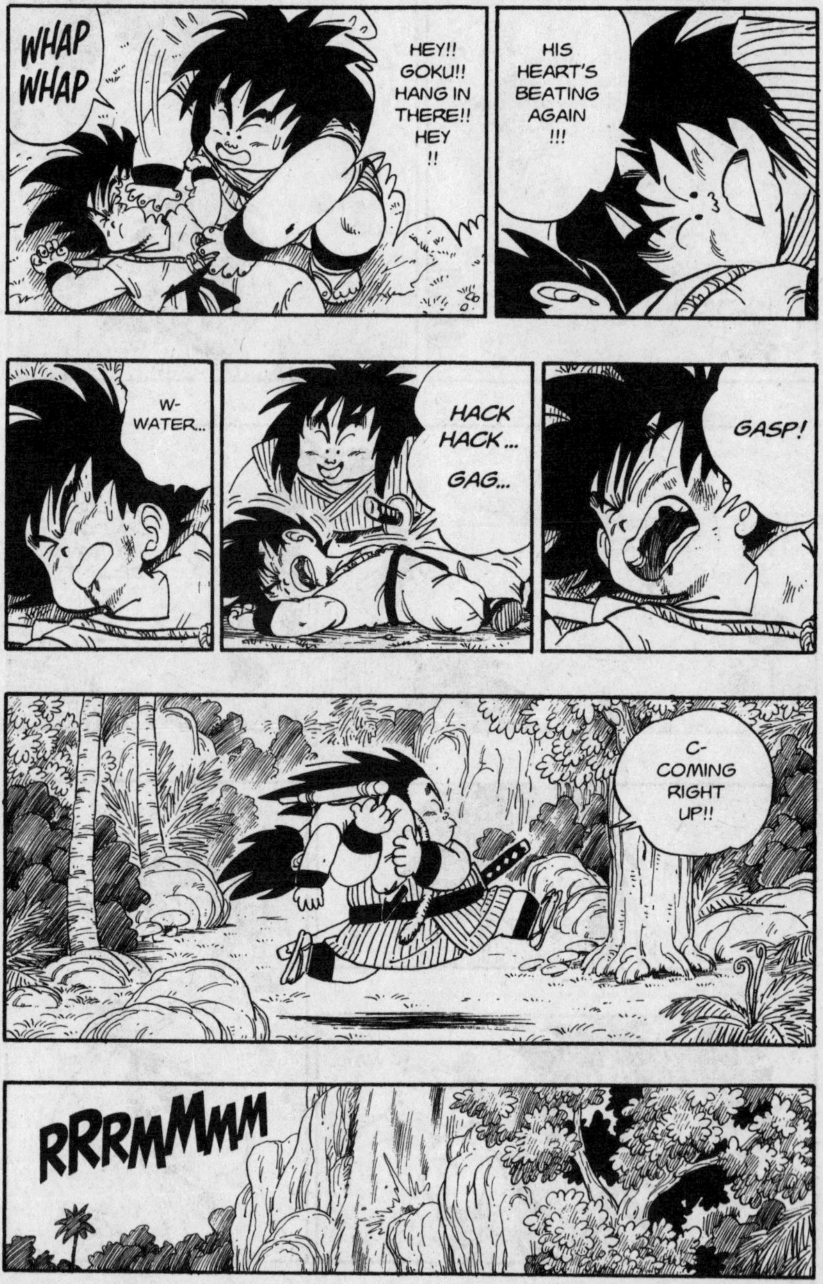
HIS HEART'S BEATING AGAIN !!!
HEY!! GOKU!! HANG IN THERE!! HEY !!
WHAP WHAP
GASP!
HACK HACK... GAG...
W-WATER..
C-COMING RIGHT UP!!
RRRMMMM

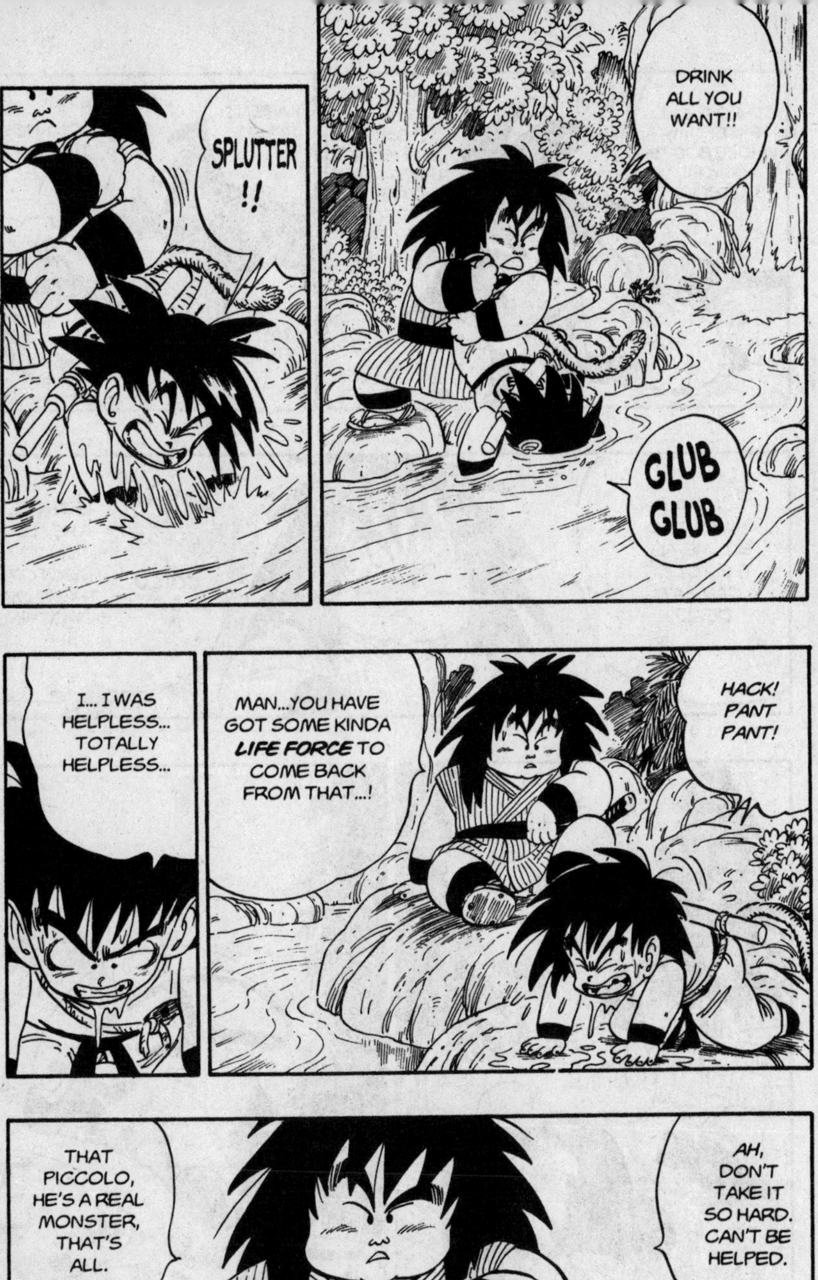
DRINK ALL YOU WANT!!
GLUB GLUB
SPLUTTER !!
HACK! PANT PANT!
MAN...YOU HAVE GOT SOME KINDA LIFE FORCE TO COME BACK FROM THAT...!
I... I WAS HELPLESS... TOTALLY HELPLESS...
AH, DON'T TAKE IT SO HARD. CAN'T BE HELPED.
THAT PICCOLO, HE'S A REAL MONSTER, THAT'S ALL.

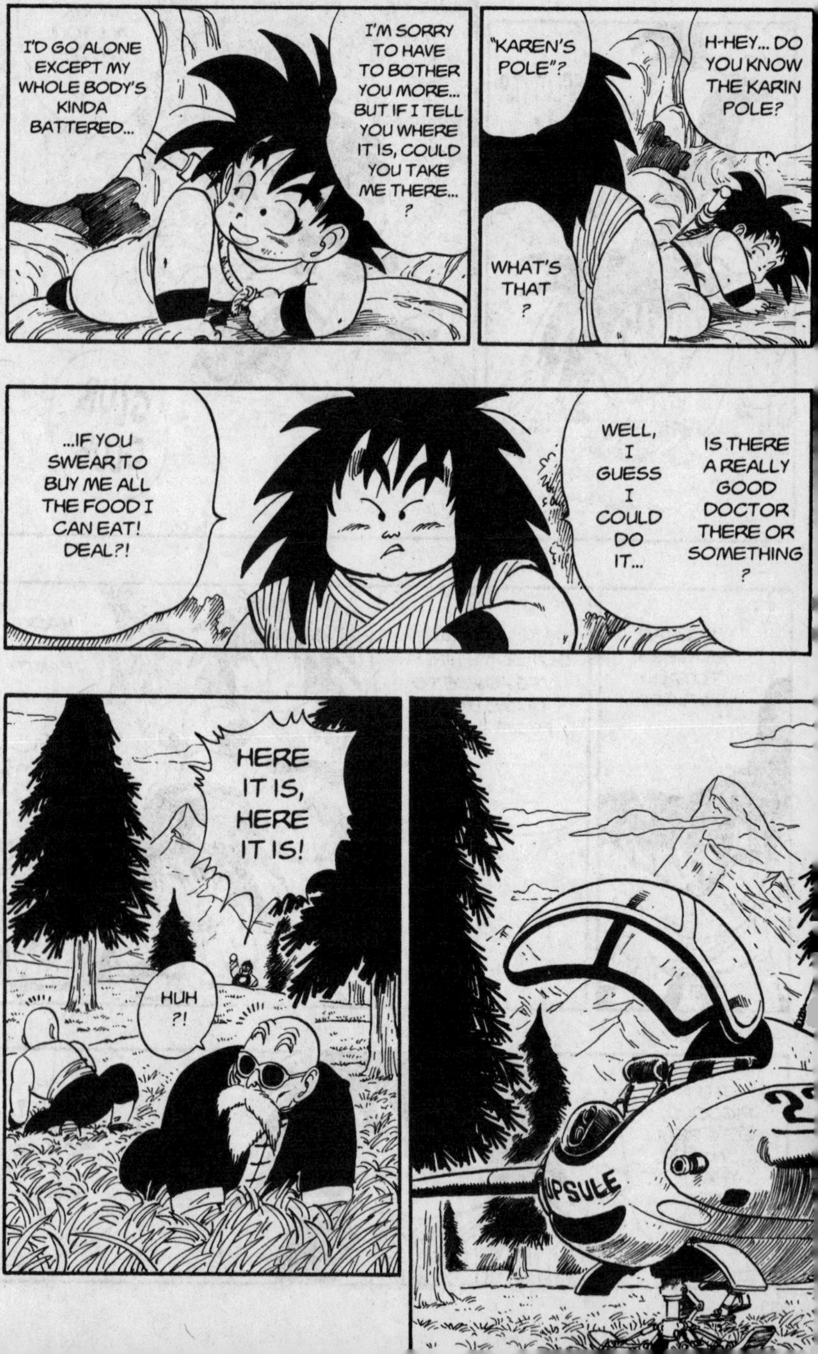
H-HEY... DO YOU KNOW THE KARIN POLE?
"KAREN'S POLE"?
WHAT'S THAT ?
I'M SORRY TO HAVE TO BOTHER YOU MORE... BUT IF I TELL YOU WHERE IT IS, COULD YOU TAKE ME THERE... ?
I'D GO ALONE EXCEPT MY WHOLE BODY'S KINDA BATTERED...
IS THERE A REALLY GOOD DOCTOR THERE OR SOMETHING ?
WELL, I GUESS I COULD DO IT...
...IF YOU SWEAR TO BUY ME ALL THE FOOD I CAN EAT! DEAL?!
UPSULE
HERE IT IS, HERE IT IS!
HUH ?!

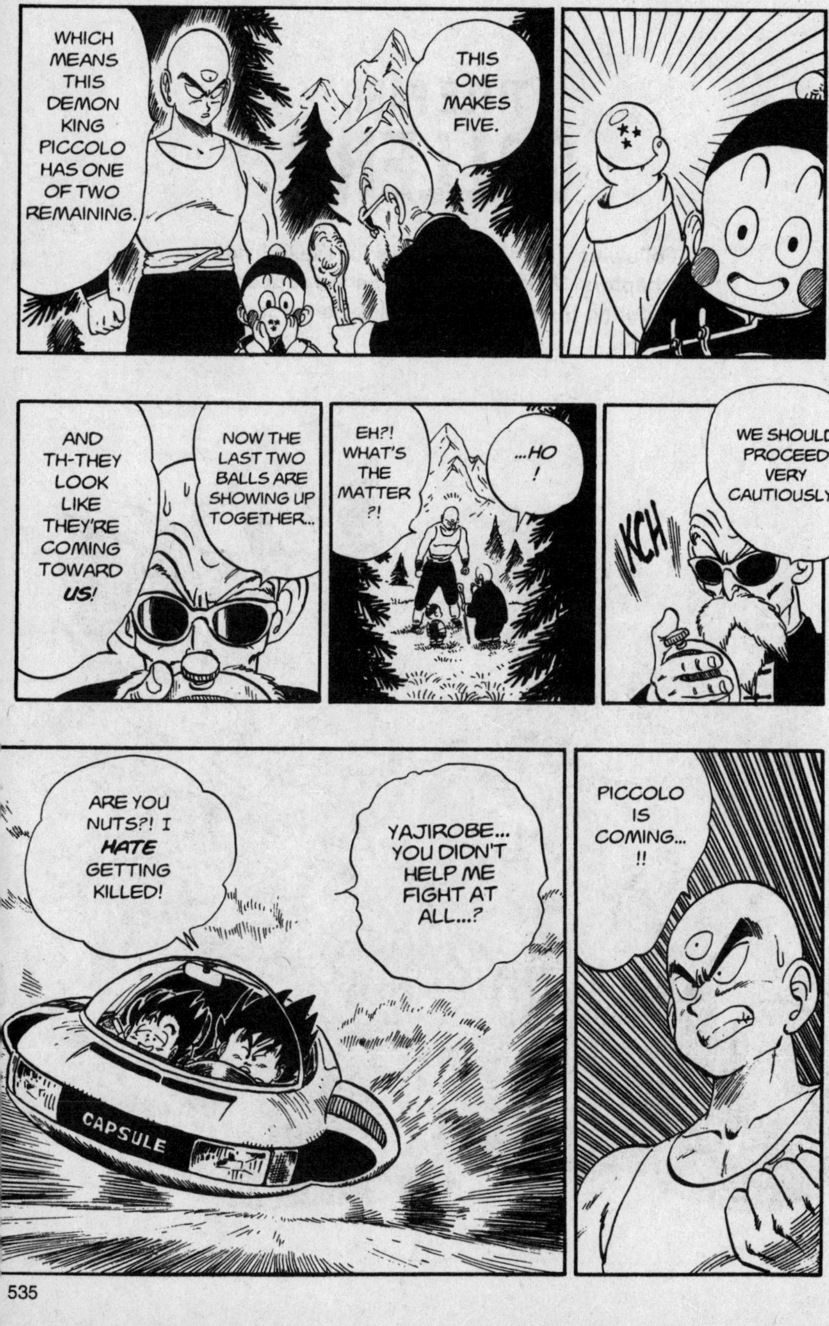
THIS ONE MAKES FIVE.
WHICH MEANS THIS DEMON KING PICCOLO HAS ONE OF TWO REMAINING.
WE SHOULD PROCEED VERY CAUTIOUSLY...
KCH
...HO!
EH?! WHAT'S THE MATTER?!
NOW THE LAST TWO BALLS ARE SHOWING UP TOGETHER...
AND TH-THEY LOOK LIKE THEY'RE COMING TOWARD *US*!
PICCOLO IS COMING... !!
YAJIROBE... YOU DIDN'T HELP ME FIGHT AT ALL...?
ARE YOU NUTS?! I *HATE* GETTING KILLED!
CAPSULE

TITLE PAGE GALLERY

Following are the title pages for the individual chapters. Most of them are as they appeared during their original serialization in Japan.

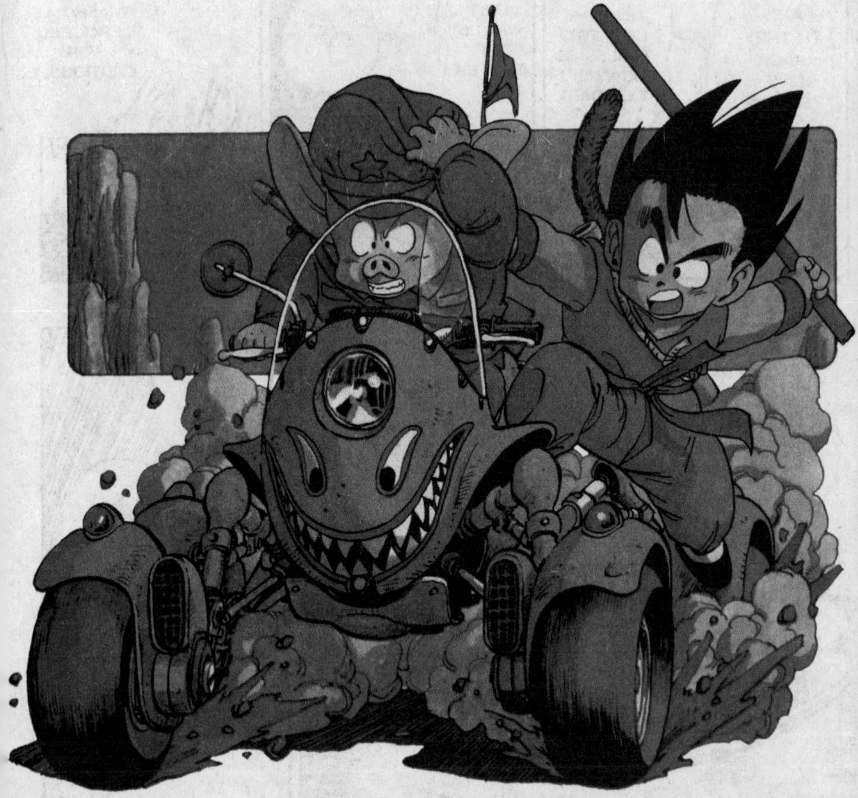

Tale 109 · A Second Helping of Pilaf

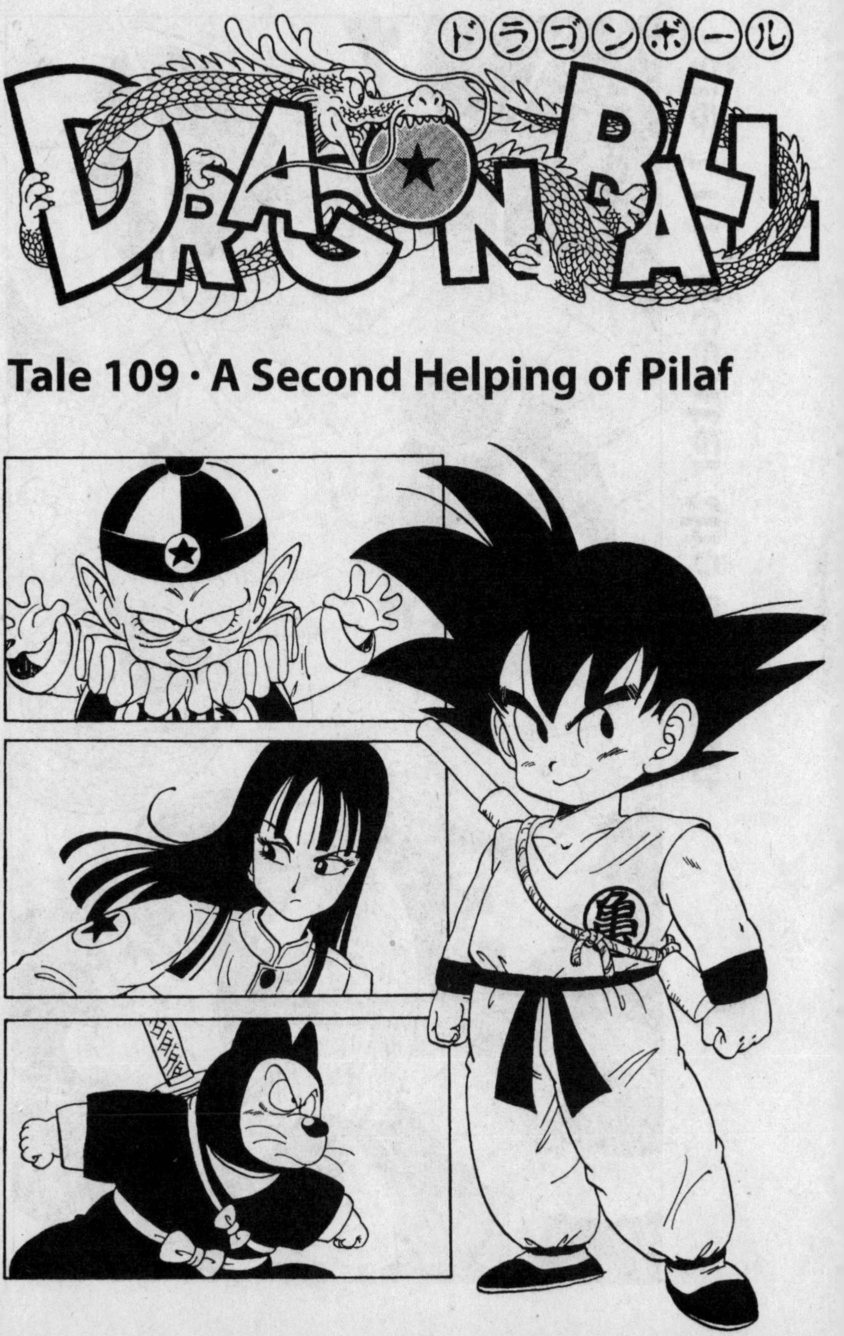

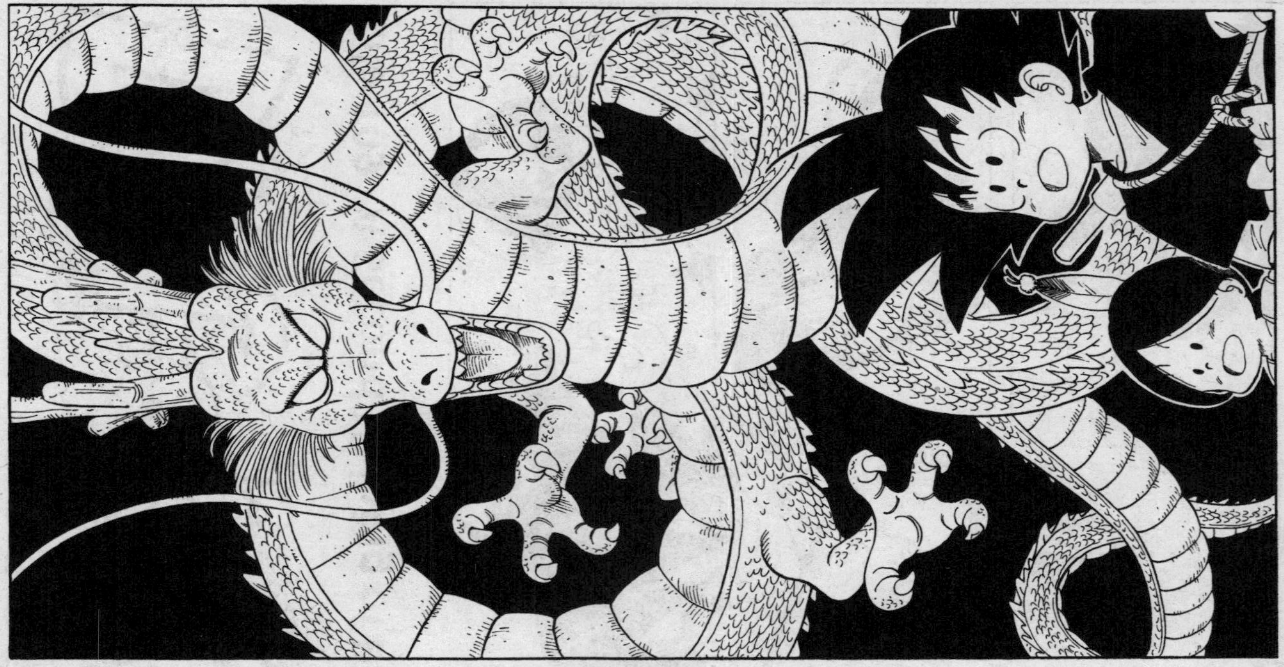

Tale 111 · Reenter the Dragon

Tale 114 · The Qualifying Round

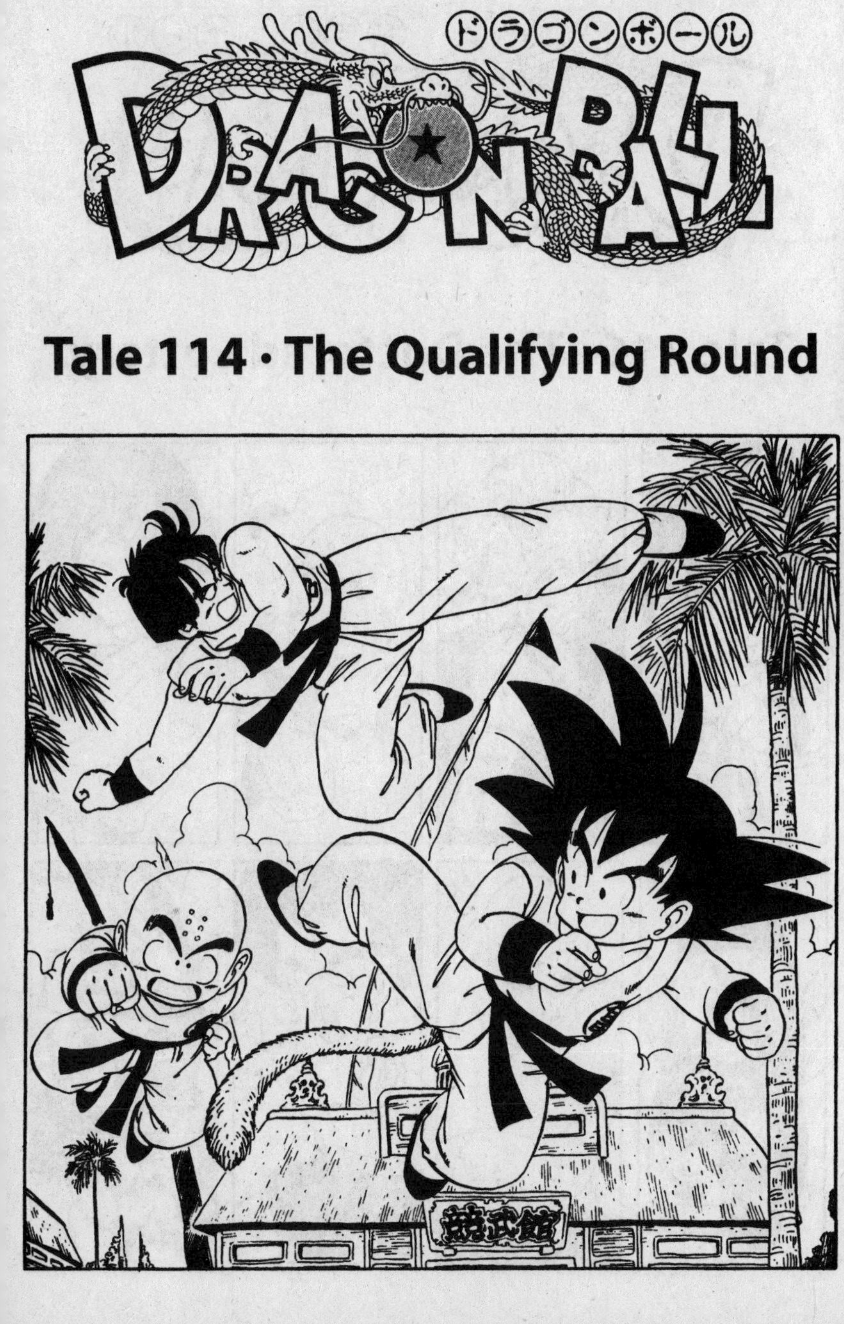

ドラゴンボール

DRAGON BALL

Tale 116 · The Doctored Lottery

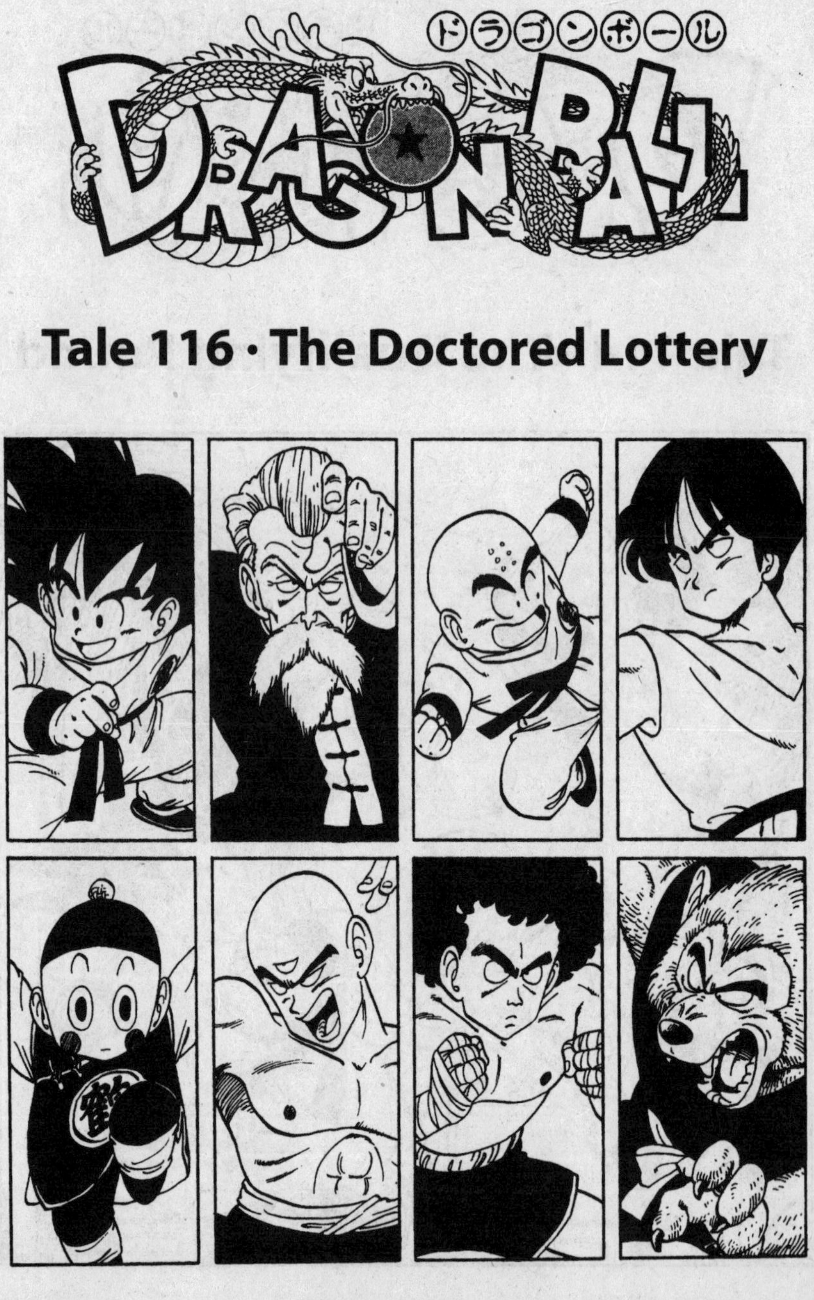

ドラゴンボール

DRAGON BALL

Tale 117 • Yamcha's Kamehameha!

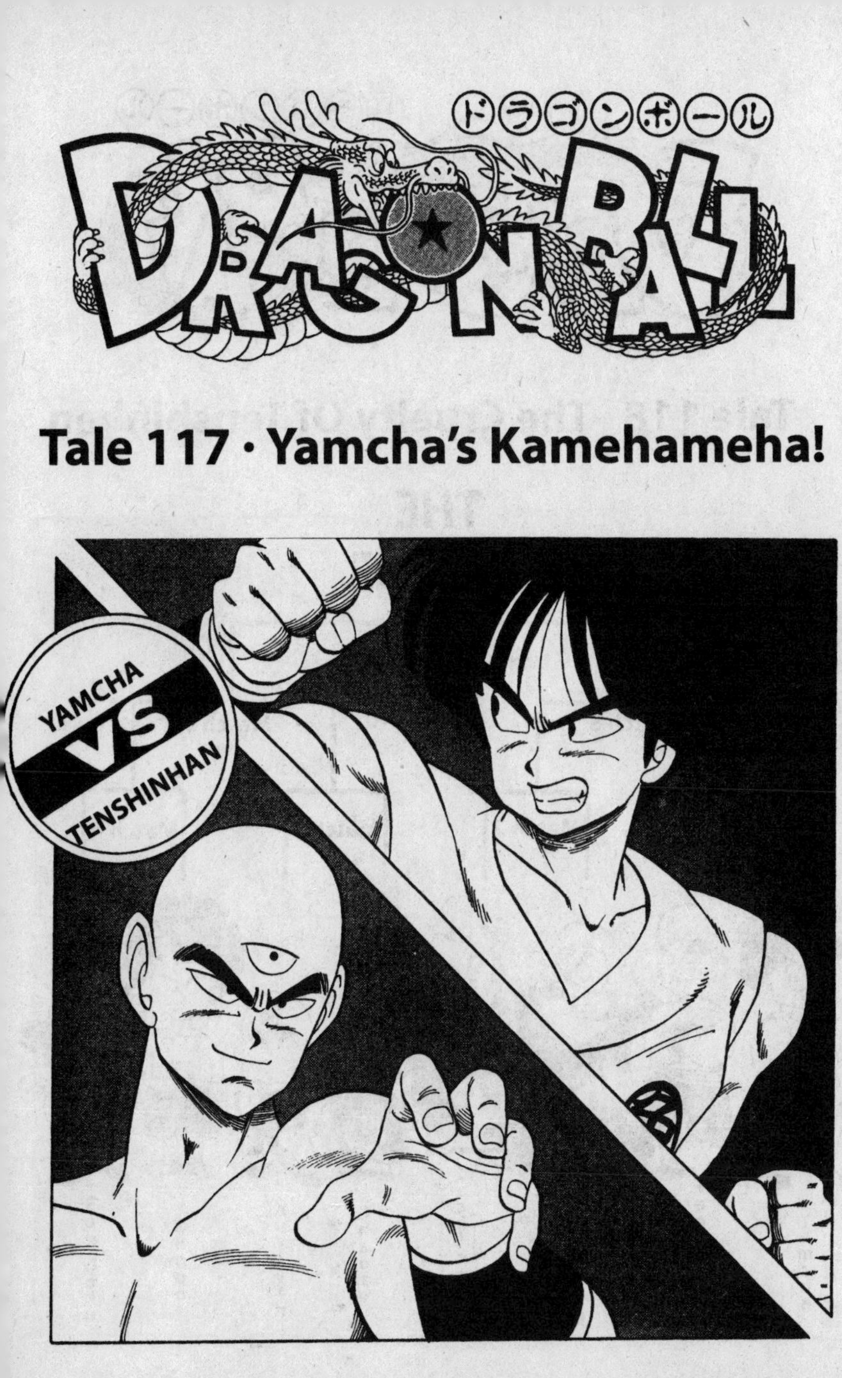
YAMCHA
VS
TENSHINHAN

ドラゴンボール

DRAGON BALL

Tale 118 • The Cruelty Of Tenshinhan

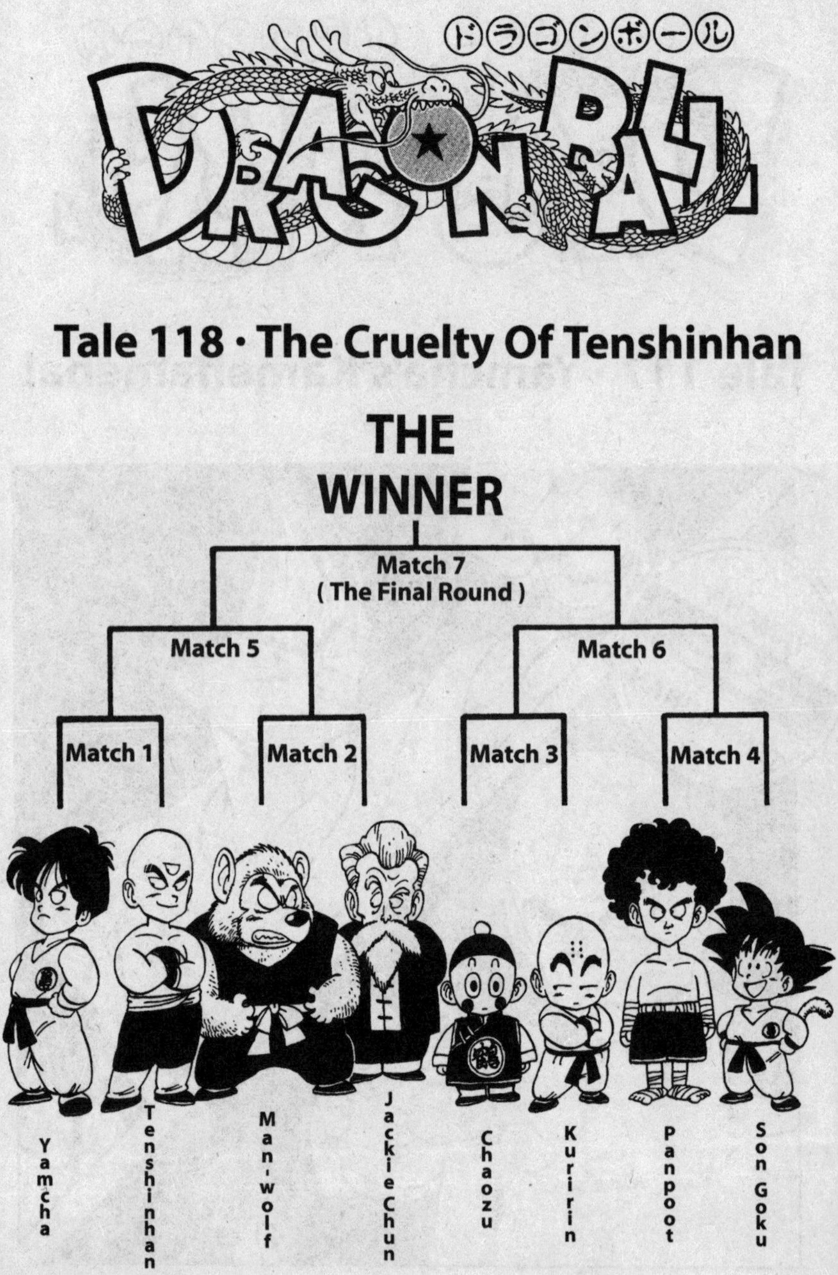
THE WINNER
Match 7
(The Final Round)
Match 5
Match 6
Match 1
Match 2
Match 3
Match 4
Yamcha
Tenshinhan
Man-wolf
Jackie Chun
Chaozu
Kuririn
Panpoot
Son Goku

Tale 119 · The Full Moon Grudge

Tale 120 · Look out! The Dodon Blast!

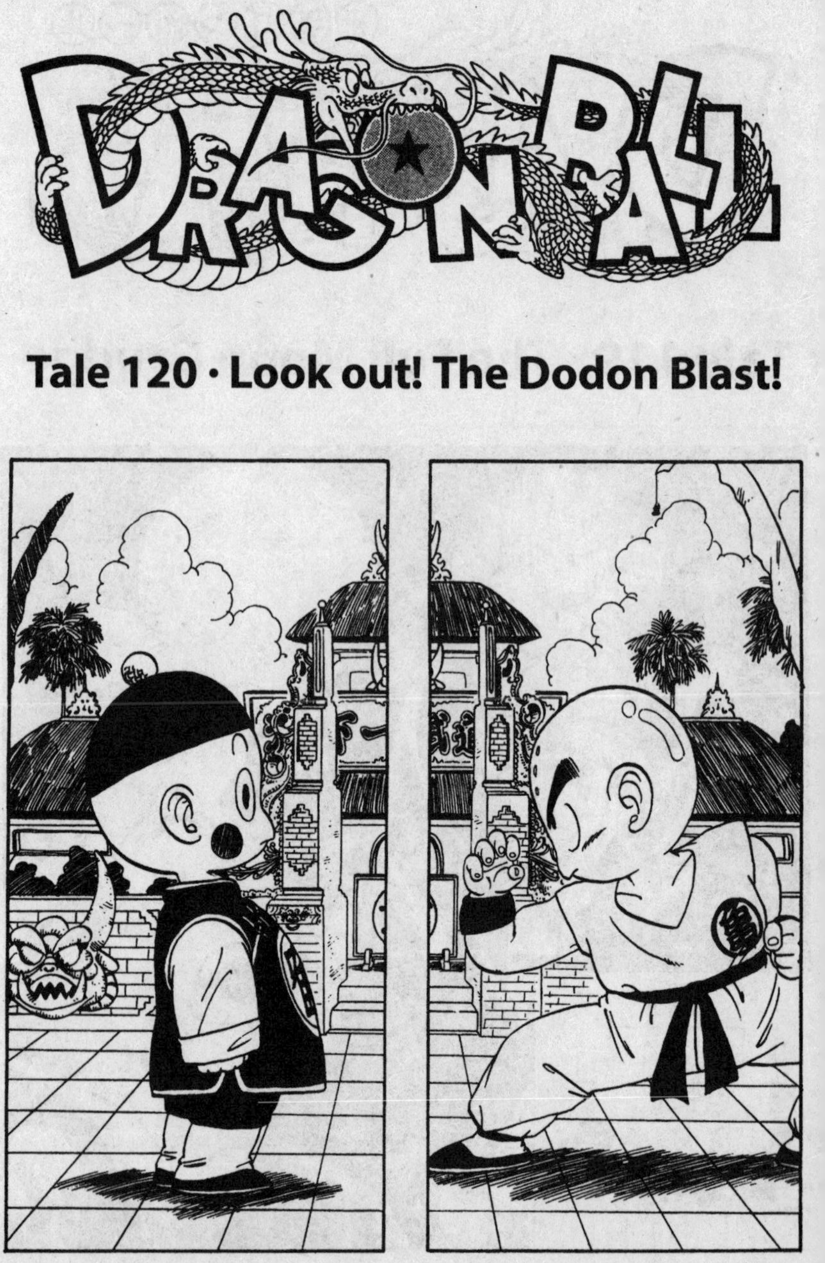

ドラゴンボール

DRAGON BALL

Tale 124 • Young Tenshinhan

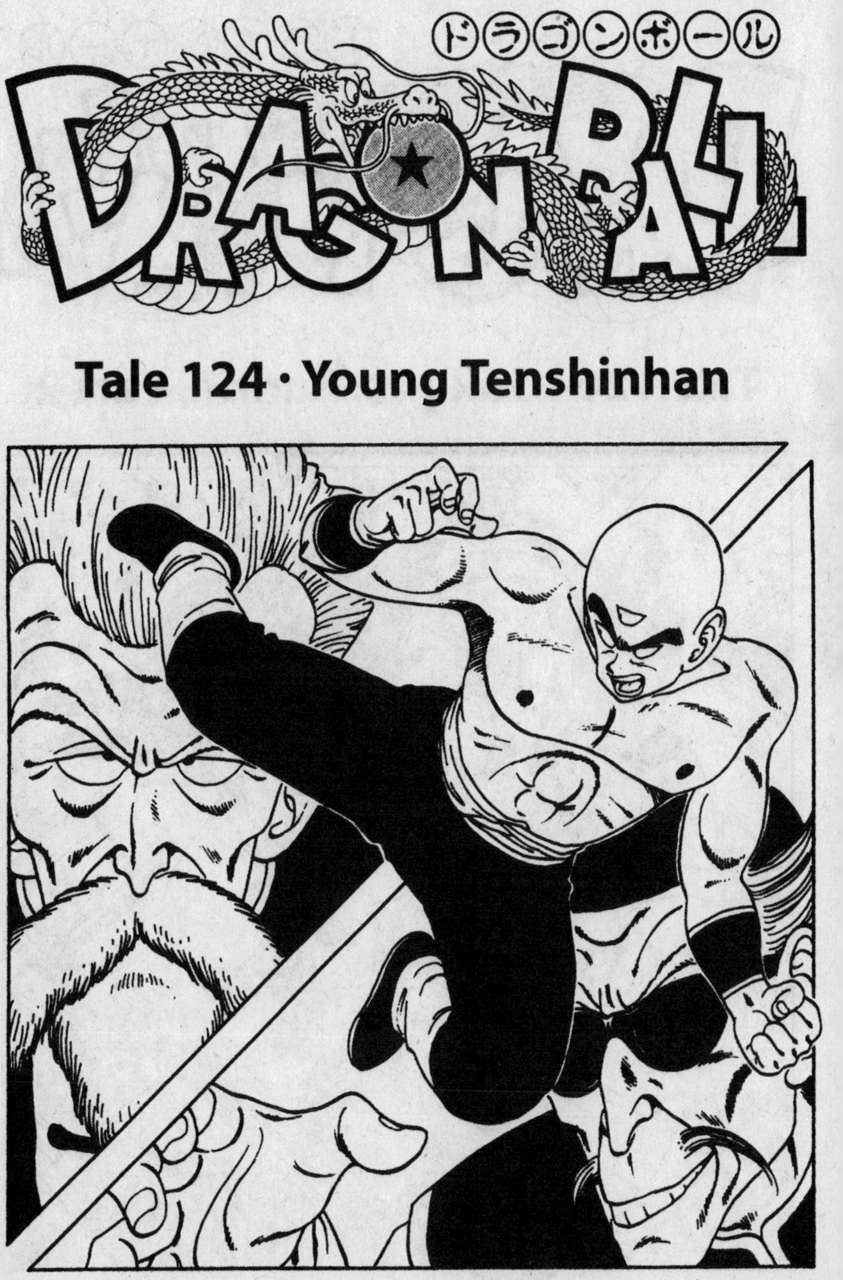

ドラゴンボール

DRAGON BALL

Tale 126 • Goku vs. Kuririn, Part 2

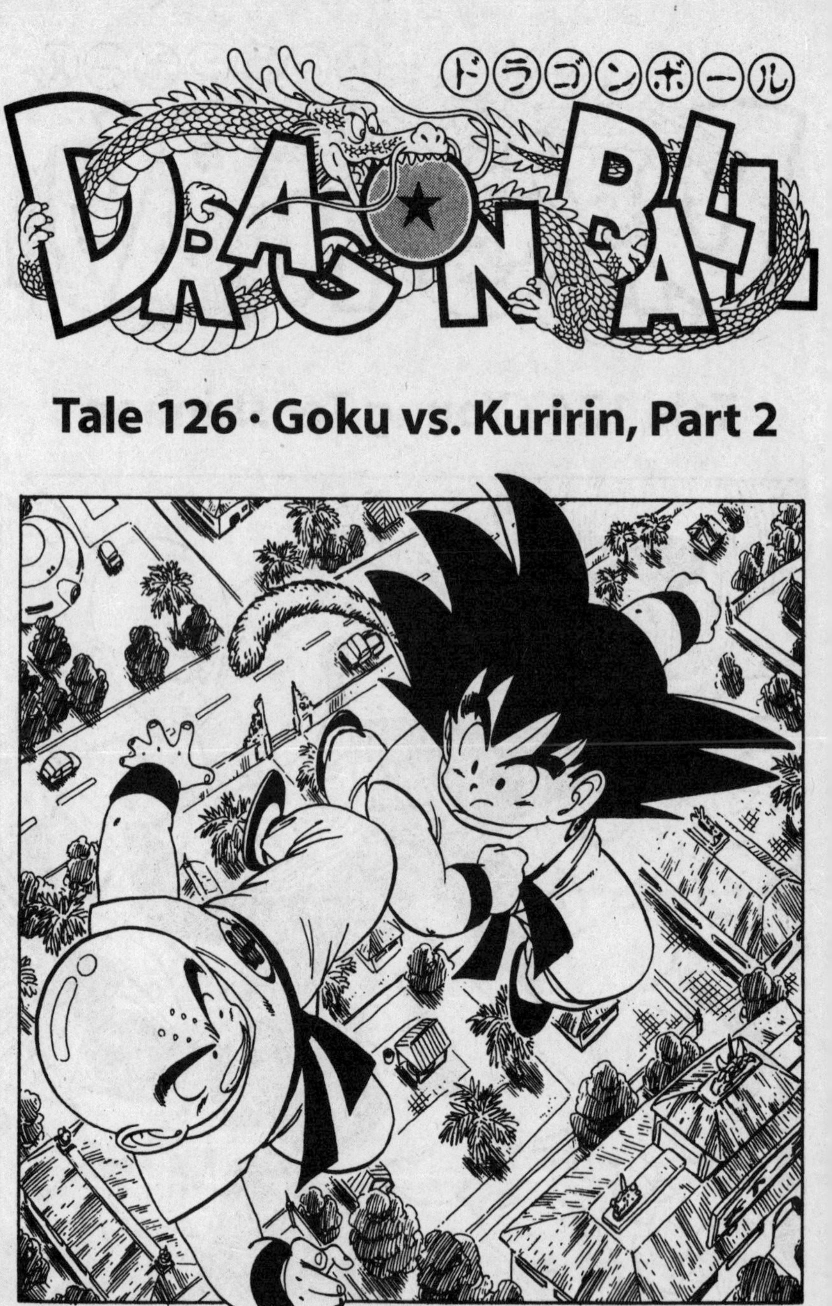

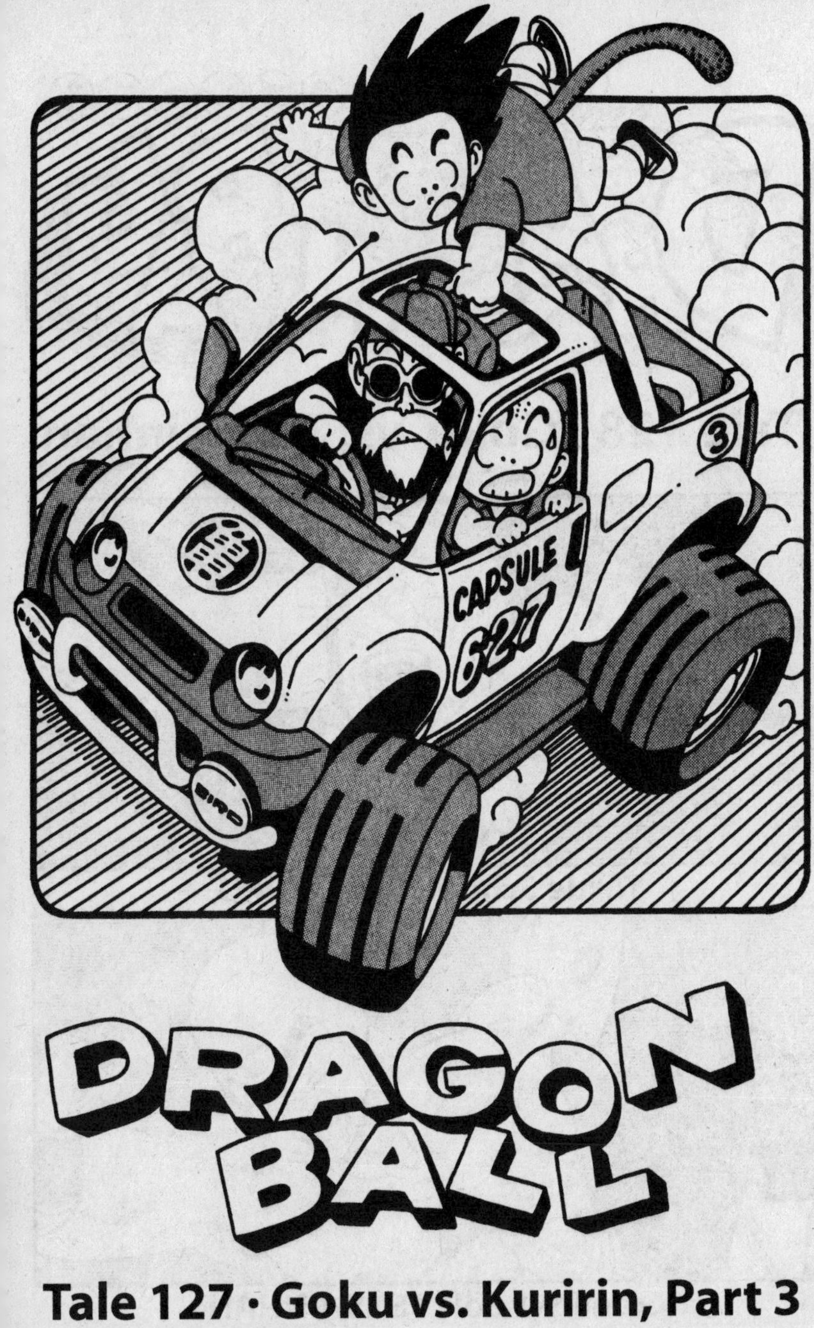
CAPSULE
627

DRAGON BALL

Tale 127 · Goku vs. Kuririn, Part 3

ドラゴンボール

DRAGON BALL

Tale 128 · Goku vs. Tenshinhan

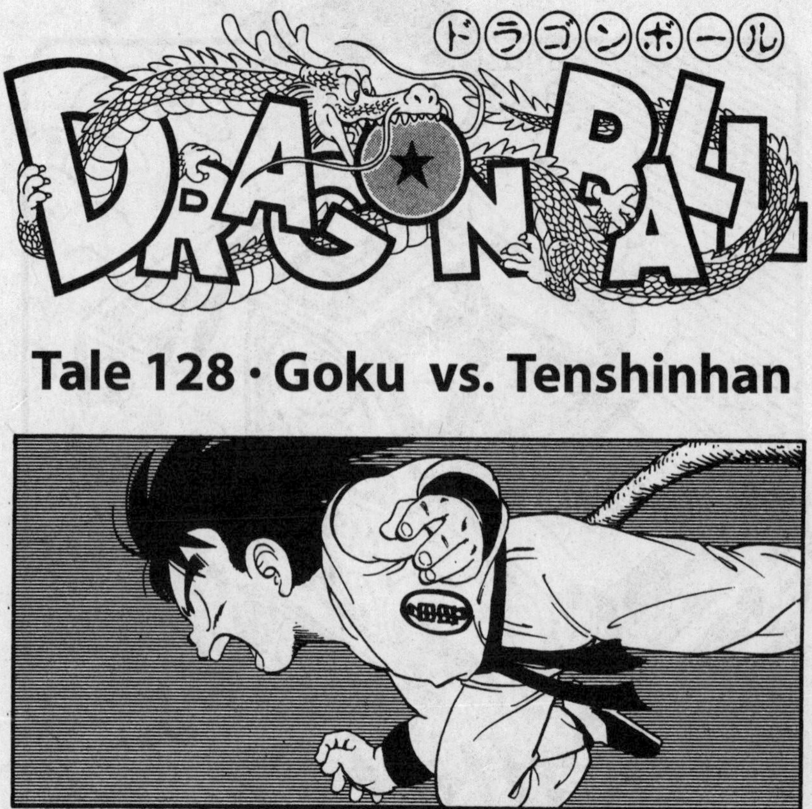

Turtle School SON GOKU

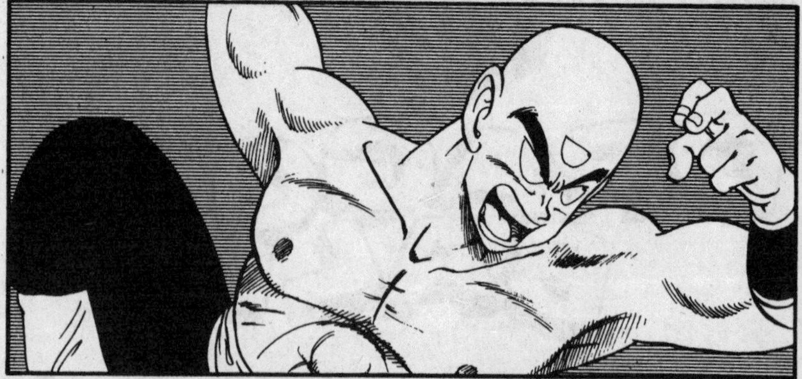

Crane School TENSHINHAN

Tale 129 · The Volleyball Play

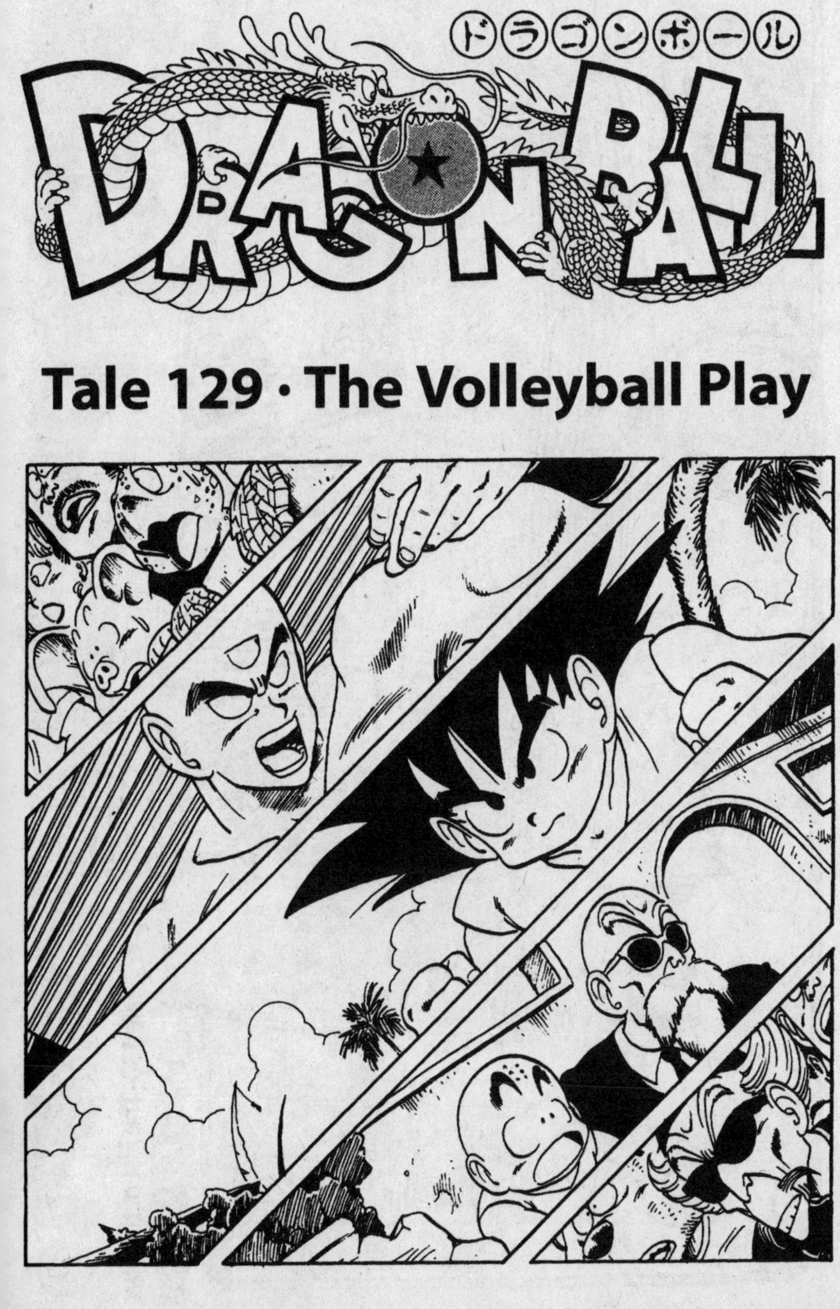

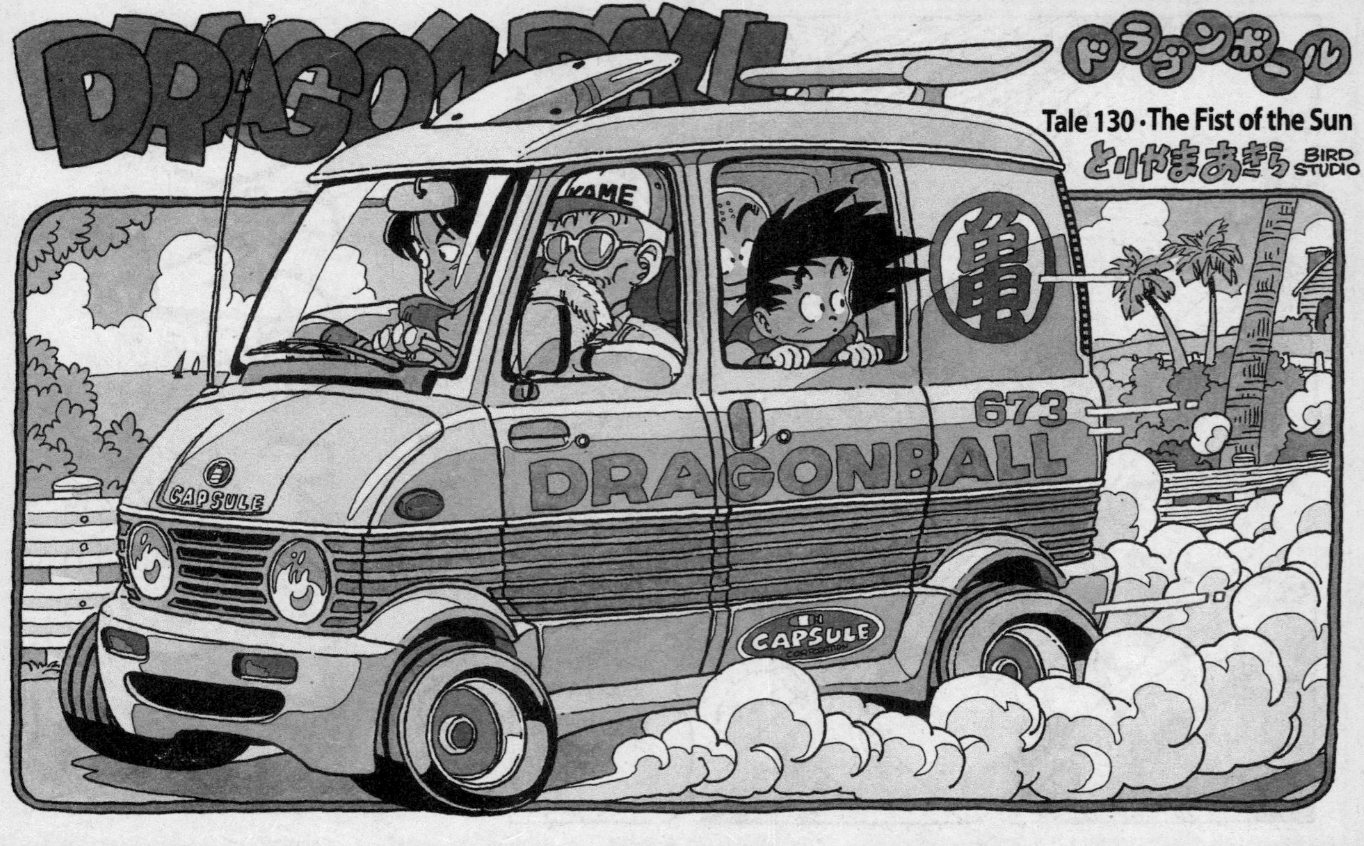
DRAGON BALL
ドラゴンボール
Tale 130 · The Fist of the Sun
とりやまあきら
BIRD STUDIO
KAME
亀
673
DRAGONBALL
CAPSULE
CAPSULE
CORPORATION

ドラゴンボール

DRAGON BALL

Tale 132 · The Arms Race

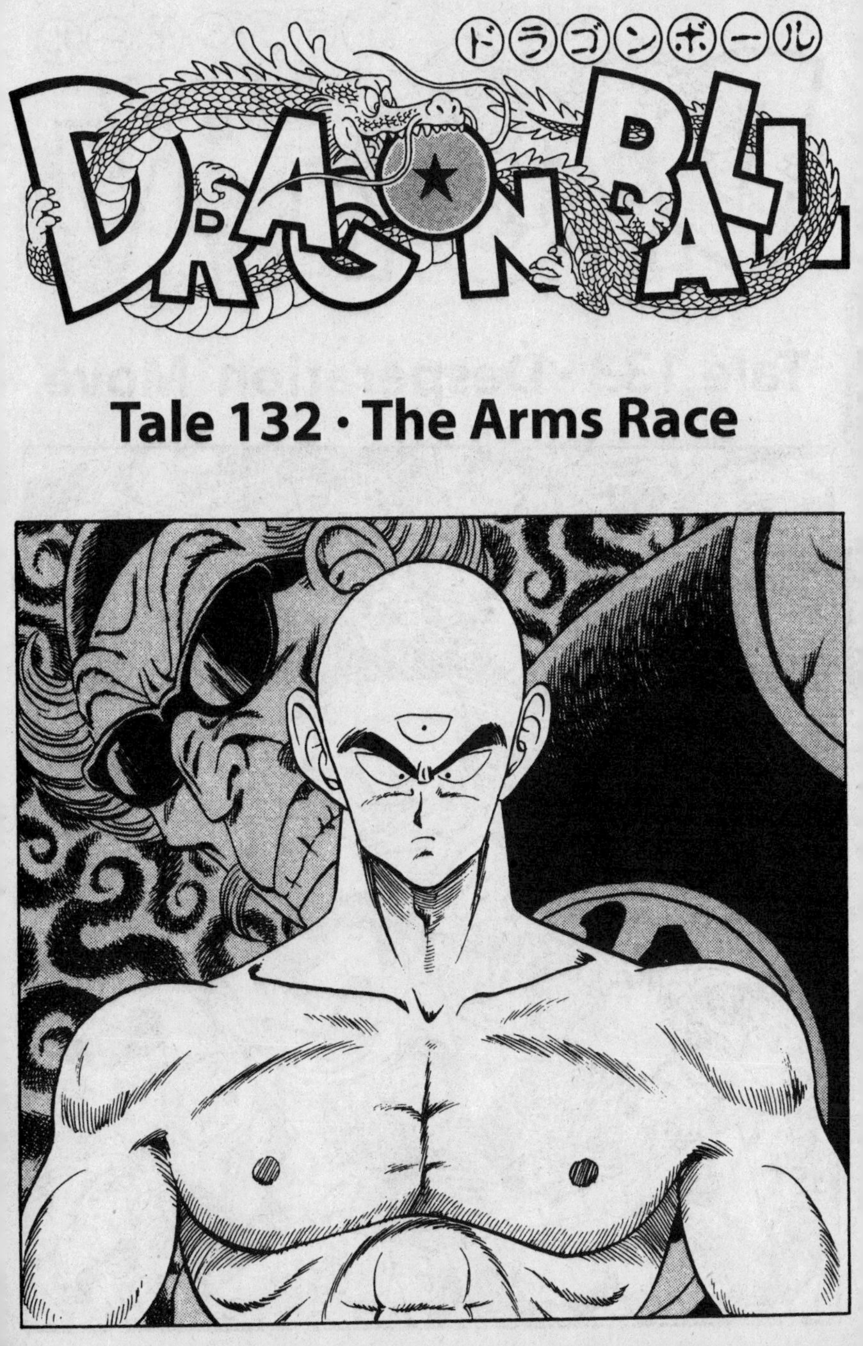

ドラゴンボール

DRAGON BALL

Tale 133 • Desperation Move

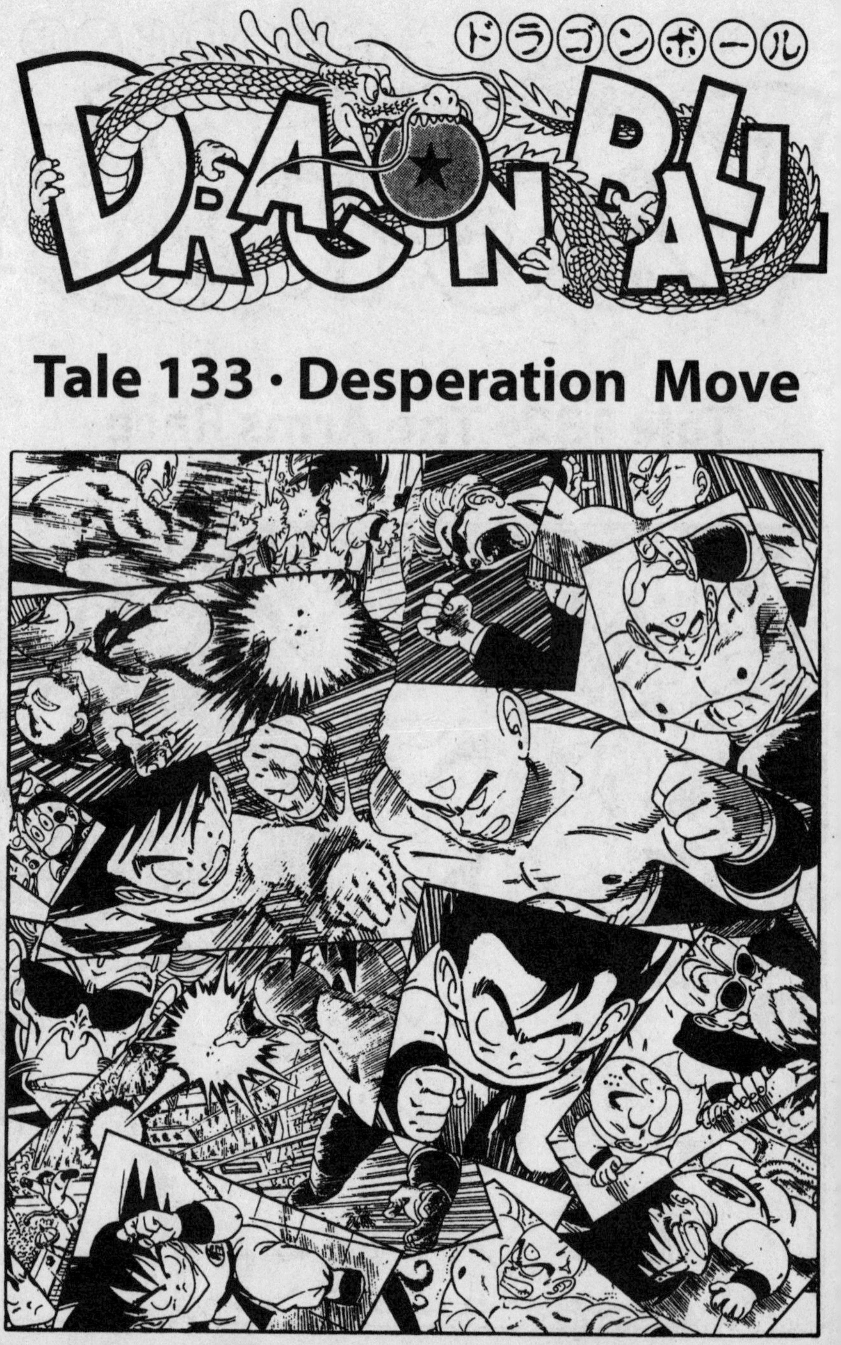

DRAGON BALL

Tale 134 • Up in the Air

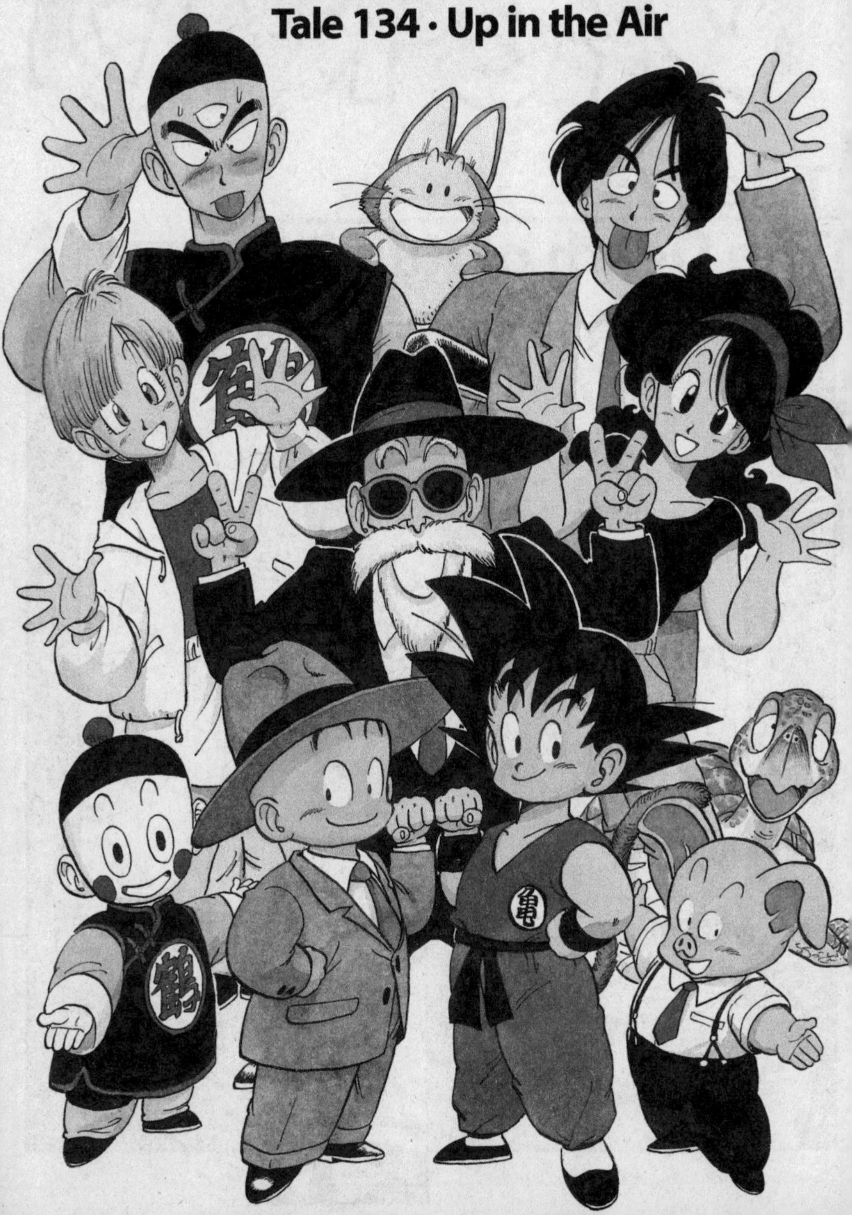

Tale 135

The Death of Kuririn

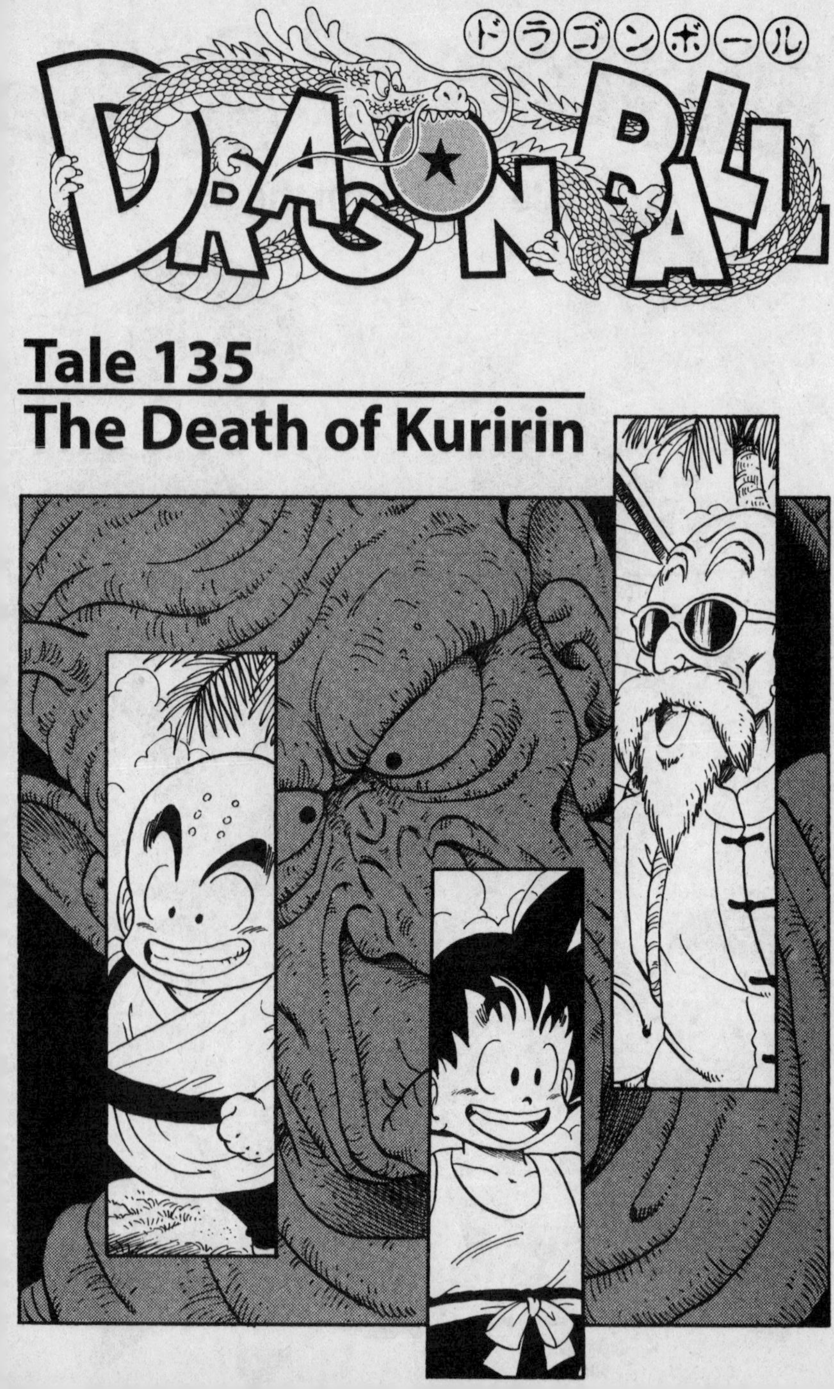

Tale 136 · Target : Tenka'ichi Budōka

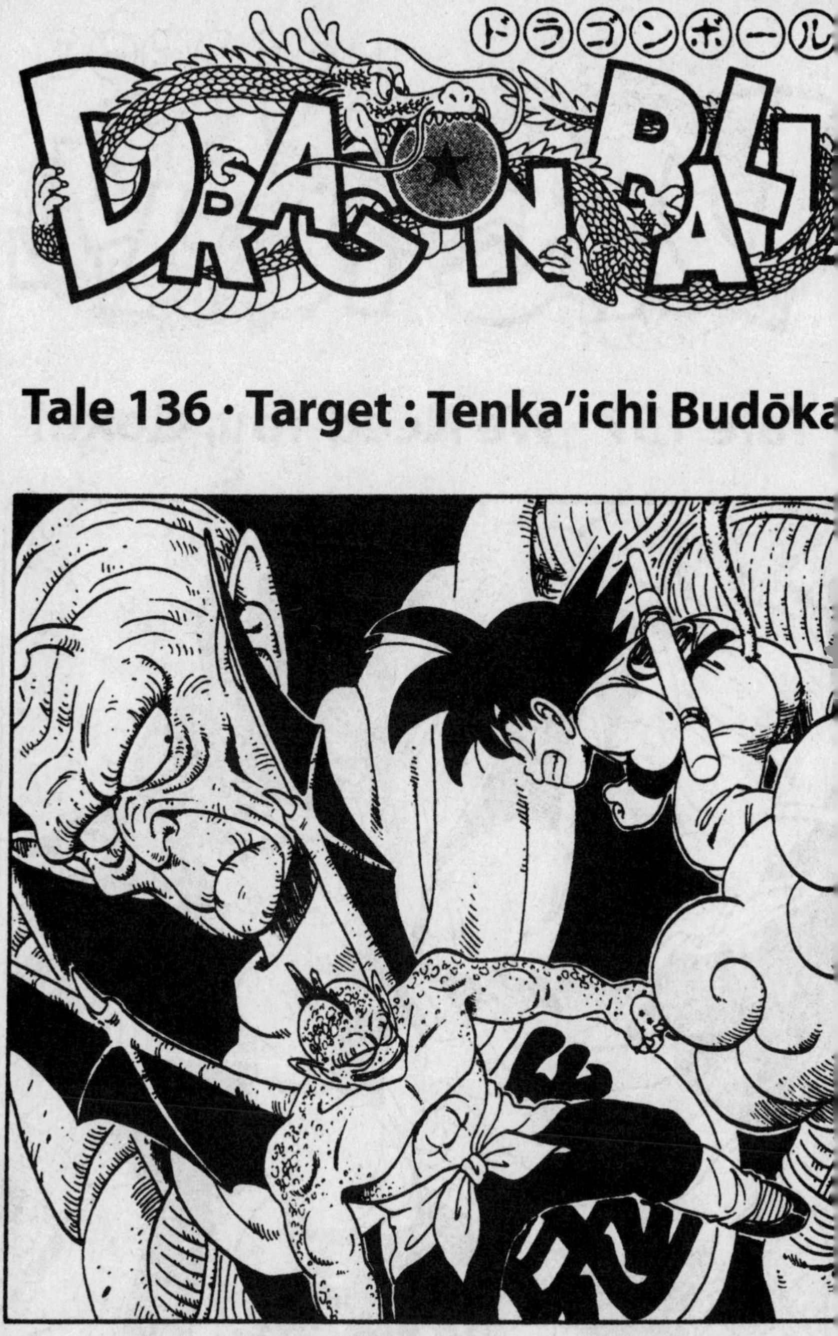

ドラゴンボール

DRAGON BALL

Tale 137 • We Need You, Goku!

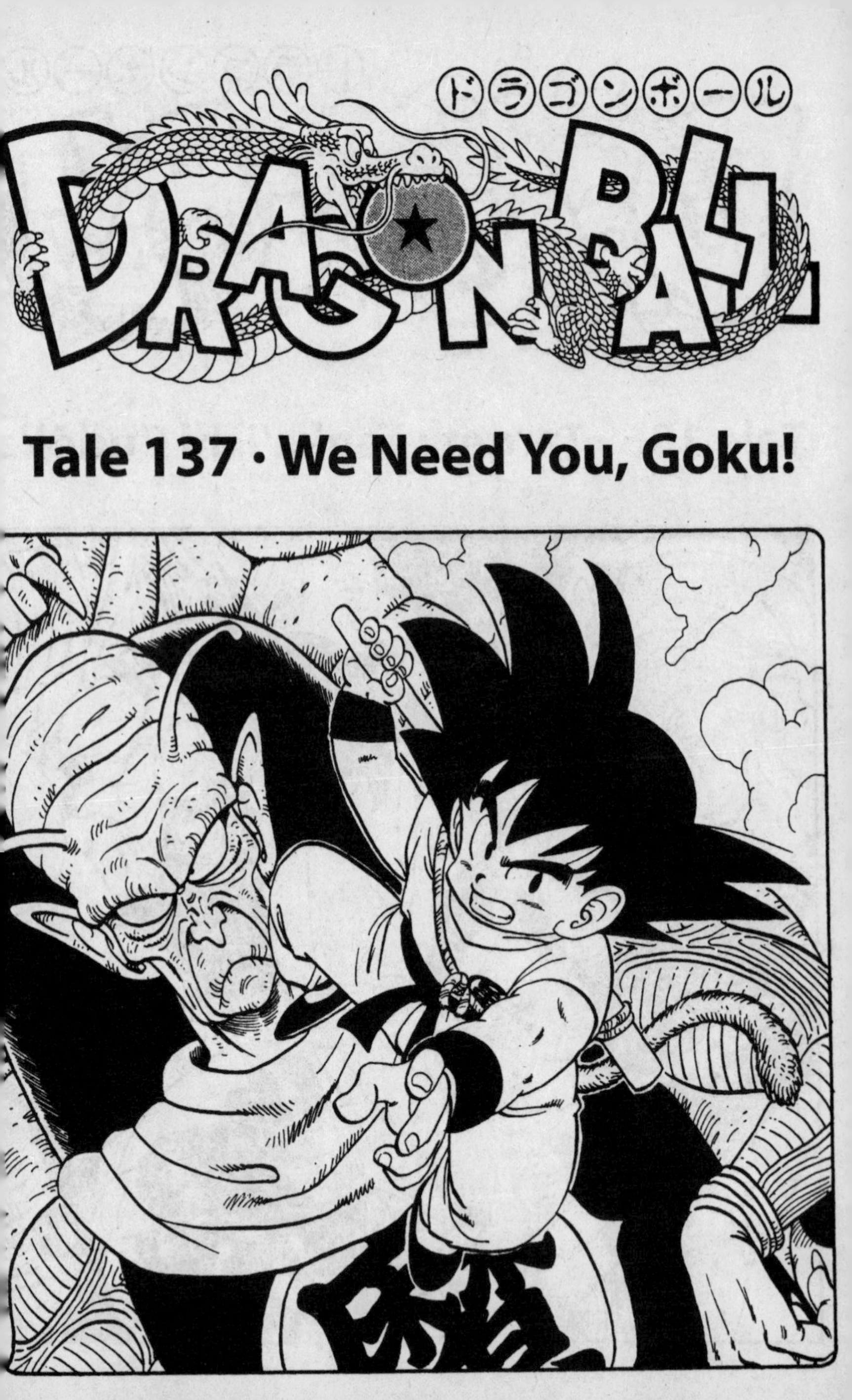

Tale 138 · The Weirdo with the Ball

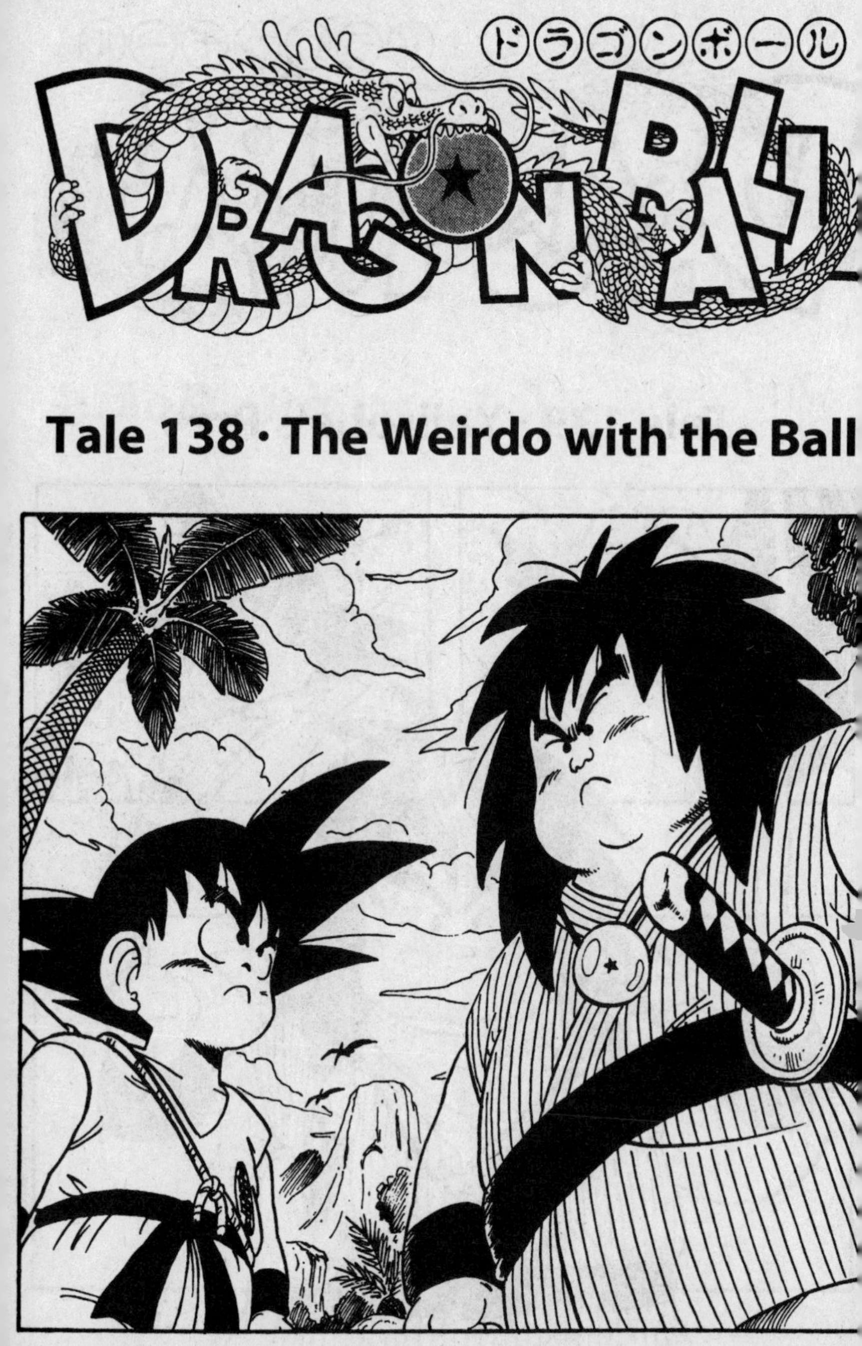

ドラゴンボール

DRAGON BALL

Tale 139 · Yajirobe's Prey

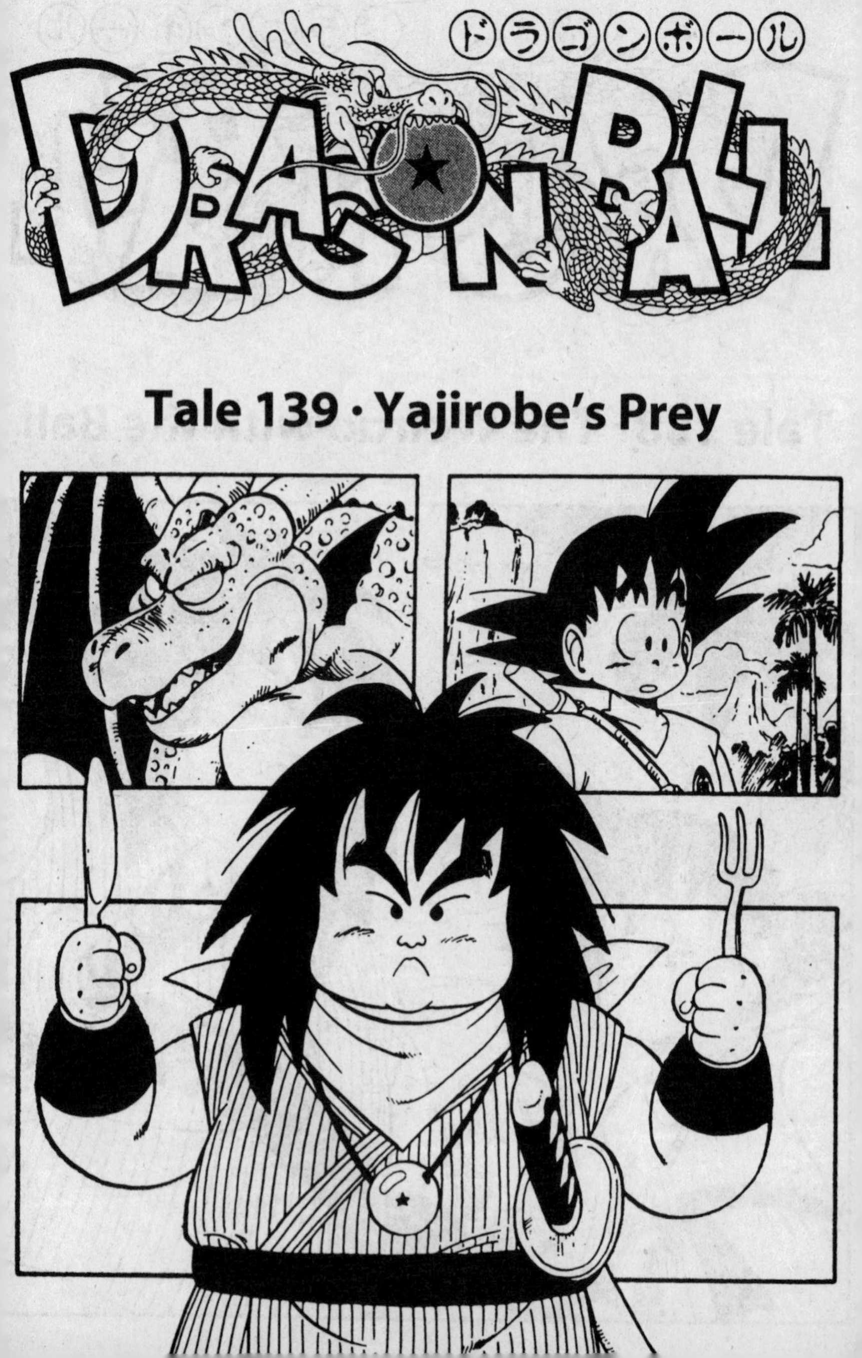

DRAGON BALL

Tale 140

The Martial Artist Hunters

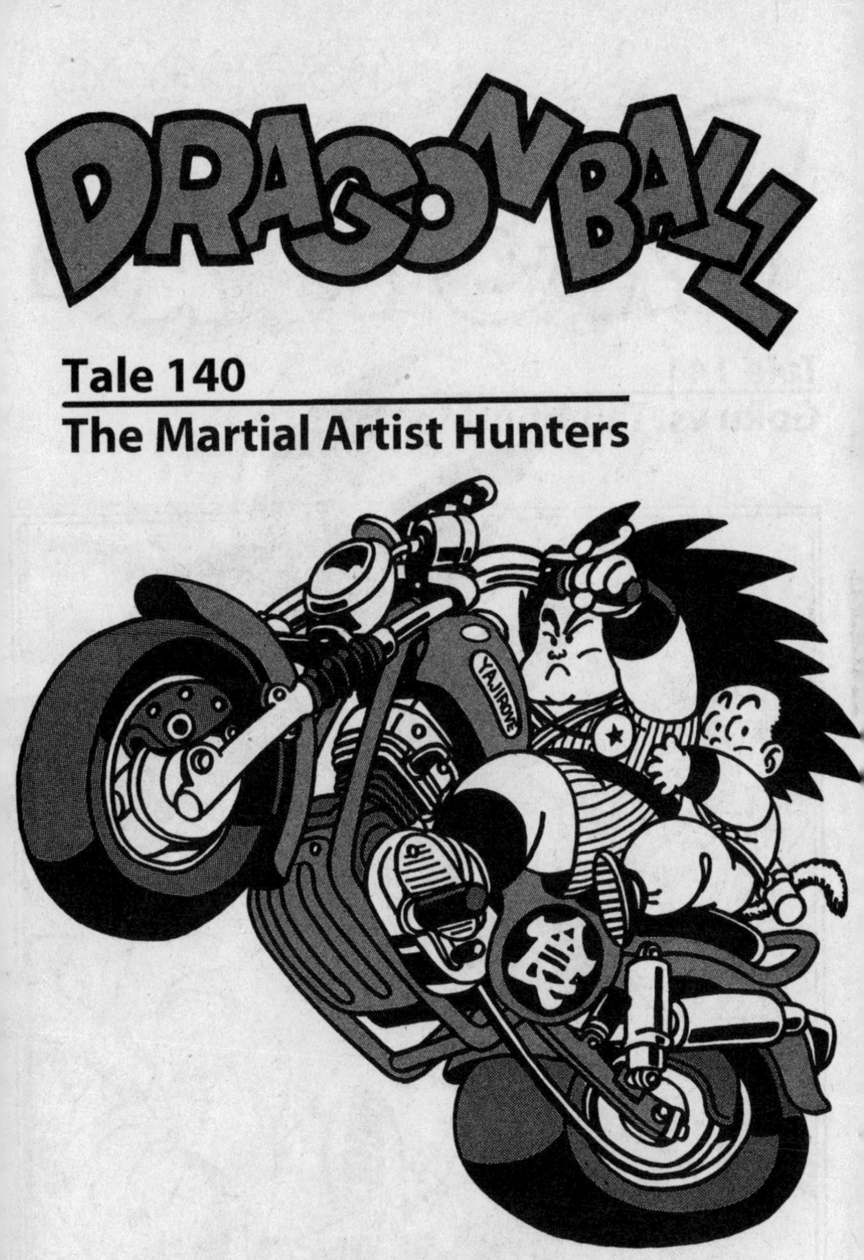
YAJIROBE

ドラゴンボール

DRAGON BALL

Tale 141

Goku vs. Tambourine

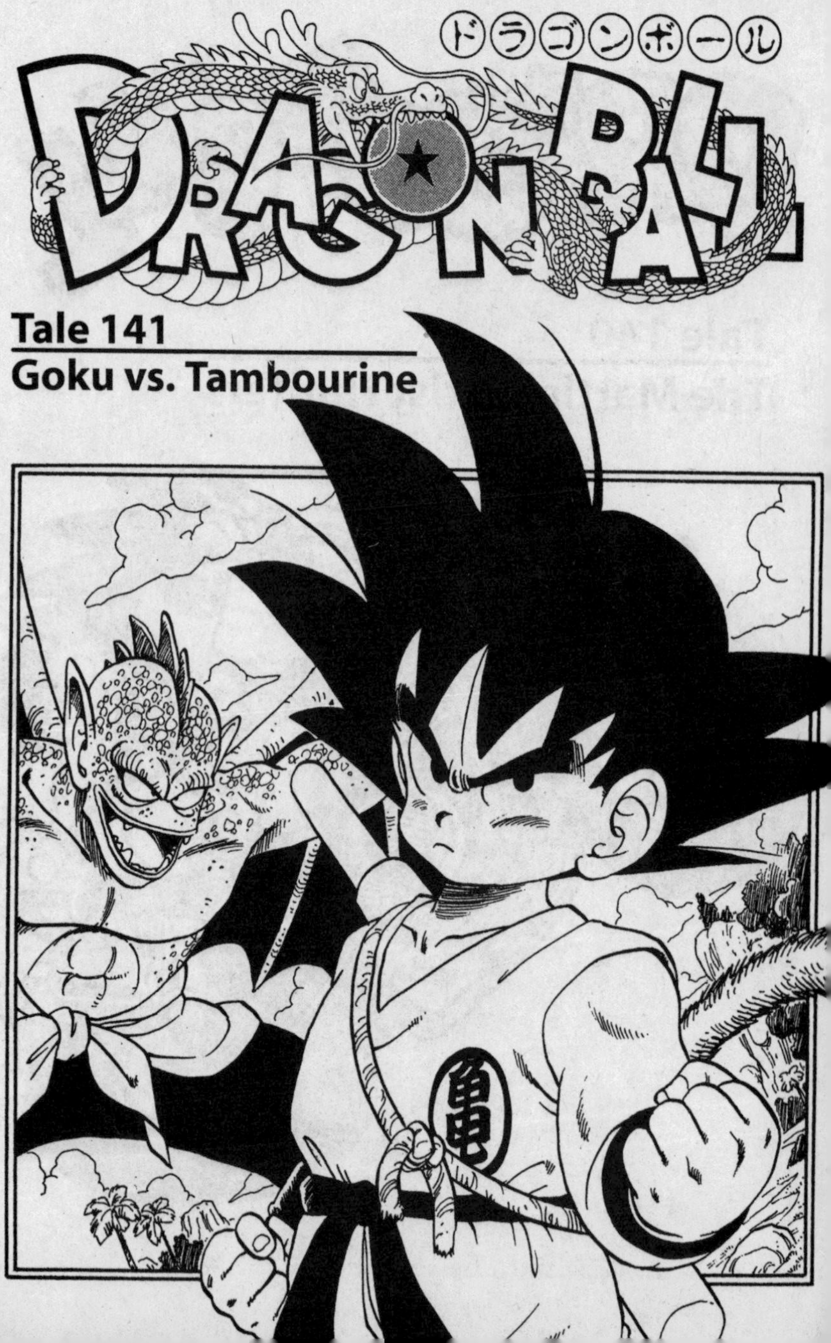

亀

ドラゴンボール

DRAGON BALL

Tale 142 · Piccolo Descends!

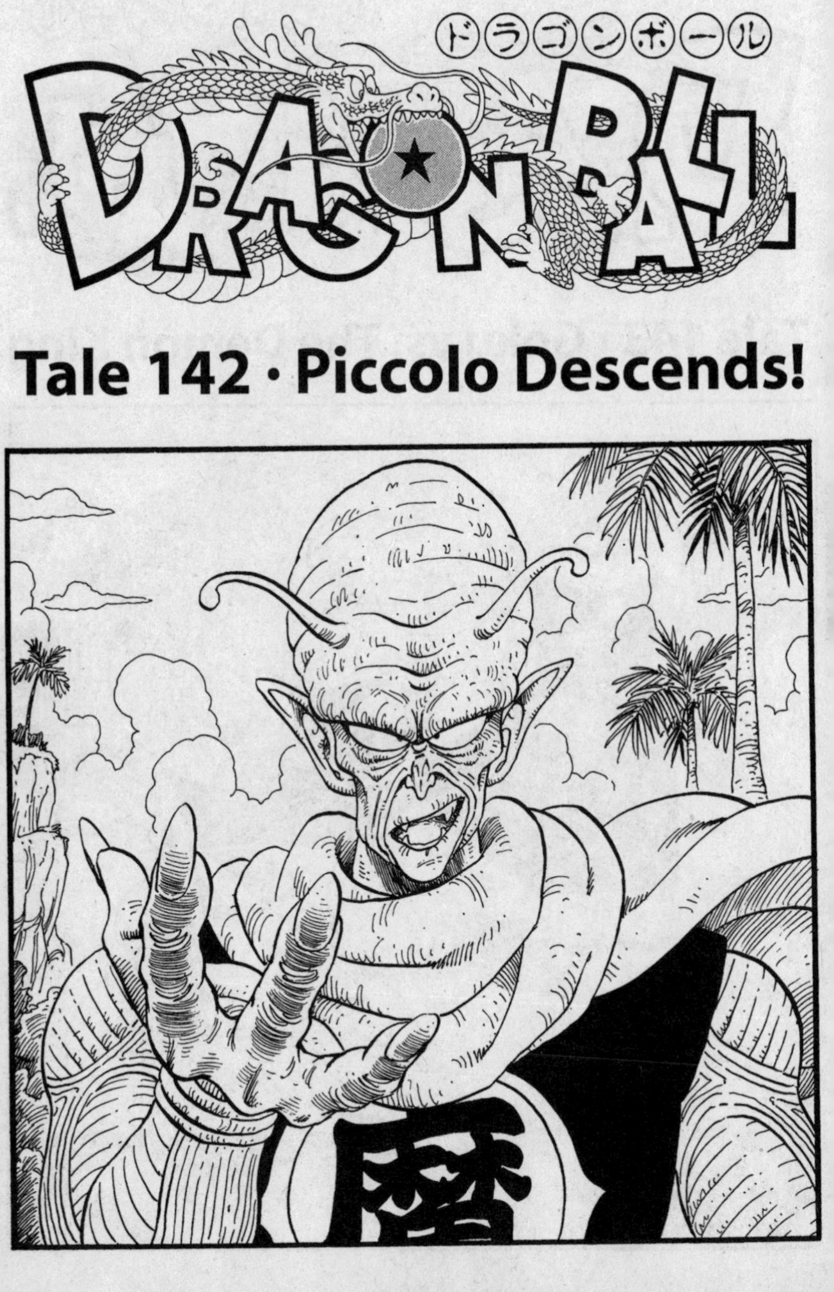
魔

ドラゴンボール

DRAGON BALL

Tale 143 · Goku vs. The Demon King

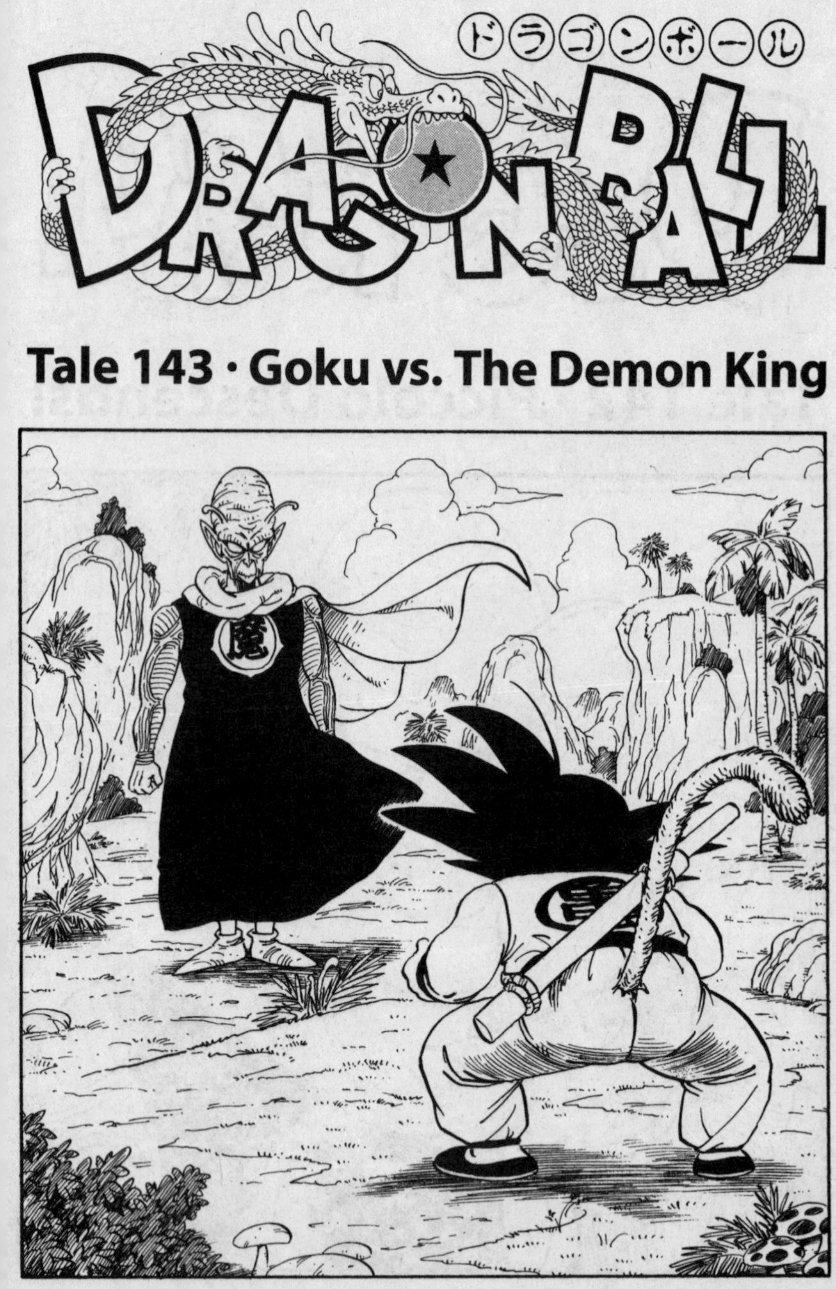

ドラゴンボール

DRAGON BALL

Tale 144 · Goku...Loses?

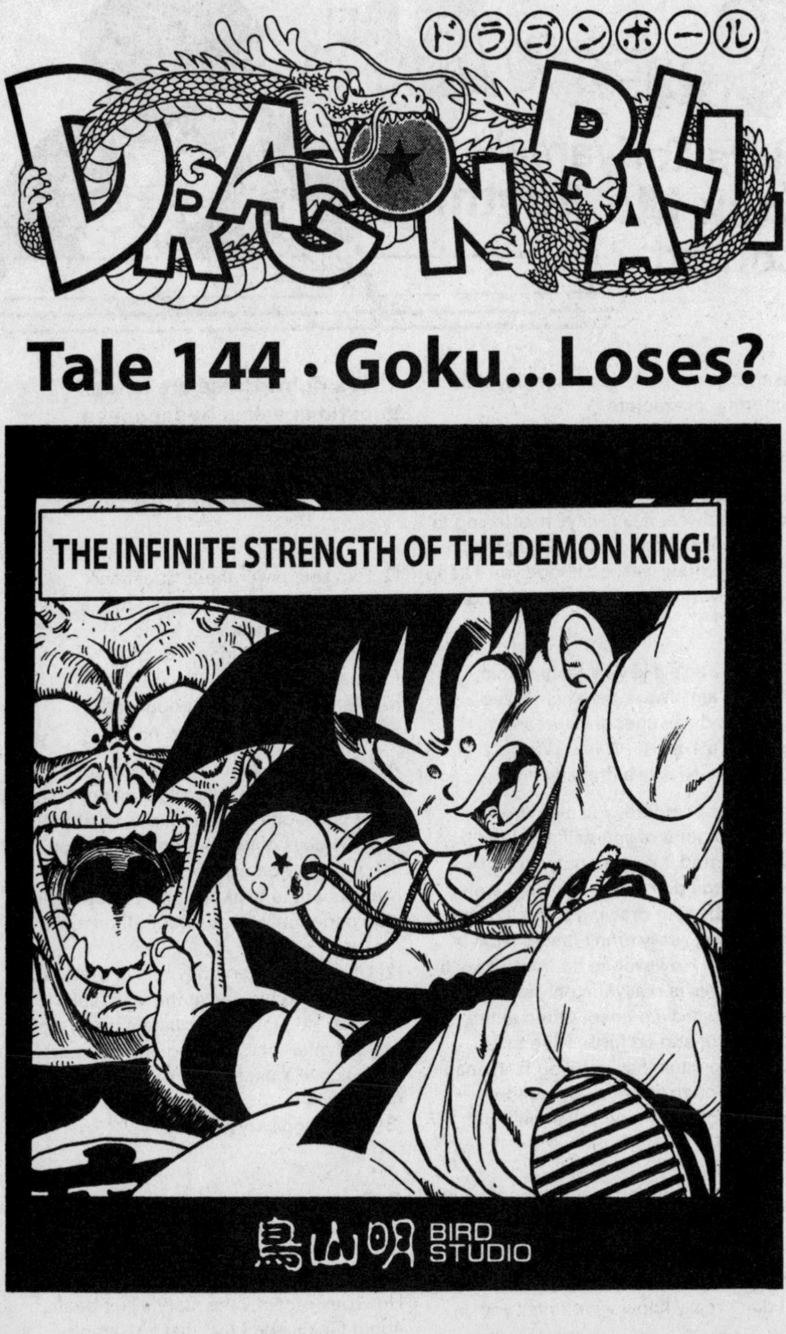
THE INFINITE STRENGTH OF THE DEMON KING!
鳥山明 BIRD STUDIO

DRAGON BALL

Akira Toriyama's "Ask Me Anything" Corner!

making the most of the personality-rich supporting characters.
–A 45-Year-Old Geezer Fan, Iwate Prefecture

A. Thank you very much for your support and your advice. It is always heartening to receive letters from older folks. I promise I'll strive to draw well, so I hope you'll keep reading it with gusto. You go too, Dad!

Q. Kame-Sen'nin is very fashionable, isn't he? I am always being criticized by my friends as uncool for wearing jeans and a T-shirt. *–Name Withheld By Request, Ishikawa Prefecture*

A. On your postcard, you also drew a full-body picture of yourself, but I realized that if I printed it your identity might be revealed, so I didn't. (I'm thinking, aren't I?) Going by your drawing alone, I'd have to agree, you really aren't fashionable at all, are you? However, to be frank, it suits you well! This is really the only style to wear with a shaved head! Often at the supermarket and so forth, I see brash youths who think they're being fashionable, but don't you think your way is more refreshing? That's how you should be!

Q. How can I get better at drawing?
–Kei Mizuno, Aichi Prefecture

A. I get tons of questions about drawing, but it's really hard to decide how to answer, so I don't really know what to tell you. In

That's right! These are actual questions asked by Japanese readers and answered by Akira Toriyama in the original *Dragon Ball* volumes 10–12!

Q. Please answer these questions.
[1] How long does it take you to create one chapter?
[2] How old are Kuririn, Oolong, Pu'ar and Yamcha?
[3] Please keep up the good work.
–Hiroko Ota, Aichi Prefecture

A. [1] Hmm…it varies depending on the chapter, but when I'm having a hard time, a good plot won't come to me even after two or three days of brainstorming. If I'm on a roll, though, sometimes it only takes about five minutes to think one up. To actually put it on paper only takes about 30 minutes a page.
[2] Uhh, how old are they…? I'm pretty sure Kuririn stated his age at the last Tenka'ichi Budōkai, so please calculate it using that as your reference. Oolong and Pu'ar are…I don't know. Yamcha is…about 20 right now, I think.
[3] Thank you very much.

Q. Sometimes when I get tired of work, I take your graphic novels off my children's bookshelf and read them with gusto. It is the best thing for a change of pace. However, recently the story's just been about Goku, and I feel that you aren't disciple. Even if you are denied entry as his disciple, the muscle you gain from your physical training will most definitely be useful later. You must continue to persevere!

Q. Dear Toriyama Sensei, your art is incredibly clean, even your backgrounds. Even though your backgrounds are so detailed, everything is really easy to read. I was wondering if you could create a *Dragon Quest* story, even if it's just a one-shot. –*Eiji Nakamura, Aichi Prefecture*

A. Thank you very much. The real reason my art is so "clean" is because it's a pain in the butt to draw tons of detail. I hate things which are a pain. Unfortunately, making a *Dragon Quest* story would also be a huge pain because there are so many characters, so I really don't want to do one. I'm sorry.

Dear Mr. Toriyama,
I hope you are well.
I always watch your shows. They are really fun. Please keep drawing fun manga.

Please write back to me.

–*Tomokazu Hirose, Toyama Prefecture*

A. Thank you very much. I hope you will cheer me on in the future too. I hope you are well too.

Q. Sensei, your work is almost always set in a country setting, but I think it really fits the image of your manga and I like it very much. –*Ayano Fujii, Aichi Prefecture*

any case you can probably guess. I think you just have to keep drawing constantly. Not just people, but landscapes and animals, all sorts of things—observe them closely and try drawing them. To practice inking, again I feel that you just need to keep drawing until you get better. But if you keep trying and you still can't draw, well, don't quit your day job.

Q. Dear Toriyama Sensei, I'm a big fan of not only *Dragon Ball*, but all your work. Manga these days seems to only be about "love" or "sports" or "fighting" or "legends"...but you're different!
–*Yuka Fujino, Kyoto Prefecture*

A. Gosh, I'm flattered. *Dragon Ball* is going to go on for quite a bit longer, but when I do finish it, I plan on creating even better and more entertaining manga. I look forward to your support then also.

Q. Exams have finally invaded my life. I'd really appreciate it (it'd be like a wish granted by Shenlong!) if you could hold off on publication of *Dragon Quest 3* until after my exams are finished.
–*Koji Iwashita, Fukuoka Prefecture*

A. I see, the exams must be really tough. I'm an adult now, so exams no longer affect my life. Bet you're jealous! But even though they are a major pain, keep up the good work! Also, *Dragon Quest 3* is insanely fun! Why don't you play it after you finish your exams?

Q. I have been doing push-ups and sit-ups in an effort to be able to use the kamehameha, but I still haven't been able to produce it. Is that move really possible?
–*Yasuhiro Kanamori, Gifu Prefecture*

A. Hmm, I am very impressed. An "A" for effort! Still, it looks like you haven't been able to produce the kamehameha, so I guess you still need more training. The fastest way may be to go to the Turtle Hermit (Kame-Sen'nin) with a girlie mag in hand and ask him to take you as his

Q. Dear Toriyama Sensei, thank you for making a great read every time. Please take care of yourself, and keep your spirits up. (I know that manga artists are very busy, so please don't worry about replying to this letter.)
—Yoshitaka Miyabe, Nagano Prefecture

A. You are the best! I have been moved by your consideration in telling me that it is unnecessary to reply, so instead I have printed it in this graphic novel. Please don't ever lose your considerate and kind nature.

Q. All the members of my family are big fans. Mom only reads manga if you wrote it. My younger brother records your anime on video and watches it.
—Ryō Mizugami, Yamanashi Prefecture

A. Thank you very much! You must be blessed to have such a wonderful mother! Make sure you are nice to her. Please give my regards to your younger brother too!

That's the end of Akira Toriyama's "Ask Me Anything!" Corner! Enjoy the rest of the Dragon Ball series!

A. Thank you very much. The reason I use a country setting so much is not only is it easy for me to draw but also because I am a total country bumpkin and I don't like the city very much. By the way, your address places you in the next town over from me.

Q. I think it's fabulous that you take care of your child and do work at the same time. Also, the character "Tanton" that appeared in the manga *Dragon Boy* from the *Shonen Jump Special* was really similar to Goku, and I thought he was a lot of fun.
—Goku, Nagano Prefecture

A. Thank you, thank you. Actually, I don't necessarily take care of the kid and work at the same time; my wife does most of it. I pretty much do stuff like playing with the kid when I feel like it and occasionally changing the diapers and feeding him, so it's really nothing much. I do most of my plotting and thinking after the baby is in bed, so it really isn't that much trouble. Anyway, *Dragon Boy* is in vol. 2 of my *Toriyama Akira Marusaki Gekijō* (Akira Toriyama's Insert-Adjective-Here Theater). Because of the popularity of the story, it ended up becoming the catalyst for *Dragon Ball*. That's why Goku is Tanton with a few modifications, and why they look so much alike.

Q. Please don't stop *Dragon Ball* even after Piccolo is defeated! Please continue the manga for at least another three years! During that time, I will study like mad to get into college, and afterwards get a job at Shueisha and become your editor.
—Tomoko Shima, Toyama Prefecture

A. When Goku was fighting Great Demon King Piccolo, there were a number of "It's going to end, isn't it?" rumors going around, but I have no intention of ending it at all. The idea of going for another three years does kind of freak me out, but I do plan on continuing it for a little longer. By the way, if you become my editor, I hope you will be kind and not reject any of my stories. I look forward to the day when this will become a reality.

AUTHOR NOTES

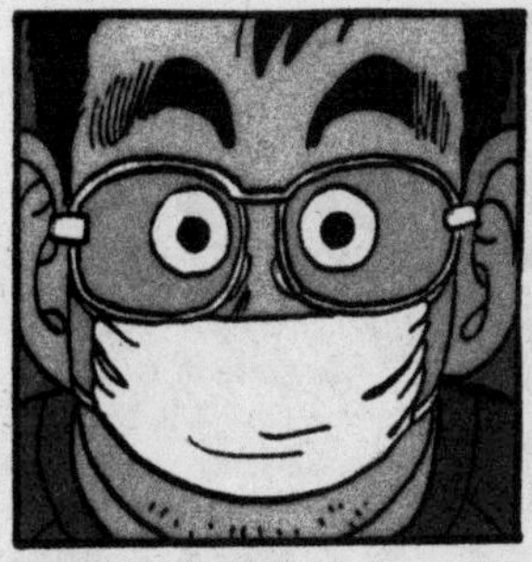

1987

VOLUME 10

I don't think there's anything good about being nearsighted. When you go to the pool or the beach, you can't see any of the girls in their bikinis! Darn it! Quickly, I'll put on my glasses, but it'll turn out the girl is actually an old lady! Then I'll take my glasses off as quickly as I can. This happens to me quite often. Once, I went to a mixed-bathing hot spring, but I couldn't see anything because I wasn't wearing my glasses! It made me want to cry. Darn this nearsightedness! Everyone, please take care of your eyes.

VOLUME 11

This is the first time I've put up my photo in this section. This is a photo of me with my son, Sasuke. I may seem like a show-off parent for including my son, but it beats having to come up with something to draw for this page. Maybe I'll start doing this from now on. Or maybe I'm just getting lazy. Let's see, next time maybe I'll use a photo of my cat Koge or my dog Mato. Hmmm...I think I'm onto something here...

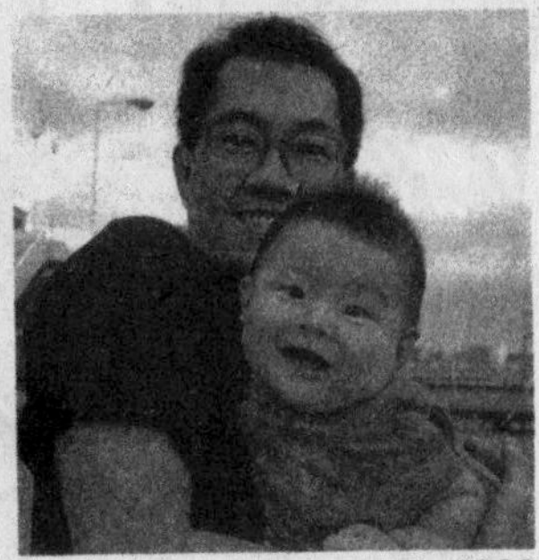

1988

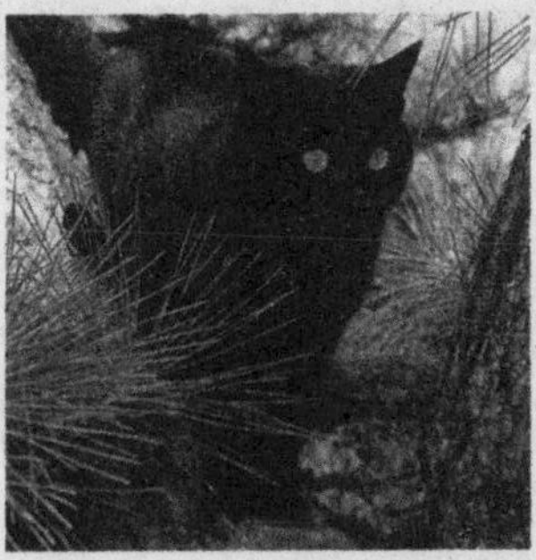

1988

VOLUME 12

This is our cat Koge (char). You probably can't tell what the heck is going on since she's so black, but here she is. We picked her up one night three years ago as a kitten, and she's a real sweetie and a total nudge. While she was giving birth to her litter, I really, really worried, and I made a huge fuss over her. But there weren't any complications, and she had four healthy (and teeny-tiny) kittens. We were so happy. By the way, my wife was the one who named her.

IN THE NEXT VOLUME

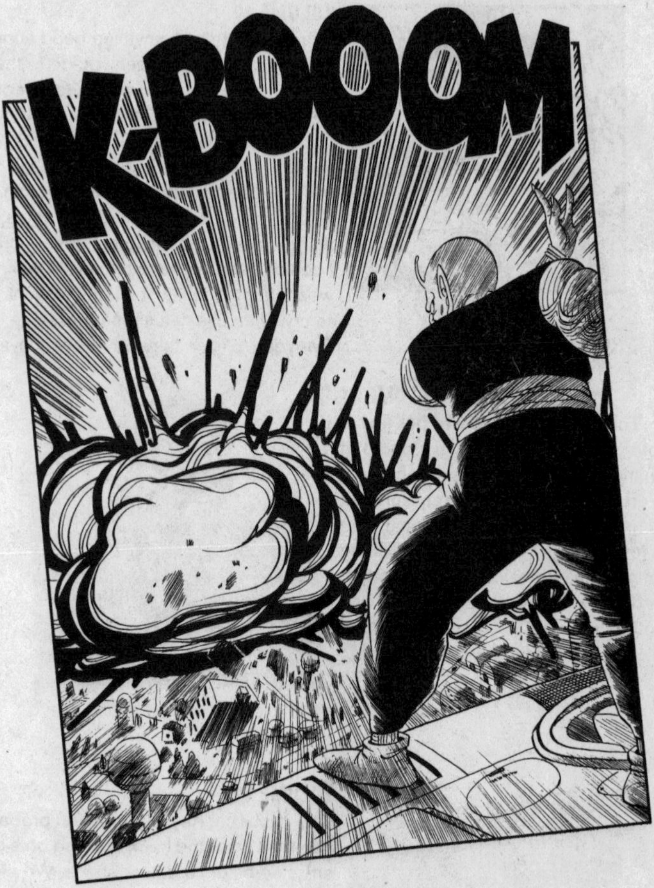
K-BOOOM

Will Goku and his friends be able to stop the diabolical Piccolo from getting his wish with the Dragon Balls? And if Piccolo does become younger and stronger again, what's in store for the rest of the world? Find out in the next *Dragon Ball* 3-in-1!